American Enterprise

Free and Not So Free

Books by Clarence H. Cramer

ROYAL BOB: THE LIFE OF ROBERT G. INGERSOLL

NEWTON D. BAKER — A BIOGRAPHY

OPEN SHELVES AND OPEN MINDS

AMERICAN ENTERPRISE: FREE AND NOT SO FREE

American Enterprise
Free and Not So Free

CLARENCE H. CRAMER

LITTLE, BROWN AND COMPANY · BOSTON · TORONTO

FIRST EDITION

T 10/72

The author is grateful for permission to reprint the following previously copyrighted material: a passage from "The Negro Is Your Brother," by Martin Luther King, Jr., published in the August 1963 issue of *The Atlantic Monthly,* copyright © 1963 by Martin Luther King, Jr., reprinted by permission of Joan Daves; excerpts from an article by Vermont Royster, which appeared in the February 8, 1950, issue of *The Wall Street Journal,* reprinted by permission of *The Wall Street Journal.*

Library of Congress Cataloging in Publication Data

Cramer, Clarence H
  American enterprise--free and not so free.

  Bibliography: p.
  1. United States--Economic conditions.
  2. United States--Commerce--History. I. Title.
  HC103.C8784   330.9'73   72-3801
  ISBN 0-316-16000-8

Published simultaneously in Canada
by Little, Brown & Company (Canada) Limited

PRINTED IN THE UNITED STATES OF AMERICA

Contents

American Enterprise

Free and Not So Free

I

"The Business of Government Is Business"

CALVIN COOLIDGE never lived down his simplistic statement that "the business of government is business." A generation later, with generous governmental support of everything from proliferating turnpikes to growing cotton to teeming bumper crops of military hardware, it was not inaccurate to say that "the business of business is government." Curiously Karl Marx, who also had a strong tendency to oversimplify, would have agreed with Coolidge. Both understood that the success or failure of a nation's business enterprises has a major influence on the character of its culture. Both apprehended that political policy would be determined, in large part, by the pride or disillusionment which a body politic has in its business accomplishment — and in the economic theories and plans supporting it.

Throughout the ages economic ideas and systems have had compulsive and strategic influence, consciously or subliminally, on every citizen from peon to plutocrat. In this volume, which will stress direct narrative history rather than complex economic theory, frequent mention will necessarily be made of economic scholars from Adam Smith to John Maynard Keynes to Gerard Piel. There will be continuing reference to ideas and battle cries important in their own heyday and later: the importance of gold and a favorable balance of trade (mercantilism), laissez-faire (Adam Smith), the iron law of wages (David Ricardo), the population problem (Thomas Malthus), socialism (Karl Marx), conspicuous consumption (Thorstein Veblen), unearned increment (Henry George), the multiplier (John Maynard Keynes), and the military-industrial complex (Gerard Piel). In 1969 the ideological warfare between economic ideas was so strong that many insisted that U.S. voyagers to the moon should take along an American flag only, and so they did — omitting the emblem of the United Nations which some favored. This was reminiscent of Nikita Khrushchev's childish glee, a decade earlier, when he learned that a Soviet rocket had deposited a Russian pennant on the moon — as though that achievement proved something about the relative advantages of socialism and capitalism. In any case, the following narrative will introduce a few of the germinal economic ideas and theories that have had such profound impact over the centuries.

Mercantilism arose out of the Commercial Revolution (circa 1500), but derived its name centuries later from Adam Smith, who was instrumental in substituting his own idea of laissez-faire for the mercantilist philosophy which had been the dominant economic philosophy in the Western world for almost three hundred years. Mercantilism was to be a prime cause of the American Revolution, and was revived in the twentieth century as the corporate state in Hitler's Germany, Mussolini's Italy, Franco's Spain, and Salazar's Portugal. Writing at the close of the eighteenth century Smith devoted about one quarter of his opus, *The Wealth of Nations*, to a relentless criticism of what he called the "commercial or mercantile system."

With the decline of feudalism, the increasing importance of merchants was accompanied by the rise of nationalism — and of national sovereigns who needed money desperately to pay for the growing cost of civil government in a period when commercial and religious wars were numerous and exhausting. It is not surprising, therefore, that mercantilism presented decided contrasts to the medieval period which preceded it. Whereas the medieval conception, based on local politics, was that the primary object of human effort was to insure a life in Heaven for the whole of society — the mercantilist saw in the subjects of the national state a means to an earthly end — and that end was the power of the state itself. Furthermore, a sovereign state no longer showed any interest in society as a whole; its concern was in its own advancement, usually at the expense of rival states. This objective required both military might and the subjection of citizens to the will of the sovereign. Philosophically, mercantilism replaced medieval religion, and the morals that went with it, with a fatalistic belief in unalterable laws of social causation. In his desire to subject the individual to the state, the mercantilist adopted an attitude toward life that was nonmoral and nonhumanitarian — whether the era was that of Henry VIII in England or Adolf Hitler in Germany.

In economics the mercantilist conception of what was good for a country centered on three closely allied aspects of economic life: the supply of money, commodities, and labor. To the mercantilist the wealth of a nation consisted of money, chiefly gold bullion. Mercantilism appeared at a time when coin was scarcer than commodities, and when specie (coin) was required not only to make up the adverse balance of trade for the luxuries of the Orient, but to provide the wherewithal with which kings hired their mercenary armies — and in time their navies. The mercantilist hoarded money, in decided contrast to the Middle Ages when the wealth of society was in the other world, and to Adam Smith (in the nineteenth century) for whom the wealth of nations was the production which resulted from labor and natural resources. Whatever the theories, bullion was all-important to the mercantilists, so much so that some of them forgot its purpose and became mere collectors. Moderns have sometimes wondered, in the same fashion, about the gold which the U.S. government has deposited at Fort Knox. The mercantilist also differed from the medievalist in regard to commodities. In the medieval period the prevalent idea was that a local community should secure plenty of food, clothing, and shelter. In order to do so imports were encouraged and obstacles were placed against exports, which were wanted for local consumption. In the feudal period, therefore, the objective was to import more than was exported. The ideal of the mercantilist was the reverse; he wanted a favorable balance of trade — to export more than he imported — so that gold would flow into the country in payment. The mercantilist went further. He came to look upon a plentiful supply of commodities *within a country* with just as much disfavor as the medievalist had regarded it with approbation. The mercantilist idea was to get rid of commodities — not to use them. In this sense the term *mercantilism* is apt, since it implies that the best policy for a nation is the same as that for an individual merchant, who seeks to take in more by selling than he pays out in buying — and thus builds a cash balance for his firm. As far as workingmen were concerned the mercantilist wanted an abundance of cheap labor in order to increase his ability to compete in price with other nations. As a consequence he was in favor of an increase in population, child labor, and employment of women. What would later be called the "iron law of wages" kept compensation at the subsistence level; it also kept workers so poverty-stricken that in Britain the terms "workers" and "the poor" were synonymous until late in the nineteenth century. Some, like Malthus later, would worry about the increase in population. Not so the mercantilists; they figured that if the population became too large the surplus could be sent to the colonies or allowed to die.

By this time it is apparent to even the casual reader that a number of faults were inherent in the mercantilist system. Politically, the creed led to wars because the mercantilist could not see that the gain of one country was not necessarily the loss of others, or that the whole family of nations — by sharing knowledge and products — might enjoy common security and a rising standard of living. Economically, it is obvious that it is impossible for *all* nations to have a favorable balance of trade, and that a continual influx of bullion will bring inflation, high prices, and the ultimate loss of one's export market. Philosophically, it is shockingly evident that the ideas of the mercantilists ran counter to the Judeo-Christian ethic in which the Western world professed to take pride.

The Industrial Revolution, which occurred first in England in the century after 1750, introduced new sources of mechanical power, new products, and new types of transportation. The new mechanical power, in turn, was generated by a new technological development, the application of steam produced first by coal and later by gas, oil, and atomic energy. This development resulted in a phenomenal increase in energy. Ancient Athens at her richest had provided, for the average member of a citizen's family, no more than the muscular power provided by five slaves. In 1962 every man, woman, and child in the United States commanded the mechanical energy generated by ten tons of coal: the equivalent of a hundred slaves. Some now consider automation the Second Industrial Revolution because this new development provides a substitute, not for human muscle but for the human nervous system. The new automational tools are expected to behave like a sensing, thinking man.

The new products of the First Industrial Revolution were largely the result of new materials used as substitutes for wood and stone. These products were made from iron and steel, from baked clay through the art of ceramics (for example, Wedgwood china), and from the plastics which came out of the developing field of physical chemistry. The new types of transportation were the steamship, which took the place of the sailing vessel — and the train, the airplane, and the automobile, which replaced the cart.

Actually the Industrial Revolution marked a slow transition from a stable agricultural and commercial society to modern industry. It was an evolution, not a revolution — and it was not restricted to England. The same transformation occurred in other countries at other times. In the United States the transition was intensified in the thirty years after the Civil War. In Japan it occurred around 1900, in Russia after World War I, in China and India after World War II. But no matter how slow and diverse the process may have been, all economic thought since the eighteenth century has represented an attempt to interpret the so-called Industrial Revolution; in actual fact the field of economics, as a major study, came into existence with the Industrial Revolution. The first interpreters were later called classical economists, and were so designated by Karl Marx, who refrained from using the term derisively, as Adam Smith had done in reference to the mercantilists. There were three classical economists of great prominence: Smith, Ricardo, and Malthus.

Adam Smith, the father of classical economics, was one of the most influential men who ever lived. This absentminded professor of moral philosophy at Glasgow University certainly did not look his part; he was troubled throughout life with a nervous affliction, his speech was odd and stumbling, and his head shook. He was a perfect exemplar of the aphorism accredited to John Stuart Mill: "One person with a belief is a force equal to ninety-nine who have only interests." Once he was invited by Prime Minister Pitt (the Younger) to attend a conference. As the old philosopher entered the chamber everyone rose, but Smith told them to be seated. "No," replied the prime minister, "we will stand until you are first seated, for we are all your scholars." Before Smith's death, his *Wealth of Nations* had been translated into Danish, French, German, Italian, and Spanish. There were interesting coincidences relating to both the time and the place of its writing. It appeared in 1776, along with the American Declaration of Independence. As Robert Heilbroner has observed (in his brilliantly written *The Worldly Philosophers*), there were two revolutionary events in that one fateful year — a political democracy was born on one side of the ocean and an economic blueprint was unfolded on the other. There is some evidence to indicate that Smith's influence was the greater; only a part of Europe became democratic, but the entire Western world was to follow the principles of laissez-faire. Smith wrote his work at Glasgow, where he was a friend of James Watt who was an instrument maker attached to the university because the local trade union would not permit him to open a workshop in the city. Watt was the founder of modern scientific industrial technique. It was a strange coincidence that these two men, working at the same time and place, produced work that revolutionized both economic thought and the technique of production.

Smith was a seminal thinker, and among the many academic seeds which he planted the following may be selected for special observation: a new definition of the wealth of nations, the self-interest of the individual in the marketplace, competition as the "invisible hand," and the concept of laissez-faire. In the feudal period the wealth of society had been in another world; to the mercantilist the worth of a nation was measured in bullion. To Smith the wealth of nations consisted of the commodities that resulted from the proper use of both labor and resources in increasing production. Smith saw that mercantilism could not survive the glut of "Things" brought about by the Industrial Revolution. There simply was not enough gold to buy the Things; in time a substitute money (in the form of paper credit) had to be created, with a quantity as variable as the supply of commodities. Credit destroyed the basic principle on which mercantilism was based — the idea of the scarcity of money. As far as the self-interest of the individual was concerned, Smith pondered the problem of how a society manages to get tasks done which are necessary for its survival. It was apparent that the people of a country must perform some work, or the society would perish. Where was the motivation for work? Smith found that this impetus to work, in past centuries, had been supplied either by tradition or authority. In primitive societies sons had inherited tasks from fathers, and the work had gone on. In totalitarian regimes the whip of autocratic rule had been used, for example, to complete the pyramids — and in recent times the Autobahn in Germany and the Five-Year Plan in Russia. Smith rejected both tradition and authority; he found the solution in the market system. In the free market, he believed, men would be motivated by the desire for monetary gain — by a quest for profit — and would need neither tradition nor authority as a spur. The lure for gain, he thought, would supply all the impetus that was needed.

There was an obvious danger of anarchy in a system in which each individual went his own way, following only his own self-interest. What was needed was a "governor" — a "regulator" — an "invisible hand" that would guide selfish individuals to a goal which served all of society. Smith found his "invisible hand" in *competition*, which would keep any one person or group from becoming too powerful, and would bind the whole of society together in such a beneficent way that social good would actually result from individual selfishness. But if the marketplace and individual self-interest and competition were to function at all, it was Smith's judgment that the government must keep hands off. In actual fact he disliked political men, and once wrote contemptuously of that "insidious and crafty animal, vulgarly called a politician." He believed that government should "let do" and "let go," that is, follow a policy of laissez-faire, laissez-aller. Actually he appropriated these phrases from a group of French economic theorists called the Physiocrats. They believed that land was the source of all wealth, that the mercantilist French state was interfering too much and should keep hands off. The founder of the physiocratic school was François Quesnay, economist and court physician of Louis XV. Asked by the dauphin what he would do if he were king, Quesnay is reported to have replied, "Nothing." Whatever the source of the phrase "laissez-faire," Smith's concern for the rights of the *individual* in this world was a far cry from the philosophy of the mercantilist who believed only in the welfare of the state, or from the religion of the medievalist who put his faith in another world. His philosophy, in time to be identified with conservatism, became the credo for businessmen, politicians, and ministers throughout U.S. history.

David Ricardo, a British economist of Dutch-Jewish parentage, was the systematizer of classical economics — a cold theorist who defined prices, rents, wages, and profits from a capitalist point of view. A brilliant entrepreneur himself, he was able to retire at twenty-five from the proceeds of his brokerage business; thereafter he devoted himself to study, to writing, and to Anglican country affairs save for a brief period in Parliament at the end of his life. He is probably best known for his "iron law of wages," with its cheerless dogma that wages cannot rise above the lowest level necessary for subsistence. Under this relentless dictate, which Ricardo enshrined as an immutable law of social causation, massive privation and inequality forecast for the working class enduring peril and hopelessness.

The third of the founding fathers, Thomas Malthus, was not only an English clergyman but an economist, sociologist, and pioneer in population study as well. In his *Essay on the Principle of Population* (1798) it was his contention that poverty and distress were inevitable because population increased geometrically while the food supply was augmented in a much more leisurely arithmetic ratio. With his theological approach Malthus could see no checks on population growth except the natural and grisly ones of war, famine, and disease. Later he concluded there might be a rational check in "moral restraint" from copulation, but this solution presented obvious difficulties because he saw sexual coitus as the privilege of the rich who could afford children. It was the poor, who were least likely to listen, who were advised to abstain. His predictions were so gloomy, and his solutions so unsatisfactory, that it was the reading of Malthus (along with that of Ricardo) that caused Thomas Carlyle to dub the two of them the "respectable Professors of the Dismal Science."

Smith, Ricardo, and Malthus had based their ideas on a "natural order" that could not be changed. Under their philosophy, as the social-gospel clergyman Washington Gladden would observe, economics became the not too gentle art of "grinding the faces of the poor" — indeed a dismal science "because of the selfishness of its maxims and the inhumanity of its conclusions." About the middle of the nineteenth century, as John Kenneth Galbraith sees it, economic theory came to a "great divide" between the classical economists and those who thought something could be done about the "natural order," even if it had to be destroyed. In the period from 1850 to 1929 the problem was one of scarcity, and writers like Karl Marx, Henry George, and Thorstein Veblen wanted to do something about the inequitable distribution of that scarcity. Since 1929 the problem has been one of abundance rather than scarcity, and theorists like John Maynard Keynes and Gerard Piel have speculated on what can be done to bring about a more equitable distribution of that abundance.

The inequitable distribution of scarcity, about which Marx and George and Veblen would write, was historically necessary during the Industrial Revolution in every country in which it occurred. In this so-called period of "carboniferous capitalism" money had to be provided for the increase of production, and this meant vast sums indeed. Where did this capital come from? It could be obtained in several ways. It could be stolen or borrowed from someone else who had it, or it could be accumulated slowly by producing *more* than one consumed — and saving the difference. The British, who first ran into the problem on a large scale, did all three. They stole from Spanish and Portuguese merchants and freebooters.

They borrowed from their aristocrats. They resorted to *forced* saving, engaging for a century in what Marx called *primitive* capital accumulation — or as most contemporary economists know it, forced saving from labor. Laborers were compelled, for survival, to work twelve to fourteen hours a day in factories and coal mines — boys and girls of eight to ten along with their parents — while all of them lived on a bare subsistence level in squalor and destitution. It was their conditions, graphically described by Hardy and Dickens, that moved Marx to remark about workers and their chains. For three or four generations the British produced a great deal and consumed just as little as possible; the difference went to pay for the railroads, mines, factories, and ships that formed the skeleton of British industrial power. The story has been the same in each industrial revolution that has followed. In the United States historians continue to celebrate the frontier, but it was 35 million steerage immigrants — a flood of humanity equal to the nation's population at the end of the Civil War — who furnished the primary capital for the Industrial Revolution that got underway in the United States at the middle of the nineteenth century.

In 1968, the 150th anniversary of the birth of Karl Marx was celebrated in various parts of the world. By that time, in terms of his impact on the twentieth century, he was regarded by many as the most influential thinker who ever lived. Communist-ruled countries with populations totaling a billion people now hail him as the founder of their fundamental ideology. Even non-Marxist historians and economists agree that his ideas have had a profound effect on the development of the modern world and have exerted a strong influence on much of the academic thinking about it. During his lifetime (1818–1883), however, he was considered a relatively minor figure and he lived most of his adult life in abject poverty. In the modern era his *Das Kapital*, a three-volume work devoted to the theory and practice of the exploitive nature of capitalism, has been compared with the Gospels and the Koran as an evangelistic document. In his own time the work was considered so boring and difficult to read that the Russian censors approved a translation for publication on the ground that so few people could understand the book that it would pose no threat to the czarist regime. Ironically Marx, the man who scoffed at moralists, who said that what counts is the evolution of material forces and not the abstract ideals in men's minds, turned out to be the most powerful moral teacher of his time.

He was a German born at Trier who was thrown out of his native land after earning his Ph.D. in philosophy at Jena; he lived most of his life in London, where he is buried in Highgate Cemetery. It seems surprising that a future agnostic and Communist should emerge from his origins, which were traditional and respectably middle class. His religious background was orthodox in *two* faiths; his family produced a long line of rabbis in

Trier, but he and his immediate family were baptized as Christians (Karl was six) because his father was a lawyer and Jews could not be admitted to the bar at that time. In the twentieth century the term "alienation" has become a favorite, and some explain Marx's reaction to society by pointing to the tension between his Jewish heritage and his Lutheran upbringing. They say his problem was one of reconciling the Jewish desire for a collective meaning in history with the Lutheran emphasis on individual man, alone and naked before God. Whatever the explanation, the Marx family was distinctly bourgeois, and the famous son married the daughter (Baroness Jenny von Westphalen) of a landed aristocrat. In exile in London, however, his poverty was so acute and the family was in such desperate straits that three of his six children died from diseases probably aggravated by malnutrition, a grievous blow because Marx was passionately fond of them. One does not wonder that his mother was reported to have said that she wished her son would spend less time writing about, and more effort in making, *Das Kapital*. In England his only regular income was his pay for articles sent to Horace Greeley's New York *Tribune* as its European correspondent. This pittance was later augmented by family legacies, and generous loans and gifts from his colleague Friedrich Engels, whose wealthy father owned an interest in a Manchester cotton mill. It is ironic that *Das Kapital*, certainly a revolutionary work, should have been financed by profits derived from a British cotton mill supported by German funds.

In his criticism of classical economics Marx made three major points:

The Economic Interpretation of History. In Marxian language this was dialectical *materialism*, a phrase which was the inverse of the German philosopher Hegel's dialectical *idealism*. To Marx, social and economic changes were the result of materialistic forces only. This meant that the entire course of history, in all its manifestations, had been determined by economic conditions only, and that important historical change took place only where strategic alterations occurred in methods of producing or exchanging goods — such as happened at the time of the Commercial and Industrial Revolutions. Intellectuals might believe there were historical factors other than economic ones — ideas centering around race, religion, culture, and fatherland — but all these were to Marx evanescent "ideological veils" which obscured the real economic forces behind them. For him dialectical materialism was the "one pass-key" that would unlock all historic secrets.

The Surplus Value Theory of Labor. To Marx labor, not bullion or commodities, was the source of all value; in fact he believed a commodity to be a mass of congealed labor-time. The tragedy, in his analysis, was that the laborer did not receive full value. Only a portion of the workday was expended in producing what the laborer actually got in wages; what he produced during the remainder of the day — "surplus value" — was siphoned off by capitalists in the form of profits. To Marx wages were, for the laborer, an illusion that he was paid for a full day's work; because of this situation the rich would become more wealthy as the poverty of the poor increased. The resultant and mounting misery would produce another sequence, namely —

THE CLASS STRUGGLE, THE DICTATORSHIP OF THE PROLETARIAT, AND A CLASSLESS SOCIETY. Marx believed that every ruling class would be replaced, until a classless society emerged — for example, from feudal lords to merchants to capitalists to the proletariat. The difference was that, after the dictatorship of the proletariat, class distinctions would ultimately disappear and the oppressive state — the instrument of the dominant class — would fade away.

There have been so many variants of Marxism that Marx himself is reputed to have said, "Thank God I am not a Marxist!" But as far as one can study *Das Kapital* a century after it appeared, two of his conclusions have been proved wrong:

The State has not withered away, and there has been no dictatorship of the proletariat. In the non-Communist world the State has begun to represent labor along with owners and other groups in society. The State has not withered away in the Communist countries either; in practice the dictatorship has been that of the Party — the political and managerial bureaucracy — or of a Stalin. In order to get capital, through forced saving, Russian workers have been forced to work long and hard, while consuming very little — to pay for Five-Year Plans and military defense. In this as in other respects, Communist states — not withered but strong — have exploited their populations as Marx bemoaned the treatment of workers by capitalists.

Labor has not developed a revolutionary, but a trade-union point of view. It has steadfastly declined to enter management, and has tried only to get for workers — through wages, pensions, and fringe benefits — the largest practicable share of national income. In the achievement of these, in highly industrialized states, it has been quite successful. Curiously Marx deserves as much credit as any man for having stimulated the reforms that have kept capitalism from destroying itself.

Marx would have destroyed the "natural order" of the classical economists. Henry George and Thorstein Veblen proposed not to annihilate, but to reform the capitalist system.

George was the single-taxer who wrote *Progress and Poverty* — of which more copies have been circulated than of any other economic work. The volume became the economic Bible of an able and articulate group of men — both abroad and in the United States. George had a profound influence on Leo Tolstoy, Sun Yat-sen, and George Bernard Shaw, who said, "Henry George set me on the economic trail, the trail of political science." In the United States, Joseph Fels — the millionaire manufacturer of Fels-Naptha Soap — founded a Single-Tax Commission, and financed it with more than a million dollars. C. H. Ingersoll, the wealthy watchmaker, contributed to the commission, and the well-known journalist Lincoln Steffens accepted a position on it. In Cleveland, Ohio, the famous reform mayor, Tom Johnson, himself a millionaire, became a convert to the single-tax philosophy, tried unsuccessfully to introduce it into Ohio, and at his death was buried near George in Brooklyn, New York.

The economic basis for George's perverse view of progress — Progress *and* Poverty — was really a legacy from Ricardo, who had pointed out that labor and capital increased in productivity, but that land supply remained constant in quality and extent. As a result, land rents increased disproportionately; this development made landlords the undeserving beneficiaries of progress. In England John Stuart Mill once remarked, "Landlords grow rich in their sleep." In the United States the first Marshall Field, who made a large part of his $100 million in Chicago land speculation, would say, "Land is not just a good way to make money . . . it is the only way to make money."

As Ricardo saw it, this was all part of the "natural order," and nothing could be done about it. George disagreed. He claimed that most of the increase in the value of land was due not to the owner, but to the growth of the surrounding community. This was true in George's time and it is true today. The Verrazano-Narrows Bridge, completed in 1964, connecting Staten Island with Brooklyn, doubled the Island's population in less than five years — with land values increasing at a minimum of 400 percent. The taxpayers of New York State spent almost half a billion dollars to build the New York Thruway, and the immediate effect was to add much more than that to land prices along the route. The federal government has played a similar role. The great boom in western land after the Civil War (which brought immense profits to some land speculators) was a direct consequence of the subsidization, by all American taxpayers, of the transcontinental railroad. Today the government's space program at Cape Kennedy, New Orleans, and Houston, has increased land values on the thousand-mile crescent which stretches from Florida's Atlantic coast to the Texas panhandle. George believed that labor and capital were productive, but that rent was an unearned increment which reduced wages (for labor) and interest (on capital) by its total amount. To him, the entrepreneur and the laborer were praiseworthy; the landlord was wicked. He said to a symbolic landlord:

> "You may sit down and smoke your pipe; . . . you may go up in a balloon or down a hole in the ground; and without doing one stroke of work, without adding one iota of wealth to the community, in ten years you will be rich! In the new city you may have a luxurious mansion, but among its public buildings will be an almshouse."

George thus equated rent with sin, and progress with poverty. He believed that unearned increment should be confiscated in the form of a single tax for the benefit of all. This unique tax would amount to all, or practically all, of economic rent; all other forms of direct and indirect taxation would be abolished.

It was a difficult theory to carry into practice, but *Progress and Poverty* was, in its day, and still is, widely read. The book "caught on" for a variety of reasons. For one thing George was optimistic. Smith, Ricardo, Malthus, and Marx were convinced that nothing could be done to reform the system. George believed progress possible because economic systems were the creations of the *minds* of men. In addition, George was eloquent and wrote with tremendous conviction. This was partly due to a religious background — his father was a vestryman in the Episcopal Church — but chiefly because of George's own poverty when he lived in California. After his second child was born, the doctor said that mother and child were starving. George stopped the first well-dressed man he met on the street and asked him for five dollars. He said later that if the stranger had not been moved by his story and had not produced the money, he was prepared to knock him down and take it. These desperate years gave him a personal knowledge of poverty which was reflected in everything he wrote.

Is George's proposal still pertinent in the present era? One real-estate authority, Daniel M. Friedenberg, has noted that the single tax would be discriminatory for an important class of investors in an economy where leasehold arrangements, long-term tenant commitments on fixed rentals, and heavy mortgages are quite common. He believes, however, that a modified single-tax policy would receive widespread support if it had two features: (1) an increase in the assessment on land to be paid by the owner as its value is augmented by extraneous factors, such as improvements in transportation, and (2) taxation of land in relation to its potential value when fully used rather than on its unimproved market value; that is, a higher levy based on the value of improved land in full use rather than the lower tax actually assessed when it stands idle. In the first case, the entire taxpaying public subsidizes the increase in value, but local individuals and speculators reap great profits although they expend little effort or energy to make them possible. Friedenberg notes that if the system were changed so that those who get unexpected "windfalls" were to bear some part of the public subsidy that made them possible, they would still come out ahead and the community would have less of a tax burden. On the second point, models exist for the taxation of land on the basis of use; Australia has provided the most impressive ones. In Sydney land is taxed as though it was improved; this has driven out both land speculators and slum owners, neither of whom can afford to pay the full-use tax. Brisbane forbids taxes on improvements but has a uniform 9 percent tax on land regardless of what is constructed on it. In Denmark both land and improvements are taxed, but land at a steeper rate. One American city, Pittsburgh, has adopted a similar formula; it taxes land at full-use value while improvements are taxed at half value. This has forced the improvement of land and has encouraged growth, as the significant building activity in that city attests. Elsewhere in the United States, however, tax policy is both discriminatory and inequitable. Those who improve the land — owners of homes, apartment buildings, and commercial property — pay higher taxes than the land speculator who simply waits for the entire community to increase the price of his land. In the late 1960's land constituted one-third of our total national wealth but carried only 5 percent of the total tax load. To Friedenberg, continuation of such an inequity could bring real trouble. He observes that "from an historical view it can be said that it was the narrow feudal policy of East European capitalists — holding land and refusing to permit its development — that helped to create an environment hospitable to the Communist take-over. This is even more true in Latin America today."

Thorstein Veblen (1857–1929) was born of Norwegian parentage on a Wisconsin farm, spent the first seventeen years of his life in Norwegian rural communities, and had to learn English as a foreign language. He was educated at Carleton, Johns Hopkins, and Yale, achieved a gargantuan and varied learning (among other things he translated sagas from the Icelandic), and was sometimes known as the "last man who knew everything."

As an eccentric he always remained aloof from society and traditional manners. He had the appearance of a Norwegian peasant, dressed in a thick and unpressed suit, and wore on his vest a large safety pin on which he moored his watch. He was never very popular with students because he gave them all the same grade of C, mumbled intricate sentences, and was given to sarcasm. He also experienced difficulty with university administrators, in part because of numerous liaisons with a variety of women; Veblen's explanation was in the form of a question, "What are you going to do if the woman moves in on you?" President Abbott Lawrence Lowell is supposed to have said at a faculty dinner for Harvard professors and their wives that if Veblen was interested in teaching at Cambridge he must promise to leave faculty wives strictly alone. As the story goes Veblen looked carefully around the room at the professorial consorts, and then assured Lowell there was nothing to worry about.

In spite of these eccentricities Veblen made a signal contribution to the development of economic thought because of his introduction of psychology into economic interpretation and his theory of a new "leisure" class. He was able to analyze social and economic institutions from a psychological base, and for this reason he is known as the founder of institutional economics. His most famous book was *The Theory of the Leisure Class* (1899). Here he drew a distinction between technology (the making of goods), which was a constructive force, and business (the making of money), which was purely predatory. Technology could produce abundance for all, but this abundance was not properly distributed because of monopolistic practices. To Veblen a modern business was open to the same censure as that applied to a barbaric chieftain. Neither had an abiding concern for the welfare and happiness of contemporaries; both were chiefly interested in a dubious personal status which was achieved through vulgar ostentation to advertise their power and wealth.

During the early stages of the Industrial Revolution — the stages which Walter Rostow called the "take-off" and the drive to maturity — the purpose was to *maximize production* and to *minimize consumption*. The first portent that there was too much production, and too little consumption, came in 1929. We were then confronted by the paradox of poverty in the midst of plenty. Since World War II this problem of abundance has become more acute because of the progress of technology, particularly the introduction of electronics and automation. Since 1929, therefore, some economists have attacked the problem, that of the equitable distribution of abundance. Keynes has done so through his "investment subterfuge." Gerard Piel and John Kenneth Galbraith have made their contributions through their insistence on investment in the public rather than in the private sector.

John Maynard Keynes, the first baron of Tilton (1883–1946), was educated at Cambridge where he studied mathematics and philosophy as well as economics. As a young official of the treasury he was largely responsible for handling Britain's financial dealings with the United States during World War I. He attended the Versailles Peace Conference and damned the treaty in a book (*Economic Consequences of the Peace*) which plunged him into a sea of controversy that continued until his death almost three decades later. He denounced the treaty and said it wouldn't work, particularly the reparations payments imposed on Germany. In the 1920's his opposition to Britain's reestablishment of the gold standard was so vigorous that his pamphlet on the subject was called *The Economic Consequences of Mr. Churchill*. During the Great Depression his theories on deficit spending influenced the governments of many nations, including that of the United States. During World War II he was again an important figure in the British treasury, and was one of the leading spirits at Bretton Woods in 1944, out of which came the establishment of the World Bank and the International Monetary Fund.

He believed in capitalism via the road of governmental assistance for investment. His studies convinced him that the "invisible hand" of Adam Smith did not always function, particularly in connection with the decision to save and the impetus to invest. Investors were lavish with savings when times were good, and the economy didn't need them; they withheld funds for investment when economic conditions were less optimistic, and when the economy sorely needed the stimulus of new investment. Keynes did not believe the economy was a seesaw that would automatically right itself; it was more like an elevator that might be going up or down *or* standing still. Most disconcerting of all was the realization that the elevator might be standing still at the bottom of the economic shaft, and would stay there indefinitely because of the disinclination of individuals to invest. In such situations (the Great Depression) governmental inducements were essential to move the elevator (the economy). This impetus was provided by governmental investment; the money would be derived initially by placing the heaviest taxes on people with the largest incomes — the very people who had withheld the funds from private investments. If the money from taxation was not sufficient, the government should borrow, through deficit financing, to meet its needs.

With this governmental stimulus to investment through taxation and, if necessary, borrowing — Keynes believed that the rest of the economy *could* and *should* be left to private initiative. He believed in capitalism provided it was prodded judiciously and in timely fashion when private initiative failed. Keynes has been called everything from Socialist to subversive; actually, as Robert Heilbroner has pointed out, he placed his faith in a *capitalism viable*. Marx had believed in *capitalism doomed*. Marx believed that the capitalist system did not and could not function; Keynes analyzed the reasons why it did not, but believed it could be made to work. The greatest tribute to the comparative conservatism of Keynes is that both the Republican party and the Democratic party in the United States, in spite of windy protestations to the contrary, are prepared to follow his precepts when the economic elevator stands at the bottom of the shaft.

Keynes was most perceptive because he realized that there was a valid reason for the reluctance of private investors to venture their funds in the 1930's. In earlier times capital for investment had been short, and was actually provided through an inequitable distribution of scarcity — laborers contributed through low wages, and capitalists were expected to plow a large part of their profits back into the plant and production. The purpose of Keynes's "investment subterfuge," in an economy which had the problem of abundance rather than scarcity, was to increase consumption without increasing production. The Keynesian theory called for an increase in the current rate of investment — but investment on roads, buildings, and relief in what John Kenneth Galbraith would call the public sector. This type of investment created consumers, but no addition to the consumable surplus.

Gerard Piel, the discerning economist who doubles as publisher of *Scientific American*, has observed that since World War II the new problem of abundance has been solved in part by what President Eisenhower referred to as the military-industrial complex, by spending in the public sector on armaments. This device helped solve the problem of abundance in two ways: it provided purchasing power through paychecks to soldiers and to workers in armament industries, and it avoided any increase in the *consumable* surplus by producing armaments which could not be consumed — except in the event of war. Apart from the morality or immorality of such a policy, Piel pointed out that spending in the public sector for armaments had not solved the problem of abundance, and was not likely to do so — unless the nation was willing to go to war. The peacetime year of 1962 was typical — idle plants and rotting surpluses and high unemployment existed in spite of a 25 percent increase in military expenditures. Furthermore, outlays on armaments were beginning to yield a diminishing economic stimulus because of what has been called the "miniaturization of violence" — the technological steps from A- to H-bombs, from manned aircraft to missiles. We were already armed with the equivalent of ten tons of TNT for every man, woman, and child on earth; little could be gained, economically or militarily, by raising that figure to twenty tons.

Piel thinks we have reached a fork in the road, a fork which will confront us with a central question — "Can We Afford Disarmament?" We can, says Piel, if in the public sector — comprising federal, state, and local governments — expenditures are such that increased purchasing power will be provided to consume the ever-growing surplus of goods. The funds released by disarmament, and more, would be invested in the enrichment of land and people — in education, mass transportation, conservation of natural resources, pollution control (both air and water), urban renewal, and problems of health. There is no economic barrier to the achievement of these goals. The chief obstacles are political. In the *international* sphere the major nations, including the United States, must be convinced that disarmament is desirable. In the *domestic* sphere the people of the United States, and their representatives in Congress, must believe that expenditures for civilian purposes in the public sector are more valid than expenditures for military purposes in the same public sector. This requires a political decision; on the economic side the choice is merely one of selecting the methods of solving the problem of abundance. Unfortunately the political obstacle is an annoying and exasperating one, and has been for a long time. After World War I the famed muckraker Lincoln Steffens would say about the fiasco at Versailles, "We do not want war; nobody in the world wants war. But some of us do want the things we can't have without war."

A half century later Senator Fred Harris of Oklahoma observed, "We always hear the farthest rumble of a distant drum but not the voice of a hungry child." In 1969 an $80 billion defense budget in which business, labor, and the Pentagon all had a direct stake, constituted a political juggernaut in search of a military mission. This was, in essence, the military-industrial complex (really the military-industrial-labor complex) against which President Eisenhower had warned when he left the White House in 1961. To many it seemed that national priorities were out of kilter.*

*In 1969 Senator William Proxmire of Wisconsin was disturbed by the easy movement of high-ranking military officers into jobs with major defense contractors, and the reverse movement of top defense contractors into high Pentagon jobs; both provided solid evidence of the military-industrial complex in operation. Proxmire issued a report showing that the number of retired officers working for the defense industry had tripled in the past ten years. A list prepared in 1959 for Paul H. Douglas, then a Democratic senator from Illinois, counted 721 retired military officers of the rank of colonel or navy captain and above working in the 88 defense industries. Proxmire's study, made with the cooperation of industry and the Pentagon in 1969, showed that 2,072 retired military officers of the rank of colonel or navy captain and above were employed by the leading military contractors. He saw this as a real threat to the public interest because it increased the chances for abuse through not-so-subtle bribery, particularly when coupled with a system of military procurement which permitted almost 90 percent of all military contracts to be negotiated rather than being awarded on the basis of competitive bidding. Proxmire did not believe that officers, looking forward to jobs in defense plants after retirement from the military, would drive very hard bargains — in the public interest — with those same industries. He listed the ten defense contractors which had the largest number of former military officers in their employ, as follows: General Dynamics (113), Lockheed (210), GE (19), United Aircraft (48), McDonnell Douglas (141), AT&T (9), Boeing (169), Ling-Temco-Vought (69), North American Rockwell (104), and GM (17).

II

A Great New Frontier for Enterprisers: The Commercial Revolution and the Age of the Reconnaissance

THE cataclysm that was ultimately responsible for the rapid development of economics and industry in western Europe and in the United States was known as the Commercial Revolution. It occurred around 1500, and was marked by a shift of trade from the Mediterranean to the Atlantic — from the interior *mare nostrum* to western open-sea ports.

In 1500 the greatest power in Europe was not England, France, or Germany. It was the Republic of Venice, which then occupied a position of primacy in world commerce and manufacturing — a position similar to that of Great Britain in later days. Around 1500 Venice had rivals in Florence and Genoa — but it was Venice that was the master of trade with the Orient, and that was Europe's chief marketplace, its major ship-building center, and one of its leading manufacturing establishments — particularly for the production of wool and silk fabrics, and in glassmaking. This preeminence, as that which came in England later, was based on a preponderant sea power and on a system of strategically placed naval bases and trading posts.

Unfortunately for Venice, the Atlantic Ocean, once a barrier, became a bridge. Europe was to turn as on a pivot from East to West; as a result renown came to heretofore obscure Atlantic states that happened to be in the heart of the rising new trade lanes and therefore benefited from the new and far-ranging *Age of the Reconnaissance*. These states were in western Europe — and ultimately in the colonies of western Europe, including what is now called the United States. On the other hand, the Commercial

Revolution brought tragedy to the Italy that had benefited so much from the older and contained *Age of the Renaissance.*

The exact causes for any decided change are always difficult to ascertain; in the case of the Commercial Revolution four of them appear to have been predominant. These can be classified as technological, economic, political, and religious.

Curiously enough, three of the technological inventions that contributed most to the Commercial Revolution came from China. These were the compass, gunpowder, and printing from movable type. Europeans had known the compass as early as the twelfth century but had used it sparingly — in part because it was not perfected, and in part because sailors looked upon it as an engine of witchcraft. Gunpowder was used in western Europe to blow up local feudal states and to accelerate the rise of national states and sovereigns, and later would make swifter the conquest of primitive peoples in the colonies of these rising national states.

Printing encouraged the rapid spread of information and the quickening of men's minds that comes from reading. The fifteenth-century John Gutenberg is known as the "inventor of printing" — but for the wrong reason. Long before Gutenberg, Orientals had cut letters by hand, either in metal or in wood, but this was far too tedious a process to produce many books. Gutenberg's actual contribution was to discover a metal alloy that neither contracted nor expanded when it went from a molten to a solid state. Previously the molten metals had either expanded too much — breaking the type box or making it impossible to get a clean piece of type free — or the alloy had contracted to the point where the product was imperfect. But Gutenberg was more than an inventor: he understood the need for mass production, the benchmark of our modern era.

In addition to inventions certain economic influences — some of them operative for a long time — were instrumental in bringing about change at the beginning of the sixteenth century. These were the stimulation of the Crusades, the salesmanship of Marco Polo, and the desire to circumvent existing high prices for Mideastern and Oriental products. As Thomas A. Bailey has pointed out so acutely, the Christian Crusaders must take high rank among the indirect discoverers of America — even though they were active three to four hundred years before Columbus discovered America. The Crusades created a desire for goods from the East; as a result European "barbarians" came to appreciate more fully "the value of spices for spoiled and monotonous food; of silk for rough skins; of drugs for aching flesh; of perfumes for unbathed bodies; and of colorful draperies for gloomy castles."

Marco Polo, a footloose Venetian, returned to Italy in 1295 after a sojourn of nearly two decades in China and dictated a travel account that became a classic. Polo was wonder-struck at Oriental splendors and was given to exaggerated descriptions of rose-tinted pearls and golden pagodas — but his volume was reasonably factual and has been of great value to historians. It fascinated Europe and when it was first printed, in 1477, became something of a best seller. Few books have so shaped and driven men's imaginations. During the Renaissance it was the chief, almost the sole, Western source of information on the East, and until the late nineteenth century there was no other European documentation on many parts of eastern Asia. As a medieval predecessor to Richard Burton and Horace Sutton, Marco Polo stirred the interests and desires of Europeans for a cheaper route to the exciting and exotic treasures of the Far East.

Alas! these treasures were expensive because of excessive costs for transportation, and because of monopolistic practices on the part of both the Turks and the Venetians. Goods had to be transported enormous distances from the Orient, often on swaying camelback; it is axiomatic that land transportation is usually much more expensive than that by water. There were also the Ottoman Turks, a new race of conquerors who made their way into Asia Minor and were nibbling at the feeble Byzantine Empire. Constantinople fell to them in 1453, and the Turks were not to be finally stopped in their advance until they were turned back at the gates of Vienna at the close of the sixteenth century. They were so influential then, and even now, that a man could and can start in Serbia — zigzag south and east through the Balkans, cross Turkey and parts of the present Soviet Union, Iran, and Afghanistan — and reach China without speaking any language but Turkish. For a long time historians contended that, in the fifteenth century, a water route to the East had become essential because the Turks had cut off the trade. In essence it was the cupidity of the Turk, who exacted excessive tariffs and tolls, rather than his hostility that turned the thoughts of Westerners to the development of new routes to the East.

If the Turks were grasping so were the Italian city-states, particularly Venice. In Christian nations the Turk was looked on theologically as the scourge of God, but the Venetians compromised their religion for material advantage. In 1479, only a few years before the discovery of America, Venice made a treaty — frequently renewed — with Turkey that effectively barred other Western powers from the East. The consequence was that Venice was to have no real commercial rival in western Europe until the Portuguese found a direct route around Africa to the Orient.

Two commodities — drugs and spices — will illustrate the Western desire for Oriental products, and Western exasperation over high prices. In relation to drugs, Europeans held to the quaint belief that whenever a disease was found somewhere a remedy would be discovered. As Louis B. Wright has observed in his delightful book *The Dream of Prosperity in Colonial America*, the hope of discovering miraculous remedies overseas became a persistent reverie — and one that still survives. In those early days adventurers and merchants returned from distant parts with bales and barrels of weeds, bark, roots, and rocks — which had a ready sale as cures. This miscellany was picked up for nothing in the Far East, but was frightfully expensive by the time it reached western Europe. Because of pyramiding transportation costs and exchanges (as many as twenty resales), and the bribes for protection from theft, a bale of dried leaves that cost one ducat in the East Indies would sell in London for one hundred ducats — or 10,000 percent of the original price.

Spices, particularly pepper, made a monotonous diet more interesting and, given the lack of refrigeration at that time, disguised its true condition. Furthermore the market for pepper and other piquant preservatives was constant because northern Europe never had an adequate supply of winter forage and had to slaughter most of its meat animals in the autumn. The result was a great autumnal surplus of meat, preserved by the use of pepper and other spices. Peppercorns which did not deteriorate readily were always in short supply, and could be easily stored and transported; in time they were to have a value equal to their weight in gold.

The Commercial Revolution was brought on by political and religious developments as well as by inventions and the demands of trade. The political change was the transition from feudalism to national states, accompanied by the appearance of strong sovereigns who allied themselves with the emerging merchant and banking classes. Merchants and bankers, opposed by the Church and the landed nobility, found an ally in the rising kings. The merchants and the bankers provided the money to hire the sovereign's mercenary armies, armies that would stay on the field of battle so long as they were paid — in decided contrast to the noble's army, which was not paid and might go home. So the nature of war changed. When knighthood was in flower war had been considered a sporting duel — a duel in which God would arm the just side. This concept the rising kings ruined, by hiring "ringers." It was small wonder that the nobles were angered and that the Church was frightened by the coalition between kings and merchant towns.

This new development also had its effect on political philosophy. In medieval Europe the king's power was severely limited by public opinion; power depended on the loyalty of subordinates who were nobles and could refuse to go to war if they thought the cause to be unjust. Now the kings had a new power, which money bought; this made possible the purchase of obedience, or at least the purchase of mercenary soldiers who could impose that obedience. It is therefore not surprising to find Niccolò Machiavelli writing *The Prince* in the early sixteenth century, claiming that national sovereignty was a purely practical matter unconnected with either religion on the one hand or morals on the other.

For more than a thousand years the Catholic Church was the most prominent single institution in western Europe. It held that economic activity was no more than a minor function, completely subordinate to the primal concern of a Christian society, which was to increase the spiritual grace of its members. The Church knew that man must eat in order to live, but beyond this necessity man's interests were concerned with an ultimate and eternal goal. As a consequence the medieval Church established a basic attitude toward temporal economics which was quite different from the mercantilist philosophy which followed it. In specific categories of human endeavor, the Church found agriculture praiseworthy because it was good to produce food by toil in the fields. Industry was reasonable — if not good — because it made sense to devote time to a handicraft for the production of clothing and shelter. By contrast, commerce was risky because it meant earning a living by merely exchanging (not producing) goods for profit — a dubious practice which "satisfied the greed for gain which knows no limit and tends to infinity." The Church, therefore, stressed the maxim that "No Christian ought to be a merchant." Finance was believed to be fatal, because it was evil for a Christian to exact profit (through loans) from others simply for the use of money. In the heyday of the medieval period, loans, if made at all, were "consumption" loans to people in distress — by contrast with modern production loans which increase the sum total of wealth. Taking interest on money was an antisocial act which was loathsome for any member of the Christian community; the practice was therefore relegated to Jews, who were outside the pale of the Establishment.

By A.D. 1500, however, commerce and finance were beginning to have some importance in the economy of Europe, and Christian entrepreneurs had appeared who wanted to share in the profits. The Church now found its economic theories out of date and religious motivation, or, at least, rationalization, for the Commercial Revolution became apparent both *within* and *without* the Catholic Church. Within the Church many began to question the traditional and dogmatic opposition to both commerce and usury. The Church had been particularly hard on usury, denouncing it a hundred times in councils and edicts, to little avail; as early as 1208 Innocent III would remark that if usurers were to be barred from church, the sanctuaries might as well be closed. One commentator, a good Catholic, sighed: "He who practiseth usury goeth to hell, and he who practiseth it not, tendeth to destitution."

There was also a revolt that took many completely away from the Church; there was an economic basis for the Protestant Reformation, apart from its purely religious causes. The Church had opposed commerce and finance — officially. It is therefore not surprising that groups appeared, groups which opposed the Church *both* religiously and economically. Perhaps the best example is that of the Calvinists. Calvinism was tailored for the rising middle classes; it glorified work *and* wealth, glossing over the danger of riches by arguing that one became wealthy because it was God's will, *not* because one desired the pleasures of the flesh that wealth might bring. In any case, Calvinists put into their everyday work the same religious fervor that Catholics in the Middle Ages had usually reserved for the monastery. They worshiped *in* business. In later generations, as their votaries became less pious *and* business became more profitable, their descendants would take the logical step from worship *in* business to worship *of* business.

This thesis, on the economic basis for the Protestant Reformation, has had two prominent proponents: the German Max Weber and the American A. Whitney Griswold. It was more than half a century ago that the great German sociologist Weber created a lively controversy when he argued, in *The Protestant Ethic and the Spirit of Capitalism*, that the newly emerging Puritan (read Calvinist) religious doctrines of the sixteenth century were peculiarly favorable to the development of capitalism in western Europe. Weber pointed out, *inter alia*, that John Calvin approved of the new gospel of wealth and defended the taking of interest on loans; it was Weber's opinion that Calvinism "released the businessman from the clutches of the priest, and sprinkled holy water on economic success."

One of the first scholars to apply Weber's thesis specifically to the United States was A. Whitney Griswold, a historian who was to become president of Yale University. Griswold attempted to show that certain doctrines were uniquely suited to encourage such values as diligence, thrift, sobriety, and concern for both material and worldly success. He found two prime examples in Cotton Mather and Benjamin Franklin. Mather was the American clergyman, scholar, and scientist who read seven languages with ease, belonged to the Royal Society, and first suggested the possibility of hybrid corn, and, disappointed that he did not succeed his father (Increase Mather) as president of Harvard, became one of the moving spirits in the founding of Yale. As a clergyman Cotton Mather was a narrow, intolerant Puritan, but (in Griswold's judgment) his praise of industry was so influential that he deserves recognition as one of the first to teach American businessmen to serve God by making money. For Mather, worship of the Lord in hymn and prayer was not enough; a man must not only be pious, he must also be useful. To him contemplation of the *good* meant nothing without some accumulation of *goods*.* By contrast, Benjamin Franklin was a rationalist and Deist with little interest in religious doctrine. He was also a canny journalist and businessman, and he shrewdly analyzed his

---

*In the 1920's Thomas J. Watson, the guiding genius of IBM, would echo the same credo. In his direction of the corporation, paternalism was raised to the level of the Godhead. "Do Right," Watson told his men, and they would do well. His grateful workers sang the company anthem ("Ever Onward I.B.M.") and Watson's praise ("He has shown us how to play the game/ And how to make the dough").

Puritan public. Any publisher knows that catering to a public taste can be profitable, and (according to Griswold) that is precisely what Franklin did. He stressed industry and frugality and all the other Puritan virtues; it is no matter for wonderment that *Poor Richard's Almanac* was a money-making venture for a quarter of a century.

There has been much speculation about the arrival of *Homo sapiens* in the New World, and who got there first. Zealous advocates have pushed claims for the Egyptians, the Phoenicians, the Irish abbot St. Brendan, and for Madoc — the illegitimate son of a Welsh king. One of the more interesting claims is that for the Buddhist priest Hwui Shan who, some believe, crossed the Pacific Ocean by following the strong and warm Japan current, landing in the wonderful Land of Fusang on the western coast of the Americas. This could have been Mexico and might explain Oriental features in the art forms of Central America. No less a person than Alexander von Humboldt, the nineteenth-century German scholar who was considered an authority on the Western Hemisphere, called Shan the Leif Ericson of China — and dubbed his discovery the Vinland of the West.

On the basis of more solid evidence we know that the first men to come to America were Asiatics, and that the first Europeans to arrive here were Norsemen. Fifteen to twenty thousand years ago, when ice had advanced to its maximum limit during the late Pleistocene period, sea level had been lowered by 300 to 500 feet, creating the Bering land bridge which connected Siberia and Alaska — allowing Arctic animals, insects, nonarboreal vegetation, and men to move freely into the New World. These predators had reached the southern tip of South America by 9000 B.C. Originally hunters — they ultimately took up farming, spreading out and establishing the Hopewell mound culture of Ohio and elsewhere about 1000 B.C. Still later, in a pre-Columbian period of approximately one thousand years (A.D. 400 to 1400), they established the civilizations of the Olmecs, Mayans, Incas, and Aztecs.

Five hundred years before Columbus the Norse discovered America. In doing so these Scandinavian voyagers with exotic names manifested the greatest of daring and courage and enterprise — and then vanished, leaving few traces!

The chief obstacles to transatlantic discovery of the New World were the prevailing *westerly* winds that drove sailing ships away from the new and unknown continent. For that reason it is logical that America was finally discovered in the two latitudes where there are periods of *easterly* winds on which sailing ships can ride — in the high latitudes of the Norse discoveries and in the trade-wind belt of the Columbian voyages. The Norse were raiders, pirates, and conquerors whose chieftains had such colorful names as Eirik Bloodaxe, Harold Bluetooth, Sven Forkbeard, and

Harold Graycloak. They were also traders whose mercantile treks and voyages took them into the heart of Russia, to Byzantium, and even to the southern shores of the Caspian Sea. Best known were their forays against England, Ireland, and the European coastal area from Normandy to Naples. The treasures they sought were silver and land. Silver was greatly coveted in Viking Scandinavia and in the primitive economy of that day the native land of the Norse was overpopulated.

The valor and boldness of the Vikings has been stressed because they sailed in open boats, had no compass or method for measuring speed, were without charts — and literally never knew where they were in the vast expanse of the ocean. But one should also note that they had very good ships, probably the best in the world at the time. One found in a large burial mound in Norway was seventy-six feet long, seventeen feet broad, a bit more than six feet in height, drew three feet of water, and (fully equipped) weighed about twenty metric tons. It had a side rudder (rather than one on the stern post), was a sailing ship which could also be rowed — with sixteen pairs of oars. It carried a crew of about thirty-five. Its seaworthiness was convincingly demonstrated in 1893 when a copy was made and was sailed across the Atlantic in less than a month.

Assuming, as current archeological findings do, that the Vikings settled in both Greenland and Newfoundland, the obvious question concerns what happened to them. They seem to have been the victims of weather. Leif Ericson made his trips in a warm weather cycle, when ice and snow were little known on the coasts of Europe and in the seas about Iceland and Greenland. Later the cycle changed, the entire Baltic froze over, and in the winters of the early 1300's packs of wolves crossed on the ice between Norway and Denmark. Ships from Iceland and Europe found it exceedingly difficult to reach Greenland or Newfoundland, the colonists were left by necessity to shift for themselves, and native Eskimos ultimately wiped them out.

Regardless of the individual courage and daring of the Vikings, their ventures had no social result, and their achievements were a thing apart from the stream of history. As Broadus and Louise Mitchell have pointed out, the grating of Viking keels on the shores of the New World sent no echoes through the centuries to Columbus or his successors. Because of lack of communication, the later discoverers knew nothing about the Norse. They had sailed out of the northern mists, and the same mists closed about them again, with the result that their bold adventures were forgotten.

As the Commercial Revolution turned the face of Europe from the Mediterranean to the open Atlantic, it was apparent that Spain and Portugal would enjoy an early advantage. Actually Portugal first took the lead and for some time was the dominant commercial nation of the world,

eclipsing the glories of Venice. This was because of the work of a remarkable succession of navigators, explorers, and administrators — beginning
with Prince Henry and extending through Dias, Gama, and Albuquerque
— who secured the Southeast Passage, by way of Africa, to the Orient.
The wealth of the Indies poured back to Portugal and its empire was early
flung across the world in Asia, Africa, and America. But the Portuguese
were merchants, not colonizers; there was a saying that they "were like
fish: remove them from the water and they straightway die." Their only
colony that was destined to support a large European population was
Brazil; Portugal never settled any significant number of Europeans in its
African and Asian outposts. The result was that in the wars with the
English and the Dutch, most of their Asian empire was permanently lost.

Prince Henry the Navigator (1394–1460) was not much of a sailor,
probably never cruised out of sight of land, and never himself traveled
farther than Morocco. But he inspired other navigators, and he combined
rare business ability with the zeal of a missionary. He set up a school at
Sagres on the southernmost point of Portugal, and there made his seamen
into navigators. By the time he died in 1460 his pilots had pushed past the
site of modern Dakar, and had rediscovered and conquered the Canary,
Madeira, and Azores Islands. In doing so they revolutionized the design
of ships. They found their broad-bottomed, single-masted ships with
square sails unsuitable for exploration; the shipwrights at Sagres produced
designs that ultimately developed into the caravel — the vessel that became the favorite of explorers in the fifteenth and sixteenth centuries. The
basic idea came from the Moslems, and the caravel, with its long and
narrow hull with three masts, carrying both square and triangular (lateen)
sails, was certainly different from and superior to its predecessors. The
Niña and *Pinta* of Columbus's first voyage were of this type, carrying a
square sail on the foremast and lateen rigs on the main- and mizzenmasts;
they were swift enough that few sailing ships since have bettered them
for speed. The change from bulkier ships to caravels, with small displace-
ment and greater maneuverability (due to lateen sails), was ideal for exploration on uncharted shores; the experimentation and achievements in
design by Henry's navigators enabled the Portuguese to take the lead in
expeditions down the coast of Africa. Prince Henry was looking for the
Rio de Oro, the River of Gold; he did not find it, although part of the
shoreline (now Ghana) would in time be called the Gold Coast. Ultimately Portugal would develop major profits from black rather than
metallic gold, that is, from human bondage, and for that reason the area
might better have been called the Slave Coast. As late as the nineteenth
century Angola, a Portuguese colony to this day, furnished most of the
slaves that were sent to Brazil.

In 1487 Bartholomeu Dias rounded and then discovered the southern
tip of Africa, calling it the Cape of Storms. The king of Portugal, who

could have written modern advertising copy, thought this designation too pessimistic, and changed it to the Cape of Good Hope. It might well have been called the Cape of Hope Deferred because no one tried to round it again for more than a decade. Then Vasco da Gama did it in 1498, completing a voyage around Africa to India. Da Gama's passage from the Cape Verde Islands (three hundred miles from the coast of West Africa) to the coast of South Africa was far and away the greatest feat of navigation to that time. Columbus's passage several years earlier to the Bahamas was over a stretch of 2,600 miles, sailed in five weeks before a fair wind. By contrast da Gama's course was 3,800 miles, across the South Atlantic, and against both adverse currents and contrary winds. He was at sea thirteen weeks, by far the longest passage that had been made by a European seaman out of sight of land.

Centuries later Adam Smith pointed out that the two greatest and most important events recorded in the history of mankind were the discovery of America *and* the discovery of the Cape Route to India. The reason, in Smith's mind, was not because of the precious metals that might be found; the importance of these events was that they provided a new and inexhaustible market for abundant European commodities. These discoveries gave rise to an enormous increase in world trade — in fact the seventeenth and eighteenth were to be the centuries of trade, just as the nineteenth would be the century of production.

Because Portugal dominated the Cape Route, Spain sent her ships to the West and found a New World. She dispatched prominent explorers: Columbus, Vespucci, Balboa, and Magellan. Interestingly, only one of this quadrumvirate was Spanish by birth and nationality. The explorers were followed by their equally famous compatriots, the conquistadores — Cortes, Pizarro, Ponce de León, de Soto, and Coronado — who fought and plundered with sword in one hand and the Bible in the other. They craved gold, and some of them found so much that it flowed into Spain in fabulous quantities. In the mother country the influx of gold had an unanticipated result; it contributed to the decline of Spanish industry and trade, and much of the precious metal ultimately found its way into other nations that could undersell the Spanish.

The importance of the Pacific Ocean, discovered by Balboa and first crossed by Magellan, was unnoticed at the time. Centuries passed before the strategic importance of the Pacific was recognized by most of the citizens of the United States, including Theodore Roosevelt, who was something of a historian. He said in 1903, with a prescience that seems prophetic in the second half of the twentieth century:

"The Mediterranean era died with the discovery of America, the Atlantic era is now at the height of its development and must soon exhaust the resources at its command; the Pacific era, destined to be the greatest of all, is just at its dawn. . . . The greatest of all the seas and the last to be used on a large scale by civilized man bids fair to become the first in importance. The empire that shifted from the Mediterranean will, in the lifetime of those now children, bid fair to shift once more westward to the Pacific."

Curiously the motivation for the famous voyage of Ferdinand Magellan came from the Fuggers — the German family of merchant princes which was allied with Venice, was centered in Augsburg, and whose members served as middlemen for the commerce between Venice and the northern cities of the Hanseatic League. The Fuggers ultimately built a fortune through a monopoly in the mining and trading of metals (silver, copper, and mercury), and by maintaining a continuous flow of pepper, spices, and dyestuffs — the latter used in the textile industry, in which they were also prominent. In the early sixteenth century this was the richest family in Europe, with a total wealth in purchasing power — at today's prices — in excess of a billion dollars. In fact, it was Jacob Fugger whose life-span encompassed the transition of European finance from medieval usury to modern industrial capitalism and international banking.

In the late fifteenth century Venice and the Fuggers were working closely with Portugal, and expected to profit from the explorations then being conducted by that country. But in 1495 there was a change of dynasty in Portugal (Manuel I succeeded John II), and the new king favored Florence and the Medicis, rather than Venice and the Fuggers. This was a serious setback because Venice would now no longer benefit from the *southeast* route around Africa, which Portugal monopolized. The Fuggers therefore envisioned the establishment of new and alternate routes to India, either through a *northwest* or a *southwest* passage. In the Northwest they were to support England and John Cabot; in the Southwest their aid went to Spain and Magellan.

Magellan was a Portuguese nobleman with a notable combat record in the Orient and North Africa. He was also an accomplished navigator and geographer, but was out of favor at the Portuguese court, and so offered his services to Spain. There the young King Charles V recognized Magellan's superior qualities and entrusted to his command the expedition that would try once more to discover a way to the East Indies by sailing westward across the Atlantic, a goal Columbus and others had failed to achieve. He left Spain on 20 September 1519 with five small ships and 265 men. Almost exactly three years later (on 6 September 1522) one of these ships — appropriately named the *Victoria* — returned with eighteen survivors. The *Victoria* had a cargo of spices that more than repaid for the loss of the other four ships; it could not recompense for the loss of 247 men, including Magellan.

The conquistadores consolidated Spanish dominion over most of South and Central, and part of North, America. As Louis B. Wright has observed (in his *Dream of Prosperity in Colonial America*) they were looking for

El Dorado, the wealth based on the legend of an Indian king who rolled in gold dust until his body was coated (El Dorado means "the gilded one") and then washed it off each night in a sacred spring. This canard haunted Spanish and other explorers, who went on numerous expeditions into the interior of the Americas hoping to find the empire of this gold-encrusted monarch. In 1520–1521 Hernando Cortes, with 700 men and 18 horses (which awed the horseless natives), defeated and killed the Emperor Montezuma, tore open the coffers of the Aztecs, and destroyed their empire — extending his control over most of Mexico and into Central America. Cortes's contemporary Francisco Pizarro began his career as an illiterate swineherd, but before his death completed the conquest of Peru. Juan Ponce de León was a wealthy entrepreneur who had conquered Puerto Rico and had made a fortune in gold, slaves, and land. In 1513 he discovered Florida, which he thought to be an island. Debauched by high living, it is claimed that Ponce de León was seeking a mythical Fountain of Youth. Historians of Florida like to think that he was up to a more serious business than looking for a miraculous fountain, but the legend persists, and has been of vast service to Florida real-estate promoters and advertisers. In all likelihood, Ponce introduced oranges to the North American mainland; for that reason the Florida Citrus Commission now promotes him as the man who was trying to find the Fountain of Youth, but actually brought it with him. In fact Ponce de León did not find youth, either from a miraculous fountain or from the fabulous orange. Instead he found death, from an Indian arrow. But no matter; 450 years later millions of Americans are still searching for a fountain of youth in Florida.

Hernando de Soto was in his late thirties when he set out, in 1539, on his ill-fated expedition into the southeastern part of what is now the United States. With six hundred armor-plated men he undertook a fantastic gold-seeking expedition in the lower Mississippi Valley. Floundering through marshes and pine barrens from Florida westward, he discovered the mighty Mississippi. He found no gold; instead he was to find misery and death.

It is interesting to note that with de Soto's failure no explorer again came through the eastern door to the Mississippi Valley for 142 years, when La Salle did. On the other hand many Spaniards pushed through the western door, via Mexico, into what is now the southwestern part of the United States.

Francisco Coronado led an expedition into this Southwest at about the same time as de Soto's to the east. He did not find the fabled wealth of the Seven Cities of Cibola, which turned out to be Indian pueblos. He did discover two impressive phenomena: the Grand Canyon of the Colorado and enormous herds of buffalo. In time others would make fortunes from sightseers and from the sale of skins.

The English also wanted a share of the good things that seemed to be in prospect in various parts of the expanding world. After an abortive attempt to find a Northwest Passage to the Orient through the voyages of John Cabot, her colonial expansion really began with the exploits of free-booters and buccaneers, of whom Drake was the most prominent example. But England had a special need for propaganda, and was particularly successful with it. In the Western Hemisphere English colonies were planted, for the most part, in areas where the native population was sparse or primitive; this was because the Spanish were already in possession of most of the territories where a docile native labor force existed. This meant that the English, at least in the early years, had to import a complete labor force of Europeans, and these migrants had to be induced and persuaded with money and special pleading. Books and pamphlets were therefore issued by editors like Richard Hakluyt for the purposes of inviting stockholders to invest and of attracting laborers to migrate.

Richard Hakluyt (1552–1616) was an English geographer, editor, and propagandist who made the doctrine of colonial expansion into a religion. He was a graduate of Oxford, where he later lectured on geography. As a scholar he was a greatly respected figure because of his immense knowledge; he was also quite accurate in his publications, well above the normal editorial standards of the time, and we owe to him the survival of nearly everything about the early American voyages. Worried about Sir Walter Raleigh's failure in Virginia during the 1580's, Hakluyt wanted to excite interest in further settlement; he did so by his writing, and by direct participation as a member of the Virginia Company in London. He was a British-colonization propagandist of persistence, imagination, and force; as such he pulled out all the stops as he played the imperial organ. On the religious side he believed sincerely that England had an obligation to carry the Protestant gospel to the Indians. As a social contribution he believed the colonies would be a useful dumping ground for excessive or undesirable population. They would be valuable economically, providing investment, trade, and customs duties for the Crown. Strategically, colonies in North America would be a counterforce to Spain and a source for ship's stores. As a maritime nation England had long been short of fir-tree poles for masts, pitch for the caulking of seams, and hemp for cordage. In the later sixteenth century, oak frames and planking were also becoming scarce; most of these came from the Baltic, where access to them could be denied by whatever power controlled the Baltic shores. The alternative was a source for naval stores in one's own colonies.

We have noted that the two southern passages to the Far East were quickly discovered and utilized. Portugal went around the African barrier, and for years monopolized the Southeast Passage. She was pleased with the American land barrier, and was not particularly happy when the Portuguese Magellan solved the Southwest Passage around it. A practical North-west Passage is still in some doubt, and it is only in very recent years that the Northeast Passage has been opened to the ships of all nations.

The chief handicap in the Northwest, if the purpose was to go to China, is the icepack in the Arctic Ocean and the Chukchi Sea. In the latter, between Bering Strait and Point Barrow at the northern tip of Alaska, the icepack locks tight that stretch of sea — except for July and early August when a southeast wind pushes it away from land, leaving a lane of open water. But in late August the wind changes to the west, and the icepack is solid again — so solid that even nuclear submarines can go under it only in midsummer. Airplanes have gone over it and the North Pole, just as nuclear submarines have gone under it and the Pole. But only half a dozen ships have gone through the Arctic Ocean to Point Barrow, not counting the trip from Alaska to the Pacific Ocean. The first was the *Gjoa*, from 1903 to 1906; its captain was the famous Arctic explorer Roald Amundsen.

In 1968 Atlantic Richfield, in a joint venture with Humble Oil & Re-fining Company (a subsidiary of Standard Oil Company of New Jersey) made a major oil discovery on Alaska's North Slope — westward of Canada and on the westward portion of the Arctic Ocean. At Prudhoe Bay the companies drilled two wells and struck a field estimated to contain 10 billion barrels of oil — surpassing Texas as the largest field in North America. The Prudhoe Bay field, however, is only one of twenty similar geological structures on the North Slope. Estimates of the oil in these Arctic fields runs as high as 50 billion barrels, a reserve gigantic enough to merit the grudging admiration even of Texas.

Following this discovery in Alaska a major problem arose: how to get the oil out. Pipelines in the northern tundra present a variety of technical and ecological problems; the one proposed from Prudhoe Bay to Valdez to southern Alaska had an estimated cost of almost a billion dollars. Ship-ment by tanker would also be expensive but original estimates indicated a saving by sea; shipment by pipeline would be $1.20 a barrel against 60¢ by sea through this Northwest Passage — this time via the Arctic icepack in reverse to the Atlantic rather than to the Chukchi Sea and the Pacific Ocean. In 1969 Humble Oil therefore spent some $40 million on the voyage of the S.S. *Manhattan*, an icebreaking tanker, to ascertain whether a reverse Northwest Passage — at very long last — was possible. The *Manhattan* had been built in 1962 with too much power for her size; dis-placing 115,000 tons, her length at more than a thousand feet was ten yards more than that of the *Queen Elizabeth*. By late September 1969 the *Manhattan* had crushed the ice and had gone through the Northwest Passage in the Arctic Ocean; she was the first commercial ship to do so, as well as the largest by a hundred thousand tons.

On the basis of this achievement there seemed to be a possibility of keeping the passage open; it was hoped that the ice would give way before the regular voyages of gigantic tankers. If so, the desired port would be Alaska — not the Cathay sought five centuries before. The sought-for gold would be black rather than yellow.

In 1551 Sebastian Cabot, son of the discoverer of Newfoundland, founded the Muscovy Company of Merchant Adventurers in London. His aim was to find the Northeast Passage, a shorter route between England and Cathay across the Arctic Sea north of Europe and Asia. Cabot's objective was not accomplished until three centuries later, when in 1878–1889 the Swedish geologist and Arctic explorer Baron Nils Nordenskjöld was the first to negotiate the passage to the Bering Strait leading to the Pacific. In the 1930's Stalin poured in the resources needed to make the waterway a commercial route; after his death these included the nuclear-powered icebreaker *Lenin*. In 1967 Russia announced its intention to open the Northeast Passage to foreign shipping; it is Russia's icebreakers that plow through 2,500 miles of frozen ice to keep the passage open 150 days a year. The saving for shipping can be enormous. The distance from the Soviet port of Archangel, in north European Russia, and Vladivostok, on the Pacific Ocean, is about 6,500 miles through the Northeast Passage. By comparison, the distance between the two ports via the Suez Canal is 15,000 miles.

The success of the Reconnaissance, in all of its magnitude, ultimately produced a lessening of geographical curiosity by the latter part of the seventeenth century. By this time, as J. H. Parry has noted, "men no longer expected to find Atlantis. Few still hoped to penetrate by a northern route to Cathay." The places still unexplored seemed to offer little prospect of immediate gain, and the freelance buccaneer who had dominated the sixteenth century became an increasingly rare exception. By contrast the seventeenth century, as Parry saw it, became "the age of consolidation overseas, of trading and planting exploitation, rather than of original exploration."

The Commercial Revolution, which began in western Europe and spread over the entire world, had proliferating economic results. What historian Walter Prescott Webb called the Great Frontier provided vast amounts of new land; it also made possible exciting profits and new capital. The windfalls on the Great Frontier made western Europe a different place. Webb was careful to distinguish between what he called primary and secondary windfalls. The primary ones were those quickly realized and gathered with a minimum of time: gold, silver, furs, ambergris, slaves. Secondary windfalls involved much more time and investment and labor; these were chiefly plantation crops and the raising of cattle. It was the primary ones that sent men off into a "frenzy of enterprises" and gave the impetus for capitalism in the sixteenth and seventeenth centuries; most of the stock companies of these two centuries, and they were numerous, were so motivated. By the eighteenth century this excitement was pretty well gone for the simple reason that most of the primary windfalls had been gathered in. In the eighteenth and nineteenth centuries the secondary windfalls would take over, providing an abundance of staple commodities such as beef and plantation crops for businessmen in western Europe to buy and sell. In this development the British colonies along the Atlantic coast, which were north of the gold and south of the furs, had to be content with secondary windfalls. Their progress depended on long-term investment and much hard work. By the time the hard labor was done the original English investors had been washed out, and the colonists they had sent over were left pretty much to shift for themselves. What these colonists really had was a little windfall of virtually free land, along with their own enterprise and initiative. They learned to shift for themselves — and in this process, and with this independent attitude, took a step toward freedom and the American Revolution.

Webb was convinced that the primary windfalls were the "exciters, the pump-primers, the cap-like detonations which set off the chain-reaction of modern capitalism." There were a number of prime and convincing examples of this reaction: the success of Bermuda as a colony, the economic benefits to England and Queen Elizabeth from Drake's *Golden Hind,* and the remarkable influence of the success of Sir William Phipps in finding sunken Spanish treasure.

Bermuda was settled in 1612 by a subsidiary of the Virginia Company. One looks for the puzzling reason for its success and the failure of the mainland colony of Virginia. The reason is that the Bermudians stumbled on a primary windfall — a fortune in ambergris. This waxlike substance, ashy in color when found floating in tropical seas, is thrown up from the bellies of whales. Ambergris is valuable as a chemical base for medicines and perfume. In the first year of the colony of Bermuda a great chunk of pure ambergris, weighing close to two hundred pounds, was found floating in the ocean. It was so valuable that it was sent to England on three different ships (lest one be lost at sea), where it brought at least the equivalent of a million dollars in present-day values. This windfall — "a golden egg laid by some indisposed whale" — launched the colony of Bermuda quite successfully. By contrast the discovery that tobacco (a secondary windfall) could be grown profitably came too late to save the mainland colony of Virginia.

The round-the-world voyage of the *Golden Hind* captained by Sir Francis Drake certainly provided the caplike detonation that set off an economic chain reaction. Drake took enough gold and silver from the Spanish to make a return of 4,700 percent to his English backers. The value of this booty was estimated to be as much as 1.5 million English pounds. With her part of the profits Queen Elizabeth paid the whole of England's foreign debt and from what was left invested £42,000 in the

Levant Company. It was the profits of the Levant Company that furnished most of the capital used in the formation of the East India Company, and it was the East India Company that established the base for England's early foreign investments. John Maynard Keynes once stated that the booty from the *Golden Hind* "may fairly be considered the fountain and origin of British foreign investment." It was England's foreign investment that made, and kept, her rich.

Drake's achievement was a magnificent one for his supporters but his record was broken a century later by Sir William Phipps, who fished up a sunken Spanish treasure near Grand Turk Island off Hispaniola and paid his backers 10,000 percent. When his vessel got back to England in 1688 it was so heavily laden with treasure that it could scarcely float. The results? Phipps reached London on the eve of the Glorious Revolution, too late to save James but just in time to enable William and Mary to meet their pressing obligations. Keynes observed drily that the arrival "must have been invaluable to the stability of the new regime," and he would wonder "how much the Glorious Revolution owed to Mr. Phipps?" But a greater effect was the stimulus given to all kinds of new enterprises, and the boom that followed this stimulus. The stockholders in the company that financed Phipps's expedition were reasonably happy with their profit of 10,000 percent. Their profits also meant a sudden injection of specie into the veins of a lagging economy. The boom that followed led to the founding of the Bank of England in 1694, to the establishment of the stock exchange, and to the reform of the currency soon brought about by philosopher John Locke and the physicist-astronomer Sir Isaac Newton. Phipps's treasure-divers off Grand Turk Island had no way of knowing how much heat they would generate in the English economic system.

These developments on the Great Frontier encouraged, as Webb pointed out so cogently, the concept of laissez-faire by making the original settler relatively free of man-made masters. He faced nature as an antagonist, but since nature was passive, the frontiersman was the only active agent and was free to proceed as he wished. Because of the great wealth of the frontier all he had to do was work hard — on his own. As a result hard work was magnified in the folk characters of Paul Bunyan in the forests and Mike Fink on the rivers; it was also advertised by Poor Richard with such statements as "God helps them that help themselves" and "Early to bed and early to rise, makes a man healthy, wealthy, and wise." In Webb's judgment laissez-faire could not exist in extreme form except in situations where wealth was abundant in proportion to population; this was certainly true on the Great Frontier. And so it was that while England was following the principles of restrictive and authoritarian mercantilism, the frontiersmen had been following the principles of laissez-faire for at least a century before the Physiocrats and Adam Smith formulated the theory. The conflict would become one of the ideological causes of the American Revolution; it is not surprising that Smith would later agree with the frontiersmen, and would urge the independence of the American colonies.

III

The Colonization of the New World: The Role of Corporations, Land Speculators, and Sweet Charity

THREE prerequisites were essential to make British colonization of the New World a success: land, labor, and capital. The land was here but the other two requirements for successful settlement came from Europe — in fact the economic history of the United States really begins with the investment of European capital and labor. Furthermore until recent times the United States continued to be dependent on European investment of capital and labor. Until the First World War the United States was in debt to Europe, and until the 1920's we had a very liberal policy on immigration, a policy that reflected our need for a supply of labor from abroad. We won political independence from Europe in 1783, but our economic independence from European capital and European labor was not to be achieved for almost a century and a half after the American Revolution.

LAND. The abundance of land was apparent but the British had some difficulty in convincing Indians that they should either work for the British or move farther back into the hinterland. When the red men declined to do either the British adopted a homicidal Indian policy which was essentially taken over by the United States in later years.

Initially the British rationalized their seizure, in major part by force, of the Indian's land on two grounds: the souls of the Indians had to be saved and the lands of the Indians had to be properly developed, and the red men were falling down on the job. On the first point the British developed the traditional rationalization that because it was the Indian's immortality that was at stake, what real difference could it make if the red man — in the form of his mortal and finite body — got cheated, or even killed, in the process? And so it was that the so-called Indian menace was met with the Bible, torch, and musket. On the second point (the proper development of land) the British argued that unless a people improved what God had given them, they lost their title to it. This was a theory that would scarcely stand up in the national courts of any nation, but has been employed frequently in international relations. The British argued that they violated no property rights because the Indian had no real title; he had only a general residency like wild beasts in the forests, who did not improve the land either. Of course, the British have no monopoly on this argument; it was, for example, used in the United States in the middle of the nineteenth century. Our Manifest Destiny divinely ordained us to take land that belonged to Indians and Mexicans. These people were dishonest, incompetent, slothful, did not develop the land properly, and should have it taken from them by someone who would. This was an echo of the usually tolerant Benjamin Franklin who once observed that rum should be regarded as an agent of Providence "to extirpate these savages in order to make room for the cultivators of the earth."

In any case the British, and later the American, policy toward Indians can only be characterized as a brutal and ruthless one. In the beginning the Indians had been regarded as pagans ripe for conversion, or as a variant of Rousseau's Noble Savage uncorrupted by civilization; later, as the economic desire for land took over, they came to be looked upon as subhuman savages without souls to be saved, fit only for extermination. As Louis Wright has observed, for most of our history the British, the Spanish, and the Americans have felt the Indian to be — like the rattlesnake and the alligator and poison ivy — a curse on Utopia. Columbus found the Arawak Indians in the Caribbean "a loving people, without covetousness" — but his Spanish successors set them to work in mines and on plantations, with the result that entire Arawak villages disappeared due to slavery, disease, warfare, and flight. When Pequot Indians in New England resisted settlement of whites in the Connecticut Valley, a party of Puritans surrounded one of the Indian villages and set fire to it (1637). About five hundred Indians were burned to death or were shot while trying to escape; the woods were then searched for any Pequots who had managed to survive and those found were sold into slavery. The white Puritans offered devout thanks to God that they had lost only two men; when the Puritan divine Cotton Mather heard about the raid, he was grateful to the Lord that "on this day we have sent six hundred heathen souls to hell." The famous Jeffrey Amherst, a renowned British general after whom a college is named, had a unique solution for the Indian problem; he would have sent them gift blankets, infected with smallpox! The Puritans of New England, and the Presbyterian Scots along the Appalachian range, often quoted out of context a passage from Joshua (13:1): ". . . and there remaineth yet very much land to be possessed." They interpreted this passage as a mandate to "move into the wilderness, to smite the Canaanites, and to seize the land that pleased them." In time, as the economic motive became all-powerful, there were but few who still talked of an obligation to convert Indians to the Christian faith. In 1790 John Adams would say that Rousseau's idea of the Noble Savage was a chimera.

In 1881 a woman named Helen Hunt Jackson, who has been dubbed the Harriet Beecher Stowe of the Indians, would publish a historical account of this record of injustice; the volume became famous under the title *A Century of Dishonor*. It might well have been called *Centuries of Dishonor*. In human annals there is no other record of the destruction of an entire race along with the violent subjugation of two whole continents. In the process of the extermination of the Indians it is discouraging to note that the most murderously effective weapons were alcohol, pestilence, warfare, broken treaties, and expropriation of land. Up to 1868 nearly four hundred treaties had been signed with various Indian groups by the U.S. government, and hardly one remained unbroken. The Indians were promised new lands — and when these lands became valuable the Indians were moved on again and again — as many as half a dozen times. This went on so routinely that the Sioux Spotted Tail once asked wearily: "Why does not the great White Father put his red children on wheels, so he can move them as he will?"

In the 1880's President Cleveland would note that the "hunger and thirst of the white man for the Indian's land is almost equal to his hunger and thirst after righteousness." By the later 1960's some 400,000 of the total 550,000 Indians left in the United States were living on approximately 200 reservations in 26 states. Ninety percent of them were housed in tin-roofed shacks, leaky adobe huts, brush shelters, even abandoned automobiles. Unemployment ranged from 40 to 75 percent, and the average Indian family was trying to live on $30 a week. The normal age of death for an Indian in 1968 was forty-three years, for a white, sixty-eight years. His education, averaging five years, was the worst of any minority group; other Americans average a bit more than eleven years.

Whatever the method of exploitation, with the arrival of the white man, the world of the Indian came to an end — whether he lived in the log houses on the Mohawk or in the tepees of the plains or on the pyramids of Mexico or in the palaces of Peru. Some nationalistic history textbooks in the United States have been critical of Spanish colonial policy but conveniently forget the elementary fact that the Indian survived in Latin America but was almost exterminated in the United States.

LABOR. Colonial labor came from three sources: freemen, indentured servants, and slaves. The freemen were by name the possessors of freeholds — they were the owners of property, usually land. The individual freeman worked hard on his own; he also augmented his labor supply by siring a large family. On the frontier a wife and children were economic assets. For that reason females were sometimes classified as good or indifferent "breeders." Biologically this meant that young women were in especial demand, so much so that (as Thomas A. Bailey notes) an "unwed girl of twenty-one could be referred to as an 'antique virgin.'" But widows were also sought after, particularly if they were not too old and had proved themselves fertile by producing children in the first or second marriages. Because of the demand there was occasionally a social and ethical problem; some widows remarried so quickly that the refreshments from the first husband's funeral could be used for the guests at the wedding which followed. On the frontier this moral issue was somewhat solved by the clergy through "delayed funerals"; this was the practice of preaching the funeral service some months after burial of the late husband in order to prevent the possibility that the "grieving" widow would ride to the graveyard behind her late husband's corpse — and ride back in the embrace of a prospective husband.

Because large families were advantageous on the frontier, babies arrived with great regularity and persistence. Benjamin Franklin was one of fifteen children by two mothers; Sir William Phipps, the successful hunter after treasure, was one of twenty-seven all by the same mother. This excessive childbearing shortened the lives of many frontier women; at the same time it resulted in a remarkable increase in the population. By the time of the American Revolution, the colonies were doubling their population every twenty-three years. In London the unfriendly and choleric Dr. Samuel Johnson would say that the colonists and rattlesnakes had similar birth rates; he found the increase undesirable for both species.

Beyond the freemen, the balance of the labor supply was made up of either indentured servants or slaves (we will reserve the discussion of slavery for a later chapter). It is possible that indentured servants accounted for as much as three-quarters of the total immigration into the thirteen American colonies before 1775; some of them came *voluntarily* and some arrived *involuntarily*. Those who signed contracts voluntarily were known as "free willers" or redemptioners. Their agreements permitted ship captains to sell their services to interested employers over a period of years, usually five to seven, for a sum of money that would pay for their passage by ship — thus *redeeming* it. Those who came involuntarily did so either as convicts or kidnappees. The kidnapped were largely children, although some were adults. The "spiriting away" of laborers became a regular business in such towns as London and Bristol, where adults would be plied with liquor and the children would be enticed with sweetmeats by the kidnappers, who were called "spirits." In the case of convicts England normally offered commutation of the death sentence to fourteen years of labor in the colonies; the commutation was usually seven years for other crimes, including imprisonment for debt. For that reason most of the convicts who were shipped to America for a period of indentured labor were known as "His Majesty's Seven-Year Passengers."

It can be noted that some of them were the luckless victims of savage laws enacted in England and on the Continent to protect the property of the ruling classes; they were peasants caught shooting rabbits on some landlord's estate, or servant girls charged with stealing a pair of stockings. At first the jailbirds were largely rogues, vagabonds, debtors, and beggars, but in the eighteenth century others with more serious crimes — murder, rape, and grand larceny — were shipped. Among the transported women, there were many whom contemporary accounts described succinctly as "lewd." Obviously the transportation of such persons enabled England to solve a penal problem and she did so until the American Revolution put a stop to the use of American colonies as social wastebaskets; in the fifty years before the Revolution, Britain sent nearly 50,000 convicts to the American colonies, certainly a large number for a country with a sparse population. Enough of them were hardened criminals to establish the nucleus, in America, of a criminal brotherhood.

The system of indentured labor could show both positive and negative aspects. For the employer this system provided cheap labor; for about twenty English pounds (for transportation, middleman's fees, and freedom dues), he acquired a laborer for a period of years. During this time the only additional charge upon him was the cost of food and shelter, usually minimal. For the employee, if he lived long enough, there was the achievement of complete freedom and something to go with it — usually some clothing and tools, occasionally a small parcel of land. The chief disadvantage was the multifarious brutality of the system, a cruelty that was extensive enough that it killed many indentured servants before they had an opportunity to become freemen. There were the appalling conditions on board the ships that transported the indentured servants, into which they were packed almost like sardines; many did not survive the trip over the ocean. There was the breakup of the family when contracts for its members were purchased by different employers in America, or when children or adults were kidnapped in England. During the period of employment, treatment of the indentured was frequently very bad; they were given inadequate food, worked frightfully long hours, could be flogged and beaten, and were sometimes at the mercy of immoral employers. Servant girls, for example, could be held in longer bondage because of bastardy, and their masters were sometimes not above conspiring to this end.

CAPITAL. Capital presented a problem; most of the American colonies were originally established as profit-making ventures. The English Crown in the sixteenth and seventeenth centuries was not able financially to engage in commerce on a large scale. Individual entrepreneurs failed, although some of them tried — particularly Sir Walter Raleigh. He was nearly bankrupted by the attempt to establish a colony at Roanoke in Virginia, and turned over the rights to his charter to nineteen London merchants. His failure taught a valuable lesson. Individuals had neither the funds nor the qualified personnel to establish a successful colony. Joint-stock companies could and did supply both in return for royal grants of monopolies.

Joint-stock companies, therefore, gave seven of the original thirteen American colonies their start: directly in the cases of Virginia, Massachusetts, New Amsterdam (New York), and New Sweden (Delaware); indirectly in the cases of Connecticut, Rhode Island, and New Hampshire. Later, land speculators known as proprietors would try their hand; they enjoyed some success in Maryland, the two Carolinas, Pennsylvania, and New Jersey. Unlike the others, Georgia was not established for the initial purpose of making a profit; it was colonized by imperialists who were impelled by both philanthropic and defense motives.

The profit motive was thus dominant in the establishment of all the American colonies save one; because of this original impulse, attempts would be made to hold settlers in the position of employees beholden for subsistence to a trading company, or in the status of liege servants to semi-feudal proprietors. This caused resentment with the result that most colonies changed over, in time, from corporate (charter) or proprietary to royal control; after their experience with corporations and proprietors, many colonists came to believe that royal governors could not be worse, and might be better. By the eve of the American Revolution Pennsylvania, Maryland, and tiny Delaware were the only surviving proprietorships — and Connecticut and Rhode Island were the only charter colonies left, although by that time in both cases the charters were held by the people and not by British corporations.

The idea of the corporation was relatively new; it had first been used in the time of Queen Elizabeth to establish what were perhaps the earliest trading companies with what came later to be called permanent capital. These were the Levant Company for trade with the Near East, the Muscovy Company for trade with Russia, and the British East India Company to exploit the Far East. Now the same corporate device would be employed in the American colonies.

During the earliest period the name Virginia embraced all North America not secured by Spain and France, and the term "Old Dominion" originally encompassed this large area. Presently a group of merchants and investors from London — and another group from Plymouth, Bristol, and other western English cities — applied for charters. They received them; the London Company was to colonize what is now North Carolina, Virginia, and Maryland. The Plymouth Company was to settle in what is now New England. The coast between the present New York City and the District of Columbia could be colonized by either company so long as their settlements were one hundred miles apart.

The site selected in 1607 by the London Company, for a tiny colony of Englishmen, was Jamestown, on the wooded banks of the James River. The early years there turned out to be a tragedy for almost all concerned; hundreds died of disease, of actual starvation, and later from Indian massacres. During the worst "starving time" in 1609–1610, according to Captain John Smith one man, his mind unhinged by slow starvation, killed his wife, "powdered [salted] her, and had eaten part of her before it was knowne," — for which he was hanged; Smith later remarked, "Now whether shee was better roasted, boyled or carbonado'd, I know not, but such a dish as powdered wife I never heard of." From hindsight we can ascertain that this loss of life was unnecessary; had the early colonists had eyes for something other than precious metals they would have observed that the woods were full of game and that the rivers were swarming with fish. A frightful Indian massacre in 1622 brought a royal investigation in the following year. It revealed that 5,500 colonists had gone to Virginia; of these, 4,000 had died, 300 had returned to England, and only 1,200 remained. The result of these shocking figures was that the king annulled the original charter in 1624, and from that time Virginia was a royal colony. The corporate life of the London Company (of Virginia) thus came to a close after seventeen years of existence, and after the original investors had sunk the present-day equivalent of more than $7 million into the venture. By 1624 they had lost everything.

There were a variety of reasons for this corporate disaster. The site had been wrong. Jamestown was embraced on one side by a swamp and on the other by the muddy waters of the James River. It was both damp and unhealthy. In London the investors had wanted a quick return on their capital, and were really interested in the primary windfalls that had made the Spanish so wealthy. Unfortunately there were no primary windfalls in Virginia, and planning based on their existence was all wrong. Ultimately profits would be found in secondary windfalls — in the lowly tobacco leaf and the humble potato. They would ultimately save Virginia, but they could not save the London Company.

In addition, there was a monumental lack of economic incentive for settlers. The initial requirement was that they were to put their produce into a common warehouse, from which they were to draw according to their needs. There are indications that this Marxist system may creak and groan in the twentieth century; it certainly did not function in Virginia. There was too much land, and settlers were perfectly aware of the agrarian opportunities which were possible. Belatedly the company allowed the colonists to have private gardens, which were promptly planted with tobacco. Finally, the type of settler sent to Virginia left much to be desired. Captain John Smith observed that the company was sending too many gentlemen, soldiers, and fortune hunters. He asked instead for immigrants who were not afraid to soil their hands. It was his observation — and the company later admitted he was right — that it had allowed too many parents to disburden themselves of lascivious sons, too many masters to get rid of bad servants, and too many wives to rid themselves of unwanted husbands.

The Virginia colony would have gone under had it not been for two men: Captain John Smith and John Rolfe. Smith was indubitably the most prominent person in the colony during its early days. As a leader he showed courage, great common sense, and a sound grasp of practical economics. Rolfe, husband of Pocahontas, was the father of the tobacco industry; by 1616 he had perfected methods of raising and curing the pungent weed, a gift (economically but not salubriously) of the Indians to the Old World. This provided Virginia with its staple export; ultimately the prosperity of the colony was built on tobacco smoke. Europe had known about the weed for some time; a half century before Jamestown was settled there was a counselor to the King of France whose name was Jean Nicot. He went to Portugal as ambassador, got hold of some tobacco plants that had lately been brought from Florida. He cultivated the herb and began to test the use of the leaves for medical properties. His cook, having nearly cut off his thumb with a chopping knife, asked Nicot for help. The ambassador put a tobacco poultice on the damaged thumb, which promptly healed — for other reasons, as we now know. Nonetheless, the fame of the herb — and of Nicot's use of it — spread to France, where tobacco became a medical remedy prescribed for almost every ailment. Thus it was that Jean Nicot gave his name to the botanical designation of the tobacco plant (*Nicotiana rustica*), and gained immortality through the noun *nicotine*.

When tobacco was first produced in Virginia it was a luxury product, high in price because of limited production. In London tobacco from the West Indies, which was considered superior, sold for more than 200 pence (18 shillings) a pound. Virginia tobacco, which was of poorer quality, nevertheless brought almost a hundred pence a pound. Under these conditions it is not surprising that tobacco was used mainly by the wealthy, and was retailed on London streets by the *pipeful*. These high prices brought on frenzied production and the inevitable drop in price. By 1627 the price paid to the planter in Virginia had fallen from almost a hundred pence to less than one penny a pound. Six years later, in 1633, the Virginia House passed a law restricting production; it limited each person who cultivated tobacco to 1,500 plants. Thus began governmental regulation of agricultural production on this continent, a practice that vexes us to this day.*

* With but few notable exceptions, all the cereals and fruits and table vegetables commonly grown in the New World originated elsewhere and were brought to these shores after Columbus's voyage. Those native plants which ultimately would be important economically are few in number. The most noteworthy are corn, tobacco, the potato, and the tomato. Curiously, two of them (the potato and the tomato) originated here but had to go abroad in order to gain acceptance in the Western Hemis-

In the southern colonies in general, and Virginia in particular, large land holdings were encouraged by the headright system, usually fifty acres per head to a promoter who transported immigrants at his own expense. This system fostered large land accumulations, along with speculation in land warrants; this frequently raised the price of land beyond the means of indentured servants who had worked out their time. Through the headright system Virginia developed into the Cavalier State, with many large landowners in the tidewater region — the FFVs (First Families of Virginia); as an example, the Byrd family alone eventually amassed almost 200,000 acres. By contrast poorer folk were forced into the wild and dangerous back country. In the tidewater region only the great planters with gangs of African slaves could make a profit, and this was limited, because tobacco exhausted the soil after seven years. Many small growers had to abandon their worn-out fields and seek their fortune on the frontier. There they were compelled to bear the full brunt of Indian massacres, although they were unrepresented (or at least underrepresented) in the Virginia House of Burgesses, where the FFVs were in control. A rebellion was clearly in the making, and it occurred in 1676 — a Virginian declaration of independence exactly a century before the one well known in U.S. history. Aristocratic old Governor William Berkeley, who was personally involved in fur trade with the Indians, was unwilling to antagonize them by fighting back. About a thousand angry back-country men broke out of control, under the leadership of twenty-nine-year-old Nathaniel Bacon whose overseer had been tomahawked. Bacon's men chastised the Indians, defeated Governor Berkeley, and burned Jamestown. In the hour of victory Bacon died of a fever; there were rumors he had been poisoned. Berkeley then crushed the uprising with great brutality, engaging in an orgy of executions until Charles II recalled his aging governor with the comment, "That old fool has hanged more men in that naked country than

---

phere. The white potato was domesticated in prehistoric times in the high Andes. To reach North America it traveled first to Spain at the end of the sixteenth century, then to the British Isles and Ireland. Ultimately Irish immigrants to New Hampshire in 1720 brought the potato to North America; this was the origin of the term *Irish* potatoes. The tomato required even more time for its return to the Western Hemisphere. It is a native of either Mexico or the Andes, was not popular here, arrived in southern Europe at the end of the seventeenth century — and caught on. Two centuries later, Thomas Jefferson, always ready to try something new, brought a few tomato plants back from Europe.

Curiously, in the early years both the potato and the tomato were considered to be aphrodisiacs. In the case of the potato it was whispered that the new product from America was a powerful love potion. Because of this belief, virtuous maids were warned against eating potatoes, and the Virgin Queen was said to look upon the new vegetable with distaste and suspicion. It was noted, however, that certain country gentlemen in England were tending their potato patches with loving care. The tomato was commonly called *la pomme d'amour*, and in this country was opposed as sinful and possibly poisonous until about 1900, when it began to attain general respectability. It now ranks third among our vegetable crops.

I have done for the murder of my father." As rebellions go this was a small one, but in the hindsight of history it was important indeed. Thomas A. Bailey has this conclusion to draw:

> The ill-fated Bacon's Rebellion was symptomatic of much that was to be American. It highlighted the cleavage between the older order of aristocracy and special privilege, on the one hand, and the emerging new order of free enterprise and equal opportunity, on the other. It arrayed the despised commoners against the lordly governing class, and the back-country frontier against the tidewater aristocracy. It showed at an early date that aroused colonists would unite and die for what they regarded as their rights as free men.

Furthermore, the struggle continues to this day. The distinguished political scientist V. O. Key has stated that Virginia is still probably the most conservative state in the Union — what he calls a "political museum piece." It has continued as an oligarchy run by gentlemanly politicians with the support of the business community and the FFVs generally.*

The second corporation that made a settlement in America was the one that financed the Pilgrim Fathers. Their leaders were Separatists who desired to withdraw entirely from the Anglican Church, and for this reason had run into trouble with the Stuart king. Ultimately they heard of Virginia and wanted to settle there; how they happened to land in New England is not exactly clear to this day. To make the trip the impecunious Pilgrims needed capital; for this purpose they got seventy "Merchant Adventurers" of London to put up seven thousand pounds to finance the expedition, and they received a charter from the London Company to settle in Virginia. The "Merchant Adventurers" had no concern for the religious aspect of the migration which, in time, was to achieve such prominence; the investors were interested in profits, which they hoped to achieve from fishing and fur trading. As with the Jamestown settlement there was to be no individual land ownership, at least in the beginning. The whole body of emigrants bound themselves to work for a period of seven years, during which time they would put all produce in a common warehouse and would receive subsistence out of a common store. There was an understanding that at the end of the period there was to be a settlement. In time adventurers and planters received one hundred acres for

---

* As David Hawke has pointed out so well (in *The Colonial Experience*, p. 273), there has been considerable disagreement among American historians in recent years about Bacon's Rebellion. In our text we have accepted the traditional point of view, well expressed by Thomas J. Wertenbaker in his *Bacon's Rebellion* (1957). On the other hand Wilcomb E. Washburn in *The Governor and the Rebel* (1957), makes Berkeley the hero and Bacon something of a villain. Wesley Frank Craven presents the rebellion as a most "complex problem" — with no simple answer — in his *Southern Colonies in the Seventeenth Century* (1949). For Bernard Bailyn it was a struggle for power between two elite groups (see James Morton Smith, ed., *Seventeenth-Century America: Essays on Colonial History* [1959]).

each person transported and every settler was assigned a garden plot plus an allotment of meadow and pasture.

The voyage itself was a curious one. The captain of the *Mayflower* was a reformed pirate by the name of Jones. He didn't take the Pilgrims to Virginia, and there is basis for the belief that he never intended to do so. There is some evidence to indicate that he was secretly in the pay of the Plymouth Company, which controlled the coast on which the ship was to land, and that his claim that he had been driven off his course was sheer poppycock. In any case the *Mayflower* sailed on 6 September 1620 with a passenger list that has been of more interest to posterity than any other in modern history. It comprised 102 persons, but the passengers were not all Pilgrims in the religious connotation of the term. There is a popular fallacy that they represented a homogeneous religious group, fired with a burning zeal to found a church of their own in the wilderness. Nothing could be farther from the truth. Only forty-four of the 102 passengers on the *Mayflower* were Pilgrims. The others, in the majority, were Strangers. They were not Separatists; in fact most of them were members of the Church of England, not from strong conviction but because they had been born in that faith. Among the fifty-eight Strangers were eighteen indentured servants, including four small waifs who were poor orphans of London, and who had been dragged off as kidnappees. The Strangers, like the tens of millions who crossed the Atlantic after them, were seeking in the New World not spiritual salvation but economic opportunity, a chance to better their worldly lot. All this led to several loud explosions between the Saints (Pilgrims) and the Strangers. By an ironic twist of fate it is among the Strangers, and not among Ye Saints, that one finds the three so-called Pilgrims who — thanks to Henry Wadsworth Longfellow — have enjoyed the greatest fame. They were Miles Standish (the Captain of the Guard), John Alden (the carpenter and suitor), and Priscilla Mullins (the sought-after damsel). But while there was a distinct cleavage between Saints and Strangers, all the passengers had one thing in common. All were from the lower classes — from the cottages and not from the castles of England.

On 11 November 1620 they all saw the "weatherbeaten face" — the "stern and rockbound" shore — of New England, rather than that of warmer Virginia. Wherever they landed — it certainly was not on Plymouth Rock — the Pilgrims finally chose as their site the inhospitable shore of Plymouth Bay. They went ashore without a charter, and to avoid anarchy they drew up the Mayflower Compact — to serve as a kind of temporary constitution until a new charter could be obtained from the Plymouth Company, which controlled from England the region where they had landed by accident or design. They never got it, with the result that the Plymouth colony was still charterless when it ultimately merged with Massachusetts Bay in 1691.

The early days of the colony were rugged ones. It was fortunate that the Indians in the area were few in number, having been wiped out by an epidemic of smallpox; even so, the winter of 1620–1621 was a terrible one, with cold and disease taking a grisly toll. Only forty-two out of the original 102 passengers survived, and at one time there were only seven who were well enough to lay the dead in their cold and forbidding graves. By the next autumn there had been good harvests, and with them the first Thanksgiving in New England.

From a corporate point of view, the settlers in the Plymouth colony in America bought out their London partners in 1626 — six years after they arrived there — for £2,400; the stockholders in England therefore liquidated their holdings and sold at a loss. The purchase sum was to be repaid at the rate of £200 a year. In order to do so William Bradford (who was governor of the colony for more than thirty years) and his associates took over a monopoly on fishing and fur-trading until the debt was paid. This was finally accomplished in 1648 — twenty-two years later — but in the process Bradford had to sell a farm and Miles Standish also took a loss. With all of its notoriety, the small and peaceful Colony of Plymouth, with a maximum population of 7,000, was never really important either economically or numerically.

Massachusetts Bay was not founded until Plymouth was nearly a decade old, but it became by far the most powerful and populous of the New England colonies. It resulted from the "Great Migration" of so-called Puritans, most of it from 1630 to 1640; the movement came to an abrupt end with the beginning of the English Civil War, after which New England's population growth was due largely to natural increase. The primary cause for the "Great Migration" was the general state of economic insecurity and unrest in England at that time. Subsidiary causes were the arbitrary rule of King Charles I and the persecutions of William Laud — the Archbishop of Canterbury who harried Nonconformists out of the kingdom so successfully that he has wryly been called "the father of New England." For whatever reason, during this decade about 75,000 refugees left England; it must be noted, however, that not all were Puritans and only a third came to the continent of North America. By comparison with Virginia or Plymouth the original expedition to Massachusetts — with its seventeen ships (led by the *Arbella*) and one thousand men and women — was a massive one; the settlement was begun on a larger scale than any of the other English colonies on the mainland. For that reason historically the *Arbella* was more important than the *Mayflower*.

The uniqueness of Massachusetts Bay was that it was not only the first self-governing colony in America, but also because it was modeled on the corporation that provided the capital. Whereas Virginia and Plymouth originally were operated by companies in England, the corporation that controlled Massachusetts Bay moved everything to the New World —

charter, officers, stockholders, capital, management. This was done largely for a religious reason; Winthrop was fearful that if the company's headquarters was left in London, interests hostile to the Puritans might gain control. So the entire corporation was moved to the New World, where it exercised the right of government over a large territory. No one seems to know how this was managed, although it is clear that it was done while the king and others were not tending to business — and that the lawyers among the Puritans (including John Winthrop) used their legal training to good advantage. In any case, the transfer of both charter and company to America gave the new colony a political structure, and established a model for later American institutions. The stockholders (freemen) were voters, provided they were church members. The company officers (eighteen assistants) were the legislators; by 1644 the deputies (executives) and assistants had separated into upper and lower houses. This structure of two legislative bodies, elected annually, took root — and in time became part of the state and federal structure of the United States. A trading company had thus given a corporate precedent to the American system of government, distinct from the parliamentary establishment of England. The company and the colony were the same until 1664, when the Crown rescinded the charter and the company ceased to exist; the colony became a royal one in 1691.

Massachusetts Bay also differed from the Plymouth colony, with which it is often confused, in two other pronounced ways: in religion and in the status of its members. In religion the emigrants to Massachusetts Bay were not radicals or Separatists; they wanted moderate reforms that would "purify" the Church of England, but no revolution that would rock the social or political boat. They were men of great and sometimes pompous piety — as the lives of the Cottons and Mathers testify. These settlers came from the middle (rather than the lower) strata of English society. A few had possessed large landed estates in England, some were wealthy merchants, others came from professional classes (doctors or lawyers), some were scholars. This is obvious from a glance at the titles on the rolls of the company: Sir Henry Roswell, Sir Richard Saltonstall, and John Winthrop — who had twenty indentured servants and was governor or deputy governor of the colony for almost two decades. These men desired to reproduce here a replica of the stratified society they had known, but they would lop off the two classes which had been above them in England — the king and the titled aristocracy — thus leaving themselves in top position. Governor Winthrop feared and distrusted the "commons" as the ignoble sort, and believed that democracy was the "meanest and worst" of all forms of government.

Essentially the Puritans also intended to establish in Massachusetts an economic structure like that in England, with large landed estates tilled by peasants and hired hands. Large estates, however, proved impossible because the gravelly soil of Massachusetts, strewn with boulders, took a long time to clear even for a small farm. In addition no staple crop was ever found for ready sale in England, like Virginia tobacco or Canadian furs. In time the forests of New England would produce lumber, and the farms would have beef for market, but these could not be sold in England — which got lumber from the Baltic and beef from her own farms. The commerce of Massachusetts with the mother country was necessarily indirect; the colony sold lumber and beef in the West Indies for sugar and rum, and used these commodities in the famed triangular trade routes.

Agriculture was disappointing; the Atlantic Ocean was not — in the sea the Puritans could farm and reap without sowing. Massachusetts began to exploit the "codfish lode" off the coast of New England; in due course the development of this secondary windfall would yield more wealth than did the Aztecs of Mexico and the Incas of Peru. As Samuel Eliot Morison has pointed out (in his classic *The Maritime History of Massachusetts*) the colony derived her ideals from the sacred book but achieved her wealth from the sacred cod — so much so that today a splendid facsimile of the fish is displayed with pride and satisfaction in the state house in Boston. The sea became so important that even the Puritan clergy were forced to recognize its existence. Once a minister told a congregation (in the famous fishing village of Marblehead) that the parishioners had come to the New World to "plant religion in the wilderness." A fisherman, with almost unanimous support from the rest of the audience, reproved him by shouting, "We did not come here for religion. Our main end is to catch fish." The clergy took the cue. In some churches the minister, as if he were on board, ascended into the pulpit by rope ladder. Men of the cloth even became interested in profits. A subsidiary feature of maritime industry — one that could provide a pleasant primary windfall — was known as "moon-cursing," the plundering of wrecks. There is a story about the Reverend Mr. Lewis of Wellfleet, Massachusetts. During his sermon one Sabbath, this entrepreneurial parson glanced out of the window and saw a vessel going ashore. He stopped his sermon, descended from the pulpit, and with a shout of "Start fair!" led his congregation pell-mell out of the meetinghouse door.

Ultimately four colonies were founded originally as a result of activities by joint-stock companies: Virginia, Massachusetts, New York, and Delaware. Three others were born because of animosity against Massachusetts: these were New Hampshire, which broke away for political reasons, and Connecticut and Rhode Island, which were settled by squatters unhappy with the theological, social, and economic climate in the Bible Commonwealth.

New Hampshire began with fishing and trading settlements, was gobbled up in 1641 by the grasping Bay Colony. In 1679 Charles II, annoyed by this display of greed, separated New Hampshire from Massachusetts and made it a royal colony. Connecticut got its start in the late 1630's largely through the influence of Thomas Hooker. He was basically a clerical autocrat of the medieval vintage, but authoritarians seldom see eye to eye and he had chafed under the restrictive laws of Massachusetts Bay. He left for the south, however, with the blessing of the Bay Colony, and it seems that the economic desire for better land was more important in the migration than any religious difference which might have developed. Like Plymouth, Connecticut was originally a squatter colony with no legal right to the lands it had usurped and no rights of government granted by the king. The latter, in the person of Charles II, had no use at all for Massachusetts Bay; he was therefore happy to grant Connecticut a royal charter in 1662.

The founding of Rhode Island in the 1630's is much more interesting than that of Connecticut or New Hampshire. The division between Massachusetts and Rhode Island was deep and wide and complex because of very real theological, social, and economic fissures. The emigrants who first went to Rhode Island, unlike those who departed for New Hampshire and Connecticut, had been banished. Roger Williams managed to get some territory south of Massachusetts from the Narragansett Indians, whose friendship he had won and whose language he had taken the trouble to learn. In 1663 he was granted a royal charter that legalized his squatter colony, in part because Charles II had a greater dislike of Massachusetts to the north.

Rhode Island turned out to be unusual in several ways: in religion, in its Indian policy, and in an economic theory that was at complete variance from the Protestant ethic. There was complete separation of church and state and freedom of religion for all — including freedom for Quakers, Jews, and Catholics. There was no compulsory attendance at church; in Williams's judgment "forced worship stinks in God's nostrils." There were no taxes to support a state religious establishment. The Puritans held firmly to the idea of the unity of church and state, and believed that the state should legislate and enforce morals among its subjects. Roger Williams and Anne Hutchinson, who had led the exodus to Rhode Island, did not believe civil authorities should have any control over conscience. Williams defended Indian claims to their soil, purchased from them instead of taking land by force. As a trader-clergyman he shared the Indian life, slept at their forest firesides, experienced their dangers; among all other Englishmen the Indians came to trust him. The old Narrangansett chief Canonicus, who distrusted whites, came to love Williams as a son; when he was dying he asked that the Englishman come to close his eyes. In his attitude toward property, Williams was as much an economic as a religious egalitarian. In Rhode Island the original distribution of land was in equal shares with Williams keeping but one share for himself; the assignment for *use* rather than *ownership*. He was devoid of self-interest; for the Protestant ethic he had no understanding at all. Wealth, success, status, power — for Williams these goals were as transient as smoke.

The Dutch, who were a leading maritime power in the seventeenth century, established two great trading companies: the Dutch East India Company and the Dutch West India Company. It was the first which sent Henry Hudson to these shores during 1609 in the *Half Moon*, to search unsuccessfully for a Northwest Passage to India. It was the second which founded New Netherland, now New York, on the North American continent.

The Dutch West India Company was chartered by the States General in 1621 for one prime purpose — to make money for its stockholders. It would earn dividends not only through trade but also by making war against Spanish and Portuguese possessions in the New World. So profitable and patriotic did the enterprise appear that by 1623, two years after its founding, subscribers had invested more than seven million guilders in the company. Here was an organization that appeared to be capable of challenging Spain and Portugal — armed as it was with its own fleet of warships, an adequate initial supply of capital, and the enthusiastic support of the home government. It became a prominent carrier of colonial trade by reason of low and attractive shipping rates, and some guile. Its plundering operations were remunerative. As an example, in 1628 — seven years after its founding — one of the company's admirals in command of a fleet of thirty-one sail, surprised and overcame a homeward-bound Spanish convoy and captured the whole fleet without firing a shot. It was a profitable theft, enough to pay a dividend of 50 percent.

In the 1630's the company seized numerous islands, including Curaçao and St. Eustatius. These were valuable chiefly as trading and smuggling depots; today Curaçao is still extremely prosperous both as a free port and as a refining center for Venezuelan oil. But outside the Caribbean the company attempted two territorial conquests, and ultimately lost both of them. It hoped to conquer Brazil and make it the principal source of sugar for Europe as well as a market for African slaves. For a brief period (1630–1650) it did control a long stretch of the Brazilian coast, but ultimately lost it for good. Curiously two countries — England and France — benefited from this effort. The Dutch so strained the resources of both Spain and Portugal during these middle years of the seventeenth century that the French and English were unmolested in their colonization of North America. As Professor John H. Parry has noted (in a perceptive volume with the intriguing title *The Age of the Reconnaissance*) the English in particular, behind this Dutch screen, had the opportunity to build their colonies along the Atlantic coast from Newfoundland to Barbados.

In New Netherland the most brilliant stroke of the company was the purchase of Manhattan Island from the Indians — after passing the bottle around — for trinkets worth about $25 (the Indian name for the area has been translated as "the Island where we all got drunk"). It turned out to be 22,000 acres of what is now the most valuable real estate in the world. This cost the company about one-tenth a cent an acre; unfortunately the company was not in existence when the time came to collect the unearned increment. Ultimately the Indians, infuriated by Dutch cruelties, would retaliate with horrible massacres. As a defensive measure the hard-pressed inhabitants erected a stout wall on Manhattan Island, a barricade from which Wall Street derived its name. The English captured the colony in 1664, renaming it New York. By this time the company's financial condition was unsound; after a reorganization in 1664 it engaged primarily in the African slave trade, although it still possessed the American colony now known as Dutch Guiana. In 1791 the charter expired and was not renewed.

During its four decades of existence New Netherland established religious and economic institutions which were to have lasting influence in the New World; it was also interesting politically as an example of authoritarian rule. The Dutch Reformed Church, Calvinistic in doctrine with a Presbyterian form of organization, became the established church of the colony; ultimately the church would found Queen's College (Rutgers) in New Jersey and today has a membership of about half a million in the United States. Economically the most interesting feature of the Dutch settlement was the patroon system, through which the company enticed large landowners to establish estates — which they did, principally along the Hudson River. Some of them were huge. Rensselaerswyck, for example, extending along both banks of the Hudson for eighteen miles, was a feudal domain facing the wilderness; it even had a private executioner. This anachronistic system continued until 1775 when the patroons became limited proprietors of their estates, but it was not completely abolished until 1846 following the Anti-Rent War in New York.

Politically the company ruled despotically through governors whose powers were similar to the autocrats in Spanish provinces. The last and most durable of their governors, who served for seventeen years (1647–1664), was the sturdy and pig-eyed and one-legged Peter Stuyvesant — remembered chiefly for his violent temper and his silver-studded wooden leg which gave him the soubriquet "Old Silver Nails." After the British threw him out in 1664 he retired to his farm or *bouwerie*, from which the name of a prominent section of lower Manhattan derives; other well-known place names — like Flushing, Brooklyn, and Flatbush — also had their origin in New Netherland. St. Nicholas was the patron saint of New Amsterdam, and the Dutch gave the Easter egg and Santa Claus to the

New World. Little did these canny enterprisers know that, three centuries later, their saints and symbols would be worth hundreds of millions of dollars for the manufacturers and merchants and advertisers of America.

Sweden wanted a share of these rising expectations in the New World and in 1633 chartered the New South Company for settlement and trade in what is now Delaware. Settlers from Finland, Holland, and Sweden were brought over, but the company did not enjoy good fortune in spite of the efforts of an impressive governor (1643–1653) of Gargantuan proportions. He was Johan Björnsson Printz, who was possibly the largest man who ever crossed the Atlantic; he was seven feet tall and weighed more than four hundred pounds. Called "Big Tub," he ran the tiny colony as he would have commanded a regiment of infantry, but he was unable either to achieve dividends for the company or to avoid conquest by the Dutch under Stuyvesant in 1655. The only permanent Swedish influence was the introduction of the log cabin to American social and architectonic life. This type of dwelling had not been used by the Pilgrims in Massachusetts, or by the early Cavaliers in Virginia. They pitched tents or took refuge in hillside caves or moved into wigwams abandoned or appropriated from the Indians. Eventually the Pilgrims, Puritans, and Cavaliers duplicated the houses they had known in England, laboriously splitting timbers to make the familiar clapboards. By contrast, the Swedes' native log cabin was to be copied by other settlers in America until it was the typical backwoods dwelling by the end of the eighteenth century. In the West it was used universally until the Great Plains were reached, where it was replaced by the sod house, only to reappear in the Rocky Mountains.

The proprietary colonies sprang from the desire of their owners to build fortunes through real estate. The Baltimores, the Penns, the various proprietors of the Carolinas and New Jersey, were all capitalist speculators and landlords who sought profits from the sale of land, the operation of their own large estates, and the collection of rent and other fees from tenants.

Six men — the Lords Baltimore — owned Maryland for 144 years. They derived their title from an estate in County Longford in the north of Ireland, where George Calvert already owned a manor of more than two thousand acres when he received his first title of nobility as Lord Baltimore. He became a Catholic in 1625, and for that reason had to resign his office as Privy Councillor. For a brief period he had a plantation in Newfoundland, but judged it to be too cold in winter and ultimately got Charles I — who had leanings toward Catholicism — to grant him what is present-day Maryland.

In the first years inducements to settle in Maryland were generous. The proprietor offered a grant of two thousand acres to every "adventurer" who took with him five men between the ages of sixteen and sixty. To those who transported less than this number he would give one hundred acres for each person within those ages, plus fifty acres for each child. For these grants the annual quitrent — a feudal due (beyond the actual rent charged by the immediate landowner) paid to the Baltimores — varied in amount but ultimately was ten pounds of good wheat for each fifty acres. The principal income for the Calverts came from sales of land, quitrents, "alienation fines" which were assessed when the property changed hands, and the resale of escheated land — land that reverted to the proprietor to pay quitrents or for other reasons. How much was all this? Toward the end of the proprietorship the income cleared annually by the Baltimores was more than £12,000, an amount in today's terms well over a quarter of a million dollars. In exchange for prerogatives which were all but royal, the Lord Proprietor of Maryland pledged the King of England — as a modern scholar has noted with some cynicism — "nothing more than his continued allegiance, one fifth of the colony's nonexistent gold and silver, and two Indian arrows to be delivered yearly during Easter week at Windsor Castle!" Unfortunately in their 144 years of possession the six Lords Baltimore decreased in vitality, generation by generation. Their ultimate problem, however, came not so much from a degeneration in the quality of the family, as in the fact that they clung with blind tenacity to feudal prerogatives which certainly were anachronistic in the New World — but which nonetheless have left their stamp upon Maryland and its people to the present day.

The interests of the Baltimores in America were predominantly economic, but collaterally they also wanted to found a refuge for English and Irish Catholics. The first Lord Baltimore earnestly desired to establish a colony free from the religious persecutions he had known as a Catholic in Protestant England, and a place of refuge that was securely beyond the reach of test-oaths. This the Baltimores did, but for Christians only; in the famed Toleration Act of 1649 Maryland prescribed the death penalty and confiscation of property for anyone denying the divinity of Christ or the concept of the Trinity.

One result of all this was that when the colonial era ended, Maryland probably sheltered more Roman Catholics than any other English-speaking colony in the New World. One of them was John Carroll, who was both the first American bishop and the founder of the first Catholic college (now Georgetown University). In retrospect it is pertinent to note that freedom of religion in America benefited because Charles I granted a colony to a Roman Catholic land speculator, and because Charles II later used land to settle a debt to a Quaker.

The two Carolinas were founded in 1670 when Charles II gave eight of his court favorites — as Lords Proprietors — the area now comprising the two states plus a wilderness that extended all the way to the Pacific, at least in theory. The philosopher John Locke, later famous as an advocate of freedom, drew up a reactionary constitution for the Carolinas which Charles Austin Beard was to characterize as one of the most fantastic now to be found moldering in the archives of government. It provided for a feudal regime based on slavery and serfdom, with a nobility possessed with such outlandish titles as palatines, admirals, chamberlains, and stewards. The proprietors were enthusiastic about it, but settlers steadfastly refused to ratify such an anachronistic government — and this fundamental conflict was one of the reasons both Carolinas became royal colonies in 1729. From the beginning there was a great difference between North and South Carolina, and the cleavage was legally recognized in 1712. South Carolina developed close economic ties with the British West Indies, was settled by English Protestants and French Huguenots, and became an aristocratic colony based on plantations (rice and indigo) *and* Charleston — a city which became the chief center of culture and wealth in the South.

North Carolina was entirely different — and still is today. The inhabitants were Scotch-Irish and Germans who came down the mountain valleys from Pennsylvania, plus a varied crew of outcasts and religious dissenters from Virginia (for that reason the North Carolinians have been called the "quintessence of Virginia's discontent"). Communication with North Carolina was difficult. By land it was almost impossible, except through Virginia, and even then swamps and forests made the attempt forbidding. By sea only vessels of light draft could negotiate the narrow and shallow passages through the island barriers. Isolated North Carolina thus developed a confident independence and a strong spirit of resistance to authority; between aristocratic Virginia and aristocratic South Carolina it was a "vale of humility between two mountains of conceit." Rhode Island and North Carolina were always two "other-minded" colonies — the most self-sufficient and the least aristocratic of the original thirteen.

The Quakers were a remarkable sect which appeared in England during the 1600's and were so-called because its members were supposed to have quaked when under the influence of deep religious emotion. They were really the anarchists of the Protestant Reformation, and were especially offensive to officials because they denied the authority of both the Bible and the Church (they relied on the "inner light"), they built simple meetinghouses and had no paid clergy, they would take no oaths because Jesus said, "Swear not at all" (this particularly angered those who believed in test-oaths), and they actively believed in peace — resorting to passive resistance and a "turning of the other cheek" in times of adversity. With all their radicalism they were the dynamic form of English Protestantism from 1650 to 1700 — just as Puritanism had been in 1600, and Methodism was to be in 1700.

William Penn was a well-born and athletic young Englishman who, in the late 1660's, had been attracted to the Quaker faith. His father, who was Admiral Sir William Penn, disapproved and administered a sound flogging. The discipline had no lasting effect; in time the youth firmly embraced the radical faith, and for his adherence was to suffer much persecution. His thoughts turned to the New World because it presented several possibilities: there he could found an asylum for his people, there he could experiment with liberal ideas of government, and there he might make a profit. He was fortunate in getting a grant because of special circumstances: Charles II owed Penn's father £16,000 and also favored religious toleration because he wanted Catholics so treated. The actual grant came from the king in 1681, and was called Penn's Woodland or Pennsylvania.

For its day Pennsylvania was liberal in the economic, political, and religious spheres. Pennsylvania was by far the best advertised of all the colonies; its founder, sometimes called the "first American advertising man," sent paid agents to Europe and distributed countless pamphlets in English, Dutch, French, and German. Unlike the lures of many another real-estate promoter, then and later, Penn's inducements were generally truthful. His liberal land policy brought a large flow of immigrants from many countries, and Pennsylvania became a melting pot of nationalities. There was, however, a paradox in all this: economically Penn was a liberal, but at the same time he retained extensive family properties in England, Ireland, and America. He was also an aristocrat in his own tastes and pleasures — as is attested by his interest in race horses, ships, good food, drink, and handsome women.

Politically Penn introduced a system that was comparatively liberal as proprietary regimes went. It had a representative assembly elected by the landowners. Here again there was a paradox; Penn himself was certainly no democrat. He believed in government *for* the people — *by* liberally educated gentlemen like himself. There was freedom of worship for all in Pennsylvania, although Jews and Catholics could not vote or hold office.

The history of New Jersey was confused and complex in the colonial era; there are some who would claim that it remains so today. When the Dutch owned New Netherland, the colony included what are now the states of New York *and* New Jersey. In 1664, when the British conquered New Netherland, Charles II granted the area to his brother the Duke of York, later James II. The duke kept the state named after him, and deeded the rest to two of his London cronies — Sir John Berkeley and

Sir George Carteret. He specified in the deed that the place be called New Jersey after the old Channel Island where Carteret had been born and had served a term as governor.

Neither Berkeley nor Carteret ever came to New Jersey because they had too many troubles, caused by their own inefficiency and greed, back in the Old Country. Ultimately the two men, or their heirs, sold to others; finally, in 1702, after much manipulation and mismanagement, New Jersey welcomed new status as a royal colony.

Alone of all the continental American colonies, Georgia was sponsored by men who were not interested in making a profit from the undertaking. This rare example of a vast enterprise with a thoroughly altruistic motive was so unusual that it has been the subject of much speculation and self-congratulation. There were certain influential and wealthy humanitarians in England who hoped to provide an asylum in America for "all the useless Poor in England, and distressed Protestants in Europe." In 1732 they managed to get a charter for Georgia (named for the king who granted it) under which they as sponsors and trustees would put up the money, but not for profit, in order to transport to the New World persons who had been imprisoned for debt. The trustees were to own no land in Georgia, but were given the right to govern the area for twenty-one years. In actual fact the trustees had three purposes in mind: military, economic, and philanthropic. They wished to protect the frontier — to provide a buffer state against the Spanish in Florida. From an economic point of view, they wanted to develop valuable semitropical products — particularly the silkworm. As philanthropists they devoutly wished to provide a "calm retreat for undeserved distress." For that reason they limited the size of land holdings in Georgia (against speculators), they forbade slavery (so the debtor-immigrants could compete), and they forbade liquor (to keep them sober and at work).

It is impossible to discuss Georgia without commenting particularly on the remarkable man who was chiefly responsible for its founding — General James Edward Oglethorpe. He was a *rara avis* indeed — a military man with liberal tendencies. A graduate of Eton and Oxford, he held a seat in Parliament for thirty-two years; in military circles he had a deservedly high reputation, gained chiefly in campaigns against the Turks. Interestingly, on the eve of the American Revolution he declined the command of the British army in America because he was not given the power of concession and conciliation. The central point is that he was vitally interested in problems which were nonmilitary, and solutions for them which avoided the employment of force. He wanted to do something for debtors in prisons; he tried to expose the evils of impressment almost a century before we went to war about it; he was opposed to Negro slavery; he was against strong drink.

It is not surprising that Oglethorpe's vision of a commonwealth of small, self-supporting, abstemious landholders did not materialize. The dream was destroyed by a number of practical developments. For one thing, the trustees' plans for land, no matter how noble, were unsound — at least for Georgia. In those pine barrens small farms were uneconomic; there was an adage that "it took three men and a quart of whiskey to raise hell on it." The original idea of fifty acres per family was therefore silly, simply because fifty acres of pine barren will not support a family. Ultimately the limitation was increased to five hundred, then to two thousand acres — and was removed entirely in 1750. This brought a demand for slaves, because the increasingly larger holdings obviously introduced a plantation economy. Reluctantly, the trustees allowed slavery in 1750.

The prohibition of liquor turned out to be both unpopular and uneconomic. Lumber from Georgia went to the West Indies, and rum was one of the few commodities that could be returned. A prohibition against the importation of rum had the effect of cutting off a vital trade with the Caribbean. The consequence could have been predicted: the trustees repealed prohibition in 1742. On top of everything else, the silkworms also refused to cooperate; however intractable the London poor were to the schemes of the trustees, the silkworms were even more so. In 1742 nearly half the silkworms in Savannah died, proving that Georgia's climate was not suited for their culture. But the trustees remained blind to a pragmatic situation; in 1751 they declared that no one could be a representative in the Georgia Assembly unless he had at least one hundred mulberry trees planted (to house and feed silkworms) on every fifty acres!

The handwriting was on the wall, in letters which were plain and large. In 1752 Georgia ceased to be a utopian settlement, and became a royal colony of the Crown of England.

IV

An Economic Interpretation of the American Revolution

THERE have been many attempts to explain the outbreak of the American Revolution — based on geography, religion, population, politics, and economics. Those who stress geography point out that distance and the Great Frontier developed in the colonies new desires and new points of view: we have already noted the development of the concepts of democracy and laissez-faire and individualism on the frontier. The religious argument is founded on the opposition of the Puritans, Presbyterians, and other colonial sects to the Church of England and the putative appointment of a resident Anglican bishop. The religious opposition appears to have been largely speculative and emotional because England had no real intention of appointing a bishop for the colonies. Nonetheless there are those who claim that the American Revolution was in reality a "Scotch-Irish Presbyterian revolt."

The argument based on population concerns the lack of national homogeneity in the English colonies on the mainland of North America. There is no question that the New World had shown a tendency toward cosmopolitanism from the very beginning. There were eight nationalities in Columbus's expedition; the very name America was established by a German geographer working in a French college — who named the New World for an Italian explorer. Although the Daughters of the American Revolution were outraged, President Franklin D. Roosevelt was quite accurate historically when he opened his remarks to their meeting with the salutation: "Fellow immigrants." The largest foreign groups in the English colonies in North America were the Scotch-Irish, the Germans, and the African slaves. The Scotch-Irish were actually Lowlanders from Scotland who had been transplanted to northern Ireland, where they developed a repugnance for the natives because of their Catholicism — and for the English because of their restrictive economic policy. For these reasons they emigrated to the American colonies in large numbers; by 1775 the Scotch-Irish comprised 7 percent of the population. They had come to these shores disliking the British with great intensity, and had gone to the frontier dreaming of a place where they would find neither Irish Papists nor Church-of-England men. On the frontier it was said that they kept the Sabbath and everything else they could lay their hands on; this observation may have been unfair but there is no question that they were pugnacious, lawless, and individualistic — or that they made a prime contribution to the rebel side of the American Revolution. The Germans were about 6 percent of the total population in 1775; so many of them had settled in Pennsylvania that Benjamin Franklin once expressed fear for the survival of the English language. As Thomas A. Bailey has pointed out, if one combines the Germans, Scotch-Irish, and miscellaneous white foreign groups (French Huguenots, Dutch, Swedes, and others) — and adds another 20 percent of the population who were African slaves — nearly 40 percent of the colonists were of non-English origin. In time of crisis this was a heavy handicap for the English as far as any expectation of a loyalty based on tradition and history and national ties was concerned.

Over the years historians by groups have been fortifying their interpretative positions both for defense and for attack on the heretical enemy. The Neo-Whigs (for example, Edmund S. Morgan and Bernard Bailyn) see the American Revolution as the defense of political freedom. The Imperialists (from Charles M. Andrews and Louis Beer to Lawrence H. Gipson) tend to view the Revolution as a disturbance of the best empire ever known to man. The Economic School (from Charles Austin Beard and Louis Hacker to Merrill Jensen and Jackson Turner Main) is inclined to emphasize the importance of the pocketbook. There are smaller splinter groups of historians manning the ramparts for their particular positions in the interpretative hinterland.

Among current historians the major argument has been between those who place major stress on political, as against those who emphasize economic reasons for the Revolution. In the early days of the Republic, and in fact until a half century ago, it was common for historians to state confidently that the American Revolution could be explained very simply; it was a struggle of Liberty against Tyranny — of the freedom-loving Americans against the wickedness of the British. In the two decades after World War I the prevalent interpretation was heavily on the economic side. In the present era the majority of American historians probably favor a political interpretation which is much more sophisticated than the one which was the conventional wisdom a century ago; it stresses the political and idealistic importance and significance of the colonial defense of democracy and civil liberties. The economic historian, including the writer, would not question the importance of democracy and civil liberties; he does occasionally wonder whether most people believe all the glittering political generalities they employ, and whether many political theories do not arise basically out of economic issues.

It is apparent that because of many reasons — geographical, nationalistic, religious, political, and economic — a psychological attitude of opposition to Britain had developed here; it was a portentous feeling compounded of ignorance, misunderstanding, ideals, interests, pride, and stubbornness — but such ugly situations can, and did, produce a revolution. This was strange because England's administration of her colonies, from both the political and economic point of view, was more liberal than that of any other power in the eighteenth century. But whatever the century there can be revolutions because of rising expectations. In Leland Baldwin's judgment it may be claimed that

> revolutions do not arise out of the desperation of misery but out of a vision of something better. . . . The American Revolution did not arise from the desperation of misery, whatever the protests made by our shrewd and highly articulate ancestors. It arose from the belief that conditions could and should be better and that self-government was the only guarantee of this betterment.

In all of the arguments about the various causes that may have brought on the American Revolution, it seems clear that the conflict would not have occurred — at least in the eighteenth century — had it not been for the British decision in 1763 to finally enforce an old mercantilist policy that had been introduced many years before, a decision that was fortified by some brand-new economic policies that angered many colonists: taxation for revenue, the prohibition against western settlement, and the Tea Act of 1773. All of these played directly into the hands of a master propagandist whose name was Sam Adams, with consequences leading directly into the American Revolution.

We have already discussed the theory of mercantilism (see pp. 4–6), the dominant economic philosophy from the sixteenth through the eighteenth centuries. It emphasized an intense nationalism in the political sphere, in economics placed stress on the acquisition of gold by means of a favorable balance of trade and cheap labor to keep prices attractive, and was at best amoral in its ethical concepts. *Vis-à-vis* America this theory could be reduced to one simple argument: that the colonies existed for the benefit of the mother country. There was nothing altruistic about the policy; mercantilism could — and did — bring incidental advantages to the colonies on occasion, but it was fundamentally designed to benefit the home nation. In the practice of mercantilism the British attempted to assure their own maximum benefit through navigation acts, trade laws, restrictions on colonial manufacturing, and limitations on issues of paper money.

A turning point in England's attitude toward its colonies came in the year 1650. During the English civil war Parliament had attempted to entice the colonies with trading privileges; the colonies (Virginia, Maryland, and Massachusetts) had responded by throwing their ports open to the ships of all nations! This was obviously heretical from a mercantilist point of view; if gold was to be kept within the Empire, payments should not be made to foreign-flag vessels. Once the civil war was over, and the king had been beheaded, the Puritans and the merchants took over. Their purpose was to tighten control over the wayward colonies. In doing so, as it happened, they struck at the English colonies through the Dutch.

By the middle of the seventeenth century Holland dominated world trade, completely overshadowing England on the high seas. Jean Baptiste Colbert (1619–1683), the French statesman who was one of the most successful advocates of mercantilism, estimated that of the 20,000 ships engaged in European commerce in his day, the Dutch owned 16,000. At that time the Dutch East India Company had a near monopoly on the spice trade, and the Dutch West India Company had captured more than five hundred Spanish vessels, had occupied large parts of the coast of Brazil, and had established settlements on the Hudson River. Amsterdam, not London, was the commercial center of the Western world. Interestingly, Holland was concerned with commerce rather than colonies. Its worldwide settlements never became much more than trading stations because, as David Hawke has observed, the Dutch "saw no reason to trade their pleasant life at home for a rude existence in the wilderness." Other nations traded with them, not because they were forced to do so but because the Dutch could usually sell and carry goods for a third less than the merchants and shippers of other nations.

In their own way the Dutch were first in the practice of automation. Their ships were designed to carry a maximum cargo with the fewest seamen. Their method of rigging sails gave them superiority in maneuvering; they used winches to speed loading and unloading; they used metal sheathing to protect hulls from shipworms (or borers). Merchants in the American colonies liked to trade with the Dutch because their vessels were stocked with a greater variety of merchandise, they extended longer credit, paid the highest prices for colonial products, and seemed to be content with a smaller profit than was the case with Londoners. This gave the Dutch a great advantage, and their superiority had increased during the English civil war. Once the fighting in that conflict had ceased, the Puritan merchants in Parliament demanded control. With internal opposition crushed by Cromwell, and with a good navy developed at long last, England was ready to challenge Dutch maritime supremacy. Her method would not be through competition, but through war and legislation restricting the colonies.

The act which insured a monopoly for English-flag ships, including thoses from the American colonies, was the Act of 1651 — commonly known as Cromwell's Act. As amended, particularly in 1660, it provided that:

No goods, except those of Europe, could be carried into any port under English sovereignty unless in ships which were British-built, British-owned, and British-manned: three-fourths of the crew must be British. This section obviously applied to goods from Asia, Africa, and the Americas.

In the case of Europe, all goods had to be brought into any part of the British Empire in ships of the country of origin — or in British-owned, British-built, and British-manned ships. This meant that no foreign vessel, meaning a Dutch ship, could carry the goods of a third European nation (for example, France or Spain) into a port of the British Empire. The Dutch were left without a large part of their shipping market.

This legislation obviously damaged the Dutch merchant marine and helped the shipbuilding industry in both the British Isles and in New England. Under the protection of these acts shipbuilding became one of the most important industries in colonial America; by 1760 one-third of the total British tonnage was built in the American colonies.

The prime examples of trade acts were the Enumerated Products Act of 1660 (as amended), the Middleman's Act of 1663, and the Molasses Act of 1733. The first two were passed to benefit business in England generally; the last was an act of very special legislation for the advantage of a particular group in the Caribbean colonies of Great Britain. All of these acts regulated trade by legislative fiat, in the finest mercantilist tradition, directing it artificially through routes which would not have been followed had the trade acts not been promulgated.

The first Enumerated Products Act of 1660 provided that certain commodities from the colonies could be shipped *only* to England. In the original act these were tobacco, sugar, cotton, and indigo. As the years went by the number of products on the enumerated list increased until it included, by the eve of the American Revolution, almost everything except fish and barrel staves. The mercantilist purpose of the act was obvious: it would insure for the mother country cheap raw materials and reexportable products, which she could reship to other countries at a good profit. The chief of these was tobacco. In 1750, when tobacco accounted for half of the total value of colonial exports to England, four-fifths of this product was reshipped to continental countries.

The Enumerated Products Act was involved with *exports* from the colonies. The Middleman's Act of 1663 concerned *imports* into the colonies. It prohibited by high duties the importation into the colonies of any European goods unless they were brought via the British Isles; this permitted duties and commissions to be collected in England before the European goods were transshipped to America. This act created, for English merchants, a national monopoly on all colonial imports. It also benefited English manufacturers. If foreign products bound for the colonies were cheaper than those manufactured in England, the solution was a simple one; they could be taxed, thus increasing their prices to the artificial point where English goods could undersell them overseas.

The problem of international trade and the balance of payments is a perennial one which has been of concern from the era of the thirteen colonies to the present day. It was aggravated in 1733 by the Molasses Act, which was passed in that year. The Caribbean colonies, and the southern ones on the mainland, were relatively well-off because England wanted their staples in return for manufactured goods. These southern colonies shipped tobacco, rice, sugar, and indigo directly to England; in return they imported dry goods, hardware, furniture, and other manufactures from England. Unfortunately, this favorable exchange did not prevail with New England and the Middle Colonies. They could ship directly to England only a limited and relatively insignificant number of commodities: these were naval stores, lumber, furs, and metals. Their great staples — fish and grain — were kept out of England by high tariffs. The direct export trade to England of New England and the Middle Colonies was therefore so small that in some years their imports — most of which by law had to come through England — were eight times their exports. New England and the Middle Colonies would obviously be on a collision course unless they found other outlets for their chief products — outlets that would enable them to earn cash (or commodities like sugar that were marketable in England) in order to compensate for the imbalance in the direct trade with the mother country. They did so, legally, by means of the famous indirect or triangular trade with the Caribbean, with southern Europe, and with Africa. They did so, illegally, through piracy. There was a solid economic basis for the illicit practice; the significant role played by piracy, in maintaining a reasonable balance of trade for the northern colonies, is little known or appreciated. Pirates fitted out in Boston, Newport, New York, and Philadelphia; backed by reputable merchants who invested openly by buying shares in the venture, they preyed on Spanish fleets in the Caribbean — and even went (as Captain Kidd did) into the Red Sea and the Indian Ocean to terrorize ships engaged in the trade with the East Indies. Their ships — heavily laden with plate and dry goods and spices — would put back into colonial ports where the loot was sold, providing good windfalls for the investors and good cash balances to make up deficits in international trade. It seems probable that the steadily diminishing supply of specie in the American colonies after 1700 came about, at least in part, because England began to exterminate piracy about that time. But in the early days some of the wisest and most respectable businessmen in the northern towns had made good profits from illegal exploits on the high seas.

Here we are concerned only with the legal triangular trade which enabled New England and the middle colonies to survive. They always had a market in the Caribbean colonies which produced sugar (with byproducts in molasses and rum) but which could not feed themselves; these island colonies were glad to buy the fish of New England and the grain of the Middle Colonies, along with lumber for barrels and staves. The trade triangle was completed by the exchange of these products for either sugar, which was taken to England and sold for manufactured goods, or for rum (produced from molasses in the Caribbean *and* in New England), which was exchanged in Africa for slaves who were sold for cash (or for commodities marketable in England) in the Caribbean colonies, or in the southern ones on the mainland. The triangular trade with southern Europe was both obvious and simple. There was a market in Spain and Portugal for grain, meat, fish, and lumber; these were exchanged for fruits and wine, which were marketable in England for manufactured goods.

The triangular trade with the Caribbean was placed in jeopardy by the Molasses Act of 1733, which levied an almost prohibitive duty of ninepence a gallon on rum, sixpence a gallon on molasses, and five shillings a hundredweight on sugar — if those commodities came from the *foreign* West Indies. There was no tax if New England skippers bought in the British West Indies, but the flourishing trade with the Dutch, Danish, and French West Indies would henceforth wither away. The Molasses Act, if enforced, would have ruined most effectively a large part of the triangular trade. First, the British West Indies could supply but a part of the rum and molasses and sugar necessary for the total trade. Second, New England would have to pay much higher prices for its rum and molasses. The *foreign* West Indies could sell sugar to their mother countries, but not molasses or rum since France had a flourishing brandy industry, and Holland produced great quantities of gin. The resulting price of these commodities in the foreign West Indies was so low that New England bought most of its supply there.

It is pertinent to note that rum was essential not alone for the African trade but also for home consumption. Eighteenth-century England and America were notorious for their alcoholism. The largest manufacturing industry in the pre-Revolutionary American colonies was distilling; rum became such an important article of commerce that on the eve of the American Revolution more than 600,000 gallons were shipped abroad annually and large quantities were consumed at home. In spite of the fact that whiskey had caught on by the early nineteenth century, as late as 1807 there were forty rum distilleries in Boston alone. The principal distilling centers were Newport and Boston, where the rum that emerged from the stills was described as "pale, potent, and paralyzing." So much was produced that John Adams called rum the "spirit of '76." The aged and infirm sipped toddies of rum and water, heavy on the rum. Babies were given heavy doses of rum and opium, and so spent their infancy in a happy fog. Students drank an amazing quota; in the middle of the seventeeth century students at Harvard, fifty in all, managed to consume 270 barrels of beer in one year. No one drank harder than the clergy and some were actually engaged in the liquor business. The Reverend Nathan Strong, pastor of the First Church at Hartford (Connecticut) about 1800, and a noted revivalist, also operated a prosperous distillery within sixty rods of his church; it was claimed that he was thus able to keep an eye on both his businesses at the same time.

In this era able-bodied men and women seldom went more than a few hours without a drink. At one time so much rum was available in Boston that it was sold for four pence a quart; it is understandable, at this price, that it became the "tipple of the poor." The custom of closing offices and business establishments at eleven o'clock each morning so that everyone could get a drink — known as "'Leven O'clock Bitters" — prevailed throughout the colonies; it was repeated at four in the afternoon. For some, in this age, drinking bouts — by the very definition — became a kind of athletic sport. Men tried for records as one-bottle or two-bottle men. Three-bottle men were looked up to with about the same reverence that we now show — probably as foolishly — to champion prizefighters and football players. Washington, for example, was a one-bottle man. This meant that at dinner he ordinarily drank a pint of Madeira, in addition to rum punch and beer; he was never known to have been intoxicated. The most famous of all colonial drinks was rum flip — made by combining rum, beer, and sugar — about two-thirds beer. The mixture was stirred with an iron poker, called a loggerhead, that had been brought to a cherry-red heat in the fireplace. When the hot loggerhead brought the flip to a boil, it was said to be potable. Properly prepared, rum flip had a slightly bitter and burned taste, and was very potent. An evening over a bowl of rum flip frequently ended in a brawl; thus the term "at loggerheads" was developed. Many have wondered, and with considerable reason, how colonials could drink so much with no visible effects. The answer appears to have been based on diet; they ate plenty of sorghum sugar and imperfectly refined flour, and thus stocked themselves with the vitamins necessary to fend off drunkenness.

In retrospect, it is apparent that the Molasses Act of 1733, if enforced, would have benefited the British West Indies, and would have seriously damaged New England and the British manufacturers and merchants who benefited from the triangular trade. A natural question arises: if the act hurt more people in the British Empire than it benefited, why was it passed in the first place? The answer is the special influence of the "sugar lords" in Parliament, a group so powerful that it was sometimes known as the "West Indian Lobby." The central point is that the really great commodity of colonial trade in the eighteenth century was sugar. By the 1760's British investment in Jamaica, Barbados, and other sugar islands amounted to the enormous sum of £60 million — six times the amount of British investment in the mainland colonies. In 1697 little Barbados, with its 166 square miles, was worth more to British capitalism than New England, New York, and Pennsylvania combined! To protect these interests seventy sugar lords sat in Parliament. Unfortunately they could not compete in price with the foreign West Indies for a variety of reasons, including the inefficiency of their absentee ownership; they therefore asked for, and got, a monopoly by legislative fiat.

The Enumerated Products and the Middleman's Acts were aggravating; the Molasses Act was abominable to the American colonies because it would have stifled their triangular trade, and because it was a piece of special legislation that benefited the few at the expense of the many. It was not enforced for more than three decades, else the American Revolution might have occurred in the 1730's. Sir Robert Walpole, the chief figure in British political life for two decades (1721–1742), believed in letting sleeping dogs lie. His period of control has been called the era of "salutary neglect for the colonies"; in fact, the phrase "salutary neglect" might well be extended to cover the entire period of colonial history down to 1764. Once Walpole responded, in reply to a suggestion that Parliament tax the colonies, with the commentary, "I will leave that to my successors, who have more courage than I have."

In addition to navigation and trade acts, the British government also imposed restrictions on colonial manufacturing and on paper money. Probably 95 percent of American colonists in 1775 were engaged in agriculture, but an iron industry was beginning, and there was some production of hats and woolens. This was not orthodox in mercantilist theory, under which the colonies were to produce raw materials and the mother country was to perform the manufacturing; such economic subordination could bring great advantages to Britain. In 1766 the *London Magazine* boasted: "The American is apparelled from head to foot in our manufactures . . . he scarcely drinks, sits, moves, labours, or recreates himself, without contributing to the emolument of the mother country." It is therefore not surprising that in 1699, Parliament passed the Woolens Act, forbidding the export of wool and woolens outside the colony where they were woven (actually the act produced no hardship in America, where most rural women carded, spun, and wove their own wool). Beaver were plentiful in America, and the primary use of the fur was in the making of hats. In 1732, Parliament enacted the Hat Act, at the insistence of London's Worshipful Company of Hatters, who feared that Americans were not importing enough of their headgear from the home country. The act limited the number of hatter apprentices and forbade exportation of hats (although they continued to be exported from New York, bearing the label "British" in them). In 1750, in order to maintain a monopoly for the iron industries of the English midland, the Iron Act prohibited the colonies from producing finished products in that metal. Enforcement of all of these acts was sporadic indeed, and they were flagrantly disregarded by the colonists; they could be, however, a most annoying nuisance in the occasional case of enforcement.

In connection with restrictions on paper money it may be helpful to comment on prevailing theory as well as the specific situation confronting the American colonies. The mercantilists of England believed that gold and silver constituted the only real money. By contrast the colonies were anticipating a laissez-faire point of view which would stress, as Adam Smith would put it, that commodities (things) were the wealth of nations. The central point is that the wealth of the Great Frontier, and in time of the Industrial Revolution, made commodities so plentiful that specie (gold and silver) became relatively scarce in spite of the efforts of the mercantilists to pile it up. Because there was not enough specie to buy all the commodities available, ultimately an extensive system of credit and substitute money had to be superimposed on specie, giving rise to the great banking systems of London, Amsterdam, and Paris. This development would provide a reasonably flexible currency that could be made to expand or contract with the expansion or contraction of commodities. In time, bank credit had to destroy the scarcity of money on which the theory of mercantilism rested. But before all of these banking developments, what were the American colonies to use for money? Under the mercantilist philosophy the exportation of British coin (specie) was restricted by law; even if it had been allowed, the unfavorable balance of trade would have taken it back to the British Isles. Banking was not established in England until 1694, and no commercial bank appeared in the New World until 1781. To meet a critical situation the American colonies avoided the use of regular money by straight barter transactions, sometimes employing Indian wampum, beaver skins, corn, rice, and lumber as legal tender. They used a great many Spanish dollars and developed substitutes known as staple money and fiat money.

As a result of the favorable West Indian trade Spanish dollars were brought in in such numbers that they were the principal coins used in the colonies. The basis of these dollars' weight was a *real* or royal — a silver coin that weighed fifty-three troy grains. Eight "reals," called a piece of eight, had about the same weight as our present silver dollar; eight bits, in the phrase of that day, equaled our dollar (to this day there are some who refer to a quarter as two bits). In Spain the piece of eight was called a peso; in English countries it was named a dollar. This came from the

Anglicization of the German *thaler*, a similar coin which had been popular in middle Europe in the early sixteenth century.

Principal commodities were used as a basis for *staple* money. In Virginia tobacco was deposited in warehouses and the *receipts* were recognized as money by the colonial government; Pennsylvania did the same with wheat. The colonials then went a step further and experimented with *fiat* money — "promise" money made legal tender by decree. Massachusetts was the first, in 1690, to use promissory notes to pay soldiers in anticipation of tax collection. This proved so successful that the device was adopted as a regular practice by all of the colonies before 1760. Time and again British mercantilists protested because paper was not bullion, and because they, as creditors, did not relish the idea of being paid in depreciated paper. Finally, in 1764, Parliament forbade all issues of paper currency by the American colonies.

In evaluating British mercantilism, the Navigation (Shipping) Acts helped New England along with the British Isles. Trade acts limited markets for colonists — but they also provided for the payment of bounties to growers of tobacco, naval stores, and providers of iron, indigo, and other products; after the American Revolution the loss of British bounties on rice, indigo, and naval stores ended flourishing enterprises in the South. It can be claimed that the prohibition of certain manufacturers was not essentially burdensome because it was fundamentally sound, at this stage in the economic development of the colonies, that they devote themselves primarily to extractive industries. To their great advantage the colonies were the beneficiaries of free military defense under the mercantilist nation state. They made some show of "training" local militia — but the real bulwark that protected them from the French, Spanish, and Dutch was provided by the mightiest navy of the world plus expeditionary forces of Redcoats that appeared from time to time. After independence the new United States had to pay for its own tiny army and navy, both of which provided inadequate protection for many decades. Finally, during most of the colonial period the British were lax and lenient about the enforcement of their mercantile system. Certainly the English version of mercantilism was less restrictive and brutal than that of other countries; France and Spain, as examples, embraced mercantilist principles completely and enforced them ironhandedly. In the American colonies smuggling, in violation of trade and other acts, was so common that it became respectable; it was like buying booze in the 1920's or like stretching deductions on a current income-tax report. The best people were involved. Probably nine-tenths of colonial merchants were smugglers; one-quarter of the signers of the Declaration of Independence were bred to contraband trade. John Hancock himself was the prince of contraband traders, and none other than future President John Adams was his counsel.

All this was true, nonetheless, mercantilism hampered the colonies. Basically, they could not carry on business under the most beneficial and profitable conditions. The Navigation Acts, no matter how good for British and New England shippers, did create a monopoly and the high rates that went with it. Manufacturing prohibitions were obviously irksome to those who wanted to exploit specific industries; bans on the issue of paper money were patently restrictive for an increasingly entrepreneurial colonial economy that wanted to expand through a "credit ease." Trade acts were probably the most burdensome of all. Virginia planters, to cite an example, got a welcome bounty on tobacco; they were also forced to sell in England, where they were at the mercy of British merchants, who often gouged them. The result was that these planters were forced into debt — so severely that some debts became hereditary and were bequeathed from father to son. There were those who thought the political slogan "Liberty or Death" had more practical meaning in its economic paraphrase, "Liberty or Debt." Finally, the entire mercantilist system was contrary to the principle of laissez-faire that was dominant on the frontier; there settlers had been practicing it for at least a century before Adam Smith formulated the theory. Later Smith himself would agree with them, and would urge independence of the American colonies.

The interests of the colonists were sacrificed to those of the home country, but the American colonists enjoyed an economic prosperity and a political liberty that was unusual in the eighteenth century. British mercantilism, no matter how annoying, would not by itself have caused the American Revolution — without the introduction of taxation for revenue and the passage of an act of very special legislation (the Tea Act of 1773).

Since the Glorious Revolution of 1688 there had been a succession of wars, in Europe and the New World, between England and her allies on the one hand and France and her allies on the other. They were known as King William's War in the 1690's, Queen Anne's War in the early eighteenth century, and King George's War in the 1740's. Now, from 1756 to 1763, there was a World War — the Seven Years' War; in the North American theater of operations it was known as the French and Indian War. In spite of the fact that there were only 80,000 French in Canada against more than a million settlers in the thirteen English colonies — the Seven Years' War began so inauspiciously for the British that defeat appeared to be highly probable. In actual fact, before the war started officially the British and the French had been at it with hammer and tongs, and the British had suffered two severe reverses near Fort Duquesne (Pittsburgh). At Fort Necessity, George Washington had found it essential to surrender his entire force of three hundred Virginians to the French in 1754. The very next year General Edward Braddock was sent out with a larger force. The French, despairing of holding the fort, laid a desperate ambush and to their surprise killed or wounded about two-thirds of the British advance force of 1,200, with Braddock himself among the slain; the French lost twenty-five men!

Affairs also went badly for England and its ally Prussia on the European continent, in the first two years of the official war. Britain, however, has not infrequently been in the habit of losing every battle but the last one, and in 1758 the entire complexion of the war changed when a remarkable man came into power as head of the ministry and virtual dictator of the Empire. He was conceited, gouty, irascible — *and* extremely able. He said, "I am sure I can save this country, and that no one else can." On this point, the egotism of William Pitt the Elder turned out to be justified.

He changed British strategy completely. In previous wars the British tactic had been to hold the French in America and to concentrate on winning the war in Europe. Pitt made America the main theater, calling for the capture of Canada. This meant that Frederick the Great would conduct a holding operation in Europe, that the British navy would bottle up the French fleet, and that British military might would be concentrated in the New World — under young and energetic generals. There were three of them. Pitt selected Lord Jeffrey Amherst as supreme commander in America, by passing over whole columns of other British officers with seniority. Amherst was in his early forties, and captured Louisbourg (on Cape Breton Island); it was the "Gibraltar" for France in the New World, and had been regarded as impregnable. Pitt picked James Wolfe, in his early thirties, for the attack on Montcalm and Quebec; Wolfe completed his mission, but lost his life in doing so. In the American West, Pitt relied on Sir William Johnson to keep the Iroquois Indians loyal; Johnson was in his forties, had a gift of blarney, and carried the Iroquois in his waistcoat pocket.

By the Treaty of Paris in 1763 France lost everything but a few scattered islands and ports; England became dominant in North America, Africa, and India. On the American continent the cession of Canada by France, and of Florida by Spain, gave England all of North America east of the Mississippi — except for a small area around New Orleans. All France had to show in America for more than two centuries of effort were two tiny islands off Newfoundland for drying fish, a handful of sugar islands in the Caribbean, and French Guiana in South America. It is little wonder that the contemporary English author, Horace Walpole, would claim that "the Romans were triflers to us"; he would urge his countrymen to "throw away your Greek and Latin books, histories of little peoples." But within a few years Benjamin Franklin was offering to provide historian Edward Gibbon with materials for a history of the *Decline and Fall of the British Empire*.

The Seven Years' War was costly in American loyalty. France and Spain were now gone as menaces on the frontier; as a result the English colonists did not feel as dependent on British defense as they once were. In addition, the Seven Years' War had been expensive in money. Britain emerged with the greatest empire, and with the largest debt in the world. It amounted to £140 million, about half of which had been incurred in defending the American colonies. British officials had no intention of asking the colonials to help pay this crushing burden from the past. But London did feel that the Americans, presumably for their own protection in the future, should be asked to defray one-third of the cost of maintaining a garrison of some 2,000 Redcoats — now necessary in America to defend a larger empire. Part of the money would come from new taxes, and these were destined to raise very real problems.

By 1763 the average British citizen was loaded with all kinds of new levies: stamp duties, taxes on the windows of their homes, excises on malt and cider. Even the king was told he must economize on household expenses. By contrast Americans were the lowest-taxed people in the world, with the surprising exception of the Poles. In England the average annual tax load was twenty-six shillings per head; in Massachusetts, which had one of the highest tax rates in the American colonies, it was only one shilling per head. When George Grenville came to power (1763–1766) as Prime Minister, the national debt had doubled from the prewar level of £75 million to almost £150 million. Britain was spending about £800,000 in America; the £200,000 collected in customs duties made but a slight dent in this total expense. Grenville proposed to relieve the burden on overtaxed Britons by collecting more money in America, directly and indirectly. He planned to do so in a threefold program: the Sugar Act of 1764, the Billeting Act of 1765, and the Stamp Act of 1765.

The Sugar Act replaced the old Molasses Act of 1733; it reduced the duty on foreign molasses from the prohibitory rate of sixpence to threepence per gallon, with the expectation that smuggling would cease and that the legal trade would yield a considerable revenue. It didn't; the American colonials said that the threepenny duty was still twopence more than the traffic would bear (two years later when it was cut to one penny under the Townshend system, they still claimed it was a confiscatory levy). Grenville figured the cost of maintaining garrisons in America at £360,000 a year; he wanted to raise one-third — or £120,000 — there. He estimated that the duties on molasses and other commodities (there were also new duties on wines, silks, and coffee) would bring in about £45,000. The difference between this amount and 120,000 pounds he expected to raise through the Billeting and Stamp acts.

The Billeting or Quartering Act (it was also called the Mutiny Act) required colonies wherein troops were stationed to provide them with barracks and certain supplies — utensils, vinegar, salt — and refreshment — rum, beer, or cider. The Stamp Act, which levied the first direct tax ever imposed by Parliament upon America, was designed to raise £60,000 annually. This form of taxation had been used in England since 1694; as introduced belatedly in the American colonies the stamp duties were to be lighter than those levied in Britain. Here it affected lawyers by requiring stamps on legal documents: licenses, wills, deeds, contracts, leases. It affected publishers by requiring a one-penny stamp on a newspaper of a whole sheet, a one-shilling stamp on pamphlets, and a two-shilling payment on advertisements. It affected tavern owners by requiring four pounds for a liquor license, a one-shilling stamp on a pack of cards, and a ten-shilling one on a pair of dice! The stamp of two pounds required for a college diploma was heavy indeed; it could be justified on the ground that it was based on ability to pay, because only the well-to-do had their children educated in that day. Curiously no one anticipated much opposition to the Stamp Act, although Grenville had announced the proposed tax a year before it was passed. All stamp collectors were to be American: Benjamin Franklin solicited positions as collectors for two of his friends, and Richard Henry Lee (later a prominent member of the Continental Congress) did the same thing for himself, much to his embarrassment when colonial opposition really broke loose.

From easy hindsight the reason for the hullabaloo which quickly developed, when the act was finally passed, is obvious. It hit hardest the three groups in the colonies which could raise the loudest howl: lawyers, editors, and tavern owners. The publisher of the Maryland *Gazette,* for example, issued his paper with broad margins in black to signify deep mourning, with a skull and crossbones on the masthead as a replica of the stamp, and with this caption: THE TIMES ARE DREADFUL, DISMAL, DOLEFUL, DOLOROUS, AND DOLLARLESS. The opposition was so vociferous and active that by 1 November 1765, when the act was to go into effect, every stamp agent had resigned — most of them out of fear. The antagonism appeared in three forms: in the Stamp Act Congress, the Non-Importation Agreement, and mob violence. The congress, which met in New York during October 1765, was the first intercolonial meeting summoned by colonial initiative, and may be regarded as the opening move in the American Revolution. Nine colonies were represented by twenty-seven delegates who met to draw up a declaration of rights and grievances for presentation to the king and to Parliament. One of these rights was that no taxes should be imposed upon them without their consent. Because circumstances seemed to preclude their representation in the House of Commons, it followed that no taxes could be levied on them except by their respective colonial assemblies. It was the Stamp Act against which they directed this argument. As to the Sugar Act, while professing "all due subordination" to Parliament, they protested against it as an unwise and oppressive trade regulation. They seemed to draw a distinction between an import duty, collected at the ports, as an *external* tax which was incidental to the primary purpose of trade regulation rather than the collection of revenue

— and the Stamp Act as an *internal* tax levied wholly for the collection of revenue. Parliament appeared to have the right to levy external, but not internal, taxes.*

James Otis, the American orator and patriot, would comment that "taxation without representation is tyranny," and the cliché caught on. Few would deny the validity of the *principle;* what Otis failed to point out was that taxation without representation, or without adequate representation, was a regular practice in both England *and* America. There was nothing unique about it; in England the suffrage was so restricted by property qualifications or antiquated districting that not more than 160,000 Englishmen (out of 2 million adults) enjoyed the right to vote. Charles Austin Beard once observed that it would not be wrong to say that ten thousand landlords and merchants ruled the England of George III. New cities like Liverpool, Manchester, and Leeds — which had grown up since the origin of Parliament several centuries before — were without any representation at all in the House of Commons. In the colonies themselves, the gerrymandering of districts by the tidewater areas, in order to deny adequate representation to the hinterland, was notorious. In actual fact the Anglo-Saxon has always been taxed without adequate representation, and is to this day, as attested by the continuing controversy over the "one-man, one-vote" decision of the Supreme Court of the United States. Before the American Revolution the radical leaders, like Sam Adams, were opposed to any plan that would give the colonies representation in Parliament; they saw clearly that thirty or forty American members sitting in London would have had little influence. In retrospect, it is apparent that Britain should have accepted the claim of her American colonies, and have given them token representation in order to quiet the clamor. Two hundred years later she did so in another area, a trifle late to change the outcome in connection with the Stamp Act. In 1956 the island of Malta was given three seats in the House of Commons, with the understanding that the Maltese would pay taxes to their own government, not to Britain. This settlement broke a seven-hundred-year-old tradition that members of Parliament represented people of the home islands only. Commenting on this

---

* There is disagreement among historians about this interpretation. Edmund S. and Helen M. Morgan, in *The Stamp Act Crisis: Prologue to Revolution*, say that Americans in 1764–1765 objected to all forms of Parliamentary taxation for revenue, and not simply to internal taxes. The Morgans state that the notion that the colonies distinguished between internal and external taxes was widely believed in England, but found no such distinction in contemporary American statements. On the other hand Bernard Knollenberg, in his *Origin of the American Revolution*, discovers evidence in Massachusetts and Connecticut of a distinction between internal and external taxes. David Hawke, in *The Colonial Experience*, points out that Benjamin Franklin drew such a distinction in his testimony before the House of Commons in February 1766. See Esmond Wright, *Causes and Consequences of the American Revolution*, 42–44, and Jack P. Greene, "The Flight from Determinism: A Review of Recent Literature on the Coming of the American Revolution," *South Atlantic Quarterly*, 61 (1962), 235–259.

break with the past, the London *Economist* observed: "Britain having lost part of its empire through insisting on taxation without representation in the eighteenth century . . . is trying to save another bit by generously agreeing to representation without taxation in the twentieth."

Opposition also appeared in the form of economic pressure and mob violence. Almost a thousand merchants in New York, Boston, and Philadelphia signed an agreement banning the purchase of European goods until the Stamp Act was repealed. As we shall see, this nonimportation agreement was the most effective of the arguments against the act. In Boston a mob looted the elegant home and library of Chief Justice Thomas Hutchinson; after throwing everything portable out of the house the crowd smashed the windows and the doors, leaving only the walls and the roof undamaged. The loss was at least $25,000. In New York a British major named James was alleged to have said, "I will cram the stamps down the throats of the people with the point of my sword." Some patriots thought the statement required an actual demonstration of the "sword-cramming" act. A large number of them went to his home, the major refused to stage the exhibition, so the mob completely destroyed his house. Such mob violence was of great concern to many colonials with property. These conservatives began to worry, with considerable reason, because they figured the dislike of the mob might be readily transferred from British men of property and position to American men of property and position. Some colonials of purse and property therefore continued as adherents of the Crown, not from affection, but simply because they feared the king less than American rioters.

By July 1765 Grenville had fallen from power, not because the American colonies opposed the stamp tax, but because he tried to remove one of the "king's friends" from his ministry. Nonetheless British merchants and manufacturers asked Parliament to repeal the Stamp Act. Their arguments were strong ones: no money from the sale of stamps was being realized in America, the colonial nonimportation agreement had brought a significant decline in British exports, several merchants had gone bankrupt, and some English manufacturers were compelled to close their mills. The economic depression in England had more influence in Parliament than vocal colonial lamentations. The Stamp Act was repealed, but Parliament childishly insisted on having the last word. It also passed a declaratory act asserting its own rights; it said it possessed authority to "bind the colonies and people of America, subjects of the crown of Great Britain, in all cases whatsoever." Pitt would have added, "with the exception of taking money out of their pockets without their consent." The rejection of his qualifying clause was ominous.

In the following year a new ministry was headed by Pitt himself, but because of his serious illness the actual leader in the critical years 1766–1767 was the Chancellor of the Exchequer, Charles Townshend. He was gifted but unstable; known as "Champagne Charley" he was alleged to have delivered brilliant speeches to Parliament while drunk. His premature death was to come in September 1767, at the age of forty-one. The Townshend program, like that of Grenville, was threefold: he proposed to collect additional customs through more rigorous enforcement, he vowed to make the Quartering Act effective over colonial opposition, and he pushed through a new revenue act (replacing the Stamp Act) which he thought to be ingenious and shrewd. To better collect customs Townshend procured the passage of a law which established a board of customs commissioners to sit in Boston; previously American customs collectors had been supervised from London, and administration had been relatively casual and easy. Four new juryless superior courts of vice-admiralty were also set up to hear appeals from provincial courts and to issue writs of assistance (general search warrants) in the pursuit of smuggled goods. Because of the latter, henceforth no man's colonial home would be his castle — inviolate from search except by specific warrant. Edmund S. Morgan has pointed out that saints chosen for the board of customs commissioners would have been unpopular in New England. Unfortunately those appointed were not saints; they were instead a "rapacious band of bureaucrats, who brought to their task an irrepressible greed and a vindictive malice, that could not fail to aggravate the antagonism." The legislation itself actually encouraged both greed and malice. Ships violating the Sugar Act were confiscated, along with their cargo. After the sale of ship and cargo, the proceeds were divided evenly in three portions: to the English treasury, to the governor of the colony, to the customs officers responsible for the seizure. For entrepreneurs bent on amassing a fortune, the act presented a grand opportunity.

The colonial opposition to the Quartering or Mutiny Act was centered in New York. It was the strategic hub of America, commanding the easiest routes to Canada and the West. For this reason General Thomas Gage had established his headquarters and had stationed several regiments of troops there, with the result that the so-called Mutiny Act bore heaviest on this province. After the Stamp Act crisis a number of Americans began to argue that the Mutiny Act was just as bad as the tax through stamps; the only difference was that colonies were now being asked to give in kind — room and board — what had been collected in cash by the Stamp Act. Many wondered why there was such a distinction between a direct levy by Parliament and one imposed by a colonial assembly in response to the "dictatorial mandate" of Parliament. In New York the legislature had refused any appropriations for Gage's forces; Townshend saw to it that it was punished by suspension, thus forcing compliance.

Townshend's Revenue Act took advantage of the distinction the Americans, including Benjamin Franklin, had drawn between internal and external taxes — when they were arguing for the repeal of the Stamp Act.

Townshend personally believed the distinction was absurd; he told Parliament that "if we have the right to impose one, we have the other." If it would please the Americans, however, he would make the distinction; he was quite willing to "indulge them and chose for that reason to confine himself to regulations of trade, by which a sufficient revenue might be raised in America." This might not be much, but the money raised was designated for the salaries of royal governors, judges, and other officials who hitherto had been dependent on the provincial assemblies for their salaries. Thus Townshend would snatch from the colonies their old control of the purse strings, a reform long overdue from the point of view of efficient administration, but one also designed to reduce the autonomy of colonial legislatures.

Following this logic Parliament enacted the Townshend Revenue Act, which imposed external taxes in the form of import duties, collected at American ports, on paint, paper, lead, glass, and tea shipped from England. As Thomas Bailey has observed, the tax on tea was especially irksome; an estimated million persons in the American colonies drank "the cup that cheers" twice a day. There was little opposition to the new levies in Parliament. George Grenville did speak against the act, stating that it would hurt British merchants more than the Stamp Act, and warning Townshend that the Americans "will laugh at you for your distinctions about regulations of trade." Grenville was right on both counts.

The death of Townshend occurred in September 1767, but the evil of his policy lived on after him. A second wave of colonial protest got under way. Once again merchants and planters drew up nonimportation agreements; again they were backed by public sentiment and by the bully boys in organized mobs. In 1768 rioting broke out in Boston when John Hancock's sloop, whose name — the *Liberty* — the mob loved, was seized. The British had every right to do so. It had come into Boston with a cargo of fine wines, the duty on which under the Grenville Act of 1764 was seven pounds per tun (a large cask holding 252 gallons). Under the time-honored bribery that had prevailed in the past, the British customs officer would have boarded the vessel, would have gone to the cabin with the captain to sample the cargo and to receive his gratuity, and then would have vanished. This time the customs officer refused the bribe. The captain of the *Liberty* was so astounded by this unorthodox procedure that, rising from his chair with an oath, he knocked the British customs officer, and his chair, end over end. The British official was then securely tied, and stowed safely below deck. As soon as the safety of darkness had descended, the cargo of wine was unloaded in record time. Hancock then entered the cargo on the customs books at a small fraction of the real amount, swearing this was a correct figure. Such shenanigans over contraband were an old story in New England and were considered respectable, rather than perjury. On this occasion, however, a British frigate took over, and seized the *Liberty*. The incident brought two regiments to Boston, along with the dissolution of the provincial assembly. The climax came in the affair known as the "Boston Massacre" of 5 March 1770.

Boston became a town virtually in siege, except that it was the British troops who were terrorized and subjected to petty persecutions. No city likes to have an army imposed on it, and Boston was no exception. On 2 March a British Redcoat was asked by a laborer if he needed part-time work. He said he did, whereupon the laborer with a laugh told him to clean out the privy. The soldier was angry, there was an altercation, and he was knocked down. For the next two days there were street brawls in Boston between soldiers and citizenry. On 5 March the sentry before the customhouse was set upon by a mob armed with stones, bricks, and snowballs. A captain and eight Redcoats came to his assistance, with bayonets fixed. They were met with taunts of "lobsterback" — the equivalent of the twentieth-century "pig."

At this point Crispus Attucks attempted to take a soldier's gun away from him, and the soldier shot him dead (Attucks was a huge mulatto or Natick Indian — the evidence about his antecedents is scant indeed). Immediately the British squad began to fire into the crowd, it appears without command; in the general confusion, five Bostonians lost their lives and several more were wounded. A young lawyer named John Adams risked his career to defend the soldiers in court; tried for manslaughter all were acquitted, though two were branded on the hand and Governor Hutchinson found it advisable to withdraw all British soldiers to the safety of an island in the harbor.

By 1770 the economic boycott by Americans against British imports had become even more effective than at the time of the Stamp Act crisis; British merchants and manufacturers were protesting again to Parliament. It was also apparent that Townshend's system, if it was for the purpose of raising revenue, was a colossal failure. In one year the net proceeds were less than £300; during the same period the military costs to British in the American colonies amounted to £170,000! By strange coincidence Parliament repealed the Townshend Revenue Act on 5 March 1770, on the same day in Boston the "Boston Massacre" occurred. Again Parliament had the last word; she repealed all of the act except the tax on tea — in order to keep the "right." The British had beat a strategic retreat, but made no concession on principle.

In the West and the South, colonists were horrified by the British prohibition against western settlement — as it developed in the Proclamation Line of 1763 and the Quebec Act of 1774.

Why did Britain restrict western settlement after the Seven Years' War? There appear to have been four groups who needed, or wanted, protection — for one reason or another. There was a very real danger from the red men, who were angered by the grasping tactics of English pioneers and who were now being organized into a general conspiracy by a chieftain named Pontiac. After conquering Canada in the Seven Years' War the English aroused the resentment of western tribes by treating them arrogantly, refusing to supply them with free ammunition as the French had done, and assuming ownership of the land. Basically, Pontiac was the first of several Indians who decided to throw the English out of the New World. He did cause great concern and considerable loss of life, and the British felt it advisable to consolidate matters before permitting additional settlers to exacerbate the situation. For that reason they cut off western settlement for the time being. American colonists were sure the prohibition would be permanent.

Another group seeking protection were the fur traders — particularly the Scottish moguls in Montreal — who wanted to reserve land for fur-bearing animals rather than human habitation. Another special-interest group consisted of land speculators, on both sides of the Atlantic, who wanted to gain all the early advantages they could. Some of these were Englishmen, who had already received large tracts in Canada and Florida, and wanted more. Some were American colonists; for example, the Illinois Company of George Croghan, which had representatives in London, and the so-called "Suffering Traders" of Pennsylvania who included Franklin and his wealthy Quaker friend Samuel Wharton. It appears that the British government was genuinely averse to turning the American West over to speculators, of whatever origin; it entertained hopes, which were thwarted, of a gradual transition from Indian occupation to colonization by small settlers. Finally, there was the French Catholic population in Quebec, which sought protection from the expanding Yankees. These French-speaking people *were* a problem for the British in Europe after 1763; they *are* a problem for the British in Canada in the 1970's.

In carrying out their prohibitory policy the British took two steps, one in establishing the Proclamation Line of 1763, and the other — a bit more than a decade later — in passing the Quebec Act of 1774. The Proclamation Line of 1763 ran along the summit of the Appalachian Mountains; white settlements were banned west of the line, and all Indian trade was placed under royal control. A decade later the British passed the Quebec Act, and considered it a liberal measure to protect the rights of a French minority. It established a highly centralized government of the type the French had always known, reestablished French civil law to assure Roman Catholics of religious freedom, and extended the old boundaries of the Province of Quebec to the Ohio River.

Colonial opposition was immediate and vociferous. There were colonial land speculators who lived chiefly in the middle and southern colonies and who would be hurt by this legislation. Speculation in western lands had provided the only methods by which the Virginia planter could balance his debt situation. Now this possibility was cut off — either by the Proclamation Line or by the denial of Virginian claims in the Old Northwest by the Quebec Act. This development explains Washington's opposition to the British; by 1773, he had achieved holdings of more than 30,000 acres west of the mountains. It also explains the fact that well-to-do planters in the South were rebels and anti-British — while most of the wealthy in the North were Tories and pro-British.

Democrats were horrified, because the government established by the Quebec Act was authoritarian; there was no representative assembly or trial by jury. If American colonists went into an expanded Quebec — that is, into what is now Ohio — they would be faced with a political situation which was hardly to their liking. Finally, Protestants were upset because the Catholic religion was given a privileged position by the Quebec Act. They said this was a gain not only for tyranny but for popery and prelacy as well, and that the purpose of the act was to establish a Catholic province to the rear of the American colonies.

In October of 1774 the First Continental Congress expressed astonishment that the British Parliament had established in the American West a Catholic religion that was marked by bigotry, impiety, persecution, and murder. Six months later the Second Continental Congress tried to gain the support of the same reprehensible French Catholics in Canada, and to wean them away from the British! In the light of what had been said previously, the Congress could not have been surprised that the French Canadians would have none of this soft talk, killed General Richard Montgomery and wounded General Benedict Arnold when the Americans tried to annex Canada, and remained loyal to Britain throughout the war.

In spite of some of the imbalances created by the practice of mercantilism, the new policy of taxation for revenue, and the prohibition of new settlement on the frontier, it is surprising but important to note that the period from 1770 to 1773 was one of relative quiet. The nonimportation agreement was largely abandoned except for a halfhearted boycott of British tea, and during these three years colonial imports from Britain actually tripled. Many conservative merchants had begun to worry about "mob rule" and for the moment, at least, chose "royal tyranny" instead. It is barely possible that the troubled quiet would have continued indefinitely, and that something akin to the Canadian solution might have been worked out in time — had not the British parliament precipitated a new crisis by passing an act to benefit an important and very large corporation, along with some of its own members who were stockholders in the company. In so doing Parliament pulled the trigger — and from this point there was a clearly recognizable chain of unexpected events leading directly into the American Revolution.

The "trigger" was the Tea Act of 1773. It was passed because the giant

British East India Company, after almost two centuries of great prosperity, was on the verge of bankruptcy, its stock down from 280 to 160 on the London exchange. The corporation had brought millions into England by its exploitation of the Orient, but its members had skimmed off too much gold and had left the company in a perilous position. It still had two promising assets: a vast surplus of 17 million pounds of tea in storage in England, and a government that was predisposed to save the corporation because of its stranglehold on India. The solution was to create an artificial market in the American colonies by enabling the company to sell its surplus tea there by reducing the price substantially and, at the same time, making a much larger profit! This would require a special act from Parliament because someone would be required to make up the loss. In the modern idiom, the government appeared to believe that what was good for the East India Company was good for the British Empire. It wasn't. Among the curious reverberations was the fact that the East India Company, by trying much too hard to sell tea here, made us a nation of coffee drinkers.

The company became a privileged private enterprise through three special kinds of financial aid: drawbacks, direct sales, and a loan. The corporation had already paid an import duty of twelvepence per pound on all the surplus tea stored in England; this would now be refunded by the government on all tea shipped to the American colonies. This drawback so far exceeded the cost of transportation across the Atlantic that, when remitted, tea would cost the consumer less in America than in England. More important was the provision giving the company (obliged up to this time to sell its tea at public auction in England) the right to sell tea directly through its own agents in the colonies, thus eliminating both English and colonial middlemen. This system of merchandising is common among large grocery chains today — it is used by the Atlantic and Pacific Tea Company, for example; in the eighteenth century it was regarded as revolutionary. The government also advanced a large loan to the company; it was expected that the money would be derived from the increase in duties paid in America (the tax of three-pence per pound still held over from the Townshend system) on vastly larger quantities of cheap tea now being offered by the East India Company. With this assistance the company was now in a position, even with the handicap of the duty, to undersell both the law-abiding colonial merchants who had bought tea through middlemen at higher prices, and the colonial smuggler who bought his tea in Holland. The British ministry also hoped to expose the allegedly shallow nature of the colonial protest against Parliamentary taxation. Let the tea be cheap enough and the colonists would buy, even if they paid a duty of threepence while doing so.

Two groups would benefit from this act, and two others would lose. Those benefiting were, obviously, the British East India Company and the

American consumer through lower prices. Those losing would be American merchants (both those engaged in legitimate trade and those involved in the smuggling of Dutch tea) and the British taxpayer (because the drawback would have to be made up from additional taxes). The old colonial device of nonimportation agreements would not be effective against this act because the tea trade was a monopoly of the East India Company — and the company was now selling directly in America. The only thing to do was to prevent the tea from reaching American consumers — by means fair or foul.

The act played directly into the hands of the master propagandist Sam Adams, who had been puzzled and worried by the quiet of the past three years. It brought the radicals and the merchants once more into alliance — the same merchants who had begun to fear mobs but some of whom were now provoked enough to join them. It also provided Adams with a popular appeal. He could argue that the act was one of special legislation to protect the largest corporation in England. He could also charge *monopoly*, always a frightening noun in American history; he would claim that if a monopoly could be granted on tea, why not on other commodities in years to come? Adams pulled all the emotional stops by presenting East India Company tea as more than a threat to American liberties. It was also a hazard to health; he quoted physicians who claimed that tea was rusting away American teeth and innards, and reducing the colonial population to a physical condition that was pitiable indeed.

It was important to keep tea from being received by the company's agents in America. Once landed, and the duty paid, Adams knew that the product at new low prices would find its way into the channels of trade and that the entire American argument against a duty for revenue would be undermined. The company's agents were therefore threatened and terrorized. At Philadelphia, New York, and Charleston the agents were persuaded to resign. When the tea arrived at the first two ports, with no one there to receive the cargo, the vessels returned to England without delivering their freight. At Charleston the tea was placed in storage, and was later sold for the benefit of the rebel cause. At Boston there was real trouble because the agents were two sons of Governor Hutchinson, whose house and library had been burned some years before by a rebel mob. The governor had no intention of giving way to popular pressure, feared that another retreat would end British sovereignty in America, and refused to issue clearance papers for the return of the ships to England. On the evening of 16 December 1773 some 8,000 people assembled in or near the Old South Church; from this large mass meeting a disciplined group of about fifty, disguised as Mohawks and using the Indian expression "ugh" as a countersign, boarded the three ships and threw overboard forty-five tons of tea. The "Indians" had been organized by Sam Adams; John Hancock was probably one of the group.

In London Lord North, who was prime minister from 1770 to 1782, was dumbfounded by the news from Boston. Tea from 342 large chests, belonging to the largest corporation in England, was now strewn along Dorchester beach in Boston harbor. There is no question that the "Indian" depredation was an aggravating example of unlawful activity by a mob. There is no question that England's reaction was coercive, heavy-handed, and foolish; it produced a chain of events leading directly into the Revolution. The Boston Tea Party occurred in December 1773; the next April Lord North was armed by the so-called Intolerable Acts. They closed the port of Boston until the tea was paid for, allowed British colonial officials to be tried in England when accused of wrongdoing, gave British commanders more power under the Quartering Act, strengthened royal control of Massachusetts, and included the ill-timed Quebec Act — which happened to be passed in 1774 and was popularly lumped in with the rest of the offensive legislation. The Boston Port Bill was to become effective on 1 June 1774; in Virginia the House of Burgesses set aside the day as one for fasting and prayer. For this act of sympathy the House was dissolved by the royal governor; a rump session continued to meet at the famed Raleigh Tavern in Williamsburg, and issued the call for the First Continental Congress to meet in Philadelphia in the following September. Twelve of the colonies sent delegates.

Out of the Continental Congress came a "Declaration of Rights and Grievances" that had no effect in England, and an "Association" that did. Unfortunately the weapon of economic boycott, which had been such an effective colonial device during the past eight years, was now virtually useless. British merchants were no longer a force putting pressure on Parliament for compromise; they were protected now by good harvests in 1774 and 1775, and by large and fortuitous increase in their exports to northern Europe, the Mediterranean, and the East Indies. They were relatively unconcerned in spite of the fact that "The Association" went far beyond previous economic boycotts; it called for nonimportation, nonexportation, and nonconsumption. It was enforced by vigilantes who used tar and feathers where necessary; by April 1775 the boycott was being enforced in twelve colonies. By the same month muskets had been collected, men were drilling, it was only a matter of time until shots were fired. The first guns went off at Lexington; who fired first, no one knows — but eight Americans were killed, ten were wounded, and one Britisher was slightly hurt. The skirmish delayed the British only fifteen minutes, but the war was on.

The stresses and strains produced in the colonies by mercantilism, taxation for revenue, restrictions on western settlement, and special legislative assistance to the East India Company could be used to great advantage by a skillful propagandist. The American radicals had one in Samuel Adams.

His own father was a brewer and a deacon in the Congregational Church who had seen his fortune largely vanish when Parliament destroyed a Massachusetts land bank which had tried to issue needed paper money. From that point the son neither forgave nor forgot. Sam Adams was a skillful writer, he initiated the network of intercolonial Committees of Correspondence, and he organized mobs consisting of the Sons of Liberty. He always had a large acquaintance in taverns where, as his cousin John Adams once said, "bastards and legislators are frequently begotten." It was Sam Adams's belief that men are ruled by their emotions rather than their reason, and it was as the organizer of irrational mobs that he made his most signal contribution to the Revolution — particularly in keeping the spirit of controversy alive during the period of comparative calm from 1770 to 1773, when the conservatives were in the ascendancy. In the decade before the Revolution, Boston was pretty much controlled by a trained mob — and Sam Adams was its keeper. It was an Adams mob that gutted Hutchinson's house in 1765. It was an Adams mob that brought about the carefully planned Boston Massacre in 1770. It was an Adams mob that brought off the Boston Tea Party.

After graduation from Harvard Sam Adams had been a magnificent failure in every business he tried except that of propagandist. His father gave him a thousand pounds to set up a business; he lent it to a friend and never saw the money again. After the father's death Sam took over the brewery and ran it into bankruptcy. He became a tax collector for Boston and was everything such an official should not be — kindly, sympathetic, a listener to every hard-luck story. He broke all previous records for *not* collecting taxes, and soon was in arrears by seven thousand pounds; Boston finally had to sue him to get some of the money. This was in 1764, one year before the passage of the Stamp Act; Adams was forty-two, and a failure. He was also neurotic; his hands were tremulous and he stuttered at times of excitement. But he had the neurotic's urge for power, and he was to find that power as a propagandist.

Nothing illustrates the Adams technique better than the Boston Massacre. To his relative John Adams, the rebel crowd there was a motley rabble, and there was fault on both sides. To Sam Adams the massacre was between vicious Bloody Backs — as he designated the English Redcoats — and holy martyrs, as he called the patriots. Paul Revere, who sold engravings whenever his silver business fell off, would execute one which showed British soldiers firing wantonly into a throng of meek and mild citizens, with dogs underneath lapping up the patriot blood. In the subsequent print the dark face of mulatto Crispus Attucks was "whitewashed" for distribution in the southern colonies. Stories were told of Boston matrons and young girls who were raped by British soldiers. Furthermore Adams saw to it that every anniversary of the Massacre was observed with proper orations, calling on every father in New England to gather his children about his knees and to tell the story "till tears of pity glisten in their eyes, and boiling passion shakes their tender frames." Ultimately, on the morning of the Battle of Lexington, Hancock and Adams were making their escape from the approaching British soldiery, and were crossing a field some distance away. The rumble of the far-off musketry reached their ears. Adams grabbed Hancock's arms, and cried: "Oh, what a glorious morning is this!"

A war requires three things: money, money, and money. Back in the golden age of mercantilism a war was paid for in specie — on the spot. This came from a "war chest," an actual chest filled with gold which was as standard a piece of war equipment as artillery. The loss of the war chest was therefore as serious as a defeat, because military operations would have to be suspended.

In our revolution the Americans obviously could not rely on a war chest simply because they were limited in specie at the beginning of the conflict, and were to receive but little more from France and Holland during the war. If the mercantilist theory of the war chest was to be followed, the American colonies would be forced to abandon the idea of armed revolution before it started. In this conflict, however, the Americans were to be inventive in a number of ways, and one of them was economic. Because they could not pay for the war in the traditional way they found other methods which are still used: taxes, loans, and paper money.

Collecting taxes was largely theoretical because the Continental Congresses had no power to tax. The states had this power; all Congress could do was to requisition the states for money, and these requests were scantily honored, with the result that only one dollar in twenty was derived from taxes to pay for the war. Loans came from two sources: foreign and domestic. Ultimately we borrowed internally by issuing certificates or bonds for cash, services (to soldiers), and goods (to farmers). Less than $30 million came to Congress from internal loans; the states borrowed almost $20 million more. This meant that something more than half of the cost of a $100 million war came from taxes and loans. The balance came from the printing presses in paper money.

It was particularly through the device of paper money that the Founding Fathers freed war from the mercantilist shackles which had bound it previously. Congress issued almost $200 million in Continental Notes; eleven states issued almost $250 million more. A typical "continental" read: "This bill entitles the Bearer to receive three Spanish milled dollars according to the Resolution to the Congress, held at Philadelphia the 10th of May, 1775." Instead of the customary coat of arms, a design engraved on the bill showed an eagle (England) fighting a subdued crane (the colonies), whose long bill seemed to be piercing the eagle's breast. The engraving was not very encouraging, and neither was the motto on the bills: *Exitus in dubio est* (The issue is in doubt). The choice of the Spanish-milled dollar, the common circulating medium in the colonies, as the specie to be redeemed — signifies the revolt against, and the scarcity of, English monetary units.

Paper money was a forced loan on the nation because too much was issued and the value declined until in 1781 it took $100 in paper money to buy a pair of shoes, $90 for a pound of tea, and more than $1,500 for a barrel of flour. The term "not worth a continental" came to represent worthlessness, then and now. Benjamin Franklin would argue that paper money was in reality a fair and progressive and gradual tax on each person in whose hands the money lost value — fair and progressive because "those people paid most, who, being richest, had most money passing through their hands." His analysis was too simple. Actually great suffering came to those with fixed incomes: the clergy, soldiers, and laborers (whose increased wages always lagged behind the increases in prices). Those benefiting were much more numerous: speculators, debtors (including Congress, who paid obligations in cheaper money), farmers (who forced the army to pay the prices they asked), and privateers who accumulated fortunes because they had goods to sell which were in demand. Altogether, about twenty thousand men sailed on these freebooting ships during the war; this was many more than served at any one time in Washington's Continental Army. Historian John Miller has said that "had Americans enlisted in the army with the alacrity with which they took to privateering, the war might have been won in the span of a few years." On the other hand it can be argued that privateering provided our only real "navy" during the war, was dangerous business indeed, and inflicted severe economic losses on England — two thousand ships and eighteen thousand English pounds in the value of goods.

Two financiers were prominent in the conflict — Robert Morris, who was known as the "financier of the American Revolution," and Haym Salomon, who deserves the title. Morris was English-born, came to this country at thirteen, and by his early thirties had become a leading merchant and banker in Philadelphia. During the Revolution he gave financial aid to the patriot cause in various ways; he also indulged in profitable speculations on his own, particularly in connection with privateering. He was an able businessman, but he never lost an opportunity to make his profit or to collect his commission; the American rebellion appealed to him because it presented grand speculative opportunities. For this reason, although Morris is still given special and patriotic recognition by hotels and credit associations that are named after him — it seems clear that the Revolution did more to finance Morris than Morris did to finance the Revolution.

Under the Confederation government Morris became superintendent of finance in 1781, held the position for three years, and during this period (when national credit was gone and the treasury was empty) was virtually a financial dictator. In this crisis he was able to specify the unusual and unique terms under which he agreed to serve: he would be allowed to retain his private commercial and financial interests (Morris did not worry about "conflict of interest") and he was permitted to name his own personnel. In his capacity as superintendent of finance he insisted on payment of taxes in specie, and got Congress to charter the Bank of North America so it could be done. This was in 1781; the institution was the first private commercial bank in the United States, and the first government-incorporated one. Later Morris served as a member of the Constitutional Convention, and as senator from Pennsylvania from 1789 to 1795. By this time he was reputedly the wealthiest man in America, but extensive speculations in western lands were complicating his life enormously. Finally he went bankrupt, spent three years in the debtor's prison on Prune Street in Philadelphia, lived out the remaining years of his life (until 1806) on his wife's annuity.

The life of Haym Salomon was more interesting and sacrificial. He was born of Jewish-Portuguese ancestry in Poland. There he was an advocate of independence, and worked with military men like Pulaski and Kosciusko to win it. The movement failed and Salomon came to the American colonies, where he would join the rebel cause in another struggle for independence and would be joined there by Pulaski and Kosciusko. Salomon himself could not be an effective soldier, although he did join the Pennsylvania militia; he was five feet in height and sickly. Others would serve on the field of battle; Salomon would contribute with great distinction in the field of finance. This would be after he had been imprisoned by the British as a spy, and in foul prisons had developed the consumption that would soon be the cause of his death at the age of forty-five.

He managed to escape from the British in 1778. He became the chief broker for the American cause (handling bills of exchange), aided Morris in securing loans from Holland and France, became the chief paymaster for French forces here, and advanced a great deal of his own money to the American cause — for supplies and to pay salaries of officers (Steuben, Kosciusko) and members of Congress (Madison and Randolph). His heavy loans to the patriot cause led to his postwar bankruptcy, and his loss of health due to imprisonment led to his early death in 1785. His heirs were left penniless. At his death Salomon owed $45,000, his bank balance was $135 — but Congress owed him more than $600,000 secured with bonds and promissory notes. Unfortunately the government at that time *could* not pay, and later governments *would* not — although there have been repeated efforts to secure a settlement of Salomon's claims. Over the years congressional committees have frequently considered the matter; one recognized the claim as valid but forgot to recommend an appropriation for payment. Friends have suggested a Haym Salomon University, or at least a statue in Washington. In 1926 Congress did publish, at public expense, a biographical sketch. It was not negotiable.

All revolutions are puzzling and complex; the American one was particularly so because it had two phases. One was the imperial revolution against Great Britain; the other was a domestic revolution that had some of the features of a civil war. The imperial phase was basically the revolt of certain propertied groups in the American colonies against English political and economic domination. These propertied groups were certainly not interested in egalitarian crusades; they simply wanted to get rid of Great Britain and to run American affairs for land and profit in their own way. Not surprisingly the Revolution was another war that made a number of rich men richer; this was particularly true of privateers, army contractors, and the *nouveaux riches* who took over from aristocratic Loyalists who found it expedient to depart. In the twentieth century President Eisenhower called it the military-industrial complex. In the era of the American Revolution it might have been designated as the military-entrepreneurial complex.

What propertied or professional groups provided the *leadership* for the American Whigs or Rebels? There were merchants who objected to many acts, enforced or unenforced, but particularly the Tea Act of 1773. There were lawyers who had no sympathy for the Stamp Act. Shipowners had been favored by the Navigation Act of 1651, had been worried by the Molasses Act of 1733, and had been horrified by the enforcement of the Sugar Act of 1764. Planters were heavily in debt to British and Scottish merchants, and objected to prohibitions against western settlement. Distillers, the most prominent manufacturing group in the Puritan American colonies, saw ruin in the Molasses and Sugar Acts.

Who were the Tories who opposed the Whigs in this imperial revolution? There were, of course, the sentimentalists who were bound by history and tradition to England. There were the officeholders, and their precinct captains, who obviously favored a status quo in which they had jobs to a new regime in which they would be unemployed. In the religious sphere there was a numerous representation: Anglicans who were faithful to the Church of England, Quakers and other pacific sects who thought — quite rightly — that there was less chance of war if they supported the Tories rather than Sam Adams and the belligerent Whigs.

One wonders — in this age of popular-opinion polls — about the numerical split between Tories and Whigs in the American Revolution. No one can be certain, but the usual figure is that one-third of the American colonists were Whigs, one-third were Tories, and the last one-third were indifferent. Many American Tories who were not in the regular service of the British military forces, organized local militia outfits — or cooperated with the Indians — carrying on a cruel warfare against the American Whigs. Away from the protection of the British army and navy, the Tory lot was a hard one: they were tarred and feathered, had their property confiscated, were sometimes driven into the back country to make certain they would not serve as a fifth column, were sometimes strung up. To avoid all these varied forms of unpleasantness, more than 70,000 Loyalists left this country during the Revolution. It comes as something of a surprise to find that, by percentage, this was a greater number than the émigrés who left France during and after the French Revolution. In France the figure was five émigrés per thousand of the population; in the United States it was twenty-four émigrés per thousand of the population. Measured in terms of human refugees and their personal deprivations, which are always infinite — the American Loyalists differed from the French émigrés only because there were more of them and because most did not return to their native land. The majority went to Canada; in fact it can be said that the makers of *British* Canada — as contrasted with the French Canada which preceded it — were the Tories who left the American colonies involuntarily during the American Revolution. How much this country lost from this exodus may be inferred directly from the fact that in the two generations after the Revolution the northern states could supply very few national leaders because they had lost a large percentage of their intellectual and economic elite. The result was that the South, where the wealthier class remained to a much larger extent than in New England and the Middle Colonies, was to furnish for half a century a far greater proportion of national leaders. The Virginia Dynasty of early Presidents may not be divorced from this particular situation.

The American Whigs certainly won the imperial revolution. By the Treaty of Paris in 1783 the British made three major concessions: independence, extensive boundaries for the new United States, and the right to fish off Newfoundland and Nova Scotia. The United States made two concessions, neither of which was carried out as the British expected. Congress promised to recommend to the states compensation to Loyalists whose estates had been confiscated; England thought such a recommendation would mean payment, but the states did not comply. The treaty also said that creditors should encounter no legal impediment in collecting prewar debts. Southerners were astounded; states did take legislative or judicial action which prevented collection, with the result that the treaty right was retarded or nullified. Apart from the details, however, it is obvious that independence freed the propertied Whigs in America (merchants, shipowners, planters, lawyers, distillers) from British economic legislation which they disliked. Swept away was British taxation for revenue, mercantile legislation of various types, prohibitions against western settlement, and the Tea Act of 1773.

The other conflict ensuing at the same time as the imperial revolution was a domestic one between certain classes and groups in the American colonies. The central point is that the American Revolution was more than a war on England. It was not merely a question of home rule — it was also a question of *who* would rule at home. The domestic revolution has sometimes been represented as a muscular rebellion of the middle and lower classes — farmers, mechanics, the landless, the politically under-represented — against the power of wealth, either British or colonial. Such a statement goes too far, but there were many illustrations of situations where the *Rebels* in the imperial revolution were *Tories* in the domestic conflict, and vice versa. In most states and regions a struggle for power and influence and land was going on: Tidewater against Piedmont, land-owner against tenant, wealth against mobs.

One would normally expect the frontier, which was known to be law-less and cantankerous and spoiling for a fight, to be against Britain in the American Revolution. But there were many areas along the Alleghenies that were loyal to Britain — for motives varying from Quaker pacifism in Pennsylvania to dislike of the Tidewater. In the South the reason was certainly not that the frontiersmen were particularly sympathetic with England but because England was three thousand miles away — whereas the planters who had gerrymandered the representation in colonial assem-blies were at hand. The choice was clear; the planters represented the most immediate danger. Because the Tidewater was Whig in the imperial revolution, many farmers of the Piedmont took the other side and became Tory. As Esmond Wright puts it, "If the dispute was over representation, they were not represented anyway; if over taxes, they paid few; if over tea, this was not a frontier beverage."

In South Carolina the aristocracy of Charleston was Whig when it looked east across the Atlantic, conservative and Tory when it faced the pine barrens to the west. Many farmers in the hinterland of the state therefore became Tories in the imperial revolution. In the interior of North Carolina a group known as Regulators had taken the law into their own hands as early as 1768, protesting lack of representation in the assem-bly for the Piedmont areas, and charging extortion and oppression by the Tidewater politicos. In 1771 the governor, with a force of 1,200 militia, met and crushed 2,000 Regulators (many of them unarmed) at Alamance Creek. The incident revealed deep-seated sectional differences; as a result the Regulators were, during the Revolution, on the Loyalist side.

In New York the landlord-dominated assembly, which had been so opposed to the Quartering Act in previous years, came to have a new appreciation of armed forces. This change in point of view was brought about because of a series of riots over land tenantry and high rents in Westchester and Dutchess counties, where the tenants hoped George III would win and give them the Whigs' possessions. It was necessary to use force against the "Levelers." As Richard Morris observes, the manor-rich Livingstons and Clintons found themselves fighting two wars — one against the British and the other against their own tenants. Gouverneur Morris had previously expressed his contempt for rioters: "The Mob begins to think and reason. Poor reptiles! It was with them a vernal morning; they are struggling to cast off their winter's slough. They bask in the sunshine, and ere long they will bite, depend upon it."

In New England John Adams himself began to wonder. There was an incident in Boston:

> I met a man who had sometimes been my client, a common horse-jockey, always in the law, who had been sued in many actions at almost every court. . . . He came up to me. "Oh, Mr. Adams, what great things have you and your colleagues done for us! We can never be grateful enough to you. There are no courts of justice now in this Province, and I hope there never will be another!"

Adams survived the shock of such statements, but a great many conservatives did not. They became Tories. They were inclined to agree with the observation of James Otis: "When the pot boils, the scum will rise."

Because of the existence of these domestic stresses and strains certain American historians of the 1920's developed the thesis that the American Revolution was far more than a political movement — that it was, like its French counterpart, a social and economic one as well. The leader of this interpretative school was John Franklin Jameson, in his *magnum opus*, *The American Revolution Considered as a Social Movement*.

Jameson and his followers discussed social and economic reforms or ferment, *inter alia*, in four prime areas: land tenure, religion, law — particularly penal reform — and slavery. In land tenure a major change was the breakup of Crown, Loyalist, and proprietary estates. These had been large, as Beard points out: Sir William Pepperell's holdings in Maine extended thirty miles along the coast, the Philipse heritage in New York embraced three hundred square miles, the property of the Penn family was worth $5 million, the Fairfax estate in Virginia — with more than 5 million acres — was provincial in extent. Tories later claimed their losses at no less than $40 million; the British parliament, after scaling down their demands to a minimum, finally granted the claimants $15 million by way of compensation. Along with the confiscation of Crown and Tory estates went the repeal of laws — particularly primogeniture and entail — designed to maintain a privileged class by keeping estates large. Much has been made of the fact that, within three months after the Declaration of Independence, its author led the way in this reform — and that within fifteen years after the close of the Revolution every state had abolished these aristocratic laws. The Revolution also brought an end to quitrents, a holdover from the feudal period. From New York southward they ranged annually from two to four shillings a hundred acres, paid to the proprietors or the king. This does not seem burdensome now, but four shillings represented the pay of a free laborer for about three days as wages were in 1770 — or for a week on the scale of a century earlier.

In recent years scholars have come to the conclusion that changes in land tenure were not as great as Jameson and Beard were inclined to believe. Among others, Richard Morris and Esmond Wright have observed that confiscated lands were not given away but sold to the highest bidder; the motive behind the entire operation was punitive and fiscal rather than egalitarian; that is, the Tories must pay for the war. Because land was sold to the highest bidder the result was not the creation of many new and small farms. Except for New York where the degree of breakup into smaller holdings was unusual, estates tended to be sold to certain individuals and already well-established families. Vitally interested in adding to their large holdings were state governors, and Revolutionary leaders like the Livingstons and the Van Rensselaers and George Washington. It has also been pointed out that entail had not been a universal custom before the Revolution, and that even in the Tidewater primogeniture had applied only when a person died intestate. As time would show, the elimination of these medieval legal relics did not produce, in Virginia or elsewhere, the "aristocracy of talent and virtue" that Jefferson had envisaged as a substitute for the existing "aristocracy of wealth." Nonetheless, as Morris observes, in this respect England waited until 1925 to reach the point to which Jefferson had brought Virginia in 1776. "That gap of one hundred and fifty years," he says, "represents the difference between a society that achieved democracy by a revolutionary process and one that reached it by glacial stages." The abolition of primogeniture and entail and quitrents dealt, at the very least, an impressive "symbolic blow against a class-structured society."

The war also appeared to encourage humanitarian advances in connection with slavery. The nefarious trade in "black ivory" had been shut off during hostilities, and many state constitutions forbade its renewal. The incongruity of slavery with the ringing phrases of the Declaration of Independence was apparent to some; by 1804 all states north of Maryland and Delaware had emancipated their slaves or had provided for gradual emancipation. On the other hand, because of the situation south of the Mason-Dixon line, a plausible brief could be written, asseverating that it was the British who fought to free slaves and the Americans who struggled to keep them in bondage. The original draft of the Declaration of Independence included a charge against George III for protecting the slave trade; it was struck from the final text because of the objections of slave-owning South Carolina *and* slave-trading Rhode Island. On this issue even the Declaration of Independence was a compromise. In 1775 the famous Royalist governor of Virginia, Lord Dunmore, had offered freedom to all indentured servants and Negroes who were able and willing to bear arms for the king. Washington was outraged and denounced the actions of that "arch-traitor to the rights of humanity, Lord Dunmore!" Dunmore later reported that very few whites, but many Negroes, had responded to his appeal. In 1779 General Henry Clinton, the British commander-in-chief in America, offered freedom for Negroes who would serve the British. He was denounced by American rebels who linked him with that "noted Negro thief, Lord Dunmore." Clinton's proclamation had some success. Jefferson believed that during Cornwallis's invasion of Virginia in 1781, the state lost 30,000 slaves. Morris concludes that "no single event did more to propel uncommitted Southern planters into the camp of rebellion than the British policy of seizing and freeing slaves. . . . What an ironic twist could have been given to the Declaration of Independence had the North Ministry been clever enough to turn the war into an antislavery crusade!"

Apart from scholarly revision of the detail of the Jameson thesis, there had been a general critique of its conclusion and implication that there was a domestic revolution that was "in truth an economic, social, and intellectual transformation of prime significance." This critical judgment is summarized with precision and force in a volume that appeared thirty years later and has a comparable title to that of the *magnum opus* of Dr. Jameson. It is *The American Revolution Reconsidered* (1967) by Richard B. Morris, by coincidence of name across the centuries the Gouverneur Morris Professor of History at Columbia University. In essence Professor Morris makes two points: that there was no conscious or planned domestic revolution, that the really revolutionary changes in the American Revolution were political in nature and that any social ferment or change was incidental, and that what economic changes occurred were conservative in degree. On the first point he insists that it is essential to distinguish between the great reforms which stemmed directly from the American Revolution, and those that were collateral to it. The direct and revolutionary reforms were political: the concept of government resting upon the consent of the people, and the idea of written constitutions. The collateral reforms, those of a social and economic nature, may have developed but were not the avowed goals of the war when it began, any more than Prohibition and the emancipation of women — which had emerged by 1920 — were the objectives of World War I.

Morris is the first to admit that in fighting for political goals which were revolutionary, we also "aroused expectations, encouraged aspirations, and created a climate conducive to a measurable degree of social reform. . . . Clearly there is something more to the Spirit of '76 than 'Redcoats go home!' " He acknowledges that in a cataclysm like the American Revolution some social changes are inevitable; he also asserts that one of the remarkable facts about this particular conflict is that the changes were so modest and conservative. There might have been a contest over who should rule at home, but there was no social revolution.

Such an American conflict — primarily political and conservative — is bound to invite comparison with the French Revolution, which occurred a few years later. Morris comments at length on two contrasts: differences in leadership and in the ultimate direction of the two revolts. Chateaubriand once wrote of the French uprising: "The patricians began the Revolution. The plebeians finished it." In America the situation was reversed. The fires of the American Revolution may have been lighted by unstable and fiery James Otis, the astute and demagogic Sam Adams, and by a first-class intellectual desperado like Tom Paine — but they were dampened by much more restrained and responsible leadership. Otis went insane from a blow on the head in 1769; after the beginning of the Revolution Adams retired into a kind of political limbo; in time Paine departed for France. In the years of construction from 1776 to 1787 the propagandists and pamphleteers of the pre-Revolutionary decade played a minor role; by 1787 men of substance were in control. Recent studies of even the lawless and violent pre-Revolutionary Sons of Liberty seem to indicate that its membership was not composed of many knowledgeable and card-carrying democrats; instead the organization appears to have been in the hands of an aristocratic leadership that knew how to agitate but championed no program of political or economic reform.

In the French conflict not only the leaders became more radical with the passage of time; so did the Revolution. It arrayed class against class and produced the Terror. The outcome was quite different in America. There was some violence arising out of fear of aristocracy but there was no anarchy, no widespread destruction, and no royal governor lost his life. At the close of the American Revolution the pro-English aristocracy had been driven away; the society that remained was middle-class — not plebeian. It was certainly no class war in the orthodox description of that term; during the American conflict the lower classes could be found on both sides of the struggle. In this connection it is interesting to note that Marx and Engels regarded the American Revolution, not as a struggle of the rich against the poor, but rather as a bourgeois movement for liberation from controls that were chiefly external. This may have been due to the fact that social grievances in America were neither as acute nor of as long duration as they were in France. It could have been due to the good fortune of the United States that Washington was willing to renounce power once the announced goals had been achieved, which was not the case with leaders in France. It could also have been due to the visible and untapped wealth of the New World, which presented many more and exciting possibilities for exploitation — once the imperial restraints had been removed.

To some degree the American Revolution affected the social and economic status of many aristocrats, bourgeois, and proletarians. There was one large group which remained *in statu quo*. Abigail Adams had written to her husband in Congress, "By the way, in the new code of laws which I suppose it will be necessary for you to make, I desire you would remember the ladies and be more generous and favorable to them than your ancestors."

Her husband, John, replied, as much in earnest as in jest, "Depend on it, we know better than to repeal our masculine systems."

The ladies would wait until 1848 for the appearance of a Declaration of the Rights of Women.

During most of the American Revolution the new United States was governed by a revolutionary *de facto* government known as the Second Continental Congress. This body did what it could — and quite well under the circumstances — in an emergency situation and without any written authorization to do so. It was obviously desirable to place these developments on a sound legal basis; therefore at the same time that the committee to draft the Declaration of Independence was chosen, another committee was appointed to draw up a permanent form of government. The latter committee performed its homework with assiduity and reported promptly, only a week after the adoption of the Declaration of Independence. The new government was to be called the Articles of Confederation, but its period of gestation was to be a long one. It would not be born for almost five years after the committee's report was made. This was due in part to the discouraging military situation in the early years of the Revolution, which indicated that the idea of a permanent government might be premature. It was due largely to the recalcitrance, for an economic reason, of Maryland — or of certain interested groups in this Old Line State. Because of their calculated delaying tactics, the Second Continental Congress would last for almost six years, until March 1781 — when the new national government under the Articles of Confederation took over at long last.

The usual story, explaining the delay in the adoption of the Articles of Confederation, is placed on a high and moral plane. It concerns ideology and equity. It is stated that the whole issue concerned an argument between Virginia, the most prominent of the six states with "sea-to-sea" charters claiming western land — and Maryland, the most prominent of the seven nonclaimant states. Virginia obviously had the best claim to western land because its original charter claims were the oldest and most extensive, and because it was the only state that could argue that it had conquered the territory. The point is that George Rogers Clark, who took Vincennes at twenty-five, represented Virginia — not the Continental Congress. According to the traditional narrative Maryland countered these good Virginian claims by stating that the West had been conquered as a result of a common effort — and for this reason all of the states, not Virginia and a few others, should benefit from subsequent land sales there.

Actually, Maryland's delay involved not ideology but real estate, often a prime influence in our history, as Henry George was to point out. A couple of private land companies, in which citizens of Maryland had invested, had made purchases from Indians in the Ohio Valley, in Virginia territory. Virginia refused to recognize the purchases, quite properly. Maryland figured that if the lands were taken away from Virginia and ceded to the United States, the claims of her citizens had some chance of being recognized. There was an additional good reason for this hope; several members of Congress also held shares in the Maryland companies.

Virginia, to her credit, finally accepted the argument that the western lands belonged to all the states. Her decision was accelerated by British military pressure from the Carolinas in January 1781; with this extra and immediate impulse, she ceded her territory north and west of the Ohio River to a national government from which she needed help. In doing so, however, she ceded it to the nation — not to individual companies. She stipulated that the land be held as a common fund for all the nation, and that *all* previous purchases from Indians in the area be declared void.

This stipulation caught Maryland, which wanted the land for individuals, *not* the nation. Maryland continued to hold out until she received a nudge from the French — just as the Virginians had received one from the British. Maryland had appealed for the protection of French naval forces against British raids in the Chesapeake. La Luzerne (the French minister) suggested that French naval aid just might not be forthcoming, unless Maryland ratified the Articles of Confederation. Maryland did so, but not from altruistic motives.

Neither Maryland nor Virginia got what they wanted, but the nation benefited. The one major loser in the entire transaction, curiously, was George Rogers Clark. He was the Virginian commissioned by that state, which paid him so slowly and inadequately that he had spent money from his own pocket for the expedition which conquered the West. After the Revolution was over, Virginia passed on his claims for compensation to the national government, which was broke. It adopted the same course that most hard-pressed debtors take; it bided its time. Finally in 1811, more than three decades after his capture of Vincennes, word came from Virginia that Clark would have an annual pension of $400 for his gallant services! Virginia also gave him a sword of honor.

By this time Clark was half-paralyzed; his sword-hand was dead and useless. He died in 1818, the year Illinois became a state, still paralyzed and sunk in poverty. One of his remaining and unsettled land claims was at the junction of the Ohio and Tennessee rivers. Much later the claim became valid, and Paducah (Kentucky) was established on it. By this time Clark had been dead many years. Today the Atomic Energy Commission has a massive development there, but Clark is not around to participate in the unearned increment which might have been his.

The Articles of Confederation established a "league of friendship" among dominant states, all of which retained and practiced their coveted sovereignty; the national Congress looked to state legislatures, not to the people of the United States, for its authority. The former colonies were not yet prepared to delegate much jurisdiction to a national body; the new Congress was really an organ for the league's "consensus," which was determined by a two-thirds vote on all important issues. The new Confederation also concentrated its functions in a one-house legislature where each state had one vote; there had been too much trouble with governors and governor's councils and admiralty courts to take a chance, at this stage, on a powerful executive or an upper house or a judicial branch. The powers of the new Congress were designated as those which had caused the states much concern in the past few years: making war and peace, foreign relations, uniform standards for weights and measures and coinage, relations with Indians to the west, and — hopefully — the payment of the debt incurred in the War for Independence.

For more than a century it was the habit of writers to be hypercritical about the Confederation era, which lasted for less than a decade in the 1780's. This was particularly true of worshipers of the successor government; they agreed with Lord Gladstone that the Constitution was "the most remarkable work . . . in modern times to have been produced by the human intellect." They wanted the Constitution to dazzle against the black background of the Confederation decade, and they painted the era accordingly; modern scholarship depicts the period as neither white nor black, but an intermediate gray.

On the brighter side there were the land ordinances of 1785 and 1787, and a variety of commercial innovations. In connection with its handling of the western situation one historian has gone so far as to say that a government that could produce the two great ordinances was entitled to universal respect. These provided for a system of land survey, and a system of territorial government that looked to the future and marked a great break with the British colonial establishment. Discussion of these contributions, which were important ideologically and pragmatically, will be reserved to a later chapter.

On the commercial side there were the beginnings of a new trade with the West Indies, with European countries, and with the Far East; the Confederation government also established a uniform system of weights and measures and coinage. The new commerce with China was the most exciting and prophetic. In 1784, with the American Revolution over by only one year, a small merchant vessel slipped out of New York Harbor with a cargo of furs, cotton, lead, and ginseng — a worthless root much prized in the Orient because it was supposed to promote fertility and the birth of boy children. One year later the *Empress of China* created a minor sensation when it returned with a cargo of exotic-smelling Oriental products. In time this trade would be a prime factor in giving Massachusetts maritime supremacy, ending in a burst of glory with the clipper ship. In 1773 a tea party in Boston Harbor, at the expense of the British East India Company, had brought on the American Revolution. Two decades later, tea and spices brought from the Far East in American vessels, were underselling the imports of the mighty East India Company, even in the ports of Europe.

The Confederation also adopted a uniform system for the coinage, and for weights and measures. The coinage was in a frightful state with no uniformity whatsoever; domestic merchants were confronted by a curious collection of coins uncertain in weight, shaven by clippers, debased by counterfeiters — along with paper notes which fluctuated in value as new issues streamed from busy printing presses. Thomas Jefferson, who was a member of Congress in 1783–1784, was responsible for the decimal system of coinage which was adopted. This system probably goes back to the factor of ten because man has ten fingers; whatever the origin it is both logical and mathematical, had been introduced into Europe around 1300, and provided a much-needed improvement over the puzzling Roman numerals that are still found on public buildings in the United States.

In weights and measures the Confederation Congress provided uniformity; unfortunately it established the wrong uniformity. It adopted the cumbersome British system — a predecimal one of Babylonian descent which incorporated inches, feet, yards, and miles for distances; ounces, pounds, and tons for weight; pints, quarts, and gallons for volume. The adoption of this awkward and unscientific Babylonian pattern, no matter how expedient at the time, was a mistake. A few years later, in 1791, the Age of Enlightenment produced a scientific reform when Revolutionary France adopted a simple — or metric — system for weights and measures. To this day the adoption of another has left the English and the Americans behind the times.

There were accomplishments, but those who assess the Confederation period can view with alarm three obvious failures — to stimulate commerce, to control public finance, and to solve the currency situation. Interstate commerce was hampered by tariff barriers; foreign trade was stunted by the absence of treaties of commerce. In the foreign sphere our diplomats and our navy did not command enough respect to encourage trade agreements. On the local scene, interstate commerce was hampered by state tariff walls which were both restrictive and silly. The city of

New York, with a population of 30,000, had long been supplied with firewood from Connecticut; it got a large part of its butter, cheese, chickens, and vegetables from the farms of New Jersey. Those who thought in parochial terms claimed that this trade carried thousands of dollars out of the city to the detested Connecticut Yankees and to despised Jerseymen; it was ruinous, they said, to domestic industry. So New York took legislative action, imposing tariff duties against New Jersey and New England — as if products from those regions had come from London or Hamburg! There was prompt retaliation. The city of New York had lately bought a small patch of Jersey soil on Sandy Hook, and had built a lighthouse there; it was eighty-five feet high and remains the oldest lighthouse in the United States. This was New York's Achilles heel. New Jersey imposed an annual tax on the lighthouse. Connecticut was equally prompt. She suspended all commercial intercourse with New York.

The Confederation government certainly failed to increase interstate and foreign commerce to its full potential. It also was derelict in handling public finance properly; there was not even a close approach to a balance in its budget. It had obvious obligations: to meet current expenses, to pay the interest on the public debt (with a first claim on that owed abroad), and to make provision for the ultimate payment of the principal of the national debt. It did not do so.

The reason was obvious. It could not levy a tax, could only requisition from the tax-levying sovereign states. In practice it meant that we had a government by supplication — supplication to sovereign states. Obviously the national government was not very successful in its supplication. During the first two years of existence it asked the states for $10 million. They responded with less than $2 million — barely enough to meet the current expenses of the national government.

The Confederation government also failed to bring order out of the chaos that existed with regard to currency. Prices had been inflated during the Revolution, fell after it was over. This was hard on debtors who had borrowed cheap dollars when prices were high, and were now expected to pay past obligations in dear dollars as prices fell. They wanted cheap money through the issue of plentiful paper money that was also legal tender for the payment of debts; prices would then rise measurably and increased income would enable debtors to pay past obligations advantageously. All of this dramatized the paper-money issue that has been perennial in our history. Paper money issued by any government and designated as legal tender for the payment of debt, if it had no adequate specie reserve for redemption (in which case it was known as "irredeemable" or "inconvertible" paper), will depreciate in value and bring an increase in the general level of prices. On the contrary, the failure of government to provide sufficient money to carry on normal business operations, will result in a decrease in prices — and a loss of income which brings very real hardships to debtors. It is obvious that debtors would prefer to repay their obligations in dollars worth less in purchasing power (when prices are higher) than those borrowed; creditors want to be repaid in dollars which are worth more (because prices have fallen) than those they lent. Ideally, the principal of a debt should be repaid in dollars of the same purchasing power as those borrowed; this is impossible in practice. Beyond the importance of the value of money used to repay debts, there was also the significance of abundant money for entrepreneurs who wanted to expand. This was vital enough that Richard Hofstadter claims that the leading advocates of paper money in the eighteenth century were not backwoods farmers; they were substantial merchants, planters, public officials, and professional men. In his judgment debt was more a sign of enterprise, perhaps daring speculation, than it was of poverty. Whatever the truth of the matter may be, it was obvious that special legislation that affected prices and the volume of money in circulation would benefit either creditors or debtors — regardless of the speculative character of their obligations.

A first-class struggle between creditors and debtors did develop in every new state. In seven of them debtors won and paper money was authorized; in six creditors triumphed and there was no paper money. In Rhode Island, for example, the debtors not only succeeded in getting legislation providing for paper money; the legislation also required creditors to accept it. This was by means of the famous "Know-Ye" law, so named from the first words of a writ; if a debtor could not find his creditor (who was in hiding to avoid payment in cheap money), or if the creditor refused to accept the paper money, the debtor could take the money to a magistrate who would issue a legal statement that the debt had been settled by the paper money so placed on deposit with the court. This resulted in a subsequent judicial decision well known because it concerned both paper money and the general principle of judicial review. It was *Trevett* v. *Weedon;* Weedon was a butcher who refused to accept paper money in payment of a bill. He sued to the state's Supreme Court, claiming that the "Know-Ye" law was unconstitutional. The court upheld his contention, a decree that made the judges unpopular indeed, but the decision stood. It was one of many contentions in American history between the legislative and judicial branches of the government.

Across the border in Massachusetts the opposite situation prevailed. There the legislature was controlled by Boston merchants who passed the burden of taxation on to western farmers by means of a poll tax, and who refused to issue paper money or to pass "stay-laws" postponing payment of debts. The result was the famous Shays' Rebellion.

Daniel Shays was no rebel in the ordinary sense of the term; he was a patriot from the American Revolution who served as the leader of hard-pressed farmers in the back country who couldn't pay their debts and did not want to lose their farms. He was thirty-nine at the time of the rebellion named after him, and had earned a fine reputation as a captain in the Fifth Massachusetts Regiment during the Revolution. He had responded to the alarm at Lexington, had been cited for gallantry at Bunker Hill, had fought with Ethan Allen at Ticonderoga and with Arnold at Saratoga and with "Mad Anthony" Wayne at Stony Point. A man of little education and no sophistication, he made up for these deficiencies by way of honesty and courage. He was convinced that in the rebellion of 1786 he was fighting the same battle for the People that he had waged in the Revolution. He and his debtor-farmer supporters first moved against the courts, to deter them from foreclosing their farms. When it appeared that state militia was going to be used by Governor Bowdoin against them, they attempted to procure arms and ammunition by attacking the state arsenal at Springfield.

Shays had approximately 1,100 men, was opposed by 1,200 state troops. But the stories grew, magnifying the number supporting Shays. It was claimed that he had 15,000 men but was only a figurehead — that the real strategy of the movement was being masterminded by a sinister power. Some believed the British fleet was offshore, ready to take over when Shays completed his rout of government forces. Others thought the mercurial Ethan Allen in Vermont was behind the movement. These stories were both false and silly because, as Marion Starkey points out so well, "Shays was no Cromwell in command of Ironsides who were willing to shed blood." In actual fact, the so-called battles in the rebellion were ludicrous. In the initial one, the state militia first fired artillery over the heads of the rebels, then lowered the barrels. Shays' men, although armed, did not fire a single shot, and ran from the field leaving three dead. Later there was a second meeting of the opposing forces during a snowstorm. Shays' forces melted away in the enveloping snow without battle. The rebellion was over; its leaders went to neighboring states or to Canada, from which extradition would be difficult. In the long run, Shays' rebellion was not in vain. At the next election Governor Bowdoin was defeated by John Hancock. When fourteen men in Shays' army were condemned to death for treason, Hancock pardoned them all. Hancock also saw to it that laws were suspended that had provided for collection of debts in specie.

The reaction of prominent contemporaries to the rebellion in Massachusetts was to have an influence on the call of the Constitutional Convention at the time. Against Shays, *inter alia*, were two prominent men: George Washington and Sam Adams. In Paris, however, Thomas Jefferson approved the rebellion with a statement that would have staggered Shays. The Sage of Monticello observed:

I hold it that a little rebellion now and then is a good thing, and as necessary in the political world as storms in the physical. . . . God forbid that we should ever be twenty years without such a rebellion. . . . The tree of liberty must be refreshed from time to time with the blood of patriots and tyrants. It is its natural manure.

Out of these economic dissatisfactions with the Articles of Confederation came two conferences that served as steps leading to the Constitutional Convention of 1787. Both preliminary conferences, which were held at Mount Vernon and Annapolis, dealt with matters purely economic. George Washington had made a trip to the West in 1784 and had come to the conclusion that the entire country, between the mountains and the Mississippi, would be open to development the moment the Ohio River was connected by canal with the Potomac and the James. If such a connection was not made, the West would still be peopled, but the Mississippi and the Gulf of Mexico would become their trade route. Both were then controlled by Spain, which would be able to offer the westerner trade and prosperity, whereas the new United States could not. This undesirable situation would have profound effects on the loyalty of the American West.

Such a prospect was to be avoided. The first step toward Washington's cherished canal scheme was to secure the cooperation of Virginia and Maryland, since the Potomac was the boundary between these states but had been a source of disputes and controversies. At Washington's invitation commissioners from the two states met at Mount Vernon in 1785 to draw up recommendations for a uniform commercial code. The conference revealed the need for a wider agreement, and accordingly Virginia invited all of the states to a convention at Annapolis in the following year, to discuss commerce amendments to the Articles — amendments that would bring uniformity in legislation dealing with internal and foreign trade. Unfortunately only five states turned up, and the conference was about to adjourn in failure, when Alexander Hamilton achieved the passage of a resolution calling upon all states to send delegates to a new convention. It would meet in Philadelphia in May 1787 to discuss, not commercial problems alone, but all matters necessary to render the federal government "adequate to the exigencies of the Union." Congress, which was the only body that could legally call such a convention, was ignored: ultimately it did issue a formal invitation when the response to the Hamilton invitation turned out to be a hearty one. The Philadelphia Convention was thus, and at long last, legitimized. According to the terms of the congressional call, following the amending clause of the Articles, recommendations would go into effect when passed by Congress and approved by the legislatures of all thirteen states.

Sixty-two delegates were chosen to attend the convention, which met from May through most of September 1787; they were from all states except Rhode Island — the stronghold of the advocates of paper money. Seven delegates never arrived, leaving the famous "fifty-five men" who participated in the writing of the Constitution. Their arguments were so bitter over the "nuts and bolts" of the government (the makeup of Congress, how to count slaves, how to elect a President) — that most of us forget that there was almost unanimous agreement on the basic design of the machinery. All were resolved to grant the necessary new powers which had been noticeable by their absence in the Articles (taxing and full authority over commerce — interstate and foreign), and to solve the problem of sovereignty. The latter was achieved by creating two sovereignties — state and national; all citizens of the United States therefore have dual citizenship in both entities. The national government was made sovereign over powers delegated in the Constitution; states retain their authority over the residual powers not delegated to the national government, or specifically prohibited to the states by the Constitution. On other issues there was compromise — or phraseology whose ambiguity and vagueness (as Richard Morris notes) posterity would try to clarify.

The resulting document was aristocratic in character. In the convention there was little faith in democracy, as we understand the term today. Indeed, as John D. Hicks has stated, one might say that it was the *fear of* — rather than the *belief in* — democracy that brought the delegates together. Gouverneur Morris had said, "Give the votes to the people who have no property and they will sell them to the rich." John Jay had commented with certainty, "The people who own the country ought to govern it." The problem of these conservatives was how to make a government that was democratic enough to be adopted by the people — but not so democratic as to constitute a serious menace to upper-class control. The Fathers really did not believe in man, but they did believe in the power of a good political constitution, which they thought they had, to control him. Madison had stated the problem succinctly when he argued that *property* and *numbers* should be balanced against each other in such a way as to prevent both the exploitation of the poor by the rich *and* the robbery of the rich by the poor.

Because of these attitudes the Fathers went to particular pains to check what Hamilton would call the "turbulence of the masses," and having written a document of which they approved, they made amendment of it difficult. To restrain public passions they provided for three coordinate branches of the government to check and balance one another — the kind of checks and balances, to curb the "lower orders," that John Winthrop had first introduced through the structure of the corporation that founded Massachusetts Bay Colony. Because the lower House of Representatives was popularly elected, a Senate selected indirectly by state legislatures was set up to restrain it. Because no one trusted the people to elect a President, a cumbersome alternative system was established to insure a wise selection — at least in theory.

Madison and Hamilton predicted that six-year terms would serve to make the Senate a stable body — while the shorter term would make the

House susceptible to the "impulse of sudden passions" from the people. In colloquial language it was claimed that the House would feel the heat but that the Senate might see the light. Each body was expected to serve the nation in its own balancing way; if the House was more responsive, the Senate would usually be more responsible. For the same reason it was assumed that the House, elected by the people, would represent little property; the Senate, elected by state legislatures, would represent the interests of big property. In retrospect, we can observe that two modern decisions of the Supreme Court have rendered illogical the bicameral system in state legislatures, and have generated considerable doubt about its wisdom at the national level. They were *Baker* v. *Carr* (1962) and *Reynolds* v. *Sims* (1964) — in which the Court held that both state legislative chambers had to be based on population alone. One statesman put it this way: "It doesn't make any sense to have two houses, both based on equal population, since they'd only be duplicating each other." In spite of this prescience, to date but a single state, Nebraska, has established a one-house legislature. The method established by the Fathers for the selection of a Chief Executive was so undemocratic that recently the American Bar Association — hardly a radical organization — characterized it as "archaic, undemocratic, complex, ambiguous, indirect, and dangerous." Nonetheless it has survived since 1789 as a monument to the distrust of the Constitutional Convention in the alleged wisdom of the masses.

Perhaps because of the impossibility of changing the Articles (because of the unanimity required), perhaps because of a desire to maintain a good thing without alteration, the Fathers made the process of constitutional amendment a difficult one. Twenty-six amendments have been added over a period of almost two centuries since the Constitutional Convention, but analysis quickly reveals that only nine of real substance have been ratified under normal circumstances. The first ten, constituting a Bill of Rights, were promised in order to get the Constitution adopted. It took a Civil War to introduce three of them into the Constitution. Two are purely procedural: the twelfth on the manner of choosing the President and Vice President, and the twentieth on the dates of their inaugural. Two, the eighteenth and the twenty-first, deal with strong drink, and cancel each other. That leaves only nine substantive amendments, added under normal circumstances — an average of approximately one every twenty years.

One wonders how such a conservative document got ratified at all. The answer is found in four explanations: not every citizen voted on it, the established system for ratification was changed, special devices were used to keep the opposition from organizing effectively, and some of the fence-sitters were won over by the promise of a Bill of Rights. There has been some scholarly attack on Beard's statement that property qualifications were such that not more than one man in six of the adult males of the country voted one way or the other on the Constitution. This appears to have been an overstatement, particularly in states like Massachusetts where the property qualification meant little. Nevertheless it is apparent that eligibility to vote was limited in the new United States as a whole by reason of property qualifications, that no Negro or indentured servant or female could vote in any election, and that the districting of the new states favored the pro-Constitution groups. In 1788 no one had heard of *Baker* v. *Carr* and the idea of "one man, one vote." The fact was that the coastal and valley commercial-city areas, which favored the Constitution, were overrepresented; the rural and agricultural areas, which opposed the Constitution, were grossly underrepresented — so much so that delegates representing less than 15 percent of the thirteen-state population could have combined to insure ratification of the Constitution by the required nine states. In addition to the limitations on voting or voting strength, the method of ratification for the Constitution was changed in two ways — by reason of sheer strategic necessity. Even with the property qualification on voting, seven state legislatures had authorized the issue of paper money. The Constitution forbids such issues. Defeat for the Constitution was therefore certain if the method of unanimous support from all thirteen state legislatures was used; it is also to be remembered that paper-money–conscious Rhode Island was absent from the convention. The Fathers therefore decreed that the new document would become effective when ratified by nine (rather than thirteen) state conventions (rather than state legislatures) specially elected for the purpose of voting on the Constitution. Beard observes that this was revolutionary, and so it was. It was in effect an appeal over the head of the Congress that had called the Philadelphia Convention, and over the heads of the legislatures that had chosen its members — an appeal over those bodies to those people who could vote. Such an operation, Beard believes, would have been called a coup d'etat had it been brought off by a Caesar or a Napoleon. He wonders what the designation would be today if the Congress of the United States should call a national convention to "revise" the Constitution, and such a convention should throw away the existing Constitution entirely — submitting a new one which would be ratified by a process of amendment completely at variance with that now in operation.

Because the Constitution was a conservative document without a Bill of Rights, some states ratified with the recommendation *and* the understanding that such guarantees would be quickly added. This assurance won the support of some of the doubtful. As many as seven states accompanied their acceptance with a series of amendments, and in the first session of the new Congress under the Constitution, twelve of them were agreed upon and were submitted to the states for adoption. Ten were subsequently ratified, and were to be designated as the Bill of Rights in the

Constitution. The Fathers were also adept in their political maneuvers, and managed to keep the opposition off-balance. To make certain that their opponents were ignorant about what was going on, the convention was held in secrecy with armed sentinels at the doors, no press reports, and a constant companion for the garrulous Franklin to see that he did not talk too much. The Fathers did not want to advertise their dissensions, and in due course would present a positive common front. In addition, elections in the states for their conventions (which would decide on ratification) were called as quickly as possible, sometimes with what the dissidents felt to be unseemly haste. The supporters of the Constitution were organized; the opposition — which had not had time to collect its thoughts or to gather supporters, many of them scattered in rural areas — did not have the advantage of much time to do so. The "unseemly haste" was apparent particularly in Pennsylvania, where two opponents of the Constitution — with torn clothes and faces white with rage — were forcibly held in their seats (in the state legislature) to complete a quorum which called early elections for the state convention. Partly as a result of such high-handed irregularities Pennsylvania would become the first large state to ratify the Constitution.

In spite of these advantages for the proponents of the Constitution, its defeat — as the Duke of Wellington once said of the Battle of Waterloo — was a "damned near thing." Delaware was the first state to ratify, and New Hampshire was the ninth and clinching one, but there were four laggards — Virginia, New York, North Carolina, and Rhode Island. Two of the four were obviously of such importance that rejoicing was premature so long as they remained out of the fold. In Virginia, the proudest and the most populous state, there was fierce opposition from Patrick Henry, George Mason, and James Monroe. But there was support from Washington, Madison, and John Marshall; the state convention finally ratified by a vote of 89 to 79. A change of six votes would have been disastrous. New York was the only state that permitted election of members to its ratifying convention by full manhood suffrage. The result was a heavy majority against the Constitution. The victory was won there — almost miraculously — by the oratory of Hamilton, the threat of secession from New York City if the Constitution was not ratified, and the sudden appearance of the *Federalist Papers*. These eighty-five essays appeared in New York newspapers, were written by Jay and Madison and Hamilton, and are notable both as propaganda and as profound treatises in political science. Even so, the vote in the New York convention was 30 to 27; a change of only two votes would have defeated ratification. North Carolina and Rhode Island, which have long provided homes for the "other-minded," did not ratify until after the new government had been established — by which time it was essential for them to do so under threat of economic boycott. As Bailey observes:

The minority had triumphed — doubly. A militant minority had engineered the military revolution which cast off the ancient British Constitution. A militant minority of conservatives — now embracing many of the earlier radicals — had engineered the peaceful revolution which overthrew the inadequate constitution known as the Articles of Confederation. Eleven states, in effect, had seceded from the Confederation, leaving two out in the cold.

Some have found the Constitution to represent a Thermidorian reaction, a defense of property rather than human rights, a conservative "backlash" from the democratic excesses unleashed during the American Revolution. If the American Revolution, as we believe, was radical politically but not economically, this would hardly be true. On these issues, however, there has been great argument and there is as yet no consensus. The controversy really started in 1913 with the appearance of a book entitled *An Economic Interpretation of the Constitution*. It was written by Charles Austin Beard, one of the greatest historians, and perhaps the most controversial, this country has produced.

An Economic Interpretation of the Constitution gave Beard a national reputation which he never relinquished. The volume shocked conservatives. The 350-pound President Taft, whom Beard called his "heaviest" critic by tonnage, suggested that Beard would have been more satisfied if the Constitution had been drafted by "deadbeats, out-at-the-elbows demagogues, and cranks who never had any money." High schools banned the book, public libraries put it on a special shelf to deter wide circulation. President Nicholas Murray Butler of Columbia, where Beard taught, stated that his misguided professor was "aping the crude, immoral, and unhistorical teaching of Karl Marx" (Beard suggested that his academic president read Federal Paper No. 10 by James Madison). Four years later in 1917 Beard was to resign from Columbia, not over the Constitution, but in protest against the dismissal of two fellow professors because they had opposed U.S. entry into World War I. Beard favored our entry into this war, but he also believed firmly that people should be allowed to oppose it if they wanted to. Always a belligerent champion of civil liberties and academic freedom, he was to join John Dewey and James Harvey Robinson during the 1920's in founding the New School for Social Research. To this point he would have been considered radical by many. Because of this early reputation it is interesting to note that in the last fifteen years of his life (he died in 1948) most liberals regarded Beard as a conservative. This was because he came to oppose President Franklin D. Roosevelt over two issues — the court-packing scheme and foreign policy.

Drawing heavily on documents from the Treasury Department, Beard substantiated his argument on lines that anticipated the massive biographical analysis by Sir Lewis Namier of British politics in the eighteenth century. This infuriated conservatives because he stated that the Fathers wrote the Constitution, at least in part, in their own economic interest. In order to identify the members of the Constitutional Convention he believed it was necessary to find what groups were dissatisfied with the Articles of Confederation. He found four of them. The first consisted of holders of public securities who had not been paid by a government that could not tax; forty of the fifty-five members of the Constitutional Convention held such securities. A second group was made up of business interests representing manufacturers, merchants, and shippers; the manufacturers wanted a protective tariff, the merchants wanted a national money and freedom from interstate tariffs and a federal system of courts to collect debts across state boundaries, the shippers wanted a government that could produce commercial treaties with new foreign governments. Beard found eleven members of the Constitutional Convention in this second group. A third contingent consisted of moneylenders and creditors who disliked the paper money being issued by states; according to Beard twenty-four members of the convention were moneylenders. Finally, there were speculators in western lands who wanted a government strong enough to suppress the Indians, and able to open their holdings both for settlement and an increase in land values. According to Beard, there were fourteen members of the convention in this group.

In Beard's judgment these were the men who dominated the Constitutional Convention. Five-sixths of those present stood to gain personally from the adoption of the Constitution because they owned securities or businesses or slaves or western land. Conspicuously absent from the convention were any members of the small farmer group in the country, any members from the laboring classes in the towns, or any of the fiery radicals of 1776. Jefferson was serving as American minister in Paris, Patrick Henry refused to attend because he said he "smelled a rat," Sam Adams had grown conservative and was not elected, Tom Paine was in Europe to exhibit an iron bridge of his invention — and to wage war on tyranny across the seas. Beard therefore concluded that the Philadelphia assembly was made up of practical men of affairs who could speak with knowledge and feeling about their personal disabilities — along with those of the nation at large — under the government of the Articles of Confederation.

At the present time, as Jackson Main has pointed out so well, no one would insist that Beard's thesis — now more than a half century old — be accepted in its entirety. On the other hand his fundamental idea that the Constitution reflected the economic interests — *inter alia* — of the large property holders who wrote it, has withstood much later research and criticism. The struggle in this nation in the waning years of the 1780's was between those who had substantial personal interests on the one hand, and the small farming-debtor interests on the other. The original commentators on the Constitutional Convention portrayed it, as Stanley Elkins has pointed out, as "an Olympian gathering of wise and virtuous men — interested *only* in the freedom and well-being of all their countrymen." Beard revised this, asserting that the convention consisted not of disinterested patriots, but of hard-fisted conservatives who were looking out for their own interests and those of their class. In later years revisionists revised Beard, and there are now revisionists who are revising the revionists. In any case, no one believes any longer that the Confederation period was one of perpetual trouble, political drift, threatening disunity, and irresponsible agitation — followed at Philadelphia by a prime example of unselfish and disinterested statesmanship.

V

The Rise and Fall of the American Merchant Marine

THE American merchant marine had been so prominent before the American Revolution that at least one-third of the tonnage under the English flag was built in America. The first effect of the Revolution was disastrous but in time American privateers increased in number until their crews had approximately as many men as Washington had in the Continental Army. Shipping declined during the Confederation period, largely because of the failure of the government to secure a treaty of commerce with Great Britain or to revive the trade with the Mediterranean. The result was that no group more ardently supported the movement for a new Constitution than did the shipping interests.

The merchant marine was to expand rapidly from 1789 until the Civil War — and was to decline steadily from that point to World War I. In its heyday from 1789 to 1860, American shipping grew in minor part because of the advantage of early tariff rebates and tonnage duties, the stimulus of European wars, and the discovery of gold in California. Chiefly responsible for the remarkable increase, however, was the growth of the whaling fleet and Yankee ingenuity as exemplified in navigation, business organization, and design.

After the War of 1812 the United States drew up reciprocal treaties with foreign nations abolishing tariff rebates and tonnage duties — but prior to that time these measures were used to benefit the American merchant marine. In fact, the second and third acts passed by Congress in 1789 provided substantial and immediate aid for shipping by permitting a discount of 10 percent in tariff duties on goods brought into the country in ships that were built and owned by American citizens. The British East India Company was dealt a double blow by a 50 percent reduction in the tariff if tea from the Far East was shipped in American vessels; there were also higher duties on tea shipped from Europe in any kind of vessel (American or foreign), because the tea was probably sold by the East India Company. In addition, tonnage duties on ships entering our ports were discriminatory; the duty imposed on foreign-built and foreign-owned ships was almost ten times as high as that for American-built ships also owned by Americans. Furthermore, after the War of 1812, the coastal trade between American ports was reserved for American ships only.

The wars arising out of the French Revolution, which lasted from 1793 to 1815, contributed both to the growth of the American merchant marine and to the ultimate involvement of the United States in the conflict. During the fighting Europe relied increasingly on the United States to furnish meat, grain, cotton, wool, and leather. American farmers and shippers prospered accordingly. The discovery of gold in California in 1848 gave a considerable lift to American shipping and to American profiteering. Thousands wanted to get to the West Coast as fast as possible; as the demand for ships grew, all possible vessels were diverted to carrying California-bound passengers. The New England whaling fleet was taken over almost in its entirety. So were merchant vessels, in spite of the fact that most of them were not designed or adapted for the comfort of passengers. Get-rich-quick operators resurrected rotten-bottomed ships from retirement, plugged up the worst of their leaks, sometimes gave command of them to incompetents or drunks who could not have held employment under normal conditions, and then sent them off on the difficult and dangerous trip around South America. It was inevitable that many of these ships went down, especially in the stormy passage around Cape Horn. How many no one knows, but diaries from the gold-run days frequently record the sighting of the wreckage of these unfortunate craft, and testify to the chilling effect on the witnesses. There was also passage by way of Panama in separate boats on both the Atlantic and Pacific oceans, plus a trip across the Isthmus. The Panama route was much shorter in miles and time, at least in theory — six to eight weeks as compared to the usual six to eight months around the Horn. The difficulty was a shortage of vessels on the Pacific side, with the result that passengers often spent several months waiting for a boat. Some of them never completed the trip; during the delay they acquired Central American maladies like malaria and cholera, and were buried in these disease-infested areas. Curiously, the most prominent American connected with the Panama route was an entrepreneur who went by the title of Commodore, but who is now chiefly remembered for his prominence in consolidating the New York Central Railroad. His name was Cornelius Vanderbilt.

In the remarkable development of the American merchant marine before the Civil War it is necessary to stress both the growth of the whaling fleet and Yankee virtuosity in navigation, business organization (packet lines), and design (the clipper ships). In the field of navigation it was Nathaniel Bowditch who, to a large extent, made possible the great age of American shipping. He was a navigator and mathematician, in physique weak, short, and spindly — but with great mental capacities that more than compensated for what he lacked in physical strength. He wrote *The New American Practical Navigator* in 1802, known as the "Bowditch." This volume became the navigator's bible and remained so until World War II brought in electronic aids such as loran, radar, the gyrocompass, and inertial guidance systems. No matter, the "Bowditch" is still going strong as the basic working and reference text on celestial navigation — in the air and on the sea. It is still published by the U.S. Hydrographic Office as HO. No. 9. It is not surprising to recall that when Bowditch died in 1838, the ships of all nations in ports throughout the world flew their flags at half-mast as the news spread, and cadets at the U.S. Naval Academy wore mourning badges.

There are two features of Bowditch's life that are significant: his self-education and his contribution to navigation. He had no formal schooling after the age of ten. When he was fourteen someone gave him a text in algebra, and he stayed up night after night with it, completely enthralled by the beauty of its unassailable logic. He found that there were books on mathematics in French, Latin, and Spanish that he wanted to read — so Bowditch learned the languages and read the books. He is the only member of the Philosophical Library of Salem (Massachusetts) whose name appears on the "charge book" as a borrower of Newton's *Principia;* he was so eager to read it in the original that he taught himself Latin. He became so competent in languages that he completed a translation of Pierre Simon La Place's *Mécanique cèleste.* By his twenties he was one of the most thoroughly educated men in America; before he died he was offered, and declined, a chair in mathematics and astronomy at Harvard.

In developing the science of navigation he carried out his studies on five long voyages, in spite of the fact that like Darwin he was subject to seasickness. The greatest difficulty in navigation at that time concerned the fixing of longitude; the problem lay in the fact that there were no accurate chronometers by which Greenwich time could be kept on ships. Bowditch solved the enigma by means of three simultaneous observations on the moon and a fixed star (or the sun), from which he was able to calculate the angular distance between them. From this calculation he could read Greenwich time, based on the angular distances and the corresponding time as published annually by the Commissioners of Longitude in London. Bowditch thus knew both the longitude and latitude of his vessel, was thus able to sail in a straight line, and could break records in taking ships all over the world. Because he saved time and money for shipowners, Bowditch was in great demand. He insisted that mariners should navigate their ships *precisely* by mathematics and celestial observations — instead of trusting to *practical* experience and luck. His greatest personal feat was in bringing the *Putnam* into Salem during a blinding blizzard and snowstorm.

Transatlantic packet ships were a testimonial to American talent in business organization, and were to be prominent for sixty years from 1820 to 1880. As sailing ships they achieved popularity and profits for several reasons: regular schedules, reliable service, and promptness of delivery. They sailed on schedule — "full or not full." This was revolutionary; previously "full and down" had been the first imperative, no matter how long a ship lay in port awaiting the last ton of cargo. They were reliable in the service offered because the ships were well maintained, and customers knew that passengers and the high-value "express" cargo would be delivered in good condition. Promptness and regularity of delivery was more important than speed, but the packet ships did manage to accelerate their schedules. In 1820 the average time from New York to Liverpool was thirty-nine days; by 1850 improved ship design had cut it to thirty-three days. For all of these reasons business came their way, and by 1845 American transatlantic packets were sailing every week to Europe. Ultimately these wooden sailing ships found it impossible to compete with iron steamships; by 1860 they had lost their passenger and steerage trade, and had become freighters only. The last regularly scheduled ocean packet sailed in 1881.

In the presteam era the saucy clipper ships, which showed their rivals a streak of foam, were America's answer to the clamor for speed. The clipper was a new type of ship — a slim, sleek, and beautiful craft that was a far cry from the Far East Indiamen that carried one-sixth as much sail, and furled even that limited spread every night. Clippers became the new aristocrats and dominated the oceans of the world in the 1850's. These fast vessels carried passengers and freight not only to California but to the Orient, to Australia, and to Europe as well. They changed seagoing freight rates by providing such fast passages that they could carry less than half the cargo of their predecessors, and charge more than twice as much for doing so. In their heyday they were so much in demand that it was an unlucky clipper ship that did not pay for itself on its first voyage to California.

The greatest designer of clipper ships was Donald McKay. Born in Nova Scotia, he was the son of a British army officer who had emigrated there after the American Revolution. The family was a farming one, producing crops and a large family of children; Donald was one of a brood of eighteen. He manifested little interest in the soil but built a fishing boat, went to New York at sixteen, and got a job in a shipyard — as an apprentice for four and a half years at $40 a year and keep. By the time he was twenty-one he was a qualified shipwright; this meant that he could command $1.25 for a fifteen-hour day, from 4:30 in the morning to 7:30 at night — with an hour off for breakfast and two hours for dinner at noon. He also managed to marry well, and within a few years had his own shipyard in Massachusetts.

McKay became celebrated as the designer and builder of the largest and swiftest ships of his time; the historian and admiral Samuel Eliot Morison is of the opinion they were the most beautiful ships that ever sailed the seas. They had wonderfully evocative names. There was the *Flying Cloud*, which made the record voyage in 1851 — eighty-nine days from Boston to San Francisco. There was the *Champion of the Seas*, appropriately designated because it held the speed record of 465 nautical miles in 24 hours — an average of almost 20 knots! On shorter runs clippers attained a speed in excess of 21 knots, records that have never been surpassed by any kind of sailing vessel; by comparison today, in America's cup-challenge races, eight knots an hour is considered good speed for the race. In the 1860's McKay was to build several ships for the Union navy; by 1873, however, the construction of iron steamships had advanced to the point that he found it necessary to close his shipyards. The advent of steam had doomed the clippers but the name was given appropriate extension: it was applied to the first great airships flying the ocean routes.

The whaling industry had begun as early as 1645, long before the United States established its independence; it ultimately developed in the first half of the nineteenth century to the point where its products surpassed in value the rest of the fishing industry — and in New England was next only to textiles, and boots and shoes. The great whaling centers in Massachusetts were at Nantucket and New Bedford. Herman Melville, the author of *Moby Dick*, is identified with New Bedford, the port out of which he shipped in 1841 on the whaler *Acushnet*.

In the early days the whaling industry had brought to New Bedford and Nantucket products which provided urgently needed foreign exchange. Whale oil was the principal illuminating fuel for homestead, village, and city. Spermaceti, the light wax found in a great cavity of the mighty sperm whale, was the substance from which good candles were made. Whalebone (or baleen) was useful in the manufacture of a variety of products from buggy whips to corsets. Ambergris was the waxy, aromatic, and extremely valuable substance formed in sperm whales by bacteria infesting peptic ulcers that came from the bony beaks and the sucker rings of the squid that made up a sizable portion of the sperm whale's diet.

The whaling industry was exciting indeed because of the size of the creatures caught, and the peril involved in killing them. The two most important types of whales were the toothless or baleen whales, and the toothed or cachelot or sperm variety. The toothless whales possessed gigantic orifices with whalebone sieves; they swam along with mouths open, taking in water and plankton at two-ton gulps. Among the toothless variety was the blue whale, one of the largest animals known to have lived on this earth.

The killing of these gargantuan whales, often after days of tedium, provided a sudden excitement and danger and booty that was exhilarating. Boats were sent out from the main vessel; they usually had five men at the oars with a harpooner at the bow. He had two harpoons, attached to the end of a whale line, usually about 1,800 feet of it. This ancient version of a modern quarterback stood in the extreme end of the bow, as the oarsmen brought the boat closer and closer to the whale. The harpooner made the basic decisions, on the basis of which the "team" won or lost. The harpoon had a razor-sharp steel barb mounted at the end of a stout ash pole; barb and pole together were about eight feet long. With this unwieldy weapon raised, the harpooner waited for close range. Because it was extremely difficult to throw a harpoon any distance at all, close range usually meant that the bow of the boat practically touched the side of the whale. Once the harpooner had driven the lance deeply into the whale's body, he probed with it to strike the lungs or arteries and cause the animal to bleed to death. At this moment there was real danger; the whale usually went into a desperate convulsion called the flurry — during which it behooved the boat to keep at a safe distance. If the ponderous flukes of the animal, thrashing in the water with enormous force, struck the boat, the vessel was usually smashed. The whale might roll over with its powerful jaw stretching out at a right angle, reaching for boat or men as an extremely dangerous antagonist. Usually, and fortunately, the animal took off for safety. If it dived, there was always the chance that it might go down too deep for the 1,800 feet of line — in which case the line had to be cut or cast adrift to keep the whale boat from being pulled under with all its crew. If the whale stayed on the surface, the crew got what they called a "Nantucket sleigh ride" — skittering along at great and dangerous speeds. When the line attached to the harpoon was pulled out too fast by reason of the speed of the whale, it smoked from the heat of friction — and someone with a water bailer would throw water on the line to keep it from bursting into flames. Ultimately the whale tired, under normal circumstances; at that point all hands would pull on the line, bringing the boat once again to the side of the animal. The harpoonist then used his second lance, giving the coup de grace to the giant mammal.

The cachelot was the superior and most valuable whale from an economic point of view; it was found in abundance in the Pacific. In 1791 an American whaler rounded Cape Horn into the South Pacific, and for the next sixty years American vessels plied those seas in search of oil and spermaceti and baleen and ambergris. Voyages were so long that they often required an absence of three or four years from the home port; the four-year cruise was common, the two-year cruise rare.

Beginning with the Civil War the American merchant marine declined rapidly for more than half a century. In 1861 its tonnage was 2.5 million; when the Confederate cruisers finally struck their colors this had been reduced to 1.5 million tons; by 1900 this figure had almost been halved to 800,000. The portion of U.S. trade carried in U.S. ships declined concurrently — from 65 percent in 1861 to 27 percent in 1865 to 9 percent in 1900. There were a number of reasons for this descent as we shall see, but a major one was our failure to realize the importance of, and to develop, the steamship built of iron and steel — as England did. In retrospect this is surprising because the United States had a head start on England in the early development of the steamship — and then lost it. We enjoyed this early leadership because of at least two inventors (Oliver Evans and Robert Fulton) among others and because of the American *Savannah* — the first steamship to cross the Atlantic.

Oliver Evans was America's first builder of the steam engine and was among the first to apply it to a ship. He was a pudgy mechanical genius whose inventions were either ignored or were shamelessly stolen. For that reason it has been said that if ever a man was born before his time it was Evans, who first saw the light of day in 1755 and died in 1819 — the same year the *Savannah* crossed the Atlantic. In 1772, when Evans was seventeen, he had never heard of Thomas Newcomen, the English blacksmith who invented the atmospheric steam engine, or of James Watt, who perfected it. But in that year Evans's brother told him how a friend had made a splendid explosion by filling a gun barrel with water, plugging both ends, and tossing it into a fire. This is understandable, because water when it is converted into steam expands 1,600 times. It suddenly occurred to Evans that here was the power to propel any engine, if only one could apply it. He did. Later when he read an account of Watt's atmospheric engine, he commented, "He's doing it the wrong way!" As a result it was Evans who developed the new high-pressure steam engine.

Without education or technical training and without patronage of any kind — but with an incredible pertinacity — he designed and constructed the first vehicle ever drawn by a high-pressure steam engine; even more, the vehicle could travel on either land or water. In 1804 he put his steamboat on wheels and drove it by steam power through the streets of Philadelphia. His contemporaries only yawned. They had also yawned in 1785 when Evans at twenty-eight had perfected machines for carding wool and had designed improvements in the machinery for making flour. These innovations made hand operation unnecessary, but at the time they were universally scorned by millers and textile manufacturers. He did live long enough to see, in old age, his machinery widely adopted in flour milling, and to observe the acceptance of his high-pressure steam engine.

Evans could make a steamboat run — but not economically. Robert Livingston and Robert Fulton could; with the steamship *Clermont* on the Hudson, they inaugurated the era of commercial navigation in 1807. Livingston was the diplomat and lawyer and entrepreneur who supplied the funds. Fulton furnished the technical skill but was not so much an inventor as the fellow who could apply the inventions of others. Born in Lancaster, Pennsylvania, he was handsome and supremely self-confident; he had been a locksmith, a gunsmith, a draftsman, and a portrait painter who had gone to England to study under the famed Benjamin West. There he did not spend much time painting; he did develop a permanent preoccupation with submarines and torpedoes — such a preoccupation that one commentator has observed that it may be doubted "whether his lifetime purpose was to put boats upon the water, or to blow them out of it." When Livingston was American minister in Paris he met Fulton; the two of them were pleased with an experimental steamboat they launched on the Seine. Fulton then bought a Watt engine in England, shipped it to the United States, and put it in a vessel named the *Clermont*, after Livingston's estate on the Hudson River. It was this paddle-wheel steamboat that created a sensation on its first voyage from New York to Albany. As she passed through the darkling highlands on her maiden voyage, like a "plangent volcano," in George Dangerfield's phrase, rustics along the banks were stricken with terror. Livingston died in 1813 and Fulton two years later; by that time they had state monopolies on steamboat navigation in New York and Louisiana, built on licenses based on their patents. The profits were enjoyed by their heirs and assigns until 1824, when Chief Justice Marshall broke the estate-authorized monopoly by asserting federal power, under the interstate commerce clause of the Constitution, in the famous case of *Gibbons* v. *Ogden*. From that point in time national trade generated by the steamboat prospered at an astonishing rate.

The first steamship to cross the Atlantic, the American steam-and-sail *Savannah*, was far from a crude beginning in ocean travel; she had private staterooms for thirty-five passengers, a separate ladies' lounge with rosewood paneling, parquet decks in public rooms, and full-length mirrors. She made the voyage in 1819, however, with neither passengers nor cargo; no one would have thought of venturing either life or property in such a craft. As a steamboat she left a great deal to be desired; her coal lasted but eighty-nine hours and she finally arrived in Liverpool three weeks later by the use of sail rather than steam power. Unfortunately the *Savannah* could make no money, whereas the new sailing packets of that era were attracting customers. Her owners could no longer afford her, and they made the *Savannah* a coastal sailing (not a steam) vessel until her destruction by fire in 1821. Europe, however, and England especially, saw the possibilities. Of about twenty-five steamers that crossed the Atlantic in the next quarter century, virtually all were British-owned or built. In the same period American ocean shipping headed swiftly, albeit for a time prosperously, toward a dead end.*

In spite of Robert Fulton and the *Savannah*, the development of the steamship contributed to the decline of the American merchant marine. Britain began with an abundance of coal and iron close to the sea, skilled mechanics and cheap labor, and the boon of a metallurgical industry that had developed to a point far in advance of the American one. In addition to these natural advantages, the British government also realized that the vessel powered by steam would be the ship of the future, and began to subsidize the shipbuilding industry heavily. This started in 1839 with aid to the four side-wheeled wooden ships which were the predecessors of the *Queen Mary* and the *Queen Elizabeth* of the Cunard Line. Subsidies later went to other companies, particularly the P. and O. (Peninsular and Oriental) in the Pacific Ocean. By contrast the New England shipbuilding industry was myopic in its stubborn refusal to build steamships. It put its faith in the clipper ships and sail when the future was with the steamship; the clipper was fast and beautiful and uneconomical — except for special reasons in a special decade, the 1850's. Steamships were superior because they were more durable (steel against wood), they were more dependable (a sailing vessel could become becalmed), and they were safer because of the reduction of fire hazard (fire at sea — in wooden vessels carrying highly inflammable sails and tarred hemp rigging — had been of great concern for centuries). Admiral Morison, who knows ships and can become misty-eyed on contemplation of the clipper, is realistic enough to say that it would have been far better if the energy that produced the clipper ships had been put into the iron-screw steamer. He writes:

> Never, in these United States, has the brain of man conceived, or the hand of man fashioned, so perfect a thing as the clipper ships. . . .
>
> "The *Flying Cloud* was our Rheims, the *Sovereign of the Seas* our Parthenon, the *Lightning* our Amiens; but they were monuments carved from snow. For

---

* In 1959, 140 years later, a second American *Savannah* was launched. It was a nuclear-powered merchant ship, again the first of its kind in the world. By contrast with the original *Savannah* and its eighty-nine hours of steam power, the new and current *Savannah* could run for three years, or about 350,000 miles, on its initial nuclear charge. The nuclear *Savannah* sailed almost 60,000 miles (including five transatlantic crossings) on less than twenty pounds of uranium. The nuclear *Savannah* also cost $35 million — enough to build 650 ships like her namesake a century and a half ago. By the late 1960's the new *Savannah* was laid up, because of a variety of problems including those involving labor and the fear of nuclear contamination. No one knew, at that point of time, whether nuclear power in merchant vessels was economically competitive or not. In the light of U.S. conservatism in 1819, however, some were concerned. The owners of the first *Savannah*, unable to see ahead to an age of steam, had sold her engines after the maiden voyage. Thereafter the United States relied for two generations on sailing ships while England turned steadily to steam and thereby made maritime history.

a brief moment of time they flashed their splendor around the world, then disappeared with the sudden completeness of the wild pigeon.

Actually, it wasn't quite that sudden. Shipping needs during World War I brought back into commission almost all of the old-time sailing vessels that were still around, including more than a hundred big schooners. They were sent mainly to the French port of Brest, carrying bulk cargo for the American Expeditionary Force. The people of Brest knew sailing vessels of the fishing type which they sent to the Grand Banks, but they had never seen anything half the size of these American four-masters. Alas! the schooners were finished by the 1930's. The last ones served out their time and timbers on Rum Row during Prohibition, sitting just beyond the twelve-mile limit, helping to smuggle whiskey into the United States. It was a sad *Götterdämmerung!*

The Civil War accentuated the industrial revolution in this country with the result that industry became more attractive to new capital than shipbuilding. The war also introduced the construction of transcontinental railroads, which competed with ships for passengers, freight, and capital, and finally the Civil War brought in a protective tariff which tended to reduce international trade. The direct effects of the Civil War were more spectacular and obvious: the Confederate commerce destroyers captured or destroyed a sizable number of Northern vessels, and forced most of the rest to change their registry to neutral flags, in order to avoid ruinous insurance rates. The Confederate government had managed to construct and purchase abroad, largely in England, some eighteen cruisers as commerce destroyers; of these the *Alabama*, the *Florida*, and the *Shenandoah* were important and lethal — these three captured upwards of two hundred Northern merchant vessels as prizes. After the war, Charles Sumner as the powerful Chairman of the Senate Foreign Affairs Committee claimed that Britain owed the United States more than $2 billion for its unneutral behavior in permitting the purchase and construction of these commerce destroyers within her territorial limits. His claim included $15 million for actual damages, $100 million for driving American merchantmen from the seas (that is, forcing them to change their registry), and $2 billion for prolonging the Civil War by at least two years. Sumner did not say so, but many assumed that he would be satisfied with the cession of Canada in payment. Ultimately the whole matter was settled in the Treaty of Washington in 1871. England expressed regret for what had happened, paid $15.5 million in damages — offset by a payment of almost $2 million for American violations of neutral rights in the Northern blockade of Southern ports.

The China trade and the American whaling fleet, once vital and important features of the American merchant marine, both declined as the nineteenth century waned. The China trade ceased to have much importance because the sea otter was no longer plentiful on the West Coast, Americans began to use European porcelain in place of Chinese pottery, a change of style in men's clothing emphasized cotton and wool rather than silk, and Brazilian coffee took the place of tea as a national drink. There were three major reasons for the decline of the whaling fleet: the influence of the Civil War; the discovery of cheaper substitutes for whale oil; and the decline in the number and availability of whales. The American Civil War saw the American whaling fleet cut in half, from 500 to approximately 250 vessels. The Union government was partly responsible; it bought a number of whalers, filled them with stone instead of whales, and sank the vessels at the entrance of Charleston and Savannah harbors — in a vain attempt to block the ship channels. The Confederate government was partly responsible because its raiders sank many whalers. This was particularly true of the *Shenandoah*, which captured thirty-eight defenseless Yankee whalers in the Pacific. There was no radio communication in those days; as a result the *Shenandoah*, unaware of the Southern defeat in April 1865, went on fighting the war by capturing whalers until August. When her captain finally learned that she no longer represented an existing government, he took the raider to England and lowered the Confederate flag in November 1865 — the last Confederate flag to come down.

Two cheaper substitutes — mineral and vegetable oils — have been found to take the place of whale oil. Mineral oil, which replaced whale oil as an illuminant, was first "discovered" in this country by Edwin L. Drake at Titusville, Pennsylvania, in 1869. Northeastern Pennsylvania seemed an unlikely milieu for the boom that occurred after the Civil War, except for the fact that it had always been afflicted with a foul-smelling, foul-looking, and foul-tasting surface liquid that polluted wells, seeped into newly plowed fields, and left a slick on ponds and canals. Locally it was called "Seneca Oil" from the Indian tribe that used it as a cure for every human ailment. Then Drake appeared, backed by the Seneca Oil Company and a group of entrepreneurs who had been impressed by the distinguished chemist Benjamin Silliman at Yale, who thought "Seneca Oil" had real potential as a substitute for whale oil in lamps. Drake struck oil at only sixty-nine feet — the first time petroleum was tapped at its source and the first proof of oil reservoirs within the earth's surface. Neither Titusville nor the world nor the whaling industry was quite the same again. Titusville got so tough that some called it a "Sodden Gomorrah." Professor Silliman spent the rest of his life discovering the chief uses which were to be made of petroleum products for the next fifty years, and outlined the principal methods of preparing and purifying these products.

In the nineteenth century the competition confronting the whaling industry came from mineral oil; in recent years the competition has been from vegetable oils. This has so reduced the price of whale oil that the only real basis for the industry now is the desire of whaling nations to conserve their foreign exchange. These are the nations, such as Norway, that do not produce enough vegetable oil for their own needs and hence must either catch whales or buy fats and oil abroad. During the past thirty years the decrease internationally in the use of whale oil, as fat, has been considerable and convincing. In the 1930's whale oil provided almost 10 percent of the world trade in fats; in 1958 it constituted less than 2 percent.

When the bark *Wanderer* broke up on the rocks off Cuttyhunk, Massachusetts, in 1924, the wild Atlantic winds brought to a dramatic close New England's most adventurous maritime enterprise. As I. T. Sanderson has pointed out, the *Wanderer* was the last square-rigged New England whaler to put to sea, and her loss marked the authentic end to an era that had lasted three hundred years. The day of the Yankee whaler was over. In the twentieth century other nations mechanized their whaling operations; the whaling and fishing business is the *one* American industry that never became modernized.* In the heyday of American whaling it had been a matter of the sea and the whale against human muscle, courage, and skill. Now there are "factory ships" with radar and sonar, extremely rapid pursuit ships with harpoons fired from cannons, and refrigerator ships to store the catch. There are only five nations (the USSR, Norway, Japan, the Netherlands, and Great Britain) prominent in the whaling industry; the United States is not one of them. The factory ships of the Big Five work for the most part in the Antarctic where 70 percent of today's whales are killed. The operation is now so efficient that many conservationists believe the whale will go the way of the North American bison or the duckbilled platypus; experts estimate that there are only a thousand giant blue whales left in all the ocean seas. There is an international agreement limiting the annual catch in theory; in practice the agreement is a bit difficult to enforce. One hundred years ago an average three-year whaling

---

* This statement requires some qualification; at the present time the U.S. fishing fleet off New England is not nearly as modern as that of the Soviet Union, which is catching more fish in the same waters. The Soviet fishing operation is sophisticated. It has trawlers capable of fishing at any depth (surface, mid-depth, and on the bottom); U.S. vessels fish at one depth only, take several weeks to shift from one type of fishing to another. The Soviet operation includes refrigerated trawlers that freeze and can fish; these vessels also serve as scout ships and direct fleets to the areas where fishing is good. American ships cannot freeze or process; they can only catch and ice fresh fish, and after five or six days must make the 100-plus–mile run back to port. This means that less than 50 percent of our vessels are actually fishing at any one time. Soviet ships operate as a fleet, constantly exchanging information by radio. Because U.S. skippers compete, if a boat finds fish it keeps the news to itself. The greatly intensified and highly efficient Soviet effort in the Northwest Atlantic has raised a serious question of overexploitation of those waters. But conservation, if it comes, will not enable American fishermen to compete with foreign fish imports. Only 1 percent of Russia's catch was exported to the United States in 1967, but an increase was expected. Seventy percent of Canada's catch, however, is shipped to the United States.

voyage would return with the oil from thirty-seven whales — about one whale caught per month. In 1970 a modern catcher-boat can kill one whale a day — or 365 in a year. Modern whalers use helicopters to spot whales, catcher-boats guided by radar, sonar to detect the surfacing of a whale, and cannon-fired harpoons fitted with grenades that explode inside the whale, killing it in five seconds. Factory ships are the largest hunting vessels in the world; some are larger than most of the aircraft carriers used in World War II. The hundred-foot blue whales were killed off first; each year the modern whalers have been forced to zero in on smaller and smaller whales — the only ones left to be killed.

Finally, the American merchant marine declined because of an attitude toward labor that was selfish and brutal and incredible. There were two practices that were particularly reprehensible: the low wages and harsh discipline that Samuel Eliot Morison documents so thoroughly in his classic, *The Maritime History of Massachusetts, 1783–1860.* These evils had appeared on the clipper ships; they were the "queens of the sea" in design and "blood boats" as far as labor policy was concerned. Wages were abysmally low on clipper ships. They could be even worse on whalers, where neither officers nor men received salaries or wages. Each man got a "lay" — a share of the net profits, if any, from the voyage. If the voyage made money, everybody got something. If the voyage did not make money, and some did not, no one made anything. Even if the voyage made money there was a variety of interesting devices for cheating American seamen. There were the high prices charged in the skipper's store on board — a very real monopoly known as the "slop chest." There were high interest rates charged for advances of wages, which sailors seem to require in every age. There were a number of fraudulent extra charges: for insurance (but if the ship was lost the owners, not the seamen, collected), for the medicine chest, for alleged "leakage" on whalers.

Over the long years the result of these practices was that Americans refused to serve on American vessels. Clipper ships and whalers therefore had crews composed mostly of men from other nations, some of them derived from the most depraved and criminal classes. If there were Americans they were apt to be habitual drunkards — as the only considerable native element in what Morison calls this "human hash." With such crews, discipline was kept only by heavy and full portions of the cat-o'-nine-tails, "belaying-pin soup," and "handspike hash." Many American captains, who qualified as pious church members on shore, were cold-blooded and heartless on the quarterdeck; there these "blubber barons" enforced conditions that no decent American could stand. It was not until the passage of the La Follette Seaman's Act of 1915 that much was done to correct these abuses; under this act for the first time seamen were given the same basic rights as factory workers. This law established wage rates and minimum standards for food and living quarters; also assured were safety measures, a nine-hour day when in port, and the right to join a union. Before the La Follette Act, however, the results were amazing and ironic because of low wages and harsh discipline. Yankees built the clippers but did not man them. Whalers never returned to New Bedford or Nantucket with the crew they shipped with; many Americans had deserted in Pacific islands from these "floating hells." By 1850, the traditional Yankee mariner — with his neat clothing and perfect seamanship — had passed into history.

There has been some growth of the American merchant marine since 1916 because of the military necessities arising from two World Wars, and because of the new policy of federal subsidies to shipping in peacetime. We found ourselves in 1914, and again in 1939, without adequate shipping. At the outbreak of World War I there were 45 million gross tons of shipping belonging to all the nations in all waters of the world. Of this tonnage, roughly 5 million were of U.S. registry — but most of this was in use on the Great Lakes, in river traffic, or in the coastal trade. Only fifteen American ships, aggregating 153,526 tons, were in active service on transatlantic or transpacific routes, and nine of these were passenger liners that carried little or no cargo. In World War I we did manage to increase our shipping measurably by an enormous amount of construction, and by the seizure and requisition of foreign ships. After our entry into the war we seized thirty German vessels that happened to be in our harbors, and placed them in operation in spite of the efforts of their crews to wreck the machinery. Conspicuous among these was the *Vaterland*, which was renamed the *Leviathan*. It became a famous transatlantic troop-carrier, and is still the largest vessel ever to fly the Stars and Stripes during its two decades as troop transport and flagship of the U.S. Lines. We requisitioned neutral ships that happened to be tied up in our waters at the time, with due compensation to the owners; in this haul were eighty-seven Dutch merchantmen. We planned and executed history's largest shipbuilding program to date, and spent more than $3 billion to deliver a total of 2,300 ships, many of which splashed into the water after the Armistice was signed. There were seven hundred steel cargo vessels and twenty-six transports, the latter a sturdy if unglamorous nucleus for our postwar passenger fleets in both oceans. Prefabricated steel ships were constructed, for the first time on a large scale. A tremendous wooden-ship program was begun, and a few concrete vessels were launched — including one appropriately christened *Faith*. By the end of the conflict we were laying down two keels for every one lost to U-boats.

In World War II it was necessary for the United States to begin construction again — in part because we were fighting in the Pacific as well as in the Atlantic. During this conflict the output of shipyards, largely because of prefabricated materials, was no less phenomenal than that of industrial plants. We built almost 5,800 merchant ships, more than twice as many as in World War I; at $15 billion the cost was five times that from 1917 to 1919. The leading miracle-man in the shipbuilding industry was Henry J. Kaiser; for his efforts he was properly dubbed "Sir Launchalot." By use of techniques involving prefabrication, he was actually able to complete a freighter of more than 10,000 tons in a bit more than four days — from keeling to launching. Kaiser managed to average a ship a day, for a total of almost 1,500 vessels. It was a marvelously integrated operation; he had seven shipyards (six on the Pacific and one on the Atlantic), plus cement and steel and magnesium plants. After the war this exciting entrepreneur was to try automobiles and fail — but was to succeed again in aluminum and prepaid medical care for his employees. Anticipating Medicare he established self-sustaining hospitals and medical centers for more than a million people on the West Coast. Unlike the industrial barons of old, his credo — in the words of an award bestowed upon him by the AFL-CIO — was: "The worker is a human being." Because of the efforts of Kaiser, and others, long before the shooting stopped in World War II, the United States had the mightiest merchant fleet the world has ever seen. In 1945 it was carrying 70 percent of our foreign trade. After that year there was another relapse. Construction virtually ceased, except for a few tankers and a scattering of passenger liners in the luxury class.

Subsidies to shipping have been both direct and indirect. Direct subsidies became important after World War I; indirect subsidies have been available throughout our history. The indirect subsidies have come from the Department of Commerce, from Congress, and from the Coast Guard. Various divisions of the Department of Commerce offer assistance to shippers. There is the Coast and Geodetic Survey, which charts the coasts. The Inland Waterways Corporation promotes, encourages, and develops transportation in the interior of the country. The Bureau of Foreign and Domestic Commerce collects data essential to the conduct of this trade. The Weather Bureau offers forecasts for both air transport and shipping.

We have already seen that Congress helped shippers in the early part of our history through tariff legislation and discriminatory tonnage duties. In 1817 Congress established a monopoly of the coastal trade for American ships only — through an absolute prohibition against foreign vessels in this trade. There are also rivers-and-harbors appropriations which have amounted to more than $25 billion since 1802; this work is supervised by the Corps of Engineers of the U.S. Army, but because these appropriations have been a prime example of political logrolling, much of the money has been spent unwisely.* The Webb Export Act of 1918 ex-

* In the 1960's approval was given for a rivers-and-harbors boondoggle that was particularly noteworthy. It is a project to build a navigation system stretching 450

empted associations of corporations engaged in such trade from the federal antitrust acts. In addition to Congress and the Department of Commerce, services to shipping are also offered through the Coast Guard. This agency, which in peacetime is under the jurisdiction of the Treasury Department, searches out smugglers and offers navigational aid through its Bureau of Lighthouses and its Life Saving Service that has 250 active stations.

In the period since World War I direct subsidies have been of three types: construction, operating, and tax exemptions. In the construction of vessels the U.S. government has assisted privately owned shipping lines in several ways: it has sold surplus vessels at bargain rates, it has provided assistance to private firms when they built their own ships, and the government itself has constructed vessels and then leased them at favorable rentals. After World War I the vast government-owned merchant fleet, more than half of which had splashed into the water in years of peace after the Armistice was signed, was offered for sale in 1923 at less than 10 percent of its original cost. American Export Lines bought $40 million worth of ships for $1 million, and Henry Ford bought vessels that had cost $1 million each — for $800 per ship. These discounts seem excessive, but they were equaled and perhaps excelled after World War II. Senator Williams of Delaware has charged that the U.S. government lost almost $3 billion in the five-year period from 1945 to 1950, selling some vessels at discounts ranging as high as 97 percent.

The government has also provided help directly to private firms through financial aid in their own construction of ships, or through advantageous lease of government vessels. In the first instance, under the Merchant Marine Act of 1936 (sometimes called the Magna Carta of the Shipping Industry), the U.S. government could pay up to 50 percent of the total cost of a vessel deemed necessary for the national defense; beyond that amount the private firm needed only to raise 25 percent of its own money because it could borrow the final 25 percent from the federal

---

miles up the Mississippi and Arkansas rivers, giving Tulsa (Oklahoma) an outlet to the sea. Estimated to cost more than a billion dollars, this project is said to be the largest since the Tennessee Valley Authority was built. It was originally engineered through Congress by the late Senator Robert Kerr of Oklahoma, a key member of two important Senate committees: Public Works, and Finance. There is a story to the effect that President Kennedy had been advised to oppose the project on the Arkansas River, but needed Kerr's help on a tax bill. The blunt Senator from Oklahoma is reported to have said, "I hope you understand how difficult I will find it to move the tax bill with the people of Oklahoma needing this river transportation." The President is said to have replied, "You know, Bob, I think I understand the Arkansas River project for the first time."

After Kerr's death, Senator John McClellan of Arkansas became the chief sponsor of the project, which reached the Arkansas-Oklahoma border in December 1969. That milestone was marked by a grand dedication. See Elizabeth B. Drew, "Dam Outrage: The Story of the Army Engineers," *Atlantic,* April 1970.

government at a favorable rate of interest — 3½ percent repayable in twenty years. In connection with lease arrangements the government could construct a vessel and lease it at an annual rental of 5 percent plus 3½ percent for depreciation — but these rates were fictitiously low because they were purposely calculated on the imaginary low cost of construction in a foreign shipyard. Such synthetic figures were half of what it would have cost to construct the vessel in the United States, and for that reason the rentals were both artificial and favorable.

In addition to subsidies for construction the U.S. government found it necessary to assist firms in operating their vessels — whatever the ships might have cost them originally. The operating subsidies were supposed to be based on the differences in cost — here and abroad. Prior to 1936, in spite of past experience, the government retained mail subsidies as the chief form of assistance to be offered. Unfortunately the mail bonuses proved to be scandalous in the celebrated hearings on merchant-marine subsidies in the U.S. Senate presided over by Senator (later Justice) Hugo Black from Alabama. This investigation brought mail subsidies into such disrepute that Black's committee recommended scrapping the entire system. It was found that American Export Lines, for example, had been paid more than $4 million for carrying a handful of mail; at the same time it was revealed that the president of this company was being paid more than a million dollars in salary and expense allowances. In 1935 the New York *Nation* figured that the entire operating cost of 282 American-flag vessels was about $29 million. The mail subsidy was exactly the same. This meant that the U.S. government was virtually paying all the operating expenses of our oceangoing fleet. The *Nation* estimated that a fair charge for carrying the mail in 1935 would have been $3 million, rather than $29 million. These revelations were so impressive that the government decided on a direct subsidy, again based theoretically on the differences in the costs here and abroad, if anyone could calculate what they really were. No one could, although many have tried. The Merchant Marine Act of 1936 required the recapture, from subsidized lines, of all profits over 10 percent; the difficulty, of course, was in determining the valuation on which the 10 percent was to be based. For this reason, throughout our entire business history, recapture has been a forlorn hope.

In addition to subsidies for construction and operation, for the past forty years shipping companies have also achieved special advantages through tax exemption, allegedly because of the difficulty they encountered in raising capital. Under the present law, the Treasury permits shipowners to deposit all or part of their earnings and capital gains in a special reserve fund, on which no taxes are paid and on which they can draw in future years for the purpose of buying extra ships. Although by 1970 the government had repealed the investment-tax-credit of 7 percent for other industries, shipping firms were permitted — in effect — to have an investment-tax-credit of 100 percent. Such a possibility permits shipping companies to defer taxes indefinitely, and there is no upper limit to the amount they can put into such reserve funds in order to avoid the payment of taxes.

Direct subsidies — construction, operating, and tax exemptions — have been paid from the U.S. Treasury for more than four decades. Regretfully, they have not restored the American merchant marine to the glory of pre-Civil-War days. In actual fact, the American maritime industry is now a sick one indeed. When the Merchant Marine Act was passed in 1936, 30 percent of American shipping was in American ships. Thirty years later less than one-tenth of U.S. foreign commerce is shipped under the American flag. By contrast, British ships carry 53 percent of that nation's trade, and the comparable figure for French ships is 62 percent.

It will be recalled that one of the major arguments in support of direct subsidies to American shipping was a military one. At the present time we have a National Naval Reserve of privately owned vessels which the U.S. government can call on in time of war. This National Naval Reserve consists of approximately 1,400 ships which are American owned, but of this number approximately 400 fly foreign flags. The U.S. oceangoing merchant marine, flying the American flag, therefore consists of about one thousand freighters, tankers, and passenger ships — operating out of western, eastern, and Gulf ports. Of these approximately one thousand vessels, 300 receive subsidies as regularly scheduled carriers and the other 700 do not. The majority of nonsubsidized ships fall into the following categories: the coastal fleet of approximately 300 vessels; the industrial fleet, numbering about 200 ships and carrying the owner's products — largely oil, steel, and fruit; and the irregularly scheduled freighters (about 200) carrying bulk freight on consignment to foreign ports. The 400 American-owned ships that do not fly the American flag sail under what are called flags of convenience: the flags of nations — Panama, Liberia, Honduras and Costa Rica — that collect few taxes and have no labor laws worthy of mention.

There has been severe criticism of the program of subsidies to American shipping, based on four main arguments: (1) that the program is unfair and discriminatory, (2) that it encourages inefficiency in American business operations, (3) that it should be discontinued for passenger vessels, and (4) that it makes no economic sense from the standpoint of balance in international payments. There are some who believe that the subsidy program, as it has been operated, has been unfair and discriminatory toward a majority of vessels in the U.S. merchant fleet. No one would assert that the coastal fleet of 300 vessels should be subsidized because it has long had a monopoly of this traffic. On the other hand, if vessels are to be held in reserve for wartime use, it would appear that the other nonsubsidized vessels should receive federal assistance. These would be identified as ships in the industrial fleet which owners could replace with foreign carriers at a saving, the irregularly scheduled freighters which are in competition with foreign vessels whose costs are lower, and the four hundred American-owned vessels sailing under flags of convenience — a practice that deprives the American treasury of taxes and American labor of wages.

The current subsidy is just under $400 million a year — $280 million for operating subsidies and $100 million for construction subsidies. More than 80 percent of the operating subsidy goes to compensate for the differential in wages paid on American and foreign ships. This averages $7,300 a year for the seaman on the three hundred ships that receive these subsidies. This is so generous that operators of the favored vessels stay in business whether their management is economical and efficient or not, and whether labor unions hold them for exorbitant wage increases — which they do. The *New York Times* has observed that there appears to be little doubt that unions representing ships' crews have been playing leapfrog at the expense of an industry that survives by grace of taxpayers' subsidies. Because the government has been paying the bill, subsidized companies have been generous with wage increases.*

If the operating subsidy has encouraged inefficiency and waste, so has the construction subsidy. There is evidence to indicate that the high cost of American ships — and they do cost twice as much to build here as in foreign ports — is largely due to the emphasis on military production with antiquated techniques. The primary difficulty is not with high wages in American shipyards, costly as they may be. Critics have observed that the automobile industry is also characterized by very high wages, and remains competitive in international markets; they also point out that during the Second World War Henry J. Kaiser, a private operator, managed to produce ships at relatively low cost. Why not now? We begin with the fact that in the United States a worker in a shipyard was paid slightly more than $3.00 an hour in 1964, whereas in Sweden the wage was half as much. This meant that in order to be competitive, American firms had to install and utilize methods of production which would be twice as fruitful as those of Swedish workers. This appears to be entirely feasible from an engineering standpoint, but the managers of American shipyards have not done it. The reason seems to be that they have been oriented to serving

---

* It is obvious that both management and labor, in the subsidized portion of the U.S. shipping industry, want this arrangement to continue. In 1969 the *Wall Street Journal* reported a situation indicating that maritime unions might be exerting improper influence on Congress through overpayment for "canned" speeches. The Maritime Trades Department of the AFL-CIO would engage a congressman for a talk; he would read a ghost-written speech of eight to ten pages and receive a fee varying from $500 to more than $1,000. The newspaper disclosed that in one recent twelve-month period legislators were paid such fees for fifty-five speeches to the maritime unions. The payments ranged up to $1,250 for a speech by the chairman of the House Merchant Marine Committee, which rules on maritime subsidies. Some wondered whether it was oratory — or votes — that the maritime unions wanted.

the U.S. Navy as their principal customer. Ships for the U.S. Navy are produced at a cost of about $5.00 a pound — and *Polaris* submarines at $12.00 per pound. By contrast a commercial tanker, to be competitive, must be manufactured at a cost of 20¢ per pound — or less, if possible. By concentrating on military work where cost is of minimal importance, the shipbuilding industry has become commercially noncompetitive in the world market. This situation cannot be altered until there is a transfer of talent and capital from the military to the civilian sphere — scarcely an immediate prospect or possibility.*

The subsidy program has also been attacked because the emphasis on passenger ships was both costly and senseless. In the 1960's a dozen passenger ships were absorbing about one-fourth of the operating subsidy, while three hundred other vessels shared the remaining three-quarters. It was claimed that American- and foreign-flag passenger lines were valid as prestige items — a showing of the flag around the world on luxury cruises. The real pinch came in the area of costs — for materials, maintenance, and operation. In the mid-1960's a jet airplane costing several million dollars, manned by a crew of eight, could move ten thousand passengers across the Atlantic each month in thirty trips. Its operating costs, not including amortization, ran a bit less than a million dollars for the month — while the total fares collected from passengers were in the neighborhood of five times as much. An ocean liner, on the other hand, had an original cost of around $60 million, required a crew of 1,000 persons, and if fortunate carried about 4,500 people a month on four round trips. Operating expenses for the month were in the neighborhood of $1.25 million, depending on whose flag was flown — while the passenger fares (if the ship was filled) did not bring in much more. The U.S. superliner, the *United States,* was able to carry fantastic loads on some trips — but the cold winter months brought on the fiscal doldrums with the result that the vessel was costing the United States Lines a deficit of nearly $5 million a year *beyond* the federal subsidy of another $12 million! In 1968 the magic Cunard queens, the *Mary* and the *Elizabeth,* were retired from the vanish-

---

* In the aerospace industry there is also evidence to indicate, unfortunately, that the Department of Defense is giving the highest profits to the poorest performances. In conventional economics the most efficient companies earn the highest rewards; the reverse appears to be true of many contracts awarded by the Pentagon. According to Bernard D. Nossiter of the *Washington Post,* in the decade from 1957 through 1966 the aerospace firms with government contracts managed to earn consistently more than American industry as a whole, piling up $9.00 in profits for every $8.00 garnered by companies not doing business with the Pentagon. This was true in spite of the fact that the efficiency of these companies left something to be desired. As an example, during the ten years cited North American did all but 2 percent of its business with the government. It produced one highly successful plane in the mid-1950's, another system that met specifications for performance, one that was canceled, and four that broke down four times as frequently as promised. Nevertheless, the company's profits were 40 percent above those of the aerospace industry and 50 percent above the average for all industries.

ing breed of transatlantic liners.* A year later six of the American-flag transatlantic liners were laid up as well — leaving only a half-dozen smaller U.S. passenger ships plying the Atlantic, but going to Latin America rather than Europe. Included in the retired group was the "Big U" — the 51,000-ton *United States* — which holds the speed record for crossing the Atlantic, is capable of carrying a division of 15,000 troops for 10,000 miles without stopping for fuel and water, has two of almost everything (including engine rooms) in order to continue operations in case of attack. She originally cost $77 million, including $25 million from the Defense Department for the extra equipment and excess speed — which could be forty-two knots, or better than forty-eight miles an hour.

These ships have given way to the big airliners that shuttle in and out of Kennedy and Dulles and other international terminals throughout the country. When the "Big U" made her debut in 1952, fewer than 15 percent of travelers on North Atlantic routes were crossing in the straining piston planes of that decade; in 1968 jets were carrying 93 percent of the same traffic. There are now hundreds of thousands of far-ranging international travelers who have never seen the inside of an ocean vessel, and who have no concept at all that leisurely ship travel can mean a great deal more than merely getting from one place to another. The modern traveler is impatient and restless, and the rush of contemporary life has given the jet airplane its great appeal. Beyond all these factors of speed and cost, there is some question as to whether maritime liners are important any longer for the movement of troops in a future war — or certainly as important as they once were. When he was Secretary of Defense from 1961 to 1968, Robert McNamara was of the opinion that they would not be, and for that reason believed that the military no longer needed subsidies for passenger ships. He pointed out that in modern war, the airlift has taken the place of traditional troopships. In the late 1960's the first Secretary of Transportation in the President's Cabinet, Alan S. Boyd, felt the same way. He stated that the governmental subvention amounted to about $275 for every passenger carried by subsidized passenger ships in 1967–1968,

---

* The 28.5-knot *Queen Elizabeth 2* made its maiden voyage to New York in 1969. A 963-foot vessel which can carry more than 2,000 passengers, it marked the end of an era that started with the first Cunard liner, the 1135-ton *Britannia* in 1840; many think it highly unlikely that another great liner will ever be built for the Atlantic. A hundred years ago passengers on Cunard passenger ships paid $30.62 for the Atlantic voyage; in 1960 passengers below deck paid about $500 for cabins, but the deluxe suites (bedroom, sitting room, two baths) on the *Elizabeth 2* cost $7,320 for the crossing. The *Elizabeth 2* has twelve decks and nine bars catering to a broad taste-range from pubcrawlers seeking company to hideaway nooks for intimate privacy. It has two cabarets, a grill room for more expensive dining, four swimming pools, shops, banks, a hospital, a newspaper, beauty salons, and laundries. The *Elizabeth 2* is more than a ship; in the words of one of its advertising brochures it is a "resort in her own right."

and that this aid was not justified; Boyd said that the defense utility of passenger ships was minimal.

Disapproval is also heard from those who assert that these subsidies make no sense from the economic standpoint of international trade and our balance of payments. Economically, if other countries can carry our goods more cheaply, we should patronize their ships. The dollars they earn in this way can then be spent for goods in the United States — thus increasing the export of goods that we can produce more cheaply than they can. To express it in other terms, they would be exchanging services for goods. There is little question, as we have seen, that they can carry the goods much more cheaply than we can. It now costs nearly twice as much to build a ship in this country as abroad. It costs a foreign line half as much to operate its ships. Subsidizing this kind of differential is an economic waste of resources. It also happens to fly in the face of our entire foreign policy, which is devoted to the principle of increasing international trade.

VI

A Money Supply for the Corporation, the Citizen, and the Government: The Uncertainties of Paper Currency in the Nineteenth Century

URING the four decades after the Constitution went into effect the
political and the economic life of the United States was dominated
by two great thinkers and statesmen — Alexander Hamilton and Thomas
Jefferson. Hamilton's contemporary, the noted French statesman and diplomat Charles Maurice de Talleyrand, once said that he considered Napoleon, Pitt, and Hamilton the three greatest men of his epoch — and he did
not hesitate to award first place to Hamilton. To Talleyrand and many
others, Hamilton was considered a Jovian philosopher. Some believe, on
the other hand, that he was also something of a reactionary — albeit an
intelligent one. That is, for example, the point of view of Claude Bowers,
historian and Democrat, in his widely read *Jefferson and Hamilton.*

He was born in the Caribbean on one of the Leeward Islands, of an
irregular connection — without benefit of clergy — between an unpros-
perous Scottish merchant and the daughter of a French Huguenot. Federalist John Adams, who did not care for his colleague Alexander Hamilton,
would explode and call him a "bastard brat of a Scotch pedlar"; he would
also comment on an "infamous birth, a more infamous life, and a con-
temptible death." Actually the unfortunate youngster was left a miserable
orphan at the age of eleven, by reason of the death of his mother and the
irresponsible wanderings of his father. When he was seventeen a hurri-
cane gave him the opportunity to emigrate from the Caribbean. In August
1772 one of the most devastating tropical cyclones in the history of the
West Indies struck St. Croix. He wrote a long letter about it, and the
description was published in the *Royal Danish American Gazette;* that

article "blew him into history." Some of his friends were so impressed that they made it possible for him to further his education in New York at King's College (now Columbia). They did not act wholly out of charity; Hamilton contemplated the study of medicine, and it was hoped that he would return to its practice in St. Croix, where physicians were needed.

The education at King's College was cut short by the outbreak of the American Revolution, in which Hamilton hoped to shine as a combat general. Washington, however, made him his aide — and virtually Secretary of War — so he was to prove his worth during the conflict not as a soldier but as a writer and constructive thinker. The war over, Hamilton practiced law in New York, where he was able to make as much as $12,000 a year, a large income in those days. He married well (Elizabeth Schuyler of the old and powerful New York family) and his family grew; in 1782 he would write: "I have been employed for the last ten months in rocking the cradle and studying the art of fleecing my neighbors." He took some time off in the 1780's to attend the Constitutional Convention, where he spoke for a government that would have been much more conservative than the one that was adopted. He wanted the President and senators appointed for life — with the President appointing the governors of states and able to veto any act of a state legislature. His President would also possess an absolute veto over acts of Congress, and would have had more power than the King of England. Hamilton's proposals were praised by a few, but supported by none. Actually, his great service to the Constitution was *before* and *after* the Philadelphia convention. He had brought dissatisfactions at the Annapolis Convention to a head and helped to produce the deliberations at Philadelphia. Afterward, by means of the *Federalist Papers* and his oratory before the New York ratifying convention, he had a leading role in installing the national government. Out of eighty-five of the *Federalist Papers* he wrote at least fifty-one, plus three more in conjunction with James Madison. He was a natural journalist and pamphleteer — one of the fathers of the American editorial. *The Federalist* has been called, without exaggeration, one of the best public-relations jobs known to history. At the ratifying convention in New York, he delivered a five-hour speech which changed the vote on the Constitution from a negative to a positive one. Allan Nevins has described this oration as "one of the few outstanding examples in American History of the decision of a deliberative body being changed by the sheer power of sustained argument."

For six years, from 1789 to 1795, he was Secretary of the Treasury. As a Cabinet member he was to father the famous financial system that bears his name, and to anger Thomas Jefferson. The latter not only objected to his policies, in connection with which he referred to the corrupt squadrons in the Treasury — but to Hamilton's personality, particularly his egotism and his vanity.

The economic and political philosophy of Alexander Hamilton was destined to have great influence. He was the *champion* of mercantilist economic planning, and of the wealthy nonagrarian classes — merchants, financiers, industrialists. He rejected the laissez-faire ideas of Adam Smith, invoked the power of the central government to promote and direct economic forces. In this respect he owed much to the mercantilist statesmen who had passed from the scene in Europe; he also offered, for modern times, an early example of economic planning. As the champion of the wealthy nonagrarian classes he has sometimes been portrayed as a sly and sinister spokesman for property against the people. Broadus Mitchell, the economist and onetime socialist who has written a definitive biography of Hamilton, says that Hamilton was not a special pleader for the rich *per se* — that he was interested primarily in the welfare of the nation as a whole. Critics phrase it differently; they say that Hamilton believed that what was good for the rich was good for the country.

With little trust in human nature, Hamilton championed a strong central government. To achieve this end he would have abolished the states. He spoke of the "constitutional imbecility" of the Confederation, said that "as well a County may alter the laws of a State as the State those of the Confederation." Perhaps he took this strong position because of his West Indian birth and the fact that he knew no native allegiance to any of the original states; he could therefore think on continental rather than state lines. His strong central state, however, was designed to conserve not only property; it would guarantee civil liberties including freedom of the press, trial by jury, and the rights of minorities. For this reason Hamilton is properly classified as an enlightened conservative, one who opposed loyalty oaths, confiscation of property, religious tests for voting, and sedition acts. At the same time, there is no question that he wanted this strong government because he had scant faith in human nature. He was reputed to have called the people the "Great Beast"; on one occasion he said that liberty (as defined by the French Revolution) was the highest "note in the gamut of nonsense." He once proposed a "Christian Constitutional Society" to combat "our real disease, which is democracy." He thus stood in decided contrast with Jefferson, who trusted human nature more than government. Jefferson believed in rights; Hamilton put his emphasis on responsibility.

At the present time a strange situation has developed in connection with the attitude of the current Democratic and Republican parties toward Jefferson and Hamilton. A century and a half after the death of these statesmen, the Democrats praise the democratic principles of Jefferson — but have out-Hamiltoned Hamilton in the establishment of elaborate controls for the guidance of economic behavior. The Republicans praise the aristocratic principles of Hamilton — but have out-Jeffersoned Jefferson in the support of states rights. *Mutatis mutandis.*

The Hamiltonian financial system was a comprehensive and forward-looking plan consisting of four essential parts. To establish the credit of the United States, which had been at an all-time low, he wanted to assume state debts incurred in support of the Revolution, and to "fund" (that is, pay at face value plus accrued interest) this consolidated debt — national and state. He wanted to establish a new and powerful financial institution — the Bank of the United States. He was particularly interested in two special types of taxation: a protective tariff and an excise tax on whiskey. He proposed a currency reform which would place the nation on a decimal and bimetallic standard.

To establish public confidence in its fiscal stability, the United States had to make certain its obligations were paid promptly and in full. This Hamilton did through the Assumption and Funding bills. Individual states had paid off part of their Revolutionary debts, but obligations remained amounting to a bit more than $20 million. In the war against England, the Second Continental Congress and the Confederation Congress had incurred a foreign debt of almost $12 million, along with an internal obligation of something more than $40 million. What Hamilton proposed to do was to provide for the regular payment of principal and interest on a consolidated debt (state and national) that amounted to almost $80 million — a colossal sum in his day.

His first challenge was to convince the Congress that it was advisable for the federal government to assume the remaining state debts. Hamilton's brief was based on two arguments: it was economically just and it was politically wise. It was economically just because the states had contracted the debts in a common cause — as the "price of liberty." It was politically wise because it would break down the esteem in which states were held as competitors of the central government. This was elementary: if the holders of the state debts looked to states for payment they would want to add to their authority and power rather than that of the federal government.

There were powerful arguments against the Assumption Bill — chiefly from the South — on the ground that it was discriminatory against two groups: southern states and southern taxpayers. Some southern states, led by Virginia, had small debts, or had already taxed their own people to pay them off. States with heavy debts, such as Massachusetts, were overjoyed by the prospect of help from the entire nation in meeting their financial obligations. Furthermore, a large portion of southern securities, which represented remaining state debts in that region, were now in the hands of northern speculators. Because a majority of federal income came from the tariff, and because the South imported a disproportionate share of the goods that came into the country, southern taxpayers would be contributing most of the taxes and would be lining the pockets of northern financiers.

The opposition was so strong that the first time the Assumption Bill came up in the House it was defeated. A compromise followed, however, involving the location of the Capital on the Potomac. At the time the location of the Capital seemed terribly important to the South. It felt that if the agricultural interest, and republicanism, was to survive, it was mandatory that the seat of government be moved away from the commercial, money-mad atmosphere of New York City — which it called *Hamiltonople*. It wanted the center of government in the South where, exposed to the purifying influence of farmers — the federal government would drop its city ways and its city slickers, and would renew its republicanism in the simple joys of country living. So an arrangement was made between Jefferson and Hamilton, in which enough Jeffersonians voted for the Assumption Bill and enough Hamiltonians voted to place the Capital on the Potomac.

Once the Assumption Bill passed, Hamilton proposed to fund the entire consolidated debt. The argument was not over the principle that the debt should be paid in full — on this issue there was general agreement — but on the question as to *whom* the debt should be paid. The major part of the debt was no longer in the hands of the soldiers, farmers, and widows who had made the original sacrifices during the Revolution. Most of them had been forced to dispose of their holdings to creditors and speculators, at a discount as low as ten cents on the dollar, during the depression of the 1780's. Furthermore, when people found that Congress was likely to redeem the old debts at par, they sent couriers into the backwoods for the purpose of buying up securities at low rates before the original patriots heard about their potential good fortune. Who participated in this feverish, last-minute speculation? Among others — twenty-nine out of sixty-five members of Congress, three secretaries of President Washington, and Robert Morris — the "financier of the American Revolution" — who was reported to have made several million dollars out of the funding operation. Secretary of the Treasury Hamilton made nothing. He did not enter public service to make money, nor did he do so. While handling the multi-million-dollar funding operations for the national government, Hamilton actually had to resort to borrowing small sums, ranging from $20 to $100, to balance his own personal budget. But the national speculative scandal, which inaugurated the new government, made a number of people angry, particularly southerners who did not have enough capital to participate in this speculation in securities. They had put their capital in the futures of human beings — slaves. Because of the overpayment to current holders contrasted with the niggardly return to original patriots, James Madison proposed to pay the speculators and creditors only what they *paid* for the securities, plus interest during the time they held them. The original holders would therefore have received the difference, plus interest during the time of their ownership. This proposal would have added up to full pay-

ment for the original holders, but Madison's scheme was difficult, and perhaps impossible to administer because of the lack of records on security
transactions in that day. Furthermore, Hamilton was not interested in paying the original holders. So Madison's proposal was defeated, and the
Funding Bill provided payment to present holders only. Some say bitterly
that the Founding Fathers had become the Funding Fathers, but the measure did establish the credit of the United States.

Hamilton then turned to the desirability of increasing banking facilities
and the control thereof. At the time there were only three commercial
banks in the nation, and none was more than a decade old. The first,
founded in 1781, was the Bank of North America which Robert Morris
asked the Confederation Congress to charter. It continued in business until
1929. The second was Hamilton's own Bank of New York, founded in
1784 and chartered by the state of New York; he organized it but owned
only one share of stock in the institution. It has continued in business
uninterruptedly since 1784, and is incontestably the oldest banking company in the United States. Third was the Bank of Massachusetts; founded
in 1784 it took a national charter in 1865 and in 1903 was absorbed by the
First National Bank of Boston.

Banks differ from other corporations because of their principal functions. They accept deposits for safekeeping — deposits which are subject
to withdrawal by check — and they make loans. Such banking in its
simple form probably started in, of all places, the temples of ancient
Egypt, Babylonia, and Greece. They accepted gold and silver for safekeeping, and sometimes loaned it at high rates of interest. It could be that
President Roosevelt was thinking of this early practice when he used an
ecclesiastical reference in his first inaugural address in 1933; he noted that
the moneychangers had fled "from their high seats in the *temple* of civilization." Apart from temples, private banking existed by 600 B.C. and was
developed to a considerable extent by the Greeks, Romans, and Byzan-
tines. In the medieval period banking was dominated by Jews and Levan-
tines because of the prejudice of the Catholic Church against usury. In the
modern period a commentary on the Bank of England is pertinent, because Hamilton admired it and built the First Bank of the United States
(BUS) on its model.

In England the early bankers had been goldsmiths who drifted into the
business by accident, just as had the early moneychangers in the temple.
Their major occupation was not banking but making jewelry and emboss-
ing pistol handles. The goldsmiths possessed large vaults which were immune from fire and theft, and because they had what amounted to facilities for safe deposit, individuals and firms began to place valuables (gold,
silver, and gems) in their vaults. These had capital value, and the goldsmiths made profits on the capital in their care (for which they paid no
interest since they were performing a service for the owners) by lending

it at astronomical rates of interest, sometimes as high as 33⅓ percent. Unlike modern banks the goldsmiths lent deposits *without* the consent of the depositors. Everything went well, and the goldsmiths prospered, if their clients paid up. If several clients did not do so, the goldsmiths went bankrupt and the depositors were surprised to find that the safekeeping they sought had been illusory. This temporary expedient for providing credit was obviously unsatisfactory, and in 1694 the Bank of England — a *private* company in spite of its national name — came into being. Its fiscal operations differed from those of the goldsmiths in the following significant respects:

On the *monetary* side it issued bank notes, i.e., currency as we know it today, "payable to the bearer on demand." This was a credit currency, like our Federal Reserve notes. Its charter enabled the Bank of England to issue such currency to a maximum equal to the amount of its capital, which was originally a bit more than a million pounds. On the *governmental* side, in return for a monopoly on deposits *by* the government, it provided special banking services for the British government. The bank provided a safe depository for governmental funds, made loans to the government, and, in time, protected the value of the pound through various banking operations. On the *commercial* side it provided needed and sound banking facilities for business.

Throughout most of its history the Bank of England functioned as both a private and a public operation, just as the BUS did; we shall see that Hamilton wanted the BUS to provide the same services — commercial, monetary, and governmental. As a private bank in the eighteenth and nineteenth centuries the Bank of England provided great impetus to British commercial and industrial expansion. This prevailed from 1694 to 1945, when it was nationalized by a Labor government. Since that time the bank has dropped its private business.

On the basis of Hamilton's proposal Congress chartered the first Bank of the United States in 1791. The charter was to run for twenty years, and the capital of the bank was to be $10 million — one-fifth of it owned by the federal government, which also appointed one-fifth of the board of directors. The stock was paid for in specie (one-fourth) and government bonds (three-fourths); this provision was necessary because in 1791 there wasn't $10 million in specie in the United States. The stock was actually subscribed for within two hours after the books were opened; this optimism was justified, because throughout its twenty-year operation the stock realized 8½ percent on the investment. The BUS could issue paper money, limited in amount to the par value of its capital stock ($10 million) and redeemable in practice in specie; Hamilton wanted a sound currency which would check the irredeemable issues of currency by state banks. The institution would act as a fiscal agent for the national government, serving as a depository for government funds and lending the government money — more than $13.5 million over the twenty-year period.

Because of this governmental connection the bank had to make reports to the Secretary of the Treasury, who was authorized to inspect its operations at any time.

The first great debate over the constitutionality of acts of Congress occurred over the bill chartering the First Bank of the United States. "Strict constructionist" Thomas Jefferson, who came from an agrarian section of the country, did not want the national bank and said it was unconstitutional because there was no specific authorization for it in the Constitution. "Loose constructionist" Alexander Hamilton, who represented the commercial interests of the nation, found a number of clauses, including the famous "elastic" one, which justified the action of Congress in chartering the bank. To Hamilton, the Constitution was an open door; to Jefferson and Madison, it was one that had been shut. The debate was high-flown and political; the basic issues, largely unmentioned, were really economic.

Hamilton wanted to establish the public credit and a central bank; he was also interested in two special types of taxation. The first was a protective tariff. In 1791 he made a statement to Congress which is known as the *Report on Manufactures*. In this document he presented his views on the status of American manufactures at that time, and advocated a protective tariff on those products which would "tend to render the United States independent of foreign nations, for military and other essential supplies." This was the doctrine of economic self-sufficiency supported in later years by ardent nationalists in all countries — including Clay and Calhoun in our own. In Hamilton's day, however, the prevailing sentiment accorded with the laissez-faire philosophy of Adam Smith, and the protectionist goals were not achieved until after Hamilton was dead.

Hamilton did achieve the second special levy in which he was interested — the excise tax on whiskey. This was a unique and unusual tax simply because, in the period before the Civil War, the federal government obtained its revenue from customs duties. In due course, some income came in from the sale of public lands, and in the first twenty-five years of our history there were a very few internal revenue taxes — of which the excise on whiskey was the first.

Because the Indian problem in the West prevented public land sales while Hamilton was in the Cabinet, his only initial source of income was from customs duties. In 1790 he found that estimated income from customs duties would fall short of meeting expenditures by almost $1 million. To raise the additional income he proposed, and Congress enacted, the excise tax of 25¢ a gallon on domestic whiskey. In those days, which some regard as halcyon and happy, the market price of whiskey was about 50¢ a gallon in the West and a dollar a gallon in the East. The excise on whiskey, amouting to approximately 50 percent of the western value of the product, was a high one.

Many wondered why the Secretary of the Treasury happened to select whiskey for the dubious honor of taxation. Hamilton reasoned that there would be less opposition to the excise tax on whiskey because it was a hidden levy. The tax was collected at the source, the stills, from a relatively few producers; it would therefore have the effect of an indirect tax which would not be recognized by the consumer who actually paid it in the form of a higher price. As it turned out, Hamilton was right as far as opposition from most consumers in the nation was involved. He was gloriously wrong in regard to opposition from the distillers and consumers in the five western counties of Pennsylvania.

Politically, Hamilton had no intention of taxing the well-born and propertied elements in the North and East, whose support he wanted for the new government, and who belonged to the Federalist party which he headed. He once said that he was opposed to taxes on profits or capital, which he regarded as contrary to the "genius of liberty" and the "maxims of industry." He was not averse to levying a tax on farmers in the West whom he regarded as stubborn Republicans and who, in his judgment, should be shown the strong arm of the law — that is, that the federal government could not only levy a tax, but collect it by force if necessary. It is not surprising that western Republicans developed the argument, as Sam Adams had in 1773, that this was just a beginning. They claimed that Congress would next extend the excise to plows at one dollar each, and after that to children at the rate of fifteen shillings for the birth of every boy and ten for each girl. In actual fact, in 1794 Hamilton did propose and get additional excises. He was then faced with the prospect of another deficit as a result of the Indian War and the naval armament program that had been adopted by Congress. He therefore proposed stamp taxes, and excises on carriages, snuff, loaf sugar, and auction sales. The stamp tax (shades of 1765!) was rejected by Congress, but the other excises were enacted over the vehement opposition of many southern members. If any additional evidence was needed for Hamilton's unique ability to infuriate Virginians, the carriage tax provided it. Although they talked like democrats, the Virginia planters rode like aristocrats in their carriages, many of the latter emblazoned with coats of arms. The excise tax on whiskey had appeared to be a levy on the poor; to Virginians the carriage tax was "soak-the-rich" legislation especially aimed at the southern gentry.

Hamilton's third purpose was moral — to discourage the consumption of strong drink. There was little question about the prevalence of overindulgence. One observer in the West reported: "An election in Kentucky lasts three days, and during that period whisky and apple toddy flow through our cities and villages like the Euphrates through ancient Babylon. . . . I turned away a confirmed believer in the doctrine of total depravity."

Whatever Hamilton's motives for the excise the distillers in the West were furious, particularly in the five western counties of Pennsylvania, a region that was proud to possess one-fourth of the 1,200 distilleries in the country. The West used whiskey to maintain its balance of trade, and for consumption. Whiskey was a commodity that was essential in the West's balance of payments with the East. The West required certain essentials from the East, such as salt, sugar, cloth, and iron products. For payment the West had grain, but on the narrow trails of that day a packhorse could carry only four bushels of rye grain over the mountains. The same packhorse could carry twenty-four bushels of rye in the form of whiskey, and the whiskey also commanded a higher price. For that reason "corn juice" from earliest times was the product traded for cash or goods. Albert Gallatin, a western Pennsylvania farmer who was to become Jefferson's Secretary of the Treasury, defended the frontiersmen as the Whiskey Rebellion erupted: "We have no means of bringing the produce of our lands to sale either in grain or in meal. We are therefore distillers through necessity, not choice, that we may comprehend the greatest value in the smallest size and weight." In this connection it is interesting to note that New Englanders, who were largely responsible for the passage of the excise tax, had been annoyed in the colonial period when England had interfered with their triangular trade in rum, with which they made up their adverse balance of trade with England.

The West also consumed a large part of the product of the stills. Bernard De Voto once claimed that "our forefathers invented self-government, the Constitution, and bourbon." Whether this is true or not, it was estimated that half of the farmers of western Pennsylvania had a still "out back" which they tended with loving care. In the country districts travelers beheld on every side smoke curling from the smokehouses, often a cheering sight to the parched and the footsore. Many found the taste pleasant, and the effect agreeable. Extravagant claims were made. It was said that whiskey kept the population cool in summer, and that in the winter months it was the old settler's equivalent of central heating. In western Pennsylvania the salaries of ministers were sometimes paid in "Monongahela Rye" — a liquid that could hardly be described as sacramental, although it may have conveyed some idea of hellfire.

The Republicans in the West regarded opposition to the excise on whiskey as a crusade of the Common People against eastern stock-jobbers, bank directors, and speculators. Most of the population in western Pennsylvania was Scotch-Irish; one conviction this group had brought with it to America was an abiding hatred of the British government and its excise laws, plus a tradition of resistance to all who attempted to enforce those laws. The new federal government in Philadelphia did not find them any more tractable than had George III. As John C. Miller has pointed out, they figured that if they succeeded in their struggle against the excise, it would be another victory by inoffensive farmers over the "knights of the funding system — headed by Lord Hamilton." Their insurrection started with protest meetings. Then vigilantes appeared and collectors were manhandled; as an example, the collector who represented Alexander Hamilton in Allegheny County was waylaid by sixteen men who cut off his hair, administered tar and feathers, and stole his horse. The opposition reached high tide in August 1794 when 7,000 militia gathered under arms and threatened to burn nearby Pittsburgh — in order to show their strength.

By this time the federal courts were unable to function. The Constitution contains a clause, reminiscent of Shays' Rebellion, empowering the national government to call out the militia to "execute the laws of the Union, suppress insurrections, and repel invasions." President Washington therefore called up 15,000 militia from neighboring states, almost as many soldiers as there were in the combined Franco-American force at Yorktown.

This large-scale punitive expedition moved west in glorious autumn weather, raiding chicken coops and consuming prodigious quantities of the commodity which lay at the heart of the controversy. Some of the inhabitants of the region were lashed, and a few were killed, largely by accident. In late November, finding no organized opposition, the army returned to the East. A few prisoners were carried back to Philadelphia, where they were paraded through the streets, with "Insurrection" labels on their caps. It was an odd Federalist version of a Roman triumph. As such it was expensive; the "army" cost a million and a half dollars, three times as much as all the money actually collected from the excise tax on whiskey. Ultimately thirty men were indicted for treason; two were sentenced to death, but President Washington had the good sense to issue pardons, thus depriving them of the dubious honor of becoming martyrs. The famous Whiskey Rebellion was over.

Hamilton had established the national credit, the Bank of the United States, and the excise tax; he also engineered a reform of the currency which placed the nation on a decimal and bimetallic standard. This was done in the Currency, or Mint, Act of 1792 which put the decimal system of coinage into practice, established the legal weight (and therefore the value) of U.S. dollars in both gold and silver, established the free and unlimited coinage of gold and silver into dollars, established a bimetallic standard at a ratio of 15 to 1, and established the first U.S. mint at Philadelphia.

Jefferson and the Confederation government had proclaimed the decimal system of coinage in theory; it was Hamilton who put it into practice. He had the Treasury weigh a random assortment of Spanish dollars and found that the average pure silver content was 371¼ grains. This weight was therefore established for the prospective American dollar in silver and remains the same today. Hamilton decided that the weight of the gold dollar should be one-fifteenth as much, or 24¾ grains. In this fashion the American dollar was finally separated from its Spanish forerunner. In the early days of the Republic there was great interest among the people over the question as to whether the dollar should carry the image of Washington or the Goddess of Liberty. The Goddess won. English coins bore the king's image, and the American populace did not wish to be reminded of the sovereign of the past or to allow the first citizen to take his place. They preferred the symbol of liberty, and this attitude persisted for more than a century. A change occurred in 1909, the centennial of Lincoln's birth, when a one-cent piece adorned with Lincoln's head — the famous Lincoln penny — was eagerly accepted. Since then commemorative coins have been engraved with the figures of great men — Franklin, Washington, Hamilton, Jefferson, Franklin Roosevelt, Kennedy — but living persons have never received the honor.

Unfortunately Hamilton's guess, on a workable bimetallic ratio, was in error. At 15 to 1 silver was overvalued and gold was undervalued — the market price of 24¾ grains was greater than a dollar, with the result that gold bullion was sold commercially and none appeared at the Treasury for coinage into dollars. Silver did appear for coinage, but the silver dollar experienced difficulties beyond our control. Spanish dollars had a slightly greater value in international exchange, with the result that U.S. silver dollars were taken on a large scale to the Spanish West Indies and there exchanged for Spanish dollars. In 1806 Jefferson recognized a practical situation by closing the Philadelphia mint; from that point until 1836 (when the ratio was changed to 16 to 1) neither silver nor gold dollars were coined. Currency needs were supplied for three decades (1806–1836) through paper money, coins of small denomination, and foreign coins.

Through this brilliantly far-reaching and ingenious financial system Hamilton had achieved almost all of his basic purposes. The fact that he had established the credit of the United States was indicated not only by domestic demand for his bonds — but by a comparable desire from abroad. This foreign demand was so great that it became the means of drawing from Europe large sums of money which were added to the active capital of the United States. This was accentuated by the outbreak of the French Revolution, during which large amounts of European capital took flight. By the close of 1794, in fact, U.S. bonds had the highest credit rating in Europe; some U.S. government securities were selling at 10 percent above par. By the middle of 1795 foreigners held more than $20 million in the U.S. domestic debt, and by 1801 their holdings had increased to $33 million. It is no wonder that Hamilton would say that a national debt, if it was not excessive, "will be unto us a national blessing." He added that the creation of a debt should always be accompanied with the means of extinguishing it — a point of view somewhat at variance from that held today. He felt that if the debt was too large to be liquidated, it would lead to "great and convulsive revolutions of empire."

He had also provided the nation's business with currency and credit. He accomplished this by transforming a well-nigh worthless paper — public securities — into fluid capital to be invested in commerce, manufacturing, and the development of western lands. Prior to Hamilton's time there had been a depressing dearth of fluid capital; as late as 1800 the amount of metallic money in circulation in the United States was estimated at about three dollars per capita — clearly insufficient for the monetary needs of the nation. Furthermore, if government bonds did not provide all the capital needed for business enterprise, the deficiency could be remedied by the valuable stock and the currency of the BUS. At last American business enterprise, which had been hamstrung by lack of currency and credit, was to be provided abundantly with both. At the same time it would also have been protected against foreign competition by a high tariff, if Hamilton had achieved all of his objectives.

He had also gained the support for the federal government of a powerful and propertied element, which was delighted with the prospects. One of Hamilton's basic objectives was to create a governing class. In his philosophy, politics and economics were inextricably intertwined. In Leland Baldwin's acute observation, he used his political control to promote an economic system, and he used his economic system to strengthen and perpetuate his political system. Hamilton's governing and economic elite happened to consist largely of manufacturers, merchants, and financiers. This led to inevitable opposition from the farmers of the West and the planters of the South, resulting in the formation of the first political parties in the United States. They were the Federalist, supporting Hamilton, with the Democratic-Republican in opposition. The planters and farmers were peeved in part because they assumed that they would pay most of the taxes to support Hamilton's financial system — through the tariff and the excise tax. Southern planters had reason to be downright jealous because — having invested their capital in land and slaves — they had no funds for investment in the good and immediate profits provided by the Hamiltonian financial system. Hamilton also wanted to strengthen the national government instead of the states. This he certainly accomplished by means of the assumption of state debts, the charter of the Bank of the United States, and the vindication — however silly and tragic and humorous — of federal authority in the Whiskey Rebellion.

The presidential election of 1800 is a prime example of a revolution at the polls, a victory by ballots rather than bullets. The Federalist party of Washington and Hamilton and John Adams went out of office, never to return; the Democratic-Republicans came into power for a quarter of a century (1801–1825) under the Virginia dynasty of Jefferson, Madison, and Monroe. Financial policy during this period was dominated by two statesmen: Jefferson, and his Secretary of the Treasury, Albert Gallatin.

Thomas Jefferson was the antithesis of Alexander Hamilton in both economics and politics. Jefferson advocated laissez-faire and championed agriculture. He distrusted the arts of commerce and industry; to him merchants, the working class, and speculators were corrupt — and cities were pestilential. For the industrial proletariat, who served the masters of commerce and industry, he had a particular dislike — once going so far as to say that the mobs of great cities were sores on the body politic, panders of vice, makers of revolution. He said that the development of urban populations was foolish because "when we pile upon one another in cities, we shall become corrupt as in Europe and go to eating one another as they do there." Jefferson placed his faith in the farmer; he believed sincerely that the only secure base for the Republic was a body of free landowning farmers looking to the sun in heaven and the labor of their own hands for their support and their independence. He was inclined to agree with Franklin, who once said that nations could acquire wealth in three ways: by war, which was cheating; by commerce, which was usually by cheating; and by agriculture. Jefferson once stated that the greatest service that could be rendered to any country was to add a useful plant to its culture. He put his advice into practice by importing olive trees from France and rice from Africa, for experimental planting in South Carolina and Georgia.

Industrial capitalism has rendered Jefferson's agrarian philosophy impractical in the era in which we now live, when at least four-fifths of the population is divorced from the soil. We now live in a Hamiltonian world, but it is the Jeffersonian one for which we yearn. It is from Jefferson's philosophy that there still evolves the myth of the honest and barefoot farmer boy, of the rugged and straight-talking backwoodsman, and of the appealing innocence and goodness of the cowboy. To this day a presidential candidate who cannot find some part of the cowbarn upon which to lean, risks the solid distrust of the American electorate. Thomas Lask of the *New York Times* has pointed out the modern paradox of

> Jefferson, who represents even today the nostalgic hankering of most Americans for pastoral acres and a handicraft way of life. The agrarian society and the sturdy individual in it — the more they recede in time, the more sanctified they appear in memory. Men live in twenty-story buildings and spend the weekend battling their way through coagulated masses of traffic, yet they yearn for the old ice-cream churn and random board floors. We see this attitude in its most classical form in the late Henry Ford, who did as much as any man to change our trails from dirt to concrete, but who hungered for log cabins and the simplicities of rural existence.

Politically Jefferson distrusted a strong central government and placed great trust in the people. He believed in as little government as possible, put his faith in militia rather than standing armies, thought regimes should be changed frequently. He also had an abiding faith that a people enlightened by free education could govern themselves, under democratic institutions, better than under any other system. He realized that in a democracy, the electorate must be educated; he said, "If a nation expects to be ignorant *and* free, . . . it expects what never was and never will be." In order to enlighten people he advocated public school systems and libraries, universities of higher learning, and newspapers (this caused Richard Hofstadter to observe that while Jefferson was planning school systems, Hamilton was scheming how to get children to work in factories). Jefferson's attitude toward newspapers shows both his belief in their important role in education and his own tolerance. During his lifetime he was accused in print of being an atheist, of having a mulatto house servant as his mistress, of having tried to seduce a friend's wife, of padding his expense account while he was minister in Paris, of selling into slavery children he had sired by his slaves. Jefferson once wrote, rather hopelessly, of his desire to escape public notice because he found "the pain of a little censure, even when it is unfounded, is more acute than the pleasure of much praise." Because of these canards, he once suggested that editors might do well to divide their papers into sections headed: Truths, Probabilities, Possibilities, Lies. Despite the attacks directed at him, Jefferson never wavered in his defense of the press. Later he would say, "Were it left to me to decide whether we should have a government without newspapers, or newspapers without a government, I should not hesitate a moment to prefer the latter."

Albert Gallatin, whose tenure as Secretary of the Treasury from 1801 to 1813 was longer than that of any other holder of the position, was born in Geneva, Switzerland. His family was prominent in the Duchy of Savoy, and gave him a splendid education. He was influenced by the writing of Jean Jacques Rousseau, who counseled that intellectuals should seek freedom from the conventions of civilization in a romantic return to nature. The young Swiss radical was so impressed with this advice that he ran away to America — after turning down with indignation a colonelcy which his family offered to get for him with the Hessian soldiers who were also coming to the New World — in the service of George III. Arriving in America in 1780, he enlisted in the Continental Army, and after the war taught French for a brief period at Harvard. He then went to Philadelphia where he bought, at the height of the land craze, vast tracts of land in southwestern Pennsylvania. Because of troubles with the Indians and the mountainous character of the terrain, Gallatin's venture was a failure.

Despite Gallatin's disappointments as a land speculator he was a great success as politician, financier, and liberal devotee of Thomas Jefferson.

He sat in the state legislature of Pennsylvania, where he not only introduced important financial reforms but in the Jeffersonian tradition worked to reform the penal code, establish a statewide system of public education, and abolish slavery. When Jefferson came to the Presidency in 1801 there was no other man in the Democratic-Republican party to dispute Gallatin's eminence in the field of finance, and he was no stranger to federal politics because he had represented Pennsylvania in the national House of Representatives for three terms prior to 1801. After twelve years in the Treasury he resigned in 1813 to become a prominent member of the peace commission which brought the War of 1812 to a close with the Treaty of Ghent — which historian Henry Adams said was the "special and peculiar triumph of Mr. Gallatin." He continued in diplomatic service for more than a decade after the war, serving as U.S. minister in both France and England. Associated with John Jacob Astor, in the 1830's he was president of the National Bank of New York, and used his great influence in banking circles to hasten return to specie payments after the panic of 1837.

It is interesting to compare the financial policies of Gallatin and Hamilton, not only because both were strong men with mature points of view but also because such a comparison reveals the fundamental differences between the Federalist policies represented by Hamilton — and the Jeffersonian Republican policies exemplified by Gallatin. The contrast is evident on the national debt, the excise taxes, and the tariff; there was agreement on the desirability of a Bank of the United States, which was strongly supported by both statesmen.

On the debt Hamilton had said, "A public debt, if it is not excessive, will be to us a national blessing." Jefferson disagreed; he characterized the debt, which Hamilton had established through the Assumption and Funding bills, as a "swindling futurity on a large scale . . . the most potent source of all political evils and the most active center of every social corruption." Gallatin felt the same way; he wanted a surplus rather than a debt — a surplus out of which a revolving fund would be created for low-interest loans to American manufacturers, and from which would come federal support for internal improvements — including a government turnpike from Maine to Georgia. He therefore instituted a policy which would have extinguished the debt ($80 million in 1801) by 1817; this required $7 million a year, three-quarters of his budget, for the payment of interest and principal. His calculations were wrecked by unforeseen developments; the purchase of Louisiana and the war against the Barbary pirates were expensive, and the embargo policy from 1807 on reduced the revenue from the tariff. Even so, he had reduced the debt to $45 million by 1811. The War of 1812, of course, was a body blow to his plans, sent the debt up to $123 million, and postponed its extinction (for twenty years) until the time of Andrew Jackson.

It is understandable that Gallatin and Jefferson would be opposed to Hamiltonian excise taxes, such as the ones on whiskey and carriages, that seemed to be aimed at Pennsylvanians and Virginians. All were repealed but, ironically, Gallatin was compelled to reintroduce internal revenue taxes temporarily in order to finance the War of 1812. He was also much opposed to the protective tariff which Hamilton wanted but did not get. His antagonism to a protective levy was so great that he once described himself as "the first free trader in the United States."

In 1791 when the first Bank of the United States was chartered, the Federalists, a moneyed minority of the population, were in control of the government and there were three banks in operation. In 1811 (when the first BUS was allowed to expire) the Federalist party had disintegrated, the Jeffersonians had long been in power, and banks — to which the Jeffersonians were traditionally opposed — had multiplied from three to ninety. In the next five years the number increased to nearly 250, and by 1820 it exceeded 300, an increase of more than a hundredfold in the first thirty years of the federal union. As Bray Hammond (the banker-historian who won a Pulitzer Prize in 1958 for his *Banks and Politics in America from the Revolution to the Civil War*) points out, it is difficult to imagine how banking could have propagated more under its alleged sponsors (the Federalists) than it actually did under its putative enemies (the Democratic-Republicans). This development indicated that business was becoming democratic, and was no longer controlled by a select aristocracy. It also reflected a close connection between banks and politics — simply because financial institutions had to go to legislatures to acquire their charters. In the United States, banks can be chartered by two sovereign agencies — federal and state. In the pre–Civil War period all new banks (except two) were chartered by states, and politics was very much involved.

A large segment of the population was unfriendly to banks — either because they were newfangled institutions or because some opponents had heard of the ill-fated South Sea Bubble. Federalist John Adams, hardly agreeing with Federalist Alexander Hamilton, wrote that "every dollar of a bank bill that is issued beyond the quantity of gold and silver in the vaults represents nothing and is therefore a cheat upon somebody." Republican Thomas Jefferson, scarcely in accord with Republican Albert Gallatin, in 1813 demonstrated with logarithms that the country could not afford banks; he stated that their object was "to enrich swindlers at the expense of the honest and industrious part of the nation." When Jefferson found that he could not stem the tide, he felt that if there *had* to be banks they should be Republican ones! Because of this opposition and suspicion, banks were sometimes chartered by guile and subterfuge. In 1799 Republican Aaron Burr took advantage of the pestilence of yellow fever in New

York to do so. To avoid a repetition of this disaster the city was desirous of a plentiful supply of fresh water; Burr's Manhattan Company was set up to supply it — along with the supposedly minor privilege of engaging in "moneyed transactions." In short order the supply of money through banking channels assumed much greater importance than making water available through the company's wooden mains. In time the Bank of Manhattan would become the oldest banking institution in the nation, until it was recently merged with Chase National — to form the second-largest commercial bank (in deposits) in the United States. The same stratagem was employed in Kentucky where a company wanted to engage in banking but was afraid that the legislature would never charter such an institution. It therefore began its operations as the Kentucky Insurance Company, which was supposed to insure boats and cargoes, but also had the privilege of engaging in a profitable discount business. In this connection it soon became a bank in everything but name — with the strong support of Henry Clay; its first year's dividend was almost 20 percent!

Because of the importance of political connections, many bankers also held political office. The most important one who did not — although he voted as a Republican — was the merchant, financier, and philanthropist Stephen Girard (1750–1831). He was born in France, went to sea as a cabin boy at fourteen, and before he was twenty-five was licensed as a captain, master, and pilot. At one time or another he was the owner of eighteen vessels, the finest of which he named after the philosophers of his native France: *Montesquieu, Rousseau, Voltaire.* For him commerce presented great speculative possibilities, and he made the most of them, becoming a very rich man. He was also a supporter of the first BUS, and when it was forced to close in 1811 he bought its building and other assets, and under a charter from the state of Pennsylvania opened the Bank of Stephen Girard — which developed a close relationship with Baring Brothers in England.

Blind in one eye, rude in manner, unhappily married (his wife became deranged and was placed in an institution), a "loner" — Girard was nonetheless a prime example of the Protestant ethic. He never tired of work and study, and once said, "To rest is to rust." He also stated, "If I thought I was to die tomorrow, I should nevertheless plant a tree today." At death, his fortune was the largest in America, amounting to $7.5 million, almost all of which he left to public benefactions. The largest portion was held in trust for the education of poor white orphan boys, and this discrimination by skin color — in what became Girard College — became a source of bitter controversy a century later.

If a bank expects to show a profit, it makes most of its loans in the form of its own credit. During our history banks have employed two methods of loaning credit: by printing and loaning bank notes, and by granting customers deposits against which the borrower can write checks. The bank-note method was developed first, and was prevalent during most of the pre–Civil War period.

These early bank notes were supposed to be redeemable in specie, but due to its chronic shortage in this country well into the 1840's, most state banks issued paper currency which was not redeemable. On occasion, specie would be accumulated and kept in the vaults long enough to satisfy the legal requirements of the state for formal inspection, after which it would be promptly withdrawn, to serve in a similar capacity in another institution. Bank examiners in Michigan once complained about the specie which was moving with rapidity from bank to bank — just ahead of their arrival! They began to recognize some of the individual coins in the collection, and reported: "Gold and silver flew around the country with the celerity of magic; its sound was heard in the depths of the forest, yet like the wind, one knew not whence it came or whither it was going."

The result was a plethora of irredeemable, or wildcat, paper money; the term "wildcat" arose from the practice of locating redemption offices, where paper could be redeemed in gold, in inaccessible spots in the depth of the forest where there were few habitations, but plenty of wildcats. There were also "saddlebag banks"; their officers loved the open road. Sometimes these banks began with very little or no investment on the part of the stockholders. In extreme form, lenient states permitted individuals to open banks with no financial risk to themselves. If the venture proved successful, the stock could be paid for out of earnings; if the bank failed, someone else lost the money. One banker said:

> Well, I didn't have much else to do and so I rented an empty store building and painted "bank" on the window. The first day I was open for business a man came in and deposited one hundred dollars. The second day another deposited two hundred fifty dollars, and so along about the third day I got confidence enough in the bank to put in a hundred myself.

In Kirtland, Ohio, Mormon Joseph Smith needed money to pay his debts, organized the Kirtland Safety Society Bank, and when the Ohio legislature refused to charter it went right ahead with a new name — the Kirtland Safety Society Anti-Banking Company. Smith ordered a quantity of crisp new bills from engravers in New York and Philadelphia and paid off the Mormon debts with alleged bank notes that cost him no more than the cost of printing. When creditors began to worry, Smith showed them his reserves — rows of boxes, glistening with silver coin and marked with the sign of $1,000. All suspicion was temporarily allayed. The holders of the bank notes did not know that under the bright layer of silver was a box full of sand, gravel, and scrap iron. Ultimately the bank failed, and Smith fled to Illinois. In all fairness it must be noted that there were Protestant, Catholic, and agnostic bankers who followed the same practices.

Such a situation was obviously very hard on merchants who did not know the value of bank notes from institutions far removed in distance from their places of business. Were the notes worth their face value? If not, how much should the discount be, without losing a sale? To help these harassed businessmen, a number of publications appeared at two dollars a year, generally called *Bank Note Detectors*. They listed the names and locations of all the banks in the United States, stating the current discount on their notes in Philadelphia — then the financial center of the nation. These publications also presented lists of broken banks, and of all counterfeit notes known to be in circulation. By consulting them a merchant might have a tentative idea of the value of the numerous state bank notes presented for payment.

Because of these developments it is not surprising that the First Bank of the United States was not renewed when its initial charter expired in 1811. The opposition came from Democratic-Republicans, nativists, and from state banks. Because the bank had been chartered by the Federalists and a majority of its directors belonged to that party, it is not surprising that many Democratic-Republicans were opposed to the recharter. The nativists argued that the bank was under foreign control. Actually in 1811 a large portion of the stock of the BUS was owned in England; it had not been originally subscribed by Englishmen, but had been remitted there in payment of debt. Although this large block of stock was held abroad, the danger of foreign control was nonexistent because foreign stockholders had no vote. But prejudice on the part of Democratic-Republicans was very strong against Britain, particularly in 1811, and for that reason the BUS was called a British bank and its potential baleful influence in this country was dreaded. The opposition from state banks was obvious because they hoped to acquire the deposits of the national government (then the monopoly of the BUS), and they wanted to stop the central bank from requiring payment of their bank notes in specie — as the central bank frequently did. Because of this situation it is not surprising that the vote on recharter was close. In the House the recharter bill lost by one vote. In the Senate the tally resulted in a tie (17 to 17). The deadlock was broken by the decisive vote of Vice-President Clinton against the bank.

Within a short time it was apparent that Clinton's vote was a monumental blunder. The absence of the BUS was responsible for additional military costs in the War of 1812 and for inflation. The national government found the war more expensive in two ways: receipts from taxes and receipts from loans. State bank notes could not be circulated beyond a limited geographical area except at a discount; the federal Treasury therefore suffered a loss of purchasing power whenever governmental receipts from taxes had to be spent outside the region in which they were collected, which was frequently the case. The national government also suffered on receipts from loans. State banks bought large amounts of national bond issues, paying for them in state bank notes at face value; these were discounted when the national government spent them on military supplies. If the government in Washington lost, so did the general public. The securities bought by the banks from the national government were used as a basis for further issues of state bank notes, flooding the country with both paper money and inflated prices. As a result of this experience it is not surprising that the second BUS was chartered in 1816. It was similar to the first bank in that its headquarters was in Philadelphia, it was chartered for twenty years, and it had the same purposes, with the national government owning one-fifth of the stock and appointing one-fifth of the board of directors. The capitalization of the second BUS was larger — $35 million instead of $10 million. In its two decades (1816–1836) the second BUS was to be attacked first by state governments and later by President Jackson. Chief Justice John Marshall managed to save the institution from the onslaught by the states but no one was able to protect it from the President sometimes called "King Andrew I."

The Second Bank had three presidents: Captain William Jones from 1816 to 1819, Langdon Cheves from 1819 to 1822, and Nicholas Biddle from 1823 to 1836. Unfortunately, the institution was badly mismanaged in its first three years. Jones was a minor and unfortunate merchant and politician who was made president of the bank although he had recently gone through bankruptcy. Under his administration the bank fell into the hands of a so-called "Baltimore Conspiracy." This cabal systematically engrossed voting power; one Baltimore director registered 1,172 shares of stock in 1,172 different names, with himself as attorney voting them all. Its members borrowed from the bank to purchase their own stock, and made loans, mostly to themselves, with no collateral of any kind. One of the worst offenders was James McCulloch, the cashier of the bank at its branch (one of twenty-five) in Baltimore, who had no means of his own but lent himself more than half a million dollars. Bray Hammond says that the dealings of this Baltimore group began as speculations, grew into frauds, and ultimately cost the bank a net loss of more than a million and a half dollars. Their chicanery, Nicholas Biddle commented, "created that solecism — a monied institution governed by those who had no money; it reduced the Bank at Philadelphia to a mere colony of the Baltimore adventurers." From this debacle the bank was saved, in the nick of time, by Cheves and Biddle. Cheves, who was its president from 1819 to 1822, was an able South Carolinian who had been Speaker of the House of Representatives. He took the presidency with some reluctance; five years before, he had refused the position of Secretary of the Treasury when it was relinquished by Gallatin, and in 1819 Monroe was ready to appoint him to the Supreme Court. When he went to Philadelphia to take over the BUS he was already dissatisfied with the want of talent in the bank, but he did not realize how little it really had.

During the period of financial reorganization after the War of 1812 state banks took advantage of popular feeling against the Second BUS to encourage legislation restricting its operations. Two states in particular were involved: Maryland and Ohio. A law in Maryland provided that all banks not chartered by the state were required to comply with restrictions on their note issues (which would drive them out of business), or pay an annual tax of $15,000. The branch of the BUS in Baltimore ignored the law on the ground that it was unconstitutional. Maryland therefore sued the cashier of the BUS, James W. McCulloch. It is ironical that when the case reached the Supreme Court, with the bank suing for its legality, it was almost bankrupt; in actual fact, a week after the Supreme Court saved the bank, McCulloch was exposed as an embezzler de luxe. This did not make John Marshall's decision very popular; at the moment the bank had barely gotten rid of Captain Jones, and Langdon Cheves had not yet taken charge.

The decision in *McCulloch* v. *Maryland* (1819) is one of the most important handed down by the Supreme Court, and the counsel on opposing sides were the greatest lawyers in the land. Maryland was represented by its attorney general for thirty-one years, Luther Martin. A graduate of Princeton, a delegate to the Constitutional Convention, eminent as a lawyer, an opponent of slavery, generous to his friends — he was his own worst enemy. He was ultimately ruined by strong drink and extravagance, and earned the unfortunate nickname of "Brandy Bottle" Martin. The bank was represented by three prominent lawyers: William Pinkney, William Wirt, and Daniel Webster. Pinkney, eminent both as diplomat and lawyer, was considered the most talented advocate of his time in spite of personal affectations and the flamboyant character of his oratory. He appeared in seventy-two cases before the Supreme Court, and reached the heights in *McCulloch* v. *Maryland*, when he spoke in Hamiltonian terms for three solid days. William Wirt was U.S. Attorney General for twelve years (1817–1829), and was the first holder of that office to organize its work. In 1832 he would be an unwilling candidate of the Anti-Masonic party for the Presidency. Webster was a rising young lawyer who would achieve great prominence in later years.

The decision of the court, delivered by John Marshall, was unanimous. Marshall was born on the frontier, one of a family of seventeen children. Appointed by fellow-Federalist President John Adams in the waning days of his administration, Marshall served on the Supreme Court for more than three decades — thirty days under the Federalists and thirty-four years under the Jeffersonian Republicans and their successors. He actually knew little law; he *did* know what he wanted and he worked very hard. Of 1,106 decisions written during his thirty-four years he wrote an incredible 519, almost half (a modern Chief Justice does well if he writes one in eight decisions). Throughout his life Marshall stood for three concepts, all of which were Hamiltonian: that the federal government should prevail over the states, that business contracts were sacred, and that the judiciary — particularly when the Jeffersonians were in control of the executive and legislative branches — should be the supreme branch of the federal government. It can be argued that Marshall did more than Hamilton himself to engraft the Hamiltonian concept upon the American political system. The Federalists left national office in 1801 never to return, but for three decades (as Thomas A. Bailey observes so well) "the ghost of Alexander Hamilton spoke through the lanky, black-robed judge." As a shaper of the Constitution in the direction of a more potent central government, Marshall ranks as the foremost of the "Moulding Fathers." In *McCulloch* v. *Maryland* he made two main points. The first was that the BUS was constitutional. Here he upheld the Hamiltonian doctrine of implied powers by saying, "Let the end be legitimate, let it be within the scope of the Constitution, and all means which are appropriate, which are plainly adapted to that end, which are not prohibited, but consistent with the letter and spirit of the Constitution, are constitutional." The second point was that the Maryland law, attacking the BUS, was unconstitutional. Marshall declared that no state possessed the right to destroy the agency (the BUS) of another sovereignty through taxation because "the power to tax is the power to destroy." Accordingly he held that the act of the Maryland legislature was unconstitutional and void.

Three years later this decision was reinforced in the case of *Osborn* v. *BUS*. The Ohio legislature had imposed a tax of $50,000 on each branch of the BUS in the state; that is, in both branches, in Chillicothe and Cincinnati. The BUS did not pay; a representative of the state entered the branch at Chillicothe, jumped over the counter "in a ruffian-like manner," took possession of the vault, and removed $120,425. The bank sued to the Supreme Court, and the decision reaffirmed *McCulloch* v. *Maryland*. Ultimately the state treasurer of Ohio was put in prison, and the purloined money was restored to the BUS.

Safe from attack by state governments, and under capable new leadership, the Second Bank of the United States became a powerful institution. Even so, in the 1830's it went down to defeat in the famous "Bank War" — a drama that demonstrated all the intensity, color, and the fury which a combination of conviction, political pageantry, and adept demagoguery could produce. The *dramatis personae* in the death struggle of the bank included Andrew Jackson, Thomas Hart Benton, Nicholas Biddle, and Daniel Webster.

Three attributes help explain the volatile Andrew Jackson: he was Prussian in personality, ambivalent in politics, and a believer in laissez-faire in economics. He had imposing arrogance: tall and thin; stern face and lantern jaw; high cheekbones and strong mouth; deepset, wild blue eyes, terrifying in anger. He fought duels, killed his man, achieved a reputation for bravery and ruthlessness. Opinions of the man varied all the way from those who were disgusted by him, to those who were afraid of him. Jefferson once said of his candidacy for the Presidency: "He is one of the most unfit men I know of for such a place — he is a dangerous man." When Harvard gave an honorary degree to Jackson, John Quincy Adams refused to attend because he could not bear "to witness her [Harvard's] disgrace in conferring her highest literary honor upon a barbarian who could . . . hardly spell his own name." Senator Abner Lacock of Pennsylvania feared for his physical well-being; he was heard to say, "How long I shall be spared mutilation I know not." Biographer Gerald Johnson believes it to be incontestably true that of all the terrifying men who have occupied the White House, the one most dreaded was "Old Hickory."

In politics he was a perplexing combination of ardent nationalist and states-rights advocate — a difficult fellow to fit into a neat category. He was a nationalist when crossed by the Indians or Great Britain or South Carolina. On other issues he was a states-rights man, fearing Big Government just as Jefferson did. In politics he was sometimes a nationalist, sometimes a states-righter — but he was not a friend of the Common Man, or a friend of Labor. Historian James L. Bugg has written a penetrating brochure entitled, *Andrew Jackson: Democratic Myth or Reality?* In it he points out that the image of Jackson as a democrat is fictitious; he had risen from the masses but was not one of them. He was not a frontier democrat; he was a frontier aristocrat who owned many slaves, cultivated many acres, and lived in one of the finest mansions in America — the Hermitage. He was a merchant, land speculator, judge, cotton planter — not a Common Man. A shrewd Nashville group — the Nashville Junto (Major W. B. Lewis, Senator John H. Eaton, and Judge John Overton) — persuaded Jackson to enter the presidential race and played him up as a mythical "Old Hickory" and the Common Man's candidate in order to get votes. Bugg insists that not one of the Nashville Junto could have been considered a man of the people; its members were interested in government for what they could get out of it — and that only. Recent attempts have been made, particularly by Arthur Meier Schlesinger, Jr., to make Jackson something of a premature New Dealer. But the New Dealers, like Hamilton, believed in a large and interventionist state. Jackson did not. It should also be noted that the New Deal was friendly to labor, and there is reason to believe that Jackson was as afraid of organized labor as he was of organized capital. The record indicates that on the only occasion when he took sides in a labor dispute, he called for federal troops to crush a strike — the first President to do so. Bray Hammond therefore makes fun of Schlesinger's attempt, in his Pulitzer Prize–winning *Age of Jackson*, to portray Jackson as a liberal. Schlesinger, he says, portrays the Jackson period as one of triumphant liberalism. It was, in Hammond's judgment, much more an age of triumphant exploitation.

If Jackson was Prussian in personality, and both ambivalent and mythical in politics, he was a believer in laissez-faire in economics — a follower of Adam Smith and Thomas Jefferson rather than Alexander Hamilton. He was himself so complete an advocate of literal laissez-faire that he was opposed to any governmental monopolies, whether through state or federal charters of special privilege to banks. He once said to Nicholas Biddle: "I do not dislike your bank more than *all* banks. But ever since the history of the South Sea Bubble I have been afraid of banks." This was his theory; in practice, as we shall see, certain entrepreneurs around Jackson used him to their advantage. They encouraged him to destroy the Second BUS, leaving state banks in control, to their own great profit.

The "Bank War" has been represented as a struggle between agrarians in the West, defended by Jackson, against the "money power" in the East, represented by Biddle and the BUS. In many history texts the bank is portrayed as Shylock lending to distressed farmers and exacting his pound of flesh — in the end having his skulduggery frustrated by Jackson. Neither frontiersmen nor farmers used bank credit to any great extent. Who did? It turns out that the "Common Men" favored by Jackson's policy were entrepreneurs in the guise of manufacturers, financiers, and land speculators. They were beginning to profit from the industrial revolution, the growth of population, and the expanding supply of state-bank credit. They resented the BUS because it stood in the way of easy credit for quick expansion; they deplored the credit restraint exercised by Biddle through the BUS.

Those opposing the BUS came from the West, which was well represented in Jackson's intimate "Kitchen" Cabinet by men who gained great profits; and from New York, where Hammond believes that Martin Van Buren's "Albany Regency" used Jackson as a tool in its own interest. The death of the BUS meant that control of the money market was shifted from Chestnut Street in Philadelphia (the headquarters of the BUS) to Wall Street in New York. In the defeat of Chestnut Street by Wall Street, Hammond is of the opinion that the general who directed political hostilities was not the President from Tennessee — but Martin Van Buren, the urbane commander of the Albany Regency.

The effective opposition to the BUS therefore came not from farmers but from businessmen. The conflict was obviously not between the rich and the poor, but between the *old* rich and the *new* rich. This was no struggle involving human rights; the "Bank War" was a struggle between two sets of capitalists. As Hammond observes, in the long run the millionaires created by the so-called Jacksonian Revolution of "agrarians" versus "capitalists" were richer and quite as numerous as those they dispossessed. Andrew Jackson had a banking theory which he thought he understood; his theory bore no resemblance to what actually happened in his presidential administrations.

On monetary policy President Jackson was supported in the Senate by

Thomas Hart Benton, who had the deserved soubriquet of "Old Bullion" and who represented Missouri as senator for thirty years (1821–1851). He was known for his extraordinary personality, his belated political devotion to Jackson, and his antiquarian theories on economics. As senator he once had the effrontery to say of the President: "Yes, sir, General Jackson was a great man, sir. . . . He was of great use to me, sir." He did become an ardent champion of Jackson, which was rather strange, because he had almost killed the future President in a brawl at a Nashville tavern just before the War of 1812. It was a lethal affair, fought with pistols and knives; only the bystanders kept the Benton brothers and Jackson from exterminating all those involved in the senseless altercation — including themselves. Jackson came out of it with a shattered left shoulder, so pulverized that he lost an incredible amount of blood and almost his arm. But Benton and Jackson were reconciled in 1824, and were boon companions from that point of time.

Benton hated the BUS, and said with his usual exaggeration: "All the flourishing cities of the West are mortgaged to this money power. They may be devoured by it at any moment. They are in the jaws of the monster! A lump of butter in the mouth of a dog! One gulp, one swallow, and all is gone."

He could only have been pleased by his soubriquet of "Old Bullion," and tried to live up to it by, first, getting Jackson to issue the Specie Circular of 1836, which required that payments for federal land be made in specie; and second, by getting Congress to enact a new Coinage Act in 1834, the first since Hamilton's in 1792. In this act Benton hoped to bring gold coinage back into circulation, and he did. It will be recalled that, as a result of the Coinage Act of 1792, gold had been undervalued and had gone out of circulation. Benton, in his Second Coinage Act of 1834, reduced the number of grains in the gold dollar from 24.75 to 23.22 — leaving the weight of the silver dollar the same at 371.25 grains. This meant, of course, that there was a new ratio — the famous one of 16 to 1. This also meant that gold was overvalued (rather than silver), and came into circulation again; this was because one could make money by having gold minted into dollars at the rate of 23.22 grains to the dollar. This overvaluation was even more apparent after 1848, when the price of the metal fell in price because of the news from California. This also meant, under the new ratio, that silver was undervalued for the first time. The result was that the silver dollar disappeared, simply because one could make more by selling one's silver commercially. This was so true that in the 1850's fractional silver was kept in circulation — as in the current era — only by debasing it. Otherwise the silver in the fractional currency would have been so valuable that it would have been melted down and sold at a profit as bullion.

Jackson and Benton did not care for the Bank of the United States;

Biddle and Webster did, for different reasons. Nicholas Biddle came from a prominent Philadelphia family which enjoyed a superfluity of social and economic advantages. There is no question about his brilliance; he entered the University of Pennsylvania at ten, was ready to graduate at thirteen but was not permitted to do so because of his youth. He immediately entered Princeton for advanced work in classics and was graduated at fifteen as the valedictorian of the class. These intellectual interests continued throughout his entire life. In 1804, when he was eighteen, he went to Paris as secretary to American Minister John Armstrong, attended the coronation in Notre Dame of Napoleon as emperor, and traveled all over Europe studying languages and history. Two years later he went to Greece and became interested in the classic glories there, the first American to do so. The interest of Biddle in Greece would appear in the architecture of the BUS in Philadelphia, visible to this day. The headquarters of the bank there was patterned after the Parthenon; the BUS moved into it in 1824, and was known thereafter as the "Greek Temple in Chestnut Street."

On his return to the United States he was in the lower house of the Pennsylvania legislature from 1811 to 1817, after which Monroe (who had always admired him) made him a director of the Second BUS. Biddle then turned his very real talents to the study of banking for the first time, and mastered that subject as quickly as he had many others. He became president of the bank in 1823 and remained in that capacity until 1839. After the struggle with Jackson he lost all of his personal fortune in the troubles that came to the bank after it took a state charter (in the place of the federal one) from Pennsylvania. His wife's fortune remained, however, and he spent his last years in elegant retirement — to the despairing anger of poet and editor William Cullen Bryant, who thought Biddle's remaining years of life should have been spent in the penitentiary.

Biddle — brilliant, arrogant, and tactless — had no awe of businessmen, understood very well how the entire banking system worked, and had a global and universal view that was singularly lacking in his colleagues and contemporaries. In Bray Hammond's opinion, under Biddle's direction the central banking function was recognized and performed in this country to a degree of effectiveness that had not at that time been attained even by the Bank of England — and was not to be reached again in the United States for a century. Hammond therefore believes that Biddle is to be ranked with Alexander Hamilton in the early days of the Republic — and with Woodrow Wilson and FDR in recent times — for their common efforts to make central banking and its control of credit the major factor that it has become in the American economy. Biddle demonstrated the monumental difference that separates an economic statesman from a mere money-maker. Biddle's difficulties came from the fact that he tried to exercise the central functions of credit-ease and credit-restraint — long before these modern practices were understood by the banking fraternity.

For this reason he did not hesitate to restrict credit when inflation threatened, or to encourage lending when depression portended — as it did in 1837. The Second BUS was not a perfect central bank, but it was the most advanced fiscal institution of its time. In Hammond's opinion Biddle was modern and Keynesian, Jackson and Benton hearkened back to an age that was past.

Daniel Webster supported Jackson during the Nullification Controversy but as Senator from Massachusetts and legal counsel for the BUS he took vehement issue with the President over fiscal policies. As an orator he was at times impressive, at times little better than a "ham" performer. He looked the part; he was known as the "God-like Daniel" who resembled a cathedral. It has been said that no man could ever be as great as Daniel Webster looked; he was the last representative to grace the Senate in a blue broadcloth coat with brass buttons. Arthur Meier Schlesinger, Jr., has noted that when inspiration lagged his oratory was simply pompous — but in the great speeches "when inspiration took charge of his booming voice, he could shake the world." Then he was, as Emerson remembered him, "the great cannon loaded to the lips."

In economics he was a standpat Hamiltonian to the point where Richard Current entitles his perceptive biography *Daniel Webster and the Rise of American Conservatism.* He wanted government to insure that property would be assisted through protective tariffs, internal improvements, and a national bank. In 1836, when he was being mentioned for the Presidency, the Jacksonian Democrats would charge that Webster had said, "Let Congress take care of the Rich, and the Rich will take care of the Poor." This is sometimes called the "drip" system of economics — what is good for the Rich is good for the country. Webster was also so acquisitive that his actions, on occasion, were venal or amoral — or both. His loose financial habits unfortunately destroyed his financial independence. At one point, when the BUS had its back to the wall, Webster forced it to send him a generous retainer, with the threat that he would quit the bank if that institution did not fork over. The bank did; Hammond thinks it was a mistake. He avers that Webster's knowledge of banking was limited, that he probably knew enough to last through one speech — but no more. Webster also passed the hat among wealthy men, cajoling the capitalists of New York and Boston into giving him special and personal support. In 1839, when he hinted that he might have to leave the Senate and devote himself to his law practice, his influential friend Edward Everett was appalled. As Current observes, Webster was indispensable to Everett's friends in Boston, as they saw it, for the protection of their houses, their lands, and their stocks. So Everett made certain that Boston businessmen were canvassed for a trust fund of a hundred thousand dollars — and the contribution was repeated in 1845.

The charter of the BUS, unless renewed, would expire in 1836. Four years earlier Biddle and Henry Clay decided that it would be strategic to bring up the rechartering of the bank during the presidential campaign of 1832. They got a recharter bill through both houses of Congress — confident that they had Andrew Jackson on a political hot seat. If he signed the bill he could be accused of inconsistency for political reasons, and would lose the support of the South and West; if he vetoed the measure he would supposedly lose the support of the East, particularly Pennsylvania — and along with it the Presidency. His opponents rather expected Jackson to sign the bill. Instead he vetoed it in a ringing message to Congress *and* to the people of the United States.

His message turned out to be a famous state paper. The first draft was prepared by Amos Kendall and put into final form by Roger Taney. Kendall was a member of the "kitchen" and regular cabinets (as Postmaster General) who became a millionaire through state banks. Taney was a future Chief Justice of the United States (1835–1864) who could be compared unfavorably with John Marshall — and who had sold his holdings of BUS stock before his decision in *McCulloch* v. *Maryland* in 1819. Taney acted more thriftily, not an unusual attribute of the Jacksonian group. While later arranging for the federal deposits to be shifted into private banks, he not only retained his state-bank stocks, but bought a few more! This is proof again that the attack on the BUS was not an attack on the rich men of the country — but was an attack on some rich men for the benefit of some other rich men.

In his spectacular veto message Jackson gave three reasons for opposing the bank: it was un-American, unconstitutional, and undemocratic. It was un-American because of a sizable number of foreign stockholders. This was a specious and demagogic argument. Actually there were 400 foreign stockholders (out of 4,000) who held eight of the $35 million of stock in the BUS. But *none* of the foreign stockholders could vote! Nonetheless, the Washington *Globe*, in an editorial which displayed complete ignorance or complete opportunism, hailed the Jacksonian veto as a "Second Declaration of Independence" — a manifesto that frustrated the plot of "the aristocracy of England to raise a revenue in America." The President also said that the bank was unconstitutional, resurrecting the argument that had been used and rejected in 1791. He clinched the negative point of view by stating that the bank was undemocratic — a monopoly that concentrated power in the hands of the few against the many. One can imagine the reaction of the proponents of the bank to what they regarded as presidential and arrant sophistry. Henry Clay, who would unsuccessfully oppose Jackson in the approaching presidential election, said of the veto message: "It has all the fury of a chained panther, biting at the bars of his cage. It is really a manifest of anarchy, such as Marat or Robespierre might have issued to the mob at the Faubourg St. Antoine."

Biddle was hopeful that the nation would soon regain its sanity: "It cannot be that our free nation can long endure the vulgar domination of ignorance and profligacy. You will live to see the laws reestablished — the banditti will be scourged back to their caverns — the penitentiary will reclaim its fugitives in office."

Biddle was a brilliant banker but a retarded political prophet. In 1832 the nation repudiated him and overwhelmingly endorsed Jackson, against Clay and Wirt. Jackson regarded this convincing success at the polls as a mandate from the country to destroy the BUS. He therefore began to withdraw the federal deposits from the BUS, and to place them in state banks. Nearly ninety, known thereafter as "pet" banks, were specially selected for this largesse. Jackson had effectively jettisoned the National Bank, which he called that "hydra of corruption." The Bank War was over.

Most modern economists think that the defeat of the Second BUS was tragic, senseless, and far-reaching in its effects. Walter B. Smith (in his *Economic Aspects of the Second Bank of the United States*) says that had the bank been continued, the United States would have had an effective banking system long before it did. Instead, because of the defeat of the recharter bill, the United States, "from being one of the most financially inventive countries in the world, . . . was transformed into one of the most backward in the years following the demise of the Second Bank of the United States." Bray Hammond stresses the selfish and entrepreneurial results of Jackson's economic policy; he says that the defeat of the Bank made the Age of Jackson a "festival of laissez-faire precursive to the Age of Grant and the Robber Barons."

The American Republic had suffered recessions before the Jacksonian period, notably in 1819, but the first really serious depression struck in 1837. In retrospect it is obvious that the Panic of 1837 was inevitable; the only question was when it would strike. The Panic was created by private speculation in companies which were selling land and railroads, and by public speculation, largely on the part of state governments, in roads and canals. Many of these investments could not count on steady profits for years to come when population and settlement had finally caught up with speculative fancy.

The Specie Circular and the Distribution Act, both in 1836, precipitated the Panic. The Specie Circular reflected the national government's concern over the dubious state-bank paper it was being paid for land. The circular simply, and logically, stated that henceforth all payments for public land would be in gold, but it brought into disrepute the unstable state-bank paper in which the West had been conducting most of its business. The Distribution Act mirrored a very strange situation in federal finances. During the 1830's the federal government found itself with no debt and with a surplus; it suffered from "the serious inconvenience of an overflowing Treasury." Furthermore the federal government found it politically inexpedient to do anything about the two major causes for the surplus: the Tariff of 1832 (which was a welcome compromise after a spirited and frightening debate between North and South), and revenue from land sales — which had to be endured because of a squabble between the East (which favored expensive lands in the West to deter laborers from moving there) and the West (which wanted cheap lands). The major problem was what to do with the surplus. The practice of depositing it in "pet" banks appeared to be unwise, because they used the deposits for more loans, accelerating speculation and inflation. The Distribution Act provided that all money in the treasury on 1 January 1837, in excess of $5 million, would be deposited with states (in proportion to their electoral vote) in four equal quarterly payments. The states could use this "dividend" in any way they chose; most planned to spend it on education and internal improvements. Federal money "in the treasury" actually meant federal money deposited in "pet" banks, and that the national government now had to ask the state banks for the return of its deposits. This had an accelerating effect; state banks were compelled to call in or restrict loans, businessmen and land speculators followed suit, and the reverberations were felt throughout the entire economy. The distribution of the surplus, amounting to $37,469,000 on 1 January 1837, was never completed, because the execution of the law was interrupted by the Panic of 1837. As if the Specie Circular and the Distribution Act were not sufficient immediate causes for a panic, the prevailing uncertainty was further aggravated by crop failures in the West in 1835 and 1837, and by the failure of certain great business houses in Great Britain which had invested heavily in American securities and now threw them on the market.

History has been unkind to Martin Van Buren, who became President in 1837; his merits were obscured by the depression and by his predecessor. Born on a farm near Kinderhook, New York (the first President *born* an American citizen), he became the head of the Democratic party that was so prominent in New York — the so-called Albany Regency. Late in life Van Buren began to develop strong ideas, particularly on slavery and the currency, but at the time of his election as President he had a reputation as a cagey compromiser.

One of the problems before Van Buren was the decision as to the disposal of government deposits in the future. The "pet-bank" system obviously made no sense. As a Democrat, particularly with Andrew Jackson still very much alive, Van Buren could not propose another BUS. He therefore devised the Independent Treasury System, which finally became effective in 1846 and remained in operation until it was superseded by the Federal Reserve System in 1913. Under the Independent Treasury the government held its own money in its own vaults. On the positive side, proponents averred that the system insured the safety of government funds, and guaranteed that they would not be used as a basis for inflationary expansion of state-bank notes. On the negative side the Independent Treasury System withdrew from circulation specie that was needed for the expansion of industry and commerce; it restricted the earnings of the federal government, because gold lying in vaults earns no income; and it restricted monetary control on the part of the federal government. It confined its monetary authority to control over coin — the minor part of the money supply — and left control over the major part (bank credit) to the state banks. The result was that by 1860 there were more than ten thousand types of state-bank money in circulation, governed by thirty-six types of state banking regulations — established by the thirty-six states then in existence. All affected the national economy, but the federal government itself had no authority or influence over this major and important type of currency.

With the failure of Biddle's first attempt to provide central banking control — an objective that was to be achieved later by Lincoln, Wilson, and FDR — a limited and partial attempt was made to accomplish the same goal through private and state regulation of bank notes. These plans did not progress very far along the road of rational and uniform monetary control, but they pointed the way, and for that reason deserve mention. The private plan was on a regional basis in New England, and was known as the Suffolk System. The Suffolk Bank of Boston established in 1819 the practice of redeeming, at its central office, notes of New England country banks at par — provided these country banks maintained a sufficient redemption fund at the Suffolk Bank. This plan proved successful; in time six other Boston banks joined, providing a Consortium of Seven which forced the country banks of New England to redeem their notes in specie. The sanction was the same as that used by the BUS. Country banks unwilling to provide a redemption fund were presented with their notes in large quantities for immediate redemption — an aggravating and embarrassing pressure that was quite effective. The Suffolk, and its colleagues, were in effect the central bank of New England. They were doing for the region what the BUS might have been doing for the country as a whole, had it been allowed to continue its operations. The result was that from 1825 to 1860 New England had an almost uniform currency, a phenomenal achievement in the early nineteenth century.

Without privileges or special sanctions from the government, the Suffolk was a prime example of laissez-faire at its best. Private enterprise, completely on its own, had developed an efficient regulation of bank credit which was quite as much in the public interest as government control could be. Its directors included members of wealthy and conservative families in New England — the Appletons, Lawrences, and Lowells — but the moving force in the system was a merchant and manufacturer and banker and rugged individualist named Nathan Appleton. He had begun his career as a merchant but made his fortune in the textile industry, particularly in Waltham and Lowell and Lawrence in Massachusetts, by helping establish its fundamental principles at that time — power machinery with cheap female labor. By 1840 he and his associates had mills in operation with a capital of $12 million. To Appleton, however, success meant not only the handsome profits which large-scale production brought; he was also an advocate of decreasing costs of textile goods for consumers and of pleasant working conditions for employees — in lieu of higher wages and shorter hours. Elected to Congress for the Boston district in 1830 he supported the tariff but did not argue for his own mills because they were competitive and needed no protection. He considered slavery a local problem, would have nothing to do with that "fanatical monomaniac" William Lloyd Garrison, and vehemently denied the charge made by Senator Charles Sumner (also from Massachusetts) that there was an "unhallowed union" between northern and southern employers — between "the lords of the lash and the lords of the loom." His resolute independence carried over into religion; he characterized all theological doctrines as "mere human opinions," and said that reason did not incline him to a belief in the immaculate conception, the Athanasian Trinity, Calvinistic dogmas, the utter iniquity of slavery, or the wickedness of possessing riches. Although he was fully occupied with business and financial affairs he found time for an interest in science, was one of the organizers of the Boston Athenaeum, and was active in the Massachusetts Historical Society. In his will he made it clear to posterity that moneymaking had not been his chief purpose in life, and that he would have been content with the first $200,000 he made in an early trading company. He asserted that he had gone into the cotton industry by chance and that it was "accident and not effort [that] made me a rich man."

In addition to the private Suffolk System, a few states made attempts to bring some order out of monetary chaos. The prime example was New York, through its Safety Fund and Free Banking Systems — although Louisiana also made progress along these lines. In 1829 the legislature of New York required all new banks to establish a safety fund, to serve as a reserve behind its note issues. This amounted to one half of one percent of its capital fund, payable each year, with a total contribution of 3 percent. The fund so accumulated was to be used to honor the notes of defaulting banks. Interestingly the person who proposed this plan was not a banker or politician; he was Joshua Forman, a lawyer and entrepreneur who first suggested it to Governor Martin Van Buren, who was so impressed that he recommended it successfully to the legislature. Forman was ingenious in many ways and found an analogy between New York and China; he wrote:

The propriety of making the banks liable for each other was suggested by the regulations of the Hong merchants of Canton, where a number of men, each acting separately, have by the grant of government the exclusive right of trading with foreigners and are all made liable for the debts of each in case of failure.

Forman had many interests beyond banks. He was one of the most influential promoters of the Erie Canal; he engaged in many enterprises in Onondaga County, New York, where he built a tavern and gristmills, and was the originator of improvements in the production of salt by evaporation. While living in Syracuse, which he founded and where he once controlled the land in the heart of the present city, he procured the passage of an act to lower the level of Lake Onondaga, making it possible to drain adjacent swamps and greatly improve health conditions in the vicinity. When his real-estate operations in Syracuse extended him financially, he moved to New Jersey and worked in a copper mine. During the last two decades of his life he owned immense tracts of wild land in North Carolina and spent the remainder of his life there. A man of wide information and character, a good lawyer, he was essentially a promoter and builder of the type who would have delighted Adam Smith. His boundless faith in the development of the United States seemed visionary to some, but his early advocacy of the Erie Canal and his idea of the Safety Fund represented solid contributions to both private and public welfare.

There was some criticism of the Safety Fund System, as proposed by Forman and enacted by New York, because the payment was based on capital rather than note issues — a device that favored the "reckless banks." Despite its faults, the Safety Fund System worked reasonably well for eight years; the numerous bankruptcies during the Panic of 1837 wrecked it. It was succeeded in 1838 by the New York Free Banking System. This plan required individual banks in the state to maintain, in their own vaults, a reserve of 12 percent for *immediate* redemption of note issues. In addition, every bank was required to deposit with the state government in Albany, for *ultimate* redemption if necessary, bonds covering the entire issue of bank notes by individual banks. This coverage was in bonds of the United States, or of the state of New York; on these the individual bank drew interest because it owned — although it did not possess — the bonds. This system provided a stable currency, and made New York the financial capital of the nation. It supplied a bond-backed currency, plus a specie reserve; Secretary of the Treasury Chase would copy the principle in establishing the bond-backed National Bank Notes in 1863.

The Secretary of the Treasury (1861–1865) who was responsible for financing the Union cause in the Civil War was Salmon Portland Chase. He was a tall, massive, handsome statesman — often compared to Webster in appearance. He also had other characteristics in common with the politician from Massachusetts; Chase was pompously religious, idealistic, ambitious, and mercenary. It was a curious combination, one that produced both its triumphs and its frustrations in politics.

He probably acquired his interest in religion from his uncle, Philander Chase, the Episcopal bishop of Ohio with whom he lived for a large part of his youth. In his private career he certainly needed the consolation of religion, because he lost by early death three wives and four of his six children. Throughout his life he repeated psalms as he was bathing and dressing, but he failed to convince some of his contemporaries. His colleague Ben Wade, also a prominent politician from Ohio, once said, "Chase is a good man but his theology is unsound. He thinks there is a fourth person in the Trinity (himself)." As a young lawyer in Cincinnati he had been idealistic. Instead of trying to get rich on corporate practice, he had taken on a most unpopular cause — the defense of runaway slaves for no fee at all. He was so active in this unusual business that he was sometimes called the "attorney general for runaway Negroes." In this activity he found what it was like to be hit on the speaker's platform — with a brick on one occasion and rotten eggs on another. This idealism happened to be beneficial politically at the particular time in which he displayed it; Chase was elected U.S. Senator from Ohio in the years 1849 to 1855, and was governor of that state for two terms from 1855 to 1859.

As a politician Chase was inordinately ambitious. He had wanted the presidential nomination in 1860, but lost it to Lincoln. Unfortunately the day Chase became a member of Lincoln's Cabinet he began to scheme for the presidential nomination in 1864. The new one-dollar Civil War greenback, obviously the piece of currency most commonly used, had Chase's portrait on the face of the bill; Lincoln's image was on the higher-priced and less commonly used notes.*

Chase's inordinate ambition led him to accept money to make up his own private deficits (because he lived beyond his means) and his political losses. The subventions came from Jay Cooke, the first American investment banker to operate on a large scale, who was known as the "Tycoon" to his partners. Cooke lent Chase money, then invested it. The investments were unusual because Chase was paid a high rate of profit without reference to the ups and downs of the market. It amounted to this: Cooke lent Chase the money, and Chase always raked in profits. It was estimated that by 1864, Cooke had invested close to $100,000 in Chase's political

---

* Ironically, with the retirement of Civil War greenbacks, Chase's image appeared only on Federal Reserve notes of $10,000 — scarcely a political boon for anyone, living or dead. In 1969 the U.S. government decided to retire all high-denomination bills of the $500 to $10,000 types. These high-denomination bills had first made their appearance in 1918 when checks — even of the certified variety — were not held in as high esteem as they are today. In recent years bills of high denomination have been used principally by black marketeers (during World War II) and gamblers who shunned any written report of their transactions. With the retirement of the high-denomination bills Chase will lose even his last remaining and token appearance on U.S. currency.

career. As the Beldens point out in their fascinating biography (*So Fell the Angels*), in all of these business transactions it should be understood that Chase did not want to become a wealthy man. He merely wanted to be President, and this required funds beyond his means. At the same time, it is shocking to contemplate that a Secretary of the Treasury was accepting gratuities from a millionaire, whose motives were obvious.

Prior to 1861 national revenue had come chiefly from tariff duties, with some helpful but sporadic income from the sale of public lands. The extraordinary financial demands of the Civil War therefore placed an enormous burden on a populace that was unaccustomed to heavy taxation. In four years, from 1861, the national government spent more than it had in the previous seventy-one years of our independence. Yet, when Lincoln was inaugurated, customs receipts were almost at a standstill, the treasury was practically empty, and public credit was nonexistent.

In a desperate effort to meet the tremendous war costs, Chase and the Congress resorted to every known device for obtaining revenue: taxation, paper money, and loans. The Secretary of the Treasury resorted to an old and new type of tax. The ancient one was the tariff, the new levy was the internal-revenue tax — which had not been used in this country since the War of 1812, and then only sparingly. In connection with the tariff, hardly a session of Congress went by during the Civil War without some increase — until the Act of 1864 advanced the average rate to 47 percent, an unprecedented figure at that time, although it was not excessive by modern standards. The major purpose behind these tariff increases was to protect Northern industrialists from foreign competition, so they could pay higher domestic taxes. Through the increased tariff duties a total of just over $300 million was raised during the Civil War — out of a total of almost $4 billion spent.

Beyond the tariff the government resorted to internal-revenue duties. Hardly anything was left untaxed — from tobacco, liquors, and billiard tables (on the moral side) to advertisements, occupations, incomes, inheritances, manufactured goods, and railroads in the practical and mundane sphere. Before the Civil War, revenue duties were unusual but not entirely new; the tax on incomes and inheritances was unprecedented. At first the income tax was all of 3 percent; by the end of the war it was graduated from 5 to 10 percent on higher incomes. Total income from internal-revenue taxes of all kinds during the war was just over $350 million. Combined with tariffs, this meant that the federal government raised during four years (1861–1865) a bit more than $650 million — still far short of the $4 billion spent.

So a second device was used. It was paper money; these were the legal-tender notes, or greenbacks, so-called because they were printed with green ink. By the simple process of working the printing presses, the government acquired extensive funds to expend for soldiers' wages and war supplies. This paper money was not unlike the Continental currency of Revolutionary days. It was fiat money, unsupported by a gold reserve. To be sure, there was a promise on the face of the greenbacks that the U.S. government would pay gold on demand; this was illusory, nor was any date announced for redemption in an uncertain future. On one occasion, at a Cabinet meeting, it was proposed to engrave on the greenbacks the hopeful statement: "In God We Trust." This suggestion produced the following comment from the Bible-reading Lincoln: "If you are going to put a legend on the greenbacks, I would suggest that of Peter and John: 'Silver and gold have I none, but such as I have I give thee.'" Altogether the national government issued $431 million in greenbacks during the four years of the Civil War. From a fiscal point of view these issues were a forced loan on the people, because the notes quickly declined in purchasing value and those who held them usually lost. Living costs rose rapidly as the greenbacks lost in value; measured in gold it took a hundred dollars' worth of greenbacks to purchase thirty-nine dollars in gold in 1864. But — as Chase once phrased it — "The war must go on until the rebellion is put down, if we have to put out paper until it takes a thousand dollars to buy a breakfast."

There was one curious corollary to the issue of greenbacks; it was the issue of fractional currency. Citizens tried to get rid of their greenbacks as quickly as possible — in the meantime holding on to the coins which comprised the only money that was worth its face value. The prevailing situation was a perfect example of Gresham's Law. People put their coins in the family sock, or under a plank in the kitchen floor, and sallied forth to get rid of the paper money which was declining in value with every passing day. The result was that there were not enough nickels, dimes, quarters, and halves — coins with valuable silver in them — left to make change. For a time stamps were used, but this was unsatisfactory because they became cracked and dirty. Finally the national government recognized the situation and issued $50 million in fractional currency — in denominations as low as three cents. They were called shinplasters.

The sum of $650 million raised by taxation, and the $431 million raised by issuing greenbacks, was insufficient to pay for a $4 billion war. The balance of the money, something more than $2.5 billion, was raised by loans — that is, by the issue of bonds. This was an expansive and an expensive project because, in order to compete with commercial and industrial investments which were booming, high interest rates had to be paid; in actual fact, the U.S. government paid more than 7 percent on one issue of bonds. But the war had to be financed, and the bonds had to be sold. In order to speed their sales, two incentives were employed: the salesmanship of Jay Cooke, and the National Banking Acts of 1863–1865.

Cooke put on the most extensive and highly organized advertising campaign the country had ever seen. His personality was perfect for the operation; he was breezy, valiant, optimistic — the perfect salesman.* What he did was most unusual for its day; he went not only to bankers but to small investors — the masses of people who could buy a $100 bond. He waged a terrific newspaper campaign, paid for advertisements, sent out news stories and canned editorials. For his trouble Cooke was paid a commission of one-quarter of 1 percent — out of which he had to pay the cost of a large sales force, and for advertising space in hundreds of papers; what his profits were, is not known. His efforts, while spectacular, did not sell enough bonds; for that reason Congress passed the National Banking Acts, which also provided a safe and uniform national-bank currency, limited or destroyed state-bank notes, and provided more federal control over banks.

The sale of bonds was facilitated by the charter of national banks in cities and towns all over the country. The banks, with federal charters, were required to invest one-third of their capital in federal bonds — but were authorized to issue national-bank notes (or currency) up to 90 percent of the current market value (not exceeding par) of the bonds. This was attractive because it meant that the new national banks could use some of their capital twice; they drew interest on the bonds *and* on the national-bank notes which cost them only the price of printing. The federal bonds were held (in their name) in the U.S. Treasury as security for the redemption of the national-bank notes if the issuing institution failed. This meant that the national government had provided a new type of national currency — a bond-backed currency similar to that previously issued in New York under the Free Banking System. It was high time. In 1861 there were in circulation almost ten thousand kinds of state-bank paper money of solvent banks; the issues of fraudulent, broken, and worthless banks — still in circulation — totaled five thousand in number. A traveler passing through several states had to change his money several times, paying heavy discounts, and sometimes commissions as well. Now in 1863 he had been given the option of using the new stable and bond-backed currency issued by the new national banks. These national-bank notes were by far the most colorful paper money ever issued in this coun-

* In making his sales "pitch" Cooke could be more than breezy and optimistic; he could also be downright dishonest. During the Civil War he achieved a reputation of having saved the Union by mounting a great advertising campaign for the sale of U.S. bonds. For his later railroad schemes he mounted an even mightier propaganda. Cooke's Northern Pacific Railroad had been given enormous federal subsidies amounting to 47 million acres of public land — a banana-shaped tract reaching from the Great Lakes to the Pacific Northwest. To encourage settlement Cooke fabricated what Peter Lyon called "the most outrageous humbug." He insisted that the Northern Pacific Railroad (from Duluth on Lake Superior to Seattle and Portland on the Pacific Ocean) went through a region with a climate that was a "cross between Paris and Venice." There were stories that orange groves and monkeys had been found by his surveyors. The public proceeded to pour money into what has been called "Jay Cooke's Banana Belt" — only to lose much of it when the spectacular failure of the Northern Pacific precipitated the national Panic of 1873. Cooke later became wealthy once again through an investment in a silver mine.

try. On them individual national banks placed elaborate historical engravings: the landing of the Pilgrims, the discovery of the Mississippi, the baptism of Pocahontas, the signing of the Declaration of Independence. Because state banks were not changing to national charters with sufficient rapidity, and out of a desire to limit further issues of dubious state-bank notes, in 1865 the Congress placed a tax of 10 percent on state-bank-note issues. This levy was properly called a "death tax"; it drove many state banks out of existence. The Civil War thus saw the demise of one type of money (the state-bank notes), and the introduction of two new national types — the unsecured Civil War greenbacks and the bond-backed national-bank notes. Interestingly, the Supreme Court in 1869 (*Veazie Bank* v. *Fenno*) upheld the constitutionality of the "death tax" — conveniently forgetting Marshall's dictum in *McCulloch* v. *Maryland* that the "power to tax is the power to destroy." Finally, the National Banking Acts enabled the federal government to exercise more control over banks. This was carried out by the Treasury which, until 1913, had administrative control over national banks. The Treasury chartered them, printed and issued their bank notes (currency), supervised them, and assumed complete charge when national banks became insolvent.

In retrospect, there are pros and cons on Salmon Portland Chase as a financier. He could point with pride to two achievements. He raised the money to finance the war; in four years he had produced more than had been raised in the entire history of the nation under the Constitution. He also introduced the National Banking Acts. These were Chase's idea, and in the monetary field were his chief merit. In so acting he looked back to Biddle and the Free Banking System of New York; he also looked forward to the Federal Reserve System. On the negative side one can view with alarm a monumental failure. Unwilling to raise enough money through taxation, he placed too much emphasis on borrowing. For a war that cost almost $4 billion, he relied on borrowing for 3 billions of the money. He borrowed $2.6 billion through bonds and he raised $431 million through Civil War greenbacks. Congress seemed willing to authorize heavier taxation, but he taxed the next generation, which would have to pay the interest and the principal on the bonds; it was the easy way out that war administrations have usually taken in our history. The issue of Civil War greenbacks happens to be a convincing example of the inequity of this policy. They helped immeasurably in producing inflation — an inflation that was particularly hard on three groups:

Those on fixed incomes who — then and now — cannot cope with rising prices.

Creditors, who had to accept greenbacks, regardless of their value, for the payment of debt. Civil War greenbacks were legal tender for everything except customs duties and interest on the federal debt; in other words, the government did not want to accept them, but expected everyone else to do so.

The federal government itself. It has been estimated that the war cost the North $500 million more than it should have — because of inflation. This was more than the benefit of the issue of $431 million in greenbacks, which were chiefly responsible for the inflation.

The financial difficulties of the South were incomparably greater than those of the North. Its Secretary of the Treasury, the counterpart to Chase, was of German extraction — Christopher Gustavus Memminger by name. He was born in Württemberg; his father, an officer in the army of the duke, was killed shortly after the birth of the son, and the mother took the lad to Charleston, South Carolina, where she soon died. Memminger was left an orphan at four. Self-educated, he developed a reputation before the war as a sound financier who favored specie payments; for that reason he must have suffered cruelly as the Confederate Secretary of the Treasury. His lasting reputation, in actual fact, is based not on his work in the Confederate Cabinet — which was doomed to failure; but on his achievements as commissioner of schools at Charleston. After the war was over he did his very best to establish public schools for both races.

Memminger used the same three methods of raising money that Chase employed — but with less satisfactory results. As far as taxation was concerned he had hoped to obtain a substantial revenue from customs duties, but the Northern blockade put an end to this aspiration. With only a trickle of income from the tariff, he asked the Southern states to levy a property tax for the Confederate Treasury — the old requisition system of the Articles of Confederation — and he got the same disappointing response. Finally, in 1863 — with the war half over — the Confederate Congress adopted an internal-revenue measure similar to that in the North, but including a 10 percent tax on farm produce, payable in kind. While this levy on farm products did supply the armies, it also caused bitter resentment among agricultural elements, which denied that the Confederate government had the power of direct taxation.

When hard pressed every government will resort to paper money, and the South was no exception. Altogether a billion dollars' worth of currency was issued by the Confederacy — plus unrecorded issues by state governments, banks, and private business firms. The inflationary effect of all this paper is apparent. Said one Southerner: "Before the war I went to market with the money in my pocket, and brought back my purchases in a basket; now I take the money in the basket and bring home the articles purchased in my pocket."

Borrowing was also resorted to, but this method proved much less successful than in the North, where money for investment was plentiful. The first bond issue in 1861 absorbed most of the specie which existed in the South; the issue of bonds in 1862 was therefore made payable in produce. As a result, the Confederacy came into possession of vast stores of cotton, tobacco, and other commodities — most of which had no sale because of the federal blockade. The South did manage to sell a bond issue of $15 million in France — the famed loan negotiated by Emil Erlanger, a Frankfurt banker then resident in Paris. Little benefit was derived because one-third of the loan was spent on vessels that were never delivered, and another third was expended in fruitless operations designed to keep the price of these bonds as high as possible on the European exchanges. Ultimately, Erlanger and two Confederate envoys in Europe (Messrs. Mason and Slidell — Erlanger's son had married Slidell's daughter) were the only ones who profited from this grand speculation.

In time, of course, the enormous war debt of the South was outlawed by the failure of the Rebellion. The Fourteenth Amendment to the Constitution, adopted in 1868, forbade either the United States or any individual state government to pay any part of it.

To Charles Austin Beard the outstanding result of the Civil War was the destruction of the planting aristocracy that had ruled the United States for a generation. In his judgment its ruin was more complete than the destruction of the clergy and nobility in the French Revolution. The Southerners saw their class destroyed — and along with it $4 billion in slave property, and all their government bonds and currency which were invalidated by the Fourteenth Amendment. To Beard this was "the most stupendous act of sequestration in the history of Anglo-Saxon jurisprudence." The destruction of the planting aristocracy also resulted in the triumph of two Northern groups which would soon be engaged in a struggle for political and economic supremacy. They were the free farmers and the capitalists, the latter those entrepreneurs who invested in business — financial or industrial. Ultimately the capitalists, particularly the Northern bankers, won out — a development which President Andrew Johnson saw clearly soon after the Civil War. He warned the American people at that time that the Civil War might result merely in the substitution of one set of masters for another. He said, "The war of finance is the next war we have to fight." It was.

The debtor West first strove to better its situation through the Greenback Movement. In theory the problem appeared in a heated argument between the creditor East which favored what was called the intrinsic-value theory of a limited currency, against the debtor West which supported the quantity theory for the currency. People commonly understand very well that the abundance or scarcity of goods affects prices, but they do not seem to understand that the abundance or scarcity of money is just as effective: if there is too much money in search of too few goods, prices will rise; if there is too little money in search of too many goods, prices should fall. In the period after the Civil War industry and agriculture were expanding, and the supply of currency did not; there simply were not enough dollars to go around, so prices went down. As Fred

Shannon has observed, from 1865 to 1870 the circulating dollars went from about a billion to three-quarters that amount, the per-capita sum declining from $31.18 to $20.10. This deflation brought a drop in the base-price index from 132 to 87 — with farm prices even lower. Agricultural prices continued their descent until they reached bottom in 1896 at 39.6; meanwhile the per-capita figure on money sank below $19 in 1875, and hovered around that mark or in the low twenties until 1897. The agrarian Populists of the 1890's would demand $50 per person. All of this explains the demand of debtors for greenbacks or free silver; they felt a deflation-ary pinch because of the static money supply. On the other hand, the few who had money could get more; they could force interest rates up, ruin borrowers, annex their assets.

The debtor West therefore favored the quantity theory of money. It was based on two principles. The first was that the issue of money was a function of sovereignty, that it never should be turned over to business-men (as had been done in the National Banking Acts), that the govern-ment instead should regulate the amount in circulation according to busi-ness needs. The second principle was that gold was too narrow a base on which to erect the monetary system of an expanding economy, and that furthermore it was notoriously susceptible to manipulation and abuse. In 1869 there happened to have been a particularly scandalous and amoral example of such misconduct. It was the attempt to corner gold by James Gould and "Jubilee Jim" Fisk. This required a policy of nonintervention by the federal government; Gould got Grant's brother-in-law to intro-duce him to the President and then lavished gifts on the naïve Grant and his wife. Grant credulously suspected nothing when Gould dropped hints that it would be ruinous to the national prosperity if the Treasury released gold in the near future. On the famous Black Friday — 24 September 1869 — the partners let the word slip out that if gold was necessary, Gould and Fisk were the only ones who could supply it. A wild panic resulted, busi-nessmen with gold obligations bid frantically against one another, and gold skyrocketed in price. At this point Grant was finally prodded into action by his Secretary of the Treasury and ordered the release of govern-ment gold. Gould had received advance notice from a White House oper-ative, and silently unloaded without saying a word to his partner. This was typical of business ethics in the Gilded Age; Fisk, though caught short, was not angry. He thought it was a good joke on himself.

Opposing the advocates of the quantity theory were those who favored the intrinsic-value one. Its intellectual background lay in England, which had adopted gold as the single monetary standard in 1821. Its proponents stressed two principles. The first was that the only real money was gold; bank notes might be used, but they must always be redeemable in gold. Their adoration for the metal has carried over into popular speech; we respect the Golden Rule, dream of the Golden Age, delight at the Golden

Wedding, reward a child who is as good as gold. The second principle was that governments cannot create money; they can acquire it only by taxes or borrowing — not by starting the printing presses. If a government should issue irredeemable paper, the advocates of the intrinsic-value theory believed that it would violate the sanctity of contracts, would cheat creditors, and would rob the widows and the orphans.

In practice there were arguments as to whether Civil War greenbacks were constitutional, and if so how many should be issued, and whether they should be redeemed or not. The question of constitutionality was decided in two famous and contradictory cases — known appropriately as the Legal Tender Cases (*Hepburn* v. *Griswold* in 1870, and *Knox* v. *Lee* in 1871). The Legal Tender Act went into effect on 25 February 1862 and authorized the issue of greenbacks, stating that they were legal tender for the payment of debts. A Mrs. Hepburn had contracted, in 1862 but before 25 February, to pay one Henry Griswold $11,500. This meant in specie at the time the debt was contracted. In 1864 she offered to pay him in greenbacks, under the authority of the Legal Tender Act of 1862. The reason for her offer was obvious; in 1864 $11,500 in greenbacks was worth only $4,500 in specie. Griswold entered a vigorous protest. The case reached the Supreme Court in 1870, when that body had only seven members because the Senate — which had not cared for former President Andrew Johnson — had refused to approve two of his nominations to fill vacancies. The Court in *Hepburn* v. *Griswold* held with the traditional view that the Constitution was a hard-money document which supported the intrinsic-value theory. It said that the government had the power to issue greenbacks to pay for the war, but that it did not have the power to make them legal tender for the payment of debts. On the latter point the Court stated specifically that all debts contracted *before* 25 February 1862 must be paid in coin (which meant that Mrs. Hepburn had lost), but left in doubt the important question as to whether debts incurred after 25 February 1862 had to be paid in greenbacks or coin. The decision was an incredible one, productive of both administrative and judicial confusion. Debtors who had contracted for money after 25 February 1862 had done so on the legal certainty that they could pay them in greenbacks. It produced judicial confusion about the integrity of the Supreme Court. The decision, by the close vote of four to three, was delivered by the Chief Justice. He was Salmon Portland Chase, who, as Secretary of the Treasury, had been responsible for the Legal Tender Act of 1862. Now he had passed adversely on it.

By coincidence, on the very day Chase announced his decision in the Hepburn case, President Grant nominated two new members of the Court, and they were subsequently approved by the Senate. The Court now had its full complement of nine, and in 1871 it reversed *Hepburn* v. *Griswold* — by a vote of five to four. The two new appointees joined with the previous three dissenters to form the majority — and one of the two new appointees (William Strong) delivered the majority decision. He said that any legal tender was valid when Congress so declared in time of emergency. Apart from the constitutional issue, the Court suffered a decided loss in prestige because in a bit more than a year it had changed sides completely, and the executive branch was accused of packing the Court. In a strict sense this was not true, but a powerful supporting brief could be written, based on circumstantial evidence. Grant had made no secret of his disapproval of the Hepburn decision. He also had studied the past records of the two new justices, and probably had a fairly good idea of the position they would take on the greenback issue.

The struggle now turned to the Treasury, which would decide how many greenbacks would be left in circulation. Creditors, who wanted to be paid in expensive dollars, favored the retirement of all the greenbacks. Debtors, who wanted to pay their debts in cheap dollars, wanted all existing Civil War greenbacks kept in circulation — and would welcome the issue of many more.

The Secretary of the Treasury from 1865 to 1869 was Hugh McCulloch, a conservative banker from Indiana who had visited Washington in 1862 to oppose national banking, was asked by Chase to become Comptroller of the Currency, agreed, and in this capacity launched the national banks which he had previously opposed. In 1866 McCulloch, who favored creditors, began to retire Civil War greenbacks as they came in for the payment of taxes. Two years later (by which time McCulloch had reduced the greenbacks from $431 to $356 million) the West was so vociferous that his policy was stopped — in part because it was a presidential campaign year, during which the question of the currency would become important.

Prominent among the Democratic candidates in 1868 was George H. Pendleton of Ohio, who favored what was called the "Ohio Idea." Pendleton was an unusual person who ultimately gave his name to federal civil-service reform; he had come from a prominent family in Virginia (his nickname was "Gentleman George"), had studied at the University of Heidelberg, and had married Alice Key — daughter of Francis Scott Key. The "Ohio Idea" proposed the payment of government bonds in greenbacks. In 1868 some Civil War bonds were beginning to fall due; they had been issued under a statute requiring interest in coin, and payment of principal in "dollars" — whatever that might mean. In 1864 an investor could change $400 in gold for $1,000 in greenbacks, then exchange this sum for a thousand-dollar government bond at 6 percent each year — 15 percent on the original investment of $400. If the principal was repaid in $1,000 in gold, rather than the greenbacks which had been used to buy the bond, the holder's profits would be phenomenal. Pendleton and western farmers did not care for this prospect; they had used the greenbacks and wanted creditors to use them too. They insisted that the Civil War had been financed with a fifty-cent dollar, and was being paid for with a one-hundred-cent dollar. They developed the slogan: "The same currency for the bondholder and the ploughholder." The "Ohio Idea" horrified eastern conservative Democrats like banker August Belmont, and they saw to it that Pendleton did not get the presidential nomination (Belmont was born Schönberg in Germany, changed his name, married a daughter of Commodore Matthew Perry, represented the Rothschilds in the United States, and is still remembered as the sportsman who gave his name to Belmont Park and the Belmont Stakes in New York). In any case, Grant won the Presidency and saw to it that both interest *and* principal on the bonds were paid in gold, to the profitable delight of the holders.

The question of security, if any, behind Civil War greenbacks was finally decided in 1875 with the passage of the Specie Resumption Act of that year. The Panic of 1873 had intensified the demand for more unsecured greenbacks, and in the congressional elections of 1874 the Republicans lost control of the House of Representatives. In the lame-duck session of Congress which met early in 1875, the Republicans got the Resumption Act passed just before they went out of office — lest something worse happen. The act was essentially a compromise, attempting to appease both the greenback notions of the West and the gold-standard sentiment of the East. The West was attracted to the measure by its denial of ultimate "cremation" for greenbacks; $346 million were left in circulation. Conservatives liked the provision for a gold reserve; it was generally believed that this reserve should have a minimum of $100 million in gold — as a reasonably safe support for $346 million in Civil War greenbacks. The Treasury was authorized to sell bonds to establish the reserve, and beginning on 1 January 1879 greenbacks would be redeemable in gold. The four-year span (between the passage of the act and the scheduled beginning of redemption) was essential because there was not $100 million in gold in the United States in 1875. The Secretary of the Treasury had a problem; he was John Sherman of Ohio, who had pushed the Specie Resumption Act through the Senate, and now had the job of finding enough gold to put it into effect. Fortune smiled; good crops and a favorable balance of trade enabled him to sell the bonds for gold, and on 1 January 1879 he actually had $140 million of the metal, about 40 percent of the greenbacks in circulation. Would it be enough? Sherman waited apprehensively; to his relief on the first day only $135,000 in greenbacks were presented for gold — while $400,000 in gold was turned in for greenbacks, which are easier to carry and handle. Confidence had been restored; the greenbacks had reached a par with gold.

The advocates of greenbacks had argued theory with their opponents, and in the practical sphere they had fought with them over questions of constitutionality, and the volume and redemption of this paper money. Beyond theory and practice they also became active in the political sphere with the Greenback party, which was organized in 1875, when it held its first national convention at Indianapolis. There they drew up a platform and nominated a presidential candidate for the campaign of 1876. The platform stressed two points: it advocated immediate repeal of the Specie Resumption Act and it favored the adoption of the Ohio Idea. The candidate was an eighty-five-year-old capitalist, inventor, manufacturer, and philanthropist. His name was Peter Cooper.

Cooper was a tall, robust, big-beaked, lantern-jawed fellow who dressed simply in black most of his life, always taking care to have with him a small pneumatic rubber cushion that he placed beneath him before he sat. He had only a year's schooling, but was a prime example of the rags-to-riches theme. In his twenties he got a corner on the glue market; subsequently he was the chief figure, in his generation, in the iron industry in America. He was most ingenious as far as inventions were concerned, and experimented with everything from washing machines to a contraption to harness the tides. Many think he would have been an early Edison had he possessed the technical training. He was also a great philanthropist; in New York City he made a great contribution toward the development of paid police and fire departments, and free public education. Ashamed at his own lack of education, he founded the Cooper Union in New York as an engineering and art school without tuition fees, for part-time evening students. The six-story building, which still stands, was noteworthy in several respects. It used iron for its frame, the first time structural iron was used to reinforce stone or brick buildings, making them stronger and fireproof. It had an auditorium seating 1,900, which became a kind of Faneuil Hall where free speech prevailed; lecturing there was an interesting array of orators including abolitionists William Lloyd Garrison and Wendell Phillips, agnostic Robert Green Ingersoll, poet William Cullen Bryant, politician Abraham Lincoln, and Victoria Woodhull — who believed in women's rights and free love.

Cooper was many things, but no politician; he got only 81,000 votes for President. Two years later, in the congressional elections, some labor organizations (embittered by the great strikes of 1877) joined him to form the Greenback-Labor party. The results were encouraging; the party polled more than 1 million votes and elected fourteen members of Congress. But by 1880 labor had pulled out and those who wanted inflation were succumbing to the rising tide of sentiment for free silver.

There were three phases in the long-lived Free-Silver Movement: the first one lasted through the 1870's, beginning with the so-called "Crime of '73" and ending with the Bland-Allison Act of 1878; the second phase began in the late 1880's and was concluded with the presidential campaign of 1896 and the Gold Standard Act of 1900; the third phase started with the New Deal of the 1930's and is still going on.

The so-called "Crime of '73" was based on the coinage acts which regulated the bimetallic ratio between silver and gold. The first was Hamilton's in 1792, which established a ratio of 15 to 1 and drove gold out of circulation. The second was Benton's Act of 1834, which established a ratio of 16 to 1 and drove silver out of circulation. The third was the Act of 1853 (recognizing the overvaluation of gold and the undervaluation of silver) which reduced the silver content of all coins except the dollar (to keep them from being melted down) and authorized the coinage of a $3 piece in the plentiful and relatively cheap gold — in the hope that it might become popular. The fourth coinage act in the history of the United States was that of 1873; it and the Gold Reserve Act of 1934 were destined to be known as the most controversial of all such laws.

The Act of 1873 demonetized silver; that is, it dropped the silver dollar from the list of standard coins, putting the United States on a single rather than a bimetallic standard — a single standard that was to last for five years. The act simply recognized an existing situation, and for that reason no one took any particular notice of its provisions at the time of passage. The point is that silver dollars had not been in circulation since 1806; in 1873 (at a ratio of 16 to 1) it took $1.02 in silver to make a silver dollar, and no sensible person presented silver bullion to make them. For this obvious reason no silver dollars were being manufactured by the U.S. mints, and no notice was taken of the demonetization in 1873. Later on, President Grant would say that he did not even remember signing the act. But the price of silver fell steadily from 1873 on — until the 371.25 grains of the metal in the legal dollar were worth commercially only 49¢ in 1894. The timing on the Fourth Coinage Act had been incredibly bad. The price of silver fell dramatically and suddenly after 1873 for reasons which are obvious now — but which were not anticipated, except by a very few, at the time. After 1873 production increased vastly in the United States because of new discoveries, particularly the Comstock lode. In addition, in the early 1870's several European countries dropped the bimetallic standard, adopted gold as the single monetary basis for their currency, and dumped their silver on the open market. Western agrarians later argued, however, that there had been a "gold conspiracy" engineered by eastern bankers and their European colleagues to remove the silver dollar from the list of standard coins and thus to make it impossible for western mine owners to flood the country with inflationary silver dollars. Historians are now agreed that there was no plot, but recent evidence indicates that the Secretary of the Treasury (George Boutwell, who had broken the attempted corner on gold by Gould and Fisk on "Black Friday") and John Sherman (chairman of the Senate Finance Committee) were aware by late

1872 that silver was about to drop in value, and they worked successfully to complete congressional action on the bill before their expert and specialized information became public knowledge. They so acted not for personal gain, but to secure a domestic gold standard before the anticipated flood of depreciated silver began arriving at government mints for coinage into legal-tender silver dollars. In doing so, there is no doubt that these officials possessed information of which most congressmen were not aware. As Professor Allen Weinstein has observed, they were not self-interested rascals as the advocates of the "Crime of '73" later charged, but neither were they the economic innocents that most historians have claimed them to be — supposedly caught without warning by a sudden and fatal decline in the silver market. Boutwell and Sherman knew what they were doing.

The leader of the western radicals was Richard P. Bland of Missouri, known by the nickname of "Silver Dick" — as a youth he had worked in the gold fields of California and the silver mines of Nevada. In 1878 he steered through the House a bill providing for the free and unlimited coinage of silver, but the measure was unacceptable to the conservative Senate. There, modifications were worked out by Senator William B. Allison of Iowa, who changed the House bill to one that allowed a specified and limited coinage, and thus gave his name to the Bland-Allison Act. It was vetoed by President Hayes, but repassed by Congress over his veto.

The measure did *not* provide for the free and unlimited coinage of silver. It *did* restore the silver dollar to the list of standard coins. It *did* provide for limited purchases of silver, and it *did* provide for a new type of currency. The Treasury was to buy not less than $2 million and not more than $4 million worth of silver each month at market prices — and this silver was to be coined into dollars. These purchases helped to retard its decline in price, but the secretaries of the Treasury followed a policy of purchasing the minimum amount each month, and the price of silver continued to drop in the world market. Mineowners were not happy, either, because the U.S. government took the seigniorage; that is, the difference between the circulating value of the coin (one dollar) and the cost of the bullion in it, plus the cost of minting. The government got the seigniorage and made money under the Bland-Allison Act. During the twelve years the measure was in effect, the U.S. government issued $378 million in silver dollars or silver certificates; it paid $308 million for the silver in, or behind, them. The new type of currency which appeared was the Bland-Allison silver certificate, issued because people objected to having pockets full of heavy "cartwheels." They were redeemable only in silver. The effect of the act was not inflationary because the increase in money barely kept pace with the increasing population and productivity, but a temporary revival of prosperity in 1879 delayed further agitation for almost a decade.

The second phase of the movement for free silver began in the late 1880's. The fiscal reason was a decline in the money supply brought about by the retirement of the federal debt, and the concomitant retirement of national-bank notes as the federal bonds which secured them were paid off. There were $359 million in national-bank notes in circulation in 1882; by 1890 there were only $186 million. The political reason for the revival of agitation was the admission of six new western states in 1889–1890; among other things this introduced twelve new senators who represented agrarian and mining interests. The economic reasons were falling agricultural and silver prices. The decline in the price of farm products agitated the farmers, one of whom observed: "There are three great crops raised in Nebraska. One is a crop of corn, one a crop of freight rates, and one a crop of interest. One is produced by farmers who by sweat and toil farm the land. The other two are produced by men who sit in their offices and farm the farmers."

In the 1880's approximately 80 percent of all Kansas farms were mortgaged, at an average interest rate of 9 percent; in the same decade one-third of these mortgages in Kansas were foreclosed. Drought aggravated the burden; after the sparse rainfall of 1887 one Kansas editor claimed that "you had to prime the mourners at a funeral so they could shed tears for the departed." In 1894 a former schoolteacher and law clerk and speculator from Arkansas named William Hope Harvey would publish a book entitled *Coin's Financial School* which became the Bible of the new faith for inflationists. It was yellow-backed and paperbound; in 1895 it was selling at the rate of 100,000 a month. In the volume Harvey was portrayed as a fictitious "Professor Coin" lecturing to classes which included Chicago's leading magnates: Joseph Medill of the *Tribune*, Lyman Gage of the city's largest bank, Marshall Field, Philip Armour, Potter Palmer, Leander McCormick. All these men had been giving out ponderous and impressive statements on the depression — very much as Hoover, Mellon and Rockefeller would do in 1930 — and many of the statements were silly or questionable. Harvey studied them carefully, incorporated them into his book, and squelched the tycoons with his own allegedly superior wisdom. Many purchasers of *Coin's Financial School* assumed that the book described a real course of lectures attended by real people. Most of them accepted the professor's bimetallic theories and agreed that currency reform spelled economic salvation. The volume also included cartoons which purportedly proved the falsity of the gold standard. There was the cripple with one leg, which indicated how handicapped the nation was without the bimetallic standard. There was also the cartoon of a cow, with western farmers industriously stuffing fodder into the animal while eastern capitalists were milking her for the benefit of New York and New England. It is no wonder that the book was enormously popular in the aggrieved West.

The campaign for "the people's money" was not solely drummed by the embattled farmers. Behind it was a wing of Wall Street composed of the great owners and speculators in western mines, especially silver. Among these men were copper kings in Montana, and silver kings in Colorado and Nevada; heir to one of the latter was William Randolph Hearst. The 371.25 grains of silver in the legal dollar were worth about 50¢ in the 1890's; the advantage of the free and unlimited coinage of silver was obvious. Because of this situation the mineowners poured hundreds of thousands of dollars into propaganda — both printed and spoken. A favorite organization was the American Bimetallic League; its favorite weapon was a young lawyer in Nebraska named William Jennings Bryan. Many of the arguments of the crusading silverites were absurd and irrelevant. Two metals are better than one, they said, just as two eyes are better for a man, two wings for a bird, and two wheels for a bicycle. They were correct in their basic contention that an increase in the money supply was necessary to carry on the business of a rapidly expanding economy; world production of gold, on which the money system rested, had fallen far behind the increase in marketable goods produced by American farms and factories. Unfortunately, their remedy amounted to uncontrolled inflation.

The revival of agitation for free silver, for all of these reasons, resulted in the passage of the Sherman Silver Purchase Act of 1890. It was named after Senator John Sherman who, as Secretary of the Treasury (1875–1879), had established the gold reserve behind Civil War greenbacks. The new act, like the Bland-Allison one, was a compromise — this time a futile one. The accommodation was between inflationist westerners voting for the high-tariff McKinley Act, which they disliked, and eastern conservatives voting for the purchase of silver, which they feared. By requiring the government to purchase twice as much silver as before, the act threatened to undermine the Treasury's gold reserve. It satisfied only a few, and after the Panic of 1893 Congress repealed it.

The Sherman Act did *not* provide for the free and unlimited coinage of silver, which the West wanted — particularly the mineowners who wanted to benefit from the seigniorage. The act *did* provide for the monthly purchase of 4,500,000 ounces of silver by the government; this would support the market because it was almost the entire output of silver in this country at the time. The act also *did* provide for a *new* type of currency — the Treasury Note of 1890 — redeemable in *either* gold or silver. This was the theory; in practice the Treasury Note of 1890 was redeemable in gold — simply because 24.75 grains in the legal gold dollar were worth twice as much as 471.25 grains in the legal silver dollar. During the three years the act was in force, the U.S. government bought $156 million worth of silver at market prices, paying for it with paper money — the Treasury Notes of 1890. Would the U.S. government have enough gold to redeem, for those who wanted the metal, $346 million in Civil War greenbacks *and* $156 million in Treasury Notes of 1890?

This issue was resolved after the Panic of 1893, but it was a close thing. The basic cause of the Panic was overspeculation in railroads and industrial corporations. Railroad building in the 1880's had been accompanied by inordinate speculation which had undermined basically strong organizations; the manner in which Fisk and Gould ruined the Erie Railroad is a good example. Many corporations on the verge of bankruptcy declared stock dividends, or paid regular dividends out of capital rather than profits — as they were to do again in 1929. Unfortunately there is no such thing as a free lunch; ultimately someone has to pay, although the lunch can be charged for a while.

The panic was inevitable; it happened to come in 1893. The failure of the famous British firm of Baring Brothers in 1890, as a result of the collapse of its goldmining enterprises in South Africa, caused English investors to sell their American securities, thus depressing prices and draining gold from the United States. Within this country the general decline was precipitated by the spectacular failures early in 1893 of the Philadelphia and Reading Railroad, and of the National Cordage Company; following them into bankruptcy were a number of railroads — the Erie, the Northern Pacific, the Union Pacific. At the same time, the Sherman Silver Purchase Act cast doubt on the stability of the currency, particularly when the U.S. gold reserve fell below — as it did in April 1893 — the $100 million mark that was considered safe. The Democratic triumph in the presidential election of 1892 caused fear and uncertainty among Republican businessmen, largely because of the inflationary sentiment in the western section of the Democratic party.

Actually President Grover Cleveland, elected in 1892, was a conservative "Gold Democrat" who followed the "conventional wisdom" in dealing with depressions — allowing the depression and deflation to run their courses. This policy required that the national government do nothing to halt bankruptcies or to stop the decline of prices, wages, and employment. Private charity was left to deal with the hungry and the homeless at a time when some 3 million laboring men were out of work. As a result of this "hands-off" policy President Cleveland acted only to maintain public order and to save the gold reserve.

The wage reductions and breadlines sowed during the Panic of 1893 brought a harvest of labor outbreaks in 1894. The most dramatic was the Pullman strike, which we will reserve for later discussion. Among the unemployed, unrest spread rapidly and some of them began to march on Washington as a personal representation of their grievances. During the summer months of 1894 probably 1,200 men straggled into Washington for this purpose; they were "petitions in boots." The *best-known* was Coxey's Army, which had about 600 recruits. Their song, harkening in exaggerated fashion back to the Civil War, was

We're coming, Grover Cleveland, 500,000 strong,
We're marching on to Washington to right the nation's wrong.

Jacob S. Coxey was no ragged Wat Tyler; he was a wealthy sand and gravel producer from Massillon, Ohio, and owner of blooded horses and a racing stable known from coast to coast. A Theosophist in religion, in politics he was successively Populist, Democrat, Republican, Farmer-Labor. In 1894 he had Senator William A. Peffer of Kansas introduce a "Good-Roads" Bill, under which the national government would issue half a billion dollars in unsecured legal-tender notes to be expended for the employment of men in a vast nationwide road-building scheme. The bill was not progressing in Washington, so Coxey decided to take his "army" to the Capital to insure its passage. Anyone was eligible to march, except "thieves, anarchists, boodlers, and bankers!"

The column moved bravely out of Massillon toward the East, with "General" Coxey riding in a phaeton drawn by a pacer (Acolyte) worth $40,000 — and accompanied by his young son who was appropriately named Legal Tender Coxey. They reached Washington on 1 May 1894. The federal government, fearing a revolution, had deployed secret service agents to cover the march, held 1,500 troops in readiness in the District of Columbia, and placed sharpshooters on the top of the Treasury Building. Down Pennsylvania Avenue went Coxey and his army; the "General" intended to make a speech from the steps of the Capitol, after a procession through the grounds. There was, however, a law against it; at the end of Pennsylvania Avenue stood a row of resolute policemen. Coxey went through them and disappeared over a wall amid some shrubbery. Mounted police spurred their horses in pursuit, caught up with him as he reached the Capitol steps, and made the arrest. He was given twenty days in jail and a fine of five dollars for carrying a banner on the Capitol grounds and for stepping on the shrubbery. In 1931, in the midst of another depression, Coxey would be elected mayor of Massillon, Ohio — on the Republican ticket! In 1944, on the fiftieth anniversary of the "March" he would stand on Capitol Hill and would complete the speech that had been interrupted a half century earlier; he was heard by two hundred curious and uncomprehending onlookers. He died in Massillon in 1951, and with him passed a radical tradition as it was preached by the "hell-raising" school of American politics: Ignatius Donnelly, General Weaver, "Pitchfork" Ben Tillman, and "Sockless" Jerry Simpson. As Russell B. Nye has observed, one can make fun of Coxey — the "General" in the stiff collar, a character out of Dickens. But he had a humanity and a dignity that commanded respect. Coxey may have been wrong, and often was — but he died fighting the same battle that he thought Jefferson had fought before him — that of the "vested interests" versus the common good.

President Cleveland maintained public order; he also maintained the gold standard through the repeal of the Sherman Act and the continuance of gold payments at any and all hazards. He called Congress in special session in August 1893 and asked it to repeal the Sherman Silver Purchase Act, which had put pressure on the gold reserve because it required the issue of Treasury Notes of 1890, redeemable in gold. The House responded to his call by passing a repeal measure on 28 August 1893. There was delay in the Senate, where the silverites from the West were strong. In the upper house there was a filibuster which finally failed, and the repeal of the Sherman Act passed the Senate in October 1894.* Long before this time the situation in the Treasury was grave. The national government had a deficit because of the depression; in order to meet its own expenses it had to dip into the gold reserve, and it also had to spend Civil War greenbacks and Treasury Notes of 1890 as they were turned in for taxes — in spite of the fact that the government knew that this currency frequently came back for redemption in gold. Two crises occurred — one in 1894 and one in 1895. In the "Crisis of 1894" the gold reserve got down to around $50 million — far below the minimum amount for safety. President Cleveland proposed a bond issue to raise more gold, but Congress — in large part because of free-silver advocates — refused to authorize it. Cleveland then acted on his own, as Presidents sometimes do. He did so under authority of an almost forgotten statute which was almost twenty years old — the Specie Resumption Act of 1875 — and under this authority he borrowed the $100 million necessary to restore confidence. Unfortunately, this bond issue brought only temporary relief because some of the gold which the national government acquired had come from the Treasury. This meant that investors had turned in their currency for gold, and had lent the gold to the government for bonds.

A new crisis was in the making, and it occurred in 1895. In January of

---

* Here there is one of those interesting "ifs" in the study of history. In June 1893, shortly after his inauguration, Cleveland had almost died. If he had passed on, his place would have been taken by a "soft-money" Vice-President, and this probably would have deepened the crisis. The "soft-money" Vice-President was Adlai E. Stevenson from Illinois, the grandfather of the Democratic candidate for the Presidency in 1952. Cleveland had a malignant growth in his mouth, and submitted to a most delicate and secret operation on a yacht in New York Harbor in late June 1893. To maintain secrecy it was necessary that the patient have no resultant impediment of speech, and no external evidence. In the clandestine surgery the entire left upper jaw was removed, and a vulcanized-rubber artificial one was put in as a replacement. While Cleveland was convalescing, he was also fussing over his speech to the special session of Congress that would repeal the Sherman Act. The operation was entirely successful as far as both speech and appearance were concerned — so successful that when Cleveland died in 1907, almost fifteen years later, it was from organic disease of the heart and kidneys in no way related to the former cancerous growth in his mouth. The secret of his operation was so well kept that it was not publicly known until half a century later.

that year the gold reserve was again approaching the low figure of $50 million — and $3 million a day of the metal was being withdrawn. At that rate, the total governmental gold reserve would last only three weeks, after which the United States could not redeem its currency. The tension in Washington was terrific; there were all-night sessions at the White House, with the Secretary of the Treasury and the Attorney General conferring with the President until dawn. Finally the government turned to the bankers, chiefly to J. P. Morgan and to August Belmont — the American representative of the European Rothschilds. A gold loan of $65 million was arranged, with unusual conditions: at least half of the metal was to be procured abroad, and the banking fraternity was to exert influence to stop the further withdrawal of gold from the Treasury; that is, to refrain from turning in currency for redemption. The arrangement was successful, but not without severe criticism of the President. William Jennings Bryan said in Congress, "I only ask that the Treasury be administered on behalf of the American people and not on behalf of the Rothschilds and other foreign bankers." The Populists charged that the bankers had made a profit of $16 million on the transaction; it was even basely whispered that Cleveland himself had benefited financially from the operation. Actually the commissions were relatively small. The American syndicate, which handled $31 million of the transaction, made a bit more than a million and a half in commissions; Morgan's personal share was around $250,000.

All of this led to the presidential campaign of 1896, in which the money issue was the prime one. This campaign not only found the two traditional parties — the Republican and Democratic — with candidates; there was also a dynamic and vigorous third party, the Populists. The latter was agrarian in its mass support, with a clientele that was frequently illiterate and unsophisticated; at the same time there was a literary and intellectual basis for its progressive aims. This was largely derived from Henry George, Edward Bellamy, and Henry Demarest Lloyd. George and his idea of the single tax, as expounded in *Progress and Poverty* (1879), has already been discussed (see pp. 12–15). Edward Bellamy achieved his prominence and reputation through the publication, in 1888, of the Utopian novel *Looking Backward, 2000–1887*. His father was a Baptist minister; at eighteen the son went to Europe and began to take great interest in social problems and to talk about "man's inhumanity to man." His novel had a hero who fell into a hypnotic sleep from which he awakened in the year A.D. 2000. He looked back, to find that the social and economic injustices of the 1880's had melted away under an idyllic government, one in which much of the economy was nationalized in a new cooperative and socialist order. Bellamy's novel never approached *Progress and Poverty* in sales, but more than a million copies of it were sold; in 1890 it was averaging 10,000 copies per week, and for years the *Farmer's Alliance* gave it away as a subscription bonus. It hit the public fancy at the right time; one commentator said that "a Jay Gould demands an Edward Bellamy." The author would organize Nationalist Clubs across the nation; in 1890 there were 150 of them. Among the members were prominent intellectuals and reformers such as Edward Everett Hale, William Dean Howells, Hamlin Garland, Julia Ward Howe, and Frances Willard. Bellamy's ideas were partly embodied in the basic platform of the Populist party. His early death in 1898 ended a meteoric career of social reform, but he had initiated a debate about state capitalism and the cooperative commonwealth that affected economic thinking throughout the world.

Henry Demarest Lloyd pleased the Populists because he was opposed to the rapacity of corporations. Like Bellamy, Lloyd's father was a penurious minister, in his case of the Dutch Reformed Church. Lloyd was brought up in a rigidly Calvinist environment, against which he later revolted. After the Civil War he got his M.A. at Columbia, and also passed the bar for the practice of law. He became the financial editor of the Chicago *Tribune,* and in this capacity familiarized himself with trusts and labor movements — and thus began the career that was to become his life. In 1885 he left the *Tribune* and devoted the balance of his career to free-lance writing and to the public welfare. In 1890 he wrote an impassioned plea for industrial justice to Illinois coal miners, entitled *A Strike of Millionaires against Miners;* four years later he published *Wealth against Commonwealth,* a classic in the literature of protest. The latter was a tremendous denunciation of monopoly, particularly that of the Standard Oil Company, based on records of courts and legislative investigations. In his discussion of the lobbying influence of the Standard Oil Company in Pennsylvania, he wrote the famous statement: "The Standard has done everything to the Pennsylvania Legislature except to refine it." Later he would be a Populist candidate for Congress in 1894, and would leave the party in 1896 because he did not think it should narrow its platform to the money issue, as was the case. He died in 1903 while engaged in an exhaustive campaign for municipal ownership of street railways in Chicago.

The organization of and the personalities in the Populist party, and its platform, were unique and highly interesting. In 1890 there was profound disappointment in the West over the Sherman Silver Purchase Act, the Sherman Antitrust Act, and the McKinley Tariff. The plan of its agrarian leaders was to cast loose from the two major parties, and to combine with the urban wage earners. This was completed in 1892, when the Populists held their first national convention at Omaha. General James B. Weaver was nominated for the Presidency, and actually received more than 1 million popular votes — which was translated into twenty-two electoral votes because he carried the western states of Colorado, Idaho, and Nevada. The Populists were so elated that they forecast the demise of the

Republican party at the next presidential election in 1896. As it turned out, their prophecy was a bit premature.

The leading personalities in the Populist party were exciting and different. From Ohio there was Clarence Darrow, the "attorney for the damned." From Georgia there was Thomas Watson, who would come to believe that he had been cheated out of the Vice-Presidency and in his later days became an embittered racist and isolationist. In Texas there was Samuel Ealy Johnson, who had fought for the Confederacy, drove herds of cattle along the Chisholm Trail to Kansas, and served in the Texas legislature as a Populist. When his grandson Lyndon B. Johnson was born he mounted a horse and took to the countryside to give the neighbors the news: "A U.S. Senator was born this morning — my grandson" (actually the grandson as President became a curious combination of the old Populist liberal who believed fiercely in "helpin' the pur folks" *and* a millionaire who respected and courted wealthy businessmen). In Kansas there was the famous trio of Peffer, Simpson, and Lease. It was Senator William A. Peffer who had supported Coxey's "Good-Roads" Bill. "Sockless Jerry" Simpson had a sharp mind and combined his Populist doctrine with a belief in the single tax. A member of the U.S. House of Representatives in the 1890's, he directed his shrewd wit at insincerity and what he considered false doctrine; Champ Clark of Missouri (later Speaker) thought him the best debater in Congress. Mary Ellen Lease was variously known as the "Carry Nation of the Populists," "The Kansas Pythoness," and Mary "Yellin" Lease. She was a curiosity in American politics; of Irish birth and upbringing she became a lawyer, went to Kansas, was married before she was twenty, and had four children. She was a woman nearly six feet tall, and with her thick torso and long legs had no figure — but she had a golden voice. William Allen White did not like her, but admitted she was quite a spellbinder. He said, "She could recite the multiplication table and set a crowd hooting and hurrahing at her will." She made stirring speeches on how Wall Street ran the country.

Some of the westerners in the Populist party may have been a bit uncouth, but basically they were no more so than those of the eastern rich who could contrive crude and vulgar and wicked ways of showing off their wealth. There was at least one respect in which the Populists were definitely modern. They favored not only free silver and greenbacks, but an income tax, postal savings, and limited government ownership. The desire for postal savings reflected suspicion of private banks, with good reason. The system was finally introduced in 1911 and lasted for more than half a century before it was liquidated in 1967. The record in deposits came in 1947 with $3 billion from 4 million depositors; over the years the Post Office made almost a quarter of a billion dollars on the use of the deposits, in large part because it paid a low interest of 2 percent. Limited government ownership of railroads and communications (telephone and telegraph) was also advocated; the Populists said that "the railroad corporations will either own the people or the people must own the railroads." In the political sphere the party favored the Australian (secret) ballot, the initiative and referendum, and popular election of U.S. Senators. On behalf of hoped-for labor support, it endorsed the eight-hour day, and equal pay for equal work by both sexes; on the latter, apart from legal guarantees, one practical feminist once said that she was only looking forward to "the day when a mediocre woman can get as far as a mediocre man." Curiously, although the Populists were identified by most people with the interests of farmers, in 1892 they derived the largest percentage of their popular vote in the mountain states, three of which Weaver carried. These were mining areas, relatively uninterested in the People's program except as it pertained to silver. As a prospective national party, therefore, the Populists were faced with the fact that they had virtually no following in the East and that they had little support in the solid South; their supposedly national ticket had done best in the silver country. On the grounds of expediency, as the decade of the 1890's wore on, they tended to emphasize the money question and to minimize the other planks in their platform — a development that turned out to be a serious mistake, as Henry Demarest Lloyd pointed out.

In any case the platform was so radical for its time that the Populists became unpopular in many places. There are records of their members being banished from churches, colleges, and universities; of being driven from their homes; of being refused credit because of their beliefs. The feeling of many people about this radical party was once expressed by Theodore Roosevelt when he declared that the Populist Movement should be suppressed as the Paris Commune was put down, "by taking ten or a dozen of their leaders out, standing . . . them against a wall, and shooting them dead." When that dread hour came, the Rough Rider continued, "I shall be found at the head of my regiment."

The three political parties held successive nominating conventions in the summer of 1896; the Republicans met first in June, the Democrats in early July, the Populists later in the month — with an opportunity to survey the work of their rivals. The Big Man for the conservatives was Marcus Alonzo Hanna, a tycoon who had developed extensive interests in coal, iron, Great Lakes shipping, banking, *and* the Republican party. Hanna was exceptionally honest and forthright; there was no dissimulation about what he wanted. He was painfully frank in his explanations of party politics, and contemptuous of those who cloaked their motives in high-sounding phrases. He once said, "Politics are one form of business, and *must* be treated strictly as a business." On another occasion he observed that in a democracy all questions of government are eventually questions of money — who has it and who gets it. In 1890 Hanna had been running the Republican party in Ohio, was instrumental in electing William McKinley as governor, and bailed him out when the governor was faced with financial ruin in 1893. In 1895 Hanna, offering vague excuses about the enjoyment of one's last years, retired from the control of his business enterprises; this freed him for full-time service to McKinley's cause. Biographer Herbert Croly put it this way: "He had come to a parting of the ways. Politics had become more absorbing than business." This was fortunate for McKinley, who would never have gone far by himself. But the two — McKinley and Hanna — in Margaret Leach's phrase, "made *one* perfect politician." McKinley was idealistic, really believed in the myth of the self-made man, was platitudinous and moralistic. Hanna was a realist who had few illusions about ideals and morality, but admired them as they appeared in McKinley because they would bring McKinley votes!

With full-time devotion to politics Hanna bought McKinley the nomination in 1896; Theodore Roosevelt was to say that Hanna advertised McKinley as though he were a patent medicine. This cost money, about $100,000 of it; it is no wonder that the Republican statesman was sometimes called "Dollar Mark" Hanna. McKinley certainly had all the traditional qualifications. He was born of Scotch-Irish stock in the pivotal state of Ohio, his antecedents were from the numerous middle class, he was a devout Methodist and a loyal husband whose wife was a chronic invalid, and he had no pretensions of learning or profundity. Everyone knew that he attended church regularly, read the Bible to his invalid wife, and would always hide his cigar when his picture was taken — lest he corrupt American youth. At the same time he had a political shrewdness; "Uncle Joe" Cannon, the Republican stalwart who was later Speaker, used to say that McKinley had his ear so close to the ground that it was full of grasshoppers. Perhaps that explains McKinley's stand on the money question in 1896. He had supported free silver until 1890, and had then voted for the Sherman Act. Speaker Tom Reed said, "McKinley isn't a gold-bug. McKinley isn't a silver-bug. McKinley is a straddle-bug." In 1896 he certainly wanted to straddle the issue, focus all attention on the tariff. Hanna agreed. Not so the eastern Republicans; they insisted on, and got, a plank in the platform calling for an inviolable gold standard. The political campaign thus became the "Battle of the Standards," whether the candidate approved or not.

When the Democrats assembled in Chicago in early July, they were sure of only one thing — they were not going to nominate Grover Cleveland again, or anyone he suggested. In the House, Democrat Champ Clark likened the Democratic President to Benedict Arnold and Aaron Burr, naming him with them as the three greatest traitors the country had ever known. In the Senate there was an irascible, blunt, and ill-mannered agrarian from South Carolina — Benjamin Ryan Tillman — who went by the nickname "Pitchfork Ben." He earned it because of his virtuosity in billingsgate. He said of his party's incumbent President:

We elected a President to give the people bread and he gave them only stones. . . . When Judas betrayed Christ his beard was not blacker than this scoundrel, Cleveland, in deceiving the Democracy. He is an old bag of beef and I am going to Washington with a pitchfork and prod him in his fat old ribs.

The hostility toward Cleveland meant that the Democratic nominee would probably come from the West. He did — in the person of William Jennings Bryan, then only thirty-six years old. He had been polishing a speech for some years, and sent the convention into a pandemonium with his attack on plutocracy and the gold standard in a rousing peroration: "You shall not press down upon the brow of labor this crown of thorns. You shall not crucify mankind upon a cross of gold." The platform called for the free and unlimited coinage of silver at a ratio of 16 to 1, and the religious Bryan would preach free silver as he preached Christ crucified — the hope of man's salvation. He would call upon eternal principles, would do obeisance to the pioneer log cabin and the little red schoolhouse, would strike the Physiocratic note that land was the source of all wealth, would assure the farmer and the shopkeeper that they were as much businessmen as those who "gambled" on Wall Street. This was too much for the eastern "gold" Democrats. Carter Glass, the peppery little Virginian who later played a prominent role in the writing and enactment of the Federal Reserve Act, found Bryan ignorant in economics; he once said, "That goddamn nincompoop thinks that any man with real goodness of heart can write a banking act." The same attitude was reflected by conservative Senator David B. Hill of New York. When he returned from the Democratic convention in July 1896, someone asked him, "Are you still a Democrat?" His reply was, "Yes, I am a Democrat still, very still." About the only effective support Bryan got in the East was from William Randolph Hearst, who had inherited millions his father made in western mines.*

---

* Bryan has a reputation of being a liberal, a progressive, in comparison with McKinley. This is doubtful. Apart from the free-silver issue on which he was wrong (the gold standard was too limited, free silver was too inflationary), Bryan was far from radical and in some respects was a reactionary. On the issue of civil liberties he was reactionary, as was indicated in his later evangelical campaigns to limit personal freedom. He opposed the appointment of Harvard's president Charles W. Eliot, a Unitarian, as minister to China on the theory that this would nullify the work of Christian missionaries who preached the Divine Birth. On the other hand he would endorse Warren G. Harding as a believer in the Scriptures, and he would temporize with the Ku Klux Klan, because most of its members were Fundamentalists. He favored Prohibition, the Noble Experiment that failed. This was ironical because Bryan could not control his own craving — for food. In old age the "Boy Orator of the Platte" would grow fat and flabby, the victim of his own insatiable appetite for hot biscuits and fried chicken and corn on the cob — and would ultimately die of disease

The Populist convention came last, at St. Louis. Some of the delegates had walked to save train fare, some could afford rooms only in the shoddiest of hotels, some bought nickel meals at cheap lunch counters. The Populists had purposely met after the conventions of the two major parties because they believed those parties would both nominate gold candidates. The Democrats, with Bryan, upset their calculations; at St. Louis they found themselves forced to nominate Bryan too, lest the vote against McKinley and Hanna be split. That made free silver the paramount issue in the election, and required the Populists to soft-pedal the more radical planks in their platform in order not to embarrass the Democrats. A group of the more radical members of the party did balk at the nomination, along with Bryan, of his Democratic running mate for the Vice-Presidency. He was Arthur Sewall, a banker and shipbuilder from Maine. Sewall belonged to a long-established New England family that had developed Bath, Maine, into a principal shipbuilding port. There, as the head of his own firm Sewall built and operated more sailing vessels than any other shipbuilder in America after the Civil War. From the standpoint of Democratic strategy Bryan and Sewall made a perfect team: Nebraska and Maine, a bank president to dilute the radicalism of Bryan's free silver. The Populists, however, found Sewall impossible. From Minnesota Ignatius Donnelly, a promoter of lost causes who was known as the "Sage of Nininger" (a farming town he had founded), said the Populists were "willing to swallow Democracy gilded with the genius of Bryan — but were unwilling to stomach plutocracy in the body of Sewall." The Populists therefore nominated their own candidate for Vice-President; he was Tom Watson from Georgia. They were hopeful that, in payment for their endorsement of Bryan, the Democrats would drop Sewall and replace him with Watson. This did not happen; Bryan never recognized Watson as his running mate during the campaign. Watson would claim that this failure defeated Bryan, that through this mistake the "Great Commoner" lost enough votes in critical states to lose the election.

During the campaign Bryan stumped the country, emphasized the issue as one between the People and the Bankers. Democratic strategy was to play up gold as the symbol of heartless greed and snobbish wealth, the same gold that had deserted the country during the Panic of 1893. Silver, on the other hand, was the symbol of honest democracy. Cartoons were drawn of Hanna as an obese man, a Mr. Moneybags with brutalized aspect — clad in a checkered suit with dollar signs all over it — leading a child on a string. The child was labeled McKinley. On the other side the Republicans portrayed Bryan as too young and crazy; it was claimed that he

---

that derived from overeating. In the field of academic freedom he opposed the teaching of evolution, thought it better to know the Rock of Ages than the age of rocks, and said, "They can't make a monkey out of me."

suffered from graphomania, oratorical monomania, paranoia reformatoria. John Hay, the biographer of Lincoln and later Secretary of State, called Bryan "a blatant ass of the prairies." The Republicans claimed that if Bryan was elected businessmen might as well close up shop, laborers and their families would starve to death, widows and orphans would lose their bank deposits, and farmers' crops would rot in the fields. On the basis of such fears Hanna was able to collect a huge campaign fund by milking the protected interests. Standard Oil gave $250,000; banks were assessed at the rate of one-fourth of one percent of their capital — and most of them paid. William Steinway, the manufacturer of pianos, announced to his employees that the factory would close if Bryan was elected. In general it can be said that American business, fearing for its privileges, acted as if the Hun were at the gates. On Wall Street there was talk of an eastern secession, in the event of a Democratic victory. Hay reported that many of his friends were preparing to buy homes in Europe if Bryan won, fearing personal harm at the hands of mobs in the United States. In retrospect this is amazing because there was no danger of a real revolution in 1896. Had Bryan won, it simply would have transferred political power from the North and Northeast, to the West and South. Democracy, Judeo-Christianity, capitalism — all would have remained intact. Bryan could be called a radical on the coinage issue only.

The Republicans won by a margin of 51 to 47 percent in popular vote, and 271 to 176 in the electoral college. It was a victory for Big Business; Alexander Hamilton had triumphed from the grave. For Hanna, with McKinley in the Presidency, God was in his heaven and the world was good. In 1899, on the eve of McKinley's second campaign, Hanna expressed his own contentment in the words: "All we need to do is 'stand pat.'" He was proud of the phrase, and by repeating it often gave the Republican party a name that became a permanent symbol. Historians have speculated over the reasons for the Democratic loss in 1896. Many have been assigned, but the major one appears to be that labor in the North and East failed to support Bryan. He failed to win the electoral vote of a single state in which the industrial working class was important, and in 1896 the struggle for the labor vote was crucial. Conversely, there seem to have been two reasons for the support, by laborers, of McKinley. For one thing, the Republicans attracted the labor vote by blaming the Democrats for the Panic of 1893 and the depression that followed. The depression had occurred in a Democratic administration, and the prosperity that was returning was seemingly due to the conservative policies of Cleveland, now repudiated by the Bryanites. The second reason was the influence of Mark Hanna. In his attitude toward labor he was much more farsighted than most industrial leaders of his day. He condemned employers who would not meet employees halfway in negotiation and regarded reasonable treatment of labor as the best security for industrial peace. He thought George Pullman a fool for refusing to arbitrate the famous strike of 1894. Not the least of Hanna's great services to his party was the reconciling of labor groups to it. He did this by convincing labor that its well-being was contingent on the prosperity of business, that McKinley was the "advance agent of prosperity," and that high protective tariffs and the "full dinner pail" went hand in hand. For a half century after the Civil War the Republican Party, although it was a party of business, enjoyed the support of three constituencies which by no means shared the economic profits of the business community. They were the wage earners mentioned above, the Negroes, and the northern farmers. After Mark Hanna was dead, the Republican party lost these groups when they finally realized that they were really not loved. From that point Presidents Wilson, Franklin Roosevelt, Truman, Kennedy, and Johnson began to capitalize on the basic dissensions within the GOP.

Somehow the dire prophecies of the free-silver orators never came to pass. After the campaign of 1896 the curtain of gloom lifted, and even before the closing month of that year there were hints of returning prosperity. The question is why — what were the forces that were to change the bitter American farmer in the years after 1896 from a flaming radical into a staid husbandman? There were two: an increase in the amount of money in circulation, and a concomitant rise in prices. The increase in money came because of an augmentation in national-bank notes and gold. New bond issues necessary to finance the war with Spain increased the amount of this bond-backed paper money; the available gold increased so rapidly that by 1914, when World War I erupted, the world's monetary stock of gold was twice that in 1896. The increase was due to new finds in the Rand of South Africa and the Klondike of Canada, and because two engineers, McArthur and Forest by name, perfected the cyanide process for extracting gold from low-grade ores not previously exploited. They had established their process in the early 1890's, when Bryan first began to talk about crucifixion on a cross of gold. As a result of the Rand, the Klondike, and the cyanide process, the advocates of free silver actually got what they wanted — cheap money — but they got it through the medium of gold. The increase in money in circulation was accompanied by an increase in prices, agricultural ones included. In the case of farm products the rise was accentuated by crop failures elsewhere in the world. The Indian wheat crop had failed in 1896, and the European was to be short in 1897.

So in 1900 Bryan could logically say that free silver was no longer necessary and that there was no reason to campaign on that dead issue, but that he should approach the American electorate on the new issue of imperialism. In actual fact, by 1920 the amount of money in circulation was beyond the wildest dreams of the most radical of the Populists. In its wildest moments the Populist party had asked for $50 per capita in the circulating medium of the country. In 1920 this mark was exceeded; it was slightly over $51. The effect on the radicalism of American farmers was regressive. In Iowa farmers had revived an ancient aphorism and given it the terminology of the 1920's: "When corn is $1 a bushel, the farmer is a radical; when it's $1.50 a bushel, he's a progressive; and when it's $2 a bushel, he's a conservative."

The Currency Act of 1900 definitely ended all fears of further silver and other "cheap money" scares. It put the country on the gold standard by definitely declaring that *all* other forms of U.S. money were redeemable in gold, and it created a Treasury reserve of $150 million — a separate and distinct fund which could be used *only* for the redemption of currency. Ironically, with the passage of the Gold Standard Act of 1900, the people of the United States were nailed to a cross of gold, and rather comfortably until 1933, when the Roosevelt administration undertook the most drastic monetary experiment in our history.

The close of the second phase of the free-silver movement presaged the end of the Populist party. In 1900 it nominated Wharton Parker, a bimetallist who received only fifty thousand votes. Although the party struggled on until 1908, it was no use; the organization had died with the demise of free silver. Henry Demarest Lloyd had been right; he had called the silver issue "the cowbird of the reform movement — likely to push all the other eggs out of the basket." As far as immediate practical results were concerned, the Populist party accomplished exactly nothing. The political system that had been in power since the Civil War, with but few exceptions, remained in power — its branches shaken by the winds of 1896 but its roots still firmly embedded. In the long run, however, the Populist platform was to have great influence. By 1940 every feature of the Populist platform had been accepted except government ownership of transportation and communications.

In 1934 a little bloc of western silver-state senators, led by the ineffable Senator Pat McCarran of Nevada, pushed through the Silver Purchase Act. They did it in the manner of all blocs — by vote-trading and logrolling and wheedling. In effect, the new act supported the price of silver through governmental purchase of all silver that was not sold in the commercial market — a program that drew horrified criticism from economists and editorial writers. Senator Paul Douglas of Illinois, a professional economist by training, was once asked, "Of what use is this silver policy?" His reply was frank and realistic: "There are only sixteen reasons for it — the sixteen senators from the mountain states."

Silver mining was a very sick industry in 1934. The Purchase Act was designed to revive it by:

Authorizing the coinage of silver dollars at any ratio the President should choose. The shades of the Populists and of William Jennings Bryan must have reappeared, in jubilant celebration. President Roosevelt chose a ratio of 27 to 1 — $1.29 per ounce for silver and $35 for gold. The new silver bought by the national government would be paid for, for those who did not want the cumbersome silver cartwheels, with a new type of paper money — the silver certificates established by this act.

Authorizing the President to buy silver until (a) the market price of the metal should reach $1.29 an ounce — as contrasted with the price of 45¢ at the time the act was passed, or (b) if this failed, until the Treasury's silver holdings should reach one-third the value of its gold stocks.

Under this legislation the U.S. government bought all the existing bullion (already mined) in the United States at 50¢ an ounce. For the next quarter of a century it also bought all newly mined silver offered, at a price which was set by the government to establish a supporting price-floor for the metal. Until the 1950's this price varied from 50¢ an ounce in 1934 to 90¢ in 1950. By that year, after sixteen years of purchases under the act, the U.S. Treasury had bought almost 3 billion ounces of silver at a total cost of $1.5 billion. It was buried at West Point, the silver counterpart of Fort Knox.

Why was all this done? According to the sixteen silver-state senators, there were three economic reasons, all of them fallacious when scrutinized and examined:

The silver industry *deserved* rehabilitation. There is no question that governmental purchases rehabilitated the industry because it assured the producers of a constant and stable market — regardless of the commercial price. As an example, in early 1934 the market price of silver was 45¢ an ounce. With the passage of the Silver Purchase Act of that year, the market price jumped immediately to 81¢ an ounce. There is a question, however, as to whether it was wise for the national government to support a small industry like silver unless, in all equity, it supported many other small industries that needed help and were just as large — or larger. Silver purchases appeared to establish a dangerous precedent because in 1934 silver mining was a piddling industry with only 3,000 employees. In annual product it was about equal with grape jelly, wire nails, and anhydrous ammonia; chewing gum was twice as valuable. In Nevada, the income from divorces was greater than that from silver. Cynics asked, "Should the national government also support divorce?"

Silver purchases would increase the purchasing power of the Orient, and of Mexico, whose monetary systems were based on silver. The argument was that an increase in the value of silver would increase their ability to buy our products, thereby increasing our exports. Actually, this claim is a prime illustration of the economic ignorance of those who made it, because the result was exactly opposite. At 81¢ an ounce the Orient and Mexico saw much of their silver, their basic money, depart from their shores. The result was deflation in both areas, forcing them off the silver standard and lowering their purchasing power.

The purchase of silver would bring inflation of *all* domestic prices, a goal devoutly desired in depression-ridden 1934. Silver advocates claimed there was a close, and mystical, connection between the price of silver and the price of all other commodities. Senator McCarran had a unique theory about this relationship. He said, "Silver is not a commodity. It is a monetary unit." This is, of course, economic twaddle. Inflation or deflation is now controlled in large part by the Federal Reserve System, and certainly not by the amount of silver we purchase. As far as inflation is concerned the purchase of tin or old tires or Fords would have been just as valuable as the purchase of silver.

On the basis of these dubious arguments the U.S. government purchased silver until the 1950's, when a change occurred that made price support for silver both silly and impossible. Silver, which had been a sick metal in the 1930's, has now become an extremely healthy one; it is an important commercial and industrial commodity for photographic film, for electronics, and for missiles — as well as for silverware. It is the best electrical conductor known — used for sophisticated batteries, switches, and other control mechanisms in everything from household appliances to spacecraft. The largest single private consumer, using about 30 million ounces a year (fifteen tons a week) for photographic supplies, is the Eastman Kodak Company. Demand exceeds supply; the world is now using three times as much silver every year as it produces. There is certainly no present need to prop up the price of silver, which was the purpose of the Silver Act of 1934.

Demand for silver is now so great that it exceeds world production by more than 200 million ounces a year. This annual deficit has been met in the United States by melting down nonmonetary silver and by freeing as much U.S. government silver as possible. To date, this has been accomplished by selling the surplus, which existed until 1963, by eliminating the silver certificates, thus freeing the reserve of silver behind them, and by debasing the silver coinage, thus reducing the need for silver in its minting.

Sale of the surplus went on from 1950 to 1963. It will be recalled that the United States had, in 1950, what seemed to be an enormous pile of silver at West Point — 2.7 billion ounces of it. At that time it was estimated that the government needed 1.3 billion ounces for new coins and as a reserve for the Bland-Allison Silver Certificates, the Treasury Notes of 1890, and the silver certificates issued under the Act of 1934. That left 1.4 billion ounces for which there seemed to be no immediate need; this surplus was sold to commercial buyers at 91¢ an ounce initially, and later at $1.29 an ounce. By 1963, however, this extraordinary surplus was gone, and other devices were necessary to free remaining reserves.

The first was to eliminate the silver certificates, and by this means to free the reserves behind them. President Kennedy asked Congress for new legislation; the response was the Silver Act of 1963. It repealed the Silver Purchase Act of 1934; demonetized the silver dollar — exactly ninety years after the "Crime of '73"; and authorized the Federal Reserve System to retire the certificates, redeemable in the Treasury silver which was behind the Bland-Allison notes, the Treasury Notes of 1890, and the silver certificates issued under the Act of 1934. The Federal was to replace these silver certificates with Federal Reserve Notes. This meant that, after 1963, the Treasury would issue coins only. The Federal would thus issue all paper money; it would have no silver behind its new notes, but they would have the usual backing of 25 percent in gold. This new legislation obviously freed the 1.3 billion ounces which was being held in reserve, so that all of it could be sold or used in the future for the production of subsidiary coins. At that time the federal government was using 300 million ounces a year in the production of these coins, for which there was an increasing demand because of the concomitant growth of population, of coin machines, and of speculative hoarding.

The next step was obviously to debase subsidiary coins, and thus relieve the Treasury of the annual obligation of putting 300 million ounces of silver into them. This was accomplished in 1965; it had been done earlier by Britain and Cuba and Mexico. For 173 years, from 1792 to 1965, the alloy in U.S. dimes, quarters, and half dollars was 90 percent silver and 10 percent copper. This became hazardous, with the increase in the price of silver. At $1.29 an ounce, the market price in 1966, silver dollars (which are pure silver) were worth their weight in silver. Subsidiary coins would be worth their weight if the market price increased to $1.38 an ounce. With this situation in mind, Congress in 1965 reduced the silver content of the half-dollar from 90 to 40 percent, the balance of 60 percent to be in copper. It also authorized what are called "sandwich" quarters and dimes, made from an alloy of copper and nickel. The Treasury had been involved for a year in a crash-research program to find nonsilver material that would work in millions of pay telephones and vending machines that are now an essential part of American society. In the nick of time it developed the cupro-nickel coins, and Congress authorized the switch to the new alloy — similar to that which had always been used in the five-cent piece. At the present time, therefore, there is no silver in any newly produced coinage except half dollars. The amount of silver in the half dollars will not be worth 50¢ commercially until the price soars to $3.38 an ounce, which seems to be unlikely in the immediate future in spite of increased demand.

This change reduced the demands on the Treasury Department for "coinage" silver from 300 million ounces in 1965 to 30 million in 1966, and to an estimated annual 15 million ounces since that time. This meant that what silver the Treasury had in its reserve could be sold or could be kept there to provide the metal for half dollars — for years to come.* It also

---

* In 1968 the Treasury was holding 165 million ounces of silver in reserve as a stockpile for future coinage, enough to produce silver half dollars for more than a decade.

meant, with world demand what it was, that the Treasury no longer needed to be ready to sell silver at $1.29 an ounce, which it had done for some years. This policy had put a ceiling (not a floor) on not only the domestic price but also on the world price of silver. The Treasury had become the "residual supplier" of silver to the world. For some time, in the 1960's, the Treasury still had enough silver to feed the market and to hold down the price — enough, it thought, to last at least until 1970. But industrial demand here and abroad began to increase rapidly, and it was obvious that the price of silver was bound to rise when the Treasury ceased its sales. Finally on 14 July 1967 (Bastille Day!) the Treasury made a key decision. It felt that enough new cupro-nickel coins had been produced to risk freeing the silver price altogether (otherwise the older silver coins would have been hoarded, and the U.S. would have been bereft of coinage). This was done through an announcement that the Treasury would no longer supply the market at $1.29 an ounce. The price immediately rose; in 1968 silver was valued commercially at more than two dollars an ounce. At this price, the new meaningless ratio with gold was approximately 16 to 1 — the goal Bryan had once thought to be so important.

After a long history as money, silver is now only a metal — more valuable in making a film emulsion or as an electronic component than as a coin. One wonders what Pat McCarran would say, were he alive to comment.

In addition, it had about 350 million ounces on hand, largely in the form of old silver coins which could be melted down. It was selling this additional amount (of 350 million ounces) on the private market at high and profitable prices, at the rate of 2 million ounces a week. This benefited the Treasury, and reduced the annual international deficit in the metal. At the rate of its sales in 1968, the Treasury could have supplied the private market for about three years.

VII

A Money Supply for the Corporation, the Citizen, and the Government: A Managed Currency in the Twentieth Century?

THE Federal Reserve System, established in 1913, had its antecedents in the Panic of 1907, the Aldrich-Vreeland Act of 1908, and the Pujo Investigation (of the "Money Power") in 1912. The nation came out of the peculiar and embarrassing "rich man's" or "banker's" Panic of 1907 with three conclusions:

First, that reserve requirements were inadequate, particularly those of the rapidly rising trust companies that were operating also as commercial banks. These trust companies had begun as managers of estates, and by branching out into commercial banking had become deeply involved in stock-market manipulations, actually becoming security affiliates to banking operations. Their reserves were inadequate; at the turn of the century in New York national banks had to keep reserves of 25 percent, state banks of 15 percent — but the requirement for trust companies was only 5 percent. It was well noted that the Panic of 1907 was precipitated by the closing of one of these trust companies, in order to prevent a run on the institution. It was the Knickerbocker Trust Company of New York City.

Second, that the currency of the nation was too inelastic. Most of the institutions that went to the wall in this crisis, though basically sound, could not weather a temporary but violent financial storm: they had no way to convert good assets into paper money during a temporary crisis.

Third, that the public interest was not considered, or at least was not thought to be very important, during the Panic of 1907. This was apparent from the fact that the most important person during the crisis was not the President of the United States, or Secretary of the Treasury George B. Cortelyou, but J. Pierpont Morgan. "Morgan the Peerless" was never more in his element than in this year, as he rallied the "money trust." He saw to it that each solvent bank was assessed to make up rescue funds, and that the federal government added at least $50 million — but that these sums were dispensed by Morgan to whomever he chose to favor, at 20 percent interest. When he drove down Broadway in his carriage the cheering crowd ran alongside to catch a glimpse of him, and when he strode into his office at 23 Wall Street it was between lines of anxious financial tycoons. It was not true, as was later charged, that Morgan and Rockefeller inspired the Panic, but it was obvious that they emerged from it stronger than ever. Rockefeller came out with rich spoils in copper and with a good share of Westinghouse. Morgan added to his steamship holdings and, with the consent of President Roosevelt, bought out at half price the Tennessee Coal and Iron Company, which had been U.S. Steel's chief competitor.

During the following year Congress reacted by passing the Aldrich-Vreeland Act, providing temporary palliatives. Edward B. Vreeland was a relatively insignificant member of the House from New York, but Nelson Wilmarth Aldrich was one of the most important — and probably one of the richest — men ever to sit in the U.S. Senate, where he represented Rhode Island for three decades, 1881–1911. When he gave up the wholesale grocery business in 1881 to enter the Senate, he was worth about $50,000. When he left the Senate thirty years later he had a fortune of more than $30 million — largely from banking, sugar, rubber, and public utilities. His power in the national arena was so great that biographer Ferdinand Lundberg once quipped that "seven Presidents served under Aldrich." The Aldrich-Vreeland Act, passed because of congressional concern over the monetary situation, provided a more elastic currency. The act permitted national banks to issue *emergency* notes on the security of bonds — those of states, counties, and towns. A tax of up to 10 percent per month was intended to discourage abundant issues, and certainly did so. It was not surprising that national banks did not take advantage of this provision for emergency notes until the dark days of 1914, when the war in Europe caused financial imbalances all over the world.

In addition, the act called for a study of the national banking system, with proposals for reform. This was to be done by a National Monetary Commission consisting of eighteen members of Congress with Aldrich as chairman. The commission reported in 1912, in thirty-eight volumes. Those who waded through it found the report to be conservative, really proposing the reestablishment of an institution similar to the old Bank of the United States as it had been in the days of Nicholas Biddle.

One of the members of the National Monetary Commission, Arsène Pujo, a member of the House of Representatives from Louisiana, was dissatisfied with the commission's report because he was worried about the existing "money power." So were a number of others. In 1911 Woodrow Wilson, then governor of New Jersey, said, "The great monopoly in this country is the money monopoly. . . . The growth of the nation and all our activities are in the hands of a few men . . . who chill and check and destroy genuine economic freedom."

Louis Brandeis, later to be a prominent member of the Supreme Court, echoed the same philosophy. He said, "We must break the money trust or the money trust will break us." So it was that in 1912 Pujo received congressional authorization to investigate the "money trust." There were two spectacular features of his investigation. One was the interrogation of J. P. Morgan by the committee's counsel, Samuel Untermyer. The other was the general finding that three banking groups — those of Morgan, Rockefeller, and Baker (First National Bank of New York) — controlled corporations with a combined capital of more than $22 billion. The country was shocked, so shocked that all candidates in the presidential campaign of 1912 promised reform. The Democrats won with Wilson, and the results were the Federal Reserve Act of 1913 and the Clayton Antitrust Act of the following year.

The most important architect of the Federal Reserve System was Carter Glass, chairman of the House Committee on Banking and Currency. In 1918 he became Secretary of the Treasury under Wilson, resigning in 1920 to serve as U.S. Senator from Virginia for more than a quarter of a century until his death in 1946. Interestingly, he was violently opposed to most of the New Deal domestic policies, including monetary ones, but supported Roosevelt's foreign policy. He was short, slight, and prickly — with the defiant and contemptuous bearing of a man who feared no one. He had a habit of talking out of the left corner of his mouth, giving his face a peculiar twisted expression that was well adapted to his snarls and his snorts. Glass wrote a banking act in 1913 that embodied Wilson's recommendations for public control, a decentralized system, and the establishment of an elastic greenback and deposit currency through control of bank reserves. Actually the final bill was a compromise. On the one side Socialists advocated government ownership, and Progressives like Robert La Follette wanted much more direct government control than was finally incorporated into the bill. On the other side the American Banker's Association campaigned bitterly against the measure. It objected to any control by a central board and spoke scornfully of asset currency — particularly of what it called "corn-tassel currency" based on farm paper. The final bill mingled some governmental control in the public interest with private ownership of banks. There had been concessions by both sides but the measure still qualified as a crucial and major step in the establishment of governmental regulation of American business enterprise. It was the first thorough overhauling of the national banking system after the Civil War, and it was long overdue.

Decentralization was insisted upon because of the historic worry in this nation over monopoly and because the Democratic party, then in control of Congress, was — in these pre–New Deal days — traditionally in favor of local control and state's rights. Rather than having one central bank in the political capital, as in central banking systems in most countries, the Federal Reserve System is divided into twelve districts, each with a Federal Reserve Bank. The district Federal Reserve Banks are "banker's banks"; by statute, their stock is held entirely by member banks, which include all national banks — and may include state banks and trust companies if they meet certain requirements. Each member bank must subscribe for stock, in the district Reserve Bank, to the extent of 6 percent of its own capital; dividends on this stock are limited to 6 percent per annum. Ownership of reserve-bank stock is in the nature of an obligation incidental to membership in the system, and does not carry with it the attributes of control and financial interest ordinarily attached to stock ownership in corporations that are operated for profit — because reserve banks are operated instead for public service. Each district reserve bank has nine directors, six of whom are chosen by member banks and three by the central board of governors of the system. At the present time member banks in the Federal Reserve System control more than 90 percent of the loans and securities of all insured commercial banks in the United States. The Federal Reserve Bank in New York is the most important of the district banks, because it is the largest in the volume of its transactions and because it is responsible for operations on the international "swap network" which deals with the complexities of foreign exchange. The president of the Federal Reserve Bank in New York earns $75,000 a year, making him the second-highest-paid quasi-federal official after the President of the United States. Federal reserve salaries in district banks are intended to be competitive in banker terms rather than those applying to the national civil service.

In this decentralized system public control is maintained through the seven members of the board of governors in Washington, appointed by the President (with the advice and consent of the Senate) for fourteen-year terms — not more than one from each district. The ideal was and is to have an intelligent, courageous, and nonpolitical board; it has been called the Supreme Court of Finance, and its chairman can be a person of tremendous power and influence. The board of governors has the power to exercise great restraint against inflation, or relief against deflation, through its extensive monetary powers. By reason of human frailty, unfortunately, this great power was not exercised very sensibly until 1951. In the late 1920's it was apparent that the board should check speculation in Wall Street; it did little or nothing. In the terrible depression of the 1930's, it was apparent that the board should provide monetary relief for the deflation that existed by lowering the rediscount rate and thus increasing the volume of money in circulation. It actually raised the rediscount rate several times in the 1930's, presumably to halt the flow of gold from the United States and to reduce inflationary pressures. At this distance in time it is difficult to understand how any informed person, much less the board of governors, could have feared inflation with 15 million unemployed. After World War II, with a great danger of inflation because of buying power in savings that had been dammed up by direct controls during the war, the board should have exercised a policy of restraint — through tighter money and higher interest rates. The Treasury, however, demanded low interest rates in order to reduce the interest charges on the huge national debt; and because of commitments the Federal had made during the war, its hands were tied from 1946 to 1951. In 1951 the two institutions reached a famous "accord," and since that time the Federal has shown more flexibility and independence and intelligence in the use of its powers.

This was due, in large part, to the fact that from 1951 until 1970 the board was to have one chairman — the most prominent and influential one in its history — William McChesney Martin. He was born in St. Louis (where his father was the first president of the Federal Reserve District Bank in that city), graduated from Yale in 1927, and early in the Depression of the 1930's moved to New York to work in a brokerage house. He was available on two occasions of great crisis when the world of finance needed a compromise candidate for a major job. The first was in the late 1930's when the Stock Exchange, already in public disrepute, had just been rocked by the Richard Whitney scandal (see pp. 216–217) and was facing an angry Securities and Exchange Commission, which was ready to pounce. Martin was the most acceptable candidate to both the "Old Guard" and the reforming "Young Turks," and became president of the Stock Exchange at thirty-one. It was under his regime from 1938 to 1941 that many of the major reforms of the Exchange occurred — converting it, as one commentator put it, "from a private club to a public utility." The second time he was on the spot, and available, was in 1951. After the war he had entered government service and by 1950 was Assistant Secretary of the Treasury. At that time there was great bitterness between Secretary of the Treasury John W. Snyder and Thomas McCabe (who was chairman of the board of governors of the Federal) over open-market operations of the board. The result was that McCabe resigned, President Truman picked Martin as his successor, and he was to remain as chairman for nineteen years. This is the longest service of any agency head in Washington, excepting the late J. Edgar Hoover of the FBI. Martin was known as the contemplative type who came as close to the "middle road" as it was possible to get. His basic philosophy was one of opposition to inflation — either galloping or creeping.

President Wilson wanted a decentralized system with public control; he also wanted to establish a more elastic currency. This meant, in practice, more flexibility in both greenback *and* deposit currency. In 1970 greenback currency in circulation, almost all of it in the form of Federal Reserve Notes, totaled about $50 billion. It is not nearly as important in our money supply as deposit currency, i.e., checks written against bank deposits which totaled $7.2 trillion in 1968. Deposit currency now comprises the major money in circulation, about 90 percent of business payments are made by check, and in the past three decades the use of checks has been increasing by about 10 percent each year. This is a relatively new development in our history. Before the Civil War bankers would not recognize a written order to pay to a third party from a depositor's account; instead the depositor had to go to the bank personally, accompanied by his creditor, and give oral instructions for the payment. There is one difference between greenback and deposit currency. Banks usually refuse to honor checks after more than six months; deposit currency thus gets "stale," whereas greenback currency does not.

Deposit currency can be *created* by banks — through loans. Let us assume a self-contained community with just one bank. Individual A asks for a loan of $1,000. It is approved. The bank puts down on one side of its books an *extra* $1,000 under "loans due," and on the other side it puts down an *extra* $1,000 under deposits credited to A. It thus adds $1,000 to A's checking account — and this $1,000 in deposit currency did not exist before. In due course A writes a check for the $1,000 to B, who adds it to his own deposit account in our one bank in the community. B pays his own laborers and suppliers by check, and they deposit them — again in our one bank. The $1,000 continues to exist until A repays the loan, at which time his deposit account and the bank's loans both decline by $1,000 — and the newly created money is extinguished. Until that time, however, the economy of the community has had a new $1,000 which people were using to buy things. With some refinements of great importance to individual bankers but not to the nation's monetary system, the same situation holds for a multiple-banking community. The only difference is that, in the national area, it is the banking *system* (of which an individual bank is only a small part) that creates the money.

For more than a century it has been apparent to students of economics that there must be some kind of governmental control over this power of private institutions to add to the supply of money. This was finally done in the United States with the Federal Reserve System. The key to the Federal's control over the money supply is its power to add or subtract from the total amount of bank reserves available to the economy. These bank reserves, which nobody ever sees, might be called "high-powered dollars" because each new dollar of reserves becomes the base upon which the banking system as a whole can increase loans, and hence deposits, by about seven dollars. The Federal can quite literally create these new reserves out of thin air; this is the modern American version of the "printing press."

But it can also extinguish reserves, with the effect that banks feel "tight" and must slow down on lending.

The Federal controls the amount — the ebb and flow — of reserves in the national banking system by three different methods:

It can *change* the percentage of reserve requirements behind deposits. In the Federal Reserve System all member banks are required to hold a fixed amount of cash at their district Federal Reserve Banks as a reserve against their total deposits. By law the Federal can set reserve requirements up to 26 percent for city banks and up to 14 percent for country banks; the average has usually been around 15 percent. Let us return again to our one-bank community where we find on a given day that our bank has $1 million of deposits and the required $150,000 in cash reserves (at the 15 percent rate) at the Federal Reserve District Bank. Our community bank cannot expand its deposits by making new loans until, somehow or other, it gets more cash for reserves. It is apparent that the Federal will impose "constraint" on lending if it increases the reserve requirements for city banks from our hypothetical 15 percent to the legal maximum of 26 percent — a ratio of 1 to 4 rather than 1 to 7 in the effectiveness of reserve or "high-powered" dollars.

It can *lend* reserves, for which it charges a rate of interest called the rediscount rate, when member banks ask for loans by presenting approved agricultural, industrial, and commercial paper; that is, short-term paper representing loans which the bank has made to private businesses in the community. This system enables a bank which is short of cash (as many were in 1907) to convert its assets, ultimately repayable in cash but not yet due, into immediate Federal Reserve Notes or deposit credits; this is the reason Federal Reserve Notes are sometimes called "asset currency." It is readily apparent that member banks will take advantage of this possibility more frequently when the charge (the rediscount rate) is low than when it is high and costly.

It can *pump* reserves into the system, or *withdraw* them, by buying or selling government securities in the market. If it buys government securities from member banks the Federal pays for them by increasing the reserves of member banks. If it sells government securities to member banks it takes payment by reducing the reserves of member banks. This operation is obviously a most important method of regulating the amount of reserves available to member banks. It is controlled by a federal Open Market Committee composed of the seven members of the board of governors plus five district-bank presidents elected annually.

The decision of when and how to use these three methods is a complicated matter, and their effect is sometimes mainly psychological. But taken together, they set the limits to the total amount of new money that the banking system can create. The fundamental purpose of the Federal is to allow enough new money to be created to permit normal growth of the economy, but not so much as to produce an inflation caused by "too much money chasing too few goods." In practice this requires the wisdom of several Solomons, and some luck.

The banking system of the United States, basically that established by the Federal Reserve Act of 1913 as amended, has been the target of critics over the years. Four major faults have been identified in the establishment: too many banks, too many systems, too many credit institutions beyond the control of the Federal, and too little coordination between the Federal and the President. There are those who say that we have had too many banks — particularly too many weak, poorly managed, and small local banks. The result has been that bank failures were not eliminated; between 1920 and 1933 fifteen thousand banks failed in the United States. Those who propose reform suggest great central banks with branches. England has only fifteen chartered banks, and the "Big Five" handle three-fourths of the banking business of that nation. Canada has but ten chartered banks, and four of them do 80 percent of the banking business. In England and Canada there have been almost no bank failures. The chief reasons appear to have been better management plus the possibility for greater diversification of assets — because the larger regional or national bank is not tied to a one-crop or a one-industry locality. The chief argument against great central banks is, of course, the fear of monopoly. Perhaps for that reason the Federal has frowned on branch banking. In 1923 it did allow city banks to establish branches in their locality. Ten years later it authorized branch banking in those states that permitted it. To date, that is as far as it has gone.

Other critics have pointed out that we also have too many systems and too many credit institutions beyond the control of the Federal. In the United States there are fifty-one systems — that of the national government plus fifty states. Because deposit currency is now so much more important than greenback currency, the 10 percent federal tax levied against state-bank notes in the Civil War is now meaningless — and state banks have increased in number. The inevitable result is that the Federal Reserve System must compete with the looser systems prevailing in many states, thus lowering banking standards the country over. This "competition in laxity" was certainly a contributing factor to the Great Depression of the 1930's. There are also many credit institutions, nonbanking in the commercial sense only, over which the Federal Reserve System has no control. These are savings and loan associations, credit unions, pension funds, insurance companies, federal credit agencies (FHA, VA, and others), and corporations — which frequently finance themselves through their own reserves. This situation has become so critical that the president of the largest bank in the United States (S. Clark Biese of the Bank of America) once joined those who think there should be another high-level inquiry — perhaps another Pujo Committee — to investigate the "money power" which has changed so much since the Federal was first established in 1913.

Finally there are those who say there has been too little coordination between the Federal controlling *monetary* policy (the supply of credit and interest rates) and the Administration (the President and Congress) controlling *fiscal* policy (spending, taxing, and debt financing through deficits or otherwise). The point is that the Federal, although its governors are appointed by the President, is an independent institution. It is not one of the many departments and agencies under the President's command; the chairman of the board of governors of the Federal is not, like the Secretary of the Treasury, a member of the President's Administration. The result is that we have had situations where the Federal was trying to hold back expansion of demand, and the Administration was trying to encourage the expansion of demand. This was particularly true during the open break between William McChesney Martin and President Johnson in 1965, when the Federal defied the Administration and raised interest rates — demonstrating effectively that it is in a position to act independently. The fact that the Federal was right in 1965 is cited by many as a powerful argument in favor of preserving its independence and permitting it to shift credit gears when it considers a shift appropriate, whether or not the President agrees.

On the other hand, there are powerful arguments for complete coordination of both monetary *and* fiscal policy by the President. Proponents of this change point out that the independence of the Federal dates from a time when the management of money and credit was the function of bankers alone, and that this traditional position was radically changed by legislation during the 1930's, the influence of John Maynard Keynes, and the Employment Act of 1946 which gives the President (not the Federal) a mandate to use his power to keep unemployment low, to keep prices reasonably steady, and to promote an adequate rate of economic growth. Because monetary policy has political implications these advocates assert that it is really too important to be left to the monetary managers; they do not believe the Federal should be considered as a supreme court of economic policy, with what amounts to a veto power over the political party in power. They argue that the President, who is charged with formulating overall economic policy and is answerable to the electorate, must not be thwarted by a small group of men shielded from the public; *he* must be responsible for the appropriate "mix" of monetary and fiscal policy necessary for business activity. They observe that as the situation now stands, responsibility is not fixed in one place — with the result that the White House takes the credit when things go right but can always blame the Federal Reserve when they go wrong. For all of these reasons they find the Federal's present independence to be an "unwarranted, anachronistic, and undemocratic element in our society."

The Panic of 1929, and the Depression that followed, were the most catastrophic and cataclysmic economic upheavals in the history of the

United States. There appear to have been four basic causes: lack of purchasing power, overspeculation, a dubious corporate structure, and lack of effective political leadership. Lack of purchasing power, necessary to keep the wheels of industry turning, was the result of unequal distribution of national income. For the decade of the 1920's output per worker increased by 43 percent. This sharp rise in productivity was not offset either by a significant price decrease or by a commensurate wage increase; wages, salaries, and prices remained comparatively stable. The immediate consequence was a rapid increase in profits. At the lower level of the economy the contrasts in family incomes were startling and tragic. In 1929 the Brookings Institution stated that a family of four with an annual income of $2,000 might be regarded, at 1929 prices, to be able to supply only basic commodities; this meant that $2,000 a year was the bare subsistence level for a family of that size. But in 1929 60 percent of American families had incomes of less than $2,000 a year, and of this 60 percent one-third had incomes of less than $1,000 per year. By contrast the richest tenth received a third of the national income. The paradox was that the poor could not consume enough because their incomes were too small, and the rich could not possibly eat, drink, or use up all their dollars because their incomes were too large. They proceeded to spend much of the surplus in undesirable speculation.*

Business attempted to circumvent this maldistribution through two procedural but basically ineffective devices: advertising and installment buying. Advertising became more than a technique; it was elevated into a gospel. Before an enthusiastic convention of businessmen President Calvin Coolidge once made the surprising claim that "advertising ministers to the spiritual side of trade." In that day there was an outstanding producer of advertising copy, by the name of Bruce Barton, who made a fortune writing it. In 1925 Barton turned to biography and published a best-selling life of Jesus entitled *The Man Nobody Knows*. Its thesis was that Jesus was really the greatest salesman of all time. The volume was a prime example of the union of church and business; Barton believed sincerely in Christ

---

* The situation was little better forty years later, in 1966, when Herman P. Miller published his *Income Distribution in the U.S.* He divided American families into five equal groups numerically, then calculated the percentage of national income each group got. He found, of course, that the national-income "pie" was not divided into five equal slices. The bottom fifth got only 5 percent of the national income, while the top fifth was receiving 45.5 percent. He also found that 5 percent got 20 percent of the national income, but that the 20 percent at the bottom received only 5 percent. This was so symmetrical that it caused TRB in the *New Republic* (for 11 May 1968) to put it in rhyme:

> *The Upper Five gets its twenty;*
> *Bangles, booze and broads a-plenty;*
> *The Lower Twenty gets its five;*
> *Just enough to stay alive.*
> *When the Pie's in such a plight,*
> *Better lock the door at night.*

and advertising, just as Rudyard Kipling believed sincerely in Christ and the British Empire.* In addition to advertising an attempt was made to extend prosperity through installment buying, obviously a mortgage on the future. By 1929 80 percent of all automobiles were sold on the installment plan, and 15 percent of all retail trade was conducted on the same basis — with the buyer paying interest rates that frequently ran as high as 20 percent and in some cases amounted to 35 percent a year. In theory it was thought that mass production *plus* advertising *plus* installment buying was the equivalent of permanent prosperity. In practice, the men and women engaged in mass production did not receive enough in wages to buy back the fruits of their toil.

The proletariat did not have enough funds to buy; the business entrepreneurs were guilty of overspeculation and of a bad corporate structure, and for these reasons were directly responsible for the Panic of 1929 and the severe economic doldrums of the 1930's. Let us consider first the problem of overspeculation in the third decade of the twentieth century. In 1927 the Federal Reserve Board *eased* the rediscount rate, because American industry sagged a bit in the summer of that year. Industry and agriculture did not need more credit; both were overexpanded and lacked markets, because of maldistribution of income at home and tariff barriers which had reduced our international trade. The result was that the additional credit, made possible by the beneficence of the Federal Reserve Board, found its way not to business and agriculture, which could not use it, but to the rising market in stocks and real estate. To put it another way, the abundant new funds — not needed in industry and agriculture — were lent into Wall Street. There, in time, the speculation got out of hand. By 1929 the Federal Reserve Board finally got around to raising the rediscount rate — all the way to 6 percent — but several years late. Speculation was then so rife, with plungers counting on capital gains rather than normal income from stocks, that banks borrowed from the Federal at the seemingly impossible rate of 6 percent, and then lent the money for speculative purposes at the outrageous figure of 12 percent. John Kenneth Galbraith observes that this was probably the most profitable arbitrage operation of all time. Overspeculation was out of hand, but the corporate structure was just as bad. This was particularly true in two areas: holding companies, which were milking operating companies in

* In 1968 the governor of Georgia, Lester G. Maddox, reflected the same philosophy. He believed in giving credit where credit was due, and averred that "the American free-enterprise system could never have been established if it were not for the birth of Christ." This was especially true at the Christmas season, when religious fervor and increased sales went hand in hand. According to Governor Maddox: "Other holidays have not expanded like Christmas. And the reason for it is found in a name — the name of Jesus. There will be more automobiles, more shoes, more record players, more television sets, more ties, more shirts, more dresses, more cosmetics, more watches and diamonds sold in the name of Christ this year than any other name."

order to support their inflated debt structure, and investment trusts — security affiliates — which were milking commercial banks in order to support their speculations on the stock market. The overall effect of watered stocks and bonds, in holding companies and investment trusts, was that they saddled industry and commerce with an interest and dividend burden which could not be borne. This had been going on, unfortunately, for a long time. Some economists insist that the depression that was scotched by Morgan in 1907, and was averted by World War I, was the one that finally arrived in 1929.

To lack of purchasing power, overspeculation, and a dubious corporate structure was added political leadership that turned out to be corrupt with Harding, apathetic with Coolidge, and stubborn with Hoover. This was a national failure on the part of successive national administrations — in spite of the sententious remark by Coolidge that "the business of America is business." * This lack of leadership and direction appeared in three areas: a high protective tariff, regressive taxation, and government by crony.

The high protective tariff, sponsored by Presidents Harding, Coolidge, and Hoover, ruined the farmer and depressed many other sections of the economy. In the field of taxation "Mellonism" was adopted: a reduction of individual income taxes, plus a reduction of corporation taxes and even some rebates to large businesses. The name is derived from Andrew Mellon, who was Secretary of the Treasury in the decade from 1921 to 1931. He was a financier and industrialist who was a millionaire many times over from companies such as Gulf Oil, Alcoa, and banks in Pittsburgh — which was his headquarters. When he became Secretary of the Treasury Mellon resigned from the boards of fifty-one corporations, and his subsequent financial policies in the national sphere were those of unabashed plutocracy.

During World War I a number of new taxes had been put into effect: heavy excise taxes had been placed on tobacco, liquor, and luxuries; the income tax had been increased to 77 percent on incomes above $1 million; corporation taxes had been levied at 12 percent, but there was an excess-profits tax of 80 percent on the largest war earnings; and estate and gift taxes had been increased. In the 1920's Mellon, seeking to succor the poor rich man, helped engineer a series of tax reductions. Congress followed his leadership by *repealing* the excess-profits and gift taxes, and by *reducing* the excise, income, and estate taxes. The result was that in 1921 a man with an income of $1 million paid $663,000 in income taxes. In 1926, five years

* Senator Hiram Johnson of California was scathing about Coolidge's ignorance of economics. He wrote: "The fact of the matter is Coolidge would not know an economic policy, if he met it on the street. He has one great virtue. Apparently he knows his limitations, and therefore, he will not talk at all. If he talked at all, the poverty of his intellect would at once be so obvious, so he sits tight, and follows implicitly what is told him, and trusts to the press of the land."

later, he paid $200,000. Mellon's spare-the-rich policies shifted a substantial part of the tax burden from the backs of the wealthy to those of the middle-income groups. The wealthy used a large part of their savings to feed the speculation of the late 1920's, thus accentuating the crash when it came.

The third example of lack of political leadership in the 1920's, was what is called "cronyism." This was represented in Harding's time by the "little green house on K. Street" where the boys drank, by numerous scandals including Teapot Dome, and by some amazing appointments. Unfortunately Harding was a misfit as President of the United States, and knew it. He was a virile fellow with a difficult and unappealing wife five years his senior. Women found him attractive and he did not limit his interests; he was capable of sending two of his mistresses boxes of candy on the same day. As Senator from Ohio from 1915 to 1921 he was conspicuous for his absence from the floor for travel, golf, and poker. His most political activity during this period was summer lecturing on the tent circuit in the bucolic America of that day, mainly on his three heroes: Hamilton, Caesar, and Napoleon — none of whom he resembled by the slightest stretch of the imagination. As President he was uneasy with the national prominence of a few in his Cabinet; he held Hughes, Hoover, and Mellon in awe. He was familiar and easy with other members who turned out badly. One of them achieved the negative distinction of being the only Cabinet officer to go to jail, another resigned under a cloud of suspicion, and the third narrowly missed criminal conviction.

In the field of finance the most dubious appointment was that of Daniel R. Crissinger to positions of great power. He was appointed to these offices by a President who came from Marion in Ohio with only the vaguest perception of the economic processes over which he presided; when Harding died it was found he owed his broker $180,000 in a blind account — he had been speculating disastrously while he was President. He brought Crissinger, an inconspicuous country lawyer who was his fellow townsman, into high financial positions. He had been trained for his financial tasks by serving as counsel for the Marion Steam Shovel Company. In 1921 he was appointed Comptroller of the Currency; when he had had enough time to demonstrate his incompetence in this post, he was kicked upstairs. This was in 1923, when he was made chairman of the Federal Reserve Board over the protest of Secretary of the Treasury Mellon; Crissinger stayed in this position during four years, and had central responsibility for action on the boom that was to culminate in the Panic of 1929. In the opinion of John Kenneth Galbraith many others including Jack Dempsey, Paul Whiteman, and F. Scott Fitzgerald would have been at least equally qualified.

The economic euphoria of the 1920's was fine while it lasted. By early October 1929 the average American saw ahead of himself an illimitable vista of prosperity. In view of the actual sledgehammer that fell within the month, it is interesting to recall the optimistic statements of the period. On the economic side the eminent Professor Irving Fisher of Yale assured all citizens that they were dwelling upon permanent "high plateaus" of prosperity. On the political side, Republican Herbert Hoover, who was sometimes known as the "Sage of Palo Alto," announced that the conquest of poverty was no longer a mirage, but that "soon with the help of God [we will] be within sight of the day when poverty will be banished from the nation." On the political side, Democrat John J. Raskob was confident that if a man saved $15 a week, allowing dividends to accumulate, at the end of twenty years he would have at least $80,000 — and an income from investments of about $400 a month. At prices of that day Raskob claimed that not only *could* everyone be rich but that everyone *ought* to be rich. On the financial side a very few saw the crash coming, put their profits in cash and government bonds, and really cashed in during the 1930's. But there were very few. There was Roger Babson of the famous Institute and the well-known *Reports*. There was Bernard M. Baruch and Joseph P. Kennedy. But the lack of foresight on the part of most financiers was indicated in a statement of Thomas Lamont, eminent in the firm of J. P. Morgan. After the crash was well under way he made what Frederick Lewis Allen called one of the most remarkable understatements of all time. He said: "There has been a little distress selling on the Stock Exchange." This was at a time when — on the floor of the Stock Exchange — the dreaded "no bid" had become commonplace. No one wanted to buy, at any price. In 1907 Morgan, Harriman, Stillman, and Frick had created a $25 million pool that saved the plunging market. It did not work in 1929. Too many had bought on margin, and now were compelled to put up the balance — to pay or to be sold out. Most were sold out. In Chicago, racketeers responded to margin calls by dynamiting the home of the broker who asked for the margin. But for the average speculator it was either pay or go broke. He went broke.

The losses on the Stock Market were colossal. The quoted value of all stocks listed on the Exchange on 1 September 1929 was almost $90 billion. Three years later the quoted value of the same stocks was a bit more than $15 billion. In this triennium stockholders had lost almost $75 billion, a figure so large that most people could not begin to grasp it. It was approximately three times what we had spent in fighting World War I; it was comparable in percentage of loss to the famous South Sea Bubble of 1720. Although individuals could not comprehend the total figure, they could understand some of the specific ones; for example, that GM had fallen from 72 to 7, and that U.S. Steel had declined from 261 to 7. The fall in national income was alarming — from $81 billion in 1929 to $41 billion in 1932. The degree of unemployment was also alarming; 13 million by 1932 with less than one-fourth of those unfortunates receiving public aid. Some of those listed as working were doing so at starvation wages — 10¢ an hour for lumber workers and $1.10 per fifty-five-hour week for girls employed in Connecticut sweatshops. There was even the spectacle of people starving to death in the richest nation on earth. In 1929 at least twenty-nine persons are known to have died of starvation in New York City alone, and by 1934 more than one hundred fatalities from starvation had been reported in the nation at large. Although farmers did not starve, they found themselves overburdened by debt, and demanded inflationary measures just as their predecessors under Daniel Shays and Peter Cooper and William Jennings Bryan had done. They had borrowed money when it took three hundred bushels of corn to pay the debt at prices as they were in the 1920's; they now found themselves at the bottom of a depression in the 1930's when, if they could stave off foreclosure, they would be compelled to sell 1,000 bushels of corn to pay the same debt. In the Corn Belt desperate farmers organized the Farmer's Holiday Association under Milo Reno, a veteran Populist, to take militant action against low farm prices and foreclosures. When mortgage sales were held on farms in western states, groups of menacing farmers appeared to overawe the representatives of mortgage holders and to prevent realistic bidding. Under these artificial circumstances the farmer's friends bought in the farm and its equipment for practically nothing, and then returned them to the farmer — for practically nothing. All this agitation, in city and on farm, was so frightening that in 1932 President Hoover secretly asked the Senate to exempt soldiers from a 10 percent cut in pay for federal employees, because he did not want to depend on disgruntled troops in case of insurrection.

The situation was so serious and tragic that for some the antidote was humor or cynicism. It was claimed that a complimentary revolver was given free with the purchase of each and every share of stock in Goldman, Sachs & Co., an investment trust whose stock soared to $326 before the bubble burst, after which it plummeted to $1.75. The penny press in London carried stories about speculators hurling themselves from the top floors of tall buildings; it was claimed that in Gotham pedestrians were picking their way, as delicately as they could, between the bodies of fallen financiers. Actually, as Galbraith has revealed, the number of suicides in New York declined during these fateful years although the stories about them increased.

The Panic of 1929 had a profound effect on the nation. On the general side a case can be made, and Galbraith makes it, that since 1789 with the single exception of the Civil War no event in our history has so deeply impressed itself upon the thoughts, attitudes, and voting behavior of the American people. The Black Thursday in late October 1929 was equal in importance to mid-April 1861 when Fort Sumter was fired on. Specifically the Panic had two significant results: it ruined the reputation of financiers and it undermined public faith in the basic philosophy of American business. In the underworld of the 1920's the terms "gangster" and "racketeer" were well known. Now, in the 1930's people began to talk about "stockateers" and "banksters," classing these erstwhile paragons of respectability with the underworld. President Roosevelt, in his inaugural address in 1933, would promise to drive the money changers from the temple. Two financiers made particular contributions, through their arrant skulduggery, to the declining reputations of financiers. They were Charles E. Mitchell and Richard Whitney.

Mitchell was chairman of the board of the National City Bank of New York City; he was also chairman of the board of the Federal Reserve District Bank in New York. His left hand did not know what the right one was doing. In 1930, at the very moment the Federal was trying to restrict credit, Mitchell was lending furiously through the National City Bank, actually borrowing money from the Federal to defeat the Federal's policy. He was later tried by the government for selling stock to his wife for the purpose of establishing a fictitious loss in order to evade payment of income taxes. He was not sent to jail, but he had to resign from his fiduciary positions and ultimately pay more than a million dollars in retarded income taxes.

In 1930, at the age of forty-one, Richard Whitney became the youngest president the New York Stock Exchange had ever had to that time. He seemed to be eminently respectable. He was the son of a Boston banker, and had been captain of both baseball and football teams at Groton. At Harvard he was treasurer of Hasty Pudding, and pulled a strong oar in the shell that beat Yale in 1909. As a gentleman farmer he lived well on his country estate of almost 500 acres at Far Hills, New Jersey, where he was master of the foxhounds at the Essex Hunt and where he raised prize chickens, pigs, and horses. At the same time, as it developed later, he was a swindler who was stealing from a great variety of people and sources — his father-in-law, his brother George (an honest man who later became president of J. P. Morgan & Co.), his yacht club, his customers, his friends. His business judgment was incredibly poor and he lost on a number of speculations, principally New Jersey applejack. To keep the price up he used clients' securities, the bonds of the New York Yacht Club, his wife's jewelry — whatever he could hock. While all this was going on he was chairman of the Exchange's Committee on Conduct, and in this capacity was making speeches at banquets and by radio, speeches in which he extolled rugged individualism and lambasted shady stockbrokers. As Harold Mehling has pointed out (in a book appropriately titled *The Scandalous Scamps*) he would have defied belief as a character in fiction — but actually existed. In 1938 the authorities finally caught up with Whitney; he received a five-to-ten-year prison sentence, was handcuffed to a rapist, and sent off to Sing Sing. There he scrubbed walls, clerked, played a creditable first base on the prison baseball team, and was parolled in 1941 — after serving three years and four months. To this day in the Stock Exchange one can see large oil paintings of past presidents — with the exception of Whitney. The official explanation is lack of space.

If the Panic of 1929 ruined the reputation of financiers, it also undermined public faith in the basic philosophy of American business. Up to this time business leaders had believed, and the majority of the voting public concurred, in the nineteenth-century idea of a self-regulating economy based on natural economic laws. This was laissez-faire — a society in which government was limited in its functions. The theory assumed that natural laws operated in such a way that the able man who worked hard would benefit society *and* himself — financially. By 1933, with 15 million unemployed, many of them able men, it was apparent that something was wrong and that the national government should do something drastic. President Hoover was to try first but would fail in the judgment of the electorate; President Roosevelt would achieve public acclaim for his policies.

Because of his early success in worldwide mining ventures Herbert Hoover was sometimes called the Great Engineer, but his four years in the White House developed into a personal disaster for him and the most tragic the American people had ever spent in peacetime. There was an oft-repeated wisecrack that Hoover, the Great Engineer, had managed to drain, ditch, and damn the country. He had a distinguished record of past service of great humanitarian merit, particularly in connection with relief work in Belgium and other European nations. What went wrong?

From the standpoint of hindsight it is obvious that he continued certain policies that had helped cause and later deepened the Depression of the 1930's. These were in particular the high protective tariff and the Mellon fiscal policies. When critics remonstrated with him, Hoover used other excuses for the nation's economic difficulties, chiefly that Europe — not the Republican party — was responsible for the Depression. In the field of inaction he refused to support direct relief even when the number of unemployed neared 15 million; he believed, like Grover Cleveland, that people should support the government — not vice versa. He was quite willing to authorize indirect relief through the "trickle-down" procedure; that is, "pump-priming" loans to commerce, industry, and agriculture by way of the Reconstruction Finance Corporation — or public works such as Hoover Dam in the Southwest. But direct relief, by the federal government, he would not support. Early in 1929 he had said that poverty would soon be abolished from the nation. In 1930 he, and his Republican friends, declared that the Depression was not serious or long-lived, that prosperity would soon come round the corner, that there would soon be two cars in every garage and two chickens in every pot. In time cartoonists would have a field day with this one, picturing garages with two chickens wandering disconsolately inside a structure that was otherwise empty. The result was that after 1929 no stock depreciated in value quite as fast as that of the Grand Old Party. The very proper noun Hoover became a prefix charged with hate: "Hoovervilles" for the shacks where the unemployed lived, "Hoover blankets" for the newspapers wrapped around cold bodies, "Hoover wagons" for the broken-down automobiles hauled by mules, "Hoover flags" for the empty pockets that were turned inside out. During the presidential campaign of 1932 the Secret Service reported that men actually ran into the streets to thumb their noses at the President of the United States as he passed in parades. He became the butt of a thousand bitter jokes. One told of Hoover's request to Mellon for the loan of a nickel (the current charge) to call a friend on the telephone; Mellon was alleged to have replied, "Here's a dime, call all your friends." The humorist Will Rogers said, in connection with the presidential campaign of 1932, that he didn't see how the Democrats could pick a candidate weak enough to lose; if their nominee lived until November he was "in." In the campaign itself the Democratic party capitalized on this feeling by advertising the ambivalent slogan, "A vote for Roosevelt is a vote against Hoover."

Hoover had been swept into office in 1928 by a landslide. In 1932 he went out the same way as Franklin Delano Roosevelt took over the responsibility of rescuing the nation from the Depression. Hoover, a gifted and kind man, had been trapped by his own beliefs.

Roosevelt was to be accused frequently of being a radical, a revolutionary. Some of the lawyers who were writing his New Deal legislation, particularly the influential Tom Corcoran and Ben Cohen, lived in a convivial house in Georgetown which was sometimes called (in contrast to the green one on K Street which had been famous in Harding's day) the "little red house on R Street." To conservatives it was the headquarters of revolution. They claimed that FDR was really carrying out the Socialist platform of 1932; this exaggerated charge so angered Socialist Norman Thomas that he said, "Roosevelt did not carry out the Socialist platform unless he carried it out on a stretcher."

Actually Roosevelt refused, by design or ignorance, to be classified as anything in the area of economic philosophy or theory. He was a pragmatist, an experimenter. He once told biographer Emil Ludwig that his only purpose was to obviate revolution. He said that civilization was like a tree which, as it grew, continually produced some rot and some dead wood: "The radical says: 'Cut it down.' The conservative says: 'Don't touch it.' The liberal compromises: 'Let's prune, so that we lose neither the *old trunk* or the *new branches.*' "

It is apparent that the pragmatic Roosevelt knew next to nothing about economics as an academic discipline. One of his early brain trusters, Raymond Moley, the political scientist from Columbia University, doubted that either Roosevelt or he could have passed an examination required of college students in elementary economics. Mackenzie King, the Prime Minister of Canada who was a trained economist and political scientist, went so far as to say that FDR knew nothing of economics and did not even understand his New Deal! One can anticipate Roosevelt's reaction to John Maynard Keynes, the mathematical theoretician. They met in 1934 and FDR was bewildered by what he called Keynes's "rigmarole of figures"; he told Perkins that the Englishman must "be a mathematician rather than a political economist." In turn Keynes was disappointed in FDR, and remarked that he had supposed the President was more literate in economics. Keynes wanted government spending on public works to promote employment and to increase purchasing power; FDR was either opposed or basically reluctant to do so. In October 1932, just before his election as President, he announced in Pittsburgh that he would reduce federal expenditures by 25 percent. He chose Lewis Douglas as his first Director of the Budget because of his fervor for economy. Rexford Tugwell, an economist and Keynesian who was also one of the Brain Trust, has commented that "with what reluctance President Roosevelt was forced into deficit spending, and how he resisted at every step — Harry Hopkins, Ickes, and numerous other New Deal administrators could testify."

Whether the pragmatic Roosevelt was a theoretician or not, he applied himself to the frightening task before him with optimism and great activity. The optimism appeared in his first inaugural address when he told the nation that it was quite capable of recovery from the Depression, that "the only thing we have to fear is fear itself." The activity and energy appeared in the famous "Hundred Days" (from 9 March through 16 June 1933) during which Roosevelt sent fifteen messages to Congress, guided fifteeen major laws to enactment, delivered ten major speeches, sponsored an international conference, made all the major decisions on domestic policy — all this without any display of panic or fright, and with only occasional evidences of bad temper. The country approved this striking contrast to Hoover's inactivity. Will Rogers would say that the people would have cheered the fire if FDR had burned the Capitol!

Roosevelt's policy toward the Depression involved Recovery and Reform — Recovery of prices and employment, and Reform to assure that we did not fall into another economic abyss. Something had to be done to get more money into circulation, to bring about a rise in prices. In May 1933 considerable light was thrown on the policy that was to come in a radio speech made by the President:

The Administration has the definite objective of raising commodity prices to such an extent that those who have borrowed money will, on the average, be able to repay the money in the same kind of dollar which they borrowed.

. . . We do not seek to let them get such a cheap dollar that they, in effect, will be able to pay back a great deal less than they borrowed.

He proposed to achieve this through an increase in currency (both deposit and greenback); provision of credit beyond that which was supplied by commercial banks; provision of additional jobs through public works; and aid to unemployables who could no longer depend on salaries and wages.

To provide deposit currency he acted with great speed. When Roosevelt came into the presidential office on 4 March 1933 not only were banks closed all over the country (by proclamation of state governors who acted to save the banks from disastrous runs by depositors) but people were hoarding what little currency there was. Several cities in the South, hearkening back to Civil War days, began to print their own currency. Stamps, telephone slugs, Mexican and Canadian currency became media of circulation. To remedy this situation, which was both tragic and absurd, FDR pushed through the complicated Emergency Banking Relief Act with incredible speed. He had been inaugurated on a Saturday, the complex measure was written by the next Wednesday, was passed by Congress on Thursday (unanimously in the House, by a vote of 73 to 7 in the Senate), and on Saturday FDR explained it to the nation in the first of his famous "fireside chats" over radio — initiating a practice that became customary during his Administration. Will Rogers commented that in this first chat the President took a complicated subject like banking and made everybody understand it, even the bankers. FDR justified the emergency act itself under the authority of the Trading-with-the-Enemy Act passed in 1917; its use in peacetime was certainly questionable but public opinion was solidly behind him. The act itself, affecting all banks in the Federal Reserve System, gave the President broad discretionary powers over credit, currency, gold and silver, including foreign exchange. Specifically, it permitted sound banks to open only under licenses from the Treasury Department, providing conservators to care for the assets of insolvent banks not permitted to reopen. About 75 percent of the banks in the Federal Reserve System were permitted to reopen; specifically 12,000 banks were reopened under license and 5,000 were left in a "state of limbo" (of the latter 300 were opened subsequently, 2,000 were consolidated under other banks or were permanently closed, and the remainder were reorganized under new names). Within two weeks after passage of the Emergency Banking Relief Act prices had risen 15 percent and hoarded currency came out of hiding as the privilege of writing checks (deposit currency) on banks again became possible. The money panic was over; in Moley's judgment "capitalism had been saved in eight days." As he reviewed the years of the Great Depression after some time had passed, Moley felt that the decisive event that turned the tide was this brilliantly successful rescue of the banks. "Surely," says Moley, "nothing so gripped the imagination of the American people and gave them assurance that their nation was sound at heart and capable of providing them once more with the means of a good life."

Getting deposit currency into circulation again was one solution for the Depression. There were also those who put their trust in the traditional panacea of greenbacks, and thought the national government should provide them in one way or another. Actually three possibilities were proposed: fiat money, silver certificates, and reduction of the gold content of the dollar to make possible additional issues of Federal Reserve notes. There were some who wanted to expand the currency simply by printing more of it; they said the government's credit was sufficient to back a large issue of fiat, or promise, money. According to their theories, the government would pay off its own obligations with printing-press money when it felt that prices ought to go up — and would cremate the stuff (as it came in for taxes) when it was thought prices should be reduced. In this connection the most absurd proposal was that the government should not only print the money but should drop it as a beneficent dew from airplanes. Roosevelt did not act on any of these proposals.

There were some, particularly from western mining states, who wanted a silver as well as a gold base for currency. They asked for silver purchases and silver certificates, and got them in the Silver Purchase Act of 1934 (see pp. 196–198). Others proposed a reduction in the gold content of the dollar to permit the issue of additional currency without a corresponding increase in the gold held in the Treasury and by the Federal Reserve System. Roosevelt certainly acted on this proposal. By the Joint Resolution of 5 June 1933 and the Gold Reserve Act of 1934, the gold clause in private and public contracts was nullified, and the dollar was reduced to 59.06 percent of its old value — from 25.8 grains to 15-plus grains in the legal dollar. This obviously was a devalued and cheaper dollar; on the basis of classical economic theory it should result in the increase in prices which was so much desired. It was suggested by some that the legend on U.S. money should be changed from "In God We Trust" to "I Hope That My Redeemer Liveth." Creditors screamed to high heaven; they said the legislation was an example of the grossest dishonesty, a breaking of the most solemn faith — disruptive of morals and ethics. They also sued, but the Supreme Court in the Gold Clause Cases of 1935 — by a close vote of 5 to 4 — upheld Roosevelt's action. It was a controversial decision. Justice McReynolds, who was in the minority, was heard to cry, "The Constitution is gone." Lewis Douglas, a conservative who had been FDR's first Director of the Budget, moaned, "Well, this is the end of Western Civilization." We now know that Roosevelt had prepared a radio speech to the nation, to be delivered if the Supreme Court had held the Gold Reserve Act unconstitutional. He did not intend to enforce such a decision. A century before President Andrew Jackson had taken exactly the same point of view in connection with the famous case of *Worcester* v. *Georgia.**

In addition to the added volume of greenback and deposit currency in circulation, more credit was demanded by those who insisted that the federal government get into this business. They pointed out that commercial banks usually performed this function, but that too many of them were either closed or were in a shaky condition — and were not inclined to be liberal with loans. This was a valid commentary, and for that reason the federal government did create many credit agencies from the Home Owner's Loan Corporation to the Reconstruction Finance Corporation (RFC). The latter was the largest and the most interesting of these governmental credit institutions; originally established to extend loans to weak railroads and banks, in time it would loan money liberally to industry and to agriculture. Actually the RFC had first been chartered in the Hoover Administration, and had proved to be Hoover's most valuable effort in dealing with the Depression. It marked the first time in our history that the federal government had come directly to the aid of all businesses, and it marked both the desertion of the idea of the self-regulating economy *and* the beginning of the concept of the "welfare state." Under Hoover, however, this new concept of a welfare state had been used for the welfare of a very few large institutions. There were a number of scandals in 1932; the most conspicuous was the loan of $90 million to the Central Republic Bank in Chicago, which was under the control of Charles Gates Dawes. Dawes was a former Vice-President of the United States who got the loan shortly after he resigned as president of the RFC and had returned to private banking. His successor as president, an Ohio politico named Atlee Pomerene, authorized an RFC loan to a bank in Cleveland of which he was a director. Both of these loans had been made originally in secret; as a result of the subsequent disclosures Roosevelt insisted that in future full publicity must be given to all loans by the

---

* There were many who compared the Court's decision, unfavorably, to that in *Knox* v. *Lee* in 1871. In that case it will be recalled that the Supreme Court had admitted that the action of the federal government in making greenbacks legal tender was unconstitutional, but had said that it would be validated as a justifiable exercise of the national government's *powers in time of emergency, not limited to war.* Chief Justice Hughes could have used the same argument in 1935, but did not. He said that the action of the federal government was unconstitutional, but that the plaintiff had suffered no more than nominal damages and therefore could not sue in the Court of Claims. Many lawyers thought the reasoning of Hughes was unsound, that it would have been better to admit the situation frankly as had been done in 1871. Justice Harlan Fiske Stone, who voted with the majority, had no doubt that the government had the right to act as it did but thought that it had behaved so amorally that for a time he could not bring himself to buy another government bond. The famous jurist and circuit-court judge, Learned Hand, said that "everybody dealing with a sovereign knows he is dealing with a creature which can welch if he wants to welch." Nonetheless he thought Hughes's opinion was sheer pettifoggery; he noted in pungent language, "It frankly makes me puke, as dear old Holmes used to say."

RFC — and from that point of time small enterprises received much more attention. In due course the RFC became the largest single investor in the American economy — and by far the largest credit institution in the country. It lasted for a quarter of a century, from 1932 to 1957, having been continued to stabilize the crises over credit in World War II and later. During its twenty-five-year period it lent $50 billion.

Roosevelt had encouraged recovery by providing more deposit and greenback currency, and by increasing the availability of credit. He also listened to those who supported public works — who said that the *volume* of money or credit was less important than the *velocity* of its circulation. They said putting money into the hands of the unemployed would circulate it rapidly, would start the wheels of industry once again. This group believed that money was like manure, good only when spread around. It was financier Marriner Eccles who once said that the only *sound* money was *used* money; this was a reflection of the old English proverb "A nimble sixpence will do the work of a lazy crown." In pursuit of this philosophy Roosevelt established a number of agencies to provide relief and meaningful work for the unemployed; the major ones were the CCC (Civilian Conservation Corps), the PWA (Public Works Administration), CWA (Civil Works Administration), and the WPA (Works Projects Administration). The CCC during its decade of existence employed 2 million persons and was a practical success because it combined relief and conservation in an ingenious way. From its inception it was one of the most popular of New Deal agencies, in spite of deep suspicions from organized labor and from pacifists — who felt that the army officers who served as camp administrators were going to militarize American youth. The PWA was particularly active from 1933 to 1939 and spent more than $4 billion on 34,000 public projects — chiefly bridges, dams, public buildings, conservation developments, and low-cost housing. It was administered by the Secretary of the Interior, the "old curmudgeon" Harold Ickes. He was so self-righteously honest that Moley observed that "he believed honesty was of his own invention and that official integrity would die with him." He was also very slow in authorizing projects.

To speed matters, CWA and WPA were authorized. The first was a temporary organization, established in the desperate winter of 1933–1934 to provide temporary work for 4 million persons at regular wages until they could be absorbed by private industry or the more permanent PWA. For this reason the projects were necessarily ephemeral in scope: laying sidewalks, patching streets, painting public buildings, improving parks, raking leaves (which caused critics to call the whole thing boondoggling of the first degree). Almost a billion dollars was spent on CWA, which ended in the spring of 1934. By contrast with PWA and CWA, the Works Projects Administration envisioned a whole new concept of government relief. Introduced in 1935, its philosophy proved that in three years the nation had come a long way from the Hoover view that *direct* aid to the victims of flood or earthquake was right and proper, but *not* to the victims of man-made economics. For a time the dole had been the answer, then work of any kind in the CWA or PWA. Now the time had come, according to the organizers of WPA, to "maintain the morale and skills" of the unemployed by paying them to perform the work they could do best — until a rejuvenated private enterprise was ready to rehire them. For its part the WPA would not build a hospital even if one was needed unless a town happened to have a pool of idle construction men looking for work *and* the maintenance of their morale and skills. But if the same town had a group of jobless musicians the WPA would launch an orchestra with pleasure. Under this philosophy, from 1935 to 1941 some $11 billion was spent on 250,000 projects to prevent idle artists, craftsmen, and professionals from losing their skills. It helped many this way; in the field of art alone it is generally acknowledged that about 80 percent of the painters and sculptors who gained world recognition in the 1940's and 1950's were supported during the Depression by U.S. government funds. As a result of this subsidy, so many artists were developed that New York City is now generally acknowledged to be the center of the visual art field, a distinction previously enjoyed by Paris. But the WPA projects in adult education went far beyond art alone; they ranged all the way from painting and sculpture to drama, music, writing — and to the construction of schoolhouses and other public buildings. Because these projects were much more permanent than those under the CWA, a scale of "security" wages was established — a scale higher than relief payments but lower than wages paid by private employers — so that workers would not become indifferent to offers of private employment; these "security" wages could vary from $15 a month for unskilled farm labor in the South to $90 for professional work in New York City. WPA workers were often discharged to encourage them to seek private employment.

If "Honest Harold" Ickes was the dominant figure in PWA — Aubrey Williams and Harry Hopkins typified CWA and WPA. Williams had a most interesting career. During World War I he served successively the YMCA, the French Foreign Legion, and the United States Army. When the war was over he became a lay minister for a time before going into welfare work. In the 1930's he was the number-two man to Hopkins in CWA and WPA, and in addition was Director of the National Youth Administration — which provided education, vocational training, and jobs for students between the ages of eighteen and twenty-four (in this organization one of the brightest and most energetic state directors was the one in Texas; his name was Lyndon B. Johnson). Because of this work and his later efforts in the National Farmers Union, Williams was charged with being a Communist. One of the allegations against him was that in sponsoring a Latin American tour by a youth symphony orchestra he had delivered 109 young Americans into the clutches of a "Communist sympathizer," who happened to be the conductor of the orchestra. His name was Leopold Stokowski. In reply to these repeated charges Williams stated, quite correctly, that the only memberships he could recall were in the Presbyterian Church, the American Legion, the Political Action Committee of the CIO, and the National Farmers Union.

Hopkins headed both the CWA and the WPA, and was to be an intimate associate of the President during World War II when he administered Lend-Lease and held high posts as special assistant to Roosevelt both at home and abroad. He was a social worker from Iowa who had been responsible for state relief in New York when FDR was governor. There was a great deal of newspaper agitation from the right against Hopkins; it was claimed that he had gloated, "We will borrow and borrow, spend and spend, and elect and elect." On the other hand an analysis of his stewardship, on the economic side, brings one to the remarkable conclusion that investigators were unable to unearth any significant evidence of corruption in WPA in spite of the expenditure of billions of dollars. On the political side there was the obvious fact that the unemployed would naturally support — without urging — an administration which believed it was the duty of the government to provide work for employables when private industry failed to do so. But there was also an obvious fact: some WPA officials, foolishly and unnecessarily, used their influence over workers to organize political support for the administration. This was authenticated by a congressional investigation, and led to the passage of the Hatch Act in 1939. This act forbade federal employees, below the policy-making level, to engage in political campaigns or to solicit or accept contributions, for example, from WPA workers.

Roosevelt also assisted *unemployables* through the Social Security Act of 1935, which is now almost universally approved as a base on which private savings, pension plans, and insurance is founded. Yet, in the 1930's it was bitterly opposed by conservatives. This included conservative college professors — the same ones who wanted tenure most of all. This included conservative business executives — the same ones who would not take a job unless it offered attractive pension arrangements. This included the conservative Chicago *Tribune*, which ran a cartoon showing a malevolent Uncle Sam wielding a branding iron on a helpless American citizen as he burned a social-security number on his back.

The act provided noncontributory assistance, matched by states, for the needy; these were mothers, children, the crippled, the blind, the aged. But the major part of the act, and of its expenditures throughout the years, concerned retirement insurance. This was the Old Age Survivors Insurance (OASI), which provided protection against economic insecurity for workers when retirement or death have cut off earnings. The act began with a payroll tax, paid by both employer and employee, of 1 percent each; this had risen to more than 4 percent each in the late 1960's, and was scheduled to go to almost 6 percent each in the late 1980's. By 1957, the twentieth anniversary of the OASI in operation, it had collected about $45 billion, had received more than $4 billion in interest on its investments in government securities, and had paid out benefits of more than $25 billion. Ten years later, in 1967, with practically all workers covered (with the exception of federal civil service employees, who have separate coverage), the payments amounted to more than $20 billion in one fiscal year. For this reason the OASI, which is located in Baltimore, has been called the world's largest bookkeeping operation. For the cynic who believes the federal government to be inefficient, a visit to Baltimore can be an eye-opener to a world of automation and electronics. In the late 1950's the files of OASI contained almost 160 million names. At that time there were more than a million Smiths, more than a thousand Americans with the name of Ditto, and close to two hundred persons over the age of one hundred. The total operation will become ever more complex as time goes by; in 1965 Medicare was added to the Social Security system to provide hospital care, extended care facilities, and other medical services for those over sixty-five.

Recently an interesting proposal has been made, as an *addition* to Social Security. This is the Negative Income Tax (NIT), or Guaranteed Annual Wage. In this system the United States would set an official "poverty line"; the one suggested in 1966 was at $3,200 for annual incomes for nonfarm families of four, and at $1,500 for individuals. If the nonfarm family of four received $2,800 rather than $3,200, it would receive $400 from the government as the "negative" tax. On anything above $3,200, the family would pay the required income tax. As of 1966 it was estimated that 34 million persons in the United States, including 15 million children, were below the "poverty line" — an extraordinary statistic for the world's richest country. It was also estimated that at least $12 billion a year would be required to close the "poverty gap," to raise all Americans above the "poverty line." One of the arguments for the NIT was the old one of increasing purchasing power for those not covered at all, or inadequately covered, by current welfare programs. Another was to save money — money now spent on charity. The poor and destitute now get charity, and this welfare tab is estimated at better than $30 billion a year. In the long run, it is argued, because of the red tape and administrative expense of welfare payments — it would be cheaper to pay people *not* to be poor — at an estimated cost of half as much. The support for NIT covers all shades in the ideological spectrum. Milton Friedman favors it. He is the professor at the University of Chicago who was one of Barry Goldwater's economic advisers during the presidential campaign of 1964. John Kenneth Galbraith favors it. He is the professor of economics at Harvard who is classified as a liberal. He thinks we can easily afford a "poverty line," although he puts a price tag of $20 billion on it. For the historians of recent U.S. history the proposal was one more example of the adage that there is nothing new under the sun. They pointed out that all this is in a utopian novel published in 1888. It was written by Edward Bellamy, and was titled *Looking Backward.*

Although FDR tried many devices to bring recovery he did not fully succeed in peacetime; it took the influence of World War II to end internal depression in the United States. In September 1939 when Hitler invaded Poland, seventeen out of every one hundred Americans willing and able to work were unemployed. By December 1941, when the Japanese bombed Pearl Harbor, unemployment was still ten per hundred. By the middle of 1943, which was also the midpoint of our participation in the war, unemployment had dropped below 2 percent of the labor force. This is a sad commentary on human irrationality and folly.

Roosevelt not only hoped to bring recovery; he also wanted reform so that another depression would be less likely to occur. In order to bring it about he proposed a triple program: reform of banking in the Acts of 1933 and 1935; reform of the stock market through the Truth-in-Securities, and Securities and Exchange Commission (SEC) Acts of 1933 and 1934; and reform of corporate structure through the Wheeler-Rayburn Act of 1935. In connection with reform in banking the Glass-Steagall Act of 1933 was the most important measure since 1913. It permitted national banks to establish branches in states which tolerated it. It separated security affiliates from commercial banks; this meant that it divorced commercial and investment banking (this made necessary a fundamental decision in the Morgan family, resulting in J. P. Morgan & Co., a commercial bank — and the completely separate Morgan, Stanley & Co., an investment trust). It established bank insurance through the Federal Deposit Insurance Corporation (FDIC) to prevent a recurrence of the tragic results of bank failures in the 1920's and early 1930's. When the FDIC was set up in 1933, deposits were insured to $2,500; the top figure is now $20,000. This means that any depositor in an insured bank will receive all the money due him, not to exceed $20,000, from a bank that has closed. Payments under the system have been unusually prompt, normally within two weeks. On its thirtieth birthday in 1963 FDIC was insuring savings and checking accounts in 99 percent of the more than 14,000 banks throughout the nation; only 394 banks are not federally insured and almost half of these are mutual savings banks in Massachusetts covered by a state insurance system. There had been 445 failures during this thirty-year period, but almost 400 of them occurred in the first ten years of the act (1933–1943). Failures have not numbered more than five in any year since 1943; in 1962 there was no bank failure for the first time in the history of the nation — a striking contrast to an average of 588 bank failures a year in the 1920's and an average of 2,277 a year in the 1930–1933 period. During its first thirty years bank failures required FDIC disbursements of $359 million, but net losses were held to $21.5 million because of subsequent recoveries. FDIC receives no appropriation from Congress; its entire income consists of assessments on insured banks and income from investments. The total fund in FDIC is now more than $3.5 billion; it is such a sound institution that interest payments on its monies amount to more than the assessments (1/31 of 1 percent of total deposits) paid annually by the member banks in support of the fund.

The Glass-Steagall Act was a major one in regard to banking; so was the Banking Act of 1935. In general this second major New Deal act in the banking field strengthened the central or federal authority in a manner of which Nicholas Biddle would have been proud.

It lessened the political influence on the board of governors of the Federal Reserve System by reconstituting it as a seven-member body — eliminating from membership two government officials who had previously held membership *ex officio*. They were the Secretary of the Treasury and the Comptroller of the Currency. It was thought that this would make the board of governors more independent of the Executive, and politically disinterested. In general, it can be said that this goal was realized. It gave the central board of governors authority over the rediscount rate, which had hitherto been controlled by the district banks. It gave the central board of governors authority, within certain limits, over reserve requirements for bank deposits. It gave the central board of governors control over the open-market operations of the entire system.

Reform of the stock market was accomplished through the Truth-in-Securities Act of 1933, followed by the more basic SEC Act of the next year. A congressional investigation (through the Senate Committee on Banking and Currency) had begun to look into the stock market's connection with the crash. Counsel for the investigation was Ferdinand Pecora, son of an Italian shoemaker and an able lawyer. Assisting him was John T. Flynn, journalist and author of a book called *Security Speculation*, in which he insisted that speculation on the stock market was the moral and practical equivalent of a crap game. Pecora turned the investigative heat on the National City Bank of New York; it was his sensational disclosures that forced the resignation of Charles E. Mitchell, the president of what was then the second-largest bank in the nation. This investigation was comparable to the one by Arsène Pujo in 1912–1913. Generally speaking the emphasis was shifted from *caveat emptor* to *caveat vendor*, and for that reason the regulatory measures were at first bitterly opposed by the financial community on the ground that they imposed such severe limitations and liabilities on security dealers as to impede the financing of industry. Congress was not impressed with this argument and the legislation (Truth-in-Securities, and the SEC Act) had the following major provisions:

It set up a SEC of five members, not more than three from the same party, with specific and authoritative functions:

a. It placed stock exchanges and over-the-counter markets under the SEC's supervision, and prohibited or severely regulated a number of shady practices hitherto widely used, and known under such names as wash sales or pools.

b. It required full disclosure from companies before securities could be offered for sale, a consequence of the suppression of vital information by fraudulent or indifferent corporations in previous years. Before an issue of securities could be offered for public sale the issuer must file with the SEC a registration statement giving complete information on the securities and the issuing company. The SEC examined the statement and might refuse registration if it appeared to be misleading, inaccurate, or incomplete. If registration was denied, the securities could not be offered for sale.

c. It gave the Federal Reserve Board the power to establish margin requirements. Back in 1927–1928 the board had asked Congress for power to control margin requirements, when it would really have counted, and was turned down. When this vital power was finally given to the board in 1934, the momentary danger of runaway speculation was nil. But in the last three decades the power has been helpful in many ways, and the board has established margin requirements all the way from 25 to 100 percent.

The Wheeler-Rayburn Public Utility Holding Company Act (named after the progressive Senator from Montana and the member of the House who was later a notable Speaker) was designed to restrict the operations of holding companies in the gas and electricity fields by placing them under the control of the SEC. A famed clause, dramatically dubbed the "death sentence" by opponents of the act, required holding companies to show cause for existing at all. If it was a "death sentence," the demise of some of these companies was slow and lingering; the act was passed in 1935, the "death sentence" was not to become effective until 1938, and the SEC did not get around to investigation until the 1940's. In time, however, it mounted a major attack on "pyramided" holding-company empires like that of Sam Insull; the purpose of the SEC was to liquidate all interstate holding companies except those in the first tier above operating companies. When the clause became effective in 1938 there were 2,152 holding companies in the public-utility field, with combined assets of more than $16 billion. By 1950, 1,510 of these companies, with assets of $8 billion, had been eliminated.

Roosevelt was reelected in 1936 with 523 electoral votes against 8 for the Republican Alf Landon. But there was opposition, symbolized by the Liberty League, a financially well-oiled machine of the far right. It represented conservatives from the Republican Duponts to Democratic ex-presidential candidates Al Smith and John W. Davis. The Liberty League not only opposed New Deal legislation; it also spread the usual lounge-car stories about a President they hated. To them FDR was an inveterate liar, a syphilitic, a tool of the Negroes and the Jews, a madman given to unprovoked gales of immoderate laughter, an alcoholic, a megalomaniac dreaming his fantasies of dictatorship, an immoralist — hadn't you heard about his affair with Fanny Perkins? A very few may have thought of a coup d'etat. There was a stormy petrel from the United States Marines, General Smedley D. Butler, who had served in imperialist ventures in various parts of the world, but after retirement had changed his point of view and was known for his strong opinions and his isolationism and his campaign against war. Butler said that he was approached by persons who had connections in the Liberty League and who insisted that a fascist government was needed in the U.S. to save the capitalist system. These persons believed that the only people sufficiently patriotic to carry it off were the soldiers, and that Butler would make an ideal leader. They averred that at least half of the American Legion and the Veterans of Foreign Wars would follow Butler if he would only accept the leadership. He refused.

It was natural that those who supported FDR would take the Liberty League for a denunciatory ride. James Farley, the Postmaster General who managed FDR's campaigns in 1932 and 1936, said that the organization ought to be called the American Cellophane League because "first, it's a Dupont product and second, you can see right through it." Harry Hopkins thought that "the League may be composed of right-thinking people but they are so far Right that no one will ever find them." Another critic stated that they had "appropriated the Liberty Bell as their symbol, but they apparently think the [American] Revolution was fought to make Long Island safe for polo players." The League failed, as historian George Wolfskill has observed, not because of what it tried to do but because of what it seemed to represent. To the nation it stood for a system that had apparently failed, a system that disappeared "under a memorial wreath of ticker tape on a certain October morning in 1929." It failed because it represented economic and political conservatism at a time when both were out of style.

In the three decades from 1938 through 1968 the purchasing power of the dollar declined in all but two of the thirty years; by 1968 the prewar dollar of 1938 (at 100 percent) was worth 39.5 percent of its former purchasing power. In 1968 William McChesney Martin, the Chairman of the Federal Reserve Board, would warn that "The nation is in the worst financial crisis since 1931. Then, the problem was deflation. Today it is inflation and equally intolerable."

Inflation, whether creeping or galloping, benefits certain groups and harms others. It is helpful to debtors because they pay back cheaper dollars than those borrowed. The ultimate example of this phenomenon was found in the runaway inflation in Germany in 1923 when the mark had depreciated to the point that it took a truckload of them to buy a loaf of bread. The same marks, however, worthless as they were for the purchase of goods, could be used at face value as legal tender for the payment of past debts. Creditors were ruined, all private debt in Germany was easily paid off. Speculators also benefit from inflation; to cite the Germany of 1923 once again, people had no faith in money and were frantic to buy things, or claims on things: that is, stocks. It is obvious that any period of inflation tends to discourage normal saving through banks or bonds, and instead encourages speculation through capital gains and real estate.

While inflation may be applauded by debtors and speculators, powerful arguments can be cited against it. Inflation prices the United States out of the export market, as has been noticeable recently in many economic areas, particularly steel. It discourages saving, because creditors are hurt. Families with savings accounts — with U.S. Savings Bonds and other types of savings — find the purchasing power of these funds subject to a discouraging and alarming erosion. In the United States such savings in the mid-1960's aggregated more than $400 billion. It was apparent that every increase of 1 percent in the price level wiped out $4 billion in the purchasing value of these savings — owned by a very large segment classified as creditors in this respect. There is a world of difference between the annual inflation of 1 to 2 percent which prevailed in the late 1950's and the early 1960's, and the annual inflation of 4 to 5 percent which developed in the late 1960's. In the latter case the value of the dollar can be cut in half in ten years or so — with the result that savers get almost no "real" return and pensioners suffer a visible and yearly loss in real spending power. It is for this reason that one cynic recently referred to a bond as a "certificate of guaranteed confiscation." Inflation is hard on exporters and creditors, but it injures most those with fixed incomes — the aged, pensioners, widows, the disabled — the very people in our society who are most helpless. In the early 1960's it was estimated that more than half of the people in the United States over sixty-five had incomes of less than $1,000 a year — and that about half in the same age bracket had assets of less than $1,000. Annual inflation of better than 4 percent, which prevailed in the late 1960's, was obviously catastrophic for such people. In 1969 the Senate Special Committee on Aging reported that millions of the elderly in the U.S. were living in poverty, and that most of them did not become poor until they became old. Low income, debased still more by inflation, was the number-one problem facing 20 million persons sixty-five years or older.

What are the causes and remedies for this creeping inflation — assuming that we really want to stop it? Its causes fall into two groups: subsidiary and major. Qualifying as subsidiary ones are the agricultural support program, high tariffs, and certain practices — such as featherbedding — indulged in by both labor and management. The major causes of creeping inflation are two: an increase in money, and an increase in costs. The increase in money results from what economists call "demand-pull" — too much money chasing too few goods. Such monetary inflation has been described as the situation where nobody has enough money because everybody has too much. This is caused basically by resort to the printing press, and now occurs through the commercial banking system, as controlled by the Federal Reserve System. This monetary inflation occurs through the process of creating debt — deposit currency — either private (private consumer or private business debt) *or* governmental debt. For this reason deficit spending by the government can be inflationary, particularly if banks participate and thus increase their volatile reserves. Those who stress the dangers of money inflation point out that the increase in bank credit has outrun the increase in productivity, and that this is the major explanation for the continued rise in prices. They point particularly to the period from 1940 to 1952 when, in supporting tremendous demands for money needed in World War II, the Federal through open-market operations became an "engine of inflation," and as such "mined" some $120 billion of new money — lifting the money supply to three times its prewar size. In each of three successive war years — 1943, 1944, and 1945 — the federal deficit exceeded $50 billion, reaching a peak in 1943; such deficits eventually produced a massive inflation, when price and wage controls were removed after the war.

Apart from money, the increase in costs results in what economists refer to as the "cost-push" type of inflation. There are two main reasons for the increase in costs: the rise in the cost of raw materials and the wage-price-profit spiral. Few of us realize how dependent the United States now is on more costly raw materials from abroad. At the beginning of this century the United States produced some 15 percent more raw materials than it consumed (excluding food); by midcentury it was consuming 10 percent more raw materials than it produced. It had completed its slow transition from a raw-materials-surplus nation to a raw-materials-deficit one. In addition, the planet on which we live is beginning to run short of some materials of great importance to a technological society; as population increases this shortage, and the high prices accompanying it, the shortage will become more critical and worrisome. Dr. Charles F. Park, a professor of geology and mineral engineering at Stanford University, has punctured one of America's most engaging and pernicious myths; this is our belief that an ever-expanding economy can go on forever. It simply cannot happen because, as Dr. Park demonstrates, the tonnage of metal in the earth's crust won't last. Already we are running short of silver, mercury, tin, copper, and cobalt — all in growing demand by the high-technology industries. The more pedestrian metals, such as iron ore, in time will become scarce metals. Beyond this frightening shortage and increasing cost for raw materials there is the wage-price-profit spiral; as Galbraith has observed, this spiral is inconvenient but is also one of the facts of modern life. It affects only a part of the economy, that part where strong corporations bargain with strong unions. This larger-than-average pay hike is followed by an even larger price hike. High company earnings then become an invitation for further wage demands; prices, wages, and profits all shove one another up. Where there are weak unions, or where businessmen are small and have no assurance that their prices can be raised (to cover higher wage costs), the spiral does not operate. This situation prevails in the cotton-textile industry, for example — an industry of weak unions and numerous companies — where prices have remained relatively stable. In steel, by contrast, the spiral has worked relentlessly. There wage advances are invariably the occasion for even larger price increases; as a result the price of steel appears to be doubling every ten years.

What are the remedies, assuming that we want to stop or at least check this creeping inflation? For the subsidiary causes, the agricultural price-support program could be dropped by a return to the free market, but Congress appears to be fearful of the farm vote. Featherbedding could be eliminated, but if this is to be accomplished it will take more statesmanship, in both management and labor, than has appeared thus far. Protection, whether through tariffs or quotas, can be reduced — but the protected industries will howl.

The subsidiary causes and the possible solutions for them, puzzling as they may be, are relatively simple compared with the difficulties involved in remedying the major causes of the creeping inflation: the increase in money and the increase in costs. The increase in money can be controlled in two ways: through monetary policy, that is, monetary restraint; and through fiscal policy, that is, fiscal restraint. Of the two, monetary restraint through the Federal is the one that has been employed most frequently through the years. In this connection Professor Milton Friedman of the University of Chicago would go further than the Federal has gone. Friedman is well known among economists for advocating the reduction, or elimination, of the Federal's discretionary powers over the money supply. He favors a policy of increasing the money supply annually by a percentage equal to the average annual percentage rise in the Gross National Product (GNP) of the United States. This is about 4 percent, and for that reason Friedman's proposal is often called the 4 percent rule. He sees two advantages in his so-called "rule": price stability because of equality of annual percentage increases in money and productivity; and the confidence of business, because businessmen would not be as uncertain about the future as they now are — simply because they would know what the Federal was going to do. Because the quantity of money rose in 1967 and 1968 at an average rate of nearly 10 percent (twice as fast as GNP), Friedman was not surprised that prices also accelerated to a rate of 5 percent in 1968. Senator William Proxmire of Wisconsin believes that the Federal should adopt as a working goal a rule holding increases in the money supply to between 2 and 6 percent a year. His proposal is based on the conviction that outsized changes in the money supply almost always precede outsized changes in the real world of incomes, jobs, and prices. When the money supply begins to rise at an annual rate of more than 6 percent, in Proxmire's judgment inflation lies ahead; when it falls below 2 percent, recession is on its way.

Fiscal restraint, by contrast with that on the monetary side, is the use of the taxing power to curb spending and to mop up excessive demand. Such austerity, however, has had little appeal in peacetime to Americans who dislike higher taxes but who adore their creature comforts. We appear to have arrived, in the United States, at a point where we puzzle our heads at Christmas over what to buy for the man who has everything. Economist John Kenneth Galbraith strongly favors the policy of fiscal restraint, to the point of applauding regressive sales taxes deplored by most other economists. Because of public needs he deplores spending for air-conditioned luxury automobiles and mink coats and gourmet foods and imported vintage wines. He would use the money not spent on excessive consumption but taken in taxes for spending in the public sector — on education, urban renewal, conservation. Governmental administrations, whether at the state or national level, do not see eye to eye with Mr. Galbraith. At the state level governors take pride in advertising how low their taxes are. Probably the most popular economic theory in the Kennedy and Johnson administrations was that known as the "fiscal drag." This held that tax receipts had a tendency to rise rapidly with economic growth, with the effect of checking that growth or even bringing on a recession. The way to prevent such a happening was to cut taxes or to increase government expenditures. The first was more popular with both Presidents and the Congress.

Something could be done about inflation caused by an increase in money — through monetary and fiscal restraint. Inflation that comes because of increases in cost presents another problem. Nothing can be done about the increases in the cost of raw materials as this nation becomes more and more dependent on imports. Something *can* be done about the wage-price-profit spiral. The most drastic remedy would be direct controls over prices and wages, such as those we had in World War II through the Office of Price Administration and the National War Labor Board — and such as Britain now has. In past years, however, Americans have not regarded direct controls, in peacetime, as respectable; those who recommended them did so at considerable risk to their reputations. When President Eisenhower got rid of them in 1953 his deed was regarded, by most of the citizens of the Republic, as an act of supreme wisdom — symbolic of enlightened Republicanism. Other proposals, short of direct controls, have been made for the purpose of stopping — or at least slowing down — the wage-price-profit spiral. Adlai Stevenson proposed compulsory arbitration of industrial wage disputes, with the public sitting in on the negotiations. Galbraith suggested a law proscribing any general price increase for at least a year following the negotiation of a new collective-bargaining contract; such an interdiction would tend to stop what are known as "soft" wage increases. This would mean that, at least for a waiting period, wage increases would be paid out of profits or productivity increases — from which they should come in any case. In the 1960's Galbraith's proposal was met with silence or cries of outrage from labor and management.

In recent years there has been a growing concern as to whether U.S. currency is being managed well enough to provide the dollar with stability sufficient to withstand the buffetings of inflationary winds. There has also been a continuing worry as to whether our balance of payments is being managed wisely enough to provide strength in international transactions sufficient to withstand pressures against the value of the dollar and the size of the U.S. gold reserve. By balance of payments is meant the ratio between U.S. earnings and expenditures abroad — the balance between U.S. sales of goods and services, and foreign investment in U.S. securities and physical property — as contrasted with U.S. purchases of goods and services from abroad, and U.S. investment of dollars in foreign securities, physical plant, wars, and aid. If a nation persists in adverse balances of payments, it can discharge its deficit by selling its currency (i.e., dollars or pounds or pesos) or gold, if it has any; if this occurs on a continuing basis, there is an inevitable decline in the value of the currency and of the size of the gold reserve.

From 1789 to the American Civil War our imports from the rest of the world were larger than our exports, and there were sizable debits in the balance of international trade. These were offset in major part, but not entirely, by foreign payments to the American merchant marine for services (the carrying of freight), by European investment of their currencies in the United States, and by the movement of specie and bullion. We have noted that the heyday of the American merchant marine was in the period down to the Civil War; during these years American flag vessels were prominent in all the ports of the world, earning foreign currency for their dependability and their speed in the day of the clipper ship. Foreigners were also interested in the possibility of attractive profits in American entrepreneurial ventures; by the time of the Civil War they had invested the equivalent, in their own currencies, of almost a billion and a half dollars in U.S. federal, state, railroad, and other securities. Specie was also a great help. Down to 1849 U.S. shippers had engaged in the reexport trade (for commissions) of gold and silver coin and bullion from Latin America and the Orient. After 1849 the United States became the greatest gold-producing nation in the world; this commodity was a fortuitous windfall and a great impetus in swinging the adverse balance of payments in the opposite direction.

From the American Civil War until 1950, a period of more than eighty years, the balance of payments was favorable to the United States. These balances were mildly advantageous until 1914, and then tipped heavily on the side of the United States from World War I until 1950. In the pre–World War I period we sold more abroad than we imported, but these earnings were easily offset by payments our citizens made abroad. With the decline of our merchant marine large sums were sent to Europe to pay for freight and insurance. American corporations paid dividends and interest to foreign holders of stocks and bonds in ventures here. Immigrants to the United States, who were coming to our shores in large numbers, sent American currency to loved ones in the "old country." American travelers and tourists, more and more inclined to make the "Grand Tour" of Europe, spent American dollars with pleasure and abandon — for services provided by the delighted natives of those countries.

Down to World War I these offsetting arrangements made for an easy and pleasant and congenial atmosphere as far as balance of payments was concerned. Beginning in 1914, however, this balance swung heavily in favor of the United States and was to remain that way until 1950. The United States suddenly became the world's banker as a result of the "New Imperialism" and two World Wars. What was called the "Old Imperialism" had been dominant in the sixteenth and seventeenth centuries when the homeland sent out conquistadores and settlers to conquer and occupy. The "New Imperialism" was the result of the Industrial Revolution. Now capitalists in the nineteenth and twentieth centuries, no longer interested in settlement, were sending out manufactured goods and investment capital. Around 1900 the United States was also converted to the "New Imperialism," and the colonies that accompany it, because of their potential for the absorption of goods and capital.

From the standpoint of investments the United States was a debtor country until World War I. In 1914 American investments abroad totaled $3.5 billion, but foreign investments here (largely European) came to $7.2 billion; we were therefore a debtor nation by almost $4 billion. The war changed this quickly. Before the United States entered the conflict in April 1917 it had become a creditor nation. This came about because more than $2 billion in foreign-owned American securities had been returned for sale in the United States, in order to develop dollar balances to pay for munitions and other supplies so urgently needed by Allied nations, and because American banks, led by J. P. Morgan, had lent Allied powers $2.6 billion. After the United States entered the fray the federal government took over the problem of financing, lending approximately $10 billion to Allied governments; these constituted the famous "war debts" of World War I. In the 1920's Europe was so exhausted economically that the United States continued to be the great source of capital as the world's financial center shifted from London to New York. Apart from government loans, American private investments abroad, which had been $3.5 billion in 1914, rose to almost $7 billion in 1919 and to $17 billion in 1929. The $17 billion in 1929 was divided evenly between two types of investments: portfolio and direct. The first represented ownership of foreign securities (stocks and bonds) by individuals and institutions in this country. Direct investment occurred when an American company built or purchased productive facilities in another country; these investments were made by American corporations in agricultural, commercial, mining, and public-utility enterprises in foreign countries.

Despite the magnitude of these dollar loans abroad, the balance of payments in favor of the United States became even heavier in the 1930's. This was due in part to a steady export surplus; there was also a flow of "scare" money into the United States from a Europe that was justifiably worried about the rise of Hitler and Mussolini. During these years we acquired a great amount of gold simply because we were running such a large and persistent surplus in our transactions with the rest of the world; under these extreme conditions foreign countries used what currency they could spare, then were compelled to sell gold to the United States Treasury to get more dollars. The result was that the U.S. gold stock, which was $4 billion in 1932, rose to $22 billion in 1940. World War II brought a temporary reversal, but the close of that conflict found the United States with its economic machinery intact — and running a heavy surplus again. Our gold stock reached its peak in 1949 when the United States held almost $25 billion; the rest of the world struggled along on the remaining $10 billion.

In the late 1940's economists worried about a "dollar gap" — referring to a financial chasm with two precipitous sides. On one of them was the United States with the dollars; on the other was the rest of the world which was short of them. Steps were taken to bridge the gap, among them the Marshall Plan (interestingly, if the Americans had treated Marshall aid as a loan instead of an outright grant, the United States would not have suffered a decline in international reserves in the past decade, and France would not have been able to hope for profits through exploitation of the dollar and gold in the late 1960's). Suddenly, in the 1950's, the seemingly omnipotent and self-satisfied United States found itself with an alarming deficit in its balance of payments. This was due to the circumstance that, in spite of a most favorable balance of trade (exports over imports) which until 1968 amounted up to $5 billion a year, the United States was also sending many, many dollars around the world to backstop Koreas and Vietnams, to finance American corporate investments abroad, and to furnish U.S. tourists with the necessary traveler's checks to meet their dollar expenditures in foreign lands. In actual fact the United States has had annual deficits in its overall balance of payments from 1950 on, with the exception of one year; during this period the United States has consistently paid out more to other countries than it has taken in — with the cumulative deficit amounting to almost $40 billion by 1969. From 1950 through 1956 the deficits, averaging about $1 billion a year, were small enough that they were not considered to be a real problem. In 1957 there was actually a change for the better. We had a tiny surplus of $5.2 million; this came from a purely temporary situation surrounding the Suez Canal crisis of 1956, as a result of which U.S. firms made massive oil shipments abroad. Then in 1958 the trouble really began. A world that once could not lay its hands on enough dollars found that it had more than it wanted.

In following years, unfortunately, the annual deficit became increasingly larger. In 1970 the United States suffered a shortage, in its transactions with foreign governments, of $10 billion — the largest such deficit in American history. While this was going on the U.S. gold reserve was halved, from $22.8 billion in 1958 to $11.8 billion in 1969. After the British devaluation of the pound in November 1967 there was an embarrassing run on the dollar by hoarders and speculators who asked for conversion into gold at the official U.S. Treasury rate of $35 an ounce. In the month of December 1967 alone, the U.S. Treasury lost almost a billion dollars worth of gold. President Johnson's balance-of-payments program, announced in January 1968 and based on restricting American bank lending and industrial investment abroad, helped to quiet the crisis for two months. But the gold rush was not to be stopped so easily. As economist John Brooks has pointed out, it was really an expression of the age-old tendency to distrust all paper currencies in time of crisis. More specifically it was the sequel to the devaluation of the pound plus a vote of no confidence in the probability that the United States would put its financial house in order. In the spring of 1968 the run on the dollar began again in real earnest and on a *single* convulsive day, Thursday 14 March, the U.S. Treasury lost more than $200 million of its gold before a temporary solution was reached on a two-price market for the metal. On the next day Americans in London, Rome, and other cities in western Europe suffered from the astonishing experience of being told they could not change their dollar traveler's checks into foreign currencies. This situation lasted only a few days but suddenly the balance of payments — and even the mysterious international monetary system itself — had become a drama that affected many, many people.

In 1948 the U.S. gold reserve had been so large that it was regarded, perhaps inaccurately, as something of a white elephant. Twenty years later it was half as large, was steadily decreasing in size, and had been metamorphosed miraculously from a white elephant into a skeleton in the closet — a mummy that rattled and was unsettling to the nerves of monetary authorities on both sides of the Atlantic. The point is that under the original Federal Reserve Act, as amended, almost $15 billion in gold was held in reserve as legal protection against bank deposits (a reserve of about $5 billion) and currency (a reserve of about $10 billion). As the U.S. gold reserve fell it was obvious that a pitifully small amount (depending on the year) — or nothing — was left for other essential purposes. What is meant by "other essential purposes"? It is simply this: by 1960 foreigners had invested about $30 billion in the United States, half of it in short-term obligations which they could cash at short notice, asking for payment in gold. If all of them asked for payment at once, it would obviously place an insupportable strain on the gold reserve of the U.S. Treasury.

What could be done to lighten this heavy burden? By the close of the 1960's four solutions had been offered, all of them controversial because they were beneficial to some and costly to others. One proposal was to *reduce* imports and to *increase* exports. A second involved the regulation of the international flow of money by means of *foreign-exchange controls*. A third provided for an increase in the *value* and *availability* of gold in the United States, to achieve its maximum use in making payments to other nations. Finally, it was suggested that we might *replace* gold with a new international monetary unit.

It is apparent that imports can be reduced in two ways: by raising the tariff or establishing quotas against foreign goods, and by reducing the amount of duty-free imports which American tourists can bring on their return to the United States. We can raise the tariff and establish quotas against foreign goods, but every educated citizen knows that international trade is a two-way street, and that if we reduce our imports we will also reduce our exports — and either lose or break even. In actual fact, President John F. Kennedy supported the Trade Expansion Act of 1962 — a low-tariff act. He did so partly because of a belief in international cooperation, but partly because he was convinced that if we increased international trade, our advantage in exports would be even greater; the trade balance of the 1960's bore him out in this assumption. A tariff or quotas against imports were therefore no solutions for this problem. We can, however, reduce imports through a limitation on the amount of duty-free goods which tourists can bring back to the United States. By 1966 American tourists were spending almost $3 billion a year while they were abroad. They spent American dollars. There are no accurate figures to show how much of this huge sum was spent for articles brought home under the duty-free allowance, but the amount was considerable. In actual fact the history of the duty-free allowance is an interesting one closely allied with the economic facts of life. Prior to 1948 the free allowance was $100. In 1948 it was raised to $500; at that time the purpose was to promote tourist expenditures of Americans in dollar-hungry countries — in order to close the "dollar gap." In recent years, however, steps have been taken to reduce these expenditures. In 1962 President Kennedy asked for and got Congress to reduce the duty-free allowance to $200. In 1965 President Johnson achieved a nominal reduction to $100 — but an actual lowering to $65 through the technical gimmick of basing valuations on retail rather than wholesale prices.

Imports cannot be decreased, in the interest of a better balance of trade, without decreasing exports commensurately. Protective tariffs and quotas against imports are therefore of little or no use; an increase in the volume of exports must be achieved in other ways. There are two of them. We could reduce prices to make our goods more attractive to foreign buyers. We could encourage foreign tourists to come to the United States in order to increase the export of our services.

As far as goods are concerned prices could be reduced through the elimination of featherbedding, of which both American labor unions and management are guilty. Labor unions are notorious because they demand, for example, firemen in diesel engines and bogus typesetting on newspapers. American business management also featherbeds through two practices. There are excessive salaries paid to executives: the salary of one American top executive frequently equals the administrative overhead of an entire European or Japanese enterprise. There are administered prices which are out of line with either real costs or demand for the product. Because of the wage-price spiral — where labor and management have agreed on increases — labor often gets a dollar, and management sees to it that the price is increased by two or even three dollars. This can be accomplished without reference to the law of supply and demand, as was illustrated in the rise of steel prices during the *recession* of 1957–1958. In 1968 economist Walter Adams of Michigan State University would say to a House committee: "The level of U.S. steel prices is uncompetitive not because of high labor costs, but because of an insensitive, monopolistic, and suicidal pricing policy, on the one hand, and technological lethargy on the other." Some consider colossal Defense Department procurement the major illustration of featherbedding by management, particularly in the highly profitable aerospace and arms industries. Under Pentagon contracting procedures, competitive bidding has been gradually disappearing, financial risks have been assumed by the taxpayers, and inefficiency has been rewarded with extra payments. According to one commentator, prices are certain to rise rapidly in a situation where a company's volume of war-production contracts "varies almost directly with the number of high-ranking retired officers it has hired."

As a result of featherbedding by both labor *and* management, American industry frequently prices itself out of world markets and can compete only by manufacturing somewhere outside the United States. It is apparent that the greater the disparity between prices here and abroad, the more exposed U.S. markets will be to invasion by a fast-industrializing world, and the greater the temptation of American industry to establish affiliates overseas instead of expanding or modernizing their facilities in this country. If this featherbedding continues with inevitably increasing prices, there will be a greater import of goods and there will be a greater export of jobs.

We can increase our export of *goods* by lowering prices. We can increase our export of *services* by encouraging foreign tourists to visit the United States. But — if we are going to increase tourism in the United States — it will be necessary to make it much easier for foreigners to come to this country. In this regard the contrast has been startling between the United States and other countries. If an American wants to go to Denmark, the Danes say, "Welcome to Denmark." If a Dane wants to come to the United States, to visit his brother in Minnesota, we say, "Why do you want to come to the U.S.?" We make the Dane submit photographs, complete a myriad of forms, and prove that he is not feebleminded, a drug addict, a polygamist or a leper (there are actually thirty-one categories that can exclude him). Someone has commented that Christopher Columbus could never have qualified, under present laws, for a U.S. tourist visa because he was a recent pauper and was insane by contemporary standards. It is certainly a demonstrable fact, in this day, that a Dane or a Swiss finds it easier to enter Communist Russia than to get within sight of our Statue of Liberty. For all of our talk about the *Iron Curtain*, the unpleasant truth is that in connection with international pleasure travel, our own Red Tape Curtain can be far harder to penetrate than iron. The *New York Times* has expressed its faith that freedom to travel belongs with freedom of speech, freedom of the press, and all of the other freedoms that make the difference between our world and the totalitarian one. Our Red Tape Curtain, by contrast, is based on fear, and stems from the McCarthy era and what many foreigners regard as a psychopathic concern for security on the part of Americans. Whatever it is, it is expensive. In 1960 Americans spent more than $2 billion on travel abroad, making tourism our largest single *import* — because we were importing foreign *services*. By contrast, in the same year the expenditures of foreigners who visited the United States were only half as much — placing tourism well down on the list of American exports (of services). The negative imbalance of 1960 was more than a billion dollars; five years later it was almost $2 billion. This loss represents a sizable percentage of our deficit in balance of payments.

We can also regulate the international flow of money through foreign-exchange controls. Such controls can be of two types — general and selective. General controls simply bar *all* American citizens from purchasing foreign exchange, *and all* foreigners from purchasing dollars (or claims on dollars) — except when permission is granted in advance to do so. This would mean, for example, that a citizen of the United States could not — without special permission — take a vacation on the Riviera, buy a factory abroad, or buy Scotch. There is nothing new or unusual about such general controls. In the 1930's the Finance Minister of Hitler's Germany, Hjalmar Horace Greeley Schacht, developed such foreign-exchange controls into a fine and complex art. His complicated and unorthodox program of currency-exchange controls and barter trade enabled Germany to secure raw materials for its rearmament and extended German economic influence in Central Europe, the Balkans, and South America. After World War II, practically every nation except the United States had to impose such controls over foreign-exchange payments.

Most Americans do not agree with the idea of *general* foreign-exchange controls. Many, however, favor *selective* controls — particularly in connection with foreign affairs, interest rates, and investments abroad (both portfolio and direct). In the field of foreign affairs the U.S. government could reduce military expenditures in foreign lands — such as those in Korea, Vietnam, Berlin, Santo Domingo, and Europe. Even when the commitment has been made, as it has in these areas, the government tries to cut the drain of dollars by supplying overseas troops from the United States, whenever possible, albeit at higher costs. Even so in 1968 the cost of maintaining troops abroad, including Vietnam, resulted in a dollar outflow of more than $4 billion. Cutting these expenditures would make complete sense from the standpoint of reducing the deficit in our balance of payments. There has been great controversy as to whether it makes complete sense from the point of view of our foreign policy. The United States could also cut foreign aid, which involves expenditures abroad in dollars. Walter Lippmann has pointed out that the United States *had* to spend a lot on foreign aid, for a period of years after World War II, to bring reconstruction and recovery to the *developed* nations of the world. In this effort we spent almost $100 billion. During this period of reconstruction, the greatest need of these *developed* countries was a supply of hard currency, of which the dollar was the most desirable unit. In these early years after World War II, our policy was brilliantly successful. Japan and western Europe not only made a full recovery — they achieved a condition of boom. As a result, for them the dollar shortage was turned into a dollar surplus. By 1960 it was evident to Lippmann that these fully recovered nations of western Europe plus Japan should now finance the cost of their own defenses and should assist the United States in the task of financing the expansion of the underdeveloped nations in Asia and Africa. Little has been accomplished along these lines. The United States now spends several billions a year on foreign aid. It tries to reduce the strain on balance of payments by requiring as many purchases as possible in the United States — and by requiring that half of the commodities shipped be carried in American-flag vessels. Even so, foreign aid contributes a billion dollars or more to the current deficit in balance of payments.

The Federal Reserve Board can keep interest rates high in the United States — thus attracting foreign capital into this country, and deterring present foreign holders of short-term bonds from cashing them and taking home either dollars or gold. In 1964 Britain increased its bank rate from 5 to 7 percent. At that time, which now seems long ago, a Swiss banker was quoted as saying, "Seven percent will drag money from the moon." The Federal Reserve Board can keep interest rates high through its control over the rediscount rate, and through its open-market operations. This it did for a number of years, and this policy was a good one from the standpoint of balance of payments. It may not have been good for the domestic economy, because high interest rates are deflationary. They keep the prospective homeowner from buying, the merchant from expanding, the industrialist from building new plants, and they cost the U.S. Treasury a lot of money on its own huge debt. (In this regard the Treasury is between Scylla and Charybdis: it applauds high interest rates because they protect and preserve our dwindling gold supply, but it deplores the same high interest rates because they are costly in funding the huge national debt.)

The United States can do, and has done, something to regulate *portfolio* investments by Americans and foreigners (as individuals and corporations) in securities. The Kennedy Administration was the first to move in this direction, and did so with great success. It asked Congress to pass, and Congress obliged, a law providing for what was called an interest equalization tax. This was a levy on foreign stocks and bonds sold in the United States; it could amount to as much as 15 percent of the purchase price. This law had a profound effect in reducing their sale in this country, and in so doing it relieved the strain on the balance of payments by reducing the export of dollars to pay for them. Prior to 1963 foreign securities were being marketed in New York at an annual rate of $2 billion. After the tax went into effect, there were few new issues of foreign securities in the United States. President Kennedy thus took successful action to restrict the purchase of foreign securities with U.S. dollars; President Johnson introduced legislation to make the purchase of American securities more attractive to foreigners, thus increasing the availability of foreign currency in this country. In 1966 Congress passed a measure known as the "Foreign Tax Bill" which provided more favorable tax treatment of foreign investors and allegedly removed tax "roadblocks which have discouraged foreign investments in this country." Specifically, the bill reduced tax rates on a foreign investor's income on U.S. securities to as low as 30 percent — as contrasted with income-tax rates of up to 70 percent for Americans.

The same degree of success was not achieved in regulating direct investments by American corporations in plants abroad. By 1968 American firms, on an increasing annual basis, had brought their overseas direct investment to almost $65 billion, more than the gross national product of many a nation, and eight times the amount foreign businessmen had invested in the United States during the almost two hundred years of the American Republic. Oil was the biggest attraction, with manufacturing and mining in second and third places, but in the specialized industries U.S. corporations now control 80 percent of Europe's computer business, 90 percent of the microcircuit industry, 40 percent of its automaking — and sizable shares of chemicals and farm machinery. Standard Oil of New Jersey, as an example, now has 54 percent of its total investments outside the United States, and of its 150,000 employees some 90,000 work in foreign countries; it sells as much gas and oil and chemicals in Europe as it does in the United States — and its business in Europe is growing at a faster rate. The same trend holds for other U.S. corporations: Colgate-Palmolive, Heinz, Woolworth, Singer, and National Cash Register do more business overseas than at home. At a time when the U.S. government was terribly worried about the deficit in balance of payments, the Ford Motor Company spent hundreds of millions of dollars buying out British Ford; U.S. Ford was simply adding to other foreign holdings — it already owned 99 percent of German Ford, and 75 percent of Ford Motor of Canada. In the automotive industry Ford is by no means alone in foreign investments; General Motors owns enough stock to control Vauxhall in Britain and the Opel Works in Germany.

Interestingly, the opportunities provided by the Common Market have been grasped by U.S. manufacturers and bankers. There is a current European joke that is considered far more true than funny. It asks who has benefited most from the Common Market; the answer is the United States. Americans have been quicker and more imaginative in making use of the opportunities for large-scale selling in the Common Market. The same is true of American banks which have developed regional facilities which few European financial institutions are in a position to offer. The central point is that U.S. businessmen, already accustomed to regionalism in their own country, grasped the significance of the Common Market long before the Europeans who had conceived it. In 1968 Jean-Jacques Servan-Schreiber, the French journalist and economist, published a best-selling book titled *The American Challenge*. He stated that within fifteen years the third industrial power in the world — after the United States and the USSR — could well be not Europe, but American Industry in Europe. Lester Pearson, the Canadian statesman who won the Nobel Peace Prize in 1957, has noted that multinational firms transcend national boundaries, not by crossing them, but by ignoring their existence through the establishment of subsidiaries in foreign countries. Their growth has been so phenomenal that one economist has predicted that by 1980 there will be 300 multinational corporations substantially controlling the business of the entire non-Communist world. This economic revolution is another reason for the erosion of national sovereignty and (as one cynic has phrased it) for the trend toward universal Americanization. Pearson believes that "the sovereign state is now becoming virtually obsolete as a satisfactory basis for rational economic organization, at least in industrially developed societies."

All of this has had a profound effect on European economic and cultural life. Reporter Tad Szulc has noted in the *New York Times* that an infinity of American products are manufactured in Europe with their own brand names under licensing arrangements, or by American-owned subsidiaries — from automobiles to home appliances, cigarettes, soft drinks, detergents, cosmetics, and foodstuffs. There are so many of these products that there has been a blurring of the line between "real" American and European goods; when an Englishman buys a new Vauxhall, he is unlikely to give any thought to the fact that Vauxhall is owned by General Motors in the United States. On her first visit to New York recently, a British housewife was heard to say — when she sighted a five-and-ten-cent store, "Oh, I see you have our Woolworth too." All this has occurred in spite of the fact that the same American advertising techniques are used abroad as in the United States; there is also "Marlboro country" in Europe. The Continental landscape is fairly covered with billboards and posters advertising, in several languages, "the pause that refreshes"; in Rome it is reported that Coca-Cola is even sold at most Communist rallies. In France some have become concerned about the future purity of the language; what is known as "Franglais" has introduced a mongrel mixture of American and French expressions including "le hamburger," "le milkshake," "le drugstore," and "le long drink." With an American materialistic appetite the affluent French family is now plunging into *la civilisation des gadgets* and wishes very much to be like its counterpart in the Western Hemisphere. The British are no better off. William Davis, the editor of the London humor magazine *Punch*, noted that in 1969 U.S.-controlled firms produced about one-tenth of everything manufactured in Britain, had a stake in more than 1,600 firms, and employed one in seventeen of all British workers. He suggested that Britain become the 51st State.

Whatever the effect of American direct investments on the economic and cultural life of Europe, there is little question that they have contributed materially to the U.S. deficit in its balance of payments. Because of this situation two proposals have been made: some have proffered the idea that we limit direct American investments abroad by requiring approval for every direct investment made, and others have suggested that we revise our tax laws, making direct investment less attractive than it has been. The first proposal has been supported particularly by labor unions. Their central point is that American direct investment abroad has been made, at least in part, to avoid *foreign* import duties against their products — and to take advantage of lower wages and costs of production abroad. This means fewer exports from the United States, for example, of automobiles, typewriters, and chemicals — constituting a direct threat to the favorable balance of trade which the United States once enjoyed. To labor, this signifies that the companies are not only exporting *capital;* they are also exporting *jobs.**

There has also been some support for the proposal that tax laws, on direct investments abroad, be strengthened and tightened. Under tax laws as they were in the early 1960's, earnings on American direct investments abroad were either slow in getting back to this country or did not get back at all. Under these laws American firms investing in foreign enterprises might postpone indefinitely the repatriation of their foreign earnings, thus delaying payment of American income and corporation taxes on them, and thus obtaining what amounted to an interest-free loan from the U.S. government on the amount of taxes which were due but deferred. These lenient laws had been devised two decades earlier to stimulate private investments abroad, when such investment was very much needed. By the 1960's this was no longer the case.

Delay is one thing; some of the earnings never return to the United States at all. American investments abroad in 1960 earned about $3.5 billion, but about $1 billion was retained for reinvestment. Some of the rest never got back either. As an example, some American companies established subsidiaries in such low-tax or tax-free areas as Switzerland, Liechtenstein, the Bahamas, Bermuda, or Monaco — and siphoned off the profits of American branch factories abroad, thereby depriving the host country of taxes and the United States of profit dollars. President Kennedy therefore proposed a tax on earnings of American subsidiaries in

---

* In 1968 Congress did limit direct investments abroad under a complex system which divided foreign nations into three categories. In Schedule A (underdeveloped countries in Asia, Africa, Latin America, and the Middle East), U.S. corporations could invest annually 110 percent of their average investment in the base years 1965–1966. For so-called Schedule B countries (Britain, Japan, Hong Kong, Iran, Australia, Ireland, and the oil-producing countries of the Middle East), the annual investment was limited to 65 percent of the base years. For Schedule C nations of western Europe, and South and West Africa, no new capital outflow was permitted, but U.S. corporations could retain earnings up to 35 percent of base-year investments. By 1970 there was considerable doubt that these limitations had had much of an impact. This was because of the availability of Eurodollars, a substantial source of investment in Europe recently. The one important difference between Eurodollars and ordinary greenbacks is that the former do not usually show up in balance-of-payments statistics. They are simply dollars held in Europe, by Europeans as well as Americans, and used in transactions that did not involve the United States directly unless they were offered for conversion into gold. The Eurodollar pool in 1969 was estimated at $13 billion, a little more than the value of the U.S. gold reserve. See F. Lewis, "To Reap a Crop of Eurodollars," Miami *Herald*, 26 Dec. 1969; H. Koshetz, "Limits on Investment Abroad Assailed," *NY Times*, 29 July 1970.

developed countries *when* they are earned — instead of waiting until they were brought home — if this occurred. He saw no justice in taxing American business operations in France or Britain or Germany any differently from American business operations in New York. He felt there were inducements enough for investment abroad, without an additional tax advantage. If his proposal had been adopted, namely, to impose a tax on foreign earnings when they were realized, it was estimated that the flow of funds *to* the United States would have been increased by half a billion dollars a year, a significant sum in the scale of international balances. Furthermore, at the rate of 52 percent, which then represented the tax on major corporate incomes, there would have been a noticeable increment for the U.S. Treasury. It is not surprising that American business mounted a major attack against this proposal. It was not passed by the Congress.

A third solution for improving the U.S. balance of payments involved the possibility of increasing the value *and* availability of U.S. gold — for use toward payment of the deficit. The *value* could be augmented by increasing the price which the government offers for gold. The *availability* could be increased by reducing or eliminating the long-established 25 percent requirement of gold against Federal Reserve System notes and deposits.

The value of our present supply of gold could be increased by the simple legislative action of devaluing the dollar. If the price of gold had been suddenly doubled, from $35 an ounce (which the U.S. government then paid to all official foreign holders of our dollars, thus making the dollar and gold interchangeable) to $70 an ounce, the value of the gold reserve would suddenly have increased (on the basis of U.S. holdings in 1965) from $15 billion to $30 billion. Correspondingly the amount of gold in the legal dollar would have been reduced from 15 plus grains, now worth a dollar in gold, to 7 plus grains, which would then be worth a dollar in gold. This operation would ease the immediate strain on the gold reserve. Devaluation is the most heroic and the most dangerous of remedies for a sick currency, and for that reason it is the most feared. By making the devaluing country's goods cheaper to others (provided those other nations do not devalue too, as frequently happens), it can boost exports, and in theory reduce or eliminate a deficit in international accounts. At the same time it makes both imports and domestic goods more expensive at home, and thus reduces the country's standard of living. As John Brooks once observed: "It is radical surgery, curing a disease at the expense of some of the patient's strength and well-being — and in many cases, some of his pride and prestige as well." If the devalued currency is one, like the pound or the dollar, which is widely used in international transactions, the effect can be disastrous. To nations or individuals holding large amounts of that particular currency in their reserve vaults, the effect of devaluation is the same as if the vaults had been burglarized.

Prior to President Nixon's bombshell of August 1971 the United States had devalued only once in a history of more than 180 years (assuming that the slight reduction of the gold content of the dollar in 1836 was a technical adjustment). That first devaluation took place in 1933 when the United States raised the price of gold from $20.67 an ounce to $35, the equivalent of a devaluation of 41 percent.* Beyond its historic reluctance to take such an action, it appeared that the nation would hesitate to repeat it for several other reasons. Devaluation would contribute to inflation — the result of a cheaper dollar — plus all the bad effects that inflation always brings in the long terms. Devaluation might also be followed by similar devaluations on the part of other nations — thus wiping out the initial advantage of increased exports. Devaluation might also be a boon to two great gold-producing nations that few U.S. citizens wanted to help. They were South Africa and Soviet Russia.

Possible devaluation of the dollar was one thing. There was also the possibility of reducing or eliminating the reserve requirement of 25 percent in gold which stood for so many years behind Federal Reserve notes and member-bank deposits. Such a step would free all, or at least part, of the approximately $15 billion in gold which was once held as a reserve for these purposes, and free it for use in settling international balances rather than domestic ones. This particular reserve had an interesting and fluctuating history. When the Federal Reserve System was created in 1913 it took over the function of issuing most of the greenback dollars which are now in our pocketbooks. At that time the Senate Banking Committee recognized that the nation was to have a "managed" money supply and that there was no longer to be any link between the amount of the nation's gold and the money in circulation. But the committee put into the law a provision for a gold cover behind the currency, for what it admitted were purely psychological reasons — to calm fears of an excessive creation of money under the new system. Interestingly, in the period of more than half a century after 1913, every time the money supply pressed on the existing gold-cover requirement, the percentage was reduced by act of Congress — to permit further growth of the money supply.

In 1913 a holder could turn in his Federal Reserve notes for gold itself.

---

* In 1933 the U.S. government took over all gold except that in jewelry and dental fillings. Since 1933 it has been illegal for an American citizen to own gold coins, gold certificates, or gold bullion within the United States; since 1961 it has been a criminal offense for U.S. citizens to own gold abroad. Nevertheless some do — in the United States, in the vaults of European bullion dealers, and in numbered Swiss bank accounts. Of the $25 billion of privately owned gold around the world in 1969, it was estimated that approximately $2 billion was being hoarded illegally in the United States.

To make sure that the gold would be there, the law required the Federal to maintain a reserve of 40 percent in gold against these paper-money notes. In 1917 commercial banks belonging to the Federal Reserve System were also required to keep a specified total of their deposits with the Federal Reserve System which, in turn, was required to hold a gold reserve of 35 percent against these deposits. Again, the key objective was to make sure that banks could redeem their deposits in gold. Then, in 1933–1934 the United States devalued the dollar. At the same time exchange of our paper money for gold was outlawed for domestic holders. Currency is not redeemable in the United States. Since 1944, however, foreign holders have enjoyed a privileged position; at the famous world monetary conference at Bretton Woods (New Hampshire) in that year, when the powerful and rich United States had the only economy that had come through the war unscathed, it promised all official foreign holders of our dollars (that is, foreign central banks) that they could turn in their dollars for gold at $35 an ounce, an assurance that automatically made the dollar the world's "reserve currency" as a supplement to limited world gold supplies. This meant that the dollar, with a status equal to gold, was used by nations to settle debts with each other; the United States became a clearinghouse for all other nations. At Bretton Woods the United States became the keystone of the world monetary arch, with U.S. gold as the foundation. This was because it was the one nation committed to sell gold in any quantity to the central banks of any other nation at the fixed price of $35 an ounce. In 1945, because of vast uncertainties about postwar international trade and payments, the gold requirement against notes and deposits was cut by the U.S. Congress from 40 to 25 percent.

There it stayed until 1965 when a change was made in relation to deposits. In that year the requirement of a gold reserve of 25 percent behind deposits was eliminated, thus freeing an estimated $5 billion in gold stocks for other purposes. There remained a gold reserve of almost $10.5 billion (in 1967) behind Federal Reserve notes valued at almost $42 billion; in the same year our gold stock had fallen to $12.4 billion. That left only $2 billion in "free gold" available to meet claims of foreign central banks, which held 14.4 billions of uncashed dollars — more than the entire U.S. stock of gold. In addition, in the same year (1967) foreign *private* dollar holdings came to another $15 billion, and these could wind up in central banks — for a total of almost $30 billion uncashed — and were potentially convertible into gold.

In all these years there were still a number of people who claimed that it was vital to retain the gold reserve behind Federal Reserve notes, as a symbol and as a restraint on the amount of paper money the Federal can issue. Many others had serious doubts about the policy. They pointed out that, in the entire history of the Federal Reserve System, there had never been an occasion when the gold-cover requirement influenced the Federal in its judgment on how much the money supply should increase. They observed that the gold cover had never acted as the theoretical check or restraint that it was supposed to be, because it applied only against greenback currency — which makes up only one-fifth of the money supply, the other 80 percent being "deposit" currency (based on checking-account deposits in banks) which had never been secured adequately with gold. They argued that, even if foreign countries never took another ounce of gold, the available gold in the United States would soon become insufficient as a reserve behind even greenback currency. No one disputes that the money supply, including its greenback-currency component, must grow with an expanding economy. The regular annual growth in greenback currency is now about $2 billion, requiring $500 million (at the 25 percent rate) of the remaining "free gold" as a cover each year. In addition, another $150 million of "free gold" was then sold annually to Americans licensed to have gold for industrial and dental uses. Obviously, the additional annual burden of $650 million on the gold stock, which is static or dwindling, would mean that "free gold" would soon cease to exist if the gold cover was retained. For all of these reasons, there was considerable wonderment as to what purpose the gold stored in Fort Knox served. One critic commented that gold is a commodity that is dug up, after much labor, from an actual hole in one part of the world, only to end up in an artificial one in Kentucky. Opponents of the currency policy insisted that the gold requirement of 25 percent behind paper currency should be eliminated simply because it served no identifiable or pragmatic purpose. Whatever the theoretical arguments pro and con, the pragmatic ones were compelling during the gold rush of early 1968. At that time the Congress of the United States, albeit with small majorities, authorized an elimination of the 25 percent gold requirement behind paper currency in the United States. This effectively freed the gold reserve, small as it was, for our monumental international requirements.

Finally there were those who believed that all the previous proposals — reducing imports and increasing exports, regulating the international flow of money through foreign exchange controls, and increasing the value and availability of gold — were not as important as the international decision to replace gold as a monetary unit. They agreed with John Maynard Keynes that gold has become a "barbarous relic," that it served no practical use except ornament — while our civilization depended for its daily operation on far more precious metals such as iron and copper and lead. In spite of the fact that some paraphrased Gertrude Stein and said that gold was acceptable because it was acceptable because it was acceptable, the critics noted that the days of the gold standard had long been numbered, and that gold was bound to be demonetized internationally, as it had long been within national boundaries. They asserted that the alternative to the gold standard was not a dollar standard unilaterally run and managed by a United States that was beginning to stagger in its monetary operations. Instead, the alternative was a true international standard calling for concerted decision and management by all participating countries. A new international monetary unit would replace sole reliance on gold and the dollar. This was essential because, in the period between 1938 and 1964, world trade increased phenomenally from $44 billion to almost $300 billion. There simply was not enough gold *and* surplus dollars in the world to compensate for such an increase. In the same period of approximately half a century, what is called foreign exchange (largely gold and dollars) increased from $27 to $70 billion. Beyond the dollars, which were hard pressed, the supply of gold was particularly limited. In 1964 the total world volume of the precious commodity in general was $42 billion. Actually, in that year, the nations of the world needed reserves alone of more than $42 billion in gold — leaving no theoretical surplus for shipment in the handling of international payments. Furthermore, the growth of world reserves in gold had ceased. A key reason was that private buying of gold, for hoarding or speculation, equaled or exceeded the whole of the annual newly mined supply, leaving none to be added to official reserves. It was no wonder that reliance on dollars and gold had been a frail one.

For this reason there were many economists who believed that an end should be brought to the arrangement under which the dollar was the world's principal reserve currency and New York its financial capital — because of free convertibility between the dollar and other currencies, and between the dollar and gold. To them the lesson was plain; no country, including the United States, could permanently escape the consequences of a chronic deficit in its international payments. They asserted that the United States should cease its pegging of the dollar by paying gold at the fixed rate of $35 an ounce for all dollars offered by foreign central banks; instead, they believed, the exchange rate of the dollar should be a realistic and flexible one established by a free market. They argued that the only reason gold was worth $35 an ounce was because the U.S. government was committed to buy at that price. If the United States were to bow out of the gold market, they theorized, the gold hoarders would soon find that they had a depreciating asset on their hands. They also believed that relief from the obligation to buy gold at a fixed rate would give the United States much greater freedom in domestic economic policy. The U.S. government would then be able to fix policy on taxes, interest rates, and governmental spending without fear of runs against the gold supply at Fort Knox. Harkening back to William Jennings Bryan they did not see why we should crucify ourselves upon a cross of gold.

There were others who saw potential trouble in such a reform. They said that once freed of the discipline of gold, the United States would abandon itself to an orgy of inflation internally and to the development of economic nationalisms (rather than international cooperation) through quotas, tariffs, and devaluations. These critics did not dispute the advisability of change; they merely questioned the timing. They said that it had long been obvious that the existing monetary system had to be replaced with something stronger and more flexible than gold. They pointed out, however, that the role of gold should not be discarded overnight, because it was an agreed and understandable method of exchanging one currency for another which made world trade and international investments and travel possible. The point is that there should be an international monetary system with a set of ground rules, because each nation has its own currency and there must be ways of exchanging one currency into another — as every trader or traveler knows. Theoretically exchange rates among currencies could fluctuate freely from day to day, like prices on the stock market or commodity exchanges. But such a system creates great uncertainty, and the one thing international financial markets hate and fear above all else is uncertainty. Traders, bankers, travelers are thoroughly convinced that steady and known exchange rates are essential to the orderly conduct and growth of international trade, investment, and travel.

Such a system of ground rules, of fixed rates, is of recent origin. John Brooks has observed that in the centuries since central banking has arisen, along with industrial capitalism, the usual attitude of central banks toward each other has been that of *sauve qui peut*. International monetary cooperation came into formal existence only in 1944 when the principle of stable and fixed exchange rates was embodied in what is, in effect, a treaty. This was done at Bretton Woods, where twenty-eight nations (grown to 111 by 1969) established the International Monetary Fund and enthroned the system of fixed exchange rates. In the judgment of many, renunciation of gold and the fixed exchange-rate system now, before there was another universally accepted medium of exchange to take its place, would invite the kind of financial and economic chaos that proved so damaging to the world in the 1930's.

As it turned out, a decision on this matter had to be made sooner than anyone expected. In June 1967 President de Gaulle, fearful of U.S. "hegemony," withdrew France from the "gold pool" of eight nations that had existed since 1961. It provided a system of emergency credits, known among central banks as the "swap network," for use in serious situations. The eight nations in the pool had been the United States and seven western European nations — Belgium, the Netherlands, Italy, West Germany, Switzerland, France, and Great Britain. They had come to the conclusion that it would be risky, in terms of the public's confidence in money, to allow the price of gold on the free markets to differ significantly from the central-bank price of $35 an ounce (this decision was always debatable and had to be abandoned on 17 March 1968). They thus declared themselves ready to buy gold, and to sell gold from their own monetary stocks if necessary, on the key London market to meet all demands at a price close to $35. The withdrawal of France left seven nations in the pool, with assets of $26 billion in gold but with the United States responsible for 59 percent of its operations. In November 1967 Britain devalued the pound for the second time since World War II. In mid-March 1968 there was such a serious run against gold at $35 an ounce in London and Paris and Zurich that the entire system was endangered; it was brought on by speculators and hoarders who were counting on a sizable increase in the price of the metal. The reason was simply that there were too many dollars floating around, by comparison with the remaining supply of gold in the United States — particularly when the annual deficit (in balance of payments) was running against the United States at $4 billion a year, largely because of the war in Vietnam. The result was that the seven-nation "gold pool" decided (March 1968) to adopt a two-price system. There would be an unchanged official price of $35 an ounce for transactions between governments — and a floating price on the world's free gold markets. The chief advantage of this agreement was that it maintained fixed and known exchange rates among national currencies. This was established by the governments in the "pool," who committed themselves to continue buying dollars on the world's foreign-exchange markets, thus holding all the main currencies at their current values against the dollar. It was hoped that eventually all 111 nations in the International Monetary Fund (IMF) would cooperate in the new two-price system under which governmental central banks would refrain from either buying or selling gold in the free markets, and would not buy (directly or indirectly) any newly mined gold.

The two-price system was a device to "buy time." The world's two kinds of gold — commodity gold and central-bank gold — look the same to a chemist. Economically they were different because central banks decreed that there should be a difference. Central-bank gold would move only at the arbitrarily fixed price of $35 an ounce; the commodity market would do as it pleased. This obviously would raise prices for jewelry and for industrial uses of gold. It would not immediately influence wages, salaries, and price — unless the United States failed to put its financial house in order by eliminating its alarming deficit in balance of payments. To accomplish this would require higher taxes, reduced federal spending, and higher interest rates in the United States. All this implied lower corporate profits and dividends; it signified that citizens would be paying more in taxes and in interest to buy homes. In essence this meant deflation; it meant that the dollar must become "dear" again — that the United States must exchange prosperity for austerity. It meant that if the United States continued the war in Vietnam a full set of wartime foreign-exchange, price, wage, and credit controls would have to be introduced. Otherwise the free-market price of gold might increase to the point, say $50 an ounce, where central banks would be tempted to cash their dollars for gold at the U.S. Treasury — to "get their gold from the U.S. while it lasted." In the summer of 1968, 33 billion U.S. dollars were at large around the world. About $18 billion were held by central banks as reserves — far more than they wanted. How could they get rid of them? Only by asking the United States for gold — from a U.S. gold stock that was down to about $10 billion. Another $15 billion were held by bankers, businessmen, and individuals. This was working capital for all kinds of commercial transactions — payments for imports and exports, the financing of new construction, the acquisition of plants and companies. Furthermore, because of the slowness of the United States in putting its fiscal and balance-of-payments houses in order, the prospect was that the number of dollars around the world would increase. This posed a very real problem for central bankers. J. A. Livingston surmised that, in their anxiety, they might soliloquize like Hamlet:

> To hold or not to hold, that is the question.
> Whether 'tis smarter for the bank to swallow
> Dollars and risk U.S. devaluation
>
> Or to draw gold and beat the others to it,
> Thus causing an embargo.
>
> To act or wait — No matter.
> No choice grants sleep at night nor rest by day.
>
> Ay, there's the rub that makes for pause. For who would take upon himself dissolution of the present system, seeing not what worse might follow?

If this occurred, it would mean that the age of the almighty dollar and the pound sterling had given way to that of the "all-flighty dollar and the pound swerling." It would mean chaos in international trade, travel, and investment. It would mean that hotel keepers, bankers, merchants, and government officials would not know how much the dollar would be worth in exchange for pounds, or French or Belgian or Swiss francs, or German marks. Americans abroad would not know in advance the price of their hotel rooms or their food in restaurants. *Sic transit gloria dollar!*

The world obviously needs *credit* in addition to gold and dollars, much more credit than is now provided through loans by the International Monetary Fund and occasional emergency packages arranged on an *ad hoc* basis by the "swap network" to help a wavering major power, as has been done for Britain and the United States. Such world credit, if it is meant to be effective, would require an International Bank along the lines of the Federal Reserve System. Back in 1943 Lord Keynes made such a proposal, which he called an International Clearing Union. Each member country would make deposits of its currency and gold in the Clearing Union, and a new international monetary unit called *Bancor* would be established. Countries suffering difficulties in balance of payments could increase their *Bancor* deposits by selling gold *to* — or borrowing *from* — the Clearing Union. In order to restrict excessive borrowing, countries would be compelled to pay progressively higher interest charges on successive loans. Keynes's plan was rejected by U.S. Treasury officials in a series of meetings that preceded the Bretton Woods Conference in 1944.

That was almost thirty years ago. There are many now who believe that the enormous changes over the past two decades prove how right Keynes was. They favor a complete overhaul of the system of meeting deficits in international payments. One of them is Professor Robert Triffin of Yale. He would use the existing IMF for the centralization of monetary reserves in the world, just as the Federal Reserve System (the FRS) serves to centralize monetary reserves on a national basis in the United States. In Triffin's plan, each member of the IMF would deposit 20 percent of its total of gold and currency reserves with the Fund, and these deposits could be increased, as need arose, through:

Sale of gold, that is, purchase of gold by the IMF from the member nation.

Loans by the IMF, in which the Fund would purchase the securities of a member country running a deficit, and would credit the amount of the loan to the member country's account in the central bank. Such loans would be given to nations running deficits for a few years, but showing reasonable prospects of improving their position in time. The central bank would *not* extend credit to nations which were not prudent in their management — as some individual countries have not been in recent years; for example, Brazil, Argentina, the Congo, and Ceylon.

This plan was supported in principle by Reginald Maulding, the former Chancellor of the Exchequer in a Conservative government in Great Britain. It received the approval of Representative Henry S. Reuss of Wisconsin, chairman of a Subcommittee on International Exchange and Credit in the U.S. House of Representatives. Until recently it had not received much support from the leading bankers of the world. For this reason there were pessimists who recalled the statement that war is too dangerous a pastime to be left to the generals; in like fashion they asserted that the international monetary situation is in too precarious a state to be left in the hands of the bankers. Nonetheless, in 1967 the finance ministers of the Group of Ten (nations in western Europe plus Japan, Canada, and the United States) did agree on a plan for the future creation of a new international money — a checking-account kind of money that no citizen would ever see or spend, usable only in the settlement of accounts among nations. This meant that at long last they had some intention of managing gold, rather than letting gold manage them. Through the IMF they would establish a new loan fund, consisting of a modified form of "paper gold" called Special Drawing Rights (SDRs). These could be used to fend off gold losses in emergencies. As it turned out the IMF in late 1969 did approve the new "paper gold" — labeled by some as "one small step," monetarily comparable to that of Neil Armstrong on the moon. It authorized $9.5 billion of SDRs over a period of three years — $3.5 billion in 1970 and $3 billion in each of the years 1971 and 1972. This $9.5 billion would compare with the current $70 billion of what is known as foreign exchange (largely gold and dollars), and would be a welcome supplement to it. As in the case with voting in the IMF, SDRs would be allocated to members in proportion to their contributions. On this basis, of any $1 billion of SDRs that were activated, the United States might receive $246 million and the Common Market countries as a group would be entitled to apply for $170 million. The creation of SDRs, however, was not to mean a lack of discipline; on the contrary it was to be the beginning of a new and managed monetary order. The negotiators especially declared that the new rights would not be available until the United States made a substantial improvement in reducing the existing chronic deficit in its transactions with the rest of the world. That world obviously wanted action, not promises.

In 1969, when the IMF celebrated its twenty-fifth birthday, it was well on the way to becoming a world superbank. It had been granted permission to issue almost $10 billion in "paper gold" in the following three years. By 1980 it appeared that SDR holdings would be as large or larger than member-bank gold reserves — the $40 billion in gold frozen in the vaults of their central banks. By 1990 it was assumed that "paper gold" controlled by the IMF would total at least $80 billion.

In real life, debts are ultimately settled with payment in goods or services. Gold is an intermediate form of payment — a way to buy time. The SDRs might enable a debtor nation to buy more time.

In 1971 the United States was faced with its first trade deficit since 1893; after seventy-eight years of favorable balances the nation would import more than it exported. Deficits in the overall balance of payments also continued to increase and by the end of 1970 the gold reserve of $11 billion was pathetically inadequate; the Germans alone had more dollars than there was gold at Fort Knox. No longer a coveted asset the dollar had become a shaky IOU; internationally it was a reserve currency without reserves. A massive run on it began once more and this time neither the United States nor its partners had the will to resist. The Bretton Woods system of fixed values for currencies began to break up as Canada, followed by Germany and others, allowed their monetary units to float where they would in a free market; they increased in value as the worth of the dollar declined.

By contrast with his immediate predecessors, President Nixon's reaction to this perennial problem was both surprising and dramatic. Beyond an internal freeze on wages and prices, on 15 August 1971 he imposed a 10 percent surcharge on all dutiable imports not subject to quotas and notified the International Monetary Fund that the United States was forthwith suspending settlement of international transactions in gold. In addition he asked Congress to authorize an investment tax credit of 10 percent on new equipment purchased in the United States. Essentially the President's policy on balance of payments had two purposes: restriction of imports by means of a tariff plus special tax credits and, through the severance of the dollar's connection with gold, abandonment of the Bretton Woods system of stable currencies under which they had been worth exactly so much in dollars within a narrow band of a few pennies.

Overnight the surcharge of 10 percent wiped out all the lower tariff rates that had been achieved during the 1960's in what was called the "Kennedy Round" of tariff negotiations. Just as disturbing to America's trading partners overseas was the proposed 10 percent investment tax credit, which would apply only to capital equipment *made in the United States.* The effect of this "Buy American" act, on top of the increase in the tariff, meant that foreign competitors would suffer a disadvantage of at least 20 percent in selling machine tools and other equipment in the United States.

As far as trade was concerned it was apparent that the real target of Nixon's moves was Japan rather than European countries. In 1971 the U.S. trade deficit with Japan was running at more than $3 billion a year; in addition the Nipponese payments balance was benefited upwards of $1 billion a year from American military expenditures, because Japan relied on the United States for security and allocated only 1 percent of its gross output for defense. After spending the equivalent of $4 billion in an attempt to maintain the old rate of exchange, in late August 1971 the Bank of Japan allowed the yen to float, which meant revaluation. It was estimated that the combination of the U.S. surcharge and investment-tax credit, plus the Japanese revaluation, could cost Japan at least $2 billion in export earnings alone. The dollar would now buy less abroad; at the same time American goods would be less expensive and more attractive to foreign buyers.

The hazard of these restrictions on imports was simply that their effect could not be limited to one or two targets like Japan and Germany whose current economic situation was strong; others, with less comparative advantage, would soon begin to retaliate with their own limitations on purchases from the United States, and a trade war would begin. Some, such as Mexico and Canada whose trade was largely concentrated in U.S. markets, seemed headed for severe depressions. In 1970, as an example, Canadians bought more from the United States than Japan, Germany, France, and Great Britain combined — and sold twice as much to the United States as did Japan. Canadian officials estimated that the first ninety days of the Nixon surcharge would cost their country $400 million in exports along with 40,000 jobs.

By far the most startling part of Nixon's new economic program was the decision to suspend gold payments against dollars, because it removed the underpinnings from the world's money. For almost a century, beginning in 1879, the United States exchanged gold for dollars at a rate which had been attractive. By 1971 no other major nation was thus committed to the redemption of its currency for gold. In his announcement of 15 August President Nixon said that the United States was joining the rest of the world; our gold was still on the shelf in the store and the theoretical price was still $35 an ounce, but the metal was not for sale right now. This had the effect of demonetizing gold and placing the world on a paper standard. Perhaps the International Monetary Fund and the monthly "Basel Club" meeting of central bankers could hasten the acceptance of SDRs, or their equivalent, as an established international paper currency. Perhaps the nations of the world, through revaluated or devaluated or floating currencies could restore some stability to the international money exchange. Whatever happened, it was a new kind of challenge.

The repercussions from the decline of the dollar were ubiquitous. Columnist George Condon knew a doctor who had been in the habit of winding up a satisfactory physical examination with a thump on the chest and the statement, "It's all right, my boy, you're as sound as a dollar." This pronunciamento would no longer do; a patient acquainted with the money market might go into a state of shock. Along with everybody else doctors would find it necessary to keep up with the world. The punchline would have to be revised. One possibility: "OK, my lad, you're chipper as a credit card." *

* Just before Christmas 1971, in the Smithsonian Agreement arranged with the Group of Ten, President Nixon canceled the 10 percent surcharge on imports and the "Buy American" investment-tax credit. He could afford to do so because, by that time, the approved devaluation of the dollar was more than compensatory. The dollar had depreciated by almost 17 percent in relation to the yen; the average depreciation of the dollar for all currencies, between August and December 1971, had been 12 percent. This meant that American goods, on the average, would cost foreign buyers 12 percent less than they did before 15 August 1971, while Americans would find that foreign merchandise and foreign travel would cost 12 percent more. In exchange for this beneficial revaluation of other currencies, the United States agreed to formal devaluation of the dollar; by late March 1972 Congress had depreciated it 8.57 percent by raising the theoretical price of gold from $35 to $38 an ounce. This gesture was purely symbolic, since the United States was no longer redeeming any dollars in gold. But the other world powers insisted that the United States recognize officially that the dollar was no longer the unique and dominant currency in the world. The United States was required to display publicly a red monetary face. See "Dollar Devaluation," editorial in *New York Times*, 15 December 1971; "Most Nations Hail Monetary Accord," *New York Times*, 20 December 1971; J. R. Slevin, "Devaluation Alone Is No Cure," Cleveland *Plain Dealer*, 24 December 1971; P. A. Samuelson, "Dollar Woes," *Newsweek*, 27 March 1972; "Devaluation Made Final by Congress," Cleveland *Plain Dealer*, 22 March 1972.

VIII

Slave Labor in the United States: The Southern Plantation Economy and Its Legacy

IN the United States slavery developed in the plantation system of the South, where it could be adapted to the simple and repetitive operations prevailing in a one-crop system, and where in a warmer climate the cost of subsistence — shelter, fuel, and clothing — was low. Laborers were hard to come by, and Africans were introduced because enslavement of native Indians presented too many disadvantages: they could not only escape easily into a wilderness they understood, but alliances with their tribes were considered essential in frontier wars against the Spanish and French. The first problem with the Negro was to transport him to the New World; after that it was necessary to utilize his labor and the land as efficiently and as profitably as possible.

For entrepreneurs the first attraction was the extraordinary profits of the African slave trade; these were enjoyed as part of what has been called the "Horrors of the Middle Passage," that is, the intermediate voyage from Africa in the triangular trade (see pp. 66–69). In this unfortunate traffic New England shippers played a prominent role; they exchanged cheap rum for slaves on the African coast, often at the low rate of 200 gallons per man. Among the shippers, regardless of nationality, there were two schools: the "loose packers" and the "tight packers." The issue concerned the methods which would bring the greatest profit; after 1750 the "tight packers" were generally in the ascendance. Slaves were wedged in so compactly that they had "not so much room as a man in his coffin." Many committed suicide, others died of disease or simply because of lack of will to live.

In this traffic there were many incongruities and paradoxes. Captain John Hawkins was a prominent Elizabethan sea dog and a good Protestant; his ship was named the *Jesus of Lubeck*. On his way to Africa he passed another English ship, also bound for the slave coast. It was named *John the Baptist*. No one seemed to find it odd that these ships with pious names were engaged in a loathsome commerce. In actual fact, in godly New England, ship captains claimed they were glad to bring black cargoes to a country of Christians, where slaves might benefit by exchanging lifelong labor for the blessings of Christian baptism and the hope of heaven. This satisfied the trader's conscience; as he rationalized it the transaction was really a boon to the slaves. Peter Faneuil of Boston thought so; he pocketed his profits from the slave traffic, salved his conscience, and built a hall named after him that was ultimately known as the "Cradle of American Liberty"!

Was slavery in the United States a profitable venture? On this issue it is essential to answer a series of questions revolving around a basic one: Profitable for whom? The slave? The poor white? The regional and national economy? The slave owner? There is little question that the answer to the first three questions is in the negative. On the fourth a perennial debate rages undiminished to this day.

The Negro could not win because slavery was degrading to him both physically and mentally. Because of the absolute power possessed by the owners of slaves, it was apparent there would be abuses, some of them spectacular. The Simon Legree type of owner would whip and torture; mobs of whites would lynch "uppity" bondsmen. The pursuit of fugitives was often with dogs, and the animals could give an escaping slave a severe mauling. Andrew Jackson, who would become a President of the United States, once offered a fifty-dollar reward for the capture of a fugitive and "ten dollars extra for every hundred lashes any person will give him to the amount of three hundred."

But these unusual and reprehensible examples were not normal for the southern Negro. It can be argued that most slaves were not too badly treated physically by comparison with what they had known previously in Africa or by contrast with northern laborers. Most bondsmen got simple but ample food, and for the most part they were not manhandled, because one does not maim or kill $1,500 worth of flesh at market value if it must be animate to be sold. Most slaves were treated about as comfortably as a well-kept farm animal of the present day, but this was not far different from the circumstances of many laborers in the North. Many southern owners developed a genuine affection for their slaves and took good care of them in infirmity and old age. This was a far advance over the wage system that applied to free labor in the North, where workers were used as long as they could produce and then were cast aside by irresponsible employers. Southerners would argue that the better care given slave labor in the South, by contrast with the harsh treatment of free labor in the North, proved that slavery was "a positive good." During the hard winter of 1855 slaveholders in Alabama infuriated the northern press by raising a subscription among their slaves for the relief of destitute workers in northern cities.

On the whole the physical side of slavery was probably not as bad as the psychological effect. With no hope of rising in the social scale, slaves became lazy and shiftless and sometimes surly.* It was said in the South that it took two slaves to help one do nothing. A candid Virginian told the Northern writer and landscape architect Frederick Law Olmsted, that one farmhand in New Jersey did as much work as four slaves in the Old Dominion. There was much malingering; thousands assured their permanent incapacity by mutilating themselves, hacking off fingers and hands that produced profit for their owners and drudgery for themselves. The religious songs of bondsmen were full of double meaning; there were songs about the children of Israel and their liberator Moses, songs pregnant with the refrain "Let my people go." The lack of incentive had a stultifying effect on both the minds and the bodies of Negroes. It still does, in an era when the Negro is legally free but considered inferior by the whites who are dominant in most American communities. Psychologists have observed that the current Negro child, by accepting the white man's prejudice against him, often becomes doubtful about himself at the age of four or five. For this reason he develops a "learned apathy," simply because he feels that he is inferior and has no chance.

Slave labor was also disastrous for the poor non-slave-owning white. If he was a farmer, he was forced onto the poor lands in the upland regions. If he was a laborer, black slavery cut down the number of job opportunities, because slaves were leased for work in mines, on railroads, in iron works, in textile factories — and even in the skilled crafts. The only advantage the poor white could get from the system was a psychological one — a sense of superiority because he believed he belonged to a superior race destined to rule over an inferior one. From an economic point of view this was amazing; Olmstead reported that a poor woman's cow on Cape Cod was better and more comfortably provided for than was the case with the majority of the white population of Georgia. In the South, however, the whites accepted a low economic status because of the

---

* According to Professor Stanley M. Elkins the slave also became childish. He equates slavery with the situation confronting Jews in German concentration camps in the 1930's and 1940's. In his judgment the concentration camp was a perverted slave system; both resulted in a patriarchy in which the inmate developed an infantile reaction to an impossible situation — attempting by juvenile guile to achieve a few small favors that might come his way. In the American South the Negro was to be a child forever; because he was an arrested youth always, he would be referred to as "boy." Whatever the validity of Professor Elkins' thesis, it is apparent that "boys" do not constitute an effective labor force.

psychic income they were able to derive from the system whose supporters, and whose dupes, they were. It is one of the great ironies of history that these were the men who freely thronged into the Confederate armies to give up their lives in defense of an institution that had victimized them for so many years.

Regionally, but with national consequences, the plantation economy resulted in a shortage of capital, retarded the development of either a home market or industry, and mined the soil of its fertility. The South had an enormous amount of capital — almost $4 billion — tied up in labor, in the human beings who served as slaves. That made it difficult for the South to compete with a North whose labor cost was only the low wage figure. The North used capital to develop industry and agriculture and commerce, with the result that the South found itself bound to the North by the "cotton triangle." The "triangle" required the South to trade with Europe through New York; in this financial arrangement the North took its toll in earnings from interest, commissions, freight, and insurance. Below the Mason-Dixon line, it was claimed that these extra charges ate up 40¢ of every dollar obtained from cotton sales.

The reason for the absence of a home market was once described by Cassius M. Clay, the Kentuckian who commented with both discernment and courage about the antebellum South in which he lived:

> Lawyers, merchants, mechanics, laborers, who are your consumers; Robert Wickliffe's two hundred slaves? How many clients do you find, how many goods do you sell, how many hats, coats, saddles, and trunks do you make for these two hundred slaves? Does Mr. Wickliffe lay out as much for himself and his two hundred slaves as two hundred freemen do? . . . All our towns dwindle, and our farmers lose, in consequence, all home markets. . . . A home market cannot exist in a slave state.

Plantation slavery so limited the purchasing power of the South that it could not sustain much industry. Without a thriving home market there was little expectation of profit from factories.

The one-crop system and slavery, whether employed in the production of tobacco or cotton, lived by exploiting the soil. The planter, in the picturesque nomenclature of the South, was a "land killer." He knew little or nothing about rotation of crops and scientific farming; Jefferson wrote that in Virginia it was possible to "buy an acre of new land cheaper than we can manure an old one." Hinton R. Helper, the prominent southern writer in antebellum days who had no sympathy for Negroes but hated the plantation economy, observed that "it must continually be fed by new fields and forests, to be wasted and wilted under the poisonous tread of the slaves." The fertility of the soil was lost partially by the planting of the same crop year after year without any efficient use of fertilizer, and partially by erosion due to poor agricultural techniques. It was estimated, during the nineteenth century, that for each bale of cotton shipped to Europe, 130 tons of topsoil were washed into the Gulf of Mexico by erosion. It was therefore no wonder that by the 1930's President Roosevelt would say that the South was the "Economic Problem No. 1" in the United States. Its resources in land had been badly damaged, so seriously that only the Tennessee Valley Authority could make a partial attempt to restore it.

In the early nineteenth century, with the exhaustion of land in Tidewater Virginia, slavery was dying as an economic institution. The old Virginia planter who raised tobacco was being ruined, as was indicated by the financial difficulties of three ex-Presidents: Jefferson, Madison, and Monroe. John Randolph of Roanoke prophesied that the time was coming when masters would be running away from their slaves, who would be advertising for them in the newspapers. Slavery might have passed out of existence in the United States during the first half of the nineteenth century had one invention not made the production of cotton possible and profitable. It is impossible to find a statesman or politician who has had more lasting influence upon our national life than that of a Yankee inventor named Eli Whitney. What he did was to prolong the life of slavery for an indefinite period of time.

Before Whitney's invention the problem of extracting seed from cotton was so difficult that in 1784 the Custom House in England had seized eight bales from this country on the ground that so much could not have been produced in America! Whitney's machine made it possible to extract the seed from the fiber cheaply and easily. It just happened that his invention coincided with the development in Europe of machines for weaving cloth. These created a great demand for cotton, with the result that the plantation economy was to expand, in the first half of the nineteenth century, first to South Carolina and then westward to Texas. Interestingly, after making the invention that changed the whole situation in the South regarding labor, Whitney returned to Connecticut and created a revolutionary method for producing firearms. He thus helped both to cause the Civil War, and to ensure that the North would win it.

Whitney's invention gave slavery a new lease on life, as long as the virgin soil held out. When it was gone, and the existing soil was exhausted, the South would be compelled to resort to scientific agriculture. When it did, the future of slavery was doubtful because it takes skilled labor to farm scientifically. Under the plantation economy the South required only simple labor and simple minds. By contrast agriculture in the free states was able to adjust itself by reducing unit costs through mechanization and greater efficiency of production. In this connection, Cyrus McCormick in 1847 began to manufacture his reaping machine. It was the North's answer to the cotton gin. But the southern agriculturist found it impossible to reduce costs through mechanization and greater efficiency

of production — neither of which he was able to employ or introduce
before the Civil War. He could decrease fixed costs only by finding
cheaper land or cheaper slaves. The latter grew dearer and dearer in price,
in large part because international opposition to slavery cut off the supply
from Africa. The South ran out of virgin land, simply because the Great
Plains presented an insurmountable barrier as far as cotton was concerned.
The northern farm system, founded on individual ownership, finally conquered the Great Plains — but in so doing it had to modify and change its
system of agriculture. The southern system, founded on slavery and cotton, was not that adaptable. It was bounded on the north by cold, and on
the west by aridity. This was the reason Daniel Webster would say in
1850, when there was an argument as to whether slavery should be permitted in the Southwest, that he would not "take pains uselessly to affirm
an ordinance of nature, nor to reenact the will of God."

The problem as to whether American Negro slavery, by the mid-
nineteenth century, was profitable for individual slave owners has been a
perennially vexing one. To this point most textbooks on American economic history aver that slavery was doomed for economic as well as moral
reasons. The late Fred A. Shannon of the University of Illinois believed
that some planters on large estates could keep their heads above the waters
of bankruptcy and might even make a small margin of profit, but that
"yeoman farmers and small slaveholders found their total receipts insufficient to meet running expenses." Harold U. Faulkner of Smith College,
whose text has been widely used, believes that the weight of evidence
"points to the fact that slave labor under the conditions present just before the Civil War was economically unsound." Like Shannon he concludes that certain plantations located on excellent land and efficiently
managed could make a profit, sometimes good ones, and did so "despite
slave labor, high interest rates, factor's commissions, and a generally dis-
advantageous economic system." But these favorable conditions were
rarely found, and the "average plantation operated on so close a margin of
profit that it was lucky in many years if it could show even a slight
profit."

In recent years this thesis has been denied with vehemence by economists and historians who contend that the plantation was indeed profitable. The most outspoken scholar of this new school is Professor Kenneth
Stampp of the University of California, whose major work *The Peculiar
Institution* was published in 1956. He insists that the plantation was profitable as a business, that if a southern planter went into debt it was because
of poor management and extravagance, that on both large *and* small plantations none but inefficient masters failed to profit from the ownership of
slaves. He also states that slave labor was cheaper than free labor, and
characterizes as "arrant nonsense" the belief that free labor under any

circumstances could be employed more cheaply than slave labor. He cites, for example, a yearly maintenance cost for a slave of about $25 a year, by contrast with the average of $135 cited by Faulkner. Stampp also asserts that slavery was not a decadent institution, that there is no convincing evidence to support the usual view that it would soon have died out if the Civil War had not brought it to an abrupt end. Indeed, Stampp says, if the slaveholder's economic self-interest were the only consideration, the institution of slavery *should* have been preserved. He contends that the pathos in the life of every master lay in the fact that slavery had no humane defense worthy of the name, that it had nothing to commend it to posterity except that it paid. Slave owners, however, did not want to place their defense of the peculiar institution on such a crass and greedy basis. As a rationalization they tried to convince everyone, and themselves, that bondsmen were the happiest people in the world, certainly much happier as Christian slaves than as pagan freemen in Africa.

Who is right? The question is maddening because records are fragmentary and plantation accounting methods were varied and frequently arcane. Nonetheless, on the basis of evidence available in 1970, the majority of scholars are inclined to conclude that slavery was profitable for the entire plantation South — even on the less productive land in the seaboard and border states by reason of profits from what was called the "breeding operation." This was a recognized livestock business in the border states of Kentucky, Maryland, and Virginia. In the peak year of this traffic, which happened to be 1836, Virginia alone sold 120,000 slaves to the lower South. They were either shipped by sea from Alexandria or marched in coffles — chain gangs — from the worn-out land in Virginia to more fertile areas in the deep South. John Randolph commented that by comparison with the slave trade from Virginia "the traffic from Africa to Charleston, or Jamaica, was mercy, was virtue." In this traffic the breakup of families was so frequent and heartrending that, asked whom he believed to be the greatest orator of the age, Randolph replied: "A slave. She was a mother, and her rostrum was the auction block."

The reconstruction of the South, following the Northern victory in the Civil War, involved problems of enormous complexity. The era after Appomattox was critical because the political, social, and economic life of the South had been totally shattered. At the close of the war manufacturing in the South had almost ceased, most banks were insolvent, and transportation was paralyzed. Schools were closed, labor was demoralized, Confederate securities were worthless, and in some areas starvation was a very real threat. The most difficult problem was the former slave, 4 million of whom had now been released from bondage with the most elementary of training for their duties and obligations in a free society.

In the early years after the Civil War the South was submissive, but no precedent existed to guide the Northern conquerors who had fought a total war to preserve national unity against seceding states. Nonetheless they were resolved to grant the Negro not only his freedom but the franchise and civil rights as well. All this would be guaranteed by the thirteenth, fourteenth, and fifteenth amendments to the Constitution. As it turned out, none of these goals were achieved by the generation that fought the war; in actual fact almost a century went by before significant progress could be recorded for Negroes in any of these areas.

The Fifteenth Amendment, added to the Constitution in 1871, was short and to the point. It seemed to give the Negro the vote by stating that the right of citizens to exercise the franchise could not be denied "on account of race, color, or previous condition of servitude." For a century, however, this was largely a paper guarantee. Southern states managed to keep the Negro, and a good many whites, from voting by a variety of devices. The major result of these voting practices was to make both the South *and* the Congress of the United States undemocratic in the political sphere and conservative in the economic one. In the southern states, particularly in rural areas, politics was controlled by small, conservative, and relatively wealthy rings or courthouse cliques. C. Vann Woodward believes that these reactionary boroughs, to this day, have been happy hunting grounds for the John Birch Society. Prime examples were found in the Byrd machine and in that begun by Eugene Talmadge in Georgia.

In the national Congress the results of these voting practices have been conservative southern control of committees when the Democratic party is in control of the Congress. Representatives of these southern political machines have been returned to Congress year after year without much difficulty. By reason of seniority, they occupy high places on important committees in Congress, and qualify as chairmen of a great many of them in Democratic administrations. The result has been that these men, some of them so conservative as to be called reactionaries, have diluted the democracy of the entire nation. A few cynics have claimed that by this means the South has achieved its revenge for Appomattox. In the fall of 1968 Russell Baker, the essayist of the *New York Times*, noted that nine of the eighteen Democrats who were returned as committee chairmen to Congress came from states carried by George Wallace. Baker went on to define the membership of Congress as follows:

The Congress of the United States consists of approximately thirty old men, most of whom are alive most of the time. They are referred to as "the leadership," a term that derives from their zealous efforts to lead the country into the golden age they remember from their boyhoods, circa 1900–1910. . . . Almost anyone can become a member of "the leadership" except women, city dwellers, members who face opposition when they stand for re-election, and persons under seventy.

Baker added that there was also a "beloved old House Boneyard Committee" (the Rules Committee) whose purpose was to "trap and bury any legislation escaped from another committee if it might have been offensive to either Mark Hanna or John C. Calhoun."

The Fourteenth Amendment, ratified in 1868, is by far the longest and most detailed of all amendments in the Constitution; it made the Negro a citizen (thus reversing the Dred Scott decision of 1857) and it seemed to guarantee civil rights to the Negro by prohibiting the states from taking them away. This was done in the famous and controversial clause which states:

No State shall make or enforce any law which shall abridge the privileges or immunities of citizens of the United States, nor shall any State deprive any person of life, liberty, or property without due process of law, nor deny to any person within its jurisdiction the equal protection of the laws.

Actually, for most of the century *after* the Civil War, this long passage was interpreted quite differently in its application to the Negro, to business, and to labor. During most of the year of this long century business would come out very well, the Negro and labor not so favorably.

One would have thought that the amendment guaranteed the Negro civil rights in at least three areas: railroads and other public areas — such as hotels, restaurants, and theaters; punishment for crime; and education. Until very recent years the Negro was discriminated against in all of them. Few stopped to calculate the cost of this widespread and flagrant prejudice. On the economic side alone, quite apart from political and moral debits, the cost came from loss of productive potential and extra burdens on the taxpayer. Segregation results in a tremendous waste of ability, a waste which the National Urban League estimated at 10 percent of the productive potential of the United States.

The central point is that if potential ability is shriveled and stunted in a sharecropper's cabin the people of the world, including the whites, are the losers. Booker T. Washington once observed: "You can't hold a man down without staying down with him." And so it is, that the low standard of Negro education in the South pulled white education down too. It was a governor of Mississippi who once remarked that to educate the Negro would be to "spoil a good field hand and to make an insolent cook"; such a philosophy also insured limited educational opportunities for whites as well. Mississippi, in fact, has had the worst record in the nation on public education for all its citizens. It was not until 1919 that its legislature provided for universal public education, the last state in the Union to do so — 116 years after Congress had reserved every sixteenth section of the state's land for school purposes. Inferior educational opportunities, however, have not been restricted to the South; President Kennedy, in sending a civil-rights act to Congress, would point out that a Negro baby at that time (as compared with a white one) had about half as much chance of completing high school, about one-third as much chance of completing college, about one-seventh as much chance of earning $10,000 a year, and a life expectancy seven years less — but twice as much chance of becoming unemployed. The President therefore concluded that "race discrimination hampers our economic growth by preventing the maximum development and utilization of our manpower."

There is loss of productive potential; there are also additional burdens for the taxpayer — in duplication of services, in additional costs for social services, in losses on the tax duplicate. In 1950 a United Press survey indicated that to duplicate *equal* facilities for the education of both Negroes and whites in the South would add another half billion dollars in expenditures. A president of a southern state university put it this way: "You can't afford to build a cyclotron for a single student." There are also additional costs for social services simply because the extraordinary charges for these services in depressed areas is a burden on the entire taxpaying public. In a study in Cleveland (Ohio), for example, it was found that taxes collected in a specific area of the poverty "flats" totaled a quarter of a million dollars. But the costs of public and private social services in this identical depressed area came to more than a million and a quarter dollars, a ratio of 5 to 1. These expenditures were for relief, juvenile delinquency, fire fighting and protection — from the police and national guard. Industries leave, or will not enter, certain areas in the South. As an example, there was no organized boycott of Little Rock after the school-integration crisis of 1957, but the city and the state suffered economically because of its undesirable reputation; in actual fact, Little Rock got no new industry during a period of four years after 1957. In Mississippi, in the mid-1960's industrial starts were down, sales-tax revenue was falling, the state had been forced to borrow to meet current expenses, tourist business on the Gulf Coast dropped drastically, salesmen from Mississippi were known to have erased the name of the state from company cars, and one factory moved across the border into Louisiana — to avoid a mailing address in Mississippi! Some believe this type of economic pressure is the only valid one; they believe there are areas in the United States where intellectual persuasion can have no influence. It has been expensive for Southerners to go into court and defend discrimination. In addition, restaurants, hotels, and motels have found that opening their doors to the total public enriched them — instead of destroying business. Stores have found that customers do not mind being waited on by Negro clerks. As Ralph McGill has observed, the myths of the old segregated order may prove to be as unsubstantial and untrue as were the myths of the old magnolia South.

Until recently the Fourteenth Amendment was of little use to Negroes, but for half a century (1890 to 1940) it provided special protection to business interests against state control. One commentator asserted that the "due process" clause became a *red* light against state regulation and a *green* light for business. Another spoke of the Fourteenth Amendment as the "eternal bulwark of property rights" and claimed that it wrote laissez-faire into the Constitution.

This novel interpretation did not appear in the decisions of the Supreme Court in the decade immediately after the Civil War, when it appeared that the amendment referred only to *Negroes* as persons — not to *corporations* as persons. The exclusion of businesses, as the "persons" protected by the initial section of the amendment, was emphasized by the Supreme Court in the Slaughterhouse Cases of 1873 and in *Munn* v. *Illinois* in 1876. In the first a carpetbag government in Louisiana, probably bribed, had granted to one company a twenty-five-year monopoly of all the slaughterhouse business in New Orleans — supposedly as a health measure under the state's police powers. This monopoly drove a thousand persons out of the enterprise, and some of these aggrieved entrepreneurs sued to the Supreme Court on the ground that they had been deprived of their property by the state of Louisiana, in violation of the Fourteenth Amendment, without due process of law. The Court said that it doubted that *any* action of a state, not *directed* against Negroes, would ever come within the purview of the amendment. Three years later, in the Munn case, the Court took the same attitude (see pp. 494–496 below). This case grew out of the Granger Laws, passed by various states in the Mississippi Valley, regulating railroads and grain elevators. The Court upheld the regulatory power of the state, indicating that the proper recourse of corporations was to the state legislatures — not the courts. There was strong dissent from the industrial East, which prophesied the destruction of property at the hands of unruly state legislatures.

From this point, between 1877 and 1900, the Court changed its collective mind — for a number of reasons. One was the cumulative effect of the Industrial Revolution in the United States after the Civil War, and its impact on the entire government in Washington, including the Supreme Court. Another was a change in the composition of the Court. Within five years, four justices in the majority which had supported the state's power to regulate corporations resigned or died. To replace them Presidents Hayes, Garfield, and Arthur appointed four conservative justices. The result was a reinterpretation of the Fourteenth Amendment by the Supreme Court. As the new meaning appeared, full-blown, in *Smyth* v. *Ames* in 1898, it had three points: a corporation is a person; a corporation is entitled to a "fair and reasonable" return on its investment; and the courts — not state legislatures — would decide the meaning of "fair and reasonable." Following this guideline, between 1899 and 1921, the Supreme Court nullified state legislation in ninety cases. What this doctrine established was a twilight zone in which state governments *could* not act and in which the federal government *did* not act — with the result that corporations did as they pleased. This was, for many, an amazing extension of the meaning of "due process." In the early view of the Court, deprivation of "life, liberty, or property" had meant the punishment for crime. The requirements of due process had been procedural: the procedure of meting out punishment must be fair — including notice to the defendant, open trial, and the right of counsel. In time, however, the Court concluded that due process was not limited to procedural considerations but had a substantive aspect as well. Thus, even if proper legal procedure was observed, the rationale on which a state legislature deprived a person of life or liberty or property might in itself violate due process — particularly if "socialistic dangers" to property interests were involved. This meant that the constitutionality of much state legislation was opened to question, with the result that so many state laws were attacked that in the early twentieth century about one-third of all cases before the Supreme Court dealt with due process under the Fourteenth Amendment. There was not to be a change until the composition of the Court changed in the late 1930's. In the meantime, according to Charles Austin Beard, the Fourteenth Amendment had subdued the states for all time to the unlimited jurisdiction of the Supreme Court.

For decades the attitude of the Court toward business, in relationship to the Fourteenth Amendment, was benign; the same kindliness did not carry over to labor. Three cases will illustrate the pronounced difference: *Lochner* v. *New York* in 1905, *Truax* v. *Corrigan* in 1921, and the New York Laundry Workers Case in 1936.

Lochner v. *New York* concerned a law passed by that state providing for a ten-hour day in bake shops; enacted under the police power of the states, it was declared unconstitutional by the Supreme Court as a violation of the Fourteenth Amendment. The Court said that laborers had a "liberty" to work any number of hours they wanted, and that no state could deprive the laborer of the "liberty" guaranteed in the amendment. As a result, the Court was portrayed by critics with sarcasm as the upholder of the God-given right of a three-year-old tenement girl to contract to make artificial flowers for as little as she pleased. Justice Oliver Wendell Holmes, in dissent, criticized the majority's decision as based "upon an economic theory which a large part of the country does not entertain. . . . The Fourteenth Amendment does not enact Mr. Herbert Spencer's Social Statics." He insisted that the Constitution was "not intended to embody a particular economic theory, whether of paternalism . . . or of laissez-faire." Three years later the Court did reverse its opinion, at least so far as women were concerned, in *Muller* v. *Oregon*. This case concerned a law in that state that limited the hours of employment for women. The case was noteworthy because the Court admitted as evidence a mass of physiological, sociological, and economic data introduced by the counsel for Oregon, Louis D. Brandeis, in a famed "Brandeis Brief." Unfortunately, in the next three decades, other Courts would not be so impressed by this monumental evidence.

In *Truax* v. *Corrigan* the issue concerned the legality of picketing. Truax owned a restaurant; his employees struck and established a picket line. All this occurred in Arizona, which had a state law that legalized picketing. Truax sued to the Supreme Court, which declared unconstitutional the picketing law of Arizona, on the ground that it was a violation of Truax's property under the due-process clause of the Fourteenth Amendment. In New York there was a state law in the 1930's guaranteeing workers in laundries, mostly Negroes and women, about $13 a week — instead of the $10 they had been earning. The Supreme Court declared the law unconstitutional as a violation of the "liberty" guaranteed to persons in the Fourteenth Amendment; that is, workers had the "liberty" to contract for whatever wages they desired. What this meant, in a practical and highly competitive world during the Depression, was the "liberty" to exploit and to be exploited. The new Court from 1937 on began to change its attitude on these matters, along with its previous restrictive interpretation of the Fourteenth Amendment.

The evolution of the Thirteenth Amendment is interesting because, at the beginning of the Civil War, the Republican party in the North had no intention of freeing the slaves in the Southern states. The Republican platform of 1860 opposed the *extension*, but not the *existence*, of slavery in the states where it already prevailed. This was because of the situation in the border states (Delaware, Maryland, Kentucky, and Missouri) where there were many slave owners who had remained loyal to the Union — and for whom abolition would be an act of ingratitude that would probably have driven them into the arms of the Confederates. This was also because of Lincoln's opportunism.

As David Donald has pointed out, one reason why Lincoln is all things to all people now is his essential ambiguity. He can be cited on all sides of all questions. He used to say, "My policy is to have no policy." Again he put it this way: "The pilots of our Western rivers steer from point to point as they call it — setting the course of the boat no farther than they can see, and that is all I propose to do myself. . . ."

A moralist might deplore Lincoln's noncommittal attitude, but it should be remembered that this fundamental opportunism has been characteristic of major American political leaders from Jefferson to FDR. Our great Presidents have joyously played the political piano by ear, making up the melody as they went. At only one time have rigid ideologists dominated our national government — the Sumners of the North and the Jefferson Davises of the South — and the result was near disaster.

Personally Lincoln felt keenly about the evils of human bondage. He was an *enemy* of slavery, but he was *no friend* of the Negro. A conservative Illinois lawyer, cautious and conventional in social matters, he never pretended to be a racial liberal or a social innovator. He shared the racial prejudice of most of his white contemporaries, and was a firm believer in white supremacy. He did not believe the Negro and the white could live together in perfect equality. He said this in his debate with Douglas in 1858:

> I have no purpose to introduce political and social equality between the white and black races. There is a physical difference between the two, which, in my judgment, will probably forever forbid their living together upon the footing of perfect equality; and inasmuch as it becomes a necessity that there must be a difference, I am in favor of the race to which I belong having the superior position.

He also worried that the emancipated Negro would provide too much competition for both the submerged whites of the South and the wage earners of the North. In this respect, he represented the caste psychology of a competitive labor market. Had he been permitted, undisturbed by men or events, to work out his own solution, he would have instituted a program of gradual emancipation with compensation to the owners, plus *removal* of the freemen to Liberia or Latin America — thus placing the Atlantic Ocean or some other large and deep body of water between the blacks and the whites. Lincoln instructed William H. Seward, his Secretary of State, to determine whether any of the governments of Latin America would agree to accept American Negroes, or whether the British or Dutch would have use for them in their Latin American possessions. The only positive result of this diplomatic correspondence was an agreement with the Republic of Haiti to permit two American promoters to settle a group of Negroes on a tiny island, called Ile à Vache, adjacent to its coast. With Lincoln's enthusiastic support, the promoters tempted several hundred Negroes to migrate by promising them a life of abundance in a tropical paradise. Instead the Negro settlers were reduced to virtual bondage and were exploited ruthlessly. Within a year, half of them were dead, and the disgraceful episode came to an end when Lincoln, discovering his error, had what survivors there were returned to the United States.

All of this seems curious from Lincoln, the humanitarian. There was the opportunism which we have already mentioned. There was also his geographical background in Kentucky and Illinois. He had been born in Kentucky, a slave state, whence he moved to Illinois — in a region largely settled by southerners. When Illinois was admitted to statehood in 1818, slavery was prohibited but there had been prolonged political struggle over the issue, and the antislavery men barely achieved their objective. From then until the Civil War, in actual fact, the small free-Negro population in Illinois had the status of an inferior caste. Illinois Negroes could not vote or hold public office, they could not attend the public schools, and additional Negro migration into the state was prohibited. Such were the racial attitudes to which Lincoln was exposed in his youth — attitudes that he was never quite able to transcend. Because of this situation as late as August 1862 he would write:

My paramount object in this struggle is to save the Union, and is not either to save or destroy slavery. If I could save the Union without freeing any slave, I would do it; and if I could save it by freeing all the slaves, I would do it; and if I could save it by freeing some and leaving others alone, I would also do that.

Initially he chose the third of these alternatives because the practical situation changed in two ways, and as a result it appeared to be expedient to issue the Emancipation Proclamation. The two new factors were the pressure of the radicals, and a foreign crisis. The radicals — Chase in the Cabinet, Sumner and Stevens in Congress, Greeley in the press — needed the appeasement that would be provided by a spectacular document. The foreign crisis came because England and France were threatening to intervene on the side of the South. The Emancipation Proclamation seemed to turn the war into a crusade, winning over European labor and liberals, and forestalling any possibility of intervention (on behalf of the South) from those countries. European laborers had not been interested in a war to save the Union. But after the Proclamation they felt that the Yankee boy was dying to make men free; as Julia Ward Howe put it in the "Battle Hymn of the Republic," "As Christ died to make men holy, let us die to make men free."

Curiously the "Great Emancipator" might never have freed a single slave through his Proclamation. Issued in late September 1862 it stated that slaves in those states still in rebellion on 1 January 1863 would be free. It would never have freed the slaves in border states which were not in rebellion. If all the Confederate states had come packing back into the Union by the deadline, not a single slave would have been freed. For the reason that the Proclamation was a bribe and a potential bargain, critics have said that it had all the moral grandeur of a bill of lading. Seward once said of it, "We show our sympathy with slavery by emancipating the slaves where we cannot reach them and holding them in bondage where we can set them free." The *London Spectator* jibed, "The principle is not that a human being cannot justly own another, but that he cannot own him unless he is loyal to the U.S." There were many things wrong with it — but diplomatically it turned out to be decisive, for it closed the door in the face of the Southern Confederacy. Europe would not intervene now, the South was limited to its own resources, and these were visibly inadequate. As Bruce Catton has pointed out, the South had been isolated, almost indiscernibly, but with grim finality.

With the Northern victory, the Thirteenth Amendment to the Constitution was ratified in December 1865. It seemed to settle the issue by stating that "neither slavery nor involuntary servitude, except as punishment for crime whereof the party shall have been duly convicted, shall exist within the United States, or any place subject to their jurisdiction." In following years slavery did disappear, for the most part; unfortunately a system of peonage took its place, and in some respects it would be difficult to determine which was worse — slavery or peonage. This new development, after the Civil War, was due to a triple revolution in land tenure, credit, and labor in the South.

The new situation in land tenure was known as the sharecropper system. It developed because of a shortage of cash. The central point is that many planters had ample land but little money for wages. At the same moment most of the former slaves *and* poor whites — uneducated and impoverished — had plenty of muscle but no money. *Both* planters and laborers were devoid of cash. Under the circumstances it was obvious that an arrangement would be made under which planters could obtain labor without paying *cash* wages — and landless farmers could obtain land without paying rent in *cash*.

This made inevitable the sharecropper system which followed. Under it the cropper brought to the farm only his own *and* his family's labor. By contrast the landlord furnished land, animals, equipment, seed — *and* credit, at the store. Under the contract the sharecropper usually received half of the value of the crop, less his debt to the merchant at the store, who was frequently the landlord. This debt was apt to be large because there were two prices at the store — one if you paid in cash, the other if the bill was charged. The latter price was never less than 30 percent higher, and sometimes was up to 70 percent in excess. This resulted in peonage, defined as a system by which debtors were kept in servitude until they had paid off their debt. Many, unfortunately, were perpetually in debt; they could not leave the land as long as they were in this condition, and if they attempted to do so, the "law" went after them. Sharecropping thus meant that the plantation system remained — but under a new form. The large holdings were now worked by families rather than gangs of slaves. The owners, as the Southern journalist Henry W. Grady commented in 1881, were "still lords of acres, though not of slaves."

How many sharecroppers were there? In the heyday of the system it was estimated that there were upwards of 4 million persons in sharecropping families in the South; curiously, by the 1930's, more of them were white than Negro families. What income did they have? In 1931 a church survey was made of 112 Negro tenants in Alabama. Of the 112, fifty ended the year in debt to the planter, and the highest annual income of the "prosperous" remainder was less than $150. In the 1930's the average sharecropper boasted of a family of seven or eight, lived in a miserable cabin, subsisted on a diet which nourished diseases like pellagra, rickets, and anemia — not men. There were two other killing diseases in the South — malaria and hookworm. These afflictions did so much damage that the eminent southern historian, Thomas D. Clark, says that they made "General Sherman appear to have been a casual visitor." Because of malaria vast fortunes were made on "chill tonics," before some of the purchasers died. Hookworm was also a killer, indirectly through the attendant diseases of anemia and tuberculosis. It was not until the 1940's that public-health programs, long known to the rest of the United States but new to the South, brought malaria under control and virtually eliminated it. Hookworm is a serious problem to this day. So is malnutrition amounting to starvation. In 1968 a group of physicians reported on conditions among impoverished Negro families in the Mississippi Delta; they said that babies were dying of hunger and that children were growing up sick and stunted. In one county in Mississippi, of every thousand Negro babies born, fifty-one died in infancy, a figure three times as high as that for white infants. Malnutrition during pregnancy and the first year of life, said the doctors, had irreversible effects on the child — harming the quality of his teeth, his bone structure, and possibly the functioning of his brain. They reported that older children were kept home from school because they had no shoes; some of the younger ones went with rags wrapped around their feet. If they survived, they grew up in shacks with no running water or toilets. Their mothers were overburdened and undereducated; their fathers were too often unemployed. Unfortunately this desperate and degrading poverty was not limited to Mississippi or to the rural South or to Negroes. It can be found in every big-city slum; it can be found among whites in Appalachia. It seemed such a disgrace in the richest nation in the world that some suggested for the United States a Marshall Plan to eradicate "hunger, poverty, desperation, and chaos" here as well as in Europe.

For the past half century sharecroppers, both Negro and white, have been leaving southern farms for urban centers in the North, to the point where (in 1967) one of every two Negroes in major northern cities was an "in-migrant," chiefly from the South. Perhaps the most dramatic effect of the rural exodus has been the conversion of America's Negroes from a country population to an urban one. Of the more than 22 million Negroes estimated to have been living in the United States in 1968, little more than a million — or about 5 percent — were living on farms. It is generally recognized that this shift of an entire racial group set the stage for some of the violent and explosive troubles of U.S. cities during the 1960's beginning with the riot in the Watts section of Los Angeles in 1965. By 1990, it was estimated, there would be Negro majorities in seven of America's

largest cities (all but New York, Los Angeles, and Houston). This movement from the South began slowly before World War I and grew to vast
proportions during and after the Second World War; in the twenty years
after 1947 there was a net decline in farm employment of nearly 4 million
jobs. There are three basic reasons for the decline of farm employment
and of the sharecropper system, which had lasted for seventy-five years
after the Civil War: the Triple-A policy of the New Deal in the 1930's;
the mechanization of southern agriculture; and the effect of federal minimum-wage laws. The Triple-A policy of the 1930's replaced sharecroppers with day laborers. Under this New Deal policy the national government specified that the landowner's share of subsidies had to be divided
with sharecroppers, while no such restriction applied to day labor. So the
landowner evicted the sharecropper, hired day laborers when he needed
them, kept the government bonus for himself. Bad as the plight of the
average sharecropper was, that of the day laborer was worse. His hours
were from sun to sun, from "kin" to "kain't." A plowhand got 75¢ a day;
a woman hoeing cotton received 60¢ for her back-breaking labor during a
very long day. Because of the Triple-A policy, many sharecroppers were
forced on relief, but that was not much help. In the cotton district of
Missouri in the 1930's, as an example, the relief allotment per person was
$1.48 a month.

The Triple A was one thing; mechanization of farms was another. In
the 1930's, in Arkansas, a machinery dealer would say: "Triple A has been
God's gift to the tractor people." The tractor permitted one man to do
the work of two or more. And so it was that a resident of Texas, looking
over his acres, said, "There used to be two families out there. The tractor
got both of them." That was in the 1930's. Since that time if one adds the
airplane (with insecticides), the flame cultivator and chemicals (to kill
weeds), and the mechanical cotton picker (which can do the work of
forty to fifty men), one can revise the statement to read: "There used to
be five families out there. Machines got all of them." The *New York
Times* would note:

> Millions of Negroes now jammed in the northern ghettos are really black
> peasants forced out by farm automation. The men and women who once picked
> cotton or tobacco or strawberries in the South fled North with little education,
> no knowledge of urban society, and none of the skills required in today's in-
> creasingly technological civilization. No wonder that they find it so difficult to
> get jobs in an era when unskilled manual labor is giving way steadily to the
> work of tending machines, building them or repairing them.

The inevitable result was racial ghettos creating a situation within northern cities comparable to the two nations once described by Benjamin Dis-
raeli — two nations living side by side, one rich and privileged and the
other poor and miserable — with no intercourse and no sympathy be-

tween them. No better formula for civil disorder could possibly be devised.

By 1967, in the Mississippi Delta, mechanization had cut the required man-hours per acre to fewer than 35, far behind the 165 needed by men and mules. More than 90 percent of the crop was picked by machine, and chemicals made hand weeding obsolete. Between 1960 and 1965 more than 60,000 Negroes between the ages of fifteen and forty-four left Mississippi. This migration was substantial, but in 1967 the federal government (with the best of intentions) added another factor that speeded the movement. Under the new minimum-wage amendment which became effective in that year, a farmer who had hired more than 500 man-days of labor during any calendar quarter of 1966 must pay his workers $1 an hour in 1967, rising to $1.30 an hour in 1968. The prevailing rate had been $3 a day. A Negro woman still living in Bolivar County (Mississippi) glanced at the fields surrounding her home and said, "They'll burn this cotton down before they'll pay that dollar-an-hour." She was partly right. In the summer of 1968 a federal judge in Greenville, Mississippi, in a decision that for the first time set standards for the application of minimum-wage provisions for farm workers, ordered payment of $50,000 in back wages by a wealthy plantation owner to 200 tenant employees. The decision went to the heart of rural poverty, underscoring the long existing fact that some rich planters were benefiting from U.S. subsidies while exploiting the poor. The case involved an eighty-seven-year-old planter named Joseph Roy Flowers who operated a 12,000-acre farm near Clarksdale, Mississippi. He drew more than $200,000 a year in federal acreage allotments while charging his Negro laborers as much as $70 a month in rental for wooden shacks with no plumbing, plus additional charges of more than $150 a year for wood to heat the cabins, and $3 for a cheap cotton sack used in the picking of cotton. The federal court found that a reasonable rental for the shacks would have been $5 a month, against Flowers' average of $20 to $40; the median value of the rude cabins was $350 (including the lot) which meant that a year's rent at $40 a month would pay the full value of the house. Evidence in the case indicated that Flowers had made no rental or other deductions before the new minimum-wage law became effective, and that he had introduced the extraordinary charges for the purpose of compensating for his payments under the new minimum-wage law. The decision in Mississippi was the first one in which back wages for farm workers were recovered under the Fair Labor Standards Act, as amended. It also represented the first occasion on which the Department of Labor held administrative hearings to determine reasonable costs of furnishing houses and other facilities for tenant farm workers. About 400,000 of them were covered by the new amendment. Apart from the 200 employees specified in the decision described above, economists of the Department of Labor did not know in 1968 how many farm workers received housing and other facilities as part of their pay — an old and traditional mode of compensation in the South.

For all of these reasons sharecroppers and day laborers, Negro and white, have been leaving farms and streaming out of the South. Sharecropping was never a heaven for the tenant; it was also no paradise for the landowner, who eagerly seized upon the Triple A and the machine to end it. The result was, in the mid-1960's, that there were only 500,000 Negroes on cotton farms in the Deep South, and most of them were there as day laborers, not as sharecroppers. There were a million other Negroes on southern and border-state farms in the tobacco belt, and they were there as sharecroppers with their families. They constituted the last stronghold for the southern system of sharecropping, but the mechanical tobacco picker, which will soon be available commercially, will wipe out this last vestige of a land system now obsolete. For these reasons the sharecropper system has been replaced in many parts of the South by the owner-renter system. In July 1965 the *New York Times* published a series of articles about a typical owner-renter — Junius Evans of North Carolina, in the heart of the bright-leaf tobacco belt. This was a description of a new breed of farmer, almost all of them white because of the amount of capital required. Evans owned tractors and other mechanized equipment, held title to fifty cultivated acres, rented fifty more in order to get the maximum advantage from his expensive equipment. On his total acreage he raised not only tobacco but corn and soybeans as well; with government subsidy he was able to gross $20,000 from tobacco alone. Before mechanization came in, four sharecroppers would have been required in Evans' farm. Now Evans did all the work himself with his machinery, plus very occasional day labor. As Ralph McGill has observed, not since the autumn of 1792 when young Eli Whitney came from New England to shake the foundations of the South with his cotton gin have so many changes confronted this region. Where only cotton was once farmed, soybeans, turnip greens, okra, and vast forests of pulpwood pines now thrive. Grain elevators are appearing in a land that man once said would produce only cotton. These were the same misguided individuals who also prophesied that no machine would ever equal two hands for picking cotton!

What should be done about this situation? Reactions have been varied and interesting. Bayard Rustin of New York, and the Reverend Martin Luther King of Atlanta, saw public works as the solution for the problem of displaced sharecroppers. Rustin said, "The machine has become as great an enemy of the Negro people as discrimination and segregation ever were." Others, including James Farmer of CORE (Congress of Racial Equality), believe public works are only part of the answer. They also favor collective or cooperative farms, like the kibbutz in Israel.

The agricultural changes were accompanied by the industrialization of the South, which has been particularly rapid in recent years. In 1965, Mississippi for the first time in its history found more of its people engaged in manufacturing than in agriculture; rural counties have been losing population in recent years, and there are predictions that by 1980 half the state's people will live in the Jackson area and along a booming urban strip on the Gulf Coast. This industrialization in the South has been brought about by two factors: cheap labor and a technological revolution. Cheap labor results from a combination of low wages, lax labor laws, and a lack of unions — a triad that has caused the migration of industries from the North into the South. Over the years, in some industrial areas, conditions existed which were comparable to the peonage in agriculture. In the 1930's, as an example, prevailing wage levels in the South were so low that WPA had to set a scale for unskilled labor down to 15¢ an hour in county after county. Laws regarding labor for women and children have been lax, and even so, inadequately enforced. In 1915 this situation elicited from Sarah Norcliffe Cleghorn the ironic stanza:

> *The golf links lie so near the mill*
> *That almost every day*
> *The laboring children can look out*
> *And watch the men at play.*

The technological revolution has brought the petrochemical industry into prominence, particularly in Texas and Louisiana. It *was* a trilogy of resources that ushered in the age of steel in the North — a trilogy found in the juxtaposition of coke, limestone, and iron ore. This gave the North its early dominance in the American economy. It *is* the trilogy of resources that has brought in the petrochemical industry in the South — a trilogy of oil and gas, sulfur, and fresh water. It was once said that the South could not industrialize because it lacked fuel. Now the South, if we include Texas in the region, produces over half the nation's oil, 100 percent of its sulfur, and has an unlimited supply of fresh water.

This industrialization has brought a number of changes and prospects for the South, prospects to which some point with pride and which others view with alarm. It has changed the political orientation of the South; once low-tariff and internationalist, the region is tending toward protection and isolationism. It has caused a few officials to realize the importance of the state's "image" in attracting new industry, and has impelled them to stress the importance of law enforcement and the amelioration of the race problem. It has encouraged urban residents, younger voters, and professionals (such as schoolteachers), who are gaining strength while traditional power blocs seem to have lost some ground. On the other hand, C. Vann Woodward challenges the optimism of southerners, both liberal and conservative, who argue that this technological revolution promises a brilliant future for the region. He avers that the South's development will be blighted by doctrines stemming from the 1870's and 1880's, doctrines which the South is still following:

Racism with an elite caste of all whites, most of whom will be exploited but will be compensated by psychic income — the belief that they are a cut above the Negro.

Low wages — encouraged by "right-to-work" and other laws.

Low taxes — which means the financial starvation of urban communities, and the neglect of needed social services. It also explains proposals, particularly prevalent in the South, for constitutional amendments to eliminate, or at least to limit, the income tax.

The continuation of these doctrines, says Woodward, will mean mint juleps for the few and pellagra for the crew — "a façade of Greek columns and a backyard full of slum."

On the question of race adjustment Negroes have divided themselves into two groups — amalgamationists and isolationists — with a few splinter groups in between. The amalgamationists believe that the Negro can integrate with the white, seeking his privileges, and eventually *disappear* as a distinct racial group. The isolationists, on the other hand, believe that the Negro should *withdraw* into himself, should separate himself from American society, should stress primarily the virtues of being black.

In the *amalgamation* group there have been two schools of thought among Negroes. Basically, they have been divided between those who were willing to progress slowly and those who wanted to move at a fast pace. They were the conservatives, led originally by Booker T. Washington, whose influence was continued by his greatest disciple, George Washington Carver; and the radicals, led originally by W. E. B. DuBois.

Booker Taliaferro Washington (1865–1915) was one of the great figures of the Negro race, regardless of what one may think of his ideas from the vantage point of hindsight. He was the son of a Negro slave and a white father. Although he worked ten hours a day in his youth at a salt furnace, he had the ambition to go to an elementary school at night and there learned to read and to write. At this school he also acquired his family designation. A teacher asked his name. Booker aimed as high as he could, said it was Washington — an appropriate answer because in time he did become a father of his people. Ultimately he completed his education at Hampton Institute, a privately endowed trade school for Negroes. In time his greatest service to the Negro would be the establishment of Tuskegee Institute, a Negro normal and trade school in Alabama. From Tuskegee his annual letter "To My People" went to them and to the press; Tuskegee became the capital of the Negro nation. The institute had begun on the Fourth of July, 1881, when thirty persons had come in, mostly from nearby cotton fields. At that time the roof leaked so badly (the one building was a small Negro church) that on rainy days the pupils held umbrellas over their heads. Before Washington died, Tuskegee had 100 substantial structures, 25,000 acres of land, an endowment of $2 million, 1,500 students, and 200 members on its faculty.

Washington emphasized three principles: a policy of "work and wait" in the field of race equality; a conservative political approach that allied him with the Republican party; and a stress on vocational training in the field of education. His policy of "work and wait" meant that he thought the Negro would solve the race problem by learning a trade and going to work; he should qualify for a job first, and later might achieve desirable political and social gains. He stated this philosophy in his famous autobiography, *Up From Slavery*, which was published in 1901. In it he said, "No race can prosper till it learns that there is as much dignity in tilling a field as in writing a poem. It is at the bottom we must begin, not at the top."

In politics Washington was a conservative Republican who believed in the gospel according to Mark Hanna. The businessman's creed of free enterprise and laissez-faire never had a more loyal exponent than the master of Tuskegee; for this reason he was never friendly toward labor unions. His personal credo made Washington popular with business tycoons — and two Presidents. The business leaders, who also contributed generously to Tuskegee, were:

H. H. Rogers of Standard Oil, on whose yacht Washington was a frequent guest,

William H. Baldwin, vice-president of the Southern Railroad, who spent hours with Washington on the texts of his speeches,

Collis P. Huntington, the railroad magnate with interests in a number of transcontinental lines, and

Andrew Carnegie, the steel magnate, who invited Washington to be his guest at Skibo Castle in Scotland.

These relationships, particularly those with railroad men, made Washington unpopular with some of his critics. They pointed out that the interest of the railroad magnates was more than philanthropic because they were large-scale employers of black labor at low wages, particularly as Pullman porters. The U.S. Presidents who cultivated Washington were Theodore Roosevelt and William Howard Taft, both Republicans. During their administrations Washington was the chief patronage referee for federal appointments in the South. He was consulted on all Negro appointments, and the merits of many whites were discussed with him as well. In 1901 he dined with TR at the White House. The reaction of the South can well be imagined. One southern editor said that no respectable southern woman could now accept an invitation to an Executive Mansion that had obviously been polluted. "Pitchfork Ben" Tillman of South Carolina said that TR's act would necessitate the killing of a thousand Negroes in the South.

This was unfortunate, but it was the only method — according to Tillman — by which Negroes would again learn their proper place in society.

In the educational field, Washington stressed a purely vocational emphasis — trade, agricultural, teacher-training; the higher education in liberal arts was not yet appropriate for Negroes. In this respect Washington's greatest pupil was George Washington Carver, the great agricultural chemist. He was born in slavery in 1864 and graduated from Iowa State in 1895; sixteen years later Henry Wallace would also graduate from the same university as an agricultural chemist. Carver joined Tuskegee immediately after his college graduation at a salary of $125 a month and was made chairman of the department of agricultural research there. He remained in this position for almost half a century, during which he achieved world renown, became the friend of three Presidents of the United States, and turned down many lucrative offers — including those from Thomas A. Edison and Henry Ford. When he died Carver, at his own insistence, was still drawing $125 a month from Tuskegee, to which he also bequeathed his life savings, which amounted to $33,000 by reason of fantastic frugality. Like Washington, Carver believed in "work and wait" and put his faith in vocational education. For this reason, even in his own day, he was considered a kind of "super–Uncle-Tom" by many civil-rights advocates. Perhaps he was, but at the same time his accomplishments and his talents were outstanding. He was a pianist of great skill, an artist of ability, and an agricultural scientist of genius. In the latter field he set out to save the South, black *and* white, from starvation. He helped unseat "King Cotton" as the tyrant of a one-crop South, coaxing farmers into planting peanuts, sweet potatoes, and soybeans as money crops. From the peanut Carver developed plastics, dyes, soap, and salad oil; in the soybean he found a valuable base for paint; he developed a hundred uses for the sweet potato. From his experiments with cotton waste came the birth of synthetics in this field. He wrenched tints and dyes from local clay. From lowly weeds he extracted healing medicines. It was little wonder that he was known as the "Wizard of Tuskegee" and the "Goober Genius" by the time he died in 1943. Ten years later his birthplace (in Missouri) was made into a national monument.

Washington and Carver belonged to the evolutionary school; for some amalgamationists their pace was much too slow and their philosophy left much to be desired. By contrast with Washington and Carver, who came from the rural South and West, the revolutionary school consisted largely of Negroes from the urban North. These radical amalgamationists were blessed with great mental ability and considerable education, and sometimes with outstanding artistic talent. Their first leader was W. E. B. (William Edward Burghardt) DuBois.

He was a mulatto of French, Dutch, and Negro ancestry who said with pride that he had a "flood of Negro blood, a strain of French, a bit of

Dutch, but, thank God *no* Anglo-Saxon." Born and educated in Massachusetts, in 1895 he was the first Negro to receive a Ph.D. from Harvard. DuBois was a striking contrast to Washington in scholarship, in appearance, in manner, and in philosophy. As a scholar he wrote beautifully, and ultimately was responsible for nineteen books. In appearance Washington looked like a sturdy farmer in his Sunday best; DuBois, with a well-trimmed goatee, pince-nez, and cane, resembled a Spanish aristocrat. In manner and personality Washington was accommodating; DuBois was fretful and aggressive. For twenty-three years he edited a journal called *The Crisis;* the analogy with the restless and revolutionary Tom Paine was obvious. Washington was a pragmatic leader; DuBois was an idea man, and his ideas were antithetical to those of Washington on race relations, on politics, and on education.

On race relations Washington had counseled "work and wait." The DuBois group found the color line an intolerable insult and demanded equal privileges at once. They raged at Washington because his evolutionary plan was too slow, and occasionally hissed him as he spoke. In 1903 DuBois published the *Souls of Black Folk*, in which he attacked Washington and decried the "veil" of prejudice that existed between whites and blacks in the United States. In 1905 he was instrumental in developing what was called the Niagara Movement. In that year a group of Negroes met at Niagara Falls, on the Canadian side, because of existing segregation in American hotels. Out of his conference came a manifesto demanding immediate suffrage for the Negro, and the abolition of "Jim Crowism." In 1910 the National Association for the Advancement of Colored People (NAACP) was founded. This occurred because of an event at Springfield, Illinois, the home of Abraham Lincoln, in 1909 — the centenary of the "Great Emancipator's" birth. Unfortunately, Springfield chose this occasion for two days of race riots, bloody days in which Negro homes were burned and Negroes were lynched. This demonstrated that the race problem was not confined to the South, and that Washington's evolutionary plan had not been very effective. Out of the revulsion from this incident came the founding of the amalgamationist NAACP, a biracial organization which represented a challenge to Washington's leadership (in the first group of officers DuBois was the only Negro; others prominent were Jane Addams, John Dewey, Rabbi Stephen Wise, Lincoln Steffens, and William Dean Howells). The nonviolent amalgamationist, Martin Luther King, later represented the same impatience when he noted that "justice too long delayed is justice denied," and went on to write, in moving words:

I guess it is easy for those who have never felt the stinging darts of segregation to say "wait." . . . But . . . when you suddenly find your tongue twisted and your speech stammering as you seek to explain to your six-year-old daughter why she cannot go to the public amusement park that has just been advertised on television, and see tears welling up in her little eyes when she is told that Funtown is closed to colored children, and see the distressing clouds of inferiority begin to form in her little mental sky, and see her begin to distort her little personality by unconsciously developing a bitterness toward white people; when you have to concoct an answer for a five-year-old son asking in agonizing pathos, "Daddy, why do white people treat colored people so mean?"; when you take a cross-country drive and find it necessary to sleep night after night in the uncomfortable corners of your automobile because no motel will accept you; when you are humiliated day in and day out by nagging signs reading "white" and "colored"; when your first name becomes "nigger" and your middle name becomes "boy" (however old you are) and your last name becomes "John," and when your wife and mother are never given the respected title "Mrs."; when you are harried by day and haunted by night by the fact that you are a Negro, living constantly at tiptoe stance, never quite knowing what to expect next, and plagued with inner fears and outer resentments; when you are forever fighting a degenerating sense of "nobodyness" — then you will understand why we find it difficult to wait.

There comes a time when the cup of endurance runs over and men are no longer willing to be plunged into an abyss of injustice where they experience the bleakness of corroding despair.

On the political side the revolutionary school has scarcely been conservative or Republican, as Washington was. They have not associated themselves with any party although, since New Deal days, they have worked more closely with Democrats (in the North, *not* the South) than any other group. Some have been far to the left. DuBois flirted with the Communists for years, and finally broke with the NAACP in 1948 (over the presidential candidacy of Henry Wallace, which he supported; the NAACP was nonpartisan in the election). He ultimately joined the Communist party in 1961, when he was ninety-three, and when he said, "Capitalism cannot reform itself; it is doomed to self-destruction. No universal selfishness can bring social good to all."

An expatriate at 94, he became a citizen of Ghana, and died in Accra in 1963 at the age of 95; his life represented a striking span of years because his birth had come only five years after the Emancipation Proclamation. Ironically, his death came on the eve of the famous March on Washington — the largest single demonstration for civil rights ever held — of which the NAACP was the principal sponsor.

Both Washington and DuBois, despite their differences, wanted to amalgamate and integrate with the whites, on the basis of equality and mutual advantage. The isolationists, by contrast, wanted to separate themselves politically and economically from the whites, and to stress the unique qualities and advantages of black skin. There is nothing particularly new about the idea of colonizing Negroes off to themselves. Monroe, Madison, John Marshall, and Henry Clay planned it, for American Negroes, in West Africa under the benevolent guidance of the young United States; this was the idea behind the American Colonization Society, which managed to establish Liberia and to settle 15,000 Negroes in Africa by 1860. Lincoln contemplated the removal of Negroes to Latin America or Liberia. Bishop Henry M. Turner (1834–1915) of the African Methodist Episcopal Church was the first Negro to be appointed an army chaplain and was also the first Negro of any prominence to support the idea of colonization. After the Civil War he became so discouraged by the lack of political and civil rights for Negroes under the Civil War Amendments that he said their only salvation was to leave the country. Interestingly, he wanted to take only the "better" Negroes to Africa. He had no use for many American Negroes, and thought that two-thirds of them would be of no help to anyone anywhere. He claimed this "lower" element came from the Congo, where they had been slaves. Turner claimed that he, by contrast, came from African nobility. His plans never materialized because of lack of money, and he spent his later days worrying that the whites would take Africa before the Negroes reclaimed it. As Edwin S. Redkey has observed, he feared that the same Europeans who once stole Africans from Africa, would now steal Africa from the Africans.

Much more spectacular, among the isolationists, were Marcus Garvey in the 1920's and the Black Muslims in the current era. Garvey's movement was strong in the decade after the First World War, probably because of the treatment of Negroes after the Armistice. Negroes had fought for the United States against Germany, but in the first year after the war seventy of them were lynched — many still in uniform. During the "Red Summer" of 1919 there were no fewer than twenty-five race riots across the country; one in the nation's capital lasted three days, and in Chicago thirty-eight were killed during two weeks of mob rule.

Garvey was a Jamaican Negro, full-blooded by contrast to Booker T. Washington. He proposed to ferry the entire Negro population of the United States *and* other lands back to Africa. He said they were coming not 200,000 strong — as Union soldiers had told Lincoln at the beginning of the Civil War — but 400 million strong, and that they meant to take every square inch of Africa. On that continent, he said, "We shall not ask England or France or Italy or Belgium, 'Why are you here?' We shall only command them, 'Get out of here.'" His real intentions were not unlike those of modern Zionism. He wanted a new state, to which Negroes would go from all over the world. To get them there he organized the UNIA (Universal Negro Improvement Association) and the Black Star Shipping Line. He had a penchant for titles, pomp, and braggadocio. He called himself, at various times, "Imperial Potentate of the Valley of the Nile," "Emperor Marcus I of Ethiopia," and "Admiral of the Black Star Line." He once billed himself in London as "The Greatest Orator of the World, the Moses of the Black Race, More Eloquent than Demosthenes, Cicero, and Marc Antony." He loved coronations with medieval trappings, and for parades had a Black Legion carrying swords in scabbards

and smartly dressed in trousers with red stripes. The official colors of the
UNIA were red, black, and green:

red — for the blood of the race, nobly shed in the past and dedicated to the
    future,
black — to symbolize pride in color of skin, and
green — for the promise of a new and better life in Africa.

He talked about a Black Christ, and a White Devil. Unfortunately for his
plans, he was apprehended by federal authorities for using the mails to
defraud — for selling stock in the bankrupt Black Star Line. He was convicted, sentenced for five years, and in 1926 sent to the penitentiary in
Atlanta; the next year President Coolidge commuted the sentence and deported him. His death in London in 1940 was scarcely noticed in the
American press. David Cronon has observed that his was a movement on
the extreme right, with intense nationalism and a narrow racial outlook.
Garvey actually hobnobbed with the Ku Klux Klan, which wanted the
same objectives, for different reasons. It is interesting to note, in retrospect, that one of his ardent supporters was the Reverend Earl Little of
Detroit, a Baptist minister. He had a son named Malcolm Little who later
assumed the name Malcolm X and achieved some prominence in another
separatist movement.

Garvey's UNIA and the Black Muslim movement were alike in that
both wanted a separate race and a separate Negro homeland. On the other
hand the Muslims are different from the UNIA in a number of other
respects: the location of the homeland, religious emphasis, intensity of
economic separatism, and intensity of racial separatism. On the homeland
the Muslims say that Garvey was right in his Negro nationalism but
wrong in telling the Negroes to return to Africa to achieve their goal. The
Muslims assert that they are going to build their society right here in the
United States; they are going to own an all-black state. Where? No one
seems to know; some say, sardonically, that Mississippi might be the solution to the problem. In 1968 militants would demand a black nation-state
that comprised the 12 seaboard states from Maryland to Florida; they
were to be emptied of whites and turned over to the black separatists. The
most spectacular leader of the Muslims, the late Malcolm X, would say
that slaves had worked 300 years without a pay day, and that the United
States could now pay them well — and not with what he called "the
phony integration stuff." He went on to assert that the United States had
helped Israel, which had never fought for this country as Negroes did; he
claimed that the United States had even helped Communist Poland and
Communist Yugoslavia. For all of these reasons, whatever their merit,
Malcolm was sure that the United States should help the Black Muslims.
He said, "We fought, died, and helped build this country, and since we

can't be citizens here, then help us to build a nation of our own. We don't need to go to Africa. We can do it right here."

There was nothing religious about the Garvey movement; the Black Muslims are enveloped in a confessional aura. They repudiate Christianity as a "white-man's religion" with a "blue-eyed God." Because Black Christians savor black-eyed peas, collard greens, corn bread, sweet potatoes, and pork, the Prophet of the movement has warned Black Muslims not to consume them. He says that this diet is productive of disease and has shortened the lives of Black Christians; he wants Black Muslims to be long-lived. The Black Muslims also have the asceticism that marks most religions. In this respect they qualify as the elite corps of *black Puritans,* because all Muslims are forbidden to gamble, smoke, drink, overeat (fines of one meal a day for violations), indulge in fripperies (such as cosmetics and fancy dress), or buy on credit. As a result most Muslims enjoy a reasonably solvent standard of living — and still have enough cash left over to tithe for the movement (one can speculate about both spiritual and economic reasons for asceticism).

The Muslims were unique in their views on the homeland and in their religious fervor; they also were much more intense in their economic and racial separatism. The Muslims say that Negroes should spend their money *only* with Negroes. They had great contempt for the Negro sit-in movement — in which black men were trying to force white merchants to take the Negro's money. A prominent Muslim once said, "There are only two languages the white folks understand — the ballot and the buck. When the cash registers keep quiet, they react." For that reason Malcolm X would call Martin Luther King a "bourgeois Uncle Tom," "a chump of chumps," and a "coward of cowards." The Reverend Adam Clayton Powell would say that it was the dollar that counted: "It's not black power, it's green power." He thought that the new Trinity in the United States was "God the Father, God the Son, and God the Almighty Dollar."

Powerful voices, both Negro and white, have been raised against black separatism. Bayard Rustin, the civil-rights activist who organized the March on Washington for Jobs and Freedom in 1963, notes that separatists — whether political or economic — represent a distinct minority among Negroes; no reliable poll has ever identified more than 15 percent of Negroes as separatists, and the actual percentage may be much lower. On the economic side Rustin points out that black capitalism is bound to fail, after it has victimized large numbers of people. A black bourgeoisie will attempt a profitable monopoly of the Negro market, but as with all small businesses there will be a high rate of failure — even greater than usual by reason of a clientele which is poor and an area of operation where the crime rate is high, resulting in a heavy burden of taxes, labor costs, and insurance. This involves the old principle of the superiority of national over local markets; in this competition the national chains will win, through lower prices, over "Buy Black" campaigns. Andrew F. Brimmer, the Negro member of the Federal Reserve Board, has noted that Negroes must enter the national rather than a parochial market established through black separatism; he says the Negroes could make much more money as hired managers and skilled craftsmen operating in the national economy than as self-employed businessmen in the ghetto. His conclusion is, "In the long run, the pursuit of black capitalism may retard the Negro's economic advancement by discouraging . . . participation in the national economy with its much broader range of challenges and opportunities."

Saul Alinsky, the peripatetic sociologist who has been active with "Back of the Yards Neighborhood Councils" in Chicago, Rochester, and elsewhere, agrees with Brimmer and Rustin but believes that the blacks must go through a painful experience before they realize that separatism is not the answer. He says that until blacks have been exploited by their own people, as they were by whites, there will be a constant source of anti-Semitism because so many businessmen in ghettos were Jews who stayed there commercially long after they had changed their residences to the suburbs. He understands that a small businessman, regardless of the color of his skin, cannot compete in terms of prices and service, and that to achieve a piece of the economic pie the blacks must become part of the national corporate economy. Their demand for separatism is wrong but

> It's one of the irrationalities you have to accept, part of life, part of growing up. After all, we've made black the color of everything ugly and shameful. Nobody is ever pinkmailed, he's blackmailed. Nobody is ever kicked out of a club on a bluelist, it's on a blacklist. We use black for mourning, for funerals; we've made it the color of tragedy, of evil. We talk about black days of infamy. So it's natural for them to react by saying black is beautiful. In the end they'll see that black is beautiful and ugly. Every color is beautiful and ugly.

Out of all these developments has come what C. Vann Woodward calls the Second Reconstruction, with many similarities to — and one striking and significant difference from — the First Reconstruction immediately after the Civil War. Woodward states that the Second Reconstruction, which is still very much with us, did not begin until 1954; prior to that year segregation was still the law of the land. *Brown* v. *Board of Education* in 1954 ended the legal claim of white monopoly in schools and other civil institutions; *Baker* v. *Carr* (the "one-man, one-vote" decision in 1962) threatened the gerrymandering that had sustained the white man's rule. This judicial "reconstruction" was supported by congressional "reconstruction" in the Civil Rights Acts of 1957, 1960, and 1964. As in the period after the Civil War the South saw Negroes at the ballot box, federal troops in the streets, the reappearance of carpetbaggers and scalawags

and abolitionists (now called integrationists) — most of them "foreigners" from the North who represented organizations like the NAACP and
CORE and SNCC and student groups.

The result, says Woodward, was that the South resurrected the old
regional syndrome of "minority psychology and rejection anxiety" that it
had felt during the First Reconstruction. A section which represented a
besieged minority could not afford the luxury of internal division; it was
necessary to close ranks against foreigners — and in the extreme instance
this paranoid impulse resulted in what Professor James W. Silver described as the "closed society" of Mississippi. The Ku Klux Klan plus the
White Citizen's Councils and other nativist organizations once more put
in an appearance. Club and gun and kerosene and dynamite again played
their roles; so did the old Confederate stratagems of nullification, interposition, congressional manifestos, and filibusters. In the Second Reconstruction the counterparts of the Wade Hamptons and the Nathan Bedford
Forrests of the decade after the Civil War, were a Thurmond of South
Carolina, a Faubus of Arkansas, a Barnett of Mississippi, and the Wallace
of Alabama who made the famous statement in his inaugural address as
governor: "I draw a line in the dust and toss the gauntlet before the feet
of tyranny."

There were indications in both North and South that another compromise like that in 1877 would bring the Second Reconstruction to a close —
with little accomplishment. There was a willingness to accept "token-
ism," a bit of integration, with the result that after ten years of school
desegregation at "deliberate speed" only 2 percent of the Negro pupils in
the old Confederate states were in schools with white children, and nearly
half of these were in Texas. In the North there was a "backlash" from neo-
Copperheads worried about the increasing numbers of Negroes in city
slums and city suburbs. The Supreme Court came under severe attack and
signs appeared across the nation asking for the impeachment of Earl Warren. Trade unions set up indignant protests against the entrance of Negroes; so did employers who talked about the fundamental freedom to
hire and to fire. Homeowners wanted to sell only to persons with the same
color of skin, and parents became militant in defending "neighborhood
schools." All the ingredients appeared to be at hand for a Compromise of
the 1960's — which might have been as much of a defeat for the Negro as
the previous one in 1877.

As Woodward points out, had it been left to the white man, North and
South, the Second Reconstruction probably would have gone the way of
the first — into frustration and into failure. But this time the Negro was
not passive as he had been in the generation after Emancipation; supported
by white allies in the northern United States and in the world outside, he
had a new consciousness of power. He now played a decisive role, varying
all the way from the moderate demonstrations organized by Martin

Luther King to the truculent aggressiveness of H. Rap Brown, who called violence "as American as apple pie." The Negro showed his power particularly through the franchise; Woodward believes the turning point was the impact of the Negro vote in the presidential election of 1964 — which went solidly for Johnson both in northern cities and in southern states; the five states Goldwater managed to carry (South Carolina, Georgia, Alabama, Mississippi, and Louisiana) were those with the lowest Negro registration. Things could never be quite the same in the South again, what with increasing Negro registration and a decided change of attitude in the border states. The First Reconstruction had had the effect of bringing the border states into the South's orbit, making them more "Confederate" after the Civil War than they were before. The Second Reconstruction had just the opposite effect; the upper South along with Texas and Florida had defected from the Goldwater group of states. With increasing Negro registration, Ralph McGill would remark about the "stark isolation" of the five southern Goldwater states — an isolation he believed "may prove in the long run to be a necessary therapy," because they have now "so isolated themselves that they cannot fail to see how terribly and irrevocably alone they are." The important Negro vote is tied to civil rights; for that reason it went on record in support of President Johnson who, as Woodward phrases it, "has gone further . . . in public commitment to the protection and extension of Negro rights than any one of his thirty-four predecessors, including all those elected by what was once known as the party of emancipation and Negro rights."

The accomplishments of the First Reconstruction were largely rhetorical. It now appears that the Negro may realize some gains from the second, but if these are achieved without strife and bloodshed both he and the white man will be required to show unprecedented understanding. In 1967 the President's National Advisory Commission on Civil Disorders, whose chairman was Governor Otto Kerner of Illinois, concluded that the United States was moving toward "two societies, one black, one white — separate and unequal." It was inclined to place major blame on the prejudices and greed of the whites. Kerner himself defined this racism as the belief that if you are white, you are superior — and if you are black, you are inferior. He said that what "white Americans have never fully understood — but what the Negro can never forget — is that white society is deeply implicated in the Ghetto. White institutions created it, white institutions maintain it, and white society condones it." These biases, baffling by reason of psychological and economic overtones, were once described by the Negro comedian Dick Gregory in tragic words: "In the South they don't mind if you get big as long as you don't get close. In the North they don't mind your getting close as long as you don't get big."

This has meant that the rate of unemployment among Negroes in urban areas has been several times that of whites, and this disquieting figure may very well be the economic reason that explains much of the tensions between the two groups. To the question asked by many whites as to why the Negro — in contrast to many European immigrants — has been unable to escape from the ghetto and from poverty, the President's National Advisory Commission on Civil Disorders said:

The immigrant who labored long hours at hard and often menial work had the hope of a better future, if not for himself then for his children. This was the promise of the "American dream" — the society offered to all a future that was open-ended.

For the Negro in the urban ghetto, there is a different vision — the future seems to lead only to a dead end.

What the American economy of the late nineteenth and early twentieth century was able to do to help the European immigrants escape from poverty is now largely impossible. New methods of escape must be found for the majority of today's poor.

IX

Free Labor in the United States

PRIOR to the Civil War the history of free labor was divided, by judicial decisions, into two periods. Before the Panic of 1837 the movement was largely political in character. There were Workingmen's parties (its members were dubbed "Workies") in several states; the movement was never national in character or organization. These parties asked state legislatures for universal education, equality in taxation, and the abolition of the militia system and of imprisonment for debt. They had little influence, and in time the membership was largely absorbed by the Democratic party. But in this early period it was necessary for the labor movement to be political because unions were illegal by court decree. The critical decision was that in the Philadelphia Cordwainers' Case of 1806. The court, basing its ruling on the conspiracy doctrine of English common law, held that unions *per se* were an illegal conspiracy. The conspiracy doctrine is interesting in many ways, one of them that it relieves a prosecutor of the necessity of proving actual wrongdoing on the part of a defendant. Clarence Darrow, who was experienced in representing defendants in such trials, once noted that if a young boy stole candy he had committed a misdemeanor. On the other hand, if two young men *planned* to steal candy, but never did so, they were guilty of conspiracy, which is a felony.* In the United States this doctrine was first used in the Philadel-

---

*In recent years Julius and Ethel Rosenberg were not executed for espionage because the government had no proof that they actually transmitted atomic secrets to Russia. They were convicted for conspiracy to commit espionage.

phia Cordwainers' Case, in which the court ruled that a strike (an agreement of journeymen shoemakers to "withhold their labor" from their masters) — for the purpose of increasing wages — was a criminal conspiracy. Curiously, if one of the shoemakers (or several) had withheld their labor, no crime would have been committed; the felony lay in the *agreement* of a group to do so. Fifteen years later in 1821, a group of journeymen made an unsuccessful attempt to reverse the charges; they tried to convict employers for a conspiracy to depress wages. This time the court held that no criminal act had been committed because the employers had combined to resist the oppression of the journeymen. Its conjectural statement was that combination was no conspiracy "when the object to be attained is meritorious"! Local unions continued to exist in the face of these decisions, but the threat of court action slowed the rate of their growth and forced laborers to attempt political action through Workingmen's parties.

After the Panic of 1837 a change came because of another court decision — that of the Massachusetts Supreme Court in *Commonwealth* v. *Hunt* in 1842. Between the Cordwainers' Case in 1806, and 1842, there had been twenty-one conspiracy trials against unions. Now there was a slight change in direction, and the beginning of legal hope for labor organizations. *Commonwealth* v. *Hunt* was the first recognition in the United States that the common law concerning conspiracy was inapplicable to labor unions and that strikes for a closed shop might be legal. In this decision the Supreme Court of Massachusetts stated that actions of unions were not illegal unless either their *intent*, or the *means* they used, were illegal. This decision, which was copied by the courts of other states, was both important and curious — curious because it held that unions were not *illegal*, but it did not say that they were legal! For the next ninety-five years labor unions in the United States existed in a limbo between legality and illegality. Decision was made by the courts alone, as the sole arbiter of the legality of a union's means and ends. It was not until 1937, in *NLRB* v. *Jones and Laughlin Steel Corp.*, that the Supreme Court finally held that unions were legal entities, and as such were entitled to the protection of the law. On a very large canvass, therefore, the history of the labor movement can be portrayed in three court decisions — Philadelphia Cordwainers', *Commonwealth* v. *Hunt*, and *NLRB* v. *Jones and Laughlin Steel Corp.* In the period of 131 years (1806–1937) the legal position of unions had shifted 180 degrees: from illegality through limbo to legality.

In spite of judicial uncertainty that lasted a very long time, *Commonwealth* v. *Hunt* strengthened labor's economic weapons and permitted the movement to turn away from politics to economic goals: wages, hours, strikes, and boycotts. By the time of the Civil War four national unions had been organized, including the Iron-Moulders International Union and the International Typographical Union.

After the Civil War the American Industrial Revolution came into its own. As a result of this transformation the American laborer saw that he needed protection, through organization, against mechanization, the rise of the large corporation, and a glutted labor market. In the long run labor-saving machines might mean more employment — but in the immediate future the replaced worker was out of a job. The large corporation was disturbing and perplexing. Before the Civil War the laborer usually toiled in a small plant where, as Thomas A. Bailey observes, the owner "hailed him in the morning by his first name and inquired after his wife's ailments." After the Civil War he was confronted by a corporation that seemed to be, and often was, depersonalized and soulless and conscienceless. The worker figured that if Big Business could combine into national trusts to raise prices, the worker should be able to combine into national unions to raise wages.

Machines and corporations were bad enough; the glutted labor market was just as bothersome. Two developments contributed to this labor surplus. One was the development of the transcontinental railroad network that could shuttle cheap labor, including Negroes and immigrants, into areas where wages were high — for the purpose of beating them down. The other was the passage of the Contract Labor Law. This law was enacted in 1864, when business interests got Congress to put through legislation permitting the advance of passage money to prospective immigrants in return for a lien upon their wages. With such encouragement corporations like the American Emigrant Company undertook to provide laborers; it was capitalized at $1 million and was backed by Cabinet members Salmon Portland Chase and Gideon Welles, Senator Charles Sumner, and the Reverend Henry Ward Beecher. In practice, unfortunately, the law often provided cheap labor — including strikebreakers — which forced wage rates down. What employers wanted were new immigrants, undemanding and submissive and eager for any kind of job. One observer asked an employer in the stockyards, where many nationalities (including Lithuanians, Slovaks, and Serbians) were working, which group gave the most trouble. The reply from the employer was immediate and surprising: "The Americans. We haven't many of them, luckily, but the few we have start more trouble than all the others."

Jim Hill, the well-known railroad magnate, echoed the same point of view: "Why should I have to pay an American fireman six dollars a day for work that a Chinaman would do for fifty cents?" Elbert Henry Gary of U.S. Steel followed the same policy. When the plant and town named for him was built in Indiana at the turn of the century it imported Poles, Serbs, Croats, Greeks, Lithuanians, and sundry others from eastern and southern Europe. It wanted malleable, inexpensive labor. These disparate nationalities (there were fifty-seven in Gary), upset this divisive strategy by supporting the great strike of 1919 against U.S. Steel. That company then turned to the American South and brought up Negroes to break the strike supported by Europeans. Forty years later these two groups (the American Negroes against the Europeans), with all of their traditional and historical animosities, faced each other across a widening chasm in that city. By rough estimate Gary now has more than 100,000 Negroes and 70,000 whites. Its Negro mayor, Richard G. Hatcher, sat on a political and ethnic volcano in 1969.

Craft unions developed rapidly after the Civil War; by 1870 there were thirty-two national ones, commanding a total membership of 300,000. It was apparent that someone would think of a national federation. That person turned out to be William H. Sylvis of the Iron-Moulders International Union, who might very well be called the first real labor leader in this country. In many ways he was very much like the later Eugene V. Debs, who became so prominent in the labor movement and the Socialist party. Sylvis had little formal education and was a wage earner from the age of eleven, yet his writings and speeches indicate a wide reading and a remarkable understanding, for his time, of economic issues. He lived like an ascetic and gave all his time to the organization of labor.

In 1866 he federated many of the unions of the country into a loose national organization, called the National Labor Union. Several annual congresses were held, and in its heyday, the federation had about 600,000 members. It was certainly a loosely knit, amorphous federation, because it included not only craft unions but farmers' unions, women's suffrage leagues, and other reform groups too numerous to mention. It failed because of its ambivalent character and because the death of Sylvis removed the only real leader it ever had. It was a divided organization — half trade union and half political. Ultimately, when the political group gained the ascendancy and went into politics, the trade unionists withdrew. Its political planks were also highly controversial. Some of them supported rights for women and Negroes; no matter how humanitarian, many trade unionists feared both as potential strikebreakers or as competitors for jobs simply because they would work for less money. Some of them favored greenbacks, on which there was great difference of opinion. The divided organization and controversial political planks placed the movement in a precarious position. When Sylvis expired suddenly in 1869, at the early age of forty-one, the steam went out of the organization.

Although it was short-lived, three contributions of the National Labor Union are worthy of mention. It was the *first* national organization of labor unions; it led the way. On a *second* front it helped the movement for an eight-hour day — by getting the federal government to adopt such a day for its own employees in 1869. This was quite an accomplishment. In the era of Andrew Jackson there had been a movement for a ten-hour day; employees demanded a working day from six in the morning until six in the evening — with an hour off for breakfast and an hour for lunch. Employers had opposed it strenuously; they said that to be idle several of the most useful hours of the morning and the evening would certainly lead to intemperance and to ruin. Finally, the National Labor Union initiated the movement that would bring repeal of the iniquitous Contract Labor Law in 1885, although the organization did not exist long enough to see the results of its initial agitation.

The American Federation of Labor (AFL) was like the National Labor Union in that both represented a federation of craft unions — local and national and international. Workingmen did not belong directly to the AFL; they belonged to their union, and the union had membership in the AFL. It got its money by collecting from each union a tax of so much per member; this began at the rate of 50¢ a year, ultimately increased to $6 a year. In 1955, at the time of the amalgamation with the CIO, the AFL claimed 10 million members in 141 affiliated unions. At that time the largest (with a few more than a million members) was the International Brotherhood of Teamsters, Chauffeurs, Warehousemen and Helpers of America.

On the other hand the American Federation of Labor was unlike the National Labor Union in its emphasis on the skilled, its cooperation with management through business unionism, and goals which were opportunistic rather than far-reaching. Its purpose was to better the status of its own members; for this reason it was sometimes called the "Labor Trust." If the status of its members had to be achieved at the expense of the rest of the laboring class, that was too bad — but it was necessary. The result of this philosophy was that the AFL abandoned the goal of labor solidarity that motivated Sylvis and Terence Powderly and "Big Bill" Haywood. The AFL was interested in *part* of the labor movement, the skilled part; it did not advance the cause of labor as a whole.

The AFL also believed in cooperation with capitalism through what is known as "business unionism." Its chief feature was the *union contract* introduced by its longtime president, Samuel Gompers; one modern commentator (Lester Velie) claims that the union contract was to modern unionism what the discovery of the wheel was to civilization. The union contract set wages, hours, overtime pay, seniority, and the training of apprentices; it even established conditions for the introduction of new machinery. It was a significant feature of free enterprise as it was being practiced in the United States during most of its history, because it guaranteed skilled labor a monopoly of jobs — just as business ownership was trying to establish a monopoly of markets. For that reason the monopolistic and grasping Dave Beck of the Teamsters' Union would say: "I run this union just like a business." A reporter who knew Beck well, put it in other words: "Dave fancies himself as the director of a huge labor-supply corporation. He is selling a product — human labor — just as Westinghouse sells refrigerators. He tries to get the best price for his product but that's as far as his ideology goes."

And so it would be, in time, that many labor leaders began to act like business leaders, and to demand the same salaries and perquisites. There was none of this in Gompers' time. As late as the 1930's it was not unusual for a union constitution to specify that the president was to earn no more than the highest-paid craftsman. After World War II the situation changed. As a result, many top labor executives came into fancy salaries, fancy offices, rode in Cadillacs, wore hand-tailored suits, joined a country club, and lived in a mansion in a restricted residential area. Their salaries ranged from James Hoffa's $75,000 on down; in 1961 Walter Reuther drew only $22,000, A. Philip Randolph $14,000, and Harry Bridges $12,000. It was not surprising, in the current generation, that one business executive would make business arrangements with another business executive — known as "sweetheart contracts" — representing labor collaboration with management. This meant that a labor executive, for a price, had guaranteed labor peace for a management executive. Such a contract was illustrative of a working partnership between two businessmen — one a representative of labor and the other of management.

As a businessman, Gompers cooperated with capitalism; he simply wanted to make capitalism serve the interest of the AFL — as well as the interests of the capitalists themselves. For that reason he had little interest in the reform of the capitalist system. He had no use for such panaceas as greenbacks, the single tax, cooperatives — reforms which so captivated the leaders of the National Labor Union and of the Knights of Labor. These represented long-range plans; by contrast one of Gompers' lieutenants (Adolf Strasser, who was president of the Cigar Makers' Union) put it this way in 1885: "We have no ultimate ends. We are going on from day to day. We fight only for immediate objectives that can be realized in a few years." With this philosophy it is not surprising that after World War I, in spite of the advantages which Gompers had gained for the labor movement through wartime *national* controls, in peacetime he opposed central control of the railroads through nationalization, compulsory national health insurance, and national unemployment insurance.

The American Federation of Labor not only failed to become the dominant American labor organization but actually witnessed a spectacular revolt against, and a secession from, its ranks in the 1930's because of weakness of the federal principle, lack of leadership, and the failure to organize along industrial lines. Gompers was proud that he could persuade his fellow unionists to pattern the AFL after the federal principle of the United States Government. He never realized that the two federations were completely different in relation to secession, preeminence, and sanctions. The U.S. government could, and did, restrain states from seceding; the AFL had no means of keeping a member union from leaving the federation. In the United States the national government is preeminent in national affairs. In the AFL the individual union was preeminent; it selected its own officers, made its own contracts with employers, called its own strikes — without any interference from the AFL at the top. The federal government in Washington has *many* sanctions; the AFL had *one*. It could expel a member union, but it had no power of subpoena to make possible the investigation of corruption among its affiliates. For this it had to rely on congressional investigators — and still does. In the absence of any real control or sanctions, the AFL had to rely heavily on superlative leadership. Unfortunately it did not get it.

During most of its history as an independent organization the AFL had but two presidents — Sam Gompers and William Green — a duo who served from 1886 to 1953. Gompers was president, save for one year, from 1886 until his death in 1924. He was a cigar maker by trade and a Jew by religious faith who was born in a London tenement, was removed from school at the age of ten, and was brought to America at the age of thirteen. He rose to the top in the Cigar Makers' Union, and in the AFL, because of several unusual attributes: physical appearance, voice, personality, and integrity. In physique he looked like a labor leader as, for example, Terence Powderly of the rival Knights of Labor did not. Depending on how one felt about Gompers, he was described as a squat frog, or a pouter pigeon. He was short (five-feet-four), and had a large chest and torso — those of a big man on a little man's legs. In the 1880's he had dark unruly hair, wore a drooping walrus moustache, had a little tuft of hair on the chin, and was not unlike many undergraduates in the current era. He was blessed with a great voice, described as rich and sonorous as a pipe organ, and quite capable of being easily heard in Madison Square Garden or a cathedral. In his early days in the cigar union, he had taken his turn at reading informative literature to his fellow cigar makers in New York as they worked; he was soon pressed into overtime service because of his strong and dramatic vocal cords. In personality he was easy, friendly, very much "one of the boys." He was completely relaxed in the back room of a saloon, a big cigar gripped in his teeth and a foaming stein of beer on the table. This conviviality shocked the straitlaced Powderly, and his Knights of Labor reported in a pamphlet that its members had "never had the pleasure of seeing Mr. Gompers sober." This was inaccurate, but there is no question that Gompers hugely enjoyed his beer. Along with physique and voice and personality, there was his integrity and honesty. It has been said, with considerable truth, that he worked eighteen hours a day to get the eight-hour day. Of the early part of his career Gompers himself would say, "There was much work, little pay, and very little honor." At that time his headquarters was an eight-by-ten-foot office made available by the cigar makers, with little furniture other than a kitchen table, some crates for chairs, and a filing case derived from tomato boxes. Impeccably honest, he was to die a poor man, and in the Depression of the 1930's his widow had to accept work from the WPA. He felt himself engaged in a holy cause; the AFL was his entire life. Given his basic premises, he was a great labor leader. Unfortunately, he merits severe criticism because some of these basic premises appear to have been wrong. His AFL was so out of touch that it would oppose unemployment compensation in the early 1930's.

William Green, who was president from 1924 until his death in 1952, had risen through the ranks of the United Mine Workers of America (UMW), of which he was secretary-treasurer; at that time, but certainly not in later years, he had the support of John L. Lewis. In physique Green was plump with a round and humorless visage; in personality he was sober and sedate. At one time he had hoped to train for the ministry, and in no fashion was he one to drink beer with the boys in the Gompers manner. He was a man of honesty and integrity; he was also dull — no one ever accused him of having a brilliant mind. On his acceptance of the AFL presidency he announced, pontifically, that he would "support the right and oppose the wrong." Later he endorsed "progressive conservatism." By May 1930 he had learned that there was considerable unemployment; all he had to offer was the sapient remark, almost Coolidgian, that "the only cure for unemployment is jobs." By September of the same year he had made another remarkable discovery; he said, "Working people must earn money in order to live . . . that is why a job is so important." With this evidence before him it is no wonder that the sardonic journalist Benjamin Stolberg would conclude: "William Green is in a permanent state of excited misunderstanding. A fluent speaker, he is never at a loss for the wrong word."

Gompers and Green, in different ways, had their weaknesses as presidents of the AFL. Although most AFL leaders were reasonably honest and democratic, there were a number of presidents of constituent unions who were either dictators or racketeers. Because of the actions of these men, a high price in money and bad public relations was paid by both the unions and the public. Among the dictators the most prominent were William Hutcheson, James Caesar Petrillo, Dave Beck, and James Hoffa. William ("Big Bill") Hutcheson was the president of the United Brotherhood of Carpenters and Joiners of America, in 1950 the fourth largest union in the nation. He was shrewd and able and a dictator. In his union, conventions were supposed to be held once every four years; in practice there were gaps of eight years between them. His control was so pervasive that someone made the famous remark: "God made the forests and gave them to Bill Hutcheson." Hutcheson himself never specifically claimed that the Deity had gone quite that far, but he did point out from time to time that Christ was a carpenter. When he retired in 1951, he turned the presidency over to his son, just as if it were a monarchical dynasty (the son was allegedly caught with soiled hands in the cookie jar, and was involved in extended litigation in connection with a high-way scandal in Indiana). James Caesar Petrillo was the profane boss of the American Federation of Musicians, and was known as the "Mussolini of Music" in the United States for twenty years. He had come out of the slums of Chicago, the son of an Italian sewer-digger. Grade school was a bit hard for him; he spent nine years getting through four years of an elementary school in Chicago. In later life he would claim that he had once read a book but didn't care much for it. He was not particularly fond of music, except brass bands. But for a fellow with a fourth-grade education he progressed well financially. As early as 1940 he received a total of more than $100,000 annually from the union that he ran dictato-rially; this was in salary ($46,000) plus perquisites (house, upkeep, garden, paid income tax, armed limousine, and bodyguards).

The Teamsters' Union provides a particularly unfortunate example of dictatorial control. It had only three presidents in the first sixty years of this century: Daniel Tobin, David Beck, and James Hoffa. Tobin ruled the Teamsters for forty-five years, and never understood why FDR did not appoint him Secretary of Labor. An immigrant from County Clare in Ireland, Tobin could make grand-sounding speeches about the necessity of keeping aliens out of the United States! He could also talk resoundingly about the evils of jazz, whiskey, college professors, and the Jewish leader-ship of the CIO. He finally became obsolete in 1952 and was shouldered aside by David Beck, who ran the union even more dictatorially. He taught backward employers the strength of Teamsters' power by way of arson, dynamite, rammed taxis, and overturned trucks. Ultimately his own venality was his undoing. The McClellan Committee of the U.S. Senate (the Select Committee on Improper Activities in the Labor and Manage-ment Fields) disclosed that in addition to his union salary of $50,000, he had purloined close to $400,000 from the Teamsters' treasury for personal use. It also developed that the union had given him a mansion in Seattle worth $163,000, complete with swimming pool and waterfall, and that Beck had sold it back to the union for the same $163,000 but had contin-ued to live in it — rent- and tax-free. The testimony before the McClellan Committee also indicated that he was the recipient of many favors from employers; for example, money, cars, planes. All of this finally caught up with him; in 1959 he was found guilty of evading income tax to the ex-tent of $56,000 in the fiscal year 1950. He had been president of the Team-sters' Union for almost six years (1952–1957) and had seen it expelled from the AFL-CIO in 1957 because of his gross misuse of union funds. In the 1960's he served two and a half years in a federal penitentiary, and emerged with the assertion that the experience had added five years to his life! He had entered the prison a puffy 211-pounder and had been released weighing 170. He credited his good health to a rigorous program of exercise and an austere prison diet. He was a millionaire when he went to prison; he was a millionaire when he came out.

James Hoffa succeeded Beck for ten years (1957–1967) before the prison gates also clanged shut behind him. Sometimes called "Labor's Dead-End Kid," his father was a miner who died early of coal-dust poisoning; the son finished the ninth grade, then left school for good. As Lester Velie has observed, he views the world only in terms of his own bitter experiences, sees it as a "hostile jungle alive with beasts of prey — of which he is one." An "instinct for the jugular" has been the foundation of Hoffa's economic strategy ever since he was eighteen and called his first strike. He was unloading freight cars on the platform of the Kroger Grocery warehouse in Detroit. The year was 1932, at the depth of the Depression, and the pay was 32¢ an hour. Hoffa decided that timing was the most essential prerequisite for a successful strike. His moment came when a carload of strawberries rolled up to the warehouse; workers folded their arms, with Hoffa notifying management that an independent union had just been formed, and that nothing would be unloaded until it was recognized. As it turned out, the company wilted before the strawberries did; the strike was over in less than an hour, and those berries became Hoffa's strange "launching pad" to the top rung of unionism. As president of the Teamsters, with a million and a half members, the "jugular" was the nation's distribution lifeline. A friend would refer to him as Napoleon or the "Little Corporal" (because of his short stature), would comment on his oversized drive for power, would recall that both Napoleon and Hoffa's wives were named Josephine. He might have added that he also had the egotism of Napoleon; Hoffa once said, "I may have faults but being wrong ain't one of them." The courts did not agree. In 1967 he was sent to jail for jury-fixing and for fraud in obtaining large loans from the pension fund of the Teamsters' Union. On 23 December 1971 President Nixon commuted the sentence, freeing the former leader of the Teamsters' Union from prison. The *New York Times* opined that "it would be nice, but naïve, to believe that the spirit of Christmas and James R. Hoffa's unblemished record as a prisoner were the only factors" that influenced the decision. As the newspaper saw it, evidence had been mounting about a "strange love affair" between the Administration in Washington and the 2 million–member truckers' union that was ousted from the rest of the labor movement in 1957 because of domination by racketeers. The *Times* found it difficult to avoid the suspicion that "the imminence of the 1972 election was a factor in Mr. Nixon's decision . . . only five months after the U.S. Parole Board had refused for the third time to let Hoffa out."

Hutcheson, Petrillo, Beck, and Hoffa may have qualified as ruthless dictators; other labor leaders, less well known, could be certified as racketeers because of their association with gangsters. In the 1930's it was the

International Alliance of Theatrical Stage Employees, AFL, whose leaders (George Brown and Willie Bioff) were tied with Capone, Costello, and Luciano. What Brown and Bioff did was to threaten strikes and personal violence; by this means they extorted more than a million dollars from film producers and from theater owners. Twenty years later it was the International Longshoreman's Association, with its shape-up and its kick-backs, and its association with Tony Anastasia — the brother of Albert Anastasia of Murder, Inc.

The emphasis and faith placed by the AFL in craft unions *only* — unions of skilled workers — was damaging for the unskilled, for the public and employers, and for the craft unions themselves by restricting their effectiveness in time of crisis. The AFL certainly damaged itself with the unskilled, whom it did not want and who were not asked to join. Unfortunately for the AFL, with the advent of the machine, the number of laborers who could continue to call themselves skilled was declining. Consider an automobile factory; the employee there who aims a paint gun at an automobile fender is not a skilled craftsman in the traditional sense of the term. In the same way, the employee who tightened a single nut on each car as it came down the assembly line could hardly be classified as a master mechanic. This meant that the AFL, if it adhered to a basic philosophy which deified skilled artisans, would never be able to organize mass-production industries such as iron and steel, food packing, rubber, automobiles, oil, and the chemical industries. The unskilled were not happy with the AFL; neither were the public and management, because of silly jurisdictional strikes. These involved arguments between rival craft unions as to which one should perform the job. In the 1930's, to cite one example from many, two craft unions in the nation's capital quarreled over which should install the radiator covers in a large new governmental building in Washington. Should it be the carpenters, or the metal workers? It was a trifling item, but both unions stood firm — with the result that the construction of the entire building was halted for weeks, throwing hundreds of other craftsmen out of work. Finally the contractor, desperate over the prospect of losing his forfeit by failure to finish the job on time, offered to pay both crafts full time, and let them divide the work between them — or to pay one union to sit and watch the other do the job. This offer was rejected too! One can understand the individual worker's immediate point of view, confronted as he is with grocery and other bills in a nation that sometimes does not have enough jobs to go around. At the same time, these jurisdictional strikes — with all their absurdities — have discredited labor with the public and with employers. They have also damaged the unions themselves, because the emphasis on skills has reduced labor's tactical strength in strikes. The unfortunate fact is that the craft organization, stressed by the AFL, has contributed to the weakness of the labor side in bargaining — because employers were astute enough to utilize the very old principle of "divide and rule." It will be recalled that the Austro-Hungarian Empire was once managed on the basis of "divide and rule." In its case the division was *racial*. In the case of labor, by contrast, the division was *craft*. Employees, if they are to pit their strength effectively against employers, obviously must organize as employers have done by — by industries. The AFL did not; its failure in the 1919 steel strike is a prime example of this weakness. That famous strike was broken partly by the tactics of steel owners and partly by the policy of the AFL — a policy that provided for *twenty-four* craft unions in this *one* industry, all of the twenty-four craft unions working at cross purposes and cutting one another's throats. It is apparent that labor must have cohesiveness and unity in time of strikes. In 1919, in steel, labor had about as much cohesiveness and unity as one would find in a load of furniture. For that reason it is not surprising to find that the International Workers of the World (IWW), a leftist labor organization, would rename the AFL the "American Separation of Labor."

The AFL stuck doggedly to its emphasis on craft unions for two basic reasons. Craft unionists fear to lose advantages they have gained in long years of struggle. Fundamentally, however, a multiplicity of craft unions creates a multiplicity of jobs for labor leaders — jobs which might disappear if the simpler form of industrial organization were established. Carpenter William Hutcheson spoke with his usual frankness on this point. He said he was opposed to industrial unions because "if all workers were organized on an industrial basis it would mean the elimination of our organization."

With the decline of the National Labor Union after the Civil War another labor organization arose immediately to take its place. It was the Knights of Labor (K. of L.), an organization founded in 1869 by Uriah Stephens and six other garment cutters; it held its first national convention in the centennial year of 1876. The K. of L. was the first national labor organization to stand for industrial unionism, and it had a most progressive platform. The Knights of Labor was based on the principle that all toilers — white and black, skilled and unskilled — should band together into one mighty partnership without distinction of trade or vocation. For that reason membership in the Knights was open to any bona fide worker eighteen years of age or over; the only groups barred were types who did not qualify as true laborers — brewers, professional gamblers, bankers, lawyers, and doctors! The purpose of the Knights of Labor was "to teach the American wage earner that he was a wage earner first, and a Catholic, Protestant, Jew, white, black, Democrat, Republican, carpenter, miner, shoemaker, after." Its ideal was "one big Union"; its slogan was "An injury to one is the injury to all." The Knights also had a platform which was as far ahead of its time as was that of the later Populist party. They favored:

The eight-hour day.

Rights for women, including equal pay for equal work.

The abolition of child labor.

An income tax.

Governmental ownership of railroads.

A federal postal-savings system — to protect investors against fraudulent private banks.

Cooperatives to protect consumers against grasping manufacturers and merchants.

Its growth was phenomenal; the K. of L. burgeoned from a minuscule society of seven journeyman tailors to a nationwide organization of 700,000 less than twenty years later, when it reached its peak in 1886. There were three major reasons for this remarkable expansion: its early secrecy, the impetus from the Panic of 1873, and its success in conducting strikes. It was a secret organization until 1879, at a time when secrecy was a very real attraction. The name of the organization was never referred to openly, and in all official documents its name was replaced by five asterisks. Why the appeal of secrecy? One reason was safety, another was the aura of fraternalism. In the 1870's it was frequently dangerous for members of labor organizations to identify themselves. In 1877 the Chicago *Tribune* advocated the poisoning of tramps and the shooting of strikers. In the same year the famous minister Henry Ward Beecher was quoted as saying, "Laborer's unions are the worst form of despotism and tyranny in the history of Christendom." The second reason for the attraction of secrecy was its role in a larger movement of American fraternalism — one that has played a perennial part in American social life. Before movies and the radio and television and the used car, there was little to relieve the drabness of life for the laboring class. For that reason, in many a city block, the saloon had been the poor man's club. Now the Knights offered another, and a more respectable club. In his working hours a member might be a garbage collector or a domestic servant; at night, he became the worshipful grand master of the K. of L., his spirit supported by sash and epaulets. It gave him a release from the drabness of life, a release to a satisfying never-never land.

Secrecy was one thing; so was the influence of the Panic of 1873 and success in conducting strikes. As a result of the Panic many national unions found it necessary to disband; they declined in number from thirty-two to six, in membership from 500,000 to 50,000. Many of their bewildered former members went into the new K. of L. There were also some notable triumphs in strikes. Particularly phenomenal was the successful strike against Jay Gould's Wabash Railroad in 1884. Gould was the ruthless entrepreneur who had boasted that he could hire, if necessary, one half of the laborers to kill the other half. During this strike there had been a series of conferences in New York City, and the nation was treated to the astounding spectacle of Gould, the mogul of one of the nation's greatest railroad systems, negotiating with the Executive Board of a nationwide labor organization. Nothing like this had ever happened before. Gould agreed to end discrimination against the K. of L., and was reputed to have said that he had come to believe in labor unions and hoped that all of his employees would join! After this, according to rumors spread by representatives of management, the membership of the K. of L. was alleged to have increased to more than 2 million, and the organization was claimed to have a "war" chest, for support of strikes, amounting to $12 million. The conservative press said that the order dominated the country, would name the next President, might overthrow the entire capitalist system. Its grand master, Terence V. Powderly, was said to be a czar, ruling his followers with "despotism and secrecy." In actual fact he was a bewildered and puzzled leader who commented ruefully, "The position I hold is too big for any ten men. It is certainly too big for me. . . ."

The Knights reached their apogee with 702,000 members in 1886, by which time they had persuaded Congress to exclude the Chinese (in 1882) and contract labor (in 1885 when a new Contract Labor Law forbade the importation of foreign labor except for professional, skilled, and domestic labor). But by 1890 its membership had fallen to 100,000, and by 1900 the K. of L. was virtually extinct. The causes of this precipitous and tragic decline are found in fumbling leadership, overemphasis on cooperatives, the presence of the unskilled, and an unfair and unfortunate association in the public mind with the Haymarket Riot. Louis Adamic once called the leaders of the K. of L. an "assembly of windbags." The first grand master, Uriah Stephens, had been a Baptist minister, couldn't make a living in the pulpit, was forced to take up tailoring. He never recovered from his early theological training; instead of stressing labor problems, he was wont to talk in high-sounding phrases about "the Fatherhood of God and the Brotherhood of Man." For this reason, as Foster Rhea Dulles has pointed out, Stephens found himself out of place in a pragmatic labor organization that needed something more than religious oratory.

His successor, Terence V. Powderly, was grand master from 1879 to 1893. In appearance he was almost the last person who would have expected to be a labor leader; he was a delicate and sensitive fellow with the vanity of a prima donna. One observer stated that one might have expected Powderly to be a poet or a philosopher, but scarcely a leader of horny-handed sons of toil. In his own personal philosophy he had little interest in wages and hours or collective bargaining, usually considered to be of some importance to labor organizations; he once told the Knights to "throw strikes, boycotts, lockouts, and *such nuisances* to the winds" —

and to concentrate on more important things. His own chief interest was in cooperatives, which he saw as the answer to most of labor's problems. He crusaded for land reform, particularly through the Single Tax. He had a great zeal for temperance. He had great difficulty in following a consistent course. During his life he supported such movements on the left as the Greenback Party, the Single Tax, and Populism. Then in the 1890's he became a conservative Republican, supporting McKinley against Bryan in 1896. He was rewarded, in 1897, by appointment as commissioner-general of immigration.

If the leadership of the Knights left something to be desired, the order was also weakened by overemphasis on cooperatives and by the presence of the unskilled in its membership. It dissipated funds and energy in cooperative ventures that were doomed to collapse because of bad management and unfair competition. At the height of the movement it had 200 producers' cooperatives, including mines and shoe factories; almost all of them failed. The presence of the unskilled, fine and benevolent as it was in theory and intention, presented weaknesses from a tactical point of view. The unskilled were easily replaced in time of strikes, making it difficult to achieve victory. The unskilled are apt to be migratory, and difficult to trace and control in an organization that wants to be permanent. The unskilled also caused considerable psychological tension within the organization; it was difficult, in a status-conscious society, for the highly skilled craft unionist to see that he had much in common with the Negro hod carrier, or for the railroad engineer to feel any bond of brotherhood between himself and the pick-and-shovel laborers along the right-of-way. Ultimately, this psychological misunderstanding would be the chief reason for the defection of the national trade unions from the K. of L. to the AFL.

The Knights of Labor received their coup de grace because the public came to the conclusion, unfairly and mistakenly, that they were involved in and associated with the violence in the Haymarket Riot and Massacre in Chicago in 1886. Through Haymarket they became intimately and wrongly connected, in the public mind, with the Black International whose members were anarchists. Throughout history anarchists have usually been harmless and idealistic dreamers like Leo Tolstoy. In 1883 at Pittsburgh, however, another brand of anarchist, inspired by the militant Russian Mikhail Bakunin, issued what was known as the "Pittsburgh Proclamation." This was regarded as the classic statement of revolutionary anarchistic doctrine; out of this came the organization in the United States of the Black International under the leadership of a German immigrant named Johann Most. His scarred and twisted face (from an untended childhood accident), deformed body, and lonely youth had provided natural soil for the nurturing of a bitter animus against society.

In 1886 the anarchists had joined the general movement in Chicago for the eight-hour day, thus associating themselves with the Knights of Labor who were the main support for the shorter workday — 80,000 Knights and 2,000 anarchists. But violence, of an unexpected and fortuitous kind, erupted. In February 1886 the McCormick Reaper Works had locked out hundreds of its men who were union members, had employed scabs, and had engaged 300 Pinkerton detectives to protect the scabs. On 3 May several workers were shot at the McCormick works when a pitched battle occurred between the locked-out former employees on the one hand and the Pinkertons and the police on the other. At this point the anarchists — *not* the K. of L. — scheduled a protest meeting for the next evening at Haymarket Square in West Chicago. At 8 P.M. on 4 May there were 3,000 persons on hand for the protest meeting, listening to the anarchists in their demand for the eight-hour day and in their denunciation of the police. By 10 P.M. it had begun to rain and only a few hundred were left in the crowd. To this point the meeting had been an orderly one, on the basis of testimony from the mayor of Chicago, who had stopped at the meeting to observe it — and had reported its peaceful nature to the police. But someone, no one knows who, ordered 180 policemen to the scene, to disperse the crowd. The last speaker had just finished when the police arrived. The police captain ordered the meeting to disperse, and the speaker cried out that this was hardly necessary because this was a peaceable meeting. At that moment a bomb exploded, wounding sixty-seven policemen, seven of whom died. The police opened fire in return, killing several in the audience and wounding at least 200. In a minute, the Haymarket tragedy had become a part of U.S. history.

Louis Adamic once observed that the resulting tension in Chicago was similar to that in a southern town at a lynching, that in California over the Mooney-Billings case, or that in Boston on the eve of the electrocution of Sacco and Vanzetti. It was never determined who threw the bomb, although a number of interesting theories have been presented. The governor of Illinois, John Peter Altgeld, thought it was someone who was embittered at the police of Chicago because of their long record for brutality. Others believed it to be an *agent provocateur*, engaged by management to discredit labor. Most newspapermen thought it was an anarchist named Rudolph Schnaubelt, who got away and escaped to Mexico. Since the actual bomb-thrower was to remain unknown, the police rounded up every known anarchist in the country, along with many prominent labor leaders. Ultimately eight of the anarchists were brought to trial on the charge of first-degree murder. It was admitted that none of the eight threw the bomb, and that only two of them had actually attended the meeting. In Chicago, however, the prevailing attitude was to "hang 'em, and try 'em afterward"; the result was that four of the eight were hanged, one committed suicide during the trial, and three were sentenced to life imprisonment. No criminal lawyer in Chicago could be found to provide defense for the accused. Ultimately three lawyers engaged in civil practice showed enough courage to withstand hostile public sentiment, and to provide the right of defense which is supposed to be an ornament of American jurisprudence. Before the four condemned men were hanged a number of prominent persons, from all over the world, tried to convince the governor of Illinois that he should commute the sentences. In England, George Bernard Shaw and Oscar Wilde circulated petitions. In this country William Dean Howells, at the risk of social ostracism, spoke courageously in the anarchists' behalf — *for a fair trial.*

The Haymarket affair broke the careers of most of those who were associated with it, directly or indirectly. It broke the Knights of Labor, through guilt by association. In actual fact, organized labor was in no way associated with the bombing at Haymarket: the Knights of Labor were as critical of anarchists as the most conservative newspapers. They said: "Let it be understood by all the world that the Knights of Labor have no affiliation, association or sympathy . . . for the band of cowardly murderers, cut-throats and robbers, known as anarchists." The Knights even clamored for the convictions of the anarchists unfairly charged with the crime. But the world did not hear their denial. It reasoned that anarchists had thrown the bomb in connection with the agitation for the eight-hour day. The Knights of Labor were in favor of the eight-hour day. Therefore, the K. of L. must be anarchistic! Because of this stigma, those members who could qualify tended to gravitate to a more conservative position, into membership in the AFL.

The Haymarket Riot also broke the career of one of the outstanding governors, on the basis of his forward-looking program, in the history of the United States. Vilified and misrepresented in his day, this governor left a remarkable record of legislation in the interest of the rank and file of citizens. He brought about a state inheritance tax, a civil-service law, a probation system, regulation of labor by women and children, factory inspection, and the establishment of machinery to arbitrate industrial disputes — all achievements of the first degree in the 1890's. He fought long franchises for privately owned utilities, worked for the welfare of the state penal and charitable institutions, and was a particular friend of the University of Illinois. He was John Peter Altgeld, born in Germany and brought to this country at the age of three. Some years after the Haymarket Riot, while Altgeld was governor from 1892 to 1896, he pardoned the three anarchists who had been given life imprisonment. To lawyer Altgeld the essential fact was that the accused had not had a fair trial, that the judge was prejudiced, that jurors frankly admitted bias, and that the record showed appalling contradictions. But when Altgeld said so in his 18,000-word pardon he was damned as a murderer, a Communist, a foreigner, a bomb-thrower, and an anarchist. Because of this, and because he had also earned the enmity of many other members of the Establishment, Altgeld was ruined.

Haymarket was in the 1880's. Forty years later, in the 1920's, there was another *cause célèbre* involving anarchists named Nicola Sacco and Bartolomeo Vanzetti. They were accused of murdering a paymaster and his guard at a shoe factory in South Braintree, Massachusetts. Although the evidence against them was insubstantial, they were convicted in 1921 and sentenced to death. There was great protest, both in the United States and abroad, because many felt that they had been tried for their radical views rather than the crime on which they were charged. In 1927, after Sacco and Vanzetti had been in a prison death house for six years, a special commission in Massachusetts, whose chairman was President Lowell of Harvard, sustained the verdict. Sacco and Vanzetti were executed. This was in August 1927.

The president of Harvard thought the two men were guilty. One of his law-school professors had some doubts. In March 1927, five months before the execution, the professor wrote an article in the *Atlantic Monthly*. The article was not so much an earnest plea for the lives of Sacco and Vanzetti as it was a criticism of the unfairness of the trial — a repetition of the argument of Altgeld four decades earlier. In the 1920's the professor pointed out that the trial of Sacco and Vanzetti had been loaded with error and judicial prejudice, and that the commission headed by the president of Harvard was also prejudiced. After this statement, relationships became difficult in Boston for the critical professor. His views split the Harvard faculty; differences became so bitter that when he would enter a room or a restaurant old friends would leave without a nod or a glance. It was claimed that he had cost the university a million dollars in contributions withheld by irate alumni. Attempts were made to remove him from the faculty. The university did not do so, to its eternal credit, and in time Harvard forgave the teacher for his unpopular but courageous struggle. He was a future Justice of the Supreme Court of the United States — Felix Frankfurter.

Another industrial union, much more radical than the Knights of Labor, was the Industrial Workers of the World — popularly called the Wobblies. It was particularly strong with migratory workers in the mines, lumber camps, and harvest fields of the West, and with textile workers in the East. The IWW had lots of enthusiasm, and songs to incite it; its members sang because when they sought the workers' attention on street corners they were challenged by those competing sidewalk hot-gospellers, the Salvation Army. By 1909 their press was able to publish the first edition of *Songs of the Workers to Fan the Flames of Discontent;* ultimately there were thirty subsequent editions, all scarlet-covered and fitted to the size of

an overalls pocket. As Bernard Weisberger once noted, this songbook and
its preamble were to the IWW membership what the hymnbooks and the
"Discipline of the Methodist Church" had been to frontier preachers; the
songwriters of the IWW wanted to chant "hymns of hope and hatred" at
the shrine of rebellion. Their most famous "hymn" was probably "Halle-
lujah, I'm a Bum" — the refrain of a song set to the old religious tune of
"Revive Us Again." The verse and the refrain of the IWW version went
as follows:

> *O, why don't you work*
> *Like other men do?*
> *How the hell can I work*
> *When there's no work to do?*

Refrain:

> *Hallelujah! I'm a bum!*
> *Hallelujah! Bum again!*
> *Hallelujah! Give us a hand-out,*
> *To revive us again.*

The IWW was organized in 1905 by William Dudley Haywood, better
known as "Big Bill" Haywood, who had been a cowboy, a homesteader,
and a miner, and was once described quite accurately as a "bundle of
primitive instincts." If the IWW had a leader Haywood merited the designation, but there was considerable suspicion of leaders in this freewheel-
ing organization. Once a sheriff shouted to a group of Wobblies, "Who's
yer leader?" He received a prompt reply: "We don't got no leader, we're
all leaders." Haywood was not averse to violence but was sometimes
falsely accused of it. In 1905 he was charged with the murder of the governor of Idaho, but was acquitted in a trial in which he was defended by
Clarence Darrow, "the attorney for the damned." In 1912 Haywood and
the IWW were accused of planting dynamite in the Lawrence (Massachusetts) textile strike. Before the strike was over it was proved that, in
collusion with mill owners, a local undertaker — apparently accustomed
to burying things — had planted the dynamite in an obvious attempt to
discredit the strikers and the IWW. The strategy backfired, and the
IWW won the strike. It was one of the few the organization won.

The IWW believed in industrial unionism, and it wanted to abolish
capitalism. It placed its faith in One Big Union and One Big Strike — the
general strike. Haywood had no use for craft unions, and thought Gompers was a "cross between a windbag and a rope of sand." Along with the
belief in industrial unionism went a desire to abolish capitalism and the
wage system that went along with it. Its program was anarchist-syndicalist-
socialist in nature, demanding the overthrow of capitalism through political and economic action. The preamble of the IWW constitution put the

matter in plain language: "The working class and the employing class have *nothing* in common." It must be remembered that the era out of which the IWW emerged was a grim one for the workingman. This was an America in which children worked a sixty-hour week in mines and factories, in which industrial accidents took a frightful toll each year because safety and sanitary regulations were virtually unknown, in which wages were set by the "marketplace" with the result that grown men with families worked ten to twelve hours a day for a dollar and stayed alive only by cramming their families into horrible tenements or company-town shacks, in which such things as pensions or paid holidays were unknown, in which workers were frequently locked out and replaced by scabs at Homestead and Pullman and Ludlow and Cripple Creek.

The IWW reached its peak membership of 100,000 in 1912; by the end of World War I it had almost disappeared. It declined because it was too radical and it was accused of treason. Its radicalism never appealed to the *mass* of American workers. Elizabeth Gurley Flynn, one of the leaders who later became a Communist, put it this way: "For the Socialists we were too radical; for the anarchists we were too conservative; for everybody else we were impossible." Because the IWW was opposed to American participation in World War I it was accused of treason. Haywood did not oppose a war against employers but he refused to participate in what he called an imperialist war against Germany. This was obviously unpopular in a United States that finally went to war in 1917, with the result that the IWW was renamed "Imperial Willie's Warriors" (a militant variant of other paraphrases such as "I Won't Work" and "I Want Whiskey"). Locally, extralegal groups resorted to whippings, clubbings, the tar-and-feathering, and even the lynching of IWW members. One sheriff told a visitor, "When a Wobblie comes to town I just knock him over the head with a night stick and throw him in the river. When he comes up he beats it out of town." Ultimately Haywood and ninety-four others were convicted of sedition in a mass trial in Chicago, and were sentenced to jail for terms running as long as twenty years. The charges of conspiring against the government were in many instances so flimsy as to be ridiculous, but the patriotic fervor of the war period sustained them. Eventually Haywood skipped bail, fled to Russia, and died there of paralysis in 1928.

Many faults can be found with Haywood and the IWW. Nonetheless, as A. H. Raskin once observed, there was a reason for the movement and some nobility in it — and some shame for the nation that treated it, and many of its members, so shabbily.

The United Mine Workers (UMW), organized in 1890, is an industrial union; every laborer in a mine belongs to it, regardless of craft. It had two famous presidents: John Mitchell from 1898 to 1908, renowned for his role in the Anthracite Strike of 1902, and John L. Lewis from 1920 to 1959, renowned for his part in the organization of the Congress of Industrial Organizations (CIO). Mitchell had begun his labors in another industrial union, the K. of L. He joined the UMW in 1890 and became its president in 1898. Four years later he was involved in the critical Anthracite Strike, which President Theodore Roosevelt called a crisis "only less serious than that of the Civil War." This was because there was a possibility that the public might freeze during the approaching winter months. Some 140,000 besooted workers in the anthracite coal mines, many of them illiterate immigrants, had long been frightfully exploited and accident-riddled. In 1902 they had struck, asking for a 20 percent increase in wages, a reduction in the working day from ten to nine hours, recognition of the UMW, and check weighmen — to reduce cheating on the amount of coal that they had mined.

The *dramatis personae* of the struggle — Theodore Roosevelt, George F. Baer, and Mitchell — were spectacular in different ways. TR was the President of the United States who talked about a "square deal" for labor; many workingmen were interested to ascertain whether he really meant it. George F. Baer was the president of the Reading Railroad, a Morgan property which had extensive interests in coal mines. Baer refused to bargain with the miners, in a very high-handed manner. In July 1902, a photographer from Wilkes-Barre named William F. Clark had written to Baer expressing a hope that "God would send the Holy Spirit of reason" into Baer's heart. This angered Baer, and in his reply to Clark he wrote, "The rights and interests of laboring men will be protected, not by the labor agitators, but by the Christian men to whom God in his infinite wisdom has given the control of the property interests of this country." A Republican stalwart, Senator Henry Cabot Lodge, had asked the President to call a meeting of all disputants at the White House, because Lodge was fearful that the continuation of the strike might defeat the Republican party in the fall elections of 1902. TR did so, and at the meeting found Baer insufferable. The President reported that he was vastly annoyed at the "extraordinary stupidity of the wooden-headed gentry" who operated the mines. He was to confess, in later years, that if it had not been for the dignity of his high office, he would have taken Baer by the seat of his breeches and "chucked him out of the window." Also present at the meeting was John Mitchell, president of the UMW and at that time a real labor statesman. At the well-publicized meeting at the White House, the President was to say there was only one gentleman present. It was not Baer, who had money but no manners; it was not TR, who lost his temper. It was Mitchell, who managed to remain cool and urbane throughout the entire performance.

The Rough Rider finally resorted to his trusty Big Stick in order to settle the impasse; he threatened to seize the mines and to operate them with federal troops. Even then the owners consented grudgingly to arbitration, insisting that the seven-man arbitration commission must *not* have a labor representative on it. TR did manage to place a representative of labor on the commission by disguising him as an "Eminent Sociologist"; his Eminence was Edgar E. Clark of the Order of Railroad Conductors. In the hearings before the commission, Mitchell made Baer look very bad, in part because Mitchell was assisted in the negotiations by his chief of Legal Staff — a fellow named Clarence Darrow. Ultimately the miners came out of the arbitration with a nine-hour day, a wage increase of 10 percent, and the employment of checkers in the weighing of coal. They did *not* achieve the recognition of their union. TR and the public had become very conscious of the increasing antagonism between labor and capital; in 1903 Congress, at TR's suggestion created the new Department of Commerce and Labor (the two segments were split into separate departments in 1913). TR's action in the strike of 1902 was the first intervention by a U.S. President — not to break labor under the guise of preserving order, but to promote the public welfare by insuring a reasonable degree of justice. For this he was severely, and unfairly, criticized.

John Llewellyn Lewis, president of the UMW from 1920 until his retirement in 1959, was the most prominent and the most controversial of the chief executives of this union. With his bulging eyebrows and black leonine mane he was to strike terror at dozens of bargaining tables; gruff and unsmiling in public, his broad-brimmed fedora tilted over his eyes, he reveled in the dramatic tensions he helped to create, and he sparkled whether he was in center stage or contributed a deep stentorian voice from the wings. The great "thunderer for labor" was born on Lincoln's birthday at Lucas, Iowa. Privately he always fancied himself as the "Great Emancipator" — of wage, rather than chattel, slaves. Lewis's Welsh parents had left mining communities in the old country. His father had been a member of the Knights of Labor, and had become active in a strike — with the result that his name had appeared on a general blacklist. The consequence was that, although the father moved from town to town, the fatal blacklist always caught up with him. The son, John L. Lewis, was therefore compelled to quit school in the seventh grade to drive mules underground. He was always conscious of his appalling lack of formal education, and by extraordinary effort was able to educate himself and to become the most intellectual, and probably the best-read, leader in the entire labor field. He developed the ability to make exciting speeches — perfect in grammar, with picturesque language — quoting Shakespeare, Homer, and Plato. Only his closest friends knew that his wife, a onetime Iowa schoolteacher, spent years straining the coarseness and the vulgarity from his diction, prodding him to soak his mind in good literature — which he did.

As an orator he was a most effective ham. As Arthur Schlesinger has observed, expressions chased themselves across his mobile face like clouds against a stormy sky. His eyes burned with fire and contempt, and his great voice, rolling out the sentences in the manner of a Welsh evangelist, alternately declaimed, bewailed, or taunted. By any standard, it was a superb act. He denounced rival labor leaders, Cabinet members, politicians. In time he came to have little use for the AFL, classified its leaders as "intellectually fat and stately asses." He was particularly hard on William Green, who reminded him "of an elderly lady with a wooden leg"; on another occasion he claimed, "I have done a lot of exploring of Bill's mind and I give my word there is nothing there." He thought Walter Reuther talked too much; he therefore dubbed him "an earnest Marxist chronically inebriated, I should think, by the exuberance of his own verbosity." Cabinet members did not escape his scorn. Of FDR's Secretary of Labor, Madam Frances Perkins, he said: "She would make an excellent housekeeper but I do not think she knows as much about economics as a Hottentot knows about the moral law." He could be just as hard on prominent politicians, particularly FDR's Vice-President, the famous "Cactus Jack" Garner — a grower of pecans from Uvalde, Texas. Garner did most of his wheeling and his dealing in a private office, to the rear of the Senate Chamber, to which he quietly invited key legislators to "strike a blow for liberty," that is, to sample his excellent bonded Bourbon. Apart from baseball and pecan-growing, his major avocation was poker; he was so good at it that his winnings in some sessions of Congress exceeded his pay of $10,000 a year. A conservative, in 1939 he opposed liberalization of the Wages and Hours Act. This angered Lewis who attacked the Vice-President as a "labor-baiting, poker-playing, whiskey-drinking, evil old man whose name is Garner. . . . I am against him officially, individually, and personally, concretely and in the abstract, when his knife searches for the heart of my people."

Lewis was a stormy petrel, a controversial figure in the labor movement for half a century. There are many arguments — pro and con, positive and negative — on the quality of his leadership and of his contributions, if any. He ran his union despotically, and would come into conflict with its members, with federal courts, and with the U.S. government and its Presidents. In addition, he was at least partly responsible for the depression in the coal industry — a depression which was largely due to competition from oil and gas, which Lewis had underestimated or ignored. His frequent strikes, particularly in the 1940's, not only increased the price of coal but also created an aggravating uncertainty about its supply, which caused former users of coal to turn to gas and oil. After his death it appeared that the union's welfare and retirement fund, long considered a model of frugal management, had not been as honest or generous as previously believed — and that the responsibility for this failure went back to Lewis. In 1972 a federal district-court judge ordered the United Mine Workers to pay $11.5 million in damages to the union's pension fund because of the misuse of the miners' money. Specifically, the union had taken $70 million from the pension fund and had placed it in a union-owned bank which paid no interest on it. The court said that this practice had stripped "thousands of sick, disabled, and aged miners of their meager pension rights."

On the positive side, he always stood for industrial unions, which appear to be the wave of the future as far as labor is concerned. He managed to get high wages and pensions for the members of his union. In the last decade of his leadership he cooperated with management — a sensible thing to do because the coal-mining industry was depressed. Lewis therefore permitted management to mechanize its mines, in order to better its competitive position, although mechanization reduced the number of miners significantly. The push-button miners and the twenty-story-high power shovels that now dig most of America's coal, have pushed tens of thousands of miners out of the coal pits. But the royalties these machines paid into Lewis's pension fund meant that by 1966 Lewis had distributed more than $2 billion in benefits to miners and their families; an industry with 100,000 active miners was able to carry 70,000 pensioners, and to spend another $50 million a year on health and hospital services. It was also these same machines, recognized and accepted by Lewis, that kept the price of coal low enough to prevent it from being squeezed out of the market by oil and natural gas.

In 1935 the Committee of Industrial Organizations (CIO) made its dramatic debut in the labor movement. At the moment it represented a significant revolt against the AFL in three respects: it stood for industrial unions, participation in politics, and progressivism. The CIO had no faith in craft unions; its stress on industrial unions brought great hope to the unskilled, who had resigned themselves to being outside the benefits of unionization in the AFL. The CIO stood for political participation, lending its support to specified candidates. The AFL had usually frowned on becoming involved politically; it stuck to this position with only two exceptions — in 1908 Gompers supported Bryan against Taft, and in 1924 he supported La Follette against Coolidge and Davis. Under the aegis of the CIO, by contrast, political activity quickly became a major operation, first under Labor's Non-Partisan League, organized by John L. Lewis; it was nonpartisan enough to work for the election of FDR. The CIO also stood for progressive and liberal policies; in practice, this meant standing for the New Deal. It was opposed to what it called the conservatism of many AFL leaders, a conservatism which was long-established and deep-rooted.

The birth of the CIO was dramatic indeed. At the national convention of the AFL in 1934 the principle of vertical (industrial) organization of unions had been approved. At the national convention at Atlantic City in 1935, however, a block of industrialists found it impossible to secure AFL charters for newly organized unions in the radio, automobile, and rubber industries — and there was a spectacular fight between John L. Lewis and "Big Bill" Hutcheson of the Carpenter's Union. In physique Lewis was just under six feet in height, and weighed in at about 225 pounds, by contrast with Hutcheson's 280. During the convention Hutcheson was heard to say, "I'll see Lewis in hell before I see industrial unions." A verbal exchange followed, during which Hutcheson mumbled a contemptuous phrase about Lewis, of which only the word "bastard" came through. The result was that Lewis hit Hutcheson and Hutcheson hit the floor, according to one excited eyewitness, with such force that half the window panes in Atlantic City were cracked and the tide went out an hour earlier than usual! With one blow Lewis had dramatized the split in the AFL. He called a meeting of leaders of industrial unions and designated his gathering the CIO (Committee for Industrial Organizations). The hierarchy of the AFL ordered the committee to disband, the committee refused, and its leaders were expelled from the AFL. Two years later, in 1938, the full name was changed to the Congress of Industrial Organizations; the congress adopted a formal constitution and took on permanent form. The CIO grew so fast — particularly in automobiles, steel, textiles, rubber, glass, and the electrical industry — that by the end of 1937 it had outstripped the AFL in total membership — 3.7 million to 3.4 million.

In addition to Lewis (who served as president from 1936 to 1940) the original leaders in the CIO comprised an able and interesting group: Philip Murray, Sidney Hillman, Walter Reuther, David Dubinsky, and Heywood Broun. Murray was born in Scotland, came to the United States in 1902, worked in Pennsylvania coal mines, had risen to the position of vice-president by 1920. A man of unimpeachable integrity and honesty, he lacked the emotionalism that marked so many labor leaders; he was amazingly quiet in personality, particularly by contrast with Lewis. Murray became vice-president of the CIO in 1936 and organized the United Steel Workers of America (USWA), with whom U.S. Steel surprisingly signed an agreement in 1937. When Lewis resigned from the CIO in 1940 Murray succeeded him as president, and remained in this position until his death in 1952. The dramatic departure of Lewis from the CIO came because of a political gamble that did not pay off. In 1936 Lewis had supported FDR mightily for the Presidency, expected FDR to treat him as his labor adviser in the second term, and expected the President to do as he was advised. FDR did not do so, relations between the two men cooled, and there was a showdown in 1940. As FDR later told his version of the story, with considerable relish, Lewis came to the White House and asked for a place on the third-term presidential ticket. Lewis was supposed to have said, "We are the two most prominent men in the nation. It will be an invincible combination." FDR is reported to have replied, "Which place will you take, John?" Lewis was not pleased and staked his CIO presidency on the election of Republican Wendell Willkie, and his own ability to get the labor vote for Willkie. When Roosevelt won, Lewis resigned and ultimately took the UMW out of the CIO.

At the time of the organization of the CIO Sidney Hillman was president of the Amalgamated Clothing Workers. Born in Lithuania, he entered a rabbinical school in Kovno, Russia; by the time he was fifteen he decided that his liberal ideas would never permit him to become a rabbi. Because of his labor sympathies he was arrested and served time in jail for his political beliefs. Ultimately he fled to England and then to the United States, settling in Chicago where he was first a clerk for Sears, Roebuck and then a cutter for Hart, Schaffner and Marx. With the break between Lewis and FDR in 1940, the isolationists and the Communists in the ranks of labor (the Communists had won control of a minority of CIO unions) supported Lewis because they did not care for FDR's interventionist foreign policy. By 1940, however, both isolationism and Communism were losing their popularity and Hillman, the spokesman for the strongly anti-Nazi Jewish unions, provided effective leadership for FDR. The result was that Hillman became the principal labor adviser to FDR, in the place of the jilted Lewis. By 1944 Hillman's influence was great enough that in the complicated negotiations at the Democratic National Convention in that year, FDR was reputed to have said, "Clear everything with Sidney."

Walter Reuther was brought up in an intensely labor-conscious home in Wheeling, West Virginia. His grandfather, Jacob Reuther, had been a dairy farmer in Mannheim, Germany; he was a strong-minded labor agitator and Socialist reformer who came to the United States in the 1840's and helped organize the brewers in the Midwest. The father, Valentine Reuther, was a close friend of Eugene V. Debs, and was a candidate for Congress on the Socialist ticket. In Walter's youth regular debates were held in the Reuther household every Sunday afternoon, when social and economic topics were perennial items of discussion. The son's early political affiliation, not surprisingly, was with the Socialist party — which he joined when he was a student at Wayne State University in Detroit. In 1932 he actively campaigned for Norman Thomas, stayed with the party until 1938, and since that time was an independent New Dealer in politics. Later he abjured the government ownership proposed by the Socialists; he once said, "I'd rather bargain with General Motors than with the government. General Motors has no army." In Detroit, while attending Wayne as a part-time student, he also worked for Ford, and was discharged for union activity. With his brother Victor, he set out on a thirty-three-month tour of the world to study European industry, unionism, and politics. Among other countries visited was Russia, where the brothers worked briefly in the Gorki automobile plant. Back in the United States in 1935, Walter plunged headlong into the great union offensive in automobiles, and in time became president of the United Automobile Workers of America (UAW). At that time the sitdown strike was the technique used by Reuther to win the initial foothold for his union. Workers in the Flint General Motors plant refused to go home in the face of company, or court, orders. When the police tried to evict them they were met with a barrage of coffee mugs, pop bottles, iron bolts, and heavy auto-door hinges. General Motors demanded that the governor of Michigan (Frank Murphy, later a Justice on the Supreme Court) order the militia to clear the plants. Murphy refused, after the workers had said they would stay, no matter how many lives were snuffed out by militia fire. Ultimately GM capitulated, and both the CIO and the UAW won their first major labor agreement. It was a dramatic victory for Reuther; he would not only become the president of the UAW but would succeed Murphy as president of the CIO in 1952.

Reuther was an unusual labor leader in many ways. One of them was in physique and habits. He was athletic in build — with the well-preserved appearance of an athlete — in contrast to most labor leaders. He drank milk (not liquor), did not smoke, play cards, or go to nightclubs. Until his death he still led picket lines from time to time, traveled second-class or coach, lived modestly with his wife (a former schoolteacher) and two children on a salary of $28,750 — not only low for major labor leaders (Meany received $70,000), but far below what his union would have paid him if he would have permitted them to do so. Because of his abstemiousness and social vision he was described by critics as one part Puritan and two parts social reformer — mixed with a pinch of Little Boy Blue. Some of his earthy colleagues considered his asceticism as juvenile. Still others regarded it as inhuman because they figured that his Spartan habits gave him an unfair advantage. One of the paradoxes about his behavior is that he conformed to the Horatio Alger formula so admired by most of the people who hated him; he worked hard, was honest and dignified, and shunned the vices that have brought downfall to so many — in both the management and the labor fields. In 1948 there was an attempt to kill him that was nearly successful. He was eating a late dinner in the kitchen of his modest cottage in Detroit, when an assassin fired a shotgun through the window. The blast shattered his right arm and injured his chest; he recovered after a long hospitalization but had little use of the arm for the rest of his life. At the time his associates wanted him to ride in a bullet-proof Cadillac which happened to cost $18,000. Said Reuther, "I'd rather drive in my old Chevy."

Apart from his unique personality, and his organization of the UAW, Reuther was noteworthy for his ideas — some fuzzy, some precise, some good, some bad, but lots of them. He had so many that he reminded some of a typical executive with one of those big THINK signs on the desk. *Inter alia*, there were the proposals for a cost-of-living escalator clause in union contracts (to guard union members against inflation), and GAW (the guaranteed annual wage) to assure workers of their own peace of mind and to assure the economic stability of the nation as a whole. As with any person who comes up with ideas, he was the subject of much criticism; it was said that he had a Reuther plan for licking his own wounds! Beyond new proposals, Reuther was known particularly for his opposition to the business unionism that attracted so many executives to the AFL. Instead Reuther favored what he called *social* unionism. He said that he had no use for a labor policy based on the "nickel-in-the-pay-envelope" idea; he was revolted by the conception of unions as slot machines into which workers dropped their dues dollars in the hope of winning a jackpot of benefits at the expense of the consumer. He always stressed labor's responsibilities, as well as its rights — responsibilities which it had to the whole community. This was, of course, a far cry from the business unionism of a Gompers or a Beck or a Hoffa. For that reason many employers feared Reuther much more than they did Hoffa. They felt certain they could buy a Hoffa, if necessary; they were convinced they could not buy Reuther.

When he was shot down in 1948, surgeons operated to save the arm that had been shattered by a thug's shotgun; afterwards Reuther forgot the pain as he began to analyze the array of cords and pulleys that held his arm in traction. When a resident appeared to check his condition, Reuther launched into a detailed analysis of what was wrong with the traction apparatus. By the time he left the hospital, it was reported that he had developed a "Reuther Plan" to reorganize the institution. When he died in a plane crash in May 1970, he was still thinking along the same lines — by this time of a much larger "Plan" for universal health insurance. Because of his abiding concern for all mankind, and the dedication so many people had to him and to the future triumph of his ideals, it was particularly appropriate that the moving service at his funeral closed with the recitation of an old and hopeful labor ballad:

> *I dreamed I saw Joe Hill last night*
> *Alive as you and me.*
> *Says I, "But Joe, you're ten years dead."*
> *"I never died," says he.*
> *"I never died," says he.**

David Dubinsky was born in Poland; until he was forty, when he became the president of the International Ladies Garment Workers' Union,

---

* Hill was born Joel Hagglund, the son of poverty-wracked Swedish immigrants to the United States; at the turn of the century he was an itinerant worker who stacked wheat, laid pipe, dug copper. Ultimately he changed his name to Joseph Hillstrom, and then to Joe Hill; he became a Wobbly in 1910. His last words to fellow members of the IWW were: "Don't waste any time in mourning — organize!" See G. M. Smith, *Joe Hill, passim.*

he spoke more Yiddish than English — because virtually all of the union's officers and most of its members were then of immigrant Jewish origin. His youth was most unusual. At fifteen he was imprisoned in Poland for leading a strike against a baker — his own father! At seventeen he was packed off by the police to Siberia, marching a good part of the time under conditions of near starvation and exhaustion; he served five months before he managed to escape. This teen-age introduction to tyranny turned many of Dubinsky's radically minded contemporaries to communism. It had the opposite effect on Dubinsky. He was disgusted with dictatorships of all kinds, including the supposedly beneficent dictatorship of the proletariat. Dubinsky resembled Walter Reuther in his disdain for dress or money or perquisites; his top salary at $26,000 was low for a prominent labor leader. As Lester Velie has observed, in appearance he had the rumpled look of the man who slept in his clothes; his baggy pants were belted precariously around an ample belly. Other labor leaders frequently arrived at conventions in limousines; Dubinsky was apt to ride to the meeting place on a bicycle. At one plush session at Miami Beach he wore sneakers. In one respect he was completely unlike Reuther; he enjoyed food and drink, and talked about his drinking as others conversed about their golf.

A good administrator, in his more than three decades as president of the ILGWU (1932–1966), he saw the membership increase eleven times, from 40,000 to 450,000 members, and during most of the period there were no strikes (he called his first general strike in 1958, a quarter of a century after taking office as president). During his administration, and long before the Landrum-Griffin Act of 1958, the ILGWU published complete financial reports. The members benefited from an extensive social program that included health centers for the sick, clubs for the care of children, a busy adult-education department, a vacation resort (Unity House) in the Poconos, and a theater division that was good enough to run a "hit" musical (*Pins and Needles*) on Broadway. One of Dubinsky's practices was unique in American unionism. When an officer was elected in the ILGWU, in a local or to the executive board, his first executive action was to sign an undated resignation; this was a constitutional requirement which was initiated by Dubinsky. The resignation would be "accepted" by a two-thirds vote of the board, which Dubinsky controlled. His reason for the practice was that it was needed to combat potential corruption; if an officer was caught cheating his official head could be lopped off quickly, with no need for a court action. Critics were not so happy with the device; they observed that Dubinsky himself signed no such "sudden-death" statement, and that the practice meant that the head of every official was placed on an administrative platter, which was then delivered to Dubinsky for possible use. Nonetheless, through such administrative practices Dubinsky, in a thirty-four-year career as president of the ILGWU, brought order into a fiercely competitive and once chaotic industry centered on Manhattan's West Side.

Heywood Broun organized the American Newspaper Guild and became its first president. He had attended Harvard but never received a degree because he flunked elementary French; he did claim that Harvard made a radical out of him, in a most unusual way. There he had taken a course in economic theories from the archconservative Thomas Nixon Carver. The professor had outlined the theories of the radicals in the fall term, and proposed to demolish them in the spring. But the Boston Red Sox commanded Broun's attention in the spring, he never heard the answer to the radicals, because "Tris Speaker was batting .348 and Carver wasn't hitting his hat. I went into the world the fervent follower of all things red, including the Boston Red Sox."

After Harvard he served as a correspondent in World War I, came out of the experience a confirmed pacifist, said "of all cleaning fluids, blood is the least effective." During the 1920's he wrote a distinguished column in the nation's greatest newspaper at that time, the New York *World;* he left the *World* in 1928 because he was too vehement in his support of Sacco and Vanzetti. In later years he wrote for the *Nation*, the Scripps-Howard press, and the New York *Evening Post*. Almost every step in his career came as a jolt to his associates and friends — from the time he appeared in a musical comedy until he joined the Roman Catholic Church late in life. He was a member of both the CIO and the Racquet and Tennis Club on Park Avenue. He enjoyed betting on horse races, but the practice cost him a lot of money; to be reasonably sure of a winner he would bet on almost every horse. In appearance he was huge, cumbersome, and unkempt; his colleagues referred to him variously as "an unmade bed" or as a "one-man slum." He had his idiosyncrasies but he was a great journalist, a great organizer, and a great fellow.

In 1937 a union between the CIO and AFL was nearly brought about, only to be torpedoed by John L. Lewis. His veto delayed the federation for eighteen years. There were three major reasons for the ultimate amalgamation of the two labor combinations: the passage of the Taft-Hartley Act in 1947, the expulsion of Communist-dominated unions from the CIO in 1949, and the fortuitous deaths of both Murray and Green in 1952. The Taft-Hartley Act obviously put labor on the defensive, inclined it to close ranks. In 1949 Murray expelled a number of Communist-dominated unions from the CIO, particularly the United Electrical Workers and the Farm Equipment Workers. After World War II probably a quarter of the CIO unions were under Communist control, in spite of the fact that only a fraction of 1 percent of the CIO members were actually card-carrying Communists. During the 1930's John L. Lewis, in his strategic tactics and maneuvers, had cooperated with the Communists to increase his own leverage in the labor movement. In the late 1940's, with the development of the Cold War, the presence of Communists in the CIO angered most of the American public and the AFL. Murray's action was one of conciliation. In 1952 both Green and Murray, presidents respectively of the AFL and the CIO, happened to die in the same year; both had thought of amalgamation but each waited for the other to make the first move. Neither did. Even in this more propitious climate the subsequent negotiations were so delicate that they almost broke down several times, once over the name. The solution to this problem — the amazingly simple one to call the combined organization AFL-CIO — was brought about by Arthur J. Goldberg, then general counsel of the CIO, later United States Ambassador to the United Nations after interim stops as Secretary of Labor and Associate Justice of the Supreme Court. Goldberg was the chief draftsman of the merger compact that ended twenty years of civil war between the two organizations, but his most delicate peacemaking involved the establishment of a rapport sufficiently cordial to induce Mr. Reuther, the crusading champion of industrial unionism, to take second place in the combined organization to George Meany, a product of the most standpat bastion of craft unionism — the New York building trades. To Goldberg's great credit he brought it off, at least for more than a decade. At the time of the merger the AFL had 141 affiliated craft unions with a claimed membership of 10 million members; the CIO had 32 affiliated unions with 5 million members. Because of its superiority in numbers the AFL got the presidency for Mr. Meany, and 19 out of the 30 members of the executive council (11 for the CIO). To finance the new organization the agreement provided that the AFL-CIO would receive from each constituent union an annual payment of 72¢ (6¢ per month) for each member. Previously the AFL had received 4¢ per month per member and the CIO rate had been 10¢ per month per member.

The new president of the combined AFL-CIO, George Meany, was born in 1894 of Irish parents and grew up in the Bronx. His origin still shows in his speech when he becomes excited ("jernt," "poissonly," and "dese"); Hoffa would call him a "dopey, thickheaded Irishman." Meany left high school before finishing his second year, has been self-educated since, and was pleased when his former public school in the Bronx was renamed the Samuel Gompers Vocational High School. He has a retentive memory, has read at a frantic clip in labor law and American history and international affairs; as a result he has developed the ability to use an extensive vocabulary and abstract ideas with ease — except when he becomes excited. He advanced from the position of business agent of the plumber's local with which he was associated to the presidency of the State Federation of Labor in New York, where he received credit for the passage of a considerable amount of legislation favorable to labor. In 1940 he had become Secretary-Treasurer of the AFL; when Murray died in 1952 he succeeded him as president.

The major objectives of the combined AFL-CIO have been elimination of racketeering, abandonment of racial discrimination, elimination of Communists, and a recruitment drive for members. Although the distinction between craft and industrial unionism is not as acute now as it was in the 1930's, the thankless job of amalgamating overlapping CIO and AFL unions was turned over to Reuther. Because mergers eliminate jobs the problem was largely a personnel one, and created many animosities. The federation has been vigorous in going after racketeers, and expelled the ILA and the Teamsters. The AFL-CIO doctrine on international affairs, under Meany's direction, has been almost indistinguishable on Vietnam and the Cold War from that of the American Legion; on occasion it has been to the right of the Pentagon. The federation has viewed with suspicion all attempts to build bridges, through cultural and educational exchanges, between the United States and the Communist countries of east Europe, Meany's anticommunism can become almost pathological; he is reported to have said that he wanted to meet Nehru — in order to tell the Indian to his face that he was a Communist. Reuther considered these policies and attitudes jingoistic and self-defeating.

On the subject of racial discrimination there has been a great difference between creed and deed. In theory labor leaders have made great advances in this regard. Gompers had refused to allow Orientals to join the AFL. In the 1880's, when white laborers in the cigar industry in California were worried about competition from Chinese labor, they originated the union label: "The cigars in this box are made by White Men." In 1919 the great steel strike of that year was broken in large part by Negro nonunion strikebreakers — who had been refused membership by the AFL Amalgamated Iron and Steel Workers' Association. Two decades later, when Philip Murray founded the USW, he remembered the lesson so well that he joined the board of the NAACP in order to encourage Negro steel workers to join the union. In general it can be said that CIO unions have been free of race prejudice. Theoretically this is true of the AFL unions too. In 1948 the AFL was holding a convention in Houston. On the first day, two officers of the all-Negro Brotherhood of Sleeping Car Porters were barred from the hotel where the convention was meeting. Meany took each official by the arm, marched to the lobby, and told the manager, "Either they get in or we all get out." They all got in. But getting into a hotel, and getting into a craft union — particularly in the building trades (including the plumbers who gave Meany his start) — are different things. Craft unions, like the medieval guilds, have a job-scarcity psychology and have always discriminated in order to keep jobs in the family. In theory anyone can join those unions regardless of color; in practice a Negro might as well forget being a plumber or an electrician or a carpenter or a printer — because of the tightly controlled apprentice system, and the competitive examinations required in order to achieve apprenticeship. This aroused the ire of the only Negro vice-president of the AFL-CIO, A. Philip Randolph, for many years president of the Brotherhood of Sleeping Car Porters. Although he administered one of the smallest unions in the AFL-CIO, he was regarded as one of the half-dozen top labor leaders in the nation. In his active days he was an eloquent orator with a melodious voice; DuBois's *Souls of Black Folk* gave him the driving idea of his life, the idea of the Talented Tenth. Denied an education in his native Florida, he finally got it by night at City College in New York City. It was Randolph who in 1941 forced FDR to set up the FEPC (Fair Employment Practices Committee); he did so by threatening to march on Washington with 100,000 Negroes unless the federal government intervened against prejudice in war plants. It was Randolph who told President Truman after World War II that Negroes would not serve in a Jim Crow army, and said that they would go to jail as an alternative to service in such an army. The volatile "Harry from Missouri" was angry at first, but ultimately had to capitulate for obvious reasons; in the face of our hopeful foreign policy in Africa and Asia he could not afford to fight Randolph on this issue. He therefore gave in and ordered the elimination of segregation in the armed forces. Randolph was obviously a worthy antagonist for Meany, who was known to talk one way and to act another. The two had many words over the subject of race discrimination in the labor movement.

On the AFL-CIO's fifth major objective, the recruitment of new members, the results have been disappointing. The general goal was to approximate the degree of organization in other countries: Sweden at 90 percent, United Kingdom at 50 percent, France at 33 percent. The percentage of union members in the total labor force has actually been dropping in the United States. In 1967 the Department of Labor reported an all-time peak of 17.9 million union members, but any satisfaction organized labor might have derived from the statistic was erased by the fact that the total growth since the merger of the AFL-CIO, in 1955, was only 400,000. In the same period the nonfarm work force grew by 11.5 million. As a result the proportion of workers carrying union cards dropped from 33.4 to 28 percent. The major reason is that in the past the labor movement has relied for membership on blue-collar wage earners in factories who have comprised the bulk of their members. Blue-collar factory workers are now 75 percent organized, but every year their number declines; the UMW is down from 700,000 to less than 200,000; the textile workers from 450,000 to less than 200,000; and the membership of the UAW has been sliding in spite of the fact it has added laborers in the aerospace and agricultural-equipment industries. As the blue-collar force shrinks, the unions have failed to find replacements among the white-collar salaried employees — the office workers, the technical and professional men — and those in service (government, trade, utilities) rather than production jobs. Traditionally, these workers have been the hardest to organize — and still are.

The prime cause of this entire problem is automation, which has labor in a pincers. On the one side it reduces the number of blue-collar workers, replaces them with hard-to-organize engineers, technicians, office workers. On the other side it tends to make business management invulnerable to strikes through push-button control and production surpluses. Through push-button control supervisors can take over in a crisis, as the Bell Telephone System and utilities have proven. Because of automation American factories can produce so much more than we (in America) can consume that a work stoppage of three or four months (in normal times) often saves an employer the necessity of ordering a forced lay-off, or a short-week schedule, in order to prevent his products from drowning the market. This was proven by the 116-day steel strike in 1959. Within six months after that strike the mills had to smother half their furnaces and furlough thousands of workers. As a result of this executive action, voluntary on the part of management (by contrast to the strike), by the end of 1960 the slackness of market demand had caused a loss of tonnage produced which was almost equal to that resulting from the dramatic strike of 1959 — over which so many journalistic tears had been wept because of loss of a mythical and unneeded production. Furthermore, in spite of the strike of 1959, steel-company earnings in 1960 increased 5 percent over the previous year — simply because steel is now able to show a profit when operating at one-third of capacity. Unfortunately, it also appears that automation reduces employment — along with job requirements for the old and traditional skills. In this connection there is the story about the automobile executive who proudly showed Walter Reuther a battery of newly installed and self-operated drilling machines. The executive said, "How are you going to collect dues from those fellows, Walter?" Reuther replied, "How are you going to sell them cars?"

If all this is true about automation, and it very well may be in spite of a number of overly optimistic reports, what can be done? There have been a number of suggestions. We could return to horse-and-buggy production methods. We could reduce the number of workers (in the face of increasing population) by lopping people off at both ends of the employment-age scale. We can provide longer schooling for youngsters through low-cost community colleges and state universities. We can require retirement at an earlier age — perhaps at fifty-five. GAW (Guaranteed Annual Wage), originally proposed — unsuccessfully — by Reuther in 1955, has been introduced in the private sector and it has been proposed, but not yet accepted, for everybody in the body politic.

Kaiser Steel and West Coast shipping pioneered with this new principle that carries blue-collar workers dramatically close to the promised land of lifetime jobs. This means that no regular employee should be jolted off the payroll because of labor savings made possible by automation. This principle is now in effect at the Kaiser Steel Plant at Fontana, California — where management can be just as efficient as it wants to be provided that no one is fired because a machine has taken his job. The Kaiser Plan was instituted after the steel strike of 1959. The job may be eliminated but the worker stays on the Kaiser payroll. He may be transferred to another job, but shrinkage in workers must be the result of normal turnover by death, retirement, or voluntary departure. Kaiser also brings the worker into the achievement and advantages of higher productivity. About one-third of every dollar the company saves through increased efficiency goes into a fund to be divided every month among workers. A. H. Raskin of the *New York Times* has noted that in spite of the substantially increased expense of these bonuses, the Kaiser Company remains enthusiastic about the plan. It has eliminated wildcat strikes; it has made employees hospitable to the introduction of new processes and machinery; it has encouraged employees to cut down on the waste of costly materials; and it has relieved the company and its customers of the necessity for the huge inventory pileups that regularly accompany the triennial contract negotiations of the rest of the steel industry. The same plan, with variations, has been introduced for Pacific coast longshoremen. It includes an assurance of full freedom for the employers to install new loading equipment, provided there is a simultaneous guarantee that no registered longshoremen will be fired. Every longshoreman must receive at least 35 hours' pay each week (a floor of $116) whether he works or not.

Reuther and the UAW had long noted that profit-sharing was a regular procedure for management through bonuses, and for stockholders through dividends. They insisted that the same method of incentive compensation should be applied to workers. Reuther put it this way:

> I say the day has to come in American industry that workers will get their basic wage and salary nailed down, and then they will stand in line with the stockholders and the executives next to the bake oven, and when that pie comes out they are going to get their share of that pie the same as everybody else.

It took a lot of futile attempts before many employers in the mass-production industries accepted such postwar innovations in collective bargaining as industry-financed pensions and supplemental unemployment benefits (SUB); yet private pension reserves exceeded $100 billion in 1968, and the SUB concept had moved so close to labor's dream of a guaranteed annual wage that laid-off GM workers drew up to 95 percent of their normal take-home pay for a full year of joblessness. In addition the profit-sharing approach can serve effectively as a brake on inflation — particularly if future union-negotiated plans are on the deferred-payment basis. These programs assign an employee a nest egg to be taken in the form of an increased pension or a lump-sum payment when and if he leaves the company. There are tax advantages for both worker and employer in such an arrangement, and it can combat inflation by tamping down immediate demand.

In 1968 Reuther took the UAW out of the AFL-CIO by withholding payment of per-capita dues for three months; under the constitution of the AFL-CIO this insubordination authorized suspension of a delinquent union by the parent organization. This was a serious loss to the federation; the UAW was its largest affiliate, and its withdrawal cost the AFL-CIO about 10 percent of its annual income and a considerable amount of political influence. Reuther and Meany had been feuding for years, particularly on civil rights and international affairs. For some time peacemakers like Arthur Goldberg and David Dubinsky had been successful in their counsel of patience to Reuther; they told him that time was on his side, that he would become president of the federation after Meany, who was thirteen years older than Reuther. By 1968 it seemed apparent that time was no longer on Reuther's side. Meany, in absolute control of the executive council, had made it plain that he would never retire in Reuther's favor. There was also increasing doubt that Reuther could be elected should Meany die. Labor no longer had the enthusiasm and devotion to causes that it had had in the 1930's — the enthusiasm and the causes in which Reuther still believed. He wanted to re-create the kind of union image that brought thousands of idealistic youngsters flocking into the old CIO at the time of the New Deal. But as A. H. Raskin has pointed out, there is a real question whether the leaders or the rank and file — in or out of the UAW — would support such an idealistic drive. For one thing, in 1967 better than half of the union-labor membership was more than forty years of age, and only 25 percent were less than thirty years old. There was also a great gulf between the social aspirations of a Reuther and the middle-class property values of much of the membership. This meant that, during the thirty years between the 1930's and the 1960's, labor's problem was not that it had failed but that it had been too successful. There was the quip that plumbers now earned so much money they no longer made house calls; by the 1960's almost half of AFL-CIO members were in the $7,500- to $15,000-a-year bracket. They lived in suburbs where they spent ten or more hours a week watching TV. They supported the welfare state by a large margin. The only theoretically labor-supported cause they frequently opposed in practice was open housing. In brief, by 1968 labor had become a full partner in the American establishment; it could hardly be expected to revolt against itself. Many union leaders were enraged when Reuther accused Meany of having made the federation the "complacent custodian of the status quo"; they *were* the status quo and were "making it big" with their country clubs and Cadillacs and large salaries. Reuther was asking for a spiritual revival and a sense of mission in the support of ideals — an uplift that had given labor *esprit de corps* and *élan* in the 1930's. Even if he had lived, by 1970 it did not appear that he was going to achieve either a spiritual revival or the presidency of the AFL-CIO.

To this point the discussion has centered on labor's point of view. Employers also had attitudes and convictions based on comparable self-interest, that is, to see how little, during most of our history, they could pay in wages and to ascertain how far they could go in keeping labor from organizing into unions. They utilized various methods in their fierce combat with labor. By their own devices and through the expenditures of their own money they employed the lockout, blacklist, ironclad oath, strikebreakers, and their own patriotic brainchild known as the American Plan. From public funds, and from the executive and judicial branches of government at various levels, they received valuable assistance from police, state militia, and the court-imposed injunction.

The lockout was the refusal by an employer to allow striking employees to enter his plant. It was obviously used to resist labor demands or to break strikes by importing new workers, and was the employer's counterpart to the strike. The blacklist was used by antiunion business firms to prevent the employment of union members; in the Anthracite Coal Strike of 1902, as an example, mine guards were armed not only with guns but also with flashlights and cameras — in order to secure pictures of strike leaders for later punitive action. The blacklist of human beings was the employer's counterpart to labor's boycott of goods. Ironclad oaths, sometimes known as "yellow-dog contracts," were agreements by which an employee contracted with his employer *not* to join a union. They were particularly prevalent and popular in the 1920's, and were enforced in the courts until invalidated by the Norris–La Guardia Anti-Injunction Act of 1932.

Strikebreakers of various kinds were furnished by an industry that was wholly a product of American capitalism, and was neither admired nor copied abroad. It was a vicious business that provided three types of strikebreakers: scabs, guards, and spies. The scab was a workman who refused to join or act with a labor union, and replaced the striker in his job. Left-wing novelist Jack London once described a scab as "a two-legged animal with a corkscrew soul, a waterlogged brain, and a backbone made of jelly and glue. Where others have hearts, he carried a tumor of rotten principles." The guards were hired to protect the scabs. Many of them were ex-gangsters from the underworld, with striking names: "Chowderhead" Cohen, "Boilermaker" Williams, "Stinkfoot" McVey. Quick on the trigger finger, they sometimes fired on each other — for the fun of it or to create disorders in order to continue their employment. The spies were sometimes called "missionaries." Their job was to break down the morale of the unions, and strikers, by spreading confusion and dissension among them. A favorite practice was to have the spy worm his way into the union and into an office therein. One spy, for example, managed to get himself elected secretary of the Hartford (Connecticut) Typewriter's local union. When he came to Hartford in 1934, the paid membership of the local was 2,500; under his biased stewardship, in less than one year it had dropped to 75. Because of the secrecy and mystery surrounding spies, there is an axiom that ultimately one needs spies to spy on spies. One of the amazing bits of testimony before the La Follette Committee of the U.S. Senate, which investigated labor and management practices in the 1930's, was that of a Lawrence Barker. At one time in 1936 he and four other officers of the UAW in the Fisher plant in Lansing, were on the Pinkerton payroll and were making daily reports to the Pinkerton office in Detroit. Through their efforts, he said, membership in the union dwindled until only the officers remained. Among other things, Barker reported that he and his colleagues had been instructed to oppose affiliation with the CIO and not to vote for FDR in 1936. Barker then brought his testimony to a dramatic climax by divulging that, soon after his employment by Pinkerton, he told the high officers of the UAW all about it — and that while the Pinkertons were paying him to spy on his fellow workers, he was actually reporting the Pinkerton activities to the UAW.

The most prominent companies providing strikebreakers, of various shapes and colors, were the Pinkerton, and the Burns, detective agencies. Less well-known, although it was the number-one strikebreaker of the 1930's, was a company run by Pearl Bergoff — a lad who outgrew his curls and girlish name to achieve this dubious distinction. He had been named Pearl by a mother disappointed in his sex; in the 1930's he would become the undisputed king of the strikebreakers. Lest one think that strikebreaking organizations were unique to the 1930's, it should be noted that Nathan Shefferman and a company known as Labor Relations Associates was active in the 1950's. In testimony before the successor to the La Follette Committee, the Senate Select Committee on Improper Activities in the Labor and Management Fields (otherwise known as the McClellan Committee because its chairman was the Senator from Arkansas), it developed that Shefferman had 1,100 clients, including Sears, Roebuck which paid him a quarter of a million dollars over a four-year period to break up unionization in the merchandizing company. It appeared that Shefferman was buying off Dave Beck and other labor leaders while working for Sears and other companies; a Sears executive would later confess that his company had engaged in "inexcusable, unnecessary and disgraceful antiunion activities." Sears was not the only corporation that patronized the Pinkertons and the Bergoffs and the Sheffermans. So did, *inter alia*, Alcoa, Westinghouse, Chase National Bank, the Pennsylvania Railroad, and the Waldorf Astoria Hotel. Before giving up the practice in 1937, General Motors had paid the Pinkertons almost half a million dollars for strikebreaking services.

The American Plan came into prominence during the 1920's, which were a rollicking good time for many businesses, and when the corporate euphoria was made no less salubrious by the friendly cooperation of the Harding and Coolidge administrations. There were two features to the American Plan, so-called patriotically by employers: the open shop and welfare capitalism. The open shop meant that there were to be no unions unless they were company unions. Because company unions almost always represented a "deal," this was the heyday of the racketeering unions — a period when union leaders sold their members down the river in the process of making deals with employers, with each other, and with gangsters (often the same gangsters with whom the employers were also making similar arrangements). Welfare capitalism, based on the idea that the employee was to look upon his employer much as sons long ago looked upon their fathers — *with* hope and *without* power — went overboard in the Depression of the 1930's, as employers were forced to withdraw the benefits granted paternally in the days of prosperity. These favors had been granted in the place of wage increases; they were profit-sharing schemes, employee stock ownership, industrial pensions, workers' health and recreation projects. While the Depression of the 1930's forced retrenchment or abandonment of these benefits, in many cases full dividends were still being paid to owners on common stock. In any case, reliance on welfare capitalism had proved, in the long run, to be a delusion for the laborer.

The partiality of police in labor disputes has been documented on many occasions. In 1919, at Duquesne, Pennsylvania, the moment labor leaders stepped into the town they were clapped into jail; the mayor boasted that no union could hold a meeting there even if Jesus Christ was the organizer. In 1933, at Homestead, Pennsylvania, Secretary of Labor Frances Perkins found that all the streets and parks and halls in the town were closed to her; the only place where she could meet with a committee of steel workers was in the U.S. post office. Probably the most spectacular use of police against workers was the famed Memorial Day Riot in Chicago in 1937. The evidence indicates that strikers and sympathizers left a mass meeting to engage in a demonstration before the main gate of the Republic Steel plant, with the object of inducing nonstriking workers to come out and join the union. Three blocks from the plant they were met by a large body of uniformed city policemen whose commanding officers ordered the marchers to turn back. After a parley lasting two or three minutes the police, without any warning, opened fire with pistols and gas grenades; eight of the demonstrators were killed or fatally wounded by pistol bullets administered by the police; nearly one hundred others were injured — but no policeman was shot and none was seriously hurt. Subsequent evidence indicated that the police pursued the fleeing and terror-stricken demonstrators, that seven of those killed were shot in the back, that one literally had his brains beaten out, and that two men were allowed to bleed to death. The chief of police tried to explain the fact that the demonstrators were shot from behind by stating that they had been shot from behind by fellow marchers who had really aimed at the police but had missed their mark. This testimony was repudiated by the La Follette Committee of the U.S. Senate; it produced a report showing that the bullets taken from the dead men were identical with those used by the Chicago police, and that the tear-gas bombs were furnished by the Republic Steel Corporation.

The use of state militia on behalf of management is well illustrated by two *causes célèbres* that happened to occur in 1892 (the Homestead Strike and the Coal Creek Rebellion), and by the famous Ludlow Massacre in 1914. The strike of the Amalgamated Association of Iron, Steel and Tin Workers against the Homestead Works of the Carnegie Steel Company, whose president was Henry Clay Frick, was one of the most bitterly fought industrial disputes in U.S. labor history. The public appeared to be on labor's side in the encounter; in 1890 Carnegie had asked for an increase in the tariff on steel in order to maintain the high standard of American living and now, in a period of prosperity two years later, he ordered a wage reduction. The Republican party was so concerned about the potential effect of this contradiction on the presidential election of 1892 that it sent its vice-presidential candidate, Whitelaw Reid, to appeal to Carnegie and Frick. The effort was in vain; in terms reminiscent of U. S. Grant, Frick replied that he would crush the union, "If it takes all summer. . . . Yes, even my life itself." He had a twelve-foot board fence, topped by barbed wire, erected around the plant; there were loopholes every twenty-five feet. Sardonically, the workers dubbed it "Fort Frick." Frick also contracted with the Pinkerton Agency in Pittsburgh for an armed force of 316 men, at five dollars per day per man, to be towed up the Monongahela River in early July 1892, where they were to be placed inside the works to protect it. The Pinkerton force was typical of agency guards, which meant that it left much to be desired; there was a hard core of Pinkerton regulars but the majority consisted of unemployed, drifters, some hoodlums, a few out-and-out criminals, and — curiously — several college lads trying to earn a little money during the summer.

The Pinkertons were confronted by 3,800 strikers who were well armed and in an ugly mood. A unique kind of double lockout soon developed: the company could not operate its mighty plant and the workers could not work. Violence occurred when the Pinkertons came up the river from Pittsburgh in two scows, which were run aground near the river entrance to the plant. Furthermore *The Little Bull*, a tug which was towing the scows, soon had to depart; it was raked with such a withering fire from the workers on the bank that it barely made it back to Pittsburgh, with the captain trying to steer while lying on his stomach. On the bank the strikers accumulated rifles, sticks of dynamite, and hauled two small cannon into position. One of the latter was a relic from Antietam; its first shot tore a hole in the roof of the outer barge but every subsequent shot went long, and when a good union man sitting innocently on a pile of beams was beheaded by a stray cannon ball, the artillery was eliminated from the workers' arsenal. The strikers then poured barrels of oil into the river and set the stream afire. Their tug gone, the Pinkertons were trapped below deck in the scow that was farthest from shore. A few managed to dive into the river and swim to the other shore but this was hazardous; the workers shot at the Pinkertons who so exposed themselves. Under the circumstances they did the only sensible thing: they shoved a white flag through a porthole (the workers immediately shot it to ribbons), surrendered, gave up their arms and ammunition in return for a promise of safe conduct back to Pittsburgh by train. But the workers, many of whom were foreigners with little knowledge of English, were angry—and union leaders had great difficulty in controlling them. As one historian describes the incident, the workers' wives "screaming in twenty-two languages and dialects, . . . grabbed their kids and took to the near hills, the better to see their men shot down." When the Pinkertons came ashore they were again attacked and were badly beaten on their way to the train. Hardly a man among the Pinkertons avoided injury; the leaders of the union tried to protect them but the workers, particularly the Slavs, were in favor of murdering all of the invaders. The death toll was ultimately nine strikers and seven Pinkertons; some forty strikers and twenty Pinkertons were shot. Labor appeared to have won the battle, but six days later the state militia came in and broke the strike. Wages in all Carnegie mills were cut even more than Frick had originally contemplated; the average slash was 50 percent. The twelve-hour day in a seven-day week was enforced with a vengeance and many union leaders were blacklisted. Company profits went up spectacularly, reaching $40 million in 1900 as against $4.3 million in 1891.

The Homestead Strike ultimately had an enormous impact on the Republican party, labor, management, and the American public. The Republicans lost the presidential election of 1892, in part because of a bad image reflected from the Homestead encounter. The Amalgamated, in November, its treasury empty, announced the end of the strike. Those members not blacklisted went back to their jobs as nonunion workers. Frick won the strike; he shattered unionism so completely that steel would not be organized by labor until the 1930's. The lasting reaction of the public was against men of the Frick mentality who were completely dedicated to profits at the expense of human values. Memories of the Homestead Strike helped leaders like Theodore Roosevelt to make plain that—if some restraints were not placed on the money-driving of the more ruthless segments of management — the whole American system of free economy might well give way to some variety of socialism.

The Coal Creek Rebellion of 1891–1892 represents an interesting example of a situation in which the use of militia boomeranged against both the company involved and the state. The Tennessee Coal, Iron and Railroad Company — later to become a subsidiary of U.S. Steel — had a combination lockout and strike in its coal mines in eastern Tennessee; the company leased some 1,500 convicts from the state of Tennessee, paying about 20¢ a day or $50 a year for the use of each ablebodied worker. There was a standard practice in the South of leasing convict labor and of keeping the penitentiaries full in order to make it possible. This was accomplished through so-called "pig" laws; they defined as grand larceny the theft of any property worth $10 or more, or of any cattle or hogs regardless of their price. Violations brought a prison term up to five years; after the passage of these laws the population of penitentiaries increased remarkably. Naturally, with such cheap labor huge profits were possible. In Tennessee at Coal Creek in 1892 the locked-out miners, Negro and white, aided by farmers from the surrounding hills, drove out the company guards, burned prison stockades throughout eastern Tennessee, and released the convicts, who escaped to the mountains. The governor sent in militia; after a pitched battle the entire force of soldiers — including a general, a colonel, and a captain — were captured, disarmed, and promised never to return. Many of the soldiers were easy to "capture" because of their open sympathy with the strikers; before the affair was over a dozen prisons had been burned to the ground and more than 1,000 convicts had been freed.

Almost a quarter of a century later, in Colorado, there was the incident known as the Ludlow Massacre. It came out of a long strike of the UMW against the Colorado Fuel and Iron Company. In 1914 the militia was called in; a detachment of this force attacked a tent village of strikers, capturing and setting the camp afire. In the encounter two strikers and a boy were killed. The major tragedy occurred the next day; two women and eleven children, seeking escape from the militia in a cave, were smothered to death. The Ludlow Massacre turned the strikers into avengers, and open warfare was waged. Strikers attacked the militia; they also attacked and destroyed half a dozen mine properties; for a week southern Colorado was a battlefield. Ultimately the governor called the federal troops and peace was restored. The major stockholder of the Colorado Fuel and Iron Company was John D. Rockefeller, who came in for bitter criticism on the part of an aroused public. But when President Wilson proposed arbitration, the company refused, and smothered the strike so successfully that the UMW was forced to call it off. Rockefeller then called in William Lyon Mackenzie King, former Canadian minister of labor and later a long-time premier, to form a plan of "friendly cooperation." His work resulted in the inevitable company union, and ushered in that favorite managerial device.

It was the executive branch of government, largely in the persons of mayors and governors, which frequently brought police and state militia to the support of management in labor disputes. For the same end, it was the judicial branch that employed the injunction as a device to break strikes. What the judges did was to issue an order enjoining or restraining the workers from doing so many things, on the ground that property might be damaged, that labor could not carry on a strike with any chance of success. Violation of an injunction is normally contempt of court; in such cases the judge, against whom the contempt was shown, can fine and imprison at will — without trial by jury. This action can be both severe and punitive.

The best example of the successful use of the injunction against labor is found in the historic Pullman Strike of 1894. The strike involved two companies or organizations on the management side (the Pullman Palace Car Company, and the railroad General Managers' Association), and one for labor (the American Railway Union). The strike involved four individuals prominently: Eugene V. Debs and John Peter Altgeld on the side of labor, Richard Olney and Grover Cleveland on the side of management. The Pullman Palace Car Company, actually controlled by the merchant-prince Marshall Field, was reputed to run a model town (Pullman, now part of Chicago) for working people. Widely advertised as a paragon of industrial benevolence, the town was actually lacking in conveniences, and was used by the company as an instrument for social control and for draining the laborer's wages; it was a company town that came as close to being a feudal estate as was possible in an industrial age. The blunt and realistic Mark Hanna thought George Pullman (who had developed the first modern sleeping car) to be a fool and scoffed at the idea that the suburb of Pullman was a model town; he advised admirers to go and live in the area, and said they would find it paid a profit to the owners. The company expended some $5 million a year in wages, at an average of $600 per worker, but contrived to get most of it back because the company owned the town. The workers lived in Pullman houses, traded at Pullman stores, used Pullman gas and water, patronized the Pullman theater and park. Despite the depression following the Panic of 1893, the company did well enough to maintain officers' salaries and to pay almost $3 million in dividends in 1894, amounting to 8 percent on an exaggerated capitalization; at the same time the wages of workers were cut on five different occasions (a total of almost 25 percent) and there was no reduction in rent. The result was a strike — followed by a lockout.

At this point Eugene V. Debs appeared onstage. He was born in Terre Haute, Indiana, and had been a close friend of James Whitcomb Riley and Eugene Field — two poets of the Midwest, sometimes known as the Valley of Democracy. In his early days Debs had been a railroad fireman, and had become a secretary-treasurer of the Locomotive Firemen, an AFL craft union. At this point he had become disgusted with the weakness of the craft union and had established his own industrial one — to be called the American Railway Union, to which anyone working around a railroad could belong. In 1893 Debs had conducted a successful strike against the Great Northern Railroad. This was so impressive that railroad workers flocked to his union; its membership rose to 150,000 — greater than the membership of the four railroad brotherhoods, which had come to regard themselves as the Establishment in rail circles. Both management and the craft unions feared that if Debs went on with his successes they could only lose. They therefore contrived to destroy him in the Pullman Strike of 1894. At the height of that crisis Debs appealed to Gompers of the AFL for help, and was turned down.

The American Railway Union, controlled by Debs and sympathetic with the locked-out workers in the Pullman plant, ordered its members to stop handling Pullman cars unless the company submitted the dispute to arbitration. At this point the American Railway Union ran into conflict with the General Managers' Association, made up of representatives of the twenty-four railroads that ran into Chicago. This association represented capital — $2 billion worth of it. It ordered the discharge of any worker who cut a Pullman car from a train, but the American Railway Union was not intimidated. Every time a worker was fired for refusing to handle a Pullman car, the entire train crew would quit. By the end of July 1894 the strike had become general, and every railroad in the Midwest was affected.

At this point the General Managers' Association was resolved to break Debs and the strike. In order to do so they had to avoid asking the governor of Illinois, John Peter Altgeld, whom they disliked, to furnish militia — because they were afraid that state militia would be impartial. They decided to rely on federal marshals and troops, who might be more partial to their interests — and so turned out to be. To get these reinforcements they needed a federal issue. They invoked it by importing strikebreakers from Canada, and secretly instructing them to connect U.S. mail cars to Pullman cars — so that when strikers cut out the Pullman cars, they could be accused of interfering with the U.S. mails. Because U.S. mail cars were now ostensibly involved, the General Managers' Association asked the Attorney General of the United States, Richard Olney, for federal marshals.

Olney was a former railroad lawyer and was a member of several railroad boards. He was also the strong man of the second Cleveland Administration. He authorized 3,400 U.S. deputy marshals, who were unusual because they were selected by the General Managers' Association, and were paid by it. They were sworn in by the U.S. Government and served both it and management. Many of the deputies so hired, perhaps by design, were thugs, thieves, and ex-convicts. At this point, not surprisingly, violence entered the conflict and some railroad property was destroyed by *agents provocateurs*. Debs implored his men not to commit violence. Later Mayor Hopkins of Chicago, Governor Altgeld of Illinois, and a Federal Investigating Commission appointed by Cleveland castigated the General Managers' Association and exculpated the American Railway Union from the charge of provoking violence. This exoneration came too late to help labor, for by that time the strike had been broken.

Now that violence had occurred the General Managers' Association asked the federal government to assist in two additional ways. The first was through the dispatch of federal troops. One would have thought that 3,400 federal deputies in Chicago would have been able to handle the situation (plus the possibility of state militia), but the railroads asked President Cleveland to send federal troops to restore order and to protect both the mails and interstate commerce. Cleveland did so; he was reported to have said that if it took every federal dollar and every federal soldier to deliver one postcard in Chicago, that postcard would be delivered. He sent 2,000 troops from the U.S. Army to Chicago.

This happened to represent an impressive extension of federal authority, since Governor Altgeld of Illinois had not asked for the troops. He insisted that the state militia could handle the situation; the central point, however, was that management had never asked for state militia. Altgeld was furious at President Cleveland, protested the invasion, and asked for the immediate withdrawal of federal troops from active duty in the state of Illinois. His protest came to nothing.

The railroads also asked Attorney General Olney whether they could proceed against the strikers under the Sherman Antitrust Act on the ground that the American Railway Union was a conspiracy in restraint of trade. Olney replied in the affirmative. The result was that a federal court issued a "blanket" injunction restraining the union from obstructing the carriage of mail, destroying property, and particularly, using threats or persuasion on any railroad workers to keep them from performing their duties. This latter prohibition in reality outlawed strikes, picketing, and boycotts.

The American Railway Union continued the strike, in the face of the injunction, with the result that Debs and hundreds of strikers were cited for contempt and jailed; in the case of Debs it was for six months. The strike was irretrievably broken. Debs's defense, which was unsuccessful, was conducted by Clarence Darrow. After his half year in jail Debs emerged a martyr, and was welcomed by a mass meeting of more than 100,000 admirers. He was not a Socialist when he entered that prison, and he was not one when he came out — but he was on the way to becoming one. Victor Berger, the Austrian-American and Socialist who later controlled Milwaukee and was elected to Congress, brought books to Debs in jail; among them were *Das Kapital* and Bellamy's *Looking Backward*. In 1896 Debs voted for Democrat William J. Bryan, but before long was running himself for the Presidency on the Socialist ticket, and in 1920, again in jail, would campaign for this office for the fifth time, piling up more than 900,000 votes.

Labor at once began a campaign against the labor injunction. It had two prime arguments against it: Olney's "Gatling gun on paper" was a wrong interpretation of the Sherman Act and it was unfair because there was no trial by jury when men were found in contempt of court. In such cases the judge acted as prosecutor, judge, and jury — a holdover from the English common law and the day, long past, when the judge was the personal representative of the king — and any criticism of the judge was a criticism of the sovereign. Labor agreed with Finley Peter Dunne when he put these words in the mouth of Mr. Dooley: "I care not who makes th' law iv th' nation if I can get out an injunction." In 1914 labor was to believe, temporarily, that it had achieved a Magna Charta in certain provisions of the Clayton Act which exempted labor from antitrust laws and limited injunctions in two ways: they could be issued only where irreparable damage (presumably defined as loss of life) was imminent, and there was provision for trial by jury in contempt cases — except where the contempt was committed in the presence of the judge. But conservative federal courts of the 1920's interpreted the Clayton Act away, and its labor provisions became a dead letter. Labor's first real triumph came with the passage of the Norris–La Guardia Act of 1932, which specifically forbade injunctions to prevent strikes, boycotts, and picketing — a prohibition that was to hold for fifteen years. Then in 1947 the Taft-Hartley Act dramatically swept away most of the gains labor had made in regard to injunctions. The use of the injunction was revived, even encouraged, in secondary boycotts, where injunctions were made mandatory. A secondary boycott is one involving a secondary employer who is attacked, by strike or other economic pressure, as a way of punishing the primary employer. Debs's move against Pullman in 1894 had been a perfect example of a secondary boycott.

In strikes imperiling the national health and safety the President can seek an injunction in federal court to restrain a union from striking for eighty days. Such requests from the President have never been denied; by 1960 this option had been used on sixteen occasions by Presidents Truman and Eisenhower.

National legislation on wages, employment, and collective bargaining is of recent origin, beginning essentially with the National Recovery Act of 1933 and extending through the Wagner Act of 1935, the Fair Labor Standards Act of 1938, the National War Labor Board during World War II, and the Landrum-Griffin Act of 1958. Section 7a of the National Recovery Act (NRA) established for the first time, by federal law, the right of *all* workers in interstate commerce to organize and bargain collectively. The principle itself was not new. During the First World War, a National War Labor Board, on which Franklin Delano Roosevelt had served, developed the doctrine that workers were entitled to choose their own representatives by majority vote. What Section 7a of NRA did was to give the tendencies of twenty years explicit legal status, by extending the same right of collective bargaining in peacetime to *all* workers in interstate commerce.

In the beginning labor hailed Section 7a as a great triumph. John L. Lewis issued posters throughout the mining areas of the nation, proclaiming that "President Roosevelt Wants You to Join the Union." Employers were worried, and called the entire effort "collective bludgeoning." Their concern was unnecessary; in the long run labor got little from the act. It had a scant voice in drawing up the codes which were vital under the NRA. In addition corporations managed to circumvent the act by establishing company unions — with the balloting taking place under company supervision and without opportunity for debate. By 1935 — two years after the NRA was passed — 43 percent of industry had no union representation, 27 percent had company unions, and a minority of 30 percent had independent unions. By this time labor was calling the NRA the "National Run Around" and was glad to see it killed by the Supreme Court in the Schechter Case (1935).

The Wagner Act (the National Labor Relations Act of 1935) was much more important. It was named after one of the great labor statesmen in the history of the United States, Robert Ferdinand Wagner (1877–1949). Born in Germany he had arrived in the United States with his family when he was eight, and grew up in a poor environment in New York City. He managed to graduate from City College of New York in 1898, nine years after Bernard Baruch was awarded a diploma by the same institution. With a law degree from the New York Law School he attached himself to Tammany Hall, and served in the New York State Senate (1910–1918) where he was noted for his investigations of factory conditions.* As a justice in the New York State Supreme Court (1919–1926) he did much to protect the rights of labor. From 1927 almost to his death in 1949 he served in the Senate in Washington, where he was one of the

---

* Wagner and Al Smith are prime examples of Tammany's realization that distinguished and popular candidates at the top of the ticket carry into office the judges, sheriffs, and local legislators who mean the life or death of a machine. Hymie Shorenstein, a Brooklyn district leader a half century ago, was once confronted by a worried assembly candidate who had not received the funds he needed to campaign actively. Shorenstein calmed him: "You see the ferryboats come in? You see them pull into the slip? You see the water suck in behind? And when the water sucks in behind the ferryboat, all kinds of dirty garbage comes smack into the slip with the ferryboat? Go home. Al Smith is the ferryboat. This year, you're the garbage."

leaders in directing New Deal legislation concerning the NRA, the National Labor Relations Act, Social Security, and the extension of federal housing. In the light of later praise for the law, it is strange to note that FDR was actually cool toward the Wagner Act — and that Wagner put the legislation through Congress almost single-handedly. The act diminished the causes of labor disputes and the number of strikes by promoting equality of bargaining power between employees and employers — by placing restrictions on employers. The restrictions on employers were three in number: they could not dominate independent unions, that is, they could not establish company unions; they could not refuse to bargain collectively with unions; and they could not dismiss an employee for belonging to a union — a legislative decree aimed lethally against the ironclad oath or "yellow-dog contract." To make certain that these new principles were enforced, a brand-new federal administrative agency was established. It was the National Labor Relations Board.

There were three results from the Wagner Act, only one of which was anticipated — the opposition of employers to the act. The unforeseen consequences were a severe siege of sitdown strikes, and the Roosevelt Court-packing scheme. Employers counted on the Supreme Court to declare the Wagner Act unconstitutional, and in the meantime refused to bargain collectively with independent unions. They did so on the basis of advice from their lawyers who decided in advance, and unilaterally, that the Wagner Act was unconstitutional; these legal cognoscenti were later horrified when the Supreme Court failed to agree with their *a priori* decision. Earl F. Reed, chief counsel of the Weirton Steel Company, wrote a report for the Lawyer's Committee of the Liberty League — a favorite right-wing organization in the 1930's. Reed stated that employers need not obey the Wagner Act; he opined that "When a lawyer tells a client that a law is unconstitutional — it is then a nullity and he need no longer obey the law."

The antagonism of employers to the act was general, but was particularly bitter from Ford and Little Steel (especially Tom Girdler of Republic Steel). Henry Ford had been a fine technician, and in the 1930's was turning out V-8 automobiles — but his labor relations clung to the Model-T period. He was so opposed to unions that he brought into the River Rouge plant the underworld of Detroit to perform spy work. They were organized by a fellow named Harry Bennett, a prizefighter who had been in the U.S. Navy in World War I. Bennett used a Detroit gang, about 800 of them, known as the Angelo Caruso gang. They were the storm troops in the Ford plants, and made no pretense of working but merely kept order — through terror. The Ford workers became so afraid that during lunch hours they would shout at the top of their voices about baseball scores lest they be suspected of talking unionism. Every man suspected of union sympathies was fired immediately, usually under the framed charge of "starting a fight." Even lunch boxes and clothes — supposedly guarded in lockers — were investigated for evidence of union literature. In Little Steel, Girdler was the leader. He had once run a so-called model town in Aliquippa (Pennsylvania), which sociologists called the Siberia of America. In 1937 his Republic Steel Company had supplies of tear and vomit gas worth almost $80,000; it was described as the largest buyer of such supplies, except for the government, in the United States. In the same year Youngstown Sheet and Tube (another company in the "Little Steel" group) had, as part of its industrial assets, 8 machine guns, 369 rifles, 190 shotguns, and 450 revolvers. Senator La Follette was to declare that the arsenals of these two steel companies "would be adequate equipment for a small war."

The wave of sitdown strikes that followed the enactment of the Wagner Act was surprising. In December 1936 the UAW asked GM to bargain, and received a negative answer. Employees in a Cleveland plant refused to operate their machines, but also refused to vacate the factory. This "sitdown" technique had spread to all the main plants of GM by New Year's Day, 1937. There was no mistake about it — sitdown strikes afforded a means of getting around strikebreakers. With laborers in possession of the plant, they could not be menaced by scabs, guards, or spies; management was more willing to negotiate because of the danger of sabotage; the solidarity of workers was maintained because they were all together in a small space; and the situation was comfortable, compared with picket lines outside a plant in the winter months. Inside the buildings the strikers wrote songs and sang them lustily.

General Motors believed, quite understandably, that agencies of law should be used on their side to eject the sitdown strikers as revolutionary trespassers on private property — which the strikers certainly were. On 2 January 1937 GM received, from Judge Edward Black of the Genesee County circuit court in Flint, an injunction ordering the strikers to evacuate two plants in that city. The strikers ignored the injunction, but both Black and his writ were discredited a few days later when it was revealed that the Flint judge held $219,900 of GM stock. Governor Frank Murphy of Michigan, a New Deal Democrat who feared bloodshed, refused to order the state militia to enforce the injunction by evicting the workers. He refused largely because of a dramatic intervention by John L. Lewis, president of the CIO. Murphy had intended to declare a state of insurrection and order the National Guard to evict the workers. The governor took a copy of his order to Lewis in his Detroit hotel in an eleventh-hour effort to get him to end the strike. After Lewis had refused, Murphy asked him what he would do if the guard were called out. Lewis replied:

You want my answer, sir? I give it to you. Tomorrow morning, I shall personally enter General Motors plant Chevrolet No. 4. I shall order the men to disregard your order. I shall then walk up to the largest window in the plant, open it, divest myself of my outer raiment, remove my shirt and bare my bosom. Then when you order your troops to fire, mine will be the first breast those bullets will strike.

And as my body falls from that window to the ground, you listen to the voice of your grandfather [he had been hanged in Ireland by the British for rebellion] as he whispers in your ear, "Frank, are you sure you are doing the right thing?"

Color draining from his face and his body quivering, the governor left the room. Shortly thereafter Murphy told his friend Mrs. Fielding H. Yost: "I am not going to do it. I'm not going down in history as 'bloody Murphy!' If I sent those soldiers right in on the men there's no telling how many would be killed. It would be inconsistent with everything I have ever stood for in my whole political life."

Later evidence also indicates that Murphy, at the outbreak of the strike, in all probability held 1,650 shares of GM stock, with a market value of more than $100,000. One wonders, with Professor Sidney Fine, if the UAW would have sought to discredit Murphy — as it had succeeded in discrediting Judge Black — had it known that the Michigan governor held this stock.

By early 1937 sitdown strikes spread to the rubber plants in Akron and to the Chrysler plants in Michigan. On 11 February 1937 GM capitulated, recognizing the UAW as the sole bargaining agent of its employees. It was a turning point in the history of modern labor unionism, and inaugurated a series of successes for the CIO. The victory was achieved by illegal strike techniques, but they represented a case of "fighting fire with fire." These practices were the direct result of the initial refusal of many employers to obey the Wagner Act — premised on the supposition that the Supreme Court would declare it unconstitutional.

This labor unrest was probably the most pressing reason for FDR's campaign to pack the Court. He believed that his Judicial Reorganization Bill was the best way to secure enforcement of the Wagner Act, as well as to end the dangerous outburst of labor militancy. He lost, in part because the Supreme Court upheld the Wagner Act on 12 April 1937 — in a famous 5 to 4 decision — resulting, according to one version, from a last-minute determination of Justice Roberts (after some prodding from Chief Justice Hughes) to vote with the majority. This was the fortuitous vote claimed to have been the "switch in time that saved Nine." Because of this decision Girdler ultimately lost before the NLRB, was ordered to reinstate 5,000 laborers with back pay, and to give up his company union. Ford lost, had to reinstate the employees he had fired, heard the NLRB refer to his methods as "ruthless" and "savage." * Ultimately labor lost,

---

* More than two decades later management made a last stand against collective bargaining during the longest major strike in the history of U.S. labor struggles. In April 1954 the United Automobile Workers began a strike against the Kohler Com-

too, in regard to the sitdown techniques. In the Fansteel case of 1939, by a 5 to 2 decision, the Supreme Court declared the sitdown practice illegal, and denied to the NLRB the right to compel the reinstatement of sitdown strikers who had been fired. The Court said that the NLRB had exceeded its authority; Chief Justice Hughes read the majority decision and said, in brief, that to justify such conduct because of unfair labor practices on the part of capital would put a premium on the use of force instead of legal remedies and would "subvert the principles of law and order which lie at the foundation of society." He added that "the employees had the right to strike, but they had no license to commit acts of violence and to seize their employer's plant."

The Fair Labor Standards Act of 1938, known also as the Wages and Hours Law, represented the first permanent legislation of its type enacted on a national scale. Basically it did three things:

Put an initial floor under wages at 25¢ an hour. This meant, in 1938, a guarantee of a minimum wage of $11 per week — far less than what was needed for a minimum standard of living. Even so, prevailing rates were so low in that year that a million and a half Americans had their wages *raised* to $11 a week. At the time the law was passed, about 1 percent of the workers to whom it applied were discharged by employers who were unable or were unwilling to obey; most of the workers discharged were in the South. By 1955 the minimum wage had been raised by Congress to $1, and by 1968 — the thirtieth anniversary of the law — the minimum wage had reached $1.60.

Put a ceiling on hours. This was to be 44 hours per week to begin with, was to reach 40 hours by 1940. Where overtime pay (at higher rates) was required, this provision could have real significance; this was soon to be the case for numerous workers in the tight labor situation during World War II.

Wiped out child labor in interstate commerce, making unnecessary the proposed Child Labor Amendment to the Constitution, which had been before the states for many years but had not been ratified. The Fair Labor Standards Act took care of the situation by prohibiting shipment in interstate commerce of goods produced in establishments where "oppressive child labor conditions

---

pany, the nation's second-largest manufacturer of plumbing equipment — mostly bathroom fixtures. The strike lasted 6 years, 4 months and 27 days. During the struggle there was considerable violence and name-calling; Herbert V. Kohler, Sr., the chief executive of the company and the brother and uncle of governors of Wisconsin, called Walter P. Reuther a "Moscow-trained socialist," and Reuther called Kohler "the most reactionary, antilabor, immoral employer in America." A Senate investigating committee disclosed that the company had purchased riot guns, rifles, pistols, tear gas, and machine guns — which were not actually used against the strikers. Reuther conceded that some of the union's tactics had been "reprehensible." For Kohler the chief issue of the strike was whether his employees had the right to decide for themselves whether to join the union. He became a symbol of embattled individualism to much of the business world; the "Old Timers' Council" of the National Association of Manufacturers named him "Man of the Year" in 1958. Ultimately the NLRB ruled that the company had prolonged the strike through unfair labor practices and the Kohler Company paid $4.5 million in back pay.

were present." This was defined as the employment of any minors under six-teen — and those between sixteen and eighteen in hazardous employment.

Unfortunately one cannot say that the act provided fair labor standards for American labor as a whole because only a little more than a third of the American labor force is covered; the national law applies only to those employees producing goods for interstate commerce. The other two-thirds is inadequately protected by state legislation. A few states come close to meeting the federal hourly rate, and Alaska had a minimum "for most industries" of $1.50 an hour as early as 1961. A quarter of a century after the enactment of the national standards on wages and hours, however, twenty-one states provided no wage floor whatever and in many others laws were inadequate. Arkansas, as an example, was covered by a mini-mum-wage act passed in 1915; it solemnly forbade paying less than 16¢ an hour — or $1.25 a day. The *New York Times* commented editorially, "It is not only unfair but inhuman not to give all our low-paid workers the equal protection of the laws."

During World War II the War Labor Board (WLB) had tremendous power and responsibility because of the no-strike pledge by labor. Shortly after Pearl Harbor labor leaders *volunteered* the no-strike pledge *provided* wage increases kept up with the rising cost of living. This pledge meant that during the war the normal processes of collective bargaining were suspended and that it was the WLB that decided the terms and conditions of employment. The board was a tripartite one of twelve — representing labor, management, and the public — with four members from each seg-ment of the economy. The public members obviously had to perform a difficult and critical role of both mediation and arbitration; they were able men and carried out their responsibilities with virtuosity and effective-ness.

Two of the decisions of the War Labor Board were basic: maintenance of union membership and the Little Steel Formula. Maintenance of union membership was granted by the Board in the International Harvester Case (April 1942). It required union members to remain union members for the life of any contract negotiated in their behalf; they were subject to discharge from their employment if at any time they failed to maintain good union standing. This assured labor that management would not be able to take advantage of the no-strike policy to destroy labor unionism. The Little Steel Formula of July 1942 concerned wage increases. The employees of the Little Steel Companies asked for an increase amounting to a dollar a day, on the ground that *before* the anti-inflation measures of the Office of Price Administration (OPA) became effective in May 1942 prices had increased that much. The problem before the board was to ascertain just how much prices had really increased between January 1941 (a time of relative stability) and May 1942 (when OPA price controls went into effect). The board decided that the increase of prices in the period was 15 percent; this amounted to 44¢ a day for Little Steel, not the dollar that had been asked. This became the Little Steel Formula that was applied to all demands for wage increases. Labor accepted it, stating that so long as the OPA was effective in keeping prices stable, it would have no quarrel with the formula. As it turned out OPA was quite effective, but prices did inch up. If January 1941 is considered the norm at 100, by May 1942 prices were at 115, and by January 1943 they were at 123.

The result of this imbalance was a few strikes, none of them sanctioned by either the AFL or the CIO. Most were "quickie" affairs, annoying but not terribly important. A few were major strikes; they were ordered by unions outside the jurisdiction of the AFL and the CIO. The brotherhoods struck the railroads, and the UMW struck the coal industry. John L. Lewis had been a party to the no-strike pledge but by 1943 had taken the UMW out of both the CIO and the AFL. The President saw to it that the government took over the operation, for necessary periods of time, of struck industries — the coal mines, the railroads, and in one exciting case Montgomery Ward, because the company refused to obey the WLB's directives (there was a dramatic and widely distributed photograph of board chairman Sewell Avery being carried out of the Montgomery Ward offices by U.S. soldiers). The War Labor Board met the crisis not by changing the Little Steel Formula on basic wages, but by granting fringe benefits instead. As an example, Lewis got portal-to-portal pay for the miners — travel time to and from the mine gate. This added $1.50 a day to wages. The railroad workers received additional emoluments in vacation pay. These fringe benefits were obviously disguised wage increases — whether they were called portal-to-portal pay, pay for vacations, bonuses, incentive payments, or generous health and insurance plans.

In spite of some strikes it can be said that labor cooperated very well during the Second World War *and* that the War Labor Board maintained their rights during the no-strike period. During previous wars labor had generally lost some of the status and power it had previously enjoyed.

The Full Employment Act of 1946 arose from contradictory fears and desires at the close of the Second World War. The public wanted demobilization of the armed forces, the reconversion of industry and agriculture to peacetime production, and an end to rationing and price controls. It was also haunted by the memory of the Great Depression — and the fact that it had been ended only by the extraordinary demands created by the war. There was genuine worry that a sudden reduction in governmental spending, plus the reappearance of millions of soldiers in the peacetime job market, might very well bring another gigantic economic slump. On the other hand there was the possibility that the shortage of civilian goods and the backlog of purchasing power dammed up during the war might very well create a runaway inflation. New Dealers remaining in President

Truman's Cabinet (particularly Henry Wallace), CIO leaders, and progressives wanted full employment — and proposed to ask Congress for the money to insure it. They did not get the funds but did achieve a statement of principles in the Full Employment Act of 1946. President Truman would say that the measure rejected laissez-faire, asserting for the first time that "our economy within reasonable limits will be what we make it, and that intelligent human action will shape our future."

The Full Employment Act of 1946, in actuality, did establish as a national policy the principle that the nation was never again to *permit* large-scale unemployment, and that it was the responsibility of the federal government to promote maximum employment. The act also created two new and important bodies, one in the Executive branch, and the other in Congress. The one in Congress was the Joint Committee on the Economic Report, which is responsible for proposing legislation. In the Executive Office it established the Council of Economic Advisors (CEA), appointed by the President. It consists of three experts who are to study the course of the economy and to make quarterly reports to the President and to the Congress — recommending action deemed necessary to insure full employment. On the basis of the CEA reports, in turn, the President is required to make an annual economic report — which in recent years has developed into one of the most valuable of state papers.

The Taft-Hartley Act of 1947 was named after two conservatives. Senator Robert Taft was the shy son of a President who graduated from Yale first in his class, and received his law degree from Harvard; although supported by the right wing of the Republican party he would lose the presidential nomination in 1952 to Dwight D. Eisenhower. Fred A. Hartley had represented New Jersey for almost two decades but was little known, except as a "good conservative Republican," until the act named for him was passed over President Truman's veto in 1947. The 80th Congress, controlled by the Republicans, placed him at the helm of the House Labor Committee, which amassed 2 million words of testimony that became the framework of the law; after its passage Hartley did not run for reelection, accepting instead a position as employer lobbyist for the Tool Owners' Association.

The purpose of the Taft-Hartley Bill was the opposite of that in the Wagner Act which Eric Goldman once called "probably the most bluntly anticorporation legislation the U.S. has ever known." The Wagner Act was designed to promote labor peace by placing restrictions on the employer. The Taft-Hartley Bill, the original draft of which appears to have been written largely by the National Association of Manufacturers and the U.S. Chamber of Commerce, was designed to promote labor peace by placing restrictions on labor; it was felt that the employer was no longer able to bargain on equal terms, and that the balance must be restored. Management would therefore call the Taft-Hartley measure "the act to free slave labor." Unions, on the other hand, would dub it the "Taft-Heartless Act" and the "slave-labor law." One thing was certain; the phraseology of the legislation was so complex that some sophisticates called it "the lawyer's full employment act of 1947."

One may very well wonder why a conservative labor law of this kind happened to be passed in 1947. Postwar periods have usually been characterized by reaction and conservatism, and the late 1940's were no exception. Wars traditionally end crusades for domestic reform simply because "the blast of the bugle drowns out the voice of the reformer." World Wars I and II blunted the impact of the New Freedom of Woodrow Wilson and the New Deal of Franklin D. Roosevelt. Furthermore, war increases the reputation and power of business leaders, who are sorely needed and who come out of the conflict with medals and profits for their effort. The confident business leader of 1946 in no way resembled his discredited colleague of 1932. Beyond the normal conservatism of postwar periods, labor was blamed — rightly or wrongly — after World War II for inflation because of the flurry of strikes. Victory found the economy dislocated, and frustration with wartime rigors and controls near the breaking point. Organized labor, whose wage demands had been tightly controlled for nearly four years, could be held back no longer. The right to strike now restored, there was a general walkout by the big unions — UAW, USWA, the packinghouse workers, the electrical workers; by the end of 1946 the total production time lost to strikes had tripled the previous annual record. Resulting wage hikes added to the pressure mounting within the business community for higher prices; finally, in the spring of 1946, Congress stripped the OPA of nearly all its power. In one month soon thereafter, 15 June to 15 July 1946, food prices soared nearly 15 percent — the largest monthly jump ever recorded by the BLS. Even so, industry could not catch up with the pent-up demand for autos, apartments, and a host of other scarce items; in desperation consumers turned to the black market, which flourished as it never had in wartime. Labor, of course, claimed that it was not responsible for all of these difficulties; it placed the blame on the purchasing power that had been dammed up during World War II, plus the precipitant end of price controls through OPA. The public, however, has little comprehension of terms such as purchasing power and economic controls, or the whys and wherefores of price indexes. It *can be* frustrated by strikes.

The Taft-Hartley Law contained new rights for employers, new prohibitions against labor, and new restrictions on the NLRB. It gave employers the right to sue unions; formerly union organizations (being unincorporated) were not subject to suit in courts of law. Now unions could be sued and fined if their members were found guilty of damaging property, or of violating a collective-bargaining contract. The act also gave employers the right to oppose unions. Under the Wagner Act any talk or other pressure by an employer against a particular union was prohibited as unfair; this provision of the Wagner Act was now voided on the ground that it was an infringement of freedom of speech. The act also placed a number of restrictions on labor. Both jurisdictional strikes and feather-bedding were outlawed. A sixty-day cooling-off period was required before any strike could occur. As we have seen, the act revived the labor injunction: it was mandatory in the case of secondary boycotts, sometimes known as sympathy strikes, and it was permissive (for an additional eighty-day cooling-off period) where the President found it necessary for the national health and safety. Finally — under the Taft-Hartley Act — the *closed* shop was outlawed, but the *union* shop was permitted. Under the closed shop an employer may not hire anyone who does not belong to a union. Under the union shop an employer may hire anyone he wishes — but the newly hired employee must join the union which has been recognized as the bargaining agent; the theory behind this obvious compromise was that the union shop might enable the employer to retain essential control over his hiring policy — a dubious assumption at best. The two co-authors of the bill, Messrs. Taft and Hartley, did not favor either the closed shop or the union shop; as died-in-the-wool conservatives they favored the open shop which employs union or nonunion labor — a halcyon situation for the management. Since they were unable to muster the votes for an endorsement of the open shop in federal legislation, they left the door ajar for state legislation. This was done through section 14b of the Taft-Hartley Act, which leaves open to states the right to pass laws restricting compulsory union membership; this section permits states to outlaw union shops even though the Taft-Hartley Act approves of them. Finally, the act placed new restrictions on the administration of the NLRB. In particular, it was denied the right to certify unions, as the bargaining agency within factories or industries, unless those unions filed financial statements and its officers took an anti-Communist oath.

The two most controversial sections of the Taft-Hartley Act have been Section 14b and the permissive eighty-day cooling-off period (by injunction) for which the President can ask in the case of strikes that imperil the national health and safety. Management wants states to pass open-shop or "right-to-work" laws; thus far nineteen states have done so, principally in the South and in the Rocky Mountain area. Labor is much opposed, and calls such legislation "right-to-wreck" and "right-to-shirk" laws. This is understandable, because there is no question that "right-to-work" laws keep wages low. Consider the situation in North and South Carolina, which have such laws. They rank thirteenth and fourteenth in the Union in the degree of their industrialization. On the other hand, in 1965 they ranked fiftieth and forty-sixth in income by wage-hour among the states of the Union; obviously North Carolina — in the position of No. 50 — could go no lower. In connection with injunctions temporarily stopping a strike that imperils the national health and safety, the proposals for reform would change the eighty-day period from one of possible mediation to one of mandatory arbitration. The current act provides that the President shall appoint a fact-finding board of inquiry which will investigate and make recommendations for settlement of the strike — during the eighty-day period. These recommendations are not mandatory; either side can turn them down. One side, or both, did so in five of the nineteen cases in which the emergency (eighty-day) injunction was used from 1947 to 1963 — more than 20 percent of the time. Bernard Baruch had once proposed a full-fledged tripartite court — with representatives of labor, management, and the public — of labor-management relations. Its decisions would be final and binding in cases sent to the court after all other possibilities under the Taft-Hartley Act had been exhausted. The Baruch proposal was a blood brother to one for an even more comprehensive Industrial Court put forward in 1946 by former mayor Fiorello La Guardia of New York. He was convinced that the rash of strikes after VJ day was bad, and that compulsory arbitration was necessary in many of them. He thought too many were waged at the public expense, and that the public should make certain that they did not continue but were settled for the greater good of all concerned.

The Landrum-Griffin Act of 1959 (also called the Labor-Management Reporting and Disclosure Act) grew out of the report of the McClellan Committee, which had specified the undemocratic practices of some labor leaders; and was passed because of the importance in the 1950's of the coalition of conservative Republicans of the North and conservative Democrats from the South. The act featured a bill of rights for labor, a requirement for full public reports, and safeguards in regard to the election of union officers. The bill of rights was aimed at union dictators. It provided that union members should be able to attend meetings and to speak and vote therein, that dues and assessments could be levied only by a majority vote in a secret ballot, that no fines or expulsions could be levied by officers against union members unless written charges had been proffered and there had been time for defense and a fair hearing, and that members were entitled to a copy of any collective-bargaining contract. The act also required a full and public report — from both unions and employers — on membership, salaries, labor-relations budgets, and any collaboration between union leaders and management that constituted the kind of conflict of interest known to exist in "sweetheart contracts." This report to the Secretary of Labor is available to the public. On elections the Landrum-Griffin Act provided that national unions must elect their officers by secret ballot on ample notice within every five-year period, and that locals must do so within every three-year period. The Act also provided that Communists, and persons convicted of crimes, could not serve as officers or agents of unions for five years after leaving the Communist party or being released from prison.

When the Landrum-Griffin measure was before Congress representatives of management and labor actually had fistfights in congressional waiting rooms, Capitol corridors, and cocktail lounges. It was thought by many, at that time, that there was not enough democracy in unions. More than a decade later some labor experts wonder whether there may not be too much democracy in unions; there are now hundreds of cases each year in which the union rank-and-file spurns agreements made by its leaders in good faith. Perhaps in the 1970's the pendulum will swing again, and another act may be needed to strengthen executive control against town-meeting democracy in unions.

Except for the American Indians it is apparent that we are a nation of outlanders. Since 1607 more than 42 million immigrants have come to what is now the United States, most of them (38 million) in the century from 1820 to 1920. In this particular hundred years there was a great difference between what was called the "old" and the "new" immigration, with the dividing line around 1890. Before that year the bulk of our immigrants came from northern Europe, chiefly from the British Isles, Germany, and Scandinavia. These "old" immigrants were usually fair-skinned Anglo-Saxon and Teutonic types, were predominantly Protestant (with some Irish and German Catholics), had a comparatively high rate of literacy — particularly in English — and had enjoyed some experience with democratic governments. During the 1850's the center of immigration to America had been the British Isles, including Ireland. In the 1870's it was Scandinavia. In 1890 the center was the border of Austria, as the source of immigration to the United States shifted to eastern and southern Europe — a shift that would continue until the quota system of the twentieth century attempted artificially to restore northern Europe as the chief source of immigrants to this country. The "new" immigrant from southern and eastern Europe was darker in complexion than the Anglo-Saxons and the Teutons, in religion he was apt to be Catholic or Judaic, he was not noticeably literate in English, and he had enjoyed little experience with democratic governments. Whereas earlier groups from northern Europe had been largely absorbed by western land, by 1890 the new concentration in eastern cities sharpened the pains of readjustment. At one time New York City boasted — whether or not correctly — that it had more Italians than any other city except Rome, more Irish than any city except Dublin, more Germans than any city except Berlin, more Greeks than any city except Athens, and more Jews than any other city in the world. In later years Mayor John Lindsay would say that "not only is New York City the nation's melting pot, it is also the casserole, the chafing dish, and the charcoal grill." The immigrant still subscribed to the "melting pot" theory that his native gifts and language would be distilled into the New American race, but by 1920 it seemed to many that this idealistic fusion had not been achieved. At the same time the "older" Americans in alarm launched a strident movement for a "quota law" lest native-born laborers be deprived of jobs. A very real "pecking order," based largely on economic considerations, had been established.

Before one can speculate on the validity of U.S. laws arbitrarily selecting or excluding immigrants, it is pertinent to ponder the basic reasons that impelled immigrants to come here in the first place. Two are economic and the other is idealistic. The economic reasons were hard conditions in the Old World and financial inducements that were offered by employers, steamship companies, and transcontinental railroads. Many sought to escape the poverty and the squalor of the Old World; unfortunately many would merely exchange one slum for another — it was their children who might ultimately profit from the transplanting. There were also the inducements offered to come to the United States — inducements that came from employers, steamship companies, and transcontinental railroads. It was the conclusion of one careful student, the famous economist J. R. Commons, that the demand for cheap labor, the competition of steerage passengers, and the need of transcontinental railroads to unload their large land holdings brought more immigrants to the New World than were sent by hard conditions in the Old World. As we have noted previously, employers induced immigrants through the Contract Labor Law; steamship and railroad companies did so through seemingly low fares and other alleged attractions. Beyond these basic economic reasons which impelled most of the immigrants to come to the United States there were some who came because they wanted not only bread but political and religious liberty as well. After the repeal of the Contract Labor Law in 1885, letters sent home by first-comers sometimes turned out to be as effective as economic inducements. One typical letter, written to a brother, read: "Michael, this is a glorious country; you have liberty to do as you will. You can read as you wish, and write as you like, and talk as you have a mind to, and no one arrests you." Sometimes a community in Europe would be virtually depopulated by such letters from a single pioneer.

Paradoxically, as a nation of immigrants we developed an increasing opposition to immigration. There was minority opposition from Protestants who worried about the large number of non-Protestants arriving on our shores; the 1920's were the years when the Ku Klux Klan would draw into its ranks some 5 million Americans frightened by the specter of the Catholic and the Jew. There were those who were more legitimately concerned about our ability — as a democracy — to assimilate large numbers of people who did not speak our language, had a low degree of literacy, and did not understand democracy. By the 1960's there was worry about numbers *per se;* with U.S. population increasing by 4 million a year there was anxiety about admitting even 300,000 additional immigrants annually, most of whom would settle in cities that were already overcrowded. The major opposition to immigration, however, was based on economic, racial, and political fears — although it should be noted that there were strong economic overtones in the racial and political frenzies. The purely economic fear came largely from organized labor, which was quick to throw its weight behind the move to choke off the rising tide of fellow foreigners. The newly arrived Europeans, frequently used as strikebreakers, were hard to unionize because of language barriers and the attraction of relatively high wages. Labor leaders argued, not illogically, that if American industry was entitled to protection from foreign goods through a tariff the American workingman was entitled to protection from foreign laborers through restriction laws. It began to get them with a vengeance in the 1920's. There were also the racists, whose convictions were based on a theory. Mankind, they held, was divided into biologically distinct races. American civilization was the work of the Anglo-Saxon branch of the great Nordic, or Aryan, family. Additions to the population of the United States from the kindred stocks of northern and western Europe were relatively harmless. On the other hand, it was assumed that contact with Latins, Slavs, Negroes, or Orientals — "beaten men from beaten races" — was dangerous. These racist assumptions were buttressed with pseudo-scientific data. Between 1890 and 1920 an entire generation of so-called sociologists laboriously turned out documents purporting to show that all the ills of American life had their sources in the wrong type of immigration (university departments of sociology have had difficulty in living down this period ever since!).* They would not listen to America's greatest anthropologist, Franz Boas, who discredited these bigoted arguments for racism. He saw clearly that races were not primitive or advanced — they simply represented different adaptations to environment and different expressions of the human potential for biological and cultural variations. Once Boas and his followers developed a sound approach to anthro-

* In 1969 it was the psychologists who were under attack over "Jensenism." Named after Professor Arthur Robert Jensen of the University of California, one of the nation's leading educational psychologists, the term meant that IQ was largely determined by the genes rather than environment; as a result the nature-versus-nurture controversy was revived with strong statements on both sides. Jensen averred that Negroes scored lower on IQ tests than whites, that they showed little ability to reason abstractly, that the Negroes brought to the United States as slaves were selected for docility and physical strength rather than mental ability, and that through selective mating their mental qualities never had a chance to flourish. His opponents accused him of reviving the idea of Aryan supremacy that had most recently been discredited by the German Nazis; his supporters charged social scientists with wishful and unscholarly thinking, of a romantic anthropological longing that all races should be equal, that all men should be born with a mental *tabula rasa* — a clean slate on which everyone could write his own destiny.

pology, no enlightened person could develop feelings of racial superiority. But many Americans did, and their fallacious and opportunistic doctrine lent support to the segregation and exploitation of the Negro and the Indian, contempt and exploitation of the "new" immigrant from southwestern Europe, and support for our imperialism in relation to "lesser breeds without the law." Curiously, the "old" immigrant groups, Germans and Irish, had no more sympathy with the "new" immigrants than they had received from natives here at the time of their own arrival. Curiously too progressives and liberals may have been more racist than conservative. This was partly because the hatred of western Populists was meshed with anti-Semitism. It was also a part of the hostility of rural America to those who settled in the city — including the latest immigrants.

The political fear — almost indistinguishable from the economic dread of anarchism and communism — came to a head in the famous Palmer Red Raids of 1919–1920. In late April and early May 1919 there were bomb scares. One was sent through the mails to Senator Thomas W. Hardwick of Georgia, the Chairman of the Committee on Immigration; a maid opened it and the resulting explosion ripped off her hands. Similar packages, stopped in the post office, had been addressed to Secretary of Labor William B. Wilson, Justice Holmes, Judge Kennesaw Mountain Landis, John D. Rockefeller, and J. P. Morgan, Jr. In June a bomb was thrown onto the front porch of the Attorney General, A. Mitchell Palmer; the thrower was so clumsy that he was torn to pieces by the explosive, on Palmer's lawn. The identity of the senders of these parcels, or of the person who placed the bomb on Palmer's porch, was never learned — but the newspapers and probably the majority of the public believed that the parcels had come from a Red bomb-shop.

All of this was in the spring of 1919. In July there were race riots in Cleveland and in Washington. In September, the Communist party and the Communist Labor party emerged from separate Chicago conventions. There were reports that their combined memberships exceeded 100,000; some accounts placed the number at upwards of a million. It is now clear that the more modest of these estimates was grossly exaggerated, but the rumors impressed the public. By this time, as Allan L. Damon has documented so well, groups like the National Security League were stating with confidence that most labor unions, the leading universities, some churches, the League of Women Voters, and many other organizations were Red-tinted. It was claimed that outspoken reformers like John Dewey, Roscoe Pound, Jane Addams, Robert M. La Follette, and Thorstein Veblen were closely allied with the growing Red menace. In the fall of 1919, in addition to the Reds, there were other worries. In September the Boston police went on strike, eliciting a remark from Calvin Coolidge that was to be of assistance in elevating him into the White House. In the same month federal troops were sent to quiet the nation's steel towns, which were involved in a nationwide strike. In November 400,000 miners left the pits. The public began to envisage a general strike, or worse. Palmer had been appointed Attorney General in March 1919. After the bomb burst outside his home he created a General Intelligence Division — a special arm of the Bureau of Investigation in the Department of Justice — to root out the Communist conspiracy, if one existed. In charge of the new bureau was J. Edgar Hoover, a twenty-four-year-old lawyer just out of the law school at George Washington University. Hoover began to put together an elaborate filing system of more than 200,000 cross-indexed cards containing information on persons, newspapers, and organizations considered dangerous to the national interest.

In October 1919 the U.S. Senate demanded an explanation of what it called Palmer's inaction in all this agitation, and in a proposed censure resolution implied that he might face removal from his post. Palmer had presidential ambitions, and began to react profoundly to the clamor that he "do something." As he later wrote:

Like a prairie-fire, the blaze of revolution was sweeping over every institution of law and order. . . . It was eating its way into the homes of the American workman, its sharp tongues of revolutionary heat were licking the altars of the churches, leaping into the belfry of the school, crawling into the sacred corners of American homes, seeking to replace marriage vows with libertine law, burning up the foundations of society.

To put out the conflagration, he decided to enforce a part of the immigration code, introduced during World War I, that outlawed anarchism in all its forms. Aliens who violated that code, even if they only read or received anarchist publications, could be arrested, and if found guilty, deported. Deportation hearings were neither lengthy nor complex. They were handled not as judicial but as executive functions by immigration officers of the Department of Labor; although aliens were supposedly protected by the Bill of Rights, in actuality only minimum proof was needed to show that some part of the immigration code had been violated. Rulings of immigration officers were arbitrary and quick; for that reason Palmer decided to test both the effectiveness of deportation as an anti-Red measure, and the public's response to it.

The Bureau of Investigation of the Department of Justice carried out two major raids, one on the night of 7 November 1919 and the other just after New Year's Day in 1920. The November date was, of course, the anniversary of the Bolshevist Revolution in Petrograd two years before; here in 1919 there were raids on Russian centers in New York and in nine other cities east of the Mississippi. In all about 450 persons were rounded up; before the night was over more than half had been released as innocent. By morning Palmer had become a national hero, now hailed by former critical newspapers as a "tower of strength to his countrymen";

one suggested that this activity might introduce a new trade program of "import-export-deport." By December Palmer had secured deportation orders for 199 Russians who had been found guilty under the immigration law; they were deported on an ancient army transport now nicknamed *The Soviet Ark*. The raid on 2 January 1919 was more comprehensive and was carried out in thirty-three cities in twenty-three states. By this time the National Council of Churches, along with the Department of Labor, was beginning to look into this activity. Their combined evidence revealed some shocking situations. One man in Newark had been apprehended simply because "he looked like a radical." In Boston, agents with drawn pistols had broken into the bedroom of a sleeping woman at 6 A.M. and had dragged her off to headquarters without a warrant — only to find that she was an American citizen with no Communist connections. A New Yorker happened to question a policeman about what was going on, and soon found himself on his way to jail. Police in Detroit arrested every diner in one foreign restaurant and jailed an entire orchestra; there 800 suspects were lodged in a corridor of the U.S. post office building — without ventilation, beds, blankets, food, or adequate toilet facilities.

By this time there was great criticism of the Palmer Raids. Twelve nationally known lawyers issued a sweeping indictment; these included Harvard's Felix Frankfurter, Roscoe Pound, and Zachariah Chafee, Jr. The real danger to the country, as they saw it, was not in the possibility of a Communist Revolution but in Palmer's obvious misuse of federal power — ignoring due process by indulging in wholesale arrests and wanton violence. At least two of the so-called radicals had been arrested because they had been photographed reading Russian-language papers; a man from New Jersey was held because agents found alleged plans for an "infernal machine" in his home — this turned out to be the blueprints for a phonograph. Palmer's defense against these accusations turned out to be weak; he claimed that "trying to protect the community against moral rats, you sometimes get to thinking more of your trap's effectiveness than of its lawful construction." By the time he made these final statements on the raids he was actually finished politically. He had been so unwise as to predict a Communist uprising in the United States in May 1920, plus a second one on the Fourth of July. At first the press took him seriously but their comments soon turned into derisive criticism; in the words of Allan L. Damon, "for many people the Fighting Quaker who had turned down the opportunity to become Secretary of War in 1913 had become a Don Quixote attacking an enemy that did not exist." Palmer made one bold and final political effort. In February 1920 he announced his candidacy for the presidential nomination of the Democratic party. When the convention opened in San Francisco in June he had considerable support from party regulars — and from those who had benefited from his patronage. But he had lost the labor vote because of his overenthusiastic endeavors, and his own failure to make a statement on the League of Nations and Prohibition hurt him. On the first convention ballot he led, but after that lost steadily and finally. There is a footnote to this entire activity, as Damon has noted so well. In 1924 J. Edgar Hoover moved up to become the director of the newly created Federal Bureau of Investigation. Hoover would warn perennially against the danger of a Red threat, but would never again resort to the slapdash techniques with which he had been associated in the Palmer days.

All of these reasons — economic, racist, and political — led inevitably to the exclusion acts of the 1920's and following. There had been intimations of what was to come. From the 1880's on, there was agitation on the West Coast against Orientals, who had a strange appearance, spoke a peculiar language, and were said to subsist on the smell of a greasy rag. In 1917 a literacy-test law was passed by Congress. It had long been the goal of the "nativists" because it would favor the "old" immigrant over the "new." It finally went into effect after three Presidents had vetoed it on the ground that literacy was more a test of opportunity than of intelligence. Then in the 1920's and following came the real exclusion acts by quota: the acts of 1921 and 1924 and the McCarran-Walter Act of 1952. These represented a significant departure from a previous American practice. It was a striking recognition of the fact that our nation, as Thomas A. Bailey has observed, was filling up — and that a "No Vacancy" sign was being hung out. Immigration would henceforth decline to a comparative trickle — with the result that the famed melting pot would have in it largely foreigners already here. By 1931, probably for the first time in our history, more foreigners left than arrived.

The first quota law in 1921 limited total immigration to 357,902 — based on 3 percent of the number of each nationality in the United States according to the census of 1910. Three years later the act of 1924 cut the total figure to 150,000 on a "national origins" basis. Each country was given a quota based on the number of their nationals here in 1920; Asians were completely disbarred, a senseless prohibition with both immediate and future consequences of serious import. The McCarran-Walter Act of 1952 (named after Senator Pat McCarran of Nevada and Representative Francis Walter of Pennsylvania) permitted certain groups to enter the country without quota; these were persons born in an independent country of the Western Hemisphere, some refugees, and a few immigrants with special skills, such as Basque shepherds (McCarran had a ranch on which he raised sheep!). Beyond this nonquota immigration, quotas on a national-origins basis were retained for all others. The total of those permitted to enter by quota was raised by 6,000 — to 156,000 — and the minimum quota for any country was to be 100; the total number of immigrants, quota and nonquota, was 321,625 in 1956. The McCarran-Walter Act eliminated the absolute ban against Orientals by granting a quota of

2,000 for the first time, and by providing that Orientals could be naturalized. On the strictly negative side the act made the deportation of aliens and naturalized citizens possible at any time — without any statute of limitations for deportable offenses; it had previously been five years, but could now be fifty! Furthermore, deportable offenses were loosely defined; among the grounds for deportation were failure to register as an alien, becoming a public charge within five years of arrival, conviction of two crimes involving moral turpitude, and advocating the doctrines of communism.

There were many criticisms of these quota laws. A minor but exasperating one was that they reduced naturalized Americans to second-class citizenship because of the clause banning the time limitation on deportable offenses. But the major assault on the laws of 1921, 1924, and 1952 was that they were based on the philosophy of national origins — a concept that encouraged the immigration of the English, Irish, Germans, and Scandinavians at the expense of other peoples. Of the 156,000 allowed to enter under quotas by the McCarran-Walter Act of 1952 — 109,531 were allotted to Great Britain, Germany, and Ireland. The result was that two-thirds of the British quota of 65,000 went unused each year. In 1956, on the other hand, 104,195 applied from Greece and more than 200,000 from Italy. The United States, however, had imposed severe restraints on immigration by men and women from Athens and Rome — two of the chief sources of glory and greatness in the Western Civilization that Americans shared and defended. The Greek people who produced Plato, Aristotle, and Demosthenes were limited to 308 quota numbers a year. The people of Dante and Michelangelo were restricted to 5,666 quota numbers; with a ratio of more than twenty applicants for each quota number, it was doubtful that the first "foreign" visitor to our shores — Christopher Columbus — could have later gotten an immigrant visa simply because he was born in Italy, whose quota was oversubscribed. China is the most populous nation in the world; under the McCarran-Walter Act its quota was 105. Furthermore, a badge of inferiority was pinned on Asians under the national-origins concept; a person was to be counted against the small Asian quota if he had "50 percent Asiatic blood," if one of his parents was Asian, regardless of his place of birth or residence. Thus a person of Chinese descent living in England had to apply under the small Chinese quota. This was obviously a discriminatory formula designed to prevent the admission of Orientals.

The assault against the national-origins concept was led by two Irish Americans who might have been expected to favor the previous laws which gave preferential treatment to their forebears. They were the Kennedy brothers. In 1958 the junior Senator from Massachusetts, John F. Kennedy, wrote a pamphlet entitled *A Nation of Immigrants;* in it he declared:

The famous words of Emma Lazarus on the pedestal of the Statue of Liberty read: "Give me your tired, your poor, your huddled masses yearning to breathe free." . . . Under present law it is suggested that there should be added: "as long as they come from northern Europe, are not too tired or too poor or slightly ill, never stole a loaf of bread . . . and can document their activities for the past two years."

The work of the Kennedys came to fruition with the passage of the Immigration Act of 1965, which abolished the forty-year-old national-origins system; for that reason it was particularly fitting that President Johnson signed the new bill at the foot of the Statue of Liberty. The new act also established a maximum of 120,000 immigrants a year from the Western Hemisphere and 170,000 from the rest of the world.

Preferences were established for the admission of immigrants from outside the Western Hemisphere; the first two, expected to provide the majority of incoming persons, were those with skills in short supply in this country and relatives of current U.S. residents. Senator Robert Kennedy had once observed that under previous acts it was easier for a man to bring a maid to the United States than to bring his mother, and that visas had not usually been available for a Korean radiologist, a Japanese microbiologist, a Greek chemist, or a skilled teacher of the deaf from the Philippines. The new preference for the skilled and for relatives replaced the former emphasis on the immigration of the unskilled and refugees — an emphasis which had been dominant throughout most of U.S. history.

As a result of this act immigration into the United States has begun to show a significant ethnic change. Increasing contingents of Italians, Greeks, Chinese, Portuguese, and Filipinos have replaced declining numbers of English, Irish, Germans, and Scandinavians.

X

The Regulation of Industrial Combinations

THE differences between *mercantile* capitalism, which was dominant in the United States before 1850, and *industrial* capitalism which became increasingly important and commanding after that time, revolved around three important aspects of the economy. They were the *use* of capital, the *type* of factory, and the *status* of labor. In the earlier period of mercantile capitalism the predominant use of capital was in nonproductive enterprise, most of it in transportation and land. In this period the possibilities for profit seemed to be greatest where capital was invested in the merchant marine, railroads, canals — or in land, which might increase in value if enough people moved west.

Before 1850, with the exception of cotton textiles, the "factory" was usually a cottage workshop on a farm or in a village. By the time of the American Revolution family workshops lined the highways of New England. Many of the Minutemen of 1775 and 1776 had been summoned to arms not from farms but from village workbenches, where for generations hats, boots, nails, chairs, and other products had been produced for general markets. Later, when Ralph Waldo Emerson eulogized at Concord the shot heard round the world from the guns of embattled farmers, he told only part of the story; embattled villagers had also left their workbenches to qualify as patriots. From its earliest days the nation had enjoyed what was known as a "homespun" industry for articles needed by the family; it produced most of the clothing, furniture, shelter, and implements that were required. In time these same homes and workbenches began to produce for sale these "homespun" items plus some associated with other markets. The sales were usually on a barter basis but sometimes were for cash; they provided the farmer or villager with the modest number of commodities he needed from the outside world. According to the census of 1820 two-thirds of all textiles, including 96 percent of woolens, were the product of household industry. Down to 1850 meat packing, canning, soap boiling, the making of butter and cheese, brewing, and distilling were practiced in the household or barnyard, or under the slope of a wooded hill. Before the Civil War the salt tub, the smokehouse, the trying-kettle, the ash-leach, and the candle-mold were necessary features of every well-conducted farm. In Kentucky flax and linen were predominant; jeans are now made from cotton or synthetic fibers but "Kentucky jeans," in the period before the Civil War, were made of linen and were reminiscent of a time when household fabrics held an important place in our domestic markets.

This early system was coordinated and controlled by merchant capitalists who had the liquid funds that made possible the financing of the various transactions involved in the collection of raw materials (where necessary), their manufacture into finished products, and their sale. Where raw materials were supplied in what was known as the "putting-out" system the merchant entrepreneur, who was more interested in commerce than in production, supplied the materials to independent artisans. Hosiery and other knit goods, for example, were made by families from homespun or factory yarn, to be sold to merchants or bartered to peddlers for other manufactures. In these early days nail making was frequently a fireside industry. Large vans circulated through New England and the central states to visit farms and villages, leaving bundles of straw plait to be sewed into hats and bonnets, and boot and shoe uppers to be closed and bound. Today garment making is an urban occupation; in pre–Civil War days it was frequently the wives and daughters on farms and in villages who finished goods, covered buttons, and fabricated the trimmings for sale by city merchants. In this system labor was blessed with relative independence. The artisan producer was not a wage laborer in the current sense of the term; he owned his own home-workshop — along with his loom and frames and tools. He also had a large garden, on the farm or in the village, and could support himself in food if the market for his manufactured goods dried up.

Under industrial capitalism, which began its great development around 1850, the predominant use of capital was in productive enterprise — in industrial production — as the investment of capital in shipping declined markedly, and as speculation in land and transportation subsided in relative importance. As far as plant was concerned, the factory system took the place of the cottage-workshop one. Labor lost its independence in part because it lived in cities and no longer had a plot of ground, and in part because handicraftsmen found it harder and harder to compete against machine-made products.

Industrial capitalism developed rapidly in the United States for both basic and unique reasons. The basic reasons were two: great natural resources in minerals and oil and land and water, and population resources — an increasing population that provided both cheap labor, and a market for millions of new consumers. But other continents — Asia, Africa, and South America — have natural resources and population resources, and have not succeeded in developing industrial capitalism. That brings us to certain immediate reasons, unique in the United States, that brought on the remarkable industrial development here. These immediate and unique reasons were four in number: the influence of the Civil War, of education, of inventors, and of great entrepreneurs.

The Civil War accelerated the transformation of the United States from an agrarian economy dominated by Southern planters into an industrial economy, dominated by the famous "robber barons" of manufacturing and finance. The point is that the military victory of the North was also a political and economic victory for the industrialists and financiers over the agrarian economy of the South.

One of the cruel ironies of our history is that the South, which cherished the Jeffersonian agrarian tradition and which had the most to fear from the industrialization of America, should have greatly accelerated its coming by her secession and the consequent Civil War. As a result of the War between the States, Hamilton — with his idea of a diversified, industrial nation — won over the Sage of Monticello. As Lewis Mumford has pointed out, when the Civil War was over the old America was — for all practical purposes — demolished. Industrialism had entered overnight.

The importance of an educated labor force was recently illustrated in Brazil. There was an experiment with two groups of farmers in the Mato Grosso. Both groups numbered more than one hundred. One was illiterate; the farmers in the second group could read and write. Both groups were given the same farm implements, seed, and advice. Both worked in the same soil and climate. The crops brought in by the literate farmers exceeded by almost three times the crops of the farmers who could neither read nor write. Time and again, this huge illiteracy is seen clearly as the largest contributor to the hunger in most Latin countries. The central point is that the economic growth of the United States and other advanced industrial countries cannot be explained in terms of natural resources and population alone. The explanation for a large, and possibly the major, part of our economic growth lies rather in our investment in the development of human resources through education. In 1966 the U.S. Director of the Budget would contend that it really pays economically to educate people and to keep them healthy. He attributed as much as one-third of the growth of U.S. productivity (1929–1957) to increased education. In the last three decades, he said, "schooling has been a larger source of growth than material capital by structures, equipment, and inventories."

There were two main crises in the struggle for an intelligent labor force: that for publicly supported schools and that for compulsory education. The opposition to tax-supported schools came from the owners of private and parochial schools; childless citizens; and the wealthy — who could send their children to private schools. The battle was actually won as early as the second quarter of the nineteenth century, primarily because it became obvious that a democracy cannot succeed without an electorate competent to inform itself. Gradually, well-to-do and conservative Americans saw the light. In the words of Thomas A. Bailey, "taxation for education was the insurance premium that the wealthy were willing to pay for stability and democracy." *Free* public education was one thing; *compulsory* education was another. Beginning about 1870, more and more states were making a grade-school education compulsory — and this movement soon spread to high schools.

In time the concept of free training spread to the field of higher education. In 1862 the federal government authorized subsidies, through appropriations of land, for the support of mechanical and agricultural colleges in various states — the famed land-grant colleges. Signed into law by Abraham Lincoln more than a century ago, the idea behind the Morrill Land-Grant Act was to establish "colleges for the benefit of agriculture and the mechanic arts . . . without excluding other scientific and classical studies . . . in order to promote the liberal and practical education of the industrial classes." In terms of the university tradition of that day, handed down from medieval Europe to the American colonies, this was sheer heresy. College education had been for the purpose of providing a literate ministry, cultured gentlemen, and a quota of doctors and lawyers. It certainly was not intended to be "practical" or for the working classes. But the American public came to the conclusion that if a university could produce *only* gentlemen in an age that called loudly for a mixture of brain and brawn, then the university might not be worth having; it was now expected to teach everything from hog cholera to Plato. And so it was that the land-grant universities — some of them private but the majority public — set up agricultural stations and engineering schools in order to carry knowledge to the people. As *agrarian* colleges they did so with great success; now the *urban* universities are asked to do as much for the renewal of cities and the uplifting of the urban poor, particularly the Negroes. In the current era there are those who believe that the United States needs sixty-seven *urban-grant* universities to stand beside the sixty-seven *land-grant* ones. This was a reminder, as Fred M. Hechinger observed in the *New York Times*, that the new urban mission seems difficult to some and offensive to others, but that it is in the tradition of the land-grant idea.

The achievement of American education was well illustrated by the wildfire success of a best seller in Europe in 1967: *The American Challenge*, by Jean-Jacques Servan-Schrieber. It was his thesis that the reason for lagging technology in Europe was not so much due to American attempts at domination; it was instead a reflection of the weaknesses in the European educational system. There was a "management gap," caused in part by a deplorable lack of places for students in higher education. In western Europe an average of 8.8 percent of the population between twenty and twenty-four was in college, compared with 43 percent in the United States. In addition the United States spent four times as much as western Europe on research and development. The result has been a very real fear in Europe that it is faced with an American take-over in all fields of advanced technology. Prime Minister Wilson of Britain was heard to comment that the west Europeans might simply become the drawers of water and the hewers of wood for Americans. If this dire eventuality ever develops, the primary reason will have been the extraordinary accomplishment of education in the United States. As Servan-Schreiber puts it, "There is no miracle at work here. America is now reaping a staggering profit from the most profitable investment of all — the education of its citizens."

Philosophers argue whether the aphorism "Necessity is the mother of invention" contains more or less truth than its opposite, that "invention is the mother of necessity." There is no question that there are now many necessities, in the world in which we live, that have been created by inventions; neither the telephone, the automobile, nor the airplane were necessities until their invention generated a social and industrial system that could no longer exist without them. The essayist and critic Joseph Wood Krutch once pondered this situation and mused that

> Perhaps these . . . devices are advantageous as well as necessary. Most people still think so. The invention of the atom bomb was the first invention which caused a considerable number of thoughtful people to wonder if the necessity which its invention had created is not too high a price to pay for any benefits we may gain. The side effects are, so to speak, not outweighed by any likely benefits.
> This is tremendously significant because it means that, for the first time, we are considering the possibility that before anything is invented we ought to ask ourselves: What necessities will this invention be the mother of?

Will we have to limit population growth, limit also the number of automobiles, and in various other ways recognize the fact that we have reached the bearable bounds of what, until yesterday, we regarded as progress?

In spite of these caveats invention stands as a formidable and indispensable part of the innovative process that brought in the highly successful Industrial Revolution in the United States. Inventor Charles Kettering once said that an ideal inventor must have the faith of a Goodyear, the creative ability of the Wrights, the patience of an Edison, the business ability of a Robert Fulton, the production knowledge of a Ford — and bundles of money to see him through recurrent failures. The surprising fact is that outstanding inventors are as rare as superior poets and painters. Each ability is unique and different, but they share certain common traits, among which are: extraordinary curiosity and capacity for self-education, persistence and tenacity, an unfettered and skeptical mind, and an ability to strip problems to their bare essentials. George Bernard Shaw once characterized inventors as "unreasonable," in a paradoxical and complimentary sense, because reasonable men accept the world as it is, while unreasonable antagonists (including inventors) persist in adapting the world to themselves. Shaw concluded: "Therefore all progress depends upon the unreasonable man." For inventors there is always the problem of the "dead hand" of the scientific and technical Establishment. Nobody is immune to dogmatism, not even distinguished inventors and innovators. Vannevar Bush, one of the nation's outstanding engineer-scientists, was wrong in 1945 when he said that a 3,000-mile-angle rocket was impossible. Lord Rutherford, the great pioneer in atomic physics, was wrong in maintaining that it was impossible to harness nuclear energy.

One of the interesting features about inventors, by type in the United States, is that prior to World War I this nation made few contributions to pure science. One of the pure scientists we did produce, the famous mathematical physicist J. Willard Gibbs (1839–1903), would testify that in a lifetime of teaching at Yale he had only a half dozen students capable of understanding his work. On the other hand the United States was in the front rank in the development of practical applications of science, and in making engineering refinements. Americans were more interested in what a thing was and how it worked than what it meant; this applied to open-pit mining for coal and ore, the use of water with no concern for its quality, or the temporary advantages of nuclear explosion. Thomas A. Edison would put it this way: "Well, I'm *not* a scientist. I'm an inventor. Faraday was a scientist. He didn't work for money . . . said he hadn't time to do so. But I do. I measure everything by the size of the silver dollar. If it don't come up to that standard then I know it's no good."

And so it was that the United States would produce not scientists but "inventors" of great significance and importance. We will mention a few of them, in the following categories:

THE STEAM ENGINE: Evans (see pp. 118–119)
TEXTILES: Slater, Whitney, Singer, Howe
AGRICULTURE: Whitney, Deere, McCormick
COMMUNICATIONS:
    Telegraph: Morse, Field, Wade
    Telephone: Bell, Edison
    Typewriter: Sholes
    Photography: Eastman
    Radio and TV: De Forest
TRANSPORTATION:
    Locomotives: Cooper, Westinghouse
    Bridges: Eads, the Roeblings
    Automobiles: Selden
    Airplanes: Wright Brothers
METALS: Kelly, Hall
CHEMICALS — PARTICULARLY PLASTICS: Gibbs

The textile industry comes logically after Evans and his steam engine, because this industry provided the first factory system in the United States — even before the Civil War, when other industries utilized the cottage-mill system. This "first" was due in part to Alexander Hamilton, who was the first to realize that water power could be used for manufacturing purposes in large factories. It was in 1778 that General George Washington lunched with a junior officer, who happened to be Hamilton, at the foot of the Great Falls in the Passaic River — now the site of Paterson, New Jersey. The brilliant and young Hamilton saw the vast power potential in the seventy-foot falls. Thirteen years later, as Secretary of the Treasury under Washington, he sent his *Report on Manufactures* to Congress. Following the philosophy in this *Report*, and on Hamilton's initiative, a company was founded in New Jersey to exploit the falls. The governor at that time was William Paterson, hence the name for the city. Paterson may therefore rightly claim to have been the first industrial city in the United States. It became preeminent in the production of cotton textiles, and later was known as the "silk city" of the United States. Today a statue of Hamilton overlooks the Great Falls of the Passaic River at Paterson; unfortunately it now surveys a decadent city and a stream that is so polluted that it has been described as a "stinking, dirty mess."

More important than Hamilton in developing the factory system in the U.S. textile industry was an Englishman named Samuel Slater who provided the complicated machinery that was required; for that reason President Jackson once graciously nominated Slater as "the Father of American Manufactures." As a boy, during the early days of his apprenticeship, he became so engrossed in the mechanics of textiles that he would go for six months without seeing his family, despite the fact that they lived only a mile away. At that time England would not let the spinning and weaving machines out of the country. Enterprising Americans tried to purchase or steal them, but in vain. Even the American minister in France was involved; machinery would be quietly purchased in England, dismantled, and sent in pieces to our Paris legation for transshipment to the United States — in boxes labeled "glassware" or "farm implements" — but the British navy managed to intercept almost all such shipments. Slater, drawn to this country by the bounties offered by the textile industry in America, reached New York in 1789 — two years before the company was established at Paterson. He kept the information about Arkwright's complicated spinning machinery in the incredible memory which he happened to have in his head. He left England in the disguise of a farmer; this was necessary because English agents carefully searched all persons leaving that country. Once in the United States Slater worked for Moses Brown, a retired Quaker merchant in Providence who was one of the founders of the university named for his family. Slater ultimately established mills at a village appropriately called Slatersville in Rhode Island, and elsewhere in New England; he prospered, became very wealthy, and when he died left an estate of more than a million dollars. In all of his business operations he exercised a strict and paternal supervision over his employees, and was a leader in the Sunday School movement in the United States.

In addition to Hamilton, who provided the initiative for the use of water power, and Slater, who provided the machinery, three other men must be mentioned in connection with the textile industry. They are Eli Whitney (who insured a supply of raw cotton), Isaac Singer, and Elias Howe. Eli Whitney, born in Massachusetts, happened to be a guest of Mrs. Nathanael Greene (the widow of the general in the American Revolution) at Mulberry Grove, her plantation near Savannah, Georgia. Whitney's mechanical bent had been evident since early childhood; he completed his model cotton gin early in 1793, after about ten days of work. He was unable to keep others from copying it. The result was that his gin, which had immense economic and social effects (see pp. 263–264), brought great wealth to many, but little to himself. Later Whitney was to build a firearms factory near New Haven, in which he introduced modern mass production with interchangeable parts. Prior to the Civil War, Singer and Howe developed the sewing machine, which moved the textile factory into the living room. Their subsequent wealth resulted primarily because of Singer's partner, Edward Clark, who was the first man to apply installment buying, the trade-in, and advertising to sell a product on a nationwide basis.

In the development of agricultural implements, in addition to Whitney, John Deere and Cyrus McCormick achieved special prominence. Deere was originally a blacksmith from Vermont; even after he became famous and wealthy, he continued to work at his forge when he could. Plows of wood and iron had been in use in America for generations before Deere came along, but the remarkably rich soil of the prairies stuck to the blade of the old iron plow like glue. In vain farmers tried to circumvent the problem by changing the shape of the plow. The rich soil still stuck to it. Deere's eye was caught by the glint from the smooth, gleaming surface of a circular steel saw. He got an idea — a simple one indeed; but when he demonstrated his new *steel* plow — from which the soil fell away cleanly, furrow after furrow — his witnesses were still skeptical. Nonetheless Deere opened a factory at Moline, Illinois, and priced the new implement at $10. Soon his steel plow, along with other agricultural machinery which he began to manufacture, became the most sought-after implements in the Midwest. It was Deere's plow, however, which was really responsible for breaking the prairie.

The mechanical reaper of Cyrus McCormick, who came originally from Virginia, was not his idea alone. His father had tried to make one, and so had a score of other men; the idea was "in the air." When McCormick did finally develop a machine that worked, the inevitable result was that other men tried to share in his profits. Never was an inventor so litigious as McCormick. In 1858 he spent more on lawsuits than he collected in royalties; implacable as the Grim Reaper himself, McCormick finally cut his competitors down. He was also a pioneer in modern business methods, among the first to introduce field demonstrations, guarantees, testimonials in advertising, and deferred payments. He insisted, as well, on the use of the latest labor-saving machinery in his plants. When his factory went up in smoke during the Chicago fire of 1871, it failed to discourage McCormick. He rebuilt it immediately, and went right back to work at the age of sixty-two. During the American Civil War his reaper had been of major importance to the Union cause. It increased the food output of the North, made possible the export of grain to help the Northern balance of payments, and released men from farms for the army and for industry. It was a curious paradox that this machine, which helped the North so much, should have been the invention of a Virginian — while the cotton gin that so thoroughly committed the South to cotton growing and the slave system, should have been invented by a Connecticut Yankee.

In addition to Samuel Finley Breese Morse, who invented the telegraph, two other prominent individuals deserve mention — more as promoters than as inventors. One was Cyrus Field, who extended the telegraph across the oceans; the other was Jeptha Homer Wade, the organizational genius behind the Western Union Telegraph Company, who extended the telegraph across the United States. Morse was originally an artist who studied painting in England, returned to the United States, gained a considerable reputation as a portrait painter, and founded in 1825 the National Academy of Design. He was also instrumental in introducing the daguerreotype to the United States. The idea for the electric telegraph occurred to him in 1832, and he spent the next twelve years developing it. In 1844 he achieved world acclaim when he demonstrated the practicality of his instrument by transmitting from Washington to Baltimore the famous biblical message (Numbers 23:23): "What hath God wrought?" In Concord, Massachusetts, Henry David Thoreau wasn't sure. When he was apprised of the prospective construction of a telegraph between Maine and Texas, he commented caustically, ". . . but Maine and Texas, it may be, have nothing important to communicate."

Cyrus Field, as head of a paper business, accumulated a modest fortune and retired in 1853. The next year he conceived the idea of an Atlantic cable. After talking to his next-door neighbor Peter Cooper, and a few other venturesome rich men, Field was sanguine enough to believe the cable could be laid across the ocean in three years. In actual fact it took twelve, and entailed protracted lobbying to get the backing of two governments and the cooperations of two navies. Field suffered an endless chain of calamitous disappointments, necessitating the formation of a new company each time a disaster ruined its predecessor; money raising was a constant problem — $9 million in all. By the time the cable was open for business Field had made more than fifty transatlantic crossings, on all of which he suffered from seasickness, and had acquired a host of influential friends on both sides of the ocean, becoming a "man of two worlds who enjoyed the best of each." Finally, in 1866 the cable's end was successfully delivered to Heart's Content, Newfoundland. Field's dream had been realized; Europe and America were linked by a telegraphic marvel. Ultimately, Field's humanity would make him a pauper. After the Civil War he bought a controlling interest in the elevated railroads of New York City; he indulged his penchant for benefiting humanity by extending the lines, improving the service, and cutting the fare from ten to five cents. This aroused the resentment of Jay Gould and Russell Sage, who were also stockholders in the elevated lines and who had anticipated larger profits. In 1887, after Field had embarked unwisely on a wild spree of buying large blocks of stocks on a 10 percent margin, Gould and Sage joined forces and wiped him out. Field died a pauper in 1892, at the age of seventy-two.

Jeptha Homer Wade deserves some mention although, like Field, he was more promoter than inventor. Born poor in New York in 1811, his father died when he was eighteen months old. In time the youngster began working as a carpenter, made and played several musical instruments, and turned into a jack-of-all-trades. For a time he worked as an itinerant portrait painter in New York, Michigan, and Louisiana. He then became interested in telegraphy, and in 1847 built the first line west of Buffalo; it was between Jackson and Detroit, Michigan. Later, with the help of governmental subsidies, he built lines to California. The Indians called the new route "the wire-rope express"; this was apt because the new device quickly spelled the end of the famous Pony Express. In 1866 Wade became president of the Western Union Telegraph Company which, by that year, had 3,000 offices and 90,000 miles of wire. He was a rugged individualist who considered himself an agnostic, and referred to ministers as "paid middlemen" and "gospel brokers." A noted philanthropist, among other benefactions was the gift of a seventy-five-acre park to the city of Cleveland, part of which ultimately became the site of its famous art museum.

Two men were prominent in the invention and development of the telephone. Both were born in the same year, 1847, and reached the fullness of their power at the same time, 1875. Both also developed the same wealth of interest, which went far beyond the telephone. They were Alexander Graham Bell and Thomas Alva Edison.

Bell was primarily a physiologist and acoustician, concerned with the teaching of speech. He was born in Scotland, the son and grandson of phoneticists; his father, Alexander Melville Bell, had invented "Visible Speech," a system of symbols indicating the position of the vocal organs in speaking. But tragedy struck the Bell family in Britain; two of his brothers died of tuberculosis, and Alexander seemed to have symptoms of it. The family had moved to London, and Bell's father decided to remove the son from the dirty and already polluted air of that city. He therefore abandoned his own career at its most prosperous peak, sold his house, and migrated to Brantford, Ontario. There the young Alexander quickly regained his health, and mastered the language of the neighboring Mohawk Indians so well that he was initiated into their tribe in a formal ceremony. Ultimately he became a professor of vocal physiology at Boston University. There he acquired a financial angel or two, one of them a man named Hubbard, whose daughter Bell married. She was deaf, having lost her hearing at the age of four because of an attack of scarlet fever.

Bell first turned his attention to the problem of telegraph wires, particularly the fact that it took one wire for every message. He tried to develop a method of sending several messages over the same wire, a process which Edison would ultimately develop. Bell thought of the harp; perhaps by sending vibrations of variable intensity, several messages could be unscrambled at the other end. His idea turned out to be too complicated. Then Bell saw a phonautograph at the Massachusetts Institute of Technology. It was a speaking trumpet, closed at the far end by a stretched membrane. Attached to the membrane was a stylus. When words were spoken into the trumpet, the membrane vibrated, causing the stylus to trace an oscillating pattern. Bell thought this instrument might be helpful in teaching the deaf to see in written form the sounds that went into a trumpet. After that he managed to procure a dead man's ear, excised from some donor to a morgue, for experimental purposes. He was particularly impressed by the fact that, in the human ear, the membrane in the ear drum could move relatively heavy bones. This gave him the idea of a larger and stouter membrane that would be able to move a piece of steel, by which he might be able to transmit speech telegraphically. He was heard to re-mark that if he could make the *dumb talk*, he could make *iron speak*.

In 1875, he went to Washington and patented his idea. While there he called upon Joseph Henry, the dean of American physicists, the inventor of the electric motor, and the director of the Smithsonian Institution from 1846 until his death in 1878. Henry had actually been the first person to develop the telegraph, but had not told anyone about it; this was two years before Morse patented it. Henry was then at Princeton, and installed the telegraph between his house and his office, which were 150 yards apart. Every afternoon he would wire his wife, letting her know whether he was coming home for lunch. In 1875 Henry became very excited over the concept of the telephone, and when Bell said that he did not have the electrical knowledge to overcome his difficulties, Henry admonished him to get that knowledge. Actually Bell did not acquire the knowledge him-self; he achieved it in the person of Thomas A. Watson, an electrical tech-nician, who provided the technical ability and the equipment that Bell lacked. And so it would be that in the nation's Centennial Year, 1876, the first complete sentence by wire was heard by Watson, who was in a room apart from Bell. Bell said, "Watson, come here, I want you," and Watson obeyed the first telephonic command.* In these early days the voice by phone was weak and indistinct; one shouted into the instrument to be heard. Watson would later recall this period as one when "all the farmers waiting in a country grocery would rush out and hold their horses when they saw anyone preparing to use the telephone." Curiously Hubbard, Bell's future father-in-law and financier, decided to sell the patent at the wrong moment; fortunately for Bell the offer was not accepted. Hubbard approached the Western Union Company, offered to sell all the Bell pat-ents for the lump sum of $100,000. The president of Western Union spurned the offer, saying that his company could not make use of an "electrical toy." In England, the *Times* called the invention the "latest American humbug." As it turned out this humbug, promoted by the Bell Telephone Company, which was formed in 1877, made the United States a nation of telephoniacs. Two years after it had rejected Hubbard's offer,

---

* Bell had been impressed by the carefully chosen words "What hath God wrought?" which Morse had tapped out on 24 May 1844. He had planned an equally imposing first message on the telephone, but it was not to be. On 10 March 1876 Bell and Watson were testing Bell's latest attempt to produce a working telephone — with Bell in his laboratory with a transmitter and Watson with a receiving unit in a room nearby. Bell prepared to recite a passage from Shakespeare, when suddenly he spilled some battery acid on his clothes. "Watson, come here, I need you," he cried in anguish, making these urgent and demanding words the first ever uttered over a tele-phone. When Bell later demonstrated his telephone at the Philadelphia Centennial Exhibition in the same year, he recited "To be or not to be . . ." from *Hamlet*, but the power of his genuine but unrehearsed first words were so great that they are the ones still remembered.

Western Union would gladly have bought Bell's patents for $25 million; in fact, they turned out to be the most valuable ever issued by the U.S. Patent Office.

In later years Bell developed teaching methods of lasting value in the improvement of education for the deaf, particularly through the audiometer and the photophone (which transmitted speech by light rays). He developed a lifetime friendship with the blind and deaf Helen Keller, whom he first knew in 1886 as a six-year-old child almost completely mute; he was tenderly considerate of his deaf wife. He would always contend that he would rather be remembered as one who helped the deaf than as the inventor of the telephone. He also worked on the photoelectric cell, the phonograph, the iron lung, and the desalinization of water. After 1897, for the remaining quarter century of his life, he turned his attention to aviation. Working with the pioneer Samuel P. Langley he made valuable contributions to aeronautical theory; on a practical level he was the inventor of the tetrahedral kite, the co-inventor of the aileron as a device to control the lateral balance of a plane, and anticipated modern developments in hydrofoil boats.

Thomas Alva Edison began the hard way; he was a hard-boiled swaggering youngster and the fastest telegraph operator of his time — so fast that he managed the telegraph facilities of the Gold Indicator Company when Gould and Fisk attempted their notorious corner on the metal in 1869. There were three features of Edison's career which deserve particular mention: his lack of formal education and training, his importance not in abstract science but in the practical application of scientific principles, and his introduction of the cooperative era of invention by surrounding himself with collaborators. The son of a Canadian rebel of 1837 who found it expedient to flee to the United States, the future inventor was born in Milan, Ohio, in 1847. The family, which later established itself in Michigan, was a prosperous one; the son did not lack for opportunities but was considered to be "addled." He was a failure in his grade school at Port Huron in Michigan, and finished only three months of it. He received part of his education at home, where he developed a passion for extensive reading on his own; he also picked up some training in the school of hard knocks by selling newspapers and candy on trains, which he built into a prosperous enterprise while still a lad. At sixteen he became a wandering telegrapher and presently began to make little labor-saving improvements in telegraphy — chiefly to give himself more time for study.

He was no abstract scientist; he was a pragmatist to the nth degree — the last great example of the earlier kind of inventor who had little scientific knowledge but a great talent for tinkering. Edison worked chiefly by the trial-and-error method, and actually possessed a vast contempt for the orderly, scientific, and mathematical processes which could have spared him much of his labor and drudgery. As a tinkerer, however, he possessed unusual powers of concentration (his deafness actually helped him in this regard) *and* the ability to inspire those who worked with him. There his genius stopped — indeed, it conformed to his own definition that "genius is 2 percent inspiration and 98 percent perspiration." Actually, he made only one significant and original scientific contribution — the so-called "Edison effect," which he stumbled on by accident and which he set aside as unimportant, although it was to become the basis for the revolutionary vacuum tube. But — working on the original ideas of others — Edison did invent a great many practical applications of these ideas. These were in the following fields: telegraph, telephone, phonograph, mimeograph, incandescent lamp, storage battery, moving picture, synthetic rubber from goldenrod, and the transmission of electric power (in 1882 from the Holburn Station in London and the Pearl Street plant in New York City, which through Edison's efforts provided the first central electric-power plant in the United States).

Edison also introduced the cooperative era in invention. A successful sale in 1870 enabled him to set up what he called an "invention factory" and to gather around him a group of young men who were to become famous engineers and inventors. In 1876 he moved this establishment to Menlo Park, New Jersey, and from that point came to be called the "Wizard of Menlo." He was quite uninterested in money except as it provided the means for more experimentation. He once said, "I want none of the rich man's usual toys. I want no horses or yachts. I have no time for them. What I want is a perfect workshop." So he took out patents, during his lifetime more than one thousand of them (more than any other person has ever been granted), and sold his products under his own name through commercial channels. His various products were manufactured by the Edison General Electric Company, which became the nucleus of the giant corporation General Electric of Schenectady, New York.

Christopher Sholes was not the first to contrive a machine that would write; at least fifty men had done so before him. He was, however, chiefly responsible for the development of the typewriter, and the machine he built was the first that would typewrite with reasonable accuracy, speed, and neatness. Most of the early machines were based on the principle of the piano and were actually called "literary pianos." Early advertisements made the extravagant claims that are not unknown to this form of enticement; one of them averred that the typewriter would protect against "pen paralysis, loss of sight, and curvature of the spine." There were interesting and prominent early purchasers of the new machine. In the United States Mark Twain used it on the manuscript of *Tom Sawyer*, which was the first book to be presented in typescript (1875). In England the best-known early user, of a Remington made by a gun company, was Lloyd George — who had learned to type when he was a struggling Welsh attorney. In Russia a promoter in St. Petersburg came up with a most spectacular sale; it was to Count Lyof Nikolayevitch Tolstoy, a man who hated modern machinery in every form. The salesman even got a photograph of Tolstoy, looking quite miserable while dictating to his daughter, who sat poised over the Remington keyboard. Sholes himself was a frail man with a wistful disposition and a tendency toward tuberculosis; he dreamed of a Utopia where there would be no greed, no poverty — only love. He once said, "All my life I have been trying to escape becoming a millionaire, and I think I have succeeded admirably." He did. True to his unworldly ambition, he sold the rights to his invention to a pair of fast-talking promoters for about $12,000.

The French physicist Louis Daguerre (1789–1851) had developed photography through a wet collodion process, and during the American Civil War Mathew B. Brady made notable use of this process in recording thousands of scenes and events. But the tremendous interest in amateur photography, which made it a very big business, followed the invention of the dry-plate process by George Eastman in 1888; he called his instrument a *kodak* because that was what it *sounded* like when the shutter was clicked. The Eastman Kodak Company, founded in 1892, was one of the first in the United States to establish a plant for large-scale production of a standardized product; to stress research it maintained a fine chemical laboratory, and to stress good labor relations the company had a progressive welfare program that included a profit-sharing plan. Eastman himself was a master of the basic administrative principle of delegation of authority; he delegated, then kept aloof from his staff. Once on a photographic expedition in Africa, he was filming a charging rhinoceros. All but one rifleman and Eastman fled, Eastman standing with the Kodak movie camera to his eye. The rifleman fired when the great animal was only fifteen paces off; fortunately his aim was accurate. Eastman was still taking pictures as the rest of the party crawled out of the bushes; they asked him why he didn't cut and run. The reply was typical of his administrative confidence: "You've got to trust your organization."

Eastman's whole life was in his factories; he remained a wifeless, childless man — had no time for any life of his own. All of the paternal feelings he might have lavished on a family and children were spent on his company, and on anonymous donations — many of them in his home city of Rochester, New York. He gave more than a hundred million dollars to the University of Rochester and to its School of Music, to the Massachusetts Institute of Technology, to Tuskegee and Hampton institutes, and to dental clinics in Europe. These benefactions were anonymous because he dreaded the public eye. Strangely, this master of mass photography rarely allowed his own photograph to be taken; in the great age of *public* millionaires, he was the least known of them all. At the age of seventy-eight, his health failing, he decided he had lived long enough. He prepared a short note, before he shot himself. It was written in a firm and regular hand, and said, "To my friends: my work is done. Why wait?"

Lee De Forest, known as the "Father of Radio," played an active role in the development of radio, television, and moving pictures with sound. He was the son of a minister who became the president of the College for the Colored at Talledega, Alabama, where he was shunned by other white boys in the neighborhood because of his father's teaching of Negroes. The young De Forest was lonely, and began to experiment with crude tools in order to pass the time; he had the unusual experience of first becoming interested in science because of racial prejudice. Later he went to Yale and entered the Sheffield Scientific School there, where he enrolled in the first course in electricity to be offered in any American college and ultimately received the Ph.D. Shy in personality, he proposed to his first wife through a "radio courtship" — the first in history. He installed a wireless apparatus in her home, and proposed from a safe distance through the electronic device. The procedure can hardly be recommended as conducive to long-term wedded bliss; initially accepted, the marriage came to an end the following year. De Forest's name is largely connected with audion — the first modern vacuum tube as we know them today. Although he was a leading pioneer in the field of wireless communication, he never reaped the full financial benefits of his work and in 1936 filed a voluntary petition of bankruptcy. In spite of much litigation, however, no one ever questioned that he was the first to invent the three-element tube — the "grid." By the time of his death in 1961 he had lived long enough to witness the development of a multi-billion-dollar electronics industry, employing more than one million persons, which had grown from the audion tube which he invented in 1906.

In the fields of invention and development Cooper and Westinghouse were prominent in connection with railroads, Eads and the Roeblings for bridges, Selden's patent was epoch-making in regard to automobiles, and the Wright brothers were authentic pioneers in aeronautics. We have already remarked on the tinkering genius of Peter Cooper, who built the first railroad locomotive in America (see p. 179). In actual fact George Westinghouse was highly important for achievements beyond the air brake with which his name is usually associated; many of his 400 patented inventions contributed to the development of electrical engineering, especially to the introduction of high-tension systems using alternating current. He became involved in a struggle with Edison known as the "Battle of the Currents"; Westinghouse favored alternating, and Edison, direct, current. Out of this came the Westinghouse Electric and Manufacturing Company, which produced lighting systems using alternating current. Some think that Westinghouse's greatest triumph was the building of the giant generators installed in 1895 at Niagara Falls, which first made hydroelectric power available on a large scale. In spite of these later achievements, there is no question that Westinghouse's first notoriety came from the air brake. Until 1869, when he introduced the new device, thirty years of railroading had developed neither adequate signaling nor a good braking system. A train was brought to a stop by the action of numerous brakemen stationed along its length, who frantically turned hand wheels on each car in response to whistle toots from the engineer; the synchronization was frequently less than perfect with the result that cars crashed end on end. Passengers clung desperately to one another when the train was being stopped in the hope that if they were thrown to the floor they would fall on one another and thus avoid fractured bones. To stop his train, Westinghouse used compressed air from a reservoir in the locomotive, which was piped to brake cylinders on the wheels of the following cars. The device worked very well, and Westinghouse capitalized the Air Brake Company in 1869. He was all of twenty-three years old, and was on the threshold of a brilliant career. His invention made high-speed travel possible on railroads.

James Buchanan Eads bridged the mighty Mississippi and made New Orleans an ocean port. Early in life Eads had invented a diving bell, and made a living salvaging wrecks in the Mississippi. He knew the river so well that during the Civil War Lincoln consulted him on military operations, and Eads built a fleet of ironclads for use on the "Father of Waters." They were so successful that Admiral David Farragut urged Washington, "Only give me the ironclads built by Mr. Eads, and I will find out how far Providence is with us." After the war he was challenged by the obstruction created by the Mississippi at St. Louis. The transcontinental railroad had made Chicago the transportation capital of the Midwest; St. Louis obviously needed a bridge over the Mississippi to replace the time-consuming job of ferrying railroad cars across the stream. Engineers regarded the project as hopeless, and financiers thought it equally impossible. Nonetheless, Eads completed the bridge in 1874, the first across the river; at its completion St. Louis honored him with a medallion that read: "The Mississippi discovered by Marquette, 1673, spanned by Captain Eads, 1874." It was more than the world's first steel-arch bridge and the largest of any kind built to that time. It was also the first important steel structure of any type in the world. Beyond this it involved the first significant use in America of compressed air in underground construction; even in the twentieth century, sandhogs seldom labor at more than the 127.5 foot depths reached in the construction of the Eads Bridge. All this took seven years to build, and cost Eads his health; he was wracked by consumption, politicians, financiers, and even by Dame Nature herself, who hurled a tornado at the half-completed structure. Later he developed a system of jetties at New Orleans by which the river dredged itself; this success made New Orleans an ocean port. He died in 1887 while working on his most visionary scheme — a railroad to haul ocean vessels across Mexico, as an alternative to a canal. At the time of his death a newspaper in New Orleans credited him with having added more than a billion dollars to the wealth of farmers and manufacturers in the Mississippi Valley; in the twentieth century he was elected to the Hall of Fame of New York University, the first and only engineer to be so honored. In 1927 the deans of U.S. engineering colleges were asked to vote on history's five greatest engineers; they honored a group that had never seen the inside of an engineering school — Leonardo da Vinci, James Watt, Ferdinand de Lesseps, Thomas A. Edison, and James Buchanan Eads. The latter's bridge still stands at St. Louis, and his jetty principles have been applied repeatedly in river channels.

The Roeblings (father John and son Washington) were responsible for suspension bridges, first at Pittsburgh then at Niagara and finally at Brooklyn. The Brooklyn Bridge, completed in 1883, had the world's first great suspension span; when it was finished it was hailed as the "Eighth Wonder of the World." John Roebling came to this country from Germany in 1831 to be a farmer, as most German immigrants of that period intended to be. For this purpose he settled in Pennsylvania. But he was to tire of farming, and went to work for the state of Pennsylvania on canal projects. There he observed the superior strength of wire cables over hemp ropes, in the hauling of canal boats. The result was that in the 1840's he began to manufacture the first wire rope in America. Before long it occurred to him that wire rope could be used to hold suspension spans — for bridges. In 1846 he completed his first suspension bridge over the Monongahela River at Pittsburgh. In the 1850's he achieved an international reputation with the completion of the breathtaking suspension bridge at Niagara Falls. Bridge-building became his life; his singlemindedness was such that when informed that his wife had given birth to a child while he was working on the Niagara Bridge, he was reported to have replied peevishly, "Why wasn't I told she was pregnant?" Unfortunately, neither Roebling, father or son, was present for the dedication of the Brooklyn Bridge for which they were responsible. Many years before the bridge was completed the father was injured in an accident, from which he died. The son was still living in 1883, but was stricken with the bends (caisson disease) from working underground, and became an invalid. Interestingly, the prominent bridges in New York City have been built by Europeans. The Roeblings were German. Now the world's greatest bridge is named after a rather elusive Italian (Verrazano) — a tribute to the power of the Italian vote in New York. It was built by the same Swiss who built the George Washington Bridge. His name: Othmar H. Amman.

There was nothing new about the automobile as a vehicle; the problem was to determine the *source* of power. At the beginning of the twentieth century no less than six propellants were in use: steam, compressed air, electricity, carbonic acid gas, alcohol, gasoline. Because most inventions are derivative, it was obvious that steam would first be used. As early as 1804 Oliver Evans had taken his fifteen-ton scow up the streets of Philadelphia — by steam power. Attempts were made in England during the early nineteenth century to develop steam-driven automobiles, and to operate them as buses on regular schedules. These plans came to naught by reason of excessive tolls and short-sighted legislation. There were laws limiting speed to four miles per hour and there was the English Red Flag Act, which was in effect until 1896. It required a man to *walk* in front of a self-propelled vehicle and to carry a red flag by day and a red lantern by night.

By 1900 gasoline had won the battle of the propellants and that is where George Baldwin Selden and the famous struggle over the Selden Patent enter the drama. He had developed a gasoline internal-combustion engine as early as 1877, several years before Benz and Daimler did the same thing in Germany. Because of difficulty in raising financial support Selden delayed the issue of the patent until 1895; this meant that all automobile manufacturers — including Buick, Winton, Franklin, Willys, Olds, and Ford — would be compelled to pay royalties to Selden. Ford said, "Tell Selden to take his patent, and go to hell"; he proceeded to build Fords without license from Selden. Selden placed advertisements in newspapers, warning owners of Ford cars not to "buy a lawsuit with your car." This was obviously intended to frighten away potential buyers; Ford retaliated with an offer to post a bond with each purchaser, for his protection. Ultimately the federal courts settled the issue in 1911. The validity of the Selden patent was upheld, but the court maintained that it covered only two-cycle engines. Ford's motor was a four-cycle one, so he really won the suit; Selden never made money from the internal-combustion engine, but Ford did. In a day without garages, when every man had to be his own mechanic, he developed the simple and durable Model T — and made a fortune. It was such an effective and reliable automobile that there was the inevitable story about the man on his deathbed, who had but one request. He asked that his Ford be buried with him, because he claimed that he had never been in a hole from which his Ford could not extricate him.

The internal-combustion engine, invented by Selden and perfected by Detroit, has been open to criticism on at least two counts: that it is notoriously inefficient in producing power and entirely too efficient in polluting the air. It utilizes only a small portion of its potential power, and is subject to constant and costly wear because of pistons and connecting rods. In Germany, during the 1960's, an inventor named Felix Wankel was attempting to develop an engine which utilized gas and compression to turn a rotary, without pistons or connecting rods. It could be a most efficient motor, at least in principle. The great ability of the internal-combustion engine to produce pollution and smog has brought many to reexamine the possibilities of substituting the electric or the steam engine for it. The difficulties of the electric have involved batteries which have sufficient range, provide adequate speed, and do not need to be recharged too frequently. The early Stanley steamers were smelly, their boiler presented an ever-present danger, they took too long to warm up (as much as forty-five minutes to develop a good head of steam), and they had to stop frequently to take on fresh supplies of water. Modern physicists and engineers believe they have solved many of the problems that plagued steam engines early in the century. They have designed an engine that starts quickly and can go 500 miles at a top speed of 100 miles an hour on ten gallons of water; more significant from the standpoint of air pollution, the car uses only one gallon of kerosene every twenty-five miles, and its emission of pollutants is negligible compared with engines using gasoline or diesel fuel. Beyond this the steam engine also eliminates the transmission, clutch, starter motor, spark plugs (except one), muffler, and carburetor; the engine would obviously be much cheaper to build and to maintain.

As far as airplanes are concerned every development was a buildup to the flight in 1903 by the Wright brothers at Kitty Hawk, North Carolina. There had been much early experimentation with lighter-than-air craft. In 1783 Frenchmen had risen in balloons, and the next year one of them made a crossing of the English channel. In 1851 another Frenchman managed to propel a balloon with a steam engine, but the experiment did not prove to be entirely practicable. Still later gasoline engines, as power plants, were attached to balloons now known as airships. The German Count Ferdinand von Zeppelin and Hugo Eckener deserve the credit for successfully developing the rigid type of airship, which had a latticework structure of aluminum or duralumin, divided into separate compartments. One of these airships, the British R34, was the first to cross the Atlantic in 1919, returning in seventy-five hours. The first rigid airship built in the United States, the *Shenandoah*, was the first such vessel to use helium (rather than hydrogen) as a lifting gas. She was wrecked in Ohio during a violent storm in 1937. A decade later the German airship *Hindenburg* and all aboard were burned at its mooring mast at Lakehurst, New Jersey. No rigid airship survived World War II.

In the realm of heavier-than-air craft, men had been trying the glider for many years; included among them was an elderly American engineer named Octave Chanute, who designed a five-planed glider that carried him a thousand feet. In 1894 Hiram Maxim, who had developed the machine gun, constructed a four-ton airplane using a 360-horse-power steam engine! He put it on rails to get the contraption off the ground, but it developed too much power; the monster ran off the rails and was wrecked. In 1903 came the famous flight of the Wright brothers at Kitty Hawk; they were bicycle manufacturers who used the trial-and-error method to develop the airplane. In 1948, when the huge six-engine B-36 bomber was introduced, newspapers would publish scale drawings that showed the Wright plane taking off from one wing of the giant B-36 and landing on the other — 120 feet being the distance of the first controlled flight. Twenty years later a flight the length of that of the original Wright plane could occur *inside* the C5-A.

In metals the names of William Kelly and Charles Martin Hall are associated with steel and aluminum. Steel is of particular importance because it accounts for more than three-quarters of all metals used in the United States, has annual sales in excess of $15 billion, employs directly more than half a million workers, indirectly makes jobs for at least 6 million more, and turned out 120 million tons in 1964 — an operating rate that produced as much steel in forty minutes as the industry poured in an entire year, its first, in 1864. The original inventor of the basic "air-boiling process" was an American from Kentucky named William Kelly, although his name is not associated with the process. It is named after an Englishman, Sir Henry Bessemer; Kelly is therefore a prophet without honor in his own country. Owner of an iron furnace in Kentucky he accidentally discovered that an air blast — when blowing directly on the uncovered molten metal — produced an even greater heat than before, thus driving out the impurities and creating steel. Bessemer had gotten a U.S. patent on the process in 1856, but one year later Kelly convinced patent officials of the priority of his invention and was declared to be the original inventor. There was a conflict between the Kelly and Bessemer interests, which was finally settled by consolidation of the rival companies — with the result that all profited handsomely. Steel, under the Kelly patent, was first blown commercially at the Wyandotte Iron Works near Detroit in the fall of 1864 — more than a century ago. Although Kelly's process is still basic, it is giving way to new processes: the electric oxygen furnace and vacuum degassing (both of which produce steel faster), and continuous casting — which eliminates the need for ingots.

Aluminum is one of the earth's most plentiful elements, but does not occur free in nature. It appears in numerous compounds — clay, bauxite, mica — and in emeralds, sapphires, and rubies. Sir Humphrey Davy recognized the existence of the metal in the early nineteenth century, but found no feasible commercial method of extracting it. This was unfortunate because aluminum, one-third as light as steel, in some alloys is stronger than steel; in particular, the alloy with magnesium would become vital for the construction of airplanes. Not until 1886 was the method discovered by which aluminum is produced today; it was discovered almost simultaneously in the United States by Charles Martin Hall and in France by Paul Héroult, working independently. The process was electrolysis. Hall discovered it at age twenty-two, eight months beyond his B.A. degree at Oberlin College in Ohio. Out of his discovery grew the giant corporation Alcoa, and $12 million which Hall left to Oberlin College. Curiously Héroult was also twenty-two and 4,000 miles away at the time of the simultaneous discovery, and both men died in 1914 at the same age of fifty-one.

Josiah Willard Gibbs was one of the very few pure scientists in America before the twentieth century. Appointed professor of mathematical physics at Yale in 1871, he lived quietly with his sister and her husband, never married. He had none of the peculiarities popularly associated with the genius which he had; he was unassuming, and gave generously of his time to simple household problems and to the encouragement of earnest students. At the same time he received and deserved many medals and honorary degrees, and belonged to many learned societies at home and abroad; the scientific world is still expounding, amplifying, and applying his ideas. In particular, as the "Newton of Chemistry," he laid the basis for physical chemistry — out of which has come the vast array of synthetics loosely known as plastics. This development led to new uses for cotton, wood, cornstalks, soybeans, and a number of other vegetable products. Agriculture found a new dimension and the chemical industry was to establish bases in the pine forests of the South, the saline pools of Michigan, the sulphur of Louisiana, the coal of the Appalachian region, and the gas and oil of Texas.

The so-called "robber barons," at least in the period immediately after the Civil War, had a few common attributes: the ability to plan large-scale operations, a lack of early advantages, a disinclination for military life, a complete lack of interest in — and even disdain for — cultural affairs, and an attitude toward ethics that was amoral at best.

Charles Austin Beard has pointed out (although he had no sympathy with their prevailing selfishness) that these entrepreneurs were masters of the administrative art, possessed with a vivid business imagination that enabled them to think imperially "of world spanning operations that lifted them above the petty moralities of the village smith or the corner grocer." As we shall see, Rockefeller and Ford are prime examples of this administrative virtuosity.

John T. Flynn once observed that for years the Rockefeller legend — spelled "Reckafellow" as Carnegie once did — was the story of little men who were crushed by the monster. Overlooked was the constructive work of Rockefeller in building a great business — one which was efficiently and ably administered. The Standard Oil Company was capitalized on the basis of its real assets. It was all oil, and most of it came from northwestern Pennsylvania. Curiously, the "oil game" has produced some millionaires and many paupers. One of the latter was Edwin L. Drake, who was responsible for the first real oil well at Titusville, Pennsylvania, in 1859. Five years earlier it had occurred to a promoter in New York that the petroleum that had been oozing from the ground in northwestern

Pennsylvania might be efficient as an illuminant. He sent Drake, who had been a railroad conductor, to Titusville largely because he had a railroad pass which would save on transportation costs. His employer dubbed him "Colonel" to help establish credit and promote respect among the locals. In spite of Drake's lack of qualifications for the job, except his availability and possession of the pass, he brought in the first oil well in the United States. In that particular terrain this was not too difficult. The well was sixty-nine feet deep; some modern wells have gone down five miles. The boom that followed changed western Pennsylvania from a backwoods region into an industrial jungle. It developed new and hideous towns named Oil City and Pithole and Petrolia and Babylon. There was some opposition, but not much. To some godly folk, Drake's drilling was interference with the Creator of the Universe. Said one preacher: "He put that oil in the bowels of the earth to heat the fires of Hell. Would you thwart the Almighty and let sinners go unpunished?"

There was also apprehension in the whaling industry of New England, where some came to the conclusion that Drake was drilling into the blubber of great shoals of whales stranded in western Pennsylvania during Noah's flood. But the boom went on, producing several memorable figures — among them Rockefeller. John Bainbridge has noted that the bonanza eluded Drake. Ultimately, he served as Justice of the Peace for Titusville at an annual salary of $2,500, then dropped out of sight to live off the earnings of his wife. In 1873 the Pennsylvania legislature awarded him, as a helpless invalid with spinal neuralgia, a pension of $1,500 a year. Drake died in 1880, leaving behind a fortune of good will; he had shaken the boughs, but others gathered the fruit.

Entrepreneurs from Cleveland, Ohio, did not invest in Pennsylvania oil — but they did *refine* the product. One of them was John Davison Rockefeller. It has been claimed that parents are a problem for their children; this was certainly the case with the young John D. His parents represented an anomalous combination. The father was big, robust, roistering, ruthless, amoral, and inconstant — with a roving eye for female flesh. The mother was small, frail, severe, industrious, and a devout Baptist. Robert L. Heilbroner is of the opinion that the son reflected most of these traits during the course of his life, with the notable exception of his father's penchant for hopping in and out of beds other than the conjugal one. The father traded with the boys, and cheated them, to make them sharp. In his first business venture John would borrow $1,000 from the elder Rockefeller — at 10 percent interest! The father was in and out of a dozen businesses in John's youth — in one of which he posed as a doctor, the Celebrated Cancer Specialist, peddling his cures on the circuit. In the end he simply disappeared. In later years the noted journalist Joseph Pulitzer offered a reward of $8,000 for news of his whereabouts, but there were no claimants. There was a rumor that for thirty-five years he had led a double life, with a second wife in Illinois — but no one knows what happened to him. The mother, by contrast, had a tired and plain face and a severe personality. The son would recall later the time when he was being whipped, and during the process finally managed to convince his mother that he was innocent. No matter; she continued the flogging with the comment, "Never mind, we have started in on this whipping and it will do for the next time." Throughout John D.'s life he would stress the importance of *gainful* work; his father may have succeeded in making him sharp, but it was the mother who strove to make him industrious. John was encouraged to raise turkeys for sale, made $50, loaned the sum to a farmer at 7 percent interest, and collected the loan at the end of one year with $3.50 in interest. The transaction made a profound impression on him; he concluded that the earning power of capital was much to be preferred to that of labor. By 1879 his Standard Oil Company was paying dividends of $3,150,000 on invested capital of $3,500,000. These profits were reinvested; by 1886 net earnings were $15 million. At the peak of his career John D. would be worth $900 million and his slogan remained constant: "Hide the profits and say nothing!"

At the time of the organization of the Standard Oil Company the moneymaking product from oil was kerosene, used as an illuminant. If one cooks crude oil, the first vapors that come off are gasoline. Warm it some more, and off comes naphtha. Next comes the illuminating oil desired in Rockefeller's early days — kerosene. He decided to produce *good* kerosene at low cost, and that is where his ability to plan large-scale operations was manifested. He allied himself with Samuel Andrews to produce kerosene of quality, with Henry Morrison Flagler to get money and promotional genius, and with Mark Hanna, who had been his schoolmate at Central High School in Cleveland, for political protection. Hanna, who was the top tiger of American politics in his heyday, was Rockefeller's servant — and so were Senators Boies Penrose of Pennsylvania, Tom Platt of New York, and Joseph Foraker of Ohio. Samuel Andrews knew how to get more and better kerosene out of crude oil — three barrels of kerosene from five of crude. Previously many an innocent buyer of "kerosene" poured it into a lamp and was met by an explosion. This meant that the refiner had spiked his kerosene with the then-useless gasoline. Andrews' product was all kerosene; that was the meaning of the word "standard" in the company name. He produced a uniform, top-quality kerosene that provided light but did not explode. Now "standard" means low-grade or garden-variety; in Andrews' time it meant a superior and uniform product.

Henry Morrison Flagler provided capital and promotional ability. He came into the firm in 1867, representing Stephen V. Harkness (the whiskey-distillery king of Ohio), whose niece he had married; at that point the firm became Rockefeller, Andrews and Flagler. He was to be Rockefeller's closest associate in the early development of the company. After 1883 he was involved in the development of Florida. He organized the Florida East Coast Railway, established steamship lines, dredged the Miami harbor, and built palatial hotels — all to encourage the development of Florida as a winter playground. Altogether he invested more than $40 million in the peninsula, and more than any other person was responsible for Florida's comparatively recent growth.

Rockefeller was a ruthless administrative genius and built a great and efficient company, with a good product. In the process he wiped out competitors without mercy. He retired in 1896 to Pocantico Hills in New York, and lived chiefly during the remainder of his life on milk and graham crackers. He read little. Perhaps it is not surprising that he once said, "It is wrong to assume that men of immense wealth are always happy." For forty years until his death at ninety-seven in 1937, his efforts were devoted chiefly to the distribution of his vast fortune. He gave away more than half a billion dollars in his own lifetime, and left the remainder to his only son and namesake who — before his death at eighty-six in 1960 — had given away $400 million more.

In spite of all his philanthropy, John D. Rockefeller was cordially hated in his day. Now the situation is turned around. Despite their wealth the four grandsons, who are worth a hundred million each, are identified with progressive causes and two of them have been elected governors of states. This may seem surprising when one recalls that the paternal grandfather of one of them (Nelson) was a conservative Hanna Republican and that his maternal grandfather was the archconservative Senator Nelson W. Aldrich of Connecticut. But the contributions of Nelson and his brothers, in time and money, to Puerto Rican housing, Negro education, Israel, conservation, and sundry liberal objectives have won them esteem from poor Democrats. A half century ago the name Rockefeller was the symbol of ruthless capitalism; now it can be a very real asset.

In some ways Henry Ford was a man of genius; he was at the same time narrow, ignorant, and mean-spirited. He carried a gun, believed in reincarnation, and hated bankers, doctors, Jews, Catholics, fat men, liquor, and tobacco. Yet for all his zaniness, as Arthur M. Schlesinger has stated, Ford had the compelling vision of a new age. He was convinced that modern mass production had created an economy that was capable of anything. This abundance, he believed, must therefore revolutionize the *philosophy* of business. The new objectives must be high output, low prices, and high wages; it was only by constantly raising wages and cutting prices that the business community would be able to maintain the buying power of the people.

Ford carried out his philosophy with three revolutionary steps in 1914; he introduced the conveyor belt assembly line, he cut the price of the Model T, and he introduced the five-dollar day. The assembly line was not new. Eli Whitney had used it with rifles, Samuel Colt with the production of revolvers, and Oliver Evans had employed the principle in his automatic flour mill. But it was Ford who perfected the idea; he studied and sped the line to the point that men had no place in it if they needed to go to the toilet before the shifts changed. Such weaklings were weeded out as soon as they were discovered. *Nature*, not the Ford line, had to make the necessary adjustment. In 1914 he reduced the price of the Model T Ford to $295. The car was a sturdy and popular one; sales were extremely good. Ford not only reduced the price but put most of the profits back into the plant for more expansion, and perhaps even cheaper prices. This peeved stockholders, who sued, and got their dividend; it amounted to $688 for each dollar invested. Ultimately Ford had his way; he bought out the stockholders, became the sole owner, ran things as he pleased.

He introduced the five-dollar day because he believed that one's own employees should be one's best customers. It is impossible, in a later generation, to comprehend fully the effect of the announcement of the five-dollar day in 1914. In actual fact, it created in the United States a sensation greater than the outbreak of World War I in the same year. The Ford wage of five dollars for eight hours of common labor was twice as much as the highest wage for such work at the time; millions of men in 1914 were glad to work nine hours for two dollars. As the word spread workers flocked to Detroit, many from hundreds of miles away. For a week thousands stormed the gates of the Ford factory. On the seventh day, company guards and police turned fire hoses on the mob; the month was February and the temperature was nine degrees above zero! If the new workers fortunate enough to get jobs were pleased, many of Ford's business colleagues were horrified by his innovation. They said Detroit would be ruined by the exodus of other employers who couldn't pay five dollars, that the Ford Company would go bankrupt, that workers would be demoralized by their sudden affluence. The *New York Times* sent a reporter to ask Ford, point-blank, if he was a Socialist; his reply was in the negative. In spite of criticism and harrassment, he went right ahead. From the vantage point of more than half a century it is easy to criticize the five-dollar day, as Ford introduced it. Turning fire hoses on eager applicants, in bitter winter weather, was brutal. The worker on the assembly line became more of a robot than ever, as portrayed by Charles Chaplin in his famous motion picture *Modern Times*, which was re-released in major cities at Christmas 1971, playing to full houses for several months. Ford also used the attractive wage as a weapon with which to control the morals of his employees; those who were divorced, drank, or stayed up late at night didn't get five dollars. Nonetheless the principle was established, and this principle of a high wage meant that the gulf between what were then known as the middle and working classes was to grow narrower and narrower.

In retrospect one can belabor most of these tycoons for their selfishness and their vulgarity. On the positive side, however, they did think globally; for that reason, as Beard has noted, one cannot get around the fact that these same "robber barons," through the *national* organization of workers and inventors, did bring "material comforts to millions of people who never could have wrung them barehanded from the hills and the forests."

Another interesting attribute common to most of these men, certainly the early and most famous of the tycoons, is that they were not born with silver spoons in their mouths. Much recent research has tended to play down the rags-to-riches theme. The sociologist C. Wright Mills made a study of the 275 richest men in America since the Civil War; he found that, of the 1900 generation, 39 percent came from lower-class families. By 1950 the "top-rich" coming from such families had shrunk to 9 percent; this seemed to indicate that the opportunities for going up the ladder to the top had declined in democratic America. But in the generation immediately after the Civil War, in the spectacular entrepreneurial class we are discussing, most of the prominent tycoons were born without inheritances. Of this early group only two, Morgan and Vanderbilt, built their fortunes on the solid basis of family inheritance. Only one had had a higher education, and he only two years of it; Morgan had spent two years at the University of Göttingen in Germany. The others came from nowhere: Carnegie began as a bobbin boy in a cotton factory; Jay Cooke as a clerk in a general store; Rockefeller as a bookkeeper in Cleveland; Huntington and Armour and Clark were farm boys.

It is no wonder that Horatio Alger was able to write over 100 novels, and sell millions of them; his heroes all won honor and fortune after a long struggle with poverty and temptation. It is too bad that Alger could not follow his own advice. He was reading Plato at nine, and wrote his first short story at thirteen. But he was dominated by a father who was a Unitarian minister and who announced that his son would be a minister rather than a writer. The result was that Horatio went off to Harvard and to divinity school. Before graduation the father forbade him to marry the girl of his dreams. Perhaps to get even, before entering the ministry Horatio went off on a year-long toot in Paris and London where, according to his diaries, he had affairs with a French café singer and an English gentlewoman. He was a small-town minister in Massachusetts for a decade, was bored with the occupation, began to hack away on the first of his novels, went to New York, and lived for thirty years at the Newsboys' Lodging House — where he could see how the city's Ragged Dicks really lived. Later he drifted from one career to another, leading antivice crusades and lecturing on the wages of sin, until he hit upon the happy literary formulas that resulted in 119 novels. This writing brought him more than a million dollars, but not happiness. He never married, and came to be so ashamed of his work that he refused to have copies of his novels in the house. He died in poverty as a result of his own spendthrift habits. One of the more interesting commentaries on Alger was allegedly made by Al Smith who, in his progress from the Fulton Fish Market in New York to the Governor's Mansion in Albany, was an authentic example of the rags-to-riches theme. He received a query, by letter, as to whether he had ever read the Alger books. A single-sentence reply came from his secretary: "Governor Smith asks me to tell you that he never read any books, and Alger's was among them."

Another common characteristic was a singular lack of military enthusiasm; someone else could fight the nation's battles. Consider the Cookes and the Mellons. The Cookes came from Revolutionary fighting stock but the love of conflict appeared to have died out in the family; none of the Cooke sons got nearer the battlefield than the Treasury Department in Washington. In the Capital they not only sold bonds for the government but got a monopoly on the streetcar lines in Washington. In Pittsburgh Judge Mellon found that one of his older sons in Wisconsin was thinking of enlisting. He wrote:

> I had hoped my boy was going to make a smart, intelligent businessman and was not such a goose as to be seduced from duty by the declamations of bun-combed speeches. It is only greenhorns who enlist. You can learn nothing in the army. . . . In time you will come to understand and believe that a man may be a patriot without risking his own life or sacrificing his health. There are plenty of other lives less valuable or others ready to serve for the love of serving.

These early entrepreneurs also lacked interest in cultural pursuits; the highly literate Carnegie was the one outstanding exception. Many of the "robber barons" could be described in the words of the American scholar Vernon Parrington about Jay Cooke. Parrington said Cooke was intellectually poverty-stricken, outside the field of banking, a child. Or one can consider Henry Ford. He learned nothing in school except a few epigrams from McGuffey's *Readers*, never learned to spell or to express himself in the simplest written sentence, could not compose or deliver a speech, was ignorant of everything except mechanics and marketing, was a man of action rather than thought. He said, "I don't read books; they muss up my mind." When he ran for the U.S. Senate in 1918 it was no wonder that the *New York Times* commented acidly, "His election would create a vacancy both in the Senate *and* in the automobile business." President Theodore Roosevelt once confessed a feeling of intense boredom in the presence of these giants:

> I am simply unable to make myself take the attitude of respect toward the very wealthy which such an enormous multitude of people evidently feel. I am delighted to show any courtesy to Pierpont Morgan . . . or James J. Hill,

but as for regarding any one of them, as for instance, I regard Professor Bury, or . . . Rhodes, the historian — why, I could not force myself to do it even if I wanted to, which I don't.

Charles Francis Adams, who came from a great family and was both a writer *and* the president of the Union Pacific Railroad, had this to say about the "money-getting" practices by his colleagues:

> It comes from rather a low instinct. . . . I have known . . . a great many "successful" men — "big" financially — men famous during the last half century, and a less interesting crowd I do not care to encounter. Not one . . . would I care to meet again either in this world or the next; nor is one associated in my mind with the idea of humor, thought, or refinement. As a set of mere money-getters and traders, they are essentially unattractive.

One reason TR and Adams disdained the tycoons of their day was that many spent their money in ways that were lavish and gaudy and senseless. They proved their economic power by orgies of spending — spending that occasioned awe, amazement, and envy from the "great unwashed." They spent it on parties, on mansions, and on treasure from Europe — which could be in the form of *objets d'art* or husbands.

There were Lucullan parties and dinners where men who had been accustomed to beer now required full baskets of champagne. At one party each lady present, opening her napkin, found a gold bracelet as a present, with the monogram of the host engraved on it. At another, cigarettes rolled in hundred-dollar bills were passed around after the coffee; the guests lit up and presumably smoked with an authentic thrill. Animals were sometimes brought in for variety; one party featured horses instead of chairs for the diners at the table, and one host gave a dinner to his dog — after the repast presenting the pet with a diamond collar worth $15,000. One of Newport's many excesses was the "Monkey" dinner at which this simian guest, in full evening dress, drank too much champagne, climbed the chandelier, and pelted his tablemates with light bulbs. For sheer bedazzlement and gastronomy none surpassed James Buchanan ("Diamond Jim") Brady, the financier and philanthropist who had begun his working career as a bellboy in New York City. He began collecting diamonds and other jewels, and ultimately had thirty complete sets of jewelry worth well over $1 million. Famed for his appetite and enormous meals, he thought nothing of going through fourteen-course dinners, finishing off with a box of chocolates, with another box in reserve for snacks at the theater. Ultimately this overindulgence caught up with him and at Johns Hopkins Hospital it was found that his stomach was six times as large as normal. This much can be said for "Diamond Jim": he was a genial soul who spent his money or gave it away — he certainly did not leave it in trust for worthless or lazy descendants or relatives. Most of what he had left when he died went to found the James Buchanan Brady Urological Institute at Johns Hopkins University.

If dinners and parties were elaborate, the mansions of the wealthy were terribly expensive architectural piles that can be used now, if at all, for museums or educational institutions or offices or dormitories. In New York City there were the large houses and grounds of Frick and Carnegie; there is the pathetic story about Carnegie, lonesome in the gardens of his palace on Fifth Avenue, sometimes going wistfully to the great iron fence hoping that some passer-by would converse with him. At Asheville, North Carolina, there was George W. Vanderbilt's massive limestone château called "Biltmore" which was copied from the Château de Blois in France. It had forty master bedrooms; from its leaded-glass windows the young owner could survey a princely and feudal domain of 130,000 acres covering 203 square miles. To plan his gardens young Vanderbilt had secured the services of Frederick Law Olmsted, the designer of Central Park in New York City. To manage his forests he employed Gifford Pinchot, who would become the greatest conservationist in the history of the United States. Here Pinchot had the first experimental forest in the country, and managed it with a staff and budget larger than that in the Department of Agriculture which he later joined.

It was in Pocantico Hills in New York that Rockefeller had his estate — with its seventy-five buildings, seventy miles of private roads, a private golf course, and employees numbering up to 1,500 depending on the season. He also had an estate at Lakewood in New Jersey for the spring, at Ormond Beach in Florida for winter, a town house on Fifty-fourth Street in New York City, and two estates or houses at Forest Hills and on Euclid Avenue in Cleveland. Rockefeller had a reputation for living simply, what with his diet of graham crackers and milk, and his penchant for bicycles. If so, as the journalist-historian Frederick Lewis Allen noted, "Never, perhaps, did any man live a more frugal life on a more colossal scale." Across the seas in Scotland, Andrew Carnegie had Skibo Castle with its 32,000 acres and two to three thousand tenants. He and his guests were awakened each morning at 8 A.M. by the Carnegie bagpiper, approaching the castle from an appropriate distance, and skirling beneath the bedroom windows. A little later everyone had breakfast, to the music of a pipe organ played by the Carnegie organist.

The favorite architect of the rich was Richard Morris Hunt, who once said that if his client wanted "you to build a house upside down standing on its chimney, it's up to you to do it." Hunt and his architectural colleagues were derivative, copying styles from the French Renaissance, the Georgian, the Gothic. The economic and tectonic mania swept the country. Even the Brooklyn Bridge was ornamented with Gothic arches and buttresses. In Washington the French Renaissance style is still seen in the executive office which was formerly the State, War, and Navy Building next to the White House. Universities followed the pattern — Duke and Princeton in Gothic, Harvard in Georgian. There is the famous story, doubtless apocryphal, that the University of Chicago wrote to Oxford University in England for advice on how to build a Gothic chemistry laboratory. The chemists at Oxford were blunt: "We cannot help you. We haven't built a Gothic building here for four hundred years."

It *was* a Gilded Age. An English comedian visiting the huge and ornate St. Nicholas Hotel in New York refused to put his shoes outside the door to be shined. He was afraid they would be gilded.

There were also the treasures imported from Europe, either in the fields of art or matrimony. Many "robber barons" showed off their wealth by ransacking art treasures in Europe, stripping medieval castles of their carvings and tapestries, and even ripping whole staircases and ceilings from the repose they had enjoyed throughout the centuries in order to transport them to this country. It was claimed that Morgan would have bought the Sistine Chapel had it been for sale. The most pathetic case of all was probably presented by Henry Clay Frick, who could claim the double designation as the toughest employer in the nation and the one most devoid of culture. He built himself a palace in New York and brought over a Renaissance throne from Italy. He was accustomed to sit in it, with Italian paintings all around him, with a copy of the *Saturday Evening Post* in his hand. On the distaff side, the wives and daughters of these tycoons made what was called the "grand tour of Europe," cultivating antiquity and culture with highest speed as they did so. Some of them, unfortunately, were gaudily dressed — which inspired the poem by Oliver Herford:

> *Ermined and minked and Persian-lambed,*
> *Be-puffed (be-painted, too, alas!)*
> *Be-decked, be-diamonded — be-damned!*
> *The women of the better class.*

It was Potter Palmer himself who once said of his wife, "There she stands with two hundred thousand dollars on her." It was no wonder that John Stuart Mill would conclude that the United States was a land where "the life of one sex is devoted to dollar hunting, and of the other to the breeding of dollar hunters."

When they came home these women imported European tutors, dancing masters, and painters who flattered them. As Matthew Josephson has observed, through well-advertised transatlantic marriages, they also imported the last lingering descendants of Europe's noblest ruling houses — "so mingling their plain American blood with the blue blood of Italian, Hungarian, and Balkan princes, not to speak of English peers." In 1910 historian Gustavus Myers calculated that more than five hundred women had married titled foreigners, and that the drain of money out of the United States as a result amounted to the princely sum of $220 million. There was the marriage of Anna Gould, one of the six children of Jay Gould who had left an estate of $100 million. She joined the parade of American girls buying coronets by marrying the penniless Count Boni de Castellane of France. At her wedding in New York City Victor Herbert, the composer, conducted a twenty-piece orchestra, and four thousand spectators thronged around the entrance to the Gould home; their trampling soon reduced the unpaved western side of Fifth Avenue to a sea of mud — an omen of the count's conduct as a husband. He abused his wife even to the point of striking her and spent her money on other women and on their pleasure yacht, inappropriately named *Valhalla*. The high point in the wave of international marriages was the union of Consuelo Vanderbilt, of the railroad family, to the Duke of Marlborough. This occurred in 1895 with the result, as Myers chronicles it, that Blenheim Castle — a useless pile with two hundred servants — "became one of the frozen assets of the New York Central Railroad." Both bride and groom were in love at the time with other persons, but love was not permitted to interfere because the marriage was dictated by money and one of the most tyrannical matriarchs in American social history. Consuelo was slim, elegant, and wealthy, and was in love with a New York society figure named Winthrop Rutherford and did not want to marry the duke. But her mother ordered it; in later years she would boast, "I forced my daughter to marry the duke. I have always had absolute power over my daughter." Soon after the marriage the duke told Consuelo that he had had to give up the "girl he loved" because "to live at Blenheim in the pomp and circumstances he considered essential" he needed money. That money was provided immediately after the marriage ceremony, when in a small room in the church itself, the bridegroom and the bride's father signed an agreement giving Marlborough a dowry of $1.6 million in cash and the income from $2 million in gilt-edged stocks; other subventions later given to the duke and duchess and their sons brought the total close to $20 million. The duke treated Consuelo miserably, and did his best to squander the money he received out of the marriage. She hated Blenheim Castle, although she liked a cousin of her husband she met there — a red-headed boy named Winston Churchill, himself the child of another unhappy transatlantic marriage. Curiously, if she had not had two sons by Marlborough, Winston would have succeeded to the title of Duke of Marlborough; her mother-in-law had once bade her have a son and heir to the title because she confided in Consuelo that "it would be intolerable to have that little upstart Winston become duke." Ultimately there was a divorce, Consuelo married again, and died in 1964 at the age of eighty-eight. Both Winston Churchill and Consuelo Vanderbilt Churchill (later Balsan) are buried in St. Martin's Churchyard at Bladon, England.

Historian Stewart H. Holbrook has pointed out that it is ironic that men who couldn't, or wouldn't, read, are remembered by most of the public now only because their names are associated with educational institutions or art galleries. Daniel Drew could barely read, Vanderbilt and Stanford wouldn't read, and Armour read precious little — but their names would have been largely forgotten except for the institutions of learning they helped found. There are also the Morgan and Huntington libraries, bequeathed by men who didn't read books — and bought them only when they were rare and costly. Except as an expensive hobby neither Henry Clay Frick nor Andrew Mellon really cared for art (although the Mellon children did); in spite of the indifference of the original donors, their galleries are memorable heritages derived from steel and aluminum. Perhaps in another century or two the recollection of Ford and Rockefeller, as Holbrook ponders it, will rest chiefly on the enormous bequests they left "for the welfare of mankind."

There are many stories to illustrate the dubious and hypocritical code of ethics of many of these businessmen. The famous showman Phineas T. Barnum had one. It was about a village grocer, shouting downstairs to his clerk:

> "John, have you watered the rum?"
> "Yes, sir."
> "And sanded the sugar?"
> "Yes, sir."
> "And dusted the pepper?"
> "Yes, sir."
> "Then come up to prayers."

There was the recollection of Joaquin Miller, the poet, about a transaction of his with Jay Gould. Miller had wanted to meet Gould and arranged to take him to dinner. In the course of the evening he asked Gould for a tip, and Gould gave him one: buy Vandalia Railroad and sell Western Union short. Miller followed the advice scrupulously, and promptly lost a major portion of his capital; the friendly advice Gould had given him was the *exact opposite* of what Gould himself was doing. It was such incidents that gave rise to the quip: "There must be some honesty in Jay Gould because none has ever come out."

Most of these men were formally religious, attended church regularly, contributed heavily to religious causes. There were a few exceptions. Carnegie was something of an agnostic. "Jubilee Jim" Fisk was a pagan, who when criticized for a particularly dishonest manipulation with other people's money would say with a wave of his fat hand, "Nothing is lost save honor." But Rockefeller and Morgan were typical — Rockefeller was a good Baptist and Morgan an active Episcopalian. Morgan was the most prominent layman in the Episcopal Church. He loved to attend its annual meetings, he gave nearly $5 million to the Cathedral of St. John the Divine, in 1904 actually persuaded the Archbishop of Canterbury to come to America. And yet, this was the same Morgan who could trace his ancestry, in more than jest, back to Henry Morgan — the seventeenth-century Caribbean pirate. In actual fact some of his business methods might have caused the pirate to blush; as it was, financier Morgan named his yacht the *Corsair.* On Wall Street they were accustomed to say that when Morgan put to sea, he flew the skull and crossbones first and the American flag in a secondary position. It was the same outwardly religious Morgan who was once told by his lawyer that he couldn't do a certain thing legally. Morgan replied: "Well, I don't know as I want a lawyer to tell me what I cannot do. I hire him to tell me how to do what I want to do." *

In regard to Baptist Rockefeller, William Jennings Bryan once heard that Rockefeller had addressed a Sunday School in Cleveland. Bryan's comment was: "Many people will wonder how Rockefeller summons courage to preach so much religion while he practices so much sin."

One wonders how these entrepreneurs could justify business skulduggery that was based more on the law of the jungle than on the Sermon on the Mount. Actually they rationalized their behavior on biological, economic, and religious grounds. The biological rationalization was based on Darwin's theory of evolution as it applied to human society — in what was known as Social Darwinism. It was preached particularly by an English philosopher named Herbert Spencer and by an American economist named William Graham Sumner. Spencer, the greatest of the Social Darwinists, coined the phrase "survival of the fittest"; he believed that, under natural Darwinian law, "fitness" to live was proved by the accumulation of wealth or by the attainment of power. Obversely, unfitness to live was proved by the person who succumbed to disease, found himself in a state of poverty, or failed to improve his status in society. Spencer believed that the whole trend in *nature* was to get *rid* of the poor. For that reason any governmental measures to protect the weak against the strong were impediments to natural progress. The "fit" must be left utterly free to overcome the "unfit." This was such an extreme laissez-faire doctrine that it

---

* In the early 1900's Morgan was a devoted senior warden at St. George's Episcopal Church in New York City. In 1969 James Forman, with both of his hands gripping a hand-carved pulpit dedicated to Morgan's memory, told worshipers at St. George's that they were "part and parcel" of an oppressive "new trinity — the church, business, and government." He noted that "Jesus Christ chased the money lenders out of the temple. But they are still there, only with more money than they had 2,000 years ago." Forman was the leader of the Black Economic Development Conference, which was demanding "reparations" of $500 million from churches and synagogues for alleged injustice suffered at the hands of white society. He was a guest speaker at Morgan's church; ironically, at the close of his unorthodox remarks, worshipers applauded — the first time this had ever happened at a regular Sunday morning service at St. George's.

carried Spencer to the point of opposing public schools and public health measures against the spread of contagious disease. In his philosophy these were unwarranted interferences with the processes of natural selection. William Graham Sumner was an American economist and sociologist who asserted that nature gave an individual but one right — that of making his way out of this world if he could not make his way within it. In Sumner's simple judgment life was "root, hog, or die." As he saw it, if progress was made only through struggle the winners were the strong and the crafty — and why should anyone subscribe to the ridiculous illusion that goodwill, mercy, and friendship were to be valued as social ideals? The state should not interfere with the natural process, or if so sparingly; it should concern itself with two main functions — the protection of the honor of women and the protection of the property of men. Rockefeller would take over the philosophy, knowingly or unknowingly, of both Spencer and Sumner. He would opine:

> The growth of a large business is merely a survival of the fittest. . . . The American Beauty Rose can be produced in the splendor and fragrance which bring cheer to its beholder only by sacrificing the early buds which grow up around it. This is not an evil tendency in business. It is merely the working out of a law of nature and a law of God.

On the economic side the corporation absorbed some of the criticism that might have been aimed at individuals. These entrepreneurs — who were good Methodists and Presbyterians and Congregationalists — may have realized that their business practices were wrong, but they let the corporation take the blame; they acted not for themselves, but "in the name of the corporation." There was a dramatic illustration of this rationalization in the 1890's at the home of J. P. Morgan in New York, where seventeen railroad presidents were meeting. One of them (A. B. Stickney of the Wisconsin, Minnesota & Pacific Railroad) delivered himself of a memorable observation: "I have the utmost respect for you gentlemen individually, but as railroad presidents I wouldn't trust you with my watch out of my sight."

And so it was that the impersonal corporation enabled men to commit, with clear conscience, acts which they would not have committed as individuals. They did not mean personally to starve children, maim workmen, defraud customers, pollute the ballot, and debauch public morals. Yet, thanks to the corporation, they frequently did these things and worse, and suffered no pangs of conscience. It recalls the old adage about the difference in penalties; one steals a bottle of milk as an individual and goes to jail, one steals a railroad through corporate practices and goes to the United States Senate. It is the essence of a corporation that it is a person for legal purposes, but not for moral ones. For that reason lawyer Ralph Nader, the current gadfly of business and business practices, has denounced corporation lawyers as men "whose agility of mind is surpassed only by their viscosity of conscience."

There were biological and economic excuses for amoral business practices; there was also a religious rationalization that developed to the point where the Establishment, particularly in the Protestant Church, was considered as scarcely more than a ceremonial ratification of the business morality that prevailed. In the Middle Ages the Church had frowned on business because it believed that the production of wealth took the minds of men off salvation. To the medievalist *godliness was in league with poverty*. By the nineteenth century religion had come to the point of believing that morality and wealth went hand in hand — that *godliness went hand in hand with riches*. Examples of this philosophizing are found in educator William Holmes McGuffey, minister Henry Ward Beecher, businessman-educator-minister Russell Conwell, and Bishop William Lawrence.

McGuffey was a Presbyterian minister, professor, and college president who compiled a series of *Eclectic Readers* which sold more than 100 million copies between 1836 and 1890. They were the basic grade-school texts in thirty-seven states and had tremendous impact in an age when schools did not have libraries and few teachers were well read. The *Readers* presented a moralistic blend of evangelical Protestantism and political reaction; on the economic side, for example, McGuffey believed in what is called the "drip" system and wrote: "God gives a great deal of money to some persons in order that they may assist those who are poor." At the present time it is not surprising that the McGuffey volumes are still best sellers at libraries of the John Birch Society.

Beecher was the pastor of the Plymouth Congregational Church in Brooklyn, had been a prominent leader in the antislavery movement, and was a proponent of women's suffrage and an early convert to the theory of evolution. He was noted for his oratory, his high salary, his extravagant tastes for driving horses, and his habit of carrying uncut gems in his pockets. As a protagonist for Social Darwinism it follows that he favored business and low wages, and was opposed to labor unions. He said: "Is not a dollar a day enough to buy bread? Water costs nothing and a man who cannot live on bread is not fit to live."

Russell Conwell was a lawyer who became a Baptist minister and the first president of Temple University. His popular sermon entitled "Acres of Diamonds" was delivered more than 6,000 times for fees totaling $8 million. The sermon expressed all too well the acclimatization of Christianity to capitalist America. In it Conwell said: "The foundation principles of business success, and the foundation principles of Christianity . . . are . . . the same. . . . I say, get rich, get rich." William Lawrence, the Episcopal Bishop of Massachusetts, was both theologian and businessman; he founded the pension system of his Church, for which he raised an

initial fund of more than $8 million. It was he who said: "In the long run
it is only to the man of morality that wealth comes. . . . Godliness is in
league with riches." Turned around, this doctrine signified that wickedness was in league with poverty; Bishop Lawrence had identified the rich
with the elect, and the poor with the damned. This meant that anyone
who attacked the rich, or urged help for the poor, automatically identified himself as an enemy of God and of the moral order.

As a result of this impressive theological support it is not surprising that
some businessmen came to believe that the Deity directed or condoned
their practices. There was George F. Baer, the spokesman in the Anthracite Strike of 1902 for the coal mineowners. They had been guilty of so
many abuses that President Roosevelt, never overly sympathetic to labor,
became disgusted with the employers. It was during this controversy that
Baer delivered his oft-quoted statement:

> The rights and interests of the laboring man will be protected and cared for,
> not by the labor agitators, but by the Christian men to whom God in his in-
> finite wisdom has given control of the property interests of this country, and
> upon the successful management of which so much depends.

There was some derisive comment, then and later. Baer was said to believe
in the "divine right of plutocrats"; William Randolph Hearst called him a
"pious pirate." Journalist Finley Peter Dunne used it as a topic of conversation between his two Irish characters:

> Mr. Hennessey: "What d'ye think iv th' man down in Pennsylvania who
> says the Lord and him is partners in a coal mine?"
> Mr. Dooley: "Has he divided th' profits?"

Henry Ford believed the Lord was with him. "I'm guided," he told his
friends, pointing to his head, "I'm guided." John D. Rockefeller believed
that God had given him his money to do with as he pleased; when John T.
Flynn wrote his biography of the oil magnate he would entitle it appropriately *God's Gold*. Later, when Rockefeller gave money to the University of Chicago, then a Baptist institution, it was claimed that students
there had revised the doxology:

> *Praise John from whom oil blessings flow;*
> *Praise Him, oil creatures here below;*
> *Praise Him above, ye heavenly host,*
> *Praise Archbold too, but John the most.*

Against this alliance of Wealth and Godliness there was a revolt within
the Church centering around what was called the Social Gospel — a decided contrast with Social Darwinism. "Father of the Social Gospel" was
Washington Gladden, the pastor of the First Congregational Church in
Columbus, Ohio, and the author of the famous hymn "O, Master, Let Me

Walk with Thee." The chief feature of the Social Gospel was emphasis on the *saving of society* rather than the *salvation of individuals*. A Christian society, its followers argued, must be based on the idea of cooperation rather than competition. The Bible, they contended, teaches not self-interest but self-sacrifice; they were unable to reconcile the doctrine of self-interest with the Golden Rule. In 1889 a group led by such prominent ministers as Gladden and such political economists as Richard T. Ely met in Boston to organize the Society of Christian Socialism, stating their belief that socialism was the logical development of Christianity, and that the accumulation of wealth was contrary to the teachings of Christ. Because the movement had much in common with the Knights of Labor and the Populist party, it became national in scope and gave rise to a vast body of writing. In this connection it is significant to note that twenty-three clergymen, most of them Social Gospelers and including Gladden, were charter members of the American Economic Association when it was founded in 1883. Interestingly, the Social Gospelers received some support from biologists who came along after Darwin. It appeared that Darwin himself had been influenced by the economic and political doctrines of free competition and laissez-faire that were current in his day. Later biologists would point out, in contrast to Darwin, that cooperation among members of a *particular* animal species was fully as important as competition. This meant that man (a species) could cooperate with man, but might fight against sharks and man-eating tigers from other species.

In retrospect, the weakness of the Social Gospelers appears to have been that their advocates believed the solution for the complex problems of the day was to be found in a vague kind of Christianity *and* social-settlement houses — the most famous of which was Hull House. It was founded in 1889 by Jane Addams on the west side of Chicago; there thousands of rootless immigrants learned to speak English (and there, in the music room, Benny Goodman learned to play the clarinet). The Social Gospelers were confident that the Kingdom of Heaven would come through the church. Time would show that it was more likely to come through remedial social legislation — through what some people call the Social Welfare State.

Many believe there has been a decided transformation from the philosophy and attitudes of the "Robber Barons" from the Great Depression of the 1930's to the present day. This was particularly the point of view of Frederick Lewis Allen, who wrote *The Big Change* in 1952. In this volume Allen discussed the evidence for this transformation and the reasons for it.

The evidence he found in two developments in business and among businessmen: a sense of responsibility for society beyond the limits of the corporation and the growing importance of public relations. The growing sense of responsibility for society appears in corporate concern for government service and international peace, civil liberties, and the laboring man. Businessmen have begun to enter governmental service, not in the usual sinecures as politically appointed ambassadors, but in posts that require very hard work as the incumbents grapple day by day with the complex administrative problems of an involved industrial and international society. There was U.S. Steel's Edward Stettinius, who accepted a difficult and thankless job as Secretary of State at the close of World War II. There was Studebaker's Paul Hoffman, who was administrator of the Marshall Plan in Europe and later headed the UN Special Fund for Technical Assistance in underdeveloped countries. More recently there has been Sol Linowitz, Chairman of the Board of the Xerox Corporation, who took the challenging position as Coordinator for the Alliance for Progress in Latin America. Linowitz has always believed that he had a responsibility not only to his company, but also to his country and to the development of world peace and progress. He insisted that Xerox support a TV program stressing the importance of the UN in spite of opposition from right-wing groups, particularly the John Birch Society. Xerox put $4 million into this TV series; as the company phrased it: "How ridiculous it would be for us to build a showroom in New York without simultaneously trying to build a peaceful world." For its idealism the company received 61,000 letters of protest, including threats of a boycott. Xerox continued to sponsor the program, and improved its public image by doing so. The John Birch letter-writing campaign against the company ended in oceans of editorial comment from every corner of the land — comment that was favorable to Xerox. This seemed to prove the point that a firm decision based on idealism and principles makes good corporate sense — by contrast with the timorous hedging and fearful compromise so often resorted to by large corporations and institutions when confronted with similar situations. It is one thing for a corporation to support education and Community Chests; it takes another kind of courage and idealism and generosity to line up behind Martin Luther King and the UN.

The new corporate sense of responsibility for society has also appeared in a new interest in the preservation of civil liberties and in a new concern for the laboring man. Some businessmen are beginning to realize that free business is an institution that shares the helm of society with the other free institutions: free press, free governments, free churches, free unions, free universities. As a result of this philosophy, to cite a few illustrations from many, Container Corporation of America ran full-page ads as tributes to Single-Taxer Henry George and other controversial economic theorists. The Ford Foundation put $15 million into the controversial Fund for the Republic. Linowitz of Xerox fought McCarthyism when it was not popular to do so in the early 1950's.

The new concern for the laboring man is seen in a comparison of the policies toward labor unions of Henry Ford I and Henry Ford II. The contrast is also seen by comparing the management ideas of Frederick Winslow Taylor with those of Elton Mayo. Taylor, known as the "Father of Scientific Management," *increased production by rationalizing it.* He was prominent in the period just prior to World War I, when he introduced time-and-motion studies and the speed-up of assembly-line production. His process, carried to its ultimate conclusion, turned the factory worker into a cog. A quarter of a century later, in the 1920's, the Australian-born psychologist Elton Mayo *increased production by humanizing it.* A professor at the Harvard Business School, he was invited by the Western Electric Company to investigate morale and to improve production at its Hawthorne Works in Chicago. He came to the absurdly simple conclusion that every worker likes to feel that his job is important, and that he will produce more if he feels that way. Working with an experimental group, he found that shortened hours, improved working conditions, and added amenities increased productivity. To double-check his conclusions he persuaded his group to revert to the original conditions only to discover that production still soared. This stupefying result led Mayo to the conclusion that where every change in conditions has been discussed in advance with laborers, they feel a sense of the dignity and importance of their work and produce more, regardless of conditions. All this once prompted Clarence Francis, Chairman of the Board of General Foods to say:

> You can buy a man's time, you can buy a man's physical presence at a given place, you can even buy a measured number of skilled muscular actions per hour a day.
> But you cannot buy enthusiasm; you cannot buy initiative; you cannot buy the devotion of heart, mind, and soul. You have to earn those things.

Evidence for the Big Change is also found in a growing realization of the importance of public relations, in the "image" of the corporation vis-à-vis the public. The old point of view had been expressed by William H. Vanderbilt in 1883 and by Mark Hanna in the late 1890's. When a reporter had asked Vanderbilt why he had taken an extra-fare mail train off the New York–Chicago run he said, "The public be damned!" In a remarkable letter dressing down a Republican Attorney General who had challenged the Standard Oil Trust Hanna declared, "There is no greater mistake for a man in or out of public place to make — than to assume that he owes any duty to the public." A half century later the attitude was entirely different. Corporations are now extremely conscious of their public image and reflect the point of view of public-relations tycoon Ivy Lee, who decreed, "The public be informed."

One can speculate on a variety of causes for the Big Change, but two major ones stand out: the influence of the Great Depression, and the influence of the technological revolution and two World Wars. The Great Depression made it necessary for the businessman to appeal to the public and to labor, on humanistic grounds, if he wanted to combat the concept of the Welfare State. Technological change and two wars made the universe smaller and much more complex, presented the possibility of destruction through nuclear bombs, and brought in the Second Industrial Revolution — that of automation and electronics. It was a New World; the old philosophers and clichés and concepts no longer applied.

Two important economic statesmen, *inter alia*, have written on the challenge and the promise of the Big Change in twentieth-century capitalism. They are Adolf Berle and Clarence Randall. Berle began as a child prodigy and went on to a brilliant career as economist, lawyer, and diplomat. In two books — *The Twentieth-Century Capitalist Revolution*, and *Power Without Property* — he documented three great contrasts between the capitalism of Adam Smith and that of the present day: the divorce of management from ownership, the divorce of investment from individuals, and the development of a mixed system in which governmental and private property are inextricably mingled. Adam Smith had assumed that those who owned the corporation would control it. He would have approved wholeheartedly of Henry Ford, the sole owner of a company which he ran dictatorially — and which he almost bankrupted in the late 1930's and early 1940's. The day of this individual entrepreneur appears to be past.

Economist John Brooks (in his book *The Great Leap*) has commented on the degeneration of the stockholder from a real force in management to a mere receiver of dividends — or a putter-in-the-wastebasket of proxy statements, an action which insures control of the company to the "official" slate of candidates. Many have commented on the disturbing parallel between the "elections" held at corporate annual meetings and political canvasses in Russia, because in each case the officially sponsored slate invariably receives at least 99 percent of the votes which happened to be cast. Berle has noted that:

> When corporations were still small, the stockholder powerfully influenced the director, but today they are so far apart that the stockholder can hardly communicate with management even by megaphone. We go through the ancient forms . . . but everyone knows that a stockholder's meeting is a kind of ancient, meaningless ritual.

Thus the managerial revolution has changed everything and has dislodged the great tycoon, replacing him with a board of skilled managers who do not own the company. In the "technostructure" of large-scale corporate enterprise today key decisions are made not by individual owners but by groups and committees of salaried scientists, technicians, engineers, and organization managers who are apt to be more interested in maximum growth than maximum profits. A new group has seized power. The Astors, Carnegies, Rockefellers, Guggenheims, Fords, Mellons, Harrimans are passé. They once dominated industry as capitalists — both owners and entrepreneurs. Nowadays the specialists, the technicians, hold strategic posts. The president of a corporation cannot make a decision without a committee.

Berle points out that there has also been a divorce of investments from individuals. Adam Smith relied on individuals to provide savings; they would be the prime source of capital. In the twentieth century, however, investment no longer comes primarily from individuals; it comes from the corporations themselves, or from fiduciary institutions and banks. At the time Berle was writing, in the 1950's, capital flowing into industry came from the following sources:

"60 percent was internally generated, by the companies themselves, through profits and funds for depreciation.

"20 percent was borrowed from banks. The tendency to borrow is increasing because tax laws permit interest paid as a tax deduction. Most of our large corporations have therefore raised cash by interest-bearing bonds instead of stocks.

"15 percent was handled through the investment staffs of insurance companies and pension trusts. This increasing institutional buying, coupled with the tendency of corporations to borrow rather than issue new stocks, is a fundamental reason for the persistent uptrend of stock prices in the last decade. There simply are not enough stocks to go around.

"5 percent — and 5 percent only — was furnished by individuals who had saved and had chosen to invest their savings directly in stocks."

This meant that individual stockholders had been reduced to impotence; it also meant, in Berle's judgment, that the stock market no longer existed for the primary purpose of raising capital. Instead it existed to exchange titles of ownership and to allow corporate managers to realize capital gains on stock options. In reality the capital system, like the price system, had become an administered one. His statement was just as true in 1969, by which time common-stock financing of corporations had become something of a lost art. Thirty years earlier (in 1928) about $7 billion of industrial stock — predominantly industrial — was sold. Since that time this method of financing companies had been abandoned as a general practice. By reason of the income-tax angle (interest on bonds is deductible), by 1969 new stock issues were at a minor $1.5 billion a year — a far cry from the $7 billion of three decades before.

Twentieth-century capitalism had divorced management from ownership, and investment from individuals; it has also produced a mixed system in which governmental and private property are inextricably mingled. There are in the world today a score of different mixtures of the capitalist and socialist tendencies; to name a few: the Swedish, French, British, and

U.S. mixes. There is no single or simple middle way. But whatever the current mix, it is a far cry from the laissez-faire ideas of Adam Smith.

In the United States there appears to be little that corporations can, or want to, do about it; for that reason it is frequently difficult to tell where corporate initiative ends and governmental contracts begin. In the aircraft-missile industry, part of the military-industrial complex, privately owned companies like Lockheed and Boeing sell 95 percent of their product to the U.S. government; some view them as governmental appendages with roughly the same status as the Post Office Department. Editor Harry Schwartz has noted in the *New York Times* that the triumphant U.S. moon program did not really represent a competition between American capitalism and Soviet socialism, as many believed; indeed, the U.S. program was as socialistic in its central direction and financing as its rival Soviet effort. The large private corporations that built the hardware for *Apollo 11* were to be complimented for their contributions — as servants of the state that paid the bills. *Luna 15* was also a reminder that Soviet enterprises can also build space hardware — as servants of the state. All this inclined Schwartz to conclude: "This ironic history is relevant because it focuses attention on a question immediately raised by the historic first manned landing on the moon. Is it to be a socialist moon or a capitalist moon?"

On the basis of the reports in the late 1960's by Senator William Proxmire of Wisconsin, testifying to exorbitant profits, it could be claimed that U.S. war production was evolving into a huge industrial welfare program — with its corporate beneficiaries showing little interest in adapting their technical knowledge to the domestic economy, exposed as it is to the rigors of a comparatively free market. By contrast, under the contracting procedures of the Pentagon, financial risks have been assumed by the taxpayers and inefficiency is often rewarded with extra payments. John Kenneth Galbraith has proposed the nationalization of any industry that, over a five-year period, does more than 75 percent of its business with the Defense Department; he says we must, as grown-up people, abandon the myth that big defense contractors are private in character; we must instead recognize them for what they are — a part of the public establishment. American capitalism may be daring, says Berle, but it never could have undertaken the Manhattan Project with its initial investment of $2 billion. American capitalism may be bold, but in the current era it does not choose to assume the costs of the Supersonic Transports. Thus the federal government plays a major role in a mixed economy, and will continue to do so. For this reason some question whether the prevailing American system is capitalism at all. Instead, they are inclined to define it as corporate socialism.

This mixed system has had interesting consequences. One of them is that corporations with too much at stake are not apt to be any more critical of the government than their Russian counterparts. Galbraith has observed that the officers of Republic Aviation, which sells all its products to the U.S. government, are no more likely to be publicly critical of obvious and serious mistakes of the air force than is the head of a Soviet state corporation to his superior. Current Ford executives will never fight Washington as did Henry I; the present head of Montgomery Ward is not apt to man the barricades in defiance of a President, as did Sewell Avery. In the same manner, government is less inclined to be critical of business; the C-5A, a huge cargo plane ordered from the Lockheed corporation, is a case in point. It was originally estimated that 120 of these planes would cost $2.9 billion, but it subsequently became clear to Pentagon officials that the actual cost would exceed $5.2 billion. Yet, according to the testimony of an air force officer before the House Government Operations Committee, that information was concealed by doctoring the records with the approval of civilian officials in the Pentagon. The excuse for concealing the information was that the Pentagon did not want news of Lockheed's lackluster performance disseminated because of the adverse effect that news would have on the market for its common stock — a striking example of the danger of the military-industrial complex about which President Eisenhower warned in his farewell address. The Pentagon had not only become Lockheed's principal customer; it also sought to shield it from the discipline of the marketplace. The C-5A was only one of a number of cases involving large cost overruns that required large additional financial outlays by the federal government.*

* The C-5A program had been destined for trouble from the beginning. The original contract, signed in 1965, contained a novel provision for a "repricing formula," called a "golden handshake" by its critics. It allowed Lockheed to offset at least part, and perhaps all, of an overrun by recomputing the price agreed on earlier. When the overrun totaled more than $2 billion, both the Pentagon and the Congress investigated. Colonel Jack W. Tooley, a former airlift expert working as a civilian adviser at Lockheed, testified on incredible inefficiency in the plant. He had observed cases where an individual was making $10 an hour, was doing nothing, and yet spent sixty hours a week doing it; he said this example could be multiplied hundreds of times. A. Ernest Fitzgerald, a management expert in the Pentagon, testified that up to $1.5 billion of the $2 billion overrun was due to gross inefficiency in the plant, and his testimony was corroborated by Colonel Joe Warren, a cost-efficiency expert with the air force. Some workers justified the waste on the ground that one should not "knock the war that feeds you." In any case, for one reason or another, the contrary witnesses became *personae non grata* to the Establishment at the Pentagon. Tooley resigned in disgust, it was decided that Colonel Warren was uniquely qualified to be an air attaché in Addis Ababa, and Fitzgerald was sent to Thailand to check the cost of an enlisted men's bowling alley. Fitzgerald said it was too high, and the air force then eliminated his job.

By the summer of 1970 it appeared that the fiscal management of Lockheed was identical with the inefficiency of its plant operations. By that time Senator Proxmire was speaking of Lockheed as a concern with an "infinite capacity for mismanagement," one that specialized in "loss plus" practices. Nonetheless Congress, by the nar-

Twentieth-century capitalism is different, but Berle is not worried about it. He says that our mixed system is not the result of any creeping socialism; instead it is a direct consequence of galloping capitalism. Will it last? Berle replies in the affirmative if the system provides growth, full employment, and equal opportunity. By growth he means not so much consumer goods, of which we have a surfeit, but expenditures in the public sector for education, medical care, urban development, conservation, and the control of pollution. In this connection the Undersecretary of Commerce, Howard Samuels, pointed out in 1968:

> We spend as much for chewing gum as for model cities. We spend as much for hair dye as for grants to urban mass transit. We spend as much for pet food as on food stamps for the poor. We spend more for tobacco than government at all levels spends on higher education. We spend $300 million for jewelry, and quarrel over $10 million for the Teachers Corps.

By full employment Berle means that the system must not only produce, through growth, but must produce continuously. Depressions were once regarded as inevitable, not unlike natural catastrophes such as droughts or tempests. Now they are regarded by the American public conscience as immoral and without reason. It is now thought depressions are due to faulty handling of resources by the power centers — Statist and non-Statist, private and public. Berle believes they can be avoided, with proper coordination of these power centers. By equal opportunity he means the freedom to participate in the growth and full employment of the economy — with no racial monopoly, with no union monopolies, and with no corporate monopolies which keep individuals from working.

Berle is quite optimistic about the prospects: Taking all elements into account he believes that twentieth-century capitalism has left every other system in recorded history immeasurably far behind — in spite of its failures and in spite of the fact that it is far from perfect. He poses an addi-

---

rowest of margins in August 1971, accepted President Nixon's recommendation to guarantee $250 million in bank loans to save the Lockheed Corporation from bankruptcy.
To many this action represented a major reversal of the philosophy underlying a competitive economy, because it removed the traditional incentives of managerial efficiency and increased labor productivity. Secretary of the Treasury John B. Connally recognized this assumption when he asserted that the free-enterprise system is in a state of transition. He said: "We sometimes kid ourselves that it is a free enterprise system, but it isn't all that free." Others carried the same idea to another conclusion. They said the bill to guarantee Lockheed's debts meant that "in the United States you have socialism for the rich and capitalism for the poor." See J. G. Phillips, "The Lockheed Scandal," *New Republic*, 1 Aug. 1970; R. F. Stock, "C-5A Critic Scores Waste in Defense," Cleveland *Plain Dealer*, 8 May 1970; "The Cup of Industry," *New York Times*, 4 Aug. 1971; "Delay of Lockheed Loan Perils Jobs, Connally Says," Cleveland *Plain Dealer*, 8 June 1971; "Socialism for the Rich," J. R. Hughes to the editor of the *New York Times*, 2 Aug. 1971; "Bailing Out Lockheed," *Newsweek*, 11 Jan. 1971.

tional caveat: If twentieth-century capitalism is to continue, corporations must think not only of their product but also about what he calls life values. Here he goes back to St. Augustine, recalling that St. Augustine talked about a moral and philosophic organization that ultimately controlled every tangible institutional organization on earth. Thus far, he says, we have thought of corporations as enterprises rather than institutions. They must now begin to think as moral and philosophical organizations; they must become institutions, assuming the role of conscience carriers for the twentieth century. Our grandfathers were inclined to quarrel with corporations because they were "soulless"; in the future, Berle believes corporations will have to become a new *City of God*, bringing economic and social happiness on this earth rather than in a future one. It is an eloquent and awesome challenge.

Clarence Randall had just as much faith in the viability of twentieth-century capitalism, but he had worked more closely with it than had Berle and his commentary on its faults were more pragmatic and less theoretical. He was a Phi Beta Kappa who graduated from Harvard College in 1912, and from the Harvard Law School in 1915. He joined Inland Steel in 1925 and spent the remainder of his life with that company, ultimately becoming chairman of the board. Perhaps the most interesting aspect of his life was the broadening of civic vision that came to him largely as a result of his governmental service; he frankly admitted that before this service some of his attitudes toward government had been "inexpressibly naïve." He was president of the board of education in Winnetka (Illinois) when it established one of the country's first school systems that was known as progressive. In 1947 Randall went to Paris as steel and coal consultant to the Economic Cooperation Administration under the Marshall Plan, and was soon plunged into Europe's problems. He wrote:

The deeper I dug and the harder I worked, the more humble I became as I came to grips with the world problems at first hand. I came to know too much to be sure anymore. . . . I came to responsibility in the business world in a period when executives customarily regarded all people in Government as congenital nitwits and all their policies as socialism blended with a dash of idiocy. Then overnight I became a Washington amphibian — half businessman, half bureaucrat.

Randall believed that if twentieth-century capitalism was to survive, reforms were overdue in two main areas and three peripheral ones. The main areas were administered prices (without regard to the law of supply and demand) and shoddy products. He was concerned by the widespread belief that corporations, through deception or fraud, were and are inducing the public to buy products that are unsafe or poorly made, or all of these things. By the late 1960's Ralph Nader would be saying that consumers were being "manipulated, defrauded and injured, not just by marginal businesses or fly-by-night hucksters but by the U.S. blue-chip business firms whose practices are unchecked by the older regulatory agencies." This view appeared to startle the business community, which had long contended that abuses and dishonesty were the result of practices of only a few unscrupulous firms. But congressional and other hearings on drug hazards, auto safety, discriminatory credit practices, price-fixing, and the disinclination of some businesses to sanction money-saving innovations raised new doubts in many minds. By that time there was little wonder that consumer legislation was being labeled "truth-in. . . ."

Beyond the main areas of administered prices and shoddy products Randall wrote voluminously on the peripheral ones of advertising, the credit racket, and expense-account cheating. Advertising had created a poor image for business — so poor that Arnold Toynbee concluded that advertising was evil, John Kenneth Galbraith said it was wasteful, and Arthur M. Schlesinger, Jr., thought it was awful to the point that Madison Avenue had succeeded Wall Street as the favorite whipping boy of the American public. But beyond the nauseating repetition and the extravagant claims, Randall would observe that there was a fundamental ethical problem in advertising, one that required much soul-searching by business. The central point is that the United States can produce far more than it can consume; the real needs of most of us were satisfied long ago, and 40 percent of what we buy today is unnecessary in terms of any real need. In addition, it is perfectly obvious that there is little difference between brands of many products: gasolines, whiskey, cigarettes, detergents. The result is, in trying to get their share of the market, advertisers have strayed pretty far from the prime function of advertising, which is supposed to be information. Instead they have attempted to influence people through psychology — they make appeals which create artificial but *meaningless* differences between products, or they appeal to anxieties. For this reason advertisers sometimes playfully call themselves "merchants of discontent." The artificial difference appears in cigarette ads — to the point where the buyer is smoking *not* a cigarette but a mythical image — one of Marlboro Country. The anxieties appealed to are based largely on health, social status, and sexual prowess. The dishonest advertising in connection with health involves cures all the way from the "tired feeling" to cancer. The appeal for social status varies from the crude stress by Listerine on the social consequences of halitosis, to the "Cadillac Syndrome" which appeals to the large middle class of America because it entitles them to show off their economic power, to the general emphasis on buying new models in cars and washing machines and refrigerators and clothing when the old product is perfectly serviceable. Advertisers call this the creation of "psychological obsolescence." The appeal to sex, based on what is called "motivation research," appears in most advertising dealing with clothing, cosmetics, and perfume. It also appeared in the advertising for toothpaste which, it was claimed, should show not only beautiful teeth — but teeth that could be used to *bite*, to express *passion*. It also appeared in the fast-sell in automobiles. A midwestern agency discovered that men could be persuaded to buy a new car by the implied promise that the more powerful car offered them a revival of flagging sexual potency. The savants of "motivation research" also convinced Detroit that it should spend millions of dollars each year to develop styles that would appeal to the psychological subconscious of American buyers. Thus they developed such styles as a "bosom" bumper and the "vaginal" look — which was applauded in the 1957 Edsel. All of this can be hard on the consumer, who buys a lot of things he doesn't need. It can be hard on the nation too, because it represents wastage in the private sector, when so much needs to be done in the public sector.

Randall was appalled by the excesses of advertising; he was even more disturbed by the credit and the expense-account rackets. The credit racket, of course, involves unscrupulous vendors who overpersuade the unwary of modest means by the pitch of no-down-payment and take-all-the-time-you-need-for-the-balance. Interest has not been revealed, and the seller normally makes more profit out of the financing of the debt than that from the profit on the product sold. Business, however, has protested mightily against "truth-in-lending" bills — and thus far legislation in this field has been disappointing.

Randall was honest in admitting that no well-informed observer can doubt for a moment that the federal government is being deprived of large sums of revenue by the unscrupulous padding of income-tax deductions claimed as business expenses. The point is that the honest citizen pays *more* than his share of the tax load — when the man who cheats pays less. The well-known broadcaster Ed Murrow once had a sensational program about the "call girls" used by business as a stimulus for sales. There was the incredible claim of one businessman that the use of prostitutes was the fastest way to establish an "intimate relationship with a buyer." The allegation was that many large corporations use "call girls" as a regular supplement to other sales techniques — frequently charging them off for tax purposes under the heading of entertainment. One madame billed a firm on a monthly basis, and some of her girls made as much as $25,000 a year.

Randall felt that all of these abuses gave private business a most unfortunate image. He was right. To a workingman, who spent 50¢ on lunch, the story was shocking of the three businessmen who had just consumed an expensive midday meal. When the time came to pay the check, Randall writes, they argued for the privilege:

Said the first: "Let me pay. I'm in the 80 percent income-tax bracket and this is deductible, so it will cost me only 20 percent."

Said the second: "I'm in a 100 percent excess-profits tax bracket. Let me pay and it won't cost me anything."

Said the third: "Gentlemen, let me pay. I'm on a cost-plus contract and I'll make a profit."

There are no neat categories in regard to government and business, from laissez-faire on the one hand to government ownership (socialism) on the other. In actual practice business does not work that way. There was a famous British economic historian at the University of London whose most famous work, written in 1926, was entitled *Religion and the Rise of Capitalism*. His name was R. H. Tawney, and he wrote: "In every human soul there is a Socialist *and* an individualist, an authoritarian and a fanatic for liberty." It was the American Thomas Jefferson who posed the same problem when he said, "That government is best which governs least." Does this mean no government at all? Obviously not. What Jefferson was expressing was both admission of the necessity of some governmental functions — and his own individual abhorrence of them. This same conflict appears in the U.S. Constitution, which both grants and prohibits governmental action — and also contains a Bill of Rights — individual rights. The same ambivalence has been found between the laissez-faire creed and the pragmatic deed of businessmen; although the policy of "hands off" seemed clear, in practice it never worked out that way. Businessmen, from Hamilton on, have never opposed government *aid* to business, only government *hindrance* in business affairs. Here is the basic dilemma in economics as well as in politics: we want governmental action, yet we abhor it. We want a free economy, but we want certain regulations. Inevitably, it has been the abuse of freedoms that leads to the demand for controls, that elicits the popular outcry, "There ought to be a law!"

Virtually since the rise of the national state from the chaos of the feudal system, state power has influenced economic life in various ways — to tax, regulate, extinguish, or promote industry and trade — according to the needs of the state. The degree of interference, or control, has varied. For three centuries, roughly 1500 to 1800, the control was extensive under the policy and doctrine of mercantilism. Then with Adam Smith came a reaction; it was laissez-faire, or "hands off." In the United States there was no time when business enterprise was completely free from governmental regulation, but by 1875 such regulation was nominal, finding expression largely in foreign commerce, Indian affairs, and land policies. By 1875 the laissez-faire philosophy had become a secular religion in the United States, accepted as completely by economists, statesmen, and businessmen as the opposite mercantilist creed had been accepted by economists, statesmen, and businessmen in its day. In the post–Civil War period the United States was comfortably isolated from troubles elsewhere in the world; few doubted that the economics of Adam Smith and the homilies of Benjamin

Franklin were the guarantors of the good life. Most of the citizens of the Republic lived on "Main Streets" in small towns; there the air was pure, the water clear, and the city park safe for young lovers at all hours. As long as the mail was delivered on time, tariffs were kept high, and diplomats avoided entangling alliances; it was thought that the federal government was serving the nation well. So pervading was the authority of this secular religion that even when the system appeared to have failed in the Great Depression, a return to government intervention (that is, to a mercantilist policy) was widely viewed as a dangerous innovation — as if it had never been done in human history. Such intervention by government, many thought, was subversive and would be destructive of the great national virtues of rugged individualism.

Another solution was government regulation — a middle way between laissez-faire and government ownership. Thus far in U.S. history government regulation has fluctuated between the enforcement of competition exemplified by Wilson's New Freedom, trust-busting, and the establishment of competitive "yardsticks" — to the recognition and regulation of existing monopolies exemplified by TR's New Nationalism and FDR's NRA. The basic idea behind Wilson's New Freedom was to maintain competition by breaking up monopoly. In this political structure his leading theorist was Louis Brandeis, who had a distinguished career in a number of fields. As a private attorney and a graduate of Harvard Law School he was a successful lawyer in Boston. As the "people's attorney" he championed human rights against property rights and argued numerous public cases in connection with fraudulent insurance companies, public transportation, and legislation dealing with wages and hours. He also revolutionized the practice and teaching of law, by minimizing legal precedents and by introducing vast amounts of sociological, economic, physiological, and psychological data. This began in *Muller* v. *Oregon* (1908) when he persuaded the U.S. Supreme Court that minimum-hours legislation for women was both reasonable and constitutional. This famous "Brandeis brief," as it came to be called, revolutionized the practice of law. In time it also changed legal education by introducing what was called sociological jurisprudence — the study of law based on much more than precedents. This concept was taken over by Dean Roscoe Pound of the Harvard Law School — and at Yale the law faculty tried to sharpen its instruction by calling in sociologists, psychologists, and economists to help train its students.

Brandeis would have achieved greatness by reason of his role in the private practice of law, as the "people's attorney," and by his influence on the practice and teaching of law. He went beyond this to a distinguished career on the Supreme Court, and he was a major architect of Wilson's New Freedom. As its advocate Brandeis proposed to end monopoly by enforcing competition. In connection with trusts he emphasized the "curse of bigness"; he said that monopoly was evil, that competition could and should be maintained in every branch of private industry. He did not believe, as TR did and FDR would for a time, that monopoly could be regulated by government. As Brandeis saw it, the regulation of monopoly was a delusion; if competition could not be enforced, and monopoly ended, there was only one alternative. It was government ownership.

The New Freedom was an example of enforcing competition through government regulation; so were trust-busting and the establishment of government yardsticks. Trust-busting was carried out, as we shall see, by various attorney generals under the Sherman and Clayton acts. Government yardsticks — the establishment of government-owned corporations to determine the validity of prices and to provide competition — have been set up by various nations. In Canada it is the government-owned Canadian National Railway versus the privately owned Canadian Pacific Railway. In France it is the government-owned Renault Company versus the private producers of automobiles. In the United States it is the Tennessee Valley Authority (TVA) in competition with the owners of private utilities.

By contrast with Wilson, Theodore Roosevelt believed that monopolies should be encouraged because they were more efficient and orderly — but should be regulated in the public interest. If Brandeis was the architect of the New Freedom, Herbert Croly and George W. Perkins were the authors of Roosevelt's New Nationalism. Croly, who gave the policy its name (the New Nationalism) was the editor of the *New Republic* from its beginning in 1914 until his own death in 1930; on this journal of opinion he had a brilliant editorial staff which included the young Walter Lippmann. Croly wrote a book (1909) entitled *The Promise of American Life;* in it he stressed the point that the "Promise" would be fulfilled if industrial monopolies were allowed to develop, but were accompanied by federal regulation. Perkins was a partner in J. P. Morgan and Company and had himself participated in the organization of trusts, particularly U.S. Steel and the International Harvester Company (IHC). He was the major financial angel behind TR's unsuccessful bid for reelection in 1912; for that reason it is not surprising that the Democrats charged that TR, with all his trustbusting, had never attacked Perkins's companies — U.S. Steel and IHC. Perkins believed, with Morgan, that competition was too destructive to be tolerated; cooperation through monopoly must be the order of the day. In order to encourage it he was willing to accept government regulation — the device Brandeis said would not work in practice.

The socialists, who come in varying degrees, favor government ownership. They believe that private ownership, at least in certain areas of our economy, will result only in exploitation. One of them put it this way:

"Cannibalism gave way to Capitalism when man discovered that it was more profitable to exploit his neighbor than to eat him."

The famed Lincoln Steffens, journalist and muckracker, is a prime example of one who ultimately came round to the socialist point of view. He was an unusual one because he was wealthy; having decided to become a socialist he first made a quick pile on the Stock Exchange so he could be a socialist in style — undisturbed by sordid material considerations. Steffens had a novel interpretation for the story of Adam and Eve. He would recall that God had established the Garden of Eden, with its tree of knowledge and of life, as the first home of man — until, eating of the forbidden fruit, Adam and Eve were banished. Steffens said that some theologians blamed Adam, that Adam blamed Eve, that Eve blamed the serpent — and that the clergy had been blaming the serpent ever since. He said the clergy were wrong; the blame should be on the apple. The economic factor was the heart of the matter. In his judgment, as long as private property kept its power, government had to be a system of bribery — and corruption became the very essence of the life of the state. By 1912 Steffens had decided that "nothing but revolution could change the system."

A corporation in law is an organization chartered by the state which enjoys *legal personality* for the purpose of carrying on certain activities. This brings up the puzzling question of the meaning of *legal personality*. Actually the *legal personality* of a corporation gives it many of the capacities of a natural person:

it can hold property,
it can sue, and be sued,
it can commit crimes — for which it can be fined, and its directors imprisoned,
it can have offspring, and often does,
it is not certain that it can make love — but it does inspire passionate affection on the part of some people, and dark hatred on the part of others.

Most corporations are businesses for profit; they are usually organized by three or more subscribers, who raise capital for the corporate activity by selling shares of stock, which represent ownership and are transferable. Most corporations are organized for profit — but not all; there are also charitable, religious, municipal, and cooperative corporations. In the United States all governmental units smaller than a state (counties, townships, cities) are municipal corporations. Cooperative corporations have more owners of shares — of a family nature — than there are owners of industrial stocks, but they involve no more than 3 percent of the nation's business.

Down to the Civil War the corporation was relatively unimportant as a type of business organization. In the pre–Civil War days businesses were owned by individuals or by partners. As long as business was conducted on a small scale, these were the dominant types of business. But after the Civil War the corporation with its variety of combinations — pools, trusts, holding companies, oligopolies — began to supersede individual ownership and partnerships. The advantages of the corporation were apparent:

1. Greater financial resources — through sale of stock.

2. Long-term policies. A corporation obviously does not depend on the life-span of individuals or partners. It can exist forever.

3. Concealment of excess profits through the "watering" of stock. Obviously 6 percent on $1 million is 3 percent on $2 million.

4. Limited liability. Individuals or partners are liable for the entire indebtedness of the firm. Stockholders of a corporation are liable only for the value of their stock. The idea of limited liability is so important that Nicholas Murray Butler, the prominent Republican who was president of Columbia University for many years, once said that the limited-liability corporation was the greatest single discovery of modern times. In Butler's opinion even steam and electricity were far less important than the limited-liability corporation in influencing modern civilization. That is an extreme statement — but it cannot be doubted that the limited-liability corporation is one of the most significant factors in the development of large-scale production — and thus of the type of civilization which now prevails.

After the Civil War businessmen formed combinations of corporations for the purpose of common action. The reason they did so was the remarkable increase in the productivity of industry. Manufacturers learned how to increase their output and to reduce their costs, but faced disaster because the market could not consume *all* they were producing. Producers at that time saw the problem as one of overproduction; modern students tend to describe it as underconsumption. Unfortunately, no businessman in the generation after the Civil War ventured, as Ford did later, to act on the principle that free competition resulting in low prices to consumers — coupled with high wages to labor — would create an *expansion* of the market to match the *expansion* in productivity. Without Ford's solution, there is no question that plants and equipment in the 1870's and 1880's were enormously overexpanded. Leading manufacturers and financial promoters believed that the risks of price collapses, and bankruptcies, resulting from the operation of free competition would be intolerable. They recalled the venerable maxim "Competition is the life of trade and the death of business." So, they turned to the easier program of making profits secure by restricting production or by dividing markets; they did so through pools, trusts, holding companies, and oligopolies.

These would maintain both high prices *and* low wages — just the opposite of Ford's solution.

Pools appeared after the Panic of 1873 and were developed extensively for about two decades. A pool was a combination of independent businesses; it was a federation, not a union. It sought to control prices by limiting output or by dividing the market. A typical example of the latter was the agreement entered into, as late as 1902, between the Imperial Tobacco Company of Great Britain and the American Tobacco Company of the United States. The former was given market control of the British Isles, and the latter was allotted market control of the United States, her colonies, and Cuba; a third corporation, British-American Tobacco Company, Ltd., was to handle the business in the rest of the world. The pool idea still prevails in Europe, where it goes under the name of cartel. Because of the prevalence of cartels on the Continent, there is much less competitive pricing in Europe than in the United States, and much more of the practice of regional division of the market between companies. But in the United States the pool did not last for reasons that were legislative, organizational, and judicial. Legislative action was particularly effective in the railroad field, where pools had been strong; the Interstate Commerce Commission Act of 1887 forbade them. Organizationally, the structure of pools was weak. This was because members retained their independence, could welch on an agreement, and frequently did. There was no legal way to force them into line. Often — as one industrialist put it — pool agreements lasted only as long as it took the quickest man in the group to get to the telegraph office, where he would quote a lower price in order to grab business from the others. Judicially, the pool agreements could not be enforced in the courts because under common law they were obviously a conspiracy in restraint of trade. A couple of Supreme Court decisions were noteworthy in this regard. In *United States* v. *Trans-Missouri Freight Association* (1897) the Court ruled, in a 5 to 4 decision, that an association of eighteen railroads which existed to fix transportation rates was a violation of the Sherman Antitrust Act. In *Addystone Pipe and Steel Co.* v. *United States* the Court was involved with a pool of pipe manufacturers; it invalidated a market allocation scheme as a violation of the Sherman Act.

The entrepreneur who led the way in the development of the trust was John D. Rockefeller; he saw this device as a method to maintain prices and restrict production. It was in 1882 that his lawyers put together the Standard Oil Trust. The owners of the stock in seventy-seven constituent companies surrendered their stock, including voting rights, to the trustees — Rockefeller and his eight partners. In return the owners of the surrendered stock received trust certificates entitling them to dividends, which were handsome, but nothing else. Under this scheme absolute power was given to the trustees. It was so obvious that trusts had been organized for the purpose of eliminating competition and controlling prices that the term has been loosely used to designate any large combination, any big business, whether it is actually a trust or not.

In the last two decades of the nineteenth century the trust idea caught on. Other industries could not help but note, and envy, the smoothness of Standard Oil's progress from one acquisition to another. Whiskey, sugar, meat, glass, tobacco — all had been suffering from overproduction, so trusts were organized to control the surplus. Populist Ignatius Donnelly even discovered an undertaker's trust in the Northwest, and claimed there was a possibility that on resurrection day the dead would awake to find Gabriel controlled by a trumpet trust "with no toots except for spot cash." The producers of cottonseed oil were in such desperate straits that they paid Standard $250,000 merely for a copy of its seemingly magical trust agreement. It was the first time the document had been seen outside the Standard board room at 26 Broadway, which had now become the most famous business address in America. Cynics sneered that U.S.A. really meant United Syndicates of America. Actually the era of the trusts, narrowly defined, was shortlived; they were the favorite form of organization in the decade from 1887 to 1897. But in 1892 the Supreme Court of Ohio ordered the Standard Oil Trust to be dissolved. Rockefeller, after delaying tactics until 1899, then turned to the holding-company device. This was to become the form popular for a long time, and particularly in the period of greatest business consolidation from 1897 to 1904.

The holding company is an organization created to dominate other corporations by owning all or a portion of the stock of constituent companies; because stock is scattered among many small holders the ownership of not more than 10 to 20 percent of the stock available may control an industry. A combination through a holding company was permissible, at least in these early days, because it was not a conspiracy in restraint of trade. There would be no conspiracy because only one holding company was involved, and this company owned enough of the stock of constituent companies to control them. The holding-company device was not possible in 1882, when Rockefeller set up his Standard Oil Trust. Standard was chartered in Ohio, and that state prohibited a company to own plants in other states. Not until 1889 would New Jersey amend its incorporation law to allow a corporation chartered within that state to hold the stock of corporations chartered elsewhere; this is one of the reasons so many holding companies are chartered in New Jersey. In time Standard Oil became a holding company. So did Bell Telephone Company, through the American Telephone and Telegraph Company (A. T. and T.). The original patents of Bell expired in the 1890's with the result that many local companies sprang up. This competitive situation led to the creation in 1900 of A. T. and T. — a holding company in which the Bell Company and lesser systems were consolidated. For many years the U.S. Steel Corporation was the largest holding company in the United States.

Though the holding company is still the most significant type of corporate organization in the United States, the vigorous enforcement of federal and state antitrust laws made the holding-company forms precarious enough that new refinements have come in under what is called community of interest. This is a looser form than the trusts and the holding companies — a throwback to the pool. The community of interest is achieved through interlocking directorates. The device is almost self-explanatory; the same men serve on the boards of directors of several companies with the result that each company knows what the other is doing, all follow a fairly uniform policy, and may even charge the same prices. It was Adam Smith who wrote in 1776 that "people in the same trade seldom meet together, even for merriment and diversion, but the conversation ends in a conspiracy against the public, or in some contrivance to raise prices."

Although interlocking directorates were knocked out by the Clayton Act, the same purpose is achieved by having dummy directors; that is, a different person represents a constituent company on each of several boards. Through this device the names on the boards may be different but behind the scenes the strings are pulled by the same men. Community of interest is sometimes known as oligopoly, once defined as a situation "where a small number of companies can control production and control prices in a friendly atmosphere of live and let live." This friendly atmosphere developed, as an example, in the stockyards in Chicago. The Big Four there (Libby, Swift, Armour, Morris) were involved in no perceptible conspiracy. But by more than coincidence only four buyers appeared in the Union Stock Yards — one from each of the Big Four — to bid on cattle and hogs. The first would offer a low price; the others were not interested in bidding. The next day, another of the four set the price and the others refused to bid higher. Stock growers grumbled, but got nowhere.

A situation has developed, under oligopoly, in which a typical manufacturing industry has a price leader with several important followers. In steel no price increase can stick unless U.S. Steel goes along with it. In farm machinery International Harvester is top dog. In electrical machinery General Electric (GE) is the leader and Westinghouse the most important follower. In automobiles General Motors (GM) is the kingpin. One might well wonder why a big competitor, like Ford, does not reduce prices to steal the market from GM. A few years ago GM announced a price increase, and Ford immediately announced a similar increase. A Ford executive was asked why; he replied that it was because Ford had to "meet competition." At this point Adam Smith must have been spinning in his grave. He believed in *competition* in price; this was the code of classical economics. The Ford executive, by contrast, believed in *competition* through *accommodation*. He believed that "meeting competition" meant touching hands with a neighbor, not struggling with him. Thus competition in the conventional sense of price competition disappears in oligopolies. What competition there is becomes a matter of advertising and salesmanship — of attempting to establish so-called unique qualities for similar or identical products.

Have the "trusts" limited competition? On this question wise and learned men have disagreed. For example, the Temporary National Economic Committee (TNEC) and Adolf Berle answer in the affirmative; John Kenneth Galbraith and Sumner Slichter say no. In the early New Deal FDR experimented with the regulation of monopoly through the NRA. This failed, and FDR came to the conclusion that the recession of 1937–1938 was caused in large part by high monopoly prices. So he asked Congress for funds for a full investigation by a special committee. The result was the TNEC, composed of various members of Congress and of Executive agencies — with ample funds and the power of subpoena. Its investigation was the most thorough examination ever made of monopoly in this country by any agency, public or private. From its report it was apparent that early New Deal policies, following the ideas of the New Nationalism (regulation of monopoly) had strengthened and encouraged monoply rather than hindering it. The Second World War was to have the same effect, and for that reason the significant studies of the TNEC were abortive.

In 1932 Berle and Gardiner Means (a Harvard-trained economist) wrote *The Modern Corporation and Private Property*. John Kenneth Galbraith has said that this volume and Keynes's *General Theory of Employment, Interest and Money* were the two most important books of the 1930's. Berle and Means stressed two points: the concentration of corporate wealth, and control without ownership. On the first issue, they stated that the two hundred largest industrial corporations controlled virtually half of the national corporate wealth. That was in 1932. Thirty-four years later in 1966, an economist for the Senate Subcommittee on Antitrust and Monopoly Policy made another report. He stated that two hundred corporations (out of a total of approximately 200,000) controlled nearly 60 percent of the country's manufacturing wealth and therefore occupied commanding positions in virtually all principal markets. Within a decade (by 1976) this economist prophesied, this group of 200 American companies — plus 50 to 100 large foreign ones — would possess most of the world's manufacturing assets, and would make the great preponderance of sales and profits, having as tight a grip on global industry as our big companies have at home. The concentration of corporate wealth worried Berle and Means; so did control without ownership. This is brought about by management, through the ownership of limited voting stock or by the control of proxies. Berle would observe that managements are not publicly accountable — and that stockholders cannot, in practice, remove them.

All of this troubled Berle. He stated that the time might come when the corporation would be equal in power to the state — or stronger than it — and that possibly the corporation would supersede the state as the dominant form of social organization. Let us consider General Motors with its three-quarters of a million employees, factories in twenty-four countries, and a line of products that includes automobiles, refrigerators, earth-moving equipment, locomotives, jet engines, and missile guidance systems. In 1965 the net profit of GM was more than $2 billion. This was greater than the general revenue of forty-eight states in the United States. In the same year GM had sales of $21 billion. This exceeded the Gross National Product (GNP) of *all* except nine foreign countries. It is no wonder that there is the quip about GM: "One of these days they're going to get sore and cut the government off without a penny." This corresponds to the statement about the Chase Manhattan Bank: "It has several subsidiaries, you know — Western Germany for one."

By contrast with Berle and the TNEC, Galbraith and Slichter think that there is some hope — that the "trusts" have not limited competition nearly as much as most economists believe. Galbraith recognizes, along with Berle, that a large share of the productivity in the United States is carried on by a comparatively small number of large corporations. He says that if you except agriculture and much retail trade, the mining of soft coal, and the manufacture of clothing — which were in the hands of small firms — that much of the rest is in the hands of the giants. The heads of the corporations that produce up to half of the national product in the United States could be seated comfortably in almost any motion-picture theater. Three companies dominate the automobile industry, two dominate aluminum, three rubber goods, and so on — even though the competitive philosophy calls for scores of companies. When Galbraith was writing — in the 1950's — he told his readers to watch television, not meaning the screen. There were scores of companies making television sets at the time. Within a few years, said Galbraith, the industry would be shaken down to a safe and sound handful of producers. He was right.

To this point Galbraith sounded like Berle. But his conclusion in *American Capitalism: The Concept of Countervailing Power* (1952) was different. Galbraith said that oligopoly, far from ruining us, had actually strengthened the American economic system. Granted that two hundred corporations had pulled out of the free market — why hadn't they enforced a kind of fascist superstate and made puppets of us all, as Berle had forecast? The reason Big Business has not enslaved us, as Galbraith sees it, is that at least four other power centers have expanded to match the power of Big Business. These countervailing powers are Big Labor, Big Agriculture, Big Distribution, and Big Government. Examples of such countervailing powers are:

if major tire companies of Big Industry wanted to boost their prices — Sears (Big Distribution) stood ready to make its own tires;
if General Foods (Big Industry) wanted to increase the prices of breakfast food — A and P (Big Distribution) stood ready to produce its own;
if U.S. Steel (Big Industry) wanted to increase prices — John F. Kennedy (Big Government) stepped in and stopped the increase.

This countervailing power, said Galbraith, served to hold Big Business in check, and therefore provided a substitute for the free competition that no longer existed in industry itself.*

Sumner Slichter was Galbraith's senior colleague at Harvard, where he was Lamont Professor of Economics for many years. He contended that one of the most widely held misconceptions about the American economy is the belief that competition is diminishing in vigor and is being supplanted in many industries by various forms of monopoly. This erroneous belief, according to Slichter, was probably accepted by a majority of economists, and certainly by a majority of the general public. He was the first to admit that there are segments of the economy where competition is not as strong as it should be, and that some groups want to limit competition through high tariff and fair-trade laws. But in spite of this, it was Slichter's view that competition was not dying. Instead it was growing in vigor and increasing because of new developments in four fields: transportation, new business methods and organizations, new products and services, emphasis on research.

The new developments in transportation concern the motor car on the one hand, and refrigeration and pipelines on the other. With the automobile and good roads the situation is entirely different from that of a century ago, when the country store in an isolated village had a monopoly. Now, with the ubiquitous automobile, buyers are able to go from one seller to another, from one town to another. Refrigeration in vessels and railroad cars and aircraft has put the winter fruits and vegetables of the

---

* Galbraith was the first to admit that his system of countervailing power had two serious flaws. It will not work in a period of continuing inflation; it will only function when there is scarcity of demand. If buyers are plentiful, both original and countervailing power tend to supplement one another in the drive for higher wages. When this situation is aggravated by the necessity for large military expenditures, and by the reluctance of government in such periods to raise taxes and reduce spending, then the entire concept of countervailing power disappears. Between wars in Asia and creeping-to-galloping inflation, many would contend that this situation describes accurately U.S. economic history in most of the years since World War II.

The second flaw is that countervailing power cannot protect the interests of certain segments of the population not included in the Big Power Centers. These are particularly white collar workers, schoolteachers, and civil servants. Their situation is apt to become worse as the better-organized groups push for advantage.

South and of the tropics in competition with the canned and preserved fruits and vegetables of the North. Gas and oil piped halfway across the continent from Oklahoma and Texas has provided real competition for the coal of West Virginia and Pennsylvania.

There are new business methods and organizations which provide competition for traditional business methods and organizations. There is the new motel against the old hotel, the new outdoor movie against the old neighborhood theater, the new vending machine against retail stores. There is the new supermarket, based on the discovery that cutting the traditional markup plus rapid turnover produces good profits. These supermarkets provide real competition for a variety of other businesses because they sell so many things — not only groceries but tobacco, drugs, hardware, clothing. There is the quip about the customer's order at a supermarket: "I want four quarts of milk, a loaf of bread, and a new car."

There are new products and services. Slichter notes that in the decade of the 1940's the output of the economy as a whole increased by 5 percent annually. But in the same period annual sales of television sets increased 113 percent, freezers 71 percent, dishwashers 21 percent, frozen foods 19 percent, electric shavers 8 percent. These new industries and services, he contended, growing faster than the average, constituted a constant competitive threat to old and established industries. They forced the old ones to keep prices down and values up, in order to compete for their share of the market. This meant that new synthetics compete with old cotton and wool, new kinds of paper compete with glass and cloth, new oleo competes with butter, new television competes with movies, new buses and automobiles and planes compete with old railroads, and new detergents compete with soap.

All this has brought great emphasis on research. Seventy-five years ago industry depended for inventions and discoveries largely on enterprising individuals like Morse, Bell, McCormick, Edison, and Goodyear. Now industries are spending billions on their own research. In Slichter's judgment industrial research is competition at its best, because it means that the producer is making systematic efforts to reduce his costs and to improve his product. Furthermore, all companies must engage in it, or find themselves left behind in the competition.

Have the "trusts" limited competition? Economists and statesmen differ in their answers to this question. What does the American public think — what is its philosophy of what business life should be? A few years ago Elmo Roper polled the citizenry of the United States on this issue. His findings revealed, first, that the vast majority of the people believe in and want a system of private ownership and operation. At the same time they were not willing to place property rights above human rights, or to regard dividends as more sacred than wages. Second, he found that a great many people believe that too much of business is at best amoral and at worst greedy. Finally, it was evident that — because they know they cannot do it themselves — many people want someone to keep an eye on business, and their candidate for that "someone" is government.

Here lies the popular basis for antitrust legislation from 1890 to the present day. It was, and is, designed to protect the consumer against high monopoly prices, the small businessman against concentrated economic power, and the public against the exploitation of natural resources.

The first steps toward regulation of corporations were taken by state governments. Most of them were in the South and West, and were under Populist influence. The first antitrust law was actually passed by Kansas in 1889, and fifteen other states followed her example within four years. But it was obvious almost as soon as this law was passed that state regulation was futile. Under the Constitution, corporations chartered in one state can trade with individuals in another one. If one state was remiss in its regulation, all the corporations would go to it for their charters. It soon developed that three states were remiss; they were New Jersey, Delaware, and West Virginia. Within a short time 95 percent of the corporations of the country were chartered in them. Actually there are fifty-six charter-granting bodies in the United States — Congress, fifty states, and five territories. Competition among states for the *business* of granting charters resulted in an almost total abolition of even minimum standards. It resulted in charter-mongering — comparable with fish-mongering and vegetable-mongering — particularly in New Jersey, Delaware, and West Virginia. Delaware and West Virginia were lavish in their bids, but New Jersey got most of the business because of its proximity to New York; it was nearby for annual meetings — the only thing directors had to do was cross the river. Furthermore the costs were low; in New Jersey a company had merely to pay a fee, maintain a dummy office, hold one annual meeting in New Jersey, and submit a meager annual report. Federal action was imperative.

The Sherman Antitrust Act, passed in 1890, had a curious origin. It had bounced around the Finance Committee of the U.S. Senate of which John Sherman of Ohio was then chairman, and finally went on to the Judiciary Committee, of which Senator George F. Hoar of Maine was the most active member. Hoar actually wrote the act, based on common law, and would later say sardonically that it was "referred to as the Sherman Act for no other reason than that Senator Sherman had nothing to do with it whatsoever." Its language was terse: "Every contract, combination in the form of trust or otherwise, or conspiracy, in restraint of trade among the several states, or foreign nations, is . . . illegal." This seemed to mean that the Sherman Act forbade combinations in restraint of trade, without any distinction as to "good" and "bad" trusts. Bigness, not badness, was sin.

There were three weaknesses in the act: its ambiguity, its lack of administrative machinery, its lack of sanctions. The ambiguous language was to be interpreted by a conservative Supreme Court. In actual fact, a number of members of Congress were purposeful in making the language ambiguous. As politicians they felt they had to do something to appease the restive masses; as conservative businessmen they knew that if they made the language equivocal enough the conservative courts would interpret it properly. Mr. Dooley put it, "What looks like a stone wall to a layman is a triumphal arch to a corporation lawyer." Beyond the puzzling language, enforcement was left up to the Presidents. During the eleven years before TR became President only eighteen antitrust suits were brought before the courts, and four of these were against labor unions. As far as punitive provisions were concerned the Sherman Act proved ineffective because it had only baby teeth, or no teeth at all. There were two types of punitive provisions: civil suits to break up the company, criminal suits to fine and imprison its officers. The fines were so light as to be ludicrous. For sixty-five years the maximum fine was $5,000 for each violation; like the $1 parking ticket, the $5,000 fine against antitrust violations was ridiculous. During one thirteen-year period General Motors was fined five times for a total of $11,000 and DuPont was fined eleven times for a total of $42,500. This was not only inconsequential to large corporations — it was also apparent that the penalties were so low that violation was regarded as a good business risk. In 1955 the fine per count (violation) was raised to $50,000, but by that time the new and increased penalty was no more realistic; Donald F. Turner, at one time the director of the antitrust division of the Department of Justice, thought a reasonable maximum would be $1 million per count. As far as imprisonment was concerned one-year jail sentences could be levied on violators, but for seventy years (1890–1960) this provision might never have been written. In 1,580 cases under the Sherman Act in this period, fines had been imposed but no business executive had been whisked away to the cooler for breaking antitrust laws. Eugene V. Debs had been sent to jail under the act not because he established a monopoly but because he violated an injunction. There were those who proposed that the possibility for imprisonment be used. In the Senate William Langer was a persistent advocate of chucking violators behind the bars. Langer was a Progressive Republican from North Dakota who had supported "Old Bob" La Follette. Time and again Langer took to the floor of the Senate to shout that a hungry man who stole a loaf of bread was carted away to jail while three or four corporations that conspired to raise the price of bread suffered no such fate. When Justice Tom C. Clarke was Attorney General (1945–1949) he had argued that jail sentences would be "one of the most wholesome things that could happen." In 1961, at long last, it did happen.

The Department of Justice had sued twenty-nine electrical companies, including General Electric and Westinghouse, and forty-six officers of these companies, for price-fixing and bid-rigging on sales of almost $2 billion a year. The indictment spelled out an elaborate conspiracy, including the use of codes for concealment, and an arrangement in which the companies took turns in submitting allegedly low bids to governmental agencies. These sales did not involve standardized products in which it is well known that GE is the price leader in the electrical field; they involved custom-made products, like generators, where there can be no standardized price because each sale is unique. After lengthy negotiations, nineteen corporations and thirty-five individuals pleaded guilty. As a result the federal judge (J. Cullen Ganey) imposed jail sentences of thirty days on seven executives, and suspended thirty-day sentences (but with probation of five years) on nineteen others. He also imposed criminal fines of almost a million dollars against the companies and individuals, and opened the door for future civil damage suits. Aggrieved buyers, who paid more because of the price-fixing and bid-rigging, subsequently sued for triple damages. In 1962, General Electric settled with two of them — TVA and the U.S. government — for approximately $7,500,000. It was estimated that if future settlements were achieved on a similar basis, by General Electric alone, with all of its aggrieved customers — that the company's total damages would be approximately $50 million in the following years.*

The real drama in the courtroom arose not from the fines, but from the

---

* All of the companies concerned then raised the question as to whether a corporation convicted of an antitrust violation should be allowed to deduct the sums paid out in settlement of civil triple-damage actions as "ordinary and necessary business expense." In a ruling that reversed its previous position and rejected a recommendation of its staff, the Internal Revenue Service decided in the summer of 1964 that such settlements indeed should be deductible. The ruling was denounced in a joint statement by the chairman of two congressional antitrust committees (Senator Philip A. Hart and Representative Emanuel Celler) for its "passive assumption that a hardcore criminal price-fixing is 'ordinary and necessary business.' " They said the ruling was "flatly contrary to existing law" and a huge "tax giveaway." The central point was that the real penalty against a guilty company, under the antitrust laws, is *not* a federal fine; it *is* the cost of triple-damage suits. They provide the real teeth of the antitrust laws. The extraordinary decision of the Internal Revenue Service was compared to telling the Mafia to deduct its expenses for bribery as a legitimate deduction from the income tax.

In 1969 there was another illustration of "deductible wrongdoing" in relation to five pharmaceutical companies which were convicted of fixing prices of tetracycline and related broad-spectrum antibiotics. To avoid suits and conceivable judgments of as much as $500 million the companies offered to settle claims out of court for $120 million. Half the money is tax deductible, saving the pharmaceutical companies — and by the same token costing taxpayers — some $60 million. IRS explained its interpretation of "necessary" (in deductions for "ordinary and necessary business expense") by stating that if these charges were not deductible the penalties would "put the companies out of business," and that it was necessary for corporations to protect themselves from losses. This was an interesting interpretation of the law, one which did not apply to the penalties individuals find it "necessary" to pay, such as traffic tickets.

corporations involved and from the men who were sentenced. GE was the corporation which had engaged Ronald Reagan, later a governor of California, as host of the "General Electric Theatre," in which he delivered "The Speech" excoriating communism, the TVA, and big government. GE appeared to be biting the hand that fed it. As one of the largest defense contractors in the country, the company depended in large measure on the risk-free, guaranteed profits of governmental orders. Furthermore, as part of a major corporate oligopoly, GE operated in a noncompetitive and administered market. The men who were sentenced were middle-aged executives in Ivy-League suits, typical businessmen described as pillars in their communities. Several were deacons or vestrymen of churches, one was president of his local chamber of commerce, another was the chief fund raiser for the Community Chest. Judge Ganey, in his statement of sentence, said that the charges were a "shocking indictment of a vast segment of our economy." He continued with a commentary on the ethics of American business as it applies to organization men. He said that he was "convinced that in the great number of these defendant cases, they were torn between conscience and an approved corporate policy, with the rewarding objectives of promotion, comfortable security, and large salaries." He classified them as "the organization or the company man, the conformist who goes along with his superiors and finds balm for his conscience in additional comforts and the security of his place in the company setup."

Most remained secure; of the fifteen executives fired by General Electric after they were convicted for conspiracy in fixing prices, twelve were subsequently reemployed elsewhere at high levels.

In spite of this spectacular suit, enforcement of the Sherman Act over the years has been unimpressive. Because of the ambiguity of the language and the lack of enforcement machinery, economist Stuart Chase once called the act "a sheet of tissue paper across Niagara Falls." Because of numerous loopholes it is sometimes referred to as the "Swiss-Cheese Act." Emanuel Celler, the longtime chairman of the House Judiciary Committee, once called it a "horse-and-buggy statute applied to a jet-propelled era." Justice Holmes was probably closest to the truth: he called it a "brooding omnipresence in the sky."

TR boldly attacked trusts in speeches and messages and he filed a large number of suits against them, but the results hardly measured up to the threats and the activity. In 1900, just before TR became President, there were 185 manufacturing combinations, with a total capitalization of over $3 billion. At the close of Roosevelt's first administration in 1905, after much huffing and puffing ostensibly against trusts on his part, there were 318 manufacturing combinations with a total capitalization of more than $7 billion. That TR's heart was not in trust-busting was shown by his confession at the close of his Presidency, "I have let up in every case where I have had any possible excuse for doing so." Ultimately he would rationalize "any possible excuse" by making an artificial distinction between "good" and "bad" trusts — just as the Supreme Court did in 1911.

The most important corporate development in the eight-year Presidency of trust-buster Theodore Roosevelt was, ironically, the formation of the first billion-dollar holding company — U.S. Steel. The new mammoth corporation came into existence under New Jersey law by acquisitions of controlling stock in eleven separate holding companies which, in turn, were the owners of 785 operating plants. In 1901 it was by far the biggest thing the American business world had seen or dreamed of. Today it is still the fourth-largest industrial company in the United States, in terms of assets. It accounts for 25 percent of the nation's steel production, compared with 65 percent when it began its operations in 1901.*

Dramatis personae in the initial formation of the company were J. Pierpont Morgan, Elbert Henry Gary, John Warne Gates, and Andrew Carnegie. All were men of ability and importance, and require special commentary at this point. Morgan had an unusual, even forbidding appearance: glowering, massive, and fierce. Everything about him bespoke solidity and permanence: his inevitable wing collar, ascot tie, severe dark suit, the enormous bloodstone that hung from a heavy gold watch chain — the very stone and chain he had worn when he entered the business world in 1857. The famous photographer Edward Steichen took a picture of Morgan in which, as one commentator put it, the eyes looked like "the headlights of a locomotive," and his clenched hands "seemed to hold an invisible dirk." More remarkable was the nose. Morgan had been troubled with skin disease from boyhood, but now acne rosacea had settled in his nose, turning it into a huge and glaring deformity that commanded the beholder's attention. The ruby nose actually added to his personal fame; with realistic humor Morgan once said, "It would be impossible for me to appear on the street without it." On another occasion he remarked that his nose was "part of the American business structure." In actual fact, under

---

* In 1952 U.S. Steel ceased to be a holding company, becoming an operating company by merger of corporate assets (plant) rather than control through ownership of stocks. The reason is that interest paid on debt is deductible for corporate income-tax purposes; dividends on preferred stock are not. This was unimportant in 1901 when the holding company induced constituent companies to join by issuing 5.5 million shares of 7 percent preferred stock — but it is important now. New Jersey law makes it extremely difficult for a holding company to retire stock, in this case 3.6 million shares of 7 percent preferred stock still remaining from the original 5.5 million shares. The 7 percent dividend on its preferred stock was costing U.S. Steel in 1952 more than $25 million in after-tax earnings. Assuming that the company could eliminate the preferred stock by offering holders new debt securities that would give them an equivalent amount of income, the saving in corporate income taxes would be roughly one half of the $25 million previously lost. The swap would benefit holders of common stock because the savings of $12 million would accrue to the benefit of common stockholders as additional earnings.

this forbidding exterior a considerable amount of sentimentality and feeling was concealed. Few knew that at the beginning of what became a lifework in business he had married a young woman who was far gone with tuberculosis, and had dropped his career to take her to the Mediterranean in a vain attempt to save her life. He was generously charitable but many of his gifts were concealed because Morgan felt that a gentleman did not advertise his philanthropies. This lost him some credit that might have provided a better balance in his general reputation with the public — a matter of complete indifference to him because he hated publicity.

Morgan possessed vast powers of concentration and had a brilliant mathematical mind. He was noted for combining businesses because, as he stated it, "I like a little competition, but I like combination better. . . . Without control you cannot do a thing." In reorganizing, or "reMorganizing," corporations he was adept in providing both the combination and the control. In the industrial field, for example, he was prominent in the organization of General Electric, International Harvester, and U.S. Steel. In railroads he kept the New York Central and the Pennsylvania from tearing each other apart in a squabble over the Albany and Susquehanna. He backed Jim Hill against Edward H. Harriman, ultimately bringing about the agreement that led to the Northern-Securities Case. All of this, particularly the formation of U.S. Steel, gave the nation the exaggerated idea that Morgan was running everything. Actually Morgan's personal fortune could not compare with others in his day; he left $68 million at the time of his death, and the value of his art collection might have raised it to $100 million.

But no matter; in 1912 the well-known congressional Pujo Investigation was directed largely at Morgan. There was the popular story about the colloquy between the teacher and pupil:

"Who made the world, Charles?"
"God made the world in 4004 B.C., but it was reorganized in 1901 by E. H. Gary, J. Pierpont Morgan, and Andrew Carnegie."

The most popular commentator of that day, Mr. Dooley, described Morgan as being able to say to one of his office boys:

"Take some change out of the damper an' r-run out and buy Europe for me. I intend to reorganize it and put it on a payin' basis. Call up the Czar and the Pope and the Sultan and the Impiror Willum, and tell them we won't need their services after next week. Give them a year's salary in advance. An' James, he says, ye better put that red-headed bookkeeper near the door in charge of the Continent. He doesn't seem to be doin' much, he says."

Elbert Henry Gary was born near Wheaton, Illinois, where he worked hard on a farm — an experience that endowed him with a robust physique and excellent health. Later he built up a wide and lucrative practice as a lawyer, earning as much as $75,000 a year before he became a steel executive in 1898 as president of the Federal Steel Company in Chicago. His legal work in constructing the corporate form of this company so impressed the elder Morgan that he turned over to Gary the major work of organizing U.S. Steel. Gary was fifty-five at the time (1901) but dominated the company until his death at eighty-one in 1927. (As late as 1969 the Gary works in Indiana were the largest in the world, and were the most modern and the most efficient in U.S. Steel.)

In manner and appearance Gary looked, and sometimes acted, like a Methodist bishop. He refused to play cards because he believed it below the dignity of the head of U.S. Steel to do so. Very religious, he was fond of reading sermons to his colleagues; this was probably a carry-over from the days when he went to Wheaton College and taught the ladies' Bible class in the Wheaton Methodist church. As an executive he was superb — with perfect self-control, unfailing tact, and extraordinary patience. On the management side he followed the policy of cooperation rather than competition; he promoted sweetness and light by founding the Iron and Steel Institute, and by staging what came to be called "Gary dinners." He believed in high profits; it was Gary who once pronounced, "A corporation is entitled to 15 percent on its money." He also believed in low wages and the open shop. His unwillingness to negotiate with organized labor led to the bitter 1919 steel strike. Labor unions and laboring men despised him; they used to say that Gary, the head of U.S. Steel, never saw a blast furnace until after his death.

Gary may have looked like a Methodist prelate, but there was no resemblance between John Warne ("Bet-a-Million") Gates and a bishop. One of the most vigorous and colorful figures in American finance, he applied the rough qualities of the frontier to the realm of Big Business. His secretary once described him as a "great boy with an extraordinary money sense attached"; no intellectual, as far as is known the only book he ever read was *David Harum*. Restless, imaginative, and more interested in floating companies than running them, he was much feared on the Stock Exchange. A manipulation of the Louisville and Nashville Railroad, which he acquired secretly and then unloaded on Morgan at an extra-fancy price, ended in his virtual ostracism from New York finance. He would bet on anything. When traveling by train during a shower, he and his companions would wager on the downward course of raindrops on the windowpanes — at a thousand dollars per race. He got his nickname from a horse race in England in 1896. There was a man-hating racer, with a tendency to sulk, named Royal Flush. Her trainer tried gentle methods for a long time, then beat Royal Flush with a cane. It floored the horse, but the beast got up a new animal. Subsequently she raced again; the odds on her, not surprisingly, were 40 to 1. Gates heard about the animal's psychological transformation, gambled $15,000, won $600,000. Some stories had his winnings at $2 million, and stated that he frequently "bet a million" in his own country. The name stuck.

Gates began his business career as a salesman for the barbed-wire industry. Rail fencing had not been able to meet the hazards of fire, wind, and cattle in the West — but ranchers were skeptical about steel wire. Gates built a corral of wire and issued a challenge to ranchers to let their most vigorous Texas steers test its endurance. The wire won, and the orders came rushing in as Gates advertised the fence as "light as air, stronger than whiskey, and cheaper than dirt." Gates was the chief figure in the consolidations that resulted in the formation of American Steel and Wire Company (1898), and was the first to talk about the billion-dollar combine that became U.S. Steel. But neither Morgan nor Carnegie could abide Gates, regarded him as an irresponsible plunger, and froze him out of the combination. Gates complained, "I only do openly what Morgan does behind closed doors." Morgan's retort became a classic: "That is what doors are for."

Andrew Carnegie was born in Scotland in a home only a few hundred yards from the resting place of Robert the Bruce. His father was a weaver and something of a radical, a believer in all sorts of social and political reforms including the liquidation of the King of England. Carnegie absorbed some of the same ideas, and later said, "As a child I could have slain king, duke, or lord, and considered their death a service to the state." The poverty of the family in Scotland was extreme, and when he was thirteen they all migrated to western Pennsylvania. Carnegie never lost his love for Scotland and in later life tried to spend six months a year at his palatial Scottish manor, Skibo Castle. He loved Burns, both for his poetry and for his democracy. In America the small (five feet, four inches, and 130 pounds), flaxen-haired Andrew began his industrial career as a bobbin boy in a cotton mill, then took a job delivering telegrams. Telegraphic impulses in that day were received on a tape that came out of a complex machine. While Carnegie was standing around the office he developed the ability to "read" the clicking tape by ear — thus becoming one of the first operators to take messages by sound. (During the early months of the Civil War he reorganized the Union telegraph system with conspicuous success.) An occasional visitor in the telegraph office was Thomas A. Scott, president of the Pennsylvania Railroad, who made Carnegie his private secretary and personal telegrapher (1853) — at the princely salary of $35 a month. Said Carnegie: "I couldn't imagine what I could even do with so much money." He advanced rapidly in the Pennsylvania Railroad, and before he resigned (1865) to devote his career to steel, was made superintendent of the Pittsburgh division of the railroad. As a steel magnate he developed the Carnegie Company into the greatest producer of crude steel in the country, enjoyed a virtual monopoly, and finally sold out to Morgan and U.S. Steel for almost $500 million.

He was a great organizer, particularly adept in selecting personnel of high caliber — men like Henry Clay Frick and Charles Schwab (who was successively president of the Carnegie Steel Company, U.S. Steel, and the Bethlehem Steel Company). Carnegie would say that the epitaph on his own tombstone should read: "Here lies the man who was able to surround himself with men far cleverer than himself." He also selected men who were less sensitive than himself; Carnegie had a great concern about public opinion and a genuine warmth toward mankind. In 1892 he retired from the active management of his company, turning it over to the tough-minded Frick. From Skibo Castle he would deplore the Homestead Strike and Massacre, writing to William E. Gladstone that "the works are not worth one drop of human blood." He also insisted on up-to-date machines, and his readiness to discard costly equipment as soon as something better appeared is a tradition in the steel industry.

But organizing ability and modern machinery were only part of the answers for Carnegie's phenomenal success. There was another factor involved in a daring gamble that he took and that paid off and gave him a tremendous advantage over the other tycoons of his day. The Carnegie gamble was expansion on the business "downswing."

In his acceptance of the risk of expanding a business during a depression or when sales and demand did not justify it, Carnegie was smart enough to capitalize on the principle that when everyone wants something and prices are high, whether for steel or automobiles, one shouldn't buy, one should sell. On the converse when no one wants chattels, whether in the form of factories or houses, and prices are low, that is the time to buy. Acting on this principle, when business was most depressed Carnegie acted. In those "downswing" years, he made immense outlays at low comparative cost to improve his plants, unlike his opponents who waited until times were flush and prices were high. The result was that Carnegie's myopic competitors, when business revived, had run-down organizations, while Carnegie was set to exploit tempting new markets to the full.

Let us take as an example the era from 1893 to 1897, which was one of great industrial depression. During this period steel plants went to seed — except Carnegie's. He developed his factories extensively at low cost, and when prosperity came back on the flood tide of the war year 1898, he had the whole steel industry at his mercy. Because of the low cost of his plant, the price at which Carnegie could sell rails and steel meant vast profits for him and absolute ruin for his competitors. The result was that in 1900 the Carnegie Company made $40 million, of which Carnegie's personal share was $25 million in an era without income taxes.

Carnegie's policy of expansion during times of depression — a kind of one-man application of Keynesian economics — was based on faith in the future prosperity of the country. Although that seems like an easy gamble to us now, because we have the advantage of hindsight, it was not an obvious gamble at the time. A curious feature was the fact that Carnegie was not a gambler in the accepted sense of the term. He never bought a share of stock on margin in his life. Yet he made a national gamble of titanic proportions and won. He wagered everything he possessed on the economic future of the United States.

In 1900 certain fabricators of steel products — such as American Steel and Wire — were so angry at Carnegie because of his virtual monopoly on crude steel that they were threatening to build their own steel mills and thus cut Carnegie out of the market. Carnegie struck back by making preparations to produce not only crude steel but finished products as well. A battle to the finish was in prospect during which it was apparent that a number of corporations would lose their lives and that Carnegie's would not be among the dead. Morgan, who did not approve of cut-throat competition, stopped it by buying out Carnegie and forming U.S. Steel. The point was that Carnegie was making steel at $12 a ton, and selling it for $23.75 a ton — behind a high tariff wall that was designed to "protect our American industry and our workers from cheap foreign steel." Carnegie could make steel more cheaply than anyone else, and Morgan knew it. For that very reason Morgan had to pay not only for the *actual value* of Carnegie's business — but also for the *value* of Mr. Carnegie's capacity to do harm to other steel companies in Mr. Morgan's tow. This capacity to do harm was capitalized, with the result that Morgan paid twice the real value of Carnegie's business. In actual fact, Morgan was bribing Carnegie to *go out* of business and the bribe was ultimately paid by the American people in higher prices.

Because Carnegie had Morgan in a corner, a most unaccustomed position for "Pierpontifex Maximus," the financier came to regard Carnegie as a brash little Scotsman — an upstart and "no gentleman." In previous years Morgan had hesitated to do business with such a fellow, but now he had no choice. There was the story about Morgan and Carnegie meeting on a transatlantic voyage after the sale, and Carnegie's statement to Morgan that he (Carnegie) should have asked for another $100 million. Morgan's alleged answer was at least typical: "If you had asked me for another $100 million, I'd have paid it, if only to be rid of you." The price Morgan did pay was almost $500 million, of which Carnegie's personal share was about $250 million. Others also profited, partners in the Carnegie Company, with the result that the term "Pittsburgh Millionaire" came into circulation. It denoted freehanded and ostentatious spending that reached a high (or perhaps a low) point in vulgarity.

In part because of the high price paid to Carnegie, U.S. Steel was half water at the time of its organization. The fair market value of the properties that went into the corporation was about $700 million, but the bonds and stock issued by U.S. Steel amounted to $1,402 million. The total cost of promotion for the new billion-dollar holding company was $150 million, of which Morgan's share, $62,500,000, was considerably less than Carnegie's profit. Not surprisingly, steel had to go up in price. Carnegie had sold steel for $23.75 a ton. The new "trust" — U.S. Steel — announced a price of $28 a ton. The reason given was "increased costs of operation" — the understatement of the year. Morgan had made the steel business *safer* for the investor, but considerably more hazardous for the consumer.

Carnegie was unusual because of his business methods and by reason of his intellectual interests. Actually steel production was an avocation with him as far as real interests were concerned; he genuinely wanted to be a writer and a scholar. From an early age Carnegie was an avid reader — in history, politics, philosophy, and science. He was a self-made man both economically and intellectually. At sixteen he was writing letters to Greeley's New York *Tribune* on the slavery question. At the same age he was borrowing books from a Colonel James Anderson of Allegheny, Pennsylvania, who opened his personal library of four hundred volumes to poor working boys, delivering the books to them on Saturday night. Carnegie was a persistent borrower; the memory of the early benefits he received from Anderson's philanthropy goes far to explain his own library gifts in later years. Even during his busy years as a steel magnate, he was the friend of intellectuals and he kept up his writing. A delightful raconteur and a man of great charm, he was on intimate terms with Mark Twain, William E. Gladstone, Lloyd George, university president Andrew White, historian-diplomat James Bryce, Matthew Arnold, and lawyer-orator-agnostic Robert G. Ingersoll.

He was a frequent contributor to magazines and he wrote one book. Two of his literary efforts created quite a stir. The first was the book *Triumphant Democracy*, published in 1886. It stressed the superiority of American republican principles over the monarchical ones found in England. The volume had a red cover with an upside-down royal crown, which was alongside an inverted pyramid. These were supposed to be symbols of the topsy-turvy characteristics of monarchical principles. The book struck some hard blows at the British royal family, and caused some scandal in Britain. Apart from his writing on the British crown, the work from his pen which was most discussed was his article "The Gospel of Wealth," which appeared in the *North American Review* in 1889. Many readers misconstrued the meaning of one sentence to signify that Carnegie had said the man who dies rich, dies disgraced. Actually he had not gone that far but he did say that the lives of rich men should be divided into two periods, one for acquiring wealth and the other for distributing it. He stood up for tycoons like himself by saying that they were valuable in stimulating industry and in organizing energies — material and human. He went on to the statement that made him a traitor to his class, in the eyes of many colleagues — whose intellectual descendants would say the same thing about Franklin D. Roosevelt a half century later — that the monetary rewards to industrialists far exceeded the value of their services. He added, in a concept that was reminiscent of Henry George and his theory of "unearned increment," that the people as a whole had created the income which was now concentrated in a few individual pockets, and that wealth which the community had thus amassed should be returned to it. The millionaire was therefore only a trustee; he merely held surplus wealth for the benefit of his fellows. Carnegie gave away $350 million — $62 million in the British Empire and $288 million in this country.

In at least one respect Carnegie's theory on wealth was open to criticism. He made money and then gave it away. He could have avoided acquiring most of it in the first place by giving labor a living wage — either through higher wages or lower prices. When Carnegie was making $15 million a year in 1895, unskilled workers were receiving less than $460 a year in the North, $300 a year in the South. Giving labor higher wages or lowering prices would merely have changed the timing on Carnegie's problem of distribution. There is no evidence, however, to indicate that Carnegie ever thought of solving the problem by distributing potential wealth before he got it.

The period of Theodore Roosevelt's Presidency (1901–1909) witnessed a great increase in the number of "trusts," and saw the formation of the world's first billion-dollar holding company. Yet TR has a great popular reputation as a trust-buster for three reasons: the spectacularity of the Northern-Securities Case; the clamor provided by TR himself; and the clamor provided by the muckrakers. The Northern-Securities Case grew out of a struggle between two gigantic financial-railroad interests: The Hill-Morgan on the one hand and the Harriman–Rockefeller–Kuhn, Loeb (Rothschild) on the other.

James J. Hill deserved the soubriquet of "Empire Builder" because he was original and different as an engineer and as a promoter of settlement. His building of the Great Northern from St. Paul to the Pacific was probably the greatest feat of railroad building in the United States. He accomplished it in spite of the most difficult terrain and *without* the federal subsidies showered so generously on other railroads. In encouraging settlers he pioneered with "farm-demonstration" trains and by his eloquent testimony persuaded thousands of farmers to settle in Montana where, unfortunately, many were later ruined by drought. His enterprise was so soundly organized that he was able to weather all financial storms.

Edward H. Harriman, the son of an Episcopal minister, became a sharp speculator in railroads, ruthless in competition and utterly without conscience as to the general welfare. At the age of twenty-one Harriman borrowed $3,000 and bought a seat on the New York Stock Exchange. At thirty-five he purchased his first railroad; at forty-nine he took over the Union Pacific, which had gone through bankruptcy. He was not satisfied with merely "taking over." He rigged up a special train, complete with observation car, and had himself *backed* over the entire UP system; when he returned to Wall Street he put $25 million into the improvement of the system. In the early 1900's he became involved in a struggle with Hill and Morgan, but came out of it with a profit of more than $50 million. By 1906 Harriman personally controlled and managed 25,000 miles of railroad and 35,000 miles of steamship lines to the Orient. TR claimed that Harriman was an "enemy of the republic" who was lost in "deep-seated corruption." There was an investigation by the ICC; Harriman began to fight back but was sick and worn, and died in 1909 before the issue could be resolved. Small and unimpressive in physique with a drooping and stringy moustache, Peter Lyon notes that "he was a man with nowhere the commanding presence of a Pierpont Morgan — but he was incontestably the most brilliant railroad executive in American history, shrewder than Gould or Sage, better informed about railroad operations than Huntington or Hill, more imaginative by far than Morgan or any of the Vanderbilts."

The Morgan-Hill interests controlled eastern railroads (the New York Central, the southern system, and lines in New England) plus the Great Northern in the Northwest. These totaled 71,000 miles. The Harriman group controlled roads from Chicago south and west to the Gulf and Pacific Coast (the Illinois Central, the Union Pacific, and the Southern Pacific). These totaled 25,000 miles of track. The bone of contention was the Northern Pacific, not because the Northern Pacific was important in itself, but because it controlled the Burlington. The Burlington went to Chicago, and Harriman had to have it or forego an entry into the highly important Windy City. The Hill-Morgan interests did not want Harriman to get into Chicago; the primary struggle between the giants therefore occurred when Harriman tried to buy the Northern Pacific (Burlington), and the Morgan-Hill group opposed him. The two well-heeled groups started buying stock, with the result that in *one hour* on 9 May 1901, Northern Pacific stock rose from $350 to $1,000 a share. Many brokers, who had sold short, were ruined.

None of the principal financiers involved had any real belief in competition, so they arranged a treaty of peace through a superconsolidation. This was the Northern Securities Company, a holding company to acquire the stock of the Great Northern and the Northern Pacific, and thus the Burlington. Such an organization meant the elimination of competition in the Northwest. TR then entered proceedings under the Sherman Act, and the Supreme Court dissolved the Northern Securities Company as an illegal combination in restraint of interstate commerce. Morgan never understood TR's attack on the merger; he had always been able to manage President McKinley and was unable to comprehend the intransigence of his successor. Morgan went to the White House and complained that the President ought to have given him advance warning of the legal action against the Northern Securities Company. Unruffled, TR replied that this was exactly what he had not wanted to do. Morgan, with wholly unconscious arrogance, expressed his *basic belief* that the financial oligarchy *and* the government of the United States were equals, and ought to be able to make a quiet arrangement in cases like this one. He said, "If we have done anything wrong send your man [the Attorney General] to my man and they can fix it up." Not many Americans at that time cared to face the wrath of Morgan, but TR simply shook his head, and said: "That can't be done." Morgan never got over his resentment against the first Roosevelt. At the time he commented, "The man's a lunatic. He is worse than a Socialist." In 1910, when TR went off to Africa to hunt lions Morgan was heard to comment, "I hope the first lion he sees does his duty."

Actually the benefit from the Northern-Securities Case, in the long run, was of little importance. Industrial bigness was not stopped. What really mattered was that the government of the United States, once and for all, had asserted its sovereignty. It *had* the power to intervene, it would *use* that power as it saw fit, and it would not *bargain* with Wall Street. The national capital *was* the national capital, and would continue to be in Washington and not in the financial district of New York. The Detroit *Free Press* summarized the situation with irony: "Wall Street is paralyzed at the thought that a President of the United States would sink so low as to try to enforce the law."

The Northern-Securities Case was one reason for TR's reputation as a trust-buster; his own histrionic clamor was another. John Morley, the English statesman and man of letters, once described Roosevelt as an interesting combination of St. Vitus and St. Paul, a wonder of nature comparable to Niagara Falls. He had a knack of doing things noisily, of creating the appearance of action whether there were any results or not. Journalist Mark Sullivan would state that when TR was in the neighborhood the public could no more look the other way than a small boy could turn his head away from a circus parade followed by a steam calliope. In retrospect it appears that he seemed to be so radical because his roar was so loud. In 1905, as President, he attended the wedding of his niece Eleanor Roosevelt to his distant cousin Franklin Delano Roosevelt. It was the President who stole the show — so much so that a relative growled, "When he goes to a wedding he wants to be the bride, and when he goes to a funeral, he wants to be the corpse."

Certainly TR incurred the hatred of rich men; he may not have weakened their power but he certainly damaged their pride. These rich men, who had been obsequiously termed "Captains of Industry," were now scornfully branded by TR as "Malefactors of Great Wealth" — and great was their psychological fall. The wrath of the deflated was great but, in the judgment of historian Gerald Johnson, the truth seems to be that TR, like his cousin a generation later, was probably performing a service for the wealthy. The period of ruthless and arrogant exploitation, both of natural resources and of labor, had come to an end. The public was fed up with it. The only question was whether wealth would dismount from its high horse feet first, or be thrown off to land on its head. TR compelled it to dismount, and thereby saved it from being overthrown violently, but his thanks consisted of bitter and reckless vituperation.

In addition to incurring the wrath of the malefactors of great wealth (the sardonic journalist Ambrose Bierce paraphrased it to "malefactors of great stealth"), TR also convinced most of the people of the nation that he — their President — was on their side. The same reaction occurred with TR's cousin a generation later; he represented a reaction from Hoover just as TR represented a reaction from McKinley. The country applauded in the 1930's just as they had approved of TR at the turn of the century. This is illustrated by the story out of North Carolina in the 1930's. A reporter from an anti-Roosevelt newspaper approached a mill worker and grilled him about his evident enthusiasm for the President. Did he realize, the reporter asked, that the New Deal was based on Socialist theories and was certain to bankrupt the nation? The mill worker squirmed and reddened but finally blurted out his answer: "Mr. Roosevelt is the only man we ever had in the White House who understood that my boss is a sonofabitch."

Theodore Roosevelt also achieved his reputation as a trust-buster because of the clamor of the muckrakers during his administration. The muckrakers represent an interesting and talented and influential group of writers in American economic history — particularly Tarbell, Steffens, Phillips, Lawson, Myers, and Sinclair.

Ida Minerva Tarbell's *History of the Standard Oil Company* (2 volumes, 1904) angered Rockefeller but pleased the public and the intellectual community. John T. Flynn, a prominent biographer of Rockefeller, would state that Tarbell's volume was the ablest document of its kind ever produced by an American writer. She had received her A.B. and M.A. degrees from Allegheny College, and had benefited from special training at the Sorbonne in the technique of historical research. Born in the oil regions of northwestern Pennsylvania, her family had been engaged as independents in the petroleum industry. She portrayed John D. Rockefeller as a cold and ruthless monster, and helped make him the most unpopular man in the United States. The supporters of Standard Oil nicknamed her "Miss Tarbarrel."

Lincoln Steffens was the journalist who in the *Shame of the Cities* (1904) not only detailed the corruption of political bosses in many municipalities, but also blamed businessmen for corrupting politicians and excoriated citizens for their inertia. David Graham Phillips, in *The Treason of the Senate* (1906), described the corrupt affiliation of state legislatures and U.S. Senators with Big Business. State legislatures then elected U.S. Senators; Phillips' evidence was so compelling that it was eventually influential in the passage (1913) of the Seventeenth Amendment, for the direct election of U.S. Senators. Phillips pointed out that at the turn of the century the U.S. Senate really represented economic principalities rather than geographic units; his conclusion was reminiscent of Mark Twain's famous remark "About all I can say for the United States Senate up on the hill is that it opens with prayer and closes with an investigation."

Thomas W. Lawson was a multimillionaire Boston stockbroker who made an important contribution to the muckraking movement in *Frenzied Finance,* when he finally decided that he could no longer endure in silence practices he viewed as wrong. Angry clients turned on him as a renegade to his class, but ultimately his sensational attacks on the "money kings," stock-market abuses, and the irresponsible practices of large insurance companies influenced significant insurance investigations in the state of New York, and other financial reforms as well. Gustavus Myers was a journalist who was first a Populist and then a Socialist. His *History of the Great American Fortunes* traced the rise to wealth of one family after another, pouring pitiless light on innumerable family skeletons. Upton Sinclair wrote an exposé of the Chicago stockyards in a novel entitled *The Jungle.* Originally rejected by five publishers, Sinclair then published it himself; after that (in 1906) Doubleday, Page became interested and published it too. The novel, which Sinclair wrote "with tears of anguish" in three months, became the nation's best-selling book for a year and was ultimately translated into seventeen languages. Within a month or two of its publication President Roosevelt was receiving a hundred letters a day demanding a federal cleanup of the meat industry and of what was then called the Beef Trust; this prodding was intense enough to annoy TR, who sent a message to Doubleday, Page: "Tell Sinclair to go home and let me run the country for a while."

TR attacked the malefactors of great wealth, and so did the muckrakers — who were in large part responsible for giving the Roosevelt Administrations a reputation of agitation for reform, including trust-busting. Because the muckrakers complemented TR, it is ironic to note that he did not like them, and gave them their name as one of derision. The orator and conservative railroad president, Senator Chauncey Depew of New York, had been attacked by the muckrakers — and Chauncey was a good friend of TR's. So in 1906, in a speech during the laying of the cornerstone for the office building of the House of Representatives, Roosevelt said:

In *Pilgrim's Progress* you may recall the description of the Man with the Muckrake, the man who could look no way but downward with the muckrake in his hands; who was offered a celestial crown for his muckrake, but who would neither look up nor regard the crown that was offered, but continued to rake to himself the filth of the floor.

TR went on to say that this figure typified some contemporary journalists, men who refused to see anything that was lofty, journalists who persistently fixed their eyes on vile and debasing things. His allusion was a pejorative one, but in time it no longer signified derision. Instead the term muckraker became one of distinction, much to TR's discomfiture.

TR had an undeserved reputation as a trust-buster. President Taft did not enjoy such acclaim, but had done much to deserve it, at least by relative standards. People thought of Taft's tonnage as they later thought of the *Leviathan* or the *Queen Mary;* he varied from 330 to 360 pounds in weight. He liked to play golf. Despite his total inability to lean far enough over to place a ball on a tee, he played the game with gusto, sometimes quitting early because he had lost all the available balls. Many would say of Taft, "He was a bad President, but a good sport." It would be fairer to say that Taft was at least an average President whose achievements tend to be overlooked because he had the historical misfortune to serve between two infinitely greater and more spectacular Presidents — TR and Wilson. The ironical truth is that the colorless Taft caused ninety legal proceedings to be brought against trusts during his four years of office, compared with forty-four for TR in seven and a half years. Furthermore, there were two sensational developments which happened to occur when Taft was President — the Rule of Reason by the Supreme Court (1911) and the Pujo Investigation of 1912.

TR had handpicked Taft as his successor, but there was a dramatic break between them which split the Republican party and induced the Rough Rider to run independently for the Presidency in 1912, thus insuring the election of Wilson. It is claimed that TR was bored by private life, wanted to return to power. It is said that he disagreed with Taft over conservation, particularly in regard to Taft's alleged conservatism over coal lands in Alaska, leading to the Pinchot-Ballinger controversy (see pp. 678–680). It is also charged that TR disagreed with Taft over antitrust policy, and this is certainly valid. In theory and practice Taft, through his trust-busting, was really enforcing the regulation of competition — the idea of the New Freedom — supported by Brandeis and Wilson. In theory TR was supporting the idea of the New Nationalism — the regulation of monopoly. In practice he was furious with Taft for initiating an antitrust suit against the U.S. Steel Corporation in 1911 for its absorption of the Tennessee Coal and Iron Company in 1908. Because TR as President had sanctioned this merger, as essential to ease the financial panic of 1907, his reaction to the antitrust suit was immediate and violent. He interpreted Taft's action against U.S. Steel as a personal affront, and felt Taft had designated him (TR) as either "a fool or a knave" — as a person who had either been "deceived by financiers or had been in league with them." So, for a variety of reasons, TR decided to run again in 1912 — thus guaranteeing the easy election of Wilson, although he received only 41 percent of the popular vote.

In the campaign of 1912 the regular Republicans, nominating Taft, asked for "clarification" of the antitrust laws. The irregular or "Bull Moose" Republicans nominated TR on a platform favoring the regulation of monopoly — the New Nationalism. In his losing campaign TR was supported by Frank Munsey and George W. Perkins — the latter a one-time partner of Morgan and an important figure in U.S. Steel and the International Harvester Company; without the financial backing of Munsey and Perkins TR might very well have refused to campaign in 1912. Under the circumstances it is not surprising that the Democrats accused TR of favoring the IHC and U.S. Steel, and much was made of his intimacy with Perkins. The Democrats, of course, nominated Woodrow Wilson on a platform favoring the regulation of competition — the New Freedom. Before the voting occurred, the cynical railroad czar Chauncey Depew pronounced: "The only question now is which [Republican] corpse gets the most flowers." It turned out to be TR. Taft carried only Vermont and Utah, and got eight electoral votes (against 88 for TR and 435 for Wilson).

The keystone of the New Freedom and of Wilson's antitrust program was found in his oft-repeated statement: "Private monopoly is indefensible and intolerable." This was carried out, during his first administration, by the Clayton Antitrust Act and the Federal Trade Commission Act, both passed in 1914. The Clayton Act was leveled at the evils of business consolidation and was supposed to fill gaps not covered by the Sherman Act of 1890. It contained three distinct types of provisions: prohibitions, sanctions, and labor clauses. The prohibitions were aimed at practices which "substantially tended" to lessen competition. These were:

Interlocking directorates, which were forbidden in concerns engaged in interstate commerce whose capital, surplus, and undivided profits aggregated more than $1 million, if such concerns were competitors.

Tying contracts; that is, a manufacturer could not sell his goods to a dealer under conditions requiring the latter not to handle the products of competitors.

Price discriminations, which were outlawed between purchasers of commodities, whenever such discrimination lessened competition or "tended to create a monopoly." Additional legislation was passed, in regard to price discriminations, in the Robinson-Patman Act of 1936 (see pp. 453–454).

Acquisition of stock in other corporations, which was forbidden where the effect was substantially to lessen competition — but the holding of stock solely for investment was allowed. This provision was supposedly strengthened by the Anti-Merger Law of 1950, which prohibited corporations from purchasing the assets (that is, plant as well as stock) of another corporation if the acquisition would substantially lessen competition or tend to create a monopoly.

The Clayton Act also provided for new sanctions and included labor clauses. Individual suits for threefold damages might be brought in the case of price discriminations and tying contracts. After its bitter disappointments in the Pullman and Danbury Hatters' cases (see pp. 441–442) labor had come to the conclusion, and rightly, that the Sherman Antitrust Act had been more effective against the workingman than corporations; it therefore regarded the Clayton Act as its "Magna Charta." Article Six of the act stated that "the labor of a human being is not a commodity or article of commerce." This meant that labor was exempted from antitrust suits. There were also clauses which outlawed injunctions except where irreparable damage was about to be done, and which required trial by jury in contempt cases — except where the contempt was in the presence of the court.

The Federal Trade Commission is a nonpartisan one consisting of five members appointed by the President for seven-year terms. Now more than a half century old, it has both powers and sanctions. Basically it is charged by law to keep the free-enterprise system from being either *stifled* or *corrupted* — stifled by monopoly, or corrupted by unfair or deceptive trade practices. From this general statement its specific powers are three in number, involving investigations, unfair trade practices, and monopolies (antitrust). It can, and has, conducted two types of investigations: continuing ones on the efficiency of antitrust laws, and special investigations at the request of the President or the Congress. On the antitrust side it is empowered to assist the Department of Justice in the enforcement of the prohibitory clauses in various antitrust acts — Sherman, Clayton, Robinson-Patman, Anti-Merger of 1950. As far as unfair competition goes, the commission prohibits unfair methods by business firms as defined by the original act of 1914, and by several others passed since that time:

unfair *advertising* of foods, drugs, and cosmetics under the Wheeler-Lea Amendment of 1938;
unfair *labeling* of wool textiles under the Wool Products Act of 1940, and of fur products under the Fur Products Act of 1946;
unfair *use* of registered trademarks under the Trade Mark Act of 1946.

Although the FTC is intended to *prevent* (through warning) rather than *punish*, it also has sanctions through its authority to issue "cease-and-desist" orders against corporations found guilty of malpractices. These punitive provisions were weak in the original act because fines were insignificant and because of judicial delays. Cease-and-desist orders did not become final unless affirmed by the courts; the burden of proof was on the

FTC. In some cases an order was found to have stood for ten years without becoming effective. Some teeth were provided for the commission by the Wheeler-Lea Amendment of 1938. Commission orders became effective within sixty days unless appealed; the burden of proof passed to the corporation. Fines of up to $5,000 could be assessed, if the order was not obeyed after it became effective.

In general, the Federal Trade Commission has been ineffective on enforcement of antitrust provisions of various acts, effective in investigations, and partly effective in curbing unfair competition. In antitrust actions it has been a woeful failure in curbing interlocking directorates, price-fixing, the development of monopolistic holding companies and mergers. Its investigations have been good; as an example there is the investigation of the electric power industry which it undertook at the request of Congress. The FTC report was seven years (1928–1935) in the making and fills ninety-four volumes; it was used as a basis for much legislation and brought rate reductions which reached a billion dollars or more. The commission's budget is little more than a thousandth of that sum.

The commission has worked hard, and with considerable frustration, to stop the *grosser* forms of unfair competition — as one critic put it, "to preserve the business of one knave from the unfair competition of another." To cite a few specific cases, under the Wheeler-Lea Amendment, it has taken the "liver" out of Carter's Little Liver Pills. In one of its most significant decisions the FTC ordered the manufacturers of the Carter laxative pills to stop using "liver" in the trade name, because these pills had no therapeutic value in the treatment of any condition, disorder, or disease of the liver. This effort took from 1943, when the FTC began its action, until 1959 when the Supreme Court finally refused to review it. In the early 1950's the commission also issued a famous cease-and-desist order against the American Tobacco Company. Specifically the order prohibited the claims that Lucky Strike cigarettes were "easy on the throat," and were preferred "two to one" by independent tobacco experts. The FTC pointed out that one brand of cigarettes was pretty much like another, that all have irritating qualities, and that the independent tobacco experts were often phonies. In 1967 the commission proposed a similar trade-regulation rule to stop drug manufacturers from making false claims about aspirin and other nonprescription analgesics. For years, on television, Americans have watched in fascination as certain aspirin brands have burbled through their telegenic anatomies, promising headache relief and balm for battered psyches. The FTC declared that, despite the advertised differences, "each of the analgesic products now offered to the consuming public is effective to essentially the same degree as all other competing products" — meaning that aspirin is still aspirin.

For the ineffectiveness of the FTC one can blame all three branches of the government. This means the Executive for poor appointments, and for lack of courage in the public interest. This means the judiciary for its delays, and for its frequent assumption that it must review not only the question of due process but also the commission's findings of fact as well. This also means the Congress for niggardly appropriations and occasionally for special interference with the FTC. In connection with the former, in 1964 there were more than 4 million business concerns in the United States, and their annual advertising budgets alone were more than $10 billion. In the same year the budget of the FTC was a bit more than $11 million, and it had slightly more than one thousand employees — including clerks and stenographers. In connection with special legislation by Congress, which impedes the FTC, there is the situation with regard to cigarette advertising. In 1964 the Surgeon General of the United States announced that cigarette smoking was a health hazard of sufficient importance to warrant remedial action. He had been impressed by the fact that in England the government itself advertises the danger of smoking cigarettes. Acting on the clear medical judgment of the Surgeon General the FTC wanted to issue regulations for cigarette advertising which would have stated that cigarette smoking was not only dangerous but might cause death from cancer and other diseases. At this point in 1965 Congress stepped in, with a bill that forbade the FTC from regulating the advertising of cigarettes, in any way, for the next four years. To distract attention from this obvious surrender to the tobacco interests, the bill directed that cigarette packages carry an innocuous warning that smoking "may be hazardous." This phrase cast doubt on the scientific certainty that it *is* dangerous. This was obviously a bill, as the *New York Times* observed, to protect the *economic health* of the tobacco industry, but not the *physical health* of American citizens. It raised the question as to what possible justification there could have been for Congress to intervene, to strip a regulatory agency of its authority over a particular industry. If Congress was going to intervene on behalf of one, presumably it should intervene on behalf of *all* industries that think they will suffer economic loss from an order of the FTC.

Roosevelt, Taft, and Wilson had tried to enforce the antitrust laws in varying ways. Under Harding, Coolidge, and Hoover (1921–1933) the energetic progressivism and reformism of the pre-World War I period was swept from the White House. The Harding-Coolidge-Hoover conservatives made no real attempt to repeal the Clayton Act or to abolish the FTC — both Wilsonian reforms — but they subtly and effectively achieved their ends by putting the courts and the administrative bureaus in the hands of fellow standpatters. The Supreme Court is a striking example of this trend. Harding was President less than three years, but he appointed four of the nine justices of the Supreme Court — all of them deep-dyed conservatives (Butler, Sutherland, Sanford, Taft); they held the dike against popular currents for two decades. The Attorney General's office, and the FTC, were friendly to corporations — and ignored or circumvented the antitrust laws. Historian Thomas A. Bailey has said that the Harding reactionaries might have boasted: "We care not what laws the Democrats pass as long as we are permitted to administer them."

The particular failures of the FTC, for whatever reason, were exasperating enough that by 1969 a study commission of distinguished lawyers and economists suggested drastic changes or its abolition. The group had been organized, at President Nixon's request, by the American Bar Association; however, only eight of its sixteen members, all of whom were recognized experts in the field of antitrust and business regulation, were members of the bar association. The study commission stated that the FTC had long since identified itself with a tradition of trivia pursued in lethargy, that its staff was characterized by incompetence, especially at the top, and that in 1969 it performed less work with more employees than it had a decade earlier. In its conclusion the commission said forthrightly that it should be the last of the long series of committees and groups which have insisted that drastic changes were essential to re-create the FTC in its intended image. The case for change was plain, and further temporizing was indefensible. The *New York Times* went further; it was so discouraged with the fifty-four-year record that it asserted that the "old lady of Pennsylvania Avenue" was probably beyond salvation and should be abolished in favor of an agency new in concept and fresh in personnel.

Before 1933 the attitude of the Supreme Court, under the antitrust laws, was quite different toward corporations on the one hand and labor unions on the other. In regard to corporations the first basic decision was that in *United States* v. *E. C. Knight Company*, in 1895. This decision severely limited congressional power under the interstate commerce clause. Previously, the Court under John Marshall (*Gibbon* v. *Ogden*, 1824) and Morrison R. Waite (*Munn* v. *Illinois*, 1876) had been very broad in interpreting the interstate commerce clause of the Constitution, and in giving the national government a great amount of power under it. The Knight case actually concerned the American Sugar Refining Company, which controlled 98 percent of the trade in sugar. The U.S. government sued under the Sherman Act to break it up. Chief Justice Melville W. Fuller, who held the position for almost a quarter of a century (1888–1910), delivered the 8 to 1 decision of the Court — with Justice Harlan dissenting. Fuller said that Congress could regulate commerce, but not manufacturing. The American Sugar Refining Company was a holding company for manufacturing concerns and "commerce succeeds to manufacturing, and is not a part of it." The Sugar Trust, he went on, was therefore a manufacturing, not a commercial, monopoly, and Congress could not control it under the Sherman Act and the interstate commerce clause of the Constitution. The assumption was that the American Sugar Refining Company made the sugar only to store it, not to sell it in interstate commerce. It was an incredible decision, reminiscent of the alleged exchange between Robert Hutchins when he was Dean of the Yale Law School, and James C. McReynolds, the conservative Justice of the Supreme Court. The Justice was said to have remarked, "I understand that at Yale you are teaching your students that the decisions of the Supreme Court of the United States are all nonsense." Dean Hutchins was reported to have replied, "Not at all, Mr. Justice. We simply give them the decisions and let them judge for themselves."

During the next three decades the Court began to change the basic decision in the Knight case.

In *United States* v. *Addystone Pipe & Steel Company*, 1899, a *group* of pipe manufacturing companies were charged with a conspiracy to restrain trade in iron pipe in thirty-six states, and with imposing excessive prices for pipe sold by the members of the group (or pool). William Howard Taft, then in the Circuit Court of Appeals, held that manufacturing was a state concern, but that these companies had solicited orders for interstate deliveries, thus constituting interstate commerce which came under the jurisdiction of the federal government. Taft's reasoning was upheld by the Supreme Court, thus reviving the Sherman Act against the debilitating effects of the Knight decision.

The Northern-Securities Case, 1904, resulted in a 5 to 4 decision against a railroad holding company (see pp. 429–431). TR regarded this decision as a reversal of the Knight case, and as important as the Dred Scott case in reversing a previous decision. This appears to be another example of the Rooseveltian gift for hyperbole; nonetheless the decision had a minor significance.

Finally, in *Swift & Co.* v. *United States*, 1905, the government charged that the "beef trust" restrained trade by means of *collusive* trade policies. Significantly, the alleged criminal activities involved only local transactions. But Justice Oliver Wendell Holmes held that these acts, although local in character, could fall under the federal commerce power if their effect formed part of a "current of commerce" among the states. This decision established the "stream of commerce" doctrine; it was a liberal interpretation of the interstate commerce clause. In time, Taft would call *Swift* a "milestone," a reaffirmation of the commerce power as the Constitution "intended it to be."

The Addystone, Northern-Securities, and Swift cases led to the "rule of reason" cases in 1911 — the first basic decision since *Knight* in 1895. In two cases in 1911 — Standard Oil and American Tobacco Company — the Supreme Court actually introduced two new ideas or concepts: first, it abandoned the doctrine that a monopoly of manufacturing was not directly a monopoly of commerce, and second, it enunciated the famous "rule of reason," that the Supreme Court would differentiate, and use its own judgment in deciding whether monopolies were in harmful restraint of trade. This meant, in other words, that some companies might be allowed to go on because they were a reasonable restraint of trade while others might be dissolved because they were an unreasonable restraint of trade. In the particular cases in 1911, the Supreme Court decided that both Standard Oil and the American Tobacco Company happened to be unreasonable restraints. This did not please the dissenting John Marshall Harlan, who said, "The statement surprises me quite as much as would a statement that black was white, or white was black. . . ." Senator John Sharp Williams would say, unfairly, that "Good trusts contributed to the party campaign, and bad trusts did not."

After this the antitrust laws became ineffective until the 1930's. In the U.S. Steel Case, 1920, the Supreme Court decided that the combination was a "good" trust. The fact that the corporation controlled almost 50 percent of the output did not constitute an unreasonable restraint of trade, because it did not exceed those of all its competitors combined. In the United Shoe Machinery Case, 1922, the Court decided that a combination that controlled more than 95 percent of the shoe-machinery business came within the "rule of reason" as a "good" trust.

After the "rule of reason" decision the antitrust laws became a dead letter as far as corporations were concerned, but such was not the case in relation to labor and labor unions, where they were enforced with rigor and strictness from 1895 on. Examples are the Pullman Strike of 1895, the Danbury Hatters' Case of 1908, *Hammer* v. *Dagenhart* of 1918, and the Bedford Stone Cutters' Case of 1927. An injunction, issued under the authority of the Sherman Antitrust Act, broke the Pullman Strike of 1895. Thirteen years later an AFL union (the United Hatters of North America) called a strike against Loewe and Company in Danbury, Connecticut, for the purpose of achieving union recognition; at the same time the union began a nationwide boycott against Loewe hats. All members of the AFL were instructed to buy only hats that had union labels, which, of course, Loewe hats did not. Employers all over the country had been worried by the concept of the union label, and the secondary boycott made possible by it; they had organized themselves into a national Anti-Boycott Association whose purpose was to come to the assistance of beleaguered employers — in this case Loewe and Company — who were harmed by national boycotts on the part of labor. The strike in Danbury therefore had implications far beyond the borders of Connecticut; it was a direct confrontation between two national organizations — the AFL for labor and the Anti-Boycott Association for management. Loewe and Company, supported by the Anti-Boycott Association, charged 191 members of the newly formed hatters' union in Danbury with conspiracy in restraint of trade, an alleged violation of the Sherman Act. In 1908 the Supreme Court upheld Loewe and Company, and triple damages of $250,000 were ultimately assessed against the local union. Because the union was not incorporated, each of the 191 defendants was liable for his share of the penalty. The president of the AFL, Sam Gompers, asked all members of the national organization to chip in an hour's pay; this voluntary contribution, however, did not bring in sufficient funds with the result that the savings of individual members of the Danbury union were attached and the homes of 140 were ordered sold. What the Court had really done was to make a distinction between primary and secondary boycotts. The former was declared legal unless accompanied by coercion, the latter — inducing collateral parties to stop patronizing or using the products of a boycotted firm — was pronounced illegal.

From the Swift decision in 1905, until 1918, the Supreme Court generally followed the broad outlines for the commerce power as set down by Taft and Holmes in the Addystone and Swift cases. But in *Hammer* v. *Dagenhart*, the Court returned to the reasoning in *Knight* by invalidating the Keating-Owen Act of 1916, which forbade interstate shipment of the products of child labor. It did so on the argument that the act was not a regulation of commerce, but an attempt to regulate the conditions of manufacture, a matter reserved to the states. (This decision was not repudiated until 1941 when, in *United States* v. *Darby*, the Court unanimously overruled the Hammer case by upholding the Fair Labor Standards Act of 1938.) In 1927 there was a strike at a quarry in Bedford, Indiana; in Colorado stone cutters refused to work on stone shipped from the Indiana quarry — obviously a secondary boycott. The Colorado stone cutters were sued, and the Supreme Court held that their refusal to work on Bedford stone constituted a conspiracy in restraint of trade under the antitrust laws. Justice Brandeis, in dissent, stated that if such reasoning was allowed to reach its final conclusion, labor would find itself in a position best labeled as involuntary servitude.

As a result of the Great Depression there were attacks from all sides of the political front. From the left there were the unemployed, Senator Huey P. Long, Francis E. Townshend, Upton Sinclair, and the Reverend Charles E. Coughlin. From the anonymous unemployed a reporter heard a talk in the early 1930's, at a meeting of the jobless in Detroit. A little man behind the reporter shouted, "They've got a better system than we've got." The reporter asked, "Are you a Communist?" The man replied, "Hell, no, I'm a Roman Catholic, how can I be a Communist? But they've got a better system than we've got. . . . Work? I've been out fifteen months. I've got four children, and I'll fight before I'll see them starve."

In Louisiana there was Huey Pierce Long (although it is possible to argue as to whether he should be classified on the left or right wing of politics). He came from the parish of Winn in the piney uplands of north central Louisiana, where poor white farmers worked the thin red soil for a meager living. It was Baptist country. Long recalled that a Methodist preacher moved to Winn, and would have starved to death had it not been for the charity of the Long family. It was claimed that the people in Winn made a living by taking in each other's washing; in that parish, as one historian described it, "a man would skin a flea for the hide and tallow." Because of this poverty it is not surprising that the major crop in Winn has been dissent; the parish has always been "other-minded." At a convention in 1861 to decide whether Louisiana should join the Confederacy, the delegate from Winn voted *against* secession. He said, "Who wants to fight to keep the Negroes for the wealthy planters?" When the Populist insurgency hit Louisiana in the 1890's, Winn was one of its centers. Twenty years later, it was a Socialist stronghold; the Socialists elected half of the parish officials in 1908, and in 1912 Eugene Debs got more than a third of its votes for President. In World War I, Huey P. Long dissented against the war. He said, "I did not go because I was not mad at anybody." Long was a notary public; he claimed, and got, draft exemption as a state official.

Politically, his slogan was adopted from Bryan: "Every man a king, but no one wears a crown." What the slogan really meant, because Long was a demagogue with an insatiable lust for power, was : "Every man a king, and Huey the kingfish." Long was elected governor of Louisiana in 1928, went to the U.S. Senate in 1931, and from that point directed his dictatorship from Washington. He was a character in every sense; Alben Barkley once told him, "You're the smartest lunatic I ever saw in my whole life." At first Long supported the New Deal, then became one of FDR's most vociferous critics. He went to see the President with a straw sailor hat perched on top of his red hair — and there it stayed during the interview — except when the Senator whipped it off and tapped it against the President's knee to drive home his complaints. When Long realized that he had no influence with FDR he began to call names. FDR became "Prince Franklin, Knight of the *Nourmahal*" (the *Nourmahal* was a yacht owned by Vincent Astor, on which the President had been a guest). The Secretary of Agriculture became "Lord Corn Wallace," and Secretary of the Interior Ickes was the "Chicago Chinch Bug." Long established the Presidency as his own next goal, and in 1935 published a book entitled *My First Years in the White House*. In the spring of that year he launched his presidential campaign with a "Share Our Wealth" program. He organized clubs all over the country to make "Every Man a King"; this would be accomplished by a federal guarantee of $5,000 a year for every family. He was shot by a political opponent in September 1935 — and thus became, as his friends pointed out, the first President of the United States who was assassinated before he was elected to office. Later John Gunther would view him as "an engaging monster," and would compare him to Hitler,

Mussolini, Goering, Goebbels, Salazar, Franco, Dollfuss, Kemal, Stalin, and Pilsudski. Actually he was the first major southern leader to put aside appeals to race-baiting and antebellum myths and to address himself to social and economic ills. When he was finished Louisiana had new schools, free textbooks, roads, mental hospitals, and bridges. But when he was finished Louisiana also had a secret police and a rubber-stamp legislature and a subservient judiciary. The democratic system had been jettisoned, and a totalitarian organization had been put in its place. An opponent had once shoved a volume before Governor Long and had said, "Maybe you've heard of this book. It's the Constitution of the State of Louisiana." Replied Long: "I'm the Constitution around here." He rested his case on rhetoric and the Scriptures. Said he, "I never read a line of Marx or Henry George or any of them economists. It's all in the law of God." And as part of the law of God he would summon Frank Costello, the famous gangster from New York, to take over the slot-machine concession in Louisiana.

In California there were Dr. Francis E. Townsend and Upton Sinclair. Townsend was a physician in Long Beach who looked out of a bathroom window while shaving. He saw in the alley below, cluttered with rubbish barrels and garbage cans, "three haggard, very old women stooped with great age, bending over the barrels, clawing into the contents." He broke into a rage of profanity; his alarmed wife rushed into the room, asking him to lower his voice lest the neighbors hear his ranting. Townsend replied, as he recalled his language later, "I want all the neighbors to hear me! I want God Almighty to hear me! I'm going to shout till the whole country hears!"

This he did. He proposed the Townsend Plan — the Old Age Revolving Pension Plan — to pay $200 a month to every retired person over sixty with the requirement that it be spent within the month. The cost was estimated at $20 billion per year; Townsend proposed to raise this sum by a universal 2 percent sales tax on all business transactions. The plan caught on and thousands of Townsend Clubs were established all over the country; by 1935 they claimed 5 million members. The doctor began to develop delusions of grandeur. He went to Washington, visited the Lincoln Monument, and said, "It might be me sitting up there." The movement progressed grandly until FDR took the steam out of it with the Social Security Act of 1935.

In California there was also ex-muckraker Upton Sinclair, an ardent Socialist who had been in and out of the American Socialist party. In 1934 he ran in the Democratic primary for governor, and garnered 436,000 votes — more than all of the other Democrats combined. He did so through the appeal of EPIC — a program to "End Poverty in California" through drastic taxes on wealth and benefits to the needy. He lost in the final election, but narrowly, by a union of forces against him which paraphrased EPIC to "End Promises in California," and called it an attempt to

"Sovietize California." The conservative Los Angeles *Times* quoted out of context from Sinclair's many books; these passages were designed to affect the sensibilities of conventional people — which most of the voters of California were. They were abbreviated quotations, carefully selected and didactically truncated, dealing with free love or Marxism or anti-Catholicism or atheism or the nationalizing of children from the moment of umbilical severing. It was a prime illustration of the validity of the wish of Job that his adversary would write a book. The Los Angeles *Times* did not comment on the stoical and exemplary code Sinclair followed in his own personal life; he was a Spartan who lived on a diet of rice and fruit, and spoke of whiskey as the devil.

In Michigan Father Charles E. Coughlin, a Canadian-born Roman Catholic priest, was ensconced in his Shrine of the Little Flower at Royal Oak, outside Detroit. A spellbinding orator, he began his disputatious radio addresses in 1930 and for the next decade as the "radio priest" was the most powerful commentator in the land with an audience that numbered 40 million. As was the case with Huey P. Long, Coughlin's opinions varied from left to right. At first he attacked the Hoover Administration and proclaimed strong support of FDR with the statement: "The New Deal is Christ's Deal." Then he developed ideological fuzziness — the ambivalence of every demagogue. On the one hand he attacked communism and socialism, and would say, "Christian parent, do you want your daughter to be the breeder of some lustful person's desires, and when the rose of her youth has withered, to be thrown upon the highways of socialism? Choose today! It is either Christ or the fog of communism." On the other hand, his own radical program went far beyond that of FDR; he wanted the nationalization of banking, currency, and natural resources. Soon he was lumping President Roosevelt with a strange assortment of godless capitalists: the Jews, Communists, international bankers, and the plutocrats. He assumed great courage in his fight and said that he would confront the Herods by name and by fact, "even though my head will be served on a golden platter, even though my body be sawed in twain." His early anti-Wall Street and "social-justice" emphasis ultimately gave way to anti-Semitic and pro-Fascist utterances. His magazine, *Social Justice*, was barred from the mails in 1942 for violating the Espionage Act; by that time he was stating dogmatically: "It is Fascism or Communism . . . I take the road of Fascism." At long last he was silenced by his clerical superiors.

There was thunder from the left; there was also rumbling from the right. In 1932 Senator David A. Reed of Pennsylvania said, "I do not often envy other countries their governments, but I say that if this country ever needed a Mussolini, it needs one now." In the same year one of the editors of *Vanity Fair* (Clare Boothe Brokaw Luce) wrote an article in which she said, "Appoint a dictator." By 1934 there was the Liberty League, an organization of conservatives to defend constitutional rights against the "statism" of the New Deal.

FDR recognized the danger of revolution. One of his admirers warned him in 1933, "Mr. President, if your program succeeds you will be the greatest President in American history. If it fails you will be the worst one." Roosevelt replied, "If it fails, I shall be the last one." Journalist Robert P. Scripps would summarize the situation by saying that if wealth was not better distributed "the alternative is the goose step, one way or another, and Lenin or Mussolini makes little difference."

The New Deal is sometimes called the Roosevelt Revolution. There were significant changes. On the political side Small Government gave way to Big Government; in order to combat Big Business and Big Agriculture and Big Labor and Big Distribution, FDR brought in Big Government. On the economic side laissez-faire gave way to the welfare state. The latter had an elaborate program of social legislation that offered protection to the entire population against the mischance of unemployment, sickness, and sudden death. In order to finance such a program the New Deal employed fiscal and financial powers to redistribute wealth and to create income. If necessary, the federal government engaged openly in business itself — as a competitor of corporations. The TVA was a prime example.

Was all of this radical or conservative? Was it revolution or evolution? Certainly, by comparison with other revolutions going on at the same time, in Russia and Germany and Italy, it was conservative. In considering the basic character of revolutions, it is essential, as Quincy Howe has observed, to consider basic American values and to ascertain how they were changed. The basic American values were democracy in the political sphere, capitalism in the economic area, and Judeo-Christian idealism in the religious field. During the 1920's and the 1930's there were, elsewhere in the world, violent and turbulent revolutions which altered significantly — or destroyed — these basic American values. Russia had turned radically to the Communist left, Germany and Italy turned radically to the Nazi and Fascist right. The New Deal, by contrast, did not destroy the fundamental American values. As Howe sees it, it was a salvage operation to restore basic values from the "big-shot plungers and the pip-squeak politicians who had disgraced American business and American government and American idealism during the 1920's." In the political sphere the New Deal drew its inspiration, not from the extreme left or right, but from the American progressive tradition. In doing so it employed a great many slogans that dated back to the Populists and to the Progressives. In the religious field the New Deal maintained the Judeo-Christian foundations of the nation; it did not substitute Thor and Woden, or the fasces, or dialectical materialism. In the economic sphere, as Howe sees it, the New Deal did not wreck Big Business; instead it tried to save Big Business from the big businessmen who were its real enemies — the Insulls, the Van Sweringens, the Mitchells.

There were radical revolutions in Russia and Germany and Italy after World War I. All of them were based on deductive plans, on blueprints carefully thought out in advance. In Russia it was the Communist state based on dialectical materialism. In Germany it was the Nazi state based on National Socialism as laid down by Adolf Hitler in *Mein Kampf*. In Italy the Fascist state was constructed by Mussolini on the basis of a preconceived plan. Our democracy has always been empirical and experimental in nature; we have always been indifferent to theory and dogma. Allan Nevins has said that our young Republic has never quite known where it was going — or how. It has marched along, veering when it saw quicksand. Other nations, by contrast, have marched by compass and map — by preconceived plan — and have often marched straight into the quicksand.

In this tradition FDR was an improviser and empiricist; he had no system except endless experimentation. He was not very well informed in business techniques and methods and was something of a plunger; he could afford to be, with the security of his own and Eleanor's income. He had a gambler's zest for new ideas, and while he never gambled very much on any single one of them, he tried a considerable number. He wildcatted for oil in Wyoming; he tried to corner the lobster market and lost $25,000 in the venture; with Owen D. Young he tried and failed to run dirigibles between New York and Chicago; he attempted to sell advertising space in taxis. Like Winston Churchill he did not know much about economic theory, although the New Deal was to have a profound effect on economics. He listened attentively to the professional economists around him, but refused to take them too seriously. As he put it, "I happen to know that professional economists have changed their definition of economic laws every five or ten years for a long time." Actually FDR had few intellectual and fewer artistic interests. He enjoyed collecting postage stamps more than he enjoyed reading; he preferred naval history to philosophy or biography. Justice Holmes was probably on the mark when he said of President Roosevelt, "A second-class intellect. But a first-rate temperament!" FDR did enjoy the company of intelligent and articulate men and women — *partly* because they interested him more than the members of New York's Four Hundred, *largely* because they aided his political fortunes. He surrounded himself with a Brain Trust — particularly professors from Columbia University — thus inaugurating the march of intellectuals on Washington that has steadily increased as a result of depression, war, and the explosion of knowledge. During the early New Deal days, the most prominent Columbia professors were: economist Rexford

Guy Tugwell; A. A. Berle, Jr., who taught and practiced law; and Raymond Moley, who had been an economic adviser to Al Smith, and who taught public law at Columbia. It was an authentic Brain Trust, although FDR preferred to call it his "Privy Council" — an expression with scatological implications that amused him.

An empiricist as far as economics was concerned, FDR was also an empiricist in politics. In 1933 he exclaimed, "No blueprints"; he wanted no preconceived plans, and expressed the American love for the pragmatic. This was revealed in his attitude toward TVA. Shortly before the TVA measure went to Congress, its chief sponsor — Senator George Norris of Nebraska — came to dinner at the White House. There the two men — one a Dutchess County patrician and the other the son of a Nebraska dirt farmer — sat talking enthusiastically about TVA's possibilities. Said Senator Norris, as he laughed, "What are you going to say when they ask you the political philosophy behind TVA?" FDR laughed, "I'll tell them it's neither fish nor fowl but whatever it is, it will taste awfully good to the people of the Tennessee Valley." During the heat of the presidential campaign of 1936, a local Democratic headquarters received a telephone call. A voice exclaimed, "Say, tell us just what the principles of the New Deal are — we're having an argument." "Hold the phone," was the answering injunction, followed by a long pause. Finally, the realistic answer came: "Sorry — we're having an argument too." Sometimes FDR would do amazing things in carrying out his pragmatism, to the exasperation of his advisers. Once when a campaign speech on the tariff was being prepared, two proposals that were utterly incompatible were placed before him. Moley asked the President which proposal he wanted incorporated into the speech; FDR left the professor speechless by airily suggesting that he "should weave the two together."

In FDR, therefore, the nation had an improviser, who also turned out to be a superb politician. He knew that his job was to "weave" what seemed to be incompatible points of view into a program that made political sense — whether it made economic sense or not. The country seemed to love it. Said humorist Will Rogers, "The whole country is with him. Even if what he does is wrong, they are with him. Just so he does something. If he burned down the Capitol, we would cheer and say, 'Well, we at least got a fire started anyway.' " It is no wonder that Professors Morison and Commager have concluded that

Historically the Franklin D. Roosevelt Administration did for twentieth-century American capitalism what the Theodore Roosevelt and Wilson administrations had done for nineteenth-century business enterprise: it saved the system by ridding it of its grosser abuses and forcing it to accommodate itself to larger public interests.

History may eventually record Franklin D. Roosevelt as the greatest American conservative since Alexander Hamilton.

In his policy toward business FDR actually did "weave" together the antithetical policies of the New Nationalism (the regulation of monopoly) and the New Freedom (the regulation of competition through trust-busting). He accomplished this *tour de force*, however, by following the principles of New Nationalism until 1938, and then resorting to trust-busting and the New Freedom until the United States entered World War II. For the first five years of the New Deal (1933–1938) there was a relaxation of antitrust laws through the NIRA (National Industrial Recovery Act), the Robinson-Patman Act, and the Miller-Tydings Act.

The NIRA was designed to revive industrial and trade activity through government-supervised business codes, and to spread employment and to provide emergency relief through pump priming. The second objective was really an advance admission that the first one was not likely to work; for that reason Title II of the NIRA authorized the President to create the PWA (Public Works Administration) (see pp. 223–224) with an authorization to expend $3.3 billion for highways, dams, federal buildings, and even naval construction. The first objective — which represented an attempt by the federal government to cooperate with business — was recognized in the act by the creation of an agency called the NRA (the National Recovery Administration). The NRA was to prescribe codes for industries which enforced fair competition between businesses, fair competition for labor, and provided for suspension of the antitrust laws while all of these advantages were supposedly being enjoyed. The codes were designed, at least in theory, in such a way that the rights of all would be protected: management, labor, and the consumer. Generally speaking the codes governed business practices, prices, wages, and hours. Each code was subject to the approval of the President; there were severe penalties, at least in theory, for noncompliance. To draw up the codes, representatives of business and management flocked to Washington — and a hectic atmosphere was created not unlike that prevailing in war days. Altogether almost 600 codes, affecting 22 million workers, were put into effect. When the President approved a code, the industry or trade concerned was permitted to display a Blue Eagle poster indicative of economic recovery rather than military triumph. Behind the Blue Eagle was the principle of industrial self-regulation — cooperation under governmental supervision. There was an assumption that the efforts of the older antitrust acts to maintain unlimited competition had brought disaster, and that in their place, at least temporarily, should be substituted an attempt to establish industrial cooperation under government control.

The specific purposes of the NRA were four in number: to relieve unemployment, to increase purchasing power, to improve the status of labor, and to eliminate unfair competition among businesses. It was designed to relieve unemployment through the child-labor and the maximum-hour provisions in codes. The child-labor provision, banning the labor of children under sixteen, opened up jobs for adults; sensational gains were made through this device. In addition, nearly all codes limited the working week to forty hours. Theoretically, this necessitated the hiring of additional employees by industry, which had been on a much longer work week than forty hours. Some gains were achieved; the AFL estimated that within a year the work week was shorter by four and a half hours. Purchasing power was to be increased, bringing prosperity around a corner that had not been sighted for four years, by establishing minimum wages. In the codes these were set at not less than $12 a week; this was a minimum annual wage amounting to the princely sum of $624. Nonetheless it represented a great improvement for many in 1933. In Pennsylvania, wages were 4¢ an hour in sawmills. In Tennessee some women were being paid $2.39 for a fifty-hour week. In sweatshops in Connecticut young girls were being paid 60¢ to $1.10 for a fifty-five-hour week. It was difficult for decent employers to continue paying 1929 wages when their competitors were cutting labor costs by one half, or more.

Relieving unemployment and increasing purchasing power was one thing, improving the status of labor and eliminating unfair business competition, was another. The former came through Section 7a, which gave labor for the first time — on a national basis — the right to bargain collectively. The establishment of the principle was valuable, but in practice it did not work out well. Many companies circumvented the principle by setting up company unions; by early 1935 workers were dubbing the NRA the "National Run Around." The elimination of unfair business competition varied in effectiveness, depending on the size of the industries involved. It worked magnificently in the large industries where unfair competition, defined always as price-cutting, had already been listed as a major sin; the codes simply legalized what they had been doing for some years. On the other hand, the elimination of competition did not work well in small trades and small industries; nine out of ten distrusted each other, and ten out of ten distrusted the government. They had not cooperated before the act was passed; there was little change after it went into effect.

The NRA was administered in spectacular fashion. During most of its two-year existence the director was Hugh Johnson, an authentic character. He was born of fine pioneer stock on the Cherokee strip in Oklahoma. His mother recalled him at the age of four, defying his playmates with the words, "Everybody in the world is a rink-stink but Hughie Johnson and he's all right." He went to West Point, in the same year with Douglas MacArthur, but ended at the foot of the class in deportment. He took a commission in the cavalry, serving in the Philippines and chasing Villa along the Mexican border — sharing a tent there with a fellow cavalry officer named George S. Patton, Jr., already known for his pearl-handled revolvers. In his spare moments Johnson wrote children's books and studied law. During the First World War he administered the draft, was the War Department's representative on the War Industries Board, and became a great friend of Bernard Baruch — the only man who inspired his complete admiration. Johnson was a whirlwind; in physique he was square-jawed, thick-necked, and indefatigable. As Arthur M. Schlesinger, Jr., has observed, no one in Washington labored so long, shouted so loudly, smoked so many cigarettes, or drank so much liquor. Johnson and his staff worked up to eighteen hours a day; Johnson himself flew all over the country in an army plane which he transformed into an office.

He was emotional, pungent, and truculent. For him all life was melodrama; he was forever rescuing the virtuous and foiling the villains. His language was so expressive and so profane that it justified his nickname of "Hugh-and-Cry" Johnson. When he was appointed he said, "It will be red fire at first and dead cats afterward. This is just like mounting the guillotine on the infinitesimal gamble that the ax won't work." He compared the crusaders for the Blue Eagle with Richard Coeur de Lion, with Moses, even with Jesus Christ. He likened the "chiselers" to Judas Iscariot and Danny Deever, denouncing critics "in whose veins there must flow something more than a trace of rodent blood." When he feuded with Donald Richberg, his general counsel, he said that Richberg was suffering from the ants of conscience in his pants; by contrast Harold Ickes, who was about the only prominent person who could match Johnson's invective, once said that Johnson was an old cavalry officer who was suffering from "mental saddle sores." Johnson ultimately created so many stresses and strains within and without NRA that he had to go; he resigned on 1 October 1934. His farewell was in character. He told assembled employees that the agency had been "as great a social advance as has occurred on this earth since a gaunt and dusty Jew in Palestine declared, as a new principle in human relationships, 'The Kingdom of Heaven is within you.'" In his peroration he quoted (in Italian) the last words of Madame Butterfly before she committed hara-kiri. When he finished tears were streaming down his cheeks, and most of the audience was sobbing. It is no wonder that FDR replaced him, not with *one* man, but with a board of five — two businessmen, two college professors, and one labor leader.

Whatever the purposes of the NRA, and whatever the spectacularity of its administration, it came under heavy criticism from economists and from the Supreme Court. Economists censured it for taking away from Congress the power to regulate Big Business, and for deepening the Depression by relaxation of the antitrust laws. On the first point, the authority of Congress was weakened because the codes were drawn up, for the most part, by the industries themselves — with labor and consumers having little or no voice in the process. In connection with the antitrust laws, economists pointed out that one of the factors causing the Depression was restriction of production by big business, bringing with it unemployment and reduced purchasing power; this created a vicious circle, from which we were partly rescued by governmental spending. They noted that the NRA codes had sanctified this procedure through price fixing and lessened production, that they really authorized administered prices.

Whether the Supreme Court listened to the criticism by economists is not known. Nonetheless on 3 June 1935 by unanimous decision in the case of *Schechter Poultry Corporation* v. *United States,* the Court declared the NRA unconstitutional on two grounds. In the first place it considered NRA to be a violation of the interstate commerce clause of the Constitution, because Congress had invaded intrastate authority through the operation of the codes. It also found, on the second count, that NRA was an unconstitutional delegation of legislative authority to code officials. This particular doctrine was an old one going back to John Locke — but until 1935 the Supreme Court had never invoked it. It appears, in retrospect, that it was the *huge number* of codes rather than the idea of delegation that appalled the justices; it was the practice rather than the principle that exercised the Court. The government was surprised at the decision because it had carefully selected the Schechter case for test purposes. The Schechter Company had brought chickens from *other* states to New York for sale, but had refused to observe the NRA Live-Poultry Code either by paying minimum wages or by observing standards of "fitness" governing chickens. Actually it was the Court's narrow definition of interstate commerce which most disturbed the government. This was because the Court's comment on legislative authority, and the delegation thereof, could have been remedied in future statutes by the inclusion of more specific details in the wording of the laws.

The Schechter decision produced extravagant statements on both sides. President Roosevelt was not happy because he had said that "History probably will record the National Recovery Act as the most far-reaching legislation enacted by the American Congress." On the other hand Justice Brandeis (who had long believed in the regulation of competition rather than monopoly) said to one of FDR's legal aides: "This is the end of centralization, and I want you to go back and tell the President that we're not going to let this government centralize everything." Huey Long, who had paraphrased the NRA into the National Ruin Association, and Nuts Running Around, said, "I raise my hand in reverence to the Supreme Court that saved this nation from fascism." The Hearst press concluded that with the end of NRA the rule of Christ had been restored!

Beyond the NRA, the Robinson-Patman and the Miller-Tydings acts were two New Deal measures enacted for the purpose of helping small business, which had taken a beating from the Depression and from the competition of chain stores. The prevailing political spirit of the 1930's was to keep everyone in business, whether it was economic to do so or not. This principle applied to farming, railroading, banking. If marginal farmers could be kept in business by putting a floor under farm prices, why not do the same thing for the small businessman? The purpose of the Robinson-Patman and Miller-Tydings acts was to keep small business in operation by maintaining prices at an artificial level. These measures were therefore at variance with the Sherman Act, which had protected the low-cost seller and competition. The Robinson-Patman and Miller-Tydings acts, by contrast, protected the high-cost seller and competitors — regardless of their economic ability to compete.

The Robinson-Patman Act was intended to provide for wholesalers and independent retailers certain protections which they had enjoyed briefly under the NRA codes. The particular objective of the act was to deny to chain stores the competitive advantages gained by quantity buying, direct from the manufacturer, at low prices. Although its backers spoke with deep emotion about the corner grocer, and the corner druggist, the bill was actually drafted by counsel for the U.S. Wholesale Grocers' Association, and was ardently backed as well by drug wholesalers. Obviously buying by chains direct from the manufacturer threatened the wholesaler quite as much as it did the retailer. For these reasons the act is sometimes called the "Chain-Store Act."

The Robinson-Patman Act amended the Clayton Act by supposedly tightening the section which forbade price discriminations. This section had always been difficult to define, and the Robinson-Patman Act did not clarify the issue. The question involves business discounts: if they are awarded for quantity purchases, when do they constitute a price discrimination? Large distributors — like the A&P — obtained advantages over competitors because of their ability to buy from manufacturers in great quantity. The manufacturer quite logically gave the A&P a larger discount than those who purchased in small quantity; he did so because he had a definite saving by selling in large quantities and he passed on this saving to the A&P — which supposedly passed it on to the consumer. The central question was this: were the manufacturer who sold the goods at a discount, and the A&P which bought them at a lower price — both guilty of price discrimination? To put it in other terms: when was a discount a legitimate discount, and when was it discriminatory? The Robinson-Patman Act prohibited discrimination in price between *large and small* purchasers of goods shipped in interstate commerce, if those discriminations promoted monopoly or reduced competition. What did this mean? No one was sure, but everyone understood that the act represented an *attempt* to prevent supermarkets, discount houses, and chains from buying more cheaply than the small retailer. This seemed to mean that quantity discounts — even though justified by cost reductions due to volume — could be limited if the FTC and the courts concluded that such discounts gave an undue advantage to large-scale marketing.

It was apparent that this act would be most difficult to enforce and would be the subject of great argument. On the pro side it could be claimed that it might eliminate the unfair practices of large and predatory companies, and that it might benefit small businessmen. On the other hand it could be charged that it contributed to inefficiency in business because it deterred the large-scale operator from passing on legitimate savings resulting from orders in volume, and that it was harmful to the consumer who for this reason had to pay higher prices.

The Miller-Tydings Act constituted a definite reversal of antitrust policy by legalizing retail-price-fixing (resale-price-maintenance) by the manufacturer on goods shipped in interstate commerce, provided the state involved had a fair-trade law. In effect, this permitted states to pass their own laws authorizing resale-price maintenance on nationally advertised products; all states except three (plus the District of Columbia) did so at the time. The measure actually squeaked through the Congress in 1937 as a rider to the Appropriation Bill for the District of Columbia. The FTC opposed it. So did FDR, who signed the bill reluctantly, condemning such legislation and expressing the fear that it would mean higher prices for the consumer. It did.

In relation to the Miller-Tydings Act the major legal controversy was over the nonsigner clause in state acts. This clause provided that a retail price established by an agreement between the manufacturer and a *single* dealer in the state applied to all dealers in the state whether or not they signed the agreement. The fight over this clause led to two decisions by the Supreme Court and one act of Congress: The first Schwegmann decision of 1951, the McGuire Act of 1952, and the second Schwegmann decision of 1953. Schwegmann ran a chain-store company in New Orleans, and had refused to sign a fair-trade agreement with Calvert and Seagram Distillers corporations. The Schwegmann stores sold Calvert Reserve for $3.35 a fifth, Seagrams for $3.51, although the fair-trade price for both was $4.24. Calvert and Seagram appealed to the courts on the ground that the nonsigner clause had the backing of federal law. In his majority decision in the Supreme Court, Justice Douglas denied that the nonsigner clause was legal under the Miller-Tydings Act. The federal law, he said, connoted a "voluntary" scheme, and that "contracts or agreements convey the idea of a cooperative arrangement, not a program whereby recalcitrants are dragged in by the heels and compelled to submit to price-fixing."

If Miller-Tydings did not authorize the nonsigner clause, a new act might do so. Manufacturers therefore turned their attention to Congress, which passed the McGuire Act in 1952. It was an enabling act authorizing the nonsigner clause; this permitted manufacturers to put clauses in resale contracts, without the necessity of signatures. The effect of the McGuire Act was limited, however, because it ran into trouble in state courts; those of seventeen states upheld the new authorization provided by the McGuire Act, but the other state courts did not. In time the attempt to aid independent businessmen through resale-price-maintenance proved a failure, because noncomplying states offered loopholes. Mail-order business permitted discount houses in states not requiring fixed prices to function in states where fair-trade laws prevailed. Thus the laws proved almost entirely futile and large companies gradually abandoned fair trade as a sales policy. This development did not save Schwegmann from a defeat in 1953 on the validity of the McGuire Act; this time the chain was fighting with Eli Lilly and Company on drugs and pharmaceuticals. Schwegmann sold insulin for $2.08 a bottle whereas Lilly had fixed the price at $2.83 under fair-trade authorization in the state of Louisiana. Schwegmann asked the Supreme Court to set aside the McGuire Act on the ground that it was being deprived of its property without due process of law as guaranteed by the Fourteenth Amendment, and that the act represented an unconstitutional delegation of congressional power over interstate commerce. The chain lost in the lower courts, and the Supreme Court refused to review their negative decisions. The reactions to the second Schwegmann decision were interesting and revealing. On the pro side a large maker of facial tissues published a full-page newspaper advertisement which ran in part as follows: "Thanks to nine wise men . . . the law of the jungle can no longer decide the price of what you buy." The "law of the jungle" is the process economists refer to as price competition. On the negative side, Schwegmann had always said that it was merely asking for the Fifth Freedom — the freedom to shop. This brought the Cleveland *Press* to comment:

One of the oldest forms of fakery is trying to sell a bad idea by giving it a pretty name. Such is the "fair trade" law — which is anything but fair.

It makes the word competition meaningless because there is no competition when every dealer sells the same goods for the same price.

Prior to 1938 the Roosevelt Administration tried to cooperate with large business corporations, as far as trust policy was concerned. This had been apparent during the period of the NRA and with the Miller-Tydings Act. Then New Deal policy changed in 1938. From that year, until FDR became occupied with World War II, it was his policy to crack down on large combinations and to enforce the antitrust laws with vigor. No one knows exactly why but it could have been the result of the recession of 1937 and the growing disillusionment of FDR with corporate tycoons. By the time 1938 rolled around the President appeared to be "fed up" with big businessmen, and was heard to say, "I get more and more convinced that most of them can't see further than the next dividend." The "first New Deal" had placed emphasis on national economic planning — with Tugwell, Moley, Johnson, and Richberg. The "Second New Deal" emphasized competition. The first manifestation of a change came with the appointment of the Temporary National Economic Committee (TNEC).

Roosevelt used Wilsonian language in his instructions to the TNEC; he said that "the power of the few to manage the economic life of the nation must be diffused among the many, or be transferred to the public." The TNEC reported in 1941 that it wanted more competition, desired more vigorous enforcement of the antitrust laws and the repeal of the Miller-Tydings Act, and hoped for stronger antitrust legislation than was found in Sherman and Clayton.

The second manifestation of the change in policy came with the inauguration of vigorous antitrust prosecutions on the part of the Department of Justice, under Thurman Wesley Arnold, who was Assistant Attorney General in charge of the Antitrust Division from 1939 to 1943. During these years Arnold became the greatest trust-buster in American history. In a bit more than four years he filed 230 suits against alleged conspiracies in restraint of trade — more than had been filed in the entire previous fifty-year history of the Sherman Act. Arnold was intelligent and unpredictable, with a highly developed sense of humor. After graduation from the Harvard Law School in 1914 he had returned to Wyoming, the state in which he was born. There he was the only Democrat elected to the Wyoming legislature in the landslide for the Republicans in 1920. When the legislature met to organize, the Republicans nominated their candidate for speaker with long-winded oratory. Then Arnold, the lone Democrat, from whom only silence was expected, rose to his feet. The Democratic minority, he announced solemnly, had also caucused the night before, and after fifteen minutes of tumultuous applause had unanimously honored that sterling leader, that true statesman, and that peerless lawmaker of the great West — Thurman W. Arnold. "I have known Arnold all my life," he went on, conveying a sense of ineffable privilege. "I would trust him as far as I would myself. I therefore nominate him to be speaker of this honorable house." Still solemn, he sat down, bobbed up again to second his nomination, and then — sensing the confusion of the old rancher who was beyond his depth in the temporary speakership — took the floor a third time to withdraw his name, complaining that it had been "placed in nomination by some irresponsible person!" He was also, in the classic mold, absentminded. There were innumerable anecdotes about occasions on which he took the wrong train, went to the wrong courtroom, or argued the wrong case. The best, surely apocryphal, related that Arnold had once delivered a masterful summation on behalf of the plaintiff, only to be reminded that he was counsel for the defendant. Thereupon, as the story had it, he made an even more powerful presentation, in which he refuted his previous arguments on every point, and won the case. Unpredictable or not, Arnold earned his reputation as the greatest trust-buster in American history. Making his own precedents as he went, he entered suits against such giants as the American Medical Association, Standard Oil of New Jersey, the Associated Press, and finally — to the horror of Democratic politicians — the building trade unions of the American Federation of Labor. He initiated many investigations and ninety-two prosecutions; decisions in these cases ultimately helped to clarify the law and to serve notice to businessmen that certain practices were forbidden. Any possibility, however, that Arnold and the TNEC would be successful was frustrated by the Second World War. By 1941 the Administration was encouraging industry to undertake all-out production under the Lend-Lease Act, and with the U.S. entry into the war the antitrust laws became moribund.

Shortly after Arnold had drawn a legal bead on union featherbedding, he suddenly found himself elevated to a judgeship in the United States Court of Appeals for the District of Columbia. Most lawyers would have been delighted with a lifetime appointment to a court which is second only to the Supreme Court in prestige and importance. Arnold was bored stiff. He complained bitterly that "all I do is to sit here and write little essays to read at the end of trials." After two years he abandoned the security of the bench to return to private practice — which he did by founding the prestigious firm of Arnold, Fortas and Porter. There he fought for both corporations and civil liberties, defending many persons accused of left-wing or Communist ties during the McCarthy era. He relished the fact that his firm's corporate clients were, in effect, paying the freight for his attacks on McCarthyism. This attitude was to be expected from a man, as the *New York Times* pointed out when he died in November 1969, who had been an Elk, a Lion, a homesteader, a sheep rancher, the mayor of Laramie, a Yale professor, and a federal judge who quit a lifetime appointment because, he said, "I'd rather speak to damn fools than listen to them."

Trust-busting was obviously called off during World War II, when cooperation between Big Government and Big Business was essential to defeat a common foe. During the Truman Administrations, there were two high points as far as Big Business was concerned: one was the continuation of antitrust suits — as illustrated by the A&P case — the other was the passage of the Anti-Merger Act of 1950. The A&P case was the most prominent antitrust action in the Truman Administrations — and in fact the most prominent one under the Robinson-Patman Act. This was because in 1950 the A&P sold more goods than any other company in the world — excepting General Motors. As the world's largest grocer at that time, the A&P sold one out of every seven cups of coffee in the United States, one out of every fourteen pounds of butter, one out of every twenty-eight eggs. Its annual sales amounted to almost $3 billion.

Against the chain store two charges were made in regard to purchases and in regard to sales. As far as purchases were concerned it was claimed that A&P (and other chain stores) received advantages from suppliers which were beyond *normal* discount rates; that is, that A&P bulldozed suppliers into giving them extra-large discounts. On the sales side it was claimed that A&P resorted to sharp price discriminations to drive rivals out of business. It would lower prices in one area, it was alleged, and make up the losses by raising them elsewhere. There was nothing new about this device; A&P could have found out all it wanted to know about it by reading the early history of the Standard Oil Company.

On behalf of A&P it was noted that the consumer and the nation had benefited: the consumer had gained because prices were low and quality was high, and the nation had advantages because the growth of Big Distribution (as exemplified by A&P) was important as a countervailing influence. The judge in the case stated that A&P's prices were low, and that its feat of selling a vast volume of goods, at a profit of only one and a half cents per dollar of sales, was an achievement of which any corporation could be proud. This had been going on from the inception of the company in 1859 when — by the elimination of middlemen — it managed to sell teas for 30¢ a pound that had previously cost a dollar.* The consumer had also benefited through several grocery improvements, notably the simple grade labeling of many products in the place of meaningless adjectival superlatives. The nation had benefited too because the growth of the giant A&P as a countervailing influence kept other corporate giants from charging too much. The individual buyer was powerless against these other corporate giants — General Foods, General Mills, Standard Brands, the Big Four in meat packing — but A&P was not.

A great deal of heat was generated during the trial. A&P charged that the "antitrust lawyers from Washington were bent on destroying the company." It claimed that the only valid charge against it was that it regularly undersold competing retailers. "To this charge," said the A&P, "we plead guilty. . . . Low prices don't hurt anyone." On the other hand Wright Patman of Texas, who had given his name to the Robinson-Patman Act, alleged that the A&P was lying and in doing so was following a technique "invented and developed by Goebbels and his Nazi masters." The federal court listened to all these arguments, and in what is known as the Danville (Illinois) decision of 1946, which settled the criminal suit, found the A&P guilty of a conspiracy to restrain and monopolize trade. As a result ten A&P corporations and fifteen of its officers were fined the maximum under the antitrust laws — a total of $175,000; this amounted to approximately $30 per A&P store, and was no more than a

* This is not the whole story. Chain-store profits based on sales are small, but based on capital investment supermarket profits are much higher, averaging 12.5 percent. In 1965 the number-one merchandiser in the United States was Sears, Roebuck, A&P ranked second (with 4,625 stores), and Safeway was in third place (with its 2,080 stores). In 1965 A&P's profits were almost 9 percent higher than those of U.S. Steel at 7.6 percent. In the same year, Safeway had a profit of almost 14 percent; by contrast Standard Oil of New Jersey made 11.9 percent.

slap on the wrist for a company with annual sales approaching $3 billion a year. The A&P decision was a basic one which affected other companies as well; in 1948 Safeway and Kroger chains pleaded no defense in similar cases. Safeway was fined $40,000 and Kroger $20,000.

There have been three great periods of business consolidation in our history: from 1897 to 1904, from 1920 to 1929, and from 1946 to the present. Current pessimists observe that the first two of these periods ended in devastating business collapses. Why the increasing number of mergers since World War II? For a variety of businesses they have provided four advantages; avoidance of bankruptcy, benefits from diversification, savings on taxes, and utilization of surplus capital. Mergers have saved some companies from bankruptcy. Woolen mills in the North, on shaky financial underpinning, have been shored up by mergers with stronger mills in the South. Mergers can provide diversification, can enable a company to offset seasonal ups and downs, or ups and downs in business generally. This is simply a device to avoid putting all one's investment eggs into one marketing basket. A business that prospers in winter (Adam, which makes hats) buys one that prospers in summer (Canada Dry and its soft drinks).

Mergers can also provide tax advantages and use for surplus capital. The companies involved in mergers are experts in tax law. They know that the federal government allows a company that has lost money in a given year to claim a *refund* for taxes paid on profits in the preceding two years, or to *deduct* the losses from any profits it may take in the next five years. Take Company A, which lost $1 million making banjos in 1955. It can claim a refund on taxes paid on $1 million of profits in 1953 and 1954 — assuming it had any — or it can keep tax-free the next $1 million it makes in 1956, 1957, 1958, 1959, and 1960. Company B buys Company A's $1 million loss. Mergers also enable corporations to utilize their superabundant cash. During the past decade many corporate treasuries were overflowing with the fruits of prosperity *and* from federal tax and depreciation benefits. In the mid-1960's government officials estimated that the cash reserves of U.S. manufacturing corporations were more than $30 billion. We have noted previously that these reserves are used by industry to finance its own expansion; the stock market now plays only a limited role.

Because of concern over the large number of mergers after World War II, the Celler-Kefauver Anti-Merger Act was passed in 1950. Both sponsors were able and public-spirited men. Emanuel Celler was the longtime Democratic Congressman from New York who was chairman of the House Judiciary Committee. He was first elected to Congress in 1923 and is obviously the dean of the House of Representatives; no one now in Congress has served as long (the late Speaker Sam Rayburn served forty-four years). In 1953 Celler wrote an autobiography entitled *You Never Leave Brooklyn;* the Republicans thought he should write a sequel, *You*

Never Leave Congress. In his eighties, with almost a half century in Congress behind him, Celler found what it takes to be a successful Congressman: "To be a successful Congressman, one must have the friendliness of a child, the enthusiasm of a teen-ager, the assurance of a college boy, the diplomacy of a wayward husband, the curiosity of a cat, and the good humor of an idiot." He once gave some advice to freshmen representatives in the House: "The good Lord gave you *two* ears and *one* mouth: listen twice as much as you speak — at least for a year or two."

Celler was known for his liberal stands in connection with trust-busting, immigration, social legislation, and civil rights. Senator Estes Kefauver, known as the fellow with the coonskin cap, represented Tennessee in the House from 1939 to 1949 and in the Senate until his death in 1964. He won the Democratic nomination for the Vice-Presidency in 1956, but was snowed under by the ticket of Eisenhower and Nixon in that year. Kefauver always stood forthrightly for three principles: opposition to political bosses — in this connection he fought the power of Boss Ed Crump (the "Red Snapper") in Memphis; civil rights, a courageous stand to take in Tennessee; and competition rather than monopoly (his last book, published posthumously in 1965, was entitled *In a Few Hands: Monopoly Power in America*).

The Anti-Merger Act of 1950, so-called, was really an amendment to Section 7 of the Clayton Act which prohibits the acquisition of *stock* in *competing* corporations — if the effect of that acquisition was to lessen competition substantially or to create a monopoly. The Clayton Act was concerned about the acquisition of *stock* only. It said nothing about buying *competing* companies outright; that is, by acquiring their assets through merger. Celler and Kefauver were concerned about mergers, and thought something should be done to stop the move toward economic combination when it began — not waiting until the merger had gathered momentum. The Celler-Kefauver Amendment therefore permitted the federal government to proceed against proposed mergers, if the effect was to lessen competition substantially or to create a monopoly.

The attitude of President Eisenhower, and of his Administrations, toward trusts is still a subject for controversy. Some claim that he went easy on them, others contend that this is not so. The former point out that he was well disposed to bigness, that he packed the administrative agencies, and that he was lenient toward mergers. In his Economic Message to Congress in January 1954 he stated that bigness would not be the test of anti-trust violations because, in his judgment, "it is clear that size alone does not preclude effective competition." This meant that ideologically, whether the President knew it or not, he had rejected the regulation (enforcement) of competition which was the core of Wilson's New Freedom, and had adopted the idea of TR's New Nationalism — the regulation of monopoly. There was considerable evidence to indicate that he packed the administrative agencies, just as Harding and Coolidge had done, with appointees who were friendly to big business. He appointed a chairman of the FTC who had spent the preceding twenty years lobbying for firms the FTC had accused of antitrust violations. Two of his appointees to the three-man board of the TVA had said that they did not care for the TVA. An ex-Congressman who did not approve of the low-tariff Trade Agreements Act, was made a member of the Tariff Commission. The official appointed as head of public housing had voted against public housing when he was a member of Congress. The new chairman of the Federal Power Commission was a gas-utility lawyer who did not like the FPC, and a Bell System lawyer who did not care for the Federal Communications Commission was made chairman of it. As far as mergers were concerned the Eisenhower Administration objected to only one — that of Bethlehem Steel and Youngstown Sheet and Tube.

On the other hand there is definite evidence of antitrust activity during Eisenhower's Presidency, particularly in the work of Robert A. Bicks and because of the Du Pont–General Motors case. The work of Bicks, who was Assistant Attorney General in charge of the Antitrust Division of the Department of Justice, was outstanding; his strong antitrust views, and his forceful leadership, confounded those who thought a Republican administration would be "soft" on antitrust enforcement. In 1960 Bicks began ninety-two *new* antitrust proceedings, the largest number of suits begun in any twelve-month period during the entire seventy-year history of the antitrust laws. In his annual report Bicks also pointed out that it was not only the number of cases, but their character and significance, that counted. In that year his prime exhibits were the criminal cases brought against the nation's major electrical manufacturers — cases which ultimately resulted in the first jail sentences for violation of the antitrust laws (see pp. 420–421).

The Du Pont–General Motors case, which concerned the clause in the Clayton Act prohibiting the acquisition of stock in another corporation where the effect was to lessen competition, involved two of the country's largest corporations. The original Éleuthère Irénée Du Pont had migrated to the United States in the 1790's; he had studied with the great French physicist and chemist Antoine Laurent Lavoisier, the founder of modern chemistry, who gave oxygen its name. Lavoisier had made gunpowder for the French government, was director of the French gunpowder commission in 1775, and was guillotined during the Reign of Terror in 1794; it is not surprising that his pupil Du Pont became a refugee — although the Du Ponts of the present day are not likely to recall that they are descendants of a refugee. Once in the United States Éleuthère Du Pont went hunting; he found that the powder he bought was high in price and inferior in quality. Encouraged by Thomas Jefferson, he built a mill to supply gunpowder for hunting, pioneering, and self-defense. It was an establishment on the Brandywine River in Delaware and cost $36,000. In 1962 the Du Pont Company would spend a quarter of a billion dollars on expansion alone of its extensive plants.

Thus it was, in 1802, that there came into being the first efficient American gunpowder factory under the name of *Du Pont de Nemours, Père et Fils et Compagnie*. It was able to sell the U.S. Government all the powder it needed in the War of 1812. In 1818 came the first major explosion. The works blew up with a roar that shook buildings in Wilmington, six miles away, and left forty employees dead. Greatly to the credit of the company, the widows and the orphans were given pension funds. In 1854 there was another spectacular explosion; this time 450 of the new metallic kegs, in which powder was being stored, went up in a mighty burst. Three employees, two innocent bystanders, and twelve horses lost their lives. During the Civil War there were a number of mystifying explosions which were easily, and perhaps inaccurately, blamed on Confederate spies. The Civil War record of the company was good; it sold to one side only (the North), and its product was effective; that is, it went off — a decided contrast to most of the shoddy goods that were sold to the U.S. government during the war, including the carbines that were purchased from J. P. Morgan.

By 1917 the Du Ponts had a monopoly on gunpowder. The company made at least $100 million during World War I and looked about for suitable investments. Its treasurer was John J. Raskob, later to become a financial angel who both helped and embarrassed FDR. Raskob put part of the surplus, about $25 million of it, in a motor concern that was to become General Motors. He bought at $2.09 a share; the value increased — both in dollars and stock split-ups — to a bit more than $3 billion (at $46 a share) in 1961. By 1957 the Du Pont investment in GM amounted to 23 percent of its stock in 63 million shares; this was enough to control the company. The antitrust question was whether the ownership of GM stock by Du Pont was for investment purposes solely (legal under the Clayton Act), or was for the purpose of controlling and directing GM's purchases — a violation of the Clayton Act because this would tend to "substantially lessen competiton." The evidence before the Supreme Court indicated that Du Pont was supplying two-thirds of the paint requirements of GM, and almost half of its needs for fabrics. The decision of the Supreme Court, written by Justice Brennan, stated that Du Pont was in violation of the Clayton Act and would be required, in due course, to divest itself of its GM stock — all 63 million shares. It was an unusual 4 to 2 decision. Justices Black, Douglas, and Warren concurred with Justice Brennan. Justices Frankfurter and Burton dissented. Justices Clark, Reid, and Harlan barred themselves from participation in the case, because of earlier connection with one of the parties in the suit.

The next question was how Du Pont was to rid itself of 63 million shares of GM stock, and how soon. The Supreme Court answered the latter question in 1961, when it told Du Pont that it must divest itself of the GM stock within the next ten years. That left the question of procedure. If the stock was thrown on the market, no matter how skillfully it was done, it was apparent that the sale of 63 million shares would depress the price of the stock. If Du Pont distributed the GM stock to its own stockholders in the form of a dividend, the problem would be neatly solved but at great cost to many of the stockholders. This would arise from the fact that many of them were in high income-tax brackets, and a dividend of that kind would be liable for income taxes under the standard progressive and expensive rates — rather than on a capital-gains basis. This would obviously cost the stockholders, and the Du Pont family, a considerable sum of money. With legal counsel from the prominent Washington attorney Clark Clifford, who later became Secretary of Defense, the company obtained congressional legislation (1962) and Treasury rulings that were claimed to have saved stockholders (including members of the Du Pont family) about $2 billion in taxes they would otherwise have had to pay. One would have thought that the Du Pont Company itself would have suffered grievously from the loss of $132 million in dividends from GM stock now distributed to stockholders, but this was not the case. In the 1960's Du Pont was a billion-dollar corporation — the largest chemical enterprise in the world. Its sales have increased so phenomenally, amounting to more than $2.5 billion in 1962, that dividends have remained constant — in spite of the so-called divestiture. In the same year (1962) Du Pont's net earnings were a quarter of a billion dollars.

There is a popular expression in the form of a question: "What's the use of power if you don't abuse it?" Antitrust lawyers have a similar phrase, reminiscent of Lord Acton: "Show me the power and I will show you its abuse." Because of this attitude critics of the New Deal and of the Fair Deal* would charge that both programs were more concerned with size

---

* There have been a number of sparkling slogans, designed by political parties to describe their programs, beginning with the euphoric adjectives "new" or "fair" or "great." We have seen TR's New Nationalism, Wilson's New Freedom, FDR's New Deal, the Fair Deal of Harry Truman, the Great Crusade of General Eisenhower, the New Frontier of John F. Kennedy, and the Great Society of Lyndon B. Johnson.

These glittering generalities have evoked some critical and cynical comment. The Republicans were inclined to rename all Democratic "Deals" by the substitution of other adjectives; they should have been called, they said, the "Fast Deal" or the "Big Deal out of Texas." Russell Baker of the *New York Times* claimed that the Democrats had given the country four deals: these were (1) the New Deal, (2) the Fair Deal, which was the New Deal with hardened arteries, (3) the New Frontier, which was the New Deal with a face-lift, and (4) the Great Society, which was the New Deal with hardened arteries, a fallen face-lift, and a Vietnamese accent. John Fischer of *Harper's* once defined the difference between a FDR New Dealer and a Truman Fair Dealer as — about thirty pounds! This was the difference in weight, he claimed,

than anything else — that they mounted attacks on efficient corporations which had done no wrong, simply because they were large in size. All this brings up the question as to how large a corporation should be. When asked how long a man's legs ought to be Abraham Lincoln had replied, "Long enough to reach the ground, I reckon." That statement may have settled the matter for male appendages, but no one has yet found such a simple way to measure the proper size of U.S. corporations.

Some hoped that the Anti-Merger Act of 1950 would provide the answer. In actual fact this act has been effective in checking horizontal mergers; it has been noticeably unsuccessful in stopping the more important conglomerate type. Horizontal mergers, so-called, involved the merger of *direct* competitors. The Department of Justice has stopped — by frowns or court actions — the proposed mergers of Humble and Tidewater Oil companies, Chrysler and Mack Truck, Bethlehem and Youngstown Steel. The first major judicial decision under the Celler-Kefauver Act did not come until 1962, a dozen years after its passage, and this decision concerned a horizontal merger. The case arose in 1955 from the acquisition by Brown Shoe Company (the fourth-largest American shoe company, manufacturing 4 percent of U.S. shoes) of G. R. Kinney Company, which operates the country's largest retail (family-style) shoe chain. Kinney had approximately 400 stores in 270 cities, accounting for a bit more than 1 percent of national retail sales in shoes. Brown Shoe argued that the combined companies did not account for enough of the nation's shoe production and sales, to "substantially" affect competition. But Chief Justice Warren, speaking for a unanimous Court, delivered an opinion that was protective of small business. He said that in passing the Anti-Merger Act of 1950, Congress was aware of the fact that "occasionally higher costs and prices might result from the maintenance of fragmented industries and markets." He added that the antimerger law had reflected a congressional belief that the economic and social values of industrial *decentralization* outweighed such considerations.

The Celler-Kefauver Act has been inadequate in retarding the new type of conglomerate merger that is now the most common. This is the merger of entirely unrelated firms, an increasingly popular type in which firms that operate in totally different industries are joined in corporate matrimony. The International Telephone and Telegraph Company (IT&T) is an excellent example of a conglomerate merger. For years it was engaged in the communications business outside the United States only. But in

---

"between the ulcerous, hot-eyed, skinny intellectuals in the New Deal — and the paunchy, good-natured courthouse politicians and settled bureaucratic types of the Truman Administration." The same difference might have been observed between the Eisenhower bureaucrats with their generous paunches, and the JFK crowd that played touch football. Or perhaps the difference was one of age. Walter Lippmann once suggested that the difference between the Eisenhower Great Crusader and the Kennedy New Frontiersman was about thirty years.

recent years IT&T has acquired an odd assortment of enterprises. It makes pies and bakes buns (it acquired Continental Baking). It runs hotels (Sheraton Corporation). It builds and equips shopping centers (Levitt & Sons). It constructs defense and space products, runs utilities, rents cars (Avis), and parks them in air terminals of the nation's largest cities (Airport Parking Company). It almost gobbled up the American Broadcasting Company but the Justice Department, at least in this case, said "No." The Columbia Broadcasting System (CBS) is another example of a conglomerate merger; it owns a book company (Holt, Rinehart & Winston), the New York Yankees baseball team, a toy company, a guitar firm, three other companies making assorted musical instruments, and two film companies.

These conglomerate combinations are now the common form of merger. In 1968 there were 4,462 mergers; that was 68 percent more than in 1967 and 300 percent more than in 1963. The FTC reported that large industrial companies having assets of $12.4 billion were acquired by new owners in 1968 and that more than 90 percent of those assets moved into the camp of the conglomerates. By that time government economists were asking seriously whether it could be true — as predicted by Nicholas Salgo, founder of the Bangor Punta conglomerate — that in a decade there would be only 200 major industrial companies left, all conglomerates. It was not a phenomenon confined to the United States; the British Board of Trade undertook monopoly investigations in that government's first major intervention in what it called the "merger mania." Some writers used euphemistic terms in describing mergers and acquisitions; they wrote of romance when negotiations were in progress, engagement when agreement had been reached, marriage when the transaction was completed. In some instances, however, the take-over of one company by another could be more aptly described as cold-blooded seduction or forcible rape. There were happy matings; there were also unhappy marriages that aroused bitterness among stockholders and consternation among ousted executives and displaced employees. What disturbed critics, *inter alia*, was that money to buy up companies was often raised through stock-market speculative fever or through lavish issue of unsecured debentures which also provided a saving on taxes through deduction of interest paid on them. This could mean that more than half of the carrying charges for acquiring a company were borne by the U.S. Treasury, thus enabling the parent company to pay in inflated price for the stock of the company being purchased; the mere rumor of a big merger might be enough to send prices of the stocks involved up 20 percent or more. By early 1969 these practices had become so worrisome that Republican Homer H. Budge, Chairman of the Securities and Exchange Commission, warned investors against being misled by the "apparent improvements" in earnings of many conglomerates; he said these had often been achieved through financial devices that created increased risks for those investing in them because "those who are engineering the present wave of takeovers appear to find the short-run profits so tempting that they ignore the long-term risks." He warned that the entire wave of creation of conglomerates, through the financial methods being used, reminded him of the utility holding companies that were created in the 1920's, many of which collapsed after the crash.

Because conglomerates account for nearly 90 percent of the assets so acquired in recent years, it is small wonder that they are the focus of attention. Senator Philip A. Hart of Michigan contended in the late 1960's that "at the present merger rate, within a few years about two-thirds of all industrial assets will be concentrated in 200 corporations. Many are far-flung conglomerates with their hundreds of arms reaching into everything from toothpicks to aerospace." Some members of Congress have been worried enough by this development that they have asked the FTC to undertake a broad fact-finding investigation. It is apparent that such mergers can lessen competition at the same time that they increase concentration, but fewer than 1 percent have been formally protested by the Department of Justice. In 1967 the Supreme Court did protest when it dealt a stiff blow against the principle behind conglomerate mergers in *FTC* v. *Procter & Gamble Company;* it said that such mergers were subject to the same strict antitrust laws that apply to other business combinations. Without dissent the Court upheld an FTC order that Procter & Gamble, the nation's largest soap manufacturer, must divest itself of the Clorox Company, which dominated the liquid bleach market when P&G acquired it in 1957. Procter & Gamble had defended the conglomerate merger on the usual ground that it would result in substantial economies. Justice Douglas delivered the 7 to 0 decision of the Court, stating that "all mergers are within the reach of Section 7 [of the Clayton Act as amended], and all must be tested by the same standard, whether they be classified as horizontal, vertical, conglomerate, or other." Douglas also specifically rejected the argument that economies could justify mergers. He stated that "Congress was aware that some mergers which lessen competition may also result in economies, but it struck the balance in favor of protecting competition." This decision could become a landmark if the Antitrust Division of the Department of Justice, in future years, follows the Court's lead.

Obviously a definitive study, if the FTC gets around to it, would attempt to determine optimum corporate size on the basis of two standards: how large should they be from the standpoint of industrial management *and* public management? As far as efficiency in industrial management is concerned no one knows the answer, although there have been a few studies and the expression of some strong opinions. Thirty years ago the FTC made a tentative study of corporate efficiency in an effort to determine whether large, medium, or small concerns were the most desirable. In this study large corporations did not come out very well; medium corporations appeared to be, on the average, the most efficient. In 1967 attacks were mounted against bigness by Barton M. Biggs writing in *Barron's*, and Donald A. Schon in his *Technology and Change*. Biggs was skeptical of conglomerate mergers and came up with some disquieting findings. Such mergers depend on men of managerial genius who are capable of operating an enterprise in five or six different markets. Biggs found such talent in very short supply, and supported his point by citing a reputable management survey to the effect that 36 percent of the corporate mergers between 1960 and 1965 were admitted to be mistakes. He also reviewed some of the questionable accounting practices used to gild the balance sheets of merging companies and thus keep their stock prices rising, and concluded that "conglomerates can't keep making two and two equal five forever." He felt that in a period of economic slowdown, the multi-market company would face multi-adversities, and that this would help end a "fad" based on the dubious assumption that the merged whole is somehow always more profitable than the sum of the parts taken independently. Schon, who is an industrial consultant with experience both in private industry and the Federal Bureau of Standards, was disturbed by the disappointing level of inventive output in big corporate enterprise. He stated that Du Pont and IBM, supposedly the paragons of creative giant enterprise, failed in initiative and original action by reason of institutional rigidities:

> Du Pont . . . owes its success more to its phenomenal ability to carry out market and engineering development of inventions derived from other sources than its own research output. IBM, the present giant of the computer field, was not the first to enter into the development of electronic computers; it waited, sticking with its older punch-card systems, until other firms had built and marketed computers and only then moved in, with great marketing and technical resources and skills, to dominate the field.

Schon observed that independent inventors and small companies are responsible for a remarkable percentage of the important inventions and innovations of this century. These include, *inter alia*, the following: the air-conditioner, power steering, xerography, cyclotron, cotton picker, helicopter, FM circuits, automatic transmissions, zipper, Polaroid camera, cellophane, continuous hot-strip rolling of steel, and the oxygen steelmaking process.

The optimum size from the standpoint of industrial efficiency is one consideration; the optimum size from the standpoint of public management is another. On this point a number of witnesses before the Celler Committee in 1950 warned that if the nation permits Big Business to exist, it will be accompanied by Big Government and Big Labor. Adolph Berle said that when business "threatens to engulf the State — it forces the State to engulf business." Morris L. Ernst, the prominent lawyer and civil libertarian, reminded the committee of the situation in Germany during the 1930's — where cartels became too big, leading to rigid government control; he also recalled Great Britain in the same period, where combinations got too large and the state took them over. Just how big is "too big"? On this question opinions vary. George Romney, a governor and Cabinet member who first achieved prominence as the manufacturer of Studebaker automobiles, feels that when a company controls more than 35 percent of its industry, it becomes too large for its own good — or that of the nation. Some economists (for example, Carl Kaysen and Robert C. Turner) say that if one firm accounts for half or more of an industry's sales, or four firms for at least 80 percent, they should be broken up.

Assuming that we can decide how large corporations should be, how can they be limited and controlled in size and power? Since the Anti-Merger Act of 1950 a number of proposals for new legislation have been made: federal incorporation, graduated taxation, prior approval for mergers, prior approval for price increases. Federal incorporation and control of all corporations would be too much of a job. It has therefore been suggested that the requirement for federal incorporation and attendant federal control, be limited to corporations that have assets totaling $100 million or more. These behemoths would continue in business under federal license only, and would be policed by the FTC. The idea of the graduated corporation tax came originally from Theodore K. Quinn, a former official of GE who turned against Big Business. He was the son of a founder of the Knights of Labor, began his career at $7 a week for GE, became head of GE's new refrigerator department in 1927 (when he was but thirty-four years of age), and made it a very prosperous division of the company. In 1936 he left GE, and began to talk and write about the evils of industrial "giantism." His particular target was GM, which he said was entirely too large, threatening countless small companies and eventually all free American institutions. To curb such "giantism" Quinn proposed a graduated corporation tax that would penalize those with net worth of $100 million or more. Others have proposed new legislation requiring prior approval for mergers and price rises. The former would prohibit corporations with combined assets of more than $10 million from merging *until* the federal government had given its approval; such a law would change the timing of the Anti-Merger Act of 1950. Prior federal approval has also been suggested for price rises by large companies — or at least a waiting period of a year or more.

Whatever the remedy, there has been increasing concern about "giantism." When Penn Central, a leviathan that owns both railroads and hotels, was reeling in 1970 — Senator Claiborne Pell called it a "constipated monster." In his recent irreverent book, *Up the Organization*, Robert Townshend intimated that Organization Men were exercising an imperium that was undesirable. The dedication of the volume was an ironic pseudo-quotation from Holy Writ:

And God created the Organization and gave It dominion over man.
—Genesis I, 30A, Subparagraph VIII

XI

The Origin and Nurture of Chaos in American Transportation

IN the early days of the Republic only the main towns along the seacoast were connected by roads, and most of them were little more than Indian paths. In wet weather they were troughs of mud; during dry spells, suffocating dust traps. In 1804 the Ohio legislature decreed that tree stumps left in the highway must not be more than a foot high! There were no bridges over rivers and creeks; when the traveler came to a stream he looked for a ford or a boatman; failing either he swam his horse across. In the 1790's there was great interest in improved transportation and this brought the construction of turnpikes or toll roads, long familiar in England. This development led to the first turnpike era in the United States (the second came after World War II), lasting until the 1840's when the competition of canals and railroads rendered them obsolete. These early roads, of gravel or planks or macadam, were built both by private corporations, and by state and federal governments. The first American turnpike was built in the 1790's between Philadelphia and Lancaster, a distance of sixty-six miles, by a private corporation at a cost of $465,000. The construction of toll bridges followed the building of toll roads, and was financed and supported in the same manner. By 1810 some three hundred turnpike corporations had been chartered in New England, New York, and Pennsylvania; they took the lead in developing the American corporate system.

There was soon a strong demand for federal aid in the transportation problem, and this led to the famous report of 1808 on internal improvements, submitted by Secretary of the Treasury Albert Gallatin at the request of Congress. Gallatin pointed out that in more developed countries, where capital was plentiful, transportation facilities could be built by private initiative without direct aid from the government; in America this was difficult because of the high cost of labor and the shortage of capital. Federal aid was therefore advisable, and Gallatin proposed a system of canals and roads. The peninsulas jutting into the Atlantic would be cut by canals across Cape Cod, New Jersey, and between the Delaware and the Chesapeake. There would be a great turnpike running north and south from Maine to Georgia; transportation east and west might be improved by building roads that would join the headwaters of key rivers. He suggested that one method of paying for this construction might come from the sale of public lands.

It was a grand plan with but one major result: the construction at the expense of the national government of the Cumberland Road, sometimes called the Old National Road. Authorized by Congress in 1806 the first 130 miles were completed, from Washington to Wheeling, West Virginia, in 1818. Subsequent extensions took the road to Columbus, Ohio, and across Indiana to Vandalia, Illinois, in 1838, but it never reached St. Louis to join the Oregon and Santa Fe trails. Until the coming of railroads the 834 miles of the "National Pike" provided one of the chief avenues to the West (automobiles would later follow its general route along U.S. Highway 40, until the Pennsylvania Turnpike supplanted it in the 1940's). So beneficial was the road that more than a hundred surveys and plans for roads, canals, and railroads were before Congress in 1830 when President Jackson called a halt by his veto of a proposed turnpike entirely in the state of Kentucky. Jackson took a strict-constructionist view and held it to be unconstitutional for the national government to use money for enterprises confined wholly to individual states. The veto was important because it ended a long struggle over the political and constitutional issue of federal aid to inland transportation; the West was thereafter opened to private enterprise under state authority.

Canals, together with the turnpikes, were the transportation facilities which first united the West with the East. A few canals had been dug before 1800 around the falls of rivers flowing into the Atlantic. The great era of canal building, however, was initiated in 1825 when the Erie Canal opened the Great Lakes to eastern markets and made New York City the gateway to the West. Until then, when a settler reached the Appalachian Mountains he broke his ties with the East so completely that many feared the trans-Appalachian West would form a separate nation. It was difficult and prohibitively expensive to ship bulk goods across the mountains; the eastern market might be only a few hundred miles away but westerners found it cheaper and easier to ship by flatboat to New Orleans and then by sea around the Atlantic coast, a distance of some three thousand miles. In the early nineteenth century western New York was so unbelievably rough and uninhabited that a canal project seemed as outrageous as one today to span the Atlantic with a bridge. But the canal was built — largely because of the political influence of Governor Dewitt Clinton *and* the mechanical genius of Canvass White. Dewitt Clinton had been secretary to his uncle George Clinton, the first governor of the state of New York. It was a good apprenticeship. Later he represented New York briefly in the U.S. Senate and served for ten years as mayor of New York City; it has been claimed that no mayor accomplished more for the city than did Clinton. He was the foremost spokesman for public education in New York at a time when private education was popular. As a naturalist, he discovered a native American wheat and a new variety of fish, and published papers on pigeons, swallows, and rice. He removed the political disabilities from Catholics, quite an accomplishment in the Protestant America of that era. He was chiefly responsible for the building of the Erie Canal, also known as "Clinton's ditch." On the technical side Canvass White was characterized as possessing the "most strict engineering mind . . . of his time." As a young man he had learned all there was to know about canals by walking two thousand miles along the towpaths of England, studying every detail of canal construction. He is also known as the "father" of the cement industry in the United States; it was in 1820 that he obtained a patent for waterproof cement.

From the St. Lawrence Valley until they dwindle away in Alabama, the Appalachian Mountains are broken in only one place — where the Hudson and Mohawk rivers flow through valleys carved in the Ice Age. This gap was an ancient Indian way, and it was Clinton's way — rough and difficult as it was. The Erie Canal, begun in 1817 and completed in 1825, was the engineering marvel of its time. Extending for 363 miles from Albany to Lake Erie, it stepped up hill and down valley to overcome a difference of 565 feet in the elevations of Lake Erie and the Hudson River; it did so with eighty-four locks and eighteen arched aqueducts that soared across eighteen rivers. The waterway cost New York $7 million; it was the best investment the state ever made. Within a decade it had more than paid for itself in toll collections. The canal not only cut the time from Buffalo to New York City from twenty to six days — it also cut costs from $100 to $10 a ton; Horace Greeley would call the Erie "old cent-and-a-half a mile, mile-and-a-half an hour." Beyond the state government in Albany, the canal converted New York City overnight into the nation's leading metropolis, as its less fortunate rivals (Boston, Philadelphia, Baltimore) watched with ill-concealed concern. In New York State, farms bordering on the route doubled and quadrupled in value, and cities like Rochester, Syracuse, and Utica burgeoned. Outside of New York State, the canal was largely responsible for the rapid development of the five states of the Old Northwest. It is still very much in operation — as the modern New York State Barge Canal System. Reconstructed in

1905, it is now three times as deep (at twelve feet) and three times as wide as the original canal. The old wooden canal steamboats and mule-propelled barges, on towpaths, have given way to powerful tugs and self-propelled motor ships specializing in bulk trade. The character of the freight carried has also changed. Grain still goes east to Albany, but three-quarters of the traffic westbound is now in oil. "Lo-o-w bridge!" — the cry of the helmsman on horse-drawn barges in the early days — is no longer heard on the Erie Canal, but its echoes resound in song and legend. In the nineteenth century canallers were rough, brawling, hard-drinking, and fun-loving men. Fistfights between barge crews often determined who passed through a lock first, and in many cities along the canal the waterfront was lined with saloons and bordellos.

In 1826 the state of Pennsylvania began a canal from Philadelphia to Pittsburgh, and two years later Maryland and Ohio financed construction of the Chesapeake and Ohio Canal. Because of mountains, and the absence of rivers flowing east and west, the construction of the canal to Pittsburgh was infinitely more difficult than the situation in New York had been. Nonetheless the state of Pennsylvania built in eight years (1826–1834) a system of canals and portages following the Susquehanna, Juniata, Conemaugh, and Allegheny rivers. The portage over mountains by railways between Hollidaysburg and Johnstown was more than thirty-three miles long, and upon its inclined planes it was possible to raise a boat 1,399 feet in ten miles and lower it 1,171 feet on the other side. The Pennsylvania Canal was almost 400 miles long, and cost $10 million; in its building an altitude of almost 2,300 feet had to be surmounted, contrasted with 566 feet on the Erie Canal. It was never as successful as the Erie, but it did bring a share of the western trade to Philadelphia. The Chesapeake and Ohio Canal ran along the north bank of the Potomac River. Work was begun in 1828, but financial and labor difficulties (the latter occasioning the first use of federal troops to settle a labor dispute, by President Andrew Jackson in 1834), along with opposition from the Baltimore & Ohio Railroad, delayed completion to Cumberland until 1850. There it stopped, unsuccessful in reaching the Ohio as its goal; in the 1870's, however, the canal was busy carrying coal from the mines near Cumberland. Traffic was actually maintained until 1924, when it was damaged by floods.

In the Middle West there was the Wabash and Erie in Indiana, and the Illinois and Michigan Canal, which connected Chicago (and still does) with the Mississippi. More interesting and important were the two canals authorized by the state of Ohio. They were the Ohio and Erie from Cleveland to Portsmouth, a distance of 308 miles with 146 locks and 14 aqueducts (over creeks and other obstacles) — and the Miami and Erie from Cincinnati to Toledo. These canals were authorized in 1825; of the two the Ohio and Erie was the more important. It made money for only a quarter of a century, but during this period it also made Cleveland and played a vital role in the development of Ohio economically and industrially — until the railroads put the canals out of business. In 1810 Cleveland had a population of fifty-seven; twenty years later the number of people in the village was only a bit more than a thousand. Then, in the next two decades, there was a period of mercantile expansion, and the foundations of Cleveland's future material prosperity were laid. The era from 1830 to 1850 was the canal period in Ohio's history, and the selection of Cleveland as the northern terminal of a vital part of the state's meandering canal system was the determining factor in the transition of a village into a city which would be known as "the Sheffield of the West."

The Ohio canals provided the same excitement and color that had been prevalent in the early history of the Erie. Canal packets left Cleveland daily on the eighty-hour trip to Portsmouth. The trip was slow and the berths were small, but the journey was luxurious compared with riding in a jolting stagecoach. Food was plentiful and whiskey was cheap; at that time a chicken sold for 5¢, corn for 8¢ a bushel, and whiskey for a modest $4 a barrel. It is not surprising that taverns and inns along the canal route did a thriving business. The mule-drivers on the towpaths were mostly boys of ten and eleven years of age; in the main they were a hard lot who swore and fought and drank. One was known as Billygoat Cole — a bully who used his head rather than his fists. Another canal boy who turned out reasonably well was James A. Garfield, in spite of the fact that he gave up the occupation after falling into the ditch eleven times. This dubious experience gave the future President a great slogan in 1880. It was "From Canal-Boy to President" — a Horatio Alger theme if there ever was one.

Most of the canals were built by state governments. The hands of the federal government had been tied by constitutional objections, and private credit was inadequate — but the credit of the states, until the Panic of 1837, seemed inexhaustible. State debts, which amounted to about $13 million in 1820, had risen to $200 million by 1840 — most of the debt for canals and roads. Because of high interest rates and ignorance of actual conditions in the American South and West, which were highly speculative, a large share of the money for canals was borrowed in England. This mania for internal improvements, especially canals, contributed to the Panic of 1837; suddenly states found themselves unable to pay interest or continue the projects they had started. Several repudiated their debts, sold the canals and roads to private concerns, and rewrote their state constitutions with clauses forbidding the use of government credit for such purposes. One result was that private individuals and corporations would do the building in the railroad era that began after 1837. Another result was extreme unhappiness in England, where most of the bonds repudiated during the Panic of 1837 and later in the post–Civil War Reconstruction period, were held. The attitude of American states in both instances was that sacred obligations were all very well in their way, but not if the people of their states, already impoverished, were going to have to pay additional taxes to redeem them. In 1852, as an example, the governor of Mississippi — expressing an anti-Semitism that is not unusual for that state — asked a rhetorical question: "Are we going to make our children serfs to Baron Rothschild, with the blood of Judas and Shylock in his veins . . . ?" Almost a century later the British were still simmering over the repudiation, and resorted to some of their own. In 1930 Lord Redesdale rose in the House of Lords to move that repudiated American state debts, which he said might amount with interest to $1 billion, be applied against the British war debt to the United States which came as a result of World War I. He said that such a solution would enable the United States to rub out a "painful and shameful page" from their history by a gesture that would "raise them from the level of Russia." Russia, in 1930, was the only sovereign nation that had repudiated its World War I debts. Nothing came from the proposal of Lord Redesdale, but three years later Britain lowered itself to the level of the United States and Russia by defaulting on its own war debts.

The American railroad industry dates from 1828 when construction began, appropriately on the Fourth of July, on the Baltimore & Ohio. But it was in the last forty years of the nineteenth century that extension of the lines was incredibly rapid — from 30,000 miles in 1860 to 193,000 miles in 1900 to 250,000 miles in 1914, the latter mileage greater than that of all Europe, and one-third of the world's total. In actual fact, the spectacular and lavish construction meant that the industry was grossly overbuilt; by 1880, according to the financial writer John Moody, the United States "had built twice as much railroad as the country could employ, and issued four times the securities it could pay interest on." The most dramatic incident was the completion of the first transcontinental railroad at Promontory Point, Utah, on 10 May 1869 — an electrifying achievement that would be compared with the Declaration of Independence and the freeing of the slaves. In the 1850's there had been a deadlock between North and South over the route; this was broken when the South seceded, leaving the field to the North. The Union Pacific Railroad (the adjective "Union" reflects the sectional controversy) was commissioned by Congress to thrust west from Omaha; its chief engineer was Thomas Clark Durant and its laborers were largely Irish. It was claimed that there was "an Irishman buried under every tie," and Americans talked jokingly about the wheelbarrow as one of the greatest inventions of all time — because it taught Irishmen to walk on their hind legs. From the West Coast, the Central Pacific was to come east; it was built largely by 10,000 pigtailed Chinese coolies, with picturesque basket hats and flapping pantaloons. As the year 1868 ended the rival railheads were so near that the point of joining became a matter of some importance; each road wanted to build as much as possible in order to cash in on government subsidies in land and money. Both sent surveyors far beyond the other's rails, and proceeded to grade potential roadbeds that paralleled each other for miles. Oscar Lewis has written about the mutual distrust with which the Chinese and Irish crews regarded each other. By accident, or design, boulders would occasionally roll down from the Central's line, which was higher on the hillside, while "startled Irishmen dropped their picks and scurried for their lives." The UP retaliated. Its powdermen sometimes laid blasts near the CP line, and once "a thousand Irishmen looked on in innocent wonderment as the earth parted and scrapers, wheelbarrows, picks, horses, and Chinese fountained upward." Later a section of the UP blew up with much loss of life; after this both sides called a truce on the wanton destruction. Ultimately preparations were made, early in May 1869, for the union of the two lines. Unfortunately there was a delay; the UP special from the East was held up by floods, and arrived three days late. In the interim the CP's Chinese and the UP's Irish amused themselves by taking potshots at one another; there were some forty casualties, including one innocent bystander from San Francisco.

Finally they got around to driving the last spike, appropriately a golden one. Leland Stanford for the Central Pacific and Durant of the Union Pacific both missed the spike on their first swings, but finally got it down in what has been described as a "burst of booze and oratory." A photograph was taken but Stanford did not care for it because he was not shown, and because numerous liquor bottles and ladies of negotiable virtue were clearly visible. Stanford thereupon commissioned Thomas Hill, an outstanding artist, to re-create a pasteurized version — which would show Stanford, always a candidate for public office, in close association with the Reverend Todd, who spoke the invocation. Hill completed the painting, and at Stanford's insistence included a number of persons who were not in attendance at the "wedding of the rails": the long-dead Theodore Judah; C. P. Huntington, who was in New York at the time; Charles Crocker and Mark Hopkins, who were in San Francisco when the ceremony at Promontory Point occurred; and Brigham Young, who was invited but refused to attend. Hill's painting hangs today at the California State Capitol in Sacramento; it has been accurately described as a "bogus re-creation of one of the epic carouses of American History." *

---

* On 10 May 1969 the centenary of the driving of the golden spike at Promontory Point was reenacted, with scrupulous adherence to historic detail, before 15,000 railroad buffs. The occasion was both nostalgic and sad. Most of the celebrants had come not by railroad but in planes and buses and automobiles driven by internal combustion engines that had devoured the railroads' passenger and express traffic, along with great bites out of their freight business. The ranking governmental dignitary at the centennial was the U.S. Secretary of Transportation John A. Volpe, a highway contractor in private life who made his mark in public affairs not as an advocate of railroads but

Because of the hastily built roadbed, and the uncertain performance of much of the early equipment — particularly locomotives and coaches — the accident rate on railroads was high; as late as 1913 a climax was reached when almost 11,000 were killed and more than 200,000 were injured in one year. Earlier the situation had been frightening enough that in 1873 a measure was actually placed before the U.S. Senate for the prevention of cruelty to travelers on railroads, not unlike the humanitarian statutes which later applied to four-legged animals. In San Francisco the *Examiner* asked for safety on railroads at least equal to that of a soldier on the battlefield. There were also the exasperating delays; according to Ambrose Bierce if you escaped with your life, arrival at a destination was frequently so late that one of the dangers of travel in California was the "peril of senility." If a train went off the track in the prairies there were few worries; in the western mountains a train might careen into a gorge with frightful loss of life. Oscar Lewis has observed that after the trip to San Francisco overimaginative travelers often decided to return east by steamer; they preferred the hazards of yellow fever at the Isthmus against those of being dashed to death in some Sierra Canyon.

There had been some opposition to any locomotives at all, poor as the early ones were. In England the gentry loved their horses. The Duke of Wellington adored horseflesh and claimed that "railroads will only encourage the lower classes to move about needlessly." It was averred that the human respiratory system could not survive a speed exceeding fifteen miles an hour, that the lungs would collapse, and that the organs of circulation would be jolted out of place; blood would also spurt from the traveler's nose, eyes, ears, and mouth. Neurological disorders would also result from excessive speed, driving men to suicide; women would lapse, it was claimed, into sexual orgies. In spite of such dire predictions, railroads were built in the United States and in Europe. The first experiments were not only with steam. Horses were placed on treadmills, inside the train. Sails were used, with the car gliding merrily along the rails until an unfriendly wind ditched the whole affair. Peter Cooper's Tom Thumb was the first locomotive built in the United States (see p. 373), but it was experimental only; Cooper built the contraption only to show that it could be done. After that an engine was constructed for the Charleston and Hamburg Railroad in South Carolina, built at the cannon works at West Point. It

---

as Federal Highway Administrator in the Eisenhower Administrations. The crowning irony, however, was that no railroad was left on which a celebration could be held at Promontory Point; it had ceased to go through that historic spot sixty-five years earlier, when the Union Pacific track was straightened and shortened in 1904. In 1969, therefore, the two locomotives that touched cowcatchers in an authentic reenactment of the scene in 1869 that had been immortalized in photograph and painting had to be hauled to Promontory Point on flatbed trucks and set down on 4,200 feet of new track specially laid for the centennial.

was called The Best Friend of Charleston, and managed to carry forty passengers in four coaches at twenty-one miles an hour. The Best Friend of Charleston established a number of "firsts" in American railroading. It was the initial full-sized, American-made engine to be used in regular service. It was the first engine to run off the track. It was also the first engine to explode; the fireman became irritated by the loss of steam from the safety valve, held it down, and was boosted to glory by the immutable laws of physics. During the early days boiler explosions were so frequent that passengers were protected by bales of cotton loaded on a flatcar just behind the engine.

The first locomotives were crude affairs operating on wood and water; woodpiles were established every six miles along the right of way, and a nearby farmer was employed to replenish the pile. Ditches paralleling the tracks were used to bring water from nearby creeks; firemen would scoop it up as the train rolled by — hence the expression "jerk-water" railroads. Smokestacks on wood-burners needed lots of draft, and were so wide, billowing out at the top, that the locomotives could not be run on rainy days. When they did run, they sent out a continuous shower of sparks, with the result that the passengers were kept occupied putting out fires in their clothing. Farmers were unhappy too, not only because the sparks set fire to their grass and buildings, but because the noise frightened the cows so much that they ceased to give milk. There was also the question of how to see the track at night. One company tried "headlights" that employed candles; the wind brought this experiment to a quick conclusion. Railroads then employed a bonfire of brightly burning pine knots, carried in a small, sand-filled boxcar that was pushed ahead of the locomotive. This device sent feeble and wavering rays down the track, at least when the fire was at its height.

In time the small wood-burners gave way to gigantic coal-burning locomotives. A number of them became famous, for one reason or another. The Illinois Central's Cannonball sent Casey Jones to immortality. The New York Central had its famous No. 999, the first American engine to run faster than 100 miles an hour. This was because the Central wanted to get to Chicago faster than the Pennsylvania, with which it was in bitter competition. No. 999 rolled out of the Central's shops in West Albany in 1893 with four driving wheels and a weight of sixty-two tons. Between Syracuse and Rochester the engineer gave 999 full throttle, and she made a bit more than 112 miles an hour. This record stood for twelve years; the current American speed record by a steam locomotive was made in 1905 by a Pennsylvania Special in Ohio, running three miles at 127 miles an hour. The steam engine is now gone — along with the open range, the buffalo, the buggy, and the surrey with the fringe on top. An American child born today will never see a steam locomotive highballing down the track, nor will he ever hear the siren song of steam-locomotive whistles in the night. The steam-engine's "fierce-throated beauty" — as Walt Whitman put it — has given way to what Lucius Beebe calls the "sullen secrecies of diesel-electric power."

If the roadbed and locomotives of the early railroads left something to be desired, so did the coaches for which passengers paid their fares. In the early days travel was on hard benches in springless cars, often with no heat and water. Iron strips, before steel rails, had the unfortunate ability to curl up — and sometimes protruded through the floor of the coach — making it necessary for the engineer to stop the train and to mend the track. There was also the serious problem of how to stop a train from its dizzying speed of twenty to thirty miles an hour; this was solved by George Westinghouse (see pp. 373–374). In time Pullman Palace Cars were developed, in the early days as a method of showing off what Thorstein Veblen would call conspicuous wealth and conspicuous consumption. These elegant cars were built to specification; the cost rose from $50,000 in the mid-1880's to $300,000 in 1929. This was for private ownership of a special car; Pullman would also rent a "consist" — an entire train of five cars — for $500 a day. The "consist" had a drawing-room car, a diner, a tonsorial car complete with barber's chair, and two sleeping cars. J. P. Morgan once rented a "consist" to take a delegation of Episcopal bishops from New York to San Francisco, after having prudently rebuilt a baggage car for his favorite Rhine wines. Beyond the palace cars for the wealthy and the coaches for the "Great Unwashed" portion of the population, there were the Pullmans, for the upper middle class, which seemed to solve the problem of sleeping outside a seat in a coach. In the late nineteenth century a great argument developed about the morality of Pullmans, as Oscar Lewis has observed. The question was a simple one: Was it moral for strangers of opposite sexes to occupy berths, separated by only a foot or two of space and a pair of denim curtains? Sermons were preached in the 1880's and 1890's advocating separate cars for males and females; as a result, part of the American public developed a confirmed idea that the sleeping car was a menace to public morals. The railroads, naturally, assumed the defensive. They assured the public that sleeping cars were pervaded with a moral atmosphere "that was no less lofty than that of a Christian American home." They also pointed out that train officials patrolled the curtain-lined corridors, with orders to "nip in the bud any breach of decorum." Nonetheless most Americans were unconvinced, and many women went to bed in a Pullman fully clothed, many armed with foot-length hatpins which they had bought especially for emergencies in such travel. Actually the Pullmans were badly designed and were one of the reasons the American traveler ultimately adopted the airplane and the motorcar in place of travel by rail. Writing in 1967, Peter

Lyon had the following commentary on Pullman cars, the vehicle that was supposed to evoke memories of the Romantic Nights of the Green Curtains:

> Only those of us who are in our forties or older can recall those sleepers, characterized so aptly as "rolling tenements." They were ugly, uncomfortable dormitories, as lacking in privacy as a jailhouse. Each passenger rocked longitudinally in a berth cloaked only by a swaying curtain of a heavy dark-green fabric that might better have been used in an upholstery for the furniture in the lobbies of commercial hotels. At one end of each sleeper was the men's room — one toilet, a pseudo-leather couch, and a meager triad of communal washbasins, inadequately equipped with mirrors, in front of which a gaggle of salesmen customarily postured and prattled, exchanging jokes of an unexampled vulgarity; at the other end was the women's room — similarly fitted, and littered with someone else's face powder and someone else's hair combings.*

A very large outlay of capital was required to build the gigantic railroad network in the United States. In Europe, national governments would take the responsibility for construction and operation of railroads; in America the job was done by private enterprise with considerable government help. By 1879 the debt of American railroads totaled $10.6 billion, compared to a total national debt of only $1.3 billion. In the three decades following the Civil War there is little question that the financial operations of the railroads had a greater effect on the economy than did those of the federal government.

In the course of this colossal railroad operation there were three sources for the money that was thrown around so lavishly: grants of land from federal and state governments, grants of money from federal and state governments, and the investments of private individuals. Until 1900 most of the private funds came from individuals in Europe; after the Spanish-American War ownership began to shift to Americans. Grants of land from federal and state governments ultimately totaled 167 million acres in 262,238 square miles; this was 15 percent of the mid-century public domain, an area approximately the size of Texas and larger than the combined size of France and Germany. An estimate of the value of this land is

---

* By 1968 the Pullman Company had reached the end of the line. During two previous decades it had made money in but one year, had less than one thousand cars in operation, had not built a new one since 1956. The sleeping-car business was so limited on the thirty-odd railroads still operating passenger trains that the Pullman Company abandoned the service, leaving it to individual railroads that still wanted to include sleeping cars in their trains. When it closed its operations in 1968 the Pullman Company had 2,900 employees, including 250 conductors and 1,200 porters. They were offered separation pay.

By this time the Pullman and parlor cars had been replaced, as far as the wealthy were concerned, by jet planes — DC-9s and Boeing 737s — costing as much as $5 million each plus annual upkeep of $200,000. Frank Sinatra was said to have wanted a jet plane roomy enough to hold a piano. Hugh Hefner, the publisher of *Playboy*, ordered a plane that was appropriately fitted with an oval bed and a step-down tiled shower.

impossible (some is still held by the railroads), but at the nominal value of $2 an acre it was worth a third of a billion dollars.* There were lavish grants of money from federal and state governments, altogether something more than $700 million dollars; of this amount local governments contributed approximately $300 million.

The justification for the early federal and state grants of land and capital, largely to western roads, was based on the fact that these lines had to get across the unpopulated Great Plains to reach the Pacific Coast. There were no people on the plains at that time; this meant that throwing a railroad across them would tie up enormous sums of capital from which no immediate return could be expected. In these areas, it was claimed, it was necessary for society to subsidize western railroads; this had not been required in the East, where settled towns came first and the railroads were built between them. In short, huge grants from the public domain, along the railroad's right of way, would protect the investments of capitalists by making the railroad companies first and foremost land companies — and only later, after regions had been settled, transportation organizations. The Illinois Central is an example. It received 2,500,000 acres of the richest lands in America. In the course of time the Illinois Central realized $25 million from the sale of these lands; the 700 miles of road built from Chicago to New Orleans cost $16,500,000. By contrast, the Pennsylvania Railroad — which traveled from New York to Philadelphia to Chicago — for many decades became, without direct federal subsidies, the best-managed and most progressive and most profitable railroad in the nation. This does not mean that the Pennsylvania did not ask for and receive favors; this it did, largely through state laws which gave it regional monopolies. For two decades during and after the Civil War the Pennsylvania legislature was almost the personal property of President Thomas Scott of the Pennsylvania Railroad. Once, after a vote had been taken on two of Scott's bills to block the B&O from entry into Pittsburgh, a member rose to ask, "Mr. Speaker, may we now go Scott free?" Scott's influence was not restricted to one state; Wendell Phillips said of him that "the members of twenty legislatures rustled like leaves in a winter's wind, as he trailed his garments across the country." Able and amoral, Scott (according to Peter Lyon) stood alone "in a time of feverish venality . . . the acknowledged master of corruption."

In the development of American railroads a great amount of money was

---

* In return for the land railroads had to carry mail, troops, and government property at rates fixed by Congress, which could be as much as 50 percent below normal. Up to the Second World War this proviso meant little. Then, with the Second World War in the Pacific, the stipulation finally caught up with the railroads. At that time they claimed that they lost so heavily on government business, which was a large part of their traffic, that they were forced to seek an adjustment. In 1947, asserting that they had remitted to the government more than they had received in original land grants, they won cancellation of the reduced rates.

involved, and this proved to be tempting to ingenious operators who resorted to bogus financing. They used two standard methods of siphoning off great sums of money for their own personal profit — one for *new* railroads, the other for *old* ones. In the case of new railroads they organized their own construction companies and drained off the assets in payment for building the roads. In the case of the Union Pacific, the construction company was known as the Credit Mobilier. It was paid almost twice the actual cost for building the railroad. In the case of the Central Pacific the construction company (Charles Crocker and Company) did even better; building costs were $22 million and the company was paid $90 million. By contrast, old and established companies were drained of available cash in the form of excessive dividends; if earnings were inadequate, more assets were created through the issue of watered stocks and bonds. As an example, the triumvirate of Gould, Fisk, and Drew looted the Erie, bringing the road and the nation to the verge of financial panic. In six years' time they issued $71 million of watered stock on a railroad worth $17 million. The Erie paid a dividend on its common stock in 1866. Seventy-six years later, in 1942, Erie again paid a dividend on common, the first since 1866. In 1951 Erie celebrated its 100th anniversary, and someone thought up an accurate slogan: "A century of operations, a decade of dividends."

On the positive side the financing of the railroads helped produce an industrialized America and boomed agriculture, mining, and the development of cities. On the negative side the financing of the railroads also produced a set of new millionaires, grasping tycoons who in the period after the Civil War were arrogant, brutal, and dishonest. They were the "Lords of the Rail" who replaced the old southern "Lords of the Lash"; both groups were prophets of the Gospel of Grab and Hold. A distinguished senator once said of them, "When they speak, they lie; when they are silent, they are stealing." The poet Stephen Vincent Benét would write about a railroad magnate:

> He toiled not, neither did he spin,
> But how he raked the dollars in.

Illustrative were the operations of the quadrumvirate (Vanderbilt, Drew, Fisk, and Gould) in milking the Erie, and of their counterparts (Stanford, Huntington, Hopkins, and Crocker) on the West Coast.

Of Dutch extraction, Cornelius Vanderbilt built the first colossal American fortune largely by the reorganization of railroads and the manipulation of their stock. As Matthew Josephson has observed, he was a big, bumptious, hard-headed, hard-swearing, hard-fighting man; his speech was loud, rustic, coarse, and interlarded with profanity and the slang of the wharves. It was Vanderbilt who, when told that a proposed step was a violation of the law, made the famous and oft-quoted statement: "What do I care about the law? Hain't I got the power?" (To his son William H. Vanderbilt was credited the equally cynical slogan: "The public be damned.") The elder Vanderbilt spent most of his life in the shipping business, from which he derived the name "Commodore." He was past seventy years of age when he acquired enduring fame in railroads; his most constructive work was the creation of the New York Central between New York and Chicago through the consolidation of shorter lines (1869–1873). In order to bring this about Vanderbilt used any means which promised results, including the bribery of legislatures and courts; like other corporations of his day the Central was full of water — as early as 1873 Charles Francis Adams said there was $53 million of watered stock and bonds in the road. Vanderbilt did cut the time of passenger service between New York and Chicago from fifty to twenty-four hours; before the Civil War passengers had to change cars seventeen times in making the same trip. At his death he left a colossal fortune of $100 million, but during his lifetime had been noteworthy for parsimony. The carpet in his home was threadbare. His wife was so badgered and browbeaten and restricted in expenditures that for a time she entered a mental institution. In spite of the fact that she had a child every two years (thirteen in all), Vanderbilt kept her busy during many of her spare moments as the manager of a hotel in which they lived, before they moved from New Jersey to Washington Square in New York. He disciplined his children severely, even brutally. His eldest son was told that he was an idiot and was consigned to a farm until middle age, a brother was disowned for extravagance. His continuing contempt for womankind was shown in his will; he left a wife and eight daughters only $4 million of a $100 million estate. In his late years there were additional signs of eccentricity. He began to attend the séances of mesmerists, and supposedly talked to the shade of Jim Fisk. He began to part with some of his money — certainly an indication of a change, and to some, of a loss of mind; his late benefactions were largely to the university that now bears his name. When he expired in New York City in 1877, it was with members of his family gathered about his bed singing the old hymn "Come Ye Sinners, Poor and Needy." At the particular moment of this musical rendition, good or bad, the deceased Vanderbilt was the richest man who had ever died in the United States.

Daniel Drew was an illiterate farm boy who rose by his own wits from cattle drover and horse trader to a dubious reputation as an operator on Wall Street. He was the first entrepreneur to drive cattle in numbers across the Alleghenies from the Midwest to New York. As the animals neared the city Drew fed them salt, followed by all the water they could drink; as a result the bovines weighed in heavily and profitably — and this fraudulent practice gave rise to the term "watering the stock." For many years Drew systematically robbed the Erie Railroad as its alleged treasurer. During this period his control was so complete that it was said on Wall Street,

"Daniel says 'up' — Erie goes up. Daniel says 'down' — Erie goes down. Daniel says 'wiggle-waggle' — it bobs both ways." He once put the basic principle behind all short selling into illiterate poetry, the only type of which he was capable:

> *He who sells what isn't his'n*
> *Must buy it back or go to prison.*

Ultimately Drew made the mistake of joining forces with Gould and Fisk, and was ruined by entrepreneurs who were smarter and even more ruthless than he. He was destroyed by the Panic of 1873 and is now remembered chiefly as the founder of a theological seminary. He had a strange and sanctimonious devotion to the Methodist Church and spent the Sabbath singing hymns; on the other six days of the week, unfortunately, he was a canting hypocrite who drank large quantities of whiskey and would cheat anyone in order to acquire money.

After scanty schooling Jim Fisk trained for a life in finance as a waiter in a hotel and as a ticket seller for a circus. He made his first fortune running cotton through the Union blockade during the Civil War. Ultimately he allied himself with Drew and Gould, staying in New York City because he was really Gould's "vice-president" in charge of Tammany Hall. In personality Fisk was genial, boastful, and flashy; these attributes earned him soubriquets as Admiral Fisk, Colonel Fisk, Jubilee Jim, and The Prince of Erie. He loved fancy clothes and swaggered as an "Admiral" of his steamboats and as the colonel of the 9th Regiment of New York militia. He wore loud checks to the racetrack, where he owned a stable of horses; he also loved canaries and put 250 of them in the staterooms of his steamboats, naming the birds after his favorite fellow thieves and corrupt judges. He had no illusions and once said, "If I've got to choose between the other world and this, I'll take this. Some people are born to be good, other people are born to be bad. I was born to be bad. As to the World, the Flesh, and the Devil, I'm on good terms with all three." As it turned out, he had no choice about the other world and this one, and his death befitted his flashy career. Involved in a triangular love affair, in 1872 he was shot by a gilded youth named Ned Stokes — a rival for his current mistress, the actress Josie Mansfield. He was given a grand funeral with every honor that the Tammany Administration could bestow; there was a cortege that included the 9th Regiment and a band of two hundred pieces. At Fisk's death the safest thing to say about him was to repeat what a character in a Mark Twain novel had said of a dead malefactor: "He made a nice, quiet corpse." Probably the most accurate obituary of Fisk appeared in the *New York Times*, which commented, "Perhaps of him it may one day be said that he was first in war, first in peace, and first in the pockets of his countrymen." A contemporary New York lawyer, George

Templeton Strong, expressed the general feeling when he wrote that although Ned Stokes well deserved hanging, yet "I would hang him on a silken rope as having rid this community of one of the worst and most dangerous scoundrels that ever disgraced it." Actually Stokes was put away in Sing Sing for four years, after three trials and heroic efforts by his attorneys; he died in 1901, still living off the bounty of women.

Jay Gould rose from lowly positions as country-store clerk and surveyor's assistant to control of the Erie, half the railroad mileage of the Southwest (Union Pacific, and Wabash), New York City's elevated railroads, and the Western Union Telegraph Company. A small man in physique, saturnine and sickly, black-bearded and black-visaged, he loved power and achieved it. He bought only to wreck, and for that reason Leland Baldwin has said that he "was probably as sinister and cold-blooded a leech as ever fastened himself on the American financial structure." His contemporaries thought of him as His Satanic Majesty, Mephistopheles; he was so cordially hated in his day that he went about like a condottiere of the old Italian cities, followed by bravos at his heels. Some modern critics believe the comparison with Satan to be unjust; they claim that the Devil was never so destructive.

The famous fight over the control of the Erie was originally between Vanderbilt on the one side and Gould, Fisk, and Drew on the other; during this struggle the operations of all parties were so notorious that "railroaded through" became a national phrase suggesting undue speed and deception. To beat Vanderbilt the trio of Gould, Fisk, and Drew printed bales of illegal stock (this was called "freedom of the press" by Fisk) and then paid the New York legislature to legitimize the action — working through a Tammany boss who was also a state senator, the infamous William Marcy Tweed. One incident in the warfare would have been ludicrous had it not been so tragic and unethical; it was the "Battle of Fort Taylor." At the Erie's main office in New York City the trio (Gould, Fisk, and Drew) had gathered some $6 million in greenbacks (the funds from sales of printing-press stock), tossed the money in a hack, and took off for the Jersey Ferry and the safety of the other shore. At the same moment another hack loaded with deputy sheriffs was placed in hot pursuit by Vanderbilt; there was a confrontation but the "Erie Trio" was protected by toughs whose clubs and brass knuckles prevailed over the law officers. Safe in Jersey City the trio took over Taylor's Hotel and mounted three small cannon to protect it; from that time the hostelry was known as Fort Taylor. Colonel Fisk was in charge of the bastion, where he passed out champagne and cigars to reporters who were fascinated by the entire drama. To the journalists Fisk explained the necessity for the operation, which was reported to the nation as follows: "Commodore Vanderbilt owns New York. He owns the Stock Exchange. He owns

New York's streets and railroads. We are ambitious young men. We saw there was no chance to expand in your city, so we came over here to Jersey to grow up with the country."

The "Erie Trio" paid more in bribery than Vanderbilt, and managed to beat him. It was claimed that "the war" cost Vanderbilt $7 million, after which he was alleged to have made the philosophical observation, "It never pays to kick a skunk." After besting Vanderbilt, Gould, and Fisk proceeded to relieve Drew of his last cent; Ned Stokes then relieved Fisk of his life, leaving Gould in control of the Erie — at least for a brief period. While all this was transpiring, the railroad, it is not surprising to find, was in frightful shape. In March 1868 the Erie's general superintendent filed a report on the condition of the road:

> The iron rails have broken, laminated and worn out beyond all precedent, until there is scarce a mile . . . between Jersey City and Buffalo . . . where it is safe to run a train at the ordinary . . . speed, and many portions of the road can only be traversed safely by reducing the speed . . . to twelve to fifteen miles an hour, solely on account of the rotten and worn-out condition of the rails. Broken wheels, rails, engines, and trains off the track, have been a daily, almost hourly, occurrence for the last two months. . . . The condition of the iron at the present is such to give me anxiety and apprehension for the safety of trains. . . .

And well it might, as Peter Lyon has noted. The very next month forty persons were killed and seventy-five were injured when the Erie's Buffalo Express plunged into a gorge northwest of New York City. At this point George Templeton Strong, the New York lawyer, made this entry in his diary:

> Another railroad accident (so-called) on the Erie Road. Scores of people smashed, burned to death, or maimed for life. We shall never travel safely till some pious, wealthy, and most beloved railroad director has been hanged for murder, with a "gentlemanly conductor" on each side of him. Drew or Vanderbilt would do to begin with. . . .

On the East Coast the quartet of Vanderbilt, Drew, Fisk, and Gould milked the Erie. On the Pacific side of the continent their counterparts were a Big Four that took its pound of flesh from the citizens of the West Coast: Leland Stanford the front man, Mark Hopkins on details, Charles Crocker as the straw boss, and Collis P. Huntington as the "Gould" of the group — and therefore its guiding force. For thirty years Stanford was one of the Pacific Coast's most conspicuous figures, in spite of the fact that he was slow in thought and speech. His own partner (Huntington) once described him as a "damned old fool," and journalist Ambrose Bierce delighted in writing his name Leland $tanford. Nonetheless he happened to make an impressive physical appearance and he had the knack of making money. By reason of these talents he served as Republican governor of California during the Civil War and helped hold that state for the Union, was president of the Central Pacific and Southern Pacific railroads, and was U.S. Senator from California from 1885 until his death in 1893 (the Senate seat cost him $100,000 and his career there was most undistinguished). The one big disappointment in his life was the death, at sixteen, of his only child and namesake. The parents had desired to raise him apart from the dreariness of the financial world, in as cultural an environment as possible; they were contemplating his college education at Harvard when the boy died in Florence, Italy. As a memorial they endowed a university in his honor and with his name. It opened in 1891 with 415 students; one of them was a lad named Herbert Hoover.

Mark Hopkins was another groceryman from New York who went west to make his pile in the Gold Rush but achieved a fortune in another way, as Treasurer of the Central Pacific and the Southern Pacific railroads. He is not to be confused with the educator with the same name who became president of Williams College, and of whom President Garfield once said that one needed in a university not buildings or equipment but a simple bench with Mark Hopkins at one end and the student at the other. On the West Coast the other Mark Hopkins was certainly no educator and spoke little — and then in monosyllables. He was tall, scrawny, long-bearded, and a rustic — with an appearance that would be commonplace on many college campuses today. He was also parsimonious, a saver of string, a blower-out of lamps, and a good man for the owners — if not the public — to have in charge of the books. His skill in this capacity was devoted, among other things, to so befuddling the accounts of his associates that they have never been disentangled; in this connection a fortuitous destruction of the books by fire was of considerable help. This is the "Top-of-the-Mark" Hopkins — now probably better known than any of his more illustrious partners. In the present day the view, from the top of the hotel named for him, is much clearer than his own accounts ever were.

Charles Crocker weighed 250 pounds, much of it muscle developed over many years as a sawmill laborer, farmhand, and blacksmith. He came to California originally to dig gold but found (as had Stanford and Hopkins and Huntington) that more money could be made in selling high-priced goods and services to the gold seekers. Crocker operated a freighting outfit in Sacramento, and the money rolled in. Ultimately he became the construction boss of the Big Four; in this capacity he was both resourceful and successful. Under his supervision records for railroad building were established that have never been broken; at one time his construction crews averaged three miles a day through rough country and he was able to complete the Central Pacific seven years ahead of the deadline established by the U.S. government. He had tremendous energy and (as Oscar Lewis has noted) was often seen running up and down the track, inhaling alkali dust and exhaling obscenities. He knew how to handle men, lived in construction camps with them, fared no better than they did — with one notable exception: Crocker made $40 million on the job. Because of his difficulty in maintaining an adequate labor force of Anglo-Saxons in the arduous work of constructing a railroad in the West, he resorted to the employment of Chinese coolies and kept them in a state of virtual slavery.

Collis Potter Huntington was a storekeeper in New York who went west in the Gold Rush of 1849. He spent one day in the gold fields, but quickly decided he could make more money in merchandising at the prevailing high prices; the result was that the "Storekeeper of Oneonta" became the "Storekeeper of Sacramento." As such he got a corner on various supplies and kept his clerks sharp by making them go to bed by nine, not because it was good morals but because it meant more sales the next day. Beyond the West his principal investment was in the Chesapeake & Ohio; this road ran from Newport News in Virginia to a western terminus, which would be named for him, on the Ohio River in West Virginia. As the smartest of the Big Four he was the "contact" man in the East, where he had unusual success in winning subsidies and favorable legislation from Congress. Huntington was selfish and grasping, and was once quoted as saying, "Whatever is not nailed down is mine. Whatever I can pry loose is not nailed down." He was so shrewd and unprincipled that enemies said he was "scrupulously dishonest," was as "ruthless as a crocodile," and "had no more soul than a shark."

The Big Four began with the Central Pacific, subsequently consolidated and expanded the Southern Pacific from San Francisco to New Orleans, then looked to the sea. In the early 1870's they organized the Oriental & Occidental Steamship Company and went into competition with the old and prosperous Pacific Mail. Stewart Holbrook has written that they were "dedicated to the proposition that California belonged by right to the Southern Pacific," and they "worked so swiftly that the people of the immense state found themselves bound hand and foot before they knew what had happened." They charged the highest tariffs in the United States and gave rebates to industries in which they had a financial interest. Not an article, animate or inanimate, moved very far in California without overpaying the Southern Pacific for the privilege. The railroad was also gouging farmers, not only in rates but also by putting squatters off land. The latter formed a Settlers' Rights League to attack by legal means the railroad's alleged right to the lands in question. They lost in courts that were also controlled by the Southern Pacific, and federal officers appeared to dispossess them. There was a fight at a place called Mussel Slough; when the smoke cleared five farmers and two officers lay dead. For this crime seventeen farmers were arrested, tried, found guilty, and sent to prison; nothing was done about the five farmers who were killed. As a result *Remember Mussel Slough!* became a rallying cry for the farmers in all of California, and two of them named Evans and Sontag began holding up trains in the San Joaquin Valley. During more than four years the duo, cheered on by virtually the entire population of the valley, held up and robbed one train after another while an army of railroad police tried in vain to catch them. Ultimately a posse of 3,000 succeeded; Sontag died in his boots and Evans, shot full of holes, was sent to prison for life. By this time both were heroes, as Holbrook observes, not because they were robbers *per se* but because they were "robbing the biggest robbers ever known." Frank Norris was inspired by the affair at Mussel Slough and the tentacular practices of the Southern Pacific to write *The Octopus*, the first important thesis-novel in the United States. For almost half a century, until his death in 1945, Hiram Johnson was the most popular politician in California because he finally shattered the domination of the Southern Pacific over state politics. Among other things, in 1911 he pardoned "Robin Hood" Evans, the popular train robber.

The Lords of the Rail contributed to the corruption of both federal and state governments. In the national sphere there was some effort on the part of railroads to disguise the skulduggery; in state capitols the venality and corruption were open and aboveboard. As a result states condoned illegal stock-and-bond issues, winked at extortionate rates, and failed to tax railroads equitably and fairly. State legislatures were sometimes bought outright. In the Erie war the Gould-Fisk-Drew trio issued bales of fraudulent stock and paid the legislature of New York to legitimize the action; assemblymen got an average of $15,000 each and the governor was down for $20,000. One legislator was reported to have been bought by Vanderbilt for $75,000 and to have later sold out to Gould for $100,000. An investigating committee discovered that the Erie in one year expended $700,000 for bribery and corruption, carried on its books as the "India Rubber Account." Gould had a custom of going to Albany with a big valise full of greenbacks. At the state capitol, as Charles Francis Adams explained it in polite language, "he assiduously cultivated a thorough understanding between himself and the legislature." Gould cared nothing about politics as such, and would say, "In a Republican district, I was a Republican; in a Democratic district, I was a Democrat; in a doubtful district, I was doubtful; But I was always for Erie."

In the national sphere railroad lobbies were strong and effective. On one occasion Senator Justin S. Morrill of Vermont, a man of rare wit, rose toward the end of a session and called attention to the presence, in the Senate's outer lobby, of the president of the Pennsylvania Railroad. Morrill moved the appointment of a committee to wait upon him and to learn if there was any further legislation desired by the railroad before adjournment! In spite of some effort at concealment, there were scandals which received great publicity, particularly those involving the Credit Mobilier and the Mulligan Letters. The Credit Mobilier had built the Union Pacific Railroad, in which the federal government was definitely involved — so much so that without its largesse the UP could never have been completed. National subsidies to the Union Pacific had amounted to 120 square miles of land plus an average loan of $32,000 for each mile of track. Altogether the UP, from government aid and the issue of stocks and bonds, managed to raise something over $100 million. Construction was then turned over to the Credit, a corporation composed chiefly of the inner circle of those who also controlled the railroad. The Union Pacific paid the Credit $93 million for building the road. The Credit then paid contractors $50 million to actually do the job. This represented a profit of $43 million for the Credit, a company that began its operations with an actual capital of only $218,000. Its major stockholders obviously became millionaires.

So much government money was involved that the UP crowd feared a congressional investigation. To keep this from happening they decided to pass enough of the "sugar" around Congress so that any demand for an investigation could be shouted down. There was a Congressman from Massachusetts by the name of Oakes Ames, whose family manufactured shovels; he was put in charge of the congressional "sugar bowl" and passed the lumps around, but was unable to dig himself out of the subsequent scandal. His basic technique was simple. No bribes were offered. Ames merely sold stock in the Credit on memorandum; favored Congressmen were told they did not need to pay until the dividends came in. It was an attractive offer; the dividends on a single share in one year amounted to $341.85. The entire transaction was finally exposed in 1872, when Horace Greeley made the most of it in his presidential campaign against U. S. Grant. It was the Teapot Dome of its day, and several high-class reputations were wrecked — at least temporarily. Among those implicated were Vice-President Schuyler Colfax, future President James A. Garfield, and several Congressmen — "Pig-Iron" Kelley of Pennsylvania, "Black Jack" Logan of Illinois, and William B. Allison of Iowa — later characterized as "a master of the arts of conciliation and construction." There was an unsuccessful attempt to expel Ames from Congress; he died soon afterward, his friends claimed of a "broken heart." The most pitiful case was that of Vice-President Schuyler Colfax, a pious fellow much given to religious lecture tours. He testified that he had never accepted any stock, nor had he received any dividends. He was then confronted with a canceled check for $1,200, made to his order by Ames, for which there was no satisfactory explanation. Because of Grant's support Colfax managed to escape official censure, no one had any belief in his innocence.

The Mulligan Letters involved James G. Blaine, sometimes called "The Plumed Knight from Maine." James Mulligan was a bookkeeper of Blaine's business partner, Warren Fisher, in Boston. Mulligan had incriminating letters indicating that Blaine, when Speaker of the House of Representatives, had received $64,000 from the Union Pacific Railroad for a nearly worthless pack of bonds in a bankrupt railroad — the Little Rock and Fort Smith Railroad. It seemed obvious that the Union Pacific, previously not known as a philanthropic institution, had taken the bonds off Blaine's hands in return for political favors which only a Speaker might bestow. Blaine went to Mulligan's room, just before the letters were to be read to a House committee that was looking into the matter in 1876. There was a conversation between the two men, during which Blaine implored Mulligan in the most moving terms to have mercy "upon his wife and children" and to lend the letters to Blaine temporarily. Mulligan did so, and never saw the letters again. Blaine did read *selected* portions before the House in a dramatic session, in a performance once described as "one of the most extraordinary exhibitions of histrionic skill, one of the most consummate pieces of acting that ever occurred upon any stage on earth." All this was in 1876, and discredited Blaine as a Republican presidential candidate in that year. Eight years later the matter came up again, when Blaine was again a presidential candidate. In 1884 Mulligan released new letters between Blaine and Fisher; from these it was apparent that, in 1876, Blaine had systematically lied and equivocated. During the campaign of 1884 the Republicans had been chanting:

> *Blaine! Blaine! James G. Blaine,*
> *The white-plumed knight from the State of Maine.*

The Democrats now paraphrased it to read:

> *Blaine! Blaine! James G. Blaine,*
> *Continental liar from the State of Maine.*

The sovereign rule of railroads was to charge all the traffic would bear. If there was competition, the rate was relatively low — if there was no competition, the rate was very high. Following this principle railroads showed discriminations based on time, place, and persons. The Erie Canal was the best example of discrimination based on time. During the summer, when the canal was in operation, railroad freight rates were lowered. During the winter, when ice stopped traffic on the canal, rail rates were raised. Discriminations between places always depended on the degree of competition — the alternatives before a shipper in transporting goods. Water transportation always provided serious competition and railroad rates from ports on rivers, especially the Mississippi, were lowered. These were made up by charging high rates from inland points, regardless of mileages; this led to what was called the long-and-short-haul abuse. At one time farmers in the Midwest were selling wheat for 50¢ a bushel; railroads were charging 72½¢ a bushel to carry it from the Mississippi Valley to the Atlantic Seaboard. The presence, or absence, of another competing railroad would result in weird situations. There was railroad competition from Cincinnati to Philadelphia; rail rates between these two cities were therefore low. There was no rail competition between Pittsburgh and Philadelphia, a route on which the Pennsylvania Railroad had a monopoly; rates were high. Shippers found that it was cheaper to ship from Pittsburgh to Philadelphia by way of Cincinnati, down the Ohio by river and thence to Philadelphia by rail. The Big Four in California charged such high rates on the monopolistic Southern Pacific that one group of merchants calculated it would be cheaper to send a cargo of nails from New York across the Atlantic to Antwerp, thence by boat around the Cape of Good Hope to San Francisco, rather than ship directly across the nation.

Discriminations between persons were of two types: those between passengers and those between shippers. The first involved the free pass, particularly to politicians from whom favors were expected. This was such an evil that in 1905 the editor of the Philadelphia *North American* wrote that "no single influence has done so much to poison the very fountains of political life as the railroad free pass." In the early decades of this century Warren G. Harding had a railway pass, then the most common political currency, which he used to travel freely around the state of Ohio. Not only politicians were favored; newspaper publishers were given free rides, a forerunner of the "junket" paid from public rather than private funds. In his early days in the South Adolph Ochs, who would ultimately bring the *New York Times* to a position of prominence, made good use of his pass as he traveled free to a variety of cities, familiarizing himself with the larger newspapers and the men who ran them. Discriminations between shippers involved both rebates and drawbacks, and John D. Rockefeller provided a prime example of the operation of this system. He went to the South Shore Railroad (which brought crude oil to Cleveland from the producing fields in Pennsylvania), demanded a secret rebate, and got it. All refiners paid 80¢ a barrel on such shipments, but Standard Oil received a 40¢ rebate from the railroad. Beyond this advantage, however, Rockefeller also received drawbacks on all oil shipped by his competitors. This meant that a competitor paid regular freight rates but that the railroad gave Standard a percentage, ranging from a fourth to one half of what the competitor had paid. It was difficult for Standard to lose on such an arrangement. Within a short time most of Rockefeller's competitors had done one of two things: gone out of business, or joined Rockefeller on his own terms.

Economic abuses almost always lead to government regulation, and the railroads were no exception. The first efforts for control came from the states, through what were known as Granger laws. One of the spectacular consequences of the Panic of 1873 was the growth of the first great farmers' movement in American history — the National Grange of the Patrons of Industry. Whereas the East recovered with reasonable speed from the Panic, in the South and West it continued throughout the 1870's — in large part because of the lack of war demands from Europe plus the opening of the Russian wheatfields. Both caused the prices of agricultural commodities to go down. The plight into which the farmer had fallen was graphically summed up in the phrase "ten-cent corn and 10 percent interest"; a sullen bitterness took possession of the prairies.

The so-called Grange, which became primarily a western movement, was actually organized in 1867 by Oliver H. Kelly, a clerk in the Department of Agriculture in the nation's capital; interestingly, Kelly's first lodge was Potomac No. 1. At first the organization was so small and poor that Kelly asserted that a five-cent stamp would have needed an introduction before it would have felt at home in the meager Treasury of the organization. The Panic of 1873 gave the organization all the impetus it needed; by 1875 there were 2,500,000 members and 30,000 separate lodges, chiefly in the upper Mississippi Valley. The main features of its program were three: social, cooperative, and legislative. Kelly believed that the lack of social opportunities made the farmer dull and conservative, simply because of the monotony of his existence. Today it is difficult, and perhaps impossible, to realize the depths of drudgery, loneliness, and futility confronting the farming family of the 1870's and 1880's. A century ago in rural America there were no hard roads, no telephones, radios, TV sets, movies, consolidated schools, rural free delivery, popular magazines, labor-saving appliances for washing and cleaning — nothing to bring the outside world to the farmer's doorstep. Life was one of bleak and unadorned toil; it is therefore little wonder that some farmers became the fanatics that they were — the cranks and zealots of the midwestern Bible Belt. Many turned their thoughts to the other world because this one was so dreary. Kelly figured that a secret society, based on the ideas of the Masons, would entertain the farmers and bind them together with arcane signs, grips, passwords, oaths, degrees, and other impressive mystic paraphernalia. There would be an ample number of lodge meetings, picnics, musicals, and lectures.

In the cooperative phase of its program the Grange hoped to alleviate price conditions through joint economic action. The organization abhorred industrial and financial monopolies, and expressed its opposition in one of its songs, the verses of which ran as follows:

> *Oppression stalks abroad, monopolies abound,*
> *Their giant hands already clutch,*
> *The tillers of the ground.*

So farmers pooled their resources and engaged in two kinds of cooperatives: *purchasing*, by buying farm implements and supplies in large quantities, and *producing*, by operating their own harvesting works, plow factories, packing plants, insurance companies, and banks. There is an interesting footnote to the cooperative feature of the Grange's program. One of the Grange's buying agents was a man named Aaron Montgomery

Ward. Through his activities for the farmers' organization, Ward became acutely conscious of the monopoly enjoyed by country stores, simply because of the lack of transportation facilities. Farmers had to patronize these stores, and buy what was offered, usually a meager variety of dubious merchandise at very high prices. He decided to attack these local retail monopolies by establishing, in 1872, a mail-order company. He used both his catalogue and newspapers to brag that he saved farmers millions of dollars, whether they bought from Ward or not. The point was that he had established a *yardstick* on prices, forcing country merchants to sell *their* goods at competitive prices. By 1880, only eight years after he had founded his company, he was grossing $2 million a year and the Ward catalogue — known as the "wishing book" — stood second only to the Holy Bible on the farmer's bookshelf. Ward was not only an acute businessman; he also had a keen sense of community responsibility, and showed it in two significant ways in connection with the Chicago lakefront and Northwestern University. Known as the "watchdog of the lakefront" he wanted a beautiful shoreline for Chicago and had such a profound passion on the matter that he kept buildings from being constructed there. Largely due to his efforts, disinterested as far as personal gain was concerned, Chicago now has a magnificent heritage in its lakefront. He also gave $9 million to Northwestern University, proving through philanthropy that selling things to Grangers by mail was not so ridiculous a business as it had seemed in 1872.

On the legislative side eleven states had Granger laws, with Illinois leading the way in 1871; these regulated railroads, grain elevators, and warehouses. A typical Granger law provided for maximum rates in such companies, the abolition of free passes and the long-and-short-haul abuse, and the establishment of a state commission for enforcement. In the financial East such laws were looked upon as communistic. Nonetheless, for a period of fifteen years until 1886, the Granger Movement was not only strong but in its heyday. Its social program was exciting and its cooperative program was flourishing. The courts also supported its Granger laws in two significant decisions in 1877: *Munn* v. *Illinois*, and *Peik* v. *Chicago and Northwestern Railroad Company*.

Munn v. *Illinois* was the result of the Illinois Granger law of 1871 regulating warehouses. To accommodate the huge quantities of grain which flowed in and out of Chicago a most lucrative business had developed, that of storing grain in warehouses until it was sold and shipped east. Built in skyscraper style they were called grain elevators; the structures could hold up to 1 million bushels in elongated perpendicular bins. Munn was a leading businessman in Chicago who diversified his investments by engaging in wholesale grain speculation and by investing in newspapers and banks. In 1868 his firm of Munn & Scott, plus four others, dominated the warehouse field; they were interlocked in a business pool which enabled them to fix prices and to force farmers to pay high storage fees. The pool not only charged excessive rates; it also cheated farmers by false reports about the condition of their grain. Munn would tell farmers that their grain was "heating," and that to avoid complete disaster they should sell the crop to a buyer at a loss of 10¢ a bushel. The farmers would do so, only to find that their perfectly sound grain had been sold by Munn at a nice profit. The farmers were peeved, and so was the Board of Trade in Chicago, which found that it could not control the fraudulent practices of these grasping warehousemen. Joseph Medill, the conservative publisher of the Chicago *Tribune*, made warehouse regulation a crusade and described Munn and his crowd as "rapacious, blood-sucking insects." Such an alliance — between the conservative Board of Trade and radical farmers — was most unusual; as a result the Illinois legislature responded with the Granger laws that declared grain elevators to be public in character, and established maximum rates therein.

Munn's lawyers developed a three-pronged attack: (1) that warehousing was *not* a *public* calling, and therefore the state had no jurisdiction; (2) that if it was a public calling, the courts rather than the legislature should determine the rates; and (3) that the Granger laws were in violation of the Fourteenth Amendment. They summarized their conclusions by stating that if the Granger laws were upheld, it would be the "beginning of the operations of the (Paris) commune in the legislation of this country."

The majority decision (7 to 2) of the Supreme Court, in favor of Illinois and against Munn, was delivered by Chief Justice Morrison R. Waite, an Ohioan appointed by President Grant who served on the Court from 1874 until his death in 1888. In his decision Waite made three points:

1. That warehousing *was* clothed with the public interest, although haberdashing was not; for that reason Illinois could regulate warehousing but not haberdashing. Waite contended that the grain elevators stood at the gateway of commerce to the East and could "take toll from all who pass"; they were similar in position to medieval nobles who controlled mountain passes. For this reason under the old English common-law principle they could be regulated, because their charge was a common one and the farmers had no choice but to pay it.

2. Maximum rates would be determined by the legislature, not the courts. Any appeal the warehousemen might want to make was therefore to the polls, not to courts of law.

3. The Fourteenth Amendment did not apply to the regulation of business.

With this striking and important decision warehousemen lowered their rates and two decades of arrogance, on their part, came to an end. The chief result of the decision, however, was the clear announcement that legislatures might regulate business on behalf of the public interest. This provided a leading precedent for future days when American big business would find itself under continuing government regulation.*

In the same year (1877) the Supreme Court upheld another Granger law in *Peik* v. *Chicago and Northwestern Railroad Company*. Here the case concerned Wisconsin, which had passed a Granger act regulating railroads. The Chicago and Northwestern claimed that its operations were interstate in character, and for that reason beyond the control of state police power. The Court said, however, that until Congress acted, states had a legal right to regulate railroads — as Wisconsin had done. The Peik and Munn decisions inaugurated a glorious decade for the structure of the Granger movement, during which it appeared that its establishment was sound and enduring. In 1886, however, the roof began to fall in, and thereafter the movement declined rapidly. Its cooperatives began to fail, because of poor management or unfair competition. Its members turned their attention away from social uplift and cooperatives and Granger laws to the panacea of inflation through greenbacks or free silver. The Supreme Court, originally so benign, now dealt the organization grievous blows in the Wabash Case of 1886 and the Minnesota Rate Case (*Chicago, Milwaukee, and St. Paul Railroad* v. *Minnesota*) of 1890. The Wabash Case concerned the long-and-short-haul abuse. Specifically, the Wabash charged more for a haul from Gilman (Illinois) to New York than from Peoria (Illinois) to New York — although Peoria was eighty-six miles more distant from New York. The reason was obvious; Peoria connected with the Mississippi by way of the Illinois River; Gilman was high and

---

* There was an immediate reaction to this decision by eastern railroad owners. The Munn decision was delivered on 1 March 1877. On 4 March a pool was organized by the presidents of four eastern trunk lines: William H. Vanderbilt of the New York Central, Hugh Jewett of the Erie, John Garrett of the B&O, and Tom Scott of the Pennsylvania. The pool agreed to boost rates by 50 percent on all westbound traffic, effective immediately, and to reduce wages by 10 percent, effective in June. At the time annual wages for trainmen, working a twelve-hour day, varied from $333 a year for the lowliest brakemen to $1,100 for some privileged conductors and engineers. According to Peter Lyon, by the late spring of 1877 the wages of thousands of poorly paid trainmen had been cut by 10 percent because of the arbitrary decision of only four men whose annual incomes ranged from Jewett's $40,000 to the $8 million that was enjoyed by William H. Vanderbilt. On the B&O Garrett insisted on reducing wages 10 percent in order to maintain dividends at 10 percent. All this led to the Railroad Strikes of 1877, the first major labor outbreaks in U.S. history, which the railroad magnates said were brought on by Communists. These strikes began on the B&O, spread quickly to other lines east of the Mississippi and eventually to western lines, with rioting in Baltimore, Pittsburgh, Chicago, and St. Louis. President Hayes sent federal troops to restore order at Martinsburg, West Virginia, after strikers had repulsed militia (nine persons killed), and at Pittsburgh, where strikers resisted militia in a pitched battle (twenty-six killed) and a mob later tore up railroad tracks and burned down machine shops, the Union Depot, and other property with losses estimated as high as $10 million. The strikes were finally broken, but they left a heritage of resentment against the national government for its use of troops, and they stimulated the first general congressional investigation of labor problems.

dry on the prairie. The Court nullified any state control over such inequity by stating that it could not exercise any control beyond its limits; such control, if any, was exclusive jurisdiction of Congress. Four years later, in the Minnesota Rate Case, the Court stated that legislatures could not establish rates and implied that the judicial branch would take over this responsibility.

From this point of time it was apparent that state regulation was illusory and that only the national Congress could act.

Prior to World War I, when the federal government took over and operated the railroads for several years, three basic regulatory acts were passed by Congress: the Interstate Commerce Commission (ICC) Act of 1887, the Hepburn Act of 1906, and the Mann-Elkins Act of 1910. Of the three the ICC Act was the first, but the Hepburn Act was by far the most important. The ICC Act of 1887 contained both affirmations *and* prohibitions. On the affirming side it said that rates should be just and reasonable, whatever that might mean, and it created the ICC, the second regulatory commission in U.S. history (the Civil Service Commission of 1883 was first). On the prohibitory side it forbade rebates and drawbacks, the long-and-short-haul abuse, and railroad pools. In spite of these brave statements two decades were to go by before the railroad problem was really brought under federal control and before the ICC became a functioning organization. The responsibility for the delay lay squarely with the Congress and with the courts. Congress was culpable because of the ambiguous phraseology of the act; specifically, it did not give the ICC clear and unequivocal power to fix rates — a power that is vital to effective railroad legislation. Under the ICC Act the commission could indicate what it thought "just and reasonable" rates should be — and then sue the railroads if they did not agree, which they emphatically did not. The burden of proof was on the ICC. The courts had their share of blame because of dubious interpretations and lengthy delays. After President Cleveland appointed Melville Fuller to be Chief Justice in 1888 (a position he retained until his death in 1910), the Supreme Court was particularly inimical to the commission; Fuller was a wealthy railroad lawyer when he took his position on the Court. In two decisions in 1897 (the Maximum Freight Rate Case and the Alabama Midland Case) a conservative Supreme Court practically interpreted the ICC Act away; the commission was denied the right to fix rates or to enforce the long-and-short-haul prohibition. Until the passage of the Hepburn Bill in 1906, the ICC became chiefly a statistical organization. After the devastating court decisions of 1897 Justice Harlan in dissent asserted that the ICC had become a "useless body for all practical purposes." The commissioners appeared to agree; in their annual report of the same year they stated that "under the law as now interpreted, there . . . can be no effective regulation of interstate carriers."

The Courts also delayed cases so long (the average time was four years) that small businessmen were out of luck; they had neither the money nor the time to prosecute cases. In the first eighteen years of the act, sixteen important cases were appealed from the commission to the Supreme Court; the Court ruled for the railroads in fifteen of them. In spite of these manifold weaknesses the ICC Act was the first major attempt by the federal government to regulate any kind of private business in the interest of society at large. It thus became a curtain-raiser for more effective railroad legislation which was to come in the future, because it established the principle of governmental control.

The Hepburn Act, enacted in 1906, as a result of Theodore Roosevelt's demand for stricter regulation of the railroads, was a real landmark. Its major clause permitted the ICC to fix rates, which would be binding unless set aside by a federal court; the burden of proof was now on the railroads. There were two minor clauses in the act: passes were abolished and the authority of the ICC was widened to include express and sleeping-car companies, and pipelines. The importance of the act was illustrated by the number of rate reductions that followed its passage; in the first five years of its operation 194,000 rates had been cut in half. Along with its merits the act also had some glaring weaknesses. The Hepburn Act stated that if an ICC order for a rate reduction was not obeyed within thirty days, penalties of $5,000 a day could be assessed thereafter. A federal circuit court, however, might annul such an order, pending appeal — and the old and higher rate, instead of the commission's decree for a new and lower one, prevailed pending a final decision in each case. This loophole encouraged railroads to institute increases and then fight for them in the courts. In the end, if the carrier lost a case, the increased revenue during the period of litigation was likely to be enough to pay the costs; if the railroad won, it was just that much ahead. The weakness in the Hepburn Act was obviously found in the fact that the ICC could only lower rates *after* they had been raised; it had no power to keep the railroads from raising them initially. This fault was corrected in the Mann-Elkins Act of 1910, which further increased the power of the commission by prohibiting any rate increases without the *prior* consent of the commission. The new act also widened the jurisdiction of the ICC to include telephone and telegraph companies.

World War I confronted the railroads with problems which they were unable to meet. As soon as the United States entered the conflict seven hundred representatives of individual roads formed the Railroads' War Board, and made some effort to minimize competition and to cooperate. They failed dismally to do so. As early as the summer of 1916 Congress had overridden the myopic policy of railroad magnates, and had thereby averted a nationwide strike, by passing the Adamson Act, providing for an eight-hour day for the industry — with increased pay for overtime. In the war crisis railroads showed little ability to utilize equipment properly. By the end of February 1917, 145,000 empty cars cluttered eastern terminals. One month later there was a freight-car shortage across the nation of the same number of cars, and by 1 November the country was short 158,000 freight cars — while nearly 200,000 of them stood idle on the tracks of eastern roads. On 1 December the ICC sadly reported to the Congress that the Railroads' War Board had failed. The reasons appear to have been psychological and monetary. For one thing, most railroad men had competed against each other all their lives; they found it difficult to change their aggressive habits overnight to cooperative ones. On the fiscal side the railroads found that they could not meet the increased costs of the war period. They needed additional funds but found that the ICC blocked their requests for increased rates, and that the loan market was monopolized by the U.S. government.

Of necessity, therefore, the U.S. government took possession of the railroads on the day after Christmas in 1917. This meant that the government now operated an industry worth more than $17 billion, owning 250,000 miles of railroad. It became the employer of more than 2 million persons, and now had to satisfy 650,000 stockholders in 400 railroad companies. President Wilson made William Gibbs McAdoo, his son-in-law who was also Secretary of the Treasury, the Director General of the U.S. Railroad Administration. It was a double assignment that would have killed a less able man, but McAdoo managed to survive it. He spent his mornings in the Treasury Department and his afternoons in the Department of Commerce. He broke but once under the strain, and was required to take an enforced rest in Maine.

The President took over the railroads, by executive order, in late December 1917. The next March Congress legalized what he had done in a Railroad Control Act that had return, rental, and loan clauses. The return clause guaranteed that the railroads would be restored to private operation not later than twenty-one months after the end of the war. In the meantime the U.S. government would pay a yearly rental for the use of the roads, a sum that would be determined by averaging the net income for the three relatively good years prior to 1917. This amounted to about a billion dollars a year, an arrangement under which bondholders were guaranteed their interest and stockholders an annual dividend of 5½ percent — so generous that railroad stocks actually rose on the market. The act also established a revolving fund of half a billion dollars for loans, so that run-down transportation facilities could be improved.

How effective was government operation of railroads? On this question there have been strong opinions on both sides. In general, it can be said that government operation increased war service immeasurably, at great expense. There is no question that efficiency and coordination were realized to an extent that would not have been possible under private management. All railroad systems were operated as one, and equipment was shifted about as needed. The most direct routes were utilized, regardless of individual roads involved. McAdoo later recalled a particularly striking instance of inefficiency under private management:

> In one instance that came to my attention it had been the custom to haul coal cars one hundred and seventy miles to a destination which was only thirteen miles from the point where the shipment originated. That miracle of inefficiency served its purpose of getting the revenue for one road even if that road did haul the coal at a loss. We stopped all that.

In addition, civilian passenger service was cut, and the public was asked to refrain from unnecessary travel — an edict that made government operation unpopular with the people. All of this was accomplished in spite of the fact that many railroad executives were guilty of what McAdoo called a "kind of sabotage" — in order to discredit government operation. After five months of tolerance he had to dismiss the railroad companies as his agents and appoint one responsible officer of each company as a federal manager to report to the regional director; from this point earnings and efficiency began to rise.

By means of this regulation and coordination under federal auspices the railroads were able to support the war effort adequately, but at considerable expense; in a little more than two years the national government had a deficit of upwards of a billion dollars. There were obvious reasons. The rental paid to private owners was too high, and operators ordered too many supplies, hoarding them against the day when the roads would be returned to private control; supplies of all kinds were squandered in the effort to discredit the government. But the chief reasons for the government deficit was the necessity of paying decent wages and of restoring the railroads to efficient operating conditions — neither of which had been done under private ownership. When he became Director General, McAdoo characterized the wages paid to railroad employees as a "long-standing national disgrace." To insure adequate wages for 2 million men and women and to bring railroad employees somewhere near parity with employees of other industries, McAdoo had to spend vast sums; in 1917 railroad labor cost $1.7 billion, in 1918 $2.6 billion. This was an increase of more than 50 percent; in the process of increasing wages McAdoo was able to guarantee for the first time that women would receive equal pay for equal work — and that Negro firemen, trainmen, and switchmen would be paid the same wages as white men in the same jobs. Vast sums also had to be spent to restore run-down roads to some semblance of operating efficiency. As an example McAdoo found the Pennsylvania Railroad to be in disgracefully shoddy shape — "in worse condition than any other railroad in the United States"; he had to spend more money on this large trunk line than on any other — ultimately $218 million of public funds in improving the road and equipping it with new rolling stock. But, as Peter Lyon points out, when the government presented a modest bill to the Pennsylvania for $187 million, "the howl of anguish could be heard all across the country." The Pennsylvania claimed that it had been sorely afflicted by the Railroad Administration, but in spite of its disabilities was ready to pay the government $53 million. After considerable negotiation, the Pennsylvania finally settled for about $90 million, or less than half of what it cost U.S. taxpayers to rebuild the road and make it an adequate transportation system.

When the war was over an argument developed concerning the future of the railroads; labor and management took positions that were diametrically opposed, with McAdoo in between. Management wanted return to private ownership but was willing to accept more government supervision *and* loans. Labor presented a plan for government ownership developed by Glenn Edward Plumb, a crusading lawyer. The "Plumb Plan" provided for purchase of the railroads by the federal government, with its securities taking the place of company stocks and bonds. The government would then lease the roads to a National Operating Corporation with fifteen directors — five each from management, labor, and the government. The National Operating Commission would pay an annual rental to the government amounting to 5 percent of the valuation of the roads, plus certain sums to be set aside for amortization of the government's investment. If there were profits beyond fixed costs, half was to go to the government and half to the National Operating Commission. McAdoo took a middle position, recommending extension of government operation of the roads for five years until 1924; he wanted to test the experiment of government operation in peacetime. He also argued that wage increases authorized by the federal government would place the roads under a heavy burden, and that the vast sums spent on improvements had given the government the right to exercise closer supervision of the transportation network.

With the nation heading toward the conservative 1920's it is not surprising that the Republican-controlled Congress carried out the wishes of the railroad magnates in the Esch-Cummins, or Transportation, Act of 1920. It had four main clauses dealing with consolidations, new and old railroads, recapture of profits, and the rate base. As far as consolidations were concerned there was an extraordinary break with previous legislation; the roads were returned to private ownership and the ICC was instructed to prepare a comprehensive plan for the unification of American railroads into a limited number of systems, which were to be exempt from former antitrust or antipooling laws (such as the ICC Act of 1887). The justification for this break with the past was the efficiency and economy that had been achieved during the war, albeit under government rather than private operation. Because the United States had reached a saturation point as far as railroads were concerned, the clause on new and old railroads stated that no new roads could be begun, nor old ones abandoned, without permission from the ICC. The recapture clause was an idealistic one founded on the principle that prosperous roads were to share their profits with less prosperous ones; one half of all profits in excess of 6 percent were to go to the ICC, which would establish a contingent fund to help the weaker roads. It was a Franciscan principle which did not work in practice because of the rate base established by the Transportation Act of 1920. Under it the old battle by Senator Robert M. La Follete for rates based exclusively on the *physical* evaluation of railroad properties was lost in favor of the companies' demand for rates based on *stock issues* — including all the watered stock left over from the past.

Two of the four main clauses of the Esch-Cummins Act, those dealing with new-old railroads and the generous rate base, were quite effective in practice. Clauses dealing with consolidations and the recapture of profits never worked, and there is some reason to doubt whether there was any initial intention that they should. It was not until 1929 that the ICC recommended a consolidation plan for the entire country. By that time the main problem before many railroads was not a plan for the future — it was how to avoid immediate bankruptcy. The recapture clause obviously turned on the answer to a simple question: 6 percent of what? The ICC used "Original Cost" as the base; the companies held out for "Reconstruction Cost New" (RCN) — at least during the 1920's when costs were high. This argument was finally settled by the Supreme Court in the O'Fallon Case of 1929. The St. Louis and O'Fallon Railroad was a tiny one carrying coal; it was only nine miles long and was worth less than a million dollars. Nonetheless the decision set a precedent for private ownership that was worth many times the value of the railroad; this was because the Supreme Court supported RCN as a basis for valuation. The result was that the ICC was unable to recapture many excess profits. Down to 1929 (the date of the O'Fallon decision), when the railroads were fighting the issue in the courts, less than $11 million had been paid to the ICC under the recapture clause. After the Panic of 1929 there was nothing to recapture. Ironically, in the 1930's the railroads came to look upon "Original Cost" with favor, although they had previously regarded this principle as confiscatory. The reason was selfish and unprincipled: with the low prices prevailing in the 1930's, valuation based on original cost was higher than RCN, and therefore better as a rate base. The hypocrisy of railroad management was completely unveiled.

In his provocative and readable book entitled *To Hell in a Day Coach*, Peter Lyon notes that in the nineteenth century U.S. railroads — in spite of a considerable amount of bogus financing and inequitable discriminations — had provided a transportation network that hauled an underdeveloped nation out of debt and helped carry it toward industrial supremacy in the world. By 1905, when American railroads were only seventy-five years old, they were both feared and respected as The Octopus. At that time it was estimated that they controlled one-sixth of the wealth of the United States, and that their capital was ten times that of the combined banks and trust companies of the nation. During the next half century the national economy expanded enormously, but the role of the railroads shrank. By the late 1960's there were several individual corporations (GM, Standard Oil of New Jersey, and AT&T) which singly boasted greater revenues than the entire railroad industry; by that time the railroads were carrying less than half the nation's freight and only 3 percent of its passengers. There were a number of reasons for this precipitous decline; one of the major ones was the sad experience of the 1930's, when it was necessary to put U.S. railroads through a financial wringer.

By 1932 one third of U.S. railroads were bankrupt, one third were tottering, and only the remaining third were making a profit. The situation would have been worse except for the fact that the government, through the Reconstruction Finance Corporation, began to administer life-saving hypodermics to the roads. The chief trouble was that profits had been drained off in the 1920's and early 1930's by financiers who headed the holding companies that dominated the railroads. One need only consider the problem of the railroad debt. Total capitalization of the railroads in the early 1930's amounted to $25 billion. One half of this was in funded debt, represented by bonds; the fixed, unpostponable charges of the funded debt, amounting annually to about $700 million, meant that American railroads were mortgaged up to their eyes. Much of this debt should have been paid off in the 1920's, when railroad profits exceeded a billion a year. Instead large dividends and generous salaries were paid, and there was speculation on the stock market that was most unfortunate and unwise. After 1927 the New York Stock Exchange was made more feverish and dangerous by speculation, on the part of large eastern railroads, in the stocks of smaller companies. These purchases were directed by the bankers and brokers of Wall Street; some of the acquisitions were recognized as violations of the Clayton Antitrust Act, but they were made anyway. From October 1929 to May 1931 the Pennsylvania Railroad spent about $25 million for stock in the New Haven, a railroad that was soon in bankruptcy. The New York Central spent $17 million to buy stock of the Lackawanna at $110 a share; a few months later the same shares were selling for $12 each. Some years later a prominent American said, with the advantage of hindsight, that "it was the crooked banking houses that looted the railroads and it was those crooked bankers who were the real authors of the Security and Exchange Commission." The "radical" who made this strong statement was Alfred M. Landon, the Republican candidate for President in 1936.

A prime example of how not to run railroads, or to protect investors therein, was the empire dominated by the Van Sweringen brothers of Cleveland, Ohio. Of this operation Lyon has the following to say:

> It is a sad duty to report that most, if not all of this empire was assembled in ways that were naughty, dishonest, and often downright illegal. It is grievous to report that the Van Sweringens were advised and assisted in their dubious career by the officers of the New York Central system; the partners of J. P. Morgan & Company; George F. Baker, the president of the First National Bank of New York; and sundry other respectable, conservative bankers, lawyers, and railroad executives of Cleveland, New York, and other cities, all of whom should have known and probably did know better.

O.P. (Oris Paxton) and M.J. (Mantis James) Van Sweringen came from Dutch colonial stock, just as Vanderbilt did. They were sons of a poor farming family in northern Ohio and left school at the eighth grade. O.P. was once asked to name his favorite authors. After some exploratory thought his careful reply was "Rand and McNally"; actually he read Westerns. O.P. was the idea man; M.J. was the technician and mechanic who carried out his brother's plans — he was interested in the how, not the why. The story is told that during childhood snowball fights, Mantis made the snowballs, and Oris threw them; this was the pattern of their business operations. The Van Sweringens were known as the "Bachelor Brothers of Daisy Hill," the 660-acre estate fifteen miles from Cleveland where "schemes came true" and on which they spent $10 million, transforming four farms into an impressive Norman barony.

They began in real estate, developing the well-planned suburb of Shaker Heights near Cleveland. They needed rapid transit to downtown Cleveland for residents of this plush area and to get a right-of-way, for only a few miles, in 1916 purchased the entire Nickel Plate Railroad (which the ICC had ordered the New York Central to sell lest it violate Section 7 of the new Clayton Antitrust Act); having purchased one railroad the Van Sweringens branched out with several more.* Needing a focal point for rapid transit and railroads in downtown Cleveland they built the Terminal Tower and surrounding buildings, a city within a city that included a large department store, a hotel, and other structures. The tower itself had fifty-two stories and was 709 feet high, the tallest building at the time outside of New York City. Unfortunately, the first train

---

* The mayor of Cleveland, Newton D. Baker, had once said of the Nickel Plate that "it was two parallel streaks of rust that ran just often enough to be dangerous." This had been true. The Nickel Plate had been built originally to blackmail the Vanderbilt-owned Lake Shore Railroad into buying it to the promoters' profit. The blackmail was paid; the name Nickel Plate supposedly was bestowed by William H. Vanderbilt who, when told the price demanded by the promoters, said that he would not pay that much if the rails were nickel-plated. The legal name of the road was the New York, Chicago & St. Louis. The Lake Shore and Vanderbilt did not need the new acquisition, except for its nuisance value, and proceded to neglect it — with the result that the Nickel Plate became a decrepit railroad. To the credit of the Van Sweringens, they made it an efficient and profitable one.

pulled into the palatial new Union Terminal — which combined facilities for five railroads previously housed in five miserable stations — on 23 October 1929. The Van Sweringen brothers were proud passengers on the train. The following day the stock market panicked; it was a bad augury, but the brothers had not anticipated — nor did they ever understand — the Panic of 1929 and the depression that followed. In all their operations they used very little money of their own; their policy was "borrow, borrow — pay tomorrow." They had learned how to use two powerful weapons: the leverage provided by pyramided holding companies (see pp. 526–527), and the use of other people's money in banks and insurance companies. By these methods they added one railroad after another until they controlled the most extensive transportation system in the country; it included the Nickel Plate, the Erie, the C&O, and the Missouri Pacific — an empire that extended 29,000 miles and was worth on paper more than $3 billion (unfortunately the Missouri Pacific went bankrupt shortly after they unwisely purchased it). Their nearest competitor, the combination organized around the Pennsylvania Railroad, controlled 23,000 miles; with the Missouri Pacific the Van Sweringens personally controlled the nation's only transcontinental system. Ultimately their financing became so complicated that no public authority or accountant could follow a wandering asset as it meandered from one of their multitudinous corporations to another. In actual fact it was so abstruse that the Van Sweringens themselves could not keep track of it, as they admitted to a Senate investigating committee.

The Van Sweringen corporate fairyland collapsed for the same reason that the credit of a persistent buyer on margin, or of a persistent installment buyer, disintegrates. Ultimately they went broke just before their deaths, within a year of each other, in 1935 and 1936. Ultimately too their empire was liquidated in 1951, fifteen years later and after many hapless investors had been forced to sell at a considerable discount; even so, in spite of the recovery of stocks and railroads during World War II, creditors in the Van Sweringen companies ultimately lost $61 million. In the meantime two major Cleveland banks had closed, at least in part because of their beneficent but fiscally unsound largesse to the Van Sweringens. For this reason it is not surprising that a Cleveland columnist named Jack Raper, who wrote for the Scripps-Howard Cleveland *Press*, would comment pointedly on the debacle of the bachelor brothers. He would write particularly about the Terminal Tower:

> . . . that wonderful tower reaching up into the clouds — the highest thing in Cleveland, except the pile of defaulted bonds they [the Van Sweringens] built; that wonderful tower in whose top there burns a powerful light, its bright rays going far across the boundaries of the city, far out into the country.

There in the tower it burns, night after night, in memory of the unknown bondholder.

Justice Louis Brandeis once commented that "the greatest factors making for communism, socialism, and anarchy among a free people are the excesses of the rich." Perhaps it was the excesses of the rich, along with the failure of many railroads, that brought a demand in the 1930's for nationalization. Those who favored this step, including John T. Flynn (later a conservative radio commentator), pointed to the successful government operation of the railroads — as they saw it — during World War I. They also pointed to government ownership elsewhere in the world; actually, with the exception of the Canadian Pacific Railroad, there is no other sizable privately owned and operated railroad in the world outside the United States. Congress did not follow the demands for public ownership but it did attempt to assist the railroads by means of extensive loans from the RFC, and by passage of the Railroad Emergency Act of 1933 and the Motor Carrier Act of 1935. The Emergency Act of 1933 recognized the inevitable by repealing the highly unsuccessful recapture clause of the Transportation Act of 1920, brought railroad holding (as well as operating) companies under the supervision of the ICC, and provided for a temporary (until 1936) Federal Railroad Coordinator to eliminate waste and promote financial organization (the coordinator's orders would be final unless they were set aside by the ICC). The Motor Carrier Act of 1935 looked good on paper but left something to be desired in practice, as we shall see. Ostensibly it brought motor carriers engaged in interstate commerce under the regulation of the ICC in regard to rates, rebates, and the long-and-short-haul abuse.

Joseph Eastman, the Federal Coordinator of Railroads from 1933 to 1936, was frank to confess that he accomplished little because of hostility of both labor and management. Labor disliked him because the elimination of waste meant the elimination of jobs; management could not abide the intervention of any federal official. In spite of the exasperations of this particular assignment, Eastman deserves recognition and praise for his great knowledge and his public service. He served on the ICC for a quarter of a century, from the time of his appointment in 1919 until his death in 1944, serving also as Federal Railroad Coordinator in the 1930's and as Chairman of the Office of Defense Transportation (ODT) in the 1940's. His life has been chronicled, in admiring but scholarly terms, by Claude M. Fuess in *Joseph Eastman — Servant of the People.*

Fuess observed that ICC members seldom emerge as personalities out of the welter of statistics and heavy technical data with which they deal. Eastman did; he won respect and confidence everywhere — a respect and confidence that amounted to reverence in some circles. He was able to achieve this reputation because of his capacity for hard work, his independence, and his devotion to duty. His work day was a killing one. Arriving at the office just before 8:30 A.M., he worked all day, took a short nap in his office at 5:30 P.M., had a brief workout at an athletic club followed by dinner, then returned to the office to work until midnight. This schedule was followed seven days a week except for Sunday, when he arrived at the office at 10:00 rather than 8:30 in the morning. His independence was manifested in every feature of his life: religion, relations with women, politics, economics. He was a minister's son but belonged to no church. Women he liked and admired, but he never married — largely because he thought that marriage would take time from his work. For this reason some claimed that he was actually married — to the ICC. In politics he was an absolute independent; again and again he found it necessary to explain, to his sponsors, that he had no party affiliations. His voting record in presidential elections certainly proves it; he voted for Taft in 1908, TR in 1912, Wilson in 1916, Cox in 1920, La Follette in 1924, Smith in 1928, FDR in 1932 and 1936, Willkie in 1940. Politically, various Presidents would have been glad to drop him from the ICC — Harding in 1922 and Hoover in 1929 because he seemed too radical, and FDR in 1936 because he seemed too independent. His relationship with FDR was an interesting and stubborn one. FDR wanted the independent commissions, including the ICC, to report to him; he really wanted the ICC to become part of the Department of Commerce, whose head (Daniel C. Roper of South Carolina) was very much connected with political patronage. The President called a conference about the advisability of attaching the ICC to Commerce and got affirmative nods from all around the table until it was Eastman's turn. Eastman said, "I'm sorry, Mr. President, but I can't go along with that. The ICC is by law a creature of Congress, and it is our duty to report directly to it." There was an awesome silence, and it was noted that the President's mouth tightened. Eastman's term expired in 1936; FDR kept him waiting until 1937 before reappointing him. When he did, the action was taken largely because the President was told, by both railroad executives and Senators, that Eastman could not be spared. In economics he not only refused to be typed but was a source of puzzlement to many. He thought socialism was a fine ideal, but in practice did not believe that the public had reached a stage of education and altruism that would permit socialism to be successful. He approved the principle of public ownership of railroads, but did not think the time had yet arrived to assure the success of the experiment; the central theme of his life was that facilities in transportation should be run primarily in the public interest, but operated economically and efficiently. Although railroad operators could not decide just where Eastman was placed in the spectrum of economic thought, they had respect for him because they knew they could count on a thorough study and a fair hearing on every case. In 1944, just before Eastman died, a silver anniversary dinner was held in honor of his quarter century on the ICC. On this occasion J. Carter Fort, the general counsel of the Association of American Railroads, told with delight the story about two railroad operators, neither of whom entirely approved of Mr. Eastman.

The first one remarked, "I think Mr. Eastman is a very fine man, but in my opinion he is a little to the left." This evoked a snort of derision from the second man, who answered, "Yes, he is a little to the left — just a little to the left of Mark Hanna."

Impressive as was Eastman's capacity for hard work and his rugged independence, the outstanding feature of his life was devotion to public service. When he assumed the tremendous burden of ODT in 1942 he was suffering from angina and his doctor told him he should have an operation. Eastman said, "I am almost sixty, with no wife or family. It makes little difference what happens to me." It is small wonder that Justice Brandeis once said of him: "Joe Eastman has more interest in public service and less in his own career than any man I have ever known."

Railroads got along reasonably well from 1942 through 1951 because of the demands of World War II and of the later Korean conflict. The Depression of the 1930's had threatened to engulf every railroad in bankruptcy and disaster; the wars of the next decade buried every railroad under an avalanche of traffic. This was an unplanned boon but the myopic roads mistook the present for the future, failed to learn from the past or to ponder tomorrow's problems, and have been on the skids ever since. In 1900 railroads carried 84 percent of the travelers between the nation's cities. By the late 1960's 88 percent went by automobile; buses and trains and planes carried the other 12 percent, but of this 12 percent the airplane carried more people than buses and trains combined. At the same time trucks were taking over the future as far as freight was concerned. As railroad freight business went down, railroad rates went up — with the inevitable result that the railroad share of freight went down still further, from 67 percent of the freight traffic in 1945 to 46 percent in 1958. Although piggybacks and auto racks, hopper cars and unit trains brightened the freight picture for railroads in the 1960's, they are still on the defensive.*

What can be done to rehabilitate railroads and to bring some order out of the chaos of the current transportation situation in the United States? The improvement of railroad management will help, but the solution of this complex problem will require reforms and new policies in areas other than railroad management: from *labor* in the elimination of featherbedding, from the *ICC* in more imaginative and equitable regulation, and

---

* Western roads have done relatively well because they have more rail freight and are sounder financially. They have more rail freight because rail freight is often more economical than trucks in the mountains of the West. They are sounder financially because of the carry-over from their large land holdings, from which many western roads have profited in recent years. As an example the UP has extensive oil- and gas-producing properties, and operates the resort at Sun Valley, Idaho. The SP has oil, gas, and mineral rights, timber land, and commercial real estate.

from the *U.S. government* in subsidies and new policies which will reduce travel by plane and motor vehicle.

There are many who believe that an improvement in stodgy railroad management could work wonders. E. B. White, the essayist on the *New Yorker*, thinks little of railroad executives and says they should stop sulking in their tents and beat the motorcar at its own game. In his judgment if the railroads would improve their passenger service by 10 percent, they would increase their business by 20 percent. But they cannot do it if they follow the philosophy of James J. Hill, who scornfully compared a passenger train (by contrast with the freight) to a "male teat" — neither useful nor ornamental. They also cannot do it with locomotives and cars that average thirty years in age, and with insolent service on trains. Railroad management counters with the claim that it loses heavily on passenger traffic which it is forced to maintain, and that this loss absorbs almost half of the total profits from freight service. Put in different language, in 1955 the railroads were claiming that they spent $1.38 to carry passengers for every dollar they took in at the ticket window. There is much controversy about these figures; Peter Lyon, for one, states that the alleged passenger deficit is a "statistical mirage." The dispute revolves around accounting procedures; for years the ICC rules provided that railroad operating expenses had to be divided between freight and passenger service. In actual fact most railroad operations (dispatching, signaling, maintenance) would go on in any case, and money would not be saved if passenger service were abandoned. For this reason, some transportation experts put the passenger loss at $100 million (or less) rather than the $700 million deficit claimed by the roads in 1957 — and a decade later the ICC asserted that profits were being made on passenger traffic. Regardless of the outcome of this controversy, there is no question that railroads relying heavily on passenger rather than freight traffic for revenue have been hard hit financially. The best examples in the East are the Long Island, and the bankrupt New York, New Haven and Hartford.

Peter Lyon questions the management of U.S. railroads against a backdrop of historic managerial greed and stupidity, and he probes the "callous deceit and disregard for the public interest that still characterizes the approach of most of our railroads toward the passenger train at the very moment in our history when it seems needed the most." By contrast in Europe, Canada, and Asia nations have built up railroad passenger traffic through nationalized roads. The Canadian National Railroad operates more than 32,000 miles of track through all ten Canadian provinces and into the United States as well. In 1965 it introduced the Rapido; this train ran the 335 miles between Toronto and Montreal in five hours (almost an hour and a half faster than the train it replaced), for a coach seat of $8 and a first-class fare (including a full-course dinner) of $15. The innovation was most successful. By contrast the New York Central took six hours to run the same distance between Cleveland and Chicago; coach fare was $16.25, and first-class travel (without dinner) was $25. Few wanted to ride on such a train, with excessive charges and poor service; travelers found it preferable to fight backache on the turnpikes or boredom in the airports, with the result that restaurants and motels replaced the dining cars and sleepers of the great trains. Japan's government-owned railways have been as successful as Canada's with high-speed travel between cities; the 320-mile line between Tokyo and Osaka has electric trains that flash at 120 miles an hour over a virtually level and curveless track. In the United States, by contrast, motorists drive long distances in autos that can roll faster than trains. The roaring big-steel railroad limited of the 1930's, sweeping past 45-mile-per-hour automobiles at a mile a minute, is a relic of the past. Automobiles and buses now cruise turnpikes and freeways at 70 miles an hour, faster than most of the passenger trains that are left. There has been much talk but limited action on high-speed travel between major cities in the United States. What little there has been is due largely to Senator Claiborne Pell of Rhode Island, who wrote a book entitled *Megalopoplis Unbound*. In it he pointed out that by 1980 it was anticipated that twenty-five urban regions containing only 10 percent of the nation's land area, from Boston to Washington, would house more than two-thirds of the people in the United States. How could they be moved about? Obviously not by car or plane, unless the populace wanted to choke. Pell envisioned an eight-state public authority which would own and operate a high-speed railroad passenger service within Megalopolis; it would be financed by long-term, tax-exempt bonds guaranteed by the U.S. government. Actually there are twenty such corridor areas in the nation (such as Milwaukee-Chicago, Chicago-Detroit, Chicago–St. Louis, Toledo-Cleveland-Buffalo, Cleveland-Pittsburgh), with such burgeoning populations that high-speed trains could make an important contribution to travel and safety by getting cars off highways and planes out of the air.

In 1965 there was a first legislative gesture toward such a plan. Congress passed a "High-speed Transportation Act" which provided $18 million a year to buy high-speed equipment, and to provide the roadbed to handle it in the corridor between Boston and Washington. In 1969 the Penn Central Company began to operate fast Metroliners between New York and Washington; this was the result of the federal government's three-year program, involving an expenditure of $90 million, for research and development of mass transportation. This was promising, but two years later (in 1971) Congress met the continuing challenge by a drastic reduction in passenger service! With the ironic goal of "getting people back on trains" it authorized a feeble subsidy of $40 million for a corporation called Amtrak, a contraction of "American" and "track." In the 1920's there had been 20,000 passenger trains. On the eve of the establishment of Amtrak only 366 noncommuter trains were still running in the United States; the new corporation cut this number in half by operating only 186 of them. Major metropolitan areas — Cleveland notably — as well as six states were left without any service at all. But the most discouraging aspect of this attempt to bring what was advertised as "the greatest business turnaround in history," was the fact that direct responsibility for train operation remained in inept hands; Amtrak was really a bill-paying organization for the same bumbling rail managements that had done their best to obliterate passenger traffic. This meant that passenger trains, in both literal and actual terms, would continue to be sidetracked to let the freight pass. The Metroliners had enjoyed some degree of success but on the other Amtrak trains, as one observer put it, passengers were confronted with the same old service: "Filthy bathrooms, decaying stations, late arrivals, surly conductors, drab coaches and no promotion left the customer with the distinct impression he was not wanted."

If railroad management has been lethargic about passenger service, on which it claims to lose money, it has been no brighter about rail freight on which it certainly has been showing a profit, but could do much better. Economist Marvin Barloon tells of an incident in April 1966 during which two small boys were inadvertently locked in a railway boxcar loaded with empty beer bottles. This was in North Carolina. Thirteen days later a workman in Milwaukee (Wisconsin) opened the car door and found the two boys alive but haggard, having subsisted for nearly two weeks on beer dregs. The urchins got a lot of attention; no one seemed to be concened with the slowness with which the boxcar had traveled. No one asked why it took thirteen days for the car to reach Milwaukee, a thousand miles away. At forty miles an hour the trip would have taken less than two days. The fact was that during most of the period the car was not moving at all; it was standing still, serving as an expensive warehouse for beer bottles. This points to the fact that the average American freight car is actually moving in a train for only two and a half out of every twenty-four hours. A freight train is quite capable of going sixty miles an hour or better; because of switching stops along the way, it averages only twenty miles an hour while actually moving between terminals. This means, unfortunately, that in an American freight car the parts least used are the wheels. It also means a severe shortage of railway cars, a shortage great enough to cut an estimated $7 billion annually from the nation's production. The reason for all this, as Barloon points out, is that rail freight today is carried in an archaic and fragmented system inherited from the nineteenth century. In 1967 there were ninety-eight separate and independent railroads still in operation, most of them less than five hundred miles long. Merger was not the only answer because freight could be moved with maximum efficiency if the lines could be consolidated into a few large regional systems. This would require the elimination of railroads, particularly some that paralleled and duplicated each other; there were six lines between Chicago and Omaha, where two were sufficient. The ninety-eight lines served reasonably well in the age of the steam locomotive; some of them were obsolete in the diesel era.

Railroad management must be improved; so must the productivity of railroad labor. Railroads have been far from happy about feather-bedding by labor, which they estimate costs them some half a billion dollars a year. Unions disagree, but concede privately that a good many practices are out of date. The central point is that railroad labor, as with labor in many industries, is faced with the problem of automation. In 1940 there were almost 41,000 locomotives in use, less than a thousand of them diesel. In 1965 there were 28,000 locomotives, all but fifty-one of them diesel. There were fewer locomotives — 28,000 as against 41,000 — but those fewer locomotives were carrying half again as much freight as was carried in 1940 — 600 billion ton-miles in 1965 as against less than 400 billion ton-miles in 1940. Meantime railroad employment was dropping sharply, from 2 million in 1920 to 1.5 million in 1945 to 1 million in 1955 to 654,000 in 1965. Railroad unions were therefore reluctant to abandon past privileges, no matter how silly and inefficient they might now be. Current work rules are essentially those in force since 1919; for engine crews they read "One hundred miles or less . . . shall constitute a day's work. . . ." For conductors and trainmen, the day's work (by 1919 standards) was 150 miles or less. This means a great deal of overtime, if they go further, as many do a half century later. Translated into wages this means that the New York Central had to employ eight engine crews — whose members divided 9½ days of basic pay — to move the Twentieth-Century Limited on its less-than-one-day trip from New York to Chicago. There was also the question of personnel no longer needed on diesel equipment; the prime example was firemen, no more necessary on a diesel locomotive than a Pullman porter would be on a cattle car. Little progress has been made on these antiquated wage and work regulations, and there has been a continuing threat of strikes over them. For a number of years railroads tried to rid themselves of 40,000 firemen who have no fires to stoke on diesels. Ultimately two presidential commissions, one congressional board, and the United States Supreme Court were needed to establish the right of railroads to eliminate firemen slowly, by attrition and reassignment.

A lethargic and unimaginative railroad management was justifiably critical of lethargic and unimaginative labor leaders; it was also unhappy about a lethargic and inequitable ICC. The railroads have asked that the ICC relax its regulations against the abandonment of unprofitable lines unless federal subsidies are forthcoming, that it lower rates for competitive purposes, and that it look favorably on mergers because railroads now compete chiefly with automobiles, river barges, trucks, and planes rather than against one another. The fact that the railroads now come hat-in-hand asking for this assistance is representative of an amazing change that has occurred during the past century. Seventy-five years ago railroad moguls were a law unto themselves. For half a century Congress and state legislatures were crowded with railroad lawyers; Lincoln himself represented the Illinois Central Railroad. Today one is hard put to name a single Senator who would make a speech for the railroads, although there are plenty of spokesmen for automobiles and highways and planes and trucks and barge lines.

In the current era railroads claim that they suffer from too much regulation by the ICC, and that the trucking industry and the inland waterways enjoy too little. The lack of regulation of the trucking industry by the ICC is due chiefly to an astonishing loophole (in the Motor Carrier Act of 1935) which frees a sizable number of trucks, carrying what are called "exempt" commodities, from regulation by the ICC. The major exemption is that of agricultural products. This loophole was originally intended to protect *farmers* who used their *own* trucks to ship their produce to market. It now keeps many *interstate carriers* by truck free from regulation, carrying anything that can be remotely considered as "agricultural" — from TV dinners to powdered milk. This exemption also encourages the "gypsies" (marginal operators) to cheat. As an example, in 1965 the ICC halted a refrigerator truck in Georgia. The driver's bill of lading showed a load of fresh vegetables. Inspection of the rig showed that it was full of frozen bathtubs. In Nevada a load of "eggs" turned out to be 44,000 pounds of paint. Because of these exemptions and violations, it is probable that only one-third of the interstate trucking industry is under the regulation of the ICC. The same absence of regulation applies to the inland waterway companies. This is due to an exemption of 1940 which frees "bulk cargoes," 90 percent of their business, from the regulation of the ICC. This means in practice that while 100 percent of the interstate traffic of railroads is regulated, and must post rates for subsequent approval — two-thirds of the truckers and 90 percent of the inland water carriers can aim their rates just under railroad rates, and thus entice shippers away from the railroads. Railroads also claim that the ICC has been slow in allowing them to merge in order to avoid bankruptcy, and it has not permitted them to abandon unprofitable lines or schedules. They can cite numerous examples of passenger runs in which the train crews regularly outnumbered the passengers, and where they could have saved money by transporting the passengers by taxis. They claim that they have not been allowed to abandon these runs because of pressure on the ICC by railroad labor and citizens in communities who normally travel by automobile but look upon trains as "foul-weather" friends — for use when travel by plane or car is limited by weather or by war. The ICC has shown some cooperation with railroads in relation to mergers, perhaps too much as critics of the Penn Central and the Great Northern–Northern Pacific amalgamations would attest. Unfortunately the ICC has developed no master plan which would delineate the kind of railroad system the United States should have ten years from now, with designation of the role (if any) that each existing railroad would have in such a combined and rational system. In 1929 the ICC had promulgated a grand plan for consolidation of railroads into twenty-one systems. This was probably too many, but in any case the Depression of the 1930's kept the proposal from being carried out. A generation later many believe we should revise and implement the "grand plan" that never came off in the 1930's.

Beyond these specific censures there have been other severe critics of the ICC on general grounds; they have attacked it as senile, stodgy, bureaucratic, and ineffective. John Kenneth Galbraith has remarked that all regulatory agencies have a marked life cycle: "In youth they are vigorous, aggressive, evangelistic, and even tolerant. Later they mellow, and in old age — after a matter of ten or fifteen years — they become, with some exceptions, either an arm of the industry they are regulating or senile." Justice Douglas, who once headed the SEC, has suggested that every regulatory agency be abolished at the end of each ten-year period. Peter Lyon notes that the ICC began in 1887 with five commissioners and a staff not much larger. It now has eleven commissioners and a secretariat of nearly 2,500; the law under which it operates has changed from a lean ten-page statute to one of more than four hundred pages. Both its responsibilities and its regulations "have multiplied like bunnies," with the bureaucratic result that today "its procedures are labyrinthine in method and glacial in dispatch." The *New York Times*, appalled that this "sleepiest and least effectual" agency has never formulated minimum standards for passenger services but is all too willing to eliminate them, had this to say about the ICC of 1968:

Made up of eleven commissioners who rotate the chairmanship each year, the ICC has a shifting membership, no executive head and few consistent policies. Its protracted procedures sometimes irritate the railroads, buslines and trucking companies, but these private interests much prefer to suffer its fussy inconsequence than to deal with a small, reformed agency which might aggressively defend the public interest.

A year later Louis Kohlmeier, a Pulitzer Prize winner who covered the ICC and other agencies for the *Wall Street Journal*, was even more blunt in his commentary. He stated that the federal agencies had reached the point where the interests they were serving were not those of the consumers but those of the businesses they were supposed to be regulating; in Kohlmeier's judgment ICC regulation of trucking, barge, and railroad industries added a billion dollars each year to the cost of transporting consumer goods.

The solution for the current crisis in regard to railroads and transportation in the United States will require more productive efforts on the part of management, labor, and the ICC; it also appears that it will necessitate, from the federal government, subsidies and new policies which will reduce travel by plane and motor vehicle. The demand for subsidies has been largely to compensate for short-haul losses. In this regard the railroads contend that they have been the victims of unfair competition because barges, planes, and trucks have been subsidized in various ways. Barge transportation is subsidized through pork-barrel legislation for the benefit of rivers and harbors, which has provided more than a billion dollars in federal aid. Transportation by aircraft has been subsidized in a variety of ways, both federally and locally. The federal government has assisted — at various times — through mail contracts, outright subsidies, and navigational assistance amounting to hundreds of millions of dollars (see pp. 608–610). The major item in local assistance comes from provision of airports. As standard practice, railroads financed their own union stations while cities provided airports at no initial cost to the airlines. In New York City the airports were built with federal and Port Authority funds; by contrast the tax bill on the Grand Central Terminal and its approaches cost the New York Central and the New Haven (soon to be bankrupt) more than $11 million a year in taxes in the late 1950's. The biggest single taxpayer in New Jersey was the Pennsylvania Railroad. In 1956 the New York Central paid a tax of $56,905 on its passenger station in Albany, New York. In the same year the operating deficit on Albany's *municipal* airport was $57,784! Truck transportation has obviously been subsidized, along with buses, because these "rubber-tired freight trains" use tracks provided at public expense. The railroads feel that motor vehicles have not paid in taxes nearly enough for this privilege. With all this in mind it is not surprising that in 1961 the ICC proposed federal subsidies for railroads — subsidies in the twentieth century. The principle was not new; it had been used in the nineteenth century for western roads. There was a major difference; subsidies in the twentieth century would go largely to eastern roads serving the most heavily populated areas along the Atlantic coastline.

Beyond subsidies for the railroads, by the early 1970's free (or nearly free) subways and buses were being proposed, all over the world, as a solution for the problem of urban transit. In Italy officials in Rome completed an experiment during which fares were eliminated on the Eternal City's buses over a period of nine days. The officials hoped that no-fare rides would lure Italian motorists out of their Fiats and into mass transportation; this might reduce gargantuan traffic jams and cleanse Rome's murky air. Paris froze the Métro fare at a low rate and levied a tax on corporate profits to pay for it. Munich had plans to provide unlimited rides on all rapid transit for only $2.50 a month. In the United States the city of Atlanta reduced bus fare from forty to fifteen cents, and paid for it by increasing the sales tax. Many believe it is only a matter of time until an American city inaugurates a no-fare policy in its public-transit system, in order to avoid "highwayitis" and to keep unwanted traffic off existing roads.

Reduction of travel by plane appears to be imperative. The United States is faced with an increasing problem of too many planes in the sky, with jets now making the situation worse — to the point where the CAB now admits that it cannot assure safety in the air because of congestion. It is apparent that little is gained by the supersonic plane, streaking across the country from coast to coast in two hours, if the plane is delayed an hour or more in takeoff and another hour or more stacked up before it can land. A 600-mile-an-hour jet can spend so much time on the runway at O'Hare Airport waiting to ascend and so much time circling over La Guardia Airport waiting to land that a traveler sometimes gets from Chicago to New York no faster than he did thirty years ago in a DC-3. This has brought the proposal that short air hops of 500 miles or less be eliminated because many of them are not profitable for airlines (and must be subsidized by the federal government) and because they are largely responsible for the congestion in the air. As an example, at peak hours about 80 percent of all air-carrier movements in Washington, D.C., are short-haul. Many transportation experts believe that railroads, rather than planes, should assume the responsibility of transporting people over these relatively short distances, up to 500 miles.

Travel by motor vehicle could be restricted by reducing public expenditures for superhighways, and by increasing taxes on automobiles and trucks. Transportation authorities have long pointed out that highways are not economic means of travel, either for short or long hauls. A double-track rail system can move ten times as many people in an hour as a multi-lane highway. In New York City 100,000 people can be moved in one direction in an hour on two subway tracks; to move the same number of persons by car would require twenty four-lane highways. If commodities rather than persons are involved, the competitive advantage of the railroad is even more startling. A diesel train averages 192 ton-miles to the gallon of fuel, while a truck gets but 58 ton-miles to the gallon. There is also a vast difference in manpower requirements; a train hauling 100 freight cars has a crew of five; to haul a comparable load by truck would involve hundreds of drivers. Few motorists realize that it costs them at least twice as much to travel by car as by public transportation; in 1967 the U.S. Department of Transportation estimated that it cost the individual owner more than 11¢ a mile to drive a $2,800 car 100,000 miles over a ten-year period. In spite of these compelling economic facts, governments at both the federal and state level have done everything to "giftwrap" highways while stalling on aid to railways and public transportation.

The pivotal year of decision for the future of transportation in the

United States was 1956. At that point in time the nation was clearly faced with a crisis in transportation as population and commerce rose rapidly. It could have turned in one of two directions: to emphasis on the privately owned automobile and truck, or to the creation of a system carefully balanced between railroads, planes, privately owned automobiles and trucks, waterways, and public transport within cities. In connection with a balanced system, transportation experts developed plans in which:

1. Railroads would specialize in long-haul freight, which they can handle most efficiently, and in high-volume passenger traffic up to five hundred miles — too short to warrant air flights but too densely traveled to be left to the private automobile. This is already the practice in Europe and Canada and Japan with fast and comfortable trains like the Rapido, the Rheingold, the Flying Scotsman, the Tokaido Line's Bullet, and Spain's speedy Talgo trains. Europe seems to improve trains as fast as the United States retires them, and offers proof that railroads can compete with and often outstrip airplanes and cars. In France the Mistral — which runs from Paris to Nice — was christened in 1950, air-conditioned in 1956, and glamorized in 1969; it packs a newsstand, a boutique, a barbershop and beauty salon, dens complete with dictating equipment and secretaries, and a gliding restaurant of epic provisions. An official of the French National Railway noted that if the distance was seven hundred miles or more Europeans might prefer to fly, but at five hundred miles the train is automatic. A businessman says to his secretary, "What's the next train to Lyons?" — not the next plane. A key advantage in Europe and Japan, of course, is a nationalized rail system that keeps trains running no matter what they cost. In 1969 British Rail, which runs 16,000 trains a day, turned its first profit since trains were nationalized in 1948. Germany runs a billion-mark deficit on its commuter and urban trains but would not think of eliminating them because of the necessity — both social and economic — for trains in their total transportation system.

2. Trucks would serve for the short-hauling of light freight loads, as feeders between rail lines, and in joint "piggy-back" operations. South Africa has already established this policy; James Michener has reported that highway travel is unbelievably pleasant there because the railroads are protected from truck competition by law; no truck may carry cargo more than 30 miles from its home garage! There is one exception; if a family moves permanently from one city to another, it can send its household goods by truck, but the truck must return empty.

3. Planes would take over the bulk of long-distance passenger carriage — certainly that of more than 500 miles.

4. Waterways would continue to handle the transportation of bulk commodities for which *time* is of less consideration than *cost*. Water carriage would comprise the economy system for coal, petroleum, grains, and chemicals; tows of barges, lashed together by cables in units larger than the *Queen Mary*, provide phenomenally low transportation costs on the Ohio, the Mississippi, and other inland waterways or coastal routes.

5. Modernization and expansion of public transport would reduce the use of the automobile within cities.

The die was cast for the motor vehicle, rather than the balanced plan, when President Eisenhower decided that new highways were essential because the existing ones were unsafe and overcrowded and — from the defense point of view with which he was so concerned — incapable of permitting quick evacuation of target areas in case of atomic attack. For these reasons in 1956 he proposed and Congress authorized a nationwide interstate highway system to provide nonstop, limited-access, high-speed car travel on 42,500 miles of new roads — estimated to cost $80 billion by the time they are completed in 1980. After the House of Representatives approved the program by a voice vote and the Senate voted for it 89 to 1, regional planner Lewis Mumford wrote gloomily:

. . . the most charitable thing to assume about this action is that they hadn't the faintest notion of what they were doing.

Within the next fifteen years they will doubtless find out, but by that time it will be too late to correct all the damage to our cities and our countryside . . . that this ill-conceived and preposterously unbalanced program will have wrought.

In 1969 the railroads had celebrated the first transcontinental line by driving a golden spike at Promontory Point in Utah; a century later a golden concrete-pouring was expected somewhere in the West as the interstate highway system announced its first transcontinental main line without a traffic light. In size and complexity this enormous public-works project dwarfs all of mankind's previous engineering undertakings including the pyramids, the Great Wall of China, the Panama Canal, and Grand Coulee Dam. This vast program has developed a highway lobby that probably commands more local and national political pressure than the more notorious "military-industrial complex." Industrial tourism has become very big business for automobile manufacturers, motel and restaurant owners, gasoline retailers, oil corporations, road-building contractors, and manufacturers of heavy equipment. It has developed a life of its own, an inherent bureaucratic momentum that is almost unstoppable. During the recession of 1957–1958 the slogan "You auto buy now" was bandied about; this may have been an atrocious use of language, but with the new highways being constructed on a colossal scale it was reasonably sound economics. In 1900 there were 8,000 automobiles on American roads; by 1960 there were 74 million and by 1969 the figure had reached 100 million. The United States had painted itself into an economic corner by allowing the national economy to become so reliant on the automobile industry.

The automobile is a problem for the railroads; it is also a problem for the nation — both *within* and *outside* cities. *Outside* cities, superhighways present a very real conservation problem for a nation that is confronted with a boom in both bulldozers and dozing babies. In the construction of highways the countryside has been leveled and rolled and graded to the point where it is estimated that an area of American land the size of the state of Louisiana now lies entombed in what is sometimes called "wall-to-wall" concrete. As neighborhoods are sliced in two and cemeteries are relocated, neither the quick nor the dead have been safe. To date most federal and state highway officials appear to have been basically indifferent to community values, natural resources, or esthetics. They have regarded as sentimental or irrelevant concern for a historic neighborhood, an ecologically important watershed, an unspoiled valley, a grove of handsome trees, or a rare stretch of wilderness. The highways must go through, no matter if they destroy precious green space on Staten Island, ram through the Vieux Carré of New Orleans, mutilate Brackenridge Park in San Antonio, or cut a multi-lane swath across the Washington Mall. They have even desecrated the national parks; in Yosemite, as an example, the current summer problem is a traffic one of what to do with all the people in automobiles creeping bumper to bumper along the roads of this confined valley. There the constant roar in the background is not a waterfall but traffic, transistor radios blare forth the latest rock tunes, campsites — pounded into dust by incessant use — are more crowded than a ghetto. Cars are sometimes backed up for twenty miles in Great Smoky Mountain Park in Tennessee and North Carolina; many national parks have found it necessary to institute one-way road systems. To those who subscribe to H. L. Mencken's definition of nature as "a place to throw beer cans on Sunday," this is laudatory; to those who have a feeling for what little remains of the wild, this is sacrilege.

Within cities automobiles have produced what is sometimes called *autosclerosis*. They have continued to invade metropolitan centers at a multiplication rate shared only by rabbits; as a result they have reduced mobility through traffic jams, have killed the central city by strangulation and saturation, and are killing its citizens through air pollution. There seems to be an inexorable rule that new roads quickly attract enough new traffic to jam them; federal and state highways proliferated and so did traffic tie-ups. Norman Cousins has observed that man's new access to the universe gives him cosmic grandeur — but a trip to the other side of town gives him the willies; the symbol of the age is really not the spaceship — it is the bottleneck. In the early 1960's San Francisco had a population of 3.3 million — with 1.3 million automobiles. By the early 1970's it was estimated that it would have 7 million people and 3.5 million motorcars. Unfortunately there is not enough room for them unless people sleep in or under their cars; if twenty square feet were allotted to each automobile, space would be required that is equal to the total area of the entire city. Columnist Art Hoppe once said that the typical resident of Los Angeles was "a well-preserved, middle-aged, middle-class, two-door Chevrolet sedan." Unless it builds a subway in the near future it is estimated that in Caracas (Venezuela), hemmed in as it is by mountains, people will soon be walking to work over the roofs of their automobiles. The automobile has also killed the *central* city by strangulation and saturation, forcing both business and people to escape to the *suburbs*. As the national flower has become the elevated cloverleaf every major city has become a tomb of concrete roads and ramps, covering their dead corpses. Not long ago the demolition of the old elevated railroads in New York was hailed as a triumph of progress; now the same citizens are told that the new construction of elevated highways is also a triumph of progress. Those left behind in the cities — chiefly the poor, the Negroes, and the aged — face a vicious spiral of spreading slums, rising crime, and increasing congestion. Los Angeles, as an example, has been turned into what has been ironically called a huge *autopia*, virtually devoid of public transportation. By making its investment in superhighways, Los Angeles isolated Negroes to the point that they had to travel two hours, transfer to several buslines, and pay half a dollar each way in order to work or even look for a job. The neglect of public transportation was a major factor in the despairing violence that broke out in Watts.

The automobile not only takes lives directly through accidents on the highways; it also kills indirectly through air pollution. In 1966 an editorial in the *New York Times* described a certain fellow:

His eyes burn and smart. His lungs turn a chic charcoal gray. From pants cuff to hat brim his clothes are nicely lined with soot. A nineteenth-century coal miner? No, these are the details in the profile of metropolitan man in the late twentieth century. The air he breathes is slowly poisoning him, defacing his buildings and destroying his environment.

The automobile is the chief offender; of the estimated 130 million tons of pollutants ejected into the air of the United States each year, automotive vehicles emit about 85 million of them. As a result the airshed over the United States is steadily filling with poisons. Only a few years ago the sky over the nation was clear except for the pall over the cities; today it extends hundreds of miles in every direction. It is not unusual for the entire eastern half of the United States, from Maine to Florida and west to Des Moines and New Orleans, to be covered by a pollution blanket. This pall is sometimes called aerial garbage; after a helicopter tour of New York City one Congressman said, "We are living under an aerial cesspool, and at hazards to our health that haven't been guessed at." This poses a hair-raising question for Norman Cousins. He asks what will happen if the rate of industrial growth, population growth, automobile growth, and highway growth goes on for the next two decades — assuming the same laggard pace of the national attack on the problem. The conclusion is inescapable that most of the large cities in the United States would be regarded as uninhabitable within a decade or two. For that reason Cousins and others have mounted an attack on the automobile; he says that the internal-combustion engine has revolutionized the way of life, not alone in the United States, but throughout the world. It has also polluted the atmosphere and literally has become "the greatest nonpolitical enemy of the human species on earth. It carries the smell of death inside it."

Cousins therefore asks the U.S. government to engage in a major program to develop the fuel cell as a substitute. A quarter of a century ago, he says, the government mounted a $2 billion project for nuclear power in the name of national survival; it must now mount a similar project to find a substitute for the internal-combustion engine — again in the name of national survival. Research chemists like Donald E. Carr have pointed out that pollution of the air in cities is a cause of cancer and emphysema, and that nothing can be done to eliminate it under driving conditions in a city (by contrast to high-speed driving on highways) because of incomplete combustion under the frequent idling conditions in the city. What to do? Carr would outlaw the internal-combustion engine in cities and permit the present smog-spewing automobile on interurban highways only. What to use in its place? Carr suggests public transportation and the electric automobile.

In consideration of these problems the ICC once issued the following warning:

A nation that is serious about propelling a man to the moon should be able to solve the mundane problem of moving its citizens dependably and comfortably some fifty miles or less from home to work without multiplying ribbons of concrete and asphalt that would strangle the central cities they are supposed to serve.

Some observers forecast, a bit prematurely, that by the time we got to the moon the earth might have become uninhabitable. Will the citizens of the Republic give serious consideration to these dire predictions? On the basis of the climate of opinion in the late 1960's, the answer was probably no. Citizens retained an overpowering affection for their "insolent chariots" and proposed to brave traffic jams, the death of cities, the death of railroads, and the death of themselves in order to retain them. According to essayist Russell Baker, the American's creed ran as follows:

I believe in the interstate highway system . . . as a Government of the traffic, by the traffic, for the traffic; whose rights-of-way are derived from the federal gasoline tax; a limited-access automopolis in a megalopolis; a perfect asphalt, one and inseparable, established upon those principles of high-speed motoring, freedom from stop lights and justice for the trucking industry for which Americans have sacrificed their farms, forests, streams, cities, and freedom from carbon monoxide.

I therefore believe it is my duty to my interstate highway system to drive it; to support its licensed hamburger concessionaires; to stay off its median strip; to respect its passing line; and to defend it against all enemies who seek to prevent its extension through their living rooms.

XII

The Control of Power

THE term "power" means varying things to different groups of people. There is *political power* at the ward level, or on the higher planes in the controversies between Kosygin and Nixon and Pompidou. There is *spiritual power*; many have sung the hymn

> *All hail the power of Jesus' name,*
> *Let angels prostrate fall.*

There is *sexual power*, as that of Helen of Troy with the face that launched a thousand ships. There is *muscular power* — in recent years the Dallas Cowboys against the rest of the league.

In this study there is no interest in political or spiritual or sexual or muscular power; here we are discussing power in the purely economic sense. This means power derived from energy provided by gas, oil, and electricity; this power is carried through lines, lines made of pipe or wire. Power that is derived directly from gas and oil comes immediately from gas and oil. Power that comes from electricity is produced commercially by heat or falling water. Hydroelectric power goes on indefinitely, as anyone who has listened to a waterfall knows; unfortunately there is not enough power in all the world's rivers to meet present electrical requirements. Power produced by heat (in the form of steam) can come from two sources: by burning coal, natural gas, and oil; or by nuclear reaction. Regardless of the sources the electricity, like aspirin or salt, is the same when it reaches the consumer. It is efficient, clean, essential, and useful. Unfortunately, it may differ greatly in price.

Coal, gas, and oil — the fossil fuels — are wasting assets. Once they are gone they cannot be replaced short of a few million years. Current estimates indicate that coal, oil, and gas will last no more than four hundred years at present rates of consumption. The new type of energy is, of course, atomic. When an atomic reaction takes place in a pile or furnace — for the generation of power for *useful* purposes — the *blast* effect is prevented, the *radiation* is checked by shields of lead or concrete, and the *heat* is transferred to a boiler. There steam is made to turn a turbine and so produce electricity. Atomic energy does not itself flow over transmission lines; it simply provides a different fuel to turn water into steam. The Atomic Energy Commission (AEC) reports that enough uranium and thorium are already available to provide the world's energy for the next 1,700 years — at the rate of consumption of energy estimated for the year A.D. 2,000.

It is obvious that two great benefits, rather than destruction, can come to mankind from atomic energy. One is through radioactive materials and their contributions to medicine, agriculture, and various kinds of research. The other advantage is the potential for extension of the world's supplies of concentrated energy. This can present difficulties, simply because atomic energy is useful only in large installations. The reason is that the cost and weight of shielding is so great that atomic energy appears to be of no use in automobiles and planes. In automobiles, as an example, it is estimated that a modest seventy-five-horsepower reactor would require a gargantuan twenty-seven tons of shielding. On the other hand atomic energy appears to be manageable in submarines, locomotives, power plants, and large surface ships — although our first nuclear ship, *Savannah*, was barred from most seaports in the world outside of the United States. Atomic energy could very well snap the ties that bind certain industries to localities where coal and water power are readily available, simply because a pound of U-235 can do the work of 1,300 tons of coal. This means that industry could now have an unprecedented freedom of movement — that Britain and India and other regions would not be required to worry about fuel shortages.

The basic question, as everyone knows and fears, is whether man will use nuclear energy for useful purposes. One remembers the Spanish parable: "God offered man all the world and said, 'Take everything you want — and pay for it.'"

The general case for federal, state, or local control of power is based on the assumption that there must be regulation of business where free competition does not exist because of limitation on the sources of supply, where there is a lack of adequate substitutes, and where the public would suffer from the construction of competing units. All of these apply to the power industry. There is certainly a limitation of the supply sources for gas, oil, and electricity through pipe and transmission lines; if one, or a few concerns gain control, the establishment of competing firms can be prevented. There are no adequate substitutes for gas, oil, and electricity; one must accept the terms of suppliers, or go without. Furthermore, the public would scarcely be served by the unwise duplication of competing companies resulting in uneconomic rate wars leading to bankruptcy and disruption of service. For these reasons governments have, in one way or another, limited the number of public-utility enterprises which may be built. They are required to obtain franchises — grants of permission to use the streets or to lay their wire or pipe lines. When this happens such enterprises become *legal* as well as *natural* monopolies.

Beyond the *general* case for governmental control at national and local levels, the *specific* case for federal control is based on (1) the inadequacy of state regulation, (2) the establishment of monopoly and minority control, (3) the imposition of excessive rates, and (4) the dubious influence exerted by the power industry on politics, the press, and education. State regulation has been inadequate from the standpoint of both the law and the consumer. It has been legally ineffective because so many oil, gas, and electrical transmission and pipe lines cross state boundaries, become interstate in character, and can only be regulated by the federal government. State regulation has also been inadequate from the standpoint of the consumer because state legislatures are more easily dominated by large corporations than is the federal government, and because many state regulatory commissions are inclined to favor RCN (Reconstruction Cost New) as a major basis for determining valuations on which the usual 7 percent return of utilities is determined.

In 1968 the Cleveland *Plain Dealer* would comment with irony on the traditional textbook statement that laws in Ohio were made by a two-house legislature. Actually, wrote two reporters for the newspaper, the General Assembly of Ohio was made up of four houses — the Senate, House, the lobbyists, and the press corps. It was noted that the insolent days were gone when lobbyists paid off legislators in cash in the halls of the statehouse after they had cast a "right" vote. Also gone were the days when "Boss" Mark Hanna sat arrogantly in his hotel suite in Columbus and pulled the strings of power — "perverting the legislative process as drunken legislators reeled among brass spittoons." Gone were the days when lobbyists thought nothing of procuring prostitutes for legislators in return for a vote. Not gone, reported the *Plain Dealer*, was the tremendous power of special-interest lobbyists lurking in legislative halls and protecting the interests of trade, business, and professional associations. Not gone was the power of the press, a power not always used with ethical detachment. The newspaper found that lobbyists representing special-interest groups outnumbered legislators; on one occasion a single monopolistic utility assigned enough men to Columbus so that each member of the

House had his own personal lobbyist (needless to add, the bill the utility wanted killed became a legislative corpse). So powerful is the utility lobby that it is a widely held belief in these legislative halls that no one can become Speaker over the veto of the Ohio utility lobby. Probably the most blatant display of raw power by this potent lobby came in the session of the Ohio General Assembly in 1959. At stake was Ohio's archaic public-utility-rate-fixing law, a heavily pro-utility statute zealously guarded by the industry against legislative tampering. In that year there was a Democratic majority in both branches of the legislature, and Democratic governor Michael V. DiSalle had vowed to repeal the old rate law and to replace it with a more public-oriented measure. Tremendous pressures were brought by the utility lobby, however, on members from both sides of the House aisle. The repealer went down to humiliating defeat. Reporters noted that "it was probably the biggest 'tank job' in the history of the House. The resounding splash dampened any further hopes of repealing the utility-rate law." The actual situation in the Ohio State Capitol was obviously an undemocratic one; nonetheless, the *Plain Dealer* was of the opinion that the Ohio Assembly was probably one of the better state legislatures. As an indication of the pathetic weakness of state regulation elsewhere, in Florida Commissioner Edwin L. Mason was frank enough to say, "The best regulation is little or no regulation." He preferred not federal, not even state, but county regulation. In New York the Joint Legislative Committee on Consumer Protection, after a yearlong study in 1968 that represented the first legislative examination of utilities' regulation in more than thirty years, charged that the state Public Service Commission's control over power utilities and the telephone industry was a "fiasco" that cost consumers millions of dollars a year. The chairman of the committee, Assemblyman Albert H. Blumenthal, claimed that the Consolidated Edison Company of New York was among the four most profitable companies in the United States, and commented that this was "not because of Consolidated Edison's superior management. Indeed, what is so paradoxically tragic about Consolidated Edison's earnings is that the more inefficient the company, the more its profit margin goes up accordingly." Most economists are agreed that RCN is a method of fleecing the public; they favor what is known as the Prudent Investment Theory. The latter means actual investment prudently made, minus depreciation plus cost of subsequent additions. The Federal Power Commission (FPC) follows the Prudent Investment Theory; many states tend toward RCN, and Ohio goes the whole way.*

The utilities prefer the RCN theory for obvious reasons. In a period of

* Thirty state utility commissions, the District of Columbia, and the FPC use original cost, less depreciation, as the rate base. Thirteen state commissions use a "fair-value" rate base — a combination of original cost, the cost of reproduction cost new, and various intangibles. The remaining states have variable formulas excepting Ohio, which uses RCN exclusively.

rising prices RCN enables the power industry to establish a higher valuation for its rate base, and thus to earn greater profits. RCN has also not infrequently enabled a company to establish fictitious valuations for its rate base. Companies have been known to count the cost of reproducing obsolete machinery. One company had a natural pond on its land, and wanted to swell the rate base. It therefore figured that the pond was not there, and that it would cost more than $2 million to reproduce it. In Cleveland the Electric Illuminating Company sold a building in the 1950's for $900,000, which appeared to be its actual value; for rate-making purposes, however, the same building had been valued at $2.7 million — three times as much. In 1961 Mayor Ralph Locher of Cleveland commented that the use of RCN as a sole basis for evaluation in Ohio meant that, by reason of this formula:

> utilities in Ohio were able to earn profits 15 percent higher than comparable companies in other states, the Ohio Bell Telephone Company was always one of the highest net earners in the entire Bell system, the East Ohio Gas Company was always the star earner of the Consolidated Natural Gas System, of which it was a constituent corporation, and the charges of the Cleveland Electric Illuminating Company were excessive by about $6 million a year.

Beyond the inadequacy of state regulation there was the problem of monopoly and minority control. In the 1920's the FPC estimated that the entire power industry was controlled by one hundred men, and that 70 percent of it was controlled by ten men. In the 1930's President Roosevelt noted that the power industry was worth $13 billion, and that control of it was vested in the hands of owners of less than $600 million of the total. This meant, as FDR phrased it, that a ninety-six-inch dog was being wagged by a four-inch tail. In 1967 Senator Lee Metcalf (of Montana) and V. Reinemer published a book entitled *Overcharge*. In it they contended that in spite of claims for wide ownership among millions of modest stockholders, the control of the privately owned power industry remained in the hands of a relatively few men.

Through the 1930's monopoly and minority control was achieved through pyramided holding companies. In theory, holding companies are supposed to provide operating companies with management, engineering, and construction services. In practice, many operating companies were milked by holding companies that were established, not because the managers wanted efficiency, but because bankers and speculators wanted profits. The ease with which concentration could be achieved was enhanced by the issue of nonvoting securities and by pyramiding. Control of a single enterprise could be accomplished by the issue of a considerable portion of nonvoting securities. As an example, the capitalization of a $500 million corporation might be composed of $250 million in bonds, $150 million in nonvoting preferred stock, and $100 million of common stock which alone had voting privileges. It is apparent that the organizers would need to invest only $50 million to control such a firm; the $400 million in bonds and preferred stock were equities which had no part in the direction of the affairs of the company. The control of ten identical operating companies could be achieved by establishing a holding company which would invest $500 million in order to control the ten operating companies (by an investment of $50 million in the common stock of each one). The funds for the holding company would be raised through $250 million in bonds, $150 million of nonvoting preferred stock, and $100 million of voting common stock. In this holding company ownership of $50 million of the common stock would insure control of the holding company *and* control of the $5 billion in assets in the ten holding companies through the investment of this same $50 million — 1 percent of the total. By means of this corporate pyramiding, minority control was a simple process.*

The art of monopoly through minority control was developed in spectacular fashion by the Van Sweringen brothers in railroading, and by Samuel Insull in public utilities. In 1878, when he was nineteen, the English-born Insull had persuaded Phineas T. Barnum — the world's foremost publicist, promoter, and circus virtuoso — to address a London literary society. Barnum delivered a speech entitled "The World Upside Down" which Insull found "screamingly funny." Four years later Insull moved to the United States, where he renewed and maintained his acquaintance with Barnum — effectively absorbing Barnum's genius for humbuggery and applying it to the fledgling electric-power industry in the United States. This relationship had such a profound effect on Insull that Forrest McDonald, a biographer who admires him, admits that the financier might well be called a link between Barnum and Madison Avenue. Insull actually came to the United States to work for Thomas A. Edison, and in this capacity performed extremely well. He often worked until the wee-small

---

* Phenomenal profits were also possible, so long as the nation remained prosperous and euphoric. This was achieved through what is known as leverage. In the case of each one of the operating companies cited above, in the power industry it could be assumed that the concern could count on a minimum profit of 7 percent; its annual profit would therefore be $35 million on the $500 million of assets. At 5 percent the $250 million in bonds would cost $12,500,000, and at 6 percent the $150 million in preferred stock would cost $9 million. This would leave $13.5 million for the $100 million in common stock — or a profit of 13.5 percent. Of this $13.5 million, $6.75 million would go to the holding company which owned $50 million of the common stock. The total income of the holding company from ten identical operating companies would thus be $67,500,000. Again, assuming the same rates of interest and dividends, the holding company would pay out $12.5 million for interest on bonds and $9 million for dividends on preferred stock, leaving a total of $46 million for the $100 million in common stock — a generous profit of 46 percent. In some instances, through leverage and pyramiding, earnings actually amounted to more than 300 percent on the relatively small amount invested in voting common stock.

In good times leverage worked beautifully and luxuriously. Unfortunately, as the Van Sweringens and the Insulls were to discover, it also incorporates an inexorable mathematical process that works equally well in reverse.

hours of the morning and Edison, a devotee of hard work, loved him for it. Some believe that the "Wizard of Menlo" owed much of his commercial success to the stubborn and wily Englishman who, as Edison's secretary, handled his financial matters, signed his checks, and (at one time) even bought his clothes. Ultimately Insull built a utilities empire in the Midwest, producing an eighth of the electricity and gas consumed in the United States. He was to initiate many new techniques and concepts which were unique in the electric-power industry, although they were being introduced at the same time by Henry Ford in the automotive field — efficient service, relatively low rates, and comparatively high wages for labor. By 1907 Chicago's electricity was entirely Insull-operated; soon thereafter he pioneered in unified rural electrification. In the 1920's he turned to large-scale public financing of his utilities, which also included gas and traction interests. He became overextended financially and the Insull empire collapsed in 1932; by that time it had a paper worth of $3 billion. Insull also built an opera house in Chicago, and had a farm near that city that comprised 4,200 acres — with a home in which the bathtub was coated with gold leaf at a cost of $30,000, and where the terraces looked out over lagoons in which there were swans and goldfish. There were so many employees on the farm that the estate had its own post office — at that time the only one operated by the U.S. government on a private farm. In spite of all this early opulence, when Insull died (in 1938) he left only $1,000 in cash and debts of many millions. When the Depression came a great many disappointed investors in his bankrupt empire were more than angry. Insull found it necessary to hire a bodyguard of thirty-six men, as Gould had done many years earlier. Once, when Insull was being driven to his office in the opera house, a bullet crashed through the limousine's window glass, and lodged in the chauffeur's shoulder. Insull himself had felt the wind of a 38-caliber missile. Shortly thereafter a new sixteen-cylinder Cadillac arrived for Insull's use. It was armor-plated from radiator cap to rear bumper, and the windows were of plate glass, one-inch thick. Even so, Insull could not ride out the storm. In 1932 he fled the country on a ship inaccurately named the *Flying Dutchman;* on his departure he resigned eighty-five directorships, sixty-five chairmanships, and eleven presidencies in his pyramided corporate empire. He went to Greece, then Turkey; sitting there disconsolately he asked, "What have I done that every banker and business magnate has not done in the course of business?" In the 1930's it was a provocative question. Later he was extradited, returned to this country, and was vindicated on charge of mail fraud and embezzlement.

In addition to the inadequacy of state regulation plus monopoly and minority control, there was also the problem of excessive profits. In the 1930's the U.S. government generated power at Muscle Shoals in Alabama for five mills (one half cent) a kilowatt hour, which was sold to privately owned companies, one of whom then charged the consumer 10¢ a kwh — a markup so generous that one commentator observed that if the utilities could meter the moonlight lovers would pay and pay and pay. Senator George Norris of Nebraska, an ardent advocate of publicly owned power, often cited comparative costs — particularly those in regard to charges for lighting on the International Bridge at Niagara Falls. It was served on the American half by a private company and on the Canadian side by Hydro, owned by the Province of Ontario. On both halves of the bridge the number of lights and the demand for current was the same, the river and the bridge were the same, and the method of production for electricity was identical. The charges were startlingly different. For the lights on the International Bridge the publicly owned Canadian company charged $8.43 per month; on the American side the charge from a privately owned corporation was $43.10 per month. Senator Metcalf of Montana has pointed out (in his book *Overcharge*) that a free-enterprise businessman makes money only if he can keep his costs low enough to make a profit by selling at prices which are competitive. By contrast independently owned utilities (the IOUs) operate on a cost-plus and monopoly basis. Governments at various levels (local, state, or national) guarantee the IOUs all expenses, including taxes and salaries, plus profit. For this obvious reason the IOUs do not fail financially, as other businesses do. It is also not surprising that, for the same reasons, the IOUs have comparative profits which are most satisfactory. In 1963, as an example, the leading manufacturing corporations in the United States averaged 6.1 percent in after-tax profit out of each sales dollar. Only two of the major groups in industry — drugs and cement — took home more than a dime in profit out of each dollar of sales. By contrast, public utilities (electric, gas, telephone, and telegraph) took home more than twice as much — 14¢ out of each revenue dollar. For the thirty-four major IOUs that happen to dominate the field of electric power in the United States, the net profits averaged 16¢ on the dollar. This development occurred in spite of the fact that the *cost*, as contrasted with the *profits*, of electrical power has been declining. In 1950 each kwh of electricity cost, on the average, a half cent — or five mills — to produce. By 1964 the average was down to four mills. In 1966 the TVA awarded GE a contract for two nuclear generators that will produce electricity at an estimated cost of 2.37 mills per kwh — less than half the cost in 1950.

Beyond excessive charges, monopoly, and the ineffectiveness of state regulation there were those who were disturbed by the methods employed by the public utilities to influence politics, the press, and education — methods that appeared to be undesirable in a democracy. In connection with politics there was the attempt to defeat George Norris in Nebraska, the attempt by Sam Insull to "elect" a U.S. Senator, and the "fake" telegrams with which the Senate was deluged at a critical time. Norris, sometimes called the "Old Roman of American Politics," represented Nebraska in both Houses of Congress for more than four decades (1901–1943). His outstanding characteristics were a progressive philosophy, fearlessness, and rugged independence; beginning his career as an insurgent Republican he once said, "I would rather be right than be regular." He opposed the conservative domestic policies of Republican Speaker "Uncle Joe" Cannon and was antagonistic to the foreign policy of Democratic President Woodrow Wilson; as a voter he supported TR in 1912, La Follette in 1924, Smith in 1928, FDR in the 1930's. The Republicans finally tired of his opposition and read him out of the party in 1936; thereafter he ran for office as an Independent. By this time Senator Arthur Capper of Kansas was describing Norris as a "perambulating Declaration of Independence." A statesman with a plethora of ideas, during his career he fathered the Twentieth ("Lame-Duck") Amendment to the Constitution, the unicameral legislature in Nebraska, and the TVA. In his own state he was opposed by the power interests, with the result that a strange development occurred when Norris was running for reelection in 1930. For a time it appeared that there would be two senatorial candidates in the Republican primary: George W. Norris of McCook (the Senator), and George W. Norris of Broken Bow (an unknown grocer). Obviously someone was financing the grocer to confuse the voters and hopefully defeat the George Norris who was a foe of power interests. The "someone" was George W. Head, chairman of the board of the Nebraska Power Company, national president of the Boy Scouts of America, and teacher of the largest Sunday School class in the state. The political ruse ultimately failed because of a technicality — late filing. Subsequently George Norris of Broken Bow was investigated by a U.S. Senate committee. He at first claimed that he had received no outside financial aid; later he admitted that he had, was indicted for perjury, and jailed for three months. George W. Head continued as head of the Boy Scouts and as a Sunday School teacher.

In Illinois during the 1920's Insull was satisfied with the demagogic William Hale ("Big Bill") Thompson as mayor of Chicago and the notorious Len Small, whose name many thought to be appropriate, as governor of Illinois. He then saw to it that Frank L. Smith was elected to the U.S. Senate, but that body refused to seat him. It appeared that Insull had contributed $285,000 to Smith's primary campaign; most of it came from public-utility companies which he controlled but which were legally subject to regulation by the Illinois Commerce Commission — of which Smith was chairman. The Senate said that Smith's use of such a large fund, from a source which represented an obvious conflict of interest, was "contrary to sound public policy, harmful to the dignity and honor of the Senate, and dangerous to the perpetuity of free government." During the 1930's Senator Hugo L. Black of Alabama (later a Justice of the Supreme Court) was chairman of a Senate committee which investigated lobbying; at the time, holding companies in the power industry were lobbying relentlessly (at a cost of $3.5 million) against the Wheeler-Rayburn Act. They called the Black Committee the "Blackguard" Committee. This committee concentrated its attention on the Associated Gas and Electric Company, a $1 billion concern centered in New York and its environs, with annual earnings of about $100 million. This company hired Western Union messenger boys in Warren, Pennsylvania, to solicit telegrams from citizens who were opposed to the Wheeler-Rayburn Act, paying them three cents for the telegrams which were then sent at the expense of the Associated Gas and Electric Company to the Congressman from that district in Washington. Unfortunately the Congressman became suspicious after he had received 816 telegrams within two days. He found that the telegrams were being sent to him, and to other Congressmen, at the rate of 4,000 an hour. He also ascertained that the company had eliminated the messenger boys as an excrescence, and was simply selecting and signing names at random from telephone books and city directories — without any authority from the constituents so selected. What had initially appeared to be a spontaneous protest against the Wheeler-Rayburn Act from an outraged citizenry turned out to be a contrived and fraudulent stratagem.

The extensive investigation by the FTC of the power industry (1928–1935) also documented its influence on the press. This was exerted in two ways: by buying newspapers outright and operating them, and by means of generous advertising contracts. About one "country" paper in ten refused the contracts, and all knew what was expected in addition to the advertisements — favorable editorials and publication of "news" favorable to the privately owned power industry. In Missouri, as an example, the utilities claimed they got their propaganda into 699 newspapers, failing only in the St. Louis *Post-Dispatch*. This was in the 1930's. Thirty years later Senator Metcalf would report a similar statement by a southern publisher whose paper had won numerous awards for excellence; he described the relationship in his state between the press and the power companies in these words:

The companies advertise fairly heavily and their representatives attend all the press-association conventions, get cozy with most publishers, foot the bills at cocktail parties, and flood the country editor's desk with ready-made editorials, editorial reprints from other newspapers that are for private power and against public power, etc.

The average weekly editor, being more of a printer, accepts this indiscriminately and usually regurgitates it on the page in one form or another. The power company officials are pleasant to work with, pay promptly and their public relations practices are much smoother and more expert than the co-op's.

The FPC investigation indicated that the influence, benign or otherwise, of the power industry was not limited to politics and journalism; it also extended to education. To influence schoolchildren the industry made sure that proper texts were written; they surveyed the colleges of the nation to locate men who were writing these books — and either encouraged or discouraged them. If schools attempted to introduce texts which were not on the approved list, pressure was put on boards of education by local utility officials or chambers of commerce. At the college level some professors were subsidized with cash and trips to Europe. These educational activities were carried out by a trade organization known as the National Electric Light Association. After it was exposed by the testimony before the FTC, the name was changed to the more euphemistic Edison Electric Institute. An acerbic reporter on the St. Louis *Post-Dispatch*, the well-known Paul Y. Anderson, was not impressed; he thought the new name might just as well have been the "George Washington and Abraham Lincoln Society." All of this was in the 1920's and 1930's. Four decades later, some commentators believe the situation remains essentially the same. They point out that in colleges in the current era, the course on public utilities — if there is one — is usually taught by an official of an IOU, by the editor of a trade publication that reflects the viewpoint of the IOUs, or by a teacher who is more interested in transportation than the basic economics of utilities.

Federal control of the power industry can be brought about through regulation of privately owned power facilities *or* through government ownership of them. Former Senator Paul Douglas of Illinois, who is an economist by profession, once pointed out the great difference between these two concepts. Federal regulation is a device to avoid public ownership by providing private ownership and operation along with governmental regulation to protect the consumer *and* the investor. Government regulation, he said, was not socialism — it was America's answer to socialism. At the federal level this regulation, during the past half century, has operated through three major acts: the Federal Water Power Act of 1920, the Federal Power Commission Act of 1930, and the Wheeler-Rayburn-Public-Utility-Holding-Company Act of 1935.

In the early part of the twentieth century conservationists had noted that water power was the only great natural resource still largely in public possession, and they proposed to keep it there. Congress first moved in 1920 when it passed the Federal Water Power Act of that year; this measure created an administrative commission and gave it certain powers. The Water Power Commission of three was to consist of Cabinet officers —

those for War, Interior, and Agriculture. It had four powers dealing with jurisdiction, development, licensing, and rate base. Jurisdiction and ownership by the federal government, over water-power sites on all navigable streams, was affirmed. In the development of these sites the commission was to give preference to state and federal governments, but it might license private companies to develop them provided it appeared to be in the public interest to do so — taking into full consideration such matters as navigation, irrigation, flood control, and power. Licenses to private companies were not to extend beyond fifty years, after which the federal government would "recapture" the development. Rates charged, whoever developed the sites, would be on the basis of original cost prudently made. On the positive side the act did establish the important principle of public ownership, but the membership of the commission left much to be desired and the recapture clause was elusive. The Cabinet members of the original commission already had too much to do; this was remedied in 1930 with the creation of a full-time Federal Power Commission of five members. It was obvious that the recapture clause was a lawyer's delight, and that it would be difficult and expensive for the federal government to recover title and possession at the end of half a century.

Much more exciting and controversial was the Wheeler-Rayburn-Public-Utilities-Holding-Company Act passed in 1935. It was named for two prominent and able Congressmen. Burton Kendall Wheeler was Senator from Montana from 1922 until 1946, for almost a quarter of a century. On the domestic side he was a progressive, fought the largest corporation in Montana (the Anaconda Copper Company), ran as a progressive for Vice-President with La Follette in the campaign of 1924, and supported much of the New Deal legislation. On foreign policy he became an isolationist, by 1940 had broken with FDR. Samuel Rayburn represented Texas in the U.S. House of Representatives for almost half a century; he entered Congress in 1913 and served continuously until his death in 1961. He was the Democratic Speaker of the House on three occasions for a total of seventeen years, more than twice as long as any of his predecessors. During the 1930's he was the tactician in the House most responsible for the passage of New Deal legislation.

The Wheeler-Rayburn Act applied only to gas and electric corporate systems. Within this framework it drew a distinction between operating and holding companies. Electric operating companies (and their interstate rates) were placed under the jurisdiction of the FPC; gas operating companies (and their interstate rates) were the responsibility of the FTC. All holding companies, gas and electric, were placed under the jurisdiction of the SEC — and were required to show cause for continued existence, which many obviously could not do. The purpose was to liquidate all interstate utility-holding companies, except those at the first level above operating companies; pyramiding would be abolished. This led to the frenetic claim, by the holding companies, that they were under a "death sentence." If there was a "death," it was a slow and leisurely one. The act went into effect in 1935; any liquidation of holding companies was forbidden before 1940. Because of World War II the actual enforcement of the act took much longer. In 1935 there were more than two thousand holding companies in the gas and electric field with assets of more than $16 billion. By 1952 more than 1,500 of them had been eliminated, with assets of approximately $10 billion.

The federal government has resorted to its own ownership of power facilities, rather than regulation of private owners because of the complexity of operations (where electrical power was only one part of a large and multi-sided project) and to provide a realistic yardstick which would measure the validity of rates charged by private companies. It should be remembered that the IOUs generate and distribute more than three times as much electricity as all the other power systems — 76 percent of the total — and almost six times as much as the 13 percent generated by the federal government (municipal systems generate 10 percent and the co-ops 1 percent). There have been two prime examples of federal ownership: those in the Tennessee and St. Lawrence valleys.

The Tennessee River has its principal headwaters in the Appalachian Mountains in Virginia and North Carolina; counting its tributaries, it serves as a river basin for five more states — making seven in all. Ranked by volume of stream flow, the Tennessee is the fifth-largest river system in the United States. The Mississippi, Columbia, and Ohio clearly outrank it; the muddy flow of the Missouri barely exceeds the Tennessee. Beyond this river system, the Tennessee Valley has two other assets: it has more rainfall than any other region in the United States except the Pacific Northwest, and it has a temperate climate, with a growing season longer than any other large area in the nation. In spite of these assets, in the 1930's the Tennessee Valley was America's Economic Problem No. 1, with depleted soil and poverty-stricken inhabitants. Its priceless assets of moderate sunshine and abundant water were not being used properly. To provide a remedy, the New Deal introduced a regional plan known as the Tennessee Valley Authority (TVA).

There had been some federal activity on the Tennessee River during World War I, when the U.S. government needed large amounts of cheap electricity to produce nitrates. This required both a dam to produce cheap electric power, and a nitrate plant. In 1918 the decision was made to construct both at Muscle Shoals in Alabama — an unnavigable portion of the Tennessee River where the drop was 130 feet in thirty-five miles. This fall is only sixty feet less than that at Niagara Falls, although the latter is more dramatic; at Muscle Shoals the river boiled over rocks and shoals for the entire thirty-five miles. As soon as World War I was over the U.S. gov-

ernment closed the nitrate plant; the electric power from the dam—
which could not be shut off—was sold at a very low price to the privately owned Alabama Power Company, which made a handsome profit
in distributing it to consumers. By the 1920's Henry Ford wanted to purchase the federal power facilities at Muscle Shoals and to operate them for
what he called the greater good of the nation. For this privilege he first
offered $1 million, later raising it to $5 million. Senator George Norris,
who wanted the installations operated by the federal government, kept
Ford from gaining control. Norris pointed out that the properties Ford
desired had cost $90 million—and that the 100-year lease Ford wanted
for electricity from the dam would yield him a profit of almost $15 billion
during the term of the contract—during which Ford claimed he would
produce cheap fertilizer for farmers. The federal operation Norris had in
mind finally came into being under the New Deal—but on a much larger
basis, that of overall planning for the entire river valley through the Tennessee Valley Authority (TVA). This was accomplished through large
multi-purpose dams, twenty-seven of which were ultimately built—in
total size twelve times the bulk of the seven great pyramids of Egypt.

For a generation the TVA has been controversial, with some pointing
with pride and others viewing with alarm. John Gunther echoed the point
of view of those who believe TVA has been highly successful. He said it
might be called the greatest single American invention of the twentieth
century because of benefits which are both regional and national, and because it has served as a model for other river-valley plans all over the
world. For the region the TVA has provided (1) flood control, (2) navigation, (3) cheap fertilizer, (4) recreation, (5) reforestation, (6) better
health, (7) revenue in lieu of taxes, and (8) cheap power. It is difficult to
calculate savings from flood control because no one knows the exact cost
of damage when streams go out of their banks. It has been estimated,
however, that the twenty-seven dams and reservoirs in the TVA, over the
past three decades, have prevented a potential half billion dollars in flood
damage on the Tennessee, Ohio, and Mississippi rivers. The dams and reservoirs also provide a nine-foot navigable channel from Knoxville to Paducah (on the Ohio); in order to achieve this depth, Muscle Shoals is now
covered with water from Wheeler and Wilson dams. By 1953, after two
decades of the TVA, navigation of the river had increased twenty-five
times. Cheap fertilizer, produced by cheap electricity, has aided farmers in
rebuilding the soil and forests so that the scarred land would not wash
away. This achievement has been a convincing one, as a mountain
preacher once confessed. He attended a TVA extension meeting for farmers in North Carolina and came away with the statement, "From now on
I'm going to preach less hellfire and brimstone, and more phosphate and
limestone." Between 1934 and 1958 the TVA planted more than 350 million seedlings which reforested more than 350,000 acres; it now produces

40 million seedlings a year, half of which are planted in the Tennessee Valley, the balance elsewhere in the nation. This planting has paid off in production. During the fiscal year 1961 the value of TVA's forest products reached a half billion dollars; they are expected to reach a billion dollars annually by the end of this century.

There have also been regional benefits in improved health, revenue, and cheap power. Malaria, once the scourge of the valley, has disappeared. By fluctuating the water levels in the reservoirs during early summer, larvae of the dreaded Anapholes mosquito have been left on the shore to die. In 1934 TVA ran blood tests to determine the incidence of malaria in the valley, came to the conclusion that 30 percent of the population showed evidence of it. By 1941 the same pattern of sampling and blood-testing showed no malaria. Much has been made of the statement that TVA pays no taxes to local governments. This is true, but it makes up for direct taxes by paying sums (in lieu of taxes), to local and state governments, which amount to 7.2 percent of its total revenues; this compares with an average of 8.2 percent in state and local taxes paid by the privately owned power companies in the area — the difference is a subsidy, albeit a small one. The TVA is the largest "taxpayer" in the state of Tennessee; similarly, most of the municipal electric systems distributing the Authority's power (including the Knoxville, Chattanooga, and Nashville systems) are the largest taxpayers to their city governments. Between 1933 and 1967 TVA paid almost a third of a billion dollars in lieu of taxes; in the fiscal year 1967, with increasing use of electricity, the payment was more than $30 million — contrasted with $4 million twenty years earlier.* Beyond the payment made by the TVA in lieu of taxes, the project has increased the tax base of the entire basin so greatly that state and local governments have benefited proportionally. Finally, cheap power has converted the entire region to the use of electricity. In the 1930's power was used there only for electric lights, because of its high price. Now it is more widely used in the valley than in the rest of the nation, both for industry and for all home appliances. The TVA now generates a little more than 8 percent of the total electricity sold in the United States.

---

* Senator Metcalf states that investor-owned (IOUs) and city-owned (municipal) power systems each pay about 10.5 percent of their operating revenue to state and local governments, as taxes or in lieu of tax payments. Unlike the municipal plants, however, the IOUs also pay federal taxes. These take an additional 13 percent of their revenue, for a total tax bill amounting to 23.5 percent of revenue, as compared with the municipals' 10.5 percent.

After allowing for the 13 percent tax differential, Senator Metcalf claims that customers of municipally owned power plants usually come out ahead of those served by the IOUs. As an example, electric service cost $12.5 million a year less in Seattle than it would if the applicable rates were those charged by the nearby investor-owned system, Puget Sound Power & Light. Puget Sound pays $4 million more in taxes than the Seattle municipal plant does — leaving a net benefit of $8.5 million to the city for providing its own power.

Beyond these *regional* benefits there have been *national* ones from flood control, navigation, construction cost, payments to the federal government, cheap power, and national defense. As far as flood control is concerned, the TVA has served well to control inundations on the Ohio and Mississippi rivers — as well as on the Tennessee. Goods carried on the newly navigable Tennessee include shipments of petroleum, automobiles, grain, and coal — not all of them from the Tennessee Valley by any means, and therefore of benefit to other areas of the United States. In constructing the TVA, of the nearly $1.5 billion used to buy equipment and materials, more than half was spent outside the states in the Tennessee Valley. The federal government has also benefited from payments — quite beyond the regular repayments made by the TVA, at 4 percent — of the more than a billion dollars originally advanced by the federal government; the TVA power system is financially self-supporting and self-liquidating. Above these direct payments to Washington, the federal government has benefited from much higher tax income; in 1933, federal income taxes from the seven states in the Tennessee Valley were 3.4 percent of the national total; in 1952 they were almost twice as much, at 6.2 percent of the national total.

There have also been national benefits from the standpoint of defense, an advantageous yardstick, and from sales of electrical equipment. On the military side, two-thirds of TVA power is now going to the Atomic Energy Commission — at Oak Ridge and elsewhere. It is a bit difficult to understand where this power would have come from if TVA had not been there. It is also estimated that the power now provided, by the TVA to AEC would have cost $50 to $60 million more each year if the power had been bought from privately owned companies rather than from the TVA. On the domestic side of the economy, TVA has provided a yardstick to judge the validity of rates charged by private companies, and it has also made possible increased sales of electrical equipment. The influence of great publicly owned power projects has been shown by the fact that electric rates become progressively higher as the distance from them increases. In 1933 consumers were paying 5.7¢ per kwh in the Tennessee Valley. In 1961 they were paying a bit less than one cent a kwh — as against a national average of 2.5¢ — and a rate in New York City of 4¢. This has resulted in a national saving simply because private utilities reduced rates to meet the competition — to an extent that saved consumers in the entire United States $50 million annually within two years after the establishment of TVA. There was also the benefit to the private sector of the economy through increased sales of electrical equipment, made outside of the Tennessee Valley but used therein because of cheap power. As an example, in the mid-1950's electric ranges were used in 27 percent of the homes of the entire nation; they were used in 62 percent of the homes in the Tennessee Valley. In the first twenty years of the TVA users of its power spent upwards of $2 billion on appliances — most of them manufactured in other regions. As a result workers in Milwaukee and Schenectady and Cleveland were living better because farmers in the Tennessee Valley were living better.

Opponents of the TVA charge that it is socialistic, and thereby bad; they had the support of President Eisenhower, who once referred to the TVA as "creeping socialism." Although the IOUs are themselves monopolies free from competition, and are assured large profits, they run advertisements alleging unfair competition from government-owned utilities; "A Socialistic USA?" was queried by one of their headlines, beneath a map dotted with government-owned dams and power plants. Norman Thomas, a six-time presidential candidate for the Socialist party, was quick to admit the charge; he said that the principle behind public power was certainly socialistic and that it was childish to deny it. And so it is. The proponents of public power counter these arguments by stressing that "socialism" is an imprecise "scare" word in an economy that is already socialist in certain areas, that the conservative population in the Tennessee Valley is hardly socialist, and that if publicly produced power is demonstrably cheaper it should be used. They point out that the United States is obviously socialist in certain areas where there is public (socialist) ownership of public schools, libraries, postal systems, streets and highways, police and fire departments, water and sewage systems, national defense (armies, navies, air forces), and atomic energy. For this reason Governor Frank G. Clement of Tennessee once said that TVA was "about as socialistic as a fleet of battleships, and twice as important to the country's defense." If the TVA is socialist it seems strange, to many, that it has been sponsored by people and politicians who are basically conservative or who bear conservative labels. It seems strange that the socialistic TVA was fathered by a Republican Senator from Nebraska — George Norris. On the same ideological plane it also seems strange that the Bonneville Dam in Oregon — a socialistic, public-power one — was fathered by a conservative Republican Senator from Oregon, Charles McNary, who was the candidate for Vice-President on the Republican ticket in 1940. It seems incredible that a socialistic TVA would be popular in the Tennessee Valley, whose conservative people would have no "truck" with Marxism and who are obviously interested only in what works — for them. In 1964 Barry Goldwater of Arizona, the Republican candidate for President, appeared in Tennessee and stated that the TVA should be sold to private enterprise. There was a sign in the crowd listening to him; it read: "Sell TVA? I'd rather sell Arizona." There is also the compelling argument that if publicly produced power is demonstrably cheaper and more beneficial, it should be used. These advocates do not agree with the assumption of President Eisenhower that privately produced power — no matter how expensive — is better than publicly produced power — no matter how cheap it may be. Unfortunately, President Eisenhower maneuvered himself into the hands of the public-power advocates — whom he disliked. He did so by involving himself in a first-class scandal that represented an attempt to bypass public power (in the TVA) by awarding a lush contract to a private company. This involved the famous — or infamous — Dixon-Yates deal, by which the AEC, which had special privileges, proposed to buy power from Dixon-Yates (a privately owned holding company) and then sell it to the TVA. Under the contract, which was unusually beneficial to private ownership, the U.S. government was to pay Dixon-Yates a guaranteed profit of 9 percent. At the end of twenty-five years, the Dixon-Yates group would have owned the plant — which by that time would have cost $140 million more than would have been the charge if the TVA had built it. This negotiation demonstrated to a number of people that the basic issue was not one of free enterprise versus socialism — it was simply a deal for the benefit of a few privileged individuals. Opponents of the Dixon-Yates proposal said there was about as much free enterprise in a guaranteed 9 percent as there was in a high tariff on wool. They called the entire transaction "Free Enterprise Without Risk," or "Creeping Capitalism," and claimed that the "Ghost of Insull Rides Again." Ultimately the Dixon-Yates arrangement was voided on the narrow base of conflict of interest — that a special consultant to the U.S. government was also a representative of the First Boston Corporation, which was financing Dixon-Yates. Beyond this legal technicality there was a broader issue: Should electric power be provided primarily in the public interest, or primarily for the benefit of private entrepreneurs?

The St. Lawrence Valley was another area where cheap power was essential and where the necessity for a waterway was complex enough to require international agreement. There was nothing new about the desire for a waterway to the West; men have been trying to find a Northwest Passage through the American continent for four hundred years. In October 1536 Jacques Cartier, in the quest of a northwest route to the Orient via the St. Lawrence, came to an abrupt halt outside of Montreal because of foaming rapids — which he named Lachine for the country he had hoped to find. In 1784 George Washington was thinking about the problem of opening the Great Lakes to the Atlantic. His conclusion was that it should *not* be done by way of the St. Lawrence. He suggested a route through Lake Erie, down the Cuyahoga at what is now Cleveland, and thence by connecting canals and creeks to the Potomac River. This would be shorter, he said, than via the St. Lawrence; one must remember that Washington came from Virginia, which might have had something to do with his southern preference. Nonetheless he must be given credit for prescience and vision; he saw the advantage of opening the Great Lakes to the Atlantic, wherever the route emerged on the eastern coast.

As far as the St. Lawrence–Great Lakes Waterway (Seaway) is concerned, the problem was to overcome a drop of slightly more than 600 feet in the 2,342 miles from Duluth (on the western end of Lake Superior) to the Atlantic Ocean. There is no problem at the extremes of this waterway. There is a drop of but twenty-two feet in the thousand miles between Montreal and the Atlantic Ocean, and this can be handled easily by the placid St. Lawrence River. There is a drop of but twenty-one feet between Lake Superior (Duluth) and Lake Huron in northern Michigan, and this has been cared for — for more than a century — by the locks at Sault Sainte Marie. The Soo, as this series of locks is called, celebrated its hundredth anniversary in 1955. In its more than a century of operations the importance of the Soo has long been underestimated. Until recently it carried more tonnage than any other canal in the world. In 1960, as an example, the Panama Canal carried 67 million tons; in the same year the Soo carried 91 million tons. Almost everyone has heard of Ferdinand de Lesseps, who built the Suez Canal, and of George Goethals, who completed the one in Panama. Few know of Charles Thompson Harvey, a twenty-two-year-old New Englander who had the vision and ability to plan and build the locks at the Soo. Harvey actually outsmarted Henry Clay, who opposed the locks in northern Michigan on the ground that they were "beyond the remotest settlement in the United States, if not the moon."

The major problem obviously arises from the drop of 560 feet between Montreal and Lake Erie. Of this, 326 feet are at Niagara and 92 feet at International Rapids on the border between Ontario and New York. To bypass Niagara there is the Welland Canal. To bypass the International Rapids, a dam 3,200 feet long and 169 feet high was necessary in order to drown the turbulence and to create a channel of 27 feet. A dam of this size obviously produces a great amount of power — 13 billion kwh annually, greater than either Boulder Dam or Grand Coulee; this is now shared by the Power Authority of the State of New York (a state-owned public corporation) and the Ontario Hydro-Electric Power Commission.

There has been a great controversy over the St. Lawrence Waterway — past and present. In the twentieth century the opposition came from four sources: the IOUs, railroads and railroad labor, coal operators and coal labor, and seacoast cities on the Atlantic. The IOUs obviously were concerned about the low price at which public power could be developed on the St. Lawrence — as the Province of Ontario already had done, an example now to be extended. In relation to railroads it is interesting to note that as late as 1950 the Pennsylvania Railroad was still growling about the Panama Canal, and the New York Central was still disturbed about the Erie Canal! In the case of coal the fear was hydroelectric power; on this issue John L. Lewis saw eyeball-to-eyeball with management — both opposed the St. Lawrence Waterway. The seacoast cities (Boston, New

York, Philadelphia, and Baltimore) obviously feared a loss of business, and for that reason opposed the St. Lawrence Waterway (Seaway).

On the side of the proponents there was support from the advocates for public power, from the shipping interests, and from a new and surprising group — certain steel interests. The public-power advocates looked longingly at the prospect of 13 billion kwh annually. The New York State Power Authority figured that consumer's savings in electricity would be upwards of $25 million a year, and that states in New England would benefit too. This seemed to be obvious. In 1920 representatives of Du Pont, GE, and Alcoa had vainly offered to spend more than a billion dollars to build the St. Lawrence Waterway — and to present the portions devoted to navigation free to the governments of Canada and the United States, in exchange for the power rights alone. These companies obviously saw the advantage of the acquisition of electric power at very low cost, and its resale at a much higher figure. At one point Cyrus Eaton, a Midwestern financier and entrepreneur, admitted that the seaway was incidental to electric power. He said, "We would have built the canal and turned it over to the government free, but we wanted the electric power that would be produced."

The shipping companies could point out, as they did, the tremendous savings in transportation by water as against transportation by rail. By railroad the cost of transportation is one dollar per ton for each 100 miles; on water the cost is one-tenth as much. The support of the steel companies, for the St. Lawrence Seaway, represented a decided change in point of view. Until the early 1950's George Humphrey, president of the M. A. Hanna Steel Company in Cleveland, called the St. Lawrence Seaway a "socialistic ditch." His statement was presumably based on the assumption that it would be sponsored by governments, and that it would develop great quantities of public power. Then a great transformation occurred — both tactically and ideologically. In the 1950's steel companies began to awaken to the fact that the Mesabi Range in Minnesota, where they had been getting their ore, was playing out and would be good for not more than twenty-five years at best — assuming there was no Third World War. The result of this realization was that U.S. Steel found ore in Venezuela at Cerro Bolívar, and developed the town of Fairless in Pennsylvania (near Philadelphia) to receive it on tidewater. The result of this realization was that Bethlehem Steel also found ore in South America and prepared to receive it at Sparrow's Point in Maryland (on the Patapsco River near Baltimore). What were Cleveland, and the M. A. Hanna Company, to do? At this point it went into Labrador and developed findings at Ungava, some four hundred miles north of the St. Lawrence. Ungava is an amazing open-pit operation, with probably 2 billion tons of exceptionally high-grade iron ore in places covered only with reindeer moss and with an average overburden of only seven feet; the overburden in the open-pit operation at Mesabi runs up to three hundred feet in depth. For the M. A. Hanna Company to transport the ore out of Ungava, two developments were necessary. One was a railroad from Seven Islands on the St. Lawrence to Ungava to the north; this the Hanna Company built. The other was the St. Lawrence Seaway from Seven Islands to Cleveland. This was ultimately built by the Canadian and U.S. governments — with considerable applause from the M. A. Hanna Company. Suddenly this company, originally opposed to the Seaway as a socialistic ditch, came to regard it as a heavenly thoroughfare. Suddenly, Ohio Senators Robert Taft and George Bender, who had previously been opposed to the Seaway, came out in favor of it. Suddenly the Cleveland Chamber of Commerce, which had been opposed to the Seaway, came out in favor of it. Suddenly President Eisenhower, who feared "creeping socialism" in the Tennessee Valley but had great respect for his Secretary of the Treasury (George Humphrey), signed the legislation authorizing the United States in constructing the Seaway. This was in 1954; some regarded the unusual sequence of events as a coincidence — others saw an invisible economic hand in the entire development.

XIII

Subsidies

SINCE their appearance almost five hundred years ago, national governments have conducted programs that seek to improve the economic
position of particular groups or industries. When such subsidy programs
work to the advantage of society as a whole — if in benefiting one group
they do not inflict a greater injury on others — little if any objection can
be raised against them. Now — a half millennium later — many current
federal subsidies fail to meet this basic test; the social costs for society as a
whole far exceed the benefits conferred on a few. At the present time
subsidies to prosperous groups appear to command indefensibly high pri-
orities at a time when the federal government is failing to provide adequate assistance to the poor. On the basis of estimates prepared for the
Joint Economic Committee of the Congress, in 1970 the government
spent at least $63 billion in direct and indirect subsidies. Since World War
II subsidies to favored groups have assumed such a wide variety of shapes
and forms that in 1950 Vermont C. Royster, editor of the conservative *Wall Street Journal*, would write a paraphrase of a then current
popular novel, *Knock on Any Door*. His observation was a sad commentary on the existing situation in relation to rugged individualism and laissez-faire:

Knock on any door and you will find a man, a man with his hand in the
public purse. Farmer, laborer, businessman, doctor, lawyer, merchant, chief,
young and old, rich or poor — we all seem to be sitting with at least one palm
outstretched. That posture personifies the politics of our times.

Businessmen, in the popular fancy, represent the more conservative thought.

They have certainly been in the forefront of those denouncing waste and extravagance. . . .

Yet when the line is formed, there are businessmen. They come seeking subsidies for this or that industry. When they find the public disinclined to risk its private money in their ventures, they trot to the government for the capital. The big and little both come; there is the big businessman seeking millions, and there is the little businessman seeking a few thousands.

There, too, is the union man who deplores those "handouts" to business. All he wants from the government is a subsidized house, subsidized food, subsidized medical care, subsidized retirement and subsidized burial. Or there is the farmer who thinks he ought to have . . . a guaranteed subsidized income. The doctor chips in to fight all these things and merely wants the government to subsidize his training and his laboratories. The professor sadly says this is the way Rome went and suggests that the government subsidize his university.

The young people have come to feel that the government owes them an education, and the old people that it owes them a rocking chair. And the veterans, young and old, are convinced that the government owes them everything.

There was nothing like this in the most wanton days of the New Deal. What began as a program to take from the "haves" and give to the "have-nots" has become a taking from everybody to give to everybody. Since everybody has to pay anyway we have developed a kind of mass hysteria to see who can get there fustest for the mostest.

From the very beginning the word *tariff* has implied a subsidy. It comes from Tarifa, a fortified seaport on the Strait of Gilbraltar which centuries ago was the rugged home of a band of pirates. These thieves were unethical but shrewd. They never took the entire cargo lest they arouse the dormant law-enforcement officers. Instead they took a portion of the cargo of every ship that passed, until shippers learned to expect a regular loss from the depredations; this *percentage of loss* they called a tariff. In spite of the clear origin of the term, most Americans do not recognize the tariff as a subsidy in the form of a *percentage of loss*. They recognize a direct payment from the Treasury — say to veterans or shipping lines or to farmers — as a subsidy. This is a subsidy paid by the public in the form of taxes. They do not recognize that the same public — as consumers — suffers a "percentage of loss" through the tariff. This loss, for the consumer, is paid through higher prices, and profits, to the protected industry.

Obviously protected manufacturers do not contend, at least openly, that the nation should pass legislation which benefits a few at the expense of the many. The arguments pro and con on the tariff have therefore been on general rather than exceptional grounds; extremists on both sides might be called the protectionists and the free traders. The protectionists have claimed that the tariff promotes nationalism, infant industries, self-sufficiency, and prosperity — and the low-tariff advocates have countered every one of these arguments. The promotion of nationalism through protection is an old cry. In the seventeenth century Parliament decreed that English dead should be buried only in woolen shrouds; the deceased would go into their graves in British woolens rather than Indian cottons. Later the cry was "Buy American." In 1961 the majority leader of the Ohio state senate was inordinately proud of the basketball team of the state university, but astounded to find that the team was riding in two German-made miniature busses. As a result he asked the Ohio legislature to enact a law requiring all departments and institutions in the state to purchase goods made only in America. It was a curious statement from an Ohioan, because in the 1960's his state exported more goods per capita than any other; the majority leader was obviously under the delusion that foreign trade is a one-way street. By contrast, low-tariff advocates point out that the evils of nationalism are so great that they more than counteract the good, if any, that comes to a few industries from a nationalistic tariff. They note two evils in particular: that tariffs breed national depressions, and that tariffs breed international tensions. In the 1780's the United States was restricted internally by nationalism — the thirteen states erected tariff walls around each other which stifled trade and were a prime factor in producing a depression after the American Revolution. The United States had the good judgment in 1787 to abolish these petty nationalisms and to establish one big economic union. Now the United States is a great and powerful nation because it is the largest free-trade area in the world. There are few who would now argue that the United States would be more prosperous if it had fifty customs barriers.

The creation of international tensions through tariffs is usually unconscious on the part of the offending country. A prime example is the passage, by the U.S. Congress, of the Wilson-Gorman Act of 1894, which became a prime cause of the Spanish-American War. This act placed high duties on foreign sugar which produced a $20 million profit for the American Sugar Trust. The same high duties so ruined Cuba that they led to the revolt of 1895 — the first link in a chain of events leading to the Spanish-American War. In the same way the Hawley-Smoot Act of 1930, which brought suspicion and retaliation from foreign countries, increased international tensions — and contributed materially to the serious problems of the 1930's which ultimately led to a world war. In the present era the nationalistic arrogance of France, in delaying British entry into the Common Market, struck many as an example of acute patriotic astigmatism. They contend that nationalism in the old sense is a childishly dangerous concept, that interdependence is now an essential fact of life for all nations.

For more than a century the tariff as a protector of infant industries has been an appealing argument — reminiscent of mother and childhood — and of bad foreign bullies who want to harm mother's boy. After the American Revolution it was claimed that we had to protect American business babies against foreign giants. The same argument was used again after the War of 1812 and the Civil War. In 1890 the most controversial part of the McKinley Tariff was a duty on tin plate, not *then* produced in the United States although large quantities were imported for canning and other industries; the Republicans wished to foster not an *infant* but an *embryo* industry by insuring a domestic market for it. After World War I it was claimed that the United States had to protect newly born "war babies," one of them Monsanto, against foreign commercial attack.

In the course of our history the foremost student of tariff policies was Frank William Taussig, who taught economics at Harvard from 1882 to 1935, and was chairman of the U.S. Tariff Commission from 1917 to 1919. Taussig concluded that, with the unimportant exception of the American silk industry and the cotton-spinning industry before 1824, U.S. tariffs had no noticeable effect upon the growth of the "infant industries" they were designed to protect. He observed that protected industries in this country have always had comparative advantages — or failed because they were so inefficient that they could not survive even with tariff protection. The free traders also comment that the tariff has been the "Mother of Trusts," and that it has been the key instrument through which these monopolies, safe from competition from abroad, have fixed prices within the United States.

The continuation of tariff protection, long after the infants are well able to fend for themselves, has been maintained through lobbyists. In the Civil War period Sam Ward, known as the "King of the Lobby," relied on entertainment; he said, "The way to a man's 'aye' is through his stomach." Some lobbyists have not been that subtle. During the debate on the Natural Gas Bill in the 1950's, a lobbyist for a large oil company characterized his company's relations with aspiring office holders in these words: "You just put good, green folding money in their lily-white hands and be goddamn sure they know why you put it there." Whatever the technique, the lobbyists do continue. In the current era it is estimated that for every member of Congress there are ten lobbyists; the most modest estimate of what they spend, in the course of working for or against specific pieces of legislation, runs to more than a billion dollars a year. In a sense the Washington representatives of special-interest groups constitute a Third House of Congress — because at least half of all the measures introduced in the Senate and the House were originally drafted in their offices.

The protective tariff has also been supported by those who believe in economic self-sufficiency. Alexander Hamilton, who believed in power politics, wanted to be self-sufficient in case of a future war. Thomas Jefferson, who believed in agrarian happiness, believed that every citizen should own a plot of land and should be self-sufficient on it. In 1812, he wrote John Adams, with great satisfaction and confidence on his part, that every family in the nation was a basic *manufactory* in itself, producing everything it needed. Simple food was abundant and Jefferson found that a sheep for every person was sufficient for clothing — in addition to the cotton, hemp, and flax which might be raised by the family. In modern times opponents of this theory have pointed out that a nation can achieve a Spartan self-sufficiency, but at the cost of a lower standard of living. Adolf Hitler tried economic self-sufficiency through what he called *autarchy*. In his Germany, the standard of living went down. This appears to be so inevitable that David L. Cohn has commented that the only truly self-contained communities in the present world are the cemeteries.

Why — under a policy of self-sufficiency which initially sounds so attractive — does the standard of living go down? The reason is an economic one: self-sufficiency violates the theory of comparative costs, a theory so compelling that it might better be called a law. According to this concept, each country should manufacture the products in which it has a comparative advantage — and buy with these products other products which it lacks. This means that each nation should develop those industries for which it is naturally suited, and in which its comparative cost is low. As examples, one can ponder the cases of watches, bananas, and sugar.

It is possible to manufacture watches in the United States. But if the Swiss can do it more cheaply, as they can, we should buy our watches in Switzerland — so that they in turn can buy from us products in which we have a comparative advantage. In 1960 the United States increased the tariff on Swiss watches. Switzerland countered by increasing the tariff on U.S. agricultural products — which they were importing. One American manufacturer commented, "We didn't gain a job. All we did, in effect, was to get another watchmaker and to lose a farmer." One could grow bananas on Pikes Peak; they would not be cheap, but they would possess a certain extravagant elegance. In effect that kind of opulence is what we now achieve under our tariffs (and import quotas) on sugar. Tropical countries are the place to grow sugarcane, but the United States can get more expensive sugar out of sugar beets — and these sugar-beet industries have powerful lobbies in Congress. Periodically the Congress allocates the controlled U.S. market between domestic and foreign producers, with high-cost domestic producers achieving a higher and higher share. On the bananas–on–Pikes Peak principle, the U.S. housewife picks up the sugar bill. The world cost of raising sugar (in 1965) was two cents a pound; the U.S. cost was four-and-a-half cents a pound — more than twice as much by any computation. Even the nontropical state of Maine has been joining the act. It intends to raise sugar beets in the Aroostook Valley, along with potatoes.

Finally, protectionists contended that the tariff was responsible for prosperity and the American high standard of living. This argument first developed in the days of Andrew Jackson. Alexander Hamilton had made no bones about the tariff being a subsidy to American industry. With the rise of Jacksonian democracy it became politically unwise to ask so boldly for a measure that would benefit the wealthy. A new rationale appeared; it was claimed, for political reasons, that the tariff benefited everyone, that it was responsible for American prosperity. This argument appeared for the first time in the 1840's; after the Civil War the Republicans made it the major principle in their political creed. They developed the faith that Republicanism, high tariffs, and prosperity went hand in hand; by implication — and sometimes by direct statement — they said that the Democratic party, low tariffs, and depressions were indissolubly connected. This argument began to carry less weight in the 1930's when it appeared, to anyone who thought about it, that the Republican party, high tariffs, and a first-class depression somehow were connected. Nonetheless, as late as 1953 a Republican member of the House of Representatives from Pennsylvania (Richard M. Simpson) would claim that low-tariff advocates were trying to "import a depression."

On the tariff-prosperity issue the free-traders ask a question: "Whose prosperity is insured by the protective tariff?" They observe that there is no question that protection is good for the protected industries, which charge higher prices and make greater profits. Because there is no such thing as a free lunch, who pays the bill? It is apparent that three groups "fork over": the consumer, the exporter, and the laborer. The consumer obviously pays through higher prices. Exporters are hit hard through loss of markets. Many citizens of the Republic do not seem to comprehend that trade is a two-way street, that the first commandment of international commerce is "As ye sell, so must ye buy." The man in the American street perceives but dimly that tariff fences not only keep foreign goods *out*, they also keep American goods *in* — and that the corollary of "Buy American" is "Sell only in America." In the early 1960's more than 3 million workers in the entire United States owed their jobs to *export* trade — about one in every seventeen then employed in the entire private sector of the nation's economy, and one in every eight farm workers. Throughout U.S. history the primary example of regional damage from loss of exports has been the South, which requires foreign markets for its perennial surplus of cotton fiber; over the long years it has been claimed that the tariff, because of its indirect effect on exports, inflicted more damage on the South than did William Tecumseh Sherman. In 1970 President Nixon asked for a restrictive quota on foreign textiles in order to fulfill a campaign promise which was part of his "southern strategy"; he appeared to be oblivious of the economic fact that this measure would destroy foreign markets for our own exports, including cotton. Republican Senator Mark Hatfield of Oregon felt so strongly about the proposal that he labeled it as "one small sop for textiles and one giant mistake for mankind."

Labor shares with consumers and exporters the cost of the American tariff. Labor has paid the tariff bill by a loss in real wages, and by a loss in jobs. Theoretically labor was supposed to benefit from the tariff through what has been called the "drip" system of economics; by way of the tariff, the manufacturer would charge higher prices and pass on the gain to both stockholders and workers. It was apparent, however, that unless labor received an increase in wages which was sufficient to offset the tariff-imposed increase in prices, it lost. This happened. Over the years prices increased more than wages with the result that, while the number of dollars in the worker's pay envelope increased, the value of those dollars was diminished. Real wages, as measured in purchasing power, tended to decline. Throughout a large part of U.S. history a large proportion of the high prices and the high profits, possible because of the high tariff, was siphoned off in the form of dividends and executive salaries rather than in wages.

Labor also lost in available jobs. The loss in employment opportunities has sometimes been the result of bad faith on the part of American employers, and has on occasion been the result of special tariff advantages which provide employment in one region at the expense of another. After the Civil War — at the very time when American employers were achieving higher tariffs on the claim that they would raise the American standard of living — the same employers were creating unemployment for Americans by sending agents across the seas to scour the countries of Europe for cheap foreign labor. On the issue of regional unemployment, one can consider the example of West Virginia. Some years ago the United States protected producers in Wisconsin by excluding Danish blue cheese; the result was that the Danes had to buy coal from Poland rather than West Virginia. Wisconsin's gain was West Virginia's loss. Where foreign countries retaliate, with tariffs of their own against those enacted by the United States, the situation can be even more catastrophic. U.S. corporations build plants abroad to evade the foreign tariff, and then hire European rather than American labor to man them.

It has been claimed that high tariffs were necessary to protect American labor against low-standard — low-wage — production abroad. In general this has not been the case; in fact, the obverse argument appears to be valid. A strong case can be made that low-standard countries actually need protection against high-standard American production. The nub of the matter is what it costs *per unit* to turn out a product — not what wages are paid per day. In the 1920's an American coal miner produced ten tons of coal a day, by comparison with one ton produced by a British miner; in the 1960's it took 170 men in Imperial Chemical Industries to turn out the same chemicals that 100 men produced at Du Pont. So, in spite of low wages, the unit cost of coal and chemicals in the United States was low. Until recently the United States, because of its resources and advanced technology, has commanded an average productivity that is twice and thrice that of any other nation.* After World War II the "economic miracle" of western Europe and Japan obscured the fact that a U.S. factory worker produced three times as much an hour as a European, and seven times as much as a Japanese. In the long run wages in *all* countries move closely with productivity, with unit cost. American workers are thus well paid because their productivity is high; foreign workers are less well paid because their productivity is relatively low. Curiously, if the argument had been valid that the tariff should give protection for plants in which wages were highest, there should have been a high tariff on automobiles, and a low one on textiles. On the contrary, in those industries where American wages have generally been highest, for example, automobiles, there has seldom been any need for protection, or much desire for it. But, in those industries where American wages have been lowest, for example, textiles, pressure for a high tariff has been insistent. There are cases where foreign workers (in Hong Kong, Singapore, the Philippines, and Pakistan) are so poorly paid that, despite the superior efficiency of American industry, foreign goods can take the market away from American concerns. As a general rule, however, this has not been the case. The result has been that the artificially high American tariff — in most industries — has enabled American manufacturers to charge artificially high prices throughout much of our history.

Throughout most of our history tariff acts have been controversial and of primary importance; the first major act passed by the initial U.S. Congress was a tariff. Down to the Civil War all federal revenue came from tariffs, save for limited income from the sale of public lands and from a very few excise taxes. After the Civil War, and until the advent of the income tax in 1914, more than half of federal revenue came from customs duties; today the tariff accounts for less than 2 percent of federal revenue. It has been customary to refer to low tariffs as those designed primarily for revenue, and to high ones as tariffs designed primarily for protection. In theory a perfect revenue tariff would offer no protection, and a perfect protective tariff would be so high that there would be no revenue. In practice, duties averaging 20 percent or below have been considered tariffs for revenue; those above 20 percent have been called protective ones.

Revenue tariffs prevailed down to the War of 1812, protective ones from the War of 1812 through the Nullification Controversy of 1833,

---

* In the late 1960's, for the first time, wage increases in the United States began to surpass productivity to a noticeable degree. This led, inevitably, to price increases and a decided drop in our exports.

revenue tariffs again from 1833 to the outbreak of the Civil War. During the first twenty years of U.S. history Alexander Hamilton, who believed in mercantilism and public assistance to the economic elite, would have preferred a high tariff. He did not get it; during these early years the tariff averaged less than 10 percent and followed the philosophy of Thomas Jefferson, who was antimercantilist and a devotee of agriculture. The Napoleonic Wars, which led the United States into the War of 1812, destroyed the Jeffersonian dream of a self-sufficient agrarian commonwealth. In the United States the War of 1812 developed a spirit of nationalism, a desire for self-sufficiency, and a willingness to protect the so-called infant industries — all arguments for high tariffs. Even Jefferson changed his mind on the tariff, at least for a brief period; he said, "We must now place the manufacturer by the side of the agriculturalist." John C. Calhoun, later a bitter opponent of high tariffs, succumbed to the conventional wisdom which prevailed in 1816; as Secretary of War he supported the protective tariff on grounds of nationalism and self-sufficiency. The result of these developments was that the first protective tariffs in U.S. history were passed — those of 1816, 1824, and 1828. The tariff went up to 25 and 33 and 41 percent in these measures; protection was given especially to woolens, cottons, and iron products. The minimum principle, a disguise for an exorbitant tariff, was introduced for the first time in the tariff of 1816 — for cottons. This principle provided that imported cotton, selling in the case of India prints for as little as 6¢ a yard, was to be valued for the tariff levy at not less than 25¢ a yard. Along with this first protective tariff came the first effective lobby in Washington. It was the Pennsylvania Society for the Encouragement of Manufacturers and the Mechanic Arts, which pressured Congress, and conducted a campaign to remove the books of low-tariff (or no-tariff) advocates — like Adam Smith and J. B. Say, his French disciple — from schools and colleges. The Pennsylvania Society even hired a German propagandist and economist, one Frederick List, to write a substitute for the subversive texts of Smith and Say. List was a staunch protectionist from Germany, where he had been released from prison on the express condition that he emigrate to the United States. Here he became a paid propagandist for a high tariff; this development led one Congressman to snap that List himself was an importation, in direct violation of the cause he espoused. List's greatest contribution, in time, was his proposal that friends of domestic industry meet annually to prepare the necessary legislation for Congress; it took seventy years for his idea to develop, but it finally came to fruition in 1895 with the organization of the National Association of Manufacturers.

In this early period the attitude of sections in the country varied. The West was protectionist largely because of Henry Clay, sometimes known as the "Cock of Kentucky," and what he called the American System. The protective tariff would develop more textile mills in the Northeast;

these mills would use more southern cotton and their employees would eat more grain and pork from the West. The sale of cotton by the South, and food by the West, would then enable the South and the West to buy more shirts and farm tools manufactured in the Northeast. The problem of transportation would be solved by turning over tariff revenue for the construction of internal improvements — roads and canals. The entire proposal had a fallacious sound to many people; it was like the argument that an entire community of people can make a living by taking in each other's washing.

The South opposed a protective tariff for obvious reasons; this section sold a large portion of its cotton and tobacco to England and the Continent, purchased goods there, and did not desire to pay a tariff on these imports. The leading spokesman for this low-tariff section was the political philosopher of the antebellum South, whom Richard Hofstadter calls the "Marx of the Master Class" — John Caldwell Calhoun, who held two Cabinet posts (Secretary of War 1817–1825, and Secretary of State 1844–1845), and two elective offices in the quarter century from 1825 to 1850 — those of Vice-President and Senator from South Carolina. In physique he was tall and cadaverous; it was said that no man could be as tragic as John C. Calhoun looked. Mentally he was a cold, merciless logician; at Yale his best subjects were metaphysics, mathematics, and the sciences. He was not interested in the humanities; once in his life he read a novel and once he tried to write a poem. The poetry was a failure because he began every sentence with "Whereas." Calhoun's hatred for the protective tariff was incorporated in his statement, "We are the serfs of the system." He shared the belief of other Southerners that because of the tariff the South would be subject to Northerners who were "lords of the spinning jenny, the lords of the loom." He said that the tariff was a certain means of making "the poor poorer and the rich richer"; after it had exhausted the planters, the contest would be between capitalists and workers — for the tariff would divide society into these two classes. Calhoun agreed with George McDuffie, South Carolinian who served that state both as governor and Senator, who claimed that the tariff, through higher prices, was giving the North forty out of every hundred bales of cotton raised in the South.

Throughout much of the antebellum period New England was ambivalent, almost schizophrenic on the issue of the tariff. Here the struggle was between the codfish aristocracy and the lords of the loom. The codfish aristocracy — the shippers and merchants — believed in low tariffs, in laissez-faire, and were internationalists. The lords of the loom were mercantilist, Hamiltonian, and nationalistic. Daniel Webster, a politician from Massachusetts who always counted noses, represented the codfish aristocracy until 1828 when (in John Randolph's phrase) he changed the trident for the distaff. In the earlier period, as a believer in laissez-faire, he criticized tariff protection as unconstitutional — even hinted at interposition and secession as justifiable courses when his section was at a disadvantage. He said that he did not favor raising American infant industries in hot-beds. He echoed Jefferson on the evils of big cities, claimed that they threatened good morals and free government, and said he was in no haste to see Sheffields and Birminghams in America. All of this was a far cry from the Webster who was a protectionist in the last twenty-five years of his political career.

It is pertinent to note that the first great crisis over the nature and permanence of the Federal Union, that is, whether the United States would continue or whether some states would secede, occurred over the question of the tariff. This happened in the Nullification Crisis of 1832–1833, which actually began with two developments in 1828: the enact-ment of a tariff by the Congress of the United States and the publication of the *South Carolina Exposition and Protest* by the legislature of that state. In actual fact, the Tariff of 1828 was introduced into Congress for the purpose of having the bill defeated; its promoters were more inter-ested in manufacturing a President than they were in protecting manufac-tures. It was the supporters of Andrew Jackson who introduced the meas-ure, expecting it to be defeated; they wanted to unhorse John Quincy Adams, who was running for reelection. The Tariff of 1828 was designed to appeal to the West, and to antagonize the South and New England. The West was pleased by the high duties on wool, flax, hemp, and iron. The South would oppose any high tariff. New England was also expected to vote against the measure because of high duties placed on raw materials which that section needed, and because the duties on foreign manufacturers were not high enough to please the "lords of the loom." If New Eng-land joined the South in defeating the measure, the West would be dis-pleased with the loss of its usual support from New England and would vote against New Englander Adams for the Presidency. To the infinite surprise of the Jacksonians, the measure passed. Enough New Englanders had voted for it — because they thought the bill at least endorsed the pro-tective principle no matter how undesirable some of the details might be — that the measure barely squeaked through. The vote in the House was 105 to 94; in the Senate it was 26 to 21. No one was happy, except the West.

The South found the bill abominable, and with that adjective gave the measure its name. It also produced the *South Carolina Exposition and Pro-test*, published by the legislature of that state but written by John C. Cal-houn. By this time Calhoun believed a *protective* tariff to be unconstitu-tional. He maintained that Congress had the right to levy taxes for revenue but not for the purpose of increasing prices for manufacturers; this would penalize agriculture for the benefit of other groups. For these reasons he claimed, in the *South Carolina Exposition and Protest*, that:

1. A single state could declare an unconstitutional act of Congress *null and void* within its boundaries.

2. Such an act would remain null and void within that state until an amendment was added to the U.S. Constitution — making legal what Congress had done. Because an amendment must be ratified by three-fourths of the states — and since the South controlled more than one-fourth of the states at that time — Calhoun and the South would dominate the situation.

The South Carolina Exposition and Protest was theory; nothing further happened in 1828. The action began four years later.

Between July 1832 and March of the next year there was a steady chain of events: (1) the passage of the Tariff of 1832 in July, (2) the Nullification Ordinance in November, (3) Jackson's Proclamation against it in December, (4) the passage of two Acts by Congress on 1 March 1833 (the Compromise Tariff of 1833 and the Force Bill), and (5) the repeal of the Nullification Ordinance. The Tariff of 1832 had reduced protective duties from 41 to 33 percent and had pared away the worst of the "abominations," but it did not satisfy the South. That section had expected a southern President, Andrew Jackson of Tennessee, to do more. Accordingly, in November a special convention in South Carolina acted on Calhoun's principle, nullified the Tariff Acts of 1828 and 1832, and asserted that any use of force by the federal government would result in secession, the nullification was to become effective on 1 February 1833; ultimately this was postponed until early March. On 10 December 1832 President Jackson issued a resounding proclamation against nullification, stating privately that he would hang the nullifiers, including the Vice-President of the United States who had just resigned; his name was John C. Calhoun. At this point a Civil War seemed likely. By 1 March of the next year, due largely to the efforts of Henry Clay, a compromise tariff and a Force Bill had passed Congress. The tariff provided for a gradual reduction from 33 to 20 percent over the next decade (by 1 January 1842). The foolish Force Bill empowered the President to do something he could already do; it authorized him to use the army and navy, if necessary, to collect federal tariff duties. Because it was unnecessary the South called this measure the "Bloody Bill." Ten days later (on 11 March 1833) South Carolina repealed the Nullification Ordinance of the preceding November; but it also had the last word in the controversy by nullifying the Force Bill which would never go into effect.

Who won the Nullification Controversy? The answer must be — everybody and nobody. Jackson could claim that he won because he vindicated the national authority; South Carolina could advertise a victory because the tariff was reduced. In retrospect it is apparent that Calhoun never got over the controversy, one that involved tariffs rather than the slavery issue usually associated with his name. In 1846 he would say, "If you should ask me the question I would wish engraved on my tombstone, it is Nullification."

In twenty-five of the twenty-eight years (1833–1861) before the Civil War the trend of the tariff was down. Three of the four bills in this period (the Compromise of 1833, the Walker Tariff of 1846, and the Tariff of 1857) provided for reductions; the only exception was a brief protectionist interlude of three years (1842–1845) made possible by the Tariff of 1842. As the minimum rates provided by the Compromise Tariff of 1833 reached 20 percent in 1842, there was a vigorous revival of protective sentiment. The propertied Whigs, led by Clay and Webster, achieved a shaky and abbreviated period of power during which they saw the enactment of the high tariff (averaging 33 percent) that protectionists desire.

The Whig policy lasted no longer than their brief period of power, which came to an end with the inauguration of Democrat James K. Polk as President in 1845; the Walker Tariff of 1846 inaugurated a low-tariff policy that continued to the Civil War. Interestingly, Robert John Walker is one of two Cabinet members and the only Secretary of the Treasury whose name has been given to a tariff act; the name of a Secretary of State would be associated with another one in the 1930's. Walker was born in Pennsylvania, graduated from the University of Pennsylvania in 1821, and became a lawyer; the balance of his life was associated with the South and with Andrew Jackson. In 1826 he moved to Natchez, Mississippi, represented that state in the U.S. Senate from 1833 to 1845, and was the Secretary of the Treasury from 1845 to 1849. In that position he supported a hard-money policy and a low tariff; his *Report* (1845) on the state of national finances took rank as a classic of free-trade literature, and his administration has been judged to have been one of the ablest in the history of the Treasury. The Walker Tariff of 1846 reduced rates to an average of 26 percent, a more moderate level than that of the principal European countries of that day; it was also both innovative and practical with regard to schedules, the rate structure, and warehousing. It introduced well-organized, classified, and graded schedules beginning with A and extending through I. The rate structure was changed from specific to much fairer ad-valorem duties (percentage of market value). The Walker Bill also introduced the system of government warehouses (still in effect), where goods could be stored until the duty was paid. A dozen years later the Tariff of 1857, the last downward revision before the Civil War, further moderated protection by reducing it to an average of 20 percent, virtually placing the United States among the free-trading nations of the world at that time.

For more than seven decades (1861–1934) the trend of the tariff was skyward, with the exception of temporary and ineffective reductions in

1882, 1894, and 1914. As soon as the Civil War broke out two arguments appeared in favor of a high tariff: the national government needed more revenue and the manufacturers needed more protection. The national need for revenue in wartime was obvious. Manufacturers in the North claimed they needed more protection as a matter of equity; this was required to pay new internal-revenue duties — duties with which foreign rivals were not burdened. When duties were raised during the war everyone thought they were temporary and that the war tariff, along with internal-revenue taxes, would come off after the conflict was terminated; this was certainly Lincoln's point of view. As it turned out, however, it proved difficult to reduce the tariff once the favored interests had experienced the delights of protection.

The name usually associated with the high Civil War tariffs is that of Justin Smith Morrill, a prominent member of the House Ways and Means Committee; he was to give his name to the tariff measures during the war and to the land-grant bill which established many state universities. An interesting and able statesman, he served the state of Vermont in both Houses of Congress for forty-three years (until his death in 1898), one of the longest terms on record. Beginning with the Morrill Bill of 1861 the tariff went up steadily during the Civil War, from 20 percent in 1861 to 47 percent at the close of the conflict. From the first, privilege reared its unpretty head. Morrill wanted wool, marble, and maple sugar protected; it was no coincidence that he represented Vermont in the Congress. Senator Charles Sumner of Massachusetts had a friend who owned a chocolate factory; Sumner therefore insisted on putting cocoa on the free list. Senator James F. Simmons of Rhode Island had a friend too; he owned the only woodscrew factory in the United States. The Senator arranged a 20 percent duty on foreign woodscrews for his domestic friend — and from that day was dubbed "Woodscrew" Simmons of Rhode Island. Thaddeus Stevens of Pennsylvania, who as chairman of the House Ways and Means Committee wielded tremendous power throughout and following the Civil War, was an iron manufacturer whose works were noted for their bad management; for this reason duties could never be high enough for him.

In the Reconstruction Period, which lasted a little more than a decade after the Civil War (1865–1877), there was a definite connection between the tariff and the policy of the dominant Republican party. Many politically astute northern Republicans were afraid that a solid Democratic South might unite with the West, for the purpose of bringing about a lower tariff. To forestall this eventuality they needed a Republican South, which they achieved by means of military occupation and the Negro (Republican) vote. By this device they had little difficulty in maintaining the high war tariffs after the conflict was over.

The Reconstruction Period also saw the appearance of a new and effective lobby, which worked with might and main to make certain that the tariff was not reduced. It was headed by an able man, the lawyer-geologist-lobbyist John Lord Hayes, the secretary of the newly formed National Association of Wool Manufacturers. It was largely through his efforts in bringing wool growers and wool manufacturers together that the West was induced to support the East in urging protection for the industry, thus fostering the passage of a special tariff bill (contrasted with a general tariff measure) providing higher protection on wool and woolens only. The association headed by Hayes was an early example of a successfully organized business lobby, and the wool-manufacturing business was the first large one to so organize. These protectionist developments so disgusted one Democratic member of the House — Samuel Sullivan (S. S. or "Sunset") Cox, who at different times represented both New York and Ohio in Congress, that he introduced resolutions against "free sunshine." These would require all windows, shutters, and curtains to be kept forever shut in the United States. The reason was, as Cox put it: "The sun is a 'foreigner.' He comes from abroad and we must gratify those gentlemen from Pennsylvania who have a monopoly on . . . coal."

If "Sunset" Cox was displeased so was David A. Wells, Special Commissioner for Revenue in the Treasury Department. Cox had always been a low-tariff Democrat; there was nothing unusual about his sustained position on the issue. On the contrary Wells had come to Washington as a Republican and as a believer in protection; he left the national capital as a Democrat and with the soubriquet of being the "Father of Tariff Reform." Wells had been educated at Williams College and at the Lawrence Technical School in Cambridge (Massachusetts); by 1861 he had achieved prominence in many fields — as inventor, as scientist, and as economist. Lincoln appointed him to the chairmanship of a special commission created to study the tax structure and in this job Wells won such high esteem that the office of Special Commissioner for Revenue was created for him in 1866. His investigations showed that the protective tariff was iniquitous. He was able to prove that, behind tariff walls, the salt industry had made a necessity of life dear in price. Monopolistic salt companies charged a high price for their product at home, and a cheap one when they sold their salt on a competitive basis abroad. According to Wells' revelations, one of the salt companies had paid six dividends in a single year — and one of the dividends was 12½ percent. He contended that the same situation was true with iron. The industry was charging $40 a ton for pig iron, $10 more than was necessary to pay American labor a higher wage and to give investors a fair profit. These exposures made the protected interests, and particularly Congressman William D. ("Pig-Iron") Kelley of Pennsylvania, furious. Kelley had the ear of President Grant; the result was that Wells' appointment was terminated in 1870.

In spite of the work of the lobby, by 1870 the demand for tariff reform was so insistent that the Republicans resorted to a subterfuge with the passage of what came to be known as the "breakfast-table" bill of 1870, claiming that it was a lower tariff. On examination it was obvious that the protected interests had not suffered at all because the major reductions in the bill were on alleged breakfast articles — tea, coffee, wines, sugar, and molasses — which did not compete with production in the United States. In spite of this stratagem, tariff dissent remained both strong and unappeased. In 1872 the Republicans made another gesture toward reform; the Tariff of 1872 provided for a horizontal reduction of 10 percent on all dutiable articles. The measure was no more than a gesture because the percentage of reduction was too small, leaving protection for major products as excessive. The following year the Panic of 1873 struck, the government soon needed revenue, and in 1875 the cut of 10 percent was quietly restored. As a result of a decade (1865–1875) of tinkering with the Tariff Bills of 1870, 1872, and 1875 the tariff remained substantially as it had been in 1865.

The tariff issue was dormant in the Administration of President Rutherford B. Hayes (1877–1881) but appeared again in the campaign of 1880 and in the Garfield-Arthur Administration that followed. In the campaign of 1880 the two major parties took their traditional stand on the tariff (the Republicans for protection and the Democrats in favor of a tariff for revenue), and the candidates made statements that indicated clearly that they knew nothing about economics and did not understand the issue. At one time during the campaign the Republican candidate, James A. Garfield, was heard to say, "Free trade can be reached only through protection." Having failed to elect civilian candidates in the past two decades, the Democrats in 1880 nominated a military man — General Winfield Scott Hancock. He had been the greatest fighting general in the Army of the Potomac; his knowledge of the tariff was minimal, if it existed at all. At one point Hancock tried to placate the fears of business and industry by stating that the tariff was a "local" rather than a national issue! Thomas Nast would draw sardonic cartoons sneering at Hancock's imposing physique ("A good man weighing two-hundred-and-forty pounds") and showing the general asking an aide, "Who is Tariff and why is he for revenue only?"

Garfield won the campaign by a whisker, less than 10,000 votes in a total of more than 9 million. His victory was shortlived; a few months after his inaugural he was mortally wounded by an assassin. His successor, Chester A. Arthur, was a spoilsman from New York whom the party never intended to be President. To the infinite surprise of all Arthur became something of a reformer, and a much better President than anyone had anticipated. Among other things there was an insistent demand for tariff reform; even protectionist Justin S. Morrill was quoted as saying, "I suppose that if the Bible has to be revised from time to time, the tariff may have to be." The chief reason for the demand was the Treasury surplus. There was a business boom in the 1880's; commencing in 1881 the surplus began to pile up in the Treasury at the rate of more than $100 million annually. This perennial surplus indicated to most people that taxes were too heavy and that money needed for business development was being kept out of circulation in government vaults of the Independent Treasury System. The Republican administrations tried to meet the problem by a policy known as "surplus financeering" — by spending excess revenue as fast as it came in. They attempted to do so by four devices: (1) early reduction of the federal debt, (2) generous pensions to veterans, (3) lavish pork-barrel legislation for internal improvements, and (4) large expenditures for the construction of a new steel navy. To the chagrin of Republicans, both the surpluses and the demand for tariff reform continued. Congress finally had to recognize it; it did so by "passing the buck" in May 1882 to a Special Tariff Commission which was packed with industrialists and whose chairman was the high-tariff lobbyist, John Lord Hayes. The commission went across the country in a special train, with industries wining and dining the members along the way. The commission's recommendation constituted a bombshell; it proposed a reduction of the tariff averaging more than 20 percent.

The only recourse for Arthur was to ask Congress to authorize the reductions. But the members of the commission did not lack shrewdness. They had received credit for a courageous report; but as lobbyists the members of the commission, and others, now descended upon Washington — and tried to defeat the very proposal that had just been made. The Democrats had captured the House in the elections of 1882, and protectionists were anxious to pass a tariff in the Republican-dominated lameduck session which would appease the populace without being as low as the Special Commission had recommended. A bill introduced by William D. Kelley was brought forward and jammed through by a coterie of brilliant leaders. Their maneuvers were successful; the Tariff of 1883 as passed by the lame-duck Congress reduced duties by only 5 percent, but cut back revenue by eliminating internal-revenue duties. When the new Congress met in December 1883 the Democrats controlled the House but found themselves unable to pass a low-tariff measure because a faction in their party formed a coalition with the Republicans against it. In this decade the dissident Democrats were from Pennsylvania rather than the South, as in later years. The rebellious faction was under the control of a high-tariff Democrat from Pennsylvania named Samuel Jackson Randall; because he controlled forty votes the group was known popularly as "Randall and his forty thieves." In 1883 there was no leader strong enough to discipline him; in 1887, however, President Cleveland would crack the whip and return the faction to the Democratic fold.

The presidential campaign of 1884 was both important and exciting —

important because it represented a revolution at the polls which brought in the first Democratic President in twenty-four years, and exciting because of the personalities involved and the closeness of the outcome. The Republicans nominated James G. Blaine, a newspaperman to whom an admirer had given the soubriquet "The Plumed Knight from Maine." In personality he was magnetic, possessed of a vivid imagination and a marvelous memory for facts, names, and faces. He was unusual as a Republican candidate in that he had not heard the whine of Confederate bullets in the Civil War; he was the first post–Civil War presidential nominee of the Grand Old Party without a battle record. But his political background in Washington was impressive; from 1863 he had served as a member of the House (for six years as Speaker), as a Senator, and as Secretary of State. The Democrats nominated Grover Cleveland, a clergyman's son who endured an early life of toil and had little formal education. He resembled Blaine in that he had no war record; he was unlike Blaine in personality and public record. In personality Cleveland was almost devoid of warmth and charm; he was brusque, unimaginative, plodding. In public record he had great knowledge and experience in local politics, knew little about the national sphere, and had never been in Washington (except for a single day) until he went there as President. Ponderous in language as well as person (he weighed over 250 pounds when inaugurated), he was one of the most independent men ever to hold office. As sheriff of Erie County in New York he had been relentless in pursuit of evildoers, and came to be known as the "Buffalo hangman." As mayor of Buffalo he achieved a reputation as the "veto mayor." As Democratic governor of New York he broke with the leader of the Democratic but corrupt Tammany Hall. Because of this rugged independence an epigram has always been associated with his name: "Public office is a public trust." Because of the same rugged independence his friends would say, "We love him most for the enemies he has made."

As it turned out the campaign, one of the most scurrilous in American history, saw Blaine's public career and Cleveland's private life besmirched. On the public side Blaine had been caught with his hands too close to the cookie jar and the country was suspicious; there was such a credibility gap that it was said that Blaine had every political asset except a reputation for honesty. Some Republicans, known as Mugwumps, were so horrified with the candidate that they bolted the party; the most prominent of this group were George William Curtis, Charles Eliot, Carl Schurz, Henry Ward Beecher, Charles Francis Adams, and Edwin L. Godkin.

It was Cleveland's private life that was attacked; as one Mugwump paper put it, the contest was one between a private immoralist and a public immoralist. Some years earlier Cleveland, who was a bachelor at the time, had known one Maria Halpin — a penniless Buffalo widow who spread her affection among a coterie of admirers, including Cleveland. Ultimately she gave birth to a child, sire unknown, but Cleveland agreed to assume the financial burden involved. The woman, who was given to drink, blackmailed him from time to time; in the end, for the child's safety, Cleveland had him removed from his mother. All this was aired in the campaign, with a Victorian profusion of detail.

The election was extremely close, turning on the vote of New York where more than a million votes were cast. Cleveland's majority in the Empire State was a meager 1,149 ballots, and on that narrowest of margins he won the Presidency. In due course Cleveland's attack on the tariff was to be spectacular and striking, but he actually knew very little about it when he took office. Carl Schurz was to testify about the President's ignorance on the issue. Shortly after his election Cleveland had asked Schurz

what big questions he ought to take up when he got to the White House. I told him I thought he ought to take up the tariff. I shall never forget what then happened. The man bent forward and buried his face in his hands on the table before him. After two or three minutes he straightened up and, with the same directness, said to me: "I am ashamed to say it, but the truth is I know nothing about the tariff. . . . Will you tell me how to go about it to learn?"

Cleveland may have known little about tariff theory but his practical sense — his sense of propriety — was outraged by two developments. One was the success of Democrat Randall and his forty thieves in defeating Democratic tariff measures. The other was the large surpluses; these were increasing — from $63 million in 1885 to $119 million in 1887. In December 1887, therefore, Cleveland devoted his entire annual address to Congress to the need for action on the tariff. In this message he observed that the two main sources of governmental income were internal-revenue taxes and the tariff. Most of the internal-revenue taxes had already been removed in the twenty years since the Civil War, except "sin taxes" on tobacco and alcoholic beverages — whose retention was supported by the public not so much for revenue as for moral effect. Reform was therefore not possible by reduction of internal-revenue duties; the tariff was the only subject for revision. The Bill of 1883 Cleveland stigmatized as the "vicious, inequitable, and illogical source of unnecessary taxation"; he added that it ought to be revised immediately. He went on to criticize trusts for maintaining high prices, and proved that the American laborer and farmer were getting very little out of the tariff. There were more than 17 million workers engaged in industry of all kinds, but only 2½ million of them were employed in the protected industries; the other 85 percent were obliged to pay higher prices on almost every necessity of life, with no compensation in increased wages. This message, a real thunderclap, cleared the air for the Democratic party — which controlled the House. A low-tariff bill (the Mills Bill) passed the House with only four Democrats — rather than the usual forty — voting against it. The Republican Senate, however, refused to pass it. Because of this impasse the tariff was to become the chief issue in the presidential campaign of 1888 — the first of two campaigns in American history in which it would be the major item of contention.

The Democrats renominated Cleveland; their platform on the tariff was a repetition of what Cleveland had said in his annual message of 1887. The Republicans nominated Benjamin Harrison, a prominent corporation lawyer and pious Presbyterian from Indiana, who was the grandson of President William Henry Harrison, the hero of Tippecanoe. The Republican platform left no doubt about its stand on protection. It read: "We are uncompromisingly in favor of the American system of protection. We protest against its destruction, as proposed by the President and his party. They serve the interests of Europe; we will support the interests of America." It is little wonder that there was a slogan in the campaign that ran, "Tippecanoe and tariff, too."

The campaign of 1888 was the first in which the tariff was the main issue; it has also been called the most corrupt election in American history. This was because the campaign of the devout Harrison was managed by the able but amoral Matthew Stanley Quay, boss of the party's machine in Philadelphia, whose manipulation of the patronage kept Pennsylvania thoroughly Republican. Curiously, he was an educated man with a passion for literature who displayed an utter contempt for ordinary political ideals and was one of the best-hated men in politics. Quay could get out the vote, by bribery and other means, and he got the manufacturers to contribute by letting them know that a high tariff was necessary for their bread and butter. Cleveland would menace their livelihood; how much would they give, asked Quay, for insurance against such a disaster as a Democratic President? Quay placed John Wanamaker, who presented a much better façade to the public, in charge of an advisory committee of businessmen. Wanamaker was the Philadelphia merchant and pioneer in the development of department stores who was both an innovative businessman and a very religious layman. In the campaign Quay and Wanamaker were engaged in what came to be called cynically, "putting businessmen over the fire and frying the fat out of them." One manufacturer gave so much that he claimed the Republicans fried out not only the fat, but part of the lean as well. No longer were officeholders expected to carry the chief burden of financing a national campaign; if businessmen felt the security of their investments depended on Republican control, they must pay a good stiff price for that assurance. Later it was not surprising that Harrison appointed a "businessman's Cabinet," with Wanamaker as Postmaster General; the connection between government and business during his administration was obvious and avowed.

Cleveland was hurt in 1888 by the "Murchison" letter and a diplomatic ass. The letter was written *ostensibly* by "Charles F. Murchison," a naturalized Englishman (in reality George A. Osgoodby, a California Republican) seeking the counsel of the British Minister in Washington, Sir Lionel Sackville-West, on how to vote in the approaching presidential election. His Lordship should have thrown the letter in the wastebasket; instead he replied, in September, intimating that "Murchison" should vote for Cleveland. The Republicans held the letter until 24 October, to ensure maximum effect just before the voting, then published it. Sackville-West was immediately handed his passports for interfering in domestic politics, but the incident cost the Democrats many Irish-American votes. The outcome of the voting was close indeed; Harrison carried the Electoral College although he received 100,000 fewer popular votes than Cleveland. The pious Harrison intoned, "Providence has given us the victory." Quay was astounded. He said, "Think of the man. He ought to know that Providence hadn't a damn thing to do with it." He added that Harrison would "never know how close a number of men were compelled to approach the gates of the penitentiary to make him President."

As soon as Harrison took office the Republicans did their best to rid themselves of the surplus. They continued to expand the steel navy. They spent money like water on payments to veterans. But the Republicans knew full well that surplus financiering dealt with symptoms rather than causes; they would have to do something about the tariff. Committed as they were to protection, there could be no lowering of it. Their problem was therefore to reduce revenue *without* reducing protection.

What seemed to be a solution was worked out by William McKinley, who was dubbed variously as "The Napoleon of Protection" and "The Advance Agent of Prosperity." The son and grandson of iron manufacturers, his family had long been protectionist in philosophy. The McKinley Tariff Act increased protection, reduced revenue, and supposedly benefited the farmer — by means of:

1. *Prohibitive duties.* Duties were raised to prohibitive levels on important commodities like cottons, woolens, iron, and steel. If the duties were high enough it was obvious there would be no imports and therefore no revenue.

2. *Reduction of internal-revenue duties.* These were further reduced by lowering the levies on tobacco and alcohol.

3. *Special provisions on raw sugar.* Revenue was further diminished by eliminating the duty on raw sugar. At the same time American producers, then chiefly in Louisiana, were given a bounty of 2¢ a pound; this took another $10 million out of the Treasury.

4. *Alleged protection for the farmer.* The McKinley Tariff made a gesture toward giving protection to the farmer by placing duties on foreign wheat, corn, potatoes, and eggs. McKinley himself said, "Let us cheerfully lend legislative assistance to the farmers." He was completely unaware of the simple economic fact that the tariff cannot lend any assistance, cheerful or otherwise, to farmers as a whole. The highly competitive American farmer does not need protection from foreign competition; his need is for a foreign market, achieved

through a low tariff which enables other countries to sell commodities here and to buy farm products with the proceeds.

The McKinley Tariff Act was pushed through Congress as the result of a bargain between western Republicans who wanted Free-Silver legislation and eastern Republicans who wanted a higher tariff. It was immensely unpopular; prices went up immediately, as did votes for Democrats; in the congressional elections in November 1890 the voters turned many Republicans out, including McKinley. It was a Democratic landslide and cost the Republicans control of the House. This meant that the tariff would again be the major issue in the presidential election of 1892. The Democrats again nominated Cleveland on a platform stating that a protective tariff was unconstitutional and denouncing the McKinley measure as "the culminating atrocity of class legislation." The Republicans renominated Harrison but without enthusiasm. Cleveland won the Presidency in 1892 because of the unpopularity of the McKinley Tariff, a large campaign fund, and the adverse effect of the Homestead Strike (see pp. 331–333) on the Republican party. For a change, in 1892, the Democrats had the largest campaign fund — $2,350,000 to the Republicans' $1,850,-000. This was because Quay did not manage Harrison's campaign, and because William C. Whitney did manage that of Cleveland. After Harrison's election in 1888 Quay had told the President that if he wanted to be reelected he had better make his appointments with an eye toward getting out the vote. The religious President replied, "I owe my election to God and prayer." Said Quay, "Well, you can trust to someone else for your votes in the next election. I'm through." Whitney was a plutocrat and Democrat who (according to Matthew Josephson) divided his time between the breeding of horses and the breeding of monopolies in whiskey, tobacco, and traction lines. He figured that if the Republicans could levy on manufacturers, he could tap the bankers. So he organized a committee of bankers of Democratic persuasion, whose chairman was August Belmont, and this group asked bankers to contribute (Josephson also believes that, as a result, Cleveland became more conservative in his second administration). The public appeared to be on labor's side in the Homestead Strike; in 1890 Carnegie had asked for an increase in the tariff on steel in order to maintain the high standard of American living and now, two years after he got it and in a period of prosperity, ordered a wage reduction. The Republicans, worried about the effect on the campaign, tried unsuccessfully to convince Carnegie and Henry Clay Frick to restore the wage cut and to end the strike; their failure undoubtedly cost Harrison many votes from a public that was shocked by the pitched battle in July 1892 between company guards and laborers at Homestead, in which ten were killed and sixty wounded.

The Republicans lost the lower branch of Congress in 1890; with Cleveland reelected in 1892 and a working majority in the Senate, it appeared that the Democrats were in a position to redeem their campaign pledge to reduce the tariff. Because of the Panic of 1893 and the depression that followed, the purpose of the reform measure, the Wilson Act, was the opposite of McKinley's in 1890: to increase the revenue, but to decrease protection. The bill which passed the House accomplished this in three provisions:

1. The free list was increased by adding basic raw materials essential to manufacturing and construction (for example, lumber, wool, sugar, and iron ore). This would enable manufacturers to reduce costs, and thus justify a corresponding reduction in their protection. For this reason —

2. Protective duties were generally lowered.

3. To compensate for anticipated loss in revenue, new internal-revenue duties were placed on liquor, tobacco, and luxuries — and an income tax was added at the basic rate of 2 percent on all incomes over $4,000. The income tax was to be the price paid for Populist support of the bill.

The Wilson Bill went to the Senate, where it was decimated. The Democrats had a small but precarious majority; a change of five votes would bring the Republicans back into control and the Senate of the 1890's was constituted in such a way that a change of five votes was extremely likely. The Senate of the 1890's represented big business; it had in it twenty-five millionaires, elected by controlled legislatures. Its members really stood for economic rather than geographic units. As examples, one stood for the Union Pacific Railroad and one for the New York Central, there was another stalwart for the insurance companies, a whole group represented the Southern Pacific, coal and iron had support from Senators in the Midwest, and cotton had half a dozen Senators.*

With this background it is possible to understand why the Senate added 634 amendments to the Wilson Bill, changing it completely. The central point is that most of the Senators — Democratic as well as Republican — favored a high tariff, at least for the products from their states. The Senate removed many of the articles from the free list and restored many duties to the levels of the McKinley Act; only the income tax and internal-revenue duties remained unchanged. This Senate bill, completely altered from the original Wilson measure, went back to the House, which finally accepted it after a bitter fight. Cleveland was furious and called the Senate's action "party perfidy and party dishonor," but there was nothing he could do. If he vetoed the bill, the nation would return to the higher (50 percent) McKinley Act of 1890, still in force. The result was that Cleve-

---

* Seventy years later, in 1968, the Associated Press estimated that one out of every five Senators were millionaires. By that year the aircraft industry was so important in the military-industrial complex that the state of Washington, where the Boeing Company was centered, was of extraordinary significance. There were those, therefore, who renamed the two representatives of that state in the Upper House of Congress the "Senators from Boeing."

land allowed the Wilson-Gorman Tariff Act of 1894 to become law without his signature; it lowered the scale of duties to a disappointing 40 percent.

The Panic of 1893 ruined Cleveland in his second administration, just as similar economic paroxysms destroyed Van Buren in 1840 and Hoover in 1932. The Republicans therefore looked forward to the campaign of 1896, particularly Mark Hanna, who intended to elect William McKinley President — and did. McKinley was born to a faith in a high tariff, but even if his parentage had been different, he had so many financial commitments and obligations by the time he became President that it would have been necessary for him to support protection. McKinley was so lovable and trusting by nature that he endorsed too many notes for an old friend in Youngstown (Ohio), banker Robert L. Walker. When Walker failed during the Panic of 1893, McKinley was caught for the payment of $130,000. This was considerably more money than he had and Hanna had to bail him out; McKinley was eternally grateful. Hanna had a reason, as he always did. After McKinley's defeat for Congress in 1890 Hanna had seen to it in 1891 that he (McKinley) was elected to the governorship of Ohio; Hanna was grooming him for the Presidency in 1896. But when McKinley and Walker were caught without funds in 1893, McKinley had talked about withdrawing from politics and going back to the private practice of law. This would upset Hanna's time schedule; he wanted McKinley reelected as governor of Ohio in 1893, to finish his term in 1895, and to run for President in 1896. In the critical year 1893, therefore, McKinley's great and good friend leaped to the rescue. Hanna took complete charge of the governor's tangled finances. He called together men of purse and property — bankers, iron and steel magnates, railroad owners, industrialists — who had benefited from McKinley's labors in promoting the protective tariff. This secret pool or syndicate subscribed the full amount of McKinley's obligations. Its members were John Hay (soon to be Secretary of State), Andrew Carnegie, Henry Clay Frick of Homestead fame, Myron T. Herrick (an Ohio banker, governor, and future ambassador), and Samuel Mather (an Ohio shipping magnate and industrialist).

Hanna succeeded in electing McKinley in the campaign of 1896 (see pp. 190–196), largely on the free-silver issue. The tariff was played down, but as soon as McKinley was inaugurated he called a special session of Congress to deal with the tariff. The reasons were obvious: pressure from protected interests who had contributed heavily in 1896 and falling revenue because of the depression that followed the Panic of 1893. The result was the Dingley Bill of 1897, named after Nelson Dingley of Maine, which raised the tariff to its highest level to that time, averaging 57 percent. Interestingly, in the first year of its operation, because many rates were prohibitive, the hoped-for increase of revenue was not realized — in fact it declined by more than $25 million. During the next decade, between the passage of the Dingley measure in 1897 and the campaign of 1908, the tariff was shelved; the public forgot about it because of the prosperity of the country, the issues surrounding imperialism brought in by the Spanish-American War, and the distraction of loud trust-busting by TR. There is also no question that Roosevelt sidestepped the tariff while he was President, from 1901 to 1909; he did not choose to devote any of his superabundant energy to the issue.

By contrast the tariff was to plague William Howard Taft, who succeeded TR as President from 1909 to 1913. By 1908 it was obvious that it would be an issue in the presidential election of that year because of the aftermath of the Panic of 1907 and because of the fear of trusts. In 1896 the Republicans had billed protectionist William McKinley as the "Advance Agent of Prosperity," in 1900 they had praised the tariff as the fount of national blessings, and in 1904 they had said the Dingley Act was responsible for prosperity. Now in 1908 there were bread lines and free soup kitchens. Certainly the Republicans could not use the "prosperity" theme in 1908; they could no longer associate the high tariff with the "full dinner pail." Fear of trusts had been engendered by TR himself. This feeling introduced protective duties as an issue in the campaign because of the widespread belief that the tariff was the "mother of trusts." In any case, the Democrats nominated William Jennings Bryan, running unsuccessfully for the Presidency for the third and last time, on a platform calling for a low tariff. The Republicans nominated Taft, and recognized the demand for tariff reform by saying that they too were in favor of revision. They wanted a "scientific" tariff, based on the difference between the costs at home and abroad, with a reasonable profit to American industry. Whether this meant that the tariff would go up or down was not clear in the platform, but the country interpreted it to mean revision downward; in actual fact, during the campaign, Bryan forced Taft to say that it meant revision downward. Few noted that the Republican plan, carried to its logical conclusion, would have meant no foreign trade at all — except in minerals that are completely nonexistent in this country. Even cocoa, coffee, and bananas could be grown in the United States, at a price ten, twenty, or thirty times what it would cost to import them; the Republican "scientific" tariff, however, was to be based on the difference between costs at home and abroad. Such a tariff would constitute a fundamental violation of the economic principle of comparative cost (see p. 547), but that is what the Republican platform on the tariff really meant, if logically analyzed.

In the elections of 1908 the Republicans won the Presidency and both Houses of Congress. The country got ready for a substantially lower tariff, and was to be deceived. After his inauguration Taft called Congress in special session (in March 1909) to consider tariff revision. The House Ways and Means Committee was headed by Sereno Elisha Payne, a Republican from New York who had helped draft the protectionist McKinley and Dingley acts. Nonetheless he carried out what he considered to be the pledges made in the presidential campaign. The Payne Bill, which passed the House, provided for sizable reductions on dutiable goods, expanded the free list, and included a progressive tax on inheritances.

The bill then went to the Senate. Chairman of the Finance Committee there was Nelson Wilmarth Aldrich, the leading spokesman in the nation for big business and the Establishment in the Republican party. With Aldrich in control the Senate added 847 amendments which changed the bill completely, including the elimination of the inheritance tax. Before this revised measure passed the Senate, however, that body witnessed and heard the greatest debate on the tariff in U.S. history. Republican Senators from the West refused to follow Aldrich and the Administration; the leading insurgents, all of them effective orators, were Robert La Follette of Wisconsin, Albert J. Beveridge of Indiana, and Albert B. Cummins and Jonathan P. Dolliver — both from Iowa. Under Dolliver's direction they divided the schedules among themselves for exhaustive study; for example, Cummins took steel, La Follette was responsible for wool, and Dolliver himself had cotton. They worked so hard that Beveridge commented that "every insurgent seriously impaired his eyesight during the session"; Dolliver so spent himself that he died shortly after the "Great Debate" was finished. To combat such careful research Aldrich and the conservative Republicans were not prepared. They had written the Aldrich Bill on data supplied to them by the specific industries protected; in fact the statistician of the National Association of Wool Manufacturers at one time had a desk in Aldrich's Senate office. Aldrich and his collaborators had never studied the schedules so provided them by industry; they now found it necessary to hire experts, in an endeavor to have their own bill explained. This situation obviously made a farce of the "scientific" tariff that the Republicans had stressed in the presidential campaign of 1908.

In spite of this thorough exposure the Senate passed the Aldrich Bill by a vote of 47 to 31 — with seven Republicans voting with Democrats against the measure; the House then accepted the Senate amendments. This raised the question as to what the President would do; he had said that he would veto any bill that did not provide for genuine downward revision. The Payne-Aldrich Tariff Act now submitted to him was patently a protective measure; there were a few reductions, but the average rate on dutiable goods was almost the same as under the Dingley Act. After some study Taft not only signed the act but made the gratuitous comment that it was the best tariff bill that the Republican party had ever passed. As a consequence the Republicans lost the House in 1910, and in 1912 lost both Houses of Congress and the Presidency! The McKinley and Payne-Aldrich bills had produced identical results.

In the presidential campaign of 1912 the Republicans were split between Taft and TR, with the result that the election of Democrat Wood-row Wilson was assured. Both Republican candidates favored a "scientific" tariff, with planks similar to that in 1908; on this economic issue TR, who liked to consider himself a progressive, was anything but progressive. The Democrats referred to the protective tariff as unconstitutional and favored immediate downward revision, but admitted that reductions should be gradual to allow industry ample time for readjustment. On this and other issues they won the Presidency and both Houses of Congress. Wilson summoned Congress in special session in April 1913, just as McKinley and Taft had done. The special session in 1913, however, was to consider trusts and the money system as well as the tariff. Wilson took the aggressive and appeared before Congress personally to deliver his message. It was the first time a President had done so since 1801.

Oscar Underwood of Alabama was chairman of the House Ways and Means Committee, wrote the low-tariff measure of 1913, and gave it his name. Underwood was a man of high character and unflagging industry, was a devout follower of Thomas Jefferson who worried about the extension of federal authority, and was courageous to the point of taking stands which would bring his own defeat. He was prominent enough to be included among the leading contenders for the Democratic presidential nomination in 1912, and again in 1924 — when he failed to get the nomination because of his uncompromising hostility to the Ku Klux Klan and national prohibition, both popular at the time, particularly in Alabama's South. In 1913, Underwood's low-tariff bill went to the Senate. There the lobby applied pressure to change the measure into a high-tariff one, as had occurred in 1894 and 1910. At this point President Wilson exercised executive leadership of a kind that had never been witnessed before. He announced that lobbyists were so thick in the capital that one could not throw a brick in any direction without hitting one, he denounced the group as the "Third House of Congress," and he told its members to get out of Washington. So stern was his warning that the capital was emptied overnight. For once the pressure groups, accustomed to working in the secrecy of committee meetings, were forced into the open.

The Underwood Tariff was a moderate one, reducing rates to a general average of 27 percent and putting iron, steel, raw wool, and sugar on the free list. To make up for loss of revenue it made provision for a small graduated tax on incomes — 1 percent of all incomes in excess of $3,000 with a surtax beginning at $20,000 and going as high as 6 percent on incomes above $500,000. This was now possible under the Sixteenth Amendment to the Constitution, ratified in 1913. Although it was in effect for eight years (1913–1921) the Underwood Act, except for the income tax, was never really tested because World War I began ten months after its passage. As a result, industries which had been catering to world markets were now diverted to the supplying of armies and navies. Imports, except in war materials, dropped off — as did foreign competition with American industry.

The tariff played a minor part in the campaign of 1920; this was a blessing for Warren G. Harding, who was not required to expose too much of his blissful ignorance of the issue. As it was, on one occasion he was heard to say, "The United States should adopt a protective tariff of such a character as will help the struggling industries of Europe to get on their feet." Nonetheless the mood of the country was protectionist, as it emerged from a war that had not ended wars and had not made the world safe for democracy. The American public was isolationist and nationalist; it wanted to "Buy American" in a return to what Harding called "Normalcy." In the period of the War of 1812, when foreign goods were cut off, new domestic industries sprang up; they demanded and got protection when peace came. In the 1920's manufacturers of articles (particularly chemicals) formerly obtained from Germany had been given opportunity to develop with little competition. It came soon after the Armistice, when the United States was flooded with imports; the "war babies," the new designation for infant industries, demanded and got protection. The old argument of maintaining employment and the high standard of American living was revived; Senator Robert N. Stanfield of Oregon boasted that he would favor duties up to 5,000 percent if necessary to equalize costs, because it "would pay the American people to be kept employed." To all of these arguments was added the old Hamiltonian one of economic self-sufficiency; it was claimed that there was a military reason for bolstering the coal-tar and chemical industries, which were valuable for explosives and poison gas in time of war.

The result was high protection under the Fordney-McCumber Act of 1922 and the Hawley-Smoot measure of 1930. Senator Porter J. McCumber of North Dakota and Representative Joseph W. Fordney, a lumberman from Michigan, were both closing a quarter century of service on the Senate Finance and the House Ways and Means committees. The chief features of the tariff act of 1922 were its effective high duties and its ineffective flexibility clause. The tariff rates were the highest in U.S. history, with increases ranging from 60 to 400 percent on some commodities. The flexibility clause represented another futile attempt to make the tariff "scientific." It gave the President the power, on recommendation of the Tariff Commission, to raise or lower duties up to 50 percent, if this was deemed necessary to compensate for the difference between foreign and U.S. costs of production. As Professor Fred Shannon once observed, this was "sheer trumpery since the cost of production, hidden as it is by false capitalization and other camouflage, cannot even be determined for American goods, much less for foreign." The supposedly nonpartisan Tariff Commission had been established in 1916 and had begun its operations impressively under Frank W. Taussig, the economist from Harvard and leading authority on the tariff who served as its chairman from 1917 to 1919. During the 1920's, unfortunately, the commission became a political football; far from taking the tariff out of politics it put the issue directly into the political arena. Under the flexibility clause in the seven-year period (1922–1929), Presidents Harding and Coolidge proclaimed thirty-seven changes; thirty-two of these were increases, including important and expensive ones for the consumer on sugar and iron. Duties were lowered on five products: mill feeds, bobwhite quail, paint-brush handles, cresylic acid, and phenol!

The Hawley-Smoot Tariff Act of 1930 was not only the highest in U.S. history, raising duties above these of the excessive Fordney-McCumber Act; it was also one of the most controversial measures ever passed by the Congress. In spite of considerable opposition — a thousand economists petitioned the President to veto it and the head of General Motors and the American Bankers' Association denounced the bill — the Hawley-Smoot Act passed the Congress because of pressures from an effective lobby and from the President of the United States.

President Hoover chose to ignore the economists, the exporters, the bankers, and the consumer. Quincy Howe has observed that when the chips were down he listened to the professional and conservative Republican politicians, who asked him to apply the traditional Republican remedy for all economic ills — a higher tariff. As a result, the President signed the bill and reaped the whirlwind. Among those defeated for reelection in 1932 were Willis C. Hawley, Reed Smoot, and Herbert Hoover.*

The Hawley-Smoot measure has been referred to as "an act of unparalleled protective ferocity"; it had immediate results on foreign trade, the gold standard, and U.S. investments abroad. The act aroused deep resentment abroad; within two years twenty-five nations had established retaliatory tariffs and foreign trade, already declining, slumped still further. From 1929 to 1932 imports into the United States fell from $4.3 to $1.3 billion; in the same years U.S. exports fell from $5.2 to $1.6 billion. Because of lack of either dollars or gold to meet her commitments England was forced off the gold standard, and other nations followed. It is little wonder that Sir Arthur Salter, the British economist, said of the Hawley-

---

* It will be recalled that manufacturers' lobbyists had played a major role in writing the Payne-Aldrich Tariff Act of 1910. This was repeated in the drafting of the Hawley-Smoot measure, and resulted dramatically in the censure by the Senate of Hiram Bingham, Republican of Connecticut — only the fourth Senator to be so censured by that body in almost a century and a half of its existence. Bingham admitted that he had engaged and had paid an employee of the Connecticut Manufacturers' Association as an adviser on the Hawley-Smoot measure, then pending. The Senate resolved that Bingham's action, "while not the result of corrupt motives," was "contrary to good morals and senatorial ethics and tends to bring the Senate into dishonor and disrepute, and such conduct is hereby condemned." Bingham was defeated for reelection in 1932. The fifth and next Senator to be censured was Joseph R. McCarthy of Wisconsin in 1954.

Smoot measure, "The ratification of that tariff was a turning point in world history." And so it was. As far as U.S. investments abroad were concerned, nations found it impossible to pay because they lacked either dollars or gold. The intergovernmental war debts became "were" debts, and the loss to private individuals and corporations in the United States was comparable and colossal. The loss of "were" debts (without interest) was $10 billion, the loss on the private side was almost $17 billion.

Since the Hawley-Smoot measure of 1930 there have been significant developments which have reduced the tariff markedly; they are the Trade Agreements Act of 1934, and the establishment of GATT (the General Agreement on Tariffs and Trade). The Trade Agreements Act of 1934, passed as a New Deal measure, is normally associated with the name of Cordell Hull — the only Secretary of State whose name has been prominently linked with an important tariff. This was unexpected for a statesman from the backwoods of Tennessee who would become the No. 1 internationalist in the United States of his day. Hull had first gone to Congress in 1906 and represented his state there almost continuously until 1933 when he became Secretary of State — to serve in the Cabinet from 1933 to 1944. In Congress, most of his service was in the House of Representatives, where he had the reputation as a great authority on all tax measures, including the tariff and income taxes. He had a slight lisp that increased his air of harmless benevolence. There was a Washington rendition of his most famous maxim: "We must eliminate these twade baa-huhs heah, theah, and ev'ywheah." When in a temper he would use the name of the Deity, which came out as "Cwist." FDR would note this anger and would occasionally comment that Hull was in a "Cwist" mood today.

Hull's Trade Agreements Act of 1934 was an amendment to the Hawley-Smoot Act, which still remains the basic law of the land, considerably amended (by 1970 the Hawley-Smoot Act had been law for forty years, longer than any other tariff in the history of the United States). The Trade Agreements Act authorized the President (for three years) to negotiate bilateral trade agreements *without* the advice and consent of the Senate, and in these agreements to raise or lower tariffs by not more than 50 percent. This act has been extended twelve times; in 1945 and 1962 the President was given authority to make reductions of an additional 50 percent, and in 1955 still another reduction of 15 percent was permitted. Such longevity is remarkable for a trade agreements act which Senator Vandenberg of Michigan characterized in 1934, at the time of its passage, as "fascist in its philosophy, fascist in its objective." The results have been spectacular. By 1951 agreements had been concluded with fifty-three nations with which the United States conducted more than 80 percent of its normal foreign trade. Because of the most-favored-nation clause (the provision in commercial treaties stating that the signatory will enjoy benefits equal to those accorded to any other state), the bilateral treaties signed by the United States actually became multilateral. Other nations therefore benefited; by the highly unsatisfactory but common index of total dutiable imports, the U.S. level of duties had fallen from 60 percent in 1931 to 37 percent in 1939 to 11 percent in 1967. An example of such a bilateral treaty, with multilateral effect, was the one signed by the United States and Switzerland in 1936. Switzerland reduced her tariffs on lard, prunes, and office machines, which the United States sold there in significant quantities. The United States reduced duties on various kinds of watch movements; as a result consumption and purchase of watches in the United States quadrupled in the next sixteen years. All this sounds most encouraging to advocates of international trade, but a warning must be sounded. There have been great reductions, but duties on 3,500 commodities remain in effect in the United States. Many of them are prohibitive. There are 500 rates that stand at 50 percent or more, those on coal-tar dyes can run to 300 and 400 percent, and those on certain watch parts are as high as 800 percent.

In the 1920's and 1930's world trade, important to the prosperity of all nations and the life blood for many, had dried to a trickle. Hoping to protect themselves against depression many nations, between the two wars, had erected high tariffs and other barriers against imports. The actual result was to make the Depression worse for everybody. At the end of World War II statesmen of all leading countries were determined not to let this happen again. They envisaged three institutions to bring world economic disarmament: the IMF (International Monetary Fund), the World Bank (actually the International Bank for Reconstruction and Development), and ITO (the International Trade Organization). The first two were quickly ratified, but ITO was stillborn; only Liberia ratified it without reservations. Because agreement on a permanent charter for ITO promised to drag on, the United States called for an immediate effort at tariff agreement through reciprocal tariff concessions. Out of these negotiations there emerged in 1948, as a temporary measure, the General Agreement on Tariffs and Trade — a specialized agency of the United Nations. Usually known as GATT, it is sometimes designated as the "Little ITO." Its opponents call it illegitimate. In GATT conferences bilateral agreements are negotiated; these are binding on all through the most-favored-nation clauses. The concessions granted on this "round-robin" basis are then incorporated into a "package" agreement accepted by all participating nations. There have been six of these major GATT conferences since the first in 1947–1948, when representatives of twenty-three nations met in Geneva to negotiate reciprocal tariff concessions. The sixth, also at Geneva, was the famous "Kennedy Round" which began in 1963 and became effective in 1968; the eighteen participating nations agreed to reduce tariffs by 35 percent over a period of five years. For a temporary organization the achievements of GATT have been remarkable. Although forces other than lower tariffs have been a factor in the growth of world trade, the reduction of import duties has certainly had a stimulating effect. As expressed in terms of exports, world trade has grown from $57 billion in 1948 to more than $200 billion in 1967 — close to a fourfold increase in twenty years.

Beyond the inflation which has priced the United States out of many markets, four new practices have contributed to the decline of foreign trade since 1930. One is a limitation on the operation of the Trade Agreements Act through what are known as peril-point and escape clauses. The remaining three practices would be classified as nontariff barriers to trade: the establishment of quotas, the Buy-American Act of 1933, and the complexity of customs regulations.

The peril-point clause, first included in the extension by a Republican Congress of the Trade Agreements Act in 1948, attempted to limit the power of the President in making bilateral treaties *before* he had signed them. It required the Tariff Commission to investigate products under negotiation for reciprocal trading, and to inform the President of the maximum concession that could be made without causing or threatening *serious injury* to a domestic industry. If the President did grant a concession beyond that peril point, he was required to explain the reason for doing so to Congress. The escape clause, added for the first time in 1951, authorized the President — again on recommendation of the Tariff Commission — to withdraw or modify a concession *after* the treaty had been signed, if the concession caused or threatened, once again, *serious injury* to a domestic industry. The escape clause had a considerable nuisance value because a number of "interested parties" demanded investigations; to the cognoscenti a "serious injury" was usually one suffered by an industry with a strong lobby.

Beyond this nuisance value, the general effect of these clauses was to stifle international trade. While an investigation by the Tariff Commission was under way, foreign exporters of the articles were stymied as far as future marketing plans were concerned. Actually the peril-point and escape clauses resulted in very few increases in the tariff on specific commodities because the Tariff Commission has seldom agreed with the "interested parties," and even when it did, the President usually refused to accept the recommendation. But in the few cases where the President did accept the recommendation, the international repercussions were loud and retaliatory. This applied particularly to the action taken by President Eisenhower against British bicycles and Swiss watches, and by President Kennedy against Belgian rugs. The action against Swiss watches was unusual because President Eisenhower issued it on the ground that the domestic watch industry should be protected because precision workers were needed for defense. This was a real "come-on" which other industries were quick to follow. On the basis of "defense essentiality":

lace manufacturers could claim that they made military mosquito nets;
wool glove manufacturers could claim that they made soldiers' gloves;
cutlery manufacturers could claim that they made military machetes;
tuna-fish producers could contend that their fleet was needed in time of war; and
lead-pencil manufacturers could claim that their product was essential for defense, in order to maintain the flow of paper turned out by the bureaucracy that dominates every large institution, including the Pentagon.

A quota is not a tariff, but it can be more effective than one in limiting foreign trade. A quota is an embargo against imports of a specific commodity, based on a percentage of total consumption of that product within the United States. In various and recent acts, Congress has authorized the President to impose quotas on agricultural products and on items deemed important for defense purposes. In 1959 President Eisenhower, acting allegedly in the interest of national defense, imposed mandatory import quotas amounting to approximately 12 percent of domestic production on low-priced crude oil and other petroleum products. It was claimed that, in the event of some future war, the United States should not be in a position of relying on foreign-produced oil.* This constraint on the growth of total supply raised petroleum prices and pleased domestic companies by compelling consumers to pay billions more than they would in a genuinely free market. In 1969 oil in the United States was selling for a little more than $3 a barrel; on the international market the price had dropped as low as $1.20 a barrel; the cost of import quotas to the consumer ranged somewhere between $4 and $7 billion a year. By the same year, by reason of these quotas and tax favoritism through the depletion allowance, the U.S. petroleum industry had been transformed into what one economist described as a "government-created cartel . . . a honeycomb of artificial restraints, privilege, and monopoly." By reason of the quota alone the cost of fuel oil was inflated in the United States by about 4¢ per gallon, the cost of gasoline by 5¢. The car owner who bought 700 gallons of gas a year, which was about the average, paid approximately $35 in overcharges. Families who heated their homes with oil

---

* The proponents of the national-defense argument make a mockery of their own argument by pressing for restrictions against *all* foreign oil, including that from neighboring Canada and Mexico. Neither is separated from this country by water, and neither is likely to become an enemy of this nation. The national-defense argument also ignores the fact that there are much cheaper methods of assuring adequate reserves of oil. The *New York Times* has observed that "the best national reserve is oil left underground, and the present policy of keeping prices artificially high works at cross-purposes to such a reserve by providing great incentive to deplete the nation's remaining oil stocks as rapidly as possible." (Editorial, "Unneeded Import Quota," *NY Times*, 16 August 1969.)

lost $59. Senator Philip Hart, whose Judiciary subcommittee made an extensive study of oil import quotas, wondered out loud why no one was upset by an oil quota that had cost the United States at least $50 billion in its first decade — more than the ABM. Beyond the cost to the consumer, American labor also faced potential losses because of the quota. The petrochemical industry opposed the oil quota and asked for cheap oil to make its synthetic fibers, plastics, and other products. If companies like Dow, Du Pont, and Union Carbide did not get enough oil at low and competitive prices they proposed to proceed with plans for overseas plants — which would mean that they would be exporting both factories and jobs. The old economic law of comparative cost (see p. 547) can be frustrated by import quotas, but only at the expense of diminishing world trade and of sacrificing the long-term interest of both American workers and consumers.

The same excessive cost has also resulted from quotas on agricultural commodities. Legislation has provided protection where foreign products can be sold at such a low price as to endanger the price-support program for U.S. farmers. These quotas have been economically absurd because they mean that in addition to costly domestic price supports, the U.S. government must help further by embargoing certain products. Nonetheless in past years the Secretary of Agriculture has imposed restrictions against Canadian, Swiss, and Danish cheese — and against Canadian, New Zealand, and Australian butter. The most spectacular example of an agricultural quota is that on sugar. This restricts imports of approximately half of U.S. consumption, basically because U.S. domestic production of sugar is approximately half of the sugar consumed in this country. During the past two decades the world price of sugar has generally been around 2¢ a pound, give or take a little. At this price, U.S. domestic sugar producers, particularly those involved in beet sugar, cannot compete. For this reason, the price in the United States has been elevated in two ways:

For domestic sugar, the Department of Agriculture has fixed a support price at 6.4¢ a pound, approximately three times the world price. This means, with markups which increase geometrically, that the American consumer pays about 12¢ a pound.

In buying from abroad, under the quota as established, the United States was paying in 1969 a premium of 5¢ a pound; the quota was bought at 7¢ in an assured market, while the free international price was 2¢ a pound in a glutted world market. It is apparent, under such a system, that the numerous tropical countries with the cane-sugar surpluses which they endure, have lobbied with vigor for a favored part of the limited U.S. sugar market — assigned by country and by tonnage.

The total cost to the American consumer for such a system, archaic for economic if not for political reasons, is estimated at about $700 million a year — above what the consumer would pay in a free market if a country devoted to free enterprise really had a free market. It has been apparent for more than half a century that there is no excuse for raising tropical sugar in the United States, except to subsidize a powerful lobby. In this area it would appear to many that if anyone needs protection, it is the consumer — not the sugar lobby.

The Buy-American Act was passed in 1933 in the heart of the Depression, when American industry could ill afford to lose a single order; in actual fact it was enacted by the lame-duck 72nd Congress, and was signed by President Hoover the day before he went out of office in 1933. It provides that the U.S. government must purchase for its own use only domestic goods or materials, but gives the President discretion to make foreign purchases if the cost of domestic products — by contrast with foreign ones — is unreasonably high. There has been considerable argument as to the meaning of "unreasonably high"; for twenty years it was administratively defined that the differential must be at least 25 percent, otherwise U.S. goods would be purchased. In 1955 President Eisenhower revised the long-standing administrative rule. He said that the normal differential was to be 6 percent, unless the company involved was in a labor-surplus area, where the differential was doubled to 12 percent. There was another loophole. A department head was permitted to award contracts to domestic firms, no matter how low the foreign bids were, if he believed it to be in the "public interest" to do so. From this point it was apparent that the purchase of foreign products by the U.S. government would be an exercise in administrative grace.

The controversy over the meaning of "public interest" has been perennial — from the bitterly disputed electrical-equipment cases for the Chief Joseph Dam in the mid-1950's that resulted in a relatively liberal policy, to the directive of President Johnson a decade later barring all foreign bidders for three huge turbine generators at Grand Coulee Dam. Opponents of the Buy-American policy fall into three categories: freetraders, taxpayers, and foreign companies and countries. Freetraders point out that such legislation is a violation of the economic theory of comparative costs. Taxpayers are losers because the deficit-ridden federal government has to pay millions of dollars more for American-made equipment. Foreign companies and countries note derisively that the United States does not really mean what it says about the virtues of free enterprise. On the other hand support for the Buy-American principle has come from nationalists, many ambitious Congressmen, and worriers about the balance-of-payments problem. It would be absurd to expect chauvinists to support a Buy-Foreign act. Congressmen want orders for plants in their districts, and will forego principle to get them. There was a query to a member of the House of Representatives: "Are you a protectionist?" The reply was direct and pragmatic: "No — but I am a survivalist!" Recently those concerned about the balance-of-payments problem have supported every policy that will keep American dollars at home — even though, in the long run, it would be self-defeating because of retaliation.

A designed complexity of customs regulations is closely associated, together with quotas and Buy-American Acts, as the third in a series of effective nontariff barriers to international trade. The complexity of customs regulations is costly to foreigners in many ways: time, classification of goods, sanitary codes, valuations. Time in transit is the equivalent of money; many goods now require a longer period to pass through U.S. customs than it took Columbus to discover America. An exasperating classification system is employed in the United States, so mystifying that the exporter does not know until many months after the event under what category his products may be classified for customs purposes. So outmoded and wild is this system in certain aspects, that the *Journal of Commerce* once observed that a shipment of Ping-Pong balls might actually be classified as ammunition. As long ago as 1913 a colossal controversy occurred over a sculptor, then relatively unknown, named Constantin Brancusi; his work appeared to be a strange assortment of polished metal and marble. The customs official decided that it was not art, which could enter the country duty-free; it belonged, he said, in the category of "kitchen utensils and hospital supplies" — dutiable at 40 percent of its value. Twelve years later Brancusi, who had achieved an international reputation by that time, won a delayed and costly lawsuit against the New York customs officials for their decision. If Brancusi was perplexed, so are the importers of musical instruments. The duty on a piano is 20 percent; on a harpsichord it is 40 percent. Musicians swear that the harpsichord is the ancestor of the piano, but get nowhere. To the customs officials it is a stringed instrument similar to a violin, on which the duty is 40 percent — and that is what is charged.

Sanitary regulations imposed by the customs service, perhaps in relation to Argentine beef and other products, may sometimes be used to exclude products that are more competitive than contaminated. Arguments over valuations go on *ad infinitum*, and always will. By now the most renowned of all obstructive valuation procedures is the American Selling Price (ASP), under which certain chemicals are evaluated at an artificially high price. In the early 1920's, when the United States had what it considered to be an "infant" chemical industry, a special system of protection was established for dyestuffs and other chemicals made from coal tar. The ASP is a system of valuing imports for duty purposes at such a high and artificial rate that it results in an exceptionally high tariff. It has been the justified target of European wrath for years. The American customs officer levies a high-percentage duty not on the price of the import but on the prevailing domestic price for the product, which in the case of chemicals is much higher. This means, as an example, that if a Swiss chemical company offers product X for sale at $1 an ounce, but the price of the same product in the United States is $4 or even $10, the tariff would be calculated on the higher U.S. price. Repeal of the ASP was one of Europe's major targets in the Kennedy Round of the 1960's. This was awkward because the ASP is a law enacted by Congress, and the U.S. chemical lobby was powerful enough to block its repeal.

The European Economic Community is a present-day version of the much older U.S. Common Market. The chief architects of the U.S. Common Market were the Fathers of the American Constitution, who came close to solving the problem of recurrent strife that had been endured in the colonial period of U.S. history. The visionary realist who was the "Father" of the European Common Market was Jean Monnet, who had long since decided that recurrent wars there — in 1871, 1914, and 1939 — could be prevented only by the same kind of economic and political unification. The European Common Market came into existence in 1957 when the "Six" (Germany, France, Italy, Belgium, the Netherlands, and Luxembourg) signed the Treaty of Rome; at that time Paul Henri Spaak, the distinguished Belgian statesman who was Secretary-General of NATO, observed that "March 25, 1957, is from a European point of view as important a date as July 14, 1789." By mid-1968 the Six had eliminated all tariff duties against each other and had brought external tariffs against other countries to a common average under 11 percent — lower than the U.S. or British level. The result in Europe was that trade tripled in the decade from 1957 to 1967. A greatly expanded home market had produced the same result in Europe as in the United States; it acted as an inciter and cap pistol to set off a number of economic explosions, creating a chain reaction which benefited the economy as a whole. There was one great difference. The United States in the early stages of its development was not engaged, as were the European Six in 1960, in a $44-billion annual trade with the rest of the world. In the 1790's the elimination of *inside* tariffs in the United States had little immediate effect on the rest of the world. In the 1960's the elimination of *inside* tariffs in western Europe could have a considerable effect on other nations.

The major strain between the United States and the European Economic Community, in its first decade, concerned agricultural surpluses. Both areas suffer from them as a result of staggering sums spent in the support of agriculture; in 1970, for dairy products alone, the Common Market laid out almost $1 billion — much of it for butter that had to be put in cold storage because no one wanted it. The central fact is that agriculture is up to its neck in politics in the nations of both groups, a reflection of the comment once made by German Chancellor Ludwig Erhard: "In agriculture, all nations are sinners." In the Common Market France is the most important and efficient farm producer, Germany the most inefficient; the Market has therefore been, in many ways, a bargain between French agriculture and German industry. All Common Market farmers receive subsidies from a community fund financed by levies on imports plus direct contributions from member states; this is of some importance because there are four times as many people dependent on agriculture in the EEC as there are in the United States. In the Common Market the Germans pay the most into the agricultural fund and the French get the most out of it. On the industrial side, by contrast, the tables are turned; the Germans have a much more efficient industrial plant than the French. In essence the Common Market enables France to sell the bulk of her basic food (wheat and meat) to the other five — protected by a tariff which keeps these products from coming in from Canada, Australia, New Zealand, Argentina, and the United States. In return Germany primarily, but also the other four nations in the EEC, have the privilege of free trade for their industrial products within France. Walter Lippmann sees this reciprocal Franco-German relation as comparable with that in the United States. He contends that the United States has been a common market in which there was an economic compact between the industrial Northeast and the agricultural South and West. Whether this analogy is exact, the agricultural situation in the EEC presents a perplexing problem for the United States.

With staggering farm surpluses and a burdensome farm-support program, the United States can ill afford to lose any export markets for agricultural products, to the Common Market or elsewhere. Many agricultural exports from the United States, such as cotton and soybeans, do not compete with the Common Market because it does not produce them. But there is real competition between the Common Market and the United States in grains, poultry, pork, and eggs. In the early 1960's there was a bitter controversy and much hard feeling between certain producers in the United States and the Common Market over — of all things — chickens. The dispute arose when the Common Market raised its tariff on poultry by 350 percent — from 4.5 to 14.2 cents a pound. Poultry sales from the United States to the Common Market promptly fell 60 percent, from $112 to $45 million. The U.S. chicken industry was both a new and a potentially profitable one. The state of Arkansas had pioneered in exports of mass-produced poultry; its example had been followed by Georgia and Alabama. It was therefore more than a coincidence that the loudest howls of anguish heard in the U.S. Senate against the action of the Common Market came from Senator Fulbright of Arkansas, Senator Russell of Georgia, and Senator Hill of Alabama. Their protestations had little effect, particularly on the French, who resented American chickens. Signs in Gallic restaurants proclaimed that French barnyard chickens were proud, were free to strut about, were happy and contented, and were most succulent when eaten. By contrast American fowl, it was claimed, were factory-produced and hormone-injected, and had neither freedom nor pride on a cramped assembly line. The conclusion was obvious: Frenchmen should eat *free* French chickens, whatever the cost, in place of *slave* fowl from the United States, no matter how cheap.

All this brought retaliation, as tariffs usually do. GATT estimated that U.S. losses, through the Common Market duties on chickens, were $26 million in 1962. President Johnson, to even the balance, ordered sharp tariff increases on French brandy, German Volkswagen trucks, and Dutch starches. What he actually did was to restore the basic act of 1930, which meant a doubling or tripling of tariffs; we were back to Hawley-Smoot on these items. This retaliation was actual; other reprisals were threatened. To a large extent the United States pays its share of European defense out of agricultural exports to the Common Market. The chairman of the Senate Foreign Affairs Committee was Senator Fulbright, who happened to come from a poultry-producing state. It was hardly surprising, therefore, to hear Fulbright proclaim that if the Common Market did not alter its trade policies, the United States — as a *quid pro quo* — might be compelled to withdraw some troops from Europe.

Beyond the problem of specific duties the United States, which established the first modern example of an effective common market, is hardly in a position to argue against the general principles of its European counterpart. Special tariff advantages are monopolistic; a common market — whether in the United States or in Europe — presents the possibility, however halting at times, for open competition and free enterprise for those in constituent nations and states who have the will and the energy to compete. In 1962, in his request for the twelfth extension of the Trade Agreements Act of 1934, President Kennedy said that the "time has come for the United States to take a giant step" — to form a trade partnership with the Common Market in the further expansion of a free-world economic community. This would represent, said Kennedy, a partnership between the United States of America and the United States of Europe — between the Americans on the one hand and the Eurocrats on the other. The coming years will witness a struggle between free enterprisers and monopolists, in both the American and European common markets, to determine if such a partnership is to be achieved.

XIV

More Subsidies

A FTER both the Napoleonic conflict and the U.S. Civil War the American farmer had been faced with serious economic crises. The same thing happened after World War I, when he was again confronted with falling prices. By 1931 corn had slid to 15¢ a bushel, cotton and wool were 5¢ a pound, hogs were 3¢, beef was 2½¢. A farmer who chewed one thick plug of Drummond a day required almost a bushel of wheat to keep him in chewing tobacco during the same twenty-four hours. It took almost sixteen bushels of wheat, more than the average yield for an entire acre at that time, to buy one of his children a pair of $4 shoes. The president of the Wisconsin's Farmers' Union said, "I am as conservative as any man could be, but any economic system that has it in power to set me and my wife on the streets, at my age — what else could I see but red." At the same time radical farm leaders staged a march on Madison and occupied the assembly chamber in the state capitol; in Iowa farmers blocked roads, overturned trucks, set bridges on fire, and poured low-priced milk along cold cement roads.

Underconsumption and overproduction were responsible. After World War I there was a falling off in normal demand for farm goods, resulting inevitably in depressed prices. Three factors were responsible: the high tariff, the tractor, and dietary changes. The protective tariff meant that foreign countries could not consume as much because they were restricted in their sales here; the farmer would ultimately learn that trade was a two-way street. The tractor did not consume grain, as horses had; this meant that acres were released — acres which had formerly been devoted to producing feed for draft animals. In 1920 there were 246,000 tractors on American farms, in 1953 the number was almost 4.5 million; this freed 70 million acres formerly used to produce food for horses and mules. American dietary changes involved the new emphasis on "slimming" — particularly on the part of the ladies; this meant less consumption of prime farm products such as meats and grains, and more emphasis on bulky but less caloric fruits and vegetables. The effect on wheat and dairy products was apparent. Our grandparents in 1910 consumed 315 pounds of wheat per person per year; a half century later their far more numerous progeny consumed half as much. With increasing farm production, it was only the rapid increase in population that kept wheat from overrunning the land. Even so, the American surplus stockpile in wheat was more than 2 billion bushels in 1960, the largest mountain of a single crop in all history; there was enough wheat in it to supply all *domestic* needs for more than four years, if not another kernel was grown in the United States. There was a decrease in the consumption of dairy products long before cholesterol and atomic fallout were heard of; people were simply eating less butterfat while milk production was increasing. In current years half-and-half has replaced heavy coffee cream and skim milk is frequently used in place of the full-bodied product. In the two decades between 1940 and 1960 consumption of butter in the United States dropped by more than half. Oldsters were worried about weight, with the result that a sizable generation has grown up hardly tasting butter at the home table; it has eaten margarine, an innovation that does not help most American farms.

Underconsumption was one cause of the fall in farm prices; overproduction was another — brought about by improved agricultural machinery, chemicals, and biological discoveries. In the long era between 3000 B.C. and A.D. 1800, only three significant advances had been made in agricultural methods; they were the horse collar, the scythe, and the cradle. This signified that down to A.D. 1800 hunger was a stark reality in the lives of men and nations; this situation required the writing of a Thomas Malthus. What the author of *An Essay on the Principle of Population* could not know was that forces would soon be released that would successfully attack the problem of starvation, at least in some countries. There was mechanization that reduced the amount of labor required for production on the farm. The United States began with the steel plow that broke the prairie — followed by the reaper, the grain drill, the twine binder, the thresher, the tractor, the combine. The "man with the hoe" was on his way out. In the forty years between 1920 and 1960 the farm worker just about doubled his productivity; in the next decade he would more than double it again. Chemicals and biologicals have vastly increased productivity per acre. Chemicals are of two kinds: fertilizers, which increase the amount of plant nutrients in the soil; and pesticides, which are used to fight insects and plant disease. It must be remembered as far as plant disease is concerned that, by contrast with animals, plants are not equipped to fight infection; for that reason infection is likely to be fatal for them. Botanists have pointed out the critical importance of stopping such disease by indicating that only fifteen plant species stand between mankind and starvation; in actual fact, 30 percent of all human energy comes from a single species of plant. It is rice; if an epidemic infection destroyed it the world would indeed be in trouble. In 1953–1954, in the United States, a difficult-to-control stem rust on wheat did destroy a quarter of the bread wheat and three-quarters of the durum (or macaroni) wheat. More spectacular, more than a century ago, was the tragic potato blight in Ireland. This disaster cost the lives of 1 million persons and forced the migration of another million and a half; the total of 2.5 million persons comprised a loss of almost a third of Ireland's population in the late 1840's. A hundred years later DDT doubled the potato crop, but with ambivalent results. It is well known that some agricultural chemicals, even when properly used, have killed large numbers of birds, fish, and other useful living organisms — thus upending the ecological balance. In addition there is no certain knowledge about the long-range effects upon human beings of continued ingestion of even small quantities of these chemicals, which can enter the human body through food, inhalation, and skin absorption. There is no question that chemical products have brought substantial benefits in the form of higher crop yields; what is inadequately understood is the possible cost and the probable hazards from heavy applications of DDT, aldrin, and dieldrin — for controlling Dutch elm disease, infestations by fire ants, and plagues of Japanese beetles, among other uses. The biologicals are discoveries that have also increased productivity per acre. The most spectacular is hybrid corn which (by 1951) had increased yield by 750 million bushels annually. This phenomenal plant also required fewer acres. In the fifteen years after World War II the United States enjoyed two bumper corn crops, one in 1948 and another in 1958; the crop of 1948 required 85 million acres, that of 1958 (almost 4 billion bushels) was raised on only 39 million acres — less than half of those needed ten years earlier. This represented a dazzling technical revolution in agriculture — a revolution like the coming of the cotton gin or Martin's process of extracting cheap aluminum from bauxite.

What were the results of these new influences — mechanical, chemical, and biological? Two will be noted here: a phenomenal increase in production on fewer farms *and* the absorption of agriculture into the industrial vortex. In 1798, when Malthus was writing his gloomy essay, the American farmer was able to feed himself and to provide one-third of the needs of a second person. In 1862, the year the U.S. Department of Agriculture began its operations with nine employees, the American farmer was feeding himself and five others. A little more than a century later (in 1966) the U.S. farmer was feeding thirty-nine others and the Department of Agriculture had more than 100,000 employees. During the same years the number of farmers in the United States has shown a steady decline. In the Civil War era more than half of the U.S. population was engaged in agriculture. By 1920 the farm population of 32 million made up more than a third of the country's 92 million people; by 1940 the number of Americans on farms had dropped only 1.5 million to 30.5 million, but this now represented only 23 percent of an increasing population of 132 million. In the next decade the decline was sharper, leaving 23 million on the farm in 1950; subsidies had not made farming attractive enough to keep many farmers from wanting to quit. By 1970 the great twentieth-century wave of farm-to-city migration appeared to be ending with a farm population of 10 million, about 5 percent of the nation's total; by that time 70 percent of the more than 200 million people in the United States were living on slightly more than 1 percent of the land — the rest lived on the remaining 99 percent in small towns, in rural areas, or on farms. In sheer magnitude this loss of 20 million people who left the farms for urban areas between 1940 and 1970 ranks in U.S. history with the wave of immigration between 1890 and 1920 in which more than 22 million aliens came to live in the United States. By 1970 the situation had reached the point where Senator Robert P. Griffin of Michigan, with tongue in cheek, proposed to Congress that "the total of employees in the Department of Agriculture shall at no time exceed the number of farmers in America." By 1969 Podunk Center in Iowa (southwest of Des Moines), the place that symbolized small-town America, was up for sale. This one-acre hamlet was deserted; its owner hoped he could realize $7,000 from it, claiming that it had "clean air, low taxes, no crime, and plenty of parking space." Its population had reached a peak of 21 in the 1930's, but had gone downhill steadily since that time. Some took consolation in the observation that phenomenal agricultural productivity did provide advantages in the Cold War; Russia requires 41 percent of its population to grow an *inadequate* amount of food.

The other major result of the new developments was that the farmer lost his self-sufficiency and came to resemble the manufacturer. In colonial days a farmer lived on a kind of Robinson Crusoe's island; the striking characteristic of the old farming unit had been its capacity for self-sufficiency. Before the Civil War the American farming community had been a complete little world in itself. Food, wearing apparel, all the essentials of life were produced on the farm; tools were simple — the plow, sickle, cradle, and flail. After the Civil War, however, the farmer came to resemble the manufacturer in two striking ways: like the manufacturer he became a producer of a special commodity or crop, and like him he began to use expensive machinery. More and more he was inclined to concentrate on a single money crop, such as wheat or corn. Many developed what were called "factories in the fields" with the result that one farmer would say, "We no longer raise wheat here, we manufacture it." As a "manufacturer" he used his profits to buy his foodstuffs and clothing at the store, instead of raising them himself, and in so doing lost a large part of his former independence. The farmer who once wore homespun from his own sheep now wore denim from Oshkosh and cotton shirts from Troy. Soap-making became a lost art; not one in a thousand farmers who grew wheat, ate his own grain. Few farmers built their own houses, and when finished they were no longer lighted with homemade candles or tallow wicks. Furthermore, farmers ordinarily did not sell or barter their product for the use of nearby townsfolk; as with the manufacturer their customers were hundreds or thousands of miles away.

In addition, the farmer and the manufacturer were both using expensive machinery. The farmer laid aside implements that cost him a few dollars and lasted a lifetime; he bought instead machines costing many times as much, in need of constant repair, and comparatively short-lived. One result was that a great amount of capital was now required to go into farming if a profit (rather than bare subsistence) was expected. The value of U.S. farms in 1967 was at a record high level of $171 billion, more than five times the value three decades before in 1935. After World War II, to set up a 160-acre farm in Iowa required at least $50,000 in capital for land and buildings and machinery. In actual fact, the use of expensive machinery tended to increase the size of farms because of the low rate at which farm machinery is normally used. A manufacturer can expect a big lathe to be in operation two thousand hours a year; a farmer can anticipate only fifty hours from his hay baler. To make the baler pay the farmer bought more land on which to use it. The result was that the average farm, which stood at 160 acres in 1935, was more than 350 acres in 1966. Furthermore, the farmer had no choice as to whether he would use this expensive machinery; he had to use it, or work for someone who owned it, because the price of agricultural commodities was determined by the most fertile and best-equipped farms.

Like the manufacturer he had become a producer and a user of expensive machinery. There the similarity ended: the manufacturer was able to fix prices by means of tariff protection and trade agreements — the farmer was unable to do so until the 1930's. The tariff did not help the farmer and he had been too much of an individualist to join with other farmers in trade agreements. For these reasons, from 1865 to 1935 he was caught; he sold in a world market at a low price and he bought in a restricted monopoly market at a higher one. For this reason it was claimed that the farmer, along with the South, lost the Civil War. This war confirmed the protectionist policies of the industrial Northeast, but left the farmer with no alternative but to buy in a protected and expensive market. In actual fact, for seventy years after the Civil War, American agriculture — although it was expanding boundlessly — was being operated at a small profit, or none at all. The only element keeping the farmer's head above water was the fact that his land was appreciating in value and he could keep borrowing on it, thus balancing his books by way of mortgages. This type of indebtedness became heavier each year; during this period it can be said that the American farmer was not interested in land, but in land values. An example from Iowa will suffice; there the average value of an acre of improved land increased from $6.09 in 1850 to $43.31 in 1900 to $255.00 in 1920. It was little wonder that the farmer counted many enemies: the railroads for high rates and rebates, the manufacturer and middleman for high prices, the bankers for high interest, and the government for high taxes on realty rather than income.

Because of these difficulties, both economic and psychological, the farmer of the 1920's demanded legislative assistance. The Republicans, who controlled the economy in this decade, proposed indirect aids through roads, warehouses, credit, and "dumping." Federal aid for roads enabled the farmer to transport his crop, a variety of warehouse acts enabled him to store it, and there were credit acts which extended dollars to tide him over. There was no question that the farmer was interested in transporting his crop to market on good roads, that he was concerned with the importance of storage until he found a market, and that he was interested in credit to carry him over hard times. All of these objectives were reasonably attractive, but what the American farmer wanted chiefly was higher prices.

Over the past half century some have believed that these higher prices could be achieved by dumping farm surpluses abroad. Dumping has been appropriately described as the equivalent, in the export field, of a high tariff in the import field. The tariff is basically uneconomic because it relieves the inefficient producer of the necessity of coping with foreign competition. By the same token the subsidizing (through dumping) of agricultural surpluses is the other side of the coin normally known as "Protectionism." It aids, artificially, the exporter and the farmer who would not be able to sell abroad except through a synthetic stimulus. Dumping is no more popular abroad than a high tariff; both alienate friendships, and if continued, result in retaliation.

Senator Charles McNary represented Oregon from 1917 to 1944; Gilbert N. Haugen was sent by Wisconsin to the House of Representatives from 1899 to 1933. The two of them combined to produce the McNary-Haugen Bills; their purpose was to skim the surplus of agricultural products off the market, thus creating an artificial scarcity which would cause prices to rise. Skimming the surplus off the market can be accomplished either by blowing up milk trucks and shooting hogs, or by dumping the surplus elsewhere in the world; the latter concept was the idea behind the McNary-Haugen Bills. The federal government would establish a gigantic corporation, backed with federal funds, which would purchase leading agricultural products at prevailing domestic prices. This would cause domestic prices to rise on what was left; in time the corporation would dump its holdings abroad for whatever they would bring, presumably less than the corporation had paid. Because there would be a loss, there was the inevitable question as to who would pay for it. The McNary-Haugen Bills provided that the producer would pay through what was known as an "equalization fee" — collected from the *farmer* as the first handler of his crop. A Federal Farm Board was supposed to set the equalization fee at a rate that would cover the federal government's losses, that is, the difference between what the government had paid and the world price at which the surpluses had been sold. It was assumed that the rise in domestic prices, through this artificial stimulus, would be much more than the equalization fee — and that the farmer would therefore benefit. The McNary-Haugen Bills passed both Houses of Congress twice; President Coolidge vetoed them twice, the first time in 1927, the second in 1928. He did so on two grounds: he said that they established the price-fixing principle (which they most assuredly did) and that they benefited certain privileged groups. The President concluded his first veto message with a statement that brought little solace to the tillers of the soil. He said, "Farmers have never made any money. I don't think there's much we can do about it." Unfortunately, on the very day he vetoed the first McNary-Haugen Bill in 1927, Coolidge also increased the tariff on pig iron by 50 percent; this was obviously price-fixing for the benefit of a special group.

The export debenture was included in a clause proposed as an addition to the Hawley-Smoot Tariff Act. The purpose was to encourage exports of farm products by giving exporters a bounty; it was to be paid on specified agricultural commodities and was to be equal to one half of the tariff duties on those commodities. Let us assume that the tariff on wheat was 50¢ a bushel. Under the proposed arrangement the exporter would sell wheat abroad for whatever he could get and would receive in addition a bounty from the federal government amounting to 25¢ a bushel. These bounties, in the form of debentures, were receivable at face value by the federal government in payment of import duties. They happened to be called debentures because, in law, a debenture is an evidence of debt and is usually issued by a corporation; in this case the corporation was the federal government. The export debenture was tied in a left-handed way to the protective tariff, which had never been protective for farm products. The export-debenture clause passed the U.S. Senate in 1929 but was defeated in the House. This outcome made little difference; President Hoover had said that he would veto the entire bill if this clause was added.

The Agricultural Marketing Act of 1929 created a Federal Farm Board to buy surpluses, store, and later market them: that is, sell them at stable prices. To do the selling separate corporations were established — for example, a Grain Stabilization Corporation, and a Cotton Stabilization Corporation. In order to purchase the surpluses a revolving fund of half a billion dollars was established by the U.S. Treasury. The Farm Board was in existence for four years and acquired many surpluses, including almost a billion bushels of wheat and more than a million bales of cotton. On the marketing side the surpluses owned by the board or its subsidiary corporations were either dumped or were ultimately given away. That which was sold was largely dumped abroad — on the world market at whatever prices it would bring — chiefly to China, Germany, and Brazil. The original intention had been to sell the surpluses rather than give them away, but in 1932 the pressure of public opinion impelled Congress to distribute a part of the reserves of wheat among the half-starving portion of people in the United States. At that time, however, suggestions that the entire surplus be disposed of in like manner among persons who could not buy, were spurned by the Hoover Administration as paternalistic and conducive to pauperization. The elections in the fall of 1932 would soon destroy this concept.

The four-year effort of the Farm Board (1929–1933) was a failure by reason of excessive cost, an administration that was plagued with scandals, and failure to stop the decline in farm prices. By the time the affairs of the board were wound up in 1933 its net loss was almost $200 million. There were allegations of scandal; in the same years when farmers were being herded into bankruptcy and people were actually starving, some officials of the board's stabilization corporations were receiving salaries of $75,000 a year. The chief indictment against the board, however, was the fact that farm prices kept falling. It was argued that prices would have gone down still further but for the purchases of the board, but this was small consolation to raisers of wheat at 25¢ a bushel and of cotton at 5¢ a pound. In the light of government expenditures of hundreds of millions of dollars to shore up prices, why did they continue to fall? The reason was apparent; as soon as farmers thought that prices *might* rise, they produced more in order to get their share of the good things. The board tried voluntary control, suggesting that farmers plow up every third row of cotton and restrict the sowing of wheat. But most farmers did not trust their neighbors and produced more, in the vain hope of earning more. It was obvious that voluntary limitation would not work because of the much-heralded "individualism" of the American farmer. It became abundantly clear that price supports would never operate efficiently without production control.

Two decades later Congress would reintroduce, with far greater success, the principle of dumping as a means of getting rid of farm surpluses. This was done in the Agricultural Act of 1954, commonly known as Public Law 480 or as the "Food for Peace" Bill. This act, which has been extended in every year since 1954, provided for sales *and* giveaways (relief) of surplus farm products. As far as gifts are concerned every disaster overseas had been seized upon as an opportunity to distribute, to those in distress, as many tons of surplus food as they can consume. Domestically, many tons of the surpluses have been given to schools for lunch programs, and to welfare institutions and agencies; these institutions have literally lived off the fat of the land because much of the pork purchased by the national government has gone to them. On the sales side, in the first decade of its operation (1954–1964) more than $12 billion worth of the surplus had been sold abroad by the U.S. government; shipments of wheat alone amounted to two bumper crops with India the principal recipient (more than $2 billion worth). Under this law payments are made by recipient countries, not in dollars but in nonconvertible currencies of the nations which purchase the products. These funds are then used *within* the country, through loans or outright grants by the U.S. government, for economic development. Many regard this device as the finest type of foreign aid because of its multiplier effect. It assists the American farmer by skimming off the surplus, thus tending to raise his prices. It feeds the hungry in the recipient country. It also provides the money for meaningful development in the recipient country. India serves as an example. One dollar's worth of nitrogen will produce $4 in additional agricultural yield; an investment of $100 million in fertilizer factories will therefore produce enough anhydrous ammonia to increase Indian food production by $400 million. Money for such fertilizer factories thus comes *from food* under Public Law 480 — a tremendous boon to India, which is short of capital and would otherwise have to raise it by enforced saving from a population already deprived. Such food not only feeds the hungry; it also serves in the place of gold for financing development, with a multiplier of four or five times in the transaction. For this reason John F. Kennedy, in his campaign for election in 1960, would say,

I don't regard . . . the agricultural surplus as a problem. I regard it as an opportunity. . . . I think the farmers can bring more credit, more lasting good will, more chance for peace, than almost any group of Americans in the next ten years, if we recognize that food is strength, and food is peace, and food is freedom, and food is a helping hand to people around the world whose good will and friendship we want.*

* The results of this agricultural aid were a decided contrast to those that sometimes developed from other types of foreign aid. Traditionally, our foreign aid after World War II emphasized the industrialization of deprived or underdeveloped countries. In those nations the educated people were frequently captivated by the vision of great steel works and textile factories; the result was that too much of the money went into these enterprises instead of into agriculture. Under the concept of foreign aid for industrialization, where the underdeveloped country had been put into a position where it could compete in the markets of the world in at least some of its industrial products, U.S. manufacturers began to complain with the result that the United States sometimes erected barriers against the reception of their goods into our own country.

Regardless of the foreign-aid benefits from this program, it must be defined as dumping from an economic point of view. The cost to the U.S. government under Public Law 480, in the first decade of its operations (1954–1964), was almost $14 billion; more than $12 billion of this amount was for "sales" to underdeveloped countries, and $1.5 billion in donations for famine and disaster relief. Specifically, the United States losses were more than $8 billion on wheat, $1.6 billion on cotton, and almost a billion on rice. Against dumping of such titanic proportions, there have been vigorous protests from friendly nations which also produce agricultural surpluses. To cite one, Canada has objected to U.S. dumping of wheat under PL 480, stating that her exports dropped 15 percent (in 1956) because of the subsidies and barter agreements under this act — with which she was unable to compete. For that reason cynics have suggested that dumping in the ocean might provide a solution; at least it would not provoke protests and possible reprisals.

Whatever the ultimate answer to the problem might be, persistent surpluses embarrass and exasperate some nations of the world. In 1969, by reason of good weather and intensive use of modern techniques, three countries (the United States, Canada, and Australia) were holding in reserve a stockpile of 2 billion bushels of wheat; the United States alone had 800 million bushels bulging its grain elevators. In the grain trade, at least, the fear of world famine resulting from the population explosion had given way to frantic worry about how to get rid of ruinous wheat surpluses. The *New York Times* observed that "the international dismay caused by this abundance of the stuff from which bread is made is ironic in the light of the persistence of hunger in every part of the world, including affluent America." Surprisingly the poor were also going hungry in the United States although the nation, in an unconscionable paradox, by that time was lavishing subsidies on its large farm operations to encourage them *not* to grow more food; the Senate Select Committee on Nutrition and Human Needs estimated in 1969 that as many as 10 million Americans — 5 percent of the population — were suffering from hunger and malnutrition and from the lassitude and disease they can cause.

By 1933 farm income had not been raised indirectly through good roads, cheap credit, and warehouses, or by dumping of surpluses abroad; in actual fact the annual "take" of the farmer had fallen steadily. He then demanded and achieved direct subsidies through two Agricultural Adjustment acts (the Triple A Acts of 1933 and 1938), the Soil Conservation Act of 1936, and a variety of price-support bills after 1942.

The architect of New Deal agricultural programs was Henry Agard

---

By so doing we effectively neutralized the industrial help we had given them; indeed we made a mockery of it.

Wallace. His grandfather, Henry Wallace, was the founder of *Wallace's Farmer* and a profound Republican. His father, Henry Wallace, was the Republican Secretary of Agriculture from 1921 until his death in 1924. The next Henry — sometimes called "Henry the Third of Iowa" — was also a Republican until 1928 when he swung to the Democratic column along with Republican George Norris of Nebraska. When FDR appointed him Secretary of Agriculture he sat in the same room that his father had occupied a decade before under different political auspices. Out of this heritage the third Henry developed great devotion to the soil and those who labored on it. From an early age he applied himself to both the science and the economics of farming. At Iowa State he had studied under a gangling Negro named George Washington Carver, and by the time of World War I he was recognized as a remarkable plant geneticist. Along with this pragmatism, which made him a millionaire because of his pioneering with hybrid corn, went a mysticism and what Arthur Schlesinger called "the aura of a prophet." He lived an ascetic life, rising at dawn, walking two-and-a-half miles through Rock Creek Park to work in Washington, exercising with violence, denying himself tobacco, liquor — and on occasion, meat. He was so unpredictable that one old-time politician said, "Henry's the sort that keeps you guessing as to whether he's going to deliver a sermon or wet the bed." Some thought of him as the Last Populist — half scientist, half mystic. Famous as Iowa editor and hybrid-corn innovator, he was also Secretary of Agriculture (1933–1940), Vice-President of the United States (1941–1945), Secretary of Commerce (1945), editor of the leftist *New Republic* (1946–1948), and a third-party candidate against President Truman in the presidential campaign of 1948. He knew and was at home with his corn and his chickens; he never really understood politicians.

The main principles behind Wallace's first Triple A were two: limitation of production and subsidy payments. Actually the subsidies were paid in order to restrict production, for the purpose of eliminating surpluses and raising prices. Wallace, in words which were reminiscent of economist Thorstein Veblen, whom he greatly admired, said that farmers would find "it necessary to practice sabotage in the same scientific, businesslike way as labor and capital." This would put them in a comparable bargaining position, and in time all three (labor, capital, farmers) might see the futility of raising prices by limiting production. He was severely criticized by those who said there was no such thing as a food surplus so long as there was a single hungry Asian. Wallace replied that those who wept because farmers were practicing the same controlled production as industry "do not suggest that clothing factories go on producing *ad infinitum* regardless of effective demand for their merchandise, until every naked Chinaman is clad." He added that no one had been morally indignant when American industry plowed under much of its potential output between 1929 and 1933 — some $20 billion worth of goods that might have fed, clothed, and housed cold and hungry Americans. He asserted that agriculture and industry were poles apart and he wanted to close the gap: "In agriculture supply sets the price. In industry, price sets the supply. . . . Agriculture cannot survive in a capitalistic society as a philanthropic enterprise."

In reality what Wallace had in mind was a government-sponsored agricultural trust, for the purposes of restricting production and raising prices. Under the first Triple A *individual* farmers would agree to limit production by reducing acreage or by destroying livestock; in return the government would pay them a subsidy. In the first year of the act more than 40 million acres of land were taken out of production and farmers received several hundred millions of dollars for doing so. The reduction applied to what were called basic commodities: wheat, cotton, corn, tobacco, rice, dairy products, and hogs. The most dramatic situations developed with three of the basic commodities: wheat, cotton, and hogs. In 1933 the carry-over in wheat was almost three and a half times as large as normal; the result was that statisticians reported that the price of wheat had not been so low since the days of Queen Elizabeth. Wallace's ironic comment was that the "United States had the largest wheat surplus and the longest breadlines in history." In cotton the carry-over from previous years was 8 million bales, in 1933 enough to satisfy the world market for American cotton without harvesting a single new plant. In addition a bumper crop was in prospect; it was apparent that the cotton market, already down to 5¢ a pound, would sink out of sight if the crop in 1933 was harvested in its entirety. For that reason the government contracted with farmers to destroy every third row of cotton; soon steel plows behind tractors were briskly uprooting a third of the anticipated yield. In the case of hogs the government bought and killed piglets and brood sows, giving the meat away as a contribution to charity. This led to a revision of the nursery rhyme:

> *This little pig went to market,*
> *While four little piggies stayed home;*
> *For the world is on a pork chop dole,*
> *And piggies must study birth control.*

> *Four little piggies, locked up in their sty,*
> *Can't meet their sweethearts in the rye;*
> *For the urgins of nature might ruin demand,*
> *By scattering pork chops all over the land.*

The subsidy payments, for what the farmer did not produce, came from two sources: (1) *directly* from the government, by means of a processing tax assessed on millers, textile manufacturers, and other processors, and

(2) *indirectly* from consumers, through higher prices. This meant that the farmer who agreed individually to limit production would profit twice — first through a subsidy for what he did not produce, and after that from higher prices on what he did raise.

Farm prices began to rise, with the result that between 1932 and 1936 gross farm income increased 50 percent. But one cannot conclude that the first Triple A had a significant influence on this phenomenon. There were other and more important factors which tended to increase prices, notably the monetary policies of the New Deal and Nature, which introduced a drought. The latter was so bad that cattle in the Texas Panhandle ran out of grass and ate so much dirt as they scratched at the remaining roots that many died from mudballs in their stomachs. Some critics saw the judgment of God in the drought and the dust — a judgment on men who had dared plow under cotton and to slaughter baby pigs. In any case, because of the drought and the Triple A, the wheat crop which had averaged 864 million bushels in the four years from 1928 to 1932 — sank to an average of 567 million bushels from 1933 to 1935. Of this reduction it has been estimated that only twenty out of a total reduction of 300 million bushels came from the first Triple A; the large balance was the result of the drought.

The first Triple A came to an end in 1936. When the act was passed in 1933 Republican Joseph Martin, later a Speaker of the House, had said, "We are on our way to Moscow." But it was not the Republicans but the Supreme Court that finally gave the deathblow to the first Triple A; it did so in the case of *United States* v. *Butler* (1936). The Court declared the act void because it was an invalid use of the taxing power and because it invaded the reserved rights of the states. The Court stated that the processing tax was not really a tax; it was instead a feature of a program to limit agricultural production and was therefore not within the purview of the taxing power given to Congress by the welfare clause in the Constitution. The Court also said that the act invaded reserved state's rights over agriculture. In this connection a commentary by novelist William Faulkner in 1956 may be pertinent: "We — Mississippi — sold our state's rights back to the federal government when we accepted the first cotton price-support subsidy twenty years ago. . . . We no longer farm in Mississippi cotton fields. We farm now in Washington corridors and congressional committee rooms."

Congress responded immediately to the negative decision in *United States* v. *Butler* by passing the Soil Conservation Act of 1936. Its purposes were procedural and conservational. On the procedural side subsidies were paid indirectly through state administrations rather than directly from the federal government — thus circumventing the objection of the Supreme Court concerning state's rights. To conserve the soil the national government indicated that it would pay subsidies of half a billion dollars a year, for the planting of *soil-conserving* crops such as clover and soybeans, in the place of *soil-depleting* crops such as corn, wheat, tobacco, and cotton; by more than coincidence the soil-depleting crops were those with surplus production. Under this act the average payment was $10 an acre. Unfortunately it failed to provide real crop curtailment and farm prices went down. It did not work simply because farmers were able to increase production on smaller acreages, by means of the new fertilizers and biologicals.

For this reason, plus the recession of 1937, Congress passed the second Triple A in 1938. Its main innovations, by contrast with the first Agricultural Adjustment Act, were five: the elimination of processing taxes, control by crop rather than through individual farmers, loan payments to farmers on surpluses, and the establishment of two new principles — one the Ever-Normal Granary and the other the concept of parity. Processing taxes were simply forgotten. Payments were now to be made from the U.S. Treasury from general revenue; this would eliminate a major objection from the Supreme Court. The second Triple A also provided much more rigid control over production through marketing quotas and acreage allotments over an entire crop, rather than by special agreements with individual farmers. When a surplus appeared, which was not unusual, the government set a maximum marketing quota for the entire crop; this quota applied to the crop anticipated in the next year provided two-thirds of the farmers agreed. If they did, each farmer was given an acreage allotment; he could plant only a given number of acres (based on preceding crops) and could market only a given quantity of the crop. If a farmer produced more than his quota, through intensive agriculture on reduced acres, he was heavily taxed on any surplus he *sold*. On the other hand, he was allowed to *store* the surplus and to receive a loan payment on it. Such loans, under the second Triple A, were restricted to certain crops: wheat, cotton, corn, tobacco, and rice — and only then if the farmers producing them had agreed to marketing quotas and acreage allotments. Under this act, in relation to the specific crops listed, the government loans were based as equitably as possible on the principle of parity (see below). The loans would vary by crop from half to three-quarters of the artificial parity price. In this connection it should be noted that excess crops would be stored in government warehouses, and that the farmer could repay the loan and both repossess and market the surplus during crop failures or war conditions when the price was at or near parity; in practice this meant 1942.

Wallace's idea of parity was based on the limitation of production through subsidy payments until the farmer had achieved equality (parity) with capital and labor — that is, until the prices he received for his goods were comparable with the prices he had to pay for the goods and the commodities he bought. Parity was thus a ratio, and the years selected as a base were the five between 1909 and 1914. It was believed that, during these years, the prices received by farmers were high enough, and those paid by him were low enough, to give him a reasonable and healthy purchasing power. In very practical terms, if a farmer could have bought a shirt with a bushel of wheat in the era of 1909–1914 and could buy a shirt with a bushel of wheat today, it would be said that he was receiving 100 percent of parity — theoretically a fair and equivalent price. Before long the principle of parity had become so basic that the farmer paraphrased the Bible: "And now let there abide Faith, Hope, and Parity, these three, but the Greatest of these is Parity."

The Ever-Normal Granary was also Wallace's idea; it was to store a surplus in good years in order to use it during drought periods or if other crises, such as wars, arose. In determining quotas and acreage allotments the Department of Agriculture was therefore to plan on a small surplus. Such excess crops were to be stored, and the farmer was to be paid for them by a loan somewhat below the parity level; such excess crops would be used, and the farmer who owned them would repossess them, when the market price was good enough to more than pay off what had been loaned. Over a long period of planned time, therefore, U.S. production would provide an Ever-Normal Granary; because of this feature the second Triple A is popularly known as the Ever-Normal Granary Act. Actually, by the end of 1942 the government had almost $2 billion tied up in such farm surpluses. The crisis, in World War II, was also at hand; the surpluses disappeared, and so did any potential losses which the Department of Agriculture might have feared.

During the 1930's farm-income supports were basically a *relief* measure designed to prevent the literal collapse of the farm economy. By contrast, during the 1940's and until 1953 they were essentially a *production* stimulus — because of the extraordinary demands of the Second World War, the reconstruction of war-torn Europe, and the Korean War. From 1953 to the present, price supports have been used primarily to counteract the income-depressing effects of the mounting agricultural surpluses.

The demands of the 1940's and the Korean War (in the first years of the next decade) were met by increased support for basic commodities, by the addition of perishables to the list of agricultural products eligible for aid, and by a new definition of parity. Encouragement for basic and storable commodities (corn, wheat, cotton, tobacco, rice, and peanuts) was achieved by guaranteeing loans on them at 90 percent of parity. In addition to basic commodities the federal government for the first time added perishables to the list of farm produce to be supported. The main ones were milk, honey, Irish potatoes, and tung nuts (produced in the South and used as a base for paints, varnish, and linoleum). The perishables were bought, at the discretion of the Secretary of Agriculture, at prices up to 90 percent of parity, but usually somewhere between 60 and

90 percent of parity. Obviously the handling of perishables was entirely different from that with basic commodities, which could be stored and loans made thereon. The Commodity Credit Corporation (CCC) bought perishables outright, paying the support level and hoping to sell them before deterioration set in. The principle of parity was also retained, but on a new basis. Henceforth it was to be based on a ratio with 1909–1914 *or* the most recent ten-year period, whichever was the most advantageous. There were additional and complex variants, designed to help some farmers. The result was, according to John Kenneth Galbraith, that the problem of figuring parity became so complicated that by 1950 there were probably not more than a hundred experts in the nation who could calculate it — on the basis of old parity, new parity, and transitional variants between the two.

The world needed all the food and raw materials it could produce at this time; in order to encourage *maximum* production, it was deemed necessary to assure the farmer a *guaranteed market* for his product. The result was that, of all economic groups, farmers benefited most from wartime prosperity. Net cash farm income increased more than four times from 1940 to 1945, and for the first time in American history most farmers shook themselves free of mortgage debt. They purchased tractors and other farm machinery, and with fertilizers and hybrid seed corn, increased production tremendously. Few contemplated that this artificial arrangement would be perpetuated in time of peace; it was thought that wartime supports would be removed as soon as the war was over. It will be recalled that the same expectancy had existed with the Civil War tariff — but the tariff had not been reduced in 1865, and agricultural price supports remained after World War II.

Interestingly the agricultural price-support program played a major role in electing Harry Truman in the close presidential race of 1948. In 1946 there was opposition from the Republicans led by Robert Taft to these payments to farmers. The result was that the Republican 80th Congress, elected in 1946 with Taft as its leader and conservative symbol, reduced the funds available to the Commodity Credit Corporation, which buys, sells, and extends loans on agricultural commodities on behalf of the Department of Agriculture. This meant that fewer cribs could be built to store the surplus grain in the farm belt, and this resulted in heavy selling by farmers at comparatively "distressed" prices; without storage places the farmer could not get a government loan on his corn and wheat. The consequent wrath of farmers, in what has been called the "green rebellion," is part of the nation's political history. All through the spring and summer of 1948 grain prices had been dropping steeply; corn, as an example, had fallen from $2.46 a bushel in January to $1.78 in September. Blaming the Republican 80th Congress for the price slide, Truman went through the Midwest telling natives that the Republicans had "stuck a pitchfork in the farmer's back." He traveled in a Presidential Special, a seventeen-car train that included a converted Pullman, luxuriously fitted and protected with armor plate and bullet-proof glass, which was set aside for the President, his wife, Bess, and his daughter, Margaret. The Pullman car was called the Ferdinand Magellan; in it Truman covered more distance than the Portuguese navigator who circled the globe. Altogether the President reckoned that he traveled 31,700 miles, made 356 prepared speeches and more than 200 extemporaneous talks, and was seen by upwards of 15 million people — before all of whom he gave the Republicans "hell." At the polls in November ten out of sixteen farm states went to Truman; even Taft's Ohio deserted the Republican column. The Republicans have never forgotten this "green rebellion" of 1948; most of them recalled it every time a farm measure came to a vote in later years.

In the 1930's the farm problem was one concerned with relief; in the 1940's the objective was more production; in the 1950's and 1960's the issue concerned mounting surpluses and what to do about them. Two Secretaries of Agriculture attacked this latter-day problem without success: Republican Ezra Taft Benson from 1953 to 1961, and Democrat Orville Freeman from 1961 to 1969. There were two features of agricultural policy in the Eisenhower Administrations: flexible rather than fixed price supports, and conservation, chiefly through the soil bank. Benson opposed rigid price supports for basic commodities at 90 percent of parity, in favor of flexible and lower price supports; after 1953 subsidy payments were reduced as Benson supported basic commodities on a flexible basis, at his discretion, at from 75 to 90 percent of parity. The Soil-Bank Bill of 1956 was obviously a variant of the Soil Conservation Act twenty years earlier. Under the Soil-Bank measure farmers were paid for retiring land from crop production, and devoting it to grass and trees. This act was certainly no solution. The poorest land was set aside for governmental payments; meanwhile the best land under the best management was made to yield bigger surpluses than ever — also to be subsidized by the public. In this way two payments were extracted from the taxpayer, where but one had been taken before. The situation reached the point where one cynic proposed that the U.S. Department of Agriculture put half of its thirty acres of prime Washington office space into the soil bank — to assist in lowering agricultural production. Benson was a conservative Mormon elder from Utah; it was claimed that underlings in the Department of Agriculture wrote no memoranda to him — instead they sent "Epistles to the Apostle." He got into his first difficulty only a few days after taking office when he was quoted as saying that he wanted to reduce the "swollen bureaucracy" of the Department of Agriculture. No matter how valid his comment might have been, the statement did not endear him to the thousands of bureaucrats over whom he was expected to preside. When he reduced parity payments, he was actually greeted with rotten eggs when he spoke in farm districts. In 1959 farm-belt members of the Republican National Committee sought his resignation; he refused, stating that he would continue the fight to oust government from agriculture. Some farmers said that Benson was the only man who could break the monopoly which the New York Yankees enjoyed in baseball in the 1950's; put him in charge of the Yankee farm system, they averred, and he would ruin the Yankees just as he had ruined farmers. Democrats contrasted him with Secretary of State John Foster Dulles, whom they also disliked. They observed that Dulles had a *fixed* foreign policy, whereas Benson had a *flexible* farm policy. The Democrats thought the roles should have been reversed: Dulles should have had a flexible policy, Benson should have adhered to a fixed policy of farm subsidies at 90 percent of parity.

Orville Freeman, who was Secretary of Agriculture under Kennedy and Johnson in the 1960's, was much more liberal in philosophy but little more popular with farmers than Benson had been. Freeman was a lawyer and Democrat who became active in politics and served three terms as governor of Minnesota from 1954 to 1960; when he was elected for his first term he was the first non-Republican governor of the state in seventeen years. The Freeman farm policy differed, at least in theory, from that of Benson in two respects: he favored higher price supports and much stricter production controls, to limit surpluses. In effect he was trying to provide an equitable policy for both farmers and urban taxpayers; that is, price supports high enough to guarantee the farmer an adequate income *and* controls effective enough to guarantee urban taxpayers a limit on the amount of farm produce they had to subsidize at high prices. Basically he told the farmer that it was satisfactory if he wanted no price supports at all — but if he did, it would be necessary to reduce production. This was accomplished by setting a national acreage allotment each year for every crop controlled by the government. Every farmer who wanted to participate got a portion of the national allotment for that crop, based primarily on what his farm had produced in past years. To oversimplify, a wheat farmer with 200 acres might be allowed to plant wheat on 100, and would be paid for leaving the remaining 100 idle. He would also be guaranteed a basic price for the wheat he grew, with the government buying and storing any that processors did not buy. If he chose not to participate he could plant all 200 acres in wheat but would take his chances on what he could get for the crop on a fluctuating open market. By 1968 this enormously complex system of governmental regulation and subsidization of farm crops was costing taxpayers more than $5 billion a year.

The Freeman program, because of the emphasis on controls, was not popular with either Congress or farmers; farmers are happiest with ineffective controls and high farm prices. They opposed stricter controls as an example of socialism and an interference with "freedom to farm"; to them socialism appeared to be a system where the government required farmers to give up something for the money they received in subsidies. By the mid-1960's a saying was going the rounds in the Farm Belt: "Benson made a Democrat out of me, and Freeman is turning me back into a Republican."

Farm subsidies have been controversial in almost every developed nation in the world, and the United States is no exception. John F. Kennedy is reported to have remarked that he didn't want to hear about agriculture from anyone but John Kenneth Galbraith, and didn't want to hear about it from him either. Nonetheless he could not escape the debate over the pros and cons of farm subsidies, and neither can his successors. Three arguments have been used in justification of them: they maintain purchasing power, the farmer deserves governmental assistance as much as manufacturers and others who receive it, and subsidies are not primarily responsible for high farm prices. On the first point it is alleged that farm purchasing power is an economic bulwark for the nation because farmers spend most of their income for goods; in the 1950's it was claimed that they bought more steel than the automobile industry, used more rubber than went into tires on new passenger cars, burned more petroleum than any other industry. When farmers could no longer afford to buy these products in quantity, the industries producing them and their employees knew it quickly. As far as equity was concerned, it was claimed that farmers were just as deserving of support from the federal government as industry; farmers argued that if manufacturers were to have a subsidy in the form of a tariff, they deserved one too. Because the tariff did not help most of them, they asked for outright payments from the Treasury. The farmer also said that if manufacturers could restrict production and keep prices up, the farmer was justified in doing the same thing. To phrase the issue in the simplest terms, the U.S. farm-support program was a political attempt, like the tariff, to give the farmer a higher share of national income than would have been his under a free-market condition of supply and demand.

It was also claimed that subsidies were not primarily responsible for higher farm prices; the farmer blamed the wholesaler, the processor, the retailer, and high wages for price increases. In 1968 a one-pound loaf of bread cost an average of 22.2¢ in the supermarket, an all-time high price; of this 22.2¢ the farmer received an average 3.3¢ for all his ingredients and 2.6¢ for the wheat alone. The gap between what the customer paid and what the farmer received was at a new peak of almost 19¢ — swallowed up in the areas of processing, packaging, transportation, and marketing. In 1967, with parity at about 75 percent, the U.S. farmer was hit by a drop of $1.5 billion in farm prices; in that year, per-capita disposable income for all U.S. farmers averaged but $1,692, about 60 percent of the income for other Americans. It was little wonder that a proposal was made to establish a National Agricultural Relations Board to serve U.S. farmers in the same way that the National Labor Relations Board served other U.S. workers — to give farmers a new way to unionize on a national scale.

On the negative side U.S. farm subsidies have been severely criticized in both principle and practice because they have been frightfully expensive, they help big farmers to the fullest but keep small ones in a state of pauperism, they are based on scarcity economics, and they operate on a principle contrary to our basic foreign policy. The excessive cost of the program has been borne by two parties — the U.S. government and the American consumer. From the standpoint of the government, in the period of almost three decades from 1933 to June 1962, the total loss was in excess of $15 billion — about $500 million each year on the average. Specifically in carrying out the farm program, in a valiant effort to absorb the *economic revolution* of agriculture's exploding production, the government purchased a food and fiber mountain — the greatest hoard of farm commodities history has ever seen. In the 1950's three crops in the government's storage bins were each valued at more than a billion dollars — wheat, cotton, and corn. The storage bill alone was several hundred million dollars a year; in 1958 *one* large storage company in Kansas collected almost $15 million for storage of surplus wheat alone. Even so, the CCC had some trouble in finding enough storage facilities and on occasion used reserve ships, wartime airplane hangars, and even caves. One commentator saw a possible solution: if we continued to use farmland as sites for storage bins, in time enough land would have been removed from farming to create a shortage of grain, causing the bins to begin to empty. This *he* called "long-range planning."

There were two dramatic examples of purchasing that went wrong — potatoes in the 1940's and butter in the 1950's. Between 1943 and 1950 the CCC spent almost $600 million on potatoes; it bought most of them at $1.25 a bushel. It had too many; as a result in 1950 it dyed them blue and sold them back to farmers at 1¢ a bushel, to be used as fertilizer. Altogether, it was estimated that the U.S. government lost half a billion dollars on the potato experiment. Under the Democrats the problem was rotting potatoes; with the Republicans in the 1950's it was rancid butter. In this decade the CCC was buying about 500 tons of butter each working day; by the end of 1954 it had almost half a billion tons of it stashed away. When butter is stored for a year it takes on an undesirable taste; after two years it is good for soap only, and without much of a market because of detergents. Furthermore, while butter prices were maintained at a high level, oleo had been stealing its market. The *Wall Street Journal*, with tongue in cheek, actually suggested that the solution to the butter problem would be a government-support program for oleo:

Why should the margarine producers be permitted to build up their volume by selling at low prices in a free market while butter producers are penalized by government price supports? With an aggressive and adequately financed margarine support program, the price of butter and margarine could soon be equalized at such a high level that consumers would find both products too expensive to buy.

The same *Journal* also suggested that the CCC buy all the butter and all the oleo, melt it down, mix it, call it butoleo — then issue it free to the people.* Regardless of the absurdity of some government purchases, they did skim the surpluses off the market, thus increasing the prices of the agricultural commodities involved; for this reason most economists estimated that the cost to the consumer was greater, in higher prices for what he bought, than the cost of the original agricultural subsidies paid by the U.S. government. This meant, on the average between 1933 and 1962, that price supports cost the consumer more than half a billion dollars a year in higher prices. This can be an interesting observation because the average American citizen is both taxpayer *and* consumer; he was caught going and coming.

A second criticism is that these expensive subsidies have benefited chiefly the more prosperous farmers who really do not need help, at the same time keeping marginal farmers in a state of poverty. An understanding of this statement requires an analysis of the 3,500,000 farms in the United States as they were classified by the census of 1960. Two million of them produced very little. Four hundred thousand of these 2 million farms formed the hard core of agricultural poverty — the small, marginal farmers who worked full time in agriculture but did not make a living at it; most of them were on small acreages in the South and Southwest, and actually should have been encouraged by subsidies to leave farming — not

---

* The situation in Wisconsin was a dramatic example of popular opposition to "free enterprise." Until 1967, when the law was repealed, Wisconsin did not permit the sale of colored (yellow) oleo; it did permit the sale of uncolored oleo, which could be made yellow if the housewife wanted to stain her hands by squeezing and mixing a bag of coloring into the pallid mess. Beyond this inconvenience, however, uncolored oleo in Wisconsin cost more because it was taxed at 15¢ a pound, bringing the lowest price there to 39¢; it was 19¢ in Illinois (butter was 79¢ and up). What happened was reminiscent of Prohibition in the 1920's. Every truck driver entering Wisconsin brought some colored oleo and sold it on the side. One "Little Old Lady of Sheboygan" became a bootlegger of colored oleo; every six months she drove south 100 miles on Highway 41, crossed into "free" Illinois, picked up her little brown box. Her contraband was yellow oleomargarine. The "Little Old Lady" told the *New York Times* that there were not enough prisons in Wisconsin to hold the smugglers. She said she had asked the local chief of police to arrest her. He replied that he would not because he was also smuggling colored oleo into the state! This gave a dentist, who had an oversupply of false teeth, an authentic idea. He wrote the House Agriculture Committee, suggesting a denture subsidy which he insisted would help the sale of corn: "Maybe you could send the surplus dentures overseas as foreign aid. This would motivate the people over there to buy our corn on the cob, solving both the problems of corn and of dentures. . . ."

to stay in it. "Forty acres and a mule" no longer make a productive farmer; they produce instead a rural pauper. The remaining 1,600,000 farms (of the 2 million that produce little) are part-time and part-retirement farms whose owners work in town or putter, but in any case produce little for sale. Because the census used a most liberal definition of the word "farmer," weekend hobbyists who grow raspberries for the gang at the office were so classified. With the elimination of these 2 million farms, one and a half million remained which were large enough to be economic and to make a profit; this was 40 percent of the total of the 3,500,000 farms so classified by the census of 1960. This 40 percent produced 91 percent of all agricultural products that were sold; with a little effort they could produce all of it, and more. In actual fact, out of the 1,500,000 farms making a profit, 300,000 made a super-profit from very large production. These super-farms, 9 percent of the total, produced as much as the other 91 percent — and received 50 percent of the price-support payments. This means that the farm-subsidy program has helped a minority of farmers who least needed it; half of our agricultural price support has gone to Big Business in Agriculture, sometimes known as "Agro-Business." Consider the situation in cotton, where production is highly mechanized and where checks for price supports can run to $1 million and more. There is an obvious reason for this; it is found in the 1909–1914 base for determining parity. This was a period before many farms were mechanized, when cotton payments were begun to aid southern farmers in earning a living from worn-out soil. This meant, in the period from 1909 to 1914, that farm costs were high. Today the cotton belt has shifted to Arizona and California, where vast irrigated operations produce three times as many bales per acre as do most southern areas. Farm costs on these mechanized farms are low, and such farms benefit mightily from farm subsidies. On the plantation, where the mule is still king (that is, where the farmer still uses the system prevailing in the period 1909–1914), it costs 28¢ a pound to grow and market a pound of cotton. With a fully mechanized operation, the cost dropped to 13¢ a pound (in 1959). The same condition prevails with wheat and corn. In 1960 the government was supporting wheat at $1.81 a bushel; this crop could be produced on mechanized farms for as little as 60¢ a bushel. In the decade of the 1960's the Department of Agriculture estimated that a corn farmer must have at least 1,000 acres, else his costs would make it impossible for him to meet competitive prices. All of this meant big profits and subsidy payments for the really efficient farmers — small profits, or none, for the least efficient ones. This situation can lead to ludicrous situations and statements. In the 1960's there was a widely publicized remark of a big farmer who was demanding price support at 90 percent of parity. He said, "Otherwise, I stand to lose $100,000." By 1967 agricultural subsidies had climbed to $4 billion a year, roughly double the expenditures on the poverty program in the same year. At the same time the Department of Agriculture reported that nine large landowners received a total of more than $14 million from one or a combination of farm programs designed, as the Department phrased it, "to encourage, promote, and strengthen the family farm." Griffin, Inc., of Fresno County (California) actually received more than $2 million in federal subsidies, exclusive of loans. Another payment was more modest, but excited political interest. Senator James O. Eastland, a member of the Senate Agriculture Committee and a strong proponent of self-reliance and individualism, got $157,000 for keeping one-third of his 5,000-acre cotton plantation out of production.

TRB in the *New Republic* has compared farm subsidies for not growing crops to the negative income tax (NIT). The latter alarms traditionalists because it proposes that the government pay out cash to families in proportion to the degree by which their income falls below an arbitrary poverty line. On the other hand many applaud the same principle when applied to farmers, usually the wealthiest, for not producing crops. This is the same thing as the NIT because it is paid for a negation — for not growing something. Some feel that it would be socialism or communism to offer income maintenance to the poor, simply for being poor. But farm payments appear to be different. As TRB sees it, this is because they reward initiative and enterprise: ". . . the more you don't grow the more NIT you get; in order not to grow a lot you have to have a large plantation to start with. Obviously you have to have a lot of initiative to have a big enough plantation not to grow anything on. It all squares with the Puritan ethic."

Agricultural subsidies have been criticized on the basis of their cost and because they are paid to farmers who do not need them; they have also been censured because they are founded on the principle of scarcity economics and are contradictory to the basic trade policies we have endeavored to encourage with foreign nations over the past three decades and more. A farm policy based on scarcity economics increases the price of farm products at the expense of the poor — both taxpayers and consumers, both here and abroad. These high prices reduce the standard of living for millions of people. The United States is inclined to think of itself as prosperous and to assume that it has few poor families, yet in 1955 there were 8 million family units in the United States with incomes of less than $2,000 a year — one in every five American families. Abroad, in Asia and parts of South America and Africa, millions are threatened with famine while in the United States surplus crops — or crops at too high a price — have filled bins and elevators and even the holds of Victory ships. It is an ironic and tragic surplus if it is true, as humanitarians have claimed, that the only real surplus in the world is a surplus of empty stomachs. In relation to trade policy, the United States has long wanted foreign nations to buy here, only to find that their purchases have been limited because of high U.S. farm prices. Because trade is a two-way street the United States has also wanted foreign countries to sell in this nation, but their opportunities have been limited by aggravating quotas on butter and cheese and sugar designed to protect American producers against foreign competition.

Proposals to alter the agricultural price-support system have come from all points of the political and economic spectrum. The extreme right would welcome a return to laissez-faire by abandoning all price supports immediately. The extreme left would solve the problem by nationalizing agriculture through state and collective farms. There have been three prominent middle-of-the-road proposals: two would reduce the surplus, the other would reduce farm prices.

The proposals from the center to reduce the surplus have come from the Committee on Economic Development (CED) and from Gunnar Myrdal. The CED was founded in 1942 by concerned and liberal businessmen and educators who were afraid that another depression, after World War II, would damage capitalism irreparably; this they wanted to avoid. Among the founders were Paul G. Hoffman of Studebaker-Packard and the UN Special Fund; Senator William Benton of Benton and Bowles (public relations) and the Encyclopaedia Britannica and both UNESCO and UN; Marion Folsom from Eastman Kodak, who was head of HEW under President Eisenhower; and Beardsley Ruml of Macy's in New York who was the inventor of the withholding tax. The proposal of the CED was to reduce the agricultural surplus through governmental purchase or rental of farms, certainly all of the marginal ones plus some of those that were really productive. Farmers so displaced would be retained and rehabilitated in industry and service occupations. Once this was done, CED proposed that price supports be reduced progressively until agriculture was returned to a free market. The national government had previously "mothballed" surplus warships and freighters, against a future day when they might be needed. The CED proposal was to "mothball" farms as well; the government would "waterproof the buildings and let hunters use the land." The second proposal for reduction of the surplus came from Gunnar Myrdal, the distinguished economist who was author of *The American Dilemma* (1944) and *Asian Drama: An Inquiry into the Poverty of Nations* (1968). He proposed a World Food Bank, to be affiliated with the UN. Myrdal observed that half the world goes to bed hungry and that developed nations have an obligation to provide surplus food, or the money to buy it. He saw no reason why the United States should be assuming most of the global burden through Public Law 480, and was convinced that other nations should assist. In his proposal he expressed the belief that, if the World Food Bank could absorb all of the American surplus at fair prices, this encouragement would result in increased agricultural production all over the world. The United States would rid itself of its price-support problems, including storage costs, and the hungry of the world would benefit as well.

The CED and Myrdal wanted to reduce the surplus; Charles Brannan wanted to reduce prices. He was from Colorado and was President Truman's Secretary of Agriculture from 1948 to 1953. The chief features of his "Plan" were the following:

1. Agricultural prices, at least on perishables such as potatoes, milk products, eggs, and pork would be allowed to seek their own level on the free market.

2. The difference between this free price, and the parity level, would be made up by the national government through a *direct* subsidy.

3. There would be a limitation on the amount of the subsidy; under Brannan's complicated formula, at prices as they were in 1949, no individual farmer could be paid in excess of $20,000 a year.

Brannan insisted that his "Plan" would provide great savings for both the taxpayer *and* the consumer. For the consumer the benefits would come because he could buy some commodities at a low (and competitive) price; he would be able to eat certain crops instead of reading about them in storage. For the taxpayer there would be economies because of (1) savings on storage and cost of sales, simply because the government would be out of the storage business, and (2) savings through the $20,000 limitation, which meant that Agro-Business would not be "cashing in." That Agro-Business was desirous of "cashing in" was apparent; by 1969 more than 16,000 "farmers" were receiving subsidy payments exceeding $25,000 a year; the total for this privileged group was more than half a billion dollars. Most of the big payments went to cotton farmers in California, Texas, Mississippi, Arkansas, and Arizona. When Congressman Paul Findley placed the names of all recipients of $25,000 a year or more in the *Congressional Record* for 1969, the list from the five largest cotton states filled twenty-one pages; the five leading grain states commandeered only four pages. It was established that the largest 1 percent of cotton growers in California and Mississippi got 25 percent of all direct federal benefits in those states.

It is not surprising that there was great and successful opposition to the Brannan Plan and that Congress refused to authorize it. Minor criticism came from liberals who pointed out that the Brannan Plan did not go far enough. They believed that the limitation of $20,000 was far too generous, and that the idea of direct subsidies should be applied to all crops, not just the perishables. (For reasons which were probably pragmatic and tactical Brannan had not included basic crops such as corn, wheat, and cotton in his Plan; they would be governed by the older techniques of loans and purchase agreements). On the other hand the major and decisive opposition came from Republicans, Big Farmers, and Big Processors. The Republicans could not stomach the concept because it was a Democratic plan. Big Farmers disliked the limitation on the maximum subsidy to be paid and charged that the Brannan Plan was socialistic. Big Processors were antagonistic to the idea because their markups are smaller as prices fall — for example, meat packers are interested in high parity because they calculate their selling price of meat as a percentage of the cost of cattle, and get more when cattle prices go up; quite obviously 10 percent of $2 is twice as much as 10 percent of $1.*

Aviation by means of lighter-than-air craft dominated the nineteenth century, culminating in dirigibles steered and driven by engines. In this development Americans participated from the earliest days. In 1785 a French aeronaut named Pierre Blanchard, accompanied by the Boston physician Dr. John Jeffries, made the first balloon flight over the English Channel. They took off from Dover Castle, landed in a forest in northern France, and later received a royal welcome at Versailles. Blanchard came to the United States in 1793, and armed with a passport signed by President Washington, who witnessed the takeoff, ascended from the courtyard of a prison in Philadelphia to a deafening volley of artillery fire and the playing of music. The landing happened to occur in New Jersey, where the passport saved Blanchard from embarrassment at the hands of suspicious rustics. It was the first actual aerial voyage in this country. Someone had asked Benjamin Franklin, "What is the use of the new invention?" He parried the query by asking one of his own, "What is the use of a new-born child?" He suggested that not even the most potent sovereign could protect his dominions from enemy troops dropped out of the sky, a development he thought might convince rulers of the folly of war (as it turned out, he was half right). In the U.S. Civil War period, an inventor named Thaddeus Sobieski Coulincourt Lowe, who experimented with both balloons and ice machines, was a prominent aeronaut. In 1859 he planned to use the prevailing Western winds for a flight to Europe, but his *Great Western* (also the name of one of the first steamboats to cross the Atlantic in 1838) was destroyed by wind before it left the ground. Two years later he did fly 900 miles over land in a balloon of his own construction. Later in the same year (1861) President Lincoln appointed

* Interestingly, the Brannan Plan caught on in certain quarters, although it was not recognized under that name. The British have long incorporated it in their own agricultural policy. So did the Republicans under President Eisenhower, without full knowledge of the similarity to a Democratic plan. Under the Wool Act of 1954, the purpose of which was to increase domestic production of wool, the parity price was set at 105 percent. Wool would be sold on the market for whatever price it would bring; the difference between the market price and the artificial one (105 percent or parity) would be paid by a direct subsidy from the U.S. Treasury. The cost (subsidy) of this plan averaged almost $50 million a year in the decade 1954–1964. For this reason Eisenhower's support of wool was sometimes called "The Brannan Plan in Sheep's Clothing."

Lowe chief of the corps of aeronauts of the U.S. Army. During the course of the Civil War he built up a fleet of observation balloons that served in many engagements.

In the field of heavier-than-air craft there were three American pioneers, one relatively unknown (Samuel Pierpont Langley) and the other two of great renown (Wilbur and Orville Wright). Langley was a physicist who became secretary of the Smithsonian Institution from 1887 to 1906. One of his small, steam-driven, and unmanned models flew almost a mile in 1896; this success induced the War Department to grant him $50,000 to construct a machine capable of carrying a man. He finished this "aerodrome" in 1903, but it failed to fly. After several alterations the attempt was renewed with success a few years later, but by this time the Wright brothers had established their prior claim as the world's first aviators. Langley died in 1906, unrecognized as the inventor in the 1890's of a power-driven heavier-than-air machine, later acknowledged as the pioneer airplane. The Wright brothers, who owned a bicycle shop and were excellent mechanics, put into flight the first such manned machine, a biplane. The flight was near Kitty Hawk, North Carolina; on the first attempt they managed to keep the plane in the air for eight seconds and to travel less than the length of a modern air transport; by 1908 they could stay aloft for an hour. In 1910 Glenn H. Curtiss flew from Albany to New York at an average speed of forty-nine miles an hour; the next year Galbraith P. Rogers flew from New York to California in sixty-eight days — forty-nine of them in the air! Although used in World War I planes were too underdeveloped to be a decisive weapon, in part because top military experts underestimated their potentialities — thought they were good for sport, useless in war; it was a civilian who devised the mechanism by which a machine gun was enabled to fire through a propeller, a rather necessary precaution. After the war, however, aviation made giant strides. In 1919 the first nonstop flight across the Atlantic was made, from Newfoundland to Ireland, by John Alcock and A. W. Brown; eight years later (in 1927) came the solo 3,600-mile nonstop flight of Charles A. Lindbergh from New York to Paris, a dramatic episode that encouraged a flood of investment. During World War II planes were a major factor in offensive and defensive strategy with air forces spelling the difference between Allied victory and defeat. In 1947 achievement of supersonic speed by jet-propelled military aircraft marked a new era in aviation history; subsonic jet propulsion was inaugurated commercially in 1958. By that time all altitude, time, and distance records were subject to continuous revision.

Subsidies to airlines, which developed after World War I, have been justified on three grounds, two practical and the other psychological. The pragmatic reasons were to provide speedy delivery of mail, and to provide a backlog of planes and pilots for national defense; the psychological justification was tied in with national prestige, which was reputedly built up by the maintenance of service on international routes. The subsidies themselves have been both indirect and direct. The indirect ones have been paid for by both the federal government (through navigation aids) and by municipalities (through the provision of airports). Federal navigation aids include the maintenance of radio facilities, airway traffic control, weather information, aids to landing, and provision of intermediate landing fields for emergencies. All of these, involving a staff of 17,000 persons in 1947, were costing the federal government $200 million a year; twenty years later the annual cost was three times as much at more than a half billion dollars a year.*

Until 1955 direct subsidies to airlines were largely derived from overpayments for the carriage of mail. This service had been inaugurated on 15 May 1918 between Washington and New York; at the Washington end the first takeoff was witnessed by President Wilson. On that occasion, after an embarrassing delay caused by a slight oversight (someone had forgotten to put gas in the plane), the pilot climbed into the open cockpit of his 150-horsepower Curtiss biplane, adjusted his goggles, and took off. He was scheduled to stop in Philadelphia on his way to New York, lost his way and crash-landed in a Maryland field, breaking the all-important propeller. The debut of aerial mail, as it was then called, was not a complete disaster; at about the same time another plane was taking off from the Belmont Park Race Track in New York. This plane, with its mail, reached Washington successfully. A half century later Postmaster General W. Marvin Watson would hail the pioneers of the mail service and the pilots "whose only beacon was a thin line of courage"; he would note that from this small beginning we had reached the point, in 1968, where almost 80 percent of all letter mail was traveling by air.

In the first decade the Post Office carried mail in its own planes and was doing so satisfactorily when, in 1927, Congress intervened. It ordered the Post Office Department to contract the business to private concerns; the result was the subsidization of American airlines, chiefly by means of generous air-mail contracts. In the 1930's the overpayment was running between $10 and $15 million a year; in the decade after World War II it was averaging $75 million a year. In 1955 President Eisenhower came to the conclusion that most of the air industry had graduated from the "infant" to the giant class, and did not need so much parental help from a paternal federal government. He saw to it that the operating subsidy was cut in half (at that time to around $35 million); these direct and lump-sum payments were made chiefly to local lines for service to communities that could not

* Navigation aids are obviously of great assistance to commercial aircraft flying on schedule. They are also of great benefit to privately owned aircraft that do not fly on schedule. It has been estimated that every one of the private and business planes flying in 1966 was subsidized, in this fashion, by the federal government at the rate of $5,000 per plane per year.

otherwise afford it, and to helicopter lines, to aid in the development of this "infant" industry. Even so, in 1968, it was estimated that commercial aviation received, directly or indirectly, about $750 million of the Federal Aviation Administration's budget of $800 million a year.

The United States Post Office Department is the largest business in the world. It has in excess of 700,000 employees drawing more than $12 million a day in salaries and wages; they are the workers eulogized, on the façade of the post office at Eighth Avenue and Thirty-third Street in New York City, in a line borrowed from Herodotus: "Neither snow nor rain nor heat nor gloom of night stays these couriers from the swift completion of their appointed rounds." The department has 45,000 post offices and branches. Every year it handles more than 80 billion pieces of mail, almost as much as the rest of the world combined; every two days it handles enough mail, if laid end to end, to completely encircle the earth. It also has one of the largest deficits in the world, in the late 1960's more than a billion dollars annually on a budget of better than $6 billion.

The source of this deficit is indicative of the subsidies involved. The Post Office makes money on first-class mail, which paid 104 percent (in 1967) of what it cost to handle it. It loses money on the balance of its operations. Half of the billion-dollar deficit is generously planned by Congress for what is known as public-service mail — congressional, diplomatic, educational mail — and rural routes. The other half comes from deficits on commercial mail in the second, third, and fourth classes. In the late 1960's the Post Office was losing more than $400 million a year on second-class mail — newspapers and magazines; postage rates in this category paid only 30 percent of the cost, the government made up the other 70 percent. Of this sizable deficit, about half was written off as a public service to education. This was not difficult to do for the scholarly magazine with a small subscription list and little if any advertising. It was harder to justify for "nonprofit" magazines with millions of dollars of revenue, such as the *National Geographic* and the *Journal of the American Medical Association.** It was difficult to explain the necessity for such subsidies to commercial magazines and newspapers with huge circulations and advertising revenues and profits, and in 1971 the new Postal Service —

---

* The American Medical Association uses its profits from advertising, at least in part, to maintain a sizable lobby in Washington. It also wants the Internal Revenue Service to exempt tax-exempt organizations (like itself) from paying taxes on income from advertisements, which the IRS had ruled "unrelated" to the educational, scientific, or charitable purposes for which the tax immunity was originally granted. The rest of the "business" press took a dim view of the claims of the AMA (and a similar one from the Chamber of Commerce) for exemption. It averred that the AMA and the C. of C. preached but did not practice free enterprise, which cannot exist "if we have one business paying an income tax on its profits and a competitor paying no income tax on its profits."

which was expected to operate on a self-sustaining basis — announced whopping increases in second-class rates for magazines and newspapers that would more than double these costs over the next five years. But in previous years, when rates were low, prominent examples of government largess could be cited to:

Life, whose subsidy was more than $10 million a year.

The Saturday Evening Post, with annual subsidies of more than $5 million.

Reader's Digest, editorially opposed to governmental handouts but glad to accept more than $3 million annually from the Post Office.

The Chicago *Tribune,* an exemplar of laissez-faire which accepted each year mail subsidies of almost $2 million.

The Post Office Department also loses heavily on third-class mail. This comprises direct-mail advertising, the unsealed letter, mail-order circulars, small catalogues and books. Much of the printed material in this category is known as "junk" mail, advertising everything from clothing to baby chicks to rose bushes. In this class the sender paid 60 percent in 1968, the government subsidy was 40 percent. Because of sheer bulk, however, this subsidy was the largest of all; in the late 1960's it amounted to $345 million, plus almost $100 million more charged off as a public service for educational catalogues and books. The companies involved in this kind of advertising enjoy their subsidy and argue that they are the bulwark of the American economy, that they account for more than $40 billion annually in sales and for upwards of 5 million jobs. No one has verified their figures but the claim is, because of this alleged importance, that they deserve postal rates which are half of those that could be justified by cost. Fourth-class mail is parcel post. The loss to the Post Office in this category has run more than $100 million annually, obviously to the advantage of mail-order houses and department stores. By the late 1960's, with increasing rates, these business establishments were paying about 80 percent of the cost of handling, much more than they had contributed a decade earlier.

It has been noted that of a deficit of more than a billion dollars in 1968, about half was defined by Congress as a "public service" for nonprofit publications, education, congressional and diplomatic mail, the sale of savings bonds, and the maintenance of rural routes. The other half, upwards of $600 million, was defined as a "hidden subsidy" by some and defended as indispensable by its beneficiaries; it comes from the failure to charge enough to cover the cost of handling. Whether the deficit is classified as a public service or as an outright subsidy it is still a deficit, and three proposals have been made to reduce or eliminate it: to cut costs, to increase rates, and to establish managerial control. It has been suggested that costs could be reduced by a cut in home deliveries, a reduction in service hours at post-office windows, and by handling the mail more efficiently. One plan would eliminate home deliveries entirely, requiring everyone to pick up his mail at neighborhood distribution centers. In the interest of efficient handling the Post Office borrowed from West Germany, where it had worked successfully, the idea of the ZIP code, which was designed to eliminate six of the existing eleven steps in the handling of mail, and thus to improve the speed of delivery by as much as twenty-four hours. All second- and third-class mailers are required to use ZIP codes; this means that mandatory ZIP-coding affects about 65 percent of all mailing. The ZIP code is merely one step toward efficiency. Much of the ever-increasing amount of mail is still being sorted and transported much as it was a century ago. An army of 700,000 is required to move it and one gloomy postal authority, taking note of the diminishing efficiency of operations in the face of an omnipresent glut, predicted that if present trends continue to the year 2000, every man, woman, and ambulant child will be delivering mail! Lawrence O'Brien, who was Postmaster General from 1965 to 1968 and who dealt at first-hand with a catastrophe in 1966 when the Chicago Post Office broke down under the sheer bulk of mail received and could not function at all for three weeks, said that his organization was in a "race with catastrophe." He pointed out that, although the annual budget of the Post Office was more than $6 billion, the percentage that went into new buildings and new machinery was 3 percent in 1961 and 2.4 percent in 1967; by contrast in 1961 AT&T had an investment rate (in new plant and machinery) of 32 percent, in 1966 of 34 percent. O'Brien said it would take an expenditure of a billion dollars a year for five years if the operators of the Post Office, including himself, were "to pull ourselves up by our bootstraps."

Others have contended that rates should be increased. They argue that three-quarters of all first-class mail is sent by businesses and institutions, particularly in the form of bills, and that these businesses should more than pay their way. They maintain that it is ridiculous to subsidize big magazines that contain fifteen minutes of reading, seventy-five minutes of advertising, and pay some of their executives $100,000 a year or more. They are convinced that, in third class, it is silly to subsidize mail that is "unread, unwanted, and unpaid for." In connection with parcel post, they are insistent that Sears and Macy's pay the full cost of carrying packages.

Historically the postal service has been at the mercy of Postmasters General more concerned with delivering votes than mail, of Congressmen whose chief interest in the enterprise was the patronage it afforded, and of postal workers' unions which have inevitably thought more intensively about job security than about quality service. In the area of managerial control Postmaster General O'Brien was the first to make the unbureaucratic proposal that his own job be abolished. He suggested that the Post Office be dropped as a department with Cabinet status and changed into a nonprofit corporation like the TVA or the Panama Canal Zone. O'Brien pointed out that the trouble with the postal system was that managerial control was vested in pressure groups rather than in the Postmaster General, to such an extent that his own "area of *no* control was almost unlimited." These pressure groups were three in number: the postal unions, whose wage scales were decided by Congress, the lobbyists for cheap second- and third- and fourth-class privileges, and (until 1969) the patronage-hungry politicos who appointed 33,000 postmasters and 31,000 rural letter carriers. During this long period of inefficient operations the Post Office Department had been forced to bargain with Congress over pay rates demanded by postal workers' unions, which had built up substantial political influence with House and Senate Post Office Committees, based on campaign contributions. These gave union leaders vast power in closed-door bargaining sessions on Capitol Hill; the unions did not choose to trade a proven political power for another system — the proposed standard bargaining between the unions and a government-owned corporation. As far as patronage is concerned, the selection of postmasters and carriers was once considered the cream of congressional political patronage; a generation ago postmasters were the political town squires who, with the help of rural mail carriers, could get out the vote. Times have changed; the small towns are disappearing and have largely assumed the anonymity of the metropolitan area. In addition the Hatch Act prohibits open political activity. It was therefore not surprising that in 1969 President Nixon placed all postmasters and letter carriers under Civil Service.

In 1968 a President's Commission on Postal Organization, headed by Frederick Kappel (former board chairman of AT&T) spent $1 million and published a report in five volumes entitled *Toward Postal Excellence*. It supported O'Brien's suggestions by proposing a self-supporting public corporation with authority to set its own postage rates, with a board of directors to keep it in the black, with the latest contrivances for handling mail, and with employees hired not through patronage but on the basis of merit. Its plan eliminated Congress — which had been setting postal rates (too low) and determining working conditions (not good), allocating money for new facilities (not enough), and wasting its time with patronage. By 1970 the situation had become so critical that the Nixon Administration achieved legislative authority for the new U.S. Postal Service, a semi-autonomous corporation which replaced the former department and was based on the principles previously enunciated by O'Brien and the Kappel Report. The new corporation began operations on 1 July 1971; government subsidies to it were initially pegged at no more than 10 percent (around $700 million) of the Service's annual budget and were to decline steadily until they reached zero in 1984. Whether that Orwellian year would mark the achievement of such a utopian goal remained to be proved.

There are two principles to support the validity of an income tax: equity and progressivity. The principle of equity signifies that every taxpayer should bear his fair share; if some avoid payment they are receiving a subsidy, and others must pay more. The principle of progressivity means that as the taxpayer's income goes up, his percentage of income tax also rises. Opponents of progressive taxes call them "soak-the-rich" legislation; Senator Barry Goldwater once said that the principle of progressivity was immoral. On the other hand proponents of progressivity base their arguments on two premises. One is that democracy will be strengthened by lessening great gaps between the rich and the poor. The other is that taxes should be based on ability to pay. This means that it is not the amount of the tax that really counts; it is the amount that is left after the tax has been paid. From this point of view a person in the 70 percent bracket who is left with $300,000 out of a net income of $1 million is still better off than a person in the 17 percent bracket who is left with $3,300 on a net income of $4000.

Before World War II the income tax could be defined, with reasonable accuracy, as a "soak-the-rich" tax. In the Civil War, although rates were low at 3 to 10 percent, only 1 percent of the population was affected and paid any income tax. In World War I, although the rates were higher (6 to 77 percent), less than 5 percent in a population of 100 million filed returns. As late as 1939, on the eve of World War II, and in spite of certain loopholes that had made their appearance by that time, an elite of 700,000 persons paid nine-tenths of the tax. By contrast, in 1964, no elite but a mass of more than 65 million persons filed income-tax returns, and those in the lower brackets paid the bulk of more than $47 billion paid; abruptly, the income tax had become a mass tax. Paul Douglas, an economist and Senator from Illinois on the Senate Finance Committee and the Joint Economic Committee, discovered that only about half of total personal income in the country was subject to taxation, while the other half escaped completely from levies. He found that the average paid by the groups with incomes above $50,000 was only a fraction of the amount they were presumed to pay, and that the uppermost group with incomes over $250,000, who according to the schedules were presumed to pay at least 70 percent, actually paid on the average 25 percent or slightly less; the "effective" rate was therefore far less than the nominal one. Moreover Douglas discovered that a considerable number of wealthy individuals paid no taxes at all; in 1965, 367 Americans with incomes over $100,000 paid no income taxes, thirty-five with incomes exceeding $500,000 escaped tax, and three taxpayers with annual incomes in excess of $5 million paid nothing.

How can these things be? Essentially there are two reasons for the discrepancies: withholding and loopholes. Withholding, through payroll deductions, is from all salaries and wages paid. This practice was authorized by Congress in 1943 and has provided a very neat system to insure payment of income tax by all those in the middle and lower brackets; this is because incomes from salaries and wages are recorded accurately, and the tax thereon is already paid. Loopholes (Senator Douglas called them "truck holes") are for those whose income is not derived from salaries and wages; these devices *save* people in the upper brackets from the inconvenience of having to pay the high rates seemingly required by the law. Among others, three prominent loopholes are through capital gains, the depletion allowance, and tax-free bonds and foundations.

Capital gains, introduced under the regime of Andrew Mellon in 1922, provides the most important loophole — so important that Philip Stern (author of *The Great Treasury Raid*) calls it "the holy grail of tax-avoidance." It provides that one half of the profits from the sale of capital assets — such as stocks, bonds, and real estate — held for more than eighteen months is not counted as income, and that the remainder of such capital gains are taxed at regular rates as long as they do not exceed 50 percent; this means that the income tax on total capital gains cannot be more than 25 percent. This established the principle of favored treatment for capital gains because it signified that money acquired through a rise in the value of investment was, for the first time, taxed at a lower rate than money earned in wages or salaries. The first break for the capital-gains groups thus came in 1922. Its second advantage was bestowed twenty years later during World War II (1942), when the time period for which stocks and other assets must be held, in order to benefit from the capital-gains provision, was reduced from eighteen to six months — another escape for the high-bracket group. The third break for the capital-gains group came in 1950 when the so-called stock option was allowed; this is an advantage enjoyed for the most part by highly paid corporate executives. Under a typical stock-option plan, corporate executives are given options to purchase, at the existing market price, large blocks of their corporations' shares. They pay nothing for these options, which are generally good for five years. If thereafter the market price of the stock rises, they can exercise their options and purchase the stock at the original (and lower) option price, giving them paper profits on which they pay no tax. If, after holding the stock for three years they wish to sell it, they pay a tax on their profits, *not* at the regular income tax applicable to high-income taxpayers, but at a much lower capital-gains rate. Through this device top executives in large publicly owned corporations have in recent years made hundreds of millions of dollars in profits. Realistically the profits made through stock options are compensation, and should be taxed at regular tax rates just as other taxpayers — salaried employees, teachers, members of professions, and other businessmen — are taxed on the compensation they receive. It has been claimed that this favored tax treatment provides an incentive to greater fidelity and diligence on the part of executives, and thereby results in increased corporate earnings. But at the hearings on the tax bill in 1963, when an unsuccessful attempt was made to eliminate the stock-option loophole, it was shown that the so-called incentive rationale was largely fictitious, and that stock options were costly to the corporations granting them and to the public shareholders whose equity they diluted. The editor of the prestigious *Commercial and Financial Chronicle* went so far as to tell the House Ways and Means Committee that a stock option was nothing but a "free stock-market ride without risk of loss that has nothing to do with management effort."

Of all loopholes favoring special groups the depletion allowance has been the most notorious, in large part because it is the oil and gas industry in Texas which has gained the greatest benefit. This brings up the great difference between the U.S. oil industry in the nineteenth and twentieth centuries. In the nineteenth century the oil industry was notable by reason of its location, the limited use of its product, and the degree of corporate concentration. Its location was in the Northeast, chiefly in Ohio and Pennsylvania; because of limited supply its use was restricted to lighting and lubrication — it was too costly for fuel. It was dominated by John D. Rockefeller, whose Standard Oil Company controlled 83 percent of all oil production in the United States. Rockefeller was so dedicated to gathering all the fruits that he was willing to do the job all by himself; anyone who tried to help was put out of business or was discouraged in other annoying ways.

These were the main characteristics of the oil industry in the nineteenth century. In its modern form the oil enterprise dates from 10 January 1901, when a remarkable gusher erupted from a hole 1,160 feet deep, dug into a marshy hillock called Spindletop one mile south of Beaumont, Texas. In its first year the initial Spindletop alone produced as much oil as all of the current 37,000 eastern wells put together. By 1902 there were 138 wells producing near Spindletop and their combined production was more than that in the rest of the world. This remarkable development ushered in the modern oil industry, whose comparable characteristics (concentration, use, and location) are quite different from those in the nineteenth century. As far as control is concerned the Rockefeller monopoly was broken; within a year after Spindletop "blew," Standard Oil was competing with Texaco, Gulf, and other incipient giants. Monopoly had given way to oligopoly. From the standpoint of use, oil as liquid fuel became a reality for the first time; Spindletop ushered in what some have called the liquid-fuel age. Suddenly oil had become a source of cheap power (as well as an illuminant and lubricator), an abundant fuel that was to break the coal monopoly, to propel automobiles and airplanes, and to alter the face of the nation. As far as location was concerned the headquarters of the oil business ceased to be the Northeast; after Spindletop it was in Texas, which for many years produced almost 40 percent of the nation's oil and had approximately half of its reserves. Texas was also well supplied with a companion product, natural gas, of which it had about half of the nation's reserves.

The move of the oil industry to the West and Southwest was dramatized by a first-class scandal in the 1920's, that known as Teapot Dome. A Senate investigating committee disclosed that the President, acting with the approval of Secretary of the Navy Edwin Denby, had transferred to Secretary of the Interior Albert B. Fall the administration of naval oil reserves at Teapot Dome, Wyoming, and Elk Hills, California. In 1922, Fall, without competitive bidding, leased the Teapot Dome reserve to oil operator Harry F. Sinclair, and the California fields to petroleum producer Edward L. Doheny. Doheny and Sinclair expected to make at least $100 million each. Fall's cut was around $400,000; because of his sudden and ostentatious wealth a Senate investigation was conducted under the able direction of Senator Thomas Walsh of Montana. The result was that Denby and Fall both resigned, the government finally recaptured the oil reserves but not until 1927, and in 1929 Fall was found guilty of accepting a bribe from Doheny and was fined $100,000 and given a sentence of a year in jail. Technicalities led to the acquittal of Sinclair and Doheny — a curious result because this implied that Fall was guilty of accepting a bribe from Doheny and Sinclair, but Doheny and Sinclair were supposedly innocent of giving a bribe to Fall. This denouement made Senator George Norris of Nebraska so angry that he said we ought to pass a law to the effect that no man with a million dollars can be confronted successfully in our courts.*

---

* In the 1970's, according to reporter Chris Welles writing in *Harper's* (August 1968), the oil-shale situation might erupt into a scandal greater than Teapot Dome. There are several thousand square miles of arid and scrub-covered land in Colorado, Wyoming, and Utah which contain the "greatest package of potential energy on the face of the globe." This treasure lies buried in the world's largest deposit of a dense and black organic mineral called "oil shale." When heated to 900 degrees Fahrenheit, the rocky substance releases crude oil. It is estimated that the shale in these three states could yield as much as 4 trillion barrels of oil — worth $10 trillion, or $50,000 for every person in the United States. In 1968 most of this shale was government-owned, but private companies were buying through a subterfuge. The Interior Department owns the shale land; there was a sudden spurt of interest which prompted prospectors to stake claims (for $2.50 an acre) for millions of acres of arid shale land. Over the years the oil industry quietly bought up thousands of the existing claims, obtaining patents on land containing one-fifth of the oil deposits. As speculation boomed, land that had been patented for $2.50 an acre was often resold for more than $2,000 an acre. Welles observed that in the mid-1950's many employees of the Department of the Interior quit to go into business for themselves. One had worked for the Bureau of the Mines, had filed claims on his own, and had ultimately leased a 21,000-acre plot to Shell Oil. This company paid him $50,000 a year for doing nothing, and had an option to buy the land for $42 million. One Senator who was worried about this development was Paul Douglas of Illinois. He described the oil-shale situation as "the most submerged issue in American domestic politics involving the greatest scandal in the history of the Republic."

The *New York Times* has observed that another important aspect of this question

In 1922 the capital-gains tax had appeared under the genial administration of Andrew Mellon as Secretary of the Treasury. In 1926, under the same auspices, came the depletion allowance which is still in effect. This was a startling revision of the original allowance, adopted shortly after passage of the income tax amendment of 1913, which enabled an oil company to recover only the actual costs incurred in the discovery of oil. This meant that if a well cost $10,000, a company could write off only that amount. In 1926, however, a much larger tax rebate was authorized. The allowance to oil companies was established at 27½ percent of *gross* income (5 percent for the man who starts a gravel pit or digs oysters or clams); as an example a company grosses $10 million on an oil well and has pre-tax profits of $3 million after expenses. Under the law for most corporations it would pay federal income taxes of 52 percent, or $1,560,000 — leaving an after-tax profit of $1,440,000. Under the depletion allowance, however, the company deducts 27½ percent of the gross, or $2,750,000 from its pre-tax net, leaving taxable income of $250,000. Its tax would be $130,000 for a satisfying after-tax profit of $2,870,000.

On the basis of prevailing taxes and costs *in 1926*, when the privilege was first authorized, it was believed that the percentage depletion figure would average out to the original cost allowance. This estimate was a colossal error. *Four decades later* a Treasury study showed that oil companies — through the depletion allowance — were recovering the cost of a well eighteen times or more. Using the Treasury's estimate, for a well that now cost $100,000, the oil company recovered $1.8 million.

On the pro side it is claimed that the depletion allowance stimulates discovery by offering an inducive for investment which may or may not produce results, and that it contributes to national defense by maintaining proved domestic reserves through continuous exploration. On the negative side powerful counterarguments have been heard: that the depletion allowance has long been an anachronism, that it has always been inimical to sound conservation, that it is not necessary for national defense, and that it makes millionaires and postpones tax cuts for all. In the early years of the twentieth century, wildcatting was widespread and the risks were considerable. Today the practice is out-of-date and wildcatters account for little of the nation's oil; improved geological studies, the pooling of company interests, and technological advances have reduced the risks. As a result, according to studies made in 1968, the oil-depletion allowance

---

concerns the conservation of land, water, and scenery in the West. Full-scale development of the oil-shale regions would require huge amounts of water in an arid area and might lead to unsightly slag heaps and erosion far surpassing the ugliness perpetrated by strip mining for coal. Because petroleum from conventional wells is more than adequate to meet fuel needs for many years to come, the *Times* saw no reason for any rush until the federal government had looked fully into both the economics and the ecology of oil-shale development.

was costing the Treasury more than a billion dollars a year in order to net $150 million in added oil reserves. As far as conservation is concerned, it has been observed for decades that the United States should shepherd its resources carefully rather than dissipating them quickly or encouraging — through tax rebates — wildcat drilling. From the standpoint of defense it is doubtful whether the growth of oil reserves within the continental boundaries of the United States is really essential to the national defense. If the next war is a nuclear one, oil would play a minor role; in a limited, non-nuclear conflict (such as that in the Middle East or Vietnam or Korea), outside sources of oil would be available in Canada, Alaska, and Latin America — and possibly in Indonesia and Australia.

There is no question that the depletion allowance encourages large fortunes. In 1963 it was estimated that the mineral industry was receiving a benefit of $3.3 billion for depletion (of which $2.2 billion was allowed to oil and gas companies), and that the U.S. government was losing about $1.5 billion in revenue as a result. A number of oil companies were paying little or no income taxes at all. In addition to the depletion allowance they could take advantage of accelerated write-offs of intangible drilling costs plus another device — the right to count as "foreign taxes" the royalties paid abroad for the extraction of government-owned oil. To most taxpayers these royalties would seem to be normal operating expenses, but they are now listed as an overseas tax to be deducted dollar for dollar from the money that would otherwise come to the Treasury. As a result, in 1966, Standard Oil of New Jersey paid only 3.8 percent on $1.8 billion in profits, and Texaco paid the same low percentage. Based on SEC reports, the Cleveland *Plain Dealer* made a study of income-tax returns of forty of the largest oil companies. Their average rate was 8.2 percent for all of the companies; by contrast, family and individual wage earners were taxed at an average rate of 14 percent, and many corporations outside the petroleum industry paid 40 to 50 percent of their profits in federal income tax. Of the forty companies, fourteen reported owing no tax at all in 1967, and eight others were taxed at an average rate of less than 5 percent. The largest of the fourteen nontaxpayers was Atlantic Richfield Company; in fact, this company and its predecessor (the Atlantic Refining Company) accumulated profits of nearly half a billion dollars in the six years from 1962 through 1967 inclusive, and paid not a penny of income tax in any of these years. In the same years J. Paul Getty, sometimes described as the richest American, paid an average income tax of 7.5 percent on the net income of the Getty Oil Company. Depletion allowances are obviously of prime importance to those in high income-tax brackets, so much so that one midwesterner whose annual income is more than a million dollars put it this way: "When a fellow is in my income bracket he automatically goes into the oil business." Because of this largess to privileged groups tax reduction for the mass of the people must be postponed. Ironic proposals have been made to extend it to others. A member of the House of Representatives from New York introduced a bill to authorize depletion allowance for individual taxpayers at the rate of 1 percent a year from age forty-five; at age seventy, the humble citizen with depleting energies would get 25 percent, almost as much as Humble Oil gets now. He had the curious notion that human resources suffer depletion too. There is also the question of feminine beauty which some claim to be a depleting asset; in actual fact twenty-five fashion models once claimed tax deductions for "the progressive loss of their only corporate asset through age, exhaustion, obsolescence, or otherwise." The Internal Revenue Service turned them down with a touch of flattery, ruling that the assets of models were "indisputable," but that "American beauty never becomes obsolete and therefore is not depreciable for tax purposes." Senator Douglas once stated that professional athletes should logically get the benefit of a depletion allowance — no less than oil, gas, sulphur, coal, iron ore, clam shells, oyster shells, sand, and gravel. The Senator also began to worry about versifiers, pointing out that the poetic impulse develops early in life as part of the ebullience of youth, that such effervescence is a wasting asset, and that a depletion allowance should be paid as it ebbs away.

Many taxpayers have saved through the capital-gains and depletion-allowance loopholes; others have benefited from the complete exemption of tax on income received from state and municipal bonds. There are approximately $100 billion of these, bearing low interest rates from 2½ to under 5 percent; they are held almost exclusively by the wealthy who, by investing heavily in these securities, obtain large tax-free incomes which they would be unable to achieve if the same funds were invested in stocks or other property — the income from which would be taxable at rates up to 70 percent. As an example, Mrs. Horace Dodge, Jr., inherited $56 million; by investing it in tax-exempt bonds she removed the entire income from federal taxation. For this reason such investment is sometimes referred to as the "cyclone cellar" into which the wealthy retreat in order to avoid the onslaught of the federal income tax. Senator Douglas estimated the loss to the Treasury as upwards of $2 billion a year.

On behalf of the tax-free exemption it is claimed that it enables state and local governments to borrow vast sums at lower rates of interest than they would normally pay. On the contrary side it is observed that the exemption is costly and inequitable to the bulk of taxpayers and to many corporations. As far as individuals are concerned it is pointed out that it is highly inequitable that one person with a portfolio in tax-exempt bonds should derive an annual income of $60,000 to $80,000 wholly free of tax while his neighbor — who receives the same income from salary, dividends, or earnings on his business — is obliged to pay $20,000 to $30,000 to the federal government in taxes. It is also observed that the savings to state and local governments (through lower interest rates) are substantially less than the cost to the general body of taxpayers, who must make up with their taxes the revenue lost to the federal government by reason of the exemption. One solution would be to abolish the exempt status of state and local bonds entirely, providing them with a federal subsidy instead — a subsidy to which all taxpayers would contribute. Senator Douglas estimated that this device would provide abundant revenue from income tax amounting to a billion dollars for the Treasury *beyond* the subsidy paid by the federal government to state and local governments as compensation for higher interest rates.* Beyond the silent individual taxpayers who must compensate for those who receive exemptions through tax-free bonds, there are corporations which suffered when local and state bonds were floated for a purpose never contemplated by Congress. The original intention had been to help states and municipalities obtain low-interest financing for needed schools, waterworks, and other public facilities. By 1968 in a number of states, particularly southern ones, municipalities and other local governments were issuing so-called industrial development bonds (tax-free IDBs) to finance the construction of plants which were then leased on advantageous terms to private firms. The bonds were then paid off by the firms through low rentals; by means of this device the municipality was simply making its federal tax exemption available to private corporations. Through this "plant piracy" municipalities financed the construction of runaway factories from other parts of the country; it was used in southern states as a means of drawing plants and employment away from the North and the Midwest. In the latter sections the practice created unemployment, depressed the tax base, and required citizens to pay higher federal income taxes because of the subsidy to their southern competitors. Finally, in March 1968 the federal Treasury, which had au-

---

* A large part of the necessity for low interest rates on the part of state and local governments derives from the fact that their tax policies are regressive by comparison with the progressive and growth-responsive federal income tax. States and local governments rely heavily on regressive property and sales and excise taxes, or bond issues, for their incomes; in 1969 fifteen states still levied no income tax at all and the other thirty-five collected a miniscule $5 billion annually from it. States, unfortunately, continually raise their regressive taxes and find them inadequate for education, welfare, and other essential services. The federal government, by contrast, in 1967 collected 64 percent of all taxes in the United States and 93 percent of the only progressive and "growth" tax — the income tax. Each year, at current levels of taxation and economic growth, the federal government can count on an extra $15 billion or so in income from progressive levies, a sum which the states could not begin to approximate with their regressive taxes. This "automatic growth dividend" represents a major tool for relocating resources to the states and localities — by direct grants from the federal government; Governor Nelson Rockefeller of New York, among other state executives, has asked for a redistribution of these federal tax bonanzas to the states. Unfortunately, the increase in federal deficits in the early 1970's lessened the chances for favorable congressional action.

thority and calculated that it was losing upwards of $30 million a year through this misuse of the tax-exempt privilege, forbade the issue of additional IDBs.

Tax-free foundations have also come under severe criticism, particularly by Wright Patman, Chairman of the House Banking and Currency Committee. In 1969 there were more than 30,000 such foundations wielding some $20 billion in money power; they were increasing at the rate of 2,000 a year without effective governmental controls. Their effect on the nation's economy was illustrated by the $1.3 billion in grants they awarded annually. They helped care for the sick, they put young people through school, and they provided millions of dollars for scientific research; they also promoted — with tax-free dollars — research into badminton, mercy-killing, and higher sense perception. There have been examples of unorthodox and unique philanthropy: tax-exempt foundations that support mistresses, divorcées, and widows; foundations used to recruit football players; foundations designed only to keep family fortunes safe from the tax collector; foundations used to pay for vacations in Europe and elsewhere in the world, or to underwrite banquets, portraits, and biographies of, by, or for the "philanthropists." Well-known foundations have been accused of unwise and irregular expenditures: it was claimed that in 1967 the Ford Foundation spent nearly half a million dollars on public relations and that the Rockefeller Foundation expended half as much on its New York office as it did on charity in the entire nation. Because tax exemption is a subsidy paid for by the taxpaying public, Patman (sometimes known as "the last of the great Populists") believed that foundations should abandon what he called "foundation foolishness," — the making of grants for the "development of trivia into nonsense." As an example of such a grant he cited a study financed by the Bollingen Foundation into the "origin and significance of the decorative types of medieval tombstones in Bosnia and Herzegovina." He pointed out that the Bollingen Foundation was a creation of the Mellon banking family of Pittsburgh, and added, "if the Mellons are more interested in tombstones than in Pittsburgh poverty . . . that is the Mellons' affair. However, there is no obligation upon either the Congress or the American citizenry to give the Mellons tax-free dollars to finance their exotic interests."

Patman was just as suspicious of the Rockefeller family as of that of the Mellons, and was worried about the proliferation of Rockefeller-controlled foundations. "Down in Houston there are some neighborhoods so rich that every flea has his own dog," said Patman. He went on to say that "the Rockefellers are like that. Everyone of them has his own foundation." (That could be an understatement. John D. Rockefeller III, testifying before a congressional committee, said he wasn't sure just how many foundations his family had, but there were at least thirteen). In 1969 Patman recommended the imposition of a 20 percent tax on the gross income of foundations, which he said would raise $200 million annually. He also proposed that no foundation be permitted to own more than 3 percent of the stock of any corporation and that foundations be required to disburse all of their net income annually.*

Because of these loopholes and other major ones (unlimited charitable deductions, farm losses, tax losses on real estate), all of which are estimated to cost the Treasury around $40 billion annually in taxable income, the evolution of our income-tax system has been a paradoxical one — *from* a low-rate tax through 1939 relying for revenue on the high-income group, *to* a high-rate tax relying on the middle and lower-income groups after 1939. We no longer have a "soak-the-rich" tax system — because the rich possess capital, and capital pays relatively little on its earnings. We do have a "soak-the-salaried" tax system, and no one with salary alone can get rich. Because of this loophole-ridden system lawyer David T. Bazelon has concluded that our income tax, in practice, is hardly progressive at all; the burden is on the lower, not the higher-income groups. Through manifold loopholes the Internal Revenue Code appears to be putting forward the policy, which appears both dubious and unjust to many, that any form of *unearned* income is more deserving than any form of *earned* income. Our present system of taxation is designed to encourage the *investment* of new capital — rather than to encourage the *expenditure* of sweat, skills, talents, or the years of one's life. What earns money fastest in modern America — is money.

There have been some proposals for reform. Presidents Kennedy and Johnson tied in their tax-cut proposals with reform (or abolition) of loopholes. The tax-cuts went through; nothing was done about the loopholes. Beyond the presidential level, Senator Russell Long of Louisiana has proposed a tax system universally applicable on *gross* income — with no loopholes and with lower rates — with a top income tax of around 50 percent. He did so for two reasons: one was equity and the other was administrative simplicity. Long believed that both Congress and the public could be persuaded to support this suggestion because, under the present exemptions, even the richest man could keep half his income for his own use; there was a simple question — Why clutter the law with complexities and tax-avoidance gimmicks? Joseph W. Barr, a former Assistant Secretary of the Treasury, not only supported Long's proposals in principle but said

* John Brooks points out in *The Great Leap* (p. 74) that astronomical inheritance taxes were the reason for the establishment of the richest charitable organization in the history of the world. When Henry Ford I and his sons made their wills around 1940, they left 90 percent of their Ford stock to the private foundation that bears their name. By so doing they avoided paying nearly all of it to the government in taxes, at the same time preserving family control of the motor company and even relieving the heirs of the other 10 percent of the necessity of paying any inheritance taxes. Brooks concluded: "The hard-shelled old Henry Ford, who had lived beyond his time, must have gone to his grave in 1947 chortling over how he had beaten the government out of its money and made philanthropy pay."

that we faced the possibility of a taxpayer revolt if the United States did not soon make major reforms in the income-tax structure. By the late 1960's the situation had reached the point where a song was written, calling attention to how good things used to be. Titled "Oh, for the Good Old Colony Days, When We Were under the King!" it went as follows:

> *Excise, income, sales tax away.*
> *Send me a tea tax — I'll gladly pay.*
>   *Of the world's biggest bargain I sing:*
>
> *Thirteen colonies under the King,*
> *We blew it, and oh, how we erred,*
>   *Overthrowing that wonderful George the Third.*

XV

Land: Its Use and Abuse

THE new United States, all thirteen of them, emerged in 1783 from a successful Revolution with boundaries extending from the Atlantic Ocean on the east to the Mississippi on the west, and from Canada on the north to the Floridas on the south. For the "West" of that day — the area immediately beyond the Appalachians — the navigation of the Ohio and Mississippi rivers was vital as an outlet for their produce; this was because it was impossible to move grain (except as whiskey) directly to the East over mountains and through wilderness. There were two general periods in transportation on these rivers: the keelboat era prior to the War of 1812 and the steamboat one after it. The keelboat was a shallow, undecked freight vessel which had a keel but no sails; it went down the river with the current and came back (if not sold for lumber in New Orleans) by the application of muscular might and main — largely expended on poles and oars. These were the picturesque days of Mike Fink, the narrator of so many "tall tales" that he ranks with Paul Bunyan in frontier legends. Fink claimed that he could "jump higher, squat lower, dive deeper, stay under longer and come up dryer . . . whip his weight in wildcats, and let a zebra kick him every fifteen minutes." So could his colleagues, with the result that:

> They fit and fit, and gouged and bit,
> And struggled in the mud.
> Until the ground for miles around
> Was kivered with their blood,

And a pile of noses, ears, and eyes,
Large and massive reached the skies.

The *New Orleans* was the first steamboat to go down the river to the mouth of the Mississippi; this was in 1811. Four years later the *Enterprise* came back up the river, from New Orleans to Louisville, in twenty-five days. As steamboats became larger and more efficient, freight rates came down. To move 100 pounds of produce from Louisville to New Orleans had cost $5 in keelboat days; the charge was down to $2 in 1820 and to 25¢ in 1840. By 1825 Cincinnati, called "Porkopolis" and the "Hog Butcher of the West," had become the steamboat capital of the Ohio Valley and its most important city. There were two interesting features of the river steamboats: their engines and their design. The rivers required a high-pressure engine to stem swift-flowing currents; this was accomplished with the adoption of a light but powerful engine whose coughing exhaust could be heard for miles, and whose rhythmic strokes set the whole ship trembling. The design was governed by the simple fact that the river required boats with little draft, drawing not more than two to four feet of water. Engineers and architects therefore made the vessels long, adding two to three upper decks to offset the loss of cargo space below the waterline. This led in time to the giant Mississippi steamboats — some 250 feet long with three decks, with pilothouses perched fifty feet above the river, and with a superstructure splendid with rococo ornaments. Such vessels carried two tons of freight for every ton of boat, while drawing two to four feet of water; some captains boasted their ships could navigate on a heavy dew. This was a bit of an exaggeration, but the river steamboats did remarkable things. In 1820 the first one ran the rapids at Louisville, with the result that the city relinquished its place as the terminus of steamboat navigation on the Ohio. In 1828 a steamboat actually ran the dangerous rapids at Muscle Shoals, thus inaugurating service on the upper Tennessee River as far as Knoxville. Soon every hamlet on a creek large enough for wading dreamed of becoming a "river port" and offered lavish rewards to the first steamboat reaching its wharves. Despite all the efforts of inventors and venturesome navigators, however, the bulk of shipments was confined to the high-water periods accompanying floods in the spring and fall. Because of this restriction on the time for navigation, too much grain reached New Orleans in a few months out of the year, resulting in glutted markets and low prices and heavy spoilage.

The Mississippi, key to all the western country beyond the Appalachians, provided a formidable diplomatic weapon for whoever controlled it. In the quarter century after the close of the Revolution the navigation of this mighty river came very close to involving the United States in war with France and Spain. The difficulties with the former were settled with the Louisiana Purchase of 1803, which represented the greatest real-estate bargain in U.S. history and also the greatest strain on the Constitution, which was silent on the acquisition of new territory or on the promise of statehood therein. "Louisiana" was then the vast region stretching north from the mouth of the Mississippi River to its source, and west to the watershed of the Rockies, a tract of 828,000 square miles which Jefferson managed to purchase at about 3¢ an acre. The northern and southern boundaries were vague and the Federalist opposition assailed Jefferson for unconstitutionally paying out a "stack of silver dollars three miles high for an enormous desert." In spite of these animadversions there was majority support for what appeared to be a pretty good bargain, from the standpoint of both economics and strategy; it increased the national territory by 140 percent and made possible the creation of thirteen states.

Difficulties with Spain were resolved by the settlement of the questions involving East and West Florida. They came to the United States as part of a swap, in what is known as the Transcontinental Treaty of 1819 between Spain and the United States; the barter involved the exchange of Texas for the Floridas. From 1810, with the outbreak of revolutions in South America, Spain had been forced to denude Florida of troops to fight the rebels. A chaotic situation rapidly developed, with much marauding into the United States by Indians and outcasts based in the swampy land of the Everglades; in 1818 General Andrew Jackson employed the dubious doctrine of "hot pursuit" and invaded Florida. Spain perceived she was going to lose Florida in any case; as Thomas A. Bailey has observed she decided to sell the alligator-infested area while she could get something for it rather than lose the region after a humiliating and costly war. The *quid pro quo* was Texas. In his negotiations Secretary of State John Quincy Adams agreed to a definitive boundary for the previously disputed southern and western boundary of Louisiana. It was to begin at the Sabine River on the Gulf of Mexico, proceeding by a stairstep progression to the forty-second parallel and the Pacific Ocean. In so doing the United States gave up its claim to Texas, and Spain surrendered her own to Florida and Oregon. Within a short time increasing American interest in Texas would cause President John Quincy Adams to regret that Secretary of State John Quincy Adams had ever relinquished so much land in the Southwest.

In 1846 the United States went to war over the area and ultimately acquired not only Texas but a large area then known as New Mexico plus California. This seems surprising in view of the fact that the Mexican War, next to that in Vietnam with which it has often been compared, was as unpopular a war as this nation has ever fought. In Massachusetts Henry David Thoreau went to jail rather than pay war taxes he thought iniquitous. In the same state, the prominent statesman Charles Sumner said that the war was "base in object. . . . It is a war of infamy, which must blot the pages of our history." Such sentiments were widespread throughout the Northeast; there the prevailing belief seemed to be that the war was a slaveholder's plot from start to finish, a scheme to acquire more land in which to cram more slaves.

If this had been the whole story the Northeast and the West would never have allowed the annexation, simply because they could have out-voted the South, which wanted the annexation of potential slave territory for cotton expansion. But the antislavery argument was not the deciding factor; there were other influences — both economic and psychological — which brought the annexation of a vast territory. On the economic side there were powerful and compelling sectional influences, favorable to annexation, in both the antislavery Northeast and the free-farming West. The West wanted more and cheaper land. In the Northeast there were strong economic influences which supported annexation whatever the antislavery forces might think. Mercantile interests wanted the prof-its of a new water traffic, in both the Gulf of Mexico and the Pacific Ocean. Speculators, particularly those who held Texan land scrip and Texan bonds, wanted profits. The point was that the Republic of Texas, which lasted from 1836 to 1845, had been conceived in debt and nourished on depreciated paper; it had issued bonds, and still more bonds, to support the original ones in their sagging condition. By 1845, when the debt was estimated to be around $10 million, Texan bonds bearing 8 percent inter-est sold for three cents on the dollar. This depreciated paper was widely disseminated in the United States; its holders realized fully that it would never appreciate until the Republic's finances were stabilized by annexa-tion and the assumption by the United States of the Texan debt (finally achieved as part of the Compromise of 1850). This list of influential northern financiers who made money out of Texan bonds, and who lob-bied zealously for annexation *and* assumption, is an interesting one. In New York City there were the Delmonico and Milbank families. In Phila-delphia there were the Drexels, the Biddles, Jay Cooke, and Charles Mac-alester — after whom a college is now named. Cooke, later a prominent financier of the Civil War, was associated with a Philadelphia banking house that was heavily involved; he said that many in the North, who would not have normally voted for the addition of potential slave terri-tory, did so because they had invested in Texan bonds. In Washington the major banking firm involved was that of Corcoran & Riggs, names that still retain artistic and financial prominence in the national capital. This highly reputable banking house, with connections in both American and European cities, had its headquarters in Washington across from the U.S. Treasury. The location was convenient because the firm took up loans required by the U.S. government to finance the Mexican War. In time the largest payment to any business institution in the country, from the as-sumption by the United States of the Texan debt, went to Corcoran &

Riggs. It is therefore not surprising that senior partner William Wilson Corcoran, a longtime friend of such leading statesmen as Clay, Buchanan, and Webster, was busy during 1850 in the entertainment of men prominent in the drama surrounding the Compromise of that year. After Webster's famous Seventh-of-March Speech ("I speak today for the Union, hear me for my cause"), which helped carry the day, Corcoran went to his office, canceled two of the improvident Webster's notes for more than $5,000, and sent them to the Massachusetts Senator with an additional check for $1,000. Some thought the orator was speaking for something beyond the Union.

In all sections of the country there were economic motives behind the annexation territory; in all sections of the nation there was also a psychological stimulus. This was wrapped up in "Manifest Destiny," a term that gained currency in the 1840's. It implied the inevitability of the continued territorial expansion of the United States into undeveloped continental areas to the west and south; many Americans believed that God had ordained that they should turn their faces toward the setting sun and acquire territory not being developed properly by Mexicans and Indians, who were dishonest, incompetent, and slothful. In such circumstances peace was folly and annexation was a virtue. There was a story about a party of northerners who were offering toasts around the festive board. Said the Bostonian in cultured accents, "Here's to the United States, bounded on the north by British America, on the south by Mexico, on the east by the Atlantic Ocean, and on the west by the Pacific."

Next came a Chicagoan, who said in his midwestern drawl: "My eastern friend has too limited a view. We must look to our Manifest Destiny. Here's to the United States, bounded on the north by the North Pole, on the south by the South Pole, on the east by the rising, and on the west by the setting, sun."

There was boisterous applause but the next gentleman, a Californian, thought the previous toasts too moderate. He cried: ". . . Why limit ourselves so narrowly? I give you the United States, bounded on the north by the Aurora Borealis, on the south by the Procession of the Equinoxes, on the east by Primeval Chaos, and on the west by the Day of Judgment!"

There were contemporaries who believed this oratory was humbug serving as a thin disguise for ignorance or greed. James Russell Lowell said that the loud talk about Manifest Destiny was half ignorance "an t'other half rum." Abraham Lincoln likened the United States, with its greed for land, to the Illinois farmer who said, "I ain't greedy about land. I only want what jines mine." To modern commentators it appears that the motivation for American continental expansion was more complex than simple greed. There was much agrarian cupidity, but included in the strange amalgam there was also the idea of mission, simple romanticism, racial prejudice, and a basic sense of insecurity felt by a still youthful republic confronting formidable rivals. All of this resulted in the eloquent bombast and the jingoistic nonsense known as Manifest Destiny.

To the surprise of everyone U.S. forces captured Mexico City; no less an authority than the Duke of Wellington, an avid student of the campaigns fought on this side of the ocean, said it couldn't be done, but General Winfield Scott, a dandy swashbuckler known as "Old Fuss and Feathers," did so in a brilliant maneuver. A treaty of peace soon followed; by this stroke of war — following the strokes of diplomacy that had gained Texas in 1845, the United States added (including Texas) an increase of two-thirds to its domain — an area larger than Louisiana. The new expanse was so varied in its riches that it gave the United States first gold, then oil, and now uranium. Curiously the peace treaty was condemned both by opponents who wanted *all* of Mexico and by opponents who wanted none of it; in that sense the settlement was a compromise because the United States took only two-fifths of its neighbor to the south! The dollar cost at the time was $118 million — $15 million for "purchased" territory in New Mexico and California, $3 million for released claims to Texas, and $100 million for the military cost of the war. Not counted was the value of lives lost, the cost of interest on debt and pensions to the present day, an intensification of the slavery issue leading to the Civil War, and the animosity of Latin America — which was unimpressed by the U.S. argument that the Mexicans were lucky not to have lost their entire domain to the "Colossus of the North."

Originally four major powers had been interested in Oregon, a name which once designated a vast territory including half of what is now British Columbia, all of the current states of Washington, Oregon, and Idaho, and substantial portions of Montana and Wyoming. The claims of Spain had been eliminated by the Transcontinental Treaty of 1819, and those of Russia by a treaty signed in 1824 which essentially restricted that nation to Alaska (north of 54° 40′). Because the population consisted largely of Indians, the two remaining powers (Great Britain and the United States) in 1818 agreed to occupy the area jointly until a division of territory seemed compelling and necessary. Before the 1840's the American public had manifested little interest in the area. In 1825 Senator Benton of Missouri said that he hoped the Rocky Mountains would be our "everlasting boundary." As late as 1843 Senator McDuffie of South Carolina thanked God for his mercy in placing the Rockies where they were. But by 1845 a member of the House of Representatives was saying, "The Rocky Mountains are mere molehills. Our destiny is onward." What had happened to increase interest in the area?

The psychological impulse was represented by Manifest Destiny. The religious one was provided by Protestant missionaries, notably Marcus

Whitman, who wished to convert the Indians; unfortunately the aborigines thought many of the evangelists, because of their grasping tendencies, were more interested in *taking* their country than in *teaching* them Christianity. There were two economic impulses, one old (furs) and the other new (farming). The American fur trade is usually associated with the name of John Jacob Astor. Born near Heidelberg in Germany he came to the United States penniless, but soon opened a small shop in New York for trade in musical instruments and furs. Shrewdness and driving ambition brought the expansion of his business until he became the prince of the China trade. He chartered the American Fur Company in 1808, established the trading post of Astoria near the mouth of the Columbia in 1811, and by the 1820's exercised a virtual monopoly of the trade in furs in U.S. territories. Remembered principally as a fur trader, Astor made most of his money as an astute investor in lands in and around New York City, at his death was the wealthiest man in the United States, and left a fortune that has continued to make his name prominent.

The first notable trek of 120 American farmers reached the Willamette Valley of Oregon in 1842; the next year an additional thousand arrived. Walter Prescott Webb, the historian who wrote a classic entitled *The Great Plains*, raised an interesting question as to why these farmers made the 2,000-mile trip in the first place — when they could have settled on land in Louisiana which was nearer and available. Webb believed there was no other phenomenon like this one in American history, and he doubted if world history could offer a parallel case. The significant point was that these immigrants went all this distance to a wooded and well-watered environment similar in practically all respects to that which they had known in the East — passing over the fertile but dryer plains of the Midwest where, as time proved, agricultural opportunities were far better than they were in Oregon. They were bound to a land where the simple plow, the scythe, and the ox or horse could be used according to the tradition that had been followed for two centuries or more; they took the long trail to Oregon because they were unwilling to adopt the new agricultural methods that would be required in the Great Plains. Many regarded their long trek to Oregon as a heroic act. Webb disagreed; in his judgment it really registered a lack of enough heroism and imagination to work out their salvation in the fertile lands through which they were passing.

The Oregon matter should have been an easy dispute to handle, but war between the two nations almost resulted because the affair got mixed up in partisan politics in both countries. In the United States it was the expansionism of the Democrats and President Polk, exemplified by chauvinistic slogans such as "54° 40′ or fight." In England there was political fear that the ministry would fall if its opponents were in a position to accuse it of "base" surrender to the Americans. Fortunately, logic prevailed on both sides and war was averted. Polk boasted that the only way to treat John Bull was to look him straight in the eye — but in private the President abandoned this eyeball-to-eyeball diplomacy because he was enough of a pragmatist to know that war in 1846, against both England and Mexico, was a bit silly. He was supported by the Atlantic-coast shipping interests of the United States, which were strong indeed before the Civil War. These interests were covetous of Puget Sound only; they were quite willing to settle on the forty-ninth parallel. The British awakened to the fact that fur trade had declined so much in the Columbia River region that the Hudson Bay Company had shifted its operations to Vancouver Island; it also realized, by reason of the potato blight in Ireland, that shipments of grain from the United States were much more important than land in Oregon. A settlement was ultimately reached along the forty-ninth parallel and the Straits of Juan de Fuca to the Pacific, thus insuring the United States both Puget Sound and the Willamette Valley.*

When the Articles of Confederation had gone into effect in 1781 the seven founding states that had claims to western land, extending as far as the Mississippi, surrendered their claims to the national government. This was in principle; in practice the cession was exasperatingly slow, particularly in the Old Southwest. The reason was obvious: in the Old Southwest the state claims were clear, in the Old Northwest they were clouded because of rival claims (Virginia and Connecticut in Ohio, Virginia and Massachusetts in Michigan). In the Southwest, therefore, it was easy for states to sell land before cession to the federal government — and they did so. North Carolina threw western land open to settlement at the low price of $5 per hundred acres; this sent Carolina land jobbers upon a speculative rampage and within seven months of the announcement 4 million acres had been sold. Once sold, eastern planters in North Carolina decided they did not want to pay taxes to protect distant frontiersmen; once this conclusion was reached the act of cession to the federal government finally went through in 1789. It conveyed little more than jurisdiction because, by that date, most of the land had been sold by the state. It was not until 1802 that Georgia, the most dilatory of the claimant states, finally turned over her western lands to the federal government — and then only after

---

* In 1867 the United States did something about the region north of 54° 40′ when Alaska was purchased from Russia. This acquisition of territory did not come because of any public demand or interest in it. Russia was then willing to sell because the area was too distant to be defended in case of war. The United States was willing to buy because Secretary of State Seward was a great believer in Manifest Destiny. The area achieved some notoriety in 1898 as a result of the gold strike in the Klondike, but it was not until World War II that it achieved lasting prominence. This was because of its military and strategic importance for the airplane; the air route from San Francisco to Japan via the Aleutians is 1,700 miles shorter than the route via Hawaii. One has only to contemplate the present implications if Alaska were a Russian beachhead in North America — instead of being the Union's forty-ninth state.

becoming involved in a disgraceful scandal. In 1795 the legislature of Georgia, anticipating the ultimate surrender of its claims to the federal government, sold the greater part of what is now Alabama and Mississippi for the sum of $500,000 to four "Yazoo" land companies made up of stockholders from different parts of the country. In this transaction, which involved 35 million acres, virtually the entire state legislature was bribed, and the backers of the new "Yazoo" companies included two U.S. Senators, one justice of the U.S. Supreme Court, and a territorial governor. There was nationwide attention and criticism with the result that a new legislature in Georgia rescinded the sale and burned all papers connected with it. Yazoo claimants appealed to Congress as well as to the courts. After years of debate, a case reached the Supreme Court (*Fletcher v. Peck*, 1810) which decided that the original state grant was an implied contract and that the rescinding law was unconstitutional ("No State shall . . . pass any bill . . . or law impairing the obligation of contract"). Ultimately Congress had to pay claimants more than $4 million — adding insult to the injury already inflicted by the prodigal state.

By contrast, in the Old Northwest (now the states of Ohio, Indiana, Illinois, Michigan, and Wisconsin) all land was turned over to the federal government except the Virginia Military Districts and the Connecticut Western Reserve. Virginia reserved 6,000 square miles, between the Scioto and Little Miami rivers in Ohio, to redeem military bounty certificates; it also reserved 150,000 acres, opposite Louisville in Indiana, which was ultimately awarded to George Rogers Clark and his men. As a small state with western land claims Connecticut was given permission by Congress to reserve 3,500,000 acres in Ohio for the purposes of reimbursing citizens who had suffered losses by fire or otherwise during the Revolution, and to provide for a permanent school fund. This area, variously known as the Western Reserve or New Connecticut, extended south from Lake Erie to the forty-first parallel and west 120 miles from the Pennsylvania line. In 1792 Connecticut set aside 500,000 of these acres on the western side of the Reserve (now Erie and Huron counties in Ohio) as a grant to 1,870 inhabitants in coastal towns whose Connecticut property had been destroyed by British raids during the Revolution. Three years later the state sold the rest of the tract (3 million acres) to a group of thirty-five speculators organized as the Connecticut Land Company. The reason for the quick sale was that it was obvious the "Firelands" to the west could never be disposed of until the region to the east was first thrown on the market; the state was not progressing with sales to individuals and therefore sold all the remaining land to the company for $1.2 million. The state used the money for its school fund; the Connecticut Land Company offered the land, which it had bought for 40¢ an acre, for sale at $1 an acre with five years to pay. Among the speculators in the company was Moses Cleaveland, who had graduated from Yale in 1777, served as a brigadier general in the Connecticut militia during the Revolution, and on behalf of the Connecticut Land Company brought the original party to the mouth of the Cuyahoga River to negotiate with the Indians. In these parleys Cleaveland was able and shrewd, plying the Indians with abundant food, ample whiskey, and exciting dancing; as a result in 1796 the red men relinquished their claims to the east of the Cuyahoga for 500 pounds of currency, two beef cattle, and 100 gallons of whiskey. Cleaveland then selected the city now named for him as the "capital" of the Western Reserve, went back to Connecticut and the legal profession for which he was trained, and never returned to the Western Reserve, leaving only his name there. Before leaving Cleveland (as the name came to be spelled after 1830) he donated the Public Square to the city. It had cost the Connecticut Land Company $1.76; by 1950 Public Square (a bit less than two acres) was valued at more than $4 million, but was not for sale. The escalation in price was what Henry George would have called "unearned increment."

The first decision before the Confederation Government (1781–1789), in relation to the western lands now coming under its jurisdiction, was whether they should be surveyed *before* or *after* sale. Here a fundamental choice had to be made between two established systems: the rectangular town system of New England, which provided for the survey of lands before settlement, and subsequent sale in orderly blocks; and the southern warrant system of indiscriminate location and subsequent survey which allowed a settler to purchase a warrant, lay out his plot wherever it suited him, and *then* have it surveyed.

There were advantages and disadvantages in both systems. The New England practice of prior survey abolished conflicting titles and assured pioneers of protection from Indians as they advanced westward in compact tiers. On the negative side the New England system forced the settler to purchase bad land along with good, in a plot that had been originally surveyed on the principles of geometry rather than special economic advantage. The southern system, by contrast, had the advantage of allowing the settler to pick his own plot, selecting the most attractive land no matter how irregular the boundaries might be. There were two disadvantages: subsequent land disputes and subsequent trouble with Indians. The latter developed because pioneers passed beyond established settlements in their search for alluring land, had no protection, and were often massacred. The irregular and inaccurate descriptions of southern land claims, based on movable rocks and trees and streams known to change their course, led to a welter of conflicting titles. Thomas Lincoln, the father of the future President, was an example of a farmer who had experience with both systems. He originally lived in Kentucky and seemed to be getting along; he paid his bills, served on juries, owned livestock, supported his family. But he had constant difficulty with the vague titles to the farms on which he lived. In 1816 he was sued, and solved the problem by moving to Indiana. There, on land previously surveyed and acquired directly from the U.S. government, he could be sure that no legal suit would cause him to lose a farm into which he had put years of hard work.

The Congress under the Articles of Confederation adopted the New England system and incorporated it into the Ordinance of 1785, one of the most important legislative measures in American history. Essentially it provided for systematic surveys and subdivisions of the public domain, along with a system of land disposal that benefited speculators. The unit was the township, six miles square divided into thirty-six numbered sections each containing one square mile (640 acres). The first base line, running from east to west, was begun where the boundary of Pennsylvania crossed the Ohio River; subsequent base lines, six miles apart, were crossed by range lines (running north and south) at similar intervals. This system of land survey certainly ended the confusion prevalent under the southern warrant system; now a prospective settler purchased a definite tract — for example, Section 20 in Township No. 3 — rather than an uncertain claim to a plot that he laid out himself. Unfortunately, the Ordinance of 1785 provided for a sales policy that could benefit speculators only; the land was to be sold at auction in minimum 640-acre sections at not less than $1 an acre — the minimum price, if there was no counterbid, was $640. This provision prevented pioneer farmers from buying government land, for no frontiersman could clear that large a plot nor did he have the money to buy on those terms. Instead the door was open for speculators who could purchase entire sections or townships at eastern auctions and then parcel them out to users in small tracts and on credit. This outcome was probably purposeful on the part of Congressmen, many of whom were land jobbers themselves.

Because of the time needed for laborious surveys, and the financial inability of frontiersmen to buy directly from the government, early sales of western land were disappointing; at the first auctions in 1787 only $176,000 in depreciated currency was taken in. Congress was both alarmed by the scant returns and desperate for money; it therefore decided to sell a few large plots to speculators. By so doing, it inadvertently set in motion the chain of events that led to the Ordinance of 1787, which provided governmental machinery for the region. It also contributed to a monumental land fraud, involving the Ohio and Scioto companies; this scandal was as notorious on the federal level as the Yazoo frauds on the state plane.

The chief organizer of the Ohio Company of Massachusetts was the Reverend Manasseh Cutler, a many-sided fellow who was Congregationalist clergyman, speculator, lawyer, physician, teacher, and botanist with an M.A. from Yale. In appearance he seemed to command confidence and respect; he was tall and portly, and was usually attired in a black velvet suit and black stockings, along with silver knee and shoe buckles. Cutler got the idea of organizing the Ohio Land Company around certificates of indebtedness held by soldiers who had fought in the Revolution. These certificates had not been paid and were selling at 12¢ on the dollar if cash was involved — but Congress might accept them at face value for land. Cutler therefore arranged for stockholders to turn in depreciated certificates of indebtedness to the Ohio Company in return for shares of its stock. He then approached Congress and proposed that it take the certificates for 1.5 million acres in what was known as the garden spot of Ohio — the valley of the Muskingum River. Because he was exchanging depreciated soldiers' certificates for this prime land, the price at which Congress was asked to sell would be about 8¢ an acre; this would seemingly guarantee good profits if the land could be resold to settlers. To his chagrin Cutler found that Congress was monumentally indifferent to his grand idea; the clergyman quickly came to the practical conclusion that it would be expedient to cut certain government officials in on the good things in prospect. A roundabout scheme, not unusual in such ventures, was developed — and that is where the Scioto Company came in. The government official with whom Cutler negotiated was William Duer, a plunger who could have taught many speculators a few tricks whatever the century in which they were operating. The idea was to have the Ohio Company receive, along with *its own* 1.5 million acres, an option to buy 5 million more — an option which would then be turned over to the Scioto Company. The obvious question at this point concerns the identity of the participants in the 5 million acres of the Scioto Company. They were: (1) Colonel Duer and associates (chiefly Congressmen), who were to receive 2 million acres, and (2) the Reverend Cutler and associates, who were to receive 2 million acres for participating in the deal. That left a million acres not accounted for; they were to be sold in Europe, where unsuspecting buyers would not know about the sordid details. By these foreign sales it was hoped that enough money could be raised to meet the corporation's preliminary down payments. The central point to be remembered is that the Scioto Company never intended to settle the land; it merely planned to make minimum down payments until the land had increased in price. By that time another purchaser would have come along to buy it, at a profit for the Scioto Company.

After this seemingly advantageous arrangement had been made between Cutler and Duer, Congress quickly approved the proposals, and the Ohio and Scioto companies began their operations. The Ohio Company soon found itself in financial difficulties, which led to cancellation of one half of the original grant. It did come through with some settlement. In 1788 Cutler traveled by sulky to Ohio, remained for a year, and helped establish Marietta — the first planned settlement in Ohio which curiously was named for Marie Antoinette. By contrast the Scioto Company made one miserable settlement by sheer accident, never made any down payments to Congress, never acquired any land, and failed; it never existed, except on paper. Nevertheless a number of Europeans were left holding the worthless paper. It will be recalled that the Scioto Company intended to sell 1 million acres in Europe in order to meet down payments in the Ohio Valley. Its representatives on the Continent were interesting indeed. One was William Playfair, an Englishman with a pleasant and inaccurate name. The other was Joel Barlow, an American poet and diplomat; he was one of the so-called Connecticut Wits, now remembered chiefly for a humorous poem called "The Hasty Pudding," after which a famous club at Harvard College is named. Barlow was no shyster, he was simply a poet who knew nothing about real estate; innocent of any chicanery, he really believed in a fictitious map that he had, purporting to depict the lands of the Scioto Company. He did use poetic license in trying to sell land which the Scioto Company did not own; he tramped the streets of Paris but made no sales. He then met Playfair, who told him that the French would never buy from an unknown foreigner, but would buy anything from a seemingly respectable company. So Barlow and Playfair now advertised sales through the *Compagnie de Scioto*, and through this device Playfair organized an intensive selling campaign. He distributed maps and pamphlets showing the land in southern Ohio as already settled, describing a gleaming white city of Gallipolis (City of the French) at the mouth of the Great Kanawha, hinted that the capital of the United States would soon be moved there, and urged Frenchmen to seize this grand opportunity to live in comfort supported by a bountiful nature. Hundreds rose to the bait (the kind offered later in Florida, the Caribbean, and around Canadian lakes) and by the end of 1789 150,000 acres had been "sold" to innocent victims who never suspected that the *Compagnie de Scioto* owned no land, and that the elaborate certificates they purchased conveyed no title whatever. Barlow, who was both proud and ignorant, gathered the unfortunate purchasers together and sent word to Duer in 1790 that he was sailing with 600 immigrants who had been promised transportation and homes in the wilderness. Duer was thunderstruck for obvious reasons; this was an unanticipated expense, the Scioto Company owned no land because the first downpayment had not been made, and the site of Gallipolis was in the grant of the Ohio Company. Hastily he bought 200,000 acres from the Ohio Company and sent a crew of axmen to build huts for the newcomers. While he was doing so 600 Frenchmen arrived in Alexandria, Virginia. Many of them were clock makers, wig makers, and dancing masters; there was a combination of high humor, pathos, and tragedy in the idea of these specialized artisans migrating to the untamed wilderness of Ohio. Some did stay on the East Coast, some went back to France, most insisted on being moved to the promised lands. What disappointments awaited them! No gleaming white city, no fertile countryside, no golden fields ripe for the harvest; there was only unbroken forest, a half-cleared village, and a few rows of ugly log cabins. Most remained, living out their lives in squalor and poverty, a fitting monument to the skulduggery of the Scioto Company. In the end almost everyone lost in its operations, except Playfair. He vanished with all funds, leaving Duer the unpleasant task of meeting expenses himself and spending his later days in debtor's prison. Barlow continued to live abroad, served in a variety of diplomatic posts, on his last one as minister to France was caught in the retreat of Napoleon's armies from Moscow and died of exposure in 1812.

Curiously, out of this speculation came the most significant act of the Confederation government — the Ordinance of 1787, or Northwest Ordinance. The Ohio Company let it be known that it would purchase its millions of acres only if Congress provided for a government organization that would attract settlers. Dazzled by the potentialities of such a large sale, plus the coincidence that many of its own members were financially interested in the Ohio Company, Congress adopted the famous ordinance. It not only organized the Northwest Territory but set the precedent for admitting new states to the Union; it provided for a preliminary system of limited self-government, evolving into an equal partnership with the older states. Men could now leave the older states assured that they were not surrendering their political privileges. This was a great contrast with the current British practice: "Once a colony, always a colony." The Ordinance of 1787 established a brand-new principle: "Once a territory, sometime a state.

From the experience of the Confederation government it was apparent that there would be two basic and contradictory purposes behind federal land policy prior to the Civil War: to promote settlement and to raise revenue. If it is remembered that most settlers were poor men with little or no capital, and that it took a decade to clear eighty acres, it is apparent that the two purposes were incompatible. If the government was primarily interested in promoting settlement it would sell in small tracts, it would sell for a low price, and it would sell for long occupancy. This was Jefferson's idea: he believed in a nation of small farmers and opposed sales of large units to speculators. If, on the other hand, the government was interested in raising quick revenue it would sell in large tracts, it would charge a high price, and it would sell for short occupancy. This was the Hamiltonian philosophy; as a conservative businessman and entrepreneur Hamilton had no objection to sales of large areas to speculative subdividers, nor did he have any objection to selling to those who might eventually create manorial estates. Furthermore, the Treasury was short of money and quick land sales to speculators represented the easiest method of raising instant money.

The Ordinance of 1785 required the purchase at auction of an entire section (640 acres) at no less than $1 an acre. The common man of that day simply did not have that kind of money; the policy therefore benefited speculators. Nonetheless, in 1796 the minimum price per acre was raised to $2, with no reduction in the minimum purchase of 640 acres; only the rich could buy land on these terms. As a result, land sales dwindled. In time, in three succeeding acts (those of 1800, 1804, and 1820) the minimum number of acres to be purchased was successively reduced from 320 to 160 to 80 acres. In the acts of 1800 and 1804 the minimum price was kept at $2 an acre but purchasers were given four to five years to pay; this was the old credit "come-on" and meant that the optimistic common man — even if he could not ultimately meet all his payments — might be able to sell to someone who could. He might cash in on "unearned increment," but still lost his land. By 1820 the minimum price for sales at auction (for a minimum eighty acres) was reduced to $1.25 per acre in cash; this plot could be purchased for a minimum outlay, if there were no counterbids, of $100. This presented opportunities which were more inviting than those provided in previous acts — with the result that sales increased.

Nonetheless, throughout the first half century under the Constitution the land policy of the Republic was undemocratic — *if* the purpose was to benefit not the speculator but the permanent farmer and settler. This was because there was no limit on the amount of land that could be purchased and because no residence was required; both "freedoms" played into the hands of the speculator. In addition, the annual *cash* incomes for laboring and farm families in this period, while difficult to estimate because of the prevalence of barter, ran from $100 to $200 a year. This meant that under the relatively liberal land act of 1820 an easterner going west had to have at hand more than the equivalent of a year's cash income, from which he had probably saved little in the passing years; under the illiberal act of 1796 he would have been required to produce the equivalent of a decade or more of his *total* income.

Before the Civil War the most important concession obtained by the impecunious frontiersman, as against the speculator, was in the Preemption Act passed in 1841. For many years settlers had "squatted" — had moved beyond surveyed public land, had cleared the forest, and had hopefully laid out farms — without land payments of any kind while they were getting a head start. Later the land surveys had an inevitable habit of catching up with them — with the result that the squatters found that their *improved* land, developed by their own sweat, was sold at auction at prices which they could not afford and with federal troops moving in to drive them from familiar areas if they refused to move. Under the circumstances, in the sparsely settled West, squatters took matters in their own hands. When the government survey got to their area and the lands were sold at auction, what were known as "Squatters' Protective Associations" were organized. They appeared at auctions en masse, with ropes coiled around arms and saddles; speculators took one look and dared not bid against the squatters, who now intended to buy at the minimum price. In 1841 the federal government finally recognized an existing situation, and spurred by the continuing thrust of the Panic of 1837, passed the Preemption (or "Log-Cabin") Act. It permitted settlers to locate a claim of 160 acres, and after residence of six months to purchase it from the government — free from competitive bids — for a minimum of $1.25 an acre. This act — which was a clear-cut frontier victory and a landmark for Jeffersonian as against Hamiltonian measures — introduced freedom from competitive bidding, a residence requirement, and a limit on the amount of land that could be purchased.

Pressure from four groups, largely economic in their motivations, ultimately brought passage of the Homestead Act in 1862, after the South had seceded from the Union. They were western farmers, northeastern industrialists, abolitionists, and labor. Western farmers were perpetually angry at speculators and loan sharks. Speculators took advantage of the Preemption Act by hiring armies of alleged squatters to preempt the best land for them. Poor westerners were the prey of loan sharks who exacted heavy tribute through ruinous interest rates. The frontiersman hoped that all these evils might vanish if a quarter section of land were given *free* to every *actual* settler. Northeastern industrialists had traditionally opposed cheap lands lest labor be drained away, causing a rise in wages; Daniel Webster had once been their spokesman, asking always for expensive lands in the West. By the 1850's, however, the same industrialists had changed their minds because of the impact of new immigration, and the realization that the West was a potential source of new customers and of new enterprises for the investment of surplus capital. In the wake of hard times in Ireland in the 1840's a flood of cheap labor inundated the Northeast; Irish immigrants drifted into mill towns in such numbers that employers no longer feared labor shortages and high wages. They also tumbled to the fact that a populated West would provide both customers and an outlet for surplus capital. In a dramatic change of position these industrialists now became enthusiastic about the growth of the West by way of attractive land laws. Abolitionists saw clearly that any measure which disposed of the public domain in small units would block the extension of the plantation system. The South saw just as clearly that a liberal land policy would do it harm. It realized that continued migration would carve the entire West into free states, bolstering the North's legislative strength; the South therefore wanted high prices for land. The chief advocate for labor, George Henry Evans, was an English-born editor and agrarian reformer who came to the United States in 1820. He had been prominent in the first labor-supported political party in the United States

— the Workingman's Party — and he edited the *Workingman's Advocate*, the first important labor paper in the Western Hemisphere. The Panic of 1837 ruined both the party and the paper, whereupon Evans began to preach a doctrine of free land. He entered the homestead movement because of his economic theory that its success would not only provide a "safety valve" to relieve the conditions of labor in eastern cities but that it would also reduce the price of land in the older states to the value of improvements on the land — which would mean that the land itself would be free (later, Henry George would borrow this argument in his theory about "unearned increment"). As a Jeffersonian agrarian Evans wanted to end the sale of public land to companies and speculators and apportion it without charge in small acreages to actual settlers only. As the best means of achieving these goals for labor he advocated pressure on politics with a slogan: "Vote yourself a farm."

After the acquisition of vast western territories as a result of the Mexican War there had been a coalition of various forces, in the presidential campaign of 1848, behind a Free Soil Party with an exciting slogan: "Free soil, free speech, free labor, and free men." It ran Martin Van Buren from New York for President and Charles Francis Adams from Massachusetts for Vice-President; this third party failed to carry a single state but it did create quite a stir. It is of interest to note that its candidates came from New York and New England, representing both antislavery forces and northeastern industrialists. By the 1850's bills providing for free homesteads passed the House but were defeated in the Senate, which was controlled by the South; in 1860 a homestead bill was finally approved by both branches of Congress only to be vetoed by the pro-Southern President James Buchanan. With the South no longer in the Union, the measure was passed and signed by President Lincoln in 1862. It provided that any adult citizen (or any alien who had filed his first papers) could, for a fee of $10, claim 160 acres of the public domain. He secured final title free of further charge after he had "resided upon or cultivated the same for a period of five years."

In principle the act was significant because it represented a major change in the philosophy of the government with regard to the disposal of the public domain. Prior to its passage the government held steadfastly to the Hamiltonian doctrine that it was the purpose of the public domain to produce revenue *directly* and to provide homes *incidentally* for the pioneer settler. The Homestead Act marked the adoption of another idea, much closer to the Jeffersonian concept, that the interests of the government might be served best by providing free homes for the settler and finding *indirect* compensation through increased national prosperity and increased property values which would serve as a basis for public revenue.

The famous act was passed with the best of intentions. It seemed to assure *every* underpaid laborer, *every* debt-ridden farmer of a chance to

secure a free farm. That was what the act was supposed to do. It did help
half a million families to carve out new homes in the vast open spaces but,
in spite of this accomplishment, the measure largely failed to achieve
its purpose. Laborers were not benefited at all, and advantages to western
farmers were limited by reason of deficiencies in the provisions of the act
and by subsequent measures which provided for gift or sale of large areas
to nonfarm groups.

Because of his lack of money and experience the laborer was not benefited at all. The wage earner, whose annual income frequently did not
exceed $250, had neither the entry fee to file a claim nor the considerable
sum necessary to move his family to the frontier, and to buy tools and
farm equipment. One worker from Massachusetts, when asked why he did
not go West, expressed with savage simplicity the laborer's attitude toward homesteading: "Well, I never saw over a $20 bill. . . . If someone
would give me $1,500 I would go." Even in rare cases where a laborer
scraped enough together, he lacked the experience needed to homestead
virgin territory *and* the resources to support himself for two or three
years before his farm became self-supporting. Historian Ray Billington
has observed (in a brilliant analysis in his *Westward Expansion*) that the
Homestead Act might have served as a "safety valve" for laborers if the
government had provided free transportation, machinery, and training —
as well as free land. Because of the failure to do so it was soon apparent
that pioneers who homesteaded were not going to be laborers; they would
be farmers who came from adjacent states and who were already skilled in
agriculture.

There were two monumental mistakes in the Homestead Act itself: the
legal acreage was unrealistic and there were loopholes through which
speculators easily crawled and even walked upright. The legal acreage was
160 acres; this would have been ideal in the Mississippi Valley but was no
good in the semi-arid Great Plains, where the homesteader had to go. He
needed much more or much less; if he was a rancher the optimum size was
50,000 acres, for extensive agriculture 640 acres was desirable, for intensive farming (by irrigation) the right size was 60 acres. The Homestead
Act was passed for benevolent reasons but its framers, who knew the
humid East, enacted a measure that was unworkable in the semi-arid
West. Some cynics claimed that Uncle Sam was betting 160 acres against
$10 that the settler could not live on his homestead for five years. One of
those unsuccessful gambles, in Greer County in Oklahoma, inspired a famous folk song:

> *Hurrah for Greer County! The land of the free,*
> *The land of the bedbug, grasshopper, and flea;*
> *I'll sing of its praises, I'll tell of its fame,*
> *While starving to death on my government claim.*

Speculators found it easy to take advantage of loopholes and lax administration. These plungers became the most unpopular of all persons in the West; they were as active there as they had always been on all frontiers — gobbling up the choice lands, engrossing potential town sites, usurping rich river bottoms — always piling up huge holdings for higher prices. They took advantage of the legal privilege of commutation; six months after filing a claim the entry could be commuted to outright ownership, by any homesteader not willing to wait five years for free land, by payment of $1.25 an acre. This loophole was of inestimable value to speculators through the use of dummy entrymen. It will be recalled that the measure had provided for a free title after the settler had "resided upon or cultivated the same for a period of five years." To satisfy the residence requirement some connivers built miniature houses, swore they had erected a "twelve by fourteen dwelling," failed to add that they meant inches rather than feet. Others rented portable cabins which were wheeled from claim to claim for a charge of $5; witnesses were hired to swear they had seen a dwelling on the property, neglecting to add that the "dwelling" would be on a neighboring homestead the next day. Some solemnly testified they lived in a shingled residence after fastening two token shingles on the side of a tent. Land Office agents could easily have detected these frauds, but their districts were large and they were both underpaid and indifferent, and most of the skulduggery went undetected. To this day there is a cliché about "doing a land-office business"; actually that governmental department was a clumsy, bureaucratic machine, rarely efficient, too often corrupt, and seemingly never up to date. Finally, there was a significant omission in the act: its failure to prohibit sale or transfer of patents. If the government was really interested in settlers, in poor laborers and farmers rather than speculators, the Homestead Act should have provided that the land would revert to the national domain if a homesteader attempted to sell or transfer it during the initial five-year period. Unfortunately the act was silent on this point, with the result that speculators used dummy entrymen and secured title to quarter section after quarter section.

Beyond the damage done by deficiencies in the Homestead Act itself, farmers were hurt by subsequent acts of Congress and transactions by the Land Office which benefited nonfarm groups. The major ones were the Desert Land Act of 1877, the Timber and Stone Act of 1878, legislation providing land grants to railroads and states, direct sales by the Land Office, and sale of Indian lands. The Desert Land Act of 1877, ostensibly designed to benefit the pioneer, actually was lobbied through Congress by cattlemen. Anticipating the end of the open range, wealthy ranchers sought some means of purchasing large tracts of land at a minimum price. Before 1877 a rancher could homestead 160 acres and purchase an additional quarter section under the Preemption Act of 1841, which remained

in force for unsurveyed land. Even if all their cowhands served as entrymen ranchers could not acquire enough land for extensive grazing.
Through the Desert Land Act anyone could make an initial payment of
25¢ an acre and acquire tentative title of 640 acres in the Great Plains and
Southwest. Three years later, if the rancher could prove that he had irrigated some of the land, he secured final title on payment of an additional
dollar an acre. Cattlemen found witnesses who would swear that water
had been seen on the claim; normally this meant that a bucket of water
had been dumped on the ground. That the act was designed to aid cattlemen, *not* homesteaders, was apparent by the size of the tract and by the
ease of transfer of claims. The alleged purpose of the measure, to encourage the development of irrigated farms, was unrealistic because no one
family could cultivate 640 acres of irrigated soil. Furthermore cowboys
could be hired to transfer claims after the first entry, thus enabling ranchers to engross huge areas.

Lumbermen were quick to learn a lesson from the cattlemen; they
profited from the Timber and Stone Act of 1878. This generous measure
applied only to lands supposedly "unfit for cultivation" and "valuable
chiefly for timber or stone in western states"; it allowed any citizen (or
alien with his first papers) to buy up to 160 acres at $2.50 an acre — about
the price of one good log. Billington notes that

> the act invited corruption; any timber magnate could use dummy entrymen
> to engross the nation's richest forest lands at trifling cost. Company agents
> rounded up gangs of alien seamen in waterfront boardinghouses, marched them
> to the courthouse to file their first papers, then to the land office to claim their
> quarter section, then to a notary public to sign over their deeds to the corpora-
> tion, and back to the boardinghouses to be paid off. Fifty dollars was the usual
> fee, although the amount soon fell to $5 or $10 and eventually to the price of a
> glass of beer. By 1900 almost 3,600,000 acres of valuable forest land were alien-
> ated under the measure.

To make matters worse from the homesteader's point of view railroads,
which were the largest land jobbers in the West, preempted vast quantities of choice land. Congress usually gave each railroad alternate sections
in a strip twenty to eighty miles wide! Normally the entire strip was
withdrawn from settlement for several years while the railroad selected
the right of way and decided which alternate sections to keep. Beyond the
railroads there were the states which controlled vast amounts of choice
land under the Morrill Land Grant of 1862 and similar measures. The
Morrill Act, designed to encourage agricultural and engineering education — the A. and M. colleges — granted each state 30,000 acres of western land for each of its Senators and Representatives in Congress, with the
understanding that the proceeds were to be used to endow vocational colleges. Apart from the economics of this measure it was also a pioneering
one from the standpoint of educational philosophy. It represented an en-

tirely new idea in higher education — as different from the tradition of classical university studies as American democracy was different from the more rigidly stratified older societies in Europe.

The older states, because of their large populations, derived the largest advantages from the Morrill Act. These elderly areas, which were in the East, were authorized to locate their acreage anywhere in the West. In all, the states received 140 million acres but curiously the provisions of this act worked to the disadvantage of most states. The act provided that the A. and M. colleges had to be established within five years, forcing many states to sell their lands in haste, unfortunately at low price, because they were in competition with land being offered by railroads and by free homesteads available from the federal government. Thus Ohio sold its lands for 50¢ an acre. The only fortunate state was New York because of the foresight and generosity of a public-spirited citizen. Ezra Cornell, who began life as a laborer, had an ingenious mechanical bent; he aided in constructing the telegraph line between Washington and Baltimore over which Samuel F. B. Morse had sent his first message. Having designed the method of stringing wires on poles, Cornell became the founder and director — and for a time the largest stockholder — in the Western Union Telegraph Company. He lived in Ithaca, was a great friend of Andrew D. White (the first and great president of Cornell University), gave half a million dollars to the university — and more important, supervised the disposal of its land under the Morrill Act. He took over most of the New York State grant at 60¢ an acre, waited for unearned increment, sold the land gradually, and turned the surplus over to Cornell University. Some of the lands in the white-pine belt of Wisconsin went for $16 an acre, with the result that the University's endowment from land sales was a handsome $5.5 million — a huge sum in those days.

It is surprising to note that until 1889 speculating companies were able to acquire western land by direct purchase. These sales obviously contradicted the philosophy behind the Homestead Act, but the Land Office went ahead with sales at $1.25 an acre and Congress made no move to stop the practice. Sales were heavy to lumber and mineral companies, and some of the best prairie lands in Kansas, Nebraska, the Dakotas, and in the Pacific states were sold to speculators in blocks of 10,000 to 600,000 acres before Congress finally ended the practice in 1889 by limiting purchases to no more than 320 acres. By that time, a bit more than a quarter century after the passage of the Homestead Act, more than 100 million acres had been disposed of through direct sales.

A similar situation prevailed in regard to Indian reservations. After the Civil War, tribe after tribe surrendered its holdings; these were either sold by the Indians themselves or disposed of by the government. In either case the speculators were the ones who benefited; the Indians were anxious to settle affairs quickly by sales in large blocs, and the U.S. government —

pledged to compensate the tribes for lands taken from them — could not open the former reservations to homesteaders. Not until the Dawes Act of 1887, which stipulated that reservation land be sold to actual settlers in 160-acre units, was the practice of selling in giant tracts stopped, but by that time 100 million acres had gone to speculators.

At the turn of the century Land Office officials, summing up the amounts of land given or sold to speculators and corporations, released the following figures:

To Railroads	181,000,000 acres
To States	140,000,000 acres
Direct Sales by the Land Office	100,000,000 acres
Sale of Indian Lands	100,000,000 acres
Total:	521,000,000 acres

Billington observes that these half a billion acres were surrendered to monopolists at the very moment that orators were boasting that the United States was giving away land to poverty-stricken masses of people. Actually patents to homesteaders totaled only 80 million acres. If every homesteader had been a bona fide farmer, only one acre in six was given away. In actual practice many alleged homesteaders were dummy entrymen for cattlemen or mining or lumbering companies; Billington believes that not more than one acre in every nine went directly to small pioneers.

Every new settler who reached the West soon learned that he could accept a free but isolated homestead on poor soil distant from transportation, but had to *buy* more advantageous land from another source which happened to have acquired it — and recently. He would see advertisements reading "Better than a Homestead," in which railroads or states or corporations would offer land at from $3 to $15 an acre. The frontiersman could acquire this good land but it was not free; he had to pay heavily for it.

When President Lincoln signed the Homestead Act into law he had written: "I am in favor of settling the land into small parcels so every man can have a home." It was a noble Jeffersonian utterance but it did not work out that way — at least not as free land.

The impetus for the first wave of migration to the West came from miners — initially from the forty-niners in California followed by the fifty-niners in Colorado and Nevada, the opening of the Black Hills in the 1870's, and the Gold Rush to the Klondike in 1896. During the Mexican period in California, which lasted until 1848, a Swiss named Johann August Sutter had received a large grant of land and had become a Mexican citizen. He had his own fort — Sutter's Fort, just outside Sacramento, which ultimately became the gateway to California for Americans who crossed the continent; he had erected this bastion, with twelve cannon and a uniformed garrison of forty men, because the Mexican government could not protect him. His hospitality and kindness were well known; for years he was a veritable feudal baron in the Sacramento Valley. Then it happened.

On 24 January 1848 a foreman on Sutter's ranch by the name of John Marshall found a lump of gold in the American River. Sutter tried to keep it a secret, but a Mormon who worked on the place rode into San Francisco hollering at the top of his voice: "Gold! On the American River." By mid-May 1848, California had gone mad. By mid-December, when President Polk mentioned the discovery in his annual message to Congress, the entire nation went mad. On the West Coast the town of San Francisco put on its collective hat and took to the hills; men abandoned their families, sailors jumped ship, some went to the fields on crutches and one was carried there on a litter. In Monterey an entire platoon of soldiers left the fort, leaving only their colors behind. In the rest of the country, after Polk's comment, word got around that gold was everywhere in California; it blew into your eyes, you breathed it into your lungs. The result was that 100,000 people went to California in 1849.

They went by three routes: around the Horn, across Panama, and overland. Within a month after Polk's message sixty-one crowded ships were on their way around South America, many of them leaky tubs rescued from well-earned retirement; a number of them never reached their destination. All were trying to exact the scandalous fees fortune hunters willingly paid for a passage to the diggings. Across the Isthmus Commodore Cornelius Vanderbilt made a fortune, not in gold but in transportation. The most dramatic trip was the overland one, the famous journey by covered wagon. In those roadless days travelers had to start from the Mississippi in June after the spring rains and arrive in California before snow set in. It was 2,100 miles; they had four months to cover them, an average of seventeen miles a day. A good many did not make it. There were accidents, many serious; in the absence of medical attention many died. They ran into Indians, sometimes with fatal results. They ran into mosquitoes, reputedly as large as crows.

Of the 100,000 who went to California in 1849 a few made money *directly* from gold or *indirectly* from the sale of transportation and goods to those who were *seeking* gold. The Crockers, Huntingtons, Hopkinses, Goldwaters, and Vanderbilts noted that prices were outrageously high and made their fortunes as merchants or shipowners. Because almost everyone was running after gold it was little wonder that eggs cost $10 a dozen, apples were $5 each, and rooms rented for $1,000 a month. The great mining period in California lasted a decade (1849–1859), and during those ten years it produced $600 million worth of gold. Today California's annual gold output comes to about $3.5 million a year, a miniscule industry in a state which now has more than 20 million people. In the present era what keeps California rolling economically is oil, citrus crops, the sale of real estate to eager newcomers, and above all — government defense contracts (if peace were to descend on earth, the California of today would suffer a hundred times more than if the gold in the ground had suddenly disappeared a century ago). Now California actually takes more from tourists visiting the old gold fields than the miners took out of the ground from 1849 to 1859. That is because of the memories and relics and legends left from that decade, which now constitute a salable commodity.

A few made money during the Great Gold Rush, but the majority got nothing from the adventure except squalor and misery. Thousands died en route; other thousands found nothing in the hills, returned to San Francisco or to the East, and lived there in destitution and misery. In this connection it is pertinent to note what happened to Sutter and Marshall. Miners overran Sutter's land, butchered his cattle, destroyed everything that he had labored to build. In 1852 he was bankrupt. He plead for redress; California granted him a pension of $250 a month, but this ended in 1878. The result was that the man who had once been known for his open hospitality spent his declining years in the East trying to get compensation from Congress; having no special political influence, he failed. He died in 1880 in a small village in Pennsylvania, still petitioning Congress for his lost acres. Marshall fared worse; he tried unsuccessfully to sell his autograph in order to support himself, and died in poverty. Sutter had been prescient when he first heard the news of gold on his property; he had then called it a disaster for California.

The fifty-niners went to Colorado and Nevada. In the former state the migration was to the Pikes Peak region; mines at Leadville yielded $300 million in silver and those at Cripple Creek a similar amount of gold. The Rush of 1859 was accentuated by the Panic of 1857; "Pikes Peak or Bust" was the motto, and not far from 100,000 reached Colorado during the migration of the first year. Although half returned, "Busted! By Gosh!" — those who remained laid the foundations of a new state which was eventually admitted to the Union in the Centennial Year 1876. In Nevada the discovery of the famed Comstock Lode occurred in 1859, but the rush did not develop until 1861 — one that was forceful enough to propel Nevada into statehood in 1864. The Comstock Lode was the greatest *single* deposit of silver ever discovered in the United States. It was found by two brothers who died under tragic circumstances before their claims were recorded. A halfwitted prospector, "Old Pancake" Comstock, took over their cabin and at least part of their claim, but sold out for $11,000. In the next twenty years the mine at Virginia City, which was near the lode, yielded more than $300 million. Out of Virginia City came great fortunes, built by men known as "silver kings," most of whom later built mansions in San Francisco. One of them was George Hearst, now remembered chiefly because he had an only son named William Randolph. The most interesting was a German engineer named Adolph Joseph Sutro, who came to the United States in 1850. He built at Virginia City the famous Sutro Tunnel, extending for several miles; it was one of the greatest engineering feats of the century and provided ventilation, drainage, and transportation for the Comstock Lode. Later Sutro went to California, continued to make money in real estate, laid out Sutro Heights in San Francisco, and was elected mayor of that city in 1890 — on the Populist ticket!

In 1875 the Black Hills in South Dakota were opened to gold seekers after that metal was reported by a U.S. military expedition headed by General George A. Custer. Fifteen thousand prospectors entered the region and the Wild West made its last glorious stand in the Black Hills mining camps. Deadwood was the rip-roaring center of frontier lawlessness; congregated there were notorious hoodlums and gunmen — Wild Bill Hickok, Calamity Jane, Poker Alice. There stagecoaches were robbed with such monotonous regularity that the local newspaper dismissed one such incident with the statement: "We have again to repeat the hackneyed phrase, 'The stage has been robbed!'" Although it provided a relatively small mining boom in the 1870's, the production of gold in the region has gone on and on. In the 1960's South Dakota was the leading producer of gold in the United States and its Homestake mine was the nation's largest gold-producing one.

Custer's report of gold in the Black Hills led to the Second Sioux War of 1876, a conflict that ended major Indian fighting in the West. The United States had ordered the miners out, failed in the effort, then decided to purchase the property from the Indians to whom it belonged. The Indians did not wish to sell. Sitting Bull, Red Cloud, Spotted Tail, Crazy Horse, and other chiefs went to Washington in 1875, said that they had no intention of selling their land, and that they would be damned if they would sign a treaty. They returned to the Black Hills, the prospectors kept coming in, and finally open war began. The Sioux Indians, defending their lands, gathered in the Valley of the Little Big Horn in 1876. The first battle was a glorious victory for the Sioux; they wiped out Custer and his entire force.

The Indian victory was short-lived. Custer was defeated on 25 June 1876. In late October General Terry defeated the Sioux and the Indians surrendered. Sitting Bull fled to Canada, remained there for five years, returned under a promise of amnesty, and appeared later in Buffalo Bill's Wild West Show. The entire episode illustrates graphically the basis for President Hayes' laconic remark in 1877: "Many, if not most, of our Indian wars had their origin in broken promises and acts of injustice on our part."

For thirty years after its purchase in 1867 Alaska, then known as Secretary of State Seward's Folly, had all but been abandoned by its new

owner. Until 1884, when it was given a governor and a feeble local administration, it had been run by the army or the navy. Most active in these
early days were missionaries who were disturbed because the Eskimos
were on the verge of starvation, due to the wholesale slaughter of whales
and seals by fleets of ships which deprived the natives of their chief source
of food — just as the destruction of the buffalo on the Great Plains had
brought starvation to American Indians. Most influential of the missionaries in Alaska was a Presbyterian named Sheldon Jackson who brought
reindeer from Siberia to feed the Eskimos. He accomplished this feat with
some aid from Congress and some money from charitable citizens. The
increasing herds of reindeer managed to save the natives, but after this
exploit the nation again lost interest in what appeared to be a valueless
"northern icebox."

Then gold was found. Paradoxically, the first finds that were to have a
tremendous influence on Alaska were across the border in Canada's Klondike region in the Yukon territory. The only practical entrance to the
Klondike was through Alaska, and this brought a stampede to the American area. The original strike was made in August 1896 in a remote and
mosquito-infested part of the interior. It was made by two Indians and a
white prospector. The Indians had interesting if unimportant names —
Skookum Jim and Tagish Charlie. The prospector was George Washington Carmack, who was more moose hunter than prospector, more interested in salmon than gold. This could have been because he had read a
lesson in his father's life; the elder Carmack had joined the rush to Califor-
naa in 1849 but had died broke. His son had come north in 1885 to prospect, had taken an Indian wife, had adopted the native customs, and spent
more time fishing than panning for gold.

When news of the discovery of gold in the Klondike reached the
United States, Seattle went stark mad — as had San Francisco in 1849.
Within ten days after the arrival of the news 1,500 people had left Seattle
for the Yukon; in the first twenty-four hours after the news reached New
York 2,000 people tried to buy tickets to Alaska. Some struck it rich but
most got nothing except blisters, sore feet, illness, and death. After the
first strike in Canada there were major gold discoveries in Alaska itself —
at Nome in 1899 and at Fairbanks in 1902. The miners and sourdoughs
took over with the result that the era of lawless and exotic mining camps,
the Alaska of Jack London and Rex Beach, was dominant.

Close on the heels of the prospectors and the miners in the West came
the cattlemen. For some two centuries longhorn cattle, which had been
known to the Southwest since the early days of the Spanish occupation,
had been bred on the Texas plains — largely for their hides. Easterners
depended on pork and poultry as primary items in their diet; before long
they would be eating beef as well. The rancher's Big Boom, which lasted

for two decades from the late 1860's to the late 1880's, was brought in by the appearance of the transcontinental railroad and the refrigerator car. It was the cross-country railroad that first opened the eyes of cattlemen to the possibilities of a market in the East for meat. After the Civil War there was a great surplus of longhorn cattle in Texas. The war had both disrupted the economy and drained the manpower of Texas; while this was going on the hardy longhorns, allowed to range freely, had multiplied like rabbits. By the end of the war there were so many of them that it was claimed a man's poverty in Texas was determined by the number of long-horns he owned — simply because the market for them had almost disap-peared. In Texas the unwanted cattle brought $3 a head. In Chicago they were worth $40. If all the 5 million longhorns in Texas could be driven north cattlemen would be enriched to the extent of almost $400 million. This was entrancing.

Before long it was discovered that cattle could be driven across the then unfenced public domain, feeding as they went, and arrive at shipping points on the transcontinental railroad in Kansas. The longhorns were driven along a Long Drive known as the Chisholm Trail, which cele-brated its 100th birthday in 1967; it went from a point north of Fort Worth in Texas to Abilene in Kansas — the original pay-end of this 1,000-mile-long route. Actually it should have been called the McCoy Trail. Jesse Chisholm, a well-known Indian trader whose "freight-route" across a part of present-day Oklahoma was used by the Kansas-bound Texas drovers, died in 1868 without ever having run a steer along the trail named for him. On the other hand Joseph G. McCoy was the twenty-nine-year-old livestock buyer who really conceived the idea of trailing surplus Texas longhorns to Kansas by way of Indian country for marketing in the East. In 1867 he looked at the map of the West to find where the cattle trail from Texas would cut the path of the railroad. The pinpoint on the map came close to the then unknown name of Abilene in Kansas.

Three months later McCoy had a yard built at Abilene for 300 head of cattle. He sent riders out on the range with the news that he would buy every steer brought to the railhead. In 1867 his offer brought in 35,000 cattle and by September of that year twenty cars of longhorns were on their way to Chicago. The next year the number of cattle shipped had increased to 300,000; in 1870 it was 750,000. Ultimately the number reached the 5 million mark. Abilene became quite a place. In previous years it had been a drowsy little village in which the one saloon keeper spent part of his plenteous spare time raising prairie dogs for tourists. Now Abilene became a beehive of industry and lawlessness. Seldom did a group of drovers leave the town without making a contribution to the population of Boot Hill, as the cemetery reserved for those who died with their boots on was called; barroom murders, drunken brawls, and chance shootings were so common that almost no one bothered to apprehend, much less to punish, the murderers. This prevailing lawlessness called, in time, for town-taming marshals; in her heyday Abilene had two of the better, or at least the more notorious ones. Tom Smith was the most efficient until he was killed in 1870. His successor was the legendary James B. Hickok; what "Wild Bill" lacked in professional qualifications he compensated for in charisma. In time, other Kansas railheads achieved prominent if questionable reputations. Dodge City was known as the "Beautiful, Bibulous Babylon of the Frontier." There were also Junction City and Salina; in the 1870's it was claimed that "there was no Sunday west of Junction City, and no God west of Salina." By whatever name it was called, the cattleman's trail from Texas had a profound influence on the region and on the nation. It brought post–Civil War prosperity to both Texas and Kansas. It helped create the western cattle industry. It greatly influenced the meat-eating habits of the nation. It also lent a hand at the birth of that legendary character the two-gun-town-tamer.

Beyond the Chisholm or McCoy Trail, the second factor bringing the Big Boom was the refrigerator car. At first meat had been laid directly on ice, but it became discolored and gave refrigerated meat a bad name in the East for some time. The advantage of the refrigerator car was that the contents of two cars, if expertly packed, were the equivalent of three cars of livestock each containing nineteen head of cattle. Because greater revenue could be derived from the shipment of live cattle, the railroads first rebelled against the introduction of refrigerator cars. When they refused to provide them the major meat packers — Swift, Cudahy, Armour, Hammond — built their own cars. This monopoly was initially forced on them; in time the packers derived great advantages from it. They used their power to force the railroads to carry the cars at rates which they set. In due course they were able to demand that railroads carry no other refrigerator cars except those furnished by members of their combine. Furthermore, as the years went by not only meat, but all fruits and vegetables as well, were shipped perforce in the monopoly's cars.

The boom was splendid while it lasted but by 1887 it was over and the so-called Cattle Kingdom was on its last legs. This was because of increasing costs, the hostility of farmers, and some bad weather in 1886 and 1887. Cattle lost so much weight in the Long Drive northward that, in time, few could be sold to eastern stockyards at attractive prices. Most of them were therefore sent as "feeders" to some farmer in Nebraska, Iowa, Wyoming, or Montana — who fattened them on corn. This increased costs, as did the charges by Indians for crossing reservations. In 1867 natives in the Indian Territory discovered that an ancient statute forbade traffic across their lands without special permission. They began to charge 10¢ a head for all steers driven through their reservations. The hostility from farmers appeared in the form of quarantine laws and barbed wire. Farmers worried about Texas Fever, carried by disease-transmitting ticks which infected

Texas cattle. At first they resorted to shooting and then, when they got control of state legislatures, to quarantine laws. Kansas was typical; in 1884 it ruled that no Texas steers could be driven into the state except in December, January, and February — when the ticks were not active. Neither were the cattle and the cowboys in these frigid months and, with adequate enforcement, the Long Drive came to an end. Its demise was also hastened by the introduction of barbed wire as fencing. As the frontier moved westward to the open plains the traditional fence materials — wooden rails and stone — became scarce and so expensive that the cost of fencing was frequently more than the land was worth. Osage-orange hedges were tried as substitutes, but they too were expensive and took years to grow; mud was tried but was found to be unstable and unattractive — thus the expression "as ugly as a mud fence." The invention of barbed wire helped to solve the problem; that designed by Joseph F. Glidden in Illinois in 1873 proved to be the most popular. Its introduction on the plains obviously ended the open range. The transformation was not made without protests; they often took the form of fence-cutters' wars and led to bloodshed. There were also battles in western state legislatures between fence men and antifence men; these were ultimately won by the more numerous farmers.

Because of increasing costs and the hostility of farmers the days of the Cattle Boom were numbered. In the early years profits had been very good with the result that eastern and European capital poured in; the demand for cattle became so great that both marginal and submarginal land was turned into pasture, much of it simply appropriated from the federal government without permission. It was apparent that only a series of abnormally wet years could keep the business going. These ended suddenly and tragically in 1886. The summer was hot and dry; as grass withered many cattlemen sold their herds in panic. As it turned out they were wise, because the ensuing winter was murderous; temperatures dropped as low as sixty degrees below zero. Cattle are able to drift with blizzards with their rumps to the tempest as long as they can paw through the snow and reach grass. In the winter of 1886–1887, unfortunately, the snow and ice were too thick, with the result that millions of cattle died. When spring came ranchers found carcass upon carcass in every ravine, there were heaps of dead bodies along the fences, and trees had been stripped of bark as the cattle made a final attempt to find sustenance. The Long Drive was over.

Farmers took over the West from the miners and the cattlemen. In one decade, 1870 to 1880, new farms were developed comprising an area equal to that of the British Isles and Sweden combined. From 1880 to the close of the century a U.S. farming domain was added which was the equivalent in size to that of the British Isles, Sweden, Norway, Denmark, Holland,

Belgium, and Switzerland. This meant the creation of new states, six of them within twelve months in 1889–1890 (North and South Dakota, Montana, Washington, Idaho, and Wyoming). They were followed in 1896 by Utah, brought into the Union after the Mormon Church had satisfied Washington that national laws against polygamy were being enforced. Seven years earlier the western section of Oklahoma, which was largely Indian Territory, was opened to white settlement. This was done with much fanfare on 22 April 1889 when prospective settlers lined up on the territorial border and at high noon the "boomers" were allowed to cross at a gallop to compete in finding and claiming the best lands. Those who had entered illegally, ahead of the set time, were dubbed the "sooners." Later other strips of Indian Territory were opened and settlers poured in from the Middle West and the South. These exciting days were described in vivid detail by Edna Ferber in her novel *Cimarron*.

The period of the sod-house frontier was an exciting, arduous, exasperating — and sometimes a tragic — one. It has been fully documented by Everett Dick in his nonfiction classic *The Sod-House Frontier*, and by novelists Ole Rolvaag and Johan Bojer in their novels *Giants in the Earth* and *The Emigrants*. Sod houses, first used by the Indians, were habitations made of thick strips of turf, and were peculiar to the prairie and plains regions of the United States where timber was sparse. During the pioneer period, in the area beyond the Missouri River, 90 percent of the settlers lived in sod houses; when they could afford frame structures, they still used the old sod houses to shelter their stock. On the positive side they were cheap, safe, and air-conditioned (cool in summer and warm in winter). In 1872 Elder Oscar Babcock, a Seventh-Day Adventist minister of North Loup, Nebraska, spent $2.78 for his fourteen-foot-square sod house. The only expense was for the glass in one window, the lumber and latch for the front door, a few nails, and a length of pipe to carry smoke out of the home. Such houses were also safe; there was no danger of the wind blowing it over, and there was no hazard from fire — either internal, or external from terrifying prairie fires.

The structures also had their drawbacks. One dweller related that, upon moving into a frame house after five years in a sod one, the change was so great from the cavelike dwelling that no one could sleep because of the excessive light. It also left a great deal to be desired from the point of view of cleanliness; dedicated housekeepers abominated them because they were so hard to keep tidy. In the early days there were no bedsteads and sleeping was on the floor — on the ground; habitants could provide a bit of comfort by making up their beds with a hoe! Dirt and straw kept dropping on everything in the house; probably the most disagreeable feature was the leaky roofs and walls. When the roof was saturated it dripped for days after the storm had cleared; dishes, pots, pans, and kettles were placed all over the floor to catch some of the continual dripping.

One pioneer woman remembered frying pancakes with another member of the family holding an umbrella over her and the stove.

Beyond the dwelling the sod-house frontier involved a number of hazards — from Indians, grasshoppers, blizzards, and ill health. Indians were so proficient in pilfering that settlers, when leaving the farm for a visit or a social function some miles away, would take with them the cow, a coop of chickens, the stove — and everything else the wagon would hold. The insatiable grasshoppers suddenly materialized in overwhelming numbers during the spring of 1874, ravaged the countryside for four successive summers, and then — without so much as a wave of their antennae — vanished mysteriously. They were actually one of four gluttonous and migratory species known to the American continent; this particular grasshopper was occasionally seen in small numbers during the remainder of the century but not a single live specimen has been reported since 1904. In the 1870's they were a frightful scourge. Had it not been for the sudden and mysterious easing of this insect plague, the course of civilization in the Great Plains might well have been changed simply because billions upon billions of grasshoppers were rendering agriculture of any kind impossible. At times the insects were four to six inches deep on the ground; the hoppers lighted in such large numbers on corn that the stalks bent toward the ground. Potato vines were smashed flat; onions were a favorite — grasshoppers ate the tops straight down into the ground to the end of the roots, leaving small hollow holes where the succulent bulbs had once been found (one observer claimed in all seriousness that when a large number of the insects flew past his cabin door, their breath was rank with the odor of onions!). Water in creeks, stained with the excrement of the hoppers, assumed the color of strong coffee. Grasshoppers gathered in such thick numbers on the warm rails of the Union Pacific that trains were actually stopped; the track had become so oily and greasy that the wheels spun. Section hands were called out to shovel enough of the insects from a specified length of track to enable the locomotive to move forward.

Cold weather and blizzards were something else. Settlers had hardly set foot on the soil of Kansas and Nebraska when they were greeted by the frightful inhospitality of one of the most severe winters recorded in the history of that region. During the winter months of 1855 and 1856, the thermometer went down to thirty degrees below zero and stayed there for days. Water froze in tumblers at breakfast and everything edible was frozen hard; bread could be cut only while thawing in front of the fire. One pioneer testified that it was not uncommon to arise in the morning and find upwards of four inches of snow on the floor, on the beds, and on everything else in the sod house. During blizzards farmers were lost between their houses and their stables ten to twelve rods away; it was prudent to run a clothesline or rope from the house to the barn, and to follow it closely. Caught in blizzards men were known — in an effort to preserve their lives — to kill their horses, rip them open, and crawl into their vitals in the hope that the warmth of the animals' intestines might preserve them from death. In such cases, unfortunately, the carcass of the pioneer's mount sometimes became his tomb.

Ill health was another hazard. If a physician was present, which was not frequent, the danger still remained because most had little training and adequate facilities were nonexistent. Many crude operations were performed on kitchen tables by the light of coal-oil lamps — or on barn doors laid across carpenter's horses. Frontier dentistry was as crude as its medicine. It consisted largely of pulling aching teeth, or the tooth that was presumed to be aching; not infrequently the wrong one was extracted. In the early days the few dentists in the West went on circuit, visiting towns periodically. If a pioneer was suffering from a toothache he tried to bear it until the perambulating dentist appeared on his appointed rounds.

In 1890 the Bureau of the Census, which had been in the habit of drawing a western line beyond which settlement had not progressed, announced that the frontier had ceased to exist. Three years later a young historian read an essay before the American Historical Association, which was meeting in Chicago in conjunction with the World's Fair of that year. His paper was to become the most widely read essay by an American historian, was to revolutionize historical thought in the United States, and was to make its author one of the most renowned of all American scholars. Like Lincoln's Gettysburg Address it was little noted at the moment; in time it would supply a theme which two generations of historians investigated and about which they wrote.

The name of the historian was Frederick Jackson Turner, who lived from 1861 to 1932. As a major historian he wrote little beyond twenty-six articles. It appears that he failed to produce a *magnum opus* because of the catholicity of his interests, his perfectionism, and his chronic ill-health. Although he was unable to write major books his influence as a teacher was phenomenal.

The title of his essay, first read in 1893, was "The Significance of the Frontier in American History"; from it was derived what is known as the Turner thesis. Essentially it included three ideas: that the frontier promoted democracy, that it encouraged nationalism as opposed to sectionalism, and that it served as a "safety valve." On the subject of frontier democracy Turner could be lyrical. For him American democracy had no foreign origin; it came from the American frontier. He wrote:

American democracy was born of no theorist's dream; it was not carried in the *Susan Constant* to Virginia, nor in the *Mayflower* to Plymouth. It came out of the American forest, and it gained a new strength each time it touched a new frontier.

In the same vein he would commend a nationalistic West as contrasted with the sectionalism of the South. He would applaud the role of the West in the War of 1812, and the part played in it by western nationalists like Clay and Jackson. He claimed that this West had a solidarity of its own with *national* tendencies, which he found good; by contrast, slavery was a *sectional* trait which would not disappear — but the West, unlike the South, could not be sectional. Therefore, for Turner it had to be the greatest of frontiersmen who declared, "I believe this government cannot endure permanently half slave and half free."

As far as the "safety valve" was concerned, Turner believed that the poor man of pluck and ambition, along with the social misfit, had always been able to escape oppressive conditions in older parts of the nation by going West to make a new start. The frontier therefore relieved excessive social pressure because it drained off restless and dissatisfied spirits from the congested centers into a land of abundant opportunity.

In recent years the Turner thesis has come under relentless and convincing attack, particularly from two economic historians, Professor Louis Hacker at Columbia and the late Professor Fred A. Shannon at the University of Illinois. These critics emphasized that the frontier frequently was not democratic at all. If there was something in the air of the frontier that produced democracy, said those who questioned Turner's major premise, how could one possibly explain the lack of democracy on the frontier in Mormon Utah, in slave-holding Oklahoma and Texas and Louisiana, and in California under authoritarian Spanish and Mexican rule. Because of these illogicalities one observer would say that democracy did not appear of its own accord on the American frontier; instead it was carried there from the East by men who had read Locke and Montesquieu, Coke and Paine. Furthermore, the vaunted individualism on the frontier was not permanent but merely a temporary and passing phase. Hacker, in particular, noted that there was really nothing unique about American development in the West, that westerners were hardly in the grip of overwhelming forces as Turner believed. In Hacker's view the United States was going through a process of settlement which all nations had experienced, and which differed in the United States only in detail. Once our western settlement was achieved the United States followed the pattern of older nations; the individual declined in importance as class lines solidified, as competitive capitalism merged into monopolistic capitalism, as the United States embarked upon an imperialistic policy. For these reasons Hacker felt that Turner made a mistake in studying western democracy in the place of more important issues such as the nature of capitalism in this country. In his judgment Turner would have been better advised to have studied Henry Demarest Lloyd's *Wealth Against Commonwealth* (1894) rather than the frontier.

The chief critic of Turner's "safety valve" theory was the greatest agricultural historian of his generation, a Scotch-Irishman from the Midwest named Fred Shannon. He pointed out that few eastern laborers took up free land in the West, and that western farmers did so in relatively small numbers. In addition Shannon stated that a "safety valve" — by its very name — was of use only when pressure reached the bursting point, as it did in the United States during the Panic of 1873 and the great strikes of 1877. Where was the "safety valve" during those critical years? There was one, but it was in the *cities*, where farmers were then going! Shannon estimated that for *every* industrial worker who moved to the country and succeeded in farming, *twenty* farm boys became urbanites. His conclusions was that "the rise of the city in the nineteenth century was a safety valve for rural discontent."

The third major criticism of Turner has been that he is basically a nativist, what would later be called an isolationist. Hacker observed that because of Turner's influence the eyes of historians were turned inward for forty years during which they should have been on events beyond this nation's borders. Turner had insisted that the advance of the frontier was a steady movement away from the influence of Europe. Hacker concluded that Turner would have been better off if he had studied, in the place of his frontier specialty, Admiral Mahan on *The Influence of Sea Power on History*.

Land is abused by erosion from water and wind, which every year takes from the farms of the nation many times as much plant food as do cultivated crops. In the dry 1930's it was estimated that in each year water and wind erosion were carrying off about 3 billion tons of topsoil at a loss of nearly half a billion dollars annually. It was apparent that if this valuable topsoil could have been saved, much less fertilizer woud have been required on what was left.

There are three basic types of water erosion: sheet, shoestring, and gully. Sheet erosion is often imperceptible except for a slight change in the color of the soil and a mysterious loss in its fertility. Cracks and wrinkles appear in the next step of shoestring erosion — followed ultimately by the inevitable gullies. During this progression the standard of living of those on the land is lowered; the incomes of entire communities go down as farm tenantry, tax delinquencies, and bankruptcies increase. It was Oliver Goldsmith who wrote, "Ill fare the men when land decays." Unfortunately, there were spectacular examples of water and gully erosion. The historic flood of 1937 in the Ohio River watershed washed away an estimated 300 million tons of fertile topsoil. Reservoirs filled up so rapidly that their usefulness was limited. In 1936 Lake Mead was completed, behind Hoover Dam, at a cost of $165 million; its primary purpose was to provide water for irrigation and power. Expected to be useful for several centuries, it is now silting from an eroded watershed so rapidly that its utility is expected to decline by 1985. Beyond plows, bulldozers, and the saws that destroy timber cover, the most dramatic producers of gullies are the giant shovels used by strip-mine operators. These have literally raped forested mountains and the rolling farmlands in the valleys of the Ohio, Kentucky, and Tennessee rivers. Spurred by expanding demand for cheap coal for steam-generating plants and by the development of Brobdingnagian earth-moving machinery, the strippers had laid waste hundreds of thousands of acres in this region. Their operations not only devastate the land under which the coal lies; they also send acidic water and landslides cascading into the valleys, where they pollute streams and destroy trees, vegetation, farmlands, and homes — sometimes wiping out entire communities. By the late 1960's state regulation of this depredation had been so ineffective that it was apparent to many that the only possibility for preservation of these natural resources was through federal legislation.

Wind erosion is the result when grass and timber areas, in which the rainfall is inadequate, are denuded of their normal ground cover. This happened along the 100th meridian in the United States, where normally arid lands had given way to the plow and the temporary production of wheat. When dry periods followed, the uncovered land blew away. It is estimated that the most famous U.S. dust storm of all time, that on 11 May 1934, blew 300 million tons of topsoil off the wheat plains in one day. The results were seen and felt as far east as the Atlantic Ocean. Visibility was reduced to a few feet, streetlights were turned on in daytime, and some families abandoned their homes. The "dust bowl" had been created by farmers who took advantage of government grants to rip out hedges and trees to establish "prairie farms." This means that men can make deserts — and have in the Middle East, in Asia, and in parts of the United States. In Australia, where the winds frequently blow at eighty miles an hour, an attempt is being made — by men — to unmake the deserts they have made. Areas are being sprayed with a mixture of latex and oil; the film prevents the land from moving but is sufficiently adaptable to allow seeds to germinate and plants to grow through it. Grass grows immediately but some time is required to develop humus; in any case, erosion is being halted and there are good prospects of recovery.

Beyond the question of what happens internally to land through various kinds of erosion there is the external problem of land pollution — garbage, junked cars, and other wastes piling up in and around cities. Some environmental scientists believe that, serious as are the hazards of air and water pollution, the current situation involving solid wastes outstrips them all. Such refuse is not only unsightly, but current and ineffective efforts to get rid of it usually causes air and water pollution as well; one expert has said that present methods of disposing of solid wastes are so primitive that we have made but one change in the system in fifty years — "putting an engine where the horse used to be." San Francisco once thought of shipping its garbage almost 400 miles away to the uncluttered deserts, inhabited by Indians, in northeastern California. This was to be done by special train — known locally as "The Twentieth Stenchery Limited" and "The Excess Express." The Indians objected, successfully. A New York businessman was supposedly thinking of building a garbage mountain somewhere upstate, equipping it with a ski run to amortize the cost. The administrator of the Consumer Protection and Environmental Health Service for the U.S. government has wondered out loud:

> Can we afford to allow ourselves the convenience of single-use bottles, plastic cups, and aluminum beer cans in the face of mounting heaps of refuse that defy destruction? Can we afford to have junked automobiles rusting away in unsightly auto graveyards just because we have not yet depleted our mineral resources? Can we afford the human cost of inadequate garbage collection in our cities?

Man has taken his litter to every new frontier — within the world and outside it. In Antarctica, something of a record was established in ruining the environment as "man the explorer turned into man the polluter at McMurdo base in a brief ten years. . . . A smoking garbage heap and a junkyard litter the shore of a once picturesque inlet." It was necessary to "jettison" electronic equipment to make possible the first landing on the moon, magnificent and epochal as it was. This produced some musing on the part of the *New York Times:*

> . . . As New Yorkers watched the discovery of a new world with awe under a smog-yellow sky, some remembered that this was once a new world, too. Americans have "jettisoned" their wastes into the waters and the skies. In three short centuries . . . the inhabitants of this land have fouled their nest to the point where it would take the major part of the country's money and resources and the redirecting of all its priorities to restore what has been spoiled. . . . Is the handwriting on the moon?

At the beginning of the Christian era world population was approximately 200 million, about that of the United States in 1970. For eighteen centuries the increase had been both slow and regular; it took until 1830 for the world to produce the first billion people. Then came a phenomenal increase; the second billion took only a hundred years more, the third billion (by 1961) only thirty-one years, while the fourth billion will require only fifteen years thereafter; at the present rate of growth more than 5 billion are predicted for the year 2,000 and within two centuries the world population would be 150 billion people. Interestingly, if the current rate of increase had begun at the time of Christ, there would not be a hundred persons for every square foot of the earth's surface. One scientist, with tongue in cheek, has established Doomsday — the one when population will reach infinity and automatically annihilate itself — on Friday the 13th of November, A.D. 2026. In his judgment "our great-great grandchildren will not starve to death. They will be squeezed to death."

The reason for this extraordinary increase in population is that we now have death control without adequate birth control. Man's sexual drives and capacities were designed for a primitive and dangerous environment in which only a small number of children survived to become adults. With the development of modern medicine this is no longer the case; we can now increase population to the point of asphyxiation. Arnold Toynbee has noted that "we have been godlike in our planned breeding of domesticated plants and animals, but . . . have been rabbitlike in our unplanned breeding of ourselves." He states that man has rescued himself from tigers and lions — and is on the verge of doing so from bacteria — but does not seem to know how to rescue himself from two enemies of his own making and breeding, the H-Bomb and the O-Bomb (the Over-population one). Others change the figure of speech; they think survival may become a stand-off between the Atomic Bomb and the Anatomic Bomb.

Observers of the current population explosion divide themselves into two groups: the cornucopians or optimists, and the neo-Malthusians or pessimists. The cornucopians include most of the physical scientists, engineers, businessmen, Catholics — and in Russia and China those who follow the religion of Marxism. They say that science will find a way, that enough food will be produced on land and in the sea — and that if necessary we may be able to move surplus populations to other planets or to artificial space satellites! * The neo-Malthusians include most biologists, social scientists, increasingly many taxpayers — and on the religious side most Protestants and members of the Jewish faith. They say that the world faces starvation, that the rapid increase in population will destroy the quality and joy of living, and that increased population will be productive of war. In relation to starvation they observe that in the battle of production versus reproduction, production cannot win. In this connection it is startling to remember that at breakfast, every morning, there are now 150,000 more mouths to be fed than there were the day before. No matter what increases can be made through miracle seeds and the plowing of the sea, there comes a time when the battle will be lost simply because the stork can outrun the plow. In 1968 President Ayub would say that "in ten years' time, human beings will eat human beings in Pakistan."

There is also the question as to whether crowded existence is worth it.

---

* The first landing on the moon did not hold out much hope in this regard, although it did convince everyone that we were more successful in outer space than we were in settling the awesome problems within the world's atmosphere. At the moment of the moon landing in July 1969 there were 203,377,182 Americans, according to the census clock in Washington. That was 24 million more persons than lived in the United States when the space program really got under way in 1960. Curiously, 24 million was almost the same number of persons living in what the U.S. government estimated to be poverty. The cost of landing men on the moon was about $25 billion; many thought the world was crying out for bread and was being offered moondust.

People may be able to live on top of one another, and in time it may be possible for them to eat wood or algae; there also may be a question as to whether they really want an existence in which they are involved in conditions similar to those in a crowded military camp, and whether they really crave algae steaks. Some claim there is a Fifth Freedom — Elbow Room — and that the world is losing it fast. Stewart L. Udall, a former member of Congress and Secretary of the Interior, has observed that beyond the dangers of starvation the population explosion confronts mankind with another more invidious hunger — the starvation of the human spirit. He notes that since the U.S. colonial era our land area has increased fourfold, our population fifty times over. From the colonial and primarily agricultural period, when population density was five persons per square mile, we have imploded toward cities so that today 70 percent of the U.S. population lives on only 1 percent of the land. This means an average density in urban areas of about 4,000 per square mile; in New York City it is 25,000 per square mile. In such circumstances society will require many controls to keep life bearable, probably so many that democracy as we now know it can no longer exist. Udall believes that, beyond economic indexes which are plentiful, we urgently need "a tranquility index, a cleanliness index, a privacy index . . . to measure the joy of living."

There are many scholars who insist that increased population will be productive of war. In the mid-1960's Gunnar Myrdal, the famed Swedish economist, said that the world was moving toward a world calamity and that mass starvation would come within ten years. Just a little more hunger, in his opinion, will push the masses over the brink in half a dozen spots in Africa, Asia, and Latin America. This mass starvation will also be accompanied by intensified racial feeling; the reason is simple — it is the white who has the food; it is the brown, the black, and the yellow who has the empty belly. In this connection Barbara Ward has said that the gap is widening between a white, complacent, highly bourgeois, very wealthy, and very small North Atlantic elite — and everybody else. The pressures are already appearing, for example, in China with a population of more than 800 million. When a hungry man has to choose between starvation and grabbing his neighbor's garden he is likely to grab, so China pushes south and El Salvador moves into Honduras. In 1963 President Kennedy, speaking before the World Food Congress, quoted the Roman philosopher Seneca: "A hungry people listens not to reason, nor cares for justice, and will be fed."

The United States is well-off, but is in a state of siege because it is surrounded by a sea of famine. The United States has about 6 percent of the people of the world; that 6 percent uses about 50 percent of the world's output of raw materials, makes about half of the world's manufactured goods, and enjoys almost half of the earth's wealth. The other 94 percent of all human beings gets along on the remaining half. For these reasons citizens of the United States can expect a world in which they will be living under pressure. Even if communism had never been invented, if Marx had never been born, and if Russia did not exist the pressure would still be great. One of the wise statesmen of the post–World War II era, the late Liaquat Ali Khan of Pakistan, said on a visit to the United States in 1950:

As I let myself ponder over this, I suddenly see the United States as an island — a fabulous, prosperous island. And round this island I see the unhealthy sea of misery, poverty, and squalor in which millions of human beings are trying to keep their heads above water. At such moments I fear for this great nation as one fears for a dear friend.

For all of these reasons there has been increasing governmental support for the neo-Malthusians. At the local level states and cities concerned about the increasing costs of welfare and relief payments to an exploding population have been distributing birth-control information and materials to mothers on relief. At the national level Congress has been disturbed with the appropriation of billions in aid to impoverished countries — which have turned this money into more hungry babies. The federal government was slow but finally got around to the dissemination of birth-control information and materials in developing countries. In this connection, ironically, it was a Catholic President who reversed his Protestant predecessor. President Eisenhower had said that the promotion of birth control in other countries was none of our business. President Kennedy said it was — if other nations requested such information. President Johnson went further — he said in 1965, "Let us act on the fact that less than $5 invested in population control is worth $100 invested in economic growth." Some say this calculation is conservative — that in some countries every dollar invested in birth control would be 200 times as productive as other forms of foreign aid.

The world has only a fixed supply of water; not one drop has been added since creation. Ninety-seven percent of the world's water is in the oceans. Another 2 percent is frozen, largely in the great ice sheet that covers Antarctica. That leaves 1 percent in the form of liquid fresh water. Unfortunately the overwhelming majority of this liquid fresh water is underground, and more than half of the water there is more than a mile deep.

Water is one natural resource in which the United States, compared with Europe, has always been badly supplied because of deficient rainfall and rapid runoff. An annual rainfall of twenty inches is essential for agriculture, and from thirty to fifty inches for ideal soil moisture. The average for the entire country runs twenty-nine inches a year, but abundant rainfall is limited to small areas in the Northwest and in the Southeast.

One spot in the state of Washington has an average of 150 inches a year; there is another in the southern Appalachians with 100 inches annually. But Nevada is a desert with less than nine inches a year, and most of the West is arid or semi-arid. California gets sixteen inches a year, when it is lucky, and so does most of Colorado.

In addition, because of the peculiar geography, geology, and soil structure of the United States, too much of the nation's rainfall is lost in runoff, instead of being stored in the subterranean water table for future use. There has been some experimentation, but not much, with the diversion of the runoff of rivers on to gravel beds (which permit percolation) or into deep wells. During the past thirty years signs have multiplied that the United States is living off its water capital, found in the underground reservoirs built up by natural processes over thousands of years. It is running the risk of repeating, with water resources, the orgy of destruction indulged in with its soil. Water tables once depleted are even more difficult to restore than eroded and depleted land. The nation is facing the tough fact that fresh water is already giving out in some sections of the country. Ground water pumping in southern California has caused the underground intrusion of salt water from the sea; the same phenomenon has occurred in New Jersey and in Florida. In the high plains of Texas ground water is being withdrawn thirty times faster than it is being replenished. This has caused Texas to be identified as "the place where there are the most cows and the least milk, and the most rivers with the least water in them, and where you can look the farthest and see the least." There is even some talk of long-distance piping of water — from the Great Lakes or from Canada. In spite of this situation, the United States continually pours new population and new industries into areas of marginal water supply, inviting new disasters — disasters it might have had the foresight to forestall. In 1965 the United States used 360 billion gallons of fresh water each day; by 1980 experts estimate that the United States will be using almost 600 billion gallons every twenty-four hours. By that year, however, the same experts estimate that the daily fresh water supply of the United States will be only 515 billion gallons a day; by 1980 it is apparent that the clouds will no longer be adequate as purveyors of water and that other sources must be found.

The major users of water are three: industry (45 percent), agriculture (45 percent), and domestic homes (10 percent). A large part of industrial use is involved in cooling, and in the process of condensation in steam generators. In these processes 300 gallons of water are required to make a barrel of beer, 750 gallons to produce a ton of cement, 65,000 gallons in the development of a ton of steel. The atomic energy plant in Pike County, Ohio, gulps 40 million gallons of water a day, and spews it forth in the form of steam from its cooling towers — 37 million gallons of it. The hottest river in the same state, and possibly in the nation, is the

Mahoning — whose waters are used eight to ten times by the steel mills in the Youngstown area; a maximum temperature of 122 degrees, for the water of this river, was recorded in August 1955. This adds the problem of thermal pollution to that from human and industrial wastes; trout don't care for such warm water but algae do. The disruption of fish and the growth of algae symptomizes a major and critical alteration of the entire ecological cycle of interrelated plant-fish-insect-animal life.

Agriculture utilizes increasing quantities of water; corn plants, to produce a bushel of grain, drink up to 20 tons of water. When a farmer grows forty bushels of corn to the acre, there is no particular strain on the water supply; when he steps up his production to eighty to a hundred bushels per acre, by the hybrid process, he is suddenly in the water business. By contrast with industry and agriculture the domestic use of water, at 10 percent of the total, is a comparatively small — although highly important — draft on our water supplies. The average man drinks a little more than a ton of water a year. Washing machines and a score of personal conveniences — including such luxuries as swimming pools, velvet green lawns, and air-conditioning devices — have added to the consumption of water. Now the average American household uses about 150 gallons of water a day — quite a change from yesteryear when on any homestead a couple of buckets per day per person was quite sufficient.

What can the United States do to make up its shortages in fresh water — to make available more than we now have? There are several solutions for the problem: the proper utilization of land, the desalinization of sea water, and the reuse of water. The most important principle to remember is that whether the source of water is above or below ground, the supply depends on the proper use of land. One can talk and write about drought and erosion, but they really amount to the same thing — uncontrolled water runoff. Before we can offer cities, farmers, and industries dependable supplies of water we must restore the abused watersheds where the water first collects. Professor Sherman of Ohio State University once put it this way: "God carries the water to the tops of the hills; it is up to us to make it walk slowly and usefully to the sea."

This takes some doing because it involves the necessary integration of forest coverage, grassland, contour plowing, and many other measures. Forest lands are particularly useful, because forest soil is both a sponge to absorb water and a blanket through which it percolates down into the minute pores of the mineral subsoil. Unfortunately the ravaging of our forests began with the pioneers; to emigrants from the settled regions of Europe, and from the American seaboard, the interior country seemed at first to be an unending, dark, and forbidding forest. Someone judged that the squirrels might then have hopped for a thousand miles without touching the ground and scarcely seeing the sunlight. To travel days on end, through the thick gloom among trees a hundred feet high, was oppressing to those who experienced it. The unfortunate result was that many Americans developed an unconquerable aversion to the trees that seemed to hem them in at every turn; they therefore cut them without mercy and without need. There were few protesting voices, but Thoreau's was one of them. He said, "Thank God they cannot cut down the clouds."

Grassland and forest lands are particularly valuable in absorbing water and reducing runoff; this is terribly important because an inch of rainfall burdens the soil with 113 tons of water to the acre. Convincing studies have been made of the amount of water that percolates into the subsoil from various kinds of areas. From grassland, where the rainfall is thirty-nine inches a year, twelve inches goes to the subsoil. In forest areas, with the same annual fall of thirty-nine inches, more than twelve inches enters the underground water supply. On corn land, by contrast, only three of the thirty-nine-inch annual rainfall finally finds its way into the underground water supply. The figures on runoff are just as dramatic: from grassland the runoff was one inch, from forest less than one inch, from cultivated areas more than fifteen inches. It is in this connection that the Tennessee Valley Authority has performed yeoman service; it has been functioning as a horticultural nursery on a breathtaking scale. In the southeastern area it was obvious that water and flood control would require extensive tree planting to prevent erosion and runoff. To meet the challenge, TVA planted seedlings. In the quarter century after 1934 it planted more than 350 million trees, reforested more than 350,000 acres in the Tennessee Valley, and became the most important source for tree seedlings in the United States. By 1958 this agency was producing 40 million seedlings annually; about half went into the valley and the remainder benefited the nation as a whole. It was a tremendous accomplishment. Gifford Pinchot, the greatest of all American conservationists, once put it this way: "The relationship between forest and rivers is like that between father and son. No forests, no rivers."

The control of land is vital to the conservation of water, but two other potential resources deserve full and complete exploration. One is the desalinization of sea water. Here the problem is not the actual accomplishment, which has long been possible, but the development of a process which is economical enough to be practical. Before World War II the cost of conversion was $4 per 1,000 gallons. By the late 1960's this had been reduced to $1 per 1,000 gallons. It still was not low enough because city water in the United States was then averaging 30¢ per 1,000 gallons. In the absence of any state planning in this area, federal foresight was obviously imperative, but conspicuously absent. During the early 1960's James Reston would comment ironically (in the *New York Times*) about a nation that could spend $5 *billion* a year on the space budget — and $8 *million* on desalinization. On Capitol Hill, he noted, it was easy to get billions for anything that flew — but almost impossible to get much of anything for anything that trickled. Beyond the control of runoff and the desalinization of sea water, there was the possible reuse of water already used and dirty. This was through treatment of sewage, an idea repellent to many people. On the contrary, the United States Public Health Service has stated that we have been like the man who turned in his Cadillac because the ashtrays were full. In this nation we have always been accustomed to using water once, and throwing it away. Sewage, in actual fact, is 99 percent plain water; all the pollutants in it amount to less than 1 percent. In sea water, interestingly, the contamination is three times as much. There are processes for removing that 1 percent — leaving water as pure as when it comes from nature. A curious commentary is that people will pump dirty water back into rivers or into the ground with a blind assurance that nature will purify, which does not always happen. It is also possible for man, as well as nature, to purify used water — if not for drinking, at least for beneficial use in industry and for lawns, golf courses, and agricultural crops.

The problem of pollution — from solid refuse, air, and water — is now so serious that there is a very real possibility that mankind will drown in its own wastes. In actual fact a strike of sanitation workers during 1968 in New York City caused that municipality to sink into an ocean of swill; it quickly became apparent that sanitation men, by staying off the job, could bury the metropolis in garbage and turn it into a heaven for rats and vermin. There is also the dangerous and catastrophic situation in rivers and lakes in the United States. The Merrimack, a fabled river in New Hampshire and Massachusetts into which textile mills are dumping their wastes, has turned a filthy brown and bubbles like soda pop with nauseating gases. The Connecticut, once regarded as among the world's most beautiful rivers, has been transformed into "the world's most beautifully landscaped cesspool," as one aggrieved New Englander has put it. The Hudson, once called the "American Rhine" and once carpeted with edible oysters, is now so deep in oil muck that any return to its previous state is — at best — a long way off. Near Troy, scavenger eels (about the only thing that can live in the Hudson's waters, befouled as they are by raw sewage) cling to wastes and have attacked sanitary engineers taking samples. The Potomac is a national disgrace; in the summer it smells and bubbles to the point that it is claimed that if a person falls in he does not drown — he dissolves. The water of Chesapeake Bay, once a grand and gracious estuary, has become "too thick to swim in and too thin to plow." The Ohio has been everybody's privy and nobody's responsibility. At Cleveland the Cuyahoga, probably the world's filthiest river, is claimed to be one-third mud, one-third sludge, and one-third pickle liquor from the great mills; in its water is found carbolic and sulfuric acid, iron, and cyanide. It is so completely devoid of oxygen that there is no fish or plant life in it; it is literally true that a person who places any part of his body in the lower part of the river runs a serious risk of harm. Because of oil slick the federal government declared the Cuyahoga a fire hazard, but the warning was unheeded; in 1969 the river caught fire and destroyed two railroad trestles. Chicago uses Lake Michigan as the tank on its municipal closet, and then flushes it into the unoffending Illinois and Mississippi rivers. As a result they had been "degraded beyond tolerance"; near St. Louis, chicken feathers and viscera collect in patches almost thick enough to stop a motorboat, and along the lower reaches of the Mississippi fish have turned belly-up and died. The Missouri has been described as a "thousand-mile sewer." Almost all recall the famous lines of Sidney Lanier about the Chattahoochee in Georgia:

> *Out of the hills of Habersham,*
> *Down the valley of Hall,*
> *I hurry amain to reach the plain,*
> *Run the rapid and leap the fall. . . .*

That was in the eighteenth century. A hundred years later it still runs the rapid and leaps the fall — but it does so as a polluted river. Lanier, looking down from Valhalla, would be horrified by the condition of the river he loved.

The problem of lake pollution is worldwide. In Russia Lake Baikal is the world's largest freshwater body, with a depth of approximately one mile and a capacity so large that all the water in the Great Lakes could be poured into it with space left over. Its purity has been menaced by gigantic pulp and paper factories which discharge millions of gallons of raw and untreated sulfate wastes into it; fish are dying and the water — once so beautifully pure — is becoming nauseous. In the northern United States, at the beginning of the twentieth century, the condition of its lakes did not differ greatly from that of 11,000 years ago when the glaciers retreated. By the late 1960's, listed in critical condition were Lakes George and Cayuga in New York, Crater Lake in Oregon, Tahoe in California-Nevada, Mendota in Wisconsin, and (among nonglacial lakes) Okeechobee in Florida. Of the Great Lakes, Erie is virtually dead and the others — particularly Lakes Ontario and Michigan — are well on their way to the same fate. This is because of "cultural eutrophication" by which man, through indiscriminate disposal of wastes, shortens the life cycles of bodies of fresh water, turning them quickly into marshes and bogs. Eutrophication is the process of aging; all lakes grow old as they collect runoff and materials from the surrounding shores. Over tens of thousands of years silt is accumulated from erosion and organic matter, eventually turning lakes into marshes and ultimately into dry land. Geologists are agreed that Lake Michigan would normally have about 1 million years of life left as a body of fresh water; they also believe it may have less than twenty years if its present rate of pollution continues. It is already over-abundant with algae and weeds; the same geologists estimate that if human polluting activity were halted immediately it would take 100 years to bring Lake Michigan back to its condition of twenty-five years ago (500 years would be required for Lake Erie if, indeed, it could be restored at all). Lake Erie is now rich in nitrates and phosphates, largely from industrial wastes; these sink to the bottom and are digested by bacteria in such volume that all oxygen in the lake is consumed. Through this process the lake has become inhospitable for fish and human beings but encouraging for plant life, primarily algae. In 1964 the U.S. Public Health Service (USPHS) found a 2,600-square-mile patch of algae — green scum — floating in Lake Erie north of Cleveland; this covered one-fourth of the total area of the lake. To provide safe swimming at Cleveland, lake water around one area was fenced in with heavy sheets of Dacron anchored to the bottom, and chlorine was piped in. Geologically Lakes Erie and Ontario (particularly the shallow Erie) are in old age, Lakes Michigan and Huron are in late maturity, and Lake Superior — deep and on a shore less populated — is in the later stages of geologic youth.

The sources of this pollution are found in domestic, industrial, and agricultural wastes. Pollution coming from domestic users is chiefly in the form of sewage; for this reason some cynics have referred to our present civilization as that of the "effluent society." In the circuit around Lake Michigan there are 310 sizable towns and cities operating sewage plants; fifty-five communities dump all their sewage directly into the lake without any treatment and eighty-eight more provide only partial treatment before dumping. Cochran Lake, once a "pure gem" set in the wilds of northern Wisconsin, has become in the last decade a "caldron of pea soup" by reason of seepage from septic tanks. The numerous lakes in Superior National Forest in Minnesota are becoming polluted from excessive use by campers. Algae fed by nutrients in human waste is beginning to form in even the remotest lakes, and forest officials are trying desperately to "toilet train" the flood of inexperienced and destructive campers. There is little industry along the Potomac River, but the sewage disposal plant that serves most of the Washington area dumps an average of 240 million gallons of ineffectively treated sewage into it every day. This situation has become so general that one scientist has remarked that "the main course of many rivers is through people's alimentary canals. In place after place, the bulk of the river's flow . . . consists of the sewage discharged just upstream." Even so, the American Chemical Society — which is in a position to know — has found the contribution from industrial waste greater than that from domestic and agricultural users. The Federal Water Pollution Administration has cited the Ford Motor Company, and the Republic and Bethlehem Steel corporations, as prime offenders in the pollution of Lake Erie. It also found that 250 industries, including steel and petroleum giants, regularly dumped huge waste deposits into Lake Michigan. There the champion polluter was the Calumet Harbor Area in Indiana, south of Chicago; industries there poured more than 35,000 gallons of oil into that harbor every day and the Gary plant of U.S. Steel alone poured sixteen tons of iron waste and 280 pounds of cyanide into the same water daily. One federal investigator has claimed that the Grand Calumet River is probably the filthiest in the world, surpassing even Ohio's Cuyahoga, which has been a main cause for the death of Lake Erie. The water of Chesapeake Bay is being threatened by the hot-water discharge from power plants, by phosphates and nitrates from sewage and farms, and by industrial wastes; the works of the Bethlehem Steel plant at Sparrow Point (Maryland) pour the equivalent of 400 tons of sulfuric acid into the bay each day. Lake Superior is already menaced with more rapid "cultural eutrophication" through what is known as the "taconite affair." In 1969 it was established that the Reserve Mining Company of Duluth (owned jointly by Republic and Armco Steel) was dumping 60,000 tons of ore wastes daily from its taconite mining operations into Lake Superior. It also appeared that Reserve was only one of a half dozen mining companies which were depositing their wastes *in* the lake rather than *on* its shore, and that on-shore disposal could have been arranged at a moderate additional cost — if the companies and the public had been so minded.

As far as agricultural wastes are concerned, quite beyond the serious pollution of rivers and lakes from manure and nitrogen fertilizers, a major concern has developed because of pesticides, particularly DDT, which has caused serious and irreparable damage to beneficial birds and fishes. In addition to DDT there are its chlorinated-hydrocarbon equivalents — dieldrin, aldrin, lindane, and endosulfan, the latter blamed for the death of millions of fish in the Rhine River in the summer of 1969. DDT (dichloro-diphenyl-trichloro-ethane) was originally synthesized in a laboratory by Othmar Zeidlar, a German chemistry student, working on a doctoral thesis in 1874. His was a lesson in pure chemistry; he had no idea what this new compound would do. The insecticidal properties of DDT did not become apparent until 1939. Then a Swiss chemist, Paul Mueller, while searching for a plant-contact insecticide — one that need not be ingested by the insect — discovered that DDT when it contacted an insect's nerve endings caused muscle spasms and eventually death. For his work, Mueller received the Nobel Prize in 1948. In 1942 the U.S. Army began testing the insecticide, and when their experiments proved successful DDT played a significant part in malaria-control programs in the South Pacific. Largely because of DDT, World War II was the first major one in history in which fewer soldiers died of typhus than from bullet wounds. DDT was ultimately used to reduce the incidence of twenty-seven diseases, saving perhaps 10 million lives and eliminating an estimated

200 million illnesses in the human population; it also saved billions of dollars in food crops from insect pests. One pound of DDT, if spread evenly over the United States, would deposit 1 billion molecules of the chemical per square foot; in 1969, the United States produced 130 million pounds a year at a cost of only 17¢ a pound! Because it does not readily break down into its constituent elements, DDT lingers for years in the air and on the surface of water, and for this reason accumulates in the fatty tissues of birds, fish, and animals. In these tissues microscopic traces ultimately build up to a dangerous level, through what is known as biological magnification, and in time attack the organism's nervous system; it is so persistent that traces have been found in the flesh of penguins in Antarctica and reindeer in Alaska, although it was applied to swamps or forests many thousands of miles away. It has had a devastating effect on marine life and birds, in the latter case illustrated by the frequent deaths of robins and the threat of the extinction of the bald eagle because of the lethal effect on its fertility. The sea plankton may store five parts of DDT per million in their tissues; fish eating the same plankton accumulate several parts per million, and sometimes die. In 1969 the Food and Drug Administration had to seize from Lake Michigan a batch of coho salmon with far higher residues of DDT than was considered safe. Shrimp have been imperiled in nursery areas, Lake George trout have failed to reproduce because of DDT in their eggs, and mallard ducks and pelicans have declined in health because they have fed on DDT-contaminated fish.

By the early 1970's increasingly severe restrictions were being placed on the use of DDT in a number of nations including the United States, Canada, Russia, and the Scandinavian countries. DDT is cheap but no longer an essential weapon in the battle for human health and food. It is less effective than it once was, for nearly 150 species of insect pests have developed a resistance to it. Many other pesticides, now available but more expensive, are less destructive to man's environment and food supply. They should be required in the place of DDT, but the problem is one that transcends local and state levels. It is both a national and an international one.

In the steel town of Gary it is claimed that, on a clear day, you can actually see your hand in front of your face. A recent cartoon in *The New Yorker* showed a woman sitting at a table on the terrace of a Manhattan apartment, calling to her husband, "Hurry, dear, your soup is getting dirty." More than soup has been getting dirty in New York. The USPHS has estimated that New Yorkers could save $800 million a year in cleaning costs if air pollution were reduced significantly. More important than the erosive effect of pollution on property is its harmful impact on human health; the Public Health Service has cited air pollution as a contributory cause of cancer and a serious irritant to lung and respiratory tissue.

Smog is a word that appeared for the first time in the twentieth century. Literally it signifies a combination of fog, smoke, and other contaminants — sometimes in toxic or lethal concentrations. It is usually identified as of two types: (1) the London variant, with air polluted by sulfur compounds produced by the burning in furnaces of coal or oil and, (2) the Los Angeles type, where the air is polluted by hydrocarbons and nitrous oxides produced by the oxidation of petroleum products in motor vehicles. When hydrocarbons and nitrous oxides are exposed to sunlight, there is a photochemical reaction resulting in the formation of ozone and still more irritating compounds. In some instances atmospheric pollutants accumulate and become concentrated when air movement is stopped by what is called thermal inversion (warm air above, holding a layer of cool air on the ground); in this case the smog usually results in reduced visibility, irritation to the eyes and respiratory system, and damage to paint, metal, rubber, and other materials. Prolonged smogs can be frightfully lethal. In 1948, one in Donora (Pennsylvania) caused the deaths of twenty persons. In 1952 a massive one in London produced 4,000 deaths.

Air pollution comes from the internal combustion engine, from furnaces (both domestic and industrial) burning coal and oil, and from the airplane. The dangers from the motor vehicle have been discussed previously (see pp. 518–521). Furnace hazards come from sulfur-dioxide gas and smoke, plus dust and fly-ash thrown into the air by combustion and industrial processes. Both "particulate matter," as pollution-control experts call the fine solids seen rising from stacks as smoke, and the invisible sulfur-dioxide gas, are harmful to health — and in combination they can become deadly. Sulfur dioxide is corrosive as well; in the presence of moisture it forms weak sulfuric acid, which can eat away stone and metal. Both "particulate matter" and sulfur dioxide can be controlled, but the remedies are expensive. Particulate matter can be washed out of stack gases with "scrubbers" or trapped by electrostatic precipitators. Sulfur dioxide can be reduced by using more expensive low-sulfur fuels or by capturing it in the stacks before the gas enters the atmosphere.

More recently scientists have begun to worry about the jet airplane and its effect on the carbon-oxygen balance in the world. The airplane is still a minor source of atmospheric pollution but it is one that in time may have disproportionate importance because much of the carbon dioxide and the water vapor produced by aircraft is released at high altitudes where they are removed from the atmosphere very slowly. In burning a ton of petroleum hydrocarbon, the resultant by-products are one-and-one-third tons of water and twice that amount of carbon dioxide. A Boeing 707 in flight accomplishes this feat every ten minutes; in a year such planes release millions of tons into the atmosphere. At the same time that the amount of carbon dioxide is increased, vast tracts of land are being removed from the cycle of photosynthetic production as millions of acres of green plants are paved under (about 1 percent of the entire United States is now under concrete and asphalt). The loss of these plants reduces drastically the rate at which oxygen enters the air, the carbon-oxygen balance is tipped, and a point could be reached at which the rate of combustion exceeds the rate of photosynthesis — with the world running out of oxygen.

Whatever the causes, every year the sky darkens as the precious envelope of air supporting life on the planet becomes more dangerously soiled and poisoned. In 1967 the federal government recognized the problem for the first time by passing the Air Quality Act of that year; unfortunately it did not provide the funds to make clean air possible. Nonetheless, when he signed the measure, President Johnson dramatized the challenge: "We are pouring at least 130 million tons of poison into the air each year. . . . Either we stop poisoning our air or we become a nation of gas masks, groping our way through dying cities and a wilderness of ghost towns." *

Conservation means the preservation of natural resources, particularly the prevention of waste of the soil, water, and air in man's physical environment. The movement for conservation was long delayed because neither the public nor the government could believe that the seemingly inexhaustible natural resources of the United States would ever be depleted; in the late 1960's Alaska was a last and belated frontier in this regard. Western Congressmen blocked governmental action because they were unwilling to revise the system that allowed the sale of public land to private interests. Economists finally began to count the cost of exploitative agriculture and found that by the 1930's 100 million acres of land had been irreparably destroyed by erosion and that much more had been rendered almost useless, that the Great Plains were turning into deserts, and that the entire nation was afflicted by recurrent floods and droughts. All of this was the inevitable consequence of a laissez-faire policy by a federal government which for many years saw no need for conservation. The beginning of a change in this attitude was brought about by two men and two events in the nineteenth century. The men were George Perkins Marsh and John Wesley Powell. The events were the establishment of the U.S. Geological Survey in 1879 and the passage of the Forest Reserve Act of 1891.

* In 1969 Dr. Gerald B. Dorman, the president-elect of the American Medical Association, recognized noise as an environmental pollutant equivalent to the "noxious gases, chemicals, and wastes that befoul our air, water, crops, and soil." Honking automobiles, screeching trains, grinding machines, and chattering jackhammers have multiplied with the millions of new residents who have jammed into the cities in the twentieth century. Environmental din is estimated to be doubling every decade; big jumps are in prospect from the mounting volume of air traffic and the advent of supersonic planes with their window- and eardrum-shattering sonic booms. One psychologist has said that "it might be a good thing if people's ears would bleed. Then people might get aroused." In any case what was once called "quiet" has become almost nonexistent in settled parts of the nation and increasingly scarce everywhere.

Marsh was a man of many talents; born in Vermont he was a diplomat, linguist, and ecologist. After graduation from Dartmouth he entered the practice of law and politics. While in Congress from 1843 to 1849 he helped organize the Smithsonian Institution. Under Presidents Taylor and Fillmore he served as minister to Turkey; at the age of sixty he was sent by President Lincoln as the first U.S. minister to Italy, a post he filled so ably that he retained it until his death more than two decades later (1882). These occupations were really subordinate to Marsh's consuming interest in linguistics and ecology. One of the prodigious American scholars of his day, he spoke twenty languages and made pioneer contributions to the study of linguistics in the United States. His volume on *The Earth as Modified by Human Action* (1874) has been described, quite justifiably, as "the fountainhead of the conservation movement."

The most important name connected with the U.S. Geological Survey was that of Major John W. Powell, its director from 1880 to 1894. He had enlisted in the Union army at the outbreak of the Civil War, lost his right arm at the elbow at the Battle of Shiloh. After the war he became a professor of geology at Illinois Wesleyan University, and in 1869 led an exploring party along some 900 miles of the Green and Colorado rivers, the first white man to make this expedition. When he started down river with four boats in May 1869, it was in the face of reports that the river vanished underground, that it plunged over falls higher than Niagara, that it was inhabited by savages. This was not altogether true but the stream was frightening enough that the initial trip stands as a tribute to the one-armed Powell's courage and scientific detachment, not to mention his salesmanship in persuading nine others to accompany him without pay on such a perilous journey; no one attempted to repeat it (except Powell in 1872) for two decades. On 30 August 1869, more than three months after the expedition had set out, Powell finished the journey with two remaining boats, a few tools and instruments, some soggy blankets, a little coffee, and a sack or two of moldy flour; they had been forced to throw away the last of their rancid bacon days before. Their clothes were in tatters, their cowhide boots water-soaked and misshapen; they were also near starvation and on the brink of total exhaustion. After they survived Lava-Falls Rapids in the Grand Canyon — the penultimate but biggest and most exciting of the 100-odd cataracts to be surmounted — three members of the party refused to listen when Powell insisted that their ordeal was nearly over. They left the river because they could see ahead another set of rapids that looked to be as bad. Climbing to the canyon's north rim, the trio was slain by Indians, the only casualties on Powell's two exploratory voyages down the river. Less than three days later the remaining members of the party emerged in what is now Lake Mead, where they encountered a Mormon family sent by Brigham Young to watch for them or for signs of their wreckage; the party had long since been given up for lost by most of the outside world.

In 1879 the U.S. Geological Survey was established to prepare geological and topographical maps, to study natural resources with a view to their development and preservation, and to analyze problems of irrigation and water power. In 1891 Congress passed the Forest Reserve Act; it repealed the malodorous Timber and Stone Act of 1878 and authorized the President to set apart forest reserve lands in any part of the public domain (subsequent legislation permitted the Presidents to withdraw mineral, water power, and oil-bearing land as well). The idea of protecting trees was an entirely new one. In the early days of the Republic timber had been so abundant that it seemed as inexhaustible as the water of the seven seas, and pioneer settlers had regarded a growth of trees as a nuisance that should be removed. Beyond the toll taken by settlers, exploitation of the nation's forests by lumber companies reached new heights of destruction and devastation after 1850; under a practice known as "chop and run" vast areas of virgin timber were cut, leaving nothing but a scarred and desolate countryside. The remaining forests were a prey to damaging fires that ravaged unchecked through winter and summer. There was also overgrazing by cattle and sheep, which was tolerated on the public domain. Under the Forest Reserve Act it was President Harrison who began to counteract these undesirable practices by setting aside the first 13 million acres. By 1950 almost 200 million acres had been reserved in national forests. In addition, mineral, water power, and oil reserves affected another large area of almost 50 million acres.

In the first six decades of the twentieth century only two were outstanding and dramatic in the history of the conservation movement. The first decade was exciting because of its accomplishments and the personalities involved. The major steps forward were the Newlands Act of 1902, the Inland Waterways Commission of 1907, the White House Conference of 1908, and a vastly increased withdrawal of public land for public use. The major personalities were Theodore Roosevelt and Gifford Pinchot.

Historian Thomas A. Bailey believes that conservation was probably TR's most enduring contribution to his countrymen as President from 1901 to 1909. The Rough Rider took "conservation out of the conversation stage" and developed the movement into a crusade by throwing the force of his colorful personality behind it. In many respects Pinchot was as unlikely a person as Roosevelt to devote his efforts to the conservation of natural resources for the common man. Both had been born with silver spoons in their mouths; in his diary, as a young man, Pinchot would note: "All day with Father counting securities and cutting off coupons." The young Gifford had boundless energy and enthusiasm, and he devoted most of it to trees and to forests. As an undergraduate at Yale some had called him "tree mad." After graduation he had gone to Europe to study forestry in France and Switzerland, returning to the United States in 1892 to undertake systematic work in the same field on George W. Vanderbilt's estate (Biltmore) in North Carolina — which at that time was employing more foresters than was the U.S. Department of Agriculture. Pinchot surprised everyone by making timber culture at Biltmore a paying proposition, his policy being "not to stop the ax but to regulate its use" — the basic principle of "sustained yields" later followed by large lumber companies like Weyerhauser and Crown-Zellerbach. From 1898 he was the distinguished head of the Division of Forestry in the Department of Agriculture; he found other Chief Executives unsympathetic but TR was a wholehearted supporter. A "man's man," Pinchot was idolized in the service because he could "outride and outshoot any man on the force." As a member of TR's tennis and boxing cabinets he had such direct access to the President that he once enjoyed the dubious distinction of knocking the Chief Executive flat on his face! There was little in the immediate impression he created to suggest his indulgent childhood spent on an estate in Pennsylvania, in a townhouse in New York, and through summers in Europe. Pinchot, however, always denied himself the leisure that his inherited wealth would have afforded him, donating both money and his valuable time to "good causes." Some years later he would visit Franklin Delano Roosevelt, one of the two Presidents most distinguished in efforts for conservation. Pinchot showed FDR his famous pair of pictures — one an old painting of a rich landscape in China, the other a photograph of the same area 400 years later after deforestation and erosion had turned it into a desert. FDR would refer again and again to the pictures during his life, would say that this incident started him on his own road to conservation, and would call Pinchot the "No. 1 conservationist" in the United States.

In the administration of the first Roosevelt the Newlands Act (the name of which was actually that of a Senator from Nevada whose moniker happened to fit the purposes of the measure) would empower the U.S. government to collect money from the sale of public lands in the sun-baked western states, and then use these funds for the development of irrigation projects. Settlers would repay the cost of reclamation from their newly productive soil, and this new money was put into a revolving fund to finance more such enterprises. Passed in 1902, by 1965 $5 billion had been spent under this measure on dams and irrigation projects. Designed to provide water when the West really needed to encourage new settlement by farm families, in time more than one-fourth of the irrigated lands in the West were developed under this program — accounting for an amazing 5 percent of all U.S. agricultural production. The most famous of the many dams constructed under this act was the Roosevelt, constructed in Arizona on the Salt River, and appropriately dedicated to the ex-President in 1911. Ultimately the sum total of the engineering projects under the Newlands Act approximated the magnitude of expenditures on the Panama Canal.* Beyond the Newlands Act, in 1907 TR appointed an Inland Waterways Commission, to emphasize the connection between forests, water supply, and stream flow. On the basis of the first report from this commission Roosevelt called the White House Conference in 1908 to educate the public on the importance of forest and water resources. Among those in attendance were the members of the Cabinet, the justices of the Supreme Court, and the governors of thirty-four states. Out of this meeting would come the National Conservation Commission, a continuing body whose chairman was Gifford Pinchot. His appointment was most appropriate because, in the absence of federal appropriations, Pinchot had paid most of the expenses for the White House Conference out of his own pocket. In addition to the Newlands Act, the Inland Waterways Commission, and the White House Conference, TR vastly increased the withdrawal of public lands for public uses. During his administrations almost 150 million acres of forest lands were set aside, all under the jurisdiction of Pinchot, to whose division in Agriculture they were transferred from the Department of Interior. Roosevelt also withdrew from private sale 80 million acres of mineral lands and 1.5 million acres of waterpower sites. This was three times the acreage set aside by his three predecessors.

Except for the establishment of the National Park Service in 1916 † and of the Federal Power Commission in 1920 (see pp. 532–533), the Conser-

---

* By the 1960's it was apparent that the Reclamation Bureau, still very active, was wasting its time and was working at cross-purposes with other agricultural policies. In 1968 John Fischer would point out from the editor's "Easy Chair" in *Harper's Magazine* that the Department of Agriculture was spending more than a billion dollars a year to bribe farmers to keep part of their cropland out of production — in all about 40 million acres. At the same time the Reclamation Bureau in the Department of the Interior was spending other billions to bring new and expensively irrigated land into production. Obviously, this made no sense. Aside from the waste of the public's money, the reclamation program has shifted much of the nation's cotton production out of the poor southeastern states and into the newly irrigated lands of the prosperous Southwest. This development pushed a couple of million southeastern farmers off their land and onto the welfare rolls of big cities, chiefly in the North. One wonders why some President did not close the Reclamation Bureau years ago. One reason, according to Fischer, was that Senator Carl Hayden, the most senior man in Congress, was chairman of the Appropriations Committee of that body for many years. Hayden came from Arizona, which lives largely on the bounty of the Reclamation Bureau.

† By 1969 the United States had almost 200 national parks with a total of upwards of 30 million acres. Because of a rapidly increasing population of both human beings and automobiles, this acreage was inadequate. By the late 1960's Japan had been much more idealistic and realistic than the United States; it had designated 5.6 percent of its limited area for national parks. The United States, with vastly greater resources, was using less than 1 percent of its land for the same purpose. It was no wonder that the Population Reference Bureau, as early as 1964, had prophesied that within a short time it might be necessary for American vacationers to make reservations, in the national parks, two to three years in advance!

vation Movement was on dead center for a quarter of a century after Roosevelt I because of a first-class scandal in Taft's administration, the influence of World War I, and the prevailing political and economic philosophy of the 1920's. It is apparent that war is the ultimate in waste and conserves nothing. It was also obvious, in the 1920's, that the reactionary administrations of Harding, Coolidge, and Hoover would make no contribution to the Conservation Movement; their consuming interest was in free enterprise, an abiding reverence for businessmen and the business system, a concomitant apathy for political action on much of anything, and a forthright rejection of society's obligation for the plight of the individual. The Ballinger-Pinchot scandal in Taft's administration was a complicated issue; the two antagonists were completely antithetical in origin, personality, and philosophy. Their controversy involved fundamental principles concerning conservation that still face the nation; for this reason the affair can be classified with Teapot Dome as a major crisis in American history. The imbroglio damaged the conservation cause and helped bring the break between TR and Taft, splitting the Republican party and insuring the election of Wilson in 1912.

The controversy arose out of charges made against the conservation policy pursued by Taft's Secretary of the Interior, Richard A. Ballinger. Under the Roosevelt Administration certain waterpower sites in Wyoming and Montana had been withdrawn from sale by Ballinger's predecessor, Secretary of the Interior James R. Garfield. Ballinger had doubts about the legality of the action and reopened the lands to public entry. At this point Pinchot publicly accused Ballinger of injuring the conservation program in order to aid corporation interests. He was supported by Louis R. Glavis, a special agent of the Interior Department, who was fired for his action; Glavis subsequently wrote an article in *Collier's* charging that Ballinger had favored the patenting of Alaskan coal claims by interests alleged to include the Morgans and the Guggenheims. Taft upheld Ballinger, and when Pinchot came to Glavis's support, he too was fired.

Ballinger was a Horatio Alger type who had grown up in the West. The father had been an abolitionist editor and the son, with little formal education but a lot of experience in the herding of cattle on the open range, had worked his way through Williams College and had gone on to become a respected lawyer and a man of substance in the Northwest. With his limited background he portrayed the strong virtues of intelligence, thrift, hard work, and Emersonian self-reliance which were admired in the Far West. In Seattle, where he had served as mayor, the emphasis was on maximum use — rather than the preservation — of lumber, minerals, and soil. Ballinger's position was similar to that of Walter J. Hickel of frontier Alaska, when he was appointed by President Nixon a half century later as Secretary of the Interior; Hickel said that he was opposed to "conservation for conservation's sake." He added that "just to withdraw a large area for conservation purposes and lock it up for no reason doesn't have any merit, in my opinion." Essentially Ballinger and Hickel were Jeffersonians who believed in state and local control; as a protagonist for Roosevelt's "New Nationalism" Pinchot put his faith in planning and regulation by a strong national government.

Pinchot was a wealthy easterner, a "preservationist" as far as natural resources were concerned. His devotion to the "Cause" — in this case Conservation — was so great that, when engaged in a controversy, he tended to ascribe to his opponent every possible shortcoming; everything was black or white, there were no intermediate grays. Usually gracious and Victorian in manner, on occasion he displayed an impetuosity and a righteousness that "bruised" both adversaries and friends. His sympathetic but fair biographer, M. Nelson McGeary, notes that he "could . . . be guilty, on occasion, of making a public charge before fully checking the facts."

A joint congressional investigating committee, by a partisan vote of 7 to 5, exonerated Ballinger of any corrupt practices, but the widely publicized hearing was a catastrophe for the Secretary of the Interior because he was branded before the public as anti-Roosevelt, anticonservation, and — in the eyes of many — personally dishonest. Actually he was no crook, but it was equally true that he had dragged his feet in conserving natural resources. Within a year he had resigned "for health and financial" reasons, to relieve the Taft Administration of political embarrassment. This denouement was the result of some tactical mistakes made in the congressional hearing, plus one great handicap. The major tactical error was Ballinger's choice, as his chief counsel for the investigation, of John J. Vertrees. Vertrees was known as a violent anticonservationist; a close friend of Taft, he was also known for his "Roosevelt-phobia." Since Ballinger was trying to prove that he was both a genuine conservationist and an admirer of Roosevelt, the appointment of Vertrees was a disaster; it was little wonder that the opposition dubbed him "Pervertrees" (by contrast Glavis was ably defended by Louis Brandeis, a future justice of the Supreme Court). The impossible handicap under which Ballinger operated was the involvement of the Morgans and the Guggenheims in Alaskan coal lands. When *Collier's* published the article by Glavis it did so with a sensational cover posing the question, "Are the Guggenheims in charge of the Department of the Interior?" This gave Ballinger's opponents the opportunity to picture him as a stooge of the "Guggies" and the "Morganheims" — the representative of the notorious Morgan-Guggenheim syndicate which, as historian James Penick observes, "had about as much standing in the hagiography of the muckraking journals as the Cosa Nostra does today." In 1911 Ballinger left government service, a sour and defeated man, never to return. Although Pinchot was also out of a federal job, he did serve two terms as governor of Pennsylvania from 1923 to 1927, and again from 1931 to 1935. As far as conservation was concerned, everyone lost.

From a lethargy of twenty-five years the Conservation Movement was finally rescued by Franklin D. Roosevelt, who ranks, with his namesake, as one of the two Presidents who were really outstanding in this endeavor. We have noted previously the contribution of the Civilian Conservation Corps (p. 223), of the TVA (pp. 534–539), and of the Soil Conservation Act (pp. 594–595). Mammoth dams were constructed during the 1930's on the Colorado and Columbia rivers, and in the Missouri River basin. There was also the Taylor Grazing Act of 1934, which provided for the segregation of some 8 million acres (later raised to 142 million acres) for grazing purposes under the jurisdiction of the Department of the Interior. In 1935 Roosevelt withdrew the remainder of the public domain for purposes of conservation. As of 1949, 455 million out of 1.9 billion acres were under federal ownership; this comprised almost a quarter of the total U.S. land area — much of it in barren areas.

Unfortunately this decade of activity in the 1930's was followed by another negative period, just as had been the case after the first Roosevelt. World War II and its long aftermath was a period of desolation rather than conservation. The Eisenhower Administration showed little interest in the movement. Presidents Kennedy and Johnson designated conservation a major crusade and made a beginning, at least in high-sounding legislation, toward the conservation of water and air — as well as soil. Unfortunately their preoccupation with foreign areas, whether in Southeast Asia or on the moon, meant that little was accomplished because of lack of money. By 1970 the air was getting dirtier and the water more polluted. On Amchitka Island in the Aleutians artificial earthquakes and the future of bald eagles, peregrine falcons, harbor seals, sea lions, and the few remaining sea otter were threatened by underground nuclear blasts. On the West Coast, every year saw more redwoods fall, the victims of power saws operated by corporations following the old practice of "cut out and get out." In Florida a new and gigantic jet airport near Miami threatened the very existence of that unique subtropical paradise for wildlife, Everglades National Park; under massive pressure from conservationists, both in and out of Congress, President Nixon stopped the project at the last moment — thus saving the Everglades from at least one of the several ecological hazards that confront it. It was a close thing; a two-mile-long runway for the training of pilots had already been completed in the park.

Many wondered if it was not already too late. Charles A. Lindbergh, a devoted conservationist, has observed that we are on the "edge of time," and that the moments are rapidly slipping away as man destroys himself. Dr. Barry Commoner, director of the Center for the Biology of Natural Systems at Washington University, has noted that "the new technological man carries strontium-90 in his bones, iodine-131 in his thyroid, DDT in his fat, and asbestos in his lungs." Biologist David W. Gates has suggested that our elegant technological society may very well be struck down for lack of ecological understanding. With these hazards in mind, some have suggested a moratorium on technological research and innovation.

The difficulty is that, to this point, the environment has been everybody's business and nobody's responsibility. But if there are no easy solutions, in the judgment of the *New York Times* there are new attitudes that can be adopted to make man prevail:

He can make population stability his ideal and actively seek it instead of passively accepting an unchecked baby boom. He can turn away from the obsession with economic growth and recognize that this planet's resource base is limited and its ecology involves many delicate balances. He can adopt a more respectful and less arrogant attitude toward the air and sea around him. Not every wilderness has to be developed or every arid acre "reclaimed" or every free-flowing river dammed and regulated by man.

Notes

These notes do not presume to provide a bibliography in depth for the legion of topics discussed in this volume. They are designed to provide the inquisitive reader with an indication of the sources that were used directly or indirectly (as general background) in the writing of this particular narrative.

1. "THE BUSINESS OF GOVERNMENT IS BUSINESS"

THE MEANING OF THE TERM "ECONOMICS": J. K. Galbraith, *The Affluent Society*, 26–27; "What Flag(s) on the Moon?" editorial in *NY Times*, 23 June 1969.

ON MERCANTILISM: S. Barr, *The Pilgrimage of Western Man*, 1–55; E. F. Heckscher, "Mercantilism," *Encyclopedia of the Social Sciences;* W. P. Webb, *The Great Frontier*, 67–69; G. Soule, *Ideas of the Great Economists*, 29 ff.; J. Dorfman, *The Economic Mind in American Civilization*, I, 9 ff.

ON THE FOUNDING FATHERS: J. Bronoseki, in *NY Times*, 15 July 1962 (on the nature of the Industrial Revolution); B. Nossiter, *The Mythmakers*, 53; J. F. Bell, *A History of Economic Thought*, 147 ff.; J. K. Galbraith, *The Affluent Society*, 26–27; R. L. Heilbroner, *The Worldly Philosophers*, 33–96; E. Heiman, *The History of Economic Doctrines*, 52 ff.

ON THE DISTRIBUTION OF SCARCITY AND ABUNDANCE: G. Piel, "Can Our Economy Stand Disarmament?" *Atlantic*, Sept. 1962 and "Abundance and the Future of Man," *Atlantic*, Apr. 1964; J. Scott, *Democracy Is Not Enough*, 99; J. K. Galbraith, *The Affluent Society*, 32 ff.; S. Fine, *Laissez-Faire and the General Welfare State*, 173 ff.

ON KARL MARX: R. L. Heilbroner, *The Worldly Philosophers*, 127 ff.; R. B. Fulton, *Original Marxism — Estranged Offspring, passim;* R. Payne, *Marx, passim;* C. Frankel, "What is the Verdict on Marx?" *Saturday Review*, 25 May 1968; H. Schwartz, in *NY Times*, 6 May 1968; A. Berle, "Marx Was Wrong and So Is Khrushchev," *NY Times Magazine*, 1 Nov. 1959.

ON HENRY GEORGE: J. Chamberlain, *Farewell to Reform*, 42 ff.; R. B. Nye, *Midwestern Progressive Politics*, 97 ff.; R. L. Heilbroner, *The Wordly Philosophers*, 179 ff.; R. H. Gabriel, *The Course of American Democratic Thought*, 203 ff.; R. G. Tugwell, "Henry George," in *Encyclopedia of the Social Sciences;* D. M. Friedenberg, "America's Land Boom: 1968," *Harper's*, May 1968, and "The Coming Bust in the Real Estate Boom," *Harper's*, June 1961.

ON VEBLEN: R. L. Heilbroner, *The Worldly Philosophers*, 205 ff.; D. Bell, "Veblen and the New Class," *American Scholar*, Autumn 1963; J. Dorfman, *Veblen and His America*, 272 ff.; H. Elsner, Jr., *The Technocrats: Prophets of Automation, passim.*

ON KEYNES AND PIEL: R. F. Harrod, *The Life of John Maynard Keynes, passim;* G. Piel, "Can Our Economy Stand Disarmament?" *Atlantic*, Sept. 1962 and "Abundance and the Future of Man," *Atlantic*, Apr. 1964; R. L. Heilbroner, *The Worldly Philosophers*, 236 ff.; Cleveland *Plain Dealer*, 12 Mar. 1969 (for statement by Senator Harris); R. H. Phelps in *NY Times*, 23 Mar. 1969 (on ex-military men in industry); J. Kaplin, in *NY Times*, 31 Aug. 1969 (quoting Steffens).

2. A GREAT NEW FRONTIER FOR ENTERPRISERS

COMMERCIAL REVOLUTION, GENERAL: C. McK. Parr, *Ferdinand Magellan, Circumnavigator*, 154 ff.

TECHNOLOGICAL INFLUENCES: B. and L. P. Mitchell, *American Economic History*, 8, 9; O. W. Fuhrmann, *The 500th Anniversary of the Invention of Printing*, 17, 18; "What Gutenberg Did," ed. in Cleveland *Plain Dealer*, 27 Feb. 1960.

ECONOMIC CAUSES: T. A. Bailey, *The American Pageant*, 5 ff.; C. McK. Parr, *Ferdinand Magellan*, 161 ff.; L. B. Wright, *The Dream of Prosperity in Colonial America*, 41 ff.; L. M. Hacker, *The Triumph of American Capitalism*, 151 ff.; F. A. Shannon, *America's Economic Growth*, 5.

RISE OF NATIONALISM: S. Barr, *The Pilgrimage of Western Man*, 27 ff.; C. W. Thayer, *Diplomat*, 45.

RELIGIOUS CAUSES: S. Barr, *The Pilgrimage of Western Man*, 6 ff.; R. L. Heilbroner, *The Quest for Wealth*, 71, 139; F. Gibney, *The Operators*, 266 ff.; G. D. Nash, *Issues in American Economic History*, 1, 2; A. W. Griswold, "Three Puritans on Prosperity," *The New England Quarterly*, Sept. 1934; C. Lehmann-Haupt, "Ever Onward I.B.M.," *N.Y. Times*, 10 Sept. 1969

WHO FIRST DISCOVERED AMERICA?: R. Larsen, "Was America the Wonderful Land of Fusang?" *American Heritage*, Apr. 1966; W. Sullivan, "Phoenicia Linked to America," *NY Times*, 16 May 1968; C. H. Farnsworth, "Now Welshman Is Called Discoverer of America," *NY Times*, 7 Oct. 1966.

THE NORSE: V. H. Cassidy, *The Seas Around Them — The Atlantic Ocean, A.D. 1250, passim*; R. D. Lyons, "How Man Came to the Americas," *NY Times*, 23 Apr. 1967; G. Jones, *A History of the Vikings, passim*; B. and L. P Mitchell, *American Economic History*, 3 ff.; P. M. Sawyer, *Age of Vikings*, 68 ff., 83; J. Lear, "What Did the Norsemen Discover?" *Saturday Review*, 6 Nov. 1965; *NY Times*, 6 Sept. 1954, 26 Jan. 1955, and 14 Aug. 1960 (on lack of archaeological evidence for settlement of Norse on the North American continent).

THE PORTUGUESE: H. Lamb, *New Found World: How America Was Discovered & Explored*, 47-48; J. H. Parry, *The Age of Reconnaissance*, 84 ff., 137 ff., 140 ff.; B. Penrose, *Travel and Discovery in the Renaissance*, 31, 51; E. E. Williams, *Capitalism and Slavery*, 51.

THE SPANISH EXPLORERS: S. E. Morison, *Christopher Columbus, Mariner, passim*; American Heritage, *The Book of the Pioneer Spirit*, 10 ff. (on Vespucci and Balboa); L. B. Wright, *The Dream of Prosperity in Colonial America*, 11; H. Sutton, *Saturday Review*, 8 Oct. 1966 (on TR and the future of the Pacific Ocean); C. McK. Parr, *Ferdinand Magellan*, 154-172 (on Magellan).

ON SPANISH CONQUISTADORES: L. B. Wright, *The Dream of Prosperity in Colonial America*, 8-16; American Heritage, *Book of the Pioneer Spirit*, 10-11; J. H. Parry, *The Age of Reconnaissance*, 172; P. Horgan, *Conquistadors in North American History*, 104; J. McPhee, "Reporter at Large," *The New Yorker*, 14 May 1966 (on Ponce de León, Florida, and the orange); T. Severn, "Passion of Hernando de Soto," *American Heritage*, Apr. 1967; B. De Voto, *The Course of Empire*, 26 ff.

ON BRITISH EXPLORERS: C. McK. Parr, *Ferdinand Magellan*, 172 ff.; E. Bradford, *The Wind Commands Me, passim*; J. H. Parry, *The Age of Reconnaissance*, 213 ff.

THE FOUR SEA PASSAGES TO THE ORIENT: J. H. Parry, *The Age of Reconnaissance*, 204-205; R. H. Anderson, "Soviet to Open Its Arctic Route," *NY Times*, 29 Mar. 1967; W. D. Smith, "Alaskan Oil Primes British Take-Overs," *NY Times*, 8 June 1969; "North Slope: An Oil Bonanza — But the Problem Is to Get It Out," *NY Times*, 21 Sept. 1969.

THE GREAT FRONTIER: W. P. Webb, *The Great Frontier, passim*; J. H. Parry, *The Age of Reconnaissance*, 324.

3. THE COLONIZATION OF THE NEW WORLD

LAND: S. Steiner, *The New Indians, passim;* A. M. Josephy, *The Indian Heritage of America, passim;* L. B. Wright, *The Dream of Prosperity in Colonial America,* 80; H. M. Jones, *O Strange New World,* 61; H. S. Commager, "A Historian Looks at Our Political Morality," *Saturday Review,* 10 July 1965; P. Farb, "American Indian: A Portrait in Limbo," *Saturday Review,* 12 Oct. 1968.

LABOR: T. A. Bailey, *The American Pageant,* 64; F. R. Dulles, *Labor in America,* 5 ff.; J. C. Furnas, *Goodbye to Uncle Tom,* 77–79; C. A. and M. R. Beard, *The Rise of American Civilization,* I, 103 ff.; E. E. Williams, *Capitalism and Slavery,* 11; L. M. Hacker, *The Triumph of American Capitalism,* 99.

IMPORTANCE OF JOINT-STOCK COMPANY: L. D. Baldwin, *The Stream of American History,* I, 174; W. F. Craven, "The Early Settlements: A European Investment of Capital and Labor," in H. F. Williamson (ed.), *The Growth of the American Economy,* 19–44.

VIRGINIA: L. D. Baldwin, *The Stream of American History,* I, 107–108; T. A. Bailey, *The American Pageant,* 14–16; I. N. Hume, "Digging up Jamestown," *American Heritage,* Apr. 1963; G. F. Willison, "Native Bounty," in *American Heritage, The American Heritage Cookbook* (1964), 18 (for narrative on "powdered wife"); L. B. Wright, *The Dream of Prosperity in Colonial America,* 49, 57, 65 (on Jean Nicot); L. C. Gray, "The Market Surplus Problems of Colonial Tobacco," *Agricultural History,* Jan. 1928; R. Froman, "Our Fellow Immigrants," *American Heritage,* Feb. 1963 (on plants in the New World); *Washington Post,* 25 Dec. 1962 (on American plants as aphrodisiacs).

PLYMOUTH COLONY: G. F. Willison, *Saints and Strangers, passim;* F. Russell, "Pilgrims and the Rock," *American Heritage,* Oct. 1962.

MASSACHUSETTS BAY: L. D. Baldwin, *The Stream of American History,* I, 122–126; C. A. and M. R. Beard, *The Rise of American Civilization,* I, 52 ff.; E. Morgan, *The Puritan Dilemma,* 46 and *passim;* S. E. Morison, *Maritime History of Massachusetts,* 11 ff., 149.

NEW AMSTERDAM: J. H. Parry, *The Age of Reconnaissance,* 188–189; American Heritage, *Book of the Pioneer Spirit,* 69.

NEW SWEDEN: D. Hawke, *The Colonial Experience,* 285; D. Wecter, *The Hero in America,* 228 (on Lincoln and Log Cabin); A. Silverman, Cleveland *Plain Dealer,* 23 Oct. 1960 (on Nixon and Log Cabin); C. A. Weslager, *The Log Cabin in America, passim.*

RHODE ISLAND: American Heritage, *Book of the Pioneer Spirit,* 63; C. Covey, *The Gentle Radical, passim.*

MARYLAND: L. M. Hacker, *The Triumph of American Capitalism,* 94–95; W. E. Wilson, "Maryland, Their Maryland," *American Heritage,* Aug. 1967; J. W. Caughey, "Our Chosen Destiny," *Journal of American History,* Sept. 1965; M. B. Davidson, *Life in America,* II, 342.

THE CAROLINAS: T. A. Bailey, *The American Pageant,* 18–19; C. A. and M. R. Beard, *The Rise of American Civilization,* I, 65–68.

PENNSYLVANIA AND NEW JERSEY: M. M. Dunn, *William Penn, Politics and Conscience, passim;* J. Brooks, "Most Improveablest Land," *American Heritage,* Oct. 1964 (on New Jersey).

GEORGIA: D. J. Boorstin, *The Americans: The Colonial Experience,* 75 ff.; T. R. Reese, *Colonial Georgia: A Study of British Imperial Policy in the Eighteenth Century, passim.*

4. AN ECONOMIC INTERPRETATION OF THE AMERICAN REVOLUTION

GENERAL: E. Wright, *Causes and Consequences of the American Revolution,* 19 and *passim* (for quotation from John Adams and general background); T. A. Bailey, *The American Pageant,* 65–67; L. M. Hacker, "The First American Revolution," *Co-*

lumbia University Quarterly, Sept. 1935; J. T. Adams, *Epic of America*, 76 ff.; L. D. Baldwin, *The Stream of American History*, I, 200–205.

NAVIGATION ACTS: R. G. Albion, "Colonial Commerce and Commercial Regulation," in H. F. Williamson (ed.), *The Growth of the American Economy*, 44–61; D. Hawke, *The Colonial Experience*, 187 ff.; F. A. Shannon, *America's Economic Growth*, 25.

TRADE ACTS: L. B. Wright, *The Dream of Prosperity in Colonial America*, 64; F. A. Shannon, *America's Economic Growth*, 25 ff.; H. U. Faulkner, *American Economic History* (Sixth Edition), 115, 120; E. L. Bogart, and D. L. Kemmerer, *Economic History of the American People*, 154 ff.; E. E. Williams, *Capitalism and Slavery*, 52–53, 79; H. Asbury, *The Great Illusion*, 3–14; W. E. Woodward, *George Washington, the Image and the Man*, 121 ff., 153 ff.; S. E. Morison, *Harvard College in the Seventeenth Century*, I, 90–93; L. M. Hacker, *The Triumph of American Capitalism*, 148–149; A. B. C. Whipple, *Pirate Rascals of the Spanish Main*, *passim*.

RESTRICTIONS ON MANUFACTURING AND PAPER MONEY: E. Wright, *Fabric of Freedom, 1763–1800*, 34–35 (for quotation from *London Magazine*); W. P. Webb, *The Great Frontier*, 67–69; F. A. Shannon, *America's Economic Growth*, 29; A. Nussbaum, *A History of the Dollar*, 9–10.

THE PROS AND CONS ON MERCANTILISM: E. L. Bogart and D. L. Kemmerer, *Economic History of the American People*, 174; H. U. Faulkner, *American Economic History*, 113; J. P. Greene, "The Flight from Determinism: A Review of Recent Literature on the Causes of the American Revolution," *South Atlantic Quarterly*, Spring 1962.

TAXATION FOR REVENUE: C. Van Doren, *Benjamin Franklin*, 321; J. M. Lee, *History of American Journalism*, 83; W. E. Woodward, *George Washington, the Image and the Man*, 196, 218 ff.; E. Morgan, *The Birth of the Republic*, 37; T. A. Bailey, *The American Pageant*, 92 ff.; C. A. and M. R. Beard, *The Rise of American Civilization*, I, 192; *NY Times*, 1 Apr. 1956 (on representation in Parliament from Malta); C. D. Bowen, *John Adams and the American Revolution*, 310, 394 ff.

PROPAGANDA AND THE AMERICAN REVOLUTION: J. C. Miller, *Sam Adams: Pioneer in Propaganda*, 5, 28, 39, 180, 188 ff.; C. D. Bowen, *John Adams and the American Revolution*, 328, 388 ff., 409 ff.; E. Forbes, *Paul Revere and the World He Lived In*, 82; F. E. Lumley, *The Propaganda Menace*, 72; W. E. Woodward, *George Washington, the Image and the Man*, 236; E. Wright, *Fabric of Freedom, 1763–1800*, 79–80.

PROHIBITION AGAINST WESTERN SETTLEMENT: D. Hawke, *The Colonial Experience*, 522–523; R. W. Van Alstyne, *Empire and Independence*, 16–19, 36 ff.

TEA ACT OF 1773: J. Street, *The American Revolution*, 48–52; L. D. Baldwin, *The Stream of American History*, I, 226.

FINANCING THE REVOLUTION: E. L. Bogart and D. L. Kemmerer, *Economic History of the American People*, 177 ff.; W. Millis, *Arms and Men*, 40; A. Nussbaum, *A History of the Dollar*, 36; D. Hawke, *The Colonial Experience*, 609; D. Wecter, *The Hero in America*, 169; C. E. Russell, *Haym Salomon and the Revolution*, *passim*.

AMERICAN REVOLUTION: IMPERIAL PHASE: A. M. Schlesinger, *Paths to the Present*, 188; J. H. Preston, *Revolution, 1776*, 72; R. R. Palmer, *Age of the Democratic Revolution*, *passim*; H. U. Faulkner, *American Economic History*, 133; J. T. Adams, *Epic of America*, 93.

AMERICAN REVOLUTION: DOMESTIC PHASE: C. D. Bowen, *John Adams and the American Revolution*, 510; R. Morris, *American Revolution Reconsidered*, 47 ff., 69, 81–85; E. Wright, *Fabric of Freedom, 1763–1800*, 145, 147, 152; F. A. Shannon, *America's Economic Growth*, 53–54; C. A. and M. R. Beard, *The Rise of American Civilization*, I, 294; R. B. Morris, "Class Struggle and the American Revolution," *William and Mary Quarterly*, Jan. 1962.

ARTICLES OF CONFEDERATION: E. Morgan, *The Birth of the Republic*, 110 ff. (on Maryland and delay in ratification); W. Havighurst, "Sword for George Rogers Clark," *American Heritage*, Oct. 1962; L. M. Hacker, *The Triumph of American Capitalism*, 180 (on trade); S. E. Morison, *Maritime History of Massachusetts*, 79 ff.; J. Fiske, *The Critical Period*, 189–205; E. Wright, *Causes and Consequences of the American Revolution*, 309 ff.; J. C. Miller, *Alexander Hamilton: Portrait in Paradox*, 88; M. Starkey, *A Little Rebellion*, 111, 114–115, 133–134, 250–251.

CONSTITUTIONAL CONVENTION: H. Agar, *The People's Choice*, 20 ff.; T. A. Bailey, *The American Pageant*, 142–147; H. Harris, "Madison and the Constitution," *Current History*, July 1936; M. Farrand, *Framing the Constitution of the United States*, 59; S. Padover, *Genius of America*, 97; J. D. Hicks, *The Federal Union: A History of the U.S. to 1865*, 198; H. B. Parkes, *The United States of America — A History*, 130; S. L. Udall, *NY Times*, 12 Jan. 1958 (on relative democracy of House and Senate); L. D. Baldwin, *The Stream of American History*, I, 293; D. Janson, "The House Nebraska Built," *Harper's*, Nov. 1964; A. Hacker, "One Man, One Vote," *NY Times*, 8 Nov. 1964; A. M. Schlesinger, *Paths to the Present*, 114; C. W. Roll, Jr., "We Some of the People: Apportionment in the Thirteen State Conventions Ratifying the Constitution," *Journal of American History*, June 1969; C. A. Beard, *The Economic Interpretation of the Constitution, passim;* E. Wright, *Causes and Consequences of the American Revolution*, 112; S. Elkins and E. McKitrick, *The Founding Fathers: Young Men of the Revolution*, 44; J. Main, "Charles A. Beard and the Constitution," *William and Mary Quarterly*, Jan. 1960; R. Hofstadter, *The Progressive Historians: Turner, Beard, Parrington* (1968), 211, 239; M. Jensen, "The American People and the American Revolution," *Journal of American History*, June 1970.

5. THE RISE AND FALL OF THE AMERICAN MERCHANT MARINE

HEYDAY, 1789–1860: P. E. Rink, "Nathaniel Bowditch," *American Heritage*, Aug. 1960; J. H. Shera, *Foundations of the Public Library: The Origins of the Public Library Movement in New England, 1629–1855* (1949), 94 — on Bowditch and *Principia;* H. U. Faulkner, *American Economic History*, 239; C. B. Mitchell, "Pride of the Seas," *American Heritage*, Dec. 1967; S. E. Morison, *Maritime History of Massachusetts*, 363–364; A. B. C. Whipple, *Tall Ships and Great Captains*, 192 ff.; R. K. Andrist, "Gold!" *American Heritage*, Dec. 1962; G. Blond, *The Great Story of Whales, passim;* I. T. Sanderson, "A-h-h B-l-o-o-w-s," *American Heritage*, Dec. 1960; J. Barbour, *In the Wake of the Whale, passim;* V. B. Scheffer, *The Year of the Whale, passim.*

DECLINE OF THE MERCHANT MARINE, 1860–1914: C. B. Mitchell, "Pride of the Seas," *American Heritage*, Dec. 1967; American Heritage, *Book of the Pioneer Spirit*, 276; G. Dangerfield, "Steamboat's Charter of Freedom," *American Heritage*, Oct. 1963; J. J. Kilpatrick, "Don't Give Up Atomic Ship," Cleveland *Plain Dealer*, 26 Feb. 1967; G. Horne, "Newest Sea Queen Marks End of Era," *NY Times*, 25 July 1968; S. E. Morison, *Maritime History of Massachusetts*, 318, 352, 369; R. Carse, *Twilight of Sailing Ships*, 53, 137–138; H. U. Faulkner, *American Economic History*, 242; I. T. Sanderson, "A-h-h B-l-o-o-w-s," *American Heritage*, Dec. 1960; E. C. Miller and T. K. Stratton, "Photographer to Oildom," *American Heritage*, Oct. 1966; I. S. Bengelsdore, "Whaling Industry Big but Dying," Cleveland *Plain Dealer*, 17 Jan. 1969; "U.S. Is Outfished by Soviet Fleets," *NY Times*, 27 Nov. 1967; *NY Times*, 1 July 1963 (on factory ships); A. B. C. Whipple, *Tall Ships and Great Captains*, 193.

GROWTH DURING TWO WORLD WARS: T. A. Bailey, *The American Pageant*, 723 ff., 885; D. Malone and B. Rauch, *Empire for Liberty*, II, 379; A. S. Link, *Wilson: The Struggle for Neutrality, 1914–15*, 81–82; "Individualist: New Style," editorial and obituary on Kaiser in *NY Times*, 25 and 26 Aug. 1967; L. W. Levine (ed.), "The 'Diary' of Hiram Johnson," *American Heritage*, Aug. 1969.

GROWTH AND SUBSIDIES SINCE 1916

(*a.*) SUBSIDIES: *NY Times*, 29 Apr. 1951; A. C. Bining and T. C. Cochran, *The Rise of American Economic Life*, 533–534; *Washington Post*, 5 June 1950; C. B. Mitchell, "Pride of the Seas," *American Heritage*, Dec. 1967; *Nation*, 5 June 1935; M. Childs in *Washington Post*, 7 June 1950.

(*b.*) CRITIQUE OF SUBSIDIES: *NY Times*, 4 Jan. 1959, 18 June and 13 July 1961, 4 May 1962, 29 Sept. and 8 Nov. 1964, 15 Feb. and 4 Apr. 1965; "End of 'Me-too' Unionism?" editorial in *NY Times*, 27 Aug. 1967; "Fat Fees Embarrass Congress," editorial in Cleveland *Plain Dealer*, 15 July 1969 (on disclosure by *Wall Street Journal*); B. D. Nossiter, "Aero Expert Slams Pentagon Fail Rate," Cleveland *Plain Dealer*, 29 Jan. 1969; G. Horne, "Rough Seas for the Queens," *NY Times*, 14 May

1967; S. Melman, "Behind the Mask of Success," *Saturday Review*, 21 July 1965; "Passenger Ships Opposed by Boyd," *NY Times*, 21 May 1968; W. Bamberger, "Once-Proud Liners of U.S. Humbled by Roar of Jets," *NY Times*, 7 Dec. 1969; G. Horne, "Superliner's Cruise Canceled; Fate of Big Ships Is Uncertain," *NY Times*, 23 Oct. 1969; B. Weinraub, "Liner United States Laid Up; Competition from Jets a Factor," *NY Times*, 15 Nov. 1969; "The Maritime Mess," editorial in *NY Times*, 18 Mar. 1970 (on tax exemptions to shipowners).

6. A MONEY SUPPLY FOR THE CORPORATION,
THE CITIZEN, AND THE GOVERNMENT: THE UNCERTAINTIES
OF PAPER CURRENCY IN THE NINETEENTH CENTURY

ALEXANDER HAMILTON: LIFE AND PHILOSOPHY: J. C. Miller, *Alexander Hamilton: Portrait in Paradox*, 5, 7, 46, 451, 534–535, 568, 577; B. Mitchell, *Alexander Hamilton*, I, x, xi, xii, 30, 47, 325, 422–423, 630; G. Johnson, *American Heroes and Hero Worship*, 54; L. D. Baldwin, *The Stream of American History*, I, 308; C. Warren, *Jacobin and Junto*, 171; H. C. Lodge, *Alexander Hamilton*, 266; B. Hammond, *Banks and Politics in America from the Revolution to the Civil War*, 120–121.

HAMILTON'S FINANCIAL SYSTEM:

(*a.*) ASSUMPTION AND FUNDING: J. C. Miller, *Hamilton*, 248, 287; F. A. Shannon, *America's Economic Growth*, 188; M. L. Ernst, *Ultimate Power*, 211; C. G. Bowers, *Jefferson and Hamilton*, 176; H. C. Lodge, *Alexander Hamilton*, 40.

(*b.*) BANK OF THE UNITED STATES: V. Cowles, *The Great Swindle: The Story of the South Sea Bubble*, 21 ff.; B. Mitchell, *Hamilton*, I, 348; B. Hammond, *Banks and Politics in America from the Revolution to the Civil War*, 67, 120, 121.

(*c.*) EXCISE TAX: S. Fine, *Laissez-Faire and the General Welfare State*, 15; G. Carson, "Tax on Whisky? Never!" *American Heritage*, Aug. 1963; R. M. Ketchum, "Appalachia, 1914," *American Heritage*, Feb. 1969; J. C. Miller, *Hamilton*, 253, 286–287, 397 ff., 411; T. Clark, "About Bourbon," *NY Times*, 8 Mar. 1964.

(*d.*) CURRENCY ACT OF 1792: A. Nussbaum, *A History of the Dollar*, 53 ff.; *NY Times*, 9 Feb. 1964 (on "trial of the pyx").

(*e.*) SUMMARY: L. D. Baldwin, *The Stream of American History*, I, 309; C. A. and M. R. Beard, *The Rise of American Civilization*, I, 342; H. Agar, *The People's Choice*, 26; E. L. Bogart and D. L. Kemmerer, *Economic History of the American People*, 319.

THOMAS JEFFERSON: LIFE AND PHILOSOPHY: C. G. Bowers, *Jefferson and Hamilton*, passim; R. Hofstadter, *The American Political Tradition and the Men Who Made It*, 18–44; A. J. Nock, *Jefferson*, 49 ff.; C. A. and M. R. Beard, *The Rise of American Civilization*, I, 378; R. Burlingame, *The American Conscience*, 4; W. von Eckhardt, "Wright Fans Mark 100th Birthday," Cleveland *Plain Dealer*, 6 July 1969; B. Hammond, *Banks and Politics in America*, 49 ff.; T. Lask, in *NY Times*, 4 July 1967, W. Lawrence, in Cleveland *Plain Dealer*, 16 Feb. 1962, and *Washington Post*, 20 Jan. 1963 (all on applicability of Jefferson's philosophy to the present era); M. L. Ernst, *Ultimate Power*, 221; S. Fine, *Laissez-Faire and the General Welfare State*, 15; D. Wecter, *The Hero in America*, 176; M. D. Peterson, *The Jeffersonian Image in the American Mind*, 356 ff., 362–363, 368, 426; D. Malone, *Jefferson and His Time* (3 vol.), *passim*.

ALBERT GALLATIN: H. M. Dater, "Albert Gallatin — Land Speculator," *Mississippi Valley Historical Review*, June 1939; H. Adams, *The Life of Albert Gallatin*, 175 and *passim*.

SECOND BUS — ESTABLISHMENT AND ATTACK BY THE STATES: B. Hammond, *Banks and Politics in America*, 145, 149 ff., 176, 195, 224, 251 ff., 262 ff., 266 ff.; E. L. Bogart and D. L. Kemmerer, *Economic History of the American People*, 319; H. F. Williamson, *Growth of the American Economy*, 263, 274, 319; W. S. Lingelbach, "Stephen Girard," DAB; B. Crane, *Getting and Spending*, 43; E. Dick, *The Sod-House Frontier*, 90; H. Hatcher, *The Western Reserve* (1966), 125 ff.; C. Sandburg, *Abraham Lincoln, The Prairie Years*, 79; R. M. Coates, *The Outlaw Years*, 201; T. A. Bailey, *The American Pageant*, 232.

JACKSON V. BIDDLE: A. M. Schlesinger, Jr., *The Age of Jackson*, 37, 40, 84, 90, 102, 108–109, 114; M. James, *Andrew Jackson: Portrait of a President*, 250 ff., 347; G. Johnson, *American Heroes and Hero Worship*, 107; J. L. Bugg, *Andrew Jackson: Democratic Myth or Reality*, 58, 102, 105; R. Hofstadter, *The American Political Tradition*, 55; H. C. Syrett, *Andrew Jackson*, 42 ff., 49; S. E. Morison and H. S. Commager, *The Growth of the American Republic*, I, 370; B. Hammond, *Banks and Politics in America*, 36 ff., 259, 270, 287 ff., 324, 345, 349, 405, 419, 518; R. B. Morris, "Andrew Jackson, Strikebreaker," *American Historical Review*, Oct. 1949; M. L. Coit, *John C. Calhoun: American Portrait*, 459; H. Agar, *The People's Choice*, 114; L. E. Davis, J. R. T. Hughes, and D. M. McDougall, *American Economic History*, 209; A. A. Cave, *Jacksonian Democracy and the Historians*, 31 and 79 (quoting Ralph C. H. Caterall and Walter B. Smith); M. James, *The Raven*, 377; G. Johnson, "Great Man Eloquent," *American Heritage*, Dec. 1957; R. Current, *Daniel Webster and the Rise of National Conservatism*, 88, 94, 136 ff., 185.

PANIC OF 1837 AND ITS AFTERMATH: A. M. Schlesinger, Jr., *The Age of Jackson*, 129; H. Agar, *The People's Choice*, 130; R. Hofstadter, "William Leggett, Spokesman of Jacksonian Democracy," *Political Science Quarterly*, Dec. 1943 (in E. N. Saveth, *Understanding the American Past*, 277–241); B. Hammond, *Banks and Politics in America*, 543, 554 ff.; L. E. Davis, J. R. T. Hughes, and D. M. McDougall, *American Economic History*, 203, 205, 210; A. Nussbaum, *A History of the Dollar*, 67, 88; A. V. Darling, "Nathan Appleton," DAB; H. Thompson, "Joshua Forman," DAB.

CIVIL WAR FINANCE IN THE NORTH: D. H. Donald, *Lincoln Reconsidered*, 73 ff.; T. G. and M. R. Belden, *So Fell the Angels*, 37 ff., 64, 104, 106 ff.; H. U. Faulkner, *American Economic History*, 542 ff.; A. C. Bining and T. C. Cochran, *The Rise of American Economic Life*, 319, 409; C. Sandburg, *Abraham Lincoln, The War Years*, II, 191 ff.; A. Nussbaum, *A History of the Dollar*, 108–114; P. Lyon, *To Hell in a Day Coach*, 43 (on Cooke's fraudulent advertising of the Northern Pacific Railroad); "A Strategist for Three Presidents: Clark McAdams Clifford," *NY Times*, 20 Jan. 1968; "Despite Inflation, Government Is Giving Heave-ho to Large Denominations," Cleveland *Plain Dealer*, 20 July 1969.

CIVIL WAR FINANCE IN THE SOUTH: C. W. Ramsdell on Memminger in *Dictionary of American Biography* (DAB); J. J. Monaghan, *Diplomat in Carpet Slippers*, 296 ff.

AGRARIAN UNREST: GOLD V. GREENBACKS: C. A. and M. R. Beard, *The Rise of American Civilization*, II, 99 ff.; T. A. Bailey, *The American Pageant*, 493, 581; L. D. Baldwin, *The Stream of American History*, II, 15; F. A. Shannon, *America's Economic Growth*, 324, 348; R. E. Riegel and D. F. Long, *The American Story*, I, 446; P. L. Bernstein, "Gold Is Still as Good as Gold," *NY Times*, 15 May 1960; B. Hammond, *Banks and Politics in America*, 108; D. Malone and B. Rauch, *Empire for Liberty*, II, 60; L. Auchincloss, "Images of Elegant New York," *American Heritage*, Oct. 1966; P. Lyon, "Honest Man," *American Heritage*, Feb. 1959 (on Peter Cooper); A. F. Harlow, *Old Bowery Days*, 531.

AGRARIAN UNREST: THE FREE SILVER MOVEMENT: F. A. Shannon, *America's Economic Growth*, 409 ff.; H. U. Faulkner, *American Economic History*, 166, 552; A. Weinstein, "Was There a Crime of 1873?" *Journal of American History*, Sept. 1967; R. B. Nye, *Midwestern Progressive Politics*, 60–69, 99, 114, 118 ff.; G. Johnson, *The Lunatic Fringe*, 175; Q. Howe, *A History of Our Own Times*, I, 115; L. D. Baldwin, *The Stream of American History*, II, 295 ff., 302; D. Malone and B. Rauch, *Empire for Liberty*, II, 162 ff., 169 ff.; A. C. Bining and T. C. Cochran, *The Rise of American Economic Life*, 399, 413, 573; R. B. Nye, "Coxey Never Surrendered," *Progressive*, July 1961; T. A. Bailey, *The American Pageant*, 590 ff.; obituary on Coxey in *NY Times*, 19 May 1951; R. B. Nye, *Baker's Dozen: Thirteen Unusual Americans*, 266 ff.; H. Hoyt, Cleveland *Plain Dealer*, 17 June 1950 (on President Cleveland's surgical operation); F. L. Allen, *The Great Pierpont Morgan*, 101, 188 ff., 124 ff.; J. Bakeless, article on Bellamy in DAB; W. J. Cooper, article on Lloyd in DAB; J. Chamberlain, *Farewell to Reform*, 281 ff.; J. Daniels, "In the Crusading Tradition," *Saturday Review*, 13 Mar. 1965 (on Lease); R. H. Luthin, *American Demagogues: Twentieth Century*, 5; O. Jensen, "We Are All Descended from Grandfathers!" *American Heritage*, June 1964 (on Lyndon B. Johnson); S. Porter, "Cash in Postal Savings," Cleveland *Plain Dealer*, 20 June 1967; N. Robertson, "Postal Savings Comes to an End," *NY Times*, 2 July 1967; C. V. Woodward, *Tom Watson, Agrarian Rebel*, 223, 305, 328 ff.; P. W. Glad, *McKinley, Bryan, and the People*, 97, 107, 141, 154, 159 ff.; M. Leach, "The Great Front Porch Campaign," *American Heritage*, Dec. 1959; M. Josephson, *The Politicos*, 618; C. V. Woodward, *Origins of the New South*, 279 ff.; C. Sandburg, *Always the Young Strangers*, 33; A. H. Raskin, "What's Wrong with American Newspapers," *NY Times*, 11 June 1967 (for comment by Glass on Bryan); D. Wecter, *The Hero in America*, 366; M. Curti, "Intellectuals and Other People," *American Historical Review*, Aug. 1964; M. Sullivan, *Our Times*, II, 377; E. F. Goldman, *Rendezvous with Destiny*, 298; A. M. Schlesinger, *Paths to the Present*, 252; *Report* of Subcommittee on Monetary, Credit, and Fiscal Policies, U.S. Senate, Jan. 1950; general articles on current situation in silver in *NY Times*, 29 Jan. and 30 Nov. 1961, 23 Jan. 1962, 29 May and 7 June 1963, 20 May 1967, 2 Mar. 1968; in *Washington Post*, 21 Mar. 1963, 5 Apr. and 5 June 1965; in Cleveland *Plain Dealer*, 29 Nov. 1961 and 24 July 1965; S. Porter, 13 and 14 Sept. 1966 in Cleveland *Plain Dealer* (on current situation in silver); J. J. Maidenberg, "Americans Joining Rush for Silver," *NY Times*, 24 Mar. 1968; E. L. Dale, Jr., "Silver — Just Another Metal," *NY Times*, 30 July 1967.

7. A MONEY SUPPLY FOR THE CORPORATION,
THE CITIZEN, AND THE GOVERNMENT:
A MANAGED CURRENCY IN THE TWENTIETH CENTURY?

The Federal Reserve System: A. C. Bining and T. C. Cochran, *The Rise of American Economic Life*, 418, 422; L. D. Baldwin, *The Stream of American History*, II, 131; L. Hacker and B. R. Kendrick, *The U.S. Since 1865*, 405; J. Brooks, *The Great Leap*; A. M. Schlesinger, Jr., *The Roosevelt Era: Politics of Upheaval*, 296; B. Baruch, *The Public Years*, 12; D. Malone and B. Rauch, *Empire for Liberty*, II, 326 ff.; E. L. Dale, Jr., in *NY Times*, 28 Jan. 1956, 19 Jan. 1958, and 30 Mar. 1967 (on Martin); L. E. Davis, J. R. T. Hughes and D. M. McDougall, *American Economic History*, 215 ff.; B. Hammond, *Banks and Politics in America*, 37; F. Gibney, *The Operators*, 145; G. Soule, *Economic Forces in American History*, 290; *NY Times*, 25 Nov. 1956 (quoting Biese on need for another Pujo Committee); M. J. Rossant, "How Much Independence for the Federal Reserve?" *NY Times*, 13 Dec. 1965 and 20 Mar. 1967; A. S. Link, *Wilson*, II, 199 ff.

1929 and After — Panic, Depression and Recovery: B. and L. P. Mitchell, *American Economic History*, 195 ff., 801 ff.; N. Weinberg, "Labor on the Hook," *Saturday Review*, 22 Jan. 1955; TRB in *New Republic*, 11 May 1968; R. L. Heilbroner, *The Worldly Philosophers*, 189; obituary on Bruce Barton, *NY Times*, 6 July 1967; C. Trilling, "U.S. Journal," *New Yorker*, 27 Jan. 1968 (on Governor Maddox of Georgia); Q. Howe, *A History of Our Own Times*, II, 205, 482 ff., 495; J. K. Galbraith, *The Great Crash*, 27 ff., 42, 98, 132 ff., 182 ff.; L. D. Baldwin, *The Stream of American History*, II, 132; S. Holbrook, *The Age of the Moguls*, 212 ff., 224; D. Malone and B. Rauch, *Empire for Liberty*, II, 375 ff., 470, 538, 565, 575; L. W. Levine (ed.), "The 'Diary' of Hiram Johnson," *American Heritage*, Aug. 1969; F. Russell, *The Shadow of Blooming Grove, Warren G. Harding in His Times, passim*; J. K. Galbraith, "Days of Boom and Bust," *American Heritage*, Aug. 1958; D. Wecter, *Age of the Great Depression*, 1, 4, 12 ff., 17, 35, 39, 45, 62; S. Terkel, "Hard Times Remembered," *American Heritage*, Apr. 1970; T. J. Fleming, "Good-bye to Everything," *American Heritage*, Aug. 1965; obituary on Sidney Weinberg in *NY Times*, 25 July 1969 (on Goldman Sachs); F. Gibney, *The Operators*, 95 ff., 116; T. Cochran, *The American Business System*, 98, 141 ff.; H. Mehling, *The Scandalous Scamps*, 2–25 (on Whitney); A. M. Schlesinger, Jr., *The Age of Roosevelt: Crisis of the Old Order*, 244 ff.; A. M. Schlesinger, Jr., *Politics of Upheaval*, 230, 259 ff., 562, 648 ff.; R. Moley, *The First New Deal*, 92 ff., 163, 224; R. M. Abrahms and L. W. Levine, *The Shaping of 20th-Century America*, 452 ff. (for quotation from Tugwell); B. Hutchinson, *loc. cit.*; R. Hofstadter, *American Political Tradition*, 185, 311 ff.; J. McG. Burns, *The Lion and the Fox*, 162; A. M. Schlesinger, Jr., *Age of Roosevelt: Coming of the New Deal*, 6 ff., 13, 21, 193, 431 ff.; C. Sandburg, *The People, Yes*, 83; C. L. Prather, *Money and Banking*, 45, 84 ff.; R. Bendiner, "The Thirties: When Culture Came to Main Street," *Saturday Review*, 1 Apr. 1967; obituary on Aubrey Williams in *NY Times*, 5 Mar. 1965; R. L. Stevens, "America's Stake in the Arts," *Saturday Review*, 28 Feb. 1970 (for contribution of WPA); *NY Times*, 7 June 1957 and 27 Dec. 1959 (on OASI); B. Nossiter, *The Mythmakers*, 143; H. Preston, Cleveland *Plain Dealer*, 14 Sept. 1966 and TRB in *New Republic*, 29 Oct. 1966 (both on NIT); S. Porter, "Deposit Insurance Taken for Granted," Cleveland *Plain Dealer*, 31 Oct. 1968; A. Nussbaum, *A History of the Dollar*, 196; *Barron's*, 29 May 1950 and *NY Times*, 22 May 1950 (on Wheeler-Rayburn Act); G. Wolfskill, *The Revolt of the Conservatives: A History of the American Liberty League*, 91, 108, 147, 160, 210 ff.

THE CURRENT PROBLEM OF INFLATION: E. L. Dale, Jr., in *NY Times*, 3 May 1959 and 4 Nov. 1968; W. Sullivan, "The World Is Running Out of Raw Materials," *NY Times*, 22 June 1969; H. H. Landsberg, L. L. Fischman, and J. L. Fisher, *Resources in America's Future: Patterns of Requirements and Availabilities, 1960–2000, passim;* "Senate Study Links Old Age to Poverty," *NY Times*, 26 Aug. 1969; J. Fischer, "The Editor's Easy Chair," *Harper's*, Sept. 1969 (quoting Dr. Park); E. L. Dale, Jr., "Reserve Disputes Economic Theory: Chicago Schools' Friedman and St. Louis Bank Called Awry on Money Supply," *NY Times*, 1 Mar. 1969; A. L. Kraus, "The Money Supply," *NY Times*, 26 Feb. 1969; J. K. Galbraith, "American Living Costs Out of Control," *Atlantic*, Feb. 1957.

A FAVORABLE BALANCE OF PAYMENTS, THE CIVIL WAR TO 1950: H. U. Faulkner, *American Economic History*, 687 ff.; E. L. Dale, Jr. in *NY Times*, 10 May 1959.

A DEFICIT OF PAYMENTS AFTER 1950: M. J. Rossant, in *NY Times*, 8 Dec. 1960; H. E. Heinemann, in *NY Times*, 3 Dec. 1967; general news articles in *NY Times* on 25 Sept. 1960, 31 May 1964, and 11 Feb. 1965; J. Brooks, "Annals of Finance," *New Yorker*, 23 and 30 Mar. 1968; "Trouble for the Dollar," editorial in *NY Times*, Apr. 1971.

CONTROL OF THE DEFICIT IN BALANCE OF PAYMENTS BY REDUCING IMPORTS AND INCREASING EXPORTS: J. P. Warburg, "Gold Crisis," *NY Times*, 8 Jan. 1961; A. H. Raskin, "Unions and Their Wealth," *Atlantic*, Apr. 1962; R. W. Dietsch, "What's The Matter with Steel?" *New Republic*, 17 Aug. 1968 (for quotation by Professor Walter Adams); C. W. Griffin, Jr., in review of J. Diebold's *Man and the Computer, Saturday Review*, 19 July 1969 (for featherbedding in Defense Department); W. Magnuson, "Columbus Couldn't Get a Visa," *NY Times*, 16 Apr. 1961; editorial on "Right to Travel," *NY Times*, 19 Sept. 1963; W. D. Patterson, "The World Is a Campus," *Saturday Review*, 1 Jan. 1966.

CONTROL OF THE DEFICIT IN BALANCE OF PAYMENTS THROUGH RESTRICTIONS ON FOREIGN EXCHANGE: W. Lippmann, in Cleveland *Plain Dealer*, 8 Oct. 1959; R. B. Semple, Jr., "President Signs Foreign Tax Bill, with Objections," *NY Times*, 14 Nov. 1966; B. Hutchinson, "Canada and the U.S.: A Centennial Retrospective," *American Heritage*, June 1967; C. H. Farnsworth, in *NY Times*, 9 Feb. 1969; L. Pearson, "Trade, Aid, and Peace," *Saturday Review*, 22 Feb. 1969; T. Szulc, "The Made-in-U.S. Label . . . Blankets Western Europe," *NY Times*, 24 Nov. 1967; *Time*, 29 Dec. 1967 (on investment and profits of U.S. firms abroad); articles on tax evasion through U.S. investment abroad in *NY Times*, 17 Nov. and 23 Dec. 1960; R. Mooney, in *NY Times*, 25 June 1961.

CONTROL OF THE DEFICIT IN BALANCE OF PAYMENTS THROUGH INCREASE IN THE VALUE AND AVAILABILITY OF GOLD: E. L. Dale, Jr., "Do We Need a Cover for the Dollar?" *NY Times*, 10 May 1959 and 28 Jan. 1968; "The Dollar Is at Bay," *NY Times*, 8 Dec. 1967; J. R. Slevin, "Germans Undersell Rivals," Cleveland *Plain Dealer*, 27 Apr. 1968; J. Brooks, *Business Adventures*, 314–389; J. A. Livingston, "Each Nation Has Different Worries," Cleveland *Plain Dealer*, 31 Mar. 1968; S. Porter, "Glitter of Gold Lures Speculators," Cleveland *Plain Dealer*, 12 May 1969.

CONTROL OF THE DEFICIT IN BALANCE OF PAYMENTS THROUGH REPLACEMENT OF GOLD AS A MONETARY UNIT: "The Role of Gold," editorial in *NY Times*, 6 Jan. 1967; R. Triffin, "Neither Gold nor the Dollar," *New Republic*, 27 Jan. 1968; R. Triffin, "Going It Alone in Monetary Reform," *NY Times*, 29 Apr. 1967; J. W. Lee, "Basel and Zurich: Opposite Symbols," *NY Times*, 13 Mar. 1968; H. E. Heinemann, "Two-

Price Gold System Is Fulfilling Its Purpose," *NY Times*, 26 Nov. 1967 and 24 Mar. 1968; J. A. Livingston, "Two-Price Gold Buys Time," Cleveland *Plain Dealer*, 24 and 31 Mar., and 28 June 1968; H. Schwartz, "Must the Dollar Be Tied to Gold?" *NY Times*, 4 Dec. 1967; J. Brooks, *Business Adventures*, 314–389.
Mr. Nixon's Bombshell: J. M. Naughton, "Nixon Orders 90-Day Wage-Price Freeze," *NY Times*, 16 Aug. 1971; A. Lewis, "Learning to Live with Monetary Flexibility," *NY Times*, 16 May 1971; ". . . And Barriers to Trade," editorial in *NY Times*, 10 Sept. 1971; "Trade War With Japan," editorial in *NY Times*, 13 Aug. 1971; P. A. Rinfret, "We Use Our Muscle," *NY Times*, 30 Aug. 1971; H. Rowen, "Yen Float Means Victory for Nixon Dollar Strategy," Cleveland *Plain Dealer*, 28 Aug. 1971; "Money: After the Crisis," *Newsweek*, 24 May 1971; "Your New Dollar," *Newsweek*, 30 Aug. 1971; "The Yen Floats," editorial in *NY Times*, 28 Aug. 1971; W. F. Miller, "Nixon Plan Perils Canadian Economy," Cleveland *Plain Dealer*, 11 Oct. 1971; R. V. Roosa, "The Import Surcharge May Boomerang," *NY Times*, 10 Sept. 1971; J. Brooks, "Mr. Nixon's Paper Standard," *NY Times*, 26 Aug. 1971; G. E. Condon, "No Buoyance for Dollar Here," Cleveland *Plain Dealer*, 26 Aug. 1971.

8. SLAVE LABOR IN THE UNITED STATES

The African Slave Trade: M. L. Starkey, *Striving to Make It My Home: The Story of Americans from Africa*, 96, 123; R. Burlingame, *The American Conscience*, 100; L. B. Wright, *Dream of Prosperity*, 24, 68; M. Cowley and D. P. Mannix, "Middle Passage," *American Heritage*, Feb. 1962.
The Profitability of Slavery for the Bondsmen and the "Poor Whites": K. M. Stampp, *The Peculiar Institution*, 188 ff., 344; H. U. Faulkner, *American Economic History*, 317; *NY Times*, 20 Aug. 1964 (for statement by psychologists on "learned apathy"); S. M. Elkins, *Slavery*, 103–140; J. C. Furnas, *Good-bye to Uncle Tom*, 334–340; B. Mandel, "The Northern Working Class and the Abolition of Slavery" (doctoral dissertation, Western Reserve University, 1952), 18–19, 73; L. M. Hacker, *The Triumph of American Capitalism*, 292.
Profitability of Slavery for the Region and the Nation: L. M. Hacker, *The Triumph of American Capitalism*, 240–241; E. D. Genovese, "The Significance of the Slave Plantation for Southern Economic Development," *Journal of Southern History*, Nov. 1962 (quoted in H. D. Woodman, *Slavery and the Southern Economy*, 232–233); E. W. Williams, *Capitalism and Slavery*, 7, 49; A. Nevins, *Ordeal of the Union*, I, 485; J. T. Adams, *Epic of America*, 112 ff., 156; S. E. Morison, *By Land and Sea*, 20; W. P. Webb, *The Great Plains*, 185.
Profitability of Slavery for the Owners of Bondsmen: F. A. Shannon, *American Economic Growth*, 301; H. U. Faulkner, *American Economic History*, 320; K. M. Stampp, *The Peculiar Institution*, 400–425; S. M. Elkins, *Slavery*, 231–237; J. D. Hicks, *The Federal Union*, 355 ff.; R. Burlingame, *The American Conscience*, 258; M. T. Finley, "Slavery," in *Encyclopedia of the Social Sciences*.
Fifteenth Amendment: R. McGill, "The South Has Many Faces," *Atlantic*, Apr. 1963; E. Garamekian, "Report from the South on the Negro Vote," *Reporter*, 27 June 1957; K. M. Stampp, *The Era of Reconstruction, 1865–1877*, 201 ff.; obituary on Harry Byrd in *NY Times*, 21 Oct. 1966; R. H. Luthin, *American Demagogues*, 188, 197; R. Baker, *NY Times*, 12 Nov. 1968.
The Fourteenth Amendment and the Negro: *Washington Post*, 1 Mar. 1963 (for quotation from President Kennedy); H. Bond and N. Puner, "Jim Crow in Education," *Nation*, 24 Nov. 1951; P. Bellamy, in Cleveland *Plain Dealer*, 5 Dec. 1963 (on additional cost of social services); *NY Times*, 20 Dec. 1964 and *New Republic*, 17 Apr. 1965 (on losses to tax duplicate); obituary on Ralph McGill, *NY Times*, 5 Feb. 1969.
Fourteenth Amendment and Business: C. W. Collins, *Fourteenth Amendment and the States, passim*; F. Rodell, *Nine Men*, 164, 186; R. Hofstadter, *American Political Tradition*, 171; J. B. James, *The Framing of the Fourteenth Amendment*, 166, 194–195; H. J. Graham, *Everyman's Constitution: Historical Essays on the Fourteenth Amendment, passim*.

The Thirteenth Amendment: D. Donald, *Lincoln Reconsidered*, 18, 136, and *passim*; R. Hofstadter, *American Political Tradition*, 111, 129 ff.; K. M. Stampp, *Reconstruction*, 32, 35, 47, 131 ff.; J. Street, *The Civil War*, 84; L. Bennett, Jr., "Was Lincoln a White Supremacist?" *Ebony*, Jan. 1968 (quoted at length in *NY Times*, 28 Jan. 1968); B. Catton, *This Hallowed Ground*, 170 ff.; C. V. Woodward, *Origins of the New South*, 178 ff.; N. Thomas, "Decline in the Cotton Kingdom," *Current History*, Apr. 1935; T. D. Clark, *The Emerging South*, *passim*; H. Bogart, "Hunger Is Still a Fact of Life among South Carolina Negroes," Cleveland *Plain Dealer*, 16 Feb. 1969; "Starvation in Mississippi," editorial in *NY Times*, 26 Mar. 1968; W. K. Stevens, "Farm-to-City Migration Is Nearing End in U.S.," *NY Times*, 23 Mar. 1969; TRB in *New Republic*, 18 Nov. 1967; R. McGill, "South's Glowing Horizon If . . . ," *Saturday Review*, 9 Mar. 1968; J. Nelson, "Tenant Pay Recovered from Plantation Owner," Cleveland *Plain Dealer*, 26 June 1968; C. Edmondson, in *St. Louis Post-Dispatch*, 9 June 1940, plus news dispatch and editorial in same newspaper on 11 June 1938 and 30 Dec. 1937 (on replacement of sharecroppers by day labor); "The Two Nations," editorial in *NY Times*, 7 Aug. 1967; *NY Times*, 19 July 1965 (on the Evans family); W. P. Webb, in *Texas Business Review*, Oct. 1959 (on petrochemical industry in South); C. V. Woodward, in *NY Times*, 18 June 1961.

Proposals for Race Adjustment: Amalgamationists and Isolationists: H. Hawkins (ed.), *Booker T. Washington and His Critics*, *passim*; S. R. Spencer, *Booker T. Washington*, *passim*; F. L. Broderick, *W. E. B. DuBois, Negro Leader in a Time of Crisis*, *passim*; M. V. S. Holt, *George Washington Carver*, *passim*; M. L. King, "The Negro Is Your Brother," *Atlantic*, Aug. 1963; C. E. Lincoln, *The Black Muslims in America*, 15 ff., 29, 56 ff., 61 ff., 190, 240 ff.; D. Malone and B. Rauch, *Empire for Liberty*, II, 335 ff.; W. Percy, "Mississippi: The Fallen Paradise," *Harper's*, Apr. 1965; obituary on DuBois, *NY Times*, 29 May 1963; H. Carter, "If All the Negroes Quit the South," *NY Times*, 29 May 1962; E. S. Redkey, "Bishop Turner's African Dream," *Journal of American History*, Sept. 1967; E. D. Cronin, *Black Moses*, *passim*.

Critique of Black Separatism: B. Rustin, "The Failure of Black Separatism," *Harper's*, Jan. 1970; "'Black Capitalism' Overrated, Negro Member of Reserve Says," *NY Times*, 30 Dec. 1969; S. Alinsky, "The Professional Radical, 1970," *Harper's*, Jan. 1970.

The First and Second Reconstructions: H. S. Ashmore, *The Other Side of Jordan*, 46 ff.; O. Kerner, "Inside Story of the Kerner Report," Cleveland *Plain Dealer*, 11 Aug. 1968; H. Brandon, "State of Affairs — Hatcher: Hostile Confrontation," *Saturday Review*, 25 May 1968; R. G. McGruder, "The Negro Struggles to Earn a Place in the Business-Economic Sun," Cleveland *Plain Dealer*, 2 June 1968; C. V. Woodward, "From the First Reconstruction to the Second," *Harper's*, Apr. 1965.

9. FREE LABOR IN THE UNITED STATES

Before the Civil War: L. E. Davis, J. R. T. Hughes, and D. M. McDougall, *American Economic History*, 130 ff.; J. Mitford, "Guilty as Charged by the Judge," *Atlantic*, Aug. 1969.

Unions Become Essential after the Civil War: T. A. Bailey, *The American Pageant*, 536 ff.; F. R. Dulles, *Labor in America*, 96 ff.; J. G. Rayback, *A History of American Labor*, 120; L. D. Baldwin, *The Stream of American History*, II, 209; A. Hamilton, "Woman of Ninety Looks at Her World," *Atlantic*, Sept. 1961.

National Labor Union: L. D. Baldwin, *The Stream of American History*, 209; H. Pelling, *American Labor*, 56; J. G. Rayback, *A History of American Labor*, 120 ff.; F. R. Dulles, *Labor in America*, 61 ff.

The American Federation of Labor: *NY Times*, 17 May 1963 (on relative size of constituent unions); F. R. Dulles, *Labor in America*, 35 ff., 150, 155 ff., 162, 254; L. Velie, *Labor U.S.A.*, 116 ff., 129, 279; J. Miller, "Dave Beck Comes out of the West," *Reporter*, 8 Dec. 1953; D. Malone and B. Rauch, *Empire for Liberty*, II, 117; H. Pelling, *American Labor*, 139; E. Levinson, *Labor on the March*, 18; E. S. Bates, "A. F. of L., Enemy of Labor," *American Mercury*, Jan. 1935; B. Stolberg, "Communist Wreckers in American Labor," *Saturday Evening Post*, 2 Sept. 1939; *NY Times*,

19 Dec. 1951, 18 Aug. 1958, 21 Feb. 1959 (on Hutcheson Dynasty); *NY Times*, 8 Jan. 1940 (on Petrillo); N. Rossiter, "The Teamsters: Corrupt Policemen of an Unruly Industry," *Harper's*, May 1959; *NY Times*, 25 July and 5 Nov. 1955, 19 May and 15 Dec. 1957 (on Beck); A. H. Raskin, "Power of James Hoffa," *Atlantic*, Jan. 1964; *NY Times*, 12 July 1961 and 18 Aug. 1964 (on Hoffa); M. Johnson, *Crime on the Waterfront*, 15 ff.; S. Yellen, *American Labor Struggles*, 282 ff.

The Knights of Labor: T. A. Bailey, *The American Pageant*, 538; E. Gertz and J. Tebbel, "The Chicago Tribune," *American Mercury*, Apr. 1944; R. Gabriel, *The Course of American Democratic Thought*, 190 ff.; H. Pelling, *American Labor*, 65; F. R. Dulles, *Labor in America*, 125, 129, 136, 140, 147 ff.; L. Adamic, *Dynamite*, 50; L. D. Baldwin, *The Stream of American History*, II, 208, 215; B. Tuchman, "Anarchists," *Atlantic*, May 1963; S. Yellen, *American Labor Struggles*, 55; G. Johnson, *The Lunatic Fringe*, 193; J. Chamberlain, *Farewell to Reform*, 67 ff.; H. Barnard, *Eagle Forgotten, passim; NY Times*, 23 Feb. 1965 (on Frankfurter and Sacco-Vanzetti).

The I.W.W.: H. Pelling, *American Labor*, 111 ff.; F. R. Dulles, *Labor in America*, 221; J. L. Kornbluh, *Rebel Voices, An IWW Anthology, passim* (reviewed by A. H. Raskin in *NY Times*, 3 Jan. 1965); B. Weisberger, "Here Come the Wobblies," *American Heritage*, June 1967.

The United Mine Workers: R. H. Wiebe, "The Anthracite Strike of 1902: A Record of Confusion," *Mississippi Valley Historical Review*, Sept. 1961; T. A. Bailey, *The American Pageant*, 650; R. L. Reynolds, "Coal Kings Come to Judgment," *American Heritage*, Apr. 1960; J. G. Rayback, *A History of American Labor*, 212; L. D. Baldwin, *The Stream of American History*, II, 217; B. Minton and J. Stuart, *Men Who Lead Labor*, 86 ff. (on Lewis); articles on Lewis in *Time*, 2 Oct. 1933, 7 Feb. 1938, 7 Aug. 1939; *NY Times*, 16 Dec. 1959 and 12 June 1969 (obituary); *Life*, 2 Dec. 1940; A. M. Schlesinger, Jr., *Coming of the New Deal*, 138, 416; A. H. Raskin, "Fresh Looks at Labor and Its Ways," *Saturday Review*, 16 Feb. 1957; obituary on Garner, in *NY Times*, 8 Nov. 1967; "Security with a Union Label," editorial in *NY Times*, 12 Aug. 1966; H. Pelling, *American Labor*, 139; L. Velie, *Labor U.S.A.*, 261 ff.

The CIO: H. U. Faulkner, *American Economic History*, 721; A. M. Schlesinger, Jr., *Coming of the New Deal*, 412 ff.; P. Y. Anderson, in *St. Louis Post-Dispatch*, 16 Feb. 1936 (on Lewis-Hutcheson fisticuffs); L. Velie, *Labor U.S.A.*, 64 ff., 77, 96 ff., 100 ff., 136, 149; F. R. Dulles, *Labor in America*, 321; B. Minton and J. Stuart, *Men Who Lead Labor*, 116 ff., 233; H. Pelling, *American Labor*, 172 ff., 178 ff.; I. Howe and B. J. Widick, *The UAW and Walter Reuther*, 187; J. Wechsler, "Labor's Bright Young Man," *Harper's*, Mar. 1948; articles on Reuther in *NY Times*, 6 and 10 Feb., 1 Dec. 1955, and 28 Aug. 1964; A. H. Raskin, *NY Times*, 22 Sept. 1952 (on Reuther); A. H. Raskin, "Reuther's Legacy for Social Stability," *NY Times*, 18 May 1970; J. M. Flint, "Reuther Praised in Funeral Rites," *NY Times*, 16 May 1970; A. H. Raskin, *NY Times*, 25 June 1952 (on Dubinsky); H. Goldberg, *American Radicals*, 68; M. Marshall, "Columnists on Parade: Heywood Broun," *Nation*, 21 May 1938; obituary on Broun in *NY Herald-Tribune*, 19 Dec. 1939.

Amalgamation of AFL-CIO: H. Pelling, *American Labor*, 192 ff., 212; articles on Meany by A. H. Raskin in *NY Times*, 10 and 20 Feb. 1955, 20 Oct. 1957, and 7 July 1961; L. Velie, *Labor U.S.A.*, 205 ff., 213 ff., 248 ff.; A. H. Raskin, "Squeeze on the Unions," *Atlantic*, Apr. 1961; W. Glazier, "Automation and Joblessness," *Atlantic*, Aug. 1962; A. H. Raskin, "Automation: Road to Lifetime Jobs?" *Saturday Review*, 28 Nov. 1964; A. H. Raskin, "Profit Sharing in the Paycheck," *Saturday Review*, 10 Feb. 1968; O. Handlin, "Man and Magic: First Encounters with the Machine," *American Scholar*, Summer 1964; A. H. Raskin, "Two-Way March in American Labor," *NY Times*, 27 Nov. 1967; W. L. Abbott, "Poppa Meany," *New Republic*, 4 May 1968.

Attitude of Employers toward Labor: S. Yellen, *American Labor Struggles*, 103, 117, 154; "Report on New York," in *Atlantic*, Oct. 1965 (on LaGuardia); "The 'Fink' Racket," editorial in *Nation*, 11 Feb. 1939; L. Huberman, *The Labor Spy Racket*, 21 ff., 29 ff.; A. Kopkind, "The Grape Pickers' Strike," *New Republic*, 29 Jan. 1966; H. Wolf, "Strikebreaker No. 1," *Nation*, 13 Nov. 1935; *NY Times*, 26 Oct. 1957 (on Shefferman); D. L. Dowd, *Modern Economic Problems in Historical Perspective*, 65; F. R. Dulles, *Labor in America*, 173, 260 ff.; P. Y. Anderson, *St. Louis Post-Dispatch*,

20, 24 June and 1 July 1937 (on Memorial Day Massacre); L. Wolf, *Lockout: The Story of the Homestead Strike of 1892, passim;* B. A. Franklin, "Frick Evalued in Book-Ban Case," *NY Times,* 3 Aug. 1965; W. Wilson, *Forced Labor in the U.S.,* 63 ff.; R. Ginger, *Age of Excess,* 33; J. G. Rayback, *A History of American Labor,* 201 ff., 257 ff.; L. D. Baldwin, *The Stream of American History,* II, 215 ff., 220; D. Malone and B. Rauch, *Empire for Liberty,* II, 121, 215; P. W. Glad, *McKinley, Bryan and the People,* 89.

NATIONAL LEGISLATION ON WAGES, EMPLOYMENT, AND COLLECTIVE BARGAINING: A. M. Schlesinger, Jr., *Coming of the New Deal,* 136 ff.; J. McG. Burns, *The Lion and the Fox,* 216, 218 ff.; J. G. Rayback, *A History of American Labor,* 329, 383; D. Malone and B. Rauch, *Empire for Liberty,* II, 597, 604, 736; G. Wolfskill, *The Revolt of the Conservatives,* 72 ff.; B. Stolberg, "Vigilantism, 1937," *Nation,* 21 Aug. 1937; L. Huberman, *The Labor Spy Racket,* 146 ff.; F. R. Dulles, *Labor in America,* 278, 307, 336, 345; obituary on Herbert Kohler, *NY Times,* 29 July 1968; R. M. Lovett, "A GM Stockholder Visits Flint," *Nation,* 30 Jan. 1937; Q. Howe, *A History of Our Own Times,* II, 655; obituary on John L. Lewis in *NY Times,* 12 June 1969; S. Fine, "The General Motors Sit-Down Strike: A Re-examination," *American Historical Review,* Apr. 1965; "Raising the Wage Floor," editorial in *NY Times,* 17 Sept. 1966; articles on inadequacy of Fair Labor Standards Act in *NY Times,* 1 Mar. 1956, 21 Mar. 1961, *New Republic,* 5 June 1961; K. Schriftgeisser, "Keeping Watch on the Economy," *Saturday Review,* 8 Jan. 1966; T. Cochran, *American Business System,* 152, 161; obituary on Fred A. Hartley, Jr., *NY Times,* 12 May 1969; K. Schriftgeisser, *The Lobbyists,* 95 ff.; R. Shogun, "1948 Election," *American Heritage,* June 1968; A. H. Raskin, "Government's Role When Bargaining Breaks Down," *Reporter,* 31 Jan. 1963; A. H. Raskin, "Labor's Crisis of Public Confidence," *Saturday Review,* 30 Mar. 1963; L. L. King, "Washington Money Birds," *Harper's,* Aug. 1965; A. H. Raskin, *NY Times,* 8 Jan. 1967 (on Landrum-Griffin).

AMERICAN ATTITUDES TOWARD IMMIGRATION: A PARADOX: T. A. Bailey, *The American Pageant,* 323 ff., 780 ff.; D. Malone and B. Rauch, *Empire for Liberty,* II, 125 ff., 292 ff., 337; C. F. Wittke, *We Who Built America, passim;* A. L. Damon, "The Great Red Scare," *American Heritage,* Feb. 1968; H. U. Faulkner, *American Economic History,* 641; J. Laikin, "Our Irrational Nationality Quotas," *Reporter,* 7 Mar. 1957; "I Lift My Lamp," editorial in *NY Times,* 14 Jan. 1965; W. Magnuson, "Columbus Couldn't Get a Visa," *NY Times,* 16 Apr. 1961; J. Corry, "Immigration Shows an Ethnic Change," *NY Times,* 18 Mar. 1968; L. Edson, "Jensenism, n. The Theory that I.Q. Is Largely Determined by the Genes," *NY Times,* 31 Aug. 1969.

10. THE REGULATION OF INDUSTRIAL COMBINATIONS

TRANSITION FROM MERCANTILE TO INDUSTRIAL CAPITALISM: L. M. Hacker, *The Triumph of American Capitalism,* 248 ff.; V. S. Clark, *History of Manufactures in the United States* (1929), I, 438–442; F. A. Shannon, *America's Economic Growth,* 230–231.

INFLUENCE OF EDUCATION: TRB in *New Republic,* 12 Feb. 1966; T. A. Bailey, *The American Pageant,* 333 ff., 550 ff.; F. M. Hechinger, "The Urban University," *NY Times,* 3 May 1968; C. H. Farnsworth, "West Europe Attributes Continuing Technology Lag behind the U.S. to Inferior Management," *NY Times,* 13 Dec. 1967.

INFLUENCE OF INVENTORS: J. W. Krutch, "Who Was Henry Thoreau?", *Saturday Review,* 19 Aug. 1967; "Some Important Inventors in the Last 100 Years," *NY Times,* 8 Jan. 1968; L. D. Baldwin, *The Stream of American History,* II, 255; *NY Times,* 27 Dec. 1966 (on Paterson, New Jersey); American Heritage, *Book of the Pioneer Spirit,* 279, 300 ff., 307, 368, 372, 376, 385; A. Welles, "Father of Our Factory System," *American Heritage,* Apr. 1958; M. B. Davidson, *Life in America,* I, 412 ff., II, 285 ff.; A. C. Clarke, *Voice Across the Sea, passim;* S. Carter, *Cyrus Field: Man of Two Worlds, passim;* C. F. Wittke, *The First Fifty Years: The Cleveland Museum of Art, 1916–1966,* 32 ff. (on Wade); L. Barnett, "The Voice Heard Round the World," *American Heritage,* Apr. 1965; S. Fox, "Armstrong Adds to the List of Historic Expressions," *NY Times,* 21 July 1969; M. Josephson, *Edison: A Biography, passim;* B. Bliven, *The*

Wonderful Writing Machine, passim; J. Dos Passos, "U.S.A. Revisited," *Atlantic,* Apr. 1964 (on Eastman); M. Wilson, *American Science and Invention,* 271 ff.; obituary on Lee De Forest, *NY Times,* 2 July 1961; J. Geis, "Mr. Eads Spans the Mississippi," *American Heritage,* Aug. 1969; M. J. Kempner, "Greatest Bridge of Them All," *Harper's,* Nov. 1964; R. Burlingame, *Henry Ford, A Great Life in Brief,* 55, 73 ff.; R. Nader, "The Infernal, Eternal, Internal Combustion Engine," *New Republic,* 27 Apr. 1968; G. E. Condon, "Steamed Up for a New Car," Cleveland *Plain Dealer,* 13 June 1968.

INFLUENCE OF ENTREPRENEURS: Beard, *op. cit.,* II, 175; J. T. Flynn, *God's Gold, passim;* Holbrook, *Age of the Moguls,* 65, 134 ff., 140, 206 ff., 363; J. Bainbridge, "The Super-American State — Oil," *New Yorker,* 18 Mar. 1961; R. L. Heilbroner, "Grand Acquisitor," *American Heritage,* Dec. 1964; G. Williams, "The Rockefeller Foundation: How It Operates," *Atlantic,* Apr. 1964; W. Manchester, "Nelson Rockefeller's Moral Heritage," *Harper's,* May 1959; A. M. Schlesinger, Jr., *Crisis of the Old Order,* 73; S. D. Smith, "Fifty Years Ago," *NY Times,* 16 Feb. 1964 (on Ford); V. Packard, *The Status Seekers,* 24, 135; American Heritage, *Book of the Pioneer Spirit,* 362; T. Meehan, "Forgettable Centenary: Horatio Alger's," *NY Times,* 28 June 1964; M. Josephson, *The Robber Barons,* 33 ff., 50 265–280; 299, 340 ff., 364; L. D. Baldwin, *The Stream of American History,* II, 173; R. Burlingame, *Ford,* 19; J. K. Galbraith, "Mystery of Henry Ford," *Atlantic,* Mar. 1958; P. Morell, *Diamond Jim: The Life and Times of James Buchanan Brady,* 18 ff., 22, 116; D. Malone and B. Rauch, *Empire for Liberty,* II, 170 ff., 178 ff., 280 ff.; R. Lynes, *The Tastemakers,* 122; F. L. Allen, *The Big Change,* 32 ff.; J. Daniels, *Prince of Carpetbaggers,* 142 (on Gilded Age); R. Edwards, "The Price of Conjugal Bliss Has Sometimes Been High," *NY Times,* 4 June 1967; obituary on Consuelo Vanderbilt Balsan in *NY Times,* 7 Dec. 1964; A. Rogers, "The Undimmed Appeal of the Gibson Girl," *American Heritage,* Dec. 1957; R. L. Heilbroner, *Quest for Wealth,* 180; E. Goldman, *Rendezvous with Destiny,* 11; F. L. Allen, *The Lords of Creation,* 87; G. Dugan, "Forman, St. George's Speaker, Praised by Rector," *NY Times,* 9 June 1969; W. H. Smith, "William Jennings Bryan and the Social Gospel," *Journal of American History,* June 1966; R. Hofstadter, *American Political Tradition,* 31; C. H. Cramer, *Royal Bob: The Life of Robert G. Ingersoll,* 124, 147; F. Gibney, *The Operators,* 6; M. Childs and D. Cater, *Ethics in a Business Society,* 136 ff., 141 ff.; C. Walsh, "Inspiration for the Modern Man," *Saturday Review,* 6 Dec. 1958 (on Conwell); R. H. Gabriel, *The Course of American Democratic Thought,* 149 ff.; I. G. Wyllie, *The Self-Made Man in America: The Myth of Rags to Riches,* 65 ff.; Adams, *Epic of America,* 347; M. Sullivan, *Our Times,* II, 426 ff.; E. Ellis, *Mr. Dooley's America,* 176; S. Fine, *Laissez-Faire,* 170 ff., 201 ff.

A POSSIBLE BIG CHANGE: L. Cherne, "Writer and the Entrepreneur," *Saturday Review,* 19 Jan. 1952; J. Brooks, "Profile: Xerox, Xerox, Xerox, Xerox," *New Yorker,* 1 Apr. 1967; J. Brooks, *The Great Leap,* 51; R. L. Tobin, "Xerox Proves a Point," *Saturday Review,* 13 Nov. 1965; *NY Times,* 17 Nov. 1963 and 19 June 1964 (on reaction to Xerox series on UN); M. Childs and D. Cater, *Ethics in a Business Society,* 89 ff.; R. Lynes, *The Tastemakers,* 289, 293; E. D. Baltzell, "Bell Telephone's Experiment in Education," *Harper's,* Mar. 1955; A. Berle, *The Twentieth-Century Capitalist Revolution,* and *Power Without Property, passim;* S. Chase, "Technological Imperative," *Saturday Review,* 16 Apr. 1960; "Critical Look at the Pentagon," editorial in *NY Times,* 12 May 1969; H. Schwartz, "Capitalist Moon or Socialist Moon," *NY Times,* 21 July 1969; S. Porter, "Demands Outpacing New Stock's Supply," Cleveland *Plain Dealer,* 1 July 1968 and 25 Mar. 1969; J. K. Galbraith, *The New Industrial State, passim;* "The Public Interest," editorial in *New Republic,* 2 Dec. 1967; C. Randall, "For a New Code of Business Ethics," *NY Times,* 8 Apr. 1962; P. Millones, "Consumer Indignation," *NY Times,* 30 June 1969; obituary on Randall in *NY Times,* 6 Aug. 1967; J. Keats, *The Insolent Chariots, passim;* V. Packard, *The Status Seekers,* 308; M. Mayer, "What Is Advertising Good For?", *Harper's,* Feb. 1958; *NY Times,* 25 Jan. 1959 (on call girls); F. Gibney, *The Operators,* 181.

RELATIONSHIP OF THE STATE TOWARD BUSINESS: LAISSEZ-FAIRE, GOVERNMENT REGULATION, GOVERNMENT OWNERSHIP: L. E. Davis, J. R. T. Hughes, and D. M. McDougall, *American Economic History,* 143 ff.; A. M. Schlesinger, Jr., *Crisis of the Old Order,*

21 ff., 31 ff., 208; A. S. Link, *Wilson*, IV, 356; E. Roseboom, *A History of Presidential Elections*, 372.

THE DEVELOPMENT OF THE CORPORATION: M. D. Lincoln, "Co-ops: How Big Can They Get?", *Reporter*, 2 Dec. 1954; D. F. Pegrum, *Regulation of Industry*, 78; D. Malone and B. Rauch, *Empire for Liberty*, II, 90 ff., 105 ff.; H. U. Faulkner, *American Economic History*, 436 ff.; M. L. Hoffman, "American in Cartel Land," *NY Times*, 9 Mar. 1952; F. L. Allen, *Big Change*, 74; R. B. Nye, *Midwestern Progressive Politics*, 93; S. H. Holbrook, *Age of the Moguls*, 109, 132; R. L. Heilbroner, "Grand Acquisitor," *American Heritage*, Dec. 1964; L. E. Davis, J. R. T. Hughes, and D. M. McDougall, *American Economic History*, 272; B. Nossiter, *The Mythmakers*, 52; U. S. Congress, House Committee on Judiciary, *Study of Monopoly Power* (Hearings before the Subcommittee on Study of Monopoly Power, 8 and 10 May 1950), Series No. 14, Part 1, 366; R. J. Barber, "New Partnership," *New Republic*, 13 Aug. 1966; A. Berle and G. C. Means, *The Modern Corporation and Private Property*, *passim*; J. K. Galbraith, *American Capitalism: The Concept of Countervailing Power*, *passim*; S. Slichter, "The Growth of Competition," *Atlantic*, Nov. 1953; E. Roper, "The Changing Face of Business," *Saturday Review of Literature*, 19 Jan. 1952.

TRUST-BUSTING BY TR AND TAFT: R. M. Abrams and L. W. Levine, *The Shaping of Twentieth-Century America*, 252; L. D. Baldwin, *The Stream of American History*, II, 109, 122 ff., 125, 389; S. E. Morison and H. S. Commager, *The Growth of the American Republic*, II, 389; R. E. Bedingfield, " 'It's Deductible' Is Big Steel's Reason for Shift," *NY Times*, 22 Aug. 1966; R. M. Ketchum, "Faces from the Past," *American Heritage*, Feb. 1963 (Morgan); S. H. Holbrook, *Age of the Moguls*, 145 ff., 153 ff., 214; F. L. Allen, *Lords of Creation*, 30, 33 ff.; Q. Howe, *A History of Our Own Times*, II, 342; L. Wendt and H. Kogan, *"Bet-A-Million" — The Life of John Warne Gates*, *passim*; R. L. Heilbroner, "Epitaph for the Steel Master," *American Heritage*, Aug. 1960 (Carnegie); B. J. Hendrick on Carnegie in DAB; R. L. Heilbroner, *Worldly Philosophers*, 225; T. Arnold, "The Law to Make Free Enterprise Free," *American Heritage*, Oct. 1960; D. Malone and B. Rauch, *Empire for Liberty*, II, 94 ff., 100 ff., 223; M. Sullivan, *Our Times*, II, 361 ff., 415, 471 ff.; A. C. Bining and T. C. Cochran, *The Rise of American Economic Life*, 329 ff.; B. Catton, "The Moment of Decision," *American Heritage*, Aug. 1964; F. L. Allen, *Big Change*, 97; G. Johnson, *The Lunatic Fringe*, 14; E. Goldman, *Rendezvous with Destiny*, 345; R. Nader, "We're Still in the Jungle," *New Republic*, 15 July 1967; TRB in *New Republic*, 18 Nov. 1967; C. C. Regier, *The Era of the Muckraker*, *passim*; A. and L. Weinberg, *The Muckrakers, 1902–1912*, *passim*; S. Hess, "Big Bill Taft," *American Heritage*, Oct. 1966; E. Roseboom, *A History of Presidential Elections*, 364 ff.

THE SHERMAN ACT: D. F. Pegrum, *Regulation of Industry*, 62 ff.; M. Sullivan, *Our Times*, II, 335; F. L. Allen, *Morgan*, 160 ff.; M. Josephson, *Robber Barons*, 359; D. Malone and B. Rauch, *Empire for Liberty*, II, 143; U.S. Congress, House Committee on Judiciary, *Study of Monopoly Power*, 33; P. G. Goulding, in Cleveland *Plain Dealer*, 9 Mar. 1952 (on Langer); *NY Times*, 8 Jan. and 7 Feb. 1961, Cleveland *Plain Dealer*, 7 Feb. 1961 (on GE case); TRB in *New Republic*, 13 Jan. 1968; M. Miles, "Reagan and the Respectable Right," *New Republic*, 20 Apr. 1968; D. Sanford, "Giving the Consumer 'Class,' " *New Republic*, 26 July 1969; M. Mintz, "The Broad-Spectrum Conspiracy," *New Republic*, 28 Sept. 1968; R. L. Heilbroner, "The Power of Big Business," *Atlantic*, Sept. 1965; B. Nossiter, *The Mythmakers*, 53; A. D. Neal, *The Antitrust Laws of the United States of America*, 395.

WILSON AND THE NEW FREEDOM: THE CLAYTON ACT AND THE FTC: L. M. Hacker and B. R. Kendrick, *The U.S. Since 1865*, 397 ff.; *NY Times*, 29 June 1964 (in commemoration of fiftieth anniversary of FTC); C. E. Egan, in *NY Times*, 5 Feb. 1953 (on unfair advertising, labeling, trademarks, fur products); Cleveland *Plain Dealer*, 10 Nov. 1959 (for FTC action against Carter's Pills); "Candor on Cigarettes . . . and Aspirin Too," editorial in *NY Times*, 6 Apr. 1965; Consumer's Union, *Reports*, Aug. 1951 and Nov. 1955; S. Blum, "Ode to the Cigarette Code," *Harper's*, Mar. 1966; *NY Times*, 9 July 1965 (on ban on cigarette advertising); T. A. Bailey, *The American Pageant*, 767; E. Shanahan, "Bar Panel Urges Changes in FTC or Its Abolition," *NY Times*, 16 Sept. 1969; "The Sluggish FTC," editorial in *NY Times*, 19 Sept. 1969.

THE SUPREME COURT AND THE ANTITRUST LAWS BEFORE 1933: Rodell, *Nine Men*, 173 and *passim;* M. Sullivan, *Our Times*, II, 417, 463; S. L. Kutler, "Chief Justice Taft, National Regulation, and the Commerce Power," *Journal of American History*, Mar. 1965; Cochran, *American Business System*, 56 ff.; D. Malone and B. Rauch, *Empire for Liberty*, II, 274; A. C. Bining and T. C. Cochran, *The Rise of American Economic Life*, 470; A. D. Neale, *Antitrust Laws, passim.*

THE GREAT DEPRESSION. ATTACKS ON THE AMERICAN ECONOMY FROM THE LEFT AND THE RIGHT: A. M. Schlesinger, Jr., *Crisis of the Old Order*, 204, 220 ff., 256, 268; A. M. Schlesinger, Jr., *Politics of Upheaval*, 17, 30, 39, 43 ff., 114, 247; S. Hess, "Long, Long, Trail . . . American Political Dynasties from Adams to Kennedy," *American Heritage*, Aug. 1966; J. McG. Burns, *The Lion and the Fox*, 210 ff.; D. Malone and B. Rauch, *Empire for Liberty*, II, 573; E. Ainsworth, "Remembering Uppie," *Saturday Review*, 30 Sept. 1967.

THE NEW DEAL AND BUSINESS, 1933–1945: A REVOLUTION OR EVOLUTION?: Q. Howe, *A History of Our Own Times*, II, 503 ff., 520 ff.; A. Nevins, in *NY Times*, 14 Mar. 1954; R. Hofstadter, *American Political Tradition*, 311 ff.; J. McG. Burns, *The Lion and the Fox*, 157; E. Goldman, *Rendezvous with Destiny*, 339; M. Keller, *The New Deal — What Was It?*, 6; S. E. Morison and H. S. Commager, *The Growth of the American Republic*, II, 630.

THE NEW DEAL AND BUSINESS: RELAXATION OF THE ANTITRUST LAWS PRIOR TO 1938: A. C. Bining and T. C. Cochran, *The Rise of American Economic Life*, 579, 695; R. Moley, *The First New Deal*, 292; A. M. Schlesinger, Jr., *Crisis of the Old Order*, 249, 414; R. Hofstadter, *American Political Tradition*, 332; S. Chase, "Government in Business," *Current History*, Mar. 1935; Q. Howe, *A History of Our Own Times*, II, 530 ff., 652; P. Ward, "NRA: Haven for Cake-Eaters," *Nation*, 10 Apr. 1935; A. M. Schlesinger, Jr., *Coming of the New Deal*, 105 ff., 157, 174 ff.; J. Strachey, "Two Wings of the Blue Eagle," *Nation*, 10 Jan. 1934; J. T. Flynn, *Country Squire in the White House*, 77 ff.; W. Berge, in S. E. Harris, *Saving American Capitalism*, 206; S. Slichter, "Sherman Act on Trial," *Atlantic*, July 1953; A. M. Schlesinger, Jr., *Politics of Upheaval*, 280 ff., 510; D. Malone and B. Rauch, *Empire for Liberty*, II, 585; H. U. Faulkner, *American Economic History*, 661; A. D. H. Kaplan and A. E. Kahn, "Big Business in a Competitive Society," *Fortune*, Feb. 1953; *NY Times*, 14 Dec. 1965 (on Patman); *NY Times*, 22 May 1951 (on first Schwegmann decision); *Wall Street Journal*, 21 Oct. 1953 and *NY Times*, 7 Jan. and 15 Nov. 1953 (on second Schwegmann decision); editorial on fair-trade laws in Cleveland *Press*, 20 Feb. 1952.

THE NEW DEAL AND BUSINESS: TRUST-BUSTING, 1938–1941: E. Goldman, *Rendezvous with Destiny*, 362; A. M. Schlesinger, Jr., in S. E. Harris, *Saving American Capitalism*, 78; J. W. Alsop and R. E. Kinter, "Trust Buster," *Saturday Evening Post*, 12 Aug. 1939; L. Cassels, "Arnold, Fortas, Porter & Prosperity," *Harper's*, Nov. 1951; obituary on Arnold in *NY Times*, 8 Nov. 1969.

TRUST-BUSTING AFTER WORLD WAR II: THE TRUMAN ADMINISTRATIONS: J. W. Andrews, "*U.S. v. A&P*: Battle of the Titans," *Harper's*, Sept. 1950; Consumer's Union, *Reports*, Jan. 1955; D. Sanford, "Gamesmanship in the Supermarkets," *New Republic*, 12 Nov. 1966; R. Butler, *NY Times*, 19 May 1955 (on business consolidations); "After Hours" in *Harper's*, Jan. 1954 (on Solid Gold Cadillac); R. Rutter, in *NY Times*, 10 Mar. 1956 (on tax advantages of mergers); articles on Celler in *NY Times*, 5 Jan. 1965 and 24 Feb. 1967.

TRUST-BUSTING AFTER WORLD WAR II: THE EISENHOWER ADMINISTRATIONS: "The I-Don't-Like-Its," editorial in *New Republic*, 23 Sept. 1957 (on packing of administrative agencies); *NY Times*, 8 and 9 Jan. 1961 (for articles on Bicks); J. Robertson, in *NY Times*, 28 Mar. 1965 (on history of Du Pont family); S. H. Holbrook, *Age of the Moguls*, 250 ff., 272; *NY Times*, 5 June 1957 (on Du Pont divestiture case); Cleveland *Plain Dealer*, 28 Jan. 1968 (on Clifford's role in Du Pont case); TRB in *New Republic*, 12 June 1961; *NY Times*, 25 May 1961, 12 May 1963, and 5 Feb. 1965 (on adjustment of income tax for Du Pont stockholders in divestiture case); Cleveland *Plain Dealer*, 28 Feb. 1967 (for dismissal of judge in El Paso Natural Gas Company case).

HOW LARGE SHOULD A CORPORATION BE?: J. W. Andrews, "*U.S. v. A&P*: Battle of the Titans," *Harper's*, Sept. 1950; "Conglomerate Mergers," editorial in *Washington*

Post, 15 Apr. 1967 (for analysis of statements by Barton M. Biggs); R. Nader, "Inventions and Their Uses," *New Republic*, 22 July 1967; D. F. Pegrum, *Regulation of Industry*, 84 ff., 435; U.S. Congress, House Committee on Judiciary, *Study of Monopoly Power*, 19 ff.; *NY Times*, 28 Feb. 1960 (for statement by Romney on optimum size for corporations); *NY Times*, 29 Aug. 1961; M. J. Rathbone, "Bias against Business," *Saturday Review*, 16 Apr. 1960; W. V. Shannon, "The Kennedy Administration: The Early Months," *American Scholar*, Fall 1961; R. Baker, in *NY Times*, 22 Aug. 1968; articles in Cleveland *Plain Dealer*, 26 June 1962 and *NY Times* 5 Aug. 1962 (on Brown Shoe case); "Conglomerates and the Free Market," Cleveland *Plain Dealer*, 15 June 1969; "Slowing the Conglomerates," editorial in *NY Times*, 4 Mar. 1969; E. Shanahan, "New S.E.C. Chief Finds Risks in Conglomerate Acquisitions," *NY Times*, 29 Feb. 1969; R. Deitsch, "The Merger Boom: Who Owns What," *New Republic*, 22 Feb. 1969; "Century's Third Wave of Mergers Peaks with $50-Billion Value," Cleveland *Plain Dealer*, 2 Feb. 1969; J. P. Mackenzie, "P&G-Clorox Merger Is Voided," *Washington Post*, 12 Apr. 1967; R. J. Barber, "New Partnership," *New Republic*, 13 Aug. 1966; TRB in *New Republic*, 23 Nov. 1968; "Bankrupt," *New Republic*, 4 July 1970 (on Penn Central); R. Townshend, *Up the Organization* (1970), frontispiece.

11. THE ORIGIN AND NURTURE OF CHAOS IN AMERICAN TRANSPORTATION

PRERAILROAD TRANSPORTATION BY ROAD AND BY CANAL: H. U. Faulkner, *American Economic History*, 270 ff., 278; L. L. Henry, "The Awkward Interval," *American Heritage*, Oct. 1968; M. S. Waggoner, *The Long Haul West*, 42, 291, 296, and *passsim*; R. K. Andrist, "The Erie Canal Passed This Way," *American Heritage*, Oct. 1968; R. Billington, *Westward Expansion*, 324; *NY Times*, 13 Apr. 1954 and 17 Aug. 1965 (on Erie Canal); E. O. Randall and D. J. Ryan, *History of Ohio*, III, 335–365; E. Roseboom and F. Weisenberger, *A History of Ohio*, 138–141, 151 ff.; C. F. Wittke, *First Fifty Years*, 2 ff., 11; P. Lyon, *To Hell in a Day Coach*, 88; G. Barman, in Cleveland *Plain Dealer*, 3 July 1961 (on Ohio Canals).

EXTENSION OF THE RAILROADS: ROADBED AND EQUIPMENT: T. A. Bailey, *The American Pageant*, 520 ff.; O. Lewis, *The Big Four*, 92 ff., 321, 329 ff., 344–349; R. E. Bedingfield, "Rail's Golden Spike Rites Reenacted," Cleveland *Plain Dealer*, 11 May 1969; O. Jensen, "Farewell to Steam: The Iron Horses That Built America," *American Heritage*, Dec. 1957; B. A. Botkin and A. F. Harlow, *A Treasury of Railroad Folklore*, 124 ff.; F. Morton, *The Rothschilds*, 110 ff.; M. Wilson, *American Science and Invention*, 151 ff., 225; M. S. Waggoner, *The Long Haul West*, 280 ff.; M. B. Davidson, *Life in America*, II, 245–249; *NY Times*, 22 Jan. 1956 and 3 Mar. 1962 (on speed records of steam locomotives); *NY Times*, 2 Mar. 1962 (for quotation from Beebe); H. U. Faulkner, *American Economic History*, 288; R. Lindsey, in *NY Times*, 20 Mar. 1969 (jet planes take place of parlor cars); "Pullman Reaches End of Line," Cleveland *Plain Dealer*, 23 Nov. 1968.

EARLY RAILROAD ABUSES: BOGUS FINANCING: A. C. Bining and T. C. Cochran, *The Rise of American Economic Life*, 328, 331, 606; W. P. Webb, *The Great Plains*, 275; P. Lyon, *To Hell in a Day Coach*, 25 ff., 53, 59; L. M. Hacker, *The Triumph of American Capitalism*, 234 ff.; *Barron's*, 23 July 1951 (on centenary of Erie); L. D. Baldwin, *The Stream of American History*, II, 139 ff., 144; T. A. Bailey, *The American Pageant*, 519 ff.; M. Josephson, *The Robber Barons*, 15 ff., 92 ff., 126 ff.; F. A. Shannon, *America's Economic Growth*, 423; F. Clark, "The Commodore Left Two Sons," *American Heritage*, Apr. 1966; S. H. Holbrook, *The Age of the Moguls*, 30 ff., 47, 56 ff., 120 ff.; J. Daniels, *Prince of Carpetbaggers*, 63 ff.; W. A. Swanberg, *Jim Fisk: The Career of an Improbable Rascal*, *passim*; O. Lewis, *The Big Four*, 156 ff., 211 ff., *passim*; R. L. Heilbroner, *Quest for Wealth*, 171 ff.; K. Schriftgiesser, *The Lobbyists*, 15; W. E. Garrison, *The March of Faith*, 42.

EARLY RAILROAD ABUSES: DISCRIMINATIONS BETWEEN PLACES: D. Malone and B. Rauch, *Empire for Liberty*, II, 101; F. A. Shannon, *America's Economic Growth*, 418; R. L. Heilbroner, *Quest for Wealth*, 196; P. Lyon, *To Hell in a Day Coach*, 127; G. Talese, "The *New York Times*: Inside a Great Newspaper," *Harper's*, Jan. 1969;

F. Russell, *Shadow of Blooming Grove, passim;* M. Sullivan, *Our Times,* II, 287; S. H. Holbrook, *The Age of the Moguls,* 66.

REGULATION OF RAILROADS: BY THE STATES: S. J. Buck, *The Granger Movement, passim;* Adams, *Epic of America,* 290 ff.; O. L. Keener, *The Background of the Country Life Movement,* 374 (unpublished doctoral dissertation at Western Reserve University); S. H. Holbrook, *The Age of the Moguls,* 115; *NY Times,* 3 Apr. 1955 (on Aaron Montgomery Ward); C. P. Magrath, *"Munn v. Illinois:* A Foot in the Door," *American Heritage,* Feb. 1964; P. Lyon, *To Hell in a Day Coach,* 176 ff.

REGULATION OF RAILROADS: BY THE FEDERAL GOVERNMENT FROM 1887 UNTIL THE GREAT DEPRESSION: P. Lyon, *To Hell in a Day Coach,* 106 ff., 138 ff., 142 ff., 148 ff.; T. A. Bailey, *The American Pageant,* 527; F. A. Shannon, *America's Economic Growth,* 577 ff.; C. M. Feuss, *Joseph B. Eastman: Servant of the People,* 106, 120, and *passim;* D. Malone and B. Rauch, *Empire for Liberty,* II, 418 ff.

THE RAILROAD CATASTROPHE OF THE 1930's: P. Lyon, *To Hell in a Day Coach,* 2 ff., 160 ff.; P. Lyon, "One-Way Ticket to Oblivion," *American Heritage,* Feb. 1968; J. T. Flynn, "The Betrayal of Cleveland," *Harper's,* Jan. 1934; C. Wertenbaker, "Mr. Ball Takes the Trains," *Saturday Evening Post,* 6 Feb. 1937; obituary on George A. Ball, *NY Times,* 23 Oct. 1955; *NY Times,* 30 Oct. 1951 (on liquidation of Van Sweringen empire); J. W. Raper, *The Soviet Table or the Rise of Civilization in Cleveland,* 12 ff.; St. Louis *Post-Dispatch,* 28 Apr. 1940 (for statement by Landon); E. K. Resseger, *The Indelible Dream, passim* (unpublished Senior Thesis, submitted at Princeton University, on Van Sweringen brothers); H. U. Faulkner, *American Economic History,* 674 ff.; C. M. Fuess, *Joseph B. Eastman,* xiv, 129 ff., 206, 246 ff., 273 ff., 299 ff., 326 ff.

THE CURRENT CRISIS OF THE RAILROADS: *NY Times,* 31 Aug. and 3 Sept. 1961 (on relative strength of western roads); W. Von Eckhardt, "Redesigning American Airports," *Harper's,* Mar. 1967; P. Lyon, *To Hell in a Day Coach,* 230 ff., 246, 256, and *passim;* R. Bendiner, "Railroads: From Overlord to Underdog," *Reporter,* 7 Aug. 1958; J. F. Stover, *American Railroads, passim;* D. Robertson and R. E. Tidyman, in Cleveland *Plain Dealer,* 6 Apr. 1965 (on "exempt" commodities); E. B. White on railroad management in *New Yorker,* 20 Feb. 1960; "Amtrak Limps on Track," *NY Times,* 2 May 1971; T. Wicker, "Euthanasia Plan for Railroads?" *NY Times,* 26 Mar. 1971; "Despair at Amtrak," *NY Times,* 22 Jan. 1972; R. Abrams, "Free Subways and Buses and All!" *NY Times,* 6 Jan. 1972; T. Wicker, "Onward and Downward," *NY Times,* 11 Jan. 1972; D. Butwin, "Booked for Travel," *Saturday Review,* 9 Jan. 1971; J. A. Michener, "The Five Warring Tribes of South Africa," *NY Times,* 23 Jan. 1972; D. I. Shipler, "New Superhighways Shaping Future of City's Suburbs," *NY Times,* 19 Aug. 1971; S. Porter, "Amtrak Still Faces a Tough, Uphill Run," Cleveland *Plain Dealer,* 22 Mar. 1972; E. B. Drew, "Is the ICC Dead?" *Atlantic,* July 1967; "Hot Foot for the ICC," editorial in *NY Times,* 13 May 1968; L. M. Kohlmeier, *The Regulators: Watchdog Agencies and the Public Interest, passim;* M. Harrington, "Taking the Great Society Seriously," *Harper's,* Dec. 1966; R. Berkvist, "The High Cost of Motoring," *NY Times,* 9 July 1967; "Highway Juggernaut," editorial in *New Republic,* 6 July 1968; J. Brooks, *The Great Leap,* 121; "Highways vs. People," editorial in *NY Times,* 20 Nov. 1966; editorial in *NY Times,* 18 Dec. 1966 (on appearance of metropolitan man in late twentieth century); N. Cousins, "There's Something in the Air," *Saturday Review,* 28 Jan. 1967; D. E. Carr, "The Poison Air Around Us," *Saturday Review,* 17 Feb. 1965; J. I. Snyder, "Unsnarling Traffic on the Roads, Rails, and Airways," *Harper's,* Nov. 1958; L. Kronenberger, "Who Shot the Iron Horse?" *Atlantic,* July 1968; M. J. Barloon, "The Coming of the Super-Railroad," *Harper's,* Apr. 1967; R. Baker, "The Observer," *NY Times,* 13 Apr. 1967 (on American creed); S. V. Roberts, "Visitors Are Swamping National Parks," *NY Times,* 1 Sept. 1969; S. V. Roberts, "Los Angeles," *Atlantic,* Sept. 1969 (quoting Art Hoppe).

12. THE CONTROL OF POWER

THE ECONOMIC MEANING OF POWER: L. Metcalf and V. Reinemer, *Overcharge,* 6; S. Chase, "Atoms and Automation," *Saturday Review,* 22 Jan. 1955; N. Weinberg, "Labor on the Hook," *Saturday Review,* 22 Jan. 1955.

Smaller capitals: GENERAL AND SPECIFIC REASONS FOR FEDERAL CONTROL OF POWER. L. Metcalf and
V. Reinemer, *Overcharge*, 21, 61, 92 ff., 130, 143 ff., 148 ff., 155; R. Zimmerman and
R. Burdock, "How the Legislature Really Works," Cleveland *Plain Dealer*, 29 Dec.
1968 and 1 Jan. 1969; H. J. Rauschenbush, *The Power Fight*, 7 ff., 112; Cleveland
Plain Dealer, 22 Jan. 1953, 22 Apr. 1961, 23 June 1962 (on cost of RCN formula to
Ohio); A. M. Schlesinger, Jr., *Politics of Upheaval*, 304; D. F. Pegrum, *The Regulation of Industry*, 162 ff.; E. K. Resseger, *The Indelible Dream*, 94 (unpublished Senior
Thesis, submitted at Princeton University on the Van Sweringen brothers); R. H.
Luthin, *American Demagogues*, 77 ff.; S. H. Holbrook, *Moguls*, 238; A. M. Schlesinger, Jr., *Coming of the New Deal*, 254 ff.; F. McDonald, *Insull, passim*; J. Rankin,
"TVA Rates as a Yardstick," *Current History*, May 1935; J. King, *The Conservation
Fight*, 128 ff.; R. L. Neuberger and S. B. Kahn, *Integrity: The Life of George W.
Norris*, 237 and *passim*; R. B. Nye, *Midwestern Progressive Politics*, 264; K. Schriftgiesser, *The Lobbyists*, 71; G. Wolfskill, *The Revolt of the Conservative*, 226 ff.;
G. Seldes, *Freedom of the Press*, 79; P. Y. Anderson, "New Year's Gift for the NRA,"
Nation, 3 Jan. 1934.

FEDERAL CONTROL THROUGH REGULATION: *Washington Post*, 29 Mar. 1950 (for statement by Senator Douglas); J. King, *The Conservation Fight*, 57; R. Baker in *NY
Times*, 1 June 1965; *Barron's*, 29 May 1950 and *NY Times*, 22 May 1950 (on liquidation of holding companies under the Wheeler-Rayburn Act).

CONTROL THROUGH FEDERAL OWNERSHIP: G. R. Clapp, *The TVA*, 1–25 and *passim*;
J. King, *The Conservation Fight*, 1, 78 ff., 112 ff.; D. Malone and B. Rauch, *Empire
for Liberty*, II, 419; F. Biddle, *In Brief Authority*, 75 ff.; Washington *Post*, 25 Mar.
1963 and *NY Times*, 31 Dec. 1957 (on TVA contribution to flood control); *NY
Times*, 29 Jan. 1958 and 17 Sept. 1961 (on value of forest products in TVA); *NY
Times*, 31 Dec. 1957 and 3 Dec. 1967 (on tax contributions of TVA); F. A. Shannon,
America's Economic Growth, 774; M. McMillan, *Progressive*, May 1959 (on cost of
electricity in Tennessee Valley, and its contribution to defense); L. Metcalf and
V. Reinemer, *Overcharge*, 5 ff., 13 ff., 96, 100; Cleveland *Plain Dealer*, 11 May 1958
(quoting Governor Clement); *NY Times*, 13 and 27 Sept. 1954, 17 Oct. 1954 (on
Dixon-Yates); Cleveland *Plain Dealer*, 12 June 1955 and *NY Times*, 10 July 1955 (on
Soo); R. Bendiner, *Progressive*, Feb. 1955 (on Dixon-Yates); C. Knowles, in *NY
Times*, 3 Feb. 1952 (on St. Lawrence Waterway); L. Freeman, "Battle of the St. Lawrence," *Fortune*, Dec. 1950; M. Gleisser, *The World of Cyrus Eaton*, 44; *Wall Street
Journal*, 3 Mar. 1952 (on Ungava).

13. SUBSIDIES

GENERAL: V. C. Royster, in *Wall Street Journal*, 8 Feb. 1950.

SUBSIDIES FOR THE MANUFACTURER THROUGH THE PROTECTIVE TARIFF — THE PROS AND
THE CONS: "Study Says Subsidies Cost $63 Billion in '70," Cleveland *Plain Dealer*, 11
Jan. 1972; F. P. Summers, *William L. Wilson and Tariff Reform*, frontispiece (on
Tarifa, Spain); D. L. Cohn, *The Life and Times of King Cotton*, 19 ff.; "Ohio Leads
All States in Exports," Cleveland *Plain Dealer*, 5 Nov. 1967; H. W. Morgan, "William
McKinley and the Tariff," *Ohio History*, Autumn 1965; L. E. Davis, J. R. T. Hughes,
and D. M. McDougall, *American Economic History*, 322; K. Schriftgiesser, *The
Lobbyists*, 122; R. Baker, *An American in Washington*, quoted in *Saturday Review*,
7 Oct. 1961; TRB in *New Republic*, 9 Oct. 1965; E. Davis, "If Roosevelt Fails,"
Harper's, Mar. 1933; D. L. Cohn, *Picking America's Pockets*, 39 and *passim*; T. A.
Bailey, *Man in the Street: The Impact of American Public Opinion on Foreign Policy*, 162; D. L. Cohn, "Southern Cotton and Japan," *Atlantic*, Aug. 1956; "Wage Increases Now Surpassing Gains in Output," *NY Times*, 24 Nov. 1966; E. T. Chase,
"Learning to Be Unemployable," *Harper's*, Apr. 1963; P. Drucker, "Japan Tries for a
Second Miracle," *Harper's*, Mar. 1963; A. H. Raskin, "John L. Lewis and the Mineworkers," *Atlantic*, May 1963; "Cue from the President," editorial in *NY Times*, 19
Nov. 1970 (quoting Senator Hatfield).

THE TARIFF BEFORE THE CIVIL WAR: Mitchell, *Hamilton*, I, x, xi; H. C. Hockett,
Political and Social Growth of the American People, 313, 453, 504–517, 550–555; R.

Hofstadter, *American Political Tradition*, 40, 69 ff.; L. D. Baldwin, *The Stream of American History*, I, 439; J. A. Barnes, *Wealth of the American People*, 271; M. L. Coit, *John C. Calhoun: American Portrait*, 40, 184, 343, 421.

SEVEN DECADES OF RISING TARIFFS, 1861–1934; I. M. Tarbell, *The Tariff In Our Times*, 1–28; M. Josephson, *The Politicos*, 114, 365 ff., 396, 432 ff., 450, 492, 513 ff.; F. P. Summers, *William L. Wilson*, 49 ff., 134 ff., 185; S. Lorant, *The Presidency*, 351; H. Agar, *The People's Choice*, 238; M. and D. Rosenberg, "The Dirtiest Election" (1884), *American Heritage*, Aug. 1962; D. Malone and B. Rauch, *Empire for Liberty*, II, 110, 135 ff.; G. T. Blodgett, "The Mind of the Boston Mugwump," *Mississippi Valley Historical Review*, Mar. 1962; D. S. Muzzey, *James G. Blaine*, 61 ff., 316, and *passim;* A. F. Harlow, *Old Bowery Days*, 444; C. Sandburg, *The Young Strangers*, 33 ff.; E. Roseboom, *History of Presidential Elections*, 279 ff., 431; T. A. Bailey, *American Pageant*, 495, 587, 591, 596; F. Lundberg, *America's Sixty Families*, 55, 60 ff.; "20% of Senators Are Millionaires," *NY Times*, Apr. 1968; H. T. Peck, *Twenty Years of the Republic, passim;* A. A. Woldman, Cleveland *Plain Dealer*, 24 Nov. 1950 (on syndicate that assumed McKinley's financial obligations); M. Sullivan, *Our Times*, IV, 358 ff., 362; J. M. Blum, *The Republican Roosevelt, passim;* M. R. Benedict, *Farm Policies in the U.S.*, 142; H. S. Merrill, *Bourbon Leader: Grover Cleveland and the Democratic Party*, 146; C. Bowers, *Beveridge and the Progressive Era, passim;* A. C. Bining and T. C. Cochran, *The Rise of American Economic Life*, 440, 564; R. A. Shannon, *America's Economic Growth*, 673, 675 ff.; K. Schriftgiesser, *The Lobbyists*, 38 ff.; Q. Howe, *A History of Our Own Times*, II, 116, 348; R. L. Neuberger and S. B. Kahn, *Integrity*, 162; R. Strout, "Foe of the Bon Mot: Politics," *NY Times*, 22 Apr. 1956; A. M. Schlesinger, Jr., *Crisis of the Old Order*, 233 ff.; R. L. Buell, "Trade Barriers," *NY Times*, 18 June 1933; L. E. Davis, J. R. T. Hughes, and D. M. McDougall, *American Economic History*, 323.

THE UNITED STATES AND FOREIGN TRADE SINCE 1930: FACTORS TENDING TO INCREASE IT: H. U. Faulkner, *American Economic History*, 697 ff.; A. C. Bining and T. C. Cochran, *The Rise of American Economic Life*, 649 ff.; A. M. Schlesinger, Jr., *Coming of the New Deal*, 190 ff.; *Time*, 8 Jan. 1940 (on Hull); letter from President Truman to Senator George and Representative Doughton, *NY Times*, 15 Aug. 1952 (on details of reciprocal trade treaties); Consumer's Union, *Reports*, Sept. 1955; *NY Times*, 27 Oct., 8 Nov., and 15 Dec. 1954 (on ITO and GATT); "Trade Mechanism Began in 1930's," *NY Times*, 16 May 1967; "Last Bell in Kennedy Round," *NY Times*, 14 May 1967.

THE UNITED STATES AND FOREIGN TRADE SINCE 1930: FACTORS TENDING TO DECREASE IT: Statement by Committee on Foreign Trade Education, Inc., in *NY Times*, 4 Mar. 1955; C. Lydon, "Oil Economist Brands Industry 'A Government-Created Cartel,'" *NY Times*, 3 Apr. 1969; *NY Times*, 4 June 1960, 21 June 1962, and 31 May 1963 — *New Republic*, 9 July 1962 — all on sugar quota; "New Wall of Jericho," editorial in *NY Times*, 18 Nov. 1968; "Footnote on Trade," editorial in *NY Times*, 6 Aug. 1968; "Oil and Inflation," *NY Times*, 8 Mar. 1969; "Cheaper Oil," editorial in *New Republic*, 19 July 1969; D. Sanford, "Jousting with Oil," *New Republic*, 30 Aug. 1969; H. F. Conn, "Sincerity Attested by Deeds," *New Republic*, 27 Apr. 1953; *NY Times*, 15 Nov. 1955, *Washington Post*, 29 May 1963, TRB in *New Republic*, 5 Feb. 1962 — on Buy-American Act; J. R. Slevin, "U.S. Is Loser by LBJ Ruling," Cleveland *Plain Dealer*, 24 July 1967 (on generators for Grand Coulee Dam); *NY Times*, 25 Nov. 1967 (on customs regulations); *NY Times*, 14 May 1967 (on "American Selling Price"); R. D. Mooney, "Non-Tariff Curbs Take Bigger Role," *NY Times*, 11 June 1967.

THE UNITED STATES AND THE COMMON MARKET: J. A. Livingston, in *Washington Post*, 12 and 14 Dec. 1962; C. Sterling, "Common Market: How Big Will It Grow?", *Reporter*, 8 Nov. 1962; C. H. Farnsworth, on accomplishments of Common Market, in *NY Times*, 10 Mar. 1967, 21 Apr., and 7 July 1968; G. Ball, "Economic Policy: Who's in Charge?", *Newsweek*, 14 Dec. 1970 (for quotation by Erhard); "Huge Farm Cost Vexing Common Market," *NY Times*, 30 Jan. 1971; *NY Times*, 2 Nov. 1961 on Kennedy and Trade Expansion Act; on agricultural tariffs and trouble over poultry, *NY Times*, 14 June, 3 and 11 Aug., and 5 Dec. 1963, C. L. Sulzberger in Cleveland

Plain Dealer, 1 July 1963, M. Childs in *Washington Post,* 30 Jan. 1963; W. Lippmann, in Cleveland *Plain Dealer,* 17 May 1962 and 1 Dec. 1966.

14. MORE SUBSIDIES

The Farmer Dreams of Subsidies: A. M. Schlesinger, Jr., *Crisis of the Old Order,* 175 ff.; A. M. Schlesinger, Jr., *Coming of the New Deal,* 65; E. W. Kenworthy, *NY Times,* 13 Nov. 1955 (on number of tractors); R. Drake, Cleveland *Plain Dealer,* 8 Jan. and 18 Mar. 1961 (on surpluses in wheat, milk, and butter); *NY Times,* 26 Apr. 1966 (on world importance of rice); E. D. Collins, in *NY Times,* 14 Dec. 1953 (on potato blight in Ireland); *NY Times,* 17 May 1963 and 27 Apr. 1965 (on pros and cons of chemical fertilizers); *NY Times,* 5 Aug. 1961 (on biologicals); "Farm to City Migration Ending," Cleveland *Plain Dealer,* 23 Apr. 1969; D. E. Kneeland, "The Growing Farm Exodus: Land Loses Its Hold," *NY Times,* 27 Nov. 1967; E. D. Collins, *NY Times,* 5 Aug. 1951 — R. Drake, Cleveland *Plain Dealer,* 13 May 1962 — D. L. Dowd, *Modern Economic Problems in Perspective,* 90 (all on percentage of population on farms); "Podunk Center? It's Yours for $7,000," Cleveland *Plain Dealer,* 11 Mar. 1969; J. Heinz, "Those Annoying Farmers: Impossible but Not Really Serious," *Harper's,* July 1963; E. Higbee, *NY Times,* 2 June 1963 (quoting Griffin); M. B. Davidson, *Life in America,* I, 363, 456; P. H. Johnstone, in Abrams and Levine, *The Shaping of Twentieth-Century America,* 173; *NY Times,* 25 Nov. 1951 and 23 Jan. 1967 (on number and size of farms); R. Hofstadter, *The Age of Reform,* 42.

The Farmer Finds Indirect Aids Disappointing: *NY Times,* 25 Feb. 1954 (on economics of dumping); M. R. Benedict, *Farm Policies in the U.S., 1790-1950,* 225 ff.; A. M. Schlesinger, Jr., *Crisis of the Old Order,* 109, 239; F. A. Shannon, *America's Economic Growth,* 746 ff., 766; G. Piel, "Abundance and the Future of Man," *Atlantic,* Apr. 1964; L. Pearson, "Trade, Aid, and Peace," *Saturday Review,* 22 Feb. 1969; A. M. Schlesinger, Jr., *A Thousand Days,* 169; *NY Times,* 13 Nov. 1957 (on Canadian protest against PL 480 to the UN Food and Agriculture Organization); "No Ceiling on Farm Subsidies," editorial in *NY Times,* 8 July 1969; "Wheat Price War," editorial in *NY Times,* 15 Aug. 1969.

The Farmer Achieves Direct Subsidies: A. M. Schlesinger, Jr., *Coming of the New Deal,* 28 ff., 35 ff., 59–65, 70 ff.; A. M. Schlesinger, Jr., *Crisis of the Old Order,* 108 ff.; L. E. Sanders, *Mother Goose in Washington* (for paraphrase of "Three Little Pigs"); W. Faulkner, "On Fear: The South in Labor," *Harper's,* June 1956; J. A. Loftus, in *NY Times,* 10 Sept. 1955; K. Gordon, "How Much Should the Government Do?" *Saturday Review,* 9 Jan. 1965; D. Malone and B. Rauch, *Empire for Liberty,* II, 691; J. K. Galbraith, "Why Be Secretary of Agriculture?" *Harper's,* July 1953; R. Shogan, "1948 Election," *American Heritage,* June 1968; W. S. White, *The Taft Story,* 63; *NY Times,* 18 Sept. 1955 and Cleveland *Plain Dealer,* 27 June 1958 (on Green Rebellion); *NY Times,* 16 May 1955, 26 July 1956, 24 Nov. 1967, and 2 June 1963 (on Benson policy); E. Higbee, "Now the Non-Farmer Asks for Parity," *NY Times,* 2 June 1963 (on Freeman policy); D. Janson, *NY Times,* 1 June 1969 (on Freeman and Hardin policy); J. Heinz, "Those Annoying Farmers," *Harper's,* July 1963.

The Pros and the Cons of Farm Policy: M. R. Benedict, *Can We Solve the Farm Problem?,* 84–123; T. Fitzimmons, "Who Has Been Hurt So Far?" *New Republic,* 25 Jan. 1954; H. Hanson, "How Are Crops in Manhattan?", *New Republic,* 30 Jan. 1956; S. Porter, "Rising Bread Prices Damage Farmers," Cleveland *Plain Dealer,* 4 Apr. and 22 July 1968; J. Heinz, "Those Annoying Farmers," *Harper's,* July 1963; Washington *Post,* 4 and 20 Feb. 1950 (on rotting potatoes); Cleveland *Plain Dealer,* 13 Mar. 1953 (on rancid butter); Cleveland *Plain Dealer,* 15 Apr. 1962 (on proposed subsidy for dentures); editorial, "On the American Farm," *New Republic,* 16 Apr. 1962; P. Drucker, "Warning to the Rich White World," *Harper's,* Dec. 1968; M. D. Reagan, "1956: Issues That Won't Be Faced," *New Republic,* 21 May 1956; E. Higbee, "Now the Non-Farmer Asks for Parity," *NY Times,* 2 June 1963; J. Brooks, *The Great Leap,* 104; D. F. Dowd, *Modern Economic Problems,* 96; TRB, "NIT-ing for a Living," *New Republic,* 5 July 1969; M. Harrington, "Will to Abolish Poverty,"

Saturday Review, 27 July 1968; *NY Times*, 27 Nov. 1966 (on "Little Old Lady from Sheboygan"); J. A. Schnittker, "The Farmer in the Till," *Atlantic*, Aug. 1969; Joint Economic Committee of Congress, *Subsidy and Subsidy Effect Programs of the U.S. Government*, Chapter IV (revised 1965).

REFORM OF AGRICULTURAL SUBSIDIES: A VARIETY OF PROPOSALS: W. Blain, *NY Times*, 11 Dec. 1955; G. Myrdal, "Can We Prevent Mass Starvation?", *New Republic*, 24 Apr. 1965; Consumer's Union, *Reports*, June 1949; M. R. Benedict, *Can We Solve the Farm Problem?*, 271–274; "House Approves Farm Curb Aid," *NY Times*, 28 May 1969; J. A. Schnittker, "The Farmer in the Till," *Atlantic*, Aug. 1969.

SUBSIDIES TO AIRLINES: M. B. Davidson, *Life in America*, II, 296 ff.; F. A. Shannon, *America's Economic Growth*, 455, 615–618; C. L. Dearing and W. Owen, *National Transportation Policy*, 44 ff.; J. Reston, *NY Times*, 7 Dec. 1966 (on subsidy to private planes); D. Bloomfield, "50th Anniversary of Air Mail Being Celebrated This Month," Cleveland *Plain Dealer*, 2 May 1968; D. Lidman, "Ceremonies in Capital Mark 50th Anniversary of U.S. Airmail," *NY Times*, 16 May 1968; H. U. Faulkner, *America's Economic History*, 630; R. S. Allen, in Cleveland *Plain Dealer*, 1 Mar. 1954; *NY Times*, 8 Sept. 1968.

SUBSIDIES THROUGH THE POST OFFICE: A. Shuster, "Swifter Completion of Their Rounds," *Saturday Review*, 21 Mar. 1964; *NY Times*, 11 Dec. 1966 (on postal deficits); *Washington Post*, 5 Apr. 1967 (on advertising revenue from second-class mail); S. V. Jones, "Who'll Pay the Postage?" *Harper's*, Jan. 1954; "Lines Form for House Hearing on Postal Rate-Rise Plan," *NY Times*, 7 May 1967; "Postal Rates," *Newsweek*, 15 Feb. 1971; *NY Times*, 22 and 28 Jan. 1952; *Washington Post*, 5 Apr. 1967 — all on third-class mail; *NY Times*, 11 Dec. 1966 (on ZIP code); "Postal Reform," editorial in *Washington Post*, 30 Apr. 1967; "Tax-Exempt Groups Score U.S. Ruling," *NY Times*, 26 Feb. 1969 (on AMA and C. of C.); *NY Times*, 11 Dec. 1966 and 9 Mar. 1967, *Washington Post*, 8 Apr. 1967 — all on pressure groups; D. Sanford, "The Post Office: Who Needs It?" *New Republic*, 31 Aug. 1968; "Hope for the Mails," editorial in *NY Times*, 28 May 1969; R. Evans and R. Novak, "Postal Reform Draws Yawns," Cleveland *Plain Dealer*, 23 July 1968; *NY Times*, 20 Mar. and 16 Apr. 1967 (on need for capital investment in new machines and new buildings); "New York Postal Unit Starts Thursday," *NY Times*, 27 June 1971.

SUBSIDIES VIA THE INCOME TAX: J. Doe, "Coming Tax Reform," *Atlantic*, Jan. 1963; TRB, "The Rich Are Always with Us," *New Republic*, 11 May 1968; P. Douglas, "The Problem of Tax Loopholes," *American Scholar*, Winter, 1967–1968; J. Brooks, "The Tax," *New Yorker*, 3 and 10 Apr. 1965; J. A. Ruskay, "Missing Taxpayers," *New Republic*, 29 Apr. 1967; J. Bainbridge, "The Super-American State: Oil," *New Yorker*, 18 Mar. 1961; D. I. Bartlett, Cleveland *Plain Dealer*, 4 Apr. 1969 (report on Prudhoe Bay and analysis of taxes paid by forty major oil companies); R. Lynes, "Take Back Your Sable," *Harper's*, June 1956; *NY Times*, 8 Dec. 1964 and TRB in *New Republic*, 29 Apr. 1957 (on depleting assets of aging, and of fashion models); "Closing the Depletion Loophole," editorial in *NY Times*, 23 July 1969; B. Bliven, "Tempest over Teapot," *American Heritage*, Aug. 1965; R. Fleming, "Oil Rush," *New Republic*, 18 Sept. 1965; C. Welles, "Oil Shale: Hidden Scandal or Inflated Myth?" *Harper's*, Aug. 1968; D. S. Broder, "Tax Revolt Hits Federal System," Cleveland *Plain Dealer*, 19 Feb. 1969; "U.S. Checks Flood of Tax-Exempt Bonds," Cleveland *Plain Dealer*, 23 Mar. 1968 (on IDBs); P. Stern, *The Great Treasury Raid, passim*; TRB, "To Them That Have," *New Republic*, 13 July 1968; J. W. Barr, "Tax Reform: The Time Is Now," *Saturday Review*, 22 Mar. 1969; R. L. Jackson, "Missing Foundation Reports Unchallenged," Cleveland *Plain Dealer*, 5 Mar. 1969; E. Shanahan, "Patman Urges Tax on All Foundations at Inquiry in House," *NY Times*, 19 Feb. 1969; R. Sherrill, "'The Last of the Great Populists' Takes on the Foundations, the Banks, the Federal Reserve, the Treasury," *NY Times*, 16 Mar. 1969 (on Patman); J. Beatty, Jr., "Trade Winds," *Saturday Review*, 19 Aug. 1967 (for poem, "Oh for the Good Old Colony Days, When We Were under the King").

15. LAND: ITS USE AND ABUSE

EARLY IMPORTANCE OF WATER TRANSPORTATION ON THE OHIO AND MISSISSIPPI RIVERS: W. Blair and F. J. Meine, *Mike Fink, King of the Mississippi Keelboatmen*, 57 ff., 105 ff., 132 ff.; M. Fishwick, "Big Search for America," *Saturday Review*, 16 Aug. 1958; R. A. Billington, *Westward Expansion*, 332 ff.; L. L. Tucker, "Cincinnati: Athens of the West, 1830–1861," *Ohio History*, Winter 1966; W. H. Goetzmann, *When the Eagle Screamed*, 4 ff.; A. De Conde, *A History of American Foreign Policy*, 48 ff.; T. A. Bailey, *A Diplomatic History of the American People*, 59–62, 80 ff., 103–115.

THE ANNEXATION OF CANADA?: R. H. Ferrell, *American Diplomacy, a History*, 60 ff.; R. A. Billington, *The Westward Movement in the United States*, 36; J. W. Pratt, "Western Aims in the War of 1812," *Mississippi Valley Historical Review*, June 1925 (in B. Perkins, *The Causes of the War of 1812*, 53–58); L. M. Hacker, "Western Land Hunger and the War of 1812," *Mississippi Valley Historical Review*, Mar. 1924 (in B. Perkins, *Causes of the War of 1812*, 46–53); W. Millis, *Arms and Men*, 65; T. A. Bailey, "The Mythmakers," *Journal of American History*, June 1968; W. H. Goetzmann, *When the Eagle Screamed*, 11; H. L. Coles, *The War of 1812*, 27–38.

THE ANNEXATIONS OF TEXAS AND THE FLORIDAS: "U.S. to Rule on Seminole Claims to Land in Florida," *NY Times*, 18 Nov. 1968; T. A. Bailey, *Diplomatic History*, 236 ff.; W. H. Goetzmann, *When the Eagle Screamed*, 13 ff.; "Personal & Otherwise," *Harper's*, Aug. 1954 (on myths about Texas); Clark, *Rampaging Frontier*, 208; T. A. Bailey, *American Pageant*, 576; R. H. Ferrell, *American Diplomacy*, 88 ff., 95; A. De Conde, *A History of American Foreign Policy*, 179 ff.

THE ACQUISITION OF MEXICO?: C. A. and M. R. Beard, *Rise of American Civilization*, I, 597; R. A. Billington, *Westward Expansion*, 505 ff.; H. Hamilton, "Texas Bonds and Northern Profits," *Mississippi Valley Historical Review*, March 1957; L. D. Baldwin, *Stream of American History*, I, 683; T. A. Bailey, *Man in the Street*, 58; R. Pollak, "Time: After Luce," *Harper's*, July 1969; W. H. Goetzmann, *When the Eagle Screamed*, 24, 40, 89 ff.

OREGON: T. A. Bailey, *Diplomatic History*, 220–235; W. P. Webb, *Great Plains*, 149; R. A. Billington, *Westward Expansion*, 511; D. Lavender, *Land of the Giants: The Drive to the Pacific Northwest, 1750–1950*, 153 ff., 236; A. De Conde, *A History of American Foreign Policy*, 165 ff.

RELINQUISHMENT OF ORIGINAL STATE CLAIMS: R. A. Billington, *Westward Expansion*, 202 ff., 263 ff.; C. P. Magrath, *Yazoo: Law and Politics in the New Republic — the Case of Fletcher vs. Peck, passim*; W. G. Rose, *Cleveland, the Making of a City*, 26 ff.

FEDERAL LAND POLICY UNDER THE ARTICLES OF CONFEDERATION: THE FAMOUS ORDINANCES AND A FIRST-CLASS SCANDAL: H. U. Faulkner, *American Economic History*, 178 ff.; F. A. Shannon, *America's Economic Growth*, 122 ff.; M. R. Benedict, *Farm Policies in the U.S., 1790–1950*, 5; C. P. Magrath, *Yazoo, passim*; R. A. Billington, *Westward Expansion*, 207 ff., 212 ff., 218; P. M. Angle, *The Lincoln Reader*, 16; R. Burlingame, *The American Conscience*, 202; R. E. Riegel, *America Moves West*, 49.

FEDERAL LAND POLICY BEFORE THE CIVIL WAR: F. A. Shannon, *America's Economic Growth*, 269 ff.; H. U. Faulkner, *American Economic History*, 180 ff.; M. R. Benedict, *Farm Policies in the U.S., 1790–1950*, 5 ff.

THE HOMESTEAD ACT: R. A. Billington, *Westward Expansion*, 385 ff., 696 ff.; W. P. Webb, *Great Plains*, 399; E. Goldman, *Rendezvous With Destiny*, 37; T. A. Bailey, *American Pageant*, 575; *NY Times*, 29 July 1962 (on land-grant universities); E. C. Kirkland, *A History of American Economic Life*, 469 ff.; P. Farb, "American Indian: Portrait in Limbo," *Saturday Review*, 12 Oct. 1968; M. Straus, "Land Reform, for Export Only," *Progressive*, Mar. 1955.

THE MINER'S FRONTIER: R. Dillon, *Fool's Gold: A Biography of John Sutter, passim*; *American Heritage, Pioneer Spirit*, 18 ff., 366 ff.; M. Minnigerode, *The Fabulous Forties*, 312 ff.; A. B. Hulbert, *The Forty Niners, passim*; J. Weld, *Don't You Cry for Me*, 217; R. L. Duffus, *NY Times*, 16 May 1965; R. A. Billington, *Westward Expan-*

sion, 631 ff.; F. F. Van de Water, *Glory Hunter: A Life of General Custer, passim;*
M. Morgan, "Off to the Klondike," *American Heritage,* Aug. 1967.

THE CATTLEMEN'S FRONTIER: R. A. Billington, *Westward Expansion,* 672 ff.;
W. Mitchell, *American Science and Invention,* 229 ff.; M. B. Davidson, *Life in America,* I, 432; E. Dick, *The Sod-House Frontier,* 334; *NY Times,* 7 May 1967 (on centennial of Chisholm Trail); W. P. Webb, *Great Plains,* 286.

THE FARMER'S FRONTIER: E. Dick, *The Sod-House Frontier,* 114 ff., 166 ff., 204, 223 ff., 243 ff., 403 ff., 443 ff.; W. G. Magnuson, "Pharaoh Had It Easy," *American Heritage,* Oct. 1960 (on plagues of locusts).

THE TURNER THESIS: F. J. Turner, *The Frontier in American History,* quoted in G. R. Taylor (ed.), *The Turner Thesis,* 1–34; L. M. Hacker, review of Turner's *The Significance of Sections in American History, Nation,* 26 July 1933 (quoted in Taylor, *op. cit.,* 43–46); R. A. Billington, "Why Some Historians Rarely Write History: A Case Study of Frederick Jackson Turner," *Mississippi Valley Historical Review,* June 1963; R. A. Billington, "How the Frontier Shaped the American Character," *American Heritage,* Apr. 1958; R. Ginger, *Age of Excess,* 83.

THE ABUSE OF LAND: S. Chase, "Old Man River," *New Republic,* 27 Mar. 1935; H. A. Wallace, "The Next Four Years in Agriculture," *New Republic,* 2 Dec. 1936; B. Frank and A. Netboy, *Water, Land, and People,* 74; "Land Erosion RX: Rubber-Oil Spray," *NY Times,* 18 Aug. 1968; "Stripping Kentucky Bare," *NY Times,* 25 July 1967; W. D. McCann, "Trash Is Bugging Cities," Cleveland *Plain Dealer,* 16 Sept. 1969 (for quotation from Charles C. Johnson, Jr., administrator of the Consumer Protection and Environmental Health Service); J. Fischer, "The Easy Chair," *Harper's,* Sept. 1969 (for attempts of San Francisco and New York to dispose of solid wastes); "Man the Polluter," *NY Times,* 23 July 1969.

THE O-BOMB AND THE MAN-LAND RATIO: C. Ogburn, "America the Expendible," *Harper's,* Aug. 1960; *NY Times,* 4 and 6 Nov. 1960 (on Doomsday); L. D. Stamp, *Land for Tomorrow,* 22, 27; B. Bliven, "Too Many People," *New Republic,* 17 Oct. 1955; on Toynbee—*NY Times,* 20 Feb. 1955 and 6 June 1963, Cleveland *Plain Dealer,* 9 June 1963; M. Frankel, "The Moon and Politics," *NY Times,* 21 July 1969; K. Sax, *Standing Room Only,* 105, 143; S. L. Udall, "Our Perilous Population Implosion," *Saturday Review,* 2 Sept. 1967; R. L. Heilbroner, "Making a Rational Foreign Policy Now," *Harper's,* Sept. 1968 (for quotation from Ayub); TRB, *New Republic,* 29 May 1965 (quoting Ward and Myrdal); *NY Times,* 5 June 1963 (President Kennedy quotes Seneca); *NY Times,* 30 May 1959 (quoting Liaquat Ali Khan); *NY Times,* 8 Aug. 1963 (on Eisenhower-Kennedy attitudes toward birth control); R. J. Crowley, Cleveland *Plain Dealer,* 6 July 1965 (on President Johnson and birth control).

THE CASE FOR CONSERVATION: A SHORTAGE OF WATER: W. Sullivan, *NY Times,* 27 Dec. 1964 (on availability of water in the world); R. and L. T. Rienow, *Moment in the Sun: A Report on the Deteriorating Quality of the American Environment, passim;* G. Hill, "Thermal Pollution Issue," *NY Times,* 10 Mar. 1969; S. Chase, *Rich Land, Poor Land,* 14; R. Nadeau, "The Water War," *American Heritage,* Dec. 1961; W. P. Webb, *Great Plains,* 367 ff.; F. Osborn, *The Limits of the Earth,* 65; B. Frank and A. Netboy, *Water, Land and People,* 19 ff.; M. B. Davidson, *Life in America,* I, 168; Federal Reserve Bank of Cleveland, *Business Trends,* 18 Apr. 1954 (on runoff from various types of land use); *NY Times,* 29 Jan. 1958 (on production of trees by TVA); J. Reston, Cleveland *Plain Dealer,* 27 May 1962; G. Hill, *NY Times,* 22 Dec. 1965 (on reuse of water).

THE CASE FOR CONSERVATION: THE POLLUTION OF WATER: E. Hill, "The Connecticut: Can It Be Saved?" *NY Times,* 12 Jan. 1969; W. Sullivan, *NY Times,* 8 June 1969 (on Hudson River); T. Wicker, *NY Times,* 9 Sept. 1967 (on Potomac); "Diseased Estuaries," *New Republic,* 1 Mar. 1969 (on Chesapeake Bay); R. McGill, "Atlanta: The Waiting Game," *Saturday Review,* 22 May 1965; R. Drake, Cleveland *Plain Dealer,* 3 Apr. 1961 and 27 Apr. 1963 (on Cuyahoga); "Cuyahoga River Put among Most Rank," Cleveland *Plain Dealer,* 3 Oct. 1968; "Cleveland River So Dirty It Burns," *NY Times,* 29 June 1969; D. J. R. Bruckner, "Political Battle Rages over Lake Michigan's Pollution," Cleveland *Plain Dealer,* 24 and 25 Oct. 1967; "Lake Erie Report Scores

Pollution," *NY Times*, 2 Oct. 1968; P. Schrag, "Life on a Dying Lake," *Saturday Review*, 20 Sept. 1969; S. V. Roberts, "Visitors Are Swamping National Parks," *NY Times*, 1 Sept. 1969; J. G. Herzberg, "A Third of U.S. Lakes Held Imperiled," *NY Times*, 3 Nov. 1968; "Politics and Pollution," *NY Times*, 16 May 1969 (on pollution of Lake Superior); *NY Times*, 1 Aug. 1966 (on Lake Baikal); *NY Times*, 1 Mar. 1965 (on American Chemical Society); "Test for DDT," editorial in *NY Times*, 1 Dec. 1968; "Welcome Action on Pesticides," editorial in Cleveland *Plain Dealer*, 23 Apr. 1969; "Scientist Fears DDT," *NY Times*, 28 Apr. 1969; "Curbing DDT," editorial in *NY Times*, 2 June 1969.

THE CASE FOR CONSERVATION: THE POLLUTION OF AIR: R. A. Bryson, "Is Man Changing the Climate of the Earth?" *Saturday Review*, 1 Apr. 1967; "The Darkening Sky," editorial in *NY Times*, 20 May 1967; "Battle for Cleaner Air," editorial in *NY Times*, 8 January 1968 (for statement by President Johnson); "City Should OK New Air Code," editorial in Cleveland *Plain Dealer*, 6 July 1969; L. C. Cole, "Can the World Be Saved?" *NY Times*, 31 Mar. 1968; G. Hill, "Experts Foresee Noisier World . . . ," *NY Times*, 30 Apr. 1969.

THE CONSERVATION MOVEMENT: THE BEGINNINGS IN THE NINETEENTH CENTURY: M. N. McGeary, *Gifford Pinchot, Forester-Politician*, 4, 34; J. V. Young, "Running the Grand Canyon Rapids 100 Years After," *NY Times*, 25 May 1969; W. C. Darrah, *Powell of the Colorado, passim*.

THE CONSERVATION MOVEMENT IN THE TWENTIETH CENTURY: M. N. McGeary, *Gifford Pinchot*, 1 ff., 47, 54, 63, 98, 125, 131, 190 ff., 260 ff., 358, 412, 430; T. A. Bailey, *American Pageant*, 653 ff.; J. Fischer, "Easy Chair," *Harper's*, Sept. 1968; J. R. Penick, *Progressive Politics and Conservation: The Ballinger-Pinchot Affair*, 19 ff., 37, 53, 114, 152 ff., 163 ff., 179; W. V. Shannon, "Hickel: His Is a Wary Constituency," *NY Times*, 26 Jan. 1969; S. V. Roberts, "Visitors Are Swamping National Parks," *NY Times*, 1 Sept. 1969; "The Lesson of the Redwoods," editorial in *NY Times*, 18 Oct. 1967; P. Brooks, "Topics: Everglades Airport — A Blueprint for Disaster," *NY Times*, 12 July 1969; W. Turner, "Amchitka Is Girding for Nuclear Blasts," *NY Times*, 14 July 1969; H. M. Schmeck, Jr., *NY Times*, 20 Mar. 1968 (quoting Dr. David M. Gates); S. Udall, "Our Perilous Population Implosion," *Saturday Review*, 2 Sept. 1967; P. Wylie, "Against All Odds, the Birds Have Won," *NY Times*, 1 Feb. 1970; "Lindberg on Taiwan Calls for Conservation," *NY Times*, 31 Oct. 1968; "By Land, Sea, and Air," editorial in *NY Times*, 3 May 1969 (quoting Dr. Barry Commoner); "A Critical Weakness," editorial in *NY Times*, 9 Mar. 1969.

Bibliography

Abrams, Richard M. and Levine, Lawrence W. (eds.). *The Shaping of Twentieth-Century America*. Boston: Little, Brown, 1965.

Adamic, Louis. *Dynamite: The Story of Class Violence in America*. New York: Viking, 1931.

Adams, Henry. *The Life of Albert Gallatin*. Philadelphia: Lippincott, 1880.

Adams, James T. *Epic of America*. Boston: Little, Brown, 1931.

Agar, Herbert. *The People's Choice*. Boston: Houghton Mifflin, 1933.

Allen, Frederick L. *The Big Change*. New York: Harper, 1952.

———. *The Great Pierpont Morgan*. New York: Harper, 1949.

———. *The Lords of Creation*. New York: Harper, 1935.

American Heritage Cookbook, Hightstown, N.J.: American Heritage, 1964.

———. *The Book of the Pioneer Spirit*. New York: American Heritage, 1959.

Angle, Paul M. *The Lincoln Reader*. New Brunswick, N.J.: Rutgers University Press, 1947.

Asbury, Herbert. *The Great Illusion: An Informal History of Prohibition*. Garden City, N.Y.: Doubleday, 1950.

Ashmore, Harry S. *The Other Side of Jordan*. New York: Norton, 1960.

Bailey, Thomas A. *The American Pageant: A History of the Republic*. Boston: Heath, 1956

———. *A Diplomatic History of the American People*. New York: Appleton-Century-Crofts, 1958.

———. *The Man in the Street: The Impact of American Public Opinion on Foreign Policy*. New York: Macmillan, 1948.

Baker, Russell. *An American in Washington*. New York: Knopf, 1961.

Baldwin, Leland D. *The Stream of American History*. 2 volumes. New York: American Book, 1952.

Barbour, John. *In the Wake of the Whale*. New York: Crowell-Collier, 1969.

Barnard, Harry. *"Eagle Forgotten": The Life of John Peter Altgeld*. Indianapolis: Bobbs-Merrill, 1938.

Barnes, James A. *Wealth of the American People*. New York: Prentice-Hall, 1949.

Barr, Stringfellow. *The Pilgrimage of Western Man*. New York: Harcourt, Brace, 1949.

Baruch, Bernard M. *The Public Years*. New York: Holt, Rinehart and Winston, 1960.

Beard, Charles A. *The Economic Interpretation of the Constitution*. New York: Macmillan, 1913.

Beard, Charles A. and Mary R. *The Rise of American Civilization*. New York: Macmillan, 1927.

Belden, Thomas G. and Marva R. *So Fell the Angels*. Boston: Little, Brown, 1956.

Bell, John F. *A History of Economic Thought*. New York: Ronald Press, 1953.

Benedict, Murray R. *Can We Solve the Farm Problem?* New York: Twentieth Century Fund, 1955.

———. *Farm Policies in the U.S., 1790–1950*. New York: Twentieth Century Fund, 1953.

Berle, Adolph. *Power Without Property*. New York: Harcourt, Brace, 1959.

―――. *The Twentieth-Century Capitalist Revolution.* New York: Harcourt, Brace, 1954.

Berle, Adolph, and Means, Gardiner C. *The Modern Corporation and Private Property.* New York: Macmillan, 1932.

Biddle, Francis B. *In Brief Authority.* Garden City, N.Y.: Doubleday, 1962.

Billington, Ray A. *Westward Expansion.* New York: Macmillan, 1949.

Bining, Arthur C., and Cochran, Thomas C. *The Rise of American Economic Life.* New York: Scribner's, 1964.

Blair, Walter, and Meine, Franklin J. *Mike Fink, King of Mississippi Keelboatmen.* New York: Holt, 1933.

Bliven, Bruce. *The Wonderful Writing Machine.* New York: Random House, 1954.

Blond, Georges. *The Great Story of Whales.* New York: Garden City Books, 1955.

Blum, John M. *The Republican Roosevelt.* Cambridge: Harvard University Press, 1954.

Bogart, Ernest L., and Kemmerer, Donald L. *Economic History of the American People.* New York: Longmans, Green, 1942.

Boorstin, Daniel J. *The Americans: The Colonial Experience.* New York: Random House, 1958.

Botkin, B. A., and Harlow, Alvin F. (eds.). *A Treasury of Railroad Folklore.* New York: Crown Publishers, 1953.

Bowen, Catherine D. *John Adams and the American Revolution.* Boston: Little, Brown, 1950.

Bowers, Claude G. *Beveridge and the Progressive Era.* Boston: Houghton Mifflin, 1932.

―――. *Jefferson and Hamilton.* Boston: Houghton Mifflin, 1925.

Bradford, Ernle. *The Wind Commands Me.* New York: Harcourt Brace & World, 1965.

Broderick, Francis L. *W. E. B. DuBois, Negro Leader in a Time of Crisis.* Stanford: Stanford University Press, 1959.

Brooks, John N. *Business Adventures.* New York: Weybright and Talley, 1969.

―――. *The Great Leap: The Past Twenty-five Years in America.* New York: Harper & Row, 1966.

Buck, Solon J. *The Granger Movement.* Cambridge: Harvard University Press, 1913.

Bugg, James L. *Andrew Jackson: Democratic Myth or Reality.* New York: Holt, Rinehart & Winston, 1963.

Burlingame, Roger. *Henry Ford, a Great Life in Brief.* New York: Knopf, 1955.

―――. *The American Conscience.* New York: Knopf, 1957.

Burns, James McG. *The Lion and the Fox.* New York: Harcourt, Brace, 1956.

Carse, Robert. *The Twilight of Sailing Ships.* New York: Grosset & Dunlap, 1965.

Carter, Samuel, III. *Cyrus Field: Man of Two Worlds.* New York: Putnam, 1968.

Cassidy, Vincent H. *The Sea around Them: The Atlantic Ocean, A.D. 1250.* Baton Rouge: Louisiana State University Press, 1968.

Catton, Bruce. *This Hallowed Ground: The Story of the Union Side of the Civil War.* Garden City, N.Y.: Doubleday, 1956.

―――. *A Stillness at Appomattox.* Garden City, N.Y.: Doubleday, 1953.

Cave, Alfred A. *Jacksonian Democracy and the Historians.* Gainesville: University of Florida Press, 1964.

Chamberlain, John. *Farewell to Reform.* New York: Liveright, 1932.

Chase, Stuart. *Rich Land, Poor Land.* New York, London: Whittlesey House, McGraw-Hill, 1936.

Childs, Marquis, and Cater, Douglas. *Ethics in a Business Society.* New York: Harper, 1954.

Clapp, Gordon R. *The TVA.* Chicago: University of Chicago Press, 1955.

Clark, Thomas D. *The Emerging South.* New York: Oxford University Press, 1961.

―――. *The Rampaging Frontier.* Indianapolis: Bobbs-Merrill, 1939.

Clark, Victor S. *History of Manufactures in the United States.* 3 vols. New York: McGraw-Hill, 1929.

Clarke, Arthur C. *Voice across the Sea.* New York: Harper, 1958.

Coates, Robert M. *Outlaw Years: The History of the Land Pirates of the Natchez Trace.* New York: Macauley, 1930.
Cochran, Thomas. *The American Business System.* Cambridge: Harvard University Press, 1957.
Cohn, David L. *The Life and Times of King Cotton.* New York: Oxford University Press, 1956.
———. *Picking America's Pockets.* New York: Harper, 1936.
Coit, Margaret L. *John C. Calhoun: American Portrait.* Boston: Houghton Mifflin, 1950.
Coles, Harry L. *The War of 1812.* Chicago: University of Chicago Press, 1966.
Collins, Charles W. *Fourteenth Amendment and the States.* Boston: Little, Brown, 1912.
Covey, Cyclone. *The Gentle Radical: A Biography of Roger Williams.* New York: Macmillan, 1966.
Cowles, Virginia S. *The Great Swindle: The Story of the South Sea Bubble.* New York: Harper, 1960.
Cramer, C. H. *Royal Bob: The Life of Robert G. Ingersoll.* Indianapolis: Bobbs-Merrill, 1952.
Crane, Burton. *Getting and Spending: An Informal Guide to National Economics.* New York: Harcourt, Brace, 1956.
Cronin, Edmund D. *Black Moses: The Story of Marcus Garvey.* Madison: University of Wisconsin Press, 1962.
Current, Richard N. *Daniel Webster and the Rise of National Conservatism.* Boston: Little, Brown, 1955.
Daniels, Jonathan. *Prince of Carpetbaggers.* New York: Lippincott, 1958.
Darrah, William C. *Powell of the Colorado.* Princeton: Princeton University Press, 1951.
Davidson, Marshall B. *Life in America.* 2 vols. Boston: Houghton Mifflin, 1951.
Davis, Lance E., Hughes, Jonathan R. T., McDougall, Duncan M. *American Economic History.* Homewood, Ill.: Irwin, 1961.
Dearing, Charles L., and Owen, Wilfred. *National Transportation Policy.* Washington: Brookings Institution, 1949.
De Conde, Alexander. *A History of American Foreign Policy.* New York: Scribner's, 1963.
De Voto, Bernard A., *The Course of Empire.* Boston: Houghton Mifflin, 1952.
Dick, Everett. *The Sod-House Frontier.* New York: D. Appleton-Century, 1937.
Dillon, Richard H. *Fool's Gold: The Decline and Fall of Captain John Sutter of California.* New York: Coward-McCann, 1967.
Donald, David H. *Lincoln Reconsidered.* New York: Random House, 1955.
Dorfman, Joseph. *The Economic Mind in American Civilization.* 5 vols. New York, Viking, 1946–1959.
———. *Thorstein Veblen and His America.* New York: Viking, 1934.
Dowd, Douglas F. *Modern Economic Problems in Historical Perspective.* Boston: Heath, 1965.
Dulles, Foster R. *Labor in America.* New York: Crowell, 1949.
Dumond, Dwight L. *Roosevelt to Roosevelt.* New York, Holt, 1937.
Dunn, Mary M. *William Penn, Politics and Conscience.* Princeton: Princeton University Press, 1967.
Elkins, Stanley M. *Slavery.* New York: Grosset & Dunlap, 1963.
Elkins, Stanley, and McKitrick, Eric. *The Founding Fathers: Young Men of the Revolution.* Washington: Service Center for Teachers of History, 1962.
Ellis, Elmer. *Mr. Dooley's America.* New York: Knopf, 1941.
Elsner, Henry, Jr. *The Technocrats: Prophets of Automation.* Syracuse, N.Y.: Syracuse University Press, 1967.
Ernst, Morris L. *Ultimate Power.* Garden City, N.Y.: Doublday, Doran, 1937.
Farrand, Max. *Framing the Constitution of the United States.* New Haven: Yale University Press, 1913.
Faulkner, Harold U. *American Economic History.* New York: Harper, 1949.

Ferrell, Robert H. *American Diplomacy*. New York: Norton, 1959.

Fine, Sidney. *Laissez-Faire and the General Welfare State: A Study of Conflict in American Thought, 1865–1901*. Ann Arbor: University of Michigan Press, 1956.

Fiske, John. *The Critical Period of American History, 1783–1789*. Boston: Houghton Mifflin, 1892.

Flynn, John T. *Country Squire in the White House*. Garden City, N.Y.: Doubleday, Doran, 1940.

———. *God's Gold: The Story of Rockefeller and His Times*. New York: Harcourt, Brace, 1932.

Forbes, Esther. *Paul Revere and the World He Lived In*. Boston: Houghton Mifflin, 1942.

Frank, Bernard, and Netboy, Anthony. *Water, Land, and People*. New York: Knopf, 1950.

Fuess, Claude M. *Joseph B. Eastman: Servant of the People*. New York: Columbia University Press, 1952.

Fuhrmann, Otto W. *The 500th Anniversary of the Invention of Printing*. New York: Philip C. Duschnes, 1937.

Fulton, Robert B. *Original Marxism — Estranged Offspring*. Boston: Christopher, 1960.

Furnas, Joseph C. *Goodbye to Uncle Tom*. New York: Sloane, 1956.

Gabriel, Ralph H. *The Course of American Democratic Thought*. New York: Ronald, 1940.

Galbraith, John K. *The Affluent Society*. Boston: Houghton Mifflin, 1958.

———. *American Capitalism: The Concept of Countervailing Power*. Boston: Houghton Mifflin, 1952.

———. *The Great Crash*. Boston: Houghton Mifflin, 1955.

———. *The New Industrial State*. Boston: Houghton Mifflin, 1967.

Gibney, Frank. *The Operators*. New York: Harper, 1960.

Ginger, Ray. *Age of Excess: The United States from 1877 to 1914*. New York: Macmillan, 1965.

Glad, Paul W. *McKinley, Bryan and the People*. Philadelphia: Lippincott, 1964.

Gleisser, Marcus. *The World of Cyrus Eaton*. New York: Barnes, 1965.

Goetzmann, William H. *When the Eagle Screamed*. New York: Wiley, 1966.

Goldberg, Harvey. *American Radicals*. New York: Monthly Review Press, 1957.

Goldman, Eric. *Rendezvous with Destiny*. New York: Knopf, 1952.

Graham, Howard J. *Everyman's Constitution: Historical Essays on the Fourteenth Amendment*. Madison, Wis.: State Historical Society, 1969.

Hacker, Louis M. *The Triumph of American Capitalism*. New York: Simon and Schuster, 1940.

Hacker, Louis M., and Kendrick, Benjamin R. *The U.S. Since 1865*. New York: Crofts, 1934.

Hammond, Bray. *Banks and Politics in America from the Revolution to the Civil War*. Princeton: Princeton University Press, 1957.

Harlow, Alvin F. *Old Bowery Days*. New York: Appleton-Century, 1931.

Harris, Seymour E. *Saving American Capitalism*. New York: Knopf, 1948.

Harrod, Roy F. *The Life of John Maynard Keynes*. London: Macmillan, 1951.

Hatcher, Harlan. *The Western Reserve*. Indianapolis: Bobbs-Merrill, 1949.

Hawke, David. *The Colonial Experience*. Indianapolis: Bobbs-Merrill, 1966.

Hawkins, Hugh (ed.). *Booker T. Washington and His Critics*. Boston: Heath, 1962.

Heilbroner, Robert L. *Quest for Wealth*. New York: Simon and Schuster, 1956.

———. *The Worldly Philosophers*. New York: Simon and Schuster, 1953.

Heimann, Eduard. *History of Economic Doctrines*. New York: Oxford University Press, 1964.

Hicks, John D. *The Federal Union: A History of the U.S. to 1865*. Boston: Houghton Mifflin, 1937.

Hockett, Homer C. *Political and Social Growth of the American People*. New York: Macmillan, 1940.

Hofstadter, Richard. *The Age of Reform*. New York: Knopf, 1955.

———. *The American Political Tradition and the Men Who Made It*. New York: Knopf, 1948.

———. *The Progressive Historians: Turner, Beard, Parrington*. New York: Knopf, 1968.

Holbrook, Stewart H. *The Age of the Moguls*. Garden City, N.Y.: Doubleday, 1953.

Holt, Margaret V. *George Washington Carver*. New York: Abington, 1966.

Horgan, Paul. *Conquistadors in North American History*. New York: Farrar, Straus, 1963.

House Committee on Judiciary. *Study of Monopoly Power*. Hearings before Subcommittee on Study of Monopoly Power, 8 and 10 May, 1950. Washington, D.C.: Government Printing Office.

Howe, Irving, and Widick, B. J. *The UAW and Walter Reuther*. New York: Random House, 1949.

Howe, Quincy. *A History of Our Own Times*. 2 vols. New York: Simon and Schuster, 1949–1953.

Huberman, Leo. *The Labor Spy Racket*. New York: Monthly Review Press, 1937.

Hulbert, Archer B. *The Forty-Niners*. Boston: Little, Brown, 1931.

James, Joseph B. *The Framing of the Fourteenth Amendment*. Urbana: University of Illinois Press, 1956.

James, Marquis. *Andrew Jackson*. Indianapolis: Bobbs-Merrill, 1937.

———. *The Raven: A Biography of Sam Houston*. Indianapolis: Bobbs-Merrill, 1929.

Johnson, Gerald W. *American Heroes and Hero Worship*. New York: Harper, 1943.

———. *The Lunatic Fringe*. Philadelphia: Lippincott, 1957.

Johnson, Malcolm M. *Crime on the Waterfront*. New York: McGraw-Hill, 1950.

Joint Economic Committee of Congress. *Subsidy and Subsidy Effect Programs of the U.S. Government*. Washington, D.C.: Government Printing Office, 1965.

Jones, Gwyn. *A History of the Vikings*. New York: Oxford University Press, 1968.

Jones, Howard M. *O Strange New World: American Culture, the Formative Years*. New York: Viking, 1964.

Josephson, Matthew. *Edison*. New York: McGraw-Hill, 1959.

———. *The Politicos*. New York: Harcourt, Brace, 1938.

———. *The Robber Barons*. New York: Harcourt, Brace, 1934.

Josephy, Alvin M. *The Indian Heritage of America*. New York: Knopf, 1968.

Keats, John. *The Insolent Chariots*. Philadelphia: Lippincott, 1958.

Keller, Morton. *The New Deal — What Was It?* New York: Holt, Rinehart and Winston, 1963.

King, Judson. *The Conservation Fight: From Theodore Roosevelt to the Tennessee Valley Authority*. Washington, D.C.: Public Affairs Press, 1959.

Kirkland, Edward C. *A History of American Economic Life*. New York: Appleton-Century-Crofts, 1951.

Kohlmeier, Louis M., Jr. *The Regulators: Watchdog Agencies and the Public Interest*. New York: Harper and Row, 1969.

Kornbluh, Joyce L. (ed.). *Rebel Voices, an I.W.W. Anthology*. Ann Arbor: University of Michigan Press, 1964.

Lamb, Harold. *New-Found World: How America Was Discovered and Explored*. Garden City, N.Y.: Doubleday, 1955.

Landsberg, Hans H., Fischman, Leonard I., and Fisher, Joseph L. *Resources in America's Future: Patterns of Requirements and Availabilities, 1960–2000*. Baltimore: Johns Hopkins University Press, 1964.

Lavender, David S. *Land of Giants: The Drive to the Pacific Northwest, 1750–1950*. Garden City, N.Y.: Doubleday, 1968.

Lee, James M. *History of American Journalism*. Boston: Houghton Mifflin, 1917.

Levinson, Edward. *Labor on the March*. New York: University Books, 1956.

Lewis, Oscar. *The Big Four*. New York: Knopf, 1938.

Lincoln, Charles E. *The Black Muslims in America*. Boston: Beacon Press, 1961.

Link, Arthur S. *Wilson*. 5 vols. Princeton: Princeton University Press, 1947.

Lodge, Henry C. *Alexander Hamilton*. Boston: Houghton Mifflin, 1886.

Lorant, Stefan. *The Presidency*. New York: Macmillan, 1951.

Lumley, Frederick E. *The Propaganda Menace*. New York: Century, 1933.

Lundberg, Ferdinand. *America's 60 Families*. New York: Vanguard, 1937.

Luthin, Richard H. *American Demagogues: Twentieth Century*. Boston: Beacon Press, 1954.

Lynes, Russell. *The Tastemakers*. New York: Harper, 1954.

Lyon, Peter. *To Hell in a Day Coach: An Exasperated Look at American Railroads*. Philadelphia: Lippincott, 1968.

McDonald, Forrest. *Insull*. Chicago: University of Chicago Press, 1962.

McGeary, Martin N. *Gifford Pinchot, Forester-Politician*. Princeton: Princeton University Press, 1960.

Magrath, C. Peter. *Yazoo: Law and Politics in the New Republic — the Case of Fletcher vs. Peck*. Providence: Brown University Press, 1966.

Malone, Dumas. *Jefferson and His Time*. 3 vols. Boston: Little, Brown, 1948–1962.

Malone, Dumas, and Rauch, Basil. *Empire for Liberty: The Genesis and Growth of the United States of America*. 2 vols. New York: Appleton-Century-Crofts, 1960.

Mehling, Harold. *The Scandalous Scamps*. New York: Holt, Rinehart and Winston, 1959.

Merrill, Horace S. *Bourbon Leader: Grover Cleveland and the Democratic Party*. Boston: Little, Brown, 1957.

Metcalf, Lee, and Reinemer, Vic. *Overcharge*. New York: McKay, 1967.

Miller, John C. *Alexander Hamilton: Portrait in Paradox*. New York: Harper, 1959.

———. *Sam Adams: Pioneer in Propaganda*. Boston: Little, Brown, 1936.

Millis, Walter. *Arms and Men: A Study in American Military History*. New York: Putnam, 1956.

Minnigerode, Meade. *The Fabulous Forties, 1840–1850*. New York: Putnam, 1924.

Minton, Bruce, and Stuart, John. *Men Who Lead Labor*. New York: Modern Age, 1937.

Mitchell, Broadus. *Alexander Hamilton*. 2 vols. New York: Macmillan, 1957–1962.

Mitchell, Broadus and Louise P. *American Economic History*. Boston: Houghton Mifflin, 1947.

Moley, Raymond. *The First New Deal*. New York: Harcourt, Brace & World, 1966.

Monaghan, James. *Diplomat in Carpet Slippers: Abraham Lincoln Deals with Foreign Affairs*. Indianapolis: Bobbs-Merrill, 1945.

Morgan, Edmund S. *The Birth of the Republic, 1763–1789*. Chicago: University of Chicago Press, 1956.

———. *The Puritan Dilemma: The Story of John Winthrop*. Boston: Little, Brown, 1958.

Morison, Samuel E. *By Land and Sea*. New York: Knopf, 1953.

———. *Christopher Columbus, Mariner*. Boston: Little, Brown, 1955.

———. *Maritime History of Massachusetts*. Boston: Houghton Mifflin, 1922.

Morison, Samuel E., and Commager, Henry S. *The Growth of the American Republic*. 2 vols. New York: Oxford University Press, 1950.

Morrell, Parker. *Diamond Jim: The Life and Times of James Buchanan Brady*. New York: Simon and Schuster, 1934.

Morris, Richard B. *American Revolution Reconsidered*. New York: Harper & Row, 1967.

Morton, Frederic. *The Rothschilds*. New York: Atheneum, 1961.

Muzzey, David S. *James G. Blaine*. Boston: Ginn, 1934.

Nash, Gerald D. *Issues in American Economic History*. Boston: Heath, 1964.

Neale, Alan D. *The Antitrust Laws of the United States of America*. Cambridge (Eng.) University Press, 1960 and 1970.

Neuberger, Richard L., and Kahn, Stephen B. *Integrity: The Life of George W. Norris*. New York: Vanguard, 1937.

Nevins, Allan. *Ordeal of the Union*. 6 vols. New York: Scribner's, 1947–1960.

Nock, Albert Jay. *Jefferson*. New York: Harcourt, Brace, 1926.

Nossiter, Bernard. *The Mythmakers*. Boston: Houghton Mifflin, 1964.

Nussbaum, Arthur. *A History of the Dollar*. New York: Columbia University Press, 1957.

Nye, Russel B. *Baker's Dozen: Thirteen Unusual Americans*. East Lansing: Michigan State University Press, 1956.
———. *Midwestern Progressive Politics*. East Lansing: Michigan State University Press, 1951.
Osborn, Fairfield. *The Limits of the Earth*. Boston: Little, Brown, 1953.
Packard, Vance O. *The Status Seekers*. New York: McKay, 1959.
Padover, Saul. *Genius of America: Men Whose Ideas Shaped Our Civilization*. New York: McGraw-Hill, 1960.
Palmer, Robert R. *Age of the Democratic Revolution*. Princeton: Princeton University Press, 1959.
Parkes, Henry B. *The United States of America*. New York: Knopf, 1953.
Parr, Charles McK. *Ferdinand Magellan, Circumnavigator*. New York: Crowell, 1964.
Parry, John H. *The Age of Reconnaissance*. Cleveland: World, 1963.
Payne, Robert. *Marx*. London: Allen, 1968.
Peck, Harry T. *Twenty Years of the Republic, 1885–1905*. New York: Dodd, Mead, 1906.
Pegrum, Dudley F. *The Regulation of Industry*. Chicago: Irwin, 1949.
Pelling, Henry. *American Labor*. Chicago: University of Chicago Press, 1960.
Penick, James L. *Progressive Politics and Conservation: The Ballinger-Pinchot Affair*. Chicago: University of Chicago Press, 1968.
Penrose, Boies. *Travel and Discovery in the Renaissance, 1420–1620*. Cambridge: Harvard University Press, 1952.
Perkins, Bradford. *The Causes of the War of 1812*. New York: Holt, Rinehart and Winston, 1962.
Peterson, Merrill D. *The Jeffersonian Image in the American Mind*. New York: Oxford University Press, 1960.
Prather, Charles L. *Money and Banking*. Homewood, Ill.: Irwin, 1957.
Preston, John H. *Revolution, 1776*. New York: Harcourt, Brace, 1933.
Randall, Emilius O., and Ryan, Daniel J. *History of Ohio*. 6 vols. New York: Century History, 1912–1915.
Raper, John W. *The Soviet Table or the Rise of Civilization in Cleveland*. Cleveland: Public Affairs Committee, 1935.
Rauschenbush, Hilmar J. *The Power Fight*. New York: New Republic, 1932.
Rayback, Joseph G. *A History of American Labor*. New York: Macmillan, 1959.
Reese, Trevor R. *Colonial Georgia: A Study of British Imperial Policy in the Eighteenth Century*. Athens: University of Georgia Press, 1963.
Regier, Cornelius C. *The Era of the Muckraker*. Chapel Hill: University of North Carolina Press, 1932.
Riegel, Robert E. *America Moves West*. New York: Holt, 1947.
Riegel, Robert E., and Long, David F. *The American Story*. 2 vols. New York: McGraw-Hill, 1955.
Rienow, Robert and Leona T. *Moment in the Sun: A Report on the Deteriorating Quality of the American Environment*. New York: Dial, 1967.
Rodell, Fred. *Nine Men: A Political History of the Supreme Court from 1790 to 1955*. New York: Random House, 1955.
Rose, William G. *Cleveland, the Making of a City*. Cleveland and New York: World, 1950.
Roseboom, Eugene. *A History of Presidential Elections*. New York: Macmillan, 1957.
Roseboom, Eugene, and Weisenberger, Francis. *A History of Ohio*. Columbus: Ohio State Archaeological and Historical Society, 1953.
Russell, Charles E. *Haym Salomon and the Revolution*. New York: Cosmopolitan Book Corporation, 1930.
Russell, Francis. *The Shadow of Blooming Grove: Warren G. Harding in His Times*. New York: McGraw-Hill, 1968.
Sandburg, Carl. *Abraham Lincoln, The Prairie Years*. New York: Harcourt, 1927.
———. *Abraham Lincoln, The War Years*. New York: Harcourt, Brace, 1929.
———. *Always the Young Strangers*. New York: Harcourt, Brace, 1953.
———. *The People, Yes*. New York: Harcourt, Brace, 1936.

Sanders, Leslie E. *Mother Goose in Washington*. New York, Harrisburg, Pa.: Telegraph Press, 1936.

Saveth, Edward (ed.). *Understanding the American Past*. Boston: Little, Brown, 1954.

Sawyer, Peter H. *The Age of the Vikings*. New York: St. Martin's Press, 1962.

Sax, Karl. *Standing Room Only: The Challenge of Overpopulation*. Boston: Beacon, 1955.

Scheffer, Victor B. *The Year of the Whale*. New York: Scribner's, 1969.

Schlesinger, Arthur M. *Paths to the Present*. New York: Macmillan, 1949.

Schlesinger, Arthur M., Jr. *The Age of Jackson*. Boston: Little, Brown, 1945.

————. *The Age of Roosevelt: Coming of the New Deal*. Boston: Houghton Mifflin, 1958.

————. *The Age of Roosevelt: Crisis of the Old Order*. Boston: Houghton Mifflin, 1957.

————. *The Age of Roosevelt: The Politics of Upheaval*. Boston: Houghton Mifflin, 1960.

————. *A Thousand Days: John F. Kennedy in the White House*. Boston: Houghton Mifflin, 1965.

Schriftgiesser, Karl. *The Lobbyists*. Boston: Little, Brown, 1951.

Scott, John. *Democracy Is Not Enough*. New York: Harcourt, Brace, 1960.

Seldes, George. *Freedom of the Press*. Indianapolis: Bobbs-Merrill, 1935.

Shannon, Fred A. *America's Economic Growth*. New York: Macmillan, 1951.

Shera, Jesse H. *Foundations of the Public Library*. Chicago: University of Chicago Press, 1949.

Soule, George H. *Economic Forces in American History*. New York: Dryden, 1952.

————. *Ideas of the Great Economists*. New York: Viking, 1952.

Spencer, Samuel R. *Booker T. Washington and the Negro's Place in American Life*. Boston: Little, Brown, 1955.

Stamp, Laurence D. *Land for Tomorrow; the Underdeveloped World*. Bloomington: Indiana University Press, 1953.

Stampp, Kenneth M. *The Era of Reconstruction, 1865–1877*. New York: Knopf, 1965.

————. *The Peculiar Institution: Slavery in the Antebellum South*. New York: Knopf, 1956.

Starkey, Marion L. *A Little Rebellion*. New York: Knopf, 1955.

————. *Striving to Make It My Home: The Story of Americans from Africa*. New York: Norton, 1964.

Steiner, Stan. *The New Indians*. New York: Harper & Row, 1968.

Stern, Philip M. *The Great Treasury Raid*. New York: Random House, 1964.

Stover, John F. *American Railroads*. Chicago: University of Chicago Press, 1961.

Street, James H. *The Civil War*. New York: Dial, 1953.

————. *The Revolutionary War*. New York: Dial, 1954.

Sullivan, Mark. *Our Times: The United States, 1900–1925*. 6 vols. New York: Scribner's, 1926–1935.

Summers, Festus P. *William L. Wilson and Tariff Reform*. New Brunswick, N.J.: Rutgers University Press, 1953.

Swanberg, William A. *Jim Fisk: The Career of an Improbable Rascal*. New York: Scribner's, 1959.

Syrett, Harold C. *Andrew Jackson*. Indianapolis: Bobbs-Merrill, 1953.

Tarbell, Ida M. *The Tariff in Our Times*. New York: Macmillan, 1911.

Taylor, George R. (ed.). *The Turner Thesis*. Boston: Heath, 1949.

Thayer, Charles W. *Diplomat*. New York: Harper, 1959.

Townshend, Robert. *Up the Organization*. New York: Knopf, 1970.

Tucker, Glenn. *Poltroons and Patriots*. 2 vols. Indianapolis: Bobbs-Merrill, 1954.

U.S. Senate Subcommittee on Monetary, Credit and Fiscal Policies. *Report, January, 1950*. Washington, D.C.: U.S. Government Printing Office.

Van Alstyne, Richard W. *Empire and Independence: The International History of the American Revolution*. New York: Wiley, 1965.

Van de Water, Frederick F. *Glory Hunter: A Life of General Custer*. Indianapolis: Bobbs-Merrill, 1934.

Van Doren, Carl C. *Benjamin Franklin*. New York: Viking, 1938.

Velie, Lester. *Labor U.S.A.* New York: Harper, 1959.

Waggoner, Madeline S. *The Long Haul West: The Great Canal Era, 1817–1850*. New York: Putnam, 1958.

Warren, Charles. *Jacobin and Junto*. Cambridge: Harvard University Press, 1931.

Webb, Walter P. *The Great Frontier*. Boston: Houghton Mifflin, 1952.

——. *The Great Plains*. Boston: Ginn, 1931.

Wecter, Dixon. *Age of the Great Depression, 1929–1941*. New York: Macmillan, 1948.

——. *The Hero in America*. New York: Scribner's, 1941.

Weinberg, Arthur and Lilo (eds.). *The Muckrakers, 1902–1912*. New York: Simon and Schuster, 1961.

Weld, John. *Don't You Cry for Me*. New York: Scribner's, 1940.

Wendt, Lloyd, and Kogan, Herman. *"Bet-A-Million" — The Life of John Warne Gates*. Indianapolis: Bobbs-Merrill, 1948.

Weslager, Clinton A. *The Log Cabin in America*. New Brunswick, N.J.: Rutgers University Press, 1969.

Whipple, A. B. C. *Pirate Rascals of the Spanish Main*. Garden City, N.Y.: Doubleday, 1957.

——. *Tall Ships and Great Captains*. New York: Harper, 1960.

White, William S. *The Taft Story*. New York: Harper, 1954.

Williams, Eric E. *Capitalism and Slavery*. New York: Russell & Russell, 1961.

Williamson, Harold F. (ed.). *The Growth of the American Economy*. New York: Prentice-Hall, 1951.

Willison, George F. *Saints and Strangers*. New York: Reynal & Hitchcock, 1945.

Wilson, Mitchell. *American Science and Invention*. New York: Simon and Schuster, 1954.

Wilson, Walter. *Forced Labor in the United States*. New York: International Publishers, 1933.

Wittke, Carl F. *The First Fifty Years: The Cleveland Museum of Art*. Cleveland: The Press of Western Reserve University, 1966.

Wolff, Leon. *Lockout, the Story of the Homestead Strike of 1892*. New York: Harper & Row, 1965.

Wolfskill, George. *The Revolt of the Conservatives: A History of the American Liberty League, 1934–1940*. Boston: Houghton Mifflin, 1962.

Woodman, Harold D. *Slavery and the Southern Economy*. New York: Harcourt, Brace & World, 1966.

Woodward, C. Vann. *Origins of the New South, 1877–1913*. Baton Rouge: Louisiana State University Press, 1951.

——. *Tom Watson, Agrarian Rebel*. New York: Macmillan, 1938.

Woodward, William E. *George Washington, the Image and the Man*. New York: Boni and Liveright, 1926.

Wright, Esmond. *Fabric of Freedom, 1763–1800*. New York: Hill & Wang, 1961.

Wright, Esmond (ed.). *Causes and Consequences of the American Revolution*. Chicago: Quadrangle, 1966.

Wright, Louis B. *The Dream of Prosperiy in Colonial America*. New York: New York University Press, 1965.

Wyllie, Irvin G. *The Self-Made Man in America: The Myth of Rags to Riches*. New Bunswick, N.J.: Rutgers University Press, 1954.

Yellen, Samuel. *American Labor Struggles*. New York: Harcourt, Brace, 1936.

Index